Visit the Web site for

A HISTORY OF
World Societies

bedfordstmartins.com/mckayworld

FREE Online Study Guide

GET INSTANT FEEDBACK ON YOUR PROGRESS WITH

- Chapter self-tests
- Key terms review
- Map quizzes
- Timeline activities
- Note-taking outlines

FREE History Research Writing Help

REFINE YOUR RESEARCH SKILLS AND FIND PLENTY OF GOOD SOURCES WITH

- A database of useful images, maps, documents, and more at *Make History*
- A guide to online sources for history
- Help with writing history papers
- A tool for building a bibliography
- Tips on avoiding plagiarism

A HISTORY OF
World Societies

■ Ito Shinsui, *Facing the Mirror*, 1916.

NINTH EDITION

A HISTORY OF
World Societies

Volume 2 | SINCE 1450

JOHN P. McKAY | *University of Illinois at Urbana-Champaign*

BENNETT D. HILL | *Late of Georgetown University*

JOHN BUCKLER | *Late of University of Illinois at Urbana-Champaign*

PATRICIA BUCKLEY EBREY | *University of Washington*

ROGER B. BECK | *Eastern Illinois University*

CLARE HARU CROWSTON | *University of Illinois at Urbana-Champaign*

MERRY E. WIESNER-HANKS | *University of Wisconsin–Milwaukee*

BEDFORD/ST. MARTIN'S
Boston • New York

FOR BEDFORD/ST. MARTIN'S

Publisher for History: Mary Dougherty
Executive Editor for History: Traci M. Crowell
Director of Development for History: Jane Knetzger
Senior Developmental Editor: Laura Arcari
Senior Production Editor: Christina Horn
Senior Production Supervisor: Dennis J. Conroy
Executive Marketing Manager: Jenna Bookin Barry
Associate Editor: Lynn Sternberger
Editorial Assistant: Arrin Kaplan
Production Assistant: Laura Winstead
Copy Editor: Sybil Sosin
Map Editor: Charlotte Miller
Indexer: Leoni Z. McVey
Cartography: Mapping Specialists, Ltd.
Page Layout: Boynton Hue Studio
Photo Researcher: Carole Frohlich and Elisa Gallagher, The Visual Connection Image Research, Inc.

Permissions Manager: Kalina K. Ingham
Senior Art Director: Anna Palchik
Text and Cover Designer: Brian Salisbury
Cover Art: Facing the Mirror, by Ito Shinsui, 1916. © Christie's Images/CORBIS.
Composition: NK Graphics
Printing and Binding: RR Donnelley and Sons

President: Joan E. Feinberg
Editorial Director: Denise B. Wydra
Director of Marketing: Karen R. Soeltz
Director of Production: Susan W. Brown
Associate Director, Editorial Production: Elise S. Kaiser
Managing Editor: Elizabeth M. Schaaf

Library of Congress Control Number: 2011925869

Manufactured in the United States of America.

1 2 3 4 5 6   15 14 13 12 11

For information, write: Bedford/St. Martin's, 75 Arlington Street, Boston, MA 02116   (617-399-4000)

ISBN: 978-0-312-66691-0 (Combined edition)
ISBN: 978-0-312-57013-2 (Loose leaf)
ISBN: 978-0-312-56969-3 (High School edition)
ISBN: 978-0-312-66692-7 (Volume 1)
ISBN: 978-0-312-57014-9 (Loose leaf)
ISBN: 978-0-312-66693-4 (Volume 2)
ISBN: 978-0-312-57051-4 (Loose leaf)
ISBN: 978-0-312-66694-1 (Volume A)
ISBN: 978-0-312-66695-8 (Volume B)
ISBN: 978-0-312-66696-5 (Volume C)

Distributed outside North America by:
PALGRAVE MACMILLAN
Houndmills, Basingstoke, Hampshire RG21 6XS
Companies and representatives throughout the world.
ISBN: 978-0-230-39436-0 (Combined edition)
ISBN: 978-0-230-39437-7 (Volume 1)
ISBN: 978-0-230-39438-4 (Volume 2)
ISBN: 978-0-230-39439-1 (Volume C)
A catalogue record for this book is available from the British Library.

□ IN MEMORIAM

JOHN BUCKLER 1945–2011

John Buckler, who authored many of the chapters in earlier editions of this book, was born in Louisville, Kentucky, on March 16, 1945. John received his B.A. summa cum laude from the University of Louisville in 1967 and his Ph.D. from Harvard University in 1973. From 1984 to 1986, he held an Alexander von Humboldt Fellowship at the Institut für Alte Geschichte at the University of Munich. In 1980 Harvard University Press published his *Theban Hegemony, 371–362 B.C.* In 1989 his *Philip II and the Sacred War* was published, and he also edited *BOIOTIKA: Vorträge vom 5. Internationalen Böotien-Kolloquium.* During the 1990s he contributed articles to the American Historical Association's *Guide to Historical Literature, The Oxford Classical Dictionary,* and *The Encyclopedia of Greece and the Hellenic Tradition.* In 2003 he published A*egean Greece in the Fourth Century B.C.* In the following year his editions of W. M. Leake's *Travels in the Morea* (three volumes) and *Peloponnesiaca* appeared. Cambridge University Press published his *Central Greece and the Politics of Power in the Fourth Century,* edited by Hans Beck, in 2007. At the time of his sudden and unexpected death, he was writing a book on the history of Greek warfare and also contributing to revisions of *Die Fragmente der Griechischen Historiker* by Felix Jacoby. Known internationally for his work, John was a scholar of great stature who will be missed by all who knew him.

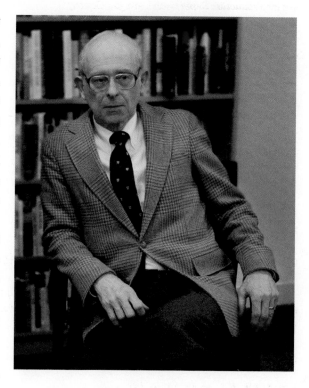

◻ BRIEF CONTENTS

◻ CONTENTS

16 The Acceleration of Global Contact

1450–1600 458

21 Continuity and Change in East Asia

1400–1800 616

22 Revolutions in the Atlantic World

1775–1815 650

27 Nation Building in the Americas and Australia
1770–1914 810

28 World War and Revolution
1914–1929 842

31 Global Recovery and Division Between Superpowers

1945 to the Present 940

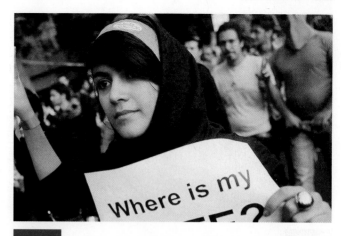

32 Independence, Progress, and Conflict in Asia and the Middle East

1945 to the Present 976

33 The Global South: Latin America and Africa

1945 to the Present 1006

34 A New Era in World History 1036

◻ MAPS, FIGURES, AND TABLES

SPECIAL FEATURES

Viewpoints

Listening to the Past

Individuals In Society

Global Trade

The ninth edition of *A History of World Societies* has been particularly significant for us because it represents important changes with the author team and with our publisher. Our new publisher, Bedford/St. Martin's, gave us the opportunity to revisit our original vision and to revitalize the text and its scholarship in exciting and fulfilling ways. Sadly, founding authors John P. McKay and John Buckler retired from the book this year, but with Merry Wiesner-Hanks and Clare Haru Crowston, who joined as authors in the last edition, and Patricia Buckley Ebrey and Roger B. Beck, who joined in the fifth and seventh editions, respectively, we continue to benefit from a collaborative team of regional experts with deep experience in the world history classroom.

In this age of global connections, with its influence on the global economy, global migration patterns, popular culture, and global warming, among other things, the study of world history is more vital and urgent than ever before. An understanding of the broad sweep of the human past helps us to comprehend today's dramatic changes and enduring continuities. People now migrate enormous distances and establish new lives far from their places of birth, yet migration has been a constant in history since the first humans walked out of Africa. Satellite and cell phones now link nearly every inch of the planet, yet the expansion of communication networks is a process that is thousands of years old. Children who speak different languages at home now sit side by side in schools and learn from one another, yet intercultural encounters have long been a source of innovation, transformation, and at times, unfortunately, conflict.

This book is designed for twenty-first-century students who will spend their lives on this small interconnected planet and for whom an understanding of only local or national history will no longer be sufficient. We believe that the study of world history in a broad and comparative context is an exciting, important, and highly practical pursuit. It is our conviction, based on considerable experience in introducing large numbers of students to world history, that a book reflecting current trends in scholarship can excite readers and inspire an enduring interest in the long human experience.

Our strategy has been twofold. First, we have made social and cultural history the core elements of our narrative. We seek to re-create the lives of ordinary people in appealing human terms and also to highlight the interplay between men's and women's lived experiences and the ways they reflect on these to create meaning. Thus, in addition to foundational works of philosophy and literature, we include popular songs and stories. We present objects along with texts as important sources for studying history, and this has allowed us to incorporate the growing emphasis on material culture in the work of many historians. At the same time we have been mindful of the need to give great economic, political, and intellectual developments the attention they deserve. We want to give individual students and instructors an integrated perspective so that they can pursue — on their own or in the classroom — the themes and questions that they find particularly exciting and significant.

Second, we have made every effort to strike an effective global and regional balance. The whole world interacts today, and to understand the interactions and what they mean for today's citizens, we must study the whole world's history. Thus we have adopted a comprehensive regional organization with a global perspective that is clear and manageable for students. For example, Chapter 7 introduces students in depth to East Asia, and at the same time the chapter highlights the cultural connections that occurred via the Silk Road and the spread of Buddhism. We study all geographical areas, conscious of the separate histories of many parts of the world, particularly in the earliest millennia of human development. We also stress the links among cultures, political units, and economic systems, for these connections have made the world what it is today. We make comparisons and connections across time as well as space, for understanding the unfolding of the human story in time is the central task of history.

Textual Changes

In preparing the ninth edition of this book, we have worked hard to keep the book up-to-date and to strengthen our comprehensive, comparative, and connective approach. We carefully revisited and reconsidered every paragraph, rewriting and expanding sections for clarity and for stronger connections and comparisons and, most important, incorporating the latest scholarship, including a new first chapter on "The Earliest Human Societies, to 2500 B.C.E." informed by the most current research available. Moreover, we revised every chapter with the goal of readability and accessibility.

Several main lines of revision have guided our many changes. As in previous editions we added significantly more discussion of groups and regions that are often shortchanged in general histories of world civilizations, and we have continued to do so in this new revision, including new material on the Minoans and Mycenaeans in Chapter 5; the Celts in Chapter 8; the Pacific Islanders and Easter Island in Chapter 12; Korea during the Koryŏ dynasty in Chapter 13; the American colonies in Chapters 17 and 22; Armenian traders in Chapter 20; the Congo Free State in Chapter 25;

the Palestinians, Kurds, and Lebanese in Chapter 32; and the countries of Latin America in Chapter 33. This expanded scope reflects the awareness within the historical profession of the enormous diversity of the world's peoples.

We have also continued to increase our coverage of social and cultural history, encouraging students to consider how life in the past was both similar to and different from our lives today. This increased emphasis is supported in every chapter by the use of artifacts that make history tangible. In addition, we enhanced the discussion of religion in many chapters, including both the central ideas and lived religious practices of world religions such as Judaism and Christianity and of local religions such as those of the Celts and Egyptians. So, for example, you will find new scholarship on Amon-Ra and Isis, Zoroastrianism, and Jewish religious beliefs in Chapter 2; expanded coverage of the Jewish background of Christianity along with new material on second- and third-century Christianity in Chapter 6; and an expanded discussion of Arian Christianity along with a new discussion of the development of the Bible as a text in Chapter 8. Students are increasingly interested in the diversity of religious practices in the world around them, and we hope these additions will help them better understand the wide range of religions in the past.

Other social and cultural additions include new sections on Life in Early India in Chapter 3, Life During the Zhou Dynasty in Chapter 4, and Life in Han China in Chapter 7; a new discussion of the *Iliad* and *Odyssey* in Chapter 5; more on Roman architecture and literature in Chapter 6; new coverage of the actual workings of the law and an expanded discussion of family structure and food in Chapter 14; a new section devoted to life in the colonies of the New World in Chapter 17; and a new in-depth section devoted to the social impact of the Atlantic world in Chapter 18, including an exciting new section on Identities and Communities of the Atlantic World, where we discuss the impact of colonization and world trade on the lives of ordinary people.

As mentioned above, in this edition we have continued to strengthen the comparative coverage within the narrative to help students see and understand the cross-cultural connections of world history. In addition, we have added an exciting **NEW Connections** feature to the end of each chapter. This feature's synthesis of main developments serves to conclude the chapter, and the connections and comparisons of countries and regions explain how events relate to larger global processes, such as the influence of the Silk Road, the effects of the transatlantic slave trade, and the ramifications of colonialism. This new feature also serves to guide students in their reading, introducing related events and cultures that they will encounter in chapters to come. In this way students are introduced to history as an ongoing process of interrelated events.

The importance of cross-cultural connections to the study of world history is reflected in new scholarship and information on the impact of writing on our understanding of the past, and the relationship between the development of writing and the growth of states in Chapter 2; attention to areas of the world in which there were significant encounters between groups, such as Nubia and Kush in eastern Africa in Chapter 2 and the Indo-Bactrian kingdoms in Chapter 3; the impact of European settlement on the lives of indigenous peoples in Chapter 16; a more global perspective on European politics, culture, and economics in the early modern period, including the global impact of the Seven Years' War and treatment of the American, French, and Haitian Revolutions as interrelated events in an Atlantic world of political debates, conflicts, and aspirations in Chapter 22; an emphasis on cross-cultural encounters along the East African coast in Chapter 19; expanded coverage of Korea in Chapter 21, allowing for more in-depth analysis of the similarities of and differences between Asian countries; coverage of early efforts at modernization and industrialization outside of Europe and a discussion of how slavery impacted worldwide industrialization in Chapter 23; connections between the early European contacts in Africa and those that occurred with the empires of Southwest Asia in Chapter 25; the worldwide effects of the Great Depression in Chapter 30; and a more global treatment of both World War I and World War II, with new coverage of the ways in which these wars affected colonial peoples, in Chapters 28 and 30.

These major aspects of revision are accompanied by the incorporation of a wealth of other new scholarship and subject areas. Additions, among others, include a new section on hieroglyphics and a discussion of gender as it relates to Mesopotamian politics in Chapter 2; a more in-depth treatment of Chinese military thought and technology in Chapter 4; new scholarship on mystery religions in Chapter 5; an updated discussion of sexuality and Christianity in Chapter 8; new scholarship on race in Chapter 10; an updated discussion of mound builders and a new discussion of environmental and political changes in Chapter 11; new coverage of China under Mongol rule in Chapter 12; new scholarship on the Crusades in Chapter 14; a revised discussion of humanism to include more about women, and an updated discussion of Machiavelli to reflect new scholarship in Chapter 15; new coverage of the Atlantic world and the ways in which Enlightenment ideas and debates circulated along with many different peoples and commodities in Chapter 18; increased attention to suffrage in Chapter 24; a new discussion of politically active emigrants and the ways in which some Asians rejected Western influence, while others embraced Western ideas and practice, in Chapter 26; and updates through 2011 in Chapters 31, 32, 33, and 34, including up-to-date coverage of the economic downturn and the 2010–2011 uprisings and protests in North Africa and the Middle East. In sum, we have tried to bring new research and interpretation into our global history, believing it essential to keep our book stimulating, accurate, and current for students and instructors.

New Chapters and Organizational Changes

To meet the demands of the evolving course, we took a close and critical look at the book's organization and have made several major changes in the organization of chapters to reflect the way the course is taught today. The most dramatic change is the addition of an entirely new first chapter, "The Earliest Human Societies, to 2500 B.C.E.," which reflects a growing awareness among world historians that the human story properly begins millions, not mere thousands, of years ago. In order to provide a more global perspective on European politics, culture, and economics in the early modern period, Chapters 17, 18, and 22 have been substantially reworked and reorganized. Chapter 17 on European absolutism and constitutionalism has been broadened in scope to include European expansion, and Chapter 18 on the scientific revolution and the Enlightenment now includes coverage of the Atlantic world. As a natural extension, Chapter 22, which used to focus on the French Revolution, now examines the age of revolution in the Atlantic world. Together, the enhanced global perspectives of these chapters help connect the different regions of the globe and, in particular, help explain the crucial period when Europe began to dominate the rest of the globe.

To increase clarity and to help students see the global connections between the events surrounding World Wars I and II, we dropped the chapter on Europe in the interwar years and integrated this material into the World War chapters. Chapter 28 now focuses on the Great War, the Russian Revolution, and the interwar years, while Chapter 30 begins with the Great Depression in order to better explain the global conditions that contributed to the outbreak of World War II. The post-1945 section has also been completely reworked. In addition to updating all of the postwar chapters through 2011, we substantially reworked the last three chapters, integrating the Epilogue on the Middle East into Chapter 32 to create a more tightly focused and accessible chapter, and moving the material on Latin America and Africa to create a new Chapter 33 on the Global South. In addition to these major organizational changes, we carefully scrutinized all chapters, reorganizing material and adding clearer heads throughout as needed for clarity and to highlight important material for students.

Features

We are proud of the diverse special features that expand upon the narrative and offer opportunities for classroom discussion and assignments. For the ninth edition we have augmented our offerings to include a new feature created in response to reviewer requests for more primary source materials. This **NEW** documents feature, **Viewpoints**, offers paired primary documents on a topic that illuminates the human experience, allowing us to provide concrete examples of differences in the ways people thought. Anyone teaching world history has to emphasize larger trends and developments, but students sometimes get the wrong impression that everyone in a society thought alike. We hope that teachers can use these passages to get students thinking about diversity within and across societies. The thirty-four Viewpoints — one in each chapter — introduce students to working with sources, encourage critical analysis, and extend the narrative while giving voice to the people of the past. Each includes a brief introduction and questions for analysis. Carefully chosen for accessibility, each pair of documents presents views on a diverse range of topics, such as Chinese and Japanese Principles of Good Government, ca. 650; Roman and Byzantine Views of Barbarians; Creation in the *Popul Vuh* and in Okanogan Tradition; Lauro Quirini and Cassandra Fedele: Women and Humanist Learning; Christian Conversion in New Spain; Ottoman Travelers in Mughal and Safavid Lands; Poetry of the Great War; Gandhi and Mao on Revolutionary Means; and Ghanaian and South African Leaders on Black Nationalism.

Each chapter also continues to include a longer primary source feature titled **Listening to the Past**, chosen to extend and illuminate a major historical issue considered in each chapter. The feature presents a single original source or several voices on the subject. Each opens with an introduction and closes with questions for analysis that invite students to evaluate the evidence as historians would. Selected for their interest and significance and carefully placed within their historical context, these sources, we hope, allow students to "hear the past" and to observe how history has been shaped by individuals. **NEW** topics include Paleolithic Venus Figures; Aristotle, On the Family and On Slavery, from *The Politics*; Cicero and the Plot to Kill Caesar; Sixth-Century Biographies of Buddhist Nuns; Felipe Guaman Poma de Ayala, *The First New Chronicle and Good Government*; A German Account of Russian Life; Denis Diderot's "Supplement to Bougainville's Voyage"; Katib Chelebi on Tobacco; Abbé de Sieyès, "What Is the Third Estate?"; Mrs. Beeton's Guide for Running a Victorian Household; Mary Seacole on Her Early Life; and Aung San Suu Kyi, "Freedom from Fear."

In addition to using documents as part of our special feature program, we have quoted extensively from a wide variety of primary sources within the narrative, demonstrating in our use of these quotations that they are the "stuff" of history. Thus primary sources appear as an integral part of the narrative as well as in extended form in the Listening to the Past and new Viewpoints chapter features. We believe that this extensive program of both integrated and separate primary source excerpts will help readers learn to interpret and think critically.

In our years of teaching world history, we have often noted that students come alive when they encounter stories about real people in the past. To give students a chance to see the past through ordinary people's lives, each chapter includes one of the popular **Individuals in Society** biographical essays, each of which offers a brief study of an individual or group, informing students about the societies in which the individuals lived. This feature grew out of our long-standing focus on people's lives and the varieties of historical experience, and we believe that readers will empathize with these human beings who themselves were seeking to define their own identities. The spotlighting of individuals, both famous and obscure, perpetuates the book's continued attention to cultural and intellectual developments, highlights human agency, and reflects changing interests within the historical profession as well as the development of "micro-history." **NEW** features include essays on the Iceman, Hatshepsut and Nefertiti, Lord Mengchang, Queen Cleopatra, Josiah Wedgwood, Henry Meiggs, Liu Xiaobo, and Eva Perón.

Rounding out the book's feature program is the popular **Global Trade** feature, two-page essays that focus on a particular commodity, exploring the world trade, social and economic impact, and cultural influence of that commodity. Each essay is accompanied by a detailed map showing the trade routes of the commodity and an illustration. Retaining the eight essays of the previous edition on pottery, silk, spices, tea, slaves, indigo, oil, and arms, we have added two **NEW** features on iron and silver. We believe that careful attention to all of these essays will enable the student to appreciate the complex ways in which trade has connected and influenced the various parts of the world.

With the goal of making this the most student-centered edition yet, we paid renewed attention to the book's pedagogy. To help guide students, each chapter opens with a **Chapter Preview** with focus questions keyed to the main chapter headings. These questions are repeated within the chapter, and again in the **Chapter Reviews**. For this edition, many of the questions have been reframed, and new summary answers have been added to the chapter reviews. Each chapter review concludes with a carefully selected list of annotated **Suggestions for Further Reading**, revised and updated to stay current with the vast amount of new work being done in many fields.

To promote clarity and comprehension, bolded **key terms** in the text are defined in the margin and listed again in the chapter review. **NEW phonetic spellings** are located directly after terms that readers are likely to find hard to pronounce. The **chapter chronologies**, each of which reviews major developments discussed in the chapter, have been improved to more closely mirror the key events covered in the chapter, and the number of topic-specific **thematic chronologies** has been expanded, with new chronologies on Major Figures of the Enlightenment, and Key Events of the American Revolution, among others. Once again we also provide a **unified timeline** at the end of the text. Comprehensive and easy to locate, this useful timeline allows students to compare developments over the centuries.

The consistently high-quality art and map program has been thoroughly revised and expanded. The new edition features more than 530 **contemporaneous illustrations**. To make the past tangible, and as an extension of our attention to social and cultural history, we include over 90 **artifacts** ranging from swords and coins to a spinning wheel and a phonograph. As in earlier editions, all illustrations have been carefully selected to complement the text, and all include captions that inform students while encouraging them to read the text more deeply. Completely redesigned and reconceptualized for the new edition, **100 full-size maps** illustrate major developments in the narrative. In addition, **82 NEW spot maps** are embedded in the narrative to show specific areas under discussion. **NEW** maps in the ninth edition highlight such topics as Human Migration in the Paleolithic and Neolithic Eras; The Settling of the Americas Before 10,000 B.C.E.; Settlement of the Pacific Islands; The Slave Coast of West Africa; The Atlantic Economy in 1701; The Muslim World, ca. 1700; Emigration Out of Asia, 1820–1914; The Spanish-American War in the Philippines, 1898; Cold War Europe in the 1950s; and Authoritarian Governments in Latin America, among others.

We recognize students' difficulties with geography and visual analysis, and the new edition includes **NEW Mapping the Past map activities** and **NEW Picturing the Past visual activities**. Included in each chapter, these activities ask students to analyze the map or visual and make connections to the larger processes discussed in the narrative, giving them valuable practice in reading and interpreting maps and images.

To showcase the book's rich art program and to signal our commitment to this thorough and deep revision, the book has been completely redesigned. The dynamic new contemporary design engages and assists students with its clear, easy-to-use pedagogy.

Acknowledgments

It is a pleasure to thank the many instructors who read and critiqued the manuscript through its development:

Alemseged Abbay, Frostburg State University
Funso Afolayan, University of New Hampshire
Maria Arbelaez, University of Nebraska
Eva S. Baham, Southern University, Baton Rouge
David S. Bovee, Fort Hays State University
Nancy Cade, Pikesville College
Stephen D. Carls, Union University
Steven Cassedy, University of California
Edward J. Chess, Pulaski Technical College
Erwin F. Erhardt III, Thomas More College
Matthew D. Esposito, Drake University
Angela Feres, Grossmont Community College
Sam Giordanengo, Hawai'i Community College
Randee Goodstadt, Asheville-Buncombe Technical
    Community College
K. David Goss, Gordon College

William W. Haddad, California State Fullerton
Susan M. Hellert, University of Wisconsin, Platteville
John S. Hill, Immaculata University
Ellen Kittell, University of Idaho
Donald McGuire, SUNY Buffalo
April Najjaj, Greensboro College
Sandra L. Norman, Florida Atlantic University
Edward Paulino, John Jay College
Carolee Pollock, Grant MacEwan University
Charlotte Power, Black River Technical College
Salvador Rivera, SUNY Cobleskill
Mark Schneider, Suffok University and Bridgewater
   State
J. M. Simpson, Pierce College
Carrie Spencer, Pikes Peak Community College
Pamela Stewart, Arizona State University
Steven A. Stofferahn, Indiana State University
Jason M. Stratton, Bakersfield College
Deborah A. Symonds, Drake University
George Watters, St. Johns River Community College
Robert H. Welborn, Clayton State University
Marc Zayac, Georgia Perimeter College

It is also a pleasure to thank the many editors who have assisted us over the years, first at Houghton Mifflin and now at Bedford/St. Martin's. At Bedford/St. Martin's, these include senior development editor Laura Arcari; freelance development editors Beth Castrodale and Arthur Johnson; associate editors Lynn Sternberger and Jack Cashman; editorial assistant Arrin Kaplan; executive editor Traci Mueller Crowell; director of development Jane Knetzger; publisher for history Mary Dougherty; map editor Charlotte Miller; photo researcher Carole Frohlich; text permissions editor Heather Salus; and senior production editor Christina Horn, with the assistance of Laura Winstead, Laura Deily, and Elise Keller and the guidance of managing editor Elizabeth Schaaf and assistant managing editor John Amburg. Other key contributors were designer Brian Salisbury, page makeup artist Cia Boynton, copyeditor Sybil Sosin, proofreaders Susan Moore and Angela Morrison, indexer Leoni McVey, cover image researcher Donna Dennison, and cover designer Brian Salisbury. We would also like to thank editorial director Denise Wydra and president Joan E. Feinberg.

Many of our colleagues at the University of Illinois, the University of Washington, the University of Wisconsin–Milwaukee, and Eastern Illinois University continue to provide information and stimulation, often without even knowing it. We thank them for it. The authors also thank the many students over the years with whom we have used earlier editions of this book. Their reactions and opinions helped shape our revisions to this edition, and we hope it remains worthy of the ultimate praise that they bestowed on it, that it is "not boring like most textbooks." Merry Wiesner-Hanks would, as always, like to thank her husband Neil, without whom work on this project would not be possible. Clare Haru Crowston thanks her husband Ali and her children Lili, Reza, and Kian, who are a joyous reminder of the vitality of life that we try to showcase in this book. Roger Beck is thankful to Ann for keeping the home fires burning while he was busy writing and to the World History Association for all past, present, and future contributions to his understanding of world history.

Each of us has benefited from the criticism of his or her coauthors, although each of us assumes responsibility for what he or she has written. In addition to writing an entirely new Chapter 1, Merry Wiesner-Hanks substantially reworked and revised John Buckler's Chapters 2, 5, and 6 and has written and revised Chapters 8, 11, 14, and 15; Patricia Buckley Ebrey has written and revised Chapters 3, 4, 7, 9, 12, 13, 20, 21, 26, and 27; Roger B. Beck took responsibility for John McKay's Chapters 24 and 25 and has written and revised Chapters 10, 19, and 28–34; Clare Haru Crowston has assumed primary responsibility for Chapters 16–18 and 22 and also built upon text originally written by John McKay to revise and expand Chapter 23.

◻ VERSIONS AND SUPPLEMENTS

Adopters of *A History of World Societies* and their students have access to abundant extra resources, including documents, presentation and testing materials, the acclaimed Bedford Series in History and Culture volumes, and much more. See below for more information, visit the book's catalog site at **bedfordstmartins.com/mckayworld/catalog**, or contact your local Bedford/St. Martin's sales representative.

Get the Right Version for Your Class

To accommodate different course lengths and course budgets, *A History of World Societies* is available in several different formats, including three-hole-punched loose-leaf Budget Books versions and e-books, which are available at a substantial discount.

- Combined edition (Chapters 1–34) — available in hardcover, loose-leaf, and e-book formats
- Volume 1: To 1600 (Chapters 1–16) — available in paperback, loose-leaf, and e-book formats
- Volume 2: Since 1450 (Chapters 16–34) — available in paperback, loose-leaf, and e-book formats
- Volume A: To 1500 (Chapters 1–14) — available in paperback
- Volume B: From 800 to 1815 (Chapters 11–22) — available in paperback
- Volume C: From 1775 to the Present (Chapters 22–34) — available in paperback

The online, interactive **Bedford e-Book** can be examined or purchased at a discount at **bedfordstmartins.com/ebooks**; if packaged with the print text, it is available at no extra cost. Your students can also purchase *A History of World Societies* in other popular e-book formats for computers, tablets, and e-readers.

Online Extras for Students

The book's companion site at **bedfordstmartins.com/mckayworld** gives students a way to read, write, and study, and to find and access quizzes and activities, study aids, and history research and writing help.

FREE **Online Study Guide.** Available at the companion site, this popular resource provides students with quizzes and activities for each chapter, including multiple-choice self-tests that focus on important concepts; flashcards that test students' knowledge of key terms; timeline activities that emphasize causal relationships; and map quizzes intended to strengthen students' geography skills. Instructors can monitor students' progress through an online Quiz Gradebook or receive e-mail updates.

FREE **Research, Writing, and Anti-plagiarism Advice.** Available at the companion site, Bedford's **History Research and Writing Help** includes **History Research and Reference Sources**, with links to history-related databases, indexes, and journals; **More Sources and How to Format a History Paper**, with clear advice on how to integrate primary and secondary sources into research papers and how to cite and format sources correctly; **Build a Bibliography**, a simple Web-based tool known as The Bedford Bibliographer that generates bibliographies in four commonly used documentation styles; and **Tips on Avoiding Plagiarism**, an online tutorial that reviews the consequences of plagiarism and features exercises to help students practice integrating sources and recognize acceptable summaries.

Resources for Instructors

Bedford/St. Martin's has developed a wide range of teaching resources for this book and for this course. They range from lecture and presentation materials and assessment tools to course management options. Most can be downloaded or ordered at **bedfordstmartins.com/mckayworld/catalog**.

NEW ***HistoryClass for A History of World Societies.*** HistoryClass, a Bedford/St. Martin's Online Course Space, puts the online resources available with this textbook in one convenient and completely customizable course space. There you and your students can access an interactive e-book and primary sources reader; maps, images, documents, and links; chapter review quizzes; interactive multimedia exercises; and research and writing help. In HistoryClass you can get all our premium content and tools and assign, rearrange, and mix them with your own resources. For more information, visit **yourhistoryclass.com**.

Bedford Coursepack for Blackboard, WebCT, Desire2Learn, Angel, Sakai, or Moodle. We have free content to help you integrate our rich content into your course management system. Registered instructors can download coursepacks with no hassle and no strings attached. Content includes our most popular free resources and book-specific content for *A History of World Societies*. Visit

bedfordstmartins.com/cms to see a demo, find your version, or download your coursepack.

Instructor's Resource Manual. The instructor's manual offers both experienced and first-time instructors tools for preparing for lecture and running discussions. It includes chapter review material, teaching strategies, and a guide to chapter-specific supplements available for the text.

Guide to Changing Editions. Designed to facilitate an instructor's transition from the previous edition of *A History of World Societies* to the current edition, this guide presents an overview of major changes as well as of changes in each chapter.

Computerized Test Bank. The test bank includes a mix of fresh, carefully crafted multiple-choice, matching, short-answer, and essay questions for each chapter. It also contains the Review, Visual Activity, Map Activity, Individuals in Society, and Listening to the Past questions from the textbook and model answers for each. The questions appear in Microsoft Word format and in easy-to-use test bank software that allows instructors to easily add, edit, re-sequence, and print questions and answers. Instructors can also export questions into a variety of formats, including WebCT and Blackboard.

PowerPoint Maps, Images, Lecture Outlines, and i>clicker Content. Look good and save time with *The Bedford Lecture Kit*. These presentation materials are downloadable individually from the Instructor Resources tab at **bedfordstmartins.com/mckayworld/catalog** and are available on *The Bedford Lecture Kit* Instructor's Resource CD-ROM. They include ready-made and fully customizable PowerPoint multimedia presentations built around lecture outlines with embedded maps, figures, and selected images from the textbook and with detailed instructor notes on key points. Also available are maps and selected images in JPEG and PowerPoint formats; content for i>clicker, a classroom response system, in Microsoft Word and PowerPoint formats; the Instructor's Resource Manual in Microsoft Word format; and outline maps in PDF format for quizzing or handing out. All files are suitable for copying onto transparency acetates.

***Make History* — Free Documents, Maps, Images, and Web Sites.** *Make History* combines the best Web resources with hundreds of maps and images, to make it simple to find the source material you need. Browse the collection of thousands of resources by course or by topic, date, and type. Each item has been carefully chosen and helpfully annotated to make it easy to find exactly what you need. Available at **bedfordstmartins.com/makehistory**.

Videos and Multimedia. A wide assortment of videos and multimedia CD-ROMs on various topics in world history is available to qualified adopters through your Bedford/St. Martin's sales representative.

Package and Save Your Students Money

For information on free packages and discounts up to 50%, visit **bedfordstmartins.com/mckayworld/catalog**, or contact your local Bedford/St. Martin's sales representative.

Bedford e-Book. The e-book for this title, described above, can be packaged with the print text at no additional cost.

***Sources of World Societies*, Second Edition.** This two-volume primary source collection provides a revised and expanded selection of sources to accompany A *History of World Societies,* Ninth Edition. Each chapter features five or six sources by well-known figures and ordinary individuals alike. Now with visual sources and two more documents per chapter, this edition offers even more breadth and depth. Headnotes and questions supplement each document, while a new Viewpoints feature highlights two or three sources per chapter that address a single topic from different perspectives. Comparative questions ask students to make connections between sources and across time. Available free when packaged with the print text.

***Sources of World Societies* e-Book.** The reader is also available as an e-book. When packaged with the print or electronic version of the textbook, it is available for free.

The Bedford Series in History and Culture. More than one hundred titles in this highly praised series combine first-rate scholarship, historical narrative, and important primary documents for undergraduate courses. Each book is brief, inexpensive, and focused on a specific topic or period. For a complete list of titles, visit **bedfordstmartins.com/history/series**. Package discounts are available.

Rand McNally Historical Atlas of the World. This collection of almost seventy full-color maps illustrates the eras and civilizations in world history from the emergence of human societies to the present. Available for $3.00 when packaged with the print text.

The Bedford Glossary for World History. This handy supplement for the survey course gives students historically contextualized definitions for hundreds of terms — from *abolitionism* to *Zoroastrianism* — that they will encounter in lectures, reading, and exams. Available free when packaged with the print text.

World History Matters: A Student Guide to World History Online. Based on the popular "World History Matters" Web site produced by the Center for History and New Media, this unique resource, edited by Kristin Lehner (The Johns Hopkins University), Kelly Schrum (George Mason University), and T. Mills Kelly (George Mason University), combines reviews of 150 of the most useful and reliable world history Web sites with an introduction that guides students in locating, evaluating, and correctly citing online sources. Available free when packaged with the print text.

Trade Books. Titles published by sister companies Hill and Wang; Farrar, Straus and Giroux; Henry Holt and Company; St. Martin's Press; Picador; and Palgrave Macmillan are available at a 50% discount when packaged with Bedford/St. Martin's textbooks. For more information, visit **bedfordstmartins.com/tradeup**.

A Pocket Guide to Writing in History. This portable and affordable reference tool by Mary Lynn Rampolla provides reading, writing, and research advice useful to students in all history courses. Concise yet comprehensive advice on approaching typical history assignments, developing critical reading skills, writing effective history papers, conducting research, using and documenting sources, and avoiding plagiarism — enhanced with practical tips and examples throughout — have made this slim reference a bestseller. Package discounts are available.

A Student's Guide to History. This complete guide to success in any history course provides the practical help students need to be effective. In addition to introducing students to the nature of the discipline, author Jules Benjamin teaches a wide range of skills, from preparing for exams to approaching common writing assignments, and explains the research and documentation process with plentiful examples. Package discounts are available.

The origins of modern societies lie deep in the past. World historians increasingly begin their exploration of the human past millions of years ago, when humans evolved from a primate ancestor in eastern Africa. Humans migrated out of Africa in several waves, walking along coasts and over land, eventually spreading across much of the earth. Their tools were initially multipurpose sharpened stones and sticks, but gradually they invented more specialized tools that enabled them to obtain food more easily, make clothing, build shelters, and decorate their surroundings. Environmental changes, such as the advance and retreat of the glaciers, shaped life dramatically.

The Earliest Human Societies, to 2500 B.C.E.

Studying the physical remains of the past, scholars constructed a model of time and gave labels to eras according to the primary materials out of which tools that survived were made. (Constructing models of time is called "periodization.") Thus the earliest human era became the Stone Age, the next era the Bronze Age, and the next the Iron Age. They further divided the Stone Age into the Old Stone Age, or Paleolithic, during which people used stone, bone, and other natural products to make tools and obtained food largely by foraging, that is, by gathering plant products, trapping or catching small animals and birds, and hunting larger prey. This was followed by the New Stone Age, or Neolithic, which saw the beginning of agricultural and animal domestication. People around the world adopted agriculture at various times, and some never did, but the transition between the Paleolithic and the Neolithic is usually set at about 9000 B.C.E., the point at which agriculture was first developed.

In the Paleolithic period, people lived in small groups of related individuals, moving through the landscape in the search for food. Most had few material possessions, and social and gender hierarchies were probably much less pronounced than they would become later. Beginning around 50,000 B.C.E. people in many parts of the world began to decorate their surroundings and the objects they made, often with vivid representations of animals and people, and sometimes with symbols. These, and careful burials of the dead, suggest that people had developed ideas about supernatural or spiritual forces beyond the visible material world.

Beginning about 9000 B.C.E. people living in the Near East, and then elsewhere, began to plant seeds as well as gather wild crops, raise certain animals instead of hunt them, and selectively breed both plants and animals to make them more useful to humans. This domestication of plants and animals, called the agricultural revolution, was the most important change in human history. Crop-raising began as horticulture, in which people—often women—used hand tools to plant and harvest. Animal domestication began with sheep and goats, which were often herded from place to place so that they could eat the available vegetation, an economic system called pastoralism. The domestication of large animals such as cattle and water buffalo led to plow agriculture, through which humans could raise much more food. Agriculture required more labor than did foraging, but it allowed the human population to grow far more quickly.

The division of labor that plow agriculture required led to growing social hierarchies between those who could afford the new tools and products and those who could not. These were reinforced over generations as children inherited goods and status from their parents, and as social norms and laws were developed that led members of the elite to marry one another. Plow agriculture also strengthened differentiation based on gender; men became more associated with the world beyond the household and women with the domestic realm. Neolithic agricultural communities developed technologies to meet their needs, including pottery, cloth-weaving, and wheeled vehicles, and they often traded with one another for products that they could not obtain locally. In some parts of the world, production and trade included copper and bronze, although most tools continued to be made of stone, bone, and wood. Religious ideas came to reflect the new agricultural society, with fertility as the most important goal and the gods, like humans, arranged in a hierarchy.

Although today's complex world seems very different from that of the earliest human societies, some aspects of life in the Neolithic, and even the Paleolithic, were very slow to change. Foraging, horticulture, pastoralism, and agriculture have been the primary economic activities of most people throughout the entire history of the world. Though today there are only a few foraging groups in very isolated areas, there are significant numbers of horticulturalists and pastoralists, and their numbers were much greater just a century ago. At that point the vast majority of the world's people still made their living directly through agriculture. The social patterns set in early agricultural societies—with most of the population farming the land, and a small number of elite who lived off their labor—lasted for millennia.

The Ancient World, 3500 B.C.E.–500 C.E.

Ten thousand years ago, humans were living in most parts of the planet. They had designed technologies to meet the challenges presented by deep forests and jungles, steep mountains, and blistering deserts. As the climate changed, they adapted, building boats to cross channels created by melting glaciers, and finding new sources of food when old sources were no longer plentiful. In some places the new sources included domesticated plants and animals, which allowed people to live much more closely to one another than they had as foragers.

That proximity created opportunities, as larger groups of people pooled their knowledge to deal with life's challenges, but it also created problems. Human history from that point on can be seen as a response to these opportunities, challenges, and conflicts. As small villages grew into cities, people continued to develop technologies and systems to handle new issues. They created structures of governance based on something beyond the kin group to control their more complex societies, along with military forces and taxation systems to support the structures of governance. In some places they invented writing to record taxes, inventories, and payments, and they later put writing to other uses, including the preservation of stories, traditions, and history.

Writing, first developed around 3000 B.C.E., was perhaps the most important of the new technologies. Written sources provide a wider range of information about past societies than is available from physical evidence alone, which means that we know much more about the societies that left written records than about those that did not. Writing was developed to meet the needs of the more complex urban societies that are often referred to as civilizations, and particularly to meet the needs of the state, a new structure of governance distinct from tribes and kinship groups. In states, a small share of the population is able to coerce resources out of everyone else, and leaders gain and maintain power through organized violence, bureaucracies, systems of taxation, and written laws. These laws generally created more elaborate social and gender hierarchies.

Mesopotamia and Egypt

States first developed in Mesopotamia, the land between the Euphrates and Tigris Rivers. Starting in the southern part of Mesopotamia known as Sumeria, sustained agriculture reliant on irrigation resulted in larger populations, a division of labor, and the growth of cities. Priests and rulers invented ways to control and organize these complex societies, including armies, taxation systems, and cuneiform writing. Conquerors from the north unified Mesopotamian city-states into larger empires and spread Mesopotamian culture over a large area. The most significant of these was the Babylonian empire, which under King Hammurabi in 1790 B.C.E. developed a written code of law and expanded trade connections.

During the third millennium B.C.E., a period known as the Old Kingdom, Egypt grew into a cohesive state under a single ruler in the valley of the Nile, which provided rich farmland and an avenue of communication. The Egyptians developed powerful beliefs in life after death, and the focal point of religious and political life was the pharaoh, a god-king who commanded the wealth, resources, and people of Egypt. For long stretches of history Egypt was prosperous and secure in the fertile Nile Valley, although at times various groups migrated in seeking better lives or invaded and conquered. Often the newcomers adopted aspects of Egyptian religion, art, and politics, and the Egyptians adopted aspects of the newcomers' cultures, such as the Hyksos's techniques for making and casting bronze. During the period known as the New Kingdom (ca. 1550–1070 B.C.E.), warrior-pharaohs expanded their power beyond the Nile Valley and created the first Egyptian empire, during which they first fought and then allied with the iron-using Hittites.

After the collapse of the New Kingdom, the Nubian rulers of Kush conquered Egypt, and another group, the Phoenicians, came to dominate trade in the Mediterranean, spreading a letter alphabet.

For several centuries after the collapse of New Kingdom Egypt, a Semitic people known as the Hebrews or the Israelites controlled a small state on the western end of the Fertile Crescent. Their most important legacy was not political, but rather a new form of religious belief, Judaism, based on the wor-

The Golden Calf According to the Bible, Moses descended from Mount Sinai, where he had received the Ten Commandments, to find the Hebrews worshipping a golden calf, which was against Yahweh's laws. In July 1990 an American archaeological team found this model of a gilded calf inside a pot. The figurine, which dates to about 1550 B.C.E., is strong evidence of the existence of the cult represented by the calf in Palestine. (Harvard Semitic Museum, Ashkelon Excavations)

ship of a single all-powerful god, Yahweh. The Hebrews wrote down their religious ideas, traditions, laws, advice literature, prayers, hymns, history, and prophecies in a series of books, which came to define the Hebrews as a people. This group of books, the Hebrew Bible, describes the Covenant between Yahweh and the Hebrew people and sets out laws and traditions that structured Hebrew society and family life. Reverence for these written texts was passed from Judaism to the other Western monotheistic religions that grew from it, Christianity and Islam.

In the ninth century B.C.E. the Assyrians began a rise to power from northern Mesopotamia, creating an empire by means of often brutal military conquest. Assyria's success was also due to sophisticated, farsighted, and effective military tactics, technical skills, and organization. From a base in what is now southern Iran, the Persians established an even larger empire, developing effective institutions of government and building roads. Though conquerors, the Persians, unlike the Assyrians, usually respected their subjects and allowed them to practice their native customs, traditions, and religions. Around 600 B.C.E. a new religion based on the teachings of the prophet Zoroaster grew in Persia. This religion emphasized the individual's responsibility to choose between good and evil.

The Greeks

The people of ancient Greece developed a culture that fundamentally shaped the civilization of the western part of Eurasia. The Greeks were the first in the Mediterranean and neighboring areas to explore most of the philosophical questions that still concern thinkers today. Going beyond mythmaking, the Greeks strove to understand the world in logical, rational terms. The result was the birth of philosophy and science, subjects as important to many Greeks as religion. Drawing on their day-by-day experiences, the Greeks also developed the concept of politics, and their contributions to literature still fertilize intellectual life today.

The history of the Greeks is divided into two broad periods: the Hellenic, roughly the time between the founding of the first complex societies in the area that is now the Greek islands and mainland, about 3500 B.C.E., and the rise of the kingdom of Macedonia in the north of Greece in 338 B.C.E.; and the Hellenistic, the years from the reign of Alexander the Great (336–323 B.C.E.) through the spread of Greek culture from Spain to India (ca. 100 B.C.E.). During the Hellenic period Greeks developed a distinctive form of city-state known as the polis and made lasting cultural and intellectual achievements. During the Hellenistic period Macedonian and Greek armies defeated the Persian Empire and built new cities and kingdoms. During their conquests they blended their ideas and traditions with those of the societies they encountered, creating a vibrant culture.

In its earliest history, Greece's mountainous terrain and lack of navigable rivers led to political fragmentation. The Greeks developed the independent city-state, known as the polis, in which individuals governed themselves without

elaborate political machinery. The two most important poleis were Sparta and Athens, which formed new social and political structures. Sparta created a military state in which men remained in the army most of their lives and women concentrated on raising healthy soldiers. After much social conflict, Athens created a democracy in which male citizens both voted for their leaders and had a direct voice in an assembly. As was the case in all democracies in ancient Greece, women, slaves, and outsiders could not be citizens.

In the classical period, between 500 and 336 B.C.E., Greek civilization reached its highest peak in politics, thought, and art, even as it engaged in violent conflicts. The Greeks successfully defended themselves from Persian invasions but nearly destroyed themselves in the Peloponnesian War, which pitted Sparta and its allies against Athens and its allies. In the last half of the fifth century B.C.E. the brilliant Athenian leader Pericles turned Athens into the showplace of Greece by sponsoring the construction of temples and other buildings. In other artistic developments, wealthy Athenians paid for theater performances in which dramatists used their art in attempts to portray, understand, and resolve life's basic conflicts. This period also saw the rise of philosophy, and Socrates, Plato, and Aristotle began a broad examination of the universe and the place of humans in it.

In the middle of the fourth century B.C.E. the Greek city-states were conquered by King Philip II and his son Alexander, rulers of Macedonia to the north of Greece. A brilliant military leader, Alexander conquered the entire Persian Empire, along with many territories to the east of Persia. He also founded new cities in which Greek and local populations mixed. His successors continued to build cities and colonies, which became powerful instruments in the spread of Greek culture and in the blending of Greek traditions and ideas with those of other peoples. The mixing of peoples in the Hellenistic era influenced religion, philosophy, and science. In the scholarly realm, advances were made in mathematics, astronomy, and mechanical design.

The Greek world was largely conquered by the Romans, and the various Hellenistic monarchies became part of the Roman Empire. In cultural terms the lines of conquest were reversed: The Romans derived their alphabet from the Greek alphabet, though they changed the letters somewhat. Roman statuary was modeled on Greek and was often made by Greek sculptors, who found ready customers among wealthy Romans. The major Roman gods and goddesses were largely the same as the Greek ones, though they had different names.

The influence of the ancient Greeks was not limited to the Romans. Art and thought in northern India was shaped by the blending of Greek and Buddhist traditions. European thinkers and writers made conscious attempts to return to classical ideals in art, literature, and philosophy during the Renaissance. In America political leaders from the revolutionary era on decided that important government buildings should be modeled on the Parthenon and other temples, complete with marble statuary of their own heroes.

The Romans

Like the Persians and the Macedonians, the Romans conquered vast territories. Their singular achievement lay in their ability to incorporate conquered peoples into the Roman system. Roman history is usually divided into two periods. The first is the republic (509–27 B.C.E.), the age in which Rome grew from a small group of cities in the middle of the Italian peninsula to a state that ruled much of the Mediterranean. The second period is the empire (27 B.C.E.–476 C.E.), when the republican constitution gave way to rule by a single individual.

In its earliest development, Roman culture was influenced by the Etruscans, people who established permanent settlements in northern and central Italy. The Etruscans introduced the Romans to urbanism, industry, trade, and the alphabet. In 509 B.C.E. the Romans won independence from Etruscan rule and continued to expand their territories. They also established a republic, which functioned through a shared government of the people directed by the senate, summarized by the expression SPQR—*senatus populusque Romanus*, meaning "the Roman senate and people." In the resolution to a social conflict known as the Struggle of the Orders, nobles and ordinary people created a state administered by magistrates elected from the entire population and established a uniform law code.

In a series of wars the Romans conquered the Mediterranean, creating an overseas empire that brought them enormous power and wealth. Yet social unrest came in the wake of the war, opening unprecedented opportunities for ambitious generals who wanted to rule Rome like an empire. Civil war ensued, and it appeared as if the great politician and general Julius Caesar would emerge victorious, but he was assassinated by a group of senators. After his assassination and another period of civil war, his grandnephew Augustus finally restored peace and order to Rome, and assumed control as a single individual.

Augustus's success in creating solid political institutions was tested by the ineptness of some leaders who followed him, but later in the first century C.E. Rome entered a period of political stability, prosperity, and relative peace that lasted until the end of the second century C.E. During this period, later dubbed the pax Romana, the city of Rome became the magnificent capital of the empire. The Roman provinces and frontiers also saw extensive prosperity in the second century through the growth of agriculture, trade, and indus-

Ara Pacis In the middle years of Augustus's reign, the Roman senate ordered a huge altar, the Ara Pacis, built to honor him and the peace he had brought to the empire. It was decorated with life-size reliefs of Augustus and members of his family, prominent Romans, and other people and deities. One side shows a goddess figure, most likely the goddess Peace herself, with twin babies on her lap and surrounded by symbols of fertility and dominance, thus linking the imperial family with continued prosperity. (Scala/Art Resource, NY)

try, among other factors. As the Roman Empire expanded eastward from Europe, it met opposition, yet even during the fighting, commerce among the Romans and peoples who lived in central and southern Asia thrived along a series of trade routes.

One of the most significant developments during the time of Augustus was the beginning of Christianity. Christianity was a religion created by the followers of Jesus of Nazareth (ca. 3 B.C.E.–29 C.E.), a Jewish man who taught that belief in his divinity led to eternal life. His followers spread their belief across the Roman Empire, transforming Christianity from a Jewish sect into a new religion. Christian groups were informal at first, but by the second century they began to develop hierarchical institutions modeled on those of Rome. At first many pagans in the Roman Empire misunderstood Christian practices and rites, and as a result Christians suffered sporadic persecution under certain Roman emperors. Gradually, however, tensions between pagans and Christians lessened, particularly as Christianity modified its teachings to make them more acceptable to wealthy and educated Romans.

In terms of politics and economics, the prosperity of the Roman Empire in the second century C.E. gave way to a period of civil war, barbarian invasions, and conflict with foreign armies in the third century. These disrupted agriculture, trade, and production and damaged the flow of taxes and troops. At the close of the third century the emperor Diocletian ended the period of chaos, in part because he recognized that the empire had become too great for one man to handle. He therefore divided it into a western and an eastern half. Diocletian and his successor, Constantine, also took rigid control of the struggling economy, but their efforts were not successful. Free tenant farmers lost control of their lands, exchanging them for security that landlords offered against barbarians and other threats. Meanwhile, tolerance of Christianity grew, and Constantine legalized the practice of the religion throughout the empire. The symbol of all the changes in the empire became the establishment of its new capital, Constantinople, the New Rome.

From the third century onward the Western Roman Empire slowly disintegrated. The last Roman emperor in the West, Romulus Augustus, was deposed by the Ostrogothic chieftain Odoacer (OH-duh-way-suhr) in 476, but much of the empire had come under the rule of various barbarian tribes long before this. Thus despite the efforts of emperors and other leaders, by the fifth century the Western Roman Empire no longer existed, a development that scholars who focus on Europe have long seen as one of the great turning points in history.

India

The vast subcontinent of India, protected from outsiders by the towering Himalayan Mountains to the north and by oceans on its other borders, witnessed the development of several early civilizations, primarily in the richly cultivated valley of the Indus River, which flows about 1,980 miles be-

fore reaching the ocean. Only in the northwest—the area between modern Afghanistan and Pakistan—was India accessible to invasion. The northwest was also the area of the earliest civilization in India, the Harappan, which built large cities mostly of brick. After the decline of this civilization, the Aryans, a nomadic Indo-European people, entered India by way of the Khyber Pass around 1500 B.C.E. They were able to establish dominance over large areas, including the eastern regions of the Ganges River. By 500 B.C.E. the Aryans ruled a number of large kingdoms in which cities were the centers of culture. The period of Aryan rule saw the evolution of a caste system designed to denote birth or descent and to distinguish Aryan from non-Aryan and rulers from the ruled. The four groups, or castes, that emerged—the *Brahman* (priests), the *Kshatriya* (warriors), the *Vaishya* (peasants), and the *Shudra* (serfs)—became the dominant features of Indian society. Persons without a place in the hierarchical strata or who lost their caste status because of some violation of ritual were *outcastes.*

Through the Khyber Pass in 513 B.C.E. the Persian king Darius I entered India and conquered the Indus Valley. The Persians introduced political administration and coin-minting techniques, and they brought India into commercial and cultural contact with the sophisticated ancient Middle East. From the Persians the Indians adopted the Aramaic language and script, which they adapted to their needs and languages. In 326 B.C.E. the Macedonian king Alexander the Great invaded the Indus Valley, but his conquests had no lasting effect. Under Ashoka (r. 269–232 B.C.E.), ancient India's greatest ruler, India enjoyed peace and stability, but from 180 B.C.E. to 200 C.E. the region suffered repeated foreign invasions. There was no dominant unifying state, and regional cultures flourished. In the northwest rulers such as the Shakas and Kushans came from outside India.

Ancient India's most enduring legacies are the three great religions that flowered in the sixth and fifth centuries B.C.E.: Hinduism, Jainism, and Buddhism. One of the modern world's largest religions, Hinduism holds that the Vedas—hymns in praise of the Aryan gods—are sacred revelations and that these revelations prescribe the caste system. Religiously and philosophically diverse, Hinduism assures believers that there are many legitimate ways to worship Brahma, the supreme principle of life. India's best-loved hymn, the *Bhagavad Gita*, guides Hindus in a pattern of life in the world and of release from it.

Jainism derives from the teachings of the great thinker Vardhamana Mahavira (ca. 540–468 B.C.E.), who held that only an ascetic life leads to bliss and that all life is too sacred to be destroyed. Nonviolence is a cardinal principle of Jainism. Thus a Jain who wishes to do the least violence to life turns to vegetarianism.

Mahavira's contemporary, Siddhartha Gautama (ca. 563–483 B.C.E.), better known as the Buddha, was so deeply distressed by human suffering that he abandoned his Hindu beliefs in a search for ultimate enlightenment. Meditation

Gandharan Frieze Depicting the Buddha This carved stone from ca. 200 C.E. is one in a series portraying scenes from the life of the Buddha. From the Gandharan kingdom located in modern Pakistan, the frieze depicts the Buddha seated below the bo tree, where he was first enlightened. (Freer Gallery of Art, Smithsonian Institution, Washington, D.C., Purchase, F1949.9b, F1954.20)

alone, he maintained, brought total enlightenment in which everything is understood. Buddha developed the "Eightfold Path," a series of steps of meditation that could lead to *nirvana*, a state of happiness attained by the extinction of self and human desires. Buddha opposed all religious dogmatism and insisted that anyone, regardless of sex or class, could achieve enlightenment. He attracted many followers, and although Buddhism split into several branches after his death, Buddhist teachings spread throughout India to China, Japan, Korea, and Vietnam. Buddhism remains one of the great Asian religions and in recent times has attracted adherents in the West.

China

Chinese civilization, which developed initially along the Huang He (Yellow) River, was much farther away from the ancient Middle East than India and had much less in the way of contact with other early civilizations. Still, the Shang Dynasty (ca. 1200 B.C.E.) shared features of other early civilizations, such as bronze technology, cities, and writing. The writing system China developed, with separate symbols for each word, had no connection to the writing systems of other parts of Eurasia and became a key feature of Chinese culture.

The Chinese always looked back on the Zhou period (ca. 1000–256 B.C.E.) as their classical age, when social and political ideas were perfected. After a few centuries, political unity was lost, and China consisted of many states, large and small, that made alliances with each other but also frequently fought each other. Political disorder seems to have stimulated philosophy, and this became the period when "one hundred schools of thought contended." Compared to Indian religious speculation, Chinese thinkers were more secular than religious in outlook. Interested primarily in social and economic problems, they sought universal rules of human conduct from the level of the family up to that of the state. Ancient China witnessed the development of Confucianism, Daoism, and Legalism, philosophies that profoundly influenced subsequent Chinese society and culture.

Confucius (551–479 B.C.E.) was interested in orderly and stable human relationships, and he focused on the proper duties and behavior of the individual. Confucius considered the family the basic unit in society. Within the family, male was superior to female and age to youth. If order was to exist in society, he taught, it must start at the level of the family. Those who help the king govern should be gentlemen, by which he meant men who exhibited the virtues of loyalty, sincerity, deference, generosity, and commitment. Only gentlemanly conduct, which involved a virtuous and ethical life, would lead to well-run government and peaceful conditions in society at large. Self-discipline, courtesy to others, punctiliousness in service to the state, and justice to the people are the obligations and behaviors expected of Confucian gentlemen. Confucius minimized the importance of class distinctions and taught that men of humble birth could achieve a high level of conduct and become gentlemen through education and self-discipline. The fundamental ingredient in the evolution of the Chinese civil service, Confucianism continued to shape Chinese government up to the twentieth century.

Daoism treated the problems of government very differently. In its two surviving books, *Laozi* and *Zhuangzi*, each named after a Daoist master, earnest efforts to perfect society were ridiculed. Daoism maintained that people would be happier only if they abandoned the world and reverted to simpler ways. Daoists insisted that the best government is the least active government. Public works and government services require higher taxes, which lead to unhappiness and popular resistance. According to the Daoists, the people should be kept materially satisfied and uneducated. A philosophy of consolation, Daoism was especially popular among those who were frustrated by the political system.

Legalism is the name given to a number of related political theories originating in the third century B.C.E. The founders of Legalism proposed pragmatic solutions to the problems of government, exalted the power of the state, and favored an authoritarian ruler who would root out dissent. They argued that laws should be made known, the penalties for infractions should be clear and harsh, and the laws and penalties should apply to everyone in society, even the close relatives of the ruler. Though Legalism seemed too harsh to many, it did contribute to the Chinese system of centralized bureaucratic rule.

In the third century B.C.E. the state of Qin adopted Legalism and then set out to defeat all the other states, thus unifying China. The Qin government attempted to achieve uniformity at many levels, standardizing weights and measures, writing systems, and laws. It even tried to do away with ideas it disapproved of by collecting and burning books. The new dynasty was called *Qin*, from which the Western term "China" derives. Under the Qin Dynasty and its successor, the Han, China achieved political and social stability and economic prosperity. On its northern border, however, Qin and Han faced tough military opponents in the Xiongnu, pastoralists who excelled at horsemanship.

The period of the Han Dynasty (206 B.C.E.–220 C.E.) witnessed notable intellectual achievements. First, many of the books that had been burned by the Qin were reconstructed from memory or hidden copies. These texts came to be known as the *Confucian Classics*. Scholars piously studied the books and worked to make them widely accessible as standards of moral behavior. Second, historical writing developed. The historian Sima Qian (145–ca. 85 B.C.E.) produced the *Records of the Grand Historian*, a massive and comprehensive survey of earlier Chinese civilization. These two sets of writings left a permanent mark on Chinese thought and peoples.

The Islamic World, 600–1400

One of the most important developments in world history—whose consequences redound to our own day—was the rise and remarkable expansion of Islam in the early Middle Ages. Muhammad (ca. 570–632), a devout merchant of

Separating Men and Women in a Mosque In this mid-sixteenth-century illustration of the interior of a mosque, a screen separates the women, who are wearing veils and tending children, from the men. The women can hear what is being said, but the men cannot see them. (Bodleian Library, University of Oxford, Ms. Ouseley Add 24, fol. 55v)

Mecca in present-day Saudi Arabia, called on his followers to return to god. Even before Muhammad's death his teachings spread through Arabia, uniting the tribes there. Within two centuries his followers controlled Syria, Palestine, Egypt, Iraq, Iran, northern India, Spain, and southern France, and his beliefs were carried eastward across Central Asia to the borders of China. In the ninth, tenth, and eleventh centuries the Muslims created a brilliant civilization centered at Baghdad in Iraq and Córdoba in Spain.

Muhammad believed that God sent him messages or revelations. These were later collected and published as the Qur'an, from an Arabic word meaning "reading" or "recitation." On the basis of God's revelations to him, Muhammad preached a strictly monotheistic faith based on the principle of the absolute unity and omnipotence of God. Since God is all-powerful, believers must submit to him. *Islam* means "submission to God," and the community of Muslims consists of those who have submitted to God by accepting the final revelation of his message as set forth by Muhammad. (Earlier revelations of God, held by Muslims to be the same God worshipped by Jews and Christians, had come from the prophets Abraham, Moses, and Jesus, whose work Muslims believe Muhammad completed.)

The Arabs carried their religion to the east and west by military conquest. Their rapid expansion was made possible by their own economic needs, the political weaknesses of their enemies, a strong military organization, and the practice of establishing army camps in newly conquered territories. In time, many of those in the conquered lands converted to Islam.

The assassination of one of the caliphs, or successors of Muhammad, led to a division within the Islamic community. When the caliph Ali (r. 656–661) was murdered, his followers claimed that, because he was related by blood to Muhammad and because Muhammad had designated him leader of the community prayer, he had been Muhammad's prescribed successor. These supporters of Ali were called *Shi'ites*, or *Shi'a*, partisans of Ali; they claimed to possess special divine knowledge that Muhammad had given his heirs. Other Muslims adhered to traditional beliefs and practices of the community based on precedents set by Muhammad. They were called *Sunnis*, a term derived from the Arabic *Sunna*, a collection of Muhammad's sayings and conduct in particular situations. This schism within Islam continues today. Sufism, an ascetic movement within Islam that sought a direct and mystical union with God, drew many followers from all classes.

Long-distance trade and commerce, which permitted further expansion of the Muslim faith, played a prominent role in the Islamic world, in contrast to the limited position it held in the heavily agricultural medieval West. The Black and Caspian Seas, the Volga River giving access deep into Russia, the Arabian Sea and the Indian Ocean, and to a lesser extent the Mediterranean Sea were the great commercial waterways of the Islamic world. Goods circulated freely over them. Muslim commercial tools such as the bill of exchange, the check, and the joint stock company were borrowed by Westerners. Many economic practices basic to capitalism were used by Muslim merchants and businessmen long before they became common in the West.

Long-distance trade brought the wealth that supported a gracious and sophisticated culture in the cities of the Muslim world. Baghdad in Iraq and Córdoba in Spain, whose streets were thronged with a kaleidoscope of races, creeds, customs, and cultures and whose many shops offered goods from all over the world, stand out as superb examples of cosmopolitan Muslim civilization. Baghdad and Córdoba were also great intellectual centers where Muslim scholars made advances in mathematics, medicine, and philosophy. The Arabs translated many ancient Greek texts by writers such as Plato and Aristotle. When, beginning in the ninth century, those texts were translated from Arabic into Latin, they came to play an important part in the formation of medieval European scientific, medical, and philosophical thought. Modern scholars consider Muslim civilization in the period from about 900 to 1200 among the most brilliant in the world's history.

Asia, 300–1400

Between about 300 and 1400 the various societies of Asia continued to evolve their own distinct social, political, and religious institutions. Also in these years momentous changes swept across Asia. Buddhism spread from India to Central Asia, China, Korea, Japan, Southeast Asia, and Tibet. Arab conquerors and their Muslim faith reached the Indian subcontinent. The Turks, moving west from the Chinese border, converted to Islam. China, under the Tang and Song Dynasties, experienced a golden age. Japan emerged into the light of written history. The Mongols formed a confederation of the tribes of the steppes of Inner Asia that had extraordinary success in conquering cities from Korea and China to Persia, Baghdad, and Russia. These centuries witnessed cultural developments that have molded and influenced later Asian societies.

India

Under the Gupta kings, who ruled from around 320 to 500, India enjoyed a great cultural flowering. Interest in Sanskrit literature—the literature of the Aryans—led to the preservation of much Sanskrit poetry. A distinctly Indian drama appeared, and India's greatest poet, Kalidasa (ca. 380–450), like Shakespeare, blended poetry and drama. Mathematicians arrived at the concept of zero, essential for higher mathematics, and scientific thinkers wrestled with the concept of gravitation.

The Gupta kings succeeded in uniting much of the subcontinent. They also succeeded in repulsing an invasion by the Huns, but the effort exhausted the dynasty. After 600

India reverted to the pattern of strong local kingdoms in frequent conflict. Between 600 and 1400, India suffered repeated invasion as waves of Arabs, Turks, and Mongols swept down through the northwest corridor. The most successful were Turks from the area of modern Afghanistan, who held power in Delhi for three centuries and managed to turn back the Mongols. By around 1400 India was as politically splintered as it had been before Gupta rule. Under the Turks Islam became dominant in the Indus Valley (modern Pakistan). Elsewhere Hinduism resisted Islam.

One other development had a lasting effect on Indian society: the proliferation and hardening of the caste system. Early Indian society had been divided into four major groups. After the fall of the Guptas, further subdivisions arose, reflecting differences of profession, trade, tribal or racial affiliation, religious belief, and even place of residence. By 800 India had more than three thousand castes, each with its own rules and governing body. As India was politically divided, the castes served to fragment it socially.

China

Scholars consider the period between 580 and 1200, which saw the rule of Tang and Song Dynasties, as China's golden age. In religion, political administration, agricultural productivity, and art, Chinese society attained a remarkable level of achievement. This era was followed by the rise of the Mongols, who in time engulfed China.

Merchants and travelers from India introduced Buddhism to China from the first century C.E. on. Scholars, rulers, the middle classes, and the poor all found appealing concepts in Buddhist teachings, and the new faith won many adherents. China distilled Buddhism to meet its own needs, and Buddhism gained a place next to Confucianism and Daoism in Chinese life.

The Tang Dynasty, which some historians consider the greatest in Chinese history, built a state bureaucracy, the political sophistication of which was unequaled until recent times. Tang emperors subdivided the imperial administration into departments of military organization, maintenance and supply of the army, foreign affairs, justice, education, finance, building, and transportation. To staff this vast administration, an imperial civil service developed in which education, talent, and merit could lead to high office, wealth, and prestige. So effective was the Tang civil service and so deeply rooted did it become in Chinese society that it lasted until the twentieth century.

Under the Song Dynasty (960–1279), greatly expanded agricultural productivity, combined with advances in the technology of coal and iron and efficient water transport, supported a population of 100 million. (By contrast, Europe did not reach this figure until the late eighteenth century.) Greater urbanization followed in China. Political stability and economic growth fostered technological innovation, the greatest being the invention of printing. Tang craftsmen invented the art of carving words and pictures into wooden blocks, inking the blocks, and then pressing them onto paper. The invention of movable type followed in the eleventh century. As would happen in Europe in the fifteenth century, the invention of printing lowered the price and increased the availability of books and contributed to the spread of literacy. Printing led to the use of paper money, replacing bulky copper coinage, and to developments in banking. The highly creative Tang and Song periods also witnessed the invention of gunpowder, originally used for fireworks, and the abacus, which permitted the quick computation of complicated sums. In the creation of a large collection of fine poetry and prose, and in the manufacture of porcelain of superb quality and delicate balance, the Tang and Song periods revealed an extraordinary literary and artistic flowering.

Shipbuilding advanced, and large ships were used both for war and for trade. Trade expanded as Japan and Korea eagerly imported Chinese silks and porcelains. The Muslims shipped Chinese goods across the Indian Ocean to East African and Middle Eastern markets. Southern China participated in a commercial network that stretched from Japan to the Mediterranean.

The thirteenth century witnessed the violent and amazingly fast creation of the Mongol Empire, the largest continuous land empire in world history. The Mongols were a steppe nomadic people in north-central Asia who had fought largely among themselves until about 1200. Their extraordinary expansion was the result of a shortage of pasture land for their sheep, goats, and cattle, and the rise of a great warrior-leader, Chinggis Khan (1162–1227), who united the steppe peoples and led them to conquer and absorb one

Woman Attendant The Song emperors were patrons of a still-extant temple in northern China that enshrined a statue of the "holy mother," the mother of the founder of the ancient Zhou Dynasty. The forty-two maids who attend her, one of whom is shown here, seem to have been modeled on the palace ladies who attended Song emperors. (© Cultural Relics Press) neighbor after another. Building a vast army of loyal followers to whom he displayed great generosity, and using a policy of terror as a weapon of war, Chinggis swept across Central Asia into northern China. In 1215, he burned Beijing, and many Chinese governors quickly submitted. Chinggis then turned westward and destroyed the Persian Empire, massacring hundreds of thousands of people. Under Chinggis's sons, the Mongols won control of Kievan Russia and Moscow, looted cities in Poland and Hungary, and established the Khanate of the Golden Horde. Chinggis's grandson Khubilai (r. 1260–1294) completed the conquest of China and overran Korea. The Mongols viewed China as their most important conquest; Mongol rule extended over most of East Asia, which they called the Great Khanate. They even invaded, but did not conquer, Japan. The Chinese called the period of Mongol rule the Yuan Dynasty. In 1368 Hungwu, the first emperor of the Ming Dynasty, restored Chinese rule.

Japan

The chain of islands that constitutes Japan entered written history only in sporadic references in Chinese writings, the most reliable set down in 297 C.E. Because the land of Japan is rugged, lacking navigable waterways, and because perhaps only 20 percent of it is arable, political unification by land proved difficult until modern times. The Inland Sea served both as the readiest means of communication and as a rich source of food; the Japanese have traditionally been fishermen and mariners.

Early Japan was divided into numerous political units, each under the control of a particular clan, a large group of families claiming descent from a common ancestor and worshipping a common deity. In the third century C.E. the Yamato clan gained control of the fertile area south of modern Kyoto near Osaka Bay and subordinated many other clans. The Yamato chieftain proclaimed himself emperor and assigned specific duties and functions to subordinate chieftains. The Yamato established their chief shrine in the eastern part (where the sun-goddess could catch the first rays of the rising sun) of Honshu, the largest of Japan's four main islands. Around this shrine local clan cults sprang up, giving rise to a native religion that the Japanese called Shinto, the "Way of the Gods." Shinto became a unifying force and protector of the nation.

Through Korea two significant Chinese influences entered Japan and profoundly influenced Japanese culture: the Chinese system of writing and record keeping, and Buddhism. Under Prince Shotoku (574–622), talented young Japanese were sent to Tang China to learn Chinese methods of administration and Chinese Buddhism. They returned to Japan to share and enforce what they had learned. The Nara era of Japanese history (710–794), so called after Japan's first capital city, north of modern Osaka, was characterized by the steady importation of Chinese ideas and methods. Buddhist monasteries became both religious and political centers, supporting Yamato rule.

Perhaps because Buddhist temples had too much power in Nara, in 794 the imperial family removed the capital to Heian (modern Kyoto), where it remained until 1867. A strong reaction against Buddhism and Chinese influences followed, symbolized by the severance of relations with China in 838. The eclipse of Chinese influences liberated Japanese artistic and cultural forces, and a new Japanese style of art and architecture appeared. In writing, Japanese scholars produced two syllabaries, sets of phonetic signs that stand for syllables instead of whole words or letters. Unshackled from Chinese forms, Japanese writers created their own literary styles and modes of expression. The writing of history and poetry flowered, and the Japanese produced their first novel, *The Tale of Genji*, a classic of court life by the court lady Lady Murasaki written over several years (ca. 1000–1010).

The later Heian period witnessed the breakdown of central authority as aristocrats struggled to free themselves from imperial control. In 1156 civil war among the leaders of the great clans erupted. By 1192 the Minamato clan had defeated all opposition. Its leader Yoritomo (1147–1199) became *shogun*, or general-in-chief. Thus began the Kamakura Shogunate, which lasted from 1185 until 1333.

In addition to the powerful shogun, a dominant figure in the new society was the *samurai*, the warrior who by the twelfth century exercised civil, judicial, and military power over the peasants who worked the land. The samurai held his land in exchange for his promise to fight for a stronger lord. In a violent society strikingly similar to that of western Europe in the early Middle Ages, the Japanese samurai, like the French knight, constituted the ruling class at the local level. Civil war among the emperor, the leading families, and the samurai erupted again in 1331. In 1338 one of the most important military leaders, Ashikaga Takauji, defeated the emperor and established the Ashikaga Shogunate, which lasted until 1573. Meanwhile, the samurai remained the significant social figure.

By 1400 the continents of Africa, Asia, and Europe experienced considerable cultural contact with one another. Chinese silks passed across the Great Silk Road to southwestern Asia and Europe. The religious ideals of Buddhism spread from India to China and Korea. The expansion of Islam across northern Africa and into the Iberian Peninsula, down the east coast of Africa, across Central Asia and into northern India, and through the Malay Archipelago led to rich commercial contacts. Religious and philosophical ideas, artistic and architectural models, and scientific and medical learning flowed across these international trade routes. The centuries that witnessed the European religious-military-imperialistic expeditions to the Middle East known as the Crusades (ca. 1100–1300) led to the slow filtering of Muslim (and ancient Greek) medical and architectural knowledge to Europe. By way of Islam, features of Chinese technology, such as paper manufacture, and nautical information, such as the compass and the astrolabe, reached Europe.

African Societies and Kingdoms, 1000 B.C.E.–1500 C.E.

Africa is a huge continent with many different climatic zones and diverse geography. The peoples of Africa are as diverse as the topography. Groups relying on herd animals developed in the drier, disease-free steppe regions well-suited to domesticated animals, while agricultural settlements developed in the wetter savanna regions. In the tropical forests of central Africa and arid zones of southern Africa, hunter-gatherers dominated. Along the coasts and by lakes and rivers grew maritime communities whose inhabitants relied on fishing and trade for their livelihood.

Because the peoples south of the Sahara are generally described as "black" Africans, the inappropriate concept of race has engendered fierce debate over just who is African. For example, since the days of ancient Greece, historians have debated whether Egypt, because of its proximity to the Mediterranean, should be identified as part of Africa or as part of the Mediterranean world. Race as a concept for determining one's "Africanness" has today generally been discredited as extremist.

Agriculture began very early in Africa. Knowledge of plant cultivation arrived in the Nile Delta in Egypt about the fifth millennium B.C.E. Settled agriculture then traveled down the Nile Valley and moved west across the Sahel to the central and western Sudan. Early societies across the western Sudan were profoundly affected as they switched from hunting and gathering in small bands to form settled farming communities. Populations increased significantly in this rich savanna zone that was ideally suited for grain production. Blood kinship brought together families in communities governed by chiefs or local councils. Animistic religions that recognized ancestral and nature spirits developed. The nature spirits were thought to dwell in nearby streams, forests, mountains, or caves.

Settled agriculture developed independently in West Africa. From there it spread to the equatorial forests. The spread of agriculture was related to the expansion of Bantu-speaking peoples, who originated in the Benue region, the borderlands of modern Cameroon and Nigeria. In the second millennium B.C.E. they began to spread south and east into the forest zone of equatorial Africa, eventually spreading across all of central and southern Africa. Possessing iron tools and weapons, domesticated livestock, and a knowledge of settled agriculture, these Bantu-speakers assimilated, killed, or drove away all the previous inhabitants of these regions.

Lines of trade and communication linked many parts of Africa with each other and with other parts of the world. The peoples of North Africa were closely connected with the Middle Eastern and European civilizations of the Mediterranean basin. Similarly, the peoples of the Swahili coast of east Africa participated in trade with Arabia, the Persian Gulf, India, China, and the Malay Archipelago.

Between 700 and 900, a network of caravan routes running south from the Mediterranean coast across the Sahara to the Sudan developed. Arab-Berber merchants exchanged manufactured goods for African gold, ivory, gum, and slaves from the West African savanna. The most essential component in the trans-Saharan trade was the camel. The camel made it possible for great loads to be hauled across vast stretches of hot, dry desert. The Berbers of North Africa endured these long treks south and then north again across the Sahara. To control this trade they fashioned camel saddles that gave them great political and military advantage. The primary items of trade were salt from the north and gold from the south, although textiles, fruit, ivory, kola nuts, gum, beads, and other goods were also prized by one side or the other. Enslaved West Africans, males and females, were also traded north to slave markets in Morocco, Algiers, Tripoli, and Cairo.

The trans-Saharan trade had three important effects on West African society. First, it stimulated gold mining. Second, it increased the demand for West Africa's second most important commodity, slaves. Third, the trans-Saharan trade stimulated the development of large urban centers in West Africa, such as Gao, Timbuktu, Koumbi Saleh, Sijilmasa, and Jenne. In the period after 700 it had a fourth major effect, introducing Islam to West African society. Conversion led to the involvement of Muslims in African governments, bringing efficient techniques of statecraft and advanced scientific knowledge and engineering skills. Between the ninth and fifteenth centuries, Islam greatly accelerated the development of the African kingdoms. Through the trans-Saharan trade, Africans living in the Sahel zone of West Africa became part of the larger world of Islam.

The period from 800 to 1450 witnessed the flowering of several powerful African states. In the western Sudan, the large empires of Ghana (ca. 900–1100) and Mali (ca. 1200–1450) arose. Each had an elaborate royal court, a massive state bureaucracy, a sizable army, a sophisticated judicial system, and a strong gold industry. The fame of Ghana rested on gold, and when the fabulously rich Mali king Mansa Musa (r. ca. 1312–1337), a devout Muslim, made a pilgrimage to Mecca, his entourage included one hundred elephants, each carrying one hundred pounds of gold.

Mali's strength resulted from two fundamental assets. First, its strong agricultural and commercial base provided for a large population and enormous wealth. Second, Mali had two rulers, Sundiata and Mansa Musa, who combined military success with exceptionally creative personalities. The city of Timbuktu developed into a great center of scholarship and learning. Architects, astronomers, poets, lawyers, mathematicians, and theologians flocked there. Intermarriage between Arab and North African Muslim intellectuals and traders and local women brought into being a group of racially mixed people. The necessity of living together harmoniously, the traditional awareness of diverse cultures, and the cosmopolitan atmosphere of Timbuktu all contributed to a rare degree of racial toleration and understanding.

Meanwhile, the East African coast gave rise to powerful city-states such as Kilwa, Mombasa, and Mogadishu, which maintained a rich maritime trade with India, China, and the Muslim cities of the Middle East. Like the western Sudan, the East African cities were much affected by Muslim influences. Like East Africa, South Africa was made up of city-states, chief among them Great Zimbabwe, which flourished between the eleventh and fifteenth centuries. Located at the southernmost reach of the Indian Ocean trade network, these city-states exchanged their gold for the riches of Arabia and Asia. Somewhat more isolated, the kingdom of Aksum in Ethiopia utilized its access to the Red Sea to trade north to the Mediterranean and south to the Indian Ocean.

The East African city-states and the kingdoms of the western Sudan were part of the world of Islam. Arabian merchants brought Islam with them as they settled along the East African coast, and Berber traders brought Islam to West Africa. Differing from its neighbors, Ethiopia was a unique enclave of Christianity in the midst of Islamic societies. The Bantu-speaking peoples of Great Zimbabwe were neither Islamic nor Christian, but practiced indigenous forms of worship such as animism.

The Americas, 2500 B.C.E.–1500 C.E.

The first humans settled in the Americas between 40,000 and 15,000 B.C.E., after emigrating from Asia. The melting of glaciers 13,000 to 11,000 years ago separated the Americas from Afroeurasia, and the Eastern and Western Hemispheres developed in isolation from one another. There were many parallels, however: In both hemispheres people initially gathered and hunted their food, and then some groups began to plant crops, adapting plants that were native to the areas they settled. Techniques of plant domestication spread, allowing for population growth. In certain parts of both hemispheres, efficient production and transportation of food supplies led to the growth of cities and to larger political entities such as states and empires.

In the Americas, all the highly varied environments, from polar tundra to tropical rain forests, came to support human settlement. About 8000 B.C.E. people in some parts of the Americas began raising crops as well as gathering wild produce. Maize became the most important crop, with knowledge about its cultivation spreading from Mesoamerica—present-day Mexico and Central America—into North and South America.

Agricultural advancement led to an increase in population, which allowed for greater concentrations of people and the creation of the first urban societies. Towns dependent on agriculture flourished in certain parts of North and South America. Some groups in North America began to build large earthwork mounds; others in Mesoamerica and South America practiced irrigation. The Olmecs created the first society with cities in Mesoamerica, with large ceremonial buildings, an elaborate calendar, and a symbolic writing.

The urban culture of the Olmecs and other Mesoamerican peoples influenced subsequent societies. Especially in what became known as the classical era (300–900 C.E.), various groups developed large states centered on cities, with high levels of technological and intellectual achievement. Of these, the Maya were the longest-lasting, creating a complex written language, multiple-crop milpas (fields) and raised beds for agriculture, roads connecting population centers, trading practices that built unity among Maya communities as well as wealth, and striking art. Peoples living in North America built communities that were smaller than those in Mesoamerica but many also used irrigation techniques to enhance agricultural production and continued to build earthwork mounds for religious purposes.

In Mesoamerica, the Aztecs, also known as the Mexica, built a unified culture based on the heritage of earlier societies and distinguished by achievements in engineering, sculpture, and architecture, including the streets, canals, public squares, and aqueduct of Tenochtitlán, the most spectacular and one of the largest cities in the world in 1500. In Mexica society, religion was the dynamic factor that transformed other aspects of the culture: economic security, social mobility, education, and especially war. War was an article of religious faith, providing riches and land, sacrificial victims for ceremonies honoring the Aztec gods, warriors for imperial expansion, and laborers. Aztec society was hierarchical, with nobles and priests having special privileges.

In the Andes, Inca achievements built on those of cultures that preceded theirs, including the Moche and Chavin civilizations. Moche, Chavin, and Inca cultures made their home in the valleys along the Peruvian coast and in the Andean highlands, cultivating food crops and cotton. The Incas, who began as a small militaristic group, eventually created the largest empire in South America in the fifteenth century and conquered surrounding groups. Their far-flung empire stretched along the Andes and was kept together by a system of roads, along which moved armies and administrators. The Incas achieved imperial unification by imposing their gods on conquered peoples, forcing local chieftains to participate in the central bureaucracy, and pursuing a policy of colonization. The imperial expansion that increased the Incas' strength also caused stress. Andean society was dominated by clan groups, and Inca measures to disrupt these groups and move people great distances created resentment.

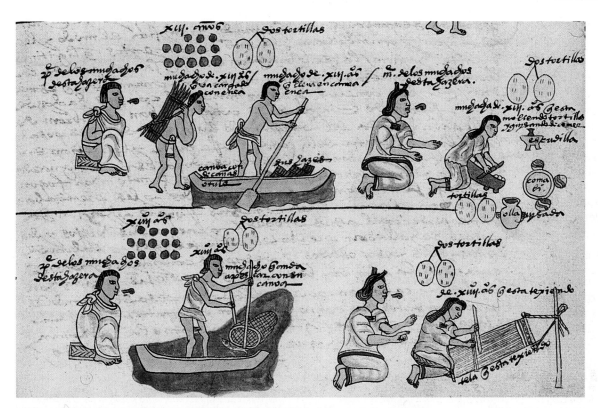

Aztec Adolescents This scene of adults supervising the tasks that young people at each age (indicated by dots) were expected to learn appeared in a painted book made by Mexica artists in the middle of the sixteenth century. It includes Nahuatl and Spanish words, including "dos [two] tortillas," the basic amount of food the artists thought was appropriate for these adolescents. (The Bodleian Library, University of Oxford, MS Arch. Selden. A.1, fol. 60r)

Europe, 500–1500

In the fifteenth century, scholars in Europe began the practice of dividing European history into different periods. They called the time of Greece and Rome the ancient or classical era, and the thousand-year period between the fall of the Western Roman Empire and their own day the Middle Ages. This three part division—ancient, medieval, and modern—has been very influential, even in areas beyond Europe.

The Middle Ages

The transition from ancient to medieval was a slow process, not a single event. The primary agents in this process of change were the barbarian tribes whose migrations broke the Roman Empire apart. The barbarians brought different social, political, and economic structures with them. Although Greco-Roman art and architecture still adorned the land and people continued to travel on Roman roads, the roads were rarely maintained, and travel itself was much less secure than during the empire. Merchants no longer traded over long distances, so people's access to goods produced outside their local area plummeted. There was inter-marriage and cultural assimilation among Romans and barbarians, but there was also violence and great physical destruction.

The Eastern Roman Empire, called the Byzantine Empire, did not fall to barbarian invasions. During the sixth and seventh centuries the Byzantine Empire survived waves of attacks, owing to effective military leadership and to fortifications around Constantinople. From this strong position Byzantine emperors organized and preserved Roman institutions, and the Byzantine Empire lasted until 1453, nearly a millennium longer than the Roman Empire in the West. In particular, the emperor Justinian oversaw creation of the *Code*, which distilled the legal genius of the Romans into a coherent whole, eliminated outmoded laws and contradictions, and clarified the law itself. Just as they valued the law, the Byzantines prized education, and because of them many masterpieces of ancient Greek literature survived to influence the intellectual life of the modern world. In mathematics and science, the Byzantines passed Greco-Roman learning on to the Arabs.

Along with Byzantium, the Christian Church was an important agent of continuity in the transition from ancient to medieval in Europe. Christianity gained the support of the fourth-century emperors and gradually adopted the Roman system of hierarchical organization. The church possessed able administrators and leaders whose skills were tested in the chaotic environment of the end of the Roman Empire in the West. Bishops expanded their activities, and in the fifth century the bishops of Rome, taking the title "pope," began to stress their supremacy over other Christian communities. Monasteries offered opportunities for individuals to develop deeper spiritual devotion and also provided a model of Christian living, methods that advanced agricultural development, and places for education and learning. Missionaries and church officials spread Christianity within and far beyond the borders of what had been the Roman Empire, transforming a small sect into the most important and wealthiest institution in Europe, North Africa, and the eastern Mediterranean.

Christian thinkers reinterpreted the classics in a Christian sense, incorporating elements of Greek and Roman philosophy and of various pagan religious groups into Christian teachings. Missionaries and priests got pagan and illiterate peoples to understand and become more accepting of Christianity by preaching the basic teachings of the religion, stressing similarities between pagan customs and beliefs and those of Christianity, and introducing the ritual of penance and the veneration of saints.

Classical and Christian traditions modified those of barbarian society, although barbarian political systems were very different from those of Rome. Barbarians generally had no notion of the state as we use the term today; they thought in social, not political, terms. The basic social unit was the tribe, made up of kin groups formed by families. Family groups lived in small agriculture-based villages, where there were great differences in wealth and status. Most barbarian kingdoms were weak and short-lived, though the kingdom of the Franks was relatively more unified and powerful. Rulers first in the Merovingian dynasty of the fifth century, and then in the Carolingian of the eighth century, used military victories, strategic marriage alliances, and the help of the church to enhance their authority.

The Frankish kingdom broke down in the late ninth century, and continental Europe was fractured politically. No European political power was strong enough to put up effective resistance to external attack, which came from many directions. Vikings from Scandinavia carried out raids for plunder along the coasts and rivers of Europe and traveled as far as Iceland, Greenland, North America, and Russia. In many places they set up permanent states, as did the Magyars, who came into central Europe from the east. From the south came Muslims, who conquered Sicily and drove northward into Italy. All these invasions as well as civil wars weakened the power of kings, and local nobles became the strongest powers against external threats. They established a new form of decentralized government, later known as feudalism, similar to that of Japan in the era of the samurai. Common people turned to nobles for protection, paying with their land, labor, and freedom.

Beginning in the last half of the tenth century, the invasions that had contributed to European fragmentation gradually ended, and domestic disorder slowly subsided. Feudal rulers began to develop new institutions of law and government that enabled them to assert their power over lesser lords and the general population. Centralized states slowly crystallized, first in western Europe in the eleventh century, and then in eastern and northern Europe. An era of relative stability and prosperity followed, generally known as the "High Middle Ages," which lasted until climate change and disease brought calamity in the fourteenth century.

At the same time that rulers expanded their authority, energetic popes built their power within the Western Christian Church. They asserted their superiority over kings and emperors, though these moves were sometimes challenged by those secular rulers. Monasteries continued to be important places of learning and devotion, and new religious orders were founded. Meanwhile, Christianity expanded into Europe's northern and eastern regions, and Christian rulers expanded their holdings in Muslim Spain. On a more personal scale, religion structured people's daily lives and the yearly calendar.

A papal call to retake the holy city of Jerusalem from the Muslims led to nearly two centuries of warfare between Christians and Muslims. Christian warriors, clergy, and settlers moved in all directions from western and central Europe, so that through conquest and colonization border regions were gradually incorporated into a more uniform European culture. The enormous popular response to the pope's call reveals the influence of the papacy and the new sense that war against the church's enemies was a duty of nobles. The Crusades were initially successful, and small Christian states were established in the Middle East. They did not last very long, however, and other effects of the Crusades were disastrous: Jewish communities in Europe were regularly attacked; relations between the Western and Eastern Christian Churches were poisoned by the Crusaders' attack on Constantinople; and Christian-Muslim relations became more uniformly hostile than they had been earlier.

For most people, the High Middle Ages did not bring dramatic change. The vast majority of medieval Europeans were rural peasants who lived in small villages and worked their own and their lords' land. Peasants led hard lives, and most were bound to the land, although there were some opportunities for social mobility. Nobles were a tiny fraction of the total population, but they exerted great power over all aspects of life. Aristocratic values and attitudes, often called chivalry, shaded all aspects of medieval culture. Medieval towns and cities grew initially as trading centers and recruited people from the countryside with the promise of greater freedom and new possibilities. They also became centers of production, and merchants and artisans formed guilds to protect their livelihoods. Not everyone in medieval towns and cities shared in the prosperity, however; many residents lived hand-to-mouth on low wages.

The towns that became centers of trade and production in the High Middle Ages also developed into cultural and intellectual centers. Trade brought in new ideas as well as merchandise, and in many cities a new type of educational institution—the university—emerged from cathedral and municipal schools. Universities developed theological, legal, and medical courses of study based on classical models and provided trained officials for the new government and church bureaucracies. People also wanted permanent visible representations of their piety, and church and city leaders supported the building of churches and cathedrals as symbols of their Christian faith and their civic pride. Cathedrals grew larger and more sumptuous, with high towers, soaring arches, and exquisite stained-glass windows in a style known as Gothic. New types of vernacular literature arose in which poems, songs, and stories were written down in local dialects.

In the fourteenth century the prosperity of the High Middle Ages ended. Bad weather brought poor harvests, which contributed to an international economic depression and fostered disease. The Black Death caused enormous population losses and had social, psychological, and economic consequences. Additional difficulties included the Hundred Years' War between England and France, which devastated much of the French countryside and bankrupted England; a schism among rival popes that weakened the Western Christian Church; and peasant and worker frustrations that exploded in uprisings. These revolts were usually crushed, though noble landlords were not always successful in reasserting their rights to labor services instead of cash rents.

The Renaissance and the Reformation

While Europe suffered greatly in the fourteenth century, a new culture was beginning to emerge in southern Europe. First in Italy and then elsewhere scholars, writers, and artists thought that they were living in a new golden age, later termed the Renaissance, French for "rebirth." The word *renaissance* was used initially to describe art that seemed to recapture, or perhaps even surpass, the glories of the classical past, and then came to be used for many aspects of life of the period. The new attitude diffused slowly out of Italy, with the result that the Renaissance "happened" at different times in different parts of Europe.

The Renaissance was characterized by self-conscious awareness among fourteenth- and fifteenth-century Italians, particularly scholars and writers known as humanists, that they were living in a new era. Key to this attitude was a serious interest in the Latin classics, a belief in individual potential, and a more secular attitude toward life. Humanists opened schools to train boys and young men for active lives of public service, but they had doubts about whether humanist education was appropriate for women. As humanism spread to northern Europe, religious concerns became more pronounced, and Christian humanists set out plans for the reform of church and society. Their ideas were spread to a much wider audience than those of early humanists as a result of the development of the printing press with movable metal type, which revolutionized communication. Interest in the classical past and in the individual shaped Renaissance art in terms of style and subject matter. Also important to Renaissance art were the wealthy patrons who helped fund it.

Social hierarchies in the Renaissance developed new features that contributed to the modern social hierarchies of race, class, and gender. The distinction between free people and slaves was one such hierarchy. Although slavery in Europe was not limited to Africans during the Renaissance, increasing numbers of black Africans entered Europe as slaves to supplement the labor force, and black skin color was increasingly viewed as a mark of inferiority. In terms of class, the medieval hierarchy of orders based on function in society intermingled with a new hierarchy that created a new social elite whose status was based on wealth. In regard to gender, the Renaissance debate about women led many to discuss women's nature and proper role in society, a discussion sharpened by the presence of a number of ruling queens in this era. Nevertheless, women continued to lag behind men in social status and earnings.

During the Renaissance the feudal monarchies of medieval Europe gradually evolved into nation-states. Beginning in the fifteenth century rulers in western Europe used aggressive methods to build up their governments, reducing violence, curbing unruly nobles, and establishing domestic order. They emphasized royal majesty and royal sovereignty and insisted on the respect and loyalty of all subjects. War and diplomacy were important ways that states increased their power, and so was marriage. Because almost all of Europe was ruled by hereditary dynasties, claiming and holding resources involved shrewd marital alliances.

Religious reformers carried out even more dramatic changes than did humanists, artists, or rulers. Calls for reform of the Christian Church began very early in its history and continued throughout the Middle Ages, but in the sixteenth century these calls gained wide acceptance. The Western Christian Church, generally known as the Roman Catholic Church, had serious problems that stretched from local parishes and monasteries to the pope in Rome. Many individuals and groups were discontented with the power and wealth of the church, and even with some basic church teachings. This discontent helps explain why the ideas of one reformer, Martin Luther, found such a ready audience. Luther and other Protestants developed a new understanding of Christian doctrine that emphasized faith, the power of God's grace, and the centrality of the Bible. Protestant ideas were attractive to the literate middle classes, and they spread rapidly through preaching, hymns, and the printing press. The progress of the Reformation was shaped by the political situation in the Holy Roman Empire, the decentralization of which allowed the Reformation to spread. In England the king's need for a church-approved divorce triggered the break with Rome, and a Protestant church was established. Protestant ideas also spread into France and eastern Europe. In all these areas, a second generation of reformers, most prominently John Calvin, developed their own theology and plans for institutional change.

The Roman Catholic Church responded slowly to the Protestant challenge, but by the middle of the sixteenth century the papacy was leading a movement for reform within the church that became known as the Catholic Reformation. Popes supported improvements in education for clergy, banned the selling of church offices, established a special court to deal with suspected heretics, and required bishops to live in their territories rather than in palaces in Rome. Every diocese, the territory governed by a bishop, was supposed to establish a seminary for training clergy. In terms of doctrine, popes and the general council of the church that met at Trent (1545–1563) reaffirmed existing Catholic teachings on the importance of tradition as well as Scripture and the importance of good works as well as faith. New religious orders such as the Jesuits and the Ursulines spread Catholic ideas through teaching, and in the case of the Jesuits through missionary work.

Religious differences led to riots, civil wars, and international conflicts in the later sixteenth century. In France and the Netherlands, Calvinist Protestants and Catholics attacked each other, and religious differences mixed with political and economic grievances. Long civil wars resulted, with the civil war in the Netherlands becoming an international conflict. War ended in France with the Edict of Nantes, in which Protestants were given some civil rights, and in the Netherlands with the division of the country into a Protestant north and a Catholic south. The era of religious wars was also marked by the most extensive witch persecutions in European history, as both Protestants and Catholics tried to rid their cities and states of people they regarded as linked to the Devil.

The Renaissance and the Reformation are often seen as key to the creation of the modern world. The radical changes of these times contained many elements of continuity, however. Artists, humanists, and religious reformers looked back to the classical era and early Christianity for inspiration, viewing those times as better and purer than their own. Political leaders played important roles in cultural and religious developments, just as they had for centuries in Europe and other parts of the world.

The events of the Renaissance and Reformation thus were linked with earlier developments, and they were also closely connected with another important element in the modern world: European exploration and colonization, which you will study in depth in Chapter 16 of this book. Renaissance monarchs paid for expeditions' ships, crews, and supplies, expecting a large share of any profits gained and increasingly viewing overseas territory as essential to a strong state. Only a week after Martin Luther stood in front of Emperor Charles V at a meeting of German rulers in the city of Worms and declared his independence in matters of religion, Ferdinand Magellan, a Portuguese sea captain using Spanish ships, was killed by indigenous people in a group of islands off the coast of southeast Asia. Charles V had provided the backing for Magellan's voyage, the first to circumnavigate the globe. Magellan viewed one of the purposes of his trip as the spread of Christianity, and later in the sixteenth century institutions created as part of the Catholic Reformation, including the Jesuit order, would operate in European colonies overseas as well as in Europe itself. The islands where Magellan was killed were later named the Philippines, in honor of Charles's son Philip. The desire for fame, wealth, and power that was central to the Renaissance and the religious zeal that was central to the Reformation were thus key to the European voyages and to colonial ventures as well.

• **Mexica Noble** This image from the early-seventeenth-century indigenous *Codex Ixtlilxochitl* shows a Mexica noble holding flowers and a tube of tobacco in his right hand. His gold necklace, turquoise bracelets, ear ornaments, and decorated cape emphasize his wealth and social standing. (Codex Ixtlilxochitl, Facsimile edition by ADEVA, Graz, Austria)

16

Before 1500 Europeans were relatively marginal players in a centuries-old trading system that linked Africa, Asia, and Europe. Elite classes everywhere prized Chinese porcelains and silks, while wealthy Chinese wanted ivory and black slaves from East Africa and exotic goods and peacocks from India. African people wanted textiles from India and cowrie shells from the Maldives. Europeans craved spices and silks, but they had few desirable goods to offer their trading partners.

The Indian Ocean was the locus of these desires and commercial exchanges, which sparked competition among Arab, Persian, Turkish, Indian, African, Chinese, and European merchants and adventurers. They fought each other for the trade that brought great wealth. They also jostled with Muslim scholars, Buddhist teachers, and Christian missionaries, who competed for the religious adherence of the peoples of Sumatra, Java, Borneo, and the Philippine Islands.

The Acceleration of Global Contact
1450–1600

The European search for better access to Asian trade goods led to a new overseas empire in the Indian Ocean and the accidental discovery of the Western Hemisphere. With this discovery South and North America soon joined an international network of trade centers and political empires, which Europeans came to dominate. The era of globalization had begun, creating new forms of cultural exchange, assimilation, conversion, and resistance. Europeans sought to impose their cultural values on the peoples they encountered while struggling to comprehend them and their societies. The Age of Discovery from 1450 to 1650, as the time of these encounters is known, laid the foundations for the modern world as we know it today. •

The Afroeurasian Trade World Before Columbus
☐ What was the Afroeurasian trade world like before the voyages of Columbus?

The European Voyages of Discovery
☐ Why and how did Europeans undertake ambitious voyages of expansion?

The Impact of Conquest
☐ How did conquest affect indigenous populations and bring about a new era of economic and cultural exchange, commercial empires, and forced migrations?

Changing Values and Beliefs
☐ How did new encounters shape cultural values and beliefs in Europe and the New World?

The Afroeurasian Trade World Before Columbus

☐ What was the Afroeurasian trade world like before the voyages of Columbus?

Historians now recognize that a type of world economy, known as the Afroeurasian trade world, linked the products and people of Europe, Asia, and Africa in the fifteenth century. Before Christopher Columbus began his voyages to the New World in 1492, the West was not the dominant player in world trade. Nevertheless, wealthy Europeans were eager consumers of luxury goods from the East, which they received through Venetian and Genoese middlemen.

The Trade World of the Indian Ocean

The Indian Ocean was the center of the Afroeurasian trade world, serving as a crossroads for commercial and cultural exchanges between China, India, the Middle East, Africa, and Europe (Map 16.1). From the seventh through the fourteenth centuries, the volume of this trade steadily increased, declining only during the years of the Black Death.

Merchants congregated in a series of multicultural, cosmopolitan port cities strung around the Indian Ocean. Most of these cities had some form of autonomous self-government, and mutual self-interest had largely limited violence and attempts to monopolize trade. The most developed area of this commercial web was made up of the ports surrounding the South China Sea. In the fifteenth century the port of Malacca became a great commercial entrepôt (AHN-truh-pôh), a trading post to which goods were shipped for storage while awaiting redistribution to other places. To Malacca came Chinese porcelains, silks, and camphor (used in the manufacture of many medications); pepper, cloves, nutmeg, and raw materials such as sandalwood from the Moluccas; sugar from the Philippines;

and Indian textiles, copper weapons, incense, dyes, and opium.

The Mongol emperors opened the doors of China to the West, encouraging Europeans like the Venetian trader and explorer Marco Polo to do business there. Marco Polo's tales of his travels from 1271 to 1295 and his encounter with the Great Khan (one of the successors of the famous Mongol ruler Chinggis Khan) fueled Western fantasies about the Orient. After the Mongols fell to the Ming Dynasty in 1368, China entered a period of agricultural and commercial expansion, population growth, and urbanization. Historians agree that China had the most advanced economy in the world until at least the beginning of the eighteenth century.

China also took the lead in exploration, sending Admiral Zheng He's fleet as far west as Egypt. (See "Individuals in Society: Zheng He," page 463.) From 1405 to 1433, each of his seven expeditions involved hundreds of ships and tens of thousands of men. In one voyage alone, Zheng sailed more than 12,000 miles, compared to Columbus's 2,400 miles on his first voyage some sixty years later.[1] Although the ships brought back many wonders, such as giraffes and zebras, the purpose of the voyages was primarily diplomatic, to enhance China's prestige and seek tribute-paying alliances. The voyages came to a sudden halt after the deaths of Zheng and the emperor who initiated his voyages, probably due to court opposition to their high cost and contact with foreign peoples.

By ending large-scale exploration on China's part, this decision marked a turning point in history. Nonetheless, Zheng He's voyages left a legacy of increased Chinese trading in the South China Sea and Indian Ocean. Following Zheng He's voyages, tens of thousands of Chinese emigrated to the Philippines, where they acquired commercial dominance of the island of Luzon by 1600.

Another center of Indian Ocean trade was India, the crucial link between the Persian Gulf and the Southeast Asian and East Asian trade networks. The subcontinent had ancient links with its neighbors to the northwest: trade between South Asia and Mesopotamia dates back to the origins of human civilization. Trade among ports bordering the Indian Ocean was revived in the Middle Ages by Arab merchants who circumnavigated India on their way to trade in the South China Sea. The need for stopovers led to the establishment of trading posts at Gujarat and on the Malabar coast, where the cities of Calicut and Quilon became thriving commercial centers.

The inhabitants of India's Coromandel coast traditionally looked to Southeast Asia, where they had ancient trading and cultural ties. Hinduism and Buddhism arrived in Southeast Asia from India during the Middle Ages, and a brisk trade between Southeast Asian and Coromandel port cities persisted from that time until the arrival of the Portuguese in the sixteenth century. India itself was an important contributor of goods to the world trading system. Most of the world's pepper was grown in India, and Indian cotton and silk textiles, mainly from the Gujarat region, were also highly prized.

Peoples and Cultures of the Indian Ocean

Indian Ocean trade connected peoples from the Malay Peninsula (the southern extremity of the Asian continent), India, China, and East Africa, among whom there was an enormous variety of languages, cultures,

and religions. In spite of this diversity, certain sociocultural similarities linked these peoples, especially in Southeast Asia.

For example, by the fifteenth century, inhabitants of what we call Indonesia, Malaysia, the Philippines, and the many islands in between all spoke languages of the Austronesian family, reflecting continuing interactions among them. A common environment led to a diet based on rice, fish, palms, and palm wine. Rice, harvested by women, is probably indigenous to the region, and it formed the staple of the diet. The seas provided many varieties of fish, crabs, and shrimp, and fishing served as the chief male occupation, well ahead of agriculture. Also, sugar cane

The Port of Calicut in India The port of Calicut, located on the west coast of India, was a center of the Indian Ocean spice trade during the Middle Ages. Vasco da Gama arrived in Calicut in 1498 and obtained permission to trade there, leading to hostilities between the Portuguese and the Arab traders who had previously dominated the port. (Private Collection/The Stapleton Collection/The Bridgeman Art Library)

CALECHVT CELEBERRI:
MVM INDIÆ EMPORIVM.

MAP 16.1 The Fifteenth-Century Afroeurasian Trading World After a period of decline following the Black Death and the Mongol invasions, trade revived in the fifteenth century. Muslim merchants dominated trade, linking ports in East Africa and the Red Sea with those in India and the Malay archipelago. The Chinese admiral Zheng He's voyages (1405–1433) followed the most important Indian Ocean trade routes, hoping to impose Ming dominance of trade and tribute.

grew in profusion, and it was chewed as a confectionery and used as a sweetener.[2]

In comparison to India, China, or even Europe after the Black Death, Southeast Asia was sparsely populated. People were concentrated in port cities and in areas of intense rice cultivation.

Another difference between Southeast Asia and India, China, and Europe was the higher status of women in the region. Their primary role in planting and harvesting rice gave them authority and economic power. At marriage, which typically occurred around age twenty, the groom paid the bride (or sometimes her family) a sum of money called **bride wealth**, which remained under her control. This practice was in sharp contrast to the Chinese, Indian, and European dowry,

which came under the husband's control. Property was administered jointly, in contrast to the Chinese principle and Indian practice that wives had no say in the disposal of family property. All children, regardless of gender, inherited equally, and when Islam arrived in the region, the rule requiring sons to receive double the inheritance of daughters was never implemented.

Respect for women carried over to the commercial sphere. Women participated in business as partners and independent entrepreneurs, even undertaking long sea voyages to accompany their wares. When Portuguese and Dutch men settled in the region and married local women, their wives continued to play important roles in trade and commerce.

In contrast to most parts of the world other than Africa, Southeast Asian peoples had an accepting attitude toward premarital sexual activity, and no premium was placed on virginity at marriage. Divorce carried no social stigma, and it was easy if a pair proved

• **bride wealth** In early modern Southeast Asia, a sum of money the groom paid the bride or her family at the time of marriage, in contrast to the husband's control of dowry in China, India, and Europe.

Individuals in Society

Zheng He

IN 1403 THE CHINESE EMPEROR YONGLE ordered his coastal provinces to build a vast fleet of ships, with construction centered at Longjiang near Nanjing. The inland provinces were to provide wood for the ships and float it down the Yangzi River. Thirty thousand shipwrights, carpenters, sailmakers, ropers, and caulkers worked in a frenzy. As work progressed, Yongle selected a commander for the fleet. The emperor chose Zheng He (1371–1433), despite fearing that the thirty-five-year-old was too old for so politically important an expedition. The decision rested on Zheng's unquestioned loyalty, strength of character, energy, ability, and eloquence. These qualities apparently were expected to compensate for Zheng's lack of seamanship.

The southwestern province of Yunnan, where Zheng was born, had a large Muslim population, and he was raised in that faith. When the then prince Zhi Di defeated the Mongols in Yunnan, Zheng's father was killed in the related disorder. The young boy was taken prisoner and, as was the custom, castrated. Raised in Zhi Di's household, he learned to read and write, studied Confucian writings, and accompanied the prince on all military expeditions. By age twenty Zheng was not the soft, effeminate stereotype of the eunuch; rather he was "seven feet tall and had a waist five feet in circumference. His cheeks and forehead were high . . . [and] he had glaring eyes . . . [and] a voice loud as a bell. . . . He was accustomed to battle." Zheng must have looked imposing. A devout Muslim, he persuaded the emperor to place mosques under imperial protection after a period of persecution. On his travels, he prayed at mosques at Malacca and Hormuz. Unable to sire sons, he adopted a nephew. When Zheng became a naval commander under Yongle, he was the first eunuch in Chinese history to hold such an important position.

The fleet for Zheng's first expedition was composed of 317 ships, including junks, supply ships, water tankers, warships, transports for horses, and patrol boats, and carried twenty-eight thousand sailors and soldiers; it was the largest naval force in world history before World War I. Because it bore tons of beautiful porcelains, elegant silks, lacquer ware, and exquisite artifacts to be exchanged for goods abroad, it was called the "treasure fleet."

Between 1405 and 1433, Zheng led seven voyages, which combined the emperor's diplomatic, political, geographical, and commercial goals (see Map 16.1). During the voyages he worked toward Yongle's goal of securing China's hegemony over tributary states and collecting pledges of loyalty from them. Zheng also sought information on winds, tides, distant lands, and rare plants and animals, and he sailed as far west as Egypt to gather it. Because smallpox epidemics had recently hit China, another purpose of his voyages was to gather pharmacological products. An Arab text on drugs and therapies was secured and translated into Chinese. He also brought back a giraffe and mahogany, a wood ideal for ships' rudders because of its hardness.

Just before his death, Zheng recorded his accomplishments on stone tablets. The expeditions had unified "seas and continents . . . the countries beyond the horizon from the ends of the earth have all become subjects . . . and the distances and routes between distant lands may be calculated," implying that China had accumulated considerable geographical information. From around the Indian Ocean, official tribute flowed to the Ming court as a result of Zheng's efforts. A vast immigration of Chinese people into Southeast Asia, sometimes called the Chinese diaspora, came into being after the expeditions. Immigrants carried with them Chinese culture, including social customs, diet, and practical objects of Chinese technology— calendars, books, scales for weights and measures, and musical instruments. With legends collected about him and monuments erected to him, Zheng became a great cult hero.

Source: Louise Levathes, *When China Ruled the Seas: The Treasure Fleet of the Dragon Throne, 1405–1433* (New York: Oxford University Press, 1996).

QUESTIONS FOR ANALYSIS

1. What do the voyages of the treasure fleet tell us about China in the fifteenth century?
2. What was Zheng He's legacy?

Zheng He (right), voyager to India, Persia, Arabia, and Africa. (From Lo Monteng, *The Western Sea Cruises of Eunuch San Pao*, 1597)

incompatible. Either the woman or the man could initiate a divorce, and common property and children were divided.

Trade with Africa and the Middle East

On the east coast of Africa, Swahili-speaking city-states engaged in the Indian Ocean trade, exchanging ivory, rhinoceros horn, tortoise shells, copra (dried coconut), and slaves for textiles, spices, cowrie shells, porcelain, and other goods. The most important cities were Mogadishu, Mombasa, and Kilwa, which had converted to Islam by the eleventh century. Peopled by confident and urbane merchants, the cities were known for their prosperity and culture.

West Africa also played an important role in world trade. In the fifteenth century most of the gold that reached Europe came from Sudan in West Africa and, in particular, from the kingdom of Mali near present-day Ghana. Transported across the Sahara by Arab and African traders on camels, the gold was sold in the ports of North Africa. Other trading routes led to the Egyptian cities of Alexandria and Cairo, where the Venetians held commercial privileges.

Inland nations that sat astride the north-south caravan routes grew wealthy from this trade. In the mid-thirteenth century the kingdom of Mali emerged as an important player on the overland trade route. In later centuries, however, the diversion of gold away from the trans-Sahara routes would weaken the inland states of Africa politically and economically.

Gold was one important object of trade; slaves were another. Slavery was practiced in Africa, as virtually everywhere else in the world, even before the arrival of Europeans. Arabic and African merchants took West African slaves to the Mediterranean to be sold in European, Egyptian, and Middle Eastern markets and also brought eastern Europeans to West Africa as slaves. In addition, Indian and Arabic merchants traded slaves in the coastal regions of East Africa.

The Middle East served as an intermediary for trade between Europe, Africa, and Asia and was also an important supplier of goods for foreign exchange, especially silk and cotton. Two great rival empires, the Persian Safavids and the Turkish Ottomans, dominated the region, competing for control over western trade routes to the East. By the mid-sixteenth century the Ottomans had established control over eastern Mediterranean sea routes to trading centers in Syria, Palestine, Egypt, and the rest of North Africa. Their power also extended into Europe as far west as Vienna.

Mansa Musa This detail from the Catalan Atlas of 1375 depicts a king of Mali, Mansa Musa, who was legendary for his wealth in gold. European desires for direct access to the trade in sub-Saharan gold helped inspire Portuguese exploration of the west coast of Africa in the fifteenth century. (Bridgeman-Giraudon/Art Resource, NY)

Genoese and Venetian Middlemen

Compared to the East, Europe constituted a minor outpost in the world trading system, for European craftsmen produced few products to rival those of Asia. However, Europeans desired luxury goods from the East, and in the late Middle Ages such trade was controlled by the Italian city-states of Venice and Genoa. Venice had opened the gateway to Asian trade in 1304, when it established formal relations with the sultan of Mamluk Egypt and started operations in Cairo. In exchange for European products like Spanish and English wool, German metal goods, Flemish textiles, and silk cloth made with imported raw materials, the Venetians obtained luxury items like spices, silks, and carpets. They accessed these from middlemen in the eastern Mediterranean and Asia Minor. Because Eastern demand for these European goods was low, Venetians made up the difference by earning currency in the shipping industry and through trade in firearms and slaves.

Venice's ancient trading rival was Genoa. By the time the Crusades ended around 1270, Genoa dominated the northern route to Asia through the Black Sea. From then until the fourteenth century, the Genoese expanded their trade routes as far as Persia and the Far East. In 1291 they sponsored a failed expedition into the Atlantic in search of India. This voyage reveals the long roots of Genoese interest in Atlantic exploration.

In the fifteenth century, with Venice claiming victory in the spice trade, the Genoese shifted focus from trade to finance and from the Black Sea to the western Mediterranean. Located on the northwestern coast of Italy, Genoa had always been active in the western Mediterranean, trading with North African ports, southern France, Spain, and even England and Flanders through the Strait of Gibraltar. When Spanish and Portuguese voyages began to explore the western Atlantic (see page 467), Genoese merchants, navigators, and financiers provided their skills to the Iberian monarchs.

A major element of both Venetian and Genoese trade was slavery. Merchants purchased slaves, many of whom were fellow Christians, in the Balkans of southeastern Europe. After the loss of the Black Sea trade routes — and thus the source of slaves — to the Ottomans, the Genoese sought new supplies of slaves in the West, eventually seizing or buying and selling the Guanches (indigenous peoples from the Canary Islands), Muslim prisoners and Jewish refugees from Spain, and by the early 1500s both black and Berber Africans. With the growth of Spanish colonies in the New World, Genoese and Venetian merchants became important players in the Atlantic slave trade.

Italian experience in colonial administration, the slave trade, and international trade and finance served as a model for the Iberian states as they pushed European expansion to new heights. Mariners, merchants, and financiers from Venice and Genoa — most notably Christopher Columbus — played crucial roles in bringing the fruits of this experience to the Iberian Peninsula and to the New World.

The European Voyages of Discovery

☐ Why and how did Europeans undertake ambitious voyages of expansion?

As we have seen, Europe was by no means isolated before its discovery of the New World. But because Europeans did not produce many products desired by Eastern elites, they were modest players in the Indian Ocean trading world. In the fifteenth and early sixteenth centuries, however, they launched new voyages of exploration, commerce, and conquest out of a desire to spread Christianity, to undo Italian and Ottoman domination of trade with the East, and to tap entirely new sources of wealth. Ultimately, their efforts landed them in the New World.

Causes of European Expansion

Europeans sought to expand their international reach for many reasons. By the middle of the fifteenth century, Europe was experiencing a revival of population and economic activity after the lows of the Black Death. This revival created demands for luxury goods, especially spices, from the East. However, the conquest of Constantinople by the Ottomans gave the Muslim empire control of trade routes to the east and blocked the fulfillment of European demands. Europeans thus needed to find new sources of precious metal to trade with the Ottomans or to find trade routes that bypassed the Ottomans.

Religious fervor was another important catalyst for expansion. The passion and energy ignited by the Christian reconquista of the Iberian Peninsula encouraged the Portuguese and Spanish to continue the Christian crusade. In 1492 Spain conquered Granada, the last remaining Muslim state on the Iberian Peninsula. Since the remaining Muslim states, such as the mighty Ottoman Empire, were too strong to defeat, Iberians turned their attention elsewhere. Just seven months after the Spanish conquest of Granada, Columbus departed across the Atlantic.

Combined with eagerness to gain wealth and to spread Christianity were the desire for glory and the urge to chart new waters. Scholars have frequently described the European discoveries as a manifestation of Renaissance curiosity about the physical universe. The detailed journals kept by European voyagers attest to their fascination with the new peoples and places they visited.

Individual explorers combined these motivations in unique ways. Columbus, a devout Christian, aimed to discover new territories where Christianity could be spread while seeking a direct trade route to Asia. The motives of Portuguese explorer Bartholomew Diaz were, in his own words, "to serve God and His Majesty, to give light to those who were in darkness and to grow rich as all men desire to do." When the Portuguese explorer Vasco da Gama reached the port of Calicut, India, in 1498 and a native asked what he wanted, he replied, "Christians and spices."[3] The bluntest of the Spanish **conquistadors** (kahn-KEES-tuh-dorz),

---

• **conquistador** Spanish for "conqueror"; Spanish soldier-explorer, such as Hernando Cortés and Francisco Pizarro, who sought to conquer the New World for the Spanish crown.

> ❝I have come to win gold, not to plow the fields like a peasant.❞
>
> **HERNANDO CORTÉS**

Hernando Cortés, announced as he prepared to conquer Mexico, "I have come to win gold, not to plow the fields like a peasant."[4]

Eagerness for exploration was heightened by a lack of opportunity at home. After the reconquista, young men of the Spanish upper classes found their economic and political opportunities greatly limited. The ambitious turned to the sea to seek their fortunes.

Whatever the reasons, the voyages were made possible by the growth of government power. The Spanish monarchy was stronger than before and in a position to support foreign ventures. In Portugal explorers also looked to the monarchy, to Prince Henry the Navigator in particular (page 467), for financial support and encouragement. Like voyagers, monarchs shared a mix of motivations, from the desire to please God to the desire to win glory and profit from trade. Competition among European monarchs was an important factor in encouraging the steady stream of expeditions that began in the late fifteenth century.

Ordinary men chose to join these voyages to escape poverty at home, to continue a family trade, to win a few crumbs of the great riches of empire, or to find better lives as illegal immigrants in the colonies. However, common sailors were ill-paid, and life at sea meant danger, unbearable stench, hunger, and overcrowding. For months at a time, 100 to 120 people lived and worked in a space of 1,600 to 2,000 square feet.

The people who stayed at home had a powerful impact on the process and a strong interest in it. Royal ministers and factions at court influenced monarchs to provide or deny support for exploration. The small number of people who could read served as an audience for tales of fantastic places and unknown peoples. Cosmography, natural history, and geography aroused enormous interest among educated people in the fifteenth and sixteenth centuries. One of the most popular books of the time was the fourteenth-century text *The Travels of Sir John Mandeville*, which purported to be a firsthand account of the author's travels in the

The Travels of Sir John Mandeville The author of this tale claimed to be an English knight who traveled extensively in the Middle East and Asia from the 1320s to the 1350s. Although historians now consider the work a skillful fiction, it had a great influence on how Europeans understood the world at the time. This illustration, from an edition published around 1410, depicts Mandeville approaching a walled city on the first stage of his voyage to Constantinople. (© British Library Board, Add 24289, f 14v)

Middle East, India, and China. Although we now know they were fictional, these fantastic tales of cannibals, one-eyed giants, men with the heads of dogs, and other marvels were believed for centuries. Columbus took a copy of Mandeville and the equally popular and more reliable *The Travels of Marco Polo* on his voyage in 1492.

Technology and the Rise of Exploration

Technological developments in shipbuilding, navigation, and weaponry provided another impetus for European expansion. Since ancient times, most seagoing vessels had been narrow, open boats called galleys, propelled largely by slaves or convicts manning the oars. Though well suited to the placid waters of the Mediterranean, galleys could not withstand the rougher conditions in the Atlantic. The need for sturdier craft,

---

- **caravel** A small, maneuverable, three-mast sailing ship developed by the Portuguese in the fifteenth century that gave the Portuguese a distinct advantage in exploration and trade.
- **Ptolemy's *Geography*** A second century C.E. work that synthesized the classical knowledge of geography and introduced the concepts of longitude and latitude. Reintroduced to Europeans in 1410 by Arab scholars, its ideas allowed cartographers to create more accurate maps.

as well as population losses caused by the Black Death, forced the development of a new style of ship that would not require much manpower to sail. In the course of the fifteenth century, the Portuguese developed the **caravel**, a small, light, three-mast sailing ship. The caravel was much more maneuverable than the galley. When fitted with cannon, it could dominate larger vessels.

Great strides in cartography and navigational aids were also made during this period. Around 1410 Arab scholars reintroduced Europeans to **Ptolemy's *Geography***. Written in the second century, the work synthesized the geographical knowledge of the classical world. It represented a major improvement over medieval cartography, showing the world as round and introducing the idea of latitude and longitude to plot position accurately. It also contained significant errors. Unaware of the Americas, Ptolemy showed the world as much smaller than it is, so that Asia appeared not very distant from Europe. Both the assets and the flaws of Ptolemy's work, combined with the latest information from mariners, became part of the new maps that European explorers would use on their voyages.

The magnetic compass enabled sailors to determine their direction and position at sea. The astrolabe, an instrument invented by the ancient Greeks and perfected by Muslim navigators, was used to determine the altitude of the sun and other celestial bodies. It permitted mariners to plot their latitude, that is, their precise position north or south of the equator.

Like the astrolabe, much of the new technology that Europeans used on their voyages was borrowed from the East. Gunpowder, the compass, and the sternpost rudder were Chinese inventions. The lateen sail, which allowed European ships to tack against the wind, was a product of the Indian Ocean trade world and was brought to the Mediterranean on Arab ships. Advances in cartography also drew on the rich tradition of Judeo-Arabic mathematical and astronomical learning in Iberia. In exploring new territories, European sailors thus called on techniques and knowledge developed over centuries in China, the Muslim world, and trading centers along the Indian Ocean.

The Expanding Portuguese Empire

For centuries Portugal was a small and poor nation on the margins of European life whose principal activities were fishing and subsistence farming. It would have been hard for a medieval European to predict Portugal's phenomenal success overseas after 1450. Yet Portugal had a long history of seafaring and navigation. Blocked from access to western Europe by Spain, the Portuguese turned to the Atlantic, whose waters they knew better than did other Europeans. Nature favored the Portuguese: winds blowing along their coast offered passage to Africa, its Atlantic islands, and, ultimately, Brazil.

In the early phases of Portuguese exploration, Prince Henry (1394–1460), a younger son of the king, played a leading role. A nineteenth-century scholar dubbed Henry "the Navigator" because of his support for the study of geography and navigation and for the annual expeditions he sponsored down the western coast of Africa.

The Portuguese Fleet Embarked for the Indies This image shows a Portuguese trading fleet in the late fifteenth century bound for the riches of the Indies. Between 1500 and 1635 over nine hundred ships sailed from Portugal to ports on the Indian Ocean in annual fleets composed of five to ten ships. Portuguese sailors used astrolabes, such as the one pictured here, to accurately plot their position. (fleet: British Museum/HarperCollins Publishers/The Art Archive; astrolabe: Courtesy of the Trustees of the British Museum)

Pepper Harvest To break the monotony of their bland diet, Europeans had a passion for pepper, which—along with cinnamon, cloves, nutmeg, and ginger—was the main object of the Asian trade. We can appreciate the fifteenth-century expression "as dear as pepper": one kilo of pepper cost 2 grams of silver at the place of production in the East Indies and from 1 to 10 grams of silver in Alexandria, Egypt; 14 to 18 grams in Venice; and 20 to 30 grams at the markets of northern Europe. Here natives fill vats, and the dealer tastes a peppercorn for pungency. (Bibliothèque nationale de France/ Archives Charmet/The Bridgeman Art Library)

Through their exploration voyages the Portuguese had several goals: to achieve military glory; to Christianize Muslims and locate a mythical Christian king of Africa, Prester John; and to find gold, slaves, and an overseas route to the spice markets of India. Portugal's conquest of Ceuta, an Arab city in northern Morocco, in 1415 marked the beginning of European overseas expansion. In the 1420s, under Henry's direction, the Portuguese began to settle the Atlantic islands of Madeira (ca. 1420) and the Azores (1427). In 1443 they founded their first African commercial settlement at Arguin in North Africa. By the time of Henry's death in 1460, his support for exploration was vindicated by thriving sugar plantations on the Atlantic islands, the first arrival of enslaved Africans in Portugal (see page 479), and new access to African gold.

The Portuguese next established trading posts and forts on the gold-rich Guinea coast and penetrated into the African continent all the way to Timbuktu (Map 16.2). By 1500 Portugal controlled the flow of African gold to Europe.

The Portuguese then pushed farther south down the west coast of Africa. In 1487 Bartholomew Diaz (ca. 1451–1500) rounded the Cape of Good Hope at the southern tip, but storms and a threatened mutiny forced him to turn back. A decade later Vasco da Gama (ca. 1469–1524) succeeded in rounding the Cape while commanding a fleet in search of a sea route to India. With the help of an Indian guide, da Gama reached the port of Calicut in India. He returned to Lisbon with spices and samples of Indian cloth, having proved the possibility of lucrative trade with the East via the Cape route. Thereafter, a Portuguese convoy set out for passage around the Cape every March.

Lisbon became the entrance port for Asian goods into Europe, but this was not accomplished without a fight. Muslim-controlled port city-states had long controlled the rich spice trade of the Indian Ocean, and they did not surrender it willingly. Portuguese cannon blasted open the port of Malacca in 1511, followed by Calicut, Hormuz, and Goa. The bombardment of these cities laid the foundation for Portuguese imperialism

Azores
1427

PORTUGAL
Lisbon

ATLANTIC
OCEAN

Madeira
ca. 1420

Ceuta
1415

MOROCCO

Canary Is.

AFRICA

Arguin
1443

1427 Date of
conquest

**Portuguese Expansion
into Africa**

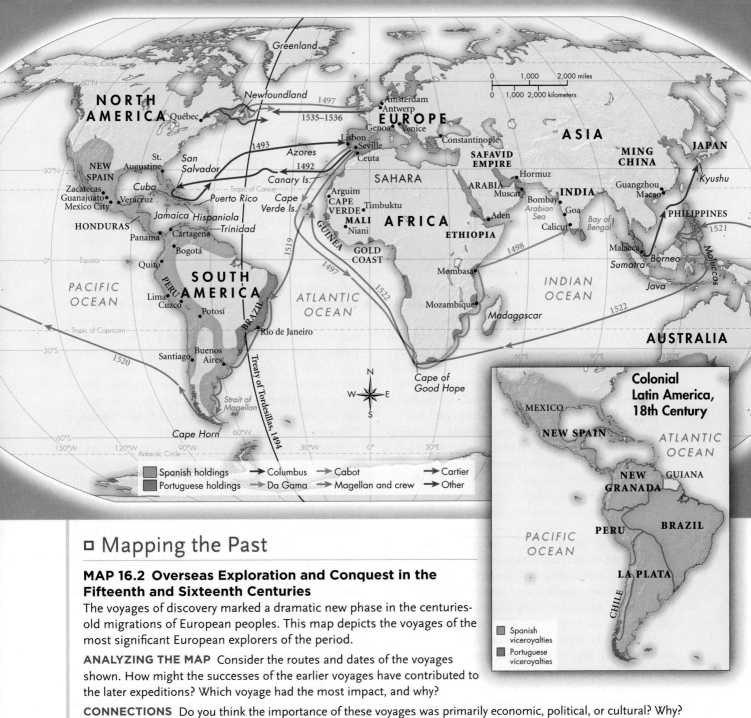

□ Mapping the Past

MAP 16.2 Overseas Exploration and Conquest in the Fifteenth and Sixteenth Centuries

The voyages of discovery marked a dramatic new phase in the centuries-old migrations of European peoples. This map depicts the voyages of the most significant European explorers of the period.

ANALYZING THE MAP Consider the routes and dates of the voyages shown. How might the successes of the earlier voyages have contributed to the later expeditions? Which voyage had the most impact, and why?

CONNECTIONS Do you think the importance of these voyages was primarily economic, political, or cultural? Why?

in the sixteenth and seventeenth centuries. The acquisition of port cities and their trade routes brought riches to Portugal but had limited impact on the lives and religious faith of Asian peoples beyond Portuguese coastal holdings. In the meantime, Spain also had begun the quest for an empire.

Christopher Columbus's Voyages to the Americas

Christopher Columbus (1451–1506) is a controversial figure in history — glorified by some as the brave discoverer of America, vilified by others as a cruel exploiter of Native Americans. Rather than judging Columbus by the debates and standards of our time, it is more important to understand him in the context of his own time. First, what kind of man was Columbus, and what forces or influences shaped him? Second, in sailing westward from Europe, what were his goals? Third, did he achieve his goals, and what did he make of his discoveries?

The westward voyages of Columbus, a native of Genoa, embodied a long-standing Genoese ambition to circumvent Venetian, and then Portuguese, domination of eastward trade. Columbus was knowledgeable about the sea. He had worked as a mapmaker, and he was familiar with such fifteenth-century Portuguese navigational aids as *portolans* — written descriptions of the courses along which ships sailed — and the use of the compass as a nautical instrument. The success of his first voyage to the Americas, which took him across the Atlantic to the Caribbean in thirty-three days, owed a great deal to his seamanship.

Columbus was also a deeply religious man. He began the *Journal* of his first voyage in the form of a letter to Ferdinand and Isabella of Spain:

Columbus's First Voyage to the New World, 1492–1493

> On 2 January in the year 1492, when your Highnesses had concluded their war with the Moors who reigned in Europe, I saw your Highnesses' banners victoriously raised on the towers of the Alhambra, the citadel of the city, and the Moorish king come out of the city gates and kiss the hands of your Highnesses and the prince, My Lord. And later in that same month, on the grounds of information I had given your Highnesses concerning the lands of India . . . your Highnesses decided to send me, Christopher Columbus, to see these parts of India and the princes and peoples of those lands and consider the best means for their conversion.[5]

Columbus had witnessed the Spanish conquest of Granada and shared fully in the religious and nationalistic fervor surrounding that event. Like the Spanish rulers and most Europeans of his age, he understood Christianity as a missionary religion that should be carried to places where it did not exist.

Although the spread of Christianity was an important goal, what was the primary object of this first voyage? Columbus gave the answer in the very title of the expedition, "The Enterprise of the Indies," *Indies* being the European word for Asia. He wanted to find a direct ocean trading route to Asia. Inspired by the stories of Mandeville and Marco Polo, Columbus also dreamed of reaching the court of the Mongol emperor, the Great Khan (not realizing that the Ming Dynasty had overthrown the Mongols in 1368). Based on Ptolemy's *Geography* and other texts, he expected to pass the islands of Japan and then land on the east coast of China.

Before Columbus could begin his voyage he needed financing. Rejected for funding by the Portuguese in 1483 and by Ferdinand and Isabella in 1486, he finally won the support of the Spanish monarchy in 1492. The Spanish crown agreed to make him viceroy over any territory he might discover and to give him one-tenth of the material rewards of the journey. With this backing, Columbus and his small fleet left Spain on August 3, 1492. He landed in the Bahamas, which he christened San Salvador, on October 12, 1492.

How did Columbus interpret what he had found, and did he think he had achieved what he had set out to do? On his arrival in the Bahamas Columbus believed he had found some small islands off the east coast of Japan. In a letter he wrote to Ferdinand and Isabella on his return to Spain, Columbus described the natives as handsome, peaceful, and primitive. Believing he was in the Indies, he called them "Indians," a name that was later applied to all inhabitants of the Americas. Columbus concluded that they would make good slaves and could quickly be converted to Christianity. (See "Listening to the Past: Columbus Describes His First Voyage," page 472.)

Scholars have identified the inhabitants of the islands as the Taino (TIGH-noh) people, speakers of the Arawak language, who inhabited Hispaniola (modern-day Haiti and the Dominican Republic) and other islands in the Caribbean. Columbus received reassuring reports from Taino villagers of the presence of gold and of a great king in the vicinity. From San Salvador, Columbus sailed southwest, believing that this course would take him to Japan or the coast of China. He landed instead on Cuba on October 28. Deciding that he must be on the mainland of China near the coastal city of Quinsay (now Hangzhou), he sent a small embassy inland with letters from Ferdinand and Isabella and instructions to locate the grand city.

The landing party found only small villages. Confronted with this disappointment, Columbus apparently gave up on his aim to meet the Great Khan. Instead, he focused on trying to find gold or other valuables among the peoples he had discovered. The sight of Taino people wearing gold ornaments on Hispaniola seemed to prove that gold was available in the region. In January, confident that its source would soon be found, he headed back to Spain to report on his discovery.

Over the next decades, the Spanish would follow a policy of conquest and colonization in the New World (see pages 474–476). On his second voyage, Columbus forcibly subjugated the island of Hispaniola and enslaved its indigenous peoples. On this and subsequent voyages, he brought with him settlers for the new Spanish territories, along with agricultural seed and livestock. Columbus himself, however, had little interest in or capacity for governing. Arriving in Hispaniola

• **Treaty of Tordesillas** The 1494 agreement giving Spain everything west of an imaginary line drawn down the Atlantic and giving Portugal everything to the east.

on this third voyage, he found revolt had broken out against his brother. A royal expedition sent to investigate returned the brothers to Spain in chains. Although Columbus was quickly cleared of wrongdoing, he did not recover his authority over the territories.

> " Those new regions which we found and explored with the fleet . . . we may rightly call a New World. "
>
> **AMERIGO VESPUCCI**

Columbus was very much a man of his times. To the end of his life in 1506, he believed that he had found small islands off the coast of Asia. He never realized the scope of his achievement: that he had found a vast continent unknown to Europeans, except for a fleeting Viking presence centuries earlier. He could not know that the lands he discovered would become a crucial new arena for international trade and colonization, with grave consequences for native peoples.

Later Explorers

The Florentine navigator Amerigo Vespucci (veh-SPOO-chee; 1454–1512) realized what Columbus had not. Writing about his discoveries on the coast of modern-day Venezuela, Vespucci stated: "Those new regions which we found and explored with the fleet . . . we may rightly call a New World." This letter, titled *Mundus Novus* (The New World), was the first document to describe America as a continent separate from

Asia. In recognition of Amerigo's bold claim, the continent was named for him.

To settle competing claims to the Atlantic discoveries, Spain and Portugal turned to Pope Alexander VI. The resulting **Treaty of Tordesillas** (tor-duh-SEE-yuhs) in 1494 gave Spain everything to the west of an imaginary line drawn down the Atlantic and Portugal everything to the east. This arbitrary division worked in Portugal's favor when in 1500 an expedition led by Pedro Alvares Cabral, en route to India, landed on the coast of Brazil, which Cabral claimed as Portuguese territory.

The search for profits determined the direction of Spanish exploration and expansion in South America. Because its profits from the Caribbean were insignificant compared to Portugal's enormous riches from the Asian spice trade, Spain renewed the search for a western passage to Asia. In 1519 Charles V of Spain commissioned Ferdinand Magellan (1480–1521) to find a direct sea route to the spices of the Moluccas, islands off the southeast coast of Asia. Magellan sailed southwest across the Atlantic to Brazil, and after a long search along the coast he located the treacherous strait off the southern tip of South America that now bears his name (see Map 16.2). After passing through the

World Map of Diogo Ribeiro, 1529 This map integrates the wealth of new information provided by European explorers in the decades after Columbus's 1492 voyage. Working on commission for the Spanish king Charles V, mapmaker Diogo Ribeiro incorporated new details on Africa, South America, India, the Malay Archipelago, and China. Note the inaccuracy in his placement of the Moluccas, or Spice Islands, which are much too far east. This "mistake" was intended to serve Spain's interests in trade negotiations with the Portuguese. (Biblioteca Apostolica Vaticana)

Listening to the Past

Columbus Describes
His First Voyage

On his return voyage to Spain in February 1493, Christopher Columbus composed a letter intended for wide circulation and had copies of it sent ahead to Isabella, Ferdinand, and others when the ship docked at Lisbon. Because the letter sums up Columbus's understanding of his achievements, it is considered the most important document of his first voyage.

❝Since I know that you will be pleased at the great success with which the Lord has crowned my voyage, I write to inform you how in thirty-three days I crossed from the Canary Islands to the Indies, with the fleet which our most illustrious sovereigns gave me. I found very many islands with large populations and took possession of them all for their Highnesses; this I did by proclamation and unfurled the royal standard. No opposition was offered.

I named the first island that I found "San Salvador," in honour of our Lord and Saviour who has granted me this miracle. . . . When I reached Cuba, I followed its north coast westwards, and found it so extensive that I thought this must be the mainland, the province of Cathay.* . . . From there I saw another island eighteen leagues eastwards which I then named "Hispaniola."† . . .

Hispaniola is a wonder. The mountains and hills, the plains and meadow lands are both fertile and beautiful. They are most suitable for planting crops and for raising cattle of all kinds, and there are good sites for building towns and villages. The harbours are incredibly fine and there are many great rivers with broad channels and the majority contain gold.‡ The trees, fruits and plants are very different from those of Cuba. In Hispaniola there are many spices and large mines of gold and other metals.§ . . .

---

*Cathay is the old name for China. In the logbook and later in this letter Columbus accepts the native story that Cuba is an island that they can circumnavigate in something more than twenty-one days, yet he insists here and during the second voyage that it is in fact part of the Asiatic mainland.

†Hispaniola is the second largest island of the West Indies; Haiti occupies the western third of the island, the Dominican Republic the rest.

‡This did not prove to be true.

§These statements are also inaccurate.

The inhabitants of this island, and all the rest that I discovered or heard of, go naked, as their mothers bore them, men and women alike. A few of the women, however, cover a single place with a leaf of a plant or piece of cotton which they weave for the purpose. They have no iron or steel or arms and are not capable of using them, not because they are not strong and well built but because they are amazingly timid. All the weapons they have are canes cut at seeding time, at the end of which they fix a sharpened stick, but they have not the courage to make use of these, for very often when I have sent two or three men to a village to have conversation with them a great number of them have come out. But as soon as they saw my men all fled immediately, a father not even waiting for his son. And this is not because we have harmed any of them; on the contrary, wherever I have gone and been able to have conversation with them, I have given them some of the various things I had, a cloth and other articles, and received nothing in exchange. But they have still remained incurably timid. True, when they have been reassured and lost their fear, they are so ingenuous and so liberal with all their possessions that no one who has not seen them would believe it. If one asks for anything they have they never say no. On the contrary, they offer a share to anyone with demonstrations of heartfelt affection, and they are immediately content with any small thing, valuable or valueless, that is given them. I forbade the men to give them bits of broken crockery, fragments of glass or tags of laces, though if they could get them they fancied them the finest jewels in the world.

I hoped to win them to the love and service of their Highnesses and of the whole Spanish nation and to persuade them to collect and give us of the things which they possessed in abundance and which we needed. They have no religion and are not idolaters; but all believe that power and goodness dwell in the sky and they are firmly convinced that I have come from the sky with these ships and people. In this belief they gave me a good reception everywhere, once they had overcome their fear; and this is not because they are stupid—far from it, they are men of great intelligence, for they navigate all those seas, and give a marvellously good account of everything—but because they have never before seen men clothed or ships like these. . . .

---

strait, his fleet sailed north up the west coast of South America and then headed west into the Pacific toward the Malay Archipelago. Some of these islands were conquered in the 1560s and named the Philippines for Philip II of Spain.

Terrible storms, disease, starvation, and violence haunted the expedition. Sailors on two of Magellan's five ships attempted mutiny on the South American

coast; one ship was lost, and another ship deserted and returned to Spain before even traversing the strait. Magellan himself was killed in a skirmish in the Philippines. At this point, the expedition had enough survivors to man only two ships, and one of them was captured by the Portuguese. Finally, in 1522 one ship with only eighteen men returned to Spain, having traveled from the east by way of the Indian Ocean, the Cape of

In all these islands the men are seemingly content with one woman, but their chief or king is allowed more than twenty. The women appear to work more than the men and I have not been able to find out if they have private property. As far as I could see whatever a man had was shared among all the rest and this particularly applies to food. . . . In another island, which I am told is larger than Hispaniola, the people have no hair. Here there is a vast quantity of gold, and from here and the other islands I bring Indians as evidence.

In conclusion, to speak only of the results of this very hasty voyage, their Highnesses can see that I will give them as much gold as they require, if they will render me some very slight assistance; also I will give them all the spices and cotton they want. . . . I will also bring them as much aloes as they ask and as many slaves, who will be taken from the idolaters. I believe also that I have found rhubarb and cinnamon and there will be countless other things in addition. . . .

So all Christendom will be delighted that our Redeemer has given victory to our most illustrious King and Queen and their renowned kingdoms, in this great matter. They should hold great celebrations and render solemn thanks to the Holy Trinity with many solemn prayers, for the great triumph which they will have, by the conversion of so many peoples to our holy faith and for the temporal benefits which will follow, for not only Spain, but all Christendom will receive encouragement and profit.

This is a brief account of the facts.

Written in the caravel off the Canary Islands.**

15 February 1493

At your orders
THE ADMIRAL "

**Actually, Columbus was off Santa Maria in the Azores.

Source: J. M. Cohen, ed. and trans., *The Four Voyages of Christopher Columbus* (Penguin Classics, 1958), pp. 115–123. Copyright © J. M. Cohen, 1969, London. Reproduced by permission of Penguin Books Ltd.

QUESTIONS FOR ANALYSIS

1. How did Columbus explain the success of his voyage?
2. What was Columbus's view of the Native Americans he met?
3. Evaluate his statements that the Caribbean islands possessed gold, cotton, and spices.
4. Why did Columbus cling to the idea that he had reached Asia?

Good Hope, and the Atlantic. The voyage — the first to circumnavigate the globe — had taken close to three years.

Despite the losses, this voyage revolutionized Europeans' understanding of the world by demonstrating the vastness of the Pacific. The earth was clearly much larger than Columbus had believed. Magellan's expedition also made Spain rethink its plans for overseas commerce and territorial expansion. Although the voyage made a small profit in spices, the westward passage to the Indies was too long and dangerous for commercial purposes. Thus Spain soon abandoned the attempt to oust Portugal from the Eastern spice trade and concentrated on exploiting its New World territories.

The English and French also set sail across the Atlantic during the early days of exploration, in their case to search for a northwest passage to the Indies. In 1497 John Cabot (ca. 1450–1499), a Genoese merchant living in London, discovered Newfoundland. The next year he returned and explored the New England coast. These forays proved futile, and at that time the English established no permanent colonies in the territories they explored. Later English efforts to find a passage to Asia focused on the extreme north. Between 1576 and 1578, Martin Frobisher (ca. 1535–1594) made three voyages in and around the Canadian bay that now bears his name. Frobisher hopefully brought a quantity of ore back to England with him, but it proved to be worthless.

Early French exploration of the Atlantic was equally frustrating. Between 1534 and 1541 Frenchman Jacques Cartier (1491–1557) made several voyages and explored the St. Lawrence region of Canada, searching for a passage to the wealth of Asia. When this hope proved vain, the French turned to a new source of profit within Canada itself: trade in beavers and other furs. French fisherman also competed with the Spanish and English for the teeming schools of cod they found in the Atlantic waters around Newfoundland.

Spanish Conquest in the New World

After Columbus's voyages Spanish explorers penetrated farther into the New World. This territorial expansion began in 1519, when the Spanish governor in Cuba sent an expedition, under the command of the conquistador Hernando Cortés (1485–1547), to what is now Mexico. Accompanied by six hundred men, sixteen horses, and ten cannon, Cortés was to launch the conquest of the **Mexica Empire**. Its people were later called the Aztecs, but now most scholars prefer to use the term *Mexica* to refer to them and their empire.

The Mexica Empire was ruled by Montezuma II (r. 1502–1520) from his capital at Tenochtitlán (tay-nawch-teet-LAHN), now Mexico City. Larger than any European city of the time, it was the heart of a sophisticated civilization with an advanced understanding of mathematics, astronomy, and engineering; with a complex social system; and with oral poetry and historical traditions.

Invasion of Tenochtitlán, 1519–1521

→ Cortés's original route, 1519
→ Cortés's retreat, 1520
→ Cortés's return route, 1520–1521

Soon after Cortés landed on the Mexican coast on April 21, 1519, his camp was visited by delegations of unarmed Mexica leaders bearing gifts and news of their great emperor. Impressed by the wealth of the local people, Cortés decided to defy his orders from the governor in Cuba, which restricted him to trading and exploration, and set up a settlement under his own authority. He thus founded the settlement of Veracruz and burned his ships to prevent any disloyal or frightened followers from returning to Cuba.

The Mexica state religion necessitated constant warfare against neighboring peoples to secure captives for religious sacrifices and laborers for agricultural and building projects. Conquered peoples were required to pay tribute to the Mexica state through their local chiefs. Realizing that he could exploit dissension over this practice to his own advantage, Cortés forged an alliance with the Tlaxcala (tlah-SKAH-lah) and other subject kingdoms, which chafed under the tribute demanded by the Mexicas. In October a combined Spanish-Tlaxcalan force occupied the city of Cholula and massacred many thousand inhabitants. Strengthened by this display of power, Cortés made alliances with other native kingdoms. In November 1519, with a few hundred Spanish men and some six thousand indigenous warriors, he marched on Tenochtitlán.

Montezuma refrained from attacking the Spaniards as they advanced toward his capital and welcomed Cortés and his men into Tenochtitlán. Other native leaders attacked the Spanish, but Montezuma relied on the advice of his state council, itself divided, and on the dubious loyalty of tribute-paying communities subjugated by the Mexica. Historians have largely discredited one long-standing explanation, that he feared the Spaniards as living gods. This idea seems to have been a myth spread by Spanish missionaries and their converts after the fact, as a way of justifying and explaining the conquest. Montezuma's long hesitation proved disastrous. When Cortés — with incredible boldness — took Montezuma hostage, the emperor's influence over his people crumbled.

During the ensuing attacks and counterattacks, Montezuma was killed. The Spaniards and their allies escaped from the city and began gathering forces and making new alliances against the Mexica. In May 1521 Cortés led a second assault on Tenochtitlán, leading an army of approximately 1,000 Spanish and 75,000 native warriors.[6] The Spanish victory in late summer 1521 was hard-won and greatly aided by the effects of smallpox, which had weakened and reduced the Mexica population. After the defeat of Tenochtitlán, Cortés and

• **Mexica Empire** Also known as the Aztec Empire, a large and complex Native American civilization in modern Mexico and Central America that possessed advanced mathematical, astronomical, and engineering technology.

• **Inca Empire** The vast and sophisticated Peruvian empire centered at the capital city of Cuzco that was at its peak from 1438 until 1532.

▫ Picturing the Past

Doña Marina Translating for Hernando Cortés During His Meeting with Montezuma

In April 1519 Doña Marina (or La Malinche as she is known in Mexico) was among twenty women given to the Spanish as slaves. Fluent in Nahuatl (NAH-wha-tuhl) and Yucatec Mayan (spoken by a Spanish priest accompanying Cortés), she acted as an interpreter and diplomatic guide for the Spanish. She had a close relationship with Cortés and bore his son, Don Martín Cortés, in 1522. This image was created by Tlaxcalan artists shortly after the conquest of Mexico and represents one indigenous perspective on the events. (The Granger Collection, New York)

ANALYZING THE IMAGE What role does Doña Marina (far right) appear to be playing in this image? Does she appear to be subservient or equal to Cortés (right, seated)? How did the painter indicate her identity as non-Spanish?

CONNECTIONS How do you think the native rulers negotiating with Cortés might have viewed Doña Marina? What about a Spanish viewer of this image? What does the absence of other women suggest about the role of women in these societies?

other conquistadors began the systematic conquest of Mexico. Over time a series of indigenous kingdoms fell under Spanish domination, although not without decades of resistance.

More surprising than the defeat of the Mexicas was the fall of the remote **Inca Empire** in Peru. Living in a settlement perched more than 9,800 feet above sea level, the Incas were isolated from other indigenous cultures. Like the Mexicas, they had created a vast empire that rivaled that of the Europeans in population

and complexity. However, by the time of the Spanish invasion the Inca Empire had been weakened by a civil war over succession and an epidemic of disease, possibly smallpox.

The Spanish conquistador Francisco Pizarro (ca. 1475–1541) landed on the northern coast of Peru on May 13, 1532, the very day Atahualpa (ah-tuh-WAHL-puh) won control of the empire after five years of fighting his brother for the throne. As Pizarro advanced across the Andes toward Cuzco, the capital of the Inca Empire, Atahualpa was also heading there for his coronation.

Like Montezuma in Mexico, Atahualpa was aware of the Spaniards' movements. He sent envoys to greet the Spanish and invite them to meet him in the provincial town of Cajamarca. His plan was to lure the Spaniards into a trap, seize their horses and ablest men for his army, and execute the rest. Instead, the Spaniards ambushed and captured him, collected an enormous ransom in gold, and then executed him in 1533. The Spanish then marched on to Cuzco, profiting once again from internal conflicts to form alliances with local peoples. When Cuzco fell in 1533, the Spanish plundered immense riches in gold and silver.

As with the Mexica, decades of violence and resistance followed the defeat of the Incan capital. Nevertheless, the Spanish conquest opened a new chapter in European relations with the New World. It was not long before rival European nations attempted to forge their own overseas empires.

The Impact of Conquest

☐ How did conquest affect indigenous populations and bring about a new era of economic and cultural exchange, commercial empires, and forced migrations?

The growing European presence in the New World transformed its land and its peoples forever. Violence and disease wrought devastating losses, while surviving peoples encountered new political, social, and economic organizations imposed by Europeans. Although the exchange of goods and people between Europe and the New World brought diseases to the Americas, it also gave both the New and Old Worlds new crops that eventually altered consumption patterns across the globe.

Also, the centuries-old Afroeurasian trade world was forever changed by the European voyages of discovery and their aftermath. For the first time, a truly global economy emerged in the sixteenth and seventeenth centuries, and it forged new links among far-flung peoples, cultures, and societies. The ancient civilizations of Europe, Africa, the Americas, and Asia confronted each other in new and rapidly evolving ways. Those confrontations often led to conquest, forced migration, and brutal exploitation, but they also contributed to cultural exchange and renewal.

• **viceroyalties** The name for the four administrative units of Spanish possessions in the Americas: New Spain, Peru, New Granada, and La Plata.

• **encomienda system** A system whereby the Spanish crown granted the conquerors the right to forcibly employ groups of Indians; it was a disguised form of slavery.

Colonial Administration

Columbus, Cortés, and Pizarro had claimed the lands they had discovered for the Spanish crown. How were these lands governed? Already in 1503, the Spanish had granted the port of Seville a monopoly over all traffic to the New World and established the House of Trade or *Casa de la Contratación* to oversee economic matters. In 1524 Spain added to this body the Royal and Supreme Council of the Indies, with authority over all colonial affairs subject to approval by the king. Spanish territories themselves were divided initially into two **viceroyalties** or administrative divisions: New Spain, created in 1535, with its capital at Mexico City, and Peru, created in 1542, with its capital at Lima. In the eighteenth century two additional viceroyalties were added: New Granada, with Bogotá as its administrative center; and La Plata, with Buenos Aires as its capital (see Map 16.2).

Within each territory, the viceroy, or imperial governor, exercised broad military and civil authority as the direct representative of Spain. The viceroy presided over the *audiencia* (ow-dee-EHN-see-ah), a board of twelve to fifteen judges that served as his advisory council and the highest judicial body. Later, King Charles III (r. 1759–1788) introduced the system of intendants to Spain's New World territories. These royal officials possessed broad military, administrative, and financial authority within their intendancies, smaller divisions within each viceroyalty, and were responsible not to the viceroy but to the monarchy in Madrid. The intendant system was pioneered by the Bourbon kings of France and was also used by the French in their overseas colonies.

The Portuguese governed their colony of Brazil in a similar manner. After the union of the crowns of Portugal and Spain in 1580, Spanish administrative forms were introduced. Local officials called *corregidores* (kuh-REH-gih-dawr-eez) held judicial and military powers. Royal policies placed severe restrictions on Brazilian industries that might compete with those of Portugal and Spain. These restrictions were just one of the many challenges native peoples faced under colonial rule.

The Impact of European Settlement on the Lives of Indigenous Peoples

Before Columbus's arrival, the Americas were inhabited by thousands of groups of indigenous peoples with different languages and cultures. These groups ranged from hunter-gatherer tribes organized into tribal confederations to large-scale agriculture-based empires connecting bustling cities and towns. The best estimate is that the peoples of the Americas numbered around 50 million in 1492.

Mixed Races The unprecedented mixing of peoples in the Spanish New World colonies inspired great fascination. An elaborate terminology emerged to describe the many possible combinations of indigenous, African, and European blood, which were known collectively as *castas*. This painting belongs to a popular genre of the eighteenth century depicting couples composed of individuals of different ethnic origin and the children produced of their unions. (Schalkwijk/Art Resource, NY)

Their lives were radically transformed by the arrival of Europeans. In the sixteenth century perhaps two hundred thousand Spaniards immigrated to the New World. Conquistadors carved out vast estates called *haciendas* (ah-see-EHN-duhz) in temperate grazing areas and imported Spanish livestock for the kinds of ranching with which they were familiar. In coastal tropical areas, the Spanish erected huge plantations to supply sugar to the European market. Around 1550 silver was discovered in present-day Bolivia and Mexico. To work the cattle ranches, sugar plantations, and silver mines, the conquistadors first turned to the indigenous peoples.

The Spanish quickly established the **encomienda system**, in which the Crown granted the conquerors the right to employ groups of Native Americans as laborers or to demand tribute from them in exchange for providing food and shelter. In practice, the encomiendas (ehn-koh-mee-EHN-duhz) were a legalized form of slavery.

The new conditions and hardships imposed by conquest and colonization resulted in enormous native population losses. The major cause of death was disease. Having little or no resistance to diseases brought from the Old World, the inhabitants of the New World fell victim to smallpox, typhus, influenza, and other illnesses. Another factor behind the decline in population was overwork. Unaccustomed to forced labor, native workers died in staggering numbers. Moreover, forced labor diverted local people from tending to their own crops, leading to malnutrition, reduced fertility rates, and starvation. Women forced to work were separated from their infants, leading to high infant mortality rates in a population with no livestock to supply alternatives to breast milk. Malnutrition and hunger in turn lowered resistance to disease. Finally, many indigenous peoples also died through outright violence in warfare.[7]

The Franciscan Bartolomé de Las Casas (1474–1566) documented the brutal treatment of indigenous peoples at the hands of the Spanish:

To these quiet Lambs . . . came the Spaniards like most c(r)uel Tygres, Wolves and Lions, enrag'd with a sharp and tedious hunger; for these forty years past, minding nothing else but the slaughter of these unfortunate wretches, whom with divers kinds of torments neither seen nor heard of before, they have so cruelly and inhumanely butchered, that of three millions of people which Hispaniola itself did contain, there are left remaining alive scarce three hundred persons.[8]

Las Casas and other missionaries asserted that the Indians had human rights, and through their persistent pressure the Spanish emperor Charles V abolished the worst abuses of the encomienda system in 1531.

The pattern of devastating disease and population loss established in the Spanish colonies was repeated everywhere Europeans settled. The best estimate is that the native population declined from roughly 50 million in 1492 to around 9 million by 1700. It is important to note, however, that native populations and cultures did survive the conquest period, sometimes by blending with European incomers and sometimes by maintaining cultural autonomy. Mixed-race populations sometimes rose to the colonial elite. The Spanish conquistadors often consolidated their power through marriage to the daughters of local rulers, and their descendants were among the most powerful inhabitants of Spanish America.

For colonial administrators the main problem posed by the astronomically high death rate was the loss of a subjugated labor force to work the mines and sugar plantations. The search for fresh sources of labor gave birth to the new tragedy of the Atlantic slave trade (see page 479).

The Columbian Exchange

The travel of people and goods between the Old and New Worlds led to an exchange of animals, plants, and diseases, a complex process known as the **Columbian exchange**. As we have seen, the introduction of new diseases to the Americas had devastating consequences. But other results of the exchange brought benefits not only to the Europeans but also to native peoples.

European immigrants wanted to eat foods familiar to them, so they searched the Americas for climatic zones favorable to crops grown in their homelands. Everywhere they settled, the Spanish and Portuguese brought and raised wheat with labor provided by the encomienda system. Grapes and olives brought over from Spain did well in parts of Peru and Chile. Perhaps the most significant introduction to the diet of Native Americans came via the meat and milk of the livestock that the early conquistadors brought with them, including cattle, sheep, and goats. The horse enabled both the Spanish conquerors and native populations to travel faster and farther and to transport heavy loads.

In turn, Europeans returned home with many food crops that became central elements of their diet. Crops originating in the Americas included tomatoes as well as many varieties of beans, squash, pumpkins, and peppers. One of the most important of such crops was maize (corn), first introduced to Europe by Columbus in 1493. Because maize gives a high yield per unit of land, has a short growing season, and thrives in climates too dry for rice and too wet for wheat, it proved an especially important crop for Europeans. By the late seventeenth century maize had become a staple in Spain, Portugal, southern France, and Italy, and in the eighteenth century it became one of the chief foods of southeastern Europe.

Even more valuable was the nutritious white potato, which slowly spread from west to east — to Ireland, England, and France in the seventeenth century, and to Germany, Poland, Hungary, and Russia in the eighteenth, contributing everywhere to a rise in popu-

Incan Women Milking Cows This illustration of Incan women milking cows is from a collection of illustrations by a Spanish bishop that offers a valuable view of life in Peru in the 1780s. (Archivo Fotografos Oronoz)

lation. Ironically, the white potato reached New England from old England in the early eighteenth century. The Portuguese quickly began exporting chili peppers from Brazil to Africa, India, and Southeast Asia along the trade routes they dominated. The chili pepper arrived in continental North America when plantation owners began to plant them as a food source for enslaved Africans, for whom they were a dietary staple.

Europeans' initial reaction to these crops was often fear or hostility. Adoption of the tomato and the potato, for example, was long hampered by belief that they were unfit for human consumption and potentially poisonous. Both plants belong to the deadly nightshade family, and both contain poison in their leaves and stems. Consequently, it took time and persuasion for these plants to win over tradition-minded European peasants, who used potatoes mostly as livestock feed. During the eighteenth-century Enlightenment, scientists and doctors played an important role in popularizing the nutritive benefits of the potato.

While the exchange of foods was a great benefit to both cultures, the introduction of European pathogens to the New World had a disastrous impact on the native population. The wave of catastrophic epidemic disease that swept the Western Hemisphere after 1492 can be seen as an extension of the swath of devastation wreaked by the Black Death in the 1300s, first on Asia and then on Europe. The world after Columbus was thus unified by disease as well as by trade and colonization.

Sugar and Early Transatlantic Slavery

Two crucial and interrelated elements of the Columbian exchange were the transatlantic trade in sugar and slaves. Throughout the Middle Ages slavery was deeply entrenched in the Mediterranean, but it was not based on race; many slaves were white. How, then, did black African slavery enter the European picture and take root in South and then North America? In 1453 the Ottoman capture of Constantinople halted the flow of white slaves from the eastern Mediterranean. Additionally, the successes of the Christian reconquest of the Iberian Peninsula drastically diminished the supply of Muslim captives. Cut off from its traditional sources of slaves, Mediterranean Europe turned to sub-Saharan Africa, which had a long history of slave trading.

As Portuguese explorers began their voyages along the western coast of Africa, one of the first commodities they sought was slaves. In 1444 the first ship returned to Lisbon with a cargo of enslaved Africans. While the first slaves were simply seized by small raiding parties, Portuguese merchants soon found that it was easier to trade with African leaders, who were accustomed to dealing in slaves captured through warfare with neighboring powers. From 1490 to 1530 Portuguese traders brought between three hundred and two thousand black slaves to Lisbon each year. There, they performed most of the manual labor and constituted 10 percent of the city's population.

In this stage of European expansion, the history of slavery became intertwined with the history of sugar. Originally sugar was an expensive luxury that only the very affluent could afford, but population increases and greater prosperity in the fifteenth century led to increasing demand. The establishment of sugar plantations on the Canary and Madeira Islands in the fifteenth century testifies to this demand.

Sugar was a particularly difficult crop to produce for profit. Seed-stems were planted by hand, thousands to the acre. When mature, the cane had to be harvested and processed rapidly to avoid spoiling, forcing days and nights of work with little rest. Moreover, sugar cane has a virtually constant growing season, meaning that there was no fallow period when workers could recuperate. The demands of sugar production were increased with the invention of roller mills to crush the cane more efficiently. Yields could be augmented, but only if a sufficient labor force was found to supply the mills. Europeans solved the labor problem by forcing first native islanders and then enslaved Africans to perform the backbreaking work.

The transatlantic slave trade began in 1518 when Spanish king Charles I authorized traders to bring African slaves to New World colonies. The Portuguese brought the first slaves to Brazil around 1550; by 1600 four thousand were being imported annually. After its founding in 1621, the Dutch West India Company transported thousands of Africans to Brazil and the Caribbean, mostly to work on sugar plantations. In the late seventeenth century, with the chartering of the Royal African Company, the English got involved in bringing slaves to Barbados and other English colonies in the Caribbean and mainland North America.

The Transatlantic Slave Trade

Before 1700, when slavers decided it was better business to improve conditions, some 20 percent of slaves died on the voyage from Africa to the Americas.[9] The most common cause of death was dysentery induced

---

• **Columbian exchange** The exchange of animals, plants, and diseases between the Old and the New Worlds.

A New World Sugar Refinery in Brazil Sugar was the most important and most profitable plantation crop in the New World. This image shows the processing and refinement of sugar on a Brazilian plantation. Sugar cane was grown, harvested, and processed by African slaves who labored under brutal and ruthless conditions to generate enormous profits for plantation owners. (The Bridgeman Art Library/Getty Images)

by poor-quality food and water, lack of sanitation, and intense crowding. (To increase profits, slave traders packed several hundred captives on each ship.) Men were often kept in irons during the passage, while women and girls were considered fair game for sailors. On sugar plantations, death rates among slaves from illness and exhaustion were extremely high, leading to a constant stream of new shipments of slaves from Africa. Driven by rising demands for sugar, cotton, tobacco, and other plantation crops, the tragic transatlantic slave trade reached its height in the eighteenth century.

The Birth of the Global Economy

With Europeans' discovery of the Americas and their exploration of the Pacific, the entire world was linked for the first time in history by seaborne trade. The opening of that trade brought into being three successive commercial empires: the Portuguese, the Spanish, and the Dutch.

The Portuguese were the first worldwide traders. In the sixteenth century they controlled the sea route to India (Map 16.3). From their fortified bases at Goa on the Arabian Sea and at Malacca on the Malay Peninsula, ships carried goods to the Portuguese settlement at Macao in the South China Sea. From Macao Portuguese ships loaded with Chinese silks and porcelains sailed to the Japanese port of Nagasaki and to the Phil-

ippine port of Manila, where Chinese goods were exchanged for Spanish silver from New Spain. Throughout Asia the Portuguese traded in slaves. They also exported horses from Mesopotamia and copper from Arabia to India; from India they exported hawks and peacocks for the Chinese and Japanese markets. Back to Portugal they brought Asian spices that had been purchased with textiles produced in India and with gold and ivory from East Africa. They also shipped back sugar from their colony in Brazil, produced by African slaves whom they had transported across the Atlantic.

Becoming an imperial power a few decades later than the Portuguese, the Spanish were determined to claim their place in world trade. This was greatly facilitated by the discovery of immense riches in silver, first at Potosí in modern-day Bolivia and later in Mexico. Silver poured into Europe through the Spanish port of Seville, contributing to steep inflation across Europe. Demand for silver also created a need for slaves to work in the mines. (See "Global Trade: Silver," page 482.)

The Spanish Empire in the New World was basically land-based, but across the Pacific the Spaniards built a seaborne empire centered at Manila in the Philippines. The city of Manila served as the transpacific bridge between Spanish America and China. In Manila, Spanish traders used silver from American mines to purchase Chinese silk for European markets. The European demand for silk was so huge that in 1597, for example, 12 million pesos of silver, almost the total

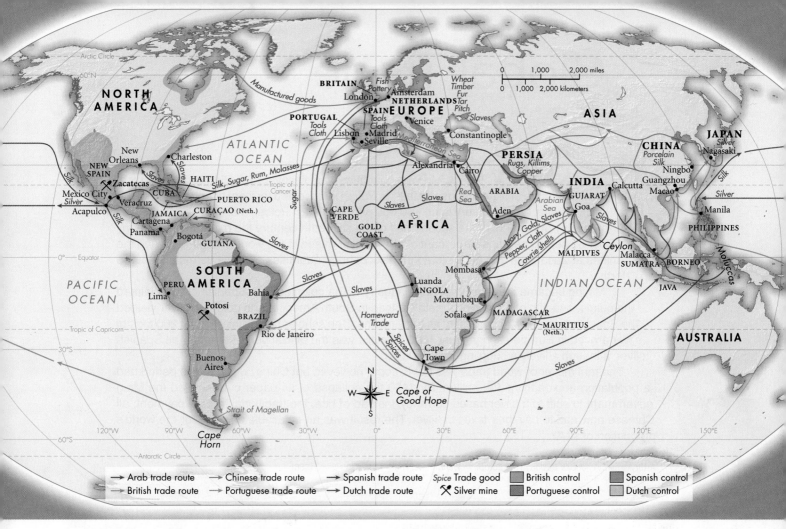

MAP 16.3 Seaborne Trading Empires in the Sixteenth and Seventeenth Centuries By the mid-seventeenth century, trade linked all parts of the world except for Australia. Notice that trade in slaves was not confined to the Atlantic but involved almost all parts of the world.

value of the transatlantic trade, moved from Acapulco in New Spain to Manila (see Map 16.4). After 1640, however, the Spanish silk trade declined in the face of stiff competition from Dutch imports.

In the seventeenth century the Dutch challenged the Spanish and Portuguese Empires. Drawing on their commercial wealth and long experience in European trade, by the end of the century the Dutch emerged as the most powerful worldwide seaborne trading power. The Dutch Empire was built on spices, and the Dutch East India Company was founded in 1602 with the stated intention of capturing the spice trade from the Portuguese.

The Dutch set their sights on gaining direct access to and control of the Indonesian sources of spices. The Dutch fleet, sailing from the Cape of Good Hope in Africa and avoiding the Portuguese forts in India, steered directly for Java (modern Indonesia; see Map 16.4). In return for assisting Indonesian princes in local squabbles and disputes with the Portuguese, the Dutch won broad commercial concessions. Through agreements, seizures, and outright war, they gained control

of the western access to the Indonesian archipelago in the first half of the seventeenth century. Gradually they achieved political domination over the archipelago itself. By the 1660s the Dutch had managed to expel the Portuguese from Ceylon and other East Indian islands, thereby establishing control of the lucrative spice trade.

Changing Values and Beliefs

□ How did new encounters shape cultural values and beliefs in Europe and the New World?

The age of overseas expansion heightened Europeans' contacts with the rest of the world. These contacts gave birth to new ideas about the inherent superiority or inferiority of different races, in part to justify European participation in the slave trade. Two great writers of the period both captured and challenged these views,

Global Trade

Silver in vast quantities was discovered in 1545 by the Spanish, at an altitude of fifteen thousand feet, at Potosí in unsettled territory conquered from the Inca Empire. A half-century later, 160,000 people lived in Potosí, making it about the size of the city of London. In the second half of the sixteenth century the mine (in present-day Bolivia) yielded perhaps 60 percent of all the silver mined in the world. From Potosí and the mines at Zacatecas and Guanajuato in Mexico, huge quantities of precious metals poured forth.

Mining became the most important industry in the colonies. The Spanish crown claimed the quinto, one-fifth of all precious metals mined in South America, and gold and silver yielded the Spanish monarchy 25 percent of its total income. One scholar has estimated that 260 tons of silver arrived in Europe each year by 1600.* Seville was the official port of entry for all Spanish silver, although a lively smuggling trade existed.

The real mover of world trade was not Europe, however, but China, which in this period had a population approaching 100 million. By 1450 the collapse of its paper currency led the Ming government to shift to a silver-based currency. Instead of rice, the traditional form of payment, all Chinese now had to pay their taxes in silver. The result was an insatiable demand for the world's production of silver.

*Artur Attman, *American Bullion in the European World Trade, 1600–1800* (Goteborg, 1986).

MAP 16.4 The Global Silver Trade

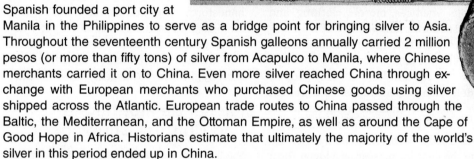

The incredibly rich silver mines at Potosí (in modern-day Bolivia) were the source of this eight-reale coin (lower right) struck at the mine during the reign of Charles II. Such coins were the original "pieces of eight" prized by pirates and adventurers. (silver mine: Courtesy of The Hispanic Society of America; coin: Hoberman Collection/SuperStock)

Japan was China's original source, and the Japanese continued to ship large quantities of silver ore until the depletion of its mines near the end of the seventeenth century. The discovery of silver in the New World provided a vast and welcome new supply for the Chinese market. In 1571 the Spanish founded a port city at Manila in the Philippines to serve as a bridge point for bringing silver to Asia. Throughout the seventeenth century Spanish galleons annually carried 2 million pesos (or more than fifty tons) of silver from Acapulco to Manila, where Chinese merchants carried it on to China. Even more silver reached China through exchange with European merchants who purchased Chinese goods using silver shipped across the Atlantic. European trade routes to China passed through the Baltic, the Mediterranean, and the Ottoman Empire, as well as around the Cape of Good Hope in Africa. Historians estimate that ultimately the majority of the world's silver in this period ended up in China.

In exchange for silver, the Chinese traded high-quality finished goods much desired by elites across the world, including fine silks, porcelain, and spices. To ensure continued demand for their products, enterprising Chinese merchants adapted them to Western tastes.

Silver had a mixed impact on the regions involved. Spain's immense profits from silver paid for the tremendous expansion of its empire and for the large armies that defended it. However, the easy flow of money also dampened economic innovation. It exacerbated the rising inflation Spain was already experiencing in the mid-sixteenth century. When the profitability of the silver mines diminished in the 1640s, Spain's power was fundamentally undercut

China experienced similarly mixed effects. On the one hand, the need for finished goods to trade for silver led to the rise of a merchant class and a new specialization of regional production. On the other hand, the inflation resulting from the influx of silver weakened the finances of the Ming Dynasty. As the purchasing power of silver declined in China, so did the value of silver taxes. The ensuing fiscal crisis helped bring down the Ming and led to the rise of the Qing in 1644. Ironically, the two states that benefited the most from silver also experienced political decline as a direct result of their reliance on it.

The consequences were most tragic elsewhere. In New Spain millions of indigenous laborers suffered brutal conditions and death in the silver mines. Demand for new sources of labor for the mines contributed to the intensification of the African slave trade.

Silver ore mined at Potosí thus built the first global trade system in history. Previously, a long-standing Afroeurasian trading world had involved merchants and consumers from the three Old World continents. Once Spain opened a trade route across the Pacific through Manila, all continents except Australia and Antarctica were linked.

Silver remained a crucial element in world trade through the nineteenth century. When Mexico won independence from Spain in 1821, it began to mint its own silver dollar, which became the most prized coin in trade in East Asia. By the beginning of the twentieth century, when the rest of the world had adopted gold as the standard of currency, only China and Mexico remained on the silver standard, testimony to the central role this metal had played in their histories.

providing insights still valued today. The essays of Michel de Montaigne epitomized a new spirit of skepticism and cultural relativism, while the plays of William Shakespeare reflected his efforts to come to terms with the cultural complexities of his day. Religion became another means of cultural contact, as European missionaries aimed to spread Christianity in both the New World and East Asia, with mixed results. While Christianity was embraced in parts of the New World, it was met largely with suspicion in China and Japan. However, the East-West contacts led to exchanges of influential cultural and scientific ideas.

New Ideas About Race

At the beginning of the transatlantic slave trade, most Europeans would have thought of Africans, if they thought of them at all, as savages because of their eating habits, religious practices, morals, clothing, and social customs, and as barbarians because of their language and methods of war. They grouped Africans into the despised categories of pagan heathens or Muslim infidels. Africans were certainly not the only peoples subject to such dehumanizing attitudes. To Christian Europeans, Jews were also an alien group and were, like Africans, naturally given to sin and depravity. More generally, elite people across Europe were accustomed to viewing the peasant masses as a lower form of humanity.

As Europeans turned to Africa for new sources of slaves, they drew on beliefs about Africans' primitiveness and barbarity to defend slavery and even argue that enslavement benefited Africans by bringing the light of Christianity to heathen peoples. In 1444 an observer defended the enslavement of the first Africans by Portuguese explorers as necessary for their salvation "because they lived like beasts, without any of the customs of rational creatures, since they did not even know what were bread and wine, nor garments of cloth, nor life in the shelter of a house; and worse still was their ignorance, which deprived them of knowledge of good, and permitted them only a life of brutish idleness."[10] Compare this with an early seventeenth-century Englishman's complaint that the Irish "be so beastly that they are better like beasts than Christians."[11]

Over time the institution of slavery fostered a new level of racial inequality. Africans gradually became seen as utterly distinct from and wholly inferior to Europeans. In a transition from rather vague assumptions about African's non-Christian religious beliefs and general lack of civilization, Europeans developed increasingly rigid ideas of racial superiority and inferiority to safeguard the growing profits gained from plantation slavery. Black skin became equated with slavery itself as Europeans at home and in the colonies convinced

themselves that blacks were destined by God to serve them as slaves in perpetuity.

Support for this belief went back to the Greek philosopher Aristotle's argument that some people are naturally destined for slavery and to biblical associations between darkness and sin. A more explicit justification was found in the story of Noah's curse upon the descendants of his disobedient son Ham to be the "servant[s] of servants." Biblical genealogies listing Ham's sons as those who peopled North Africa and Kush (which includes parts of modern Egypt and Sudan) were interpreted to mean that all inhabitants of those regions bore Noah's curse. From the sixteenth century onward, many defenders of slavery cited this story as justification for the enslavement of an entire race.

After 1700 the emergence of new methods of observing and describing nature led to the use of science to define race. From referring to a nation or an ethnic group, henceforth "race" would be used to describe supposedly biologically distinct groups of people whose physical differences produced differences in culture, character, and intelligence. Biblical justifications for inequality thereby gave way to allegedly scientific ones.

Michel de Montaigne and Cultural Curiosity

Racism was not the only possible reaction to the new worlds emerging in the sixteenth century. Decades of religious fanaticism, bringing civil anarchy and war, led both Catholics and Protestants to doubt that any one faith contained absolute truth. Added to these doubts was the discovery of peoples in the New World who had radically different ways of life. These shocks helped produce ideas of skepticism and cultural relativism in the sixteenth and seventeenth centuries. Skepticism is a school of thought founded on doubt that total certainty or definitive knowledge is ever attainable. Cultural relativism suggests that one culture is not necessarily superior to another, just different. Both notions found expression in the work of Frenchman Michel de Montaigne (MEE-shel duh mahn-TAYN; 1533–1592).

Montaigne developed a new literary genre, the essay — from the French *essayer*, meaning "to test or try" — to express his thoughts and ideas. Published in 1580, Montaigne's *Essays* consisted of short personal reflections. Intending to be accessible to ordinary people, Montaigne wrote in French rather than in Latin and used an engaging conversational style.

Montaigne's essay "On Cannibals" reveals the impact of overseas discoveries on his consciousness. In contrast to the prevailing views of the time, he rejected the notion that one culture is superior to another. Speaking of native Brazilians, he wrote:

I find that there is nothing barbarous and savage in this nation [Brazil], . . . except, that everyone gives the title of barbarism to everything that is not according to his usage; as, indeed, we have no other criterion of truth and reason, than the example and pattern of the opinions and customs of the place wherein we live. . . . They are savages in the same way that we say fruits are wild, which nature produces of herself and by her ordinary course; whereas, in truth, we ought rather to call those wild whose natures we have changed by our artifice and diverted from the common order.[12]

In his own time and throughout the seventeenth century, few would have agreed with Montaigne's challenging of European superiority. The publication of his ideas, however, contributed to a basic shift in attitudes. Montaigne inaugurated an era of doubt. "Wonder," he said, "is the foundation of all philosophy, research is the means of all learning, and ignorance is the end."[13]

William Shakespeare and His Influence

In addition to marking the introduction of the essay as a literary genre, the period fostered remarkable creativity in other branches of literature. England — especially in the latter part of Queen Elizabeth I's reign

and in the first years of her successor, James I (r. 1603–1625) — witnessed remarkable literary expression.

The undisputed master of the period was the dramatist William Shakespeare, whose genius lay in the originality of his characterizations, the diversity of his plots, his understanding of human psychology, and his unsurpassed gift for language. Born in 1564, Shakespeare was a Renaissance man with a deep appreciation of classical culture, individualism, and humanism.

Like Montaigne's, Shakespeare's work reveals the impact of new connections between Europeans and peoples of other cultures. The title character of *Othello* is described as a "Moor of Venice." In Shakespeare's day, the word *moor* referred to Muslims of Moroccan or North African origin, including those who had migrated to the Iberian Peninsula. It could also be applied, though, to natives of the Iberian Peninsula who converted to Islam or to non-Muslim Berbers in North Africa. To complicate things even more, references in the play to Othello as "black" in skin color have led many to believe that Shakespeare intended him to be a sub-Saharan African, and he is usually depicted as such in modern performances. This confusion in the play reflects the uncertainty in Shakespeare's own day about racial and religious classifications.

The character of Othello is both vilified in racist terms by his enemies and depicted as a brave warrior, a key member of the city's military leadership, and a

Titus Andronicus With classical allusions, fifteen murders and executions, a Gothic queen who takes a black lover, and incredible violence, this early Shakespearean tragedy (1594) was a melodramatic thriller that enjoyed enormous popularity with the London audience. The shock value of a dark-skinned character on the English stage is clearly shown in this illustration. (Reproduced by permission of the Marquess of Bath, Longleat House, Warminster, Wilts)

Viewpoints

Christian Conversion in New Spain

• *In justifying their violent conquest of the Mexica and Inca civilizations, Spanish conquistadors emphasized the need to bring Christianity to heathen peoples. For the conquered, the imposition of Christianity and repression of their pre-existing religions were often experienced as yet another form of loss. The first document describes the response of the recently vanquished Mexica leaders of Tenochtitlán to Franciscan missionaries. Despite resistance, missionaries eventually succeeded in converting much of the indigenous population to Catholicism. In his firsthand account of the Spanish conquest, written a few decades after the fall of Tenochtitlán, Bernal Díaz del Castillo expressed great satisfaction at the Catholic piety of some indigenous communities.*

Mexica Response to the Franciscans' Explanation of Their Mission in 1524

"You have told us that we do not know the One who gives us life and being, who is Lord of the heavens and of the earth. You also say that those we worship are not gods. This way of speaking is entirely new to us, and very scandalous. We are frightened by this way of speaking because our forebears who engendered and governed us never said anything like this. On the contrary, they left us this our custom of worshiping our gods, in which they believed and which they worshiped all the time that they lived here on earth. They taught us how to honor them. And they taught us all the ceremonies and sacrifices that we make. They told us that through them [our gods] we live and are, and that we were beholden to them, to be theirs and to serve countless centuries before the sun began to shine and before there was daytime. They said that these gods that we worship give us everything we need for our physical existence: maize, beans, chia seeds, etc.

. . . All of us together feel that it is enough to have lost, enough that the power and royal jurisdiction have been taken from us. As for our gods, we will die before giving up serving and worshiping them."

Bernal Díaz del Castillo, from *The True History of the Conquest of New Spain*

"It is a thing to be grateful for to God, and for profound consideration, to see how the natives assist in celebrating a holy Mass. . . . There is another good thing they do [namely]

that both men, women and children, who are of the age to learn them, know all the holy prayers in their own languages and are obliged to know them. They have other good customs about their holy Christianity, that when they pass near a sacred altar or Cross they bow their heads with humility, bend their knees, and say the prayer "Our Father," which we Conquistadores have taught them, and they place lighted wax candles before the holy altars and crosses, for formerly they did not know how to use wax in making candles. In addition, to what I have said, we taught them to show great reverence and obedience to all the monks and priests, and, when these went to their pueblos, to sally forth to receive them with lighted wax candles and to ring the bells, and to feed them very well. . . . Beside the good customs reported by me they have others both holy and good, for when the day of Corpus Christ comes, or that of Our Lady, or other solemn festivals when among us we form processions, most of the pueblos in the neighbourhood of this city of Guatemala come out in procession with their crosses and lighted wax tapers, and carry on their shoulders, on a litter, the image of the saint who is the patron of the pueblo."

Sources: Mexica Response: "The Lords and Holy Men of Tenochtitlan Reply to the Franciscans Bernardino de Sahagún, Coloquios y doctrina Cristiana," ed. Miguel León-Portilla, in *Spanish Colonial America: A Documentary History*, ed. Kenneth Mills and William B. Taylor. Copyright 1998. Reproduced with permission of SR BOOKS in the format Textbook and Other Book via Copyright Clearance Center; Bernal Díaz del Castillo: Bernal Diaz, *The True History of the Conquest of New Spain*, in Stuart B. Schwarz, *Victors and Vanquished: Spanish and Nahua Views of the Conquest of Mexico*, pp. 218–219.

QUESTIONS FOR ANALYSIS

1. What reasons do the leaders of Tenochtitlán offer for rejecting the teachings of Franciscan missionaries? What importance do they accord their own religious traditions?

2. What evidence does Bernal Diaz provide for the conversion of the indigenous people in the city of Guatemala?

3. How and why do you think indigenous peoples might have evolved from the attitudes expressed in the first document to those described in the second? Do you think the second document tells the whole story of religious attitudes under Spanish rule?

man capable of winning the heart of an aristocratic white woman. In contrast to the prevailing view of Moors as inferior, Shakespeare presents Othello as a complex human figure. Shakespeare's play thus demonstrates both the intolerance of contemporary society and the possibility for some individuals to look beyond racial stereotypes.

Shakespeare's last play, *The Tempest*, displays a similar interest in race and race relations. The plot involves the stranding on an island of sorcerer Prospero and his daughter, Miranda. There Prospero finds and raises Caliban, a native of the island, whom he instructs in his own language and religion. After Caliban's attempted rape of Miranda, Prospero enslaves him, earning the rage and resentment of his erstwhile pupil. Modern scholars often note the echoes between this play and the realities of imperial conquest and settlement in Shakespeare's day. It is no accident, they argue, that the playwright portrayed Caliban as a monstrous dark-skinned island native who was best-suited for slavery. However, Shakespeare himself borrows words from Montaigne's essay "On Cannibals," suggesting that he may have intended to criticize, rather than endorse, racial intolerance. Shakespeare's work shows us one of the finest minds of the age struggling to come to terms with the racial and religious complexities around him.

Religious Conversion in the New World

Converting indigenous people to Christianity was a key ambition for all European powers in the New World. Galvanized by the desire to spread their religion and prevent any gains by Protestants, Catholic powers actively sponsored missionary efforts. Franciscans, Dominicans, Jesuits, and members of other religious orders who accompanied the conquistadors and subsequent settlers established Catholic missions throughout Spanish and Portuguese colonies. Later French explorers were also accompanied by missionaries who preached to the Native American tribes with whom they traded.

Rather than a straightforward imposition of Christianity, conversion entailed a complex process of cultural exchange. Catholic friars were among the first Europeans to seek understanding of native cultures and languages as part of their effort to render Christianity comprehensible to indigenous people. In addition to spreading Christianity, missionaries taught indigenous peoples European methods of agriculture and instilled loyalty to colonial masters. In turn, Christian ideas and practices in the New World took on a distinctive character. For example, a sixteenth-century apparition of the Virgin Mary in Mexico City, known as the Virgin of Guadalupe, became a central icon of Spanish-American Catholicism.

Missionaries' success in the New World varied over time and space. In Central and South America large-scale conversion forged enduring Catholic cultures in Portuguese and Spanish colonies. (See "Viewpoints: Christian Conversion in New Spain," page 486.) For example, it is estimated that missionaries had baptized between four and nine million indigenous people in New Spain by the mid-1530s.[14] Conversion efforts in seventeenth-century North America were less effective due to the scattered nature of settlement and the lesser integration of native people into the colonial community. On the whole, Protestants were less active than Catholics as missionaries, although some dissenters like Quakers and Methodists did seek converts among native people. Efforts to Christianize indigenous peoples in the New World were paralleled by missionary work by the Jesuits and other orders in the Far East.

CONNECTIONS

Just three years separated Martin Luther's attack on the Catholic Church in 1517 and Ferdinand Magellan's discovery of the Pacific Ocean in 1520. Within a few short years western Europeans' religious unity and notions of terrestrial geography were shattered. Old medieval certainties about Heaven and earth collapsed. In the ensuing decades Europeans struggled to come to terms with religious differences among Protestants and Catholics at home and with the multitudes of new peoples and places they encountered abroad. While some Europeans were fascinated and inspired by this new diversity, too often the result was violence. Europeans endured decades of religious civil war, and indigenous peoples overseas suffered massive population losses as a result of European warfare, disease, and exploitation. Tragically, both Catholic and Protestant religious leaders condoned the trade in slaves that was to bring suffering and death to millions of Africans.

Even as the voyages of discovery contributed to the fragmentation of European culture, they also factored into state centralization and consolidation in the longer term.

Henceforth, competition to gain overseas colonies became an integral part of European politics. Spain's investment in conquest proved spectacularly profitable, and yet, the ultimate result was a weakening of its power. Over time the Netherlands, England, and France also reaped tremendous profits from colonial trade, which helped them build modernized, centralized states.

The most important consequence of the European voyages of discovery was the creation of enduring contacts among five of the seven continents of the globe — Europe, Asia, Africa, North America, and South America. From the sixteenth century onward, the peoples of the world were increasingly entwined in divergent forms of economic, social, and cultural exchange. Our modern era of globalization had begun.

◻ CHAPTER REVIEW

KEY TERMS

bride wealth (p. 462)
conquistador (p. 465)
caravel (p. 467)
Ptolemy's *Geography* (p. 467)
Treaty of Tordesillas (p. 471)
Mexica Empire (p. 474)
Inca Empire (p. 475)
viceroyalties (p. 476)
encomienda system (p. 477)
Columbian exchange (p. 478)

◻ What was the Afroeurasian trade world like before the voyages of Columbus? (p. 460)

Prior to Columbus's voyages, well-developed trade routes linked the peoples and products of Africa, Asia, and Europe. The Indian Ocean was the center of the Afroeurasian trade world, ringed by cosmopolitan commercial cities such as Mombasa in Africa, Calicut in India, and Malacca in Southeast Asia. Among the goods traded were silk, porcelain, spices, textiles, gold, and slaves. Overall, Europe played a minor role in the Afroeurasian trade world because it did not produce many products desired by Eastern elites. Nevertheless, Europeans — especially Venetian and Genoese merchants — sought to tap into the goods and wealth of Afroeurasian commerce.

◻ Why and how did Europeans undertake ambitious voyages of expansion? (p. 465)

A revival of populations and economies after the time of the Black Death created markets for spices and other goods from the East. In addition to searching for routes that would undo the Italian and Ottoman dominance of trade in the East, Europeans were motivated by intellectual curiosity, driving ambition, religious zeal, and a lack of opportunities at home. Strengthened monarchies possessed sufficient resources to back ambitious seafarers like Christopher Columbus, Vasco da Gama, and Ferdinand Magellan. Technological developments such as the invention of the caravel and magnetic compass enabled Europeans to undertake ever more ambitious voyages. Driven by desires for conquest and wealth, Europeans — first Hernando Cortés and then Francisco Pizarro — eventually penetrated farther into the New World than Columbus had.

◻ How did conquest affect indigenous populations and bring about a new era of economic and cultural exchange, commercial empires, and forced migrations? (p. 476)

In the aftermath of conquest, the Spanish established new forms of governance to dominate native peoples and exploit their labor. The arrival of Europeans also brought enormous population losses to native communities, primarily through the spread of infectious diseases. Disease was one element of the Columbian exchange, a complex transfer of germs, plants, and animals between the Old and New Worlds. Although this exchange brought diseases to the Americas, it also gave both the New and Old Worlds new crops that eventually altered consumption patterns internationally. These new cultural linkages were part of the creation of the first truly global economy. Tragically, a major component of global trade was the transatlantic slave trade, in which Europeans transported, under horrific conditions, many thousands of Africans to labor in the sugar plantations and silver mines of the New World. European nations vied for supremacy in global trade, with early Portuguese success in India and Asia being challenged first by the Spanish and then by the Dutch, who took control of trade with the East in the mid-seventeenth century.

☐ **How did new encounters shape cultural values and beliefs in Europe and the New World? (p. 481)**

Increased contact with the outside world led Europeans to develop new ideas about cultural and racial differences. Europeans had long held negative attitudes about Africans; as the slave trade grew, they began to express more rigid notions of racial inequality and to claim that Africans were inherently suited for slavery. Most Europeans, with some important exceptions, shared such views. In his essays, Michel de Montaigne challenged the idea that natives of the Americas were inferior barbarians, while William Shakespeare's plays contain ambivalent attitudes toward complex non-European characters. Religion became another means of cultural contact, as European missionaries aimed to spread Christianity in the New World, with mixed results. Christianity was especially embraced in Central and South America, where large-scale conversion led to the development of distinct and enduring Catholic cultures. Missionaries were less successful in North America because of the distance between settlements and the lesser integration of native populations into colonial society.

SUGGESTED READING

Crosby, Alfred W. *The Columbian Exchange: Biological and Cultural Consequences of 1492.* 30th anniversary ed. 2003. An innovative and highly influential account of the environmental impact of Columbus's voyages.

Elliot, J. H. *Empires of the Atlantic World: Britain and Spain in America, 1492–1830.* 2006. A masterful account of the differences and similarities between the British and Spanish Empires in the Americas.

Fernández-Armesto, Felip. *Columbus.* 1992. An excellent biography of Christopher Columbus.

Greenblatt, Stephen. *Marvelous Possessions: The Wonder of the New World.* 1991. Describes the cultural impact of New World discoveries on Europeans.

Menard, Russell. *Sweet Negotiations: Sugar, Slavery, and Plantation Agriculture in Early Barbados.* 2006. Explores the intertwined history of sugar plantations and slavery in seventeenth-century Barbados.

Northrup, David, ed. *The Atlantic Slave Trade.* 1994. Collected essays by leading scholars on many different aspects of the slave trade.

Pérez-Mallaína, Pablo E. *Spain's Men of the Sea: Daily Life on the Indies Fleet in the Sixteenth Century.* 1998. A description of recruitment, daily life, and career paths of ordinary sailors and officers in the Spanish fleet.

Pomeranz, Kenneth, and Steven Topik. *The World That Trade Created: Society, Culture, and the World Economy, 1400 to the Present.* 1999. Explores the creation of a world market through the rich and vivid stories of merchants, miners, slaves, and farmers.

Restall, Matthew. *Seven Myths of Spanish Conquest.* 2003. A re-examination of common ideas about why and how the Spanish conquered native civilizations in the New World.

Scammell, Geoffrey V. *The World Encompassed: The First European Maritime Empires, c. 800–1650.* 1981. A detailed overview of the first European empires, including the Italian city-states, Portugal, and Spain.

Schmidt, Benjamin. *Innocence Abroad: The Dutch Imagination and the New World, 1570–1670.* 2001. Examines changing Dutch attitudes toward the New World, from criticism of the cruelty of the Spanish conquest to eagerness for their own overseas empire.

Subrahamanyam, Sanjay. *The Career and Legend of Vasco da Gama.* 1998. A probing biography that places Vasco da Gama in the context of Portuguese politics and society.

NOTES

1. Thomas Benjamin, *The Atlantic World: Europeans, Africans, Indians and Their Shared History, 1400–1900* (Cambridge, U.K.: Cambridge University Press, 2009), p. 56.
2. A. Reid, *Southeast Asia in the Age of Commerce, 1450–1680.* Vol. 1: *The Land Under the Winds* (New Haven, Conn.: Yale University Press, 1988), pp. 3–20.
3. Quoted in C. M. Cipolla, *Guns, Sails, and Empires: Technological Innovation and the Early Phases of European Expansion, 1400–1700* (New York: Minerva Press, 1965), p. 132.
4. Quoted in F. H. Littell, *The Macmillan Atlas: History of Christianity* (New York: Macmillan, 1976), p. 75.
5. Quoted in R. L. Kagan, "The Spain of Ferdinand and Isabella," in *Circa 1492: Art in the Age of Exploration*, ed. J. A. Levenson (Washington, D.C.: National Gallery of Art, 1991), p. 60.
6. Benjamin, *The Atlantic World*, p. 141.
7. Ibid., pp. 35–59.
8. Quoted in C. Gibson, ed., *The Black Legend: Anti-Spanish Attitudes in the Old World and the New* (New York: Knopf, 1971), pp. 74–75.
9. Herbert S. Klein, "Profits and the Causes of Mortality," in *The Atlantic Slave Trade*, ed. David Northrup (Lexington, Mass.: D. C. Heath and Co., 1994), p. 116.
10. Quoted in James H. Sweet, "The Iberian Roots of American Racist Thought," *The William and Mary Quarterly*, Third Series, 54 (Jan. 1997): 155.
11. Quoted in Sean J. Connolly, *Contested Island: Ireland, 1460–1630* (Oxford, U.K.: Oxford University Press, 2007), p. 397.
12. C. Cotton, trans., *The Essays of Michel de Montaigne* (New York: A. L. Burt, 1893), pp. 207, 210.
13. Ibid., p. 523.
14. David Carrasco, *The Oxford Encyclopedia of Mesoamerican Cultures* (Oxford: Oxford University Press, 2001), p. 208.

For practice quizzes and other study tools, visit the **Online Study Guide** at bedfordstmartins.com/mckayworld.

For primary sources from this period, see *Sources of World Societies*, **Second Edition**.

For Web sites, images, and documents related to topics in this chapter, visit **Make History** at bedfordstmartins.com/mckayworld.

• **Louis XIV** Representations of royal power emphasized the aristocratic bearing, elegance, and innate authority of absolutist kings. This was one of Louis XIV's favorite portraits of himself. He liked it so much that he had many copies of the portrait made, in full and half-size format. (Louvre/Giraudon/ The Bridgeman Art Library)

17

European Power and Expansion

1500–1750

The seventeenth century was a period of crisis and transformation in Europe. What one historian described as the long European "struggle for stability" that originated with conflicts sparked by the Reformation in the early sixteenth century and continued with economic and social breakdown was largely resolved by 1680.[1] To meet the demands of war, armies grew larger, taxes increased, and new bureaucracies came into being. Thus at the same time that powerful governments were emerging and evolving in Asia—such as the Qing Dynasty in China, the Tokugawa Shogunate in Japan (see Chapter 21), and the Mughal Empire in India (see Chapter 20)—European rulers also increased the power of the central state.

Important differences existed, however, in terms of which authority within the state possessed sovereignty—the Crown or privileged groups. Between roughly 1589 and 1715 two basic patterns of government emerged in Europe: absolute monarchy and the constitutional state. Almost all subsequent European governments have been modeled on one of these patterns, which have also influenced greatly the rest of the world in the past three centuries.

Constitutional or absolutist, European states sought to further increase their power through colonial expansion. Jealous of the silver that had flowed into Spain from the New World, England, France, and the Netherlands vied for new acquisitions on the mainland and in the Caribbean. •

Estonian Serfs in the 1660s The Estonians were conquered by German military nobility in the Middle Ages and reduced to serfdom. The German-speaking nobles ruled the Estonian peasants with an iron hand, and Peter the Great reaffirmed their domination when Russia annexed Estonia. (Mansell Collection/Time Life Pictures/Getty Images)

Seventeenth-Century Crisis and Rebuilding

□ What were the common crises and achievements of seventeenth-century European states?

Historians often refer to the seventeenth century as an "age of crisis." After the economic and demographic growth of the sixteenth century, Europe was challenged by population losses, economic decline, and social and political unrest. These difficulties were partially due to climate changes that reduced agricultural productivity. But they also resulted from religious divides, increased taxation, and war. Peasants and the urban poor were hit especially hard by the economic problems, and peasants took action against rising food prices, sometimes rioting for food to obtain relief. In the long run, however, governments proved increasingly able to impose their will on the populace. This period witnessed a spectacular growth in army size as well as increased taxation, expansion of government bureaucracies, and strides toward state sovereignty.

Crises Among Peasants and the Urban Poor

In the seventeenth century a period of colder and wetter climate throughout Europe, dubbed the "little ice age" by historians, meant a shorter growing season with lower yields. The result was recurrent famines that significantly reduced the population of early modern Europe. Most people did not die of outright starvation, but rather of diseases brought on by malnutrition and exhaustion. Facilitated by the weakened population, outbreaks of the Black Death (bubonic plague) continued in Europe until the 1720s.

In 1651 the estates of Normandy, a provincial assembly, reported on the dire conditions in northern France during an outbreak of plague in which disease was compounded by the disruption of agriculture and a lack of food:

> Of the 450 sick persons whom the inhabitants were unable to relieve, 200 were turned out, and these we saw die one by one as they lay on the roadside. A large number still remain, and to each of them it is only possible to dole out the least scrap of bread. We only give bread to those who would otherwise die. The staple dish here consists of mice, which the inhabitants hunt, so desperate are they from hunger. They devour roots which the animals cannot eat; one can, in fact, not put into words the things one sees.[2]

When food prices were high, industry also suffered because consumers had little money to purchase goods.

The result was low wages and widespread unemployment, which further exacerbated economic problems. The output of woolen textiles, one of the most important manufactured products from Europe, declined sharply in many parts of Europe in the first half of the seventeenth century. This economic crisis was not universal: it struck various regions at different times and to different degrees. In the middle decades of the century, Spain, France, Germany, and England all experienced great economic difficulties. In the Netherlands, however, an influx of foreign capital, among other factors, made these years a golden age (see page 515).

The urban poor and peasants were the hardest hit. When the price of bread rose beyond their capacity to pay, they frequently expressed their anger by rioting. In towns they invaded bakers' shops to seize bread and resell it at a "just price." In rural areas they attacked convoys taking grain to the cities. Women often led these actions, since their role as mothers gave them some protection against punishment by authorities. Historians have labeled this vision of a world in which community needs predominate over competition and profit a moral economy.

The Return of Serfdom in Eastern Europe

While economic and social hardship was common across Europe, important differences existed between east and west. In the west the demographic losses of the Black Death allowed peasants to escape the bonds of working the landed estate of a lord (serfdom) as they acquired enough land to feed themselves and the livestock and ploughs necessary to work their land. In eastern Europe, however, the Black Death had the opposite effect, and peasants largely lost their ability to own land independently. Before the arrival of the plague, starting in about 1050, rulers and nobles in eastern Europe had attracted new settlers to their sparsely populated estates by offering them land on excellent terms and granting them much personal freedom. But in the fourteenth century eastern lords addressed labor shortages caused by the Black Death by restricting the right of their peasants to move to take advantage of better opportunities elsewhere. Moreover, lords steadily took

□ **CHRONOLOGY**

ca. 1500–1650 Consolidation of serfdom in eastern Europe

1533–1584 Reign of Ivan the Terrible in Russia

1589–1610 Reign of Henry IV in France

1598–1613 Time of Troubles in Russia

1612–1697 Caribbean islands colonized by France, England, and the Netherlands

1620–1740 Growth of absolutism in Austria and Prussia

1642–1649 English civil war, ending with the execution of Charles I

1643–1715 Reign of Louis XIV in France

1651 First of the Navigation Acts

1653–1658 Oliver Cromwell's military rule in England (the Protectorate)

1660 Restoration of English monarchy under Charles II

1665–1683 Jean-Baptiste Colbert applies mercantilism to France

1670 Charles II agrees to re-Catholicize England in secret agreement with Louis XIV

1670–1671 Cossack revolt led by Stenka Razin

1682 Louis XIV moves court to Versailles

1682–1725 Reign of Peter the Great in Russia

1683–1718 Habsburgs push the Ottoman Turks from Hungary

1685 Edict of Nantes revoked

1688–1689 Glorious Revolution in England

1701–1713 War of the Spanish Succession

more and more of their peasants' land and arbitrarily imposed heavier and heavier labor obligations. By the early 1500s lords in many eastern territories could command their peasants to work for them without pay for as many as six days a week.

The power of the lord reached far into serfs' everyday lives. Not only was their freedom of movement restricted, but they required permission to marry or could be forced to marry. Lords could reallocate the lands worked by their serfs at will or break up serf families by selling individual members. The local lord also monopolized the legal system, acting as prosecutor, judge, and jailer. There were no independent royal officials to provide justice or uphold the common law.

Between 1500 and 1650 the consolidation of serfdom in eastern Europe was accompanied by the growth of commercial agriculture, particularly in Poland and eastern Germany. As economic expansion and population growth resumed after 1500, eastern lords increased the production of their estates by squeezing sizable surpluses out of the impoverished peasants. They then sold these surpluses to foreign merchants, who exported them to the growing cities of wealthier western Europe.

The worsened conditions for serfs in eastern Europe reflected the fact that eastern lords enjoyed much greater political power than their western counterparts. In the late Middle Ages, when much of eastern Europe was experiencing innumerable wars and general public chaos, the noble landlord class had greatly increased its political power at the expense of the ruling monarchs. Moreover, the western concept of a king as one who protects the interests of all his people was not well developed in eastern Europe before 1650.

With the approval of weak kings, landlords in eastern Europe systematically undermined the medieval privileges of the towns and the power of the urban classes. For example, eastern towns lost their medieval right to provide refuge to runaways and were compelled to return escaped peasants to their lords. The populations of the towns and the urban middle classes declined greatly. This development both reflected and promoted the supremacy of noble landlords in most of eastern Europe in the sixteenth century. Although noble landlords held onto their powers in the seventeenth century, kings increased their authority during this period (see pages 501–509).

The Thirty Years' War

In the first half of the seventeenth century, the fragile balance of life was violently upturned by the ravages of the Thirty Years' War (1618–1648). Leading up to the war were conflicts between Catholics and Protestants in the Holy Roman Empire, a confederation of hundreds of principalities, independent cities, duchies, and other polities loosely united under an elected emperor. Although the emperor was Catholic, Protestantism had started to take hold in parts of the empire, including Germany, and clashes resulted. In 1555 the two religious groups came to an uneasy truce under the Peace of Augsburg, which officially recognized Lutheranism and allowed political authorities in each German territory to decide whether the territory would be Catholic or Lutheran. But the truce deteriorated as the faiths of various areas shifted. Lutheran princes felt compelled to form the Protestant Union (1608), and Catholics retaliated with the Catholic League (1609). Each alliance was determined that the other should make no religious

or territorial advance. Dynastic interests were also involved; the Spanish Habsburgs strongly supported the goals of their Austrian relatives: the unity of the empire and the preservation of Catholicism within it.

The war is traditionally divided into four phases. The first, or Bohemian, phase (1618–1625) was characterized by civil war in Bohemia (part of the present-day Czech Republic) between the Catholic League and the Protestant Union. In 1620 Catholic forces defeated Protestants at the Battle of the White Mountain. The second, or Danish, phase of the war (1625–1629) — so called because of the leadership of the Protestant king Christian IV of Denmark (r. 1588–1648) — witnessed additional Catholic victories.

The third, or Swedish, phase of the war (1630–1635) began with the arrival in Germany of the Swedish king Gustavus Adolphus (r. 1594–1632) and his army. The ablest administrator of his day and a devout Lutheran, he intervened to support the empire's Protestants. The French chief minister, Cardinal Richelieu, subsidized the Swedes, hoping to weaken Habsburg power in Europe. Gustavus Adolphus won two important battles but was fatally wounded in combat. The final, or French, phase of the war (1635–1648) was prompted by Richelieu's concern that the Habsburgs, France's greatest rival for power, would rebound after the death of Gustavus Adolphus. Richelieu declared war on Spain and sent military as well as financial assistance. Finally, in October 1648 peace was achieved.

The 1648 **Peace of Westphalia** that ended the Thirty Years' War marked a turning point in European history. The treaties that established the peace not only ended conflicts fought over religious faith but also recognized the independent authority of more than three hundred German princes (Map 17.1), reconfirming the emperor's severely limited authority. The Augsburg agreement of 1555 became permanent, adding Calvinism to Catholicism and Lutheranism as legally permissible creeds. The north German states remained Protestant; the south German states, Catholic.

The Thirty Years' War was probably the most destructive event for the central European economy and society prior to the world wars of the twentieth century. Perhaps one-third of urban residents and two-fifths of the rural population died, leaving entire areas depopulated. Trade in southern German cities was virtually destroyed. Agricultural areas also suffered catastrophically. Many small farmers lost their land, allowing nobles to enlarge their estates and consolidate their control.[3]

Achievements in State Building

In this context of economic and demographic depression, monarchs began to make new demands on their people. Traditionally, historians have distinguished be-

• **Peace of Westphalia** The name of a series of treaties that concluded the Thirty Years' War in 1648 and marked the end of large-scale religious violence in Europe.

MAP 17.1 Europe After the Thirty Years' War Which country emerged from the Thirty Years' War as the strongest European power? What dynastic house was that country's major rival in the early modern period?

tween the absolutist governments of France, Spain, eastern and central Europe, and Russia and the constitutionalist governments of England and the Dutch Republic. Whereas absolutist monarchs gathered all power under their personal control, English and Dutch rulers were obliged to respect laws passed by representative institutions. More recently, historians have emphasized commonalities among these powers. Despite their political differences, all these states sought to protect and expand their frontiers, raise new taxes, consolidate central control, and compete for the colonies opening up in the New and Old Worlds.

Rulers who wished to increase their authority encountered formidable obstacles. Without paved roads, telephones, or other modern technology, it took weeks to convey orders from the central government to the provinces. Rulers also suffered from lack of information about their realms, making it impossible to police and tax the population effectively. Local power structures presented another serious obstacle. Nobles, the church, provincial and national assemblies, town councils, guilds, and other bodies held legal privileges that could not easily be rescinded. In some kingdoms many people spoke a language different from the Crown's, further diminishing their willingness to obey the Crown's commands.

Nonetheless, over the course of the seventeenth century both absolutist and constitutional governments achieved new levels of central control. This increased authority focused on four areas in particular: greater taxation, growth in armed forces, larger and more efficient bureaucracies, and the increased ability to compel obedience from subjects. Over time, centralized power added up to something close to sovereignty. A state may be termed sovereign when it possesses a monopoly over the instruments of justice and the use of force within clearly defined boundaries. In a sovereign state, no nongovernmental system of courts, such as ecclesiastical tribunals, competes with state courts in the dispensation of justice. Also, private armies, such as those of feudal lords, present no threat to central authority. While seventeenth-century states did not acquire total sovereignty, they made important strides toward that goal.

Absolutism in France and Spain

□ Why and how did the French absolutist state arise under Louis XIV, and why did absolutist Spain experience decline in the same period?

Kings in absolutist states asserted that, because they were chosen by God, they were responsible to God alone. They claimed exclusive power to make and enforce laws, denying any other institution or group the authority to check their power. Louis XIV of France is often seen as the epitome of an absolute monarch. In truth, his success relied on collaboration with nobles, and thus his example illustrates both the achievements and the compromises of absolutist rule.

As French power rose in the seventeenth century, the glory of Spain faded. Once the fabulous revenue from American silver declined, Spain's economic stagnation could no longer be disguised, and the country faltered under weak leadership.

The Foundations of Absolutism

Louis XIV's absolutism had long roots. In 1589 his grandfather Henry IV (r. 1589–1610), the founder of the Bourbon dynasty, acquired a devastated country. Civil wars between Protestants and Catholics had wracked France since 1561. Poor harvests had reduced peasants to starvation, and commercial activity had declined drastically.

Henry IV inaugurated a remarkable recovery by keeping France at peace during most of his reign. Although he had converted to Catholicism, he issued the Edict of Nantes, allowing Huguenots (French Protestants) the right to worship in 150 traditionally Protestant towns throughout France. He sharply lowered taxes and instead charged royal officials an annual fee to guarantee the right to pass their positions down to their heirs. He also improved the country's infrastructure, building new roads and canals and repairing the ravages of years of civil war. Despite his efforts at peace, Henry was murdered in 1610 by a Catholic zealot.

After the death of Henry IV his wife, the queen-regent Marie de' Medici, headed the government for their eldest son, nine-year-old Louis XIII (r. 1610–1643). In 1628 Armand Jean du Plessis — Cardinal Richelieu (1585–1642) — became first minister of the French crown. Richelieu's maneuvers allowed the monarchy to maintain power within Europe and within its own borders despite the turmoil of the Thirty Years' War.

Cardinal Richelieu's domestic policies were designed to strengthen royal control. He extended the use of intendants, commissioners for each of France's thirty-two districts who were appointed directly by the monarch, to whom they were solely responsible. They recruited men for the army, supervised the collection of taxes, presided over the administration of local law, checked up on the local nobility, and regulated economic activities in their districts. As the intendants' power increased under Richelieu, so did the power of the centralized French state.

Under Richelieu, the French monarchy also acted to repress Protestantism. Louis XIII personally supervised the siege of La Rochelle, an important port city and a major commercial center with strong ties to Protestant Holland and England. The fall of La Rochelle in October 1628 was one step in the removal of Protestantism as a strong force in French life.

Richelieu did not aim to wipe out Protestantism in the rest of Europe, however. His main foreign policy goal was to destroy the Catholic Habsburgs' grip on territories that surrounded France. Consequently, Richelieu supported Habsburg enemies, including Protestants (see page 494). For the French cardinal, interests of state outweighed religious considerations.

In 1642 Cardinal Jules Mazarin (1602–1661) succeeded Richelieu as chief minister for the next child-king, the four-year-old Louis XIV. Along with the regent, Queen Mother Anne of Austria, Mazarin continued Richelieu's centralizing policies. His struggle to increase royal revenues to meet the costs of the Thirty Years' War led to the uprisings of 1648–1653 known as the **Fronde**. In Paris, magistrates of the Parlement of Paris, the nation's most important law court, were outraged by the Crown's autocratic measures. These so-called robe nobles (named for the robes they wore in court) encouraged violent protest by the common people. As rebellion spread outside Paris and to the sword nobles (the traditional warrior nobility), civil order broke down completely, and young Louis XIV had to flee Paris for his safety. In 1651 Anne's regency

Louis XIV Receiving Ambassadors from Siam The kings of France and Siam (today's Thailand) sent ambassadors to each other's courts in the 1680s. This engraving commemorates Louis XIV's reception of the second Siamese diplomatic mission at Versailles, a visit that aroused great excitement and enthusiasm throughout western Europe. (Private Collection/Photo © Luca Tettoni/The Bridgeman Art Library)

ended with the declaration of Louis as king in his own right. Much of the rebellion died away, and its leaders came to terms with the government.

The twin evils of noble rebellion and popular riots left the French wishing for peace and for a strong monarch to reimpose order. This was the legacy that Louis XIV inherited when he assumed personal rule of the largest and most populous country in western Europe. Humiliated by his flight from Paris during the Fronde, he was determined to avoid any recurrence of rebellion when he assumed personal rule at Mazarin's death in 1661.

Louis XIV and Absolutism

In the long reign of Louis XIV (r. 1643–1715) the French monarchy reached the peak of absolutist development. Louis believed in the doctrine of the divine right of kings: God had established kings as his rulers on earth, and they were answerable ultimately to him alone. However, though kings were divinely anointed and shared in the sacred nature of divinity, they could

not simply do as they pleased. They had to obey God's laws and rule for the good of the people. To symbolize his central role in the divine order, when he was fifteen years old Louis danced at a court ballet dressed as the sun, thereby acquiring the title "Sun King."

Louis worked very hard at the business of governing. He ruled his realm through several councils of state and insisted on taking a personal role in many of the councils' decisions. He selected councilors from the recently ennobled or the upper middle class because he believed "that the public should know, from the rank of those whom I chose to serve me, that I had no intention of sharing power with them."[4] Despite increasing financial problems, Louis never called a meeting of the Estates General, the traditional French representative assembly composed of the three estates of clergy, nobility, and commoners. The French people, and its noble leaders, therefore, had no means to form united views or exert joint pressure on the monarch.

• **Fronde** A series of violent uprisings early in the reign of Louis XIV triggered by growing royal control and oppressive taxation.

Also, Louis freed himself from the inordinate power of a Richelieu by not appointing a first minister.

Although personally tolerant, Louis hated division within the realm and insisted that religious unity was essential to his royal dignity and to the security of the state. He thus pursued the policy of Protestant repression launched by Richelieu. In 1685 Louis revoked the Edict of Nantes and took steps to suppress the Huguenots.

Despite his claims to absolute authority, there were multiple constraints on Louis's power. As a representative of divine power, he was obliged to rule in a way that seemed consistent with virtue and benevolent authority. He had to uphold the laws issued by his royal predecessors. Moreover, he also relied on the collaboration of nobles, who maintained authority in their ancestral lands. Without their cooperation, it would have been impossible for Louis to extend his power throughout France or wage his many foreign wars (see page 499). His need to elicit noble cooperation led him to revolutionize court life at his palace at Versailles.

Life at Versailles

Through most of the seventeenth century, the French court had no fixed home, following the monarch to his numerous palaces and country residences. In 1682 Louis moved his court and government to the newly renovated palace at Versailles, in the countryside southwest of Paris. The palace quickly became the center of political, social, and cultural life. The king required all great nobles to spend at least part of the year in attendance on him there. Since he controlled the distribution of state power and wealth, nobles had no choice but to obey and compete with each other for his favor at Versailles.

Louis further revolutionized court life by establishing an elaborate set of etiquette rituals to mark every moment of his day, from waking up and dressing in the morning to removing his clothing and retiring at night. He required nobles to serve him in these rituals, and they vied for the honor of doing so. Endless squabbles broke out over what type of chair one could sit on at court and the order in which great nobles entered and were seated in the chapel for Mass.

These rituals may seem absurd, but they were far from meaningless or trivial. The king controlled immense resources and privileges; access to him meant favored treatment for government offices, military and religious posts, state pensions, honorary titles, and a host of other benefits. The Duke of Saint-Simon wrote

of the king's power at court in his memoirs:

> No one understood better than Louis XIV the art of enhancing the value of a favour by his manner of bestowing it; he knew how to make the most of a word, a smile, even of a glance. If he addressed any one, were it but to ask a trifling question or make some commonplace remark, all eyes were turned on the person so honored; it was a mark of favour which always gave rise to comment.[5]

Courtiers sought these rewards for themselves and their family members and followers. A system of patronage — in which a higher-ranked individual protected a lower-ranked one in return for loyalty and services — flowed from the court to the provinces. Through this mechanism Louis gained cooperation from powerful nobles.

Although they were denied public offices and posts, women played a central role in the patronage system. At court the king's wife, mistresses, and other female relatives recommended individuals for honors, advocated policy decisions, and brokered alliances between noble factions. Noblewomen played a similar role among courtiers, bringing their family connections into their marriages to form powerful social networks.

Louis XIV was also an enthusiastic patron of the arts. He commissioned many sculptures and paintings for Versailles as well as performances of dance and music. Louis loved the stage, and in the plays of Molière and Racine his court witnessed the finest achievements in the history of the French theater.

With Versailles as the center of European politics, French culture grew in international prestige. French became the language of polite society and international diplomacy, gradually replacing Latin as the language of scholarship and learning. The royal courts of Sweden, Russia, Poland, and Germany all spoke French. France inspired a cosmopolitan European culture in the late seventeenth century that looked to Versailles as its center.

French Finances

France's ability to build armies and fight wars depended on a strong economy. Fortunately for Louis, his controller general, Jean-Baptiste Colbert (1619–1683), proved to be a financial genius. Colbert's central principle was that the wealth and the economy of France should serve the state. To this end, from 1665 to his death in 1683, Colbert rigorously applied mercantilist policies to France.

Mercantilism is a collection of governmental policies for the regulation of economic activities by and for the state. It derives from the idea that a nation's international power is based on its wealth, specifically its

---

• **mercantilism** A system of economic regulations aimed at increasing the power of the state based on the belief that a nation's international power was based on its wealth, specifically its supply of gold and silver.

supply of gold and silver. To accumulate wealth, a country always had to sell more goods abroad than it bought. Thus, to reduce imports Colbert insisted that French industry should produce everything needed by the French people.

To increase exports, Colbert supported old industries and created new ones. He enacted new production regulations, created guilds to boost quality standards, and encouraged foreign craftsmen to immigrate to France. To encourage the purchase of French goods, he abolished many domestic tariffs and raised tariffs on foreign products. In 1664 Colbert founded the Company of the East Indies with (unfulfilled) hopes of competing with the Dutch for Asian trade. Colbert also sought to increase France's control over and presence in New France (Canada) — rich in untapped minerals and some of the best agricultural land in the world (see page 516).

During Colbert's tenure as controller general, Louis was able to pursue his goals without massive tax increases and without creating a stream of new offices.

The constant pressure of warfare after Colbert's death, however, undid many of his economic achievements.

Louis XIV's Wars

Louis XIV kept France at war for thirty-three of the fifty-four years of his personal rule. François le Tellier, Marquis de Louvois, Louis's secretary of state for war, equaled Colbert's achievements in the economic realm. Louvois created a professional army in the employ of the French state. The French army grew in size from roughly 125,000 men in the Thirty Years' War (1630–1648) to 250,000 during the Dutch War (1672–1678) and 340,000 during the War of the League of Augsburg (1688–1697).[6] Uniforms and weapons were standardized, and a rational system of training and promotion was devised. As in so many other matters, Louis's model was followed across Europe.

During this long period of warfare Louis's goal was to expand France to what he considered its natural borders. His armies managed to extend French borders

Spanish Troops The long wars that Spain fought over Dutch independence, in support of Habsburg interests in Germany, and against France left the country militarily exhausted and financially drained by the mid-1600s. In this detail from a painting by Peeter Snayers, Spanish troops — thin, emaciated, and probably unpaid — straggle away from battle. (Prado, Madrid/Index/The Bridgeman Art Library)

Legend:
- French Bourbon lands
- Spanish Bourbon lands
- Austrian Habsburg lands
- Prussian lands
- Great Britain
- Russian Empire
- Boundary of the Holy Roman Empire

☐ Mapping the Past

MAP 17.2 Europe After the Peace of Utrecht, 1715 The series of treaties commonly called the Peace of Utrecht ended the War of the Spanish Succession and redrew the map of Europe. A French Bourbon king succeeded to the Spanish throne. France surrendered the Spanish Netherlands (later Belgium), then in French hands, to Austria and recognized the Hohenzollern rulers of Prussia. Spain ceded Gibraltar to Great Britain, for which it has been a strategic naval station ever since. Spain also granted Britain the *asiento*, the contract for supplying African slaves to America.

ANALYZING THE MAP Identify the areas on the map that changed hands as a result of the Peace of Utrecht. How did these changes affect the balance of power in Europe?

CONNECTIONS How and why did so many European countries possess scattered or discontiguous territories? What does this suggest about European politics in this period? Does this map suggest potential for future conflict?

to include important commercial centers in the Spanish Netherlands and Flanders as well as the entire province of Franche-Comté between 1667 and 1678. In 1681 Louis seized the city of Strasbourg, and three years later he sent his armies into the province of Lorraine. At that moment the king seemed invincible. In fact, Louis had reached the limit of his expansion. The wars of the 1680s and 1690s brought no additional territories but placed unbearable strains on French resources. Colbert's successors resorted to desperate measures to finance these wars, including devaluation of the currency and new taxes.

Louis's last war was endured by a French people suffering high taxes, crop failure, and widespread malnutrition and death. This war resulted from a dispute over the rightful successor to the Spanish throne. In 1700 the childless Spanish king Charles II (r. 1665–1700) died. His will bequeathed the Spanish crown and its empire to Philip of Anjou, Louis XIV's grandson (Louis's wife, Maria-Theresa, had been Charles's sister). The will violated a prior treaty by which the European powers had agreed to divide the Spanish possessions between the king of France and the Holy Roman emperor, both brothers-in-law of Charles II. Claiming that he was following both Spanish and French interests, Louis broke with the treaty and accepted the will, thereby triggering the War of the Spanish Succession (1701–1713).

In 1701 the English, Dutch, Austrians, and Prussians formed the Grand Alliance against Louis XIV. War dragged on until 1713, when it was ended by the **Peace of Utrecht**. This series of treaties allowed Louis's grandson Philip to remain king of Spain on the understanding that the French and Spanish crowns would never be united. France surrendered large territories overseas to England (Map 17.2; see also page 519).

The Peace of Utrecht marked the end of French expansion. Thirty-three years of war had given France the rights to all of Alsace (on France's present-day border with Germany and Switzerland) and some commercial centers in the north. But at what price? In 1714 an exhausted France hovered on the brink of bankruptcy. It is no wonder that when Louis XIV died on September 1, 1715, many subjects felt as much relief as they did sorrow.

The Decline of Absolutist Spain

At the beginning of the seventeenth century, France's position appeared extremely weak. Struggling to recover from decades of religious civil war, France could not compete with Spain's European and overseas empire or its mighty military. Yet by the end of the century the countries' positions were reversed.

By the early seventeenth century the seeds of Spanish disaster were sprouting. Between 1610 and 1650 Spanish trade with the colonies in the New World fell 60 percent due to competition from local industries in the colonies and from Dutch and English traders. At the same time, frightful epidemics of disease reduced the number of native Indian and African slaves who toiled in the South American silver mines. Ultimately, the mines that filled the Spanish Empire's treasury started to run dry, and the quantity of metal produced steadily declined after 1620.

In Madrid, royal expenditures constantly exceeded income. To meet mountainous state debt, the Spanish crown repeatedly devalued the coinage and declared bankruptcy, which resulted in the collapse of national credit. Meanwhile, commerce and manufacturing shrank. In the textile industry manufacturers were forced out of business by steep inflation that pushed their production costs to the point where they could not compete in colonial and international markets.[7] To make matters worse, the Crown expelled some three hundred thousand Moriscos, or former Muslims,

in 1609, significantly reducing the pool of skilled workers and merchants.

Spanish aristocrats, attempting to maintain an extravagant lifestyle they could no longer afford, increased the rents on their estates. High rents and heavy taxes drove the peasants from the land, leading to a decline in agricultural productivity. In cities wages and production stagnated.

The Spanish crown had no solutions to these dire problems. Philip III (r. 1598–1621) handed the running of the government over to the duke of Lerma, who used the position to increase his personal and familial wealth. Philip IV (r. 1621–1665) left the management of his several kingdoms to Gaspar de Guzmán, Count-Duke of Olivares. Olivares was an able administrator who has often been compared to Richelieu. He did not lack energy and ideas, and he succeeded in devising new sources of revenue. But he clung to the belief that the solution to Spain's difficulties rested in a return to the imperial tradition of the sixteenth century. Unfortunately, the imperial tradition demanded the revival of war with the Dutch at the expiration of a twelve-year truce in 1622 and a long war with France over Mantua (1628–1659). These conflicts, on top of an empty treasury, brought disaster.

Spain's situation worsened with internal conflicts and fresh military defeats through the remainder of the seventeenth century. In 1640 Spain faced serious revolts in Catalonia and Portugal. In 1643 the French inflicted a crushing defeat on the Spanish army at Rocroi in what is now Belgium. By the Treaty of the Pyrenees of 1659, which ended the French-Spanish conflict, Spain was compelled to surrender extensive territories to France. And in 1688 the Spanish crown reluctantly recognized the independence of Portugal. With these losses the era of Spanish dominance in Europe ended.

Absolutism in Austria, Prussia, and Russia

☐ How did Austrian, Prussian, and Russian rulers transform their nations into powerful absolutist monarchies?

Rulers in eastern and central Europe and in Russia also labored to build strong absolutist states in the seventeenth century. But they built on social and economic foundations far different from those in western Europe, namely serfdom and the strong nobility who

• **Peace of Utrecht** A series of treaties, from 1713 to 1715, that ended the War of the Spanish Succession, ended French expansion in Europe, and marked the rise of the British Empire.

MAP 17.3 The Growth of Austria and Brandenburg-Prussia to 1748 Austria expanded to the southwest into Hungary and Transylvania at the expense of the Ottoman Empire. It was unable to hold the rich German province of Silesia, however, which was conquered by Brandenburg-Prussia.

benefited from it. The endless wars of the seventeenth century allowed monarchs to increase their power by building large armies, increasing taxation, and suppressing representative institutions. In exchange for their growing political authority, monarchs allowed nobles to remain unchallenged masters of their peasants, a deal that appeased both king and nobility but left serfs at the mercy of the lords.

There were important variations on the absolutist theme in eastern Europe, central Europe, and Russia. The royal absolutism created in Prussia was stronger and more effective than that established in Austria. As for Russia, it developed its own form of absolutism, which was quite different from that of France or even Prussia.

The Austrian Habsburgs

In 1521 Habsburg emperor Charles V ceded power over his Austrian territories to his brother Ferdinand I,

thus permanently separating the dynasty into Austrian and Spanish branches. Like all of central Europe, the Austrian Habsburgs emerged from the Thirty Years' War impoverished and exhausted. Their efforts to destroy Protestantism in the German lands and to turn the weak Holy Roman Empire into a real state had failed. Defeat in central Europe encouraged the Austrian Habsburgs to turn away from a quest for imperial dominance and to focus inward and eastward in an attempt to unify their diverse holdings.

Habsburg victory over Bohemia during the Thirty Years' War was an important step in this direction. Ferdinand II (r. 1619–1637) drastically reduced the power of the Bohemian Estates, the largely Protestant representative assembly. He also confiscated the landholdings of Protestant nobles and gave them to loyal Catholic nobles and to the foreign aristocratic mercenaries who led his armies. After 1650 a large portion of the Bohemian nobility was of recent origin and owed its success to the Habsburgs.

With the support of this new nobility, the Habsburgs established direct rule over Bohemia. Under their rule the condition of the enserfed peasantry worsened substantially, and Protestantism was stamped out. These changes were important steps in creating absolutist rule in Bohemia.

Ferdinand III (r. 1637–1657) continued to build state power. He centralized the government in the empire's German-speaking provinces, which formed the core Habsburg holdings. For the first time, a permanent standing army was ready to put down any internal opposition.

The Habsburg monarchy then turned east toward Hungary, which had been divided between the Ottomans and the Habsburgs in the early sixteenth century. Between 1683 and 1699 the Habsburgs pushed the Ottomans from most of Hungary and Transylvania. The recovery of all the former kingdom of Hungary was completed in 1718 (Map 17.3).

The Hungarian nobility, despite its reduced strength, effectively thwarted the full development of Habsburg absolutism. Throughout the seventeenth century Hungarian nobles rose in revolt against the Habsburgs. They never triumphed decisively, but neither were they crushed. In 1703, with the Habsburgs bogged down in the War of the Spanish Succession, the Hungarians rose in one last patriotic rebellion under Prince Francis Rákóczy (RAH-cohtsee).

Rákóczy and his forces were eventually defeated, but the Habsburgs agreed to restore many of the traditional privileges of the Hungarian aristocracy in return for the country's acceptance of hereditary Habsburg rule. Thus Hungary was never fully integrated into a centralized, absolute Habsburg state. Despite checks on their ambitions in Hungary, the Habsburgs made significant achievements in state-building elsewhere by forging consensus with the church and the nobility.

Prussia in the Seventeenth Century

In the fifteenth and sixteenth centuries the Hohenzollern family ruled parts of eastern Germany as the

A Prussian Giant Grenadier Frederick William I wanted tall, handsome soldiers. He dressed them in tight bright uniforms to distinguish them from the peasant population from which most soldiers came. He also ordered several portraits of his favorites, such as this one, from his court painter, J. C. Merk. Grenadiers wore the miter cap instead of an ordinary hat so that they could hurl their heavy grenades unimpeded by a broad brim. (The Royal Collection © 2011, Her Majesty Queen Elizabeth II)

imperial electors of Brandenburg and the dukes of Prussia, but they had little real power. Although the elector of Brandenburg enjoyed the right to help choose the Holy Roman emperor, nothing would suggest that the Hohenzollern territories would come to play an important role in European affairs.

When he came to power, twenty-year-old Frederick William (r. 1640–1688), later known as the Great Elector, was determined to unify his three provinces and enlarge them by diplomacy and war. These provinces were Brandenburg; Prussia, inherited in 1618; and scattered holdings along the Rhine inherited in 1614 (see Map 17.3). Each had its own representative assembly, or estates, and taxes could not be levied without their consent. The estates of Brandenburg and Prussia were dominated by the nobility and the landowning classes, known as the **Junkers**.

In 1660 Frederick William persuaded Junkers in the estates to accept taxation without consent in order to fund a permanent army. They agreed to do so in exchange for reconfirmation of their own privileges, including authority over the serfs. Opposition from the towns was crushed ruthlessly.

Thereafter, the estates' power declined rapidly, for the Great Elector had both financial independence and superior force. State revenue tripled during his reign, and the army expanded dramatically. In 1688 a population of one million supported a peacetime standing army of thirty thousand. In 1701 the elector's son, Frederick I, received the elevated title of king of

Junkers The nobility of Brandenburg and Prussia; they were reluctant allies of Frederick William in his consolidation of the Prussian state.

> "A formidable army and a war chest large enough to make this army mobile in times of need can create great respect for you in the world, so that you can speak a word like the other powers."
>
> **KING FREDERICK WILLIAM I**

Prussia (instead of elector) as a reward for aiding the Holy Roman emperor in the War of the Spanish Succession.

The Consolidation of Prussian Absolutism

The son of the first king of Prussia, Frederick William I (r. 1713–1740), completed his grandfather's work, eliminating the last traces of parliamentary estates and local self-government. Known as "the Soldiers' King," Frederick William firmly established Prussian absolutism and transformed Prussia into a military state. He summed up his life's philosophy in his instructions to his son: "A formidable army and a war chest large enough to make this army mobile in times of need can create great respect for you in the world, so that you can speak a word like the other powers."[8]

Twelfth in Europe in population, Prussia had the fourth largest army by 1740. The Prussian army was the best-trained in Europe, astonishing foreign observers with its precision, skill, and discipline. As one western traveler put it:

> There is no theatre in Berlin whatsoever, diversion is understood to be the handsome troops who parade daily. A special attraction is the great Potsdam Grenadier Regiment . . . when they practice drill, when they fire and when they parade up and down, it is as if they form a single body.[9]

In spite of his restrictive rule, Frederick William and his ministers built an exceptionally honest and conscientious bureaucracy to administer the country and foster economic development. Nevertheless, Prussians paid a heavy and lasting price for bureaucratic and military achievements. Civil society became rigid and highly disciplined. As a Prussian minister later summed up, "To keep quiet is the first civic duty."[10] Thus the policies of Frederick

William I, combined with harsh peasant bondage and Junker tyranny, laid the foundations for a highly militaristic country.

Frederick II (r. 1740–1786), commonly known as Frederick the Great, built masterfully on the work of his father. When the young Maria Theresa of Austria inherited the Habsburg dominions upon the death of her father Charles VI, Frederick was quick to make use of the splendid army his own father had left him. He invaded Austria's rich, mainly German province of Silesia, defying solemn Prussian promises to respect the Pragmatic Sanction, a diplomatic agreement that had guaranteed Maria Theresa's succession. In 1742, as other powers vied for her lands in the European War of the Austrian Succession (1740–1748), Maria Theresa was forced to cede almost all of Silesia to Prussia. In one stroke Prussia had doubled its population to 6 million people. Now Prussia unquestionably towered above all the other German states and stood as a European Great Power.

Mongol Rule in Russia and the Rise of Moscow

Absolutism in Russia had its roots in two hundred years of rule under the king (khan) of the Mongols, a group of nomadic tribes from present-day Mongolia. These tribes had come together under Chinggis Khan (ca. 1162–1227). In the thirteenth century the Mongols conquered Kievan Rus, the medieval Slavic state centered first at Novgorod and then at Kiev, a city on the

Dnieper River, which included most of present-day Ukraine, Belarus, and part of northwest Russia. The Mongols forced the Slavic princes to submit to their rule and to give them tribute and slaves. The princes of the Grand Duchy of Moscow, a principality within Kievan Rus, became particularly adept at serving the Mongols. They loyally put down uprisings and collected the khan's taxes. Eventually the Muscovite princes were able to destroy the other princes who were their rivals for power. Ivan III (r. 1462–1505), known as Ivan the Great, successfully expanded the principality of Moscow eastward toward the Baltic Sea and westward to the Ural Mountains and the Siberian frontier.

By 1480 Ivan III felt strong enough to stop acknowledging the khan as his supreme ruler. To legitimize their new autonomy, he and his successors

The Expansion of Russia, to 1725

Map legend:
- Moscow, ca. 1300
- Gains by 1505
- Gains by 1584
- Gains by 1725
- Major battle

SWEDEN
FINLAND
St. Petersburg
Novgorod
POLAND-LITHUANIA
Moscow
Kiev
Cossacks
Poltava 1709
Cossacks
URAL MTS.
CAUCASUS MTS.

Russian Peasant An eighteenth-century French artist visiting Russia recorded his impressions of the daily life of the Russian people in this etching of a fish merchant pulling his wares through a snowy village on a sleigh. Two caviar vendors behind him make a sale to a young mother standing at her doorstep with her baby in her arms. (From Jean-Baptiste Le Prince's second set of Russian etchings, 1765. Private Collection/www.amis-paris-petersbourg.org)

declared themselves to be autocrats, meaning that they were the sole source of power. The Muscovite state also borrowed Mongol institutions such as the tax system, postal routes, and the census. Loyalty from the highest-ranking nobles, or **boyars**, helped the Muscovite princes consolidate their power.

Another source of legitimacy lay in Moscow's claim to the political and religious inheritance of the Byzantine Empire. After the empire's capital, Constantinople, fell to the Turks in 1453, the princes of Moscow saw themselves as the heirs of both the caesars (or emperors) and of Orthodox Christianity. Ivan III's marriage to the daughter of the last Byzantine emperor enhanced Moscow's claim to have inherited imperial authority. The title *tsar*, first taken by Ivan IV in 1547, is a contraction of *caesar*.

The Tsar and His People

Developments in Russia took a chaotic turn with the reign of Ivan IV (r. 1533–1584), the famous Ivan the Terrible, who ascended to the throne at age three. His mother died, possibly poisoned, when he was eight,

leaving Ivan to suffer insults and neglect from the boyars at court. At age sixteen he suddenly pushed aside his hated advisers and crowned himself tsar.

Ivan's reign was successful in defeating the remnants of Mongol power, adding vast new territories to the realm, and laying the foundations for the huge multiethnic Russian empire. After the sudden death of his beloved first wife, Anastasia Romanov, however, Ivan began a campaign of persecution against those he suspected of opposing him. Many were intimates of the court from leading boyar families, whom he killed along with their families, friends, servants, and peasants. To further crush the power of the boyars, Ivan created a new service nobility, who received noble titles and estates in return for serving in the tsar's army.

Ivan also moved toward making all commoners servants of the tsar. (See "Listening to the Past: A German Account of Russian Life," page 506.) As landlords demanded more from the peasants who survived the wars and persecutions, growing numbers of them fled

• **boyars** The highest-ranking members of the Russian nobility.

Listening to the Past

A German Account of Russian Life

Seventeenth-century Russia remained a remote and mysterious land for western and even central Europeans, who had few direct contacts with the tsar's dominion. Westerners portrayed eastern Europe as more "barbaric" and less "civilized" than their homelands. Thus they expanded eastern Europe's undeniably harsher social and economic conditions to encompass a very debatable cultural and moral inferiority.

Knowledge of Russia came mainly from occasional travelers who had visited Muscovy and sometimes wrote accounts of what they saw. The most famous of these accounts was by the German Adam Olearius (ca. 1599–1671), who was sent to Moscow on three diplomatic missions in the 1630s. These missions ultimately proved unsuccessful, but they provided Olearius with a rich store of information for his Travels in Muscovy, *from which the following excerpts are taken. Published in German in 1647 and soon translated into several languages (but not Russian), Olearius's unflattering but well-informed study played a major role in shaping European ideas about Russia.*

❝The government of the Russians is what political theorists call a "dominating and despotic monarchy," where the sovereign, that is, the tsar or the grand prince who has obtained the crown by right of succession, rules the entire land alone, and all the people are his subjects, and where the nobles and princes no less than the common folk—townspeople and peasants—are his serfs and slaves, whom he rules and treats as a master treats his servants. . . .

If the Russians be considered in respect to their character, customs, and way of life, they are justly to be counted among the barbarians. . . . The vice of drunkenness is so common in this nation, among people of every station, clergy and laity, high and low, men and women, old and young, that when they are seen now and then lying about in the streets, wallowing in the mud, no attention is paid to it, as something habitual. If a cart driver comes upon such a drunken pig whom he happens to know, he shoves him onto his cart and drives him home, where he is paid his fare. No one ever refuses an opportunity to drink and to get drunk, at any time and in any place, and usually it is done with vodka. . . .

The Russians being naturally tough and born, as it were, for slavery, they must be kept under a harsh and strict yoke and must be driven to do their work with clubs and whips, which they suffer without impatience, because such is their station,

and they are accustomed to it. Young and half-grown fellows sometimes come together on certain days and train themselves in fisticuffs, to accustom themselves to receiving blows, and, since habit is second nature, this makes blows given as punishment easier to bear. Each and all, they are slaves and serfs. . . .

Because of slavery and their rough and hard life, the Russians accept war readily and are well suited to it. On certain occasions, if need be, they reveal themselves as courageous and daring soldiers. . . .

Although the Russians, especially the common populace, living as slaves under a harsh yoke, can bear and endure a great deal out of love for their masters, yet if the pressure is beyond measure, then it can be said of them: "Patience, often wounded, finally turned into fury." A dangerous indignation results, turned not so much against their sovereign as against the lower authorities, especially if the people have been much oppressed by them and by their supporters and have not been protected by the higher authorities. And once they are aroused and enraged, it is not easy to appease them. Then, disregarding all dangers that may ensue, they resort to every kind of violence and behave like madmen. . . . They own little; most of them have no feather beds; they lie on cushions, straw, mats, or their clothes; they sleep on benches and, in winter, like the non-Germans [natives] in Livonia, upon the oven, which serves them for cooking and is flat on the top; here husband, wife, children, servants, and maids huddle together. In some houses in the countryside we saw chickens and pigs under the benches and the ovens. . . . Russians are not used to delicate food and dainties; their daily food consists of porridge, turnips, cabbage, and cucumbers, fresh and pickled, and in Moscow mostly of big salt fish which stink badly, because of the thrifty use of salt, yet are eaten with relish. . . .

The Russians can endure extreme heat. In the bathhouse they stretch out on benches and let themselves be beaten and rubbed with bunches of birch twigs and wisps of bast (which I could not stand); and when they are hot and red all over and so exhausted that they can bear it no longer in the bathhouse, men and women rush outdoors naked and pour cold water over their bodies; in winter they even wallow in the snow and rub their skin with it as if it were soap; then they go back into the hot bathhouse. And since bathhouses are usually near rivers and brooks, they can throw themselves straight from the hot into the cold bath. . . .

● **The brutality of serfdom is shown in this illustration from Olearius's *Travels in Muscovy*.**
(University of Illinois Library, Champaign)

Generally noble families, even the small nobility, rear their daughters in secluded chambers, keeping them hidden from outsiders; and a bridegroom is not allowed to have a look at his bride until he receives her in the bridal chamber. Therefore some happen to be deceived, being given a misshapen and sickly one instead of a fair one, and sometimes a kinswoman or even a maidservant instead of a daughter; of which there have been examples even among the highborn. No wonder therefore that often they live together like cats and dogs and that wife-beating is so common among Russians. . . .

In the Kremlin and in the city there are a great many churches, chapels, and monasteries, both within and without the city walls, over two thousand in all. This is so because every nobleman who has some fortune has a chapel built for himself, and most of them are of stone. The stone churches are round and vaulted inside. . . . They allow neither organs nor any other musical instruments in their churches, saying: Instruments that have neither souls nor life cannot praise God. . . .

In their churches there hang many bells, sometimes five or six, the largest not over two hundredweights. They ring these bells to summon people to church, and also when the priest during mass raises the chalice. In Moscow, because of the multitude of churches and chapels, there are several thousand bells, which during the divine service create such a clang and din that one unaccustomed to it listens in amazement. ”

Source: G. Vernadsky and R. T. Fisher, Jr., eds., *A Source Book for Russian History from Early Times to 1917*, vol. 1 (New Haven: Yale University Press, 1972), pp. 249–251. Reprinted by permission of Yale University Press.

QUESTIONS FOR ANALYSIS

1. How did Olearius characterize the Russians in general? What evidence did he offer for his judgment?

2. How might Olearius's account help explain Stenka Razin's rebellion (page 508)?

3. On the basis of these passages, why do you think Olearius's book was so popular and influential in central and western Europe?

Peter the Great This compelling portrait by Grigory Musikiysky captures the strength and determination of the warrior-tsar in 1723, after more than three decades of personal rule. In his hand Peter holds the scepter, symbol of royal sovereignty, and across his breastplate is draped an ermine fur, a mark of honor. In the background are the battleships of Russia's new Baltic fleet and the famous St. Peter and St. Paul Fortress that Peter built in St. Petersburg. Peter the Great commissioned this magnificent new crown (left) for himself for his 1682 joint coronation with his half-brother Ivan. (crown: Bildarchiv Preussischer Kulturbesitz/Kremlin Museums, Moscow/The Bridgeman Art Library; portrait: Bildarchiv Preussischer Kulturbesitz/The Bridgeman Art Library)

toward wild, recently conquered territories to the east and south. There they joined free groups and warrior bands known as **Cossacks**. In the 1580s Ivan's government began to forbid peasants to leave their masters, a first step toward the imposition of serfdom on all peasants. (Formerly only those who could not repay debts to their landlords fell into the category of serfs.)

Simultaneously, Ivan bound urban traders and artisans to their towns and jobs so that he could tax them more heavily. These restrictions checked the growth of the Russian middle classes and stood in sharp contrast to developments in western Europe. From nobles down to merchants and peasants, all the Russian people were thus brought into the tsar's service. Ivan even made use of Cossack armies in forays to the southeast, forging a new alliance between Moscow and the Cossacks.

Following Ivan's death, Russia entered a chaotic period known as the Time of Troubles (1598–1613). While Ivan's relatives struggled for power, the Cossacks and peasants rebelled against nobles and officials. This social explosion from below brought the nobles together. They crushed the Cossack rebellion and elected Ivan's

grandnephew, Michael Romanov, the new hereditary tsar (r. 1613–1645).

Although the new tsar successfully reconsolidated central authority, social and religious uprisings continued. One of the largest rebellions was led by the Cossack Stenka Razin, who in 1670 attracted a great army of urban poor and peasants, killing landlords and government officials and proclaiming freedom from oppression. In 1671 this rebellion was defeated.

Despite the turbulence of the period, the Romanov tsars, like their Western counterparts, made several important achievements during the second half of the seventeenth century. After a long war, Russia gained land in Ukraine from Poland in 1667 and completed the conquest of Siberia by the end of the century. Territorial expansion was accompanied by growth of the bureaucracy and the army. The great profits from Siberia's natural resources funded the Romanovs' bid for Russia's status as a Great Power. Thus, Russian imperialist expansion to the east paralleled the Western powers' exploration and conquest of the Atlantic world in the same period.

The Reforms of Peter the Great

Heir to Romanov efforts at state-building, Peter the Great (r. 1682–1725) embarked on a tremendous campaign to accelerate and complete these processes. Possessing enormous energy and willpower, Peter was determined to continue the tsarist tradition of territorial expansion.

In 1697 the tsar, who was fascinated by foreign technology, led a group of 250 Russian officials and young nobles on an eighteen-month tour of western European capitals. Traveling unofficially to avoid lengthy diplomatic ceremonies, Peter met with foreign kings and experts. He was particularly impressed with the growing power of the Dutch and the English, and he considered how Russia could profit from their example. He soon had reason to apply what he had learned.

Suffering initial defeat in war with Sweden in 1701, Peter responded with measures designed to increase state power, strengthen his armies, and gain victory. He required all nobles to serve in the army or in the civil administration — for life. Peter also created schools and universities to produce skilled technicians and experts. Furthermore, he established an interlocking military-civilian bureaucracy with fourteen ranks, and he decreed that all had to start at the bottom and work toward the top. Drawing on his experience abroad, Peter sought talented foreigners and placed them in his service. These measures gradually combined to make the army and government more powerful and efficient.

Peter also greatly increased the service requirements of commoners. He established a regular standing army of more than two hundred thousand peasant-soldiers commanded by officers from the nobility. Taxes on peasants to fund the military and other government spending increased threefold during Peter's reign. Serfs were arbitrarily assigned to work in the growing number of factories and mines that supplied the military.

In 1709 Peter's new war machine was able to crush the army of Sweden in Ukraine at Poltava in one of the most significant battles in Russian history. Russia's victory against Sweden was conclusive in 1721, and Estonia and present-day Latvia came under Russian rule for the first time. The cost was high: warfare consumed 80 to 85 percent of all revenues. But Russia became the dominant power in the Baltic and very much a great European power.

After his victory at Poltava, Peter channeled enormous resources into building a new Western-style capital on the Baltic to rival the great cities of Europe. Originally a desolate and swampy Swedish outpost, the magnificent city of St. Petersburg was designed to reflect modern urban planning with wide, straight avenues, buildings set in a uniform line, and large parks. Each summer, twenty-five to forty thousand peasants were sent to provide construction labor in St. Petersburg without pay.

There were other important consequences of Peter's reign. For Peter, modernization meant westernization, and both Westerners and Western ideas flowed into Russia for the first time. He required nobles to shave their heavy beards and wear Western clothing. He also required them to attend parties where young men and women would mix together and freely choose their own spouses, in defiance of the traditional pattern of strictly controlled marriages. From these efforts a new elite class of Western-oriented Russians began to emerge.

Peter's reforms were unpopular with many Russians. For nobles, one of Peter's most detested reforms was the imposition of unigeniture — inheritance of land by one son alone — cutting off daughters and other sons from family property. For peasants, the reign of the tsar saw a significant increase in the bonds of serfdom, and the gulf between the enserfed peasantry and the educated nobility increased.

Peter's reforms were in some ways a continuation of Russia's distinctive history. He built on the service obligations of Ivan the Terrible and his successors, and his monarchical absolutism can be seen as the culmination of the long development of a unique Russian civilization.

Alternatives to Absolutism in England and the Dutch Republic

☐ Why and how did the constitutional state triumph in England and the Dutch Republic?

While France, Prussia, Russia, and Austria developed absolutist states, England and the Netherlands evolved toward **constitutionalism**, which is the limitation of government by law. Constitutionalism also implies a balance between the authority and power of the government, on the one hand, and the rights and liberties of the subjects, on the other.

- **Cossacks** Free groups and outlaw armies originally comprising runaway peasants living on the borders of Russian territory from the fourteenth century onward. By the end of the sixteenth century they had formed an alliance with the Russian state.

- **constitutionalism** A form of government in which power is limited by law and balanced between the authority and power of the government, on the one hand, and the rights and liberties of the subject or citizen, on the other; it includes constitutional monarchies and republics.

A nation's constitution may be written or unwritten. It may be embodied in one basic document, like the Constitution of the United States. Or it may be only partly formalized and include parliamentary statutes, judicial decisions, and a body of traditional procedures and practices, like the English and Dutch constitutions.

Despite their common commitment to constitutional government, England and the Dutch Republic represented significantly different alternatives to absolute rule. After decades of civil war and an experiment with **republicanism**, the English opted for a constitutional monarchy in 1688. Under this system of government, England retained a monarch as the titular head of government but vested sovereignty in an elected parliament. For their part, the Dutch rejected monarchical rule in 1648, when their independence from Spain was formally recognized. Instead, they adopted a republican form of government in which elected estates (assemblies) held supreme power.

> "There are no privileges and immunities which can stand against a divinely appointed King."
>
> **KING JAMES I**

Absolutist Claims in England

Queen Elizabeth I of England (r. 1558–1603) exercised very great personal power. A rare female monarch, she was able to maintain control over her realm in part by refusing to marry and submit to a husband. Elizabeth was immensely popular with her people but left no immediate heir to continue her legacy.

In 1603 Queen Elizabeth's Scottish cousin James Stuart succeeded her as James I (r. 1603–1625). King James was well educated and had thirty-five years' experience as king of Scotland. But he was not as interested in displaying the majesty of monarchy as Elizabeth had been. Urged to wave at the crowds who waited to greet their new ruler, James complained that he was tired and threatened to drop his breeches "so they can cheer at my arse."[11]

James's greatest problem stemmed from his absolutist belief that a monarch has a divine right to his authority and is responsible only to God. James went so far as to lecture the House of Commons (part of the English Parliament): "There are no privileges and immunities which can stand against a divinely appointed King." Such a view ran counter to the long-standing English idea that a person's property could not be taken away without due process of law. James I and his son Charles I (r. 1625–1649) considered such constraints a threat to their divine-right prerogative. Consequently, at every meeting of Parliament between 1603 and 1640, bitter squabbles erupted between the Crown and the House of Commons. Charles I's attempt to govern without Parliament (1629–1640) and to finance his government by emergency taxes brought the country to a crisis.

Religious Divides and Civil War

Religious issues also embittered relations between the king and the House of Commons. In the early seventeenth century increasing numbers of English people felt dissatisfied with the Church of England established by Henry VIII and reformed by Elizabeth. Many **Puritans** believed that the Reformation had not gone far enough. They wanted to "purify" the Anglican Church of Roman Catholic elements — elaborate vestments and ceremonials, bishops, and even the giving and wearing of wedding rings.

James I responded to such ideas by declaring, "No bishop, no king." For James, bishops were among the chief supporters of the throne. His son and successor, Charles I, further antagonized subjects with opposing religious views. Not only did Charles marry a Catholic princess, but he also supported the policies of Archbishop of Canterbury William Laud (1573–1645). In 1637 Laud attempted to impose two new elements on church organization in Scotland: a new prayer book, modeled on the Anglican *Book of Common Prayer*, and bishoprics. The Presbyterian Scots rejected these elements and revolted. To finance an army to put down the Scots, King Charles was compelled to summon Parliament in November 1640.

Charles had ruled from 1629 to 1640 without Parliament, financing his government through extraordinary stopgap levies considered illegal by most English people. Most members of Parliament believed that such taxation without consent amounted to despotism. Consequently, they were not willing to trust the king with an army. Moreover, many supported the Scots' resistance to Charles's religious innovations. Accordingly, this Parliament, called the Long Parliament because it sat from 1640 to 1660, enacted legislation that limited the power of the monarch and made government without Parliament impossible.

In 1641 the House of Commons passed the Triennial Act, which compelled the king to summon Parlia-

---

- **republicanism** A form of government in which there is no monarch and power rests in the hands of the people as exercised through elected representatives.
- **Puritans** Members of a sixteenth- and seventeenth-century reform movement within the Church of England that advocated purifying it of Roman Catholic elements, such as bishops, elaborate ceremonials, and wedding rings.

ment every three years. The Commons also impeached Archbishop Laud and then threatened to abolish bishops. King Charles, fearful of a Scottish invasion — the original reason for summoning Parliament — reluctantly accepted these measures. The next act in the conflict was precipitated by the outbreak of rebellion in Ireland, where English governors and landlords had long exploited the people. In 1641 the Catholic gentry of Ireland led an uprising in response to a feared invasion by anti-Catholic forces of the British Long Parliament.

Without an army, Charles I could neither come to terms with the Scots nor respond to the Irish rebellion. After a failed attempt to arrest parliamentary leaders, Charles left London for the north of England, where he recruited an army. In response, Parliament formed its own army, the New Model Army. During the spring of 1642 both sides prepared for war.

The English civil war (1642–1649) pitted the power of the king against that of the Parliament. After three years of fighting, Parliament's New Model Army defeated the king's armies at the battles of Naseby and Langport in the summer of 1645. Charles refused to concede defeat. Both sides jockeyed for position, waiting for a decisive event. This arrived in the form of the army under the leadership of Oliver Cromwell, a member of the House of Commons and a devout Puritan. In 1647 Cromwell's forces captured the king and dismissed members of the Parliament who opposed Cromwell's actions. In 1649 the remaining representatives, known as the Rump Parliament, put Charles on trial for high treason. Charles was found guilty and beheaded

The English Civil War, 1642–1649

Puritan Occupations
These twelve engravings depict typical Puritan occupations and show that the Puritans came primarily from the artisan and lower middle classes. The governing classes and peasants made up a much smaller percentage of Puritans, and most generally adhered to the traditions of the Church of England.
(Visual Connection Archive)

on January 30, 1649, an act that sent shock waves around Europe.

The Puritan Protectorate

With the execution of Charles, kingship was abolished. The question then became how the country would be governed. One answer was provided by philosopher Thomas Hobbes (1588–1679). Hobbes held a pessimistic view of human nature and believed that, left to themselves, humans would compete violently for power and wealth. The only solution, as he outlined in his 1651 treatise *Leviathan*, was a social contract in which all members of society placed themselves under the absolute rule of a monarch who would maintain peace and order. Hobbes imagined society as a human body in which the monarch served as head and individual subjects together made up the body. Just as the body cannot sever its own head, so Hobbes believed that society could not, having accepted the contract, rise up against its king. For this reason he was deeply shocked by Charles's execution.

Hobbes's longing for a benevolent absolute monarch was not widely shared in England. Instead, a commonwealth, or republican government, was proclaimed. Theoretically, legislative power rested in the surviving members of Parliament, and executive power was lodged in a council of state. In fact, the army that had defeated the king controlled the government, and Oliver Cromwell controlled the army. Though called the **Protectorate**, the rule of Cromwell (1653–1658) was a form of military dictatorship.

The army prepared a constitution, the Instrument of Government (1653), that invested executive power in a lord protector (Cromwell) and a council of state. It provided for triennial parliaments and gave Parliament the sole power to raise taxes. But after repeated disputes, Cromwell dismissed Parliament in 1655, and the instrument was never formally endorsed. Cromwell continued the standing army and proclaimed quasi-martial law. He divided England into twelve military districts, each governed by a major general. Reflecting Puritan ideas of morality, Cromwell's state forbade sports, kept the theaters closed, and rigorously censored the press.

On the issue of religion, Cromwell favored some degree of toleration, and the Instrument of Government gave all Christians except Roman Catholics the right

to practice their faith. Cromwell had long associated Catholicism in Ireland with sedition and heresy, and he led an army there to reconquer the country in August 1649. One month later, his forces crushed a rebellion at Drogheda and massacred the garrison. Following Cromwell's reconquest, the English banned Catholicism in Ireland, executed priests, and confiscated land from Catholics for English and Scottish settlers. These brutal acts left a legacy of Irish hatred for England and had little success in discouraging Catholicism.

The Protectorate collapsed when Cromwell died in 1658 and his ineffectual son succeeded him. Fed up with military rule, the English longed for a return to civilian government and, with it, common law and social stability. By 1660 they were ready to restore the monarchy.

Restoration of the English Monarchy

The Restoration of 1660 brought to the throne Charles II (r. 1660–1685), eldest son of Charles I, formerly exiled in the Netherlands. Both houses of Parliament were also restored, together with the established Anglican Church. The Restoration failed to resolve two serious problems, however. What was to be the attitude of the state toward Puritans, Catholics, and dissenters from the established church? And what was to be the relationship between the king and Parliament?

To answer the first question, Parliament enacted the **Test Act** of 1673 against those outside the Church of England, denying them the right to vote, hold public office, preach, teach at or attend the universities, or even assemble for meetings. In politics Charles II set out to work with Parliament, but this resolve did not last. Finding that Parliament did not grant him an adequate income, in 1670 Charles entered into a secret agreement with his cousin Louis XIV. Under this pact, the French king would give Charles two hundred thousand pounds annually, and in return Charles would relax the laws against Catholics, gradually re-Catholicize England, and convert to Catholicism himself. When the details of this treaty leaked out, a great wave of anti-Catholic sentiment swept England.

When James II (r. 1685–1688) succeeded his brother, the worst fears of English anti-Catholics were realized. In violation of the Test Act, James appointed Roman Catholics to positions in the army, the universities, and local government. And he went further; attempting to broaden his base of support with Protestant dissenters and nonconformists, James granted religious freedom to all.

Seeking to prevent the return of Catholic absolutism, a group of eminent persons in Parliament and the Church of England offered the English throne to James's

---

• **Protectorate** The English military dictatorship established by Oliver Cromwell following the execution of Charles I (1653–1658).

• **Test Act** Legislation passed by the English parliament in 1673 to secure the position of the Anglican Church by stripping Puritans, Catholics, and other dissenters of the right to vote, preach, assemble, hold public office, and attend or teach at the universities.

The Massacre at Drogheda In September 1749 English forces under Oliver Cromwell laid siege to Drogheda, a town on the east coast of Ireland and killed approximately three thousand soldiers and civilians when they entered the town. The Drogheda massacre long fostered hatred of Cromwell and English rule in Ireland. (The Granger Collection, New York)

Protestant daughter Mary and her Dutch husband, Prince William of Orange. In December 1688 James II, his queen, and their infant son fled to France. Early in 1689 William and Mary were crowned king and queen of England.

Constitutional Monarchy

The English call the events of 1688 and 1689 the Glorious Revolution because it replaced one king with another with a minimum of bloodshed. It also represented the destruction, once and for all, of the idea of divine-right monarchy. The revolution established the principle that sovereignty, the ultimate power in the state, was divided between king and Parliament and that the king ruled with the consent of the governed.

The men who brought about the revolution framed their intentions in the Bill of Rights, which was formulated in direct response to the attempts by the Stuart kings to impose absolute rule on England. Law was to be made in Parliament; once made, it could not be suspended by the Crown. Parliament had to be called at least once every three years, and no taxes could be im-

posed without its approval. The independence of the judiciary was also established, and there was to be no standing army in peacetime. In terms of laws regarding religion, Protestants could possess arms, but the Catholic minority could not. No Catholic could ever inherit the throne. Additional legislation granted freedom of worship to Protestant dissenters, but not to Catholics.

The Glorious Revolution and the concept of representative government found its best defense in political philosopher John Locke's *Second Treatise of Civil Government* (1690). Locke (1632–1704) maintained that a government that oversteps its proper function — protecting the natural rights of life, liberty, and property — becomes a tyranny. (See "Viewpoints: The Debate over the Extent of Royal Power in England," page 514.) By "natural rights" Locke meant rights basic to all men because all have the ability to reason. Under a tyrannical government, he argued, the people have the natural right to rebellion.

Although the events of 1688 and 1689 brought England closer to Locke's ideal, they did not constitute a democratic revolution. The Glorious Revolution placed sovereignty in Parliament, and Parliament represented

Viewpoints

The Debate over the Extent of Royal Power in England

• *In 1688 King James II of England, fearing a revolution like the one that led to the trial and execution of his grandfather, Charles I, fled to France. The crisis was resolved when Parliament invited James's daughter Mary and her husband, William of Orange, to take the throne. Although the Glorious Revolution shed little blood, it did generate furious debate over the extent of royal power in England. Thomas Cartwright, a bishop of the Church of England, spoke out in defense of James and his God-given right to rule. Taking the opposite side, John Locke argued that sovereign power resided in the people, who could reject a monarch if he set himself above the law. In 1689 William and Mary settled the debate by signing the Petition of Right, which enshrined the rights of Parliament and limited the authority of the monarch.*

Thomas Cartwright, A Sermon Preached upon the Anniversary Solemnity of the Inauguration of Our Dread Sovereign Lord King James II

Our religion will never suffer us to dispense with our loyalty, to serve any worldly interest or advantage; no, not for its own defense. It sets the crown fast and easy upon the King's head, without catechizing him: for be his heart inclinable to any religion, or none, it leaves him no rival, none to insult or lord it over him. It disclaims all usurpation, popular or papal; neither pope nor presbyter may control him; none but the great God, the only ruler of princes, can over-rule him; to whom 'tis his duty, glory and happiness to be subject. Though the King should not please or humor us; though he should rend off the mantle from our bodies (as Saul did from Samuel) nay though he should sentence us to death (of which, blessed be God and the King, there is no danger), yet if we are living members of the Church of England, we must neither open our mouths, nor lift our hands against him; but honor him before the people and elders of Israel.

John Locke, *Two Treatises of Government*

But government into whosesoever hands it is put, being as I have before shown, entrusted with this condition, and for this end, that men might have and secure their properties, the prince or senate, however it may have power to make laws for the regulation of property between the subjects one amongst another, yet can never have a power to take to themselves the whole, or any part of the subjects' property without their own consent. For this would be in effect to leave them no property at all.

. . . The constitution of the legislative is the first and fundamental act of society, whereby provision is made for the continuation of their union, under the direction of persons, and bonds of laws, made by persons authorized thereunto, by the consent and appointment of the people, without which no one man, or number of men, amongst them, can have authority of making laws that shall be binding to the rest. When any one, or more, shall take upon them to make laws, whom the people have not appointed so to do, they make laws without authority, which the people are not therefore bound to obey; by which means they come again to be out of subjection, and may constitute to themselves a new legislative, as they think best, being in full liberty to resist the force of those, who, without authority, would impose any thing upon them.

Source: Steven C. A. Pincus, *England's Glorious Revolution, 1688–1689: A Brief History with Documents* (Boston: Bedford/St. Martin's, 2006), pp. 71–72 (Cartwright), 161–164 (Locke).

QUESTIONS FOR ANALYSIS

1. How does Cartwright justify James's right to rule England? Are there any limitations on royal authority according to Cartwright?
2. What is the reason for people forming a government, according to Locke? What would be the justification for disobeying laws and rejecting the authority of government?

MAP 17.4 Seventeenth-Century Dutch Commerce Dutch wealth rested on commerce, and commerce depended on the huge Dutch merchant marine, manned by perhaps forty-eight thousand sailors. The fleet carried goods from all parts of the globe to the port of Amsterdam.

the upper classes. Aristocratic government lasted in England at least until 1832 and in many ways until 1928, when women received full voting rights.

The Dutch Republic in the Seventeenth Century

In the late sixteenth century the seven northern provinces of the Netherlands fought for and won their independence from Spain. The independence of the Republic of the United Provinces of the Netherlands was recognized in 1648 in the treaty that ended the Thirty Years' War. In this period, often called the "golden age of the Netherlands," Dutch ideas and attitudes played a profound role in shaping a new and modern worldview. At the same time, the United Provinces developed its own distinctive model of a constitutional state.

Rejecting the rule of a monarch, the Dutch established a republic, a state in which power rests in the hands of the people and is exercised through elected representatives. Other republics of the time included

the Swiss Confederation and several autonomous city-states of Italy and the Holy Roman Empire. Among the Dutch, an oligarchy of wealthy businessmen called regents handled domestic affairs in each province's estates, or assemblies. The provincial estates held virtually all the power. A federal assembly, or States General, handled foreign affairs and war, but it did not possess sovereign authority. All issues had to be referred back to the local estates for approval, and each of the seven provinces could veto any proposed legislation.

In each province, the estates appointed an executive officer, known as the **stadholder**, who carried out ceremonial functions and was responsible for military defense. Although in theory freely chosen by the estates, in practice the reigning prince of Orange usually held the office of stadholder in several of the seven provinces of the republic. Tensions persisted between supporters of the House of Orange and those of the staunchly

• **stadholder** The executive officer in each of the United Provinces of the Netherlands, a position often held by the princes of Orange.

republican estates, who suspected the princes of harboring monarchical ambitions. When one of them, William III, took the English throne in 1689 with his wife, Mary, the republic simply continued without stadholders for several decades.

The political success of the Dutch rested on their commercial prosperity. The moral and ethical bases of that commercial wealth were thrift, frugality, and religious toleration. Jews enjoyed a level of acceptance and assimilation in Dutch business and general culture unique in early modern Europe. (See "Individuals in Society: Glückel of Hameln," page 517.) In the Dutch Republic, toleration paid: it attracted a great deal of foreign capital and investment.

The Dutch came to dominate the shipping business by putting profits from their original industry — herring fishing — into shipbuilding. They boasted the lowest shipping rates and largest merchant marine in Europe, allowing them to undersell foreign competitors (Map 17.4). Trade and commerce brought the Dutch the highest standard of living in Europe, perhaps in the world.

Colonialism in the Americas

☐ How did European nations compete to build new colonies in the Americas?

Absolutist or constitutional, European powers deeply envied the fabulous wealth and glory Spain acquired from her American colonies. As Spain's power began to weaken in the early seventeenth century, the Dutch, English, and French seized their opportunity, ruthlessly vying to claim their own territories in the New World. Competition among them was encouraged by mercantilist economic doctrine, which dictated that foreign trade was a zero-sum game in which one country's gains necessarily entailed another's loss. Conflicts over access to trade mounted in the seventeenth century, but by the early eighteenth century England had won a series of concessions that enabled it to dominate trade across the Atlantic.

Life in the colonies was shaped by many factors, including the absence or presence of European women. Complex ethnic and cultural identities emerged due to the mixing of European, indigenous, and African peoples.

Colonial Expansion of Northern European Powers

For a century after the fall of the Mexica (Aztec) capital of Tenochtitlán, the Spanish and Portuguese domi-

nated colonization of the Americas (see Chapter 16). In the early seventeenth century, however, England, France, and the Netherlands profited from Spain's weakness to challenge its dominion. Unlike Spain, where the royal government financed exploration and directly ruled the colonies, England, France, and the Netherlands left colonization largely to chartered companies endowed with monopolies over settlement and trade in a given area.

The first English colony was founded at Roanoke (in what is now North Carolina) in 1585. After a three-year loss of contact with England, the settlers were found to have disappeared; their fate remains a mystery. The colony of Virginia, founded at Jamestown in 1607, had better luck and gained a steady hold, producing tobacco for a growing European market. Indentured servants obtained free passage to the colony in exchange for several years of work and the promise of greater opportunity than in England. In the 1670s Carolina was settled by English colonists from the Caribbean island of Barbados, who found conditions suitable for large rice plantations. During the late seventeenth century enslaved Africans replaced indentured servants as laborers on tobacco and rice plantations, and a harsh racial divide was imposed.

For the first settlers on the coast of New England, the reasons for seeking a new life in the colonies were more religious than economic. Many of these colonists were radical Protestants escaping Anglican repression. The small and struggling outpost of Plymouth Colony (1620) was followed by Massachusetts Bay Colony (1630), which grew into a prosperous settlement. Religious disputes in Massachusetts led to the dispersion of settlers into the new communities of Providence, Connecticut, Rhode Island, and New Haven. Because New England lacked the conditions for plantation agriculture, slavery was always a minor element of life there.

Whereas the Spanish established wholesale dominance over Mexico and Peru, English settlements hugged the Atlantic coastline. This did not prevent conflict with the indigenous inhabitants over land and resources. The haphazard nature of English colonization also led to conflicts of authority within the colonies. As the English crown grew more interested in colonial expansion, efforts were made to acquire the territory between New England in the north and Virginia in the south. The goal was to unify English holdings and minimize French and Dutch competition on the Atlantic seaboard. The results of these efforts were the mid-Atlantic colonies: the Catholic settlement of Maryland (1632); New York, captured from the Dutch in 1664; and the Quaker colony of Pennsylvania (1681).

The French established colonies in present-day Canada and then moved farther south. In 1608 Samuel de Champlain founded the first permanent French

Glückel of Hameln

IN 1690 A JEWISH WIDOW IN THE SMALL German town of Hameln in Lower Saxony sat down to write her autobiography. She wanted to distract her mind from the terrible grief she felt over the death of her husband and to provide her twelve children with a record "so you will know from what sort of people you have sprung, lest today or tomorrow your beloved children or grandchildren came and know naught of their family." Out of her pain and heightened consciousness, Glückel (1646–1724) produced an invaluable source for scholars.

She was born in Hamburg two years before the end of the Thirty Years' War. In 1649 the merchants of Hamburg expelled the Jews, who moved to nearby Altona, then under Danish rule. When the Swedes overran Altona in 1657–1658, the Jews returned to Hamburg "purely at the mercy of the Town Council." Glückel's narrative unfolds against a background of the constant harassment to which Jews were subjected—special papers, permits, bribes—and in Hameln she wrote, "And so it has been to this day and, I fear, will continue in like fashion."

When Glückel was "barely twelve," her father betrothed her to Chayim Hameln, and they married when she was fourteen. She describes him as "the perfect pattern of the pious Jew," a man who stopped his work every day for study and prayer, fasted, and was scrupulously honest in his business dealings. Only a few years older than Glückel, Chayim earned his living dealing in precious metals and in making small loans on pledges (pawned goods). This work required constant travel to larger cities, markets, and fairs, often in bad weather, always over dangerous roads. Chayim consulted his wife about all his business dealings. As he lay dying, a friend asked if he had any last wishes. "None," he replied. "My wife knows everything. She shall do as she has always done." For thirty years Glückel had been his friend, full business partner, and wife. They had thirteen children, twelve of whom survived their father, eight then unmarried. As Chayim had foretold, Glückel succeeded in launching the boys in careers and in providing dowries for the girls.

Glückel's world was her family, the Jewish community of Hameln, and the Jewish communities into which her children married. Her social and business activities took her across Europe, from Amsterdam to Berlin, from Danzig to Vienna; thus her world was far from narrow or provincial. She took great pride that Prince Frederick of Cleves, later king of Prussia, danced at the wedding of her eldest daughter. The rising prosperity of Chayim's businesses allowed the couple to maintain up to six servants.

Glückel was deeply religious, and her culture was steeped in Jewish literature, legends, and mystical and secular works. Above all, she relied on the Bible. Her language, heavily sprinkled with scriptural references, testifies to a rare familiarity with the Scriptures.

Students who wish to learn about seventeenth-century business practices, the importance of the dowry in marriage, childbirth, Jewish life, birthrates, family celebrations, and even the meaning of life can gain a good deal from the memoirs of this extraordinary woman who was, in the words of one of her descendants, the poet Heinrich Heine, "the gift of a world to me."

Source: *The Memoirs of Glückel of Hameln* (New York: Schocken Books, 1977).

QUESTIONS FOR ANALYSIS

1. Consider the ways in which Glückel of Hameln was both an ordinary and an extraordinary woman of her times. Would you call her a marginal or a central person in her society? Why?
2. How might Glückel's successes be attributed to the stabilizing force of absolutism in the seventeenth century?

• **Although no images of Glückel exist, Rembrandt's *The Jewish Bride* suggests the mutual devotion of Glückel and her husband for one another.** (Rijksmuseum-Stichting Amsterdam)

The Fur Trade In the early seventeenth century, European fur traders relied on Native Americans' expertise and experience, leading to the equal relations depicted in this scene from the colony of New Sweden (in modern-day Pennsylvania). The action in the background shows violence among indigenous groups, rivalries exacerbated by contact with Europeans and their trade goods. Hudson's Bay Company, the English colonial trading company, issued its own tokens as currency in the fur trade. This token, dating from the mid-nineteenth century, displays the company's crest, which says "a skin for a skin" in Latin. Two stags face each other, with a fox at the top and four beavers on the shield. Traders received tokens for the pelts they sold and could use them to purchase goods from the company's store. European demand for beaver hats, made from the felted pelts of beavers, drove the tremendous expansion of the North American fur trade in the beginning of the seventeenth century. (engraving: Fur trade in New Sweden in the early 1600s, Peter Lindestrom, artist. From *Geographia Americae with An Account of the Delaware Indians, Based on Surveys and Notes Made 1654–1656*, by Peter Lindestrom, published by The Swedish Colonial Society; token: © National Maritime Museum/The Image Works; hat: Picture Research Consultants and Archives)

settlement at Quebec as a post for trading beaver pelts with local Algonquin and Huron peoples. Settlement of Ville-Marie, later named Montreal, followed in 1642. Louis XIV's capable economic minister, Jean-Baptiste Colbert, established direct royal control over New France (Canada) and sent colonists to enlarge its population. Although the population of the French settlements was always minuscule compared with that of British North America, the French were energetic and industrious traders and explorers. Following the waterways of the St. Lawrence River, the Great Lakes, and the Mississippi River, they ventured into much of North America in the 1670s and 1680s. In 1673 the Jesuit Jacques Marquette and the merchant Louis Joliet sailed down the Mississippi and claimed possession of the land on both sides of the river as far south as present-day Arkansas. In 1682 Robert de La Salle traveled the Mississippi to the Gulf of Mexico, opening the way for French occupation of Louisiana.

In the first decades of the seventeenth century, English and French captains also defied Spain's hold over the Caribbean Sea (see Map 18.2 on page 548). The English seized control of Bermuda (1612), Barbados (1627), and a succession of other islands. The French took Cayenne (1604), St. Christophe (1625), Martinique and Guadeloupe (1635), and, finally, Saint-Domingue (1697) on the western half of Spanish-occupied Hispaniola. These islands acquired new importance after

1640, when the Portuguese brought sugar plantations to Brazil. Sugar and slaves quickly followed in the West Indies (see pages 479–480), making the Caribbean plantations the most lucrative of all colonial possessions.

Not content with challenging the Portuguese in the Indian Ocean (see page 481), the Dutch also aspired to a role in the Americas. Founded in 1621 in a period of war with Spain, the Dutch West India Company aggressively sought to open trade with North and South America and to take possession of Spanish territories there. The company captured or destroyed hundreds of Spanish ships, seized a fleet carrying Spanish silver in 1628, and gained control of portions of Brazil and the Caribbean. The Dutch also successfully interceded in the transatlantic slave trade, bringing much of the west coast of Africa under their control.

Dutch efforts to colonize North America were less successful. The colony of New Netherland, governed from New Amsterdam (modern-day New York City), was hampered by lack of settlement and weak governance and was easily captured by the English.

Mercantilism and Colonial Wars

European powers in the seventeenth century shared a mercantilist view of economics (see page 498). In England the desire to increase both military power and private wealth resulted in the mercantile system of the **Navigation Acts**. Oliver Cromwell established the first of these laws in 1651, and the restored monarchy of Charles II extended them in 1660 and 1663. The acts required most goods imported into England and Scotland (Great Britain after 1707) to be carried on British-owned ships with British crews or on ships of the country producing the article. Moreover, these laws gave British merchants and shipowners a virtual monopoly on trade with British colonies. The colonists were required to ship their products on British (or American) ships and to buy almost all European goods from Britain. It was believed that these economic regulations would eliminate foreign competition, thereby helping British merchants and workers as well as colonial plantation owners and farmers. It was hoped, too, that the emerging British Empire would develop a shipping industry with a large number of experienced seamen who could serve when necessary in the Royal Navy.

European Claims in North America, 1714

Claims
- British
- French
- Spanish

The Navigation Acts were a form of economic warfare. Their initial target was the Dutch, who were far ahead of the English in shipping and foreign trade in the mid-seventeenth century. In conjunction with three Anglo-Dutch wars between 1652 and 1674, the Navigation Acts seriously damaged Dutch shipping and commerce. By the late seventeenth century the Netherlands was falling behind England in shipping, trade, and settlement.

Thereafter France was England's most serious rival in the competition for overseas empire. Rich in natural resources, allied with Spain, and home to a population three or four times that of England, France was continental Europe's leading military power. It was already building a powerful fleet and a worldwide system of rigidly monopolized colonial trade. But the War of the Spanish Succession, the last of Louis XIV's many wars (see page 500), tilted the balance in favor of England. The 1713 Peace of Utrecht forced France to cede its North American holdings in Newfoundland, Nova Scotia, and the Hudson Bay territory to Britain. Spain was compelled to give Britain control of its West African slave trade — the so-called *asiento* (ah-SYEN-toh) — and to let Britain send one ship of merchandise into the Spanish colonies annually. These acquisitions primed Britain to take a leading role in the growing Atlantic trade of the eighteenth century, including the transatlantic slave trade (discussed in Chapter 19).

Life in the Colonies

Many factors helped shape life in European colonies, including locations of settlements, indigenous cultures and practices, and the cultural attitudes and official policies of the European colonizers. Women played a crucial role in the creation of new identities and the continuation of old ones. The first explorers formed unions with native women, through coercion or consent, and relied on them as translators, guides, and intermediaries in the formation of alliances with indigenous powers. As settlement developed, the character of each colony was influenced by the presence or absence of European women. Where women and children accompanied male colonists, as in the British colonies

• **Navigation Acts** Mid-seventeenth-century English mercantilist laws that greatly restricted other countries' rights to trade with England and its colonies.

and the Spanish mainland colonies, new settlements took on European languages, religion, and ways of life that have endured, with input from local cultures, to this day. Where European women did not accompany male settlers, as on the west coast of Africa and most European outposts in Asia, local populations largely retained their own cultures, to which male Europeans acclimatized themselves.

Most women who crossed the Atlantic were Africans, who constituted four-fifths of the female newcomers before 1800.[12] Wherever slavery existed, masters profited from their power to engage in sexual relations with enslaved women. One important difference among European colonies was in the status of children born of such unions. In some colonies, mostly those dominated by the Portuguese, Spanish, or French,

◻ Picturing the Past

Mulatto Painting The caption in the upper left corner of this mid-eighteenth-century painting identifies the family as being composed of a Spanish father and a black mother, and their child is described as "mulatto." The painting was number six in a series of sixteen images by the painter José de Alcibar, each showing a different racial and ethnic combination. The series belonged to a popular genre in the Spanish Americas known as *castas* paintings, which commonly depicted sixteen different forms of racial mixing. (Attrib. Jose de Alcibar, 6, De *Espano y Negra, Mulato*, ca. 1760–1770. Denver Art Museum: Collection of Frederick and Jan Mayer. Photo © James O. Milmoe)

ANALYZING THE IMAGE How would you characterize the relations among mother, father, and child as shown in this painting? Does the painter suggest power relations within the family? What attitude does the painter seem to have toward the family?

CONNECTIONS Why do you think such paintings were so popular? Who do you think the audience might have been, and why would viewers be fascinated by such images?

substantial populations of free blacks descended from the freed children of the unions. In English colonies, masters were less likely to free children they fathered with female slaves.

The mixing of indigenous people with Europeans and Africans created whole new populations and ethnicities and complex self-identities. In Spanish America the word *mestizo*—*métis* in French— described people of mixed Native American and European descent. The blanket terms "mulatto" and "people of color" were used for those of mixed African and European origins. With its immense slave-based plantation system, large indigenous population, and relatively low Portuguese immigration, Brazil developed a particularly complex racial and ethnic mosaic.

CONNECTIONS

The seventeenth century represented a difficult passage between two centuries of dynamism and growth in Europe. On one side lay the sixteenth century's religious enthusiasm and strife, overseas discoveries, rising populations, and vigorous commerce. On the other side stretched the eighteenth century's renewed population growth, economic development, and cultural flourishing. The first half of the seventeenth century was marked by the spread of religious and dynastic warfare across Europe, resulting in death and widespread suffering. Recurring crop failure, famine, and epidemic disease contributed to a stagnant economy and population loss. In the middle decades of the seventeenth century, the very survival of the European monarchies established in the Renaissance appeared in doubt.

With the re-establishment of order in the second half of the century, maintaining stability was of paramount importance to European rulers. While a few nations placed their trust in constitutionally limited governments, many more were ruled by monarchs proclaiming their absolute and God-given authority. The ability to actually assume such power depended on cooperation from local elites, who acquiesced to state authority in exchange for privileges and payoffs. In this way, both absolutism and constitutionalism relied on political compromises forged from decades of strife.

As Spain's power weakened, other European nations bordering the Atlantic Ocean sought their own profits and glory from overseas empires. Henceforth, war among European powers would include high-stakes conflicts over territories and trade in the colonies. European rulers' increased control over their own subjects thus went hand in glove with the expansion of European power in the world.

The eighteenth century was to see these power politics thrown into question by new Enlightenment aspirations for human society, which themselves derived from the inquisitive and self-confident spirit of the scientific revolution. These movements — both of which would have long-lasting influence worldwide — are explored in the next chapter. By the end of the eighteenth century, demands for real popular sovereignty, colonial self-rule, and slave emancipation challenged the very bases of order so painfully achieved in the seventeenth century. Chapter 22 recounts the revolutionary movements that swept the late-eighteenth-century Atlantic world, while Chapters 25, 26, and 27 follow the story of European imperialism and the resistance of colonized peoples into the nineteenth century.

CHAPTER REVIEW

□ **What were the common crises and achievements of seventeenth-century European states?** (p. 492)

Most parts of Europe experienced the seventeenth century as a period of severe economic, social, and military crisis. Across the continent, rulers faced popular rebellions from desperate subjects, who were pushed to the brink by poor harvests, famine, disease, poor wages, high prices, and more. In eastern Europe, lords addressed labor shortages by increasing peasants' work burdens and reducing their rights. The Thirty Years' War also had devastating consequences, drastically reducing urban and rural populations and harming trade and agriculture. Despite these obstacles, both absolutist and constitutional European states emerged from the seventeenth century with increased powers and more centralized control. Whether they ruled through monarchical fiat or parliamentary negotiation, European governments strengthened their bureaucracies, raised more taxes, and significantly expanded their armies.

□ **Why and how did the French absolutist state arise under Louis XIV, and why did absolutist Spain experience decline in the same period?** (p. 496)

Louis XIV rose to power in the wake of noble rebellion and popular riots that left the French wishing for a strong monarch to reimpose order. Using the doctrine of the divine right of kings to justify his hold on power, Louis ruled France by securing the collaboration of high nobles in exchange for confirmation of their ancient privileges. To build armies and fight wars, Louis relied on the wealth brought in through mercantilist policies. In Spain, where monarchs made similar claims to absolute power, the seventeenth century witnessed economic catastrophe and a decline in royal capacities. This decline resulted from a fall in colonial trade revenue, massive state debt, and a decline in manufacturing and agricultural productivity. Adding to these problems were internal conflicts and military defeats.

□ **How did Austrian, Prussian, and Russian rulers transform their nations into powerful absolutist monarchies?** (p. 501)

Within a framework of resurgent serfdom and entrenched nobility, Austrian and Prussian monarchs fashioned strong absolutist states in the seventeenth and early eighteenth centuries. These monarchs won absolutist control over standing armies, taxation, and representative bodies, but left intact the underlying social and economic relationships between the nobles and their peasants. In exchange, nobles cooperated with the growth of state power. In Russia, Mongol conquest and rule set the stage for absolutism, and a harsh tsarist autocracy was firmly in place by the time of the reign of Ivan the Terrible in the sixteenth century. Ivan's brutal rule brought all segments of Russian society into state service, sparking resentment and revolt. The reign of Ivan and his successors saw a great expansion of Russian territory, laying the foundations for a huge multiethnic empire. More than a century later, Peter the Great succeeded in modernizing Russia's traditional absolutism by reforming the army and the bureaucracy.

□ **Why and how did the constitutional state triumph in England and the Dutch Republic?** (p. 509)

England and the Netherlands defied the general trend toward absolute monarchy. In England, opposition arose against the monarchy for a number of reasons, including the Crown's resistance to religious reform, its skirting of parliamentary oversight, and its levying of taxes that most people considered illegal. Civil war resulted, and the country eventually came under what amounted to a military dictatorship. Eventually, however, England emerged with a constitutional monarchy. After the Glorious Revolution of 1688–1689, power was divided between king and Parliament, Parliament had to be called at least once every three years, and the independence of the judiciary was established. By contrast, the Dutch rejected monarchical rule after winning independence from Spain. Instead, the United Provinces of the Netherlands adopted a decentralized republican government in which local affairs were run by provincial estates and the national States General handled foreign affairs and war.

KEY TERMS

Peace of Westphalia (p. 494)
Fronde (p. 496)
mercantilism (p. 498)
Peace of Utrecht (p. 501)
Junkers (p. 503)
boyars (p. 505)
Cossacks (p. 508)

constitutionalism (p. 509)
republicanism (p. 510)
Puritans (p. 510)
Protectorate (p. 512)
Test Act (p. 512)
stadholder (p. 515)
Navigation Acts (p. 519)

□ How did European nations compete to build new colonies in the Americas? (p. 516)

As Spain's power weakened in the early seventeenth century, England, France, and the Netherlands competed with one another to gain territories in and wealth from the Americas. English settlement took on distinct characteristics in different regions, with religious dissenters establishing colonies in New England, while plantations with slave labor dominated in the South. New France had a small population, but its industrious traders explored and claimed for France vast territories along the waterways of the interior. In the early seventeenth century the Dutch successfully rivaled Spain's control of trade by disrupting shipping and by seizing portions of territories in Brazil and the Caribbean. Mercantilist competition among European powers led to conflict, with England emerging in the early eighteenth century as the most advantaged power. Life in the colonies was shaped by many factors, especially by the extent of immigration by European women. Throughout the Americas, new ethnic identities were formed by the mixing of European, indigenous, and African populations.

SUGGESTED READING

Benedict, Philip, and Myron P. Gutmann, eds. *Early Modern Europe: From Crisis to Stability.* 2005. A helpful introduction to the many facets of the seventeenth-century crisis.

Burke, Peter. *The Fabrication of Louis XIV.* 1992. Explains the use of architecture, art, medals, and other symbols to promote the king's image.

Clark, Christopher. *Iron Kingdom: The Rise and Downfall of Prussia, 1600–1947.* 2006. A fascinating long-term account tracing Prussia's emergence as an international power and the impact of Prussian history on later political developments in Germany.

Collins, James B. *The State in Early Modern France.* 1995. A detailed and well-argued survey of French administration from Louis XIII to Louis XVI.

Elliott, John H. *Imperial Spain, 1469–1716,* 2d ed. 2002. An authoritative account of Spain's rise to imperial greatness and its slow decline.

Gaunt, Peter, ed. *The English Civil War: The Essential Readings.* 2000. A collection showcasing leading historians' interpretations of the civil war.

Hagen, William W. *Ordinary Prussians: Brandenburg Junkers and Villagers, 1500–1840.* 2002. A fascinating look at the people of a Prussian estate, with first-person accounts.

Hughes, Lindsey, ed. *Peter the Great and the West: New Perspectives.* 2001. Essays by leading scholars on the reign of Peter the Great and his opening of Russia to the West.

Ingrao, Charles W. *The Habsburg Monarchy, 1618–1815,* 2d ed. 2000. An excellent synthesis of the political and social development of the Habsburg empire in the early modern period.

Parker, Geoffrey. *The Thirty Years' War,* 2d ed. 1997. The standard account of the Thirty Years' War.

Schama, Simon. *The Embarrassment of Riches: An Interpretation of Dutch Culture in the Golden Age.* 1987. A lengthy but vivid and highly readable account of Dutch culture in the seventeenth century, including a chapter on the mania for speculation on the tulip market.

NOTES

1. Theodore K. Rabb, *The Struggle for Stability in Early Modern Europe* (Oxford: Oxford University Press, 1975).
2. Quoted in Cecile Hugon, *Social France in the XVII Century* (London: McMilland, 1911), p. 189.
3. H. Kamen, "The Economic and Social Consequences of the Thirty Years' War," *Past and Present* 39 (April 1968): 44–61.
4. Quoted in John A. Lynn, *Giant of the Grand Siècle: The French Army, 1610–1715* (Cambridge, U.K.: Cambridge University Press, 1997), p. 74.
5. F. Arkwright, ed., *The Memoirs of the Duke de Saint-Simon,* vol. 5 (New York: Brentano's, n.d.), p. 276.
6. John A. Lynn, "Recalculating French Army Growth," in *The Military Revolution Debate: Readings on the Military Transformation of Early Modern Europe,* ed. Clifford J. Rogers (Boulder, Colo.: Westview Press, 1995), p. 125.
7. J. H. Elliott, *Imperial Spain, 1469–1716* (New York: Mentor Books, 1963), pp. 306–308.
8. H. Rosenberg, *Bureaucracy, Aristocracy, and Autocracy: The Prussian Experience, 1660–1815* (Boston: Beacon Press, 1966), p. 43.
9. Cited in Giles MacDonogh, *Frederick the Great: A Life in Deed and Letters* (New York: St. Martin's, 2001), p. 23.
10. Rosenberg, *Bureaucracy, Aristocracy, and Autocracy,* p. 40.
11. For a revisionist interpretation, see J. Wormald, "James VI and I: Two Kings or One?" *History* 62 (June 1983): 187–209.
12. Geoffrey Vaughn Scammel, *The First Imperial Age: European Overseas Expansion, c. 1400–1715* (London and New York: Routledge, 2002), p. 432.

For practice quizzes and other study tools, visit the **Online Study Guide** at bedfordstmartins.com/mckayworld.

For primary sources from this period, see *Sources of World Societies*, **Second Edition**.

For Web sites, images, and documents related to topics in this chapter, visit **Make History** at bedfordstmartins.com/mckayworld.

• **Free People of Color** A sizable mixed-race population emerged in many European colonies in the Americas, often descendants of unions between masters and enslaved African women. The wealthiest of the free people of color, as they were called, were plantation owners with slaves of their own. (Unknown artist, *Portrait of a Young Woman*, late 18th century, pastel, 16 × 12 inches, Saint Louis Art Museum, Museum Purchase 186:1951)

18

Intellectual developments of the sixteenth through eighteenth centuries created the modern worldview that the West continues to hold—and debate—to this day. Beginning in the sixteenth century, European scholars developed fundamentally new ways of understanding the natural world, later characterized as a "scientific revolution." Whereas medieval scholars looked to classical works and the Bible, seventeenth-century natural philosophers, as they called themselves, performed experiments and relied on complex mathematical calculations. The resulting conception of the universe and its laws remained in force until Albert Einstein's discoveries in the first half of the twentieth century.

New Worldviews and Ways of Life

1540–1790

Eighteenth-century philosophers extended the use of reason from nature to human society. Self-proclaimed members of an "Enlightenment" movement, they wished to bring the same progress to human affairs that their predecessors brought to the understanding of the natural world. While the scientific revolution ushered in modern science, the Enlightenment created concepts of human rights, equality, progress, and tolerance that still guide Western societies. At the same time, some Europeans used their new understanding of reason to explain their own superiority, thus rationalizing attitudes now regarded as racist and sexist.

The expression of new ideas was encouraged by changes in the material world. With the growth of population, the revitalization of industry and growing world trade, Europeans began to consume at a higher level. Feeding the growth of consumerism was the expansion of transatlantic trade and lower prices for colonial goods, often produced by slaves. During the eighteenth century, ships crisscrossing the Atlantic circulated commodities, ideas, and people to all four continents bordering the ocean. As trade became more integrated and communication intensified, an Atlantic world of mixed identities and shared debates emerged. •

The Scientific Revolution

□ What was revolutionary in the new attitudes toward the natural world?

The Enlightenment

□ How did a new spirit of critical and rational thinking affect ideas about society and human relations?

Enlightened Absolutism

□ What impact did new ways of thinking have on monarchical absolutism and those under its rule?

The Growth of Consumerism and the Atlantic World

□ How did the growth of consumerism and the Atlantic economy interact with Enlightenment ideas?

The Scientific Revolution

□ What was revolutionary in the new attitudes toward the natural world?

A noted historian has said that the scientific revolution, which lasted roughly from 1540 to 1690, was "the real origin both of the modern world and the modern mentality."[1] Through new methods of investigating the physical world, Western society began to come to a new understanding of astronomy, physics, and medicine based on both experimentation and reasoning.

Scientific Thought Through the Early 1500s

The term *science* as we use it today came into use only in the nineteenth century. Prior to the scientific revolution, many different scholars and practitioners were involved in aspects of what came together to form science. One of the most important disciplines was **natural philosophy**, which focused on fundamental questions about the nature of the universe, its purpose, and how it functioned. In the early 1500s natural philosophy was still based primarily on the ideas of Aristotle, the great Greek philosopher of the fourth century B.C.E. Medieval theologians such as Thomas Aquinas brought Aristotelian philosophy into harmony with Christian doctrines. According to the revised Aristotelian view, a motionless earth was fixed at the center of the universe and was encompassed by ten separate concentric crystal spheres in which were embedded the moon, sun, planets, and stars. Beyond the spheres was Heaven, with the throne of God and the souls of the saved. Angels kept the spheres moving in perfect circles.

Aristotle's cosmology made intellectual sense, but it could not account for the observed motions of the stars and planets and, in particular, provided no explanation for the apparent backward motion of the planets (which we now know

The Aristotelian Universe as Imagined in the Sixteenth Century A round earth is at the center, surrounded by spheres of water, air, and fire. Beyond this small nucleus, the moon, the sun, and the five planets were embedded in their own rotating crystal spheres, with the stars sharing the surface of one enormous sphere. Beyond, the heavens were composed of unchanging ether. (Image Select/Art Resource, NY) occurs as planets closer to the sun periodically overtake the earth on their faster orbits). The great second-century Greek scholar Ptolemy offered a theory for this phenomenon. According to Ptolemy, the planets moved in small circles, called epicycles, each of which moved in turn along a larger circle or deferent. Ptolemaic astronomy was less elegant than Aristotle's neat nested circles and required complex calculations, but it provided a surprisingly accurate model for predicting planetary motion.

Aristotle's views, revised by medieval philosophers, also dominated thinking about physics and motion on earth. Aristotle had distinguished sharply between the world of the celestial spheres and that of the earth — the sublunar world. The sublunar realm was made up of four imperfect, changeable elements: air, fire, water, and earth. The spheres, however, consisted of a perfect, incorruptible "quintessence," or fifth essence. Aristotle and his followers also believed that a uniform force moved an object at a constant speed and that the object would stop as soon as that force was removed. Both of these views would be challenged based on new observations and analysis of the physical world.

Origins of the Scientific Revolution

Why did Aristotelian teachings give way to new views about the universe? The first important driver of the scientific revolution was the medieval university. By the thirteenth century permanent universities had been established in western Europe. In the fourteenth and fifteenth centuries leading universities established new professorships of mathematics, astronomy, and physics (natural philosophy) within their faculties of philosophy. Although the prestige of the new fields was low, a permanent community of scholars was now focused on investigating scientific problems

Medieval scholarship in the universities was based on the study of ancient texts, whose wisdom was considered authoritative. Contact with Muslims in Spain and Sicily brought awareness of many ancient texts that survived only in Arabic versions, and these were translated into Latin in the twelfth century. In some instances, such as mathematics and astronomy, the translations were accompanied by learned commentaries that went beyond ancient learning. Arabic and Persian mathematicians, for example, invented algebra, the

concept of the algorithm, and decimal point notation, while Arabic astronomers improved on measurements recorded in ancient works.

Second, the Renaissance also stimulated scientific progress. Renaissance patrons played a role in funding scientific investigations, as they did art and literature. The goal of exploration in late fifteenth and sixteenth centuries was not only to find wealth and Christian converts, but also to increase Europeans' knowledge about the wider world. In addition, Renaissance artists' turn toward realism and their use of geometry to convey three-dimensional perspective encouraged scholars to practice close observation and to use mathematics to describe the natural world. Furthermore, the Renaissance rise of printing provided a faster and less expensive way to circulate knowledge across Europe.

The navigational problems of long sea voyages in the age of overseas expansion were a third factor in the scientific revolution. To help solve these problems, inventors developed many new scientific instruments, such as the telescope, barometer, thermometer, pendulum clock, microscope, and air pump. Better instruments, which permitted more accurate observations, often led to important new knowledge.

natural philosophy An early modern term for the study of the nature of the universe, its purpose, and how it functioned; it encompassed what we call "science" today.

Finally, recent historical research has focused on the contribution of practices now regarded as far beyond the realm of science. For most of human history, interest in astronomy was inspired by the belief that the changing relationships between planets and stars influenced events on earth. Many of the most celebrated astronomers were also astrologers. Used as a diagnostic tool in medicine, astrology formed a regular part of the curriculum of medical schools. Centuries-old practices of magic and alchemy also remained important traditions for participants in the scientific revolution. The idea that objects possessed hidden or "occult" qualities that allowed them to affect other objects was a particularly important legacy of the magical tradition. Such hidden qualities helped inspire an important new law of physics (see page 530).

Copernican Hypothesis

The first great departure from the medieval understanding of the physical world system was the work of the Polish cleric Nicolaus Copernicus (1473–1543). After studying at the university of Kraków, Copernicus departed for Italy, where he studied astronomy, medicine, and church law at the famed universities of Bologna, Padua, and Ferrara. In the course of his study of astronomy, Copernicus came to believe that Ptolemy's cumbersome and occasionally inaccurate rules detracted from the majesty of a perfect creator. He preferred an ancient Greek idea: that the sun, rather than the earth, was at the center of the universe.

Finishing his university studies and returning to a church position in East Prussia, Copernicus worked on his hypothesis from 1506 to 1530. Without questioning the Aristotelian belief in crystal spheres or the idea that circular motion was divine, Copernicus theorized that the stars and planets, including the earth, revolved around a fixed sun. Fearing the ridicule of other astronomers, Copernicus did not publish his *On the Revolutions of the Heavenly Spheres* until 1543, the year of his death.

The **Copernican hypothesis** presented a revolutionary view of the universe and brought sharp attacks from religious leaders, especially Protestants, who objected to the idea that the earth moved but the sun did not. Protestant leaders John Calvin and Martin Luther condemned Copernicus. Luther noted that the theory was counter to the Bible: "as the Holy Scripture tells us, so did Joshua bid the sun stand still and not the earth."[2] Catholic reaction was milder at first. The Catholic Church had never held to literal interpretations of the Bible, and not until 1616 did it officially declare the Copernican hypothesis false.

Other events were almost as influential in creating doubts about traditional astronomical ideas. In 1572 a new star appeared and shone very brightly for almost two years. The new star, which was actually a distant exploding star, seemed to contradict the idea that the heavenly spheres were unchanging and therefore perfect. In 1577 a new comet suddenly moved through the sky, cutting a straight path across the supposedly impenetrable crystal spheres. It was time, as a sixteenth-century scientific writer put it, for "the radical renovation of astronomy."[3]

Proving Copernicus Right

One astronomer who agreed with Copernicus was the Danish astronomer Tycho Brahe (TEE-koh BRAH-hee; 1546–1601). Brahe established himself as Europe's leading astronomer with his detailed observations of the new star of 1572. Aided by grants from the king of Denmark, Brahe built the most sophisticated observatory of his day.

Upon the king's death, Brahe acquired a new patron in the Holy Roman emperor Rudolph II and built a new observatory in Prague. In return for the emperor's support, he pledged to create new and improved tables of planetary motions, dubbed the *Rudolfine Tables*. For twenty years Brahe observed the stars and planets with his naked eye, compiling much more complete and accurate data than ever before. His limited understanding of mathematics and his sudden death in 1601, however, prevented him from making much sense out of his mass of data.

It was left to Brahe's young assistant, Johannes Kepler (1571–1630), to rework Brahe's mountain of observations. A brilliant mathematician, Kepler was inspired by his belief that the universe was built on mystical mathematical relationships and a musical harmony of the heavenly bodies.

Kepler's examination of his predecessor's findings convinced him that they could not be explained by Ptolemy's astronomy. Abandoning the notion of epicycles and deferents, Kepler developed three revolutionary laws of planetary motion. First, he demonstrated that the orbits of the planets around the sun are elliptical rather than circular. Second, he demonstrated that the planets do not move at a uniform speed in their orbits. When a planet is close to the sun it moves more rapidly, and it slows as it moves farther away from the sun. Finally, Kepler's third law stated that the time a planet takes to make its complete orbit is precisely related to its distance from the sun.

• **Copernican hypothesis** The idea that the sun, not the earth, was the center of the universe.

• **law of inertia** A law formulated by Galileo that states that motion, not rest, is the natural state of an object, and that an object continues in motion forever unless stopped by some external force.

Kepler's contribution was monumental. Whereas Copernicus had speculated, Kepler proved mathematically the precise relations of a sun-centered (solar) system. His work demolished the old system of Aristotle and Ptolemy, and in his third law he came close to formulating the idea of universal gravitation (see page 530). In 1627 he also fulfilled Brahe's pledge by completing the *Rudolfine Tables* begun so many years earlier. These tables were used by astronomers for many years.

Kepler was not, however, the consummate modern scientist that his achievements suggest. His duties as court mathematician included casting horoscopes, and his own diary was based on astrological principles. He also wrote at length on cosmic harmonies and explained, for example, elliptical motion through ideas about the beautiful music created by the combined motion of the planets. His career exemplifies the complex interweaving of rigorous empirical observations and mystical beliefs in the emerging science of his day.

While Kepler was unraveling the mysteries of planetary motion, a young Florentine named Galileo Galilei (1564–1642) was challenging old ideas about motion on earth. Galileo's achievement was the elaboration and consolidation of the experimental method. That is, rather than speculate about what might or should happen, Galileo conducted controlled experiments to find out what actually did happen.

In some of his experiments Galileo measured the movement of a rolling ball across a surface, repeating the action again and again to verify his results. In his famous acceleration experiment, he showed that a uniform force—in this case, gravity—produced a uniform acceleration. Through another experiment, he formulated the **law of inertia**. According to this law, rest is not the natural state of objects. Rather, an object continues in motion forever unless stopped by some external force,

such as friction. His discoveries thus proved Aristotelian physics wrong.

Galileo also applied the experimental method to astronomy. On hearing details about the invention of the telescope in Holland, Galileo made one for himself. He quickly discovered the first four moons of Jupiter, which clearly suggested that Jupiter could not possibly be embedded in an impenetrable crystal sphere as Aristotle and Ptolemy maintained. This discovery provided new evidence for the Copernican theory, in which Galileo already believed. Galileo then pointed his telescope at the moon. He wrote in 1610 in *Siderus Nuncius*:

> By the aid of a telescope anyone may behold [the Milky Way] in a manner which so distinctly appeals to the senses that all the disputes which have tormented philosophers through so many ages are exploded by the irrefutable evidence of our eyes, and we are freed from wordy disputes upon the subject.[4]

Galileo's Telescopic Observations of the Moon Among the many mechanical devices Galileo invented was a telescope that could magnify objects twenty times (other contemporary telescopes could magnify objects only three times). Using this telescope, he obtained the empirical evidence that proved the Copernican system. He sketched many illustrations of his observations, including the six phases of the moon, two of which are shown here. (Scala/Art Resource, NY)

Reading these famous lines, one feels a crucial corner in Western civilization being turned. A new method of learning and investigating was being developed, in which scholars relied more on observable evidence and critical thinking than on established authority. This method proved useful in any field of inquiry. A historian investigating documents of the past, for example, is not so different from a Galileo studying stars and rolling balls.

As early as 1597, when Johannes Kepler sent Galileo an early publication defending Copernicus, Galileo wrote back agreeing with his position and confessing he lacked the courage to follow Kepler's example. Within the Catholic world, expressing public support for Copernicus was increasingly dangerous. In 1616 the Holy Office placed the works of Copernicus and his supporters, including Kepler, on a list of books Catholics were forbidden to read.

Out of caution Galileo silenced his beliefs for several years, until in 1623 he saw new hope with the ascension of Pope Urban VIII, a man sympathetic to developments in the new science. However, Galileo's 1632 *Dialogue on the Two Chief Systems of the World* went too far. Published in Italian and widely read, this work openly lampooned the traditional views of Aristotle and Ptolemy and defended those of Copernicus. In 1633 Galileo was tried for heresy by the papal Inquisition. Imprisoned and threatened with torture, the aging Galileo recanted, "renouncing and cursing" his Copernican errors.

Newton's Synthesis

Despite the efforts of the church, by about 1640 the work of Brahe, Kepler, and Galileo had been largely accepted by the scientific community. But the new findings failed to explain what forces controlled the movement of the planets and objects on earth. That challenge was taken up by English scientist Isaac Newton (1642–1727).

Although he was a genius who united the experimental and theoretical-mathematical sides of modern science, Newton—like Kepler and other practitioners of the scientific revolution—was far from being the perfect rationalist so glorified by writers in the eighteenth and nineteenth centuries. For example, he was intensely religious and also fascinated by alchemy, whose practitioners believed (among other things) that base metals could be turned into gold.

Nevertheless, Newton dedicated himself to scientific pursuits from a young age. Born into the lower English gentry, he enrolled at Cambridge University in 1661. He arrived at some of his most basic ideas about physics in 1666 at age twenty-four but was unable to prove them mathematically. In 1684, after years of studying optics, Newton returned to physics for eighteen extraordinarily intensive months. The result was his towering accomplishment, a single explanatory system that integrated the astronomy of Copernicus, as corrected by Kepler's laws, with the physics of Galileo and his predecessors. Newton did this through a set of mathematical laws that explain motion and mechanics. These laws were published in 1687 in Newton's *Mathematical Principles of Natural Philosophy* (also known as the *Principia*). Because of their complexity, it took scientists and engineers two hundred years to work out all their implications.

The key feature of the Newtonian synthesis was the **law of universal gravitation**. According to this law, each body in the universe attracts every other body in a precise mathematical relationship, whereby the force of attraction is proportional to the quantity of matter of the objects and inversely proportional to the square of the distance between them. The whole universe—from Kepler's elliptical orbits to Galileo's rolling balls—was unified in one majestic system. Newton's synthesis prevailed until the twentieth century.

Bacon, Descartes, and the Scientific Method

One of the keys to achieving a better understanding of the world was the development of better ways of obtaining knowledge. Two important thinkers, Francis Bacon (1561–1626) and René Descartes (day-KAHRT; 1596–1650), were influential in describing and advocating for improved scientific methods based, respectively, on experimentation and mathematical reasoning.

The English politician and writer Francis Bacon was the greatest early propagandist for the new experimental method. Rejecting the Aristotelian and medieval method of using speculative reasoning to build general theories, Bacon argued that new knowledge had to be pursued through empirical research. The researcher who wants to learn more about leaves or rocks, for example, should not speculate about the subject but should rather collect a multitude of specimens and then compare and analyze them to derive general principles. Bacon's contribution was to formalize the empirical method, which had already been used by Brahe and Galileo, into the general theory of inductive reasoning known as **empiricism**.

• **law of universal gravitation** Newton's law that all objects are attracted to one another and that the force of attraction is proportional to the object's quantity of matter and inversely proportional to the square of the distance between them.

• **empiricism** A theory of inductive reasoning that calls for acquiring evidence through observation and experimentation rather than reason and speculation.

• **Cartesian dualism** Descartes's view that all of reality could ultimately be reduced to mind and matter.

On the continent, more speculative methods retained support. In 1619, as a twenty-three-year-old soldier serving in the Thirty Years' War (1618–1648), the French philosopher René Descartes experienced a life-changing intellectual vision one night. Descartes saw that there was a perfect correspondence between geometry and algebra and that geometrical spatial figures could be expressed as algebraic equations and vice versa. A major step forward in the history of mathematics, Descartes's discovery of analytic geometry provided scientists with an important new tool.

Descartes used mathematics to elaborate a highly influential vision of the workings of the cosmos. Drawing on ancient Greek atomist philosophies, Descartes developed the idea that matter was made up of identical "corpuscules" (tiny particles) that collided together in an endless series of motions. All occurrences in nature could be analyzed as matter in motion, and, according to Descartes, the total "quantity of motion" in the universe was constant. Descartes's mechanistic view of the universe depended on the idea that a vacuum was impossible, so that every action had an equal reaction, continuing in an eternal chain reaction. Although Descartes's hypothesis about the vacuum was proved wrong, his notion of a mechanistic universe intelligible through the physics of motion proved highly influential.

Descartes's greatest achievement was to develop his initial vision into a whole philosophy of knowledge and science. The Aristotelian cosmos was appealing in part because it corresponded with the evidence of the human senses. However, Descartes acknowledged that impressions of the world gained through the senses can sometimes be proved wrong. Thus, they can be doubted. Only things about which there can be no doubt should be accepted as truths, Descartes argued, and from these truths, or general principles, people can arrive at additional truths. This process of moving from general principles to specific truths is known as deductive reasoning. Descartes's reasoning ultimately reduced all substances to "matter" and "mind"—that is, to the physical and the spiritual. Descartes believed that God had endowed man with reason for a purpose and that rational speculation could provide a path to the truths of creation. His view of the world as consisting of two fundamental entities is known as **Cartesian dualism**. Descartes's thought was highly influential in France and the Netherlands but less so in England, where an emphasis on experimentation won the day.

Both Bacon's inductive experimentalism and Descartes's deductive mathematical reasoning had faults. Bacon's inability to appreciate the importance of mathematics and his obsession with practical results clearly showed the limitations of antitheoretical empiricism. Likewise, some of Descartes's positions—he believed, for example, that it was possible to deduce the whole science of medicine from a set of foundational first principles—demonstrated the inadequacy of rigid, dogmatic rationalism. Although insufficient on their own, Bacon's and Descartes's extreme approaches are combined in the modern scientific method, which began to crystallize in the late seventeenth century.

☐ MAJOR CONTRIBUTORS TO THE SCIENTIFIC REVOLUTION

Nicolaus Copernicus (1473–1543)	Published *On the Revolutions of the Heavenly Spheres* (1543); theorized that the sun, rather than the earth, was the center of the galaxy
Paracelsus (1493–1541)	Pioneered the use of chemicals and drugs to address perceived chemical imbalances
Andreas Vesalius (1514–1564)	Published *On the Structure of the Human Body* (1543)
Tycho Brahe (1546–1601)	Built observatories and compiled data for the *Rudolfine Tables*, a new table of planetary data
Francis Bacon (1561–1626)	Advocated experimental method, formalizing theory of inductive reasoning known as empiricism
Galileo Galilei (1564–1642)	Used telescopic observation to provide evidence for Copernican hypothesis; experimented to formulate laws of physics, such as inertia
Johannes Kepler (1571–1630)	Used Brahe's data to mathematically prove the Copernican hypothesis; his new laws of planetary motion united for the first time natural philosophy and mathematics; completed the *Rudolfine Tables* in 1627
William Harvey (1578–1657)	Discovered blood circulation (1628)
René Descartes (1596–1650)	Used deductive reasoning to formulate theory of Cartesian dualism
Robert Boyle (1627–1691)	Founded the modern science of chemistry; created the first vacuum; discovered Boyle's law on the properties of gases
Isaac Newton (1642–1727)	Introduced the law of universal gravitation, synthesizing the theories of Copernicus and Galileo

Medicine, the Body, and Chemistry

The scientific revolution, which began with the study of the cosmos, soon inspired renewed study of the microcosm of the human body. For many centuries the ancient Greek physician Galen's explanation of the body carried the same authority as Aristotle's account of the universe. According to Galen, the body contained four humors: blood, phlegm, black bile, and yellow bile. Illness was believed to result from an imbalance of these humors.

Swiss physician and alchemist Paracelsus (1493–1541) was an early proponent of the experimental method in medicine and pioneered the use of chemicals and drugs to address what he saw as chemical,

Frontispiece to *De Humani Corporis Fabrica* (*On the Structure of the Human Body*) The frontispiece to Vesalius's pioneering work, published in 1643, shows him dissecting a corpse before a crowd of students. This was a revolutionary new hands-on approach for physicians, who usually worked from a theoretical, rather than a practical, understanding of the body. Based on direct observation, Vesalius replaced ancient ideas drawn from Greek philosophy with a much more accurate account of the structure and function of the body. (© SSPL/Science Museum/The Image Works)

rather than humoral, imbalances. Another experimentalist, Flemish physician Andreas Vesalius (1514–1564), studied anatomy by dissecting human bodies. In 1543, the same year Copernicus published *On the Revolutions of the Heavenly Spheres*, Vesalius issued *On the Structure of the Human Body*. Its two hundred precise drawings revolutionized the understanding of human anatomy. The experimental approach also led English royal physician William Harvey (1578–1657) to discover the circulation of blood through the veins and arteries in 1628. Harvey was the first to explain that the heart worked like a pump and to explain the function of its muscles and valves.

Irishman Robert Boyle (1627–1691) founded the modern science of chemistry. Following Paracelsus's lead, he undertook experiments to discover the basic elements of nature, which he believed was composed of infinitely small atoms. Boyle was the first to create a vacuum, thus disproving Descartes's belief that a vacuum could not exist in nature, and he discovered Boyle's law (1662), which states that the pressure of a gas varies inversely with volume.

Science and Society

The rise of modern science had many consequences. First, it led to the rise of a new and expanding social group — the international scientific community. Members of this community were linked together by common interests and shared values as well as by journals and learned scientific societies. The personal success of scientists and scholars depended on making new discoveries, and as a result science became competitive. Second, as governments intervened to support and sometimes direct research, the new scientific community became closely tied to the state and its agendas. National academies of science were created under state sponsorship in London in 1662, Paris in 1666, Berlin in 1700, and later across Europe. At the same time, some scientists developed a critical attitude toward established authority that would inspire thinkers to question traditions in other domains as well, such as politics and religion.

Some things did not change in the scientific revolution. For example, new "rational" methods for approaching nature did not question traditional inequalities between the sexes — and may have worsened them in some ways. When Renaissance courts served as centers of learning, talented noblewomen could find niches in study and research. But the rise of a professional scientific community raised barriers for women because the new academies that furnished professional credentials did not accept female members.

There were, however, a number of noteworthy exceptions. In Italy, universities and academies did offer posts to women. Moreover, women across Europe were allowed to work as makers of wax anatomical models and as botanical and zoological illustrators. They were also very much involved in informal scientific communities, attending salons (see page 539), participating in scientific experiments, and writing learned treatises. Some female intellectuals were recognized as full-fledged participants in the philosophical dialogue.

The scientific revolution had few consequences for economic life and the living standards of the masses until the late eighteenth century, when its insights helped create new manufacturing technologies. Instead, it was first and foremost an intellectual revolution. For more than a hundred years its greatest impact was on how people thought and believed.

Finally, there is the question of the role of religion in the development of science. All Western religious authorities — Catholic, Protestant, and Jewish — opposed the Copernican system to a greater or lesser extent until about 1630, by which time the scientific revolution was definitely in progress. The Catholic Church was initially less hostile than Protestant and Jewish religious leaders, and Italian scientists played a crucial role in scientific progress right up to the trial of Galileo in 1633. Thereafter, the Counter-Reformation church became more hostile to science, a change that helped account for the decline of science in Italy (but not in Catholic France) after 1640. At the same time, Protestant countries — especially those lacking a strong religious authority capable of imposing religious orthodoxy on scientific questions — became quite "pro-science." Such countries included the Netherlands, Denmark, and England.

The Enlightenment

☐ How did a new spirit of critical and rational thinking affect ideas about society and human relations?

The scientific revolution was the single most important factor in the creation of the new worldview of the eighteenth-century **Enlightenment**. This worldview grew out of a rich mix of diverse and often conflicting ideas. For the writers who espoused them, the ideas competed vigorously for the attention of a growing public of well-educated readers, who remained a minority of the population.

Despite the diversity, three concepts stand at the core of Enlightenment thinking. The most important and original idea was that the methods of natural science could and should be used to examine and understand all aspects of life. This was what intellectuals meant by *reason*, a favorite word of Enlightenment thinkers. Nothing was to be accepted on faith; every-

Popularizing Science The frontispiece illustration of Fontenelle's *Conversations on the Plurality of Worlds* (1686) invites the reader to share the pleasures of astronomy with an elegant lady and an entertaining teacher. The drawing shows the planets revolving around the sun. (© Roger-Viollet/The Image Works)

thing was to be submitted to rationalism, a secular, critical way of thinking. A second important Enlightenment concept was that the scientific method was capable of discovering the laws of human society as

> • **Enlightenment** The influential intellectual and cultural movement of the late seventeenth and eighteenth centuries that introduced new ways of thinking based on the use of reason, the scientific method, and progress.

Metamorphoses of the Caterpillar and Moth Maria Sibylla Merian (1647–1717), the stepdaughter of a Dutch painter, became a celebrated scientific illustrator in her own right. Her finely observed pictures of insects in the South American colony of Surinam introduced many new species. For Merian, science was intimately tied with art: she not only painted but also bred caterpillars and performed experiments on them. Her two-year stay in Surinam, where she was accompanied by a teenage daughter, was a daring feat for a seventeenth-century woman. (Bildarchiv Preussischer Kulturbesitz/Art Resource, NY)

well as those of nature. This second concept led to the third key idea, that of progress: the goal of creating better societies and better people by discarding outmoded traditions and embracing rationalism.

The Emergence of the Enlightenment

An intellectual movement based on the core concepts just mentioned, the European Enlightenment (ca. 1690–1789) gained strength gradually and did not reach maturity until about 1750. Yet it was the generation that came of age between the publication of Newton's *Principia* in 1687 and the death of French king Louis XIV in 1715 that tied the crucial knot between the scientific

revolution and a new outlook on life. Talented writers of that generation popularized hard-to-understand scientific achievements for the educated elite.

This new generation came to believe that the human mind itself is capable of making great progress. Medieval and Reformation thinkers had been concerned primarily with the abstract concepts of sin and salvation. The humanists of the Renaissance had emphasized worldly matters (especially art and literature), but their inspiration came from the classical past. By contrast, Enlightenment thinkers came to believe that their era had gone far beyond antiquity and that fresh intellectual progress was possible.

The excitement of the scientific revolution also generated doubt and uncertainty, as Europeans of the late seventeenth century began to question long-standing religious assumptions and practices. In the wake of the devastation wrought by the Catholic-Protestant struggle of the Thirty Years' War, some people asked whether ideological conformity in religious matters was really necessary. Others skeptically asked if religious truth could ever be known with absolute certainty and concluded that it could not.

The most famous of these skeptics was the French Huguenot Pierre Bayle (1647–1706). Bayle critically examined the religious beliefs and persecutions of the past in his *Historical and Critical Dictionary* (1697). Demonstrating that human beliefs had been extremely varied and often mistaken, he concluded that nothing can ever be known beyond all doubt, a view known as skepticism.

Some Jewish scholars participated in the early Enlightenment movement. The philosopher Baruch Spinoza (1632–1677) was excommunicated by the relatively large Jewish community of Amsterdam for his controversial religious ideas. Spinoza believed that mind and body are united in one substance and that God and nature were two names for the same thing. He envisioned a deterministic universe in which good and evil were merely relative values. Few of Spinoza's radical writings were published during his lifetime, but he is now recognized as among the most original thinkers of the early Enlightenment.

Out of this period of intellectual turmoil came John Locke's *Essay Concerning Human Understanding* (1690), often viewed as the first major text of the Enlightenment. In this work Locke (1632–1704) set forth a new theory about how human beings learn and form their ideas. Whereas Descartes based his deductive logic on the conviction that certain first premises, or innate ideas, are imbued in all humans by God, Locke insisted that all ideas are derived from experience. According to Locke, the human mind at birth is like a blank tablet, or tabula rasa, on which the environment writes the individual's understanding and beliefs. Human development is therefore determined by education and social institutions, for good or for evil. Locke's essay contributed to the theory of sensationalism, the idea that all human ideas and thoughts are produced as a result of sensory impressions. The *Essay Concerning Human Understanding* passed through many editions and translations and, along with Newton's *Principia*, was one of the dominant intellectual inspirations of the Enlightenment.

The rapidly growing literature about non-European lands and cultures was another cause of questioning among thinkers. In the wake of the great discoveries, Europeans were learning that the peoples of the world had their own very different beliefs and customs. Whereas Europeans shaved their faces and let their hair grow, Turks shaved their heads and let their beards grow. In Europe a man bowed before a woman to show respect, while in Siam (now Thailand) a man turned his back on a woman when he met her because it was disrespectful to look directly at her. Countless similar examples discussed in travel accounts helped change the perspective of educated Europeans. They began to look at truth and morality in relative, rather than absolute, terms. If anything was possible, who could say what was right or wrong?

The Influence of the Philosophes

By the time Louis XIV died in 1715, many of the ideas that would soon coalesce into the new worldview had been assembled. Yet Christian Europe was still strongly attached to its established political and social structures and its traditional spiritual beliefs. By 1775, however, a large portion of western Europe's educated elite had embraced many of the new ideas. This acceptance was largely the work of the **philosophes**, a group of influential intellectuals in France who proudly proclaimed that they were bringing the light of knowledge to their ignorant fellow creatures.

To appeal to the public and get around the censors, the philosophes wrote novels and plays, histories and philosophies, dictionaries and encyclopedias, all filled with satire and double meanings to spread their message. One of the greatest philosophes, the baron de Montesquieu (mahn-tuhs-KYOO; 1689–1755), pioneered this approach in *The Persian Letters*, an extremely influential social satire published in 1721. This work consisted of letters supposedly written by two Persian travelers, Usbek and Rica, who as outsiders see European customs in unique ways and thereby allow Montesquieu a vantage point for criticizing existing practices and beliefs.

Having gained fame by using wit as a weapon against cruelty and superstition, Montesquieu settled down on his family estate to study history and politics. Disturbed by royal absolutism under Louis XIV and inspired by the example of the physical sciences, Montesquieu set out to apply the critical method to the problem of government in *The Spirit of Laws* (1748).

> " I would reform an abuse which cuts off, so to speak, half the human race. I would make women participate in all the rights of humankind, and above all in those of the intellect. "
>
> **MADAME DU CHÂTELET**

Showing that forms of government were shaped by history, geography, and customs, Montesquieu identified three main types: monarchies, republics, and despotisms. Admiring greatly the English balance of power among the king, the houses of Parliament, and the independent courts, he argued for a separation of powers, with political power divided among a variety of classes and legal estates holding unequal rights and privileges. Montesquieu was no democrat; he was apprehensive about the uneducated poor, and he did not question the overarching sovereignty of the French monarch. But he was concerned that royal rule in France was drifting into tyranny and believed that strengthening the influence of intermediary powers was the best way to prevent it. Decades later, his theory of separation of powers had a great impact on the constitutions of the young United States in 1789 and of France in 1791.

The most famous philosophe was François-Marie Arouet, who was known by the pen name Voltaire (1694–1778). In his long career, Voltaire wrote more than seventy witty volumes, hobnobbed with kings and queens, and died a millionaire because of shrewd business speculations. His early career, however, was turbulent, and he was arrested on two occasions for insulting noblemen. To avoid a prison term in France, Voltaire moved to England for three years, and there he came to share Montesquieu's enthusiasm for English liberties and institutions.

Returning to France, Voltaire met Gabrielle-Emilie Le Tonnelier de Breteuil, marquise du Châtelet (1706–1749), a gifted woman from the high aristocracy. Madame du Châtelet invited Voltaire to live in her country house at Cirey in Lorraine and became his long-time companion (under the eyes of her tolerant husband). Passionate about science, she studied physics and mathematics and published scientific articles and translations, including the first French translation of Newton's *Principia*. Excluded from the Royal Academy of Sciences because she was a woman, Madame du Châtelet had no doubt that women's limited role in science was due to their unequal education. She once wrote that if she were a ruler, "I would reform an abuse which cuts off, so to speak, half the human race. I would

• **philosophes** A group of French intellectuals who proclaimed that they were bringing the light of knowledge to their fellow creatures in the Age of Enlightenment.

Voltaire and Philosophes This painting belongs to a series commissioned by Catherine the Great to depict daily life at the philosopher's retreat at Ferney in Switzerland. It shows Voltaire seated at the dinner table surrounded by his followers, including *Encyclopedia* editors Diderot and d'Alembert. The scene is imaginary, for Diderot never visited Ferney. (Photo by permission of the Voltaire Foundation, University of Oxford)

make women participate in all the rights of humankind, and above all in those of the intellect."[5]

While living at Cirey, Voltaire wrote works praising England and popularizing English scientific progress. Yet, like almost all of the philosophes, Voltaire was a reformer, not a revolutionary, in social and political matters. He pessimistically concluded that the best form of government was a good monarch, since human beings "are very rarely worthy to govern themselves." (For a discussion of monarchs influenced by Enlightenment ideals, see page 540.) Nor did Voltaire believe in social and economic equality. The only realizable equality, Voltaire thought, was that "by which the citizen only depends on the laws which protect the freedom of the feeble against the ambitions of the strong."[6]

Voltaire's philosophical and religious positions were much more radical than his social and political beliefs. Voltaire believed in God, but his was a distant, noninterventionist, deistic God. Drawing on Newton, he envisioned a mechanistic universe in which God acted like a great clockmaker who built an orderly system and then stepped aside and let it run. Above all, Voltaire and most of the philosophes hated all forms of religious intolerance, which they believed often led to fanaticism and savage, inhuman action.

The ultimate strength of the philosophes lay in their number, dedication, and organization. Their greatest and most representative intellectual achievement was a group effort — the seventeen-volume *Encyclopedia: The Rational Dictionary of the Sciences, the Arts, and the Crafts,* edited by Denis Diderot (1713–1784) and Jean le Rond d'Alembert (1717–1783). The two men set out in 1751 to find coauthors who would examine the rapidly expanding whole of human knowledge. Even more fundamentally, they set out to teach people how to think critically and objectively about all matters.

The *Encyclopedia* survived initial resistance from the French government and the Catholic Church. Completed in 1765, it contained hundreds of thousands of articles by leading scientists, writers, skilled workers, and progressive priests, and it treated every aspect of life and knowledge. Science and the industrial arts were exalted, religion and immortality questioned. Intoler-

economic liberalism The theory that the pursuit of self-interest in a competitive market suffices to improve living conditions, rendering government intervention unnecessary and undesirable, associated with Adam Smith.

ance, legal injustice, and out-of-date social institutions were openly criticized. The *Encyclopedia* also included thousands of articles describing non-European cultures and societies, including acknowledgment of Muslim scholars' contribution to the development of Western science. Summing up the new worldview of the Enlightenment, the *Encyclopedia* was widely read, especially in less-expensive reprint editions, and it was extremely influential.

Enlightenment Across Europe

Enlightenment thought took on distinctive forms in different European countries. Even within each nation, reform-minded philosophers and writers formed their own societies and cliques with contrasting interests and points of view. Overall, England and the Netherlands were the most accepting of philosophical ideas, and they served as a beacon of tolerance and limited government for the rest of Europe.

The Scottish Enlightenment, centered in Edinburgh, was marked by an emphasis on pragmatic and scientific reasoning. Intellectual revival there was stimulated by the creation of the first public educational system in Europe. A key figure in Edinburgh was David Hume (1711–1776), whose carefully argued religious skepticism had a powerful impact at home and abroad. Building on Locke's teachings on learning, Hume argued that the human mind is really nothing but a bundle of impressions. These impressions originate only in sense experiences and our habits of joining these experiences together. Since our ideas ultimately reflect only our sense experiences, our reason cannot tell us anything about questions that cannot be verified by sense experience, such as questions about the origin of the universe or the existence of God. Paradoxically, Hume's rationalistic inquiry ended up undermining the Enlightenment's faith in the power of reason.

Another Scottish philosopher, Adam Smith (1723–1790), was a pioneer of the new field of political economy. Inspired by the possibilities of growing world trade, Smith developed the general idea of freedom of enterprise and established the basis for modern economics in his groundbreaking work, *Inquiry into the Nature and Causes of the Wealth of Nations* (1776). In keeping with his deep-seated fear of political oppression and with the "system of natural liberty" that he advocated, Smith argued that government should limit itself to "only three duties": defending against foreign invasion, maintaining civil order with courts and police protection, and sponsoring certain indispensable public works and institutions that private investors would never fund because such ventures would not be profitable. He believed that the pursuit of self-interest in a competitive market would be sufficient to improve the living conditions of citizens, a

view that quickly emerged as the classic argument for **economic liberalism**.

In most of central and eastern Europe, reform-minded thinkers rejected the deism of Voltaire and the skepticism of Hume. Instead, they tried to integrate the findings of the scientific revolution with the teachings of established churches. In Germany, Gottfried Leibniz (GAHT-freed LIGHB-nuhtz; 1646–1716) was a founding father of the Enlightenment. His work spanned many disciplines, including mathematics, physics, history, and rationalist philosophy. Leibniz attempted to

◻ MAJOR FIGURES OF THE ENLIGHTENMENT

Baruch Spinoza (1632–1677)	Early Enlightenment thinker excommunicated from the Jewish community for his concept of a deterministic universe
John Locke (1632–1704)	*Essay Concerning Human Understanding* (1690)
Gottfried Leibniz (1646–1716)	Early German rational philosopher and scientist
Pierre Bayle (1647–1706)	*Historical and Critical Dictionary* (1697)
Montesquieu (1689–1755)	*The Persian Letters* (1721); *The Spirit of Laws* (1748)
Voltaire (1694–1778)	Renowned French philosophe and author of more than seventy works
Gabrielle-Emilie Le Tonnelier de Breteuil, marquise du Châtelet (1706–1749)	French scholar and supporter of equal education for women
David Hume (1711–1776)	Central figure of the Scottish Enlightenment
Jean-Jacques Rousseau (1712–1778)	*The Social Contract* (1762)
Denis Diderot (1713–1784) and Jean le Rond d'Alembert (1717–1783)	Editors of *Encyclopedia: The Rational Dictionary of the Sciences, the Arts, and the Crafts* (1765)
Adam Smith (1723–1790)	Pioneering political economist and author of *Inquiry into the Nature and Causes of the Wealth of Nations* (1776)
Immanuel Kant (1724–1804)	*What Is Enlightenment?* (1784); *On the Different Races of Man* (1775)

reconcile philosophy with faith by arguing that God allowed evil to exist as a means of allowing imperfect humans to exercise free will. He further argued that, despite the existence of pain and suffering, our world must be the best of all possible worlds since it was created by an omnipotent and benevolent God, a position later mocked as naively optimistic by Voltaire. Leibniz's last years were overshadowed by a dispute over whether he or Newton had invented calculus. Leibniz's opponents argued, probably incorrectly, that he had plagiarized Newton's work.

Immanuel Kant (1724–1804), a professor in East Prussia and the greatest German philosopher of his day, took up the question of the age when he published a pamphlet in 1784 titled *What Is Enlightenment?* Kant answered, "*Sapere Aude* (dare to know)! 'Have the courage to use your own understanding' is therefore the motto of enlightenment." He argued that if serious thinkers were granted the freedom to exercise their reason publicly in print, enlightenment would almost surely follow. Kant nonetheless epitomized the cautious eastern European attitude toward state authority. He insisted that in their private lives, individuals must obey all laws, no matter how unreasonable, and should be punished for "impertinent" criticism. Kant thus tried to reconcile absolute monarchical authority with a critical public sphere.

Urban Culture and Life in the Public Sphere

A major stimulant to Enlightenment thought was urbanization. More and more people migrated to the city, especially after 1750. London and Paris swelled to over 500,000 people, while Naples and Amsterdam had populations of more than 100,000. Urban life gave rise to new institutions and practices that encouraged the spread of Enlightenment ideas. From about 1700 to 1789, the production and consumption of books grew significantly, and the types of books people read changed dramatically. The proportion of religious and devotional books published in Paris declined after 1750; history and law held constant; the arts and sciences surged.

Reading more books on many more subjects, the educated public increasingly approached reading in a new way. The result was what some scholars have called a reading revolution. The old style of reading was centered on a core of sacred texts. Reading was patriarchal and communal, with the father of the family slowly reading texts aloud. Now reading involved a broader field of books that constantly changed. Reading became individual and silent, and texts could be

• **salons** Regular social gatherings held by talented and rich Parisian women in their homes, where philosophes and their followers met to discuss literature, science, and philosophy.

questioned. Subtle but profound, the reading revolution ushered in new ways of relating to the written word.

The conversation, discussion, and debate encouraged by an urban milieu also played a critical role in the Enlightenment. Paris set the example that other French and European cities followed. In Paris from about 1740 to 1789, a number of talented, wealthy women presided over regular social gatherings named after their elegant private drawing rooms, or **salons**. There they encouraged the exchange of observations on literature, science, and philosophy with great aristocrats, wealthy middle-class financiers, high-ranking officials, and noteworthy foreigners. Talented hostesses, or *salonnières* (sah-lahn-ee-EHRZ), mediated the public's examination of Enlightenment thought. As one philosophe described his Enlightenment hostess and her salon:

> She could unite the different types, even the most antagonistic, sustaining the conversation by a well-aimed phrase, animating and guiding it at will. . . . Politics, religion, philosophy, news: nothing was excluded. Her circle met daily from five to nine. There one found men of all ranks in the State, the Church, and the Court, soldiers and foreigners, and the leading writers of the day.[7]

◻ Picturing the Past

Enlightenment Culture An actor performs the first reading of a new play by Voltaire at the salon of Madame Geoffrin in this painting from 1755. Voltaire, then in exile, is represented by a bust statue. (Réunion des Musées Nationaux/Art Resource, NY)

ANALYZING THE IMAGE Which of these people do you think is the hostess, Madame Geoffrin, and why? Using details from the painting to support your answer, how would you describe the status of the people shown?

CONNECTIONS What does this image suggest about the reach of Enlightenment ideas to common people? To women? Does the painting of the bookstore on page 538 suggest a broader reach? Why?

Elite women also exercised great influence on artistic taste. Soft pastels, ornate interiors, sentimental portraits, and starry-eyed lovers protected by hovering cupids were all hallmarks of the style they favored. This style, known as rococo, was popular throughout Europe from 1720 to 1780. During this period, women were also closely associated with the rise of the novel as a literary genre, both as authors and readers. The novel helped popularize a new cult of sensibility, which celebrated strong emotions and intimate family love. Some philosophes championed greater rights and expanded education for women, claiming that the position and treatment of women were the best indicators of a society's level of civilization and decency.[8]

While salon membership and artistic pursuits were largely restricted to the well-born and the exceptionally talented, a number of institutions emerged for the rest of society. Lending libraries served an important function for people who could not afford their own books. The coffeehouses that first appeared in the late seventeenth century became meccas of philosophical discussion. In addition, book clubs, Masonic lodges (groups of Freemasons, a secret egalitarian society that existed across Europe), and journals all played a part in creating a new **public sphere** that celebrated open debate informed by critical reason. The public sphere was an idealized space where members of society came together to discuss the social, economic, and political issues of the day.

What of the common people? Did they participate in the Enlightenment? Enlightenment philosophes did not direct their message to peasants or urban laborers. They believed that the masses had no time or talent for philosophical speculation and that elevating them would be a slow and potentially dangerous process.

There is some evidence, however, that ordinary people were not immune to the words of the philosophes. At a time of rising literacy, book prices were dropping in cities and towns, and many philosophical ideas were popularized in cheap pamphlets. Moreover, even illiterate people had access to written material through the practice of public reading. Although they were barred from salons and academies, ordinary people were nonetheless exposed to the new ideas in circulation.

Late Enlightenment

After about 1770 a number of thinkers and writers began to attack the Enlightenment's faith in reason and progress. The most famous of these was the Swiss intellectual Jean-Jacques Rousseau (1712–1778). Rousseau was both one of the most influential voices of the Enlightenment and, in his rejection of rationalism and social discourse, a harbinger of reaction against En-lightenment ideas. Like other Enlightenment thinkers, Rousseau was passionately committed to individual freedom. Unlike them, however, he attacked rationalism and civilization as destroying, rather than liberating, the individual. Warm, spontaneous feeling, Rousseau believed, had to complement and correct cold intellect. Moreover, he asserted, the basic goodness of the individual and the unspoiled child had to be protected from the cruel refinements of civilization. Rousseau's ideals greatly influenced the early romantic movement, which rebelled against the culture of the Enlightenment in the late eighteenth century.

Rousseau also called for a rigid division of gender roles, arguing that women and men were radically different beings. According to Rousseau, because women were destined by nature to assume a passive role in sexual relations, they should also be passive in social life. Additionally, he believed that women's love for displaying themselves in public, attending salons, and pulling the strings of power was unnatural and had a corrupting effect on both politics and society. Rousseau thus rejected the sophisticated way of life of Parisian elite women. His criticism led to broader calls for privileged women to renounce what he regarded as frivolous behavior and stay at home to care for their children.

Rousseau's contribution to political theory in *The Social Contract* (1762) was based on two fundamental concepts: the general will and popular sovereignty. According to Rousseau, the **general will** is sacred and absolute, reflecting the common interests of all people, who have displaced the monarch as the holder of sovereign power. The general will is not necessarily the will of the majority, however. At times the general will may be the authentic, long-term needs of the people as correctly interpreted by a farseeing minority. Little noticed before the French Revolution, Rousseau's concept of the general will appealed greatly to democrats and nationalists after 1789.

Enlightened Absolutism

❑ What impact did new ways of thinking have on monarchical absolutism and those under its rule?

Although Enlightenment thinkers were often critical of untrammeled despotism and eager for reform, their impact on politics was mixed. Outside of England and the Netherlands, especially in central and eastern Europe, most believed that political change could best come from above — from the ruler — rather than from below. Nevertheless, government officials' daily involvement in complex affairs of state made them natu-

Maria Theresa The empress and her husband pose with eleven of their sixteen children at Schönbrunn palace in this family portrait by court painter Martin Meytens (1695–1770). Joseph, the heir to the throne, stands at the center of the star on the floor. Wealthy women often had very large families, in part because they, unlike poor women, seldom nursed their babies. (Réunion des Musées Nationaux/Art Resource, NY)

rally attracted to ideas for improving human society. Encouraged and instructed by these officials, some absolutist rulers tried to reform their governments in accordance with Enlightenment ideals. The result was what historians have called the **enlightened absolutism** of the later eighteenth century.

Reforms in Prussia, Russia, and Austria

Frederick II (r. 1740–1786) of Prussia, known as Frederick the Great, sought to improve the standing of his nation within Europe (see page 503). In 1740 he initiated the War of the Austrian Succession (1740–1748) to contest the right of a woman, Maria Theresa, to inherit the Habsburg throne. After a bold military victory, Frederick the Great acquired almost all of the province of Silesia from Austria, albeit without unseating Maria Theresa from her throne. Influenced by the philosophes, Frederick tolerantly allowed his subjects to believe as they wished in religious and philosophical matters. He promoted the advancement of knowledge, improving his country's schools and

- **public sphere** An idealized intellectual space that emerged in Europe during the Enlightenment. Here, the public came together to discuss important social, economic, and political issues.
- **general will** A concept associated with Rousseau, referring to the common interests of all the people, who have replaced the power of the monarch.
- **enlightened absolutism** Term coined by historians to describe the rule of eighteenth-century monarchs who, without renouncing their own absolute authority, adopted Enlightenment ideals of rationalism, progress, and tolerance.

> "I must enlighten my people, cultivate their manners and morals, and make them as happy as human beings can be, or as happy as the means at my disposal permit."
>
> **FREDERICK THE GREAT**

permitting scholars to publish their findings. He also sought to improve life for ordinary people with innovations in agriculture and industry. As he wrote to his friend Voltaire, "I must enlighten my people, cultivate their manners and morals, and make them as happy as human beings can be, or as happy as the means at my disposal permit."

Frederick's most fundamental reforms were to the legal system. Under his reign, Prussia's laws were simplified, torture of prisoners was abolished, and judges decided cases quickly and impartially. Prussian officials became famous for their hard work and honesty. However, Frederick did not free the serfs of Prussia; instead, he extended the privileges of the nobility over them.

Frederick's reputation as an enlightened prince was rivaled by that of Catherine the Great of Russia (r. 1762–1796), one of the most remarkable rulers of her time. When she was fifteen years old Catherine's family ties to the Romanov dynasty made her a suitable bride for the heir to the Russian throne. Catherine profited from her husband's unpopularity, having him murdered so that she could be declared empress of Russia.

Never questioning that absolute monarchy was the best form of government, Catherine set out to rule in an enlightened manner. She had three main goals. First, she worked hard to continue Peter the Great's efforts to bring the culture of western Europe to Russia (see page 509). To do so, she patronized Western architects, sculptors, musicians, and philosophes and encouraged Russian nobles to follow her example. Catherine's second goal was domestic reform. She restricted the practice of torture and allowed limited religious toleration. She also tried to improve

The War of Austrian Succession, 1740–1748

- Prussia, 1740
- Prussian gains, 1742
- Austria, 1740
- Boundary of the Holy Roman Empire

education and strengthen local government. The philosophes applauded these measures and hoped more would follow.

These hopes were dashed by a massive uprising of serfs in 1733 under the leadership of a common Cossack soldier named Emelian Pugachev. Although Pugachev was ultimately captured and executed, his rebellion shocked Russian rulers and put an end to any intentions Catherine might have had about reforming the system. After 1775 Catherine gave the nobles absolute control of their serfs and extended serfdom into new areas. In 1785 she formally freed nobles from taxes and state service. Therefore, under Catherine the Russian nobility attained its most exalted position, and serfdom entered its most oppressive phase.

Catherine's third goal was territorial expansion, and in this respect she was extremely successful. Her armies subjugated the last descendants of the Mongols and the Crimean Tartars, and began the conquest of the Caucasus, on the border between Europe and Asia. Her greatest coup was the partition of Poland, which took place in stages from 1772 to 1795 (Map 18.1).

Maria Theresa (r. 1740–1780) of Austria also established reforms in her nation, although traditional power politics was a more important motivation for her than were Enlightenment teachings. Her more radical son, Joseph II (r. 1780–1790), drew on Enlightenment ideals, earning the title of "revolutionary emperor." Most notably, Joseph abolished serfdom in 1781, and in 1789 he decreed that peasants could pay landlords in cash rather than through compulsory labor. This measure was rejected not only by the nobility but also by the peasants it was intended to help, because they lacked the necessary cash. When Joseph died at forty-nine, the Habsburg empire was in turmoil. His brother Leopold II (r. 1790–1792) canceled Joseph's radical edicts in order to reestablish order.

Jewish Life and the Limits of Enlightened Absolutism

Perhaps the best example of the limitations of enlightened absolutism are the debates surrounding the possible emancipation of the Jews. Europe's small Jewish populations lived under highly discriminatory laws. For the most part, Jews were confined to tiny, overcrowded ghettos, excluded by law from most business and professional activities, and could be ordered out of a kingdom at a moment's notice. Still, a very few did manage to succeed and to obtain the right of permanent settlement, usually by performing some special service for the state, such as money lending. Also, because of their large and closely knit communities, Jewish merchants and traders were prominent in international trade.

Individuals in Society

Moses Mendelssohn and the Jewish Enlightenment

IN 1743 A SMALL, HUMPBACKED JEWISH BOY with a stammer left his poor parents in Dessau in central Germany and walked eighty miles to Berlin, the capital of Frederick the Great's Prussia. According to one story, when the boy reached the Rosenthaler Gate, the only one through which Jews could pass, he told the inquiring watchman that his name was Moses and that he had come to Berlin "to learn." The watchman laughed and waved him through. "Go Moses, the sea has opened before you."*

In Berlin the young Mendelssohn studied Jewish law and eked out a living copying Hebrew manuscripts in a beautiful hand. But he was soon fascinated by an intellectual world that had been closed to him in the Dessau ghetto. There, like most Jews throughout central Europe, he had spoken Yiddish—a mixture of German, Polish, and Hebrew. Now, working mainly on his own, he mastered German; learned Latin, Greek, French, and English; and studied mathematics and Enlightenment philosophy. Word of his exceptional abilities spread in Berlin's Jewish community (the dwelling of 1,500 of the city's 100,000 inhabitants). He began tutoring the children of a wealthy Jewish silk merchant, and he soon became the merchant's clerk and later his partner. But his great passion remained the life of the mind and the spirit, which he avidly pursued in his off-hours.

Gentle and unassuming in his personal life, Mendelssohn was a bold thinker. Reading eagerly in works of Western philosophy dating back to antiquity, he was, as a pious Jew, soon convinced that Enlightenment teachings need not be opposed to Jewish thought and religion. He concluded that reason could complement and strengthen religion, although each would retain its integrity as a separate sphere.† Developing this idea in his first great work, "On the Immortality of the Soul" (1767), Mendelssohn used the neutral setting of a philosophical dialogue between Socrates and his followers in ancient Greece to argue that the human soul lived forever. In refusing to bring religion and critical thinking into conflict, he was strongly influenced by contemporary German philosophers who argued similarly on behalf of Christianity. He reflected the way the German Enlightenment generally supported established religion, in contrast to the French Enlightenment, which attacked it.

Mendelssohn's treatise on the human soul captivated the educated German public, which marveled that a Jew could have written a philosophical masterpiece. In the excitement, a Christian zealot named Lavater challenged Mendelssohn in a pamphlet to accept Christianity or to demonstrate how the Christian faith was not "reasonable." Replying politely but pas-

sionately, the Jewish philosopher affirmed that his studies had only strengthened him in his faith, although he did not seek to convert anyone not born into Judaism. Rather, he urged toleration in religious matters and spoke up courageously against Jewish oppression.

Orthodox Jew and German philosophe, Moses Mendelssohn serenely combined two very different worlds. He built a bridge from the ghetto to the dominant culture over which many Jews would pass, including his novelist daughter Dorothea and his famous grandson, the composer Felix Mendelssohn.

QUESTIONS FOR ANALYSIS

1. How did Mendelssohn seek to influence Jewish religious thought in his time?
2. How do Mendelssohn's ideas compare with those of the French Enlightenment?

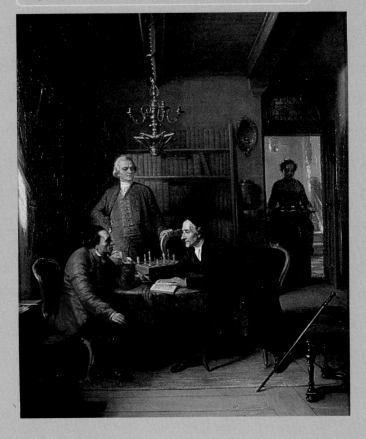
Lavater (right) attempts to convert Mendelssohn, in a painting of an imaginary encounter by Moritz Oppenheim. (akg-images)

*H. Kupferberg, *The Mendelssohns: Three Generations of Genius* (New York: Charles Scribner's Sons, 1972), p. 3.

†D. Sorkin, *Moses Mendelssohn and the Religious Enlightenment* (Berkeley: University of California Press, 1996), pp. 8 ff.

▢ Mapping the Past

MAP 18.1 The Partition of Poland, 1772–1795 In 1772 the threat of war between Russia and Austria arose over Russian gains from the Ottoman Empire. To satisfy desires for expansion without fighting, Prussia's Frederick the Great proposed dividing parts of Poland among Austria, Prussia, and Russia. In 1793 and 1795 the three powers partitioned the remainder, and Poland ceased to exist as an independent nation.

ANALYZING THE MAP Of the three powers that divided the kingdom of Poland, which benefited the most? How did the partition affect the geographical boundaries of each state, and what was the significance? What border with the former Poland remained unchanged? Why do you think this was the case?

CONNECTIONS Why was Poland vulnerable to partition in the later half of the eighteenth century? What does it say about European politics at the time that a country could simply cease to exist on the map? Could that happen today?

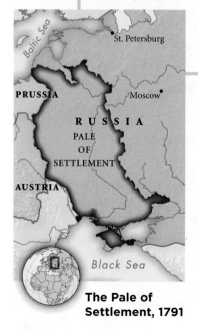

The Pale of Settlement, 1791

In the eighteenth century, an Enlightenment movement known as the **Haskalah** emerged from within the European Jewish community. This movement was led by the Prussian philosopher Moses Mendelssohn (1729–1786). Christian and Jewish Enlightenment philosophers, including Mendelssohn, began to advocate for freedom and civil rights for Eu-

ropean Jews. In an era of growing reason and tolerance, they argued, restrictions on religious grounds could not stand. (See "Individuals in Society: Moses Mendelssohn and the Jewish Enlightenment," page 543.)

Arguments for tolerance won some ground, especially under Joseph II of Austria. Most monarchs, however, refused to entertain the idea of emancipation. In 1791 Catherine the Great established the Pale of Settlement, a territory including modern-day Belarus, Lithuania, Latvia, Moldava, Ukraine, and parts of Poland, in which most Jews were required to live until the Russian Revolution of 1917.

The Growth of Consumerism and the Atlantic World

☐ How did the growth of consumerism and the Atlantic economy interact with Enlightenment ideas?

The new practices of debate and sociability brought by the Enlightenment took place within a rapidly evolving material world. A rising European population in the eighteenth century furnished more skilled hands to produce finished goods as well as more consumers to purchase these products. Scientific instruments for making discoveries, and books and newspapers for publicizing them; coffee and tea for stimulating thought; hats, ribbons, and stockings for embellishing sociable urbanites — material goods like these set the stage for the lively exchange of ideas.

Consumerism in the eighteenth century was fed by an increasingly integrated Atlantic economy that circulated finished European products, raw materials from the colonies, and enslaved peoples from Africa. Over time, distinctive Atlantic communities and identities were constituted by the peoples, goods, and ideas that crisscrossed the ocean.

In turn, the contents of Enlightenment thought were shaped by the material world in which they emerged. Enlightenment thinkers drew inspiration from accounts of New World encounters as well as from the economic possibilities of colonial trade. As Adam Smith himself declared, "The discovery of America and that of a passage to the East Indies by the Cape of Good Hope, are the two greatest and most important events recorded in the history of mankind."[9] Enlightenment thinkers also used science and reason to establish a racial hierarchy that placed whites at the top, helping to justify slavery.

> "The discovery of America and that of a passage to the East Indies by the Cape of Good Hope, are the two greatest and most important events recorded in the history of mankind."
>
> **ADAM SMITH**

A Revolution in Consumption and Daily Life

One of the most important developments of eighteenth-century Europe was the emergence of a fledgling consumer culture. Many purchasers of consumer goods were from the upper and upper-middle classes, but a boom in cheap reproductions of luxury items provided affordable goods for people of modest means. From food to ribbons and from coal stoves to umbrellas, the material worlds of city dwellers grew richer and more diverse. This "consumer revolution," as it has been called, created new expectations for comfort and self-expression, dramatically changing European daily life in the eighteenth century.

Food was one of the chief areas of advance. Using Enlightenment techniques of observation and experimentation, a group of scientists, government officials, and a few big landowners devised new agricultural practices and tools that raised crop yields dramatically, especially in England and the Netherlands. These included new forms of crop rotation, better equipment, and selective breeding of livestock. The controversial process of **enclosure**, fencing off common land to create privately owned fields, allowed a break with traditional methods, but at the cost of reducing poor farmers' access to land.

Colonial plants also provided new sources of calories and nutrition. Introduced into Europe from the Americas — along with corn, squash, tomatoes, and many other useful plants — the humble potato provided an excellent new food source. Containing a good supply of carbohydrates and vitamins A and C, the potato offset the lack of fresh vegetables and fruits in common people's winter diet. After initial resistance, the potato became an important dietary supplement in much of Europe by the end of the eighteenth century. Together, these improvements in agriculture led to a rapid growth of population, especially after 1750.

One of the most remarkable dietary changes in the eighteenth century was the greater consumption of sugar, tea, coffee, tobacco, and chocolate. Previously expensive and rare luxury items, they became dietary staples for people of all social classes, especially in Britain. This was possible because new surpluses in production provided by slave labor in the New World lowered the price of many of these items.

No commodities grew as quickly in popularity as sugar and tea. There were significant class distinctions in the consumption of tea. Whereas the gentry took tea as a leisurely and genteel ritual, the lower classes usually drank it at work to fight monotony or fatigue. With the widespread adoption of these products (which turned out to be mildly to extremely addictive), working people in Europe became increasingly dependent on faraway colonial economies and slave labor. What they now saw as daily necessities linked them to global trade networks beyond their ability to shape or control.

- **Haskalah** A Jewish Enlightenment movement led by Prussian philosopher Moses Mendelssohn.
- **enclosure** The controversial process of fencing off common land to create privately owned fields that increased agricultural production at the cost of reducing poor farmers' access to land.

The Consumer Revolution From the mid-eighteenth century on, the cities of western Europe witnessed a new proliferation of consumer goods. Items once limited to the wealthy few—such as fans (lower right), watches, snuffboxes, umbrellas, ornamental containers (right), and teapots—were now reproduced in cheaper versions for middling and ordinary people. The fashion for wide hoopskirts was so popular that the armrests of the chairs of the day, known as Louis XV chairs (left), were specially designed to accommodate them. (fan: Scala/White Images/Art Resource, NY; jar: Victoria & Albert Museum, London/The Bridgeman Art Library; chair: Louvre/Réunion des Musées Nationaux/Art Resource, NY)

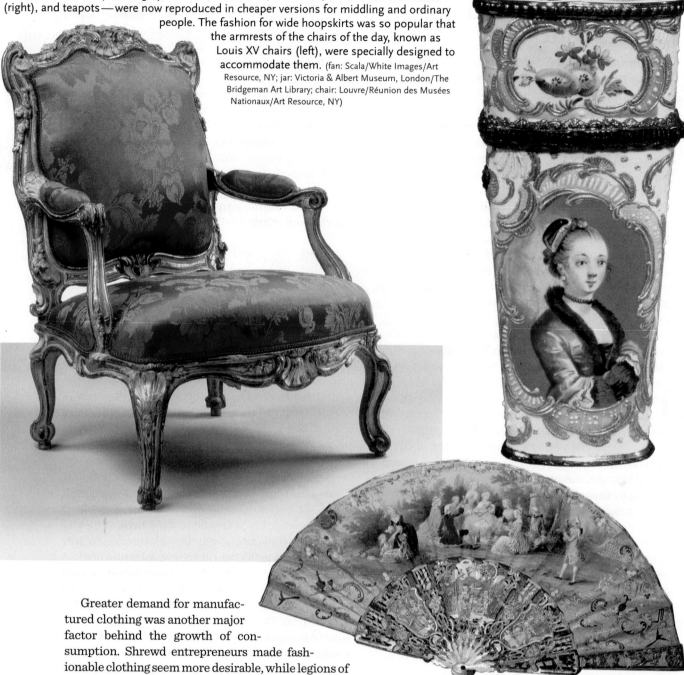

Greater demand for manufactured clothing was another major factor behind the growth of consumption. Shrewd entrepreneurs made fashionable clothing seem more desirable, while legions of women entering the textile and needle trades made it ever cheaper. As a result, eighteenth-century western Europe witnessed a dramatic rise in the consumption of clothing, particularly in large cities. One historian has documented a large growth in the size and value of Parisians' wardrobes from 1700 to 1789, as well as a new level of diversity in garments and accessories, colors, and fabrics.[10] Colonial economies again played an important role in lowering the cost of materials, such as cotton and vegetable dyes, largely due to the unpaid toil of enslaved Africans. Cheaper copies of elite styles made it possible for working people to as-

pire to follow fashion for the first time. Elite onlookers were bemused by the sight of lower-class people in fashionable dress. In 1784 Mrs. Fanny Cradock described encountering her milkman during an evening stroll "dressed in a fashionable suit, with an embroidered waistcoat, silk knee-breeches and lace cuffs."[11]

Mrs. Cradock's milkman notwithstanding, the spread of fashion was primarily a female phenomenon. Parisian women significantly out-consumed men, acquiring larger and more expensive wardrobes than those of their husbands, brothers, and fathers. Whereas traditionally fashion had belonged as much to men as to women, henceforth it was increasingly identified with women and the perceived frivolity of the "fair sex."

Changes in outward appearances were reflected in inner spaces as new attitudes about privacy and individuality also emerged. In 1700 the cramped home of a modest family consisted of a few rooms, each of which had multiple functions. For example, the same room might be used for sleeping, receiving friends, and working. In the eighteenth century rents rose sharply, making it impossible to gain more space, but families began attributing specific functions to specific rooms and putting barriers up to divide rooms into separate spaces.

New levels of comfort and convenience accompanied this trend toward more individualized ways of life. In 1700 a meal might be served in a common dish, with each person dipping his or her spoon into the pot. By the end of the eighteenth century even humble households contained a much greater variety of cutlery and dishes, making it possible for each person to eat from his or her own plate. More books and prints, now available at lower prices, decorated the shelves and walls. Improvements in glassmaking provided more transparent glass, which allowed daylight to penetrate into gloomy rooms. Cold and smoky hearths were replaced by more efficient and cleaner coal stoves, which also eliminated the backache of cooking over an open fire. All these changes made rooms warmer, better lit, more comfortable, and more personalized.

The scope of the new consumer economy should not be exaggerated. These developments were concentrated in large cities in northwestern Europe and in the colonial cities of North America. Even in these centers elites benefited the most from new modes of life. This was not yet the society of mass consumption that emerged toward the end of the nineteenth century with the full expansion of the Industrial Revolution. The eighteenth century did, however, lay the foundations for one of the most distinctive features of modern Western life: societies based on the consumption of goods and services obtained through global markets in which many individuals' identities and self-worth are shaped through the goods they consume.

The Atlantic Economy

The consumer revolution fed on the dynamic growth of trade across the Atlantic Ocean. Commercial exchange in the Atlantic is often referred to as the triangle trade, designating a three-way transport of goods: European commodities, like guns and textiles, to Africa; enslaved Africans to the colonies; and colonial goods, such as cotton, tobacco, and sugar, back to Europe. This model highlights some of the most important flows of trade but significantly oversimplifies the picture. For example, a brisk intercolonial trade also existed, with the

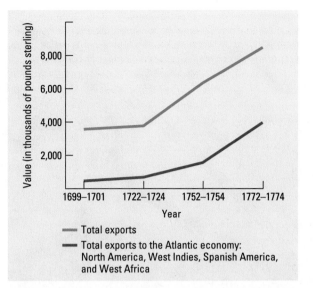

FIGURE 18.1 Exports of English Manufactured Goods, 1700–1774 While trade between England and Europe stagnated after 1700, English exports to Africa and the Americas boomed and greatly stimulated English economic development. (Source: Data from R. Davis, "English Foreign Trade, 1700–1774," *Economic History Review*, 2nd ser., 15 [1962]: 302–303.)

Caribbean slave colonies importing food in the form of fish, flour, and livestock from the northern colonies and rice from the south, in exchange for sugar and slaves (Map 18.2).

Moreover, the Atlantic economy was inextricably linked to trade with the Indian and Pacific Oceans. An outstanding example is the trade in cowrie shells. These seashells, originating in the Maldives in the Indian Ocean, were used as a form of currency in West Africa. European traders obtained them in Asia, packing them alongside porcelains, spices, and silks for the journey home. The cowries were then brought from European ports to the West African coast to be traded for slaves. Indian cotton cloth was also prized in Africa and played a similar role in exchange. The rising economic and political power of Europeans in the eighteenth century thus drew on the connections they established between the long-standing Asian and Atlantic trade worlds.

Across the eighteenth century the economies of European nations bordering the Atlantic Ocean relied more and more on colonial exports. In England, sales to the mainland colonies of North America and the West Indian sugar islands — with an important assist from West Africa and Latin America — soared from £500,000 to £4 million (Figure 18.1). Exports to England's colonies in Ireland and India also rose substantially from 1700 to 1800.

At the core of this Atlantic world was the misery and profit of the Atlantic slave trade (see pages 572–582). The brutal practice intensified dramatically after 1700 and especially after 1750 with the growth of

MAP 18.2 The Atlantic Economy in 1701 The growth of trade encouraged both economic development and military conflict in the Atlantic basin. Four continents were linked together by the exchange of goods and slaves.

trade and demand for slave-produced goods. English dominance of the slave trade provided another source of large profits to the home country.

The French also profited enormously from colonial trade in the eighteenth century, even after losing their vast North American territories to England in 1763. The Caribbean colonies of Saint-Domingue (modern-day Haiti), Martinique, and Guadeloupe, which remained in French hands, provided immense fortunes in plantation agriculture and slave trading. By 1789 the population of Saint-Domingue (sehn daw-MEHNG) included five hundred thousand slaves, whose labor had allowed the colony to become the world's leading producer of coffee and sugar and the most profitable plantation colony in the New World.[12] The wealth generated from colonial trade fostered the confidence of the merchant classes in Nantes, Bordeaux, and other large cities, and merchants soon joined other elite groups clamoring for more political power.

The third major player in the Atlantic economy, Spain, also saw its colonial fortunes improve during the eighteenth century. Its mercantilist goals were boosted by a recovery in silver production, which had dropped significantly in the seventeenth century. Spanish territory in North America expanded significantly in the second half of the eighteenth century. At the close of the Seven Years' War (1756–1763), Spain gained Louisiana from the French, and its influence extended westward all the way to northern California through the efforts of Spanish missionaries and ranchers.

Identities and Communities of the Atlantic World

As contacts among the Atlantic coasts of the Americas, Africa, and Europe became more frequent, and as European settlements grew into well-established colonies, new identities and communities emerged. The term *Creole* referred to people of Spanish ancestry born in the Americas. Wealthy Creoles and their counterparts throughout the Atlantic colonies prided themselves on following European ways of life. In addition to their agricultural estates, they maintained townhouses in colonial cities built on the European model, with theaters, central squares, churches, and coffeehouses. They purchased luxury goods made in Europe, and their children were often sent to be educated in the home country.

Over time, however, the colonial elite came to feel that their circumstances gave them different interests

Plantation Zones, ca. 1700

> "A turn of mind peculiar to the planter, occasioned by a physical difference of constitution, climate, customs, and education, tends . . . to repress the remains of his former attachment to his native soil."
>
> **EUROPEAN OBSERVER**

and characteristics from those of their home population. As one observer explained, "a turn of mind peculiar to the planter, occasioned by a physical difference of constitution, climate, customs, and education, tends . . . to repress the remains of his former attachment to his native soil."[13] Colonial elites became "Americanized" by adopting native foods, like chocolate and potatoes, and sought relief from tropical disease in native remedies. Also, they began to turn against restrictions from their home countries: Creole traders and planters increasingly resented the regulations and taxes imposed by colonial bureaucrats, and such resentment would eventually lead to revolutions against colonial powers (discussed in Chapter 27).

Enlightenment ideas thrived in the colonies, although with as much diversity and disagreement as in Europe. The colonies of British North America were deeply influenced by the Scottish Enlightenment, with its emphasis on pragmatic approaches to the problems of life. Following the Scottish model, leaders in the colonies adopted a moderate, "common-sense" version of the Enlightenment that emphasized self-improvement and ethical conduct. In most cases, this version of the Enlightenment was perfectly compatible with religion and was chiefly spread through the growing colleges and universities of the colonies, which remained church-based institutions.

Some thinkers went even further in their admiration for Enlightenment ideas. Benjamin Franklin's writings and political career provide an outstanding example of the combination of the pragmatism and economic interests of the Scottish Enlightenment with the constitutional theories of Locke, Montesquieu, and Rousseau. Franklin was privately a lifelong deist, but he continued to attend church and respect religious proprieties, a cautious pattern followed by fellow deist Thomas Jefferson and other leading thinkers of the American Enlightenment.

Northern Enlightenment thinkers often depicted the Spanish American colonies as the epitome of the

Viewpoints

Malachy Postlethwayt and Olaudah Equiano on the Abolition of Slavery

● *As Britain took control of transatlantic commerce during the eighteenth century, debate arose over the morality of the slave trade and the country's involvement in it. Malachy Postlethwayt, an economist, rejected criticism of slavery by arguing that African nations treated their subjects much worse than slave traders did and that the benefits of Christianity by far outstripped any disadvantages slaves might endure. In his famous autobiography, former slave Olaudah Equiano emphasized the cruelties of slavery. He argued, against authors like Postlethwayt, that trade with free peoples in Africa promised much more economic benefit to Britain than did slavery.*

Malachy Postlethwayt, *The National and Private Advantages of the African Trade Considered*

❝Many are prepossessed against this trade, thinking it a barbarous, inhuman and unlawful traffic for a Christian country to trade in Blacks; to which I would beg leave to observe; that though the odious appellation of slaves is annexed to this trade, it being called by some the slave-trade, yet it does not appear from the best enquiry I have been able to make, that the state of those people is changed for the worse, by being servants to our British planters in America; they are certainly treated with great lenity and humanity: and as the improvement of the planter's estates depends upon due care being taken of their healths and lives, I cannot but think their condition is much bettered to what it was in their own country.

Besides, the negro princes in Africa, 'tis well known, are in perpetual war with each other, and since before they had this method of disposing of their prisoners of war to Christian merchants, they were wont not only to be applied to inhuman sacrifices, but to extreme torture and barbarity, their transportation must certainly be a melioration [improvement] of their condition; provided living in a civilized Christian country, is better than living among savages; Nay, if life be preferable to torment and cruel death, their state cannot, with any color or reason, be presumed to be worsened.❞

Olaudah Equiano, Appeal for the Abolition of Slavery

❝Tortures, murder, and every other imaginable barbarity and iniquity, are practiced upon the poor slaves with impunity. I hope the great slave trade will be abolished. I pray it may be an event at hand. The great body of manufacturers, uniting in the cause, will considerably facilitate and expedite it; and as I have already stated, it is most substantially their interest and advantage, and as such the nation's at large (except those persons concerned in the manufacturing neck yokes, collars, chains, handcuffs, leg bolts, drags, thumb screws, iron muzzles, and coffins; cats, scourges, and other instruments of torture used in the slave trade). In a short time one sentiment will alone prevail, from motives of interest as well as justice and humanity.... If the blacks were permitted to remain in their own country, they would double themselves every fifteen years. In proportion to such increase will be the demand for manufactures. Cotton and indigo grow spontaneously in most parts of Africa; a consideration this of no small consequence to the manufacturing towns of Great Britain. It opens a most immense, glorious and happy prospect—the clothing, &c. of a continent ten thousand miles in circumference, and immensely rich in productions of every denomination in return for manufactures.❞

Sources: Malachy Postlethwayt, *The National and Private Advantages of the African Trade Considered* (London: Jon and Paul Knapton, 1746), pp. 4–5; Olaudah Equiano, *The Interesting Narrative of the Life of Olaudah Equiano,* Second Edition, ed. Robert J. Allison (Boston: Bedford/St. Martin's, 2007), pp. 194–195.

QUESTIONS FOR ANALYSIS

1. What contrast does Postlethwayt draw between the treatment of African people under slavery and in their home countries? What conclusion does he draw from this contrast?

2. To whom does Equiano address his appeal for abolition of the slave trade? What economic reasons does he provide for trading goods rather than slaves with Africa?

---

superstition and barbarity they contested. The Catholic Church strictly controlled the publication of books there, just as it did on the Iberian Peninsula. Nonetheless, educated elites were well aware of the new currents of thought, and the universities, newspapers, and salons of Spanish America produced their own reform ideas. The establishment of a mining school in Mexico City in 1792, the first in the Spanish colonies, illumi-

nates the practical achievements of reformers. In all European colonies, one effect of Enlightenment thought was to encourage colonists to criticize the policies of the mother country and aspire toward greater autonomy.

Not all Europeans in the colonies were wealthy or well-educated. Numerous poor and lower-middle-class whites worked as clerks, shopkeepers, craftsmen, and plantation managers. Whether rich or poor, however, white Europeans usually made up a small proportion of the population. Since most European migrants were men, much of the colonial population of the Atlantic world descended from unions—forced or through consent—of European men and indigenous or African women. Colonial attempts to establish and systematize racial categories greatly influenced developing Enlightenment thought on racial differences (see below).

In the Spanish and French Caribbean, as in Brazil, many masters acknowledged and freed their mixed-race children, leading to sizable populations of free people of color. Advantaged by their fathers, some became wealthy landowners and slaveholders in their own right. In the second half of the eighteenth century, the prosperity of some free people of color brought a backlash from the white population of Saint-Domingue in the form of new race laws prohibiting nonwhites from marrying whites and forcing them to adopt distinctive attire. In the British colonies of the Caribbean and the southern mainland, by contrast, masters tended to leave their mixed-race progeny in slavery, maintaining a stark discrepancy between free whites and enslaved people of color.[14] British colonial law forbade marriage between Englishmen and women and Africans or Native Americans.

Some mixed-race people sought to enter Creole society and obtain its many official and unofficial privileges by passing as white. Where they existed in any number, though, free people of color established their own proud social hierarchies based on wealth, family connections, occupation, and skin color.

Restricted from owning land and holding many occupations in Europe, Jews were eager participants in the new Atlantic economy and established a network of mercantile communities along its trade routes. As in the Old World, Jews in European colonies faced discrimination; for example, restrictions existed on the number of slaves they could own in Barbados in the early eighteenth century.[15] Jews were considered to be white Europeans and thus ineligible to be slaves, but they did not enjoy equal status with Christians. The status of Jews adds one more element to the complexity of Atlantic identities.

Race and the Enlightenment

Encounters in the Atlantic world—either personal or experienced through memoirs, travel literature, and other sources—had a strong impact on Enlightenment philosophers' views on race. Although most Europeans had little direct contact with Africans, educated writers were well aware of the growth of the slave trade and may have come across the increasing numbers of individuals of African descent living in European cities. Some Enlightenment thinkers took part in the slave

trade. John Locke invested significant sums in slaving enterprises and served for many years as an administrator to colonial trade bodies. Among other activities, he coauthored the constitution for the Carolina colony, which included a clause dictating that Christian baptism would not endow freedom on slaves. Scholars still debate how this champion of freedom from tyranny could be personally involved in slavery.

Alongside intensified interaction with non-European peoples, another primary catalyst for new ideas about race was the urge to classify nature unleashed by the scientific revolution and its insistence on empirical observation. As scientists developed more elaborate taxonomies of plant and animal species, they also began to classify humans into hierarchically ordered "races" and to investigate the origins of race. The French naturalist Georges-Louis Leclerc, Comte de Buffon (1707–1788), argued that humans originated with one species that then developed into distinct races due largely to climatic conditions. Enlightenment thinkers such as David Hume and Immanuel Kant (see page 537) helped popularize these ideas.

In *On the Different Races of Man* (1775), Kant claimed that there were four human races, each of which had derived from a supposedly original race of "white brunette" people. According to Kant, the closest descendants of the original race were the white inhabitants of northern Germany. As they acquired new physical characteristics from their local climate and geography, the other races had degenerated both physically and culturally from this origin.

Using the word *race* to designate biologically distinct groups of humans was new. Previously, Europeans grouped other peoples into "nations" based on their historical, political, and cultural affiliations, rather than on supposedly innate physical differences. Unsurprisingly, when European thinkers drew up a hierarchical classification of human species, their own "race" was placed at the top. Europeans had long believed they were culturally superior. The new idea that racial difference was physical and innate rather than cultural taught them they were biologically superior as well. In turn, scientific racism helped legitimate and justify the tremendous growth of slavery that occurred during the eighteenth century. If one race of humans was fundamentally different and inferior, its members could be seen as particularly fit for enslavement. (See "Viewpoints: Malachy Postlethwayt and Olaudah Equiano on the Abolition of Slavery," page 550.)

Racist ideas did not go unchallenged. *Encyclopedia* editor Denis Diderot penned a scathing critique of European arrogance and exploitation in the voice of Tahitian villagers. (See "Listening to the Past: Denis Diderot's 'Supplement to Bougainville's Voyage,'" page 552.) Scottish philosopher James Beattie (1735–1803) responded directly to claims of white superiority by

Listening to the Past

Denis Diderot's "Supplement to Bougainville's Voyage"

Denis Diderot (1713–1784) was born in a provincial town in eastern France and educated in Paris. Rejecting careers in the church and the law, he devoted himself to literature and philosophy. In 1749, sixty years before Charles Darwin's birth, Diderot was jailed by Parisian authorities for publishing an essay questioning God's role in the creation and suggesting the autonomous evolution of species. Following these difficult beginnings, Diderot's editorial work and writing on the Encyclopedia *were the crowning intellectual achievements of his life and, according to some, of the Enlightenment itself.*

Like other philosophes, Diderot disseminated Enlightenment ideas through various types of writing, ranging from scholarly articles in the Encyclopedia *to philosophical treatises, novels, plays, book reviews, and erotic stories. His "Supplement to Bougainville's Voyage" (1772) was a fictional account of a European voyage to Tahiti inspired by the writings of traveler Louis-Antoine de Bougainville. In this passage, Diderot expresses his own loathing of colonial conquest and exploitation through the voice of an elderly Tahitian man. The character's praise for his own culture allows Diderot to express his Enlightenment idealization of natural man, free from the vices of civilized societies.*

❝He was the father of a large family. When the Europeans arrived he looked upon them with scorn, showing neither astonishment, nor fear, nor curiosity. On their approach he turned his back and retired into his hut. Yet his silence and anxiety revealed his thoughts only too well; he was inwardly lamenting the eclipse of his countrymen's happiness. When Bougainville was leaving the island, as the natives swarmed on the shore, clutching his clothes, clasping his companions in their arms and weeping, the old man made his way forward and proclaimed solemnly, "Weep, wretched natives of Tahiti, weep. But let it be for the coming and not the leaving of these ambitious, wicked men. One day you will know them better. One day they will come back, bearing in one hand the piece of wood you see in that man's belt, and, in the other, the sword hanging by the side of that one, to enslave you, slaughter you, or make you captive to their follies and vices. One day you will be subject to them, as corrupt, vile and miserable as they are. . . ."

Then turning to Bougainville, he continued, "And you, leader of the ruffians who obey you, pull your ship away swiftly from these shores. We are innocent, we are content, and you can only spoil that happiness. We follow the pure instincts of nature, and you have tried to erase its impression from our hearts. Here, everything belongs to everyone, and you have preached I can't tell what distinction between 'yours' and 'mine.' . . . If a Tahitian should one day land on your shores and engrave on one of your stones or on the bark of one of your trees, *This land belongs to the people of Tahiti*, what would you think then? You are stronger than we are, and what does that mean? When one of the miserable trinkets with which your ship is filled was taken away, what an uproar you made, what revenge you exacted! At that moment, in the depths of your heart, you were plotting the theft of an entire country! You are not a slave, you would rather die than be one, and yet you wish to make slaves of us. Do you suppose, then, that a Tahitian cannot defend his own liberty and die for it as well? This inhabitant of Tahiti, whom you wish to ensare like an

pointing out that Europeans had started out as savage as nonwhites and that many non-European peoples in the Americas, Asia, and Africa had achieved high levels of civilization. German thinker Johann Gottfried von Herder (1744–1803) criticized Kant, arguing that humans could not be classified into races based on skin color and that each culture was as intrinsically worthy as any other.

One popular idea, among Rousseau and others, was that indigenous peoples of the Americas represented prime examples of "natural man," the being who embodied the essential goodness of humanity uncorrupted by decadent society. Other popular candidates for utopian natural man were the Pacific Island societies explored by Captain James Cook and others from the 1770s on (see pages 834–835).

There are clear parallels between the use of science to propagate racial hierarchies and to defend social inequalities between men and women. As we have noted, French philosopher Jean-Jacques Rousseau used women's "natural" passivity to argue for their passive role in society, just as other thinkers used non-Europeans' "natural" inferiority to defend slavery and colonial domination. The new powers of science and reason were thus marshaled to imbue traditional stereotypes with the force of natural law.

animal, is your brother. You are both children of Nature. What right do you have over him that he does not have over you? You came; did we attack you? Have we plundered your ship? Did we seize you and expose you to the arrows of our enemies? Did we harness you to work with our animals in the fields? We respected our own image in you.

"Leave us our ways; they are wiser and more decent than yours. We have no wish to exchange what you call our ignorance for your useless knowledge. Everything that we need and is good for us we already possess. Do we merit contempt because we have not learnt how to acquire superfluous needs? When we are hungry, we have enough to eat. When we are cold, we have enough to wear. You have entered our huts; what do you suppose we lack? Pursue as far as you wish what you call the comforts of life, but let sensible beings stop when they have no more to gain from their labours than imaginary benefits. If you persuade us to go beyond the strict bounds of necessity, when will we finish our work? When will we enjoy ourselves? We have kept our annual and daily labours within the smallest possible limits, because in our eyes nothing is better than rest. Go back to your own country to agitate and torment yourselves as much as you like. But leave us in peace. Do not fill our heads with your factitious needs and illusory virtues." 99

Source: Edited excerpts from pages 41–43 in Denis Diderot, *Political Writings*, translated and edited by John Hope Mason and Robert Wokler. © 1992 by Cambridge University Press.

QUESTIONS FOR ANALYSIS

1. On what grounds does the speaker argue for the Tahitians' basic equality with the Europeans?

2. What is the good life, according to the speaker, and how does it contrast with the European way of life? Which do you think is the better path, and why?

3. In what ways could Diderot's thoughts here be seen as representative of Enlightenment ideas? Are there ways in which they are not?

4. How realistic do you think this account is? Does it matter? How might defenders of colonial expansion respond to Diderot's criticism?

● **This image depicts the meeting of French explorer Louis-Antoine de Bougainville with Tahitians in April 1768. Of his stay on the island, Bougainville wrote: "I felt as though I had been transported to the Garden of Eden. . . . Everywhere reigned hospitality, peace, joy, and every appearance of happiness." Diderot's philosophical tract was a fictional sequel to Bougainville's account.** (Unknown artist, Tahitians presenting fruit to Bougainville attended by his officers. PIC T2996 NK5066 LOC7321, National Library of Australia)

CONNECTIONS

Hailed as the origin of modern thought, the scientific revolution must also be seen as a product of its past. Borrowing in part from Arabic translators and commentators, medieval universities gave rise to important new scholarship. In turn, the ambition and wealth of Renaissance patrons nurtured intellectual curiosity and encouraged scholarly research and foreign exploration. Religious faith also influenced the scientific revolution, inspiring some thinkers to understand the glory of God's creation, while bringing censure and personal tragedy to others. Natural philosophers following Copernicus pioneered new methods of observing and explaining nature while drawing on centuries-old traditions of mysticism, astrology, alchemy, and magic.

Enlightenment ideas of the eighteenth century were a similar blend of past and present, progressive and traditional, homegrown and influenced by other cultures. Enlightenment thinkers advocated universal rights and liberties but also preached the biological inferiority of non-Europeans. Their principles served as much to bolster authoritarian regimes as to inspire revolutionaries to fight for human rights. Although the Enlightenment fostered critical thinking about everything from science to religion, most Europeans, including many prominent thinkers, remained devout Christians.

Key Western values of rationalism, human rights, and open-mindedness were born from the scientific revolution and the Enlightenment. With their new notions of progress and social improvement, Europeans would embark on important revolutions in politics and industry (see Chapters 22 and 23). Nonetheless, some critics have seen a darker side. For them, the mastery over nature permitted by the scientific revolution now threatens to overwhelm the earth's fragile equilibrium, and the Enlightenment belief in the universal application of reason can lead to intolerance of other people's spiritual, cultural, and political values. Such vivid debate about the legacy of these intellectual and scientific developments testifies to their continuing importance in today's world.

As the era of European exploration and conquest gave way to empire-building, the eighteenth century witnessed increased consolidation of global markets and bitter competition among Europeans. The eighteenth-century Atlantic world thus tied the shores of Europe, the Americas, and Africa in a web of commercial and human exchange, including the tragedy of slavery, discussed in Chapter 19. The Atlantic world maintained strong ties with trade in the Pacific and the Indian Ocean.

□ CHAPTER REVIEW

KEY TERMS

natural philosophy (p. 526)	philosophes (p. 535)
Copernican hypothesis (p. 528)	economic liberalism (p. 537)
law of inertia (p. 529)	salons (p. 539)
law of universal gravitation (p. 530)	public sphere (p. 540)
empiricism (p. 530)	general will (p. 540)
Cartesian dualism (p. 531)	enlightened absolutism (p. 541)
Enlightenment (p. 533)	Haskalah (p. 544)
	enclosure (p. 545)

□ What was revolutionary in the new attitudes toward the natural world? (p. 526)

Decisive breakthroughs in astronomy and physics in the seventeenth century demolished the medieval synthesis of Aristotelian philosophy and Christian theology. One of the most notable discoveries was that the sun, not the earth, was the center of the universe. Although the early scientists considered their ideas to be in line with religion, their discoveries ran counter to long-held beliefs about the design of the universe by a creator; therefore, the findings of Copernicus, Kepler, Galileo, and others were opposed by religious authorities, and Galileo was tried for heresy. Meanwhile, Bacon promoted an experimental method that drew conclusions based on empirical evidence, and Descartes championed deductive reasoning, which speculated truths based on known principles. These two important methods eventually combined to form the modern scientific method, which relies on both experimentation and reason. Following these early innovators, Newton devised the law of universal gravitation, which for the first time synthesized the orbiting planets of the solar system with the motion of objects on earth. The impact of these scientific breakthroughs on intellectual life was enormous, nurturing a new critical attitude in many disciplines. In addition, an international scientific community arose, and state-sponsored academies, which were typically closed to women, advanced scientific research.

□ How did a new spirit of critical and rational thinking affect ideas about society and human relations? (p. 533)

Interpreting scientific findings in a manner that questioned long-standing traditions and religious beliefs, Enlightenment philosophes extolled the superiority of rational, critical thinking. This new method, they believed, promised not just increased knowledge but

even the discovery of the fundamental laws of human society. Believing that all aspects of life were open to question and skepticism, Enlightenment thinkers opened the doors to religious tolerance, representative government, and general intellectual debate. Among the influential Enlightenment thinkers were Locke, who asserted that all human ideas are produced as a result of sensory impressions; Montesquieu, who argued for the separation of powers based on a critical and comparative study of governments; Voltaire, who drew on Newton to envision a mechanistic universe; Hume, who through rationalistic inquiry concluded that reason can be applied only to phenomena that can be verified by the human senses; and Rousseau, who described a general will reflecting the common interests of all people.

□ What impact did new ways of thinking have on monarchical absolutism and those under its rule? (p. 540)

The ideas of the Enlightenment were an inspiration for monarchs, particularly absolutist rulers in central and eastern Europe, who saw in them important tools for reform. In Prussia and Russia, rulers became more religiously tolerant and made efforts to improve education and government, among other changes. However, conditions for serfs worsened under their rule. In

Austria, Joseph II abolished serfdom, but his reform efforts were ultimately unsuccessful. All in all, the influence of Enlightenment ideas on monarchies was limited, as perhaps is best illustrated by most rulers' refusal to support emancipation of the Jews.

□ **How did the growth of consumerism and the Atlantic economy interact with Enlightenment ideas? (p. 545)**

The eighteenth century witnessed rising levels of consumption and increased comfort and privacy within the home, particularly in the cities and towns of northwestern Europe and British North America. These achievements were made possible in part by the expansion of transatlantic trade and the lowering of prices on colonial goods due to the growth of slave labor. Atlantic trade involved the exchange of commodities among Europe, Africa, and the Americas, but it was also linked in important ways with trade in the Indian and Pacific Oceans. The movement of people and ideas across the Atlantic in the eighteenth century helped shape the identities of colonial inhabitants. At first colonial elites prided themselves on following European ways of life. With time, however, they developed customs and attitudes apart from those of their homeland. Enlightenment ideas circulated in the colonies with as much diversity as in the mother countries. In turn, Enlightenment thinkers drew inspiration from the new peoples and cultures Europeans encountered. One important development was new ideas about race, defined as biologically distinct groups of people with innate differences and inequalities. When European thinkers created a hierarchical classification of humans, they placed their own race at the top, helping to justify the enslavement of peoples they saw as their inferiors.

SUGGESTED READING

Alexander, John T. *Catherine the Great: Life and Legend.* 1989. The best biography of the famous Russian tsarina.

Delborgo, James, and Nicholas Dew, eds. *Science and Empire in the Atlantic World.* 2008. A collection of essays examining the relationship between the scientific revolution and the imperial expansion of European powers across the Atlantic.

Ellis, Markman. *The Coffee-House: A Cultural History.* 2004. An engaging study of the rise of the coffeehouse and its impact on European cultural and social life.

Eze, E. Chukwudi, ed. *Race and the Enlightenment: A Reader.* 1997. A pioneering source on the origins of modern racial thinking in the Enlightenment.

Goodman, Dena. *The Republic of Letters: A Cultural History of the Enlightenment.* 1994. An innovative study of the role of salons and salon hostesses in the rise of the Enlightenment.

MacDonogh, Giles. *Frederick the Great.* 2001. An outstanding biography of the Prussian king.

Mannin, Susan, and Francis D. Cogliano. *The Atlantic Enlightenment.* 2008. A series of essays examining the exchange of Enlightenment ideas, authors, and texts across the Atlantic Ocean.

Osler, Margaret J., ed. *Rethinking the Scientific Revolution.* 2000. A collection of essays focusing on new historical approaches to the scientific revolution.

Outram, Dorinda. *The Enlightenment,* 2d ed. 2006. An outstanding and accessible introduction to Enlightenment debates that emphasizes the Enlightenment's social context and global reach.

Shapin, Steven. *The Scientific Revolution.* 2001. A concise and well-informed general introduction to the scientific revolution.

Sorkin, David. *Moses Mendelssohn and the Religious Enlightenment.* 1996. A brilliant study of the Jewish philosopher and of the role of religion in the Enlightenment.

NOTES

1. H. Butterfield, *The Origins of Modern Science* (New York: Macmillan, 1951), p. viii.
2. Quoted in A. G. R. Smith, *Science and Society in the Sixteenth and Seventeenth Centuries* (New York: Harcourt Brace Jovanovich, 1972), p. 97.
3. Quoted in Butterfield, *The Origins of Modern Science,* p. 47.
4. Ibid., p. 120.
5. L. Schiebinger, *The Mind Has No Sex? Women in the Origins of Modern Science* (Cambridge, Mass.: Harvard University Press, 1989), p. 64.
6. Quoted in G. L. Mosse et al., eds., *Europe in Review* (Chicago: Rand McNally, 1964), p. 156.
7. Quoted in G. P. Gooch, *Catherine the Great and Other Studies* (Hamden, Conn.: Archon Books, 1966), p. 149.
8. See E. Fox-Genovese, "Women in the Enlightenment," in *Becoming Visible: Women in European History,* 2d ed., ed. R. Bridenthal, C. Koonz, and S. Stuard (Boston: Houghton Mifflin, 1987), esp. pp. 252–259, 263–265.
9. R. Heilbroner, *The Essential Adam Smith* (New York: W. W. Norton, 1986), p. 281.
10. Daniel Roche, *The Culture of Clothing: Dress and Fashion in the Ancien Regime,* trans. Jean Birrell (Cambridge, U.K.: Cambridge University Press, 1996).
11. Quoted in Cissie Fairchilds, "The Production and Marketing of Populuxe Goods in Eighteenth-Century Paris," in *Consumption and the World of Goods,* ed. John Brewer and Roy Porter (London: Routledge, 1993), p. 228.
12. Laurent Dubois and John D. Garrigus, *Slave Revolution in the Caribbean, 1789–1904* (New York: Palgrave, 2006), p. 8.
13. Pierre Marie François Paget, *Travels Round the World in the Years 1767, 1768, 1769, 1770, 1771* (London, 1793), vol. 1, p. 262.
14. Orlando Patterson, *Slavery and Social Death* (Cambridge, Mass.: Harvard University Press, 1982), p. 255.
15. Erik R. Seeman, "Jews in the Early Modern Atlantic: Crossing Boundaries, Keeping Faith," in *The Atlantic in Global History, 1500–2000,* ed. Jorge Canizares-Esguerra and Erik R. Seeman (Upper Saddle River, N.J.: Pearson Prentice-Hall, 2007), p. 43.

For practice quizzes and other study tools, visit the **Online Study Guide** at bedfordstmartins.com/mckayworld.

For primary sources from this period, see *Sources of World Societies,* **Second Edition.**

For Web sites, images, and documents related to topics in this chapter, visit **Make History** at bedfordstmartins.com/mckayworld.

• **Waist Pendant of Benin Worn by Royalty** European intrusion in Africa during the early modern period deeply affected the diverse societies of Africa. The facial features, the beard, and the ruffled collar on this Edo peoples' artifact dating from the sixteenth to the nineteenth centuries are clearly Portuguese, but the braided hair is distinctly African, probably signifying royalty. (Image copyright © The Metropolitan Museum of Art/Art Resource, NY)

19

Africa and the World
1400-1800

African states and societies of the early modern period — from the fifteenth through the eighteenth centuries — comprised a wide variety of languages, cultures, and kinds of economic and political development. Kingdoms and stateless societies coexisted throughout Africa, from the small villages of the Senegambia to the kingdom of Songhai and its renowned city of Timbuktu in West Africa, and from the Christian state of Ethiopia to the independent city-states of the Swahili coast in East Africa. So too by the fifteenth century had Africans developed a steady rhythm of contact and exchange. Across the great Sahara, trade goods and knowledge passed back and forth from West Africa to North Africa and beyond to Europe and the Middle East. The same was true in East Africa, where Indian Ocean traders touched up and down the African coast to deliver goods from Arabia, India, and Asia and to pick up the ivory, gold, spices, and other products representing Africa's rich natural wealth. In the interior as well, extensive trading networks linked African societies across the vast continent.

Modern European intrusion into Africa beginning in the fifteenth century profoundly affected these diverse societies and ancient trading networks. The intrusion led to the trans-atlantic slave trade, one of the greatest forced migrations in world history, through which Africa made a substantial, though involuntary, contribution to the building of the West's industrial civilization. In the seventeenth century an increasing desire for sugar in Europe resulted in an increasing demand for slave labor in South America and the West Indies. In the eighteenth century Western technological changes created a demand for cotton and other crops that required extensive human labor, thus intensifying the West's "need" for African slaves. •

West Africa in the Fifteenth and Sixteenth Centuries
☐ What different types of economic, social, and political structures were found in the kingdoms and states along the west coast and in the Sudan?

Cross-Cultural Encounters Along the East African Coast
☐ How did the arrival of Europeans and other foreign cultures impact the East African coast, and how did Ethiopia and the Swahili city-states respond to these incursions?

The African Slave Trade
☐ What role did slavery play in African societies before the transatlantic slave trade began, and what was the effect of European involvement?

West Africa in the Fifteenth and Sixteenth Centuries

☐ What different types of economic, social, and political structures were found in the kingdoms and states along the west coast and in the Sudan?

In mid-fifteenth-century Africa, Benin and a number of other kingdoms flourished along the two-thousand-mile west coast between Senegambia and the northeastern shore of the Gulf of Guinea. Because much of that coastal region is covered by tropical rain forest, in contrast to the western Sudan, it is called the West African Forest Region (Map 19.1). Further inland, in the region of the Sudan, the kingdoms of Songhai, Kanem-Bornu, and Hausaland benefited from the trans-Saharan caravan trade, which along with goods brought Islamic culture to the region. These West African kingdoms maintained their separate existences for centuries. Stateless societies such as those in the region of Senegambia (modern-day Senegal and the Gambia) existed alongside these more centralized states. Despite their political differences and whether they were agricultural, pas-

toral, or a mixture of both, the cultures of West Africa equally faced the challenges presented by famine, disease, and the slave trade.

The West Coast: Senegambia and Benin

The Senegambian states possessed a homogeneous culture and a common history. For centuries Senegambia—named for the Senegal and Gambia Rivers—served as an important entrepôt for desert caravan contact with North African and Middle Eastern Islamic civilizations. Through the transatlantic slave trade, Senegambia came into contact with Europe and the Americas. Thus Senegambia felt the impact of Islamic culture to the north and of European influences from the maritime West.

The Senegambian peoples spoke Wolof, Serer, and Pulaar, which all belong to the West African language group. Both the Wolof-speakers and the Serer-speakers had clearly defined social classes: royalty, nobility, warriors, peasants, low-caste artisans such as blacksmiths and leatherworkers, and enslaved persons. This enslaved class consisted of individuals who were pawned for debt, house servants who could not be sold, and people who were acquired through war or purchase. Senegambian slavery varied from society to society but generally was not a benign institution. In some places, slaves were considered chattel property and were treated as harshly as they would be later in the Western Hemisphere.

The word **chattel** originally comes from a Latin word meaning head, as in "so many head of cattle." It

The Oba of Benin The oba's palace walls were decorated with bronze plaques that date from about the sixteenth to the eighteenth centuries. This plaque vividly conveys the oba's power, majesty, and authority. The necklace (or choker) is his symbol of royalty. His warrior attendants surround and protect him and carry his royal regalia. (Museum für Völkerkunde/Kunsthistorisches Museum, Vienna)

reflects the notion that enslaved people are not human, but subhuman, like beasts of burden, like animals. Thus, they can be treated like animals — whipped, beaten, worked to exhaustion, and forced to live in conditions no better than those provided for animals. But in Senegambia and other parts of Africa, many enslaved people were not considered chattel property. That is, unlike livestock or other common property, they could not be bought and sold. Some even served as royal advisers and enjoyed great power and prestige.[1] What is more, unlike in the Americas, where slave status passed forever from one generation to the next, in Africa the enslaved person's descendants were sometimes considered free, although the stigma of slave could attach to the family.

Senegambia was composed of stateless societies, culturally homogeneous ethnic societies where kinship and lineage groups tended to fragment communities. These societies comprised small groups of villages without a central capital. Among these stateless societies **age-grade systems** evolved. Age-grades were groups of teenage males and females whom the society initiated into adulthood at the same time. Age-grades cut across family ties, created community-wide loyalties, and provided a means of local law enforcement, because each age-grade was responsible for the behavior of all its members.

The typical Senegambian community was a small, self-supporting agricultural village of closely related families. Fields were cut from the surrounding forest, and the average six- to eight-acre farm supported a moderate-size family. Millet and sorghum were the staple grains in northern Senegambia; farther south, forest dwellers cultivated yams as a staple. Senegambians supplemented their diet with plantains, beans, bananas, fish, oysters, and small game such as rabbits and monkeys. Village markets for produce exchange offered opportunities for receiving outside news and for social diversion. Social life was centered around the family, and government played a limited role, interceding mostly to resolve family disputes and conflicts between families.

Alongside West African stateless societies like the Senegambia were kingdoms and states ruled by kings who governed defined areas through bureaucratic hierarchies. The great forest kingdom of Benin emerged in the fifteenth and sixteenth centuries in what is now

southern Nigeria (see Map 19.1). Over time the position of its **oba**, or king, was exalted, bringing stability to the state. In the later fifteenth century the oba Ewuare, a great warrior himself, strengthened his army and pushed Benin's borders as far as the Niger River in the east, westward into Yoruba country, and south to the Gulf of Guinea. During the late sixteenth and seventeenth centuries the office of the oba evolved from a warrior-kingship to a position of spiritual leadership.

At its height in the late sixteenth century, Benin controlled a vast territory, and European visitors described a sophisticated society. A Dutch visitor in the early 1600s, possibly Dierick Ruiters, described the capital, Benin City, as possessing a great, wide, and straight main avenue down the middle, with many side streets crisscrossing it. The visitor entered the city through a high, well-guarded gate framed on each side

---

- **chattel** An item of personal property; a term used in reference to enslaved people that conveys the idea that they are subhuman, like animals, and therefore may be treated like animals.
- **age-grade systems** Among the societies of Senegambia, groups of men and women whom the society initiated into adulthood at the same time.
- **oba** The title of the king of Benin.

◻ Mapping the Past

MAP 19.1 West African Societies, ca. 1500–1800
The coastal region of West Africa witnessed the rise of a number of kingdoms in the sixteenth century.

ANALYZING THE MAP What geographical features defined each of the kingdoms shown here? Consider rivers, lakes, oceans, deserts, and forests. How might they have impacted the size and shape of these kingdoms?

CONNECTIONS Compare this map to the spot map of the slave coast of West Africa on page 576. Consider the role that rivers and other geographical factors played in the development of the West African slave trade. Why were Luanda and Benguela the logical Portuguese sources for slaves?

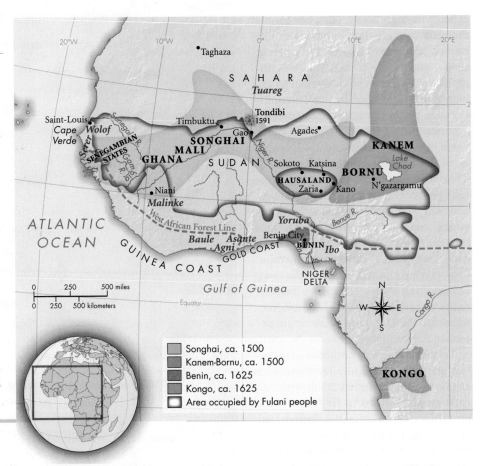

by a very tall earthen bulwark, or wall, with an accompanying moat. There was also an impressive royal palace, with at least four large courtyards surrounded by galleries leading up to it. William Bosman, another Dutch visitor writing a hundred years later, in 1702, described the prodigiously long and broad streets "in which continual Markets are kept, either of Kine [cattle], Cotton, Elephants Teeth, European Wares; or, in short, whatever is to be come at in this Country."[2] Visitors also noted that Benin City was kept scrupulously clean and had no beggars and that public security was so effective that theft was unknown. The period also witnessed remarkable artistic creativity in ironwork, carved ivory, and especially bronze portrait busts. Over nine hundred brass plaques survive, providing important information about Benin court life, military triumphs, and cosmological ideas.

In 1485 Portuguese and other Europeans began to appear in Benin in pursuit of trade, and over the next couple of centuries Benin grew rich from the profits made through the slave trade and the export of tropical products, particularly pepper and ivory. Its main European trading partners along this stretch of the so-called slave coast were the Dutch and Portuguese. In the early eighteenth century tributary states and stronger neighbors nibbled at Benin's frontiers, challenging its power. Benin, however, survived as an independent entity

until the British conquered and burned Benin City in 1898 as part of the European imperialist seizure of Africa (discussed in Chapter 25).

The Sudan: Songhai, Kanem-Bornu, and Hausaland

The Songhai kingdom, a successor state of the kingdoms of Ghana (ca. 900–1000) and Mali (ca. 1200–1450), dominated the whole Niger region of the western and central Sudan (see Map 19.1). The imperial expansion of Songhai (song-GUY) began during the reign of the Songhai king Sonni Ali (r. ca. 1464–1492) and continued under his eventual successor, Muhammad Toure (r. 1493–1528). From his capital at Gao, Toure extended his rule as far north as the salt-mining center at **Taghaza** in the western Sahara and as far east as Agades and Kano. A convert to Islam, Toure returned from a pilgrimage to Mecca impressed by what he had seen there. He tried to bring about greater centralization in his own territories by building a strong army, improving taxation procedures, and replacing local Songhai officials with more efficient Arabs in an effort to substitute royal institutions for ancient kinship ties.

We know little about daily life in Songhai society because of the paucity of written records and surviv-

Islamic law for African tribunals and ancient customary law. His eighteenth-century successors lacked his vitality and military skills, however, and the empire declined.

Between Songhai and Kanem-Bornu were the lands of the Hausa, an agricultural people who lived in small villages. Hausa merchants carried on a heavy trade in slaves and kola nuts with North African communities across the Sahara, and obscure trading posts evolved into important Hausa city-states like Kano and Katsina, through which Islamic influences entered the region. Kano and Katsina became Muslim intellectual centers and in the fifteenth century attracted scholars from Timbuktu. The Muslim chronicler of the reign of King Muhammad Rimfa of Kano (r. 1463–1499) records that the king introduced the Muslim practices of purdah, or seclusion of women; of the *idal-fitr*, the festival after the fast of Ramadan; and of assigning eunuchs to high state offices.[5] As in Songhai and Kanem-Bornu, however, Islam made no strong imprint on the Hausa masses until the nineteenth century.

The Lives of the People of West Africa

The negative effects of the transatlantic slave trade (see page 580) on West Africa's population profoundly affected marriage patterns and family structure. Wives and children were highly desired because they could clear and cultivate the land and because they brought prestige, social support, and security in old age. The result was intense competition for women, inequality of access to them, an emphasis on male virility and female fertility, and serious tension between male generations. Polygyny was almost universal; as recently as the nineteenth century two-thirds of rural wives were in polygynous marriages.

Men acquired wives in two ways. First, some couples simply eloped and began their union. More commonly, a man's family gave bride wealth to the bride's family as compensation for losing the fruits of her productive and reproductive abilities. She was expected to produce children, to produce food through her labor, and to pass on the culture in the raising of her children. Because it took time for a young man to acquire the bride wealth, all but the richest men delayed marriage until about age thirty. Women married at about the onset of puberty.

The easy availability of land in Africa reduced the kinds of generational conflict that occurred in western Europe, where land was scarce. Competition for wives between male generations, however, was fierce. On the one hand, myth and folklore stressed respect for the elderly, and the older men in a community imposed their authority over the younger ones by including painful rites of initiation into adulthood, such as circumcision. On the other hand, West African societies were not based on rule by elders, as few people lived much beyond forty. Young men possessed the powerful asset of their labor, which could easily be turned into independence where so much land was available.

"Without children you are naked" goes a Yoruba proverb, and children were the primary goal of marriage. Just as a man's virility determined his honor, so barrenness damaged a woman's status. A wife's infidelity was considered a less serious problem than her infertility. A woman might have six widely spaced pregnancies in her fertile years; the universal practice of breast-feeding infants for two, three, or even four years may have inhibited conception. Long intervals between births due to food shortages also may have limited pregnancies and checked population growth. The harsh

Queen Mother and Attendants As in Ottoman, Chinese, and European societies, the mothers of African rulers sometimes exercised considerable political power because of their influence on their sons. African kings granted the title Queen Mother as a badge of honor. In this figure, the long beaded cap, called "chicken's beak," symbolizes the mother's rank, as do her elaborate neck jewelry and attendants. (Image copyright © The Metropolitan Museum of Art/Art Resource, NY)

climate, poor nutrition, and infectious diseases also contributed to a high infant mortality rate.

Both nuclear and extended families were common in West Africa. Nuclear families averaged only five or six members, but the household of a Big Man (a local man of power) included his wives, married and unmarried sons, unmarried daughters, poor relations, dependents, and scores of children. Extended families were common among the Hausa and Malinke peoples. On the Gold Coast in the seventeenth century, a well-to-do man's household might number 150 people, in the Kongo region several hundred. Where one family cultivated extensive land, a large household of young adults, children, and slaves probably proved most efficient. Still, although many children might be born, many also died. Families rarely exceeded five or six people; high infant mortality rates and short life spans kept the household numbers low.

In agriculture men did the heavy work of felling trees and clearing the land; women then planted, weeded, and harvested. Between 1000 and 1400, cassava (manioc), bananas, and plantains came to West Africa from Asia. Cassava required little effort to grow and became a staple food, but it had little nutritional value. In the sixteenth century the Portuguese introduced maize (corn), sweet potatoes, and new varieties of yams from the Americas. Fish supplemented the diets of people living near bodies of water. According to Olaudah Equiano (oh-lah-OO-dah ay-kwee-AH-noh), the Ibo people in the mid-eighteenth century ate plantains, yams, beans, and Indian corn, along with stewed poultry, goat, or bullock (castrated steer) seasoned with peppers.[6] Such a protein-rich diet was probably exceptional.

Disease posed perhaps the biggest obstacle to population growth. Malaria, spread by mosquitoes and rampant in West Africa (except in cool, dry Cameroon), was the greatest killer, especially of infants. West Africans developed a relatively high degree of immunity to malaria and other parasitic diseases, including hookworm (which enters the body through shoeless feet and attaches itself to the intestines), yaws (contracted by nonsexual contact and recognized by ulcerating lesions), sleeping sickness (the parasite enters the blood through the bite of the tsetse [SEHT-see] fly; symptoms are enlarged lymph nodes and, at the end, a comatose state), and a mild nonsexual form of syphilis. Acute strains of smallpox introduced by Europeans certainly did not help population growth, nor did venereal syphilis, which possibly originated in Latin America. As in Chinese and European communities in the early modern period,

the sick depended on folk medicine. African medical specialists, such as midwives, bonesetters, exorcists using religious methods, and herbalists, administered a variety of treatments, including herbal medications like salves, ointments, and purgatives. Still, disease was common where the diet was poor and lacked adequate vitamins.

The devastating effects of famine, often mentioned in West African oral traditions, represented another major check on population growth. Drought, excessive rain, swarms of locusts, and rural wars that prevented the cultivation of land all meant later food shortages. In the 1680s famine extended from the Senegambian coast to the Upper Nile, and many people sold themselves into slavery for food. In the eighteenth century "slave exports" reached their peak in times of famine, and ships could fill their cargo holds simply by offering food. The worst disaster occurred from 1738 to 1756, when, according to one chronicler, the poor were reduced to cannibalism, an African metaphor for the complete collapse of civilization.[7]

Because the Americas had been isolated from the Eurasian-African landmass for thousands of years, parasitic diseases common in Europe, Africa, and Asia were unknown in the Americas before the arrival of the Europeans. Enslaved Africans taken to the Americas brought with them the diseases common to tropical West Africa, such as yellow fever, dengue fever, malaria, and hookworm. Thus, the hot, humid disease environment in the American tropics, where the majority of enslaved Africans lived and worked, became more "African." On the other hand, cold-weather European diseases, such as chicken pox, mumps, measles, and influenza, prevailed in the northern temperate zone in North America and the southern temperate zone in South America. This difference in disease environment partially explains why Africans made up the majority of the unskilled labor force in the tropical areas of the Americas, and Europeans made up the majority of the unskilled labor force in the temperate zones of the Western Hemisphere, such as the northern United States and Canada.

Trade and Industry

As in all premodern societies, West African economies rested on agriculture. There was some trade and industry, but population shortages encouraged local self-sufficiency, slowed transportation, and hindered exchange. There were very few large markets, and their relative isolation from the outside world and failure to attract large numbers of foreign merchants limited technological innovation.

For centuries, black Africans had exchanged goods with North African merchants in centers such as Gao and Timbuktu. That long-distance trans-Saharan trade was conducted and controlled by Muslim-Berber mer-

• **Tuareg** Along with the Moors, warriors who controlled the north-south trans-Saharan trade in salt.

• **cowrie shells** Imported from the Maldives, they served as the medium of exchange in West Africa.

chants using camels. The two primary goods exchanged were salt, which came from salt mines in North Africa, and gold, which came mainly from gold mines in modern-day Mali.

As elsewhere around the world, water was the cheapest method of transportation, and many small dugout canoes and larger trading canoes plied the Niger and its delta region (see Map 19.1). On land West African peoples used pack animals (camels or donkeys) rather than wheeled vehicles; south of the Sahara, only a narrow belt of land was suitable for animal-drawn carts. When traders reached an area infested with tsetse flies, they transferred each animal's load to human porters. Such difficulties in transport severely restricted long-distance trade, so most people relied on the regional exchange of local specialties.

West African communities had a well-organized market system. At informal markets on riverbanks, fishermen bartered fish for local specialties. More formal markets existed within towns and villages or on neutral ground between them. Markets also rotated among neighboring villages on certain days. People exchanged cotton cloth, thread, palm oil, millet, vegetables, and small articles for daily living. Local sellers were usually women; traders from afar were men.

Salt had long been one of Africa's most critical trade items. Salt is essential to human health; the Hausa language has more than fifty words for it. The salt trade dominated the West African economies in the fifteenth, sixteenth, and seventeenth centuries. The main salt-mining center was at Taghaza (see Map 19.1) in the western Sahara. In the most wretched conditions, slaves dug the salt from desiccated lakes and loaded heavy blocks onto camels' backs. **Tuareg** warriors and later Moors (peoples of Berber and Arab descent) traded their salt south for gold, grain, slaves, and kola nuts, which were used by Muslims as stimulants or aphrodisiacs. **Cowrie shells**, imported from the Maldives in the Indian Ocean by way of Gujarat (see page 609) and

West African Trade Routes

North Africa, served as the medium of exchange (and continued to do so long after European intrusion). Gold continued to be mined and shipped from Mali until South American bullion flooded Europe in the sixteenth century (see page 480). Thereafter, its production in Africa steadily declined. In the late twentieth and early twenty-first centuries gold mining revived in Mali, to the point that gold briefly was Mali's number-one export in 2002. Mali is now Africa's third largest gold producer, after South Africa and Ghana.

West African peoples engaged in many crafts, such as basket weaving and pottery making. Ironworking, a specialized skill producing articles useful to hunters, farmers, and warriors, became hereditary in individual families; such expertise was regarded as family property. The textile industry had the greatest level of specialization. The earliest fabric in West Africa was made of vegetable fiber. Muslim traders introduced cotton

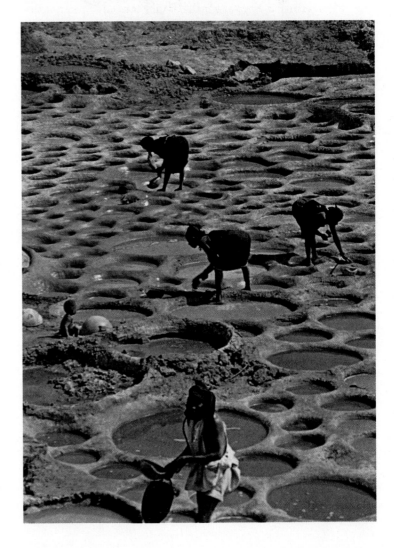

Salt Making in the Central Sahara For centuries camel caravans transported salt south across the Sahara to the great West African kingdoms, where it was exchanged for gold. Here at Tegguida-n-Tessum, Niger, in the central Sahara, salt is still collected by pouring spring water into small pools dug out of the saline soil. The water leaches out the salt before evaporating in the desert sun, leaving deposits of pure salt behind, which are then shaped into blocks for transport. (Afrique Photo, Cliché Naud/Visual Connection Archive)

MAP 19.2 East Africa in the Sixteenth Century In early modern times, the Christian kingdom of Ethiopia, first isolated and then subjected to Muslim and European pressures, played an insignificant role in world affairs. But the East African city-states, which stretched from Sofala in the south to Mogadishu in the north, had powerfully important commercial relations with Mughal India, China, the Ottoman world, and southern Europe.

and its weaving in the ninth century, as the fine-quality fabrics found in Mali reveal. By the fifteenth century the Wolof and Malinke regions had professional weavers producing beautiful cloth, but this cloth was too expensive to compete in the Atlantic and Indian Ocean markets after 1500. Women who spun cotton used only a spindle and not a wheel, which slowed output. Women wove on inefficient broadlooms, men on less clumsy but narrow looms. Although the relatively small quantities of cloth produced on these narrow looms (one to two inches wide) could not compete in a world market, they are the source of the famous multicolored African kente cloth made from threads of cotton, or cotton and silk, by the Akan people of Ghana and the Ivory Coast. The area around Kano, in northern Nigeria, was famous for the deeply dyed blue cloth produced on the narrowest looms in the world and favored by the Tuareg Berber peoples of North Africa.

Cross-Cultural Encounters Along the East African Coast

☐ How did the arrival of Europeans and other foreign cultures impact the East African coast, and how did Ethiopia and the Swahili city-states respond to these incursions?

East Africa in the early modern period faced repeated incursions from foreign powers. At the beginning of the sixteenth century Ethiopia faced challenges from the Muslim state of Adal, and then from Europeans. Jesuit attempts to substitute Roman liturgical forms met with fierce resistance and ushered in a centuries-long period of hostility to foreigners. The wealthy Swahili city-states along the southeastern coast of Africa also resisted European intrusions in the sixteenth century, with even more disastrous results. Cities such as Mogadishu, Kilwa, and Sofala used Arabic as the language of communication, and their commercial economies had long been tied to the trade of the Indian Ocean. The arrival of the Portuguese in 1498 proved catastrophic for those cities, and the Swahili coast suffered economic decline as a result.

Muslim and European Incursions in Ethiopia, ca. 1500–1630

At the beginning of the sixteenth century the powerful East African kingdom of Ethiopia extended from Massawa in the north to several tributary states in the south (Map 19.2), but the ruling Solomonic dynasty in Ethiopia, in power since the thirteenth century, faced

Saint George in Ethiopian Art This wall painting of Saint George slaying a dragon resides in the stone-carved Church of St. George at Lalibela, Ethiopia, and attests to the powerful and pervasive Christian influence on Ethiopian culture. (Galen R. Frysinger)

serious external threats. Alone among the states in northeast and eastern Africa, Ethiopia was a Christian kingdom that practiced **Coptic Christianity**, an orthodox form of the Christian faith that originated in Egypt in 451. Christianity had first come to Ethiopia from Egypt when the archbishop in Alexandria appointed Saint Frumentius the first bishop of Ethiopia in 328. By the early 1500s Ethiopia was an island of Christianity surrounded by a sea of Muslim states.

Adal, a Muslim state along the southern base of the Red Sea, began incursions into Ethiopia, and in 1529 the Adal general Ahmad ibn-Ghazi inflicted a disastrous defeat on the Ethiopian emperor Lebna Dengel (r. 1508–1540). Ahmad followed up his victory with systematic devastation of the land; destruction of many Ethiopian artistic and literary works, churches, and monasteries; and the forced conversion of thousands to Islam. Lebna Dengel fled to the mountains and appealed to Portugal for assistance. A Portuguese force of four hundred men under Christovao da Gama came to his aid, but Dengel was killed in battle before the Portuguese arrived. The Muslim occupation of Christian Ethiopia, which began around 1531, ended in 1543, after a joint Ethiopian and Portuguese force defeated a larger Muslim army at the battle of Wayna Daga on February 21. During the battle Ahmad ibn-Ghazi was killed by a Portuguese musketeer, leaving a horrific legacy of destruction and death that continues to resonate in Ethiopia today.

In the late twelfth century tales of Prester John, rumored to be a powerful Christian monarch ruling a vast and wealthy African empire, reached western Europe. The search for Prester John, as well as for gold and

spices, spurred the Portuguese to undertake a series of trans-African expeditions that reached Timbuktu and Mali in the 1480s and the Ethiopian court by 1508. Although Prester John was a totally mythical figure, Portuguese emissaries triumphantly but mistakenly identified the Ethiopian emperor as Prester John.[8] Desirous of converting Ethiopians from Coptic Christianity to Roman Catholicism, the Portuguese responded to Lebna Dengel's request for help with a force of musketeers. In 1543 they decisively defeated the Muslims near Lake Tana.

No sooner had the Muslim threat ended than Ethiopia encountered three more dangers. The Galla, Cushitic-speaking peoples, moved northward in great numbers, occupying portions of Harar, Shoa, and Amhara. The Ethiopians could not defeat them militarily, and the Galla were not interested in assimilation. For the next two centuries the two peoples lived together in an uneasy truce. Simultaneously, the Ottoman Turks seized Massawa and other coastal cities. Then the Jesuits arrived and attempted to force Roman Catholicism on a proud people whose Coptic form of Christianity long antedated the European version. The overzealous Jesuit missionary Alphonse Mendez tried to revamp the Ethiopian liturgy, rebaptize the people, and

• **Coptic Christianity** Orthodox form of Christianity from Egypt practiced in Ethiopia.

replace ancient Ethiopian customs and practices with Roman ones. Since Ethiopian national sentiment was closely tied to Coptic Christianity, violent rebellion and anarchy ensued.

In 1633 the Jesuit missionaries were expelled. For the next two centuries, hostility to foreigners, weak political leadership, and regionalism characterized Ethiopia. Civil conflicts between Galla and Ethiopia erupted continually. The Coptic Church, though lacking strong authority, survived as the cornerstone of Ethiopian national identity.

The Swahili City-States and the Arrival of the Portuguese, ca. 1500–1600

The word **Swahili** means "People of the Coast" and refers to the people living along the East African coast and on the nearby islands. Although predominantly a Bantu-speaking people, the Swahili have incorporated significant aspects of Arabic culture. The Arabic alphabet was used for the first written works in Swahili (although the Latin alphabet is now standard), and roughly 35 percent of Swahili words come from Arabic. Surviving texts in Swahili — from the earliest known Swahili documents dating from 1711 — provide historians with a glimpse of early Swahili history that is not possible when studying early nonliterate African societies. By the eleventh century the Swahili had accepted Islam, which provided a common identity and unifying factor for all the peoples along coastal East Africa. Living on the Indian Ocean coast, the Swahili also felt the influences of Indians, Indonesians, and Persians.

Swahili civilization was overwhelmingly maritime. A fertile, well-watered, and intensely cultivated stretch of land extending down the coast yielded rice, grains, citrus fruit, and cloves. The region's considerable prosperity, however, rested on trade and commerce. The Swahili acted as middlemen in an Indian Ocean–East African economy that might be described as early capitalism. They exchanged ivory, rhinoceros horn, tortoise shells, inlaid ebony chairs, copra (dried coconut meat that yields coconut oil), and inland slaves for Arabian and Persian perfumes, toilet articles, ink, and paper and for Indian textiles, beads, and iron tools. In the fifteenth century the cosmopolitan city-states of Mogadishu, Pate, Lamu, Mombasa, and especially Kilwa enjoyed a worldwide reputation for commercial prosperity and high living standards.[9]

The arrival of the Portuguese explorer Vasco da Gama (see Map 16.2 on page 469) in 1498 spelled the end of the Swahili cities' independence. Lured by the spice trade, da Gama wanted to build a Portuguese maritime empire in the Indian Ocean. Swahili rulers responded in different ways to Portuguese intrusion. Some, such as the sultan of Malindi, quickly agreed to a trading alliance with the Portuguese. Others, such as the sultan of Mombasa, were tricked into commercial agreements. Still other Swahili rulers totally rejected Portuguese overtures, and their cities were subjected to bombardment. To secure alliances made between 1502 and 1507 the Portuguese erected forts at the southern port cities of Kilwa, Zanzibar, and Sofala. These fortified markets and trading posts served as the foundation of Portuguese commercial power on the Swahili coast. (See "Listening to the Past: Duarte Barbosa on the Swahili City-States," page 570.) The better-fortified northern cities, such as Mogadishu, survived as important entrepôts for goods to India.

The Portuguese presence in the south did not yield the expected commercial fortunes. Rather than accept Portuguese commercial restrictions, the residents deserted the towns, and the town economies crumbled. Large numbers of Kilwa's people, for example, immigrated to northern cities. The gold flow from inland mines to Sofala slowed to a trickle. Swahili noncooperation successfully prevented the Portuguese from gaining control of the local coastal trade.

In 1589 Portugal finally won an administrative stronghold near Mombasa. Called Fort Jesus, it remained a Portuguese base for over a century. In the late seventeenth century pressures from the northern European maritime powers — the Dutch, French, and English, aided greatly by Omani Arabs — combined with local African rebellions to bring about the collapse of Portuguese influence in Africa. A Portuguese presence remained only at Mozambique in the far south and Angola on the west coast.

The Portuguese had no religious or cultural impact on the Swahili cities. Their sole effect was the cities' economic decline.

The African Slave Trade

☐ What role did slavery play in African societies before the transatlantic slave trade began, and what was the effect of European involvement?

The exchange of peoples captured in local and ethnic wars within sub-Saharan Africa, the trans-Saharan slave trade with the Mediterranean Islamic world beginning in the seventh century, and the slave traffic across the Indian Ocean all testify to the long tradition and continental dimensions of the African slave trade before European intrusion. The enslavement of human beings was practiced in some form or another all over

• **Swahili** Meaning "People of the Coast," the term used for the people living along the East African coast and on nearby islands.

□ Picturing the Past

Chinese Porcelain Plates Embedded in an eighteenth-century Kunduchi pillar tomb, these Chinese plates testify to the enormous Asian-African trade that flourished in the fourteenth to sixteenth centuries. Kunduchi, whose ruins lie north of Dar es Salaam in present-day Tanzania, was one of the Swahili city-states. (Werner Forman/Art Resource, NY)

ANALYZING THE IMAGE How many Chinese plates can you identify? What features identify this as a tomb?

CONNECTIONS Why would a Muslim African want a Chinese plate embedded in his tomb? What does this suggest about his status, occupation, and wealth?

Africa—indeed, all over the world. Sanctioned by law and custom, enslaved people served critical and well-defined roles in the social, political, and economic organization of many African societies. Domestically these roles ranged from concubines and servants to royal guards and advisers. As later in the Americas, some enslaved people were common laborers. Economically, slaves were commodities for trade, more or less important than other trade items, such as gold and ivory.

The trans-Saharan slave trade became less important than the transatlantic trade, which witnessed an explosive growth during the seventeenth and eighteenth centuries. The millions of enslaved Africans forcibly exported to the Americas would have a lasting impact on African society and would lead ultimately to a wider use of slaves within Africa itself.

The Institution of Slavery in Africa

Islamic practices strongly influenced African slavery. African rulers justified enslavement with the Muslim argument that prisoners of war could be sold and that

Listening to the Past

Duarte Barbosa on the Swahili City-States

The Portuguese writer, government agent, and traveler Duarte Barbosa made two voyages to India. Arriving first in 1500, he acted for five years as interpreter and translator in Cochin and Cananor in Kerala (in southwestern India on the Malabar Coast), returning to Lisbon in 1506. On his second trip to India in 1511, he served the Portuguese government as chief scribe in the factory of Cananor (a factory was a warehouse for the storage of goods, not a manufacturing center) and as the liaison with the local Indian rajah (prince). Barbosa returned to Portugal around 1516. In September 1519 he began his greatest adventure, setting off with Ferdinand Magellan to circumnavigate the globe. Magellan was killed in a battle with native forces in the Philippines. Barbosa then took joint command of the expedition, but was himself killed in the Philippines less than a week after Magellan, on May 1, 1521.

On the basis of his trips around the Indian Ocean in 1518, Barbosa completed his Libro de Duarte Barbosa *(The Book of Duarte Barbosa), a geographical and ethnographic survey of peoples, lands, and commerce from the Cape of Good Hope to China. It was based largely on his personal observations. First published in Italian, the book won wide acclaim in Europe, and modern scholars consider its geographical information very accurate. The excerpts below describe some of the city-states along the East African coast of Swahili.*

Sofala

66And the manner of their traffic was this: they came in small vessels named *zambucos* from the kingdoms of Kilwa, Mombasa, and Malindi, bringing many cotton cloths, some spotted and others white and blue, also some of silk, and many small beads, grey, red, and yellow, which things come to the said kingdoms from the great kingdom of Cambaya [in northwest India] in other greater ships. And these wares the said Moors who came from Malindi and Mombasa paid for in gold at such a price that those merchants departed well pleased; which gold they gave by weight.

The Moors of Sofala kept these wares and sold them afterwards to the Heathen of the Kingdom of Benametapa, who came thither laden with gold which they gave in exchange for the said cloths without weighing it. These Moors collect also great store of ivory which they find hard by Sofala, and this also they sell in the Kingdom of Cambaya at five or six cruzados the quintal. They also sell some ambergris, which is brought to them from the Hucicas, and is exceeding good. These Moors are black, and some of them tawny; some of them speak Arabic, but the more part use the language of the country. They clothe themselves from the waist down with cotton and silk cloths, and other cloths they wear over their shoulders like capes, and turbans on their heads. Some of them wear small caps dyed in grain in chequers and other woollen clothes in many tints, also camlets and other silks.

Their food is millet, rice, flesh and fish. In this river as far as the sea are many sea horses, which come out on the land to graze, which horses always move in the sea like fishes; they have tusks like those of small elephants in size, and the ivory is better than that of elephants, being whiter and harder, and it never loses colour. In the country near Sofala are many wild elephants, exceeding great (which the country-folk know not how to tame) ounces, lions, deer and many other wild beasts. It is a land of plains and hills with many streams of sweet water. . . . 99

Kilwa

66Going along the coast from this town of Mozambique, there is an island hard by the mainland which is called Kilwa, in which is a Moorish town with many fair houses of stone and mortar, with many windows after our fashion, very well arranged in streets, with many flat roofs. The doors are of wood, well carved, with excellent joinery. Around it are streams and orchards and fruit-gardens with many channels of sweet water. It has a Moorish king over it. From this place they trade with Sofala, whence they bring back gold, and from here they spread all over . . . the seacoast [which] is well-peopled with villages and abodes of Moors.

Before the King our Lord sent out his expedition to discover India the Moors of Sofala, Cuama, Angoya and Mozambique

captured people were considered chattel, or personal possessions, to be used any way the owner saw fit. Between 650 and 1600, black as well as white Muslims transported perhaps as many as 4.82 million black slaves across the trans-Saharan trade route.[10] In the fourteenth and fifteenth centuries the rulers and elites of Mali and Benin imported thousands of white Slavic slave women, symbols of wealth and status, who had been seized in slave raids from the Balkans and Caucasus regions of the eastern Mediterranean by Turks, Mongols, and others.[11] In 1444, when Portuguese caravels landed 235 slaves at Algarve in southern Portugal, a contemporary observed that they seemed "a marvelous (extraordinary) sight, for, amongst them, were some were all subject to the King of Kilwa, who was the most mighty king among them. And in this town was great plenty of gold, as no ships passed towards Sofala without first coming to this island. . . .

This town was taken by force from its king by the Portuguese, as, moved by arrogance, he refused to obey the King our Lord. There they took many prisoners and the king fled from the island, and His Highness ordered that a fort should be built there, and kept it under his rule and governance. Afterwards he ordered that it should be pulled down, as its maintenance was of no value nor profit to him, and it was destroyed by Antonio de Saldanha. . . . "

Malindi

" . . . Journeying along the coast towards India, there is a fair town on the mainland lying along a strand, which is named Malindi. It pertains to the Moors and has a Moorish king over it; the which place has many fair stone and mortar houses of many storeys, with great plenty of windows and flat roofs, after our fashion. The place is well laid out in streets. The folk are both black and white; they go naked, covering only their private parts with cotton and silk cloths. Others of them wear cloths folded like cloaks and waist-bands, and turbans of many rich stuffs on their heads.

They are great barterers, and deal in cloth, gold, ivory, and divers other wares with the Moors and Heathen of the great kingdom of Cambaya; and to their haven come every year many ships with cargoes of merchandize, from which they get great store of gold, ivory and wax. In this traffic the Cambay merchants make great profits, and thus, on one side and the other, they earn much money. There is great plenty of food in this city (rice, millet, and some wheat which they bring from Cambaya), and divers sorts of fruit, inasmuch as there is here abundance of fruit-gardens and orchards. Here too are plenty of round-tailed sheep, cows and other cattle and great store of oranges, also of hens.

The king and people of this place ever were and are friends of the King of Portugal, and the Portuguese always find in them great comfort and friendship and perfect peace, "and there the ships, when they chance to pass that way, obtain supplies in plenty." "

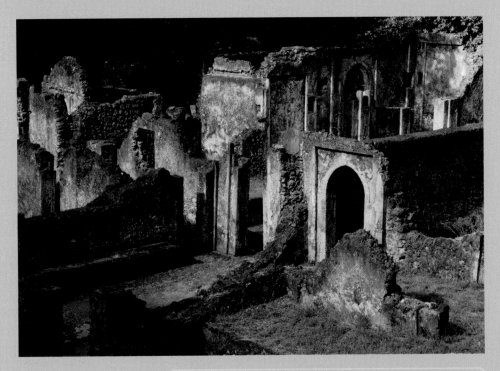

The walls of the sultan's palace sit silently amidst the ruins at Gedi, a historic Swahili site a few miles south of Malindi on the Kenyan coast. Founded in the late thirteenth or early fourteenth century, it survived as a thriving trading community until the early seventeenth century. Although it was not a major Swahili town, excavations have uncovered iron lamps from India, scissors from Spain, a Chinese Ming vase, Persian stoneware, and Venetian beads. Some homes had bathrooms with running water and flush toilets, and the streets had drainage gutters. The dated tomb in the cemetery has 1399 incised in its plaster wall. (Ariadne Van Zandbergen/Lonely Planet Images)

Source: Dames, Mansel Longworth, trans., *The Book of Duarte Barbosa, Volume 1* (London: Bedford Press, 1918).

QUESTIONS FOR ANALYSIS

1. What seems to have impressed Barbosa? What was his attitude toward the various peoples he saw? What Portuguese or Western prejudices do you discern?
2. What was the Portuguese relationship to the Swahili city-states at the time Barbosa saw them?
3. What was the source of Sofala's gold? Of Sofala's and Malindi's ivory? What did the Indian kingdom of Cambaya use ivory for?

white enough, fair enough, and well-proportioned; others were less white, like mulattoes; others again were black as Ethiops."[12]

Meanwhile, the flow of black people to Europe, begun during the Renaissance, continued. In the seventeenth and eighteenth centuries as many as two hundred thousand Africans entered European societies.

Some arrived as slaves, others as servants; the legal distinction was not always clear. Eighteenth-century London, for example, had more than ten thousand blacks, most of whom arrived as sailors on Atlantic crossings or as personal servants brought from the West Indies. In England most were free, not slaves. Initially, a handsome black was a fashionable accessory, a rare status symbol. Later, English aristocrats considered black servants too ordinary. The duchess of Devonshire offered her mother an eleven-year-old boy, explaining that the duke did not want a Negro servant because "it was more original to have a Chinese page than to have a black one; everybody had a black one."[13] London's black population constituted a well-organized, self-conscious subculture, with black pubs, black churches, and black social groups assisting the black poor and unemployed. Some black people attained wealth and position, the most famous being Francis Barber, manservant of the sixteenth-century British literary giant Samuel Johnson and heir to Johnson's papers and to most of his sizable fortune. Barber had helped Johnson in revising Johnson's famous *Dictionary of the English Language*, published in 1755, and he is frequently mentioned in the celebrated biography of Johnson by James Boswell. He was a contemporary of another well-known African who lived in London for a while, Olaudah Equiano.

In 1658 the Dutch East India Company (see page 481) began to allow the importation of slaves into the Cape Colony, which the company had founded on the southern tip of Africa in 1652. Over the next century and a half about 75 percent of the slaves brought into the colony came from Dutch East India Company colonies in India and Southeast Asia or from Madagascar; the remaining 25 percent came from Africa. Some of those enslaved at the Cape served as domestic servants or as semiskilled artisans, but most worked long and hard as field hands and at any other menial or manual forms of labor needed by their European masters.

The Dutch East India Company was the single largest slave owner in the Cape Colony, employing its slaves on public works and company farms. Initially, individual company officials collectively owned the most slaves, working them on their wine and grain estates, but by about 1740 urban and rural free burghers owned the majority of the slaves. In 1780 half of all white men at the Cape had at least one slave, as slave ownership fostered a strong sense of racial and economic solidarity in the white master class.

The slave population at the Cape was never large, although from the early 1700s to the 1820s it outnumbered the European free burgher population. When the British ended slavery in the British Empire in 1834, there were around thirty-six thousand slaves in

Cape Colony, ca. 1750

the Cape Colony. In comparison, over three hundred thousand enslaved Africans labored on the Caribbean island of Jamaica, also a British slaveholding colony at the time.

Although in the seventeenth and eighteenth centuries Holland enjoyed a Europe-wide reputation for religious toleration and intellectual freedom (see page 515), in the Cape Colony the Dutch used a strict racial hierarchy and heavy-handed paternalism to maintain control over enslaved native and foreign-born peoples. Early accounts of slavery at the Cape often gave the impression that it was a relatively benign institution in comparison with slavery in the Americas. Modern scholars, however, consider slavery in the Cape Colony in many ways as oppressive as slavery in the Americas and the Muslim world. In Muslim society, the offspring of a freeman and an enslaved woman were free, but in southern Africa such children remained enslaved. Because enslaved males greatly outnumbered enslaved females in the Cape Colony, marriage and family life were almost nonexistent. Because there were few occupations requiring special skills, those enslaved in the colony lacked opportunities to earn manumission. And in contrast with North and South America and with Muslim societies, in the Cape Colony only a very small number of those enslaved won manumission; most of them were women, suggesting sexual or close personal relationships with their owners.[14]

The savanna and Horn regions of East Africa experienced a great expansion of the slave trade in the late eighteenth century and the first half of the nineteenth century. Exports of slaves from these areas and from the eastern coast of Africa amounted to perhaps thirty thousand a year. Why this demand? Merchants and planters wanted slaves to work the sugar plantations on the Mascarene Islands, located east of Madagascar, the clove plantations on Zanzibar and Pemba, and the food plantations along the Kenyan coast. The eastern coast also exported enslaved people to the Americas, particularly to Brazil. In the late eighteenth and early nineteenth centuries, precisely when the slave trade to North America and the Caribbean declined, the Arabian and Asian markets expanded. Only with colonial conquest of Africa by Great Britain, Germany, and Italy after 1870 did suppression of the trade begin. Enslavement, of course, persists even today. (See "Global Trade: Slaves," page 574.)

The Transatlantic Slave Trade

Although the trade in African people was a worldwide phenomenon, the transatlantic slave trade involved the largest number of enslaved Africans. This forced

KITCHIN STUFF.

Below Stairs The prints and cartoons of Thomas Rowlandson (1756–1827) testify to the sizable numbers of blacks in eighteenth-century London, where they worked in naval and military as well as domestic service. Here the household cook, maid, and footman relax before the kitchen fire. Interracial marriages were not uncommon. (Courtesy of the Trustees of the British Museum)

migration of millions of human beings, extending from the early sixteenth to the late nineteenth centuries, represents one of the most inhumane, unjust, and shameful tragedies in human history. It also immediately provokes a troubling question: Why Africa? Why, in the seventeenth and eighteenth centuries, did enslavement in the Americas become exclusively African?

European settlers first enslaved indigenous peoples, the Amerindians, to mine the silver and gold discovered in the New World (see page 480). When they proved ill suited to the harsh rigors of mining, the Spaniards brought in Africans. Although the Dutch had transported Indonesian peoples to work as slaves in the Cape Colony in South Africa, the cost of transporting Chinese or Pacific island peoples to the Americas was far too great.

One scholar has argued that a pan-European insider-outsider ideology prevailed across Europe. This cultural attitude permitted the enslavement of outsiders but made the enslavement of white Europeans taboo. Europeans could not bear the sight of other Europeans doing plantation slave labor. According to this theory, a similar pan-African ideology did not exist, as Africans had no problem with selling Africans to Europeans.[15] Several facts argue against the validity of this theory. English landlords exploited their Irish peasants with merciless severity; French aristocrats often looked on their peasantry with cold contempt; and Russian boyars treated their serfs with casual indifference and harsh brutality. These and other possible examples contradict the existence of a pan-European ideology or culture that opposed the enslavement of white Europeans. Moreover, the flow of white enslaved Slavic peoples from the Balkans into the eastern Mediterranean continued unabated during the same period.

Another theory holds that in the Muslim and Arab worlds by the tenth century, an association had developed between blackness and menial slavery. The Arab word *abd*, or "black," had become synonymous with *slave*. Although the great majority of enslaved persons in the Islamic world were white, a racial element existed in Muslim perceptions: not all slaves were black, but blacks were identified with slavery. In Europe, after the arrival of tens of thousands of sub-Saharan Africans in the Iberian Peninsula during the fifteenth century, Christian Europeans also began to make a strong association between slavery and black Africans. Therefore, Africans seemed the "logical" solution to the labor shortage in the Americas.[16]

Another important question relating to the African slave trade is this: Why were African peoples enslaved in a period when serfdom was declining in western Europe, and when land was so widely available and much of the African continent had a labor shortage? The answer seems to lie in a technical problem related to African agriculture. Partly because of the tsetse fly, which causes sleeping sickness and other diseases, and partly because of easily leached lateritic soils (containing high concentrations of oxides), farmers had great difficulty using draft animals. Tropical soils responded poorly to plowing, and most work had to be done with the hoe. Productivity, therefore, was low. Economists maintain that in most societies, the value of a worker's productivity determines the value of his or her labor. In precolonial Africa, the individual's agricultural productivity was low, so his or her economic value to society was less than the economic value of a European peasant in Europe. Enslaved persons in the Americas were more productive than free producers in Africa. And European slave dealers were very willing to pay a price higher than the value of an African's productivity in Africa.

The incidence of disease in the Americas also helps explain African enslavement. Smallpox took a terrible toll on Native Americans (see page 577), and between 30 and 50 percent of Europeans exposed to malaria succumbed to that sickness. Africans had developed some

Global Trade

Slaves

are people who are bound to servitude and often traded as property or as a commodity. The traffic in human persons bought and sold for the profits of their labor cannot decently be compared to the buying and selling of other commodities; people are not goods. But most societies, with the remarkable exception of the Aborigines in Australia, have treated people as goods and have engaged in the slave trade. Those who have been enslaved include captives in war, persons convicted of crimes, persons sold for debt, and persons bought and sold for sex. The ancient Greek philosophers, notably Aristotle, justified slavery as "natural." The Middle Eastern monotheistic faiths—Judaism, Christianity, and Islam—while professing the sacred dignity of each individual, and the Asian religious and sociopolitical ideologies of Buddhism and Confucianism, while stressing an ordered and harmonious society, all tolerated slavery and urged slaves' obedience to established authorities. Until the Enlightenment of the eighteenth century, most people everywhere accepted slavery as a "natural phenomenon." It is not without irony that the Thirteenth Amendment to the U.S. Constitution (ratified in 1865), popularly interpreted as abolishing slavery, allows slavery "as a punishment for crime whereof the party shall have been duly convicted."

Between 1500 and 1900 the transatlantic African slave trade accounted for the largest number of people bought and sold. As such, and because of ample documentation, it has attracted much of the attention of scholars, and it also has tended to identify the institution of slavery with African blacks. From a global perspective, however, the trade was far broader.

MAP 19.3 The International Slave Trade

The revolting conditions on slave ships sailing to Caribbean and North American ports pale in barbarity beside conditions on the southern route to Brazil, where slaves were literally packed like sardines in a can. (Visual Connection Archive)

Slaves came from all over the world and included people of all races. The steady flow of white women and children from the Crimea, the Caucasus, and the Balkans in the fourteenth to eighteenth centuries for domestic, military, or sexual services in Ottoman lands, Italy, and sub-Saharan Africa; the use of convicts as galley slaves in the Venetian, French, Spanish, and Turkish navies; the enslavement of peoples defeated in war by Aztec, Inca, Sioux, Navajo, and other indigenous peoples of the Americas; the various forms of debt slavery in China and in Russia (where the legal distinction between serf and slave before 1861 was very hazy); the traffic of Indonesian and Pacific island peoples for slave labor in Dutch South Africa; and the trans-Saharan stream of Africans to Mediterranean ports that continued at medieval rates into the late nineteenth century—all were different forms of a worldwide practice. Although these forms sometimes had little in common with one another, they all involved the buying and selling of human beings who could not move about freely or enjoy the fruits of their labor.

The price of slaves varied widely over time and from market to market, according to age, sex, physical appearance, buyers' perceptions of the social characteristics of each slave's ethnic background, and changes in supply and demand. The Mediterranean and Indian Ocean markets preferred women for domestic service; the Atlantic markets wanted strong young men for mine and plantation work, for example. We have little solid information on prices for slaves in the Balkans, Caucasus, or Indian Ocean region. Even in the Atlantic trade, it is difficult to determine, over several centuries, the value of currencies, the cost and insurance on transported slaves, and the cost of goods exchanged for slaves. Yet the gold-encrusted cathedrals of Spain and the elegant plantation houses of the southern United States stand as testimony to the vast fortunes made in the slave trade.

How is the human toll of slavery measured? Transformations within societies occurred not only because of local developments but also because of interactions among regions. For example, the virulent racism that in so many ways defines the American experience resulted partly from medieval European habits of dehumanizing the enemy (English versus Irish, German versus Slav, Christian versus Jew and Muslim) and partly from the movement of peoples and ideas all over the globe. American gold prospectors in the 1850s carried the bigotry they had heaped on blacks in the Americas to Australia, where it conditioned attitudes toward Asians and other peoples of color. Racism, like the slave trade, is a global phenomenon.

For all the cries for human rights today, the slave trade continues on a broad scale. The ancient Indian Ocean traffic in Indian girls and boys for "service" in the Persian Gulf oil kingdoms persists, as does the sale of African children for work in Asia. In 2011 an estimated 12 to 27 million people globally are held in one form of slavery or another. The U.S. State Department estimates that 15,000 to 18,000 enslaved foreign nationals are brought to the United States each year and, conservatively, perhaps as many as 50,000 people, mostly women and children, are in slavery in America at any given time. They have been bought, sold, tricked, and held in captivity, and their labor, often as sex slaves, has been exploited for the financial benefit of masters in a global enterprise.

immunity to both diseases, and in the Americas they experienced the lowest mortality rate of any people, making them, ironically, the most suitable workers for the environment.

In 1500 a Portuguese fleet en route to India around Africa sailed too far west into the Atlantic and made landfall on the coast of modern Brazil. Although its commander, Pedro Cabral, did not know where he was, he followed the common practice (see page 465) and immediately claimed the land for King Manuel I, the Portuguese monarch. Colonization began in the early 1530s, and in 1551 the Portuguese founded a sugar colony at Bahia. Between 1551 and 1575, before the North American slave traffic began, the Portuguese delivered more African slaves to Brazil than would ever reach British North America (see Figure 19.1). Portugal essentially monopolized the slave trade until 1600 and continued to play a large role in the seventeenth century, though the trade was in-

The Slave Coast of West Africa

creasingly taken over by the Dutch, French, and English. From 1690 until the British House of Commons abolished the slave trade in 1807, England was the leading carrier of African slaves.

Population density and supply conditions along the West African coast and the sailing time to New World markets determined the sources of slaves. As the demand for slaves rose, slavers moved down the West African coast from Senegambia to the more densely populated hinterlands of the Bight of Benin and the Bight of Biafra. The abundant supply of Africans to enslave in Angola, the region south of the Congo River, and the quick passage from Angola to Brazil and the Caribbean established that region as the major coast for Portuguese slavers.

Transatlantic wind patterns partly determined exchange routes. Shippers naturally preferred the swiftest crossing — that is, from the African port nearest the latitude of the intended American destination. Thus Portuguese shippers carried their cargoes from Angola to Brazil, and British merchants sailed from the Bight of Benin to the Caribbean. The great majority of enslaved Africans were intended for the sugar and coffee plantations extending from the Caribbean islands to Brazil. Angola produced 26 percent of all African slaves and 70 percent of all Portuguese slaves. Trading networks extending deep into the interior culminated at two major ports on the Angolan coast, Luanda and Benguela. The Portuguese acquired a few slaves through warfare but secured the vast majority through trade with African dealers. Whites did not participate in the inland markets, which were run solely by Africans.

Almost all Portuguese shipments went to satisfy the virtually insatiable Brazilian demand for slaves. The so-called **Middle Passage** was the horrific journey experienced by Africans from freedom to enslavement in the Americas. Here is an excerpt from a Portuguese doctor's 1793 report on conditions in Luanda before the voyage across the Atlantic had begun. Be sure to note in this and subsequent quotations how the enslaved peoples are clearly considered, and treated, as chattel:

> The dwelling place of the slave is simply the dirt floor of the compound, and he remains there exposed to harsh conditions and bad weather, and at night there are only a lean-to and some sheds . . . which they are herded into like cattle.
>
> Their food continues scarce as before . . . limited at times to badly cooked beans, at other times to corn. . . .

FIGURE 19.1 Estimated Slave Imports by Destination, 1501–1866 Brazil was the single largest importer of African slaves from 1501 to 1866. But when taken cumulatively, the British, French, Dutch, and Danish colonies of the Caribbean rivaled the much larger colony of Brazil for numbers of slaves imported from Africa. (Source: Data from Emory University. "Assessing the Slave Trade: Estimates," in *Voyages: The Trans-Atlantic Slave Trade Database.* 2009. http://www.slavevoyages.org.)

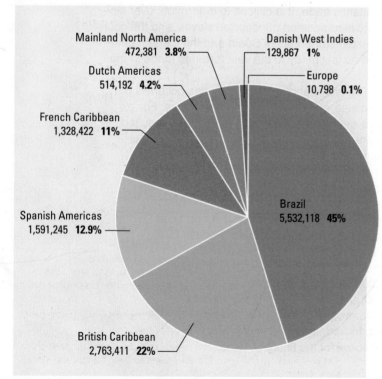

And when they reach a port . . . , they are branded on the right breast with the coat of arms of the king and nation, of whom they have become vassals. . . . This mark is made with a hot silver instrument in the act of paying the king's duties, and this brand mark is called a *carimbo*. . . .

In this miserable and deprived condition the terrified slaves remain for weeks and months, and the great number of them who die is unspeakable. With some ten or twelve thousand arriving at Luanda each year, it often happens that only six or seven thousand are finally transported to Brazil.[17]

Conditions during the Middle Passage were even worse. Olaudah Equiano (see "Individuals in Society: Olaudah Equiano," page 578) describes the experience of his voyage as a captured slave from Benin to Barbados in the Caribbean:

At last, when the ship we were in had got in all her cargo [of slaves], they made ready with many fearful noises, and we were all put under deck so that we could not see how they managed the vessel. . . . The stench of the hold while we were on the coast was so intolerably loathsome that it was dangerous to remain there for any time, and some of us had been permitted to stay on the deck for the fresh air; but now that the whole ship's cargo were confined together it became absolutely pestilential. The closeness of the place and the heat of the climate, added to the number in the ship, which was so crowded that each had scarcely room to turn himself, almost suffocated us. This produced copious perspirations, so that the air soon became unfit for respiration from a variety of loathsome smells, and brought on a sickness among the slaves, of which many died, thus falling victims to the improvident avarice, as I may call it, of their purchasers. This wretched situation was again aggravated by the galling of the chains, now become insupportable, and the filth of the necessary tubs [of human waste], into which the children often fell and were almost suffocated. The shrieks of the women and the groans of the dying rendered the whole a scene of horror almost inconceivable.[18]

Although the demand was great, Portuguese merchants in Angola and Brazil sought to maintain only a steady trickle of slaves from the African interior to Luanda and across the ocean to Bahia and Rio de Janeiro: a flood of slaves would have depressed the American market. Rio, the port capital through which most enslaved Africans passed, commanded the Brazilian trade. Planters and mine operators from the provinces traveled to Rio to buy slaves. Between 1795 and 1808, approximately 10,000 Angolans per year stood in the Rio slave market. In 1810 the figure rose to 18,000; in 1828 it reached 32,000.[19]

The English ports of London, Bristol, and particularly Liverpool dominated the British slave trade. In the eighteenth century Liverpool was the world's greatest slave-trading port. In all three cities, small and cohesive merchant classes exercised great public influence. The cities also had huge stores of industrial products for export, growing shipping industries, and large amounts of ready cash for investment abroad. Merchants generally formed partnerships to raise capital and to share the risks; each voyage was a separate enterprise or venture.

Slaving ships from Bristol plied back and forth along the Gold Coast, the Bight of Benin, Bonny, and Calabar looking for African traders who were willing to supply them with slaves. Liverpool's ships drew enslaved people from Gambia, the Windward Coast, and the Gold Coast. British ships carried textiles, gunpowder and flint, beer and spirits, British and Irish linens, and woolen cloth to Africa. A collection of goods was grouped together into what was called the **sorting**. An English sorting might include bolts of cloth, firearms, alcohol, tobacco, and hardware; this batch of goods would be traded for an enslaved individual or a quantity of gold, ivory, or dyewood.[20]

European traders had two systems for exchange. First, especially on the Gold Coast, they established factory-forts (for more on factory-forts, see page 608). These fortified trading posts were expensive to maintain but proved useful for fending off European rivals. Second, they used **shore trading**, in which European ships sent boats ashore or invited African dealers to bring traders and enslaved Africans out to the ships. The English captain John Adams, who made ten voyages to Africa between 1786 and 1800, described the shore method of trading at Bonny:

This place is the wholesale market for slaves, as not fewer than 20,000 are annually sold here; 16,000 of whom are natives of one nation called Ibo. . . . Fairs where the slaves of the Ibo nation are obtained are held every five or six weeks at several villages, which are situated on the banks of the rivers and creeks in the interior, and to which the African traders of Bonny resort to purchase them.

. . . The traders augment the quantity of their merchandise, by obtaining from their friends, the captains of the slave ships, a considerable quantity

- **Middle Passage** African slaves' voyage across the Atlantic to the Americas, a long and treacherous journey during which slaves endured appalling and often deadly conditions.

- **sorting** A collection or batch of British goods that would be traded for a slave or for a quantity of gold, ivory, or dyewood.

- **shore trading** A process for trading goods in which European ships sent boats ashore or invited African dealers to bring traders and slaves out to the ships.

Individuals in Society

Olaudah Equiano

THE TRANSATLANTIC SLAVE TRADE WAS A MASS movement involving millions of human beings. It was also the sum of individual lives spent partly or entirely in slavery. Most of those lives remain hidden to us. Olaudah Equiano (1745–1797) represents a rare ray of light into the slaves' obscurity; he is probably the best-known African slave.

In his autobiography, *The Interesting Narrative of the Life of Olaudah Equiano* (1789), Equiano says that he was born in Benin (modern Nigeria) of Ibo ethnicity.* His father, one of the village elders (or chieftains), presided over a large household that included "many slaves," prisoners captured in local wars. All people, slave and free, shared in the cultivation of family lands. One day, when all the adults were in the fields, two strange men and a woman broke into the family compound, kidnapped the eleven-year-old Olaudah and his sister, tied them up, and dragged them into the woods. Brother and sister were separated, and Olaudah was sold several times to various dealers before reaching the coast. As it took six months to walk there, his home must have been far inland. The sea, the slave ship, and the strange appearance of the white crew terrified the boy (see page 577). Equiano's master took him to Jamaica, to Virginia, and then to England, where he placed him in the custody of a kind family. They gave him the rudiments of an education, and he was baptized a Christian.

Equiano soon went to sea as a captain's boy (servant), serving in the Royal Navy during the Seven Years' War. On shore at Portsmouth, England, after one battle, Equiano was urged by his master to read, study, and learn basic mathematics. This education served him well, for after a voyage to the West Indies, his master sold him to a Philadelphia Quaker, Robert King, who was a rum and sugar merchant. Equiano worked as a clerk in King's warehouse, as a longshoreman loading and unloading cargo ships, and at sea where he developed good navigational skills; King paid him for his work. Equiano became an entrepreneur himself, buying and selling small goods in the islands and mainland ports. Determined to buy his freedom, Equiano had amassed enough money by 1766, and King signed the deed of manumission. Equiano was twenty-one years old; he had been a slave for ten years.

Equiano returned to London and used his remaining money to hire tutors to teach him hairdressing, mathematics, and how to play the French horn. When money was scarce, he found work as a merchant seaman, traveling to Portugal, Nice, Genoa, Naples, and Turkey. He even participated in an Arctic expedition.

Equiano's *Narrative* reveals a complex and sophisticated man. He had a strong constitution and an equally strong character. His Christian faith undoubtedly sustained him. On the title page of his book, he cited a verse from Isaiah (12:2): "The Lord Jehovah is my strength and my song." The very first thought that came to his mind the day he was freed was a passage from Psalm 126: "I glorified God in my heart, in whom I trusted."

Equiano loathed the brutal slavery he saw in the West Indies and the vicious racism he experienced in the North American colonies. He respected the fairness of Robert King, admired British navigational and industrial technologies, and had many close white friends. He once described himself as "almost an Englishman." He was also involved in the black communities in the West Indies and in London. Equiano's *Narrative* is a well-documented argument for the abolition of slavery and a literary classic that went through nine editions before his death.

Olaudah Equiano's *Narrative*, with its horrific descriptions of slavery, proved influential, and after its publication Equiano became active in the abolition movement. He spoke to large crowds in the industrial cities of Manchester and Birmingham in England, arguing that it was in the business interests of manufacturers to support abolition, as Africa was a huge, virtually untapped market for English cloth. Though he died in 1797, ten years before its passage, Equiano significantly advanced the abolitionist cause that led to the Slave Trade Act of 1807.

Source: *Equiano's Travels: The Interesting Narrative of the Life of Olaudah Equiano*, ed. Paul Edwards (Portsmouth, N.H.: Heinemann, 1996).

Olaudah Equiano, 1789, dressed as an elegant Englishman, his Bible open to the book of Acts. (National Portrait Gallery, Smithsonian Institution/Art Resource, NY)

*Recent scholarship has re-examined Equiano's life and raised some questions about his African origins and his experience of the Middle Passage. To explore the debate over Equiano's authorship of the African and Middle Passage portions of his autobiography, see Vincent Carretta, *Equiano, the African: Biography of a Self-Made Man* (New York: Penguin, 2007).

QUESTIONS FOR ANALYSIS

1. How typical was Olaudah Equiano's life as a slave? How atypical?
2. Describe Equiano's culture and his sense of himself.

Peddlers in Rio de Janeiro A British army officer sketched this early-nineteenth-century scene of everyday life in Rio de Janeiro, Brazil. The ability to balance large burdens on the head meant that the person's hands were free for other use. Note the player (on the left) of a musical instrument originating in the Congo. On the right a woman gives alms to the man with the holy image in return for being allowed to kiss the image as an act of devotion. We do not know whether the peddlers were free and self-employed or were selling for their owners. (From "Views and Costumes of the City and Neighborhood of Rio de Janeiro, Brazil," in *Drawings Taken by Lieutenant Henry Chamberlain, During the Years 1819 and 1820* [London: Columbian Press, 1822])

of goods on credit. . . . Evening is the period chosen for the time of departure, when they proceed in a body, accompanied by the noise of drums, horns, and gongs. At the expiration of the sixth day, they generally return bringing with them 1,500 or 2,000 slaves, who are sold to Europeans the evening after their arrival, and taken on board the ships. . . .

It is expected that every vessel, on her arrival at Bonny, will fire a salute the instant the anchor is let go, as a compliment to the black monarch who soon afterwards makes his appearance in a large canoe, at which time, all those natives who happen to be alongside the vessel are compelled to proceed in their canoes to a respectful distance, and make way for his Majesty's barge. After a few compliments to the captain, he usually enquires after brother George, meaning the King of England, George III, and hopes he and his family are well. He is not pleased unless he is regaled with the best the ship affords. . . . His power is absolute; and the surrounding country, to a considerable distance, is subject to his dominion.[21]

The shore method of buying slaves allowed the ship to move easily from market to market. The final prices of those enslaved depended on their ethnic origin, their availability when the shipper arrived, and their physical health when offered for sale in the West Indies or the North or South American colonies.

Supplying slaves for the foreign market was controlled by a small, wealthy African merchant class, or it was a state monopoly. By contemporary standards, slave raiding was a costly operation: gathering a band of raiders and the capital for equipment, guides, tolls, and supplies involved considerable expense. Only black African entrepreneurs with sizable capital and labor could afford to finance and direct raiding drives. They exported enslaved men and women because the profits on exports were greater than the profits to be made from using labor in the domestic economy.

The transatlantic slave trade that the British, as well as the Dutch, Portuguese, French, Americans, and others, participated in was part of a much larger trading network that is known in history as the "triangle trade." European merchants sailed to Africa on the first leg of the voyage to trade European manufactured goods for enslaved Africans. When they had filled their ships' holds with enslaved peoples, they headed across the Atlantic on the second leg of the voyage, the Middle Passage. When they reached the Americas the merchants unloaded and sold their human cargoes and used the profits to purchase raw materials — cotton, sugar, indigo — that they then transported back to Europe, completing the third leg of the commercial triangle.

Enslaved African people had an enormous impact on the economics of the Portuguese and Spanish colonies of South America and in the Dutch, French, and British colonies of the Caribbean and North America. For example, on the sugar plantations of Mexico and the Caribbean; on the cotton, rice, and tobacco plantations of North America; and in the silver and gold mines of

The African Slave Trade Enslaved African men, women, and children, captured in the interior, are marched to the coast by their African captors. The guards carry guns obtained from Europeans in the slave trade. The enslaved men are linked together by heavy wooden yokes, making it impossible to escape. (The Granger Collection, New York)

Peru and Mexico, enslaved Africans not only worked in the mines and fields but also filled skilled, supervisory, and administrative positions and performed domestic service. In the United States, enslaved Africans and their descendants influenced many facets of American culture, such as language, music (ragtime and jazz), dance, and diet. Even the U.S. Capitol building, where Congress meets, was built partly by slave labor.[22] But the importance of the slave trade extended beyond the Atlantic world. The expansion of capitalism, as well as the industrialization of Western societies, Egypt, and the nations of West, Central, and South Africa — all related in one way or another to the traffic in African people.

Impact on African Societies

What economic impact did European trade have on African societies? Africans possessed technology well suited to their environment. Over the centuries, they had cultivated a wide variety of plant foods; developed plant and animal husbandry techniques; and mined, smelted, and otherwise worked a great variety of metals. Apart from firearms, American tobacco and rum, and the cheap brandy brought by the Portuguese, European goods presented no novelty to Africans. They found foreign products desirable because of their low prices.

Traders of handwoven Indian cotton textiles, Venetian imitations of African beads, and iron bars from European smelters could undersell African manufacturers. Africans exchanged slaves, ivory, gold, pepper, and animal skins for those goods. African states eager to expand or to control commerce bought European firearms, although the difficulty of maintaining guns often gave gun owners only marginal superiority over skilled bowmen.[23] The kingdom of Dahomey (modern-day Benin in West Africa), however, built its power on the effective use of firearms.

The African merchants who controlled the production of exports gained the most from foreign trade. Dahomey's king, for example, had a gross income in 1750 of £250,000 (almost U.S. $33 million today) from the overseas export of his fellow Africans. A portion of his profit was spent on goods that improved his people's living standard. Slave-trading entrepôts, which provided opportunities for traders and for farmers who supplied foodstuffs to towns, caravans, and slave ships, prospered. But such economic returns did not spread very far.[24] International trade did not lead to Africa's economic development. Africa experienced neither technological growth nor the gradual spread of economic benefits in early modern times.

As in the Islamic world, women in sub-Saharan Africa also engaged in the slave trade. In Guinea these

Queen Njiga Mbandi Ana de Sousa
Njiga (also known as Nzinga) of Ndongo (r. 1624–1629) is the most important female political figure in the history of early modern Angola. She used military force in her expansionist policy and participated fully in the slave trade, but she fiercely resisted Portuguese attempts to control that trade. Here she sits enthroned, wearing her crown (the cross a sign of her Christian baptism) and bracelets, giving an order. She has become a symbol of African resistance to colonial rule. (Courtesy, Luigi Araldi, Modena)

women slave merchants and traders were known as *nhara*, a corruption of the Portuguese term *senhora*, a title used for a married woman. They acquired considerable riches, often by marrying the Portuguese merchants and serving as go-betweens for these outsiders who were not familiar with the customs and languages of the African coast. One of them, Mae Aurélia Correia (1810?–1875?), led a life famous in the upper Guinea coastal region for its wealth and elegance. Between the 1820s and 1840s she operated her own trading vessels and is said to have owned several hundred slaves. Some of them she hired out as skilled artisans and sailors. She and her sister (or aunt) Julia amassed a fortune in gold, silver jewelry, and expensive cloths while living in European-style homes. Julia and her husband, a trader from the Cape Verde Islands, also owned their own slave estates where they produced peanuts.

The intermarriage of French traders and Wolof women in Senegambia created a métis, or mulatto, class. In the emerging urban centers at Saint-Louis, members of this small class adopted the French language, the Roman Catholic faith, and a French manner of life, and they exercised considerable political and economic power. However, European cultural influences did not penetrate West African society beyond the seacoast.

The political consequences of the slave trade varied from place to place. The trade enhanced the power and wealth of some kings and warlords in the short run but promoted conditions of instability and collapse over the long run. In the Kongo kingdom, which was located in parts of modern Angola, the Republic of the Congo, and the Democratic Republic of the Congo, the perpetual Portuguese search for Africans to enslave undermined the monarchy, destroyed political unity, and led to constant disorder and warfare; power passed to the village chiefs. Likewise in Angola, which became a Portuguese

proprietary colony (a territory granted to one or more individuals by the Crown for them to govern at their will), the slave trade decimated and scattered the population and destroyed the local economy. By contrast, the military kingdom of Dahomey, which entered into the slave trade in the eighteenth century and made it a royal monopoly, prospered enormously. Dahomey's economic strength rested on the slave trade. The royal army raided deep into the interior, and in the late eighteenth century Dahomey became one of the major West African sources of slaves. When slaving expeditions failed to yield sizable catches and when European demand declined, the resulting depression in the Dahomean economy caused serious political unrest. Iboland, inland from the Niger Delta, from whose great port cities of Bonny and Brass the British drained tens of thousands of enslaved Africans, experienced minimal political effects. A high birthrate kept pace with the incursions of the slave trade, and Ibo societies remained demographically and economically strong.

What demographic impact did the slave trade have on Africa? Between approximately 1501 and 1866, more than 12 million Africans were forcibly exported to the Americas, 6 million were traded to Asia, and 8 million were retained as slaves within Africa. Figure 19.2 shows the estimated number of slaves shipped to the Americas in the transatlantic slave trade. Export figures do not include the approximately 10 to 15 percent who died during procurement or in transit.

The early modern slave trade involved a worldwide web of relationships among markets in the Middle East,

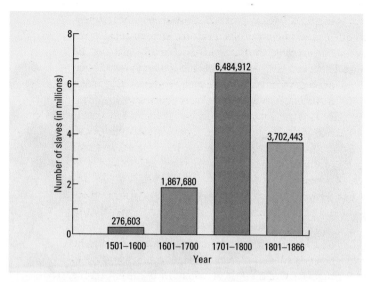

FIGURE 19.2 The Transatlantic Slave Trade, 1501–1866
The volume of slaves involved in the transatlantic slave trade peaked
during the eighteenth century. These numbers show the slaves who
embarked from Africa, and do not reflect the 10 to 15 percent of
enslaved Africans who died in transit. (Source: Data from Emory University.
"Assessing the Slave Trade: Estimates," in *Voyages: The Trans-Atlantic Slave Trade
Database.* 2009. http://www.slavevoyages.org.)

Sapi-Portuguese Saltcellar Contact with the Sapi people of
present-day Sierra Leone in West Africa led sixteenth-century
Portuguese traders to commission this ivory saltcellar, for
which they brought Portuguese designs. But the object's basic
features—a spherical container and separate lid on a flat base, with
men, women, and supporting beams below—are distinctly African.
An executioner, holding an ax with which he has beheaded five men,
stands on the lid. This piece was probably intended as an example
of Sapi artistic virtuosity, rather than for practical table use. (Courtesy,
Museo Nazionale Preistorico ed Etnografico, Rome)

Africa, Asia, Europe, and the Americas. But Africa was
the crucible of the trade. There is no small irony in the
fact that Africa, which of all the continents was most
desperately in need of population because of its near
total dependence on labor-intensive agriculture and
pastoralism, lost so many millions to the trade. Although
the British Parliament abolished the slave trade in 1807
and traffic in Africans to Brazil and Cuba gradually declined, within Africa the trade continued at the levels
of the peak years of the transatlantic trade, 1780–1820.
In the later nineteenth century, developing African industries, using slave labor, produced a variety of products for domestic consumption and export. Again, there
is irony in the fact that in the eighteenth century European demand for slaves expanded the trade (and wars)
within Africa, yet in the nineteenth century European
imperialists defended territorial aggrandizement by
arguing that they were "civilizing" Africans by abolishing slavery. But after 1880 European businessmen (and
African governments) did not push abolition; they
wanted cheap labor.

Markets in the Americas generally wanted young
male slaves. Asian and African markets preferred young
females. Women were sought for their reproductive
value, as sex objects, and because their economic productivity was not threatened by the possibility of physical rebellion, as might be the case with young men. Consequently, two-thirds of those exported to the Americas
were male, one-third female. As a result, the population on the western coast of Africa became predominantly female; the population in the East African savanna and Horn regions was predominantly male. The
slave trade therefore had significant consequences for
the institutions of marriage, the local trade in enslaved
people (as these local populations became skewed with
too many males or too many females), and the sexual
division of labor. Although Africa's overall population
may have shown modest growth from roughly 1650 to
1900, that growth was offset by declines in the Horn
and on the eastern and western coasts. While Europe
and Asia experienced considerable demographic and
economic expansion in the eighteenth century, Africa
suffered a decline.[25]

CONNECTIONS

During the period from 1400 to 1800 many parts of Africa experienced a profound transition with the arrival of Europeans all along Africa's coasts. Ancient trade routes, such as those across the Sahara Desert or up and down the East African coast, were disrupted. In West Africa trade routes that had been purely internal now connected with global trade networks at European coastal trading posts. Along Africa's east coast, the Portuguese attacked Swahili city-states in their effort to take control of the Indian Ocean trade nexus.

The most momentous consequence of the European presence along Africa's coast, however, was the introduction of the transatlantic slave trade. For more than three centuries Europeans, with the aid of African slave traders, enslaved millions of Africa's healthiest and strongest men and women. Although many parts of Africa were untouched by the transatlantic slave trade, at least directly, areas where Africans were enslaved experienced serious declines in agricultural production, little progress in technological development, and significant increases in violence.

As we will see in Chapters 20 and 21, early European commercial contacts with the empires of the Middle East and of South and East Asia were similar in many ways to those with Africa. Initially, the Portuguese, and then the English, Dutch, and French, did little more than establish trading posts at port cities and had to depend on the local people to bring them trade goods from the interior. Tropical diseases, particularly in India and in Southeast Asia, took heavy death tolls on the Europeans as they did in tropical Africa. What is more, while it was possible for the Portuguese to attack and conquer the individual Swahili city-states, Middle Eastern and Asian empires — such as the Ottomans in Turkey, the Safavids in Persia, the Mughals in India, and the Ming and Manchu Dynasties in China — were, like the West African kingdoms, economically and militarily powerful enough to dictate terms of trade with the Europeans.

Resistance to enslavement took many forms on both sides of the Atlantic. In Haiti, as discussed in Chapter 22, resistance led to revolution and independence, marking the first successful uprising of non-Europeans against a colonial power. At the end of the nineteenth century, as described in Chapter 25, Europeans used the ongoing Arab-Swahili slave raids from Africa's eastern coast far into the interior as an excuse to invade and eventually colonize much of central and eastern Africa. The racial discrimination that accompanied colonial rule in Africa would set the stage for a struggle for equality that would lead to eventual independence after World War II.

☐ CHAPTER REVIEW

☐ What different types of economic, social, and political structures were found in the kingdoms and states along the west coast and in the Sudan? (page 558)

In the early modern world, kingdoms and stateless societies in West Africa existed side by side. Stateless societies like the Senegambia were oriented around a single village or group of villages without a central capital. Age-grade systems, which passed on societal norms to successive generations and unified communities, were a common feature of many of these societies. Benin and other kingdoms were ruled by obas, kings who governed defined areas through bureaucratic hierarchies. The economies of both the kingdoms and the stateless societies were predominantly agricultural.

KEY TERMS

chattel (p. 558)
age-grade systems
  (p. 559)
oba (p. 559)
Taghaza (p. 560)
Tuareg (p. 565)
cowrie shells (p. 565)

Coptic Christianity
  (p. 567)
Swahili (p. 568)
Middle Passage
  (p. 576)
sorting (p. 577)
shore trading (p. 577)

Village markets served as sites for the exchange of produce and news and for social interaction. The transatlantic slave trade, along with disease and famine, had a negative effect on population throughout West Africa, resulting in intense competition for women.

The Sudanic empires immediately south of the Sahara, such as Songhai, Kanem-Bornu, and Hausaland, controlled the north-south trans-Saharan trade in gold, salt, cloth, and other items. The rulers of the kingdoms of the Sudan were predominantly Muslim. Being part of the Islamic world gave these societies not only commercial links to Europe, the Middle East, and beyond, but also access to some of the most advanced scholarship in the world at the time. As a result, Timbuktu became a Muslim intellectual center, as did Kano and Katsina. Still, although West African societies experienced strong Islamic influences, Muslim culture affected primarily the royal and elite classes and seldom reached the masses.

□ How did the arrival of Europeans and other foreign cultures impact the East African coast, and how did Ethiopia and the Swahili city-states respond to these incursions? (page 566)

Europeans came to believe that the Christian kingdom of Ethiopia was ruled by a wealthy (mythical) Christian monarch named Prester John. The Prester John fable attracted Europeans to Ethiopia for centuries. The myth partly explains why, when the Ethiopians called for European assistance in fighting off Muslim incursions by the Red Sea state of Adal in the sixteenth century, the Portuguese came to their aid, soundly defeating a Muslim force at Lake Tana in 1543. Jesuit missionaries soon followed and tried to convert Ethiopians to Roman Catholicism, but the Ethiopians fiercely resisted, expelling the Jesuits in 1633.

The wealthy Swahili city-states on the southeastern coast of Africa possessed a Muslim and mercantile culture. The Swahili acted as middlemen in the East African–Indian Ocean trade network, and had long felt the influence of Indians, Indonesians, Persians, and Arabs. When the Portuguese arrived in the Indian Ocean in the late fifteenth and early sixteenth centuries, they sought to conquer and control this network. Some Swahili rulers agreed to form trading alliances with the Portuguese, while others refused and faced bombardment. Although the Portuguese had little effect on Swahili culture or religion, their presence caused the economic decline and death of many Swahili cities as people along the coast deserted their cities rather than face Portuguese control.

□ What role did slavery play in African societies before the transatlantic slave trade began, and what was the effect of European involvement? (page 568)

Many African societies had long used some form of slavery. Generally, slaves were obtained as payment for debt, in war, or through simple purchase. Slaves were treated relatively benignly in some societies, serving as wives, house servants, royal guards, or even royal advisers. But other slaves were considered chattel possessions, little more than animals, and suffered under harsh and brutal treatment as field hands, common laborers, sex objects, or miners. European involvement in the slave trade began around 1550 with the Portuguese importation of slaves to work in Brazil. The Dutch East India Company used enslaved Africans to work Cape Colony, supplemented with slaves from Southeast Asia. As the labor demands in the colonies of the New World grew, the transatlantic slave trade run by Europeans exploited millions of Africans to work in the often harsh conditions of the New World. African entrepreneurs and merchants played an important role in the slave trade, capturing and selling slaves from the interior to the Portuguese in Angola and to the British along the Gold Coast of West Africa. Africans exchanged slaves for firearms and inexpensive foreign products. Influences were variable, with some kingdoms experiencing a rise of wealth and power, though over time the influence was largely destabilizing. As a result of the demand in the New World for young male slaves, the West African population became predominately female, further destabilizing African society and leading to economic decline.

SUGGESTED READING

Berger, Iris, E. Frances White, and Cathy Skidmore-Heiss. *Women in Sub-Saharan Africa: Restoring Women to History*. 1999. Necessary reading for a complete understanding of African history.

Cooper, Frederick. *Plantation Slavery on the East Coast of Africa*. 1997. Useful study of slavery as practiced in Africa.

Fredrickson, G. M. *Racism: A Short History*. 2002. Contains probably the best recent study of the connection between African slavery and Western racism.

Klein, Martin, and Claire C. Robertson. *Women and Slavery in Africa*. 1997. From the perspective that most slaves in Africa were women.

Law, Robin. *Oyo Empire, c. 1600–c. 1836: A West African Imperialism in the Era of the Atlantic Slave Trade*. 1977. Remains the definitive study of the powerful Oyo Empire in what is today southwestern Nigeria.

Lovejoy, Paul E. *Transformation in Slavery: A History of Slavery in Africa*. 2d ed. 2000. Essential for an understanding of slavery in an African context.

Middleton, J. *The World of Swahili: An African Mercantile Civilization*. 1992. Introduction to East Africa and the Horn region.

Northrup, D. *Africa's Discovery of Europe, 1450–1850*. 2002. Offers a unique perspective on African-European contact.

Oliver, Roland, and Anthony Atmore. *Medieval Africa, 1250–1800*. 2001. A history of premodern Africa by two renowned historians of the continent.

Pearson, Michael N. *Port Cities and Intruders: The Swahili Coast, India, and Portugal in the Early Modern Era.* 2002. Comprehensive introduction to the Swahili coast and the Indian Ocean trade network.

Powell, Eve Troutt, and John O. Hunwick. *The African Diaspora in the Mediterranean Lands of Islam.* 2002. Important study of Islam and the African slave trade.

Robinson, David. *Muslim Societies in African History.* 2004. Valuable introduction to Islam in Africa by a renowned Africanist.

Shell, R. *Children of Bondage: A Social History of the Slave Society at the Cape of Good Hope, 1652–1938.* 1994. A massive study of Cape slave society filled with much valuable statistical data.

Shillington, K. *History of Africa.* 2005. Provides a soundly researched, highly readable, and well-illustrated survey.

Thorton, J. *Africa and Africans in the Making of the Atlantic World, 1400–1680.* 1992. Places African developments in an Atlantic context.

NOTES

1. P. D. Curtin, *Economic Change in Precolonial Africa: Senegambia in the Era of the Slave Trade* (Madison: University of Wisconsin Press, 1975), pp. 34–35; J. A. Rawley, *The Transatlantic Slave Trade: A History* (Lincoln: University of Nebraska Press, 2005).

2. Pieter de Marees, *Description of the Gold Kingdom of Guinea* (Dantzig, 1602), Albert van Dantzig and Adam Jones, trans. and eds. (Oxford, U.K.: Oxford University Press, 1987), pp. 226–228; William Bosman, *A New Description of the Coast of Guinea*, ed. John Ralph Willis (London: Frank Cass, 1967), p. 461.

3. Quoted in R. Hallett, *Africa to 1875* (Ann Arbor: University of Michigan Press, 1970), p. 151.

4. A. ibn-Fartura, "The Kanem Wars," in *Nigerian Perspectives*, ed. T. Hodgkin (London: Oxford University Press, 1966), pp. 111–115.

5. "The Kano Chronicle," quoted in *Nigerian Perspectives*, ed. T. Hodgkin (London: Oxford University Press, 1966), pp. 89–90.

6. *Equiano's Travels: The Interesting Narrative of the Life of Olaudah Equiano*, ed. P. Edwards (Portsmouth, N.H.: Heinemann, 1996), p. 4.

7. J. Iliffe, *Africans: The History of a Continent* (Cambridge, U.K.: Cambridge University Press, 2007), p. 68.

8. See A. J. R. Russell-Wood, *The Portuguese Empire: A World on the Move* (Baltimore: Johns Hopkins University Press, 1998), pp. 11–13.

9. Ibid., pp. 35–38.

10. P. E. Lovejoy, *Transformations in Slavery: A History of Slavery in Africa* (Cambridge, U.K.: Cambridge University Press, 1992), p. 25, Table 2.1, "Trans-Saharan Slave Trade, 650–1600."

11. Iliffe, *Africans*, p. 77.

12. Quoted in H. Thomas, *The Slave Trade* (New York: Simon and Schuster, 1997), p. 21.

13. G. Gerzina, *Black London: Life Before Emancipation* (New Brunswick, N.J.: Rutgers University Press, 1995), pp. 29–66, passim; quotation from p. 53.

14. C.-H. Shell, *Children of Bondage: A Social History of the Slave Society at the Cape of Good Hope, 1652–1838* (Hanover, N.H.: University Press of New England, 1994), pp. 285–289.

15. See D. Eltis, *The Rise of African Slavery in the Americas* (Cambridge, U.K.: Cambridge University Press, 2000), Chap. 3; and the review/commentary by J. E. Inikori, *American Historical Review* 106, no. 5 (December 2001): 1751–1753.

16. R. Blackburn, *The Making of New World Slavery: From the Baroque to the Modern, 1492–1800* (New York: Verso, 1998), pp. 79–80.

17. R. E. Conrad, *Children of God's Fire: A Documentary History of Black Slavery in Brazil* (Princeton, N.J.: Princeton University Press, 1983), pp. 20–23.

18. *Equiano's Travels*, pp. 23–26.

19. Rawley, *The Transatlantic Slave Trade*, pp. 45–47.

20. Robert W. July, *A History of the African People* (Prospect Heights, Ill.: Waveland Press, 1998), p. 171.

21. J. Adams, "Remarks on the Country Extending from Cape Palmas to the River Congo," *Nigerian Perspectives*, ed. T. Hodgkin (London: Oxford University Press, 1966), pp. 178–180.

22. J. Thornton, *Africa and Africans in the Making of the Atlantic World* (New York: Cambridge University Press, 1992), pp. 138–142.

23. Robert W. July, *Precolonial Africa: An Economic and Social History* (New York: Scribner's, 1975), pp. 269–270.

24. A. G. Hopkins, *An Economic History of West Africa* (New York: Columbia University Press, 1973), p. 119.

25. P. Manning, *Slavery and African Life: Occidental, Oriental, and African Slave Trades* (New York: Cambridge University Press, 1990), pp. 22–23 and Chap. 3, pp. 38–59.

For practice quizzes and other study tools, visit the **Online Study Guide** at bedfordstmartins.com/mckayworld.

For primary sources from this period, see *Sources of World Societies*, **Second Edition**.

For Web sites, images, and documents related to topics in this chapter, visit **Make History** at bedfordstmartins.com/mckayworld.

● **Persian Princess** The ruling houses of the Islamic empires were great patrons of art and architecture. This depiction of a princess in a garden is from an early-seventeenth-century palace built by Shah Abbas of the Safavid Dynasty in Persia. (Giraudon/The Bridgeman Art Library)

20

After the decline of the Mongol Empire in the mid-fourteenth century, powerful new Islamic states emerged in south and west Eurasia. By the sixteenth century the Ottoman Empire, centered in Anatolia; the Safavid (sah-FAH-weed) Empire in Persia; and the Mughal (MOO-guhl) Empire in India controlled vast territories from West Africa to Central Asia, from the Balkans to the Bay of Bengal.

Lasting more than six centuries (1299–1922), the Ottoman Empire was one of the largest, best-organized, and most enduring political entities in world history. In Persia (now Iran) the Safavid Dynasty created a Shi'a state and presided over a brilliant culture. In India the Mughal leader Babur and his successors gained control of much of the Indian subcontinent. Mughal rule inaugurated a period of radical administrative reorganization in India and the flowering of intellectual and architectural creativity. Although these three states were often at war with each other, they shared important characteristics and challenges. For instance, their ruling houses all emerged from Turkish tribal organizations, and they all had to adapt their armies to the introduction of firearms. Over time, they became strongly linked culturally, as merchants, poets, philosophers, artists, and military advisers moved relatively easily across their political boundaries. Before the end of this period, Europeans were also active in trade in these empires, especially in India.   •

The Islamic World Powers
1300–1800

The Turkish Ruling Houses: The Ottomans, Safavids, and Mughals

☐ How were the three Islamic empires established, and what sorts of governments did they set up?

Cultural Flowering

☐ What cultural advances occurred under the rule of the Ottoman, Safavid, and Mughal empires?

Non-Muslims Under Muslim Rule

☐ How did Christians, Jews, Hindus, and other non-Muslims fare under these Islamic states?

Shifting Trade Routes and European Penetration

☐ How were the Islamic empires affected by the gradual shift toward trade routes that bypassed their lands?

Political Decline

☐ Did any common factors lead to the decline of central power in the Islamic empires in the seventeenth and eighteenth centuries?

The Turkish Ruling Houses: The Ottomans, Safavids, and Mughals

☐ How were the three Islamic empires established, and what sorts of governments did they set up?

Before the Mongols arrived in Central Asia and Persia, another nomadic people from the region of modern Mongolia, the Turks, had moved west, gained control over key territories from Anatolia to Delhi in north India, and contributed to the decline of the Abbasid caliphate in the thirteenth century. The Turks had been quick to join the Mongols and were important participants in the armies and administrations of the Mongol states in Persia and Central Asia. In these regions, Turks far outnumbered ethnic Mongols.

As Mongol strength in Persia and Central Asia deteriorated in the late thirteenth to mid-fourteenth centuries, the Turks resumed their expansion. In the late fourteenth century the Turkish leader Timur (1336–1405), also called Tamerlane, built a Central Asian em-

pire from his base in Samarkand that reached into India and through Persia to the Black Sea. Timur campaigned continuously from the 1360s until his death in 1405, his goal to repeat the achievements of Chinggis Khan. He did not get involved in administering the new territories but rather appointed lords and let them make use of existing political structures. His conquests were exceptionally destructive and benefited only Samarkand, where craftsmen and other specialists were forced to move to work for the new rulers. After his death his sons and grandson fought each other for succession. By 1450 his empire was in rapid decline, and power devolved to the local level. Meanwhile, Sufi orders (groups of Islamic mystics) thrived, and Islam became the most important force integrating the region. It was from the many small Turkish chiefs that the founders of the three main empires emerged.

The Ottoman Turkish Empire's Expansion

The **Ottomans** took their name from Osman (r. 1299–1326), the chief of a band of seminomadic Turks that had migrated into western **Anatolia** while the Mongols still held Persia. The Ottomans gradually expanded at the expense of other small Turkish states and the Byzantine Empire (Map 20.1). The Ottoman ruler called himself "border chief," or leader of the *ghazis* (GAH-zeez), frontier raiders. Although temporarily slowed by defeat at the hands of Timur in 1402, the Ottomans quickly reasserted themselves after Timur's death in 1405.

Osman's campaigns were intended to subdue, not to destroy. The Ottomans built their empire by absorbing the Muslims of Anatolia and by becoming the protector of the Orthodox Church and of the millions of Greek Christians in Anatolia and the Balkans. In 1326 they took Bursa in western Anatolia, and in 1352 they gained

Empire of Timur, ca. 1405

a foothold in Europe by seizing Gallipoli. Their victories led more men, including recent converts, to join them as ghazis. In 1389 at Kosovo in the Balkans, the Ottomans defeated a combined force of Serbs and Bosnians. And in 1396 on the Danube River in modern Bulgaria, they crushed King Sigismund of Hungary, who was supported by French, German, and English knights. After the victories in the Balkans, the Ottomans added to their military strength by obtaining slave troops. These troops were outfitted with guns and artillery and trained to use them effectively.

In 1453, during the reign of Sultan Mehmet II (r. 1451–1481), the Ottomans conquered Constantinople, capital of the Byzantine Empire, which had lasted a thousand years. The Byzantine emperor, Constantine IX Palaeologus (r. 1449–1453), with only about ten thousand men, relied on Constantinople's magnificent system of circular walls and stone fortifications for defense. Although Mehmet II had more than a hundred thousand men and a large fleet, iron chains spanning the city's harbor kept him out. Nevertheless, Turkish ingenuity and up-to-date technology eventually decided the battle. Mehmet's army carried boats over steep hills to come in behind the chains blocking the harbor and then bombarded the city from the rear. A Transylvanian cannon maker who had deserted the Greeks for the Turks cast huge bronze cannon on the spot (bringing raw materials to the scene of military action was easier than moving guns long distances), and these guns were used to weaken the defensive walls.

Once Constantinople was theirs, the Ottoman **sultans** considered themselves successors of both the Byzantine and Seljuk Turk emperors, and they quickly absorbed the rest of the Byzantine Empire. In the sixteenth century they continued to expand through the Middle East and into North Africa.

To begin the transformation of Constantinople (renamed Istanbul) into an imperial Ottoman capital, Mehmet ordered the city cleaned up and the walls repaired. He appointed officials to adapt the city administration to Ottoman ways and ordered wealthy residents to participate in building mosques, markets, fountains, baths, and other public facilities. The city's

☐ CHRONOLOGY

1299–1326	Reign of Osman, founder of the Ottoman Dynasty
1299–1922	Ottoman Empire
1336–1405	Life of Timur
ca. mid-1400s	Coffeehouses become center of Islamic male social life
1453	Ottoman conquest of Constantinople
1501–1524	Reign of Safavid Shah Isma'il
1501–1722	Safavid empire
1520–1558	Hürrem wields influence in the Ottoman Empire as Suleiman's concubine and then wife
1520–1566	Reign of Ottoman sultan Suleiman I; period of artistic flowering in Ottoman Empire
1521	Piri Reis produces *Book of the Sea*, a navigational map book
1526–1857	Mughal Empire
1556–1605	Reign of Akbar in Mughal Empire
1570	Ottomans take control of Cyprus
1571	First major Ottoman defeat by Christians, at Lepanto
1587–1629	Reign of Shah Abbas; height of Safavid power; carpet weaving becomes major Persian industry
1631–1648	Construction of Taj Mahal under Shah Jahan in India
1658–1707	Reign of Aurangzeb; Mughal power begins to decline
1763	Treaty of Paris recognizes British control over much of India

population had declined in the decades before the conquest, and warfare, flight, and the sale of many survivors into slavery had decreased it further. Therefore, Mehmet transplanted inhabitants of other territories to the city, granting them tax remissions and possession of empty houses. He wanted them to start businesses, make Istanbul prosperous, and transform it into a microcosm of the empire.

Gunpowder, which was invented by the Chinese and adapted to artillery use by the Europeans, played an influential role in the expansion of the Ottoman

- **Ottomans** Ruling house of the Turkish empire that lasted from 1299 to 1922.
- **Anatolia** The region of modern Turkey.
- **sultan** An Arabic word originally used by the Seljuk Turks to mean authority or dominion; it was used by the Ottomans to connote political and military supremacy.

Map legend:

- Ottoman state, ca. 1300
- Ottoman Empire under Suleiman, 1566
- Tributary states of the Sultan, 1566
- → Major Ottoman campaign, 1530–1584
- Habsburg Empire, ca. 1550

◻ Mapping the Past

MAP 20.1 The Ottoman Empire at Its Height, 1566 The Ottomans, like their great rivals the Habsburgs, rose to rule a vast dynastic empire encompassing many different peoples and ethnic groups. The army and the bureaucracy served to unite the disparate territories into a single state.

ANALYZING THE MAP Trace the coastlines of the Ottoman Empire. What were the major port cities of the empire? Which regions were encompassed within the empire at its height?

CONNECTIONS If the Ottoman Empire is compared to Europe of the same period (see Map 17.1 on page 495), which had more of its territory near the sea? How did proximity to the Mediterranean shape the politics of Ottoman-European relations in this period?

state. In the first half of the sixteenth century, thanks to the use of this technology, the Ottomans gained control of shipping in the eastern Mediterranean, eliminated the Portuguese from the Red Sea and the Persian Gulf, and supported Andalusian and North African Muslims in their fight against the Christian reconquest of Muslim Spain. In 1514, under the superb military leadership of Selim (r. 1512–1520), the Ottomans turned the Safavids back from Anatolia. In addition, the Ottomans added Syria and Palestine (1516) and Egypt (1517) to their empire, giving them control of

the holy cities of Islam. Next they extended their rule across North Africa to Tunisia and Algeria. Selim's rule marks the beginning of four centuries when most Arabs were under Ottoman rule.

Suleiman (r. 1520–1566) extended Ottoman dominion to its widest geographical extent (see Map 20.1). Suleiman's army crushed the Hungarians at Mohács in 1526, killing the king and thousands of his nobles. Three years later the Turks besieged the Habsburg capital of Vienna. This target proved impossible to attain, however, perhaps because the Ottomans had reached the logistical limit of their expansion, as some scholars argue.

From the late fourteenth to the early seventeenth centuries, the Ottoman Empire was a key player in European politics. In 1525 Francis I of France and Suleiman struck an alliance; both believed that only their collaboration could prevent Habsburg domination of Europe. The Habsburg emperor Charles V retaliated by seeking an alliance with Safavid Persia. Suleiman renewed the French agreement with Francis's son, Henry II (r. 1547–1559), and this accord became the cornerstone of Ottoman policy in western Europe. Suleiman also allied with the German Protestant princes, forcing the Catholic Habsburgs to grant concessions to the Protestants. Ottoman pressure thus contributed to the official recognition of Lutheran Prot-

estants at the Peace of Augsburg in 1555 and the consolidation of the national monarchy in France.

In eastern Europe to the north of Ottoman lands stood the Grand Duchy of Moscow. In the fifteenth century Ottoman rulers did not regard it as a threat; in 1497 they even gave Russian merchants freedom of trade within the empire. But in 1547 Ivan IV (the Terrible) brought the entire Volga region under Russian control (see Map 20.1). In 1557 Ivan's ally, the Cossack chieftain Dimitrash, tried to take Azov, the northernmost Ottoman fortress. Ottoman plans to recapture the area succeeded in uniting Russia, Persia, and the pope against the Turks.

Though usually victorious on land, the Ottomans did not enjoy complete dominion on the seas. Competition with the Habsburgs and pirates for control of the

Battle of Mohács The *Süleymanname* (Book of Suleiman), a biography, contains these wonderful illustrations of the battle that took place in Hungary on August 29, 1526. In the right panel, Suleiman in a white turban sits on a black horse surrounded by his personal guard, while janissaries fire cannon at the enemy. In the left panel, the Europeans are in disarray, in contrast to the Turks' discipline and order. Suleiman inflicted a crushing defeat and absorbed Hungary into the Ottoman Empire. (Private Collection/Archives Charmet/The Bridgeman Art Library)

Mediterranean led the Ottomans to conquer Cyprus in 1570 and settle thousands of Turks from Anatolia there. (Thus began the large Turkish presence on Cyprus that continues to the present day.) In response, Pope Pius V organized a Holy League against the Turks, which had a victory in 1571 at Lepanto off the west coast of Greece with a squadron of more than two hundred Spanish, Venetian, and papal galleys. Still, the Turks remained supreme on land and quickly rebuilt their entire fleet.

To the east, war with Safavid Persia occupied the sultans' attention throughout the sixteenth century. Several issues lay at the root of the long and exhausting conflict: religious antagonism between the Sunni Ottomans and the Shi'a Persians, competition to expand at each other's expense in Mesopotamia, desire to control trade routes, and European alliances. (For more on the Shi'a faith, see page 595.) Finally, in 1638 the Ottomans captured Baghdad, and the treaty of Kasr-I-Shirim established a permanent border between the two powers.

The Ottoman political system reached its classic form under Suleiman I. All authority flowed from the sultan to his public servants: provincial governors, police officers, military generals, heads of treasuries, and **viziers**. In Turkish history, Suleiman is known as "the Lawgiver" because of his profound influence on the civil law. He ordered Lütfi Paşa (d. 1562), a poet and juridical scholar of slave origin, to draw up a new general code of laws that prescribed penalties for routine criminal acts such as robbery, adultery, and murder. It also sought to reform bureaucratic and financial corruption, such as foreign merchants' payment of bribes to avoid customs duties, imprisonment without trial, and promotion in the provincial administration because of favoritism rather than ability. The legal code also introduced the idea of balanced government budgets. The head of the religious establishment was given the task of reconciling sultanic law with Islamic law. Suleiman's legal acts influenced many legal codes, including that of the United States. Today, Suleiman's image appears in the chamber of the U.S. House of Representatives, along with the images of the Athenian lawmaker Solon, Moses, and Thomas Jefferson.

- **viziers** Chief assistants to caliphs.
- **devshirme** A process whereby the sultan's agents swept the provinces for Christian youths to become slaves.
- **janissaries** Turkish for "recruits"; they formed the elite army corps.
- **concubine** A woman who is a recognized spouse but of lower status than a wife.
- **shah** Persian word for "king."
- **Safavid** The dynasty that encompassed all of Persia and other regions; its state religion was Shi'ism.
- **Qizilbash** Nomadic Sufi tribesmen who were loyal to and supportive of the early Safavid state.

The Ottomans ruled their more distant lands, such as those in North Africa, relatively lightly. Governors of distant provinces collected taxes and maintained trade routes, but their control did not penetrate deeply into the countryside.

The Ottoman Empire's Use of Slaves

The power of the Ottoman central government was sustained through the training of slaves. Slaves were purchased from Spain, North Africa, and Venice; captured in battle; or drafted through the system known as **devshirme**, by which the sultan's agents compelled Christian families in the Balkans to sell their boys. As the Ottoman frontier advanced in the fifteenth and sixteenth centuries, Albanian, Bosnian, Wallachian, and Hungarian slave boys filled Ottoman imperial needs. The slave boys were converted to Islam and trained for the imperial civil service and the standing army. The brightest 10 percent entered the palace school, where they learned to read and write Arabic, Ottoman Turkish, and Persian in preparation for administrative jobs. Other boys were sent to Turkish farms, where they acquired physical toughness in preparation for military service. Known as **janissaries** (Turkish for "recruits"), they formed the elite army corps. Thoroughly indoctrinated and absolutely loyal to the sultan, the janissary slave corps threatened the influence of fractious old Turkish families. They played a central role in Ottoman military affairs in the sixteenth century, adapting easily to the use of firearms. The devshirme system enabled the Ottomans to apply merit-based recruitment to military and administrative offices at little cost and provided a means of assimilating Christians living in Ottoman lands. Some Muslims, however, doubted whether janissary converts could be viewed as reliably Muslim.

The Ottoman ruling class consisted partly of descendants of Turkish families that had formerly ruled parts of Anatolia and partly of people of varied ethnic origins who rose through the bureaucratic and military ranks, many beginning as the sultan's slaves. All were committed to the Ottoman way: Islamic in faith, loyal to the sultan, and well versed in the Turkish language and the culture of the imperial court. In return for their services to the sultan, they held landed estates for the duration of their lives. The ruling class had the legal right to use and enjoy the profits, but not the ownership, of the land. Because all property belonged to the sultan and reverted to him on the holder's death, Turkish nobles, unlike their European counterparts, did not have a local base independent of the ruler. The absence of a hereditary nobility and private ownership of agricultural land differentiates the Ottoman system from European feudalism.

Music in a Garden This illustration of a courtly romance depicts several women in a garden, intently listening to a musician, with cups of a beverage in their hands. (Biblioteca Vaticana Apostolica)

Another distinctive characteristic of the Ottomans was the sultan's failure to marry. From about 1500 on, the sultans did not contract legal marriages but perpetuated the ruling house through concubinage. A slave **concubine** could not expect to exert power the way a local or foreign noblewoman could (with a notable exception; see "Individuals in Society: Hürrem," page 594). When one of the sultan's concubines became pregnant, her status and her salary increased. If she delivered a boy, she raised him until the age of ten or eleven. Then the child was given a province to govern under his mother's supervision. She accompanied him there, was responsible for his good behavior, and worked through imperial officials and the janissary corps to promote his interests. Because succession to the throne was open to all the sultan's sons, fratricide often resulted upon his death, and the losers were blinded or executed.

Slave concubinage paralleled the Ottoman development of slave soldiers and slave viziers. All held positions entirely at the sultan's pleasure, owed loyalty solely to him, and thus were more reliable than a hereditary nobility, as existed in Europe. Great social prestige, as well as the opportunity to acquire power and

wealth, was attached to being a slave of the imperial household. Suleiman even made it a practice to marry his daughters to top-ranking slave-officials.

The Safavid Empire in Persia

With the decline of Timur's empire after 1450, Persia was controlled by Turkish lords, with no single one dominant until 1501, when fourteen-year-old Isma'il (1487–1524) led a Turkish army to capture Tabriz and declared himself **shah** (king).

The strength of the early **Safavid** state rested on three crucial features. First, it had the loyalty and military support of Turkish Sufis known as **Qizilbash** (KIH-zil-bahsh; a Turkish word meaning "redheads" that was applied to these people because of the red hats they wore). The shah secured the loyalty of the Qizilbash by granting them vast grazing lands, especially on the troublesome Ottoman frontier. In return, the Qizilbash supplied him with troops. Second, the Safavid state utilized the skills of urban bureaucrats and made them an essential part of the civil machinery of government.

The third source of Safavid strength was the Shi'a faith, which became the compulsory religion of the

Individuals in Society

Hürrem

HÜRREM (1505?–1558) WAS BORN IN THE western Ukraine (then part of Poland), the daughter of a Ruthenian priest, and was given the Polish name Aleksandra Lisowska. When Tartars raided, they captured and enslaved her. In 1520 she was given as a gift to Suleiman on the occasion of his accession to the throne. The Venetian ambassador (probably relying on secondhand or thirdhand information) described her as "young, graceful, petite, but not beautiful." She was given the Turkish name Hürrem, meaning "joyful."

Hürrem apparently brought joy to Suleiman. Their first child was born in 1521. By 1525 they had four sons and a daughter; sources note that by that year Suleiman visited no other woman. But he waited eight or nine years before breaking Ottoman dynastic tradition by making Hürrem his legal wife, the first slave concubine so honored. For the rest of her life, Hürrem played a highly influential role in the political, diplomatic, and philanthropic life of the Ottoman state. First, great power flowed from her position as mother of the prince, the future sultan Selim II (r. 1566–1574). Then, as the intimate and most trusted adviser of the sultan, she was Suleiman's closest confidante. During his frequent trips to the far-flung corners of his multiethnic empire, Hürrem wrote him long letters filled with her love and longing for him and her prayers for his safety in battle. She also shared political information about affairs in Istanbul, the activities of the grand vizier, and the attitudes of the janissaries. At a time when some people believed that the sultan's absence from the capital endangered his hold on the throne, Hürrem acted as his eyes and ears for potential threats.

Hürrem was the sultan's contact with her native Poland, which sent more embassies to Istanbul than any other power. Through her correspondence with King Sigismund I, peace between Poland and the Ottomans was maintained. When Sigismund II succeeded his father in 1548, Hürrem sent congratulations on his accession, along with two pairs of pajamas (originally a Hindu garment but commonly worn in southwestern Asia) and six handkerchiefs. Also, she sent the shah of Persia gold-embroidered sheets and shirts that she had sewn herself, seeking to display the wealth of the sultanate and to keep peace between the Ottomans and the Safavids.

The enormous stipend that Suleiman gave Hürrem permitted her to participate in his vast building program. In Jerusalem (in the Ottoman province of Palestine), she founded a hospice for fifty-five pilgrims that included a soup kitchen that fed four hundred pilgrims a day. In Istanbul Suleiman built and Hürrem endowed the Haseki (meaning "royal favorite concubine") mosque complex and a public bath for women near the Women's Market.

Perhaps Hürrem tried to fulfill two functions hitherto distinct in Ottoman political theory: those of the sultan's favorite and of mother of the prince. She also performed the conflicting roles of slave concubine and imperial wife. Many Turks resented Hürrem's interference at court. They believed she was behind the execution of Suleiman's popular son Mustafa on a charge of treason to make way for her own son to succeed as sultan.

Source: Leslie P. Pierce, *The Imperial Harem: Women and Sovereignty in the Ottoman Empire* (New York: Oxford University Press, 1993).

QUESTIONS FOR ANALYSIS

1. How does Hürrem compare to powerful women in other places, such as Empress Wu in China, Isabella of Castile, Catherine de' Medici of France, Elizabeth I of England, Mary Queen of Scots, or any other you know about?
2. What was Hürrem's "nationality"? What role did it play in her life?

Hürrem and her ladies in the harem.
(Bibliothèque nationale de France)

MAP 20.2 The Safavid Empire, 1587–1629 In the late sixteenth century the power of the Safavid kingdom of Persia rested on its strong military force, its Shi'a Muslim faith, and its extraordinarily rich trade in rugs and pottery. Many of the cities on the map, such as Tabriz, Qum, and Shiraz, were great rug-weaving centers.

empire. The Shi'a believed that leadership among Muslims rightfully belonged to the Prophet Muhammad's descendants. Because Isma'il claimed descent from a line of twelve infallible imams (leaders) beginning with Ali (Muhammad's cousin and son-in-law), he was officially regarded as their representative on earth. Isma'il's own beliefs were messianic and not mainstream, but he took steps that ended up promoting standard Shi'ism. For example, he recruited Shi'a scholars outstanding in learning and piety from other lands to instruct and guide his people, and he persecuted and exiled Sunni **ulama**. To this day, Iran remains the only Muslim state in which Shi'ism is the official religion.

Safavid power reached its height under Shah Abbas (r. 1587–1629), who moved the capital from Qazvin to Isfahan. His military achievements, support for trade and commerce, and endowment of the arts earned him the epithet "the Great." In the military realm, he adopted the Ottoman practice of building an army of slaves, primarily captives from the Caucuses (especially Arme-

nians and Georgians), who could serve as a counterweight to the Qizilbash, who had come to be considered a threat. He also increased the use of gunpowder weapons and made alliances with European powers against the Ottomans and Portuguese. In his campaigns against the Ottomans, Shah Abbas captured Baghdad, Mosul, and Diarbakr in Mesopotamia (Map 20.2).

Conflict between the Ottomans and the Safavids was not an even match. The Safavids did not have as many people or as much wealth as the Ottomans and continually had to defend against encroachments on their western border. Still, they were able to attract some of the Turks in Ottoman lands who felt that their government had shifted too far from its nomadic roots. After Shah Abbas, Safavid power was sapped by civil war between tribal factions vying for control of the court.

• **ulama** Religious scholars whom Sunnis trust to interpret the Qur'an and the Sunna, the deeds and sayings of Muhammad.

The Mughal Empire in India

Of the three great Islamic empires of the early modern world, the **Mughal** Empire of India was the largest, wealthiest, and most populous. Extending over 1.2 million square miles at the end of the seventeenth century, with a population between 100 and 150 million, and with fabulous wealth and resources, the Mughal Empire surpassed the other two by a wide margin. In the sixteenth century, only the Ming Dynasty in China could compare.

In 1504 Babur (r. 1483–1530), a Turkish ruler forced out of a small territory in Central Asia, captured Kabul and established a kingdom in Afghanistan. An adventurer who claimed descent from Chinggis Khan and Timur, Babur moved southward in search of resources to restore his fortunes. In 1526, with a force that was small (twelve thousand in number) but was equipped with firearms, Babur defeated the sultan of Delhi at Panipat. Babur's capture of the cities of Agra and Delhi, key fortresses of the north, paved the way for further conquests in northern India. Although many of his soldiers wished to return north with their spoils, Babur decided to stay in India. A gifted writer, Babur wrote an autobiography in Turkish that recounts his military campaigns, describes places and people he encountered, recounts his difficulties giving up wine, and shows his wide-ranging interests in everything from fruit and swimming to a Turkish general who excelled at leapfrog. He was not particularly impressed by India, as can be inferred from this description in his memoirs:

> Hindustan is a country which has few pleasures to recommend it. The people are not handsome. They have no idea of the charms of friendly society, of frankly mixing together, or familiar discourse. They have no genius, no comprehension of mind, no politeness of manner, no kindness or fellow-feeling, no ingenuity or mechanical invention in planning or executing their handicraft works, no skill or knowledge in design or architecture; they have no horses, no good flesh, no grapes or muskmelons, no good fruits, no ice or cold water, no good food or bread in their bazaars, no baths or colleges, no candles, no torches, not a candlestick.[1]

During the reign of Babur's son Humayun (r. 1530–1540 and 1555–1556), the Mughals lost most of their territories in Afghanistan. Humayun went into temporary exile in Persia, where he developed a deep appreciation for Persian art and literature. The reign of Humayun's son Akbar (r. 1556–1605) may well have been the greatest in the history of India. A boy of thirteen when he succeeded to the throne, Akbar pursued expansionist policies. Under his dynamic leadership, the Mughal state took definitive form and encompassed most of the subcontinent north of the Godavari River. No kingdom or coalition of kingdoms could long resist Akbar's armies. The once independent states of northern India were forced into a centralized political system under the sole authority of the Mughal emperor.

Akbar replaced Turkish with Persian as the official language of the Mughal Empire, and Persian remained the official language until the British replaced it with English in 1835. To govern this vast region, Akbar developed an administrative bureaucracy centered on four co-equal ministers: for finance and revenue; the army and intelligence; the judiciary and religious patronage; and the imperial household, whose jurisdiction included roads, bridges, and infrastructure throughout the empire. Under Akbar's Hindu finance minister, Raja Todar Mal, a uniform system of taxes was put in place. In the provinces, imperial governors, appointed by and responsible solely to the emperor, presided over administrative branches modeled on those of the central government. The government, however, rarely interfered in the life of village communities. Whereas the Ottoman sultans and Safavid shahs made extensive use of slaves acquired from non-Muslim lands for military and administrative positions, Akbar used the services of royal princes, nobles, and warrior-aristocrats. Initially these men were Muslims from Central Asia, but to reduce their influence, Akbar vigorously recruited Persians and Hindus. No single ethnic or religious faction could challenge the emperor.

Akbar's descendants extended the Mughal Empire further. His son Jahangir (r. 1605–1628) lacked his father's military abilities and administrative genius, but he did succeed in consolidating Mughal rule in Bengal. Jahangir's son Shah Jahan (r. 1628–1658) launched fresh territorial expansion. Faced with dangerous revolts by the Muslims in Ahmadnagar and the resistance of the newly arrived Portuguese in Bengal, Shah Jahan not only crushed this opposition but also strengthened his northwestern frontier. Shah Jahan's son Aurangzeb (r. 1658–1707), unwilling to wait for his

The Mughal Empire, 1526–1857

Mughal territory
- In 1525
- Added, by 1539
- Added, by 1605
- Added, by 1707
- Lost, by 1707

HIMALAYA MTS.

Panipat
Delhi
Agra

Arabian Sea

Bay of Bengal

Persian "Ardabil" Carpet, ca. 1540 The Persians were among the first carpet weavers of ancient times and perfected the art over thousands of years. This wool carpet, reputably from the Safavid shrine at Ardabil, is one of only three signed and dated carpets from the Safavid period, when Persian carpet making was at its zenith. Hand-knotted and hand-dyed, it was royally commissioned with a traditional medallion design, consisting of a central sunburst medallion surrounded by radiating pendants. Mosque lamps project from the top and bottom of the medallion. Inscribed on the carpet is an ode by the fourteenth-century poet Hafiz: "I have no refuge in this world other than thy threshold / My head has no resting place other than this doorway." (Victoria & Albert Museum/The Art Archive)

father to die, deposed him and confined him for years in a small cell. A puritanically devout and strictly orthodox Muslim, as well as a skillful general and a clever diplomat, Aurangzeb ruled more of India than did any previous Mughal emperor, having extended the realm deeper into south India. His reign, however, also marked the beginning of the empire's decline. His non-Muslim subjects were not pleased with his religious zealotry, and his military campaigns were costly. In the south resistance to Mughal rule led to major uprisings. (For more on Aurangzeb's rule, see page 607.)

Cultural Flowering

☐ What cultural advances occurred under the rule of the Ottoman, Safavid, and Mughal empires?

All three Islamic empires presided over an extraordinary artistic and intellectual flowering in everything from carpet making to architecture and gardening, from geography and astronomy to medicine. At the same time, new religious practices (and conflicts) emerged,

and new gathering places — coffeehouses — became popular outlets for socializing and exchanging ideas. Artistic and intellectual advances spread from culture to culture, probably because of the common Persian influence on the Turks since the tenth century. This exchange was also aided by common languages. Persian was used as the administrative language by the Mughals in India, and Arabic was a lingua franca of the entire region because of its centrality in Islam. In Ottoman lands both Persian and Arabic were literary languages, but Turkish slowly became the lingua franca of the realm. (For Ottoman perceptions of the other major Islamic empires, see "Viewpoints: Ottoman Travelers in Mughal and Safavid Lands," page 598.)

The Arts

One of the arts all three empires shared was carpet making. Carpet designs and weaving techniques demonstrate both cultural integration and local

• **Mughal** A term meaning "Mongol," used to refer to the Muslim empire of India, although its founders were primarily Turks, Afghans, and Persians.

Viewpoints

Ottoman Travelers in Mughal and Safavid Lands

• As the Ottoman Empire expanded, soldiers, officers, and administrators were dispatched to distant lands. Just as European travelers wrote of their adventures and the unusual customs they encountered, so too did Ottoman travelers.

The first excerpt from such travel writing comes from Sidi Ali Reis (1498–1563), an Ottoman admiral whose ship was blown off course and shipwrecked in northwest India. With the winds against him, he returned overland through India, Afghanistan, and Persia, the journey taking three years (1554–1556). The second excerpt is from Mustafa Ali's "Description of Cairo," written in 1599. Ali was a career official who held a series of posts as a financial administrator and worked on a history of the world. Although he had requested an assignment in Egypt, thinking it would help him with his world history, he found much of which he did not approve there. The final excerpt is from the lengthy travel writings of Evilya Celebi (1611–1682). In this passage he reports on Tabriz, then under Safavid control, which he visited in 1640 in the entourage of an envoy. This region was predominantly Shi'a, which attracted Celebi's attention.

Sidi Ali Reis on His Journey Across India, 1554–1556

"The Sultan offered to give me an escort by the way of Lahore, warning me to be on my guard against the Djats, a hostile tribe which had its abode there. But whichever route I chose I should have to wait a while yet, and as a matter of fact I waited for a whole month. One night in my dream I saw my mother, who told me that she had seen her highness Fatima in a dream, and had learned from her the glad news that I should soon be coming home, safe and sound.

When next morning I told this dream to my companions they were full of good courage. Sultan Mahmud, when he heard of it, at once consented to my departure. He gave me a beautiful horse, a team of camels, a large and a small tent, and money for the journey. He also provided me with a letter of recommendation to Humayun, and an escort of 250 mounted camel-drivers from Sind. . . . On the second day we came to the spring, but found no water, and many of my companions nearly succumbed with heat and thirst. I gave them some Teriak [opium], of the very best quality, and on the second day they were recovered. After this experience we deemed it advisable to leave the desert and to return to Mav, for the proverb says truly, "A stranger is an ignorant man."

The people of Sind gave us permission to proceed as far as the Machvara, and this river was crossed by boats. On the other side we found 500 Djats awaiting us, but our firearms frightened them and they did not attack. We advanced unmolested, and reached the town of Multan on the fifteenth of Ramazan."

Mustafa Ali's Description of Cairo, 1599

"Their women, all of them, ride donkeys! Even the spouses of some notables ride on donkeys to the Bulak promenade. Week after week they mount their donkeys and dismount like soldiers. Moreover, when they marry a daughter off they let her ride on a donkey and seventy or eighty women ride [with her], while the only things visible in terms of weapons are their shields. People of intelligence find that this unbecoming behavior constitutes a serious defect for the city of Cairo, because in other lands they put prostitutes on a donkey as a punishment. In Cairo the women mount donkeys by their own free will and expose themselves [to the eyes of the public]; therefore it appears appropriate that for punishment they be put on camels."

Evilya Celebi on His 1640 Visit to Tabriz

"Painters, architects, goldsmiths, and tailors are nowhere to be found so perfect as here. Precious stuffs manufactured here go all over the world; the velvet is much renowned. . . . Among the abundance of delicious fruits are particularly the pears and exquisite apricots; they are not found in such perfection even at Constantinople.

On New Year's day or the beginning of spring, battles are fought in this place by horses trained in the dark during forty or fifty days, by camels, buffaloes, sheep, asses, dogs, and cocks. These fights are peculiar to Persia. Every year on the tenth of the first month, being the feast of A'ashura, all the population of the town assemble under tents. . . . The finest show is in the variegated tent of the Khân, where all the great men of Tabriz are assembled, and where a Hymn on the death of Hussein is recited, in the same manner as the Hymn on the Prophet's birthday is in the Turkish mosques. The hearers listen, sighing and lamenting, but when the reciter arrives at the passage where Hussein is killed by accursed Shabr, a curtain opens behind him, and a severed head and trunk of a body, representing that of the Imam when dead, is thrown on the ground, when there rises such an uproar of cries and lamentations that everybody loses his wits. At this moment some hundred men mingle in the crowd with razors, with which they cut the arms and breasts of all loving believers, who desire to shed their blood on this day in remembrance of the blood shed by the Imam; they make such deep incisions and scars, that the ground appears as if it was blooming with tulips."

Sources: Ármin Vámbéry, trans., *The Travels and Adventures of the Turkish Admiral Sidi Ali Reïs in India, Afghanistan, Central Asia, and Persia, During the Years 1553–1556* (London: Luzac, 1899); Andreas Tietze, trans., *Mustafa Ali's Description of Cairo of 1599* (Vienna: Verlag der Österreichischen Akademie der Wissenschaften, 1975), p. 41; Evliya Effendi, *Narrative of Travels in Europe, Asia, and Africa in the Seventeenth Century*, trans. Joseph von Hammer (London: William H. Allen, 1834), pp. 137–138, slightly modified.

QUESTIONS FOR ANALYSIS

1. Why do you think these authors wrote about their experiences? Who was their likely audience?
2. Do you see any common themes or issues in these writings?

distinctiveness. Turkic migrants carried their weaving traditions with them as they moved but also readily adopted new motifs, especially from Persia. In Anatolia the town of Usak began its rise as a center of commercial carpet production in the fifteenth century. In Safavid Persia Shah Abbas was determined to improve his country's export trade and built the small cottage business of carpet weaving into a national industry. In the capital city of Isfahan alone, factories employed more than twenty-five thousand weavers who produced woolen carpets, brocades, and silks of brilliant color, design, and quality. Women and children often were employed as weavers, especially of the most expensive rugs, because their smaller hands could tie tinier knots.

Another art that spread from Persia to both Ottoman and Mughal lands was miniature painting, especially for book illustration. This tradition had been enriched by the many Chinese artists brought to Persia during the Mongol period. There was also an interplay between carpets and miniature painting. Naturalistic depictions of lotus blossoms, peonies, chrysanthemums, tulips, carnations, birds, and even dragons appear in both book illustrations and carpets.

Akbar enthusiastically supported artists who produced magnificent paintings and books in the Indo-Persian style. In Mughal India, as throughout the Muslim world, books were regarded as precious objects. Time, talent, and expensive materials went into their production, and they were highly coveted because they reflected wealth, learning, and power. Akbar reportedly possessed twenty-four thousand books when he died. Abu-l-Fazl describes Akbar's library and love of books:

> His Majesty's library is divided into several parts. . . . Prose works, poetical works, Hindi, Persian, Greek, Kashmirian, Arabic, are all separately placed. In this order they are also inspected. Experienced people bring them daily and read them before His Majesty, who hears every book from beginning to end . . . and rewards the readers with presents of cash either in gold or silver, according to the number of leaves read out by them. . . . There are no historical facts of past ages, or curiosities of science, or interesting points of philosophy, with which His Majesty, a leader of impartial sages, is unacquainted.[2]

City and Palace Building

In all three empires strong rulers built capital cities and imperial palaces as visible expressions of dynastic majesty. Europeans called Suleiman "the Magnificent" because of the grandeur of his court. With annual state revenues of about $80 million (at a time when

> "There are no historical facts of past ages, or curiosities of science, or interesting points of philosophy, with which His Majesty, a leader of impartial sages, is unacquainted."
>
> **ABU-L-FAZL**

Elizabeth I of England could expect $150,000 and Francis I of France perhaps $1 million) and thousands of servants, he had a lifestyle no European monarch could begin to rival. He used his fabulous wealth to adorn Istanbul with palaces, mosques, schools, and libraries, and the city reached about a million in population. The building of hospitals, roads, and bridges and the reconstruction of the water systems of the great pilgrimage sites at Mecca and Jerusalem benefited his subjects. Safavid Persia and Mughal India produced rulers with similar ambitions.

The greatest builder under the Ottomans was Mimar Sinan (1491–1588), a Greek-born devshirme recruit who rose to become imperial architect under Suleiman. A contemporary of Michelangelo, Sinan designed 312 public buildings, including mosques, schools, hospitals, public baths, palaces, and burial chapels. His masterpieces, the Shehzade and Suleimaniye mosques in Istanbul, which rivaled the Byzantine church of Hagia Sophia, were designed to maximize the space under the dome. His buildings expressed the discipline, power, and devotion to Islam that characterized the Ottoman Empire under Suleiman.

Shah Abbas made his capital, Isfahan, the jewel of the Safavid Empire. He had his architects place a polo ground in the center and surrounded it with palaces, mosques, and bazaars. A seventeenth-century English visitor described one of Isfahan's bazaars as "the surprisingest piece of Greatness in Honour of commerce the world can boast of." Besides splendid rugs, stalls displayed pottery and fine china, metalwork of exceptionally high quality, and silks and velvets of stunning weave and design. A city of perhaps 750,000 people, Isfahan also contained 162 mosques, 48 schools where future members of the ulama learned the sacred Muslim sciences, 273 public baths, and the vast imperial palace. Mosques were richly decorated with blue tile. Private houses had their own garden courts, and public gardens, pools, and parks adorned the wide streets. Tales of the beauty of Isfahan circulated worldwide, attracting thousands of tourists annually in the seventeenth and eighteenth centuries.

Akbar in India was also a great builder. The birth of a long-awaited son, Jahangir, inspired Akbar to build a new city, Fatehpur-Sikri, to symbolize the regime's

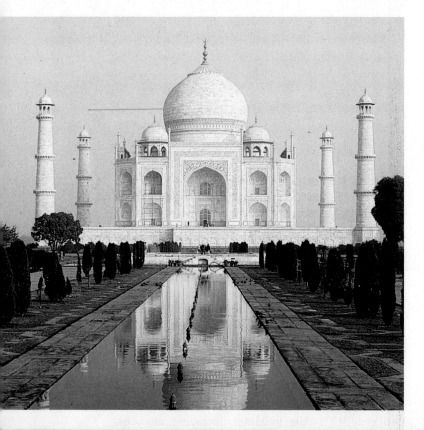

Islamic foundations. He personally supervised the construction of the city, which combined the Muslim tradition of domes, arches, and spacious courts with the Hindu tradition of flat stone beams, ornate decoration, and solidity. According to the historian Abu-l-Fazl, "His Majesty plans splendid edifices, and dresses the work of his mind and heart in the garment of stone and clay."[3] Completed in 1578, the city included an imperial palace, a mosque, lavish gardens, and a hall of worship, as well as thousands of houses for ordinary people. Unfortunately because of its bad water supply, the city was soon abandoned.

Of Akbar's successors, Shah Jahan had the most sophisticated interest in architecture. Because his capital at Agra was cramped, in 1639 he decided to found a new capital city at Delhi. In the design and layout of the buildings, Persian ideas predominated, an indication of the number of Persian architects and engineers who had flocked to the subcontinent. The walled palace-fortress alone extended over 125 acres. Built partly of red sandstone, partly of marble, it included private chambers for the emperor; mansions for the wives, widows, and concubines of the imperial household; huge audience rooms for the conduct of public business (treasury, arsenal, and military); baths; and vast gardens filled with flowers, trees, and thirty silver fountains spraying water. In 1650, with living quarters for guards, military officials, merchants, dancing girls, scholars, and hordes of cooks and servants, the palace-fortress housed 57,000 people. It also boasted a covered public bazaar (comparable to a modern mall), 270 feet long and 27 feet wide, with arcaded shops. It was probably the first roofed shopping center in India, although such centers were common in western Asia. The sight of the magnificent palace left contemporaries speechless. Shah Jahan had a Persian poetic couplet inscribed on the walls:

> If there is a paradise on the face of the
>   earth,
> It is this, it is this.

Two Masterpieces of Islamic Architecture
Istanbul's Suleimaniye Mosque, designed by Sinan and commissioned by Suleiman I, was finished in 1557. Its interior (left), is especially spacious. The Taj Mahal (above), built about a century later in Agra in northern India, is perhaps the finest example of Mughal architecture. Its white marble exterior is decorated with Arabic inscriptions and floral designs. (mosque: Flirt/SuperStock; Taj Mahal: John Elk/Stock, Boston)

Beyond the walls, princes and aristocrats built mansions and mosques on a smaller scale. With its fine architecture and its population of between 375,000 and 400,000, Delhi gained the reputation of being one of the great cities of the Muslim world.

For his palace, Shah Jahan ordered the construction of the Peacock Throne. This famous piece, encrusted with emeralds, diamonds, pearls, and rubies, took seven years to fashion and cost the equivalent of $5 million. It served as the imperial throne of India until 1739, when the Persian warrior Nadir Shah seized it as plunder and carried it to Persia.

Shah Jahan's most enduring monument is the Taj Mahal. Between 1631 and 1648 twenty thousand workers toiled over the construction of this memorial in Agra to Shah Jahan's favorite wife, who died giving birth to their fifteenth child. One of the most beautiful structures in the world, the Taj Mahal is both an expression of love and a superb architectural blending of Islamic and Indian culture.

Gardens

Many of the architectural masterpieces of this age had splendid gardens attached to them as well. Gardens represent a distinctive and highly developed feature of Persian culture. They commonly were walled, with a pool in the center and geometrically laid-out flowering plants, especially roses. Identified with paradise in Arabic tradition, gardens served not only as centers of prayer and meditation but also as places of leisure and revelry. A ruler might lounge near his pool as he watched the ladies of his harem bathe in it. Although first limited to the ruler's court, gardening soon spread among the wealthy citizens.

After the incorporation of Persia into the caliphate in the seventh century, formal gardening spread west and east through the Islamic world, as illustrated by the magnificent gardens of Muslim Spain, southern Italy, and later southeastern Europe. The Mongol followers of Timur took landscape architects from Persia back to Samarkand and adapted their designs to nomad encampments. In 1396 Timur ordered the construction of a garden in a meadow, called House of Flowers. When Timur's descendant Babur established the Mughal Dynasty in India, he adapted the Persian garden to the warmer southern climate. Gardens were laid out near palaces, mosques, shrines, and mausoleums, including the Taj Mahal, which had four water channels symbolizing the four rivers of paradise.

Because it evoked paradise, the garden played a large role in Muslim literature. Some scholars hold that to understand Arabic poetry, one must study Arabic gardening. The literary subjects of flowers and gardens provided basic themes for Hispano-Arab poets. The secular literature of Muslim Spain, rife with references

Isfahan Tiles The embellishment of Isfahan under Shah Abbas I created an unprecedented need for tiles, as had the rebuilding of imperial Istanbul after 1453, the vast building program of Suleiman the Magnificent, and a huge European demand. Persian potters learned their skills from the Chinese. By the late sixteenth century Italian and Austrian potters had imitated the Persian and Ottoman tile makers. (© Victoria & Albert Museum, London/ V&A Images)

Polo Two teams of four on horseback ride back and forth on a grass field measuring 200 by 400 yards, trying to hit a 4½-ounce wooden ball with a 4-foot mallet through the opponents' goal. Because a typical match involves many high-speed collisions among the horses, each player has to maintain a string of expensive ponies in order to change mounts several times during the game. Students of the history of sports believe the game originated in Persia, as shown in this eighteenth-century miniature, whence it spread to India, China, and Japan. Brought from India to England, where it became very popular among the aristocracy in the nineteenth century, polo is a fine example of cross-cultural influences. (Private Collection)

such as "a garland of verses," influenced the lyric poetry of southern France, the troubadours, and the courtly love tradition.

Gardens, of course, are seasonal. To remind themselves of paradise during the cold winter months, rulers, city people, and nomads ordered Persian carpets, most of which use floral patterns and have formal garden designs.

Intellectual Advances and Religious Trends

Between 1400 and 1800, the culture of the Islamic empires underwent many changes. Particularly notable were new movements within Islam as well as advances in mathematics, geography, astronomy, and medicine. Building on the knowledge of earlier Islamic writers and

stimulated by Ottoman naval power, the geographer and cartographer Piri Reis produced a map incorporating Islamic and Western knowledge that showed all the known world (1513); another of his maps detailed Columbus's third voyage to the New World. Piri Reis's *Book of the Sea* (1521) contained 129 chapters, each with a map incorporating all Islamic (and Western) knowledge of the seas and navigation and describing harbors, tides, dangerous rocks and shores, and storm areas. In the field of astronomy, Takiyuddin Mehmet (1521–1585), who served as the sultan's chief astronomer, built an observatory at Istanbul. He also produced *Instruments of the Observatory*, which catalogued astronomical instruments and described an astronomical clock that fixed the location of heavenly bodies with greater precision than ever before.

There were also advances in medicine. Under Suleiman the imperial palace itself became a center of medical science, and the large number of hospitals established in Istanbul and throughout the empire testifies to his support for medical research and his concern for the sick. Abi Ahmet Celebi (1436–1523), the chief physician of the empire, produced a study on kidney and bladder stones. He also founded the first Ottoman medical school, which served as a training institution for physicians of the empire.

Recurrent outbreaks of the plague posed a challenge for physicians in Muslim lands. Muhammad had once said not to go to a country where an epidemic existed but also not to leave a place because an epidemic broke out. As a consequence, when European cities began enforcing quarantines to control the spread of the plague, early Muslim rulers dismissed such efforts. By the sixteenth century, however, a better understanding of contagion led to a redefinition of the proper response to a plague epidemic and allowed for leaving the city in search of clean air.

In the realm of religion, the rulers of all three empires drew legitimacy from their support for Islam, at least among their Muslim subjects. The Sunni-Shi'a split between the Ottomans and Safavids led to efforts to define and enforce religious orthodoxy on both sides. For the Safavids this entailed suppressing Sufi movements and Sunnis, even marginalizing—sometimes massacring—the original Qizilbash warriors, who had come to be seen as politically disruptive. Sectarian conflicts within Islam were not as pronounced in Mughal lands, perhaps because even though the Mughals ruled over both Sunni and Shi'a subjects, these subjects were greatly outnumbered by non-Muslims, mostly Hindus.

Sufi fraternities thrived throughout the Muslim world in this era, even when the states tried to limit them. In India, Sufi orders also influenced non-Muslims. The mystical Bhakti movement among Hindus involved dances, poems, and songs reminiscent of Sufi practice. The development of the new religion of the Sikhs (seeks) also was influenced by Sufis. The Sikhs traced themselves back to a teacher in the sixteenth century who argued that God did not distinguish between Muslims and Hindus but saw everyone as his children. Sikhs rejected the caste system (division of society into hereditary groups) and forbade alcohol and tobacco, and men did not cut their hair (covering it instead with a turban). The Sikh movement was most successful in northwest India, where Sikh men armed themselves to defend their communities.

Despite all the signs of cultural vitality in the three Islamic empires, none of them adopted the printing press or went through the sorts of cultural expansion associated with it in China and Europe. Until 1729 the Ottoman authorities prohibited printing books in Turkish or Arabic (Jews, Armenians, and Greeks could establish presses and print in their own languages). Printing was not banned in Mughal India, but neither did the technology spread, even after Jesuit missionaries printed Bibles in Indian languages beginning in the 1550s. The Islamic authorities in each of these empires did not want to see writings circulate that might unsettle society and religious teachings. Nevertheless, the copying of manuscripts was permitted, and those who made their living this way sometimes organized to keep competition at bay.

Coffeehouses and Their Social Impact

In the mid-fifteenth century a new social convention spread throughout the Islamic world — drinking coffee. Arab writers trace the origins of coffee drinking to Yemen Sufis, who sought a trancelike concentration on God to the exclusion of everything else and found that coffee helped them stay awake (similarly, Buddhist monks drank tea to stay awake during long meditation sessions, a practice responsible for the spread of tea in East Asia). Most Sufis were not professional holy men but were employed as tradesmen and merchants. Therefore, the use of coffee for pious purposes led to its use as a business lubricant — an extension of hospitality to a potential buyer in a shop. Merchants carried the Yemenite practice to Mecca in about 1490. From Mecca, where pilgrims were introduced to it, coffee drinking spread to Egypt and Syria. In 1555 two Syrians opened a coffeehouse in Istanbul.

Coffeehouses provided a place for conversation and male sociability; there a man could entertain his friends

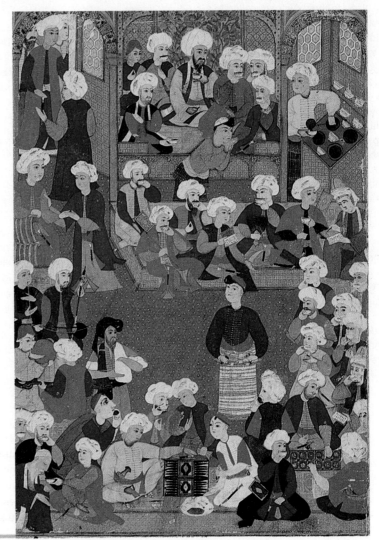

◻ Picturing the Past

Turkish Coffeehouse This sixteenth-century miniature depicts a crowded coffeehouse. (Reproduced by kind permission of the Trustees of the Chester Beatty Library, Dublin, Ms 439, folio 9)

ANALYZING THE IMAGE What activities are people engaged in? How does the artist convey differences in the ages of those drinking coffee?

CONNECTIONS Why would religious and political authorities have worried about what went on in coffeehouses?

Listening to the Past

Katib Chelebi on Tobacco

Katib Chelebi (1609–1657) was an Ottoman civil servant who spent much of his time as an accountant for the Turkish army, accompanying it on several important campaigns. Over time he became passionate about learning and pursued not only Islamic law but also ancient Greek philosophy, geography, and modern European sciences. He wrote several important books, including a bibliographical encyclopedia. The book of essays from which the following extract comes also discusses such contemporary issues as coffee, singing, opium, shaking hands, bowing, and bribery.

"Sometime in the latter half of the ninth century of the Hijra, after some Spanish ships had discovered the New World, the Portuguese and English were exploring its shores to find a passage from the Eastern to the Western Ocean. They came to an island close to the mainland, called in the Atlas "Gineya." A ship's doctor, who had been smitten with a lymphatic disorder, due to the influence of the sea air on his natural temperament, decided to try and cure it with hot and dry things, in accordance with the laws of treatment by opposites. When his ship reached that island, he noticed a kind of leaf was burning. He smelled it, and as it was hot of scent he began to inhale it, using an instrument resembling a pipe. It did him good, so he took a large quantity of the leaf and used it throughout their stay. The ship's company saw this and, regarding it as a beneficial medicine, followed the doctor's example and loaded themselves up with the leaf. One saw another and they all began to smoke. When the ship arrived in England, the habit spread, through France to the other lands. People tried it, not knowing its origin, and not considering that it was smoked for a serious purpose. Many became addicts, putting it in the category of stimulating drugs. It has become a thing common to East and West, and no one has succeeded in suppressing it.

From its first appearance in Turkey, which was about the year 1010/1601, to the present day, various preachers have spoken against it individually, and many of the Ulema [ulama] have written tracts concerning it, some claiming that it is a thing forbidden, some that it is disapproved. Its addicts have replied to the effect that it is permissible. After some time had elapsed, the eminent surgeon Ibrāhīm Efendi devoted much care and attention to the matter, conducting great debates in the Abode of the Sultanate, that is, in the city of Istanbul, giving warning talks at a special public meeting in the mosque of Sultan Mehmed, and sticking copies of fetwas [fatwas] onto walls. He troubled himself to no purpose. The more he spoke, the more people persisted in smoking. Seeing that it was fruitless, he abandoned his efforts. After that, the late Sultan Murad IV, towards the end of his reign, closed down the coffeehouses in order to shut the gate of iniquity, and also banned smoking, in consequence of certain outbreaks of fire. People being undeterred, the imperial anger necessitated the chastisement of those who, by smoking, committed the sin of disobedience to the imperial command. Gradually His Majesty's severity in suppression increased, and so did people's desire to smoke, in accordance with the saying, "Men desire what is forbidden," and many thousands of men were sent to the abode of nothingness.

When the Sultan was going on the expedition against Baghdad, at one halting-place fifteen or twenty leading men of the Army were arrested on a charge of smoking, and were put to death with the severest torture in the imperial presence. Some of the soldiers carried short pipes in their sleeves, some in their pockets, and they found an opportunity to smoke even during the executions. At Istanbul, no end of soldiers used to go into the barracks and smoke in the privies. Even during this rigorous prohibition, the number of smokers exceeded that of the non-smokers.

After that Sultan's death, the practice was sometimes forbidden and sometimes allowed, until the Sheykh al-Islam, the late Baha'i Efendi, gave a fetwa ruling that it was permissible, and the practice won renewed popularity among the people of the world. Occasional reprimands from the Throne to smokers have generally been disregarded, and smoking is at present practiced all over the habitable globe. Such are the vicissitudes undergone by tobacco.

Now there are a number of possible ways of considering the subject, which we shall briefly set forth.

(1) The first possibility is that the people may be effectively prevented from smoking and may give it up. This possibility must be set aside, for custom is second nature. Addicts are not made to give up in this way. . . .

cheaply and more informally than at home. But coffeehouses encountered religious and governmental opposition based on the following arguments: (1) because of its composition, coffee is intoxicating, making it analogous to wine, prohibited to Muslims; (2) coffee drinking was an innovation and therefore a violation of Islamic law; (3) coffeehouses encouraged political discussions, facilitating sedition; (4) coffeehouses attracted unemployed soldiers and other low types, encouraging immoral behavior, such as gambling, using drugs, and soliciting prostitutes; and (5) music at coffeehouses encouraged debauchery. Thus coffeehouses drew the attention of government officials, who considered themselves the guardians of public morality.

A man is smoking a long pipe in one of the stalls in a bazaar depicted in this seventeenth-century Turkish painting. (The Granger Collection, New York)

(2) Is this tobacco found to be good or bad by the intelligence? If we set aside the fact that addicts think it good, common sense judges it to be bad. . . .

(3) Its good and harmful effects. As to its harmful effects there is no doubt. It ends by becoming a basic need of the addict, who does not consider its evil consequences. Its harmful physical effect too is established, for tobacco is medically noxious in that it makes turbid the aerial essence. . . .

(4) Is it innovation? It may be conceded that it is innovation in the eyes of the sacred law, for it appeared in recent times, nor is it possible to class it as "good innovation." That it is innovation in the light of intelligence is sure, for it is not a thing that has been seen or heard of by the intelligent ever since the time of Adam. . . .

(5) Is it abominable? There is no word of justification for this, in reason or in law. . . . It is perhaps not irrelevant to point out that the scent of burning tobacco has curative uses as an inhalant. But an evil odor arises in the mouth of the heavy smoker. . . .

(6) Is it canonically forbidden? It is written in the manuals of jurisprudence that in any particular matter where there is no decisive ruling in the law, the jurisconsult may exercise his own discretion. He may, according to one point of view, bring together all relevant circumstances, consider them, and make his own deductions. Yet the following course is preferable: not to declare things forbidden, but always to have recourse to any legal principle that justifies declaring them permitted, thus preserving the people from being laden with sins and persisting in what has been prohibited.

(7) Is it canonically indifferent? As the rise of smoking is of recent occurrence, there is no explicit treatment or mention of it in the legal manuals. This being so, some say that in accordance with the principle that permissibility is the norm—i.e., that in the absence of a clear prohibition things are permitted—smoking is permitted and lawful. ❞

Source: Katib Chelebi, *The Balance of Truth*, trans. G. L. Lewis (London: George Allen and Unwin, 1957), pp. 50–58.

QUESTIONS FOR ANALYSIS

1. What do you learn about social life in the Ottoman Empire from this essay?

2. What can you infer about the sorts of arguments that were made by Islamic jurists in Katib Chelebi's day?

3. How open-minded was Katib Chelebi? What evidence from the text led you to your conclusion?

On the other hand, the coffee trade was a major source of profit that local notables sought to control.

Although debate over the morality of coffeehouses continued through the sixteenth century, their eventual acceptance represented a revolution in Islamic life: socializing was no longer confined to the home. Ultimately, because the medical profession remained divided on coffee's harmful effects and because religious authorities could not prove that coffeehouses violated religious law, coffee drinking could not be forbidden. In the seventeenth century coffee and coffeehouses spread to Europe. (For reaction to another new product that spread quickly despite opposition, see "Listening to the Past: Katib Chelebi on Tobacco," above.)

Non-Muslims Under Muslim Rule

☐ How did Christians, Jews, Hindus, and other non-Muslims fare under these Islamic states?

Drawing on Qur'anic teachings, Muslims had long practiced a religious toleration unknown in Christian Europe. Muslim rulers for the most part guaranteed the lives and property of Christians and Jews on their promise of obedience and the payment of a poll tax. In the case of the Ottomans, this tolerance was extended not only to the Christians and Jews who had been living under Muslim rule for centuries but also to the Serbs, Bosnians, Croats, and other Orthodox Christians in the newly conquered Balkans. The Ottoman conqueror of Constantinople, Mehmet, nominated the Greek patriarch as official representative of the Greek population. This and other such appointments recognized non-Muslims as functioning parts of the Ottoman society and economy. In 1454 Rabbi Isaac Sarfati sent a letter to the Jews in the Rhineland, Swabia, Moravia, and Hungary, urging them to move to Turkey because of the good conditions for Jews there. A massive migration to Ottoman lands followed. When Ferdinand and Isabella of Spain expelled the Jews in 1492 and later, many immigrated to the Ottoman Empire.

The Safavid authorities made efforts to convert Armenian Christians in the Caucuses, and many seem to have embraced Islam, some more voluntarily than others. Nevertheless, the Armenian Christian Church retained its vitality, and under the Safavids Armenian Christians were prominent merchants in long-distance trade (see page 610).

Babur and his successors acquired even more non-Muslim subjects with their conquests in India, which had not only Hindus but also substantial numbers of Jains, Zoroastrians, Christians, and Sikhs. Over time, the number of Indians who converted to Islam increased, but the Mughal rulers did not force conversion. The Ganges plain, the area of the Indian subcontinent most intensely exposed to Mughal rule and for the longest span of time, had, when the first reliable census was taken in 1901, a Muslim population of only 10 to 15 percent. Accordingly, some scholars have argued that in the Indian subcontinent there was an inverse relationship between the degree of Muslim political penetration and conversion to Islam.

Akbar went the furthest in promoting Muslim-Hindu accommodation. He celebrated important Hindu festivals, such as Diwali, the festival of lights, and he wore his uncut hair in a turban as a concession to Indian practice. Also, Akbar twice married Hindu princesses, one of whom became the mother of his heir, Jahangir, and he appointed the Spanish Jesuit Antonio Monserrate (1536–1600) as tutor to his second son, Prince Murad. Eventually, Hindus totaled 30 percent of the imperial bureaucracy. In 1579 Akbar abolished the **jizya**, the poll tax on non-Muslims that guaranteed their protection. These actions, especially the abolition

Emperor Akbar in the City of Fatehpur-Sikri In 1569 Akbar founded the city of Fatehpur-Sikri (the City of Victory) to honor the Muslim holy man Shaykh Salim Chishti, who had foretold the birth of Akbar's son and heir Jahangir. Akbar is shown here seated on the cushion in the center overseeing the construction of the city. The image is contained in the *Akbarnama*, a book of illustrations Akbar commissioned to officially chronicle his reign. (Victoria & Albert Museum/The Bridgeman Art Library)

of the jizya, infuriated the ulama, and serious conflict erupted between them and the emperor. Ultimately, Akbar issued an imperial decree declaring that the Mughal emperor had supreme authority, even above the ulama, in all religious matters. This statement, resting on a policy of benign toleration, represented a severe defeat for the Muslim religious establishment.

Some of Akbar's successors, above all Aurangzeb, sided more with the ulama. Aurangzeb appointed censors of public morals in important cities to enforce Islamic laws against gambling, prostitution, drinking, and the use of narcotics. He forbade sati — the self-immolation of widows on their husbands' funeral pyres — and the castration of boys to be sold as eunuchs. He also abolished all taxes not authorized by Islamic law. This measure led to a serious loss of state revenues. To replace them, in 1679 Aurangzeb reimposed the tax on non-Muslims. Aurangzeb's reversal of Akbar's religious toleration and cultural cosmopolitanism extended further. He ordered the destruction of some Hindu temples and tried to curb Sikhism. He also required Hindus to pay higher customs duties than Muslims. Out of fidelity to Islamic law, he even criticized his mother's tomb, the Taj Mahal: "The lawfulness of a solid construction over a grave is doubtful, and there can be no doubt about the extravagance involved."[4] Aurangzeb's attempts to enforce rigid Islamic norms proved highly unpopular with the majority of his subjects and aroused resistance that weakened Mughal rule. Aurangzeb himself died on an unsuccessful military campaign in 1707 to suppress a rebellion by the Marathas in the southern highlands.

Shifting Trade Routes and European Penetration

☐ How were the Islamic empires affected by the gradual shift toward trade routes that bypassed their lands?

It has widely been thought that a decline in the wealth and international importance of the Muslim empires could be directly attributed to the long-term shift in trading patterns that resulted from the discoveries of Columbus, Magellan, and other European explorers. The argument is that new sea routes enabled Europeans to acquire goods from the East without using Muslim intermediaries, so that the rise of Europe associated with exploration and the creation of colonial powers beginning in the sixteenth century led directly and indirectly to the eclipse of the Ottomans, Safavids, and Mughals. Recent scholars have challenged these

> " It is true that there does exist a common right to all to navigate the seas and in Europe we recognize the rights which others hold against us; but the right does not extend beyond Europe. "

PORTUGUESE HISTORIAN BARRÕES

ideas as too simplistic. Turkish, Persian, and Indian merchants remained very active as long-distance traders into the eighteenth century and opened up many new routes themselves. Moreover, it was not until the eighteenth century that there were many signs of political decline in the three Islamic empires. As well, government revenue came more from taxes on farmers than from trade.

Agriculture benefited from the spread of new crops, such as coffee and sugar, from elsewhere in the Old World, but New World crops like potatoes and sweet potatoes played a relatively minor role in the economy and do not seem to have fueled population increases as rapid as those in western Europe and East Asia. By 1800 the population of India was about 190 million, that of Safavid lands about 8 million, and that of Ottoman lands about 24 million. (By comparison, China's population stood at about 300 million in 1800, greater than that of all three Islamic empires put together.)

Still, the importance of trade to the economies of the three Islamic empires should not be discounted. Over the centuries covered in this chapter, trading patterns and practices evolved, and European penetration increased.

European Rivalry for Trade in the Indian Ocean

Shortly before Babur's invasion of India, the Portuguese had opened the subcontinent to Portuguese trade. In 1510 they established the port of Goa on the west coast of India as their headquarters and through an aggressive policy took control of Muslim shipping in the Indian Ocean and Arabian Sea, charging high fees to let ships through. The Portuguese historian Barrões attempted to justify Portugal's seizure of commercial traffic that the Muslims had long dominated:

> It is true that there does exist a common right to all to navigate the seas and in Europe we recognize the rights which others hold against us; but the right does not extend beyond Europe and therefore the Portuguese as Lords of the Sea are justified in confiscating the goods of all those who navigate the seas without their permission.[5]

• **jizya** A poll tax on non-Muslims.

MAP 20.3 India, 1707–1805
In the eighteenth century Mughal power gradually yielded to the Hindu Marathas and to the British East India Company.

In short, the Portuguese decided that Western principles of international law should not restrict them in Asia. As a result, they controlled the spice trade over the Indian Ocean for almost a century.

In 1602 the Dutch formed the Dutch East India Company with the stated goal of wresting the enormously lucrative spice trade from the Portuguese. In 1685 they supplanted the Portuguese in Ceylon (Sri Lanka). The scent of fabulous profits also attracted the English. With a charter signed by Queen Elizabeth, eighty London merchants organized the British East India Company. In 1619 Emperor Jahangir granted a British mission important commercial concessions. Soon, by offering gifts, medical services, and bribes to Indian rulers, the British East India Company was able to set up twenty-eight coastal forts/trading posts. By 1700 the company had founded the cities that became Madras and Calcutta (today called Chennai and Kolkata) and had taken over Bombay (today Mumbai), which had been a Portuguese possession (Map 20.3).

The British called their trading posts **factory-forts**. The term *factory* did not signify manufacturing; it designated the walled compound containing the residences, gardens, and offices of British East India Company officials and the warehouses where goods were stored before being shipped to Europe. The company president exercised political authority over all residents.

Factory-forts existed to make profits from Asian-European trade, which was robust due to the popularity of Indian and Chinese wares in Europe in the late seventeenth and early eighteenth centuries. The European middle classes wanted Indian textiles, which were colorful, durable, cheap, and washable. The upper classes desired Chinese wallpaper and porcelains and Indian silks and brocades. Other Indian goods in demand included pepper and other spices, sugar, and opium. To pay for these goods, the British East India Company sold silver, copper, zinc, lead, and fabrics to the Indians. Profits grew even larger after 1700, when the company began to trade with China.

Merchant Networks in the Islamic Empires

The shifting trade patterns associated with European colonial expansion brought no direct benefit to the Ottomans and the Safavids, whose merchants could now be bypassed by Europeans seeking goods from India, Southeast Asia, or China. Yet merchants from these

• **factory-forts** A term first used by the British for their trading post at Surat that was later applied to all European walled settlements in India.

English Factory-Fort at Surat
The factory-fort began as a storage place for goods before they were bought and transported abroad; it gradually expanded to include merchants' residences and some sort of fortification. By 1650 the English had twenty-three factory-forts in India. Surat, in the Gujarat region, was the busiest factory-fort and port until it was sacked by the Marathas in 1664. (Mansell Collection/Getty Images)

Islamic empires often proved adaptable, finding ways to benefit from the new trade networks.

In the case of India, the appearance of European traders led to a rapid increase in overall trade, helping Indian merchants and the Indian economy. Some Indian merchants in Calcutta and Bombay, for instance, made gigantic fortunes from trade within Asia carried on European ships. Block-printed cotton cloth, produced by artisans working at home, was India's chief export. Through an Islamic business device involving advancing payment to artisans, banker-brokers supplied the material for production and money for the artisans to live on while they worked; the cloth brokers specified the quality, quantity, and design of the finished products. This procedure resembles the later English "domestic" or "putting-out" system (see page 687), for the very good reason that the English took the idea from the Indians.

Within India, the demand for cotton cloth, as well as for food crops, was so great that Akbar had to launch a wide-scale road-building campaign. From the Indian region of Gujarat, Indian merchant bankers shipped their cloth worldwide: across the Indian Ocean to Aden and the Muslim-controlled cities on the east coast of Africa; across the Arabian Sea to Muscat and Hormuz and up the Persian Gulf to the cities of Persia; up the Red Sea to the Mediterranean; by sea also to Malacca, Indonesia, China, and Japan; by land across Africa to Ghana on the west coast; and to Astrakhan, Poland, Moscow, and even the Russian cities on the distant Volga River. Indian businessmen had branch offices in many of these places, and all this activity produced fabulous wealth for some Indian merchants. Some scholars have compared India's international trade in

English Dress Made of Indian Printed Cotton Cloth Early British traders in India were impressed with the quality of the textiles made there and began ordering designs that would be popular with the English. This dress, created around 1770–1780 in England, is made of printed cotton (chintz) from the southeastern part of India. Chintz became so popular in England that it was eventually banned because it was threatening local textile industries. (© Victoria and Albert Museum, London/V&A Images)

the sixteenth century with that of Italian firms, such as the Medici. Indian trade actually extended over a far wider area, however. Indian merchants were often devout Hindus, Muslims, Buddhists, or Jains, evidence that undermines the argument of some Western writers, notably Karl Marx (see page 721), that religion retarded Asia's economic development.

Throughout Muslim lands both Jews and Christians were active in commerce. A particularly interesting case involves the Armenian Christians in the Safavid empire in the sixteenth to eighteenth centuries. Armenian merchants had been trading from their base in Armenia for centuries and were especially known for their trade in Persian silk. When the Portuguese first appeared on the western coast of India in 1498 and began to settle in south India, they found many Armenian merchant communities already there. A few decades later Akbar invited Armenians to settle in his new capital, Agra. In 1603 Shah Abbas captured much of Armenia, taking it from the Ottomans. Because defending this newly acquired border area was difficult, he forced the Armenians to move more deeply into Persia. Among them was the merchant community of Julfa, which was moved to a new suburb of Isfahan that was given the name New Julfa. The old city of Julfa was burned down so that they could not return. Shah Abbas made use of the Armenian merchants as royal merchants and financiers, but their economic mainstay continued to be long-distance trade.

Surviving letters and account books have allowed scholars to reconstruct the expanding trading networks of the Armenian merchants — networks that stretched from Venice and Amsterdam in western Europe, Moscow in Russia, Ottoman-controlled Aleppo and Smyrna, to all the major trading cities of India and even regions farther east, including Guangzhou in southern China and Manila in the Philippines. Many Armenian communities in these cities became quite substantial, built churches, and recruited priests. Kinship connections were regularly used to cement commercial relations, and members of the community living in these scattered cities would return to New Julfa to marry, creating new kinship connections. Business, though, was conducted through contracts. The merchant about to take a journey would borrow a sum of money to purchase goods and would contract to pay it back with interest on his return. Using couriers, these Armenian merchants sent long letters describing the trade environment and the prices that could be realized for given goods. These letters were written in a dialect of Armenian known to few outside their community, making it easier to maintain confidentiality in reports on trade conditions.

The Armenian merchants would sail on whatever ships were available, including Dutch and Italian ones. The goods they dealt in included silver, gold, precious stones, indigo and other dyestuffs, silk, cotton cloth, and tea. The merchants often could speak half a dozen languages and were comfortable in both Islamic and Christian lands. In India Armenian merchants reached an agreement with the British East India Company that recognized their rights to live in company cities and observe their own religion. By the 1660s they had settled in Manila, and a few decades later they entered what is now Malaysia and Indonesia. By the end of the seventeenth century a small group of Armenian merchants had crossed the Himalayas from India and established themselves in Lhasa, Tibet. By the mid-eighteenth century they had also settled in the Dutch colony of Batavia (Indonesia). Clearly the Armenian merchants were able to operate profitably in cities European powers dominated.

In the mid-eighteenth century the Armenian community lost its center in New Julfa because of religious

Armenian Brass Bowl The inscription on this bowl dates it to 1616 and places it in New Julfa, the Armenian quarter of Isfahan. It would have been used by an Armenian Christian priest to wash his hands. (© Ana A. Melikian 2007)

persecution by a zealous shah, and the community scattered. Still, Armenian merchants remained prominent in many trading centers, including Russia, the Mediterranean, and especially India, well into the nineteenth century.

From the British East India Company to the British Empire in India

Britain's presence in India began with the British East India Company and its desire to profit from trade. Managers of the company in London discouraged all unnecessary expenses and financial risks and thus opposed missionary activities or interference in local Indian politics. Nevertheless, the company responded to political instability in India in the early eighteenth century by extending political control. When warlords appeared or an uprising occurred, people from the surrounding countryside flocked into the company's factory-forts, which gradually came to exercise political authority over the territories around them. The company's factories evolved into defensive installations manned by small garrisons of native troops — known as **sepoys** — trained in Western military weapons and tactics.

Britain eventually became the dominant foreign presence in India, despite challenges from the French. The French arrived in India in the 1670s and established factories in Bengal, Pondicherry, and elsewhere. They made allies of Indian princes and built an army of native troops who were trained as infantrymen. From 1740 to 1763, Britain and France were engaged in a tremendous global struggle, and India, like North America in the Seven Years' War, became a battlefield and a prize. The French won land battles, but English sea power proved decisive by preventing the landing of French reinforcements. The Treaty of Paris of 1763 recognized British control of much of India, marking the beginning of the British Empire in India.

How was Britain to govern so large a territory? Eventually, the East India Company was pushed out of its governing role because the English Parliament distrusted the company, believing it was corrupt. The Regulating Act of 1773 created the office of governor general to exercise political authority over the territory controlled by the company. The India Act of 1784 required that the governor general be chosen from outside the company, and it made company directors subject to parliamentary supervision.

Implementation of these reforms fell to three successive governors, Warren Hastings, (r. 1774–1785), Lord Charles Cornwallis (r. 1786–1794), and the marquess Richard Wellesley (r. 1797–1805). Hastings sought allies among Indian princes, laid the foundations for the first Indian civil service, abolished tolls to facilitate internal trade, placed the salt and opium trades under government control, and planned a codification of Muslim and Hindu laws. Cornwallis introduced the British style of property relations, in effect converting a motley collection of former Mughal officers, tax collectors, and others into English-style landlords. The result was a new system of landholding in which the rents of tenant farmers supported the landlords. Wellesley was victorious over local rulers who resisted British rule, vastly extending British influence in India. Like most nineteenth-century British governors of India, Wellesley believed that British rule strongly benefited the Indians. With supreme condescension, he wrote that British power should be established over the Indian princes in order

> to deprive them of the means of prosecuting any measure or of forming any confederacy hazardous to the security of the British empire, and to enable us to preserve the tranquility of India by exercising a general control over the restless spirit of ambition and violence which is characteristic of every Asiatic government.[6]

Political Decline

□ Did any common factors lead to the decline of central power in the Islamic empires in the seventeenth and eighteenth centuries?

By the end of the eighteenth century, all three of the major Islamic empires were on the defensive and losing territory (Map 20.4). They faced some common problems — succession difficulties, financial strain, and loss of military superiority — but their circumstances differed in significant ways as well.

The first to fall was the Safavid empire. Persia was exceptionally difficult to govern, and it did not have the revenue base to maintain the sort of standing armies that the Ottomans and the Mughals had. Decline in the strength of the army encouraged increased foreign aggression. In 1722 the Afghans invaded from the east, seized Isfahan, and were able to repulse an Ottoman invasion from the west. In Isfahan thousands of officials and members of the shah's family were executed. In the following century some potential leaders emerged, but none were able to reunite all of Persia. In this political vacuum, Shi'a religious institutions grew stronger.

• **sepoys** The native Indian troops who were trained as infantrymen.

MAP 20.4 The Muslim World, ca. 1700 The three great Islamic empires were adjacent to each other and of similar physical size. Many of their other neighbors were Muslim as well.

The Ottoman Empire also suffered from poor leadership. Early Ottoman practice had guaranteed that the sultans would be forceful men. The sultan's sons gained administrative experience as governors of provinces and military experience on the battlefield as part of their education. After the sultan died, any son who wanted to succeed had to contest his brothers to claim the throne, after which the new sultan would have his defeated brothers executed. Although bloody, this system led to the succession of capable, determined men. After Suleiman's reign, however, the tradition was abandoned. To prevent threats of usurpation, sons of the sultan were brought up in the harem and confined there as adults, denied roles in government. The result was a series of rulers who were incompetent or minor children, leaving power in the hands of high officials and the mothers of the heirs. Political factions formed around viziers, military leaders, and palace women. In the contest for political favor, the devshirme was abandoned, and political and military ranks were filled by Muslims.

The Ottoman Empire's military strength also declined. The defeat of the Turkish fleet by the Spanish off the coast of Greece at Lepanto in 1571 marked the loss of Ottoman dominance in the Mediterranean, and the empire's political and military setbacks continued. By the terms of a peace treaty with Austria signed at Karlowitz (1699), the Ottomans lost the major European provinces of Hungary and Transylvania, along with the tax revenues they had provided. Also, the Ottoman armies were depending more on mercenaries, and they did not keep up with the innovations in drill, command, and control that were then transforming European armies. From the late seventeenth century Ottoman armies began losing wars and territory along both northern and eastern borders. In 1730 the empire gave up territory along its eastern border. And in 1774 it lost the lands on the northern bank of the Black Sea to Russia. In North Africa the local governors came to act more independently, sometimes starting hereditary dynasties.

In Mughal India the old Turkish practice of letting heirs fight for the throne persisted, leading to frequent struggles over succession, but also to strong rulers. Yet military challenges proved daunting there as well. After defeating his father and brothers, Aurangzeb pushed the conquest of the south. The stiffest opposition came from the Marathas, a militant Hindu group centered in the western Deccan. From 1681 until his death in 1707, Aurangzeb led repeated sorties through the Deccan. He took many forts and won several battles, but total destruction of the Maratha guerrilla bands eluded him.

Aurangzeb's death led to thirteen years of succession struggles, shattering the empire. His eighteenth-century successors were less successful than the Ottomans in making the dynasty the focus of loyalty. Mughal provincial governors began to rule independently, giving only minimal allegiance to the throne at Delhi. Meanwhile, the Marathas pressed steadily northward, constituting the gravest threat to Mughal authority. In 1857 the Mughal Dynasty came to an end.

In 1739 the Persian adventurer Nadir Shah invaded India, defeated the Mughal army, looted Delhi, and after a savage massacre carried off a huge amount of treasure, including the Peacock Throne. When Nadir Shah withdrew to Afghanistan, he took with him the Mughal government's prestige. Constant skirmishes between the Afghans and the Marathas for control of the Punjab and northern India ended in 1761 at Panipat, where the Marathas were crushed by the Afghans. At that point, India no longer had a state strong enough to impose order on the subcontinent or check the penetration of the Europeans.

In all three empires economic difficulties also put strain on the state. A long period of peace in the late sixteenth century and again in the mid-eighteenth century, as well as a decline in the frequency of visits of the plague, led to a doubling of the population. Increased population, coupled with the "little ice age" of the mid-seventeenth century, meant that the land could not sustain so many people; nor could the towns provide jobs for the thousands of agricultural workers who fled to them. The return of demobilized soldiers aggravated the problem. Inflation, famine, and widespread revolts resulted. The economic center of gravity shifted from the capital to the provinces, and politically the empire began to decentralize as well. Power was seized by local notables and military strongmen at the expense of central government officials. There was a positive side to increasing provincial autonomy, however, because it drew more people into political participation, thus laying a foundation for later nationalism. At the time, however, it was perceived in negative terms.

CONNECTIONS

From 1300 to 1800 and from North Africa to India, Islamic civilization thrived under three dynastic houses: the Ottomans, the Safavids, and the Mughals. All three empires had a period of expansion when territory was enlarged, followed by a high point politically and culturally, and later a period of contraction, when territories broke away. Two of the empires had large non-Muslim populations. India, even under Mughal rule, remained a predominantly Hindu land, and the Ottomans, in the process of conquering the Balkans, acquired a population that was predominantly Greek Orthodox Christians. Though all three states supported Islam, the Safavids took Shi'a teachings as orthodox, and the other two favored Sunni teachings. At the cultural level, the borders of these three states were porous, and people, ideas, art motifs, languages, and trade flowed back and forth.

In East Asia the fifteenth through eighteenth century also saw the creation of strong, prosperous, and expanding states, though in the case of China (under the Qing Dynasty) and Japan (under the Tokugawa Shogunate) the eighteenth century was a cultural high point, not a period of decline. The Qing emperors were Manchus, from the region northeast of China proper, reminiscent of the Mughals, who began in Afghanistan. As in the Islamic lands, during these centuries the presence of European powers became an issue in East Asia, though the details were quite different. Although one of the commodities that the British most wanted was the tea produced in China, Britain did not extend political control in China the way it did in India. Japan managed to refuse entry to most European traders after finding their presence and their support for missionary activity disturbing. The next chapter takes up these developments in East Asia.

■ CHAPTER REVIEW

□ **How were the three Islamic empires established, and what sorts of governments did they set up? (p. 588)**

After the decline of the Mongols in Central Asia and Persia, many small Turkic-ruled states emerged. Three of them went on to establish large empires: the Ottomans in Anatolia, the Safavids in Persia, and the Mughals in India. The Ottoman Empire's political system reached its classic form under Suleiman I. All authority flowed from the sultan to his public servants: provincial governors, police officers, military generals, heads of treasuries, and viziers. In Persia power was held for some time by Turkish lords, no single one dominant until 1501, when a fourteen-year-old military leader declared himself shah. The strength of the Safavid state rested in part on the skills of urban bureaucrats, who were an essential part of the civil machinery of government. One of the great leaders of the Mughal Empire, Akbar, developed an administrative bureaucracy centered on four co-equal ministers: for finance and revenue; the army and intelligence; the judiciary and religious patronage; and the imperial household. Whereas the Ottoman sultans and Safavid shahs made extensive use of slaves acquired from non-Muslim lands for military and administrative positions, Akbar used the services of royal princes, nobles, and warrior-aristocrats. All three empires responded to the shift in military technology away from the mounted archer toward the use of gunpowder weapons. The Ottomans in particular made effective use of guns and artillery.

□ **What cultural advances occurred under the rule of the Ottoman, Safavid, and Mughal empires? (p. 597)**

All three Islamic empires presided over an extraordinary artistic and intellectual flowering in everything from carpet making and book illustration to architecture and gardening, from geography and astronomy to medicine. At the same time, new religious practices and conflicts emerged, and new gathering places — coffeehouses — became popular outlets for socializing and exchanging ideas. In the realm of religion, the rulers of all three empires drew legitimacy from their support for Islam, at least among their Muslim subjects; however, there were key differences: the Ottomans and Mughals supported the Sunni tradition, the Safavids the Shi'a tradition.

□ **How did Christians, Jews, Hindus, and other non-Muslims fare under these Islamic states? (p. 606)**

All the Islamic empires had a substantial number of non-Muslim subjects. Drawing on Qur'anic teachings, Muslims had long practiced a religious toleration unknown in Christian Europe. Most Muslim rulers guaranteed the lives and property of Christians and Jews who promised obedience and paid a poll tax. The Ottomans ruled over the Balkans, where most of the people were Christian, and Muslims in India were greatly outnumbered by Hindus. Although the Safavid authorities made efforts to convert Armenian Christians in the Caucuses, the Armenian Christian Church retained its vitality.

□ **How were the Islamic empires affected by the gradual shift toward trade routes that bypassed their lands? (p. 607)**

European exploration and colonization of foreign lands opened new trade routes and enabled Europeans to acquire goods from the East without using Muslim intermediaries. Nevertheless, enterprising merchants from India and Persia frequently found ways to profit from the new trade relations, showing considerable adaptability. Within India, British merchants took on more and more political control in politically unstable areas, leading before the end of the eighteenth century to a colonial empire in India recognized by the British Parliament.

□ **Did any common factors lead to the decline of central power in the Islamic empires in the seventeenth and eighteenth centuries? (p. 611)**

By the end of the eighteenth century all three of the major Islamic empires were on the defensive and losing territory. Common challenges included succession difficulties, economic problems, and loss of military superiority. The first to fall was the Safavid Empire, which did not have the revenue base to maintain the sort of standing armies that the Ottomans and the Mughals had. Decline in the strength of its armies encouraged increased foreign aggression. The Ottoman Empire suffered from weakened leadership and military strength. From the late seventeenth century, Ottoman armies began losing wars and territory along both the northern and eastern borders, eventually giving up northern and eastern territories entirely. Military challenges proved daunting in Mughal India as well. The stiffest opposition came from the Marathas, a militant Hindu group in the south. India also suffered from succession struggles that shattered the empire. All three empires faced decentralization of authority. Power was seized by local notables and military strongmen at the expense of central government officials.

SUGGESTED READING

Atil, Esin. *The Age of Sultan Suleyman the Magnificent*. 1987. A splendidly illustrated celebration of the man and his times.

Barkey, Karen. *Empire of Difference*. 2008. Places the history of the Ottomans in comparative perspective.

Bridge, Antony. *Suleiman the Magnificent*. 1983. Lively, accessible account of the sultan's impact.

Dale, Stephen Frederic. *The Garden of the Eight Paradises: Babur and the Culture of Empire in Central Asia, Afghanistan and India, 1483–1750*. 2004. A scholarly biography that draws on and analyzes Babur's autobiography.

Dale, Stephen Frederic. *The Muslim Empires of the Ottomans, Safavids, and Mughals*. 2010. A comparative study of the three empires, with much on religion and culture.

Findley, Carter Vaughn. *The Turks in World History*. 2005. Takes a macro look at the three Islamic empires as part of the history of the Turks.

Finkel, Caroline. *Osman's Dream: A History of the Ottoman Empire*. 2006. A new interpretation that views the Ottomans from their own perspective.

Inalcik, Halil, and Renda Günsel. *Ottoman Civilization*. 2002. A huge, beautifully illustrated, government-sponsored overview, with an emphasis on the arts and culture.

Jackson, Peter, and Lawrence Lockhart, eds. *The Cambridge History of Iran*, Vol. 6, *The Timurid and Safavid Periods*. 1986. A set of essays by leading scholars on the social and cultural as well as the political and economic history of Iran.

Keay, John. *India: A History*. 2000. A comprehensive history, rich in insights.

Lapidus, Ira M. *A History of Islamic Societies*, 2d ed. 2002. A comprehensive, yet lucid survey.

Mukhia, Harbans. *The Mughals of India: A Framework for Understanding*. 2004. A short but thoughtful analysis of the Mughal society and state.

Pierce, Leslie. *The Imperial Harem: Women and Sovereignty in the Ottoman Empire*. 1993. A fresh look at the role of elite women under the Ottomans.

Richards, John F. *The Mughal Empire*. 1993. A coherent narrative history of the period 1526–1720.

Ruthven, Malise, and Azim Nanji. *Historical Atlas of Islam*. 2004. Provides numerous maps illustrating the shifting political history of Islamic states.

NOTES

1. *Memoirs of Zehir-Ed-Din Muhammed Baber: Emperor of Hindustan*, trans. John Leyden and William Erskine (London: Longman and Cadell, 1826), p. 333.
2. Quoted in M. C. Beach, *The Imperial Image: Paintings for the Mughal Court* (Washington, D.C.: Freer Gallery of Art, Smithsonian Institution, 1981), pp. 9–10.
3. Quoted in V. A. Smith, *The Oxford History of India* (Oxford, U.K.: Oxford University Press, 1967), p. 398.
4. Quoted in S. K. Ikram, *Muslim Civilization in India* (New York: Columbia University Press, 1964), p. 202.
5. Quoted in K. M. Panikkar, *Asia and Western Domination* (London: George Allen & Unwin, 1965), p. 35.
6. Quoted in W. Bingham, H. Conroy, and F. W. Iklé, *A History of Asia*, vol. 2 (Boston: Allyn and Bacon, 1967), p. 74.

For practice quizzes and other study tools, visit the **Online Study Guide** at bedfordstmartins.com/mckayworld.

For primary sources from this period, see *Sources of World Societies*, **Second Edition**.

For Web sites, images, and documents related to topics in this chapter, visit **Make History** at bedfordstmartins.com/mckayworld.

• Kabuki Actor Urban entertainment flourished in Japan under the rule of the Tokugawa shoguns. This late-eighteenth-century woodblock print was made for the many fans of the Kabuki actor Matsumoto Yonesaburo, who specialized in performing female roles. (Private Collection/Photo © Boltin Picture Library/ The Bridgeman Art Library)

21

The four centuries from 1400 to 1800 were a time of growth and dynamic change throughout East Asia. Although both China and Japan suffered periods of war, each ended up with expanded territories. The age of exploration brought New World crops to the region, leading to increased agricultural output and population growth. It also brought new opportunities for foreign trade and new religions. Another link between these countries was the series of massive Japanese invasions of Korea in the late sixteenth century, which led to war between China and Japan.

Continuity and Change in East Asia
1400–1800

In China, the native Ming Dynasty brought an end to Mongol rule. Under the Ming, China saw agricultural reconstruction, commercial expansion, and the rise of a vibrant urban culture. In the early seventeenth century, after the Ming Dynasty fell into disorder, the non-Chinese Manchus founded the Qing Dynasty (1644–1911) and added Taiwan, Mongolia, Tibet, and Xinjiang to their realm. The Qing Empire thus was comparable to the other multiethnic empires of the early modern world, such as the Ottoman, Russian, and Habsburg empires. In China itself the eighteenth century was a time of peace and prosperity.

In the Japanese islands the fifteenth century saw the start of civil war that lasted a century. At the end of the sixteenth century the world seemed to have turned upside down when a commoner, Hideyoshi (HEE-deh-YOH-shee), became the supreme ruler. He did not succeed in passing on his power to an heir, however. Power was seized by Tokugawa Ieyasu (toe-koo-GAH-wuh ee-yeh-YAH-soo). Under the Tokugawa Shogunate (1603–1867), Japan restricted contact with the outside world and social mobility among its own people. Yet Japan thrived, as agricultural productivity increased and a lively urban culture developed. •

Ming China, 1368–1644

□ What sort of state and society developed in China after the Mongols were ousted?

The story of Ming China begins with the rise of a poor boy to emperor of a new dynasty. This individual, Zhu Yuanzhang (JOO-yoowan-JAHNG) — known as Taizu as emperor — proved to be one of the most despotic emperors in Chinese history. Still, peace brought prosperity and a lively urban culture. By the beginning of the seventeenth century, however, the Ming government was beset by fiscal, military, and political problems.

The Rise of Zhu Yuanzhang and the Founding of the Ming Dynasty

The founder of the **Ming Dynasty**, Zhu Yuanzhang (1328–1398), began life in poverty during the last decades of the Mongol Yuan Dynasty. His home region was hit by drought and then plague in the 1340s, and when he was only sixteen years old, his father, oldest brother, and that brother's wife all died, leaving two penniless boys with three bodies to bury. With no relatives to turn to, Zhu Yuanzhang asked a monastery to accept him as a novice. The monastery itself was short of funds, and the monks soon sent Zhu out to beg for food. For three or four years he wandered through central China. Only after he returned to the monastery did he learn to read.

A few years later, in 1351, members of a religious sect known as the Red Turbans rose in rebellion against the government. Red Turban teachings drew on Manichaean ideas about the incompatibility of the forces of good and evil as well as on the cult of the Maitreya Buddha, who according to believers would in the future bring his paradise to earth to relieve human suffering. The Red Turbans met with considerable success, even defeating Mongol cavalry. When the temple where Zhu Yuanzhang was living was burned down in the fighting, Zhu joined the rebels and rose rapidly.

Zhu and his followers developed into brilliant generals, and gradually they defeated one rival after another. In 1356 Zhu took the city of Nanjing and made it his base. In 1368 his armies took Beijing, which the Mongol emperor and his closest followers had vacated just days before. Then forty years old, Zhu Yuanzhang declared himself emperor of the Ming ("Bright") Dynasty. As emperor, he was known as Taizu (TIGH-dzoo) or the Hongwu emperor.

Taizu started his reign wanting to help the poor. To lighten the weight of government taxes and compulsory labor, he ordered a full-scale registration of cultivated land and population so that these burdens could be assessed more fairly. He also tried persuasion. He issued instructions to be read aloud to villagers, telling them to be obedient to their parents, live in harmony with their neighbors, work contentedly at their occupations, and refrain from evil.

Although in many ways anti-Mongol, Taizu retained some Yuan practices. One was setting up provinces as the administrative layer between the central government and the prefectures (local governments a step above counties). Another was hereditary service obligations for both artisan and military households. Any family classed as a military household had to supply a soldier at

Ming China, ca. 1600

all times, replacing those who were injured, who died, or who deserted.

Garrisons were concentrated along the northern border and near the capital at Nanjing. Each garrison was allocated a tract of land that the soldiers took turns cultivating to supply their own food. Although in theory this system should have supplied the Ming with a large but inexpensive army, the reality was less satisfactory. Garrisons were rarely self-sufficient. Furthermore, men compelled to become soldiers did not necessarily make good fighting men, and desertion was difficult to prevent. Consequently, like earlier dynasties, the Ming turned to non-Chinese northerners for much of its armed forces. Many of the best soldiers in the Ming army were Mongols in Mongol units. Taizu did not try to conquer the Mongols, and Ming China did not extend into modern Inner Mongolia.

Taizu had deeply ambivalent feelings about men of education and sometimes brutally humiliated them in open court, even having them beaten. His behavior was so erratic that it is most likely that he suffered from some form of mental illness. As Taizu became more literate, he realized that scholars could criticize him in covert ways, using phrases that had double meanings or that sounded like words for "bandit," "monk," or the like. Even poems in private circulation could be used as evidence of subversive thoughts. When literary men began to avoid official life, Taizu made it illegal to turn down appointments or to resign from office. He began falling into rages that only the empress could stop, and after her death in 1382 no one could calm him. In 1376 Taizu had thousands of officials killed because they were found to have taken shortcuts in their handling of paperwork for the grain tax. In 1380 Taizu concluded that his chancellor was plotting to assassinate him, and thousands only remotely connected to the chancellor were executed. From then on, Taizu acted as his own chancellor, dealing directly with the heads of departments and ministries.

The next important emperor, called Chengzu or the Yongle emperor (r. 1403–1425), was also a military man. One of Taizu's younger sons, he took the throne by force from his nephew and often led troops into battle against the Mongols. Like his father, Chengzu was willing to use terror to keep government officials in line.

Early in his reign, Chengzu decided to move the capital from Nanjing to Beijing, which had been his own base as a prince and the capital during Mongol times. Constructed between 1407 and 1420, Beijing was a planned city. Like Chang'an in Sui-Tang times (581–

907), it was arranged like a set of boxes within boxes built on a north-south axis. The main outer walls were forty feet high and nearly fifteen miles around, pierced by nine gates. Inside was the Imperial City, with government offices, and within that the palace itself, called the Forbidden City, with close to ten thousand rooms. Because the Forbidden City survives today, people can still see the series of audience halls with vast courtyards between them where attending officials would stand or kneel.

The areas surrounding Beijing were not nearly as agriculturally productive as those around Nanjing. To supply Beijing with grain, the Yuan Grand Canal connecting the city to the rice basket of the Yangzi River regions was broadened, deepened, and supplied with more locks and dams. The 15,000 boats and the 160,000 soldiers of the transport army who pulled loaded barges from the towpaths along the canal became the lifeline of the capital.

Problems with the Imperial Institution

Taizu had decreed that succession should go to the eldest son of the empress or to the son's eldest son if the son predeceased his father, the system generally

---

• **Ming Dynasty** The Chinese dynasty in power from 1368 to 1644; it marked a period of agricultural reconstruction, foreign expeditions, commercial expansion, and a vibrant urban culture.

Forbidden City The palace complex in Beijing, commonly called the Forbidden City, was built in the early fifteenth century when the capital was moved from Nanjing to Beijing. Audience halls and other important state buildings are arranged on a north-south axis with huge courtyards between them, where officials would stand during ceremonies. (Vincent Loy, photographer)

followed by earlier dynasties. In Ming times, the flaws in this system became apparent as one mediocre, obtuse, or erratic emperor followed another. There were emperors who refused to hold audiences, who fell into irrational fits, and who let themselves be manipulated by palace ladies.

Because Taizu had abolished the position of chancellor, emperors turned to secretaries and eunuchs to manage the paperwork. Eunuchs were essentially slaves. Many boys and young men were acquired by dubious means, often from non-Chinese areas in the south, and after they were castrated they had no option but to serve the imperial family. Zheng He, for instance (see page 639), was taken from Yunnan as a boy of ten by a Ming general assigned the task of securing boys to be castrated. Society considered eunuchs the basest of servants, and Confucian scholars heaped scorn on them. Yet Ming emperors, like rulers in earlier dynasties, often preferred the always compliant eunuchs to highminded, moralizing civil service officials.

In Ming times the eunuch establishment became huge. By the late fifteenth century the eunuch bureaucracy had grown as large as the civil service, each with roughly twelve thousand positions. After 1500 the eunuch bureaucracy grew even more rapidly, and by the mid-sixteenth century seventy thousand eunuchs were in service throughout the country, ten thousand in the

capital. Tension between the two bureaucracies was high. In 1420 Chengzu set up a eunuch-run secret service to investigate cases of suspected corruption and sedition in the regular bureaucracy. Eunuch control over vital government processes, such as appointments, became a severe problem.

In hope of persuading emperors to make reforms, many Ming officials risked their careers and lives by speaking out. In 1376, when Taizu asked for criticism, one official criticized harsh punishment of officials for minor lapses. Incensed, Taizu had him brought to the capital in chains and let him starve to death in prison. In 1519, when an emperor announced plans to make a tour of the southern provinces, over a hundred officials staged a protest by kneeling in front of the palace. The emperor ordered the officials to remain kneeling for three days, then had them flogged; eleven died. The Confucian tradition celebrated these acts of political protest as heroic. Rarely, however, did they succeed in moving an emperor to change his mind.

Although the educated public complained about the performance of emperors, no one proposed or even imagined alternatives to imperial rule. High officials were forced to find ways to work around uncooperative emperors, but they were not able to put in place institutions that would limit the damage an emperor could do. Knowing that strong emperors often acted their own editions of these novels, sometimes adding new illustrations or commentaries.

The Chinese found recreation and relaxation in many ways besides reading. The affluent indulged in an alcoholic drink made from fermented and distilled rice, and once tobacco was introduced from the Americas, both men and women took up pipes. Plays were also very popular. The Jesuit missionary Matteo Ricci, who lived in China from 1583 to 1610, described resident troupes in large cities and traveling troupes that "journey everywhere throughout the length and breadth of the country" putting on plays. The leaders of the troupes would purchase young children and train them to sing and perform. Ricci thought too many people were addicted to these performances:

> These groups of actors are employed at all imposing banquets, and when they are called they come prepared to enact any of the ordinary plays. The host at the banquet is usually presented with a volume of plays and he selects the one or several he may like. The guests, between eating and drinking, follow the plays with so much satisfaction that the banquet at times may last for ten hours.[1]

People not only enjoyed play performances but also avidly read the play scripts. The love stories and social satires of Tang Xianzu, the greatest of the Ming playwrights, were very popular. One of his plays tells the story of a young man who falls asleep while his meal is cooking. In his dream he sees his whole life: he comes in first in the civil service examinations, rises to high office, is unfairly slandered and condemned to death, and then is cleared and promoted. At the point of death, he wakes up, sees that his dinner is nearly ready, and realizes that life passes as quickly as a dream.

More than bread in Europe, rice supplied most of the calories of the population in central and south China. (In north China, wheat, made into steamed or baked bread or into noodles, served as the dietary staple.) In the south, terracing and irrigation of mountain slopes, introduced in the eleventh century, had increased rice harvests. Other innovations also brought good results. Farmers began to stock the rice paddies with fish, which continuously fertilized the rice fields, destroyed malaria-bearing mosquitoes, and enriched the diet. Farmers also developed commercial cropping in cotton, sugar cane, and indigo. New methods of crop rotation allowed for continuous cultivation and for more than one harvest per year from a single field.

The Ming rulers promoted the repopulation and colonization of war-devastated regions through reclamation of land and massive transfers of people. Immigrants to these areas received large plots and exemption from taxation for many years. Reforestation played a dramatic role in the agricultural revolution. In 1391 the Ming government ordered 50 million trees planted

> " The guests, between eating and drinking, follow the plays with so much satisfaction that the banquet at times may last for ten hours. "
>
> **MATTEO RICCI**

in the Nanjing area to produce lumber for the construction of a maritime fleet. In 1392 each family holding colonized land in Anhui province had to plant two hundred mulberry, jujube, and persimmon trees. In 1396 peasants in the present-day provinces of Hunan and Hubei in central China planted 84 million fruit trees. Historians have estimated that 1 billion trees were planted during Taizu's reign.

Increased food production led to steady population growth and the multiplication of markets, towns, and small cities. Larger towns had permanent shops; smaller towns had periodic markets — some every five days, some every ten days, some only once a month. They sold essential goods — such as pins, matches, oil for lamps, candles, paper, incense, and tobacco — to country people from the surrounding hamlets. Markets usually included moneylenders, pawnbrokers, a tearoom, and sometimes a wine shop where tea and rice wine were sold and entertainers performed. Tradesmen carrying their wares on their backs and craftsmen — carpenters, barbers, joiners, locksmiths — moved constantly from market to market. Itinerant salesmen depended on the city market for their wares.

Ming Decline

Beginning in the 1590s the Ming government was beset by fiscal, military, and political problems. The government went nearly bankrupt helping defend Korea against a Japanese invasion (see pages 642–643). Then came a series of natural disasters: floods, droughts, locusts, and epidemics ravaged one region after another. At the same time, a "little ice age" brought a drop in average temperatures that shortened the growing season and reduced harvests. In areas of serious food shortages, gangs of army deserters and laid-off soldiers began scouring the countryside in search of food. Once the gangs had stolen all their grain, hard-pressed farmers joined them just to survive. The Ming government had little choice but to try to increase taxes to deal with these threats, but the last thing people needed was heavier taxes.

Adding to the hardship was a sudden drop in the supply of silver. In place of the paper money that had circulated in Song and Yuan times, silver ingots came into general use as money in Ming times. Even agricultural taxes came to be paid in silver rather than in grain. Much of this silver originated in either Japan or the

New World and entered China as payment for the silk and porcelains exported from China (see pages 482–483). When events in Japan and the Philippines led to disruption of trade, silver imports dropped. This led to deflation in China, which caused real rents to rise. Soon there were riots among urban workers and tenant farmers. In 1642 a group of rebels cut the dikes on the Yellow River, causing massive flooding. A smallpox epidemic soon added to the death toll. In 1644 the last Ming emperor, in despair, took his own life when rebels entered Beijing, opening the way for the start of a new dynasty.

The Manchus and Qing China, to 1800

☐ Did the return of alien rule with the Manchus have any positive consequences for China?

The next dynasty, the **Qing Dynasty** (1644–1911), was founded by the Manchus, a non-Chinese people who were descended from the Jurchens who had ruled north China during the Jin Dynasty (1127–1234), when south China was controlled by the Song. Manchu men shaved the front of their heads and wore their hair in a long braid called a queue. In the late sixteenth century the Manchus began expanding their territories, and in 1644 they founded the Qing Dynasty, which brought peace and in time prosperity. Successful Qing military campaigns extended the borders into Mongol, Tibetan, and Uighur regions, creating a multiethnic empire that was larger than any earlier Chinese dynasty.

The Rise of the Manchus

In the Ming period the Manchus lived in dispersed communities in what is loosely called Manchuria (the northeast of modern-day China). In the more densely populated southern part of Manchuria, the Manchus lived in close contact with Mongols, Koreans, and Chinese (Map 21.1). They were not nomads but rather hunters, fishers, and farmers. Like the Mongols, they also were excellent horsemen and archers and had a strongly hierarchical social structure, with elites and slaves. Slaves, often Korean or Chinese, were generally acquired through capture. A Korean visitor described many small Manchu settlements, most no larger than twenty households, supported by fishing, hunting for

pelts, collecting pine nuts or ginseng, or growing crops such as wheat, millet, and barley. Villages were often at odds with each other over resources, and men did not leave their villages without arming themselves with bows and arrows or swords. Interspersed among these Manchu settlements were groups of nomadic Mongols who lived in tents.

The Manchus credited their own rise to Nurhaci (1559–1626). Over several decades, he united the Manchus and expanded their territories. Like Chinggis Khan, who had reorganized the Mongol armies to reduce the importance of tribal affiliations, Nurhaci created a new social basis for his armies in units called **banners**. Each banner was made up of a set of military companies and included the families and slaves of the soldiers. Each company had a hereditary captain, often from Nurhaci's own lineage. Over time new companies and new banners were formed, and by 1644 there were eight each of Manchu, Mongol, and Chinese banners. When new groups were defeated, their members were distributed among several banners to lessen their potential for subversion.

The Manchus entered China by invitation of the distinguished Ming general Wu Sangui, himself a native of southern Manchuria, who was near the eastern end of the Great Wall when he heard that the rebels had captured Beijing. The Manchus proposed to Wu that they join forces and liberate Beijing. Wu opened the gates of the Great Wall to let the Manchus in, and within a couple of weeks they occupied Beijing. When the Manchus made clear that they intended to conquer the rest of the country and take the throne themselves, Wu and many other Chinese generals joined forces with them. Before long, China was again under alien rule.

In the summer of 1645 the Manchus ordered all Chinese serving in Manchu armies to shave the front of their heads in the Manchu fashion, presumably to make it easier to recognize whose side they were on. Soon this order was extended to all Chinese men. Because so many of those newly conquered by the Qing refused to shave off their hair, Manchu commanders felt justified in ordering the slaughter of defiant cities. After quelling resistance, the Qing put in place policies and institutions that gave China a respite from war and disorder. However, most of the political institutions of the Ming Dynasty were taken over relatively unchanged, including the examination system.

After peace was achieved, population growth took off. Between 1700 and 1800 the Chinese population seems to have nearly doubled, from about 150 million to over 300 million. Population growth during the eighteenth century has been attributed to many factors: global warming that extended the growing season, expanded use of New World crops, slowing of the spread of new diseases that had accompanied the sixteenth-century expansion of global traffic, and the efficiency

• **Qing Dynasty** The dynasty founded by the Manchus that ruled China from 1644 to 1911.

• **banners** Units of the Qing army, composed of soldiers, their families, and slaves.

◻ Mapping the Past

MAP 21.1 The Qing Empire, ca. 1800 The sheer size of the Qing Empire in China almost inevitably led to its profound cultural influence on the rest of Asia.

ANALYZING THE MAP How many different cultural groups are depicted? Which occupied the largest territories? Where was crop agriculture most prevalent?

CONNECTIONS What geographical and political factors limited the expansion of the Qing Empire?

---

of the Qing government in providing relief in times of famine.

Some scholars have recently argued that China's overall standard of living in the mid-eighteenth century was comparable to Europe's and that the standards of China's most developed regions, such as the lower Yangzi region, compared favorably to the most developed regions of Europe at the time, such as England and the Netherlands. Life expectancy, food consumption, and even facilities for transportation were at similar levels.

Competent and Long-Lived Emperors

For more than a century, China was ruled by only three rulers, each of them hard-working, talented, and com-

mitted to making the Qing Dynasty a success. Two, the Kangxi and Qianlong emperors, had exceptionally long reigns.

Kangxi (r. 1661–1722) proved adept at meeting the expectations of both the Chinese and the Manchu elites. At age fourteen he announced that he would begin ruling on his own and had his regent imprisoned. Kangxi (KAHNG-shee) could speak, read, and write Chinese and made efforts to persuade educated Chinese that the Manchus had a legitimate claim to rule, even trying to attract Ming loyalists who had been unwilling to serve the Qing. He undertook a series of tours of the south, where Ming loyalty had been strongest, and he held a special exam to select men to compile the official history of the Ming Dynasty.

Kangxi's son and heir, the Yongzheng emperor (r. 1722–1735), was also a hard-working ruler who took an interest in the efficiency of the government. Because his father had lived so long, he did not come to the throne until his mid-forties and reigned only thirteen years. His successor, however, the Qianlong emperor (r. 1736–1796), like Kangxi had a reign of sixty years, with the result that China had only three rulers in 135 years.

Qianlong (chyan-loong) put much of his energy into impressing his subjects with his magnificence. He understood that the Qing's capacity to hold the multiethnic empire together rested on their ability to appeal to all those they ruled. Besides speaking Manchu and Chinese, Qianlong learned to converse in Mongolian, Uighur, Tibetan, and Tangut, and he addressed envoys in their own languages. He became as much a patron of Tibetan Buddhism as of Chinese Confucianism. He initiated a massive project to translate the Tibetan Buddhist canon into Mongolian and Manchu and had huge multilingual dictionaries compiled.

To demonstrate to the Chinese scholar-official elite that he was a sage emperor, Qianlong worked on affairs of state from dawn until early afternoon and then turned to reading, painting, and calligraphy. He was ostentatious in his devotion to his mother, visiting her daily and tending to her comfort with all the devotion of the most filial Chinese son. He took several tours down the Grand Canal to the southeast, in part to emulate his grandfather, in part to entertain his mother, who accompanied him on these tours.

Despite these displays of Chinese virtues, the Qianlong emperor was not fully confident that the Chinese supported his rule, and he was quick to act on any suspicion of anti-Manchu thoughts or actions. During a project to catalogue nearly all the books in China, he began to suspect that some governors were holding back books with seditious content. He ordered full searches for books with disparaging references to the Manchus or to previous alien conquerors like the Jurchens and Mongols. Sometimes passages were deleted or rewritten, but when an entire book was offensive, it was destroyed. So thorough was this book-burning that no copies survive of more than two thousand titles.

Through Qianlong's reign, China remained an enormous producer of manufactured goods and led the way in assembly-line production. The government operated huge textile factories, but some private firms were even larger. Hangzhou had a textile firm that gave work to four thousand weavers, twenty thousand spinners, and ten thousand dyers and finishers. The porcelain kilns at Jingdezhen employed the division of labor on a large scale and were able to supply porcelain to much of the world. The growth of the economy benefited the Qing state, and the treasury became so full that the Qianlong emperor was able to cancel taxes on several occasions. When he abdicated in 1796, his treasury had 400 million silver dollars in it.

Imperial Expansion

The Qing Dynasty put together a multiethnic empire that was larger than any earlier Chinese dynasty. Taiwan was acquired in 1683 after Qing armies pursued a rebel there. Mongolia was acquired next. In 1696 Kangxi led an army of eighty thousand men into Mongolia, and within a few years Manchu supremacy was accepted there. Cannon and muskets gave Qing forces military superiority over the Mongols, who were armed only with bows and arrows. Thus the Qing could dominate the steppe cheaply, effectively ending two thousand years of Inner Asian military advantage.

Presenting a Horse to the Emperor This detail from a 1757 hand scroll shows the Qianlong emperor, seated, receiving envoys from the Kazakhs. Note how the envoy, presenting a pure white horse, is kneeling to the ground performing the kowtow, which involved lowering his head to the ground as an act of reverence. The artist was Guiseppe Castiglione (1688–1768), an Italian who worked as a painter in Qianlong's court. (Qing, 1757. Handscroll, ink and colors on paper [45 cm × 2.67 m]. Musée Guimet, Paris/Art Resource, NY)

In the 1720s the Qing established a permanent garrison of banner soldiers in Tibet. By this time, the expanding Qing and Russian empires were nearing each other. In 1689 the Manchu and the Russian rulers approved a treaty — written in Russian, Manchu, Chinese, and Latin — defining their borders in Manchuria and regulating trade. Another treaty in 1727 allowed a Russian ecclesiastical mission to reside in Beijing and a trade caravan to make a trip from Russia to Beijing once every three years.

The last region to be annexed was Chinese Turkestan (the modern province of Xinjiang). Both the Han and the Tang Dynasties had stationed troops in the region, exercising loose overlordship, but neither Song nor Ming had tried to control the area. The Qing won the region in the 1750s through a series of campaigns against Uighur and Dzungar Mongol forces.

Both Tibet and Turkestan were ruled lightly. The local populations kept their own religious leaders and did not have to wear the queue.

Japan's Middle Ages, ca. 1400–1600

☐ How did Japan change during this period of political instability?

In the twelfth century Japan entered an age dominated by military men, an age that can be compared to Europe's feudal age. The Kamakura Shogunate (1185–1333) had its capital in the east, at Kamakura. It was succeeded by the Ashikaga Shogunate (1336–1573), which returned the government to Kyoto (KYOH-toh) and helped launch, during the fifteenth century, the great age of Zen-influenced Muromachi culture. The sixteenth century brought civil war over succession to the shogunate, leading to the building of massive castles and the emergence of rulers of obscure origins who eventually unified the realm.

Muromachi Culture

The headquarters of the Ashikaga shoguns were on Muromachi Street in Kyoto, and the refined and elegant style that they promoted is often called Muromachi culture. The shoguns patronized Zen Buddhism, the school of Buddhism associated with meditation and mind-to-mind transmission of truth. Because Zen monks were able to read and write Chinese, they often assisted the shoguns in handling foreign affairs. Many of the Kyoto Zen temples in this period had rock gardens, seen as aids to Zen meditation.

Zen ideas of simplicity permeated the arts. The Silver Pavilion built by the shogun Yoshimasa (r. 1449–1473) epitomizes Zen austerity. A white sand cone constructed in the temple garden was designed to reflect moonlight. Yoshimasa was also influential in the development of the tea ceremony, practiced by warriors, aristocrats, and priests, but not by women. Aesthetes celebrated the beauty of imperfect objects, such as plain or misshapen cups or pots. Spare monochrome paintings fit into this aesthetic, as did simple asymmetrical flower arrangements.

The shoguns were also patrons of the **Nō theater**. Nō drama originated in popular forms of entertainment, including comical skits and dances directed to the gods. It was transformed into high art by Zeami (1363–1443), an actor and playwright who also wrote on the aesthetic theory of Nō. Nō was performed on a bare stage with a pine tree painted across the backdrop. One or two actors wearing brilliant brocade robes would perform, using stylized gestures and stances. One actor would wear a mask indicating whether the character he was portraying was male or female, old or young, a god, a ghost, or a demon. The actors would be accompanied by a chorus and a couple of musicians playing drums and flute. Many of the stories concerned ghosts consumed by jealous passions or the desire for revenge. Zeami argued that the most meaningful moments came during silence, when the actor's spiritual presence allowed the audience to catch a glimpse of the mysterious and inexpressible.

Civil War

Civil war began in Kyoto in 1467 as a struggle over succession to the shogunate. Rival claimants and their followers used arson as their chief weapon and burned down temples and mansions, destroying much of the city and its treasures. In the early phases defeated opponents were exiled or allowed to retire to monasteries. As the conflict continued, violence escalated; hostages and prisoners were slaughtered and corpses mutilated. Once Kyoto was laid waste, war spread to outlying areas. When the shogun could no longer protect cities, merchants banded together to hire mercenaries. In the political vacuum, the Lotus League, a commoner-led religious sect united by faith in the saving power of the Lotus Sutra, set up a commoner-run government that collected taxes and settled disputes. In 1536, during eight days of fighting, the powerful Buddhist monastery Enryakuji attacked the League and its temples, burned much of the city, and killed men, women, and children thought to be believers.

• **Nō theater** A type of Japanese theater in which performers convey emotions and ideas as much through gestures, stances, and dress as through words.

In these confused and violent circumstances, power devolved to the local level, where warlords, called **daimyo** (DIGH-mee-oh), built their power bases. Unlike earlier power holders, these new lords were not appointed by the court or shogunate and did not send taxes to absentee overlords. Instead they seized what they needed and used it to build up their territories and recruit more samurai. To raise revenues they surveyed the land and promoted irrigation and trade. Many of the most successful daimyo were self-made men who rose from obscurity.

The violence of the period encouraged castle building. The castles were built not on mountaintops but on level plains, and they were surrounded by moats and walls made from huge stones. Inside a castle was a many-storied keep. Though relatively safe from incendiary missiles, the keeps were vulnerable to Western-style cannon, introduced in the 1570s. Many of the castles had splendid living quarters for the daimyo; leading painters embellished interior sliding doors and screens.

Hideyoshi's Campaigns in Japan and Korea, 1537–1598

MING CHINA

KOREA

Sea of Japan

JAPAN

Edo

Kyoto

Takamatsu

Kagoshima

→ Reunification campaign
→ Campaign against Korea

The Victors: Nobunaga and Hideyoshi

The first daimyo to gain a predominance of power was Oda Nobunaga (1534–1582). A samurai of the lesser daimyo class, he recruited followers from masterless samurai who had been living by robbery and extortion. After he won control of his native province in 1559, he immediately set out to extend his power through central Japan. A key step was destroying the military power of the great monasteries. To increase revenues, he minted coins, the first government-issued money in Japan since 958. Also to raise revenues, he promoted trade by eliminating customs barriers and opening the little fishing village of Nagasaki to foreign commerce; it soon became Japan's largest port.

In 1582, in an attempted coup, Nobunaga was forced by one of his vassals to commit suicide. His general and staunchest adherent, Toyotomi Hideyoshi (1537–1598), avenged him and continued the drive toward unification of the daimyo-held lands.

Like the Ming founder, Hideyoshi was a peasant's son who rose to power through military talent. Hideyoshi succeeded in bringing northern and western Japan under his control. In 1582 he attacked the great fortress at Takamatsu. When direct assault failed, his troops flooded the castle to force its surrender. A successful siege of the town of Kagoshima then brought the southern island of Kyushu (KYOO-shoo) under his domination. Hideyoshi soothed the vanquished daimyo as Nobunaga had done—with lands and military positions—but he also required them to swear allegiance and to obey him down to the smallest particular. For

Matsumoto Castle Hideyoshi built Matsumoto Castle between 1594 and 1597. Designed to be impregnable, it was surrounded by a moat and had a base constructed of huge stones. In the sixteenth and early seventeenth centuries Spanish and Portuguese missionaries compared Japanese castles favorably to European castles of the period. (Adina Tovy/ Robert Harding World Imagery)

MAP 21.2 Tokugawa Japan, 1603–1867 The lands that the shogunate directly controlled were concentrated near its capital at Edo. The daimyo of distant places, such as the island of Kyushu, were required to make long journeys to and from Edo every year.

the first time in over two centuries, Japan had a single ruler.

Hideyoshi did his best to ensure that future peasants' sons would not be able to rise as he had. His great sword hunt of 1588 collected weapons from farmers, who were no longer allowed to wear swords. Restrictions were also placed on samurai; they were prohibited from leaving their lord's service or switching occupations. To improve tax collection, Hideyoshi ordered a survey of the entire country. His agents collected detailed information about each daimyo's lands and about towns, villages, agricultural produce, and industrial output all over Japan. His surveys not only tightened tax collection, but also registered each peasant household, tied the peasants to the land, and tightened the collection of the land tax. With the country pacified, Hideyoshi embarked on an ill-fated attempt to conquer Korea and China that ended only with his death, discussed below (see page 643).

The Tokugawa Shogunate, to 1800

☐ What was life like in Japan during the Tokugawa peace?

On his deathbed, Hideyoshi set up a council of regents to govern during the minority of his infant son. The strongest regent was Hideyoshi's long-time supporter

Tokugawa Ieyasu (1543–1616), who ruled vast territories around Edo (AY-doh; modern-day Tokyo). In 1600 at Sekigahara, Ieyasu smashed a coalition of daimyo defenders of the heir and began building his own government. In 1603 he took the title "shogun." The **Tokugawa Shogunate** that Ieyasu fashioned lasted until 1867. This era is also called the Edo period after the location of the shogunate, starting Tokyo's history as Japan's most important city (Map 21.2). Peace brought many benefits. Towns and cities thrived and became centers for the theater and publishing.

Tokugawa Government

In the course of the seventeenth century the Tokugawa shoguns worked to consolidate relations with the daimyo. In a scheme resembling the later residency requirements imposed by Louis XIV in France (see page 497) and Peter the Great in Russia (see page 509), Ieyasu set up the **alternate residence system**, which compelled the lords to live in Edo every other year and to leave their wives and sons there—essentially as hostages. This arrangement had obvious advantages:

- **daimyo** Regional lords in Japan; many had built their power by seizing what they needed and promoting irrigation and trade to raise revenues.
- **Tokugawa Shogunate** The Japanese government founded by Tokugawa Ieyasu that lasted from 1603 until 1867; it is also called the Edo period because the shogunate was located at Edo.
- **alternate residence system** Arrangement in which lords lived in Edo every other year and left their wives and sons there as hostages.

Daimyo Procession The system of alternate residence meant that some daimyo were always on the road. Daimyo's travel with their attendants between their domains and Edo, the shogun's residence, stimulated construction of roads, inns, and castle towns. (Tokugawa Art Museum, © The Togugawa Art Museum Image Archives/DNPartcom)

the shogun could keep tabs on the daimyo, control them through their wives and children, and weaken them financially with the burden of maintaining two residences.

The peace imposed by the Tokugawa Shogunate brought a steady rise in population to about 30 million people by 1800 (making Tokugawa Japan about one-tenth the size of Qing China). To maintain stability, the early Tokugawa shoguns froze social status. Laws rigidly prescribed what each class could and could not do. Nobles, for example, were strictly forbidden to go sauntering, whether by day or by night, through the streets or lanes in places where they had no business to be. Daimyo were prohibited from moving troops outside their frontiers, making alliances, and coining money. As intended, these rules protected the Tokugawa shoguns from daimyo attack and helped ensure a long era of peace.

The early Tokugawa shoguns also restricted the construction and repair of castles — symbols, in Japan as in medieval Europe, of feudal independence. Continuing Hideyoshi's policy, the Tokugawa regime enforced a policy of complete separation of samurai and peasants. Samurai were defined as those permitted to carry swords. They had to live in castles (which evolved into castle-towns), and they depended on stipends from their lords, the daimyo. Samurai were effectively prevented from establishing ties to the land, so they could not become landholders. Likewise, merchants and artisans had to live in towns and could not own land. Japanese castle-towns evolved into bustling, sophisticated urban centers.

After 1639 Japan limited its contacts with the outside world because of concerns about both the loyalty of subjects converted to Christianity by European missionaries and about the imperialist ambitions of European powers (discussed below). However, China remained an important trading partner and source of ideas. For example, Neo-Confucianism gained a

stronger hold among the samurai-turned bureaucrats, and painting in Chinese styles enjoyed great popularity. The Edo period also saw the development of a school of native learning that rejected Buddhism and Confucianism as alien and tried to identify a distinctly Japanese sensibility.

Commercialization and the Growth of Towns

During the civil war period, warfare seems to have promoted social and economic change, much as it had in China during the Warring States Period (403–221 B.C.E.). Trade grew, and greater use was made of coins imported from Ming China. Markets began appearing at river crossings, at the entrances to temples and shrines, and at other places where people congregated. Towns and cities sprang up all around the country, some of them around the new castles. Traders and artisans dealing in a specific product — such as comb makers, sesame oil producers, or metalworkers — began forming guilds. Money-lending was a very profitable business — annual interest rates reached 300 percent. In Kyoto the powerful monastery Enryakuji licensed the moneylenders, in essence running a lucrative protection racket. Foreign trade also flourished, despite chronic problems with pirates who raided the Japanese, Korean, and Chinese coasts (see pages 642–643).

Recent scholarship demonstrates that the Tokugawa era witnessed the foundations of modern Japanese capitalism: the development of a cash economy, the use of money to make more money, the accumulation of large amounts of capital for investment in factory or technological enterprises, the growth of business ventures operating over a national network of roads, and the expansion of wage labor. That these developments occurred simultaneously with, but entirely independent of, similar changes in Europe fascinates and challenges historians.

In most cities, merchant families with special privileges from the government controlled the urban economy. Frequently, a particular family dominated the trade in a particular product and then branched out into other businesses. The family of Kōnoike Shinroku is an example. In 1600 he established a sake (SAH-kee) brewery in the village of Kōnoike (sake is an alcoholic beverage made from fermented rice). By 1604 he had opened a branch office in Edo, and in 1615 he opened an office in Osaka and began shipping tax-rice (taxes paid in rice) from western Japan to Osaka. In 1656 one of Shinroku's sons founded a banking or money-changing business in Osaka. Forty years later the Kōnoike family was doing business in thirty-two daimyo domains. Eventually, the Kōnoike banking house made loans to and handled the tax-rice for 110 daimyo families. In 1705, with the interest paid from daimyo loans, the Kōnoike bought a tract of ponds and swampland, turned the land into rice paddies, and settled 480 households on the land. (Land reclamation under merchant supervision became a typical feature of Tokugawa business practices.) Involved by this time in five or six business enterprises, the house of Kōnoike had come a long way from brewing sake.

Japanese merchant families also devised distinct patterns and procedures for their business operations. What today is called "family-style management principles" determined the age of apprenticeship (between eleven and thirteen); the employee's detachment from past social relations and adherence to the norms of a particular family business; salaries; seniority as the basis of promotion, although job performance at the middle rungs determined who reached the higher ranks; and the time for retirement. All employees in a family business were expected to practice frugality, resourcefulness, self-denial, and careful accounting. These values formed the basis of what has been called the Japanese "industrious revolution." They help to explain how, after the Meiji (MAY-jee) Restoration of 1867 (see page 797), Japan was able to industrialize rapidly and compete successfully with the West. (In both Japan and China, there was a market for books giving advice on how to get ahead. See "Viewpoints: Chinese and Japanese Financial Advice," page 634.)

In the seventeenth century underemployed farmers and samurai, not to mention the ambitious and adventurous, thronged to the cities. As a result, Japan's cities grew tremendously. Kyoto became the center for the manufacture of luxury goods like lacquer, brocade, and fine porcelain. Osaka was the chief market, especially for rice. Edo was a center of consumption by the daimyo, their vassals, and government bureaucrats. Both Osaka and Edo reached about a million residents.

Two hundred fifty towns came into being in this period. Most ranged in size from 3,000 to 20,000 people, but a few, such as Hiroshima, Kagoshima, and Nagoya, had populations of between 65,000 and 100,000. In addition, perhaps two hundred towns along the main road to Edo emerged to meet the needs of men traveling on the alternate residence system. In the eighteenth century perhaps 4 million people, 15 percent of the Japanese population, resided in cities or towns.

Interior of Nijo Castle To assert control over the imperial court and the city of Kyoto, Tokugawa Ieyasu built palace-like Nijo Castle there in 1601–1603. He had the sliding doors painted by leading artists of the period, making the castle as elegant as the imperial palace. (From Fujioka Michio, *Genshoku Nihon no Bijutsu*, Vol. 12: Shiro to Shoin [Tokyo: Shogakkan, 1968])

Viewpoints

Chinese and Japanese Financial Advice

> • *The two passages below offer advice on how to prosper and avoid common mistakes. The first is a short passage from a longer work by a Chinese official, Zhang Ying (1638–1708), addressed to his son. The second, also from a longer work, is by his Japanese contemporary, Ihara Saikaku (1642–1693), and is aimed as much to entertain as to inform its audience.*

Zhang Ying, *On Permanent Property*

" All worldly things that once were new will eventually age. A house that has stood for a long time will decay; clothes worn for a long time will become shabby. Cattle, slaves, and horses are costly when purchased, yet ten years later they are no longer the same, and after another ten years they do not even exist. Only land remains new through hundreds and thousands of years. Even if, due to negligence, the soil becomes barren, once fertilizer is applied, it becomes rich again. With cultivation desolate land becomes productive; with irrigation dry land becomes arable; with weeding neglected soil becomes fertile. Since time immemorial man has not had to worry about the land becoming worn out or ruined, nor about its running away or becoming scarce. Indeed, land is truly precious.

Nowadays the young heirs of large estates wear fancy clothes, ride strong horses, and seek pleasure to their hearts' content in song and dance. A fur garment easily costs scores of gold taels; a feast, several taels. The price of grain in our area has been low for the past decade so that now ten piculs of grain will barely pay for a feast and a hundred piculs will scarcely buy a fur garment; but the young heirs act ignorant of this. They do not wish to know that the peasants, bodies soaked and feet muddy, toil all year round to produce a hundred piculs of grain. "

Ihara Saikaku, *This Scheming World*

" When a man becomes rich, people always say he's lucky. But this is merely a conventional expression, for in reality he becomes rich and his household thrives solely on account of his own ability and foresight. Even Ebisu, the god of wealth, is unable at will to exercise power over riches.

But be that as it may, our wealthy merchants, for whom the discussion of a pending loan to a feudal lord is a far more engaging pastime than carousing or any other form of merry-making, have recently organized themselves into the Daikoku Club. Shunning a rendezvous in the red-light district, they gather in the guest room of the Buddhist temple in Shimotera, Ikutama. There they meet every month to discuss the financial condition of each individual applicant for a loan. Though they are all well along in years, they take pleasure only in ever-increasing interest and in mounting capital, utterly heedless of the life to come. Although it's quite true that there's nothing more desirable than plenty of money, the proper way for a man to get along in the world should be this: in his youth until the age of twenty-five to be ever alert, in his manly prime up to thirty-five to earn a lot of money, in the prime of discretion in his fifties to pile up his fortune, and at last in his sixties—the year before his sixty-first birthday—to turn over all his business to his eldest son. Thereafter it is proper for him to retire from active affairs and devote the remainder of his days to visiting temples for the sake of his soul. "

Sources: Zhang Ying from Patricia Buckley Ebrey, *Chinese Civilization: A Sourcebook*, 2nd ed., Revised and Enlarged. Reprinted with the permission of The Free Press, a Division of Simon & Schuster, Inc. Copyright © 1993 by Patricia Buckley Ebrey. Copyright © 1981 by The Free Press. All rights reserved; Ihara Saikaku, *This Scheming World*, trans. Masanori Takatsuka and David C. Stubbs (Rutland, Vt.: Tuttle, 1965), p. 42. Copyright © 1965 by Charles E. Tuttle Publishing Co., Inc. Used by permission of Tuttle Publishing, a member of the Periplus Publishing Group.

QUESTIONS FOR ANALYSIS

1. How does the advice of these two authors reflect the ways one could get ahead in their respective societies?

2. Do you see any common elements in the advice offered in these two passages?

3. Do you think the difference in intended audience explains some of the differences in these two passages?

Life in the Japanese Entertainment Quarters This detail from a seventeenth-century six-panel Japanese screen depicts men and women playing instruments and enjoying games. The women are probably professional entertainers (geisha). (Courtesy, Hikone Castle Museum)

The Life of the People in the Edo Period

The Tokugawa shoguns brought an end to civil war by controlling the military. Stripped of power and required to spend alternate years at Edo, many of the daimyo and samurai passed their lives in idle pursuit of pleasure. They spent extravagantly on fine silks, paintings, concubines, boys, the theater, and the redecoration of their castles. Around 1700 one scholar observed that the entire military class was living "as in an inn, that is, consuming now and paying later."[2] Eighteenth-century Japanese novels, plays, and histories portray the samurai engrossed in tavern brawls and sexual orgies. These temptations, as well as more sophisticated pleasures and the heavy costs of maintaining alternate residences at Edo, gradually bankrupted the warrior class.

All major cities contained places of amusement for men — teahouses, theaters, restaurants, and houses of prostitution. Desperately poor parents sometimes sold their daughters to entertainment houses (as they did in China and medieval Europe), and the most attrac-

tive or talented girls, trained in singing, dancing, and conversational arts, became courtesans, later called geishas (GAY-shuhz), "accomplished persons."

Another form of entertainment in the cities was **kabuki theater**, patronized by both merchants and samurai. An art form created by townspeople, kabuki originated in crude, bawdy skits dealing with love and romance. Performances featured elaborate costumes, song, dance, and poetry. Because actresses were thought to corrupt public morals, the Tokugawa government banned them from the stage in 1629. From that time on, men played all the parts. Male actors in female dress and makeup performed as seductively as possible to entice the burly samurai who thronged the theaters. Homosexuality, long accepted in Japan, was widely practiced among the samurai, who pursued the actors and spent profligately on them. Some moralists and bureaucrats complained from time to time, but the

• **kabuki theater** A popular form of Japanese drama that brings together dialogue, dance, and music to tell stories. The actors wear colorful costumes and dramatic makeup.

◻ Picturing the Past

Interior View of a Theater Complex kabuki plays, which dealt with heroes, loyalty, and tragedy and which included music and dance, became the most popular form of entertainment in Tokugawa Japan for all classes. Movable scenery and lighting effects made possible the staging of storms, fires, and hurricanes. (Tokyo National Museum/image: TNM Image Archives)

ANALYZING THE IMAGE How many people are performing in this scene? Are there more men or women in the audience? How do you distinguish them? Are any of the men samurai?

CONNECTIONS What connections do you see between the popularity of kabuki plays and other aspects of Japanese life in this period?

Tokugawa government decided to accept kabuki and prostitution as necessary evils. The samurai paid for their costly pleasures in the way their European counterparts did — by fleecing the peasants and borrowing from the merchants.

Cities were also the center for commercial publishing. As in contemporary China, the reading public eagerly purchased fiction and the scripts for plays. Ihara Saikaku (1642–1693) wrote stories of the foibles of townspeople in such books as *Five Women Who Loved Love* and *The Life of an Amorous Man*. One of the

puppet plays of Chikamatsu Monzaemon (1653–1724) tells the story of the son of a business owner who, caught between duty to his family and love of a prostitute, decides to resolve the situation by double suicide. The art of color woodblock printing also was perfected during this period. Many of the surviving prints, made for a popular audience, depict the theater and women of the entertainment quarters.

Almost as entertaining was watching the long processions of daimyo, their retainers, and their luggage as they passed back and forth to and from Edo twice a year. The shogunate prohibited travel by commoners, but they could get passports to take pilgrimages, visit relatives, or seek the soothing waters of medicinal hot springs. Setting out on foot, groups of villagers would travel to such shrines as Ise, often taking large detours to visit Osaka or Edo to sightsee or attend the theater. Older women with daughters-in-law to run their households were among the most avid pilgrims.

According to Japanese tradition, farmers deserved respect. In practice, however, peasants were often treated callously. It was government policy to tax them to the level of bare subsistence, and official legislation repeatedly redefined their duties. In 1649 every village in Japan received these regulations:

> Peasants are people without sense or forethought. Therefore they must not give rice to their wives and children at harvest time, but must save food for the future. They should eat millet, vegetables, and other coarse food instead of rice. Even the fallen leaves of plants should be saved as food against famine. . . . During the seasons of planting and harvesting, however, when the labor is arduous, the food taken may be a little better. . . .
>
> They must not buy tea or sake to drink nor must their wives. The husband must work in the fields, the wife must work at the loom. Both must do night work. However good-looking a wife may be, if she neglects her household duties by drinking tea or sightseeing or rambling on the hillsides, she must be divorced.
>
> Peasants must wear only cotton or hemp — no silk. They may not smoke tobacco. It is harmful to health, it takes up time, and costs money. It also creates a risk of fire.[3]

During the seventeenth and eighteenth centuries the extravagant lifestyles of the daimyo and upper-level samurai were paid for by raising taxes on their subordinate peasants, from 30 or 40 percent of the rice crop to 50 percent. Not surprisingly, this angered peasants, and peasant protests became chronic during the eighteenth century. For example, oppressive taxation provoked eighty-four thousand farmers in the province of Iwaki to revolt in 1739; after widespread burning and destruction, their demands for lower taxes were met. Natural disasters also added to the peasants' misery. In 1783 Mount Asama erupted, spewing volcanic ash that darkened the skies all summer; the resulting crop failures led to famine. When famine recurred again in 1787, commoners rioted for five days in Edo, smashing merchants' stores and pouring sake and rice into the muddy streets. The shogunate responded by trying to control the floating population of day laborers without families in the city. At one point they were rounded up and transported to work the gold mines in an island off the

> "Peasants must wear only cotton or hemp — no silk. They may not smoke tobacco. It is harmful to health, it takes up time, and costs money. It also creates a risk of fire."
>
> **JAPANESE VILLAGE REGULATIONS, 1649**

north coast, where most of them died within two or three years.

This picture of peasant hardship tells only part of the story. Agricultural productivity increased substantially during the Tokugawa period. Peasants who improved their lands and increased their yields continued to pay the same assessed tax and could pocket the surplus as profit. As those without land drifted to the cities, peasants left in the countryside found ways to improve their livelihoods. At Hirano near Osaka, for example, 61.7 percent of all arable land was sown in cotton. The peasants ginned the cotton locally before transporting it to wholesalers in Osaka. In many rural places, as many peasants worked in the manufacture of silk, cotton, or vegetable oil as in the production of rice.

In comparison to farmers, merchants had a much easier life, even if they had no political power. By contemporary standards anywhere in the world, the Japanese mercantile class lived well. In 1705 the shogunate confiscated the property of a merchant in Osaka "for conduct unbecoming a member of the commercial class." In fact, the confiscation was at the urging of influential daimyo and samurai who owed the merchant gigantic debts. The government seized 50 pairs of gold screens, 360 carpets, several mansions, 48 granaries and warehouses scattered around the country, and hundreds of thousands of gold pieces. Few merchants possessed such fabulous wealth, but many lived in comfort, if not luxury.

Within a village, some families would be relatively well-off, others barely able to get by. The village headman generally came from the richest family, but he consulted a council of elders on important matters. Women in better-off families were much more likely to learn to read than women in poor families. Daughters of wealthy peasants studied penmanship, the Chinese classics, poetry, and the proper forms of correspondence, and they rounded out their education with travel. By contrast, girls from middle-level peasant families might have had from two to five years of formal schooling, but they were thought incapable of learning the difficult Chinese characters, so their education focused on moral instruction intended to instill virtue.

By the fifteenth and sixteenth centuries Japan's family and marriage systems had evolved in the

Edo Craftsmen at Work Less than 3 inches tall, the ivory figure below shows a parasol maker seated on the floor (the typical Japanese practice) eating his lunch, his tools by his side. The painting on the left shows a family of dyers, with men, women, and children all sharing the labor. (ivory: Private Collection/Photo © Boltin Picture Library; painting: Werner Forman/Art Resource, NY)

direction of a patrilocal, patriarchal system more like China's, and Japanese women had lost the prominent role in high society that they had occupied during the Heian period. It became standard for women to move into their husbands' homes, where they occupied positions subordinate to both their husbands and their mothers-in-law. In addition, elite families stopped dividing their property among all of their children; instead they retained it for the sons alone or increasingly for a single son who would continue the family line. Marriage, which now had greater consequence, also had a more public character and was marked by greater ceremony. Wedding rituals involved both the exchange of betrothal gifts and the movement of the bride from her parents' home to her husband's home. She brought with her a trousseau that provided her with clothes and other items she would need for daily life, but not with

land, which would have given her economic autonomy. On the other hand, her position within her new family was more secure, for it became more difficult for a husband to divorce his wife. She also gained authority within the family. If her husband was away, she managed family affairs. If her husband fathered children with concubines, she was their legal mother.

A peasant wife shared responsibility for the family's economic well-being with her husband. If of poor or middling status, she worked alongside her husband in the fields, doing the routine work while he did the heavy work. If they were farmhands and worked for wages, the wife invariably earned a third or a half less than her husband. Wives of prosperous farmers never worked in the fields, but they reeled silk, wove cloth, helped in any family business, and supervised the maids. When cotton growing spread to Japan in the sixteenth century, women took on the jobs of spinning and weaving it. Whatever their economic status, Japanese women, like women everywhere in the world, tended the children. Families were growing smaller in this period in response to the spread of single-heir inheritance. From studies of household registers, demographic historians have shown that Japanese families restricted the number of children they had by practicing abortion and infanticide, turning to adoption when no heir survived.

How was divorce initiated, and how frequent was it? Customs among the upper class differed considerably from peasant practices. Among the elite, the husband alone could initiate divorce; all he had to do was order his wife to leave or send her possessions to her parents' home. For the wife, divorce carried a stigma, but she could not prevent it or insist on keeping her children. Widows and divorcées of the samurai elite — where female chastity was the core of fidelity — were expected not to remarry. Among the peasant classes, by contrast, divorce seems to have been fairly common — at least 15 percent in the villages near Osaka in the eighteenth century. A poor woman wanting a divorce could simply leave her husband's home. It was also possible to secure divorce through a temple. If a married woman entered the temple and performed rites there for three years, her marriage bond was dissolved. Sometimes Buddhist temple priests served as divorce brokers: they went to the village headman and had him force the husband to agree to a divorce. News of the coming of temple officials was usually enough to produce a letter of separation.

Maritime Trade, Piracy, and the Entry of Europe into the Asian Maritime Sphere

☐ How did the sea link the countries of East Asia, and what happened when Europeans entered this maritime sphere?

In the period 1400–1800, maritime trade and piracy connected China and Japan to each other and also to Korea, Southeast Asia, and Europe. All through the period China and Japan traded extensively with each other as well as with Korea. Both Korea and Japan relied on Chinese coinage, and China relied on silver from Japan. During the fifteenth century China launched overseas expeditions. Japan was a major source of pirates. In the sixteenth century European traders appeared, eager for Chinese porcelains and silks. Christian missionaries followed, but despite initial suc-

cesses, they were later banned, first by the Japanese government and then by the Chinese government. Political changes in Europe changed the international makeup of the European traders in East Asia, with the dominant groups first the Portuguese, next the Dutch, and then the British.

Zheng He's Voyages

Early in the Ming period the Chinese government tried to revive the tribute system of the Han (202–220 c.e.) and Tang Dynasties (618–907), when China had dominated East Asia and envoys had arrived from dozens of distant lands. To invite more countries to send missions, the third Ming emperor (Chengzu or Yongle) authorized an extraordinary series of voyages to the Indian Ocean under the command of the Muslim eunuch Zheng He (1371–1433; see also the "Individuals in Society" feature on page 463).

Zheng He's father had made the trip to Mecca, and the seven voyages that Zheng led between 1405 and 1433 followed old Arab trade routes. The first of the seven was made by a fleet of 317 ships, of which 62 were huge, 440 feet long. Each expedition involved from twenty thousand to thirty-two thousand men. Their itineraries included stops in Vietnam, Malaysia, Indonesia, Sri Lanka, India, and, in the later voyages, Hormuz (on the coast of Persia) and East Africa (see Map 16.1 on page 462). At each stop Zheng He went ashore to visit rulers, transmit messages of China's peaceful intentions, and bestow lavish gifts. Rulers were invited to come to China or send envoys and were offered accommodation on the return voyages. Near the Straits of Malacca, Zheng He's fleet battled Chinese pirates, bringing them under control. Zheng He made other shows of force as well, deposing rulers deemed unacceptable in Java, Sumatra, and Sri Lanka.

On the return of these expeditions, the Ming emperor was delighted by the exotic things the fleet brought back, such as giraffes and lions from Africa, fine cotton cloth from India, and gems and spices from Southeast Asia. Ma Huan, an interpreter who accompanied Zheng He, collected data on the plants, animals, peoples, and geography that they encountered and wrote a book titled *The Overall Survey of the Ocean's Shores*. Still, these expeditions were not voyages of discovery; they followed established routes and pursued diplomatic rather than commercial goals.

Why were these voyages abandoned? Officials complained about their cost and modest returns. As a consequence, after 1474, all of the remaining ships with three or more masts were broken up and used for lumber. Chinese did not pull back from trade in the South China Sea and Indian Ocean, but the government no longer promoted trade, leaving the initiative to private merchants and migrants.

Listening to the Past

Keinen's Poetic Diary of the Korea Campaign

The Buddhist priest Keinen (1534?–1611) was ordered in 1597 to accompany the local daimyo on Hideyoshi's second campaign in Korea and spent seven months there. As a Buddhist, he did not revel in military feats but rather deplored the death and suffering that he observed. Adopting the time-honored form of the poetic diary, Keinen ends each day's entry with a short poem. The excerpt quoted here begins about six weeks after he left home.

"Eighth month, 4th day. Every one is trying to be the first off the ship; no one wants to lag behind. They fall over each other in trying to get at the plunder, to kill people. It is a sight I cannot bear to see.

> A hubbub rises
> as from roiling clouds and mist
> where they swarm about
> in their rage for the plunder
> of innocent people's goods.

VIII.5.
They are burning the houses. As I watched them go up in smoke, I thought that my own existence was like this and was seized by sympathy.

> The "Red Country" is
> what they call it, but black is
> the smoke that rises
> from the burning houses
> where you see flames flying high.

VIII.6.
The very fields and hillsides have been put to the fire, not to speak of the forts. People are put to the sword, or they are shackled with chains and bamboo tubes choking the neck. Parents sobbing for their children, children searching for their parents—never before have I seen such a pitiable sight.

> The hills are ablaze
> with the cries of soldiers
> intoxicated
> with their pyrolatry—
> the battleground of demons.

VIII.7.
Looking at the various kinds of plunder amassed by them all, I formed a desire for such things. Could I really be like this, I thought, and felt ashamed. How can I attain salvation like this, I thought.

> How ashamed I am!
> For everything that I see
> I form desires—

a creature of delusions,
my mind full of attachments.

On the same day, as I exerted myself in reflections on my spiritual state, I felt myself more and more ashamed. And yet the Buddha has vowed not to give weight to the weightiest of evil deeds, not to abandon the most abandoned and intemperate!

> Unless it be through
> reliance on the vow of
> Amida Buddha,
> who could obtain salvation
> with such wicked thoughts as mine?

VIII.8.
They are carrying off Korean children and killing their parents. Never shall they see each other again. Their mutual cries—surely this is like the torture meted out by the fiends of hell.

> It is piteous;
> when the four fledglings parted,*
> it must have been thus—
> I see the parents' lament
> over their sobbing children.

VIII.11.
As night fell, I saw people's houses go up in smoke. They have lost everything to the fire, all their grain and all their property.

> How wretched it is!
> Smoke lingers still where the grain
> was burned and wasted;
> so that is where I lay my
> head tonight: on the scorched earth.

VIII.13.
His lordship has set up camp about five leagues this side of Namwon. Unless this fortress is taken, our prospects are dubious; so we are to close in and invest it this evening. The word is that fifty or sixty thousand soldiers from Great Ming are garrisoning the place.

> We'll solve the challenge
> posed even by this fortress
> of the Red Country!—
> The troops rejoice to hear this,
> and they rest their weary feet.

*An allusion to the proverbial tale of a mother bird's sorrow at her fledglings' departure to the four directions.

VIII.14.

Rain has been falling steadily since the evening. It comes down in sheets, like a waterfall. We have put up a makeshift tent covered with oil paper only, and it is frightening how the rain pours in. It is impossible to sleep. I had to think of the story "The Devil at One Gulp" in *Tales of Ise*.† The night described in that tale must have been just like this.

> Inexorably,
> fearsome torrents beating down
> remind me of that
> dreadful night when the devil
> at one gulp ate his victim.

VIII.15.

The fortress is to be stormed before dawn tomorrow. Fascines of bamboo have been distributed to the assault troops. The sun was about to set as they worked their way close in, right up against the edge of the castle's bulwarks, and gunfire opened up from the several siege detachments, accompanied by arrows shot from short-bows. Unthinkable numbers of men were killed. As I saw them dying:

> From the fortress, too,
> from their short-bows, too.
> How many killed? Beyond count
> is the number of the dead.

The castle fell to the assault in the course of the night. Lord Hishu's troops were the first inside the walls. Needless to say, he is to get a vermilion-seal letter of commendation.

VIII.16.

All in the fortress were slaughtered, to the last man and woman. No prisoners were taken. To be sure, a few were kept alive for exchange purposes.

> How cruel! This world
> of sorrow and inconstancy
> does have one constant—
> men and women, young and old
> die and vanish; are no more.

VIII.17.

Until yesterday they did not know that they would have to die; today, they are transformed into the smoke of impermanence, as is the way of this world of constant change. How can I be unaffected by this!

> Look! Everyone, look!
> Is this, then, to be called the human condition?—
> a life with a deadline,
> a life with a limit: today. "

†This is a story of an abduction that ends badly. The lady in question, sequestered in a broken-down storehouse to keep her safe from the elements on a dark and stormy night, is devoured "at one gulp" by an ogre who dwells there.

• **Although the Japanese invasion failed, some of the warriors who fought in it were celebrated, like Kato Kiyomasa, shown here fighting a tiger in the hills of Korea.** (Courtesy, Stephen Turnbull)

Source: *Sources of Japanese Tradition*, by Wm. Theodore de Bary, Donald Keene, George Tanabe, and Paul Varley. Copyright © 2001 by Columbia University Press. Reproduced with permission of the publisher.

QUESTIONS FOR ANALYSIS

1. Buddhism teaches the impermanence of phenomena, the need to let go of attachments, and it opposes the taking of life. Can any of Keinen's responses be identified as specifically Buddhist?

2. Does Keinen's use of poetry seem natural, or do you think it seems forced?

3. What would be the purpose of bringing a Buddhist priest opposed to killing on a military campaign?

Piracy and Japan's Overseas Adventures

One goal of Zheng He's expeditions was to suppress piracy, which had become a problem all along the China coast. Already in the thirteenth century social disorder and banditry in Japan had expanded into seaborne banditry, some of it within the Japanese islands around the Inland Sea (Map 21.3), but also in the straits between Korea and Japan. Japanese "sea bandits" would raid the Korean coast, seizing rice and other goods to take home. In the sixteenth century bands several hundred strong would attack and loot Chinese coastal cities or hold them hostage for ransom. As maritime trade throughout East Asia grew more lively, sea bandits also took to attacking ships to steal their cargo. Although the pirates were called the "Japanese pirates" by both the Koreans and the Chinese, pirate gangs in fact recruited from all countries. The Ryūkyū (ryoo-kyoo) Islands and Taiwan became major bases.

Possibly encouraged by the exploits of these bandits, Hideyoshi, after his victories in unifying Japan, decided to extend his territory across the seas. In 1590, after receiving congratulations from Korea on his victories, Hideyoshi sent a letter asking the Koreans to allow his armies to pass through their country, declaring that his real target was China: "Disregarding the distance of the sea and mountain reaches that lie in between, I shall in one fell swoop invade Great Ming. I have in mind to introduce Japanese customs and values to the four hundred and more provinces of that country and bestow upon it the benefits of imperial rule and culture for the coming hundred million years."[4] He also sent demands for submission to countries of Southeast Asia and to the Spanish governor of the Philippines.

In 1592 Hideyoshi mobilized 158,000 soldiers and 9,200 sailors for his invasion, and equipped them with muskets and cannon, which had recently been introduced into Japan. His forces overwhelmed Korean defenders and reached Seoul within three weeks and Pyongyang in two months. A few months later, in the middle of winter, Chinese armies arrived to help defend Korea, and Japanese forces were pushed back

MAP 21.3 East Asia, ca. 1600 Pirates and traders often plied the same waters as seaborne trade grew in the sixteenth century. The Portuguese were especially active in setting up trading ports.

from Pyongyang. A stalemate lasted till 1597; when Hideyoshi sent new troops. This time the Ming army and the Korean navy were more successful in resisting the Japanese. For years the Korean navy had to defend against Japanese pirates, and it was able to keep the Japanese from supplying or reinforcing their troops. In 1598, after Hideyoshi's death, the Japanese army withdrew, but Korea was left devastated. (See "Listening to the Past: Keinen's Poetic Diary of the Korea Campaign," page 640.)

After recovering from the setbacks of these invasions, Korea began to advance socially and economically. During the Choson Dynasty (1392–1910), the Korean elite (the yangban) turned away from Buddhism and toward strict Neo-Confucian orthodoxy. As agricultural productivity improved, the population grew from about 4.4 million in 1400, to about 8 million in 1600, 10 million in 1700, and 14 million in 1810 (or about half as big as Japan's population and one-twentieth as big as China's). With economic advances slavery declined. When slaves ran away, landowners found that it was less expensive to replace them with sharecroppers than to recapture them. Between 1750 and 1790 the

> "I have in mind to introduce Japanese customs and values to the four hundred and more provinces of that country [China] and bestow upon it the benefits of imperial rule and culture for the coming hundred million years."
>
> **HIDEYOSHI**

slave population dropped from 30 percent to 5 percent of the population. The hold of the yangban elite, however, remained strong. Through the eighteenth century about two dozen yangban families dominated the civil service examinations, leaving relatively few slots for commoners to rise to through study.

Europeans Enter the Scene

In the sixteenth century Portuguese, Spanish, and Dutch merchants and adventurers began to participate in the East Asian maritime world. The trade between Japan, China, and Southeast Asia was very profitable,

Dutch in Japan The Japanese were curious about the appearance, dress, and habits of the Dutch who came to the enclave of Deshima to trade. In this detail from a long hand scroll, Dutch traders are shown interacting with a Japanese samurai in a room with Japanese tatami mats on the floor. Note also the Western musical instruments. (Private Collection/The Bridgeman Art Library)

and the European traders wanted a share of it. They also wanted to develop trade between Asia and Europe.

The Portuguese and Dutch were not reluctant to use force to gain control of trade, and they seized many outposts along the trade routes, including Taiwan. Moreover, they made little distinction between trade, smuggling, and piracy. In 1521 the Ming tried to ban the Portuguese from China. Two years later an expeditionary force commissioned by the Portuguese king to negotiate a friendship treaty defeated its mission by

Missionary Publication To appeal to a Chinese audience, the Jesuits illustrated some of their publications in a distinctly Chinese style. This book illustration shows Mary during the annunciation in a Chinese-style room with a Chinese landscape painting on the wall, and the descent from Heaven of the angel Gabriel signaled in Chinese fashion by stylized clouds. (Courtesy, Archivum Romanum Societatis Iesu [ARSI], Rome)

firing on Chinese warships near Guangzhou. In 1557, without informing Beijing, local Chinese officials decided that the way to regulate trade was to allow the Portuguese to build a trading post on uninhabited land near the mouth of the Pearl River. The city they built there — Macao — became the first destination for Europeans going to China until the nineteenth century, and it remained a Portuguese possession until 1999.

European products were not in demand in China, but silver was. Japan had supplied much of China's silver, but with the development of silver mines in the New World, European traders began supplying large quantities of silver to China, allowing the expansion of China's economy.

Chinese were quick to take advantage of the new trading ports set up by European powers. In Batavia harbor (now Jakarta, Indonesia) Chinese ships outnumbered those from any other country by two or three to one. Manila, under Spanish control, and Taiwan and Batavia, both under Dutch control, all attracted thousands of Chinese colonists. Local people felt the intrusion of Chinese more than of Europeans, and riots against Chinese led to massacres on several occasions.

A side benefit of the appearance of European traders was New World crops. Sweet potatoes, maize, peanuts, tomatoes, chili peppers, tobacco, and other crops were quickly adopted in East Asia. Sweet potatoes and maize in particular facilitated population growth because they could be grown on land previously thought too sandy or too steep to cultivate. Sweet potatoes became a common poor people's food.

Christian Missionaries

The Spanish and Portuguese kings supported missionary activity, and merchant vessels soon brought Catholic missionaries to East Asia. The first to come were Jesuits, from the order founded by Ignatius Loyola in 1534 to promote Catholic scholarship and combat the Protestant Reformation.

The Jesuit priest Francis Xavier had worked in India and the Indies before China and Japan attracted his attention. In 1549, after many misadventures, he landed on Kyushu, Japan's southernmost island (see Map 21.2). After he was expelled by the local lord, he traveled throughout western Japan as far as Kyoto, proselytizing wherever warlords allowed. He soon made many converts among the poor and even some among the daimyo. Xavier then set his sights on China but died on an uninhabited island off the China coast in 1552.

Other missionaries carried on his work, and by 1600 there were three hundred thousand baptized Christians in Japan. Most of them lived on Kyushu, where the shogun's power was weakest and the loyalty of the daimyo most doubtful. In 1615 bands of Christian samurai supported Tokugawa Ieyasu's enemies at the fierce Battle of Osaka. A couple of decades later, thirty thousand peasants in the heavily Catholic area of northern Kyushu revolted. The Tokugawa shoguns thus came to associate Christianity with domestic disorder and insurrection. Accordingly, what had been mild persecution of Christians became ruthless repression after 1639. Foreign priests were expelled or tortured, and thousands of Japanese Christians suffered crucifixion.

Meanwhile, in China the Jesuits concentrated on gaining the linguistic and scholarly knowledge they would need to convert the educated class. The Jesuit Matteo Ricci studied for years in Macao before setting himself up in Nanjing and trying to win over members of the educated class. In 1601 he was given permission to reside in Beijing, where he made several high-placed conversions. He also interested educated Chinese men in Western geography, astronomy, and Euclidean mathematics.

Ricci and his Jesuit successors believed that Confucianism was compatible with Christianity. Both shared similar concerns for morality and virtue, and they viewed making food offerings to ancestors as an expression of filial reverence rather than as a form of worship. The Franciscan and Dominican mendicant orders that arrived in China in the seventeenth century disagreed with the Jesuit position. In 1715 religious and political quarrels in Europe led the pope to decide that the Jesuits' accommodating approach was heretical. Angry at this insult, the Kangxi emperor forbade all Christian missionary work in China.

Porcelain Vase Among the objects produced in China that were in high demand in Europe in the seventeenth and eighteenth centuries were colorful porcelains. In this period Chinese potters perfected the use of overglaze enamels, which allowed the application of many colors to a single object. Blue, green, yellow, orange, and red all appear on this 18-inch-tall (45.7 cm) vase. (Image copyright © The Metropolitan Museum/Art Resource, NY)

Learning from the West

Although both China and Japan ended up prohibiting Christian missionary work, other aspects of Western culture were seen as impressive and worth learning. The closed-country policy that Japan instituted in 1639 restricted Japanese from leaving the country and kept European merchants in small enclaves. Still, Japanese interest in Europe did not disappear. Through the Dutch enclave of Deshima on a tiny island in Nagasaki harbor, a stream of Western ideas and inventions trickled into Japan in the eighteenth century. Western writings, architectural illustrations, calendars, watches, medicine, weapons, and paintings deeply impressed the Japanese. Western portraits and other paintings introduced the Japanese to perspective, shading, and other strategies for bringing more realism to art.

In China, too, both scholars and rulers showed an interest in Western learning. The Kangxi emperor frequently discussed scientific and philosophical questions with the Jesuits at court. When he got malaria, he accepted the Jesuits' offer of the medicine quinine. In addition, he had translations made of a collection of Western works on mathematics and the calendar. The court was impressed with the Jesuits' skill in astronomy and quickly appointed them to the Board of Astronomy. In 1674 the emperor asked them to re-equip the observatory with European instruments. In the visual arts the emperor and his successors employed Italian painters to make imperial portraits. Qianlong also took a fancy to European-style gardens and palaces. Firearms and mechanical clocks also were widely admired. The court established its own clock and watch factory, and in 1673 the emperor insisted that the Jesuits manufacture cannon for him and supervise gunnery practice.

Admiration was not one-sided. In the early eighteenth century China enjoyed a positive reputation in Europe. Voltaire wrote of the rationalism of Confucianism and saw advantages to the Chinese political system because the rulers did not put up with parasitical aristocrats or hypocritical priests. Chinese medical practice also drew

European interest. One Chinese practice that Europeans adopted was "variolation," an early form of smallpox inoculation.

The Shifting International Environment in the Eighteenth Century

The East Asian maritime world underwent many changes from the sixteenth to the eighteenth centuries. As already noted, the Japanese pulled back their own traders and limited opportunities for Europeans to trade in Japan. In China the Qing government limited trading contacts with Europe to Guangzhou in the far south in an attempt to curb piracy. Portugal lost many of its bases to the Dutch, and by the eighteenth century the British had become as active as the Dutch. In the seventeenth century the British and Dutch sought primarily porcelains and silk, but in the eighteenth century tea became the commodity in most demand. By the end of the century tea made up 80 percent of Chinese exports to Europe.

By the late eighteenth century Britain had become a great power and did not see why China should be able to dictate the terms of trade. Wanting to renegotiate its relations with China, in the 1790s King George III sent Lord George Macartney on a mission there. Macartney was instructed to secure a place for British traders to live near the tea-producing areas, negotiate a commercial treaty, create a desire for British products, arrange

• **kowtow** The ritual of kneeling on both knees and bowing one's head to the ground performed by children to their parents and by subjects to the Chinese ruler.

for diplomatic representation in Beijing, and open Japan and Southeast Asia to British commerce. He traveled with an eighty-four-person entourage and six hundred cases packed with British goods that he hoped would impress the Chinese court and attract trade: clocks, telescopes, knives, globes, plate glass, Wedgwood pottery, landscape paintings, woolen cloth, and carpets. The only member of the British party able to speak Chinese, however, was a twelve-year-old boy who had learned a bit of the language by talking with Chinese passengers on the long voyage.

After Lord Macartney arrived in Guangzhou in 1793, he proceeded overland. Because he would not perform the **kowtow** (kneeling on both knees and bowing his head to the ground), he was denied a formal audience in the palace. He was permitted to meet more informally with the Qianlong emperor at his summer retreat, but no negotiations followed this meeting because Qianlong saw no merit in Macartney's requests. As he pointed out in his formal reply, the Qing Empire "possesses all things in prolific abundance and lacks no product within its own borders"; thus trading with Europe was a kindness, not a necessity.[5] The Qing court was as intent on maintaining the existing system of regulated trade as Britain was intent on doing away with it.

Several members of the Macartney mission wrote books about China on their return, updating European understanding of China. These books, often illustrated, described many elements of Chinese culture and social customs — accounts less rosy than the reports written by the Jesuits a century or two earlier. The British writers, for instance, introduced the idea that Chinese women were oppressed, unable even to sit at the same table with their husbands to eat dinner.

CONNECTIONS

During the four centuries from 1400 to 1800, the countries of East Asia became increasingly connected. On the oceans trade and piracy linked them, and for the first time a war involved all three East Asian countries. In all three this was a time of economic advance. At the same time, their cultures and social structures were in no sense converging. The elites of the three countries were very different: in both Korea and Japan elite status was hereditary, while in China the key route to status and power involved doing well on a written examination. In Japan the samurai elite were expected to be skilled warriors, but in China and Korea the highest prestige went to men of letters. The Japanese woodblock prints that capture many features of the entertainment quarters in Japanese cities show a world distinct from anything in China and Korea.

By the end of this period, East Asian countries found themselves in a rapidly changing international environment, mostly because of revolutions occurring far from their shores. The next two chapters take up the story of these revolutions, first the political ones in America, France, and Haiti, and then the Industrial Revolution that began in Britain. In time these revolutions would profoundly alter East Asia as well.

☐ CHAPTER REVIEW

☐ **What sort of state and society developed in China after the Mongols were ousted? (p. 618)**

After the fall of the Mongols, China was ruled by the native Ming Dynasty for nearly three centuries. The dynasty's founder, who knew poverty firsthand, ruled for thirty years, becoming more paranoid and despotic over time. Very few of his successors were particularly good rulers, yet China thrived in many ways. Population grew as food production increased. Educational levels were high as more and more men prepared for the civil service examinations. Urban culture was lively, and publishing houses put out novels, short stories, and plays in the vernacular language for large audiences.

☐ **Did the return of alien rule with the Manchus have any positive consequences for China? (p. 626)**

The Ming suffered a series of disasters, beginning with a Japanese invasion of Korea at the end of the sixteenth century, and in 1644 the dynasty fell to a force from beyond the Great Wall, the Manchus. The Manchu rulers proved more competent than the Ming emperors and were able to both maintain peace and expand the empire to its maximum extent, bringing in Mongolia, Tibet, and Central Asia. Population grew steadily under Manchu rule, probably reaching around 300 million.

☐ **How did Japan change during this period of political instability? (p. 629)**

During the fifteenth and sixteenth centuries Japan was fragmented by civil war. New power holders emerged in the daimyo, who built stone castles to defend their territories. As daimyo attacked and defeated each other, power was gradually consolidated, until Hideyoshi gained control of most of the country. Japan also saw many cultural developments during this period, including the increasing influence of Zen ideas on the arts and the rise of Nō theater.

☐ **What was life like in Japan during the Tokugawa peace? (p. 631)**

After Hideyoshi's death, power was seized by Tokugawa Ieyasu, the founder of the Tokugawa Shogunate. In this shogunate's first two centuries (the seventeenth and eighteenth centuries), Japan reaped the rewards of peace. Steady economic growth and increased agri-cultural productivity swelled the population to approximately 30 million. But as the wealth of the business classes grew, the samurai, now dependent on fixed stipends, became progressively poorer. Samurai and others in search of work and pleasure fled to cities, where amusements of many kinds flourished.

☐ **How did the sea link the countries of East Asia, and what happened when Europeans entered this maritime sphere? (p. 639)**

Between 1400 and 1800 maritime trade connected the countries of Asia, in particular China and Japan. Piracy was a perpetual problem. Early in this period China sent out seven naval expeditions looking to promote diplomatic contacts, and these went as far as Africa. In the sixteenth century European traders arrived in China and Japan. The first European traders often acted like pirates, but profitable trading relationships soon developed. The Chinese economy became so dependent on huge imports of silver acquired through this trade that when supplies were cut off, it caused severe hardship. Trade with Europe also brought New World crops and new ideas. The Catholic missionaries who began to arrive in Asia introduced Western science and learning as well as Christianity, until they were banned in both Japan and China. Although the shogunate severely restricted trade, some Western scientific ideas and technology entered Japan through the port of Nagasaki. Chinese, too, took an interest in those elements of Western technology and science that seemed advanced, such as firearms, clockwork, astronomy, and oil painting. Because Europeans saw much to admire in East Asia in this period, ideas also flowed from East to West.

SUGGESTED READING

Berry, Mary Elizabeth. *The Culture of Civil War in Kyoto*. 1994. Uses diaries and other records to examine how people made sense of violence and social change.

Crossley, Pamela. *The Manchus*. 2002. A lively account that lets one think about Qing history from the rulers' point of view.

Elman, Benjamin. *A Cultural History of Civil Examinations in Late Imperial China*. 2000. Provides fascinating detail on how the examination system worked.

Elvin, Mark. *The Pattern of the Chinese Past*. 1973. Offers an explanation of China's failure to maintain its technological superiority in terms of a "high-level equilibrium trap."

Handley, Susan B. *Everyday Things in Premodern Japan*. 1999. Shows that the standard of living during the Edo period was comparable to that in the West at the same time.

Hegel, Robert E., trans. *True Crimes in Eighteenth-Century China: Twenty Case Histories*. 2009. Describes various crimes (including neighborhood feuds, murder, and sedition) and how the Chinese government dealt with them at several levels.

Keene, Donald. *Yoshimasa and the Silver Pavilion: The Creation of the Soul of Japan*. 2003. A lively introduction to the aesthetic style associated with Zen and its connection to shogunate patrons.

Mann, Susan. *Precious Records: Women in China's Long Eighteenth Century*. 1997. A well-written analysis of women's lives in the educated class.

McDermott, Joseph. *A Social History of the Chinese Book: Books and Literati Culture in Late Imperial China*. 2006. Places Chinese printing in a comparative perspective.

Mote, Frederic. *Imperial China*. 1999. An overview that analyzes the strengths and weaknesses of both the Ming and Qing Dynasties.

Mungello, David. *The Great Encounter of China and the West, 1500–1800*. 1999. A short but stimulating examination of the various dimensions of the first phase of Chinese-European relations.

Pomeranz, Kenneth. *The Great Divergence: China, Europe, and the Making of the Modern World Economy*. 2000. Argues that the most advanced areas of China were on a par with the most advanced regions of Europe through the eighteenth century.

Rowe, William T. *China's Last Empire: The Great Qing*. 2009. An up-to-date and thoughtful narrative of the Manchu rulers and the empire over which they presided.

Totman, Conrad. *A History of Japan*. 2000. An excellent, well-balanced survey.

Vaporis, Constantine Komitos. *Breaking Barriers: Travel and the State in Early Modern Japan*. 1994. An examination of recreational and religious travel.

Waldron, Arthur. *The Great Wall of China: From History to Myth*. 1990. Places the construction of the current Great Wall in the context of Ming-Mongol relations.

NOTES

1. L. J. Gallagher, trans., *China in the Sixteenth Century: The Journals of Matthew Ricci: 1583–1610* (New York: Random House, 1953), p. 23.
2. Quoted in D. H. Shively, "Bakufu Versus Kabuki," in *Studies in the Institutional History of Early Modern Japan*, ed. J. W. Hall (Princeton, N.J.: Princeton University Press, 1970), p. 236.
3. Quoted in G. B. Sansom, *A History of Japan, 1615–1867*, vol. 3 (Stanford, Calif.: Stanford University Press, 1978), p. 99.
4. W. T. de Bary et al., eds., *Sources of Japanese Tradition from Earliest Times to 1600* (New York: Columbia University Press, 2001), p. 467.
5. Pei-kai Cheng and M. Lestz, with J. Spence, ed., *The Search for Modern China: A Documentary History* (New York: W.W. Norton, 1999), p. 106.

For practice quizzes and other study tools, visit the **Online Study Guide** at bedfordstmartins.com/mckayworld.

For primary sources from this period, see *Sources of World Societies*, **Second Edition**.

For Web sites, images, and documents related to topics in this chapter, visit **Make History** at bedfordstmartins.com/mckayworld.

• **Liberty** The figure of Liberty bears a copy of the Declaration of the Rights of Man and of the Citizen in one hand and a pike to defend them in the other in this painting by the female artist Nanine Vallain. The painting hung in France's Jacobin club until its fall from power. (Nanine Vallain, *La Liberté*, oil on canvas, 1794/Musée de la revolution française de Vizille, © Conseil général de l'Isère/Domaine de Vizille)

22

A great wave of revolution rocked the Atlantic world in the last decades of the eighteenth century. As trade goods, individuals, and ideas circulated in ever greater numbers across the Atlantic Ocean, debates and events in one locale soon influenced those in another. Enlightenment ideals of freedom and equality flourished, inspiring reformers in many places to demand an end to the old ways. At the same time, wars fought for dominance of the Atlantic economy left European governments weakened by crushing debts, making them vulnerable to calls for reform.

Revolutions in the Atlantic World 1775–1815

The revolutionary era began in North America in 1775. Then in 1789 France became the leading revolutionary nation. It established first a constitutional monarchy, then a radical republic, and finally a new empire under Napoleon that would last until 1815. During this period of constant domestic turmoil, French armies violently exported revolution throughout much of Europe. Inspired both by the ideals of the revolution on the continent and by internal colonial conditions, the slaves in the French colony of Saint-Domingue rose up in 1791. Their rebellion would eventually lead to the creation of the independent nation of Haiti in 1804. The relationship between Europe and its colonies was fundamentally altered by this wave of revolution and by subsequent independence movements in Spanish North America. In Europe and its colonies abroad, the world of modern politics was born. •

Background to Revolution
□ What were the factors behind the age of revolution in the Atlantic world?

The American Revolutionary Era, 1775–1789
□ Why and how did American colonists forge a new, independent nation?

Revolution in France, 1789-1791
□ How did the events of 1789 result in a constitutional monarchy in France, and what were the consequences?

World War and Republican France, 1791–1799
□ Why and how did the French Revolution take a radical turn entailing terror at home and war with European powers?

Napoleon's Europe, 1799–1815
□ Why did Napoleon Bonaparte assume control of France and much of Europe, and what factors led to his downfall?

The Haitian Revolution, 1791–1804
□ How did slave revolt on colonial Saint-Domingue lead to the creation of the independent state of Haiti in 1804?

The Three Estates French inhabitants were legally divided into three orders, or estates: the clergy, the nobility, and everyone else. In this political cartoon from 1789 a peasant of the third estate struggles under the weight of a happy clergyman and a plumed nobleman. The caption—"Let's hope this game ends soon"—sets forth a program of reform that any peasant could understand. (Réunion des Musées Nationaux/Art Resource, NY)

Background to Revolution

□ What were the factors behind the age of revolution in the Atlantic world?

The origins of the revolutions in the Atlantic world were complex. No one cause lay behind them, nor was revolution inevitable or foreordained. However, certain important factors helped set the stage for reform. Among them were fundamental social and economic changes and political crises that eroded state authority. Another significant cause of revolutionary fervor was the impact of political ideas derived from the Enlightenment. Even though major intellectuals of the Enlightenment, the philosophes, were usually cautious about political reform themselves, the confidence in reason and progress that they fostered helped inspire a new generation to fight for greater freedom from repressive governments. Perhaps most important, financial crises generated by war expenses brought European states to their knees and allowed abstract discussions of reform to become pressing realities.

Social Change

Eighteenth-century European society was still legally divided into groups with special privileges, such as the nobility and the clergy, and groups with special burdens, such as the peasantry. Nobles in France enjoyed not only exemption from taxation but also exclusive rights to hunt game, bear swords, and wear gold ribbon in their clothing. In most countries, various middle-class groups — professionals, merchants, and guild masters — enjoyed privileges that allowed them to monopolize all sorts of economic activity.

Traditional privileges persisted in societies undergoing dramatic and destabilizing change. Due to increased agricultural production, Europe's population rose rapidly after 1750, and its cities and towns swelled in size. Inflation kept pace with demography, making it ever more difficult for urban people to find affordable food and living space. One way they kept up, and even managed to participate in the new consumer revolution (see pages 545–547), was by working harder and for longer hours. More women and children entered the paid labor force. In another change, men and women in jostling European cities were freer from the constraints of village life, and the rate of illegitimate births soared. A more positive development was increased schooling and a rise in literacy rates, particularly among urban men.

The growth of the economy created new inequalities between rich and poor. While the poor struggled with rising prices, investors who sponsored overseas trade or the spread of manufacture in the countryside reaped great profits. Old distinctions between landed aristocracy and city merchant began to fade as enterprising nobles put money into trade and rising middle-class bureaucrats and merchants bought landed estates and noble titles. Marriages between proud nobles and wealthy, educated commoners (often called the *bourgeoisie* [boorzh-wah-ZEE] in France) served both groups' interests, and a mixed-caste elite began to take shape. In the context of these changes, ancient privileges seemed to pose an intolerable burden to many observers.

Another social change involved the racial regimes established in European colonies to enable and protect slavery. By the late eighteenth century European law accepted that only Africans and people of African descent were subject to slavery. Even free people of color — a term for non-slaves of African or mixed African-European descent — were subject to special laws restricting the property they could own, whom they could marry, and what clothes they could wear. Racial privilege conferred a new dimension of entitlement on European settlers in the colonies, and they used extremely brutal methods to enforce it. The contradiction between slavery and the Enlightenment ideals of liberty and equality was all too evident to slaves and free people of color.

Growing Demands for Liberty and Equality

In addition to destabilizing social changes, the ideals of liberty and equality helped fuel revolutions in the Atlantic world. What did these concepts mean to eighteenth-century politicians and other people, and why were they so radical and revolutionary in their day?

The call for liberty was first of all a call for individual human rights. Before the revolutionary period, even the most enlightened monarchs believed they needed to regulate what people wrote and believed. Opposing this long-standing practice, supporters of the cause of individual liberty (who became known as "liberals" in the early nineteenth century) demanded freedom to worship according to the dictates of their consciences, an end to censorship, and freedom from arbitrary laws and from judges who simply obeyed orders from the government. The Declaration of the Rights of Man and of the Citizen, issued at the beginning of the French Revolution, proclaimed that "Liberty consists in being able to do anything that does not harm another person." In the context of the monarchical and absolutist forms of government then dominating Europe, this was a truly radical idea.

The call for liberty was also a call for a new kind of government. Reformers believed that the people had sovereignty — that is, that the people alone had the

> "Liberty consists in being able to do anything that does not harm another person."
>
> **DECLARATION OF THE RIGHTS OF MAN**

authority to make laws limiting an individual's freedom of action. In practice, this system of government meant choosing legislators who represented the people and were accountable to them. Monarchs might retain their thrones, but their rule should be constrained by the will of the people.

Equality was a more ambiguous idea. Eighteenth-century liberals argued that, in theory, all citizens should have identical rights and liberties and that the nobility had no right to special privileges based on birth. However, they accepted a number of distinctions. First, most eighteenth-century liberals were men of their times, and they generally believed that equality between men and women was neither practical nor desirable. Women played an important political role in the French Revolution at several points, but the men of the French Revolution limited formal political rights — the right to vote, to run for office, to participate in government — to men. Second, few questioned the inequality between blacks and whites. Even those who believed that the slave trade was unjust and should be abolished, such as Thomas Jefferson, usually felt that abolition was so socially and economically dangerous that it needed to be indefinitely postponed.

Finally, liberals never believed that everyone should be equal economically. Although Jefferson wrote in an early draft of the American Declaration of Independence that everyone was equal in "the pursuit of property," liberals certainly did not expect equal success in that pursuit. (Jefferson later changed "property" to the more noble-sounding "happiness.") Great differences in wealth and income between rich and poor were perfectly acceptable. The essential point was that every free male should have a legally equal chance at economic gain. However limited they appear to modern eyes, these demands for liberty and equality were revolutionary, given that a privileged elite had long existed with little opposition.

The two most important thinkers to use Enlightenment goals of personal freedom and legal equality to justify liberal self-government were John Locke and the baron de Montesquieu. Locke maintained that England's long political tradition rested on "the rights of Englishmen" and on representative government through Parliament. He argued that if a government oversteps its proper function of protecting the natural rights of life, liberty, and private property, it becomes a tyranny. Montesquieu was also inspired by English constitutional history and the Glorious Revolution, which placed sovereignty in Parliament (see pages 510–515). He, too, believed that powerful "intermediary groups" — such as the judicial nobility of which he

was a proud member — offered the best defense of liberty against despotism.

The belief that representative institutions could defend their liberty and interests appealed powerfully to the bourgeoisie. Yet liberal ideas about individual rights and political freedom also appealed to members of the hereditary nobility, at least in western Europe and as formulated by Montesquieu. Representative government did not mean democracy, which liberal thinkers tended to equate with mob rule. Rather, they envisioned voting for representatives as being restricted to men who owned property — those with "a stake in society." The blurring of practical distinctions between landed aristocrats and wealthy commoners meant that there was no clear-cut opposition between nobles and non-nobles on political issues. The poor themselves usually had little time to plan for reform, given the challenges of earning their daily bread.

Revolutions thus began with aspirations for equality and liberty among the social elite. Soon, however, dissenting voices emerged as some revolutionaries became frustrated with the limitations of classical liberal notions of equality and liberty and clamored for a fuller realization of these concepts. Depending on location, their demands included political rights for women and free people of color, the emancipation of slaves, and government regulation to guarantee fair access to resources and to impose economic equality. The age of revolution was thus characterized as much by conflicts over how far reform should go as by the arguments for change that launched this age in the first place.

The Seven Years' War

The roots of revolutionary ideology could be found in the writings of Locke or Montesquieu, but it was by no means inevitable that their ideas would result in revolution. Many members of the educated elite were satisfied with the status quo or too intimidated to challenge it. Instead, events — political, economic, and military — created crises that opened the door for radical action. One of the most important was the global conflict known as the Seven Years' War (1756–1763).

The war's battlefields stretched from central Europe to India to North America (where the conflict was known as the French and Indian War), pitting a new alliance of England and Prussia against the French and Austrians. Its origins were in conflicts left unresolved at the end of the War of the Austrian Succession in 1748 (see pages 502–503). In central Europe, Austria's Maria Theresa vowed to win back Silesia, which Prussia took in the war of succession, and to crush Prussia, thereby re-establishing the Habsburgs' traditional leadership in German affairs. By the end of the Seven Years' War Maria Theresa had almost succeeded, but Prussia survived with its boundaries intact.

• **Treaty of Paris** The 1763 peace treaty that ended the Seven Years' War, according vast French territories in North America and India to Britain and Louisiana to Spain.

Unresolved tensions also lingered in North America, particularly regarding the border between the French and British colonies. The encroachment of English settlers into territory claimed by the French in the Ohio Valley resulted in skirmishes that soon became war. Although the inhabitants of New France were greatly outnumbered — Canada counted fifty-five thousand inhabitants, compared to 1.2 million in the thirteen English colonies — French forces achieved major victories until 1758. Then, the British diverted resources from the war in Europe, using superior sea power to destroy the French fleet and choke off French commerce around the world. In 1759 the British laid siege to Quebec for four long months, finally defeating the French in a battle that sealed the fate of France in North America.

British victory on all colonial fronts was ratified in the 1763 **Treaty of Paris**. Canada and all French territory east of the Mississippi River passed to Britain, and France ceded Louisiana to Spain as compensation for Spain's loss of Florida to Britain. France also gave up most of its holdings in India, opening the way to British dominance on the subcontinent (Map 22.1).

By 1763 Britain had realized its goal of monopolizing a vast trading and colonial empire, but at a tremendous cost in war debt. France emerged from the conflict humiliated and broke, but with its profitable Caribbean colonies intact. In the aftermath of war, both British and French governments had to raise taxes to repay loans, raising a storm of protest and demands for fundamental reform. Since the Caribbean colony of Saint-Domingue remained French, revolutionary turmoil in

MAP 22.1 European Claims in North America and India Before and After the Seven Years' War, 1755–1763 As a result of the war, France lost its vast territories in North America and India. In an effort to avoid costly conflicts with Native Americans living in the newly conquered territory, the British government in 1763 prohibited colonists from settling west of the Appalachian Mountains. One of the few remaining French colonies in the Americas, Saint-Domingue (on the island of Hispaniola) was the most profitable plantation in the New World.

the mother country would directly affect its population. The seeds of revolutionary conflict in the Atlantic world were thus sown.

The American Revolutionary Era, 1775–1789

☐ Why and how did American colonists forge a new, independent nation?

Increased taxes were one factor behind colonial protests in the New World, where the era of liberal political revolution began. After revolting against their home country, the thirteen mainland colonies of British North America succeeded in establishing a new unified government. Participants in the revolution believed they were demanding only the traditional rights of English men and women. But those traditional rights were liberal rights, and in the American context they had very strong democratic and popular overtones. Thus the American Revolution was fought in the name of ideals that were still quite radical for their time. In founding a government firmly based on liberal principles, the Americans set an example that would have a forceful impact on France and its colonies.

The Origins of the Revolution

The high cost of the Seven Years' War doubled the British national debt. Anticipating further expenses to defend newly conquered territories, the government in London imposed bold new administrative measures. Breaking with tradition, the British announced that they would maintain a large army in North America and tax the colonies directly. In 1765 Parliament passed the Stamp Act, which levied taxes on a long list of commercial and legal documents, diplomas, newspapers, almanacs, and playing cards. A stamp glued to each article indicated that the tax had been paid.

These measures seemed perfectly reasonable to the British, for a much heavier stamp tax already existed in Britain, and proceeds from the tax were to fund the defense of the colonies. Nonetheless, the colonists vigorously protested the Stamp Act by rioting and by boycotting British goods. Thus Parliament reluctantly repealed it.

This dispute raised important political questions. To what extent could the British government reassert its power while limiting the authority of elected colonial bodies? Who had the right to make laws for Americans? The British government replied that Americans were represented in Parliament, albeit indirectly (like most British people), and that Parliament ruled throughout the empire. Many Americans felt otherwise. In the words of John Adams, a major proponent of colonial independence, "A Parliament of Great Britain can have no more rights to tax the colonies than a Parliament of Paris." Thus British colonial administration and parliamentary supremacy came to appear as grave threats to existing American liberties.

Americans' resistance to these threats was fed by the great degree of independence they had long enjoyed. In British North America, unlike in England and Europe, no powerful established church existed, and religious freedom was taken for granted. Colonial assemblies made the important laws, which were seldom overturned by the British government. Also, the right to vote was much more widespread than in England. In many parts of colonial Massachusetts, for example, as many as 95 percent of adult males could vote.

Moreover, greater political equality was matched by greater social and economic equality, at least for the free population. No hereditary nobility exercised privileges over peasants and other social groups. Instead, independent farmers dominated colonial society. This was particularly true in the northern colonies, where the revolution originated.

In 1773 disputes over taxes and representation flared up again. Under the Tea Act of that year, the British government permitted the financially hard-pressed East India Company to ship tea from China directly to its agents in the colonies rather than through London middlemen, who sold to independent merchants in the colonies. Thus the company secured a profitable monopoly on the tea trade, and colonial merchants were excluded. The price on tea was actually lowered for colonists, but the act generated a great deal of opposition because of the monopoly it gave to the East India Company.

Commemorative Teapot Manufacturers were quick to bring products to the market celebrating weighty political events, like this British teapot heralding "Stamp Act Repeal'd." By purchasing such items, ordinary people could champion political causes of the day and bring public affairs into their private lives. (Gift of Richard C. Manning/Peabody Essex Museum, Salem, Massachusetts. Acquired 9/16/1933)

In protest, Boston men disguised as Native Americans had a rowdy Tea Party in which they boarded East India Company ships and threw tea from them into the harbor. In response, the so-called Coercive Acts of 1774 closed the port of Boston, curtailed local elections, and expanded the royal governor's power. County conventions in Massachusetts urged that such measures be "rejected as the attempts of a wicked administration to enslave America." Other colonial assemblies joined in the denunciations. In September 1774, the First Continental Congress—consisting of colonial delegates who sought at first to peacefully resolve conflicts with Britain—met in Philadelphia. The more radical members of this assembly argued successfully against concessions to the English crown. The British Parliament also rejected compromise, and in April 1775 fighting between colonial and British troops began at Lexington and Concord.

Independence from Britain

As fighting spread, the colonists moved slowly toward open calls for independence. The uncompromising attitude of the British government and its use of German mercenaries did much to dissolve loyalties to the home country and to unite the separate colonies. *Common Sense* (1775), a brilliant attack by the recently arrived English radical Thomas Paine (1737–1809), also mobilized public opinion in favor of independence. A runaway bestseller with sales of 120,000 copies in a few months, Paine's tract ridiculed the idea of a small island ruling a great continent. In his call for freedom and republican government, Paine expressed Americans' growing sense of separateness and moral superiority.

On July 4, 1776, the Second Continental Congress adopted the **Declaration of Independence**. Written by Thomas Jefferson and others, this document boldly listed the tyrannical acts committed by George III (r. 1760–1820) and confidently proclaimed the natural rights of mankind and the sovereignty of the American states. The Declaration of Independence in effect universalized the traditional rights of English people and made them the rights of all mankind. It stated that "all Men are created equal, that they are endowed by their Creator with certain unalienable Rights, that among these are Life, Liberty, and the Pursuit of Happiness." No other American political document has ever caused such excitement, either at home or abroad.

☐ KEY EVENTS OF THE AMERICAN REVOLUTION

1765	Britain passes the Stamp Act
1773	Britain passes the Tea Act
1774	Britain passes the Coercive Acts in response to the Tea Party in the colonies; the First Continental Congress refuses concessions to the English crown
April 1775	Fighting begins between colonial and British troops
July 4, 1776	The Second Continental Congress adopts the Declaration of Independence
1777–1780	The French, Spanish, and Dutch side with the colonists against Britain
1783	The Treaty of Paris recognizes the independence of the American colonies
1787	The U.S. Constitution is signed
1791	The first ten amendments to the Constitution are ratified (the Bill of Rights)

Loyalist stronghold
Patriot stronghold
Strongly contested area

Québec
Montréal
VT.
N.H.
MASS.
Boston
N.Y.
Newport
R.I.
CONN.
Philadelphia
PA.
New York
N.J.
DEL.
MD.
VA.
Norfolk
N.C.
ATLANTIC OCEAN
S.C.
Wilmington
GA.
Charleston
Savannah

Loyalist Strength in the Colonies, ca. 1774–1776

After the Declaration of Independence, the conflict often took the form of a civil war pitting patriots against Loyalists, those who maintained an allegiance to the Crown. The Loyalists tended to be wealthy and politically moderate. Many patriots—such as John Hancock and George Washington—were also wealthy, but they willingly allied themselves with farmers and artisans in a broad coalition. This coalition harassed the Loyalists and confiscated their property to help pay for the war, causing more than thirty thousand of them to flee, mostly to Canada. The broad social base of the revolutionaries tended to make the revolution democratic. State governments extended the right to vote to many more men, including free African American men in many cases, but not to women.

On the international scene, the French wanted revenge against the British for the humiliating defeats of the Seven Years' War. Thus they sympathized with the rebels and supplied guns and gunpowder from the

• **Declaration of Independence** The 1776 document in which the American colonies declared independence from Great Britain and recast traditional English rights as universal human rights.

The Signing of the Declaration of Independence, July 4, 1776 John Trumbull's famous painting shows the dignity and determination of America's revolutionary leaders. An extraordinarily talented group, they succeeded in rallying popular support without losing power to more radical forces in the process. (Photo © Boltin Picture Library/The Bridgeman Art Library)

beginning of the conflict. By 1777 French volunteers were arriving in Virginia, and a dashing young nobleman, the marquis de Lafayette (1757–1834), quickly became one of the most trusted generals of George Washington, who was commanding American troops. In 1778 the French government offered a formal alliance to the American ambassador in Paris, Benjamin Franklin, and in 1779 and 1780 the Spanish and Dutch declared war on Britain. Catherine the Great of Russia helped organize the League of Armed Neutrality to protect neutral shipping rights and succeeded in hampering Britain's naval power. Thus by 1780 Britain was engaged in an imperial war against most of Europe as well as the thirteen colonies. In these circumstances, and in the face of severe reverses in India, in the West Indies, and at Yorktown in Virginia, a new British government decided to cut its losses and end the war.

American officials in Paris were receptive to negotiating a deal with England alone, for they feared that France wanted a treaty that would bottle up the new United States east of the Allegheny Mountains and give British holdings west of the Alleghenies to France's ally, Spain. Thus the American negotiators deserted their French allies and accepted the extraordinarily favorable terms Britain offered.

Under the Treaty of Paris of 1783, Britain recognized the independence of the thirteen colonies and ceded all its territory between the Allegheny Mountains and the Mississippi River to the Americans. Out of the bitter rivalries of the Old World, the Americans snatched dominion over a vast territory.

Framing the Constitution

The liberal program of the American Revolution was consolidated by the federal Constitution, the Bill of Rights, and the creation of a national republic. Assembling in Philadelphia in the summer of 1787, the

Antifederalists Opponents of the American Constitution who felt it diminished individual rights and accorded too much power to the federal government at the expense of the states.

delegates to the Constitutional Convention were determined to end the period of economic depression, social uncertainty, and leadership under a weak central government that had followed independence. The delegates thus decided to grant the federal, or central, government important powers: regulation of domestic and foreign trade, the right to tax, and the means to enforce its laws.

Strong rule would be placed squarely in the context of representative self-government. Senators and congressmen would be the lawmaking delegates of the voters, and the president of the republic would be an elected official. The central government would operate in Montesquieu's framework of checks and balances, under which authority was distributed across three different branches — the executive, legislative, and judicial branches — that would systematically balance one another, preventing one interest from gaining too much power. The power of the federal government would in turn be checked by that of the individual states.

When the results of the secret deliberations of the Constitutional Convention were presented to the states for ratification, a great public debate began. The opponents of the proposed Constitution — the **Antifederalists** — charged that the framers of the new document had taken too much power from the individual states and made the federal government too strong. Moreover, many Antifederalists feared for the individual freedoms for which they had fought. To overcome these objections, the Federalists promised to spell out these basic freedoms as soon as the new Constitution was adopted. The result was the first ten amendments to the Constitution, which the first Congress passed shortly after it met in New York in March 1789. These amendments, ratified in 1791, formed an effective Bill of Rights to safeguard the individual. Most of them — trial by jury, due process of law, the right to assemble, freedom from unreasonable search — had their origins in English law and the English Bill of Rights of 1689. Other rights — the freedoms of speech, the press, and religion — reflected natural-law theory and the strong value colonists had placed on independence from the start.

Like the French republic that was soon to emerge, the early American republic also sought to advance the rights of African Americans, and many free people of color voted in elections to ratify the Constitution. Congress banned slavery in federal territory in 1789, then the export of slaves from any state, and finally, in 1808, the import of slaves to any state. These early measures, along with voting rights for free people of color, were eroded in the early nineteenth century as abolitionist fervor waned.

The American Constitution and the Bill of Rights exemplified the great strengths and the limits of what

came to be called classical liberalism. Liberty meant individual freedoms and political safeguards. Liberty also meant representative government but did not necessarily mean democracy, with its principle of one person, one vote. Equality meant equality before the law, not equality of political participation or wealth. It did not mean equal rights for women, slaves, or indigenous peoples.

Revolution in France, 1789–1791

◻ How did the events of 1789 result in a constitutional monarchy in France, and what were the consequences?

No country felt the consequences of the American Revolution more deeply than France. Hundreds of French officers served in America and were inspired by the experience. The most famous of these, the young and impressionable marquis de Lafayette, left home as a great aristocrat determined to fight France's traditional foe, England. He returned with a love of liberty and firm republican convictions. French intellectuals and publicists engaged in passionate analysis of the federal Constitution as well as the constitutions of the various states of the new United States. The American Revolution undeniably fueled dissatisfaction with the old monarchical order in France. Yet the French Revolution did not mirror the American example. It was more radical and more complex, more influential and more controversial, more loved and more hated. For Europeans and most of the rest of the world, it was the great revolution of the eighteenth century, the revolution that opened the modern era in politics.

Breakdown of the Old Order

As did the American Revolution, the French Revolution had its immediate origins in the financial difficulties of the government. The efforts of the ministers of King Louis XV (r. 1715–1774) to raise taxes to meet the expenses of the War of the Austrian Succession and the Seven Years' War were thwarted by the high courts, known as the parlements. The noble judges of the parlements resented this threat to their exemption from taxation and decried the government's actions as a form of royal despotism.

When renewed efforts to reform the tax system met a similar fate in 1776, the government was forced to finance its enormous expenditures during the American war with borrowed money. As a result, the national debt soared. By the 1780s fully 50 percent of France's annual budget went to interest payments on the ever-increasing debt. Another 25 percent went to maintain the military, while 6 percent was absorbed by the royal family and the court at Versailles. Less than 20 percent of the national budget was available for the productive functions of the state, such as transportation and general administration. This was an impossible financial situation.

Nor could the king and his ministers print money and create inflation to cover their deficits, as modern governments do. Unlike England and Holland, which had far larger national debts relative to their populations, France had no central bank, no paper currency, and no means of creating credit. Therefore, when a depressed economy and a lack of public confidence made it increasingly difficult for the government to obtain new loans in 1786, it had no alternative but to try increasing taxes. Because France's tax system was unfair and out-of-date, increased revenues were possible only through fundamental reforms. Such reforms, which would affect all groups in France's complex and fragmented society, were guaranteed to create social and political unrest.

These crises struck a monarchy that had lost much of its mantle of royal authority. Kings had always maintained mistresses, who were invariably chosen from the court nobility. Louis XV broke that pattern with Madame de Pompadour, daughter of a disgraced bourgeois financier. As the king's favorite mistress from 1745 to 1750, Pompadour exercised tremendous influence that continued even after their love affair ended. She played a key role, for example, in bringing about France's break with Prussia and its new alliance with Austria in the mid-1750s. Pompadour's low birth and hidden political influence generated a stream of resentful and illegal pamphleteering. The king was being stripped of the sacred aura of God's anointed on earth (a process called desacralization) and was being reinvented in the popular imagination as a degenerate.

Despite the progressive desacralization of the monarchy, Louis XV would probably have prevailed had he lived longer, but he died in 1774. The new king, Louis XVI (r. 1774–1792), was a shy twenty-year-old with good intentions. Taking the throne, he is reported to have said, "What I should like most is to be loved."[1] The eager-to-please monarch Louis waffled on political reform and the economy, and he proved unable to quell the rising storm of opposition.

The Formation of the National Assembly

Spurred by a depressed economy and falling tax receipts, Louis XVI's minister of finance revived old proposals to impose a general tax on all landed property as well as to form provincial assemblies to help administer the tax, and he convinced the king to call an assembly of notables in 1787 to gain support for the idea. The assembled notables, mainly important noblemen and high-ranking clergy, declared that such sweeping tax changes required the approval of the **Estates General**, the representative body of all three estates, which had not met since 1614.

Facing imminent bankruptcy, the king tried to reassert his authority. He dismissed the notables and established new taxes by decree. In stirring language, the judges of the Parlement of Paris promptly declared the royal initiative null and void. When the king tried to exile the judges, a tremendous wave of protest swept the country. Frightened investors refused to advance more loans to the state. Finally in July 1788, a beaten Louis XVI bowed to public opinion and called for a spring session of the Estates General. Absolute monarchy was collapsing.

As its name indicates, the Estates General was a legislative body with representatives from the three orders of society: the clergy, nobility, and commoners. Following centuries-old tradition each order met separately to elect delegates, first at a local and then at a regional level. Results of the elections reveal the mindset of each estate on the eve of the revolution. The local assemblies of the clergy, representing the first estate, elected mostly parish priests rather than church leaders, demonstrating their dissatisfaction with the church hierarchy. The nobility, or second estate, voted in a majority of conservatives, primarily from the provinces, where nobles were less wealthy and more numerous. Nonetheless, fully one-third of noble representatives were liberals committed to major changes. Commoners of the third estate, who constituted over 95 percent of the population, elected primarily lawyers and government officials to represent them, with few delegates representing business and the poor.

The petitions for change drafted by the newly elected assemblies showed a surprising degree of consensus about the key issues confronting the realm. In all three estates, voices spoke in favor of replacing absolutism with a constitutional monarchy in which laws and taxes would require the consent of the Estates General in regular meetings. There was also the strong feeling that individual liberties would have to be guaranteed by law and that economic regulations should be loosened.

On May 5, 1789, the twelve hundred delegates of the three estates gathered in Versailles for the opening ses-

• **Estates General** Traditional representative body of the three estates of France that met in 1789 in response to imminent state bankruptcy.

• **National Assembly** French representative assembly formed in 1789 by the delegates of the third estate and some members of the clergy, the second estate.

sion of the Estates General. Despite widespread hopes for serious reform, the Estates General was almost immediately deadlocked due to arguments about voting procedures. Controversy had begun during the electoral process itself, when the government confirmed that, following precedent, each estate should meet and vote separately. During the lead-up to the Estates General, critics had demanded a single assembly dominated by the third estate. In his famous pamphlet "What Is the Third Estate?" the abbé Emmanuel Joseph Sieyès (himself a member of the first estate) argued that the nobility was a tiny, overprivileged minority and that the neglected third estate constituted the true strength of the French nation. (See "Listening to the Past: Abbé de Sieyès, 'What Is the Third Estate?'" page 664.) The government conceded that the third estate should have as many delegates as the clergy and the nobility combined, but then upheld a system granting one vote per estate instead of one vote per person. This meant that the two privileged estates could always outvote the third, even if the third estate had a majority by head count.

The issue came to a crisis in June 1789 when delegates of the third estate refused to meet until the king ordered the clergy and nobility to sit with them in a single body. Finally, after six weeks, a few parish priests began to go over to the third estate, which on June 17 voted to call itself the **National Assembly**. On June 20 the delegates of the third estate, excluded from their hall because of "repairs," moved to a large indoor tennis court where they swore the famous Oath of the Tennis Court, pledging not to disband until they had been recognized as a national assembly and had written a new constitution.

The king's response was disastrously ambivalent. On June 23 he made a conciliatory speech to a joint session in which he urged reforms, and four days later he ordered the three estates to meet together. At the same time, Louis apparently followed the advice of relatives and court nobles who urged him to dissolve the National Assembly by force. The king called an army of eighteen thousand troops toward the capital to bring the delegates under control, and on July 11 he dismissed his finance minister and other more liberal ministers. It appeared that the monarchy was prepared to renege on its promises for reform and to use violence to restore its control.

Popular Uprising and the Rights of Man

While delegates at Versailles were pressing for political rights, economic hardship gripped common people in the towns and countryside. Conditions were already tough, due to the disastrous financial situation of the Crown. A poor grain harvest in 1788 caused the price of

☐ KEY EVENTS OF THE FRENCH REVOLUTION

May 5, 1789	Estates General meets at Versailles
June 17, 1789	Third estate declares itself the National Assembly
June 20, 1789	Oath of the Tennis Court
July 14, 1789	Storming of the Bastille
July–August 1789	Great Fear
August 4, 1789	National Assembly abolishes feudal privileges
August 27, 1789	National Assembly issues Declaration of the Rights of Man
October 5, 1789	Women march on Versailles; royal family returns to Paris
November 1789	National Assembly confiscates church lands
July 1790	Civil Constitution of the Clergy establishes a national church; Louis XVI agrees to a constitutional monarchy
June 1791	Royal family is arrested while attempting to flee France
August 1791	Austria and Prussia issue the Declaration of Pillnitz
April 1792	France declares war on Austria
August 1792	Mob attacks the palace, and Legislative Assembly takes Louis XVI prisoner
September 1792	National Convention declares France a republic and abolishes monarchy
January 21, 1793	Louis XVI is executed
February 1793	France declares war on Britain, Holland, and Spain; revolts take place in some provinces
March 1793	Struggle between Girondists and the Mountain
June 1793	Sans-culottes invade the National Convention; Girondist leaders are arrested
September 1793	Price controls are instituted to aid the poor
1793–1794	Reign of Terror
Spring 1794	French armies are victorious on all fronts
July 1794	Robespierre is executed; Thermidorian reaction begins
1795	Economic controls are abolished, and suppression of the sans-culottes begins
1795–1799	Directory rules
1798	Austria, Britain, and Russia form the Second Coalition against France
1799	Napoleon Bonaparte overthrows the Directory and seizes power

The Tennis Court Oath, June 20, 1789 Painted two years after the event shown, this dramatic painting by Jacques-Louis David depicts a crucial turning point in the early days of the Revolution. On June 20 delegates of the third estate arrived at their meeting hall in the Versailles palace to find the doors closed and guarded. Fearing the king was about to dissolve their meeting by force, the deputies reassembled at a nearby indoor tennis court and swore a solemn oath not to disperse until they had been recognized as the National Assembly. (Musée de la Ville de Paris, Musée Carnavalet, Paris/Giraudon/The Bridgeman Art Library)

bread to soar suddenly and inflation spread quickly through the economy. As a result, demand for manufactured goods collapsed, and many artisans and small traders lost work. In Paris perhaps 150,000 of the city's 600,000 people were unemployed by July 1789.

Against this background of poverty and political crisis, the people of Paris entered decisively onto the revolutionary stage. They believed that, to survive, they should have steady work and enough bread at fair prices. They also feared that the dismissal of the king's liberal finance minister would put them at the mercy of aristocratic landowners and grain speculators. At the beginning of July, knowledge spread of the massing of troops near Paris. On July 14, 1789, several hundred people stormed the Bastille (ba-STEEL), a royal prison, to obtain weapons and gunpowder for the city's defense. Faced with popular violence, Louis soon announced the reinstatement of his finance minister and the withdrawal of troops from Paris. The National Assembly

was now free to continue its work without the threat of royal military intervention.

Just as the laboring poor of Paris had been roused to a revolutionary fervor, the struggling French peasantry had also reached a boiling point. In the summer of 1789, throughout France peasants began to rise in insurrection against their lords, ransacking manor houses and burning feudal documents that recorded their obligations. In some areas peasants reoccupied common lands enclosed by landowners and seized forests. Fear of marauders and vagabonds hired by vengeful landlords — called the Great Fear by contemporaries — seized the rural poor and fanned the flames of rebellion.

Faced with chaos, the National Assembly responded to peasant demands with a surprise maneuver on the night of August 4, 1789. By a decree of the assembly, all the old noble privileges — peasant serfdom where it still existed, exclusive hunting rights, fees for having legal cases judged in the lord's court, the right to make peasants work on the roads, and a host of other dues — were abolished along with the tithes paid to the church. From this point on, French peasants would seek mainly to protect and consolidate this victory.

Having granted new rights to the peasantry, the National Assembly moved forward with its mission of reform. On August 27, 1789, it issued the Declaration of the Rights of Man and of the Citizen. This clarion call of the liberal revolutionary ideal guaranteed equality before the law, representative government for a sovereign people, and individual freedom. This revolutionary credo, only two pages long, was disseminated throughout France, the rest of Europe, and around the world.

The National Assembly's declaration had little practical effect for the poor and hungry people of Paris. The economic crisis worsened after the fall of the Bastille, as aristocrats fled the country and the luxury market collapsed. Foreign markets also shrank, and unemployment among the urban working class grew. In addition, women — the traditional managers of food and resources in poor homes — could no longer look to the church, which had been stripped of its tithes, for aid.

On October 5 some seven thousand women marched the twelve miles from Paris to Versailles to demand action. This great crowd, "armed with scythes, sticks and pikes," invaded the National Assembly. Interrupting a delegate's speech, an old woman defiantly shouted into the debate, "Who's that talking down there? Make the chatterbox shut up. That's not the point: the point is that we want bread."[2] Hers was the genuine voice of the people, essential to any understanding of the French Revolution.

The women invaded the royal apartments, killed some of the royal bodyguards, and searched for the queen, Marie Antoinette, who was widely despised for her frivolous and supposedly immoral behavior. "We are going to cut off her head, tear out her heart, fry her liver, and that won't be the end of it," they shouted. It seems likely that only the intervention of Lafayette and the National Guard saved the royal family. But the only way to calm the disorder was for the king to live closer to his people in Paris, as the crowd demanded.

Liberal elites brought the revolution into being and continued to lead politics. Yet the people of France were now roused and would henceforth play a crucial role in the unfolding of events.

A Constitutional Monarchy and Its Challenges

The day after the women's march on Versailles, the National Assembly followed the king to Paris, and the next two years, until September 1791, saw the consolidation of the liberal revolution. In June 1790 the

The Women of Paris March to Versailles On October 5, 1789, a large group of poor Parisian women marched to Versailles to protest the price of bread. For the people of Paris, the king was the baker of last resort, responsible for feeding his people during times of scarcity. The angry women forced the royal family to return with them and to live in Paris, rather than remain isolated from their subjects at court. (Erich Lessing/Art Resource, NY)

Listening to the Past

Abbé de Sieyès, "What Is the Third Estate?"

In the flood of pamphlets that appeared after Louis XVI's call for a meeting of the Estates General, the most influential was written in 1789 by a Catholic priest named Emmanuel Joseph Sieyès. In "What Is the Third Estate?" the abbé Sieyès vigorously condemned the system of privilege that lay at the heart of French society. The term privilege *combined the Latin words for "private" and "law." In Old Regime France, no one set of laws applied to all; over time, the monarchy had issued a series of particular laws, or privileges, that enshrined special rights and entitlements for select individuals and groups. Noble privileges were among the weightiest.*

Sieyès rejected this entire system of legal and social inequality. Deriding the nobility as a foreign parasite, he argued that the common people of the third estate, who did most of the work and paid most of the taxes, constituted the true nation. His pamphlet galvanized public opinion and played an important role in convincing representatives of the third estate to proclaim themselves a National Assembly in June 1789. Sieyès later helped bring Napoleon Bonaparte to power, abandoning the radicalism of 1789 for an authoritarian regime.

1. What is the Third Estate? Everything.
2. What has it been until now in the political order? Nothing.
3. What does it want? To become something.

. . . What is a Nation? A body of associates living under a *common* law and represented by the same *legislature*.

Is it not more than certain that the noble order has privileges, exemptions, and even rights that are distinct from the rights of the great body of citizens? Because of this, it [the noble order] does not belong to the common order, it is not covered by the law common to the rest. Thus its civil rights already make it a people apart inside the great Nation. It is truly *imperium in imperio* [a law unto itself].

As for its *political* rights, the nobility also exercises them separately. It has its own representatives who have no mandate from the people. Its deputies sit separately, and even when they assemble in the same room with the deputies of the ordinary citizens, the nobility's representation still remains essentially distinct and separate: it is foreign to the Nation by its very principle, for its mission does not emanate from the people, and by its purpose, since it consists in defending, not the general interest, but the private interests of the nobility.

The Third Estate therefore contains everything that pertains to the Nation and nobody outside of the Third Estate can claim to be part of the Nation. What is the Third Estate? EVERYTHING. . . .

By Third Estate is meant the collectivity of citizens who belong to the common order. Anybody who holds a legal privilege of any kind leaves that common order, stands as an exception to the common law, and in consequence does not belong to the Third Estate. . . . It is certain that the moment a citizen acquires privileges contrary to common law, he no longer belongs to the common order. His new interest is opposed to the general interest; he has no right to vote in the name of the people. . . .

In vain can anyone's eyes be closed to the revolution that time and the force of things have brought to pass; it is none the less real. Once upon a time the Third Estate was in bondage and the noble order was everything that mattered. Today the Third is everything and nobility but a word. Yet under the cover of this word a new and intolerable aristocracy has slipped in, and the people has every reason to no longer want aristocrats. . . .

What is the will of a Nation? It is the result of individual wills, just as the Nation is the aggregate of the individuals who com-

National Assembly abolished the nobility and in July the king swore to uphold the as-yet-unwritten constitution, effectively enshrining a constitutional monarchy. The king remained the head of state, but all law-making power now resided in the National Assembly, elected by the wealthiest half of French males. The constitution finally passed in September 1791 and, reluctantly recognized by Louis XVI, was the first in French history. It broadened women's rights to seek divorce, to inherit property, and to obtain financial support for illegitimate children from fathers, but excluded women from political office and voting.

This decision was attacked by a small number of men and women who believed that the rights of man should be extended to all French citizens. Olympe de Gouges (1748–1793), a self-taught writer and woman of the people, protested the evils of slavery as well as the injustices done to women. In September 1791 she published her "Declaration of the Rights of Woman." This pamphlet echoed its famous predecessor, the Declaration of the Rights of Man and of the Citizen, proclaiming, "Woman is born free and remains equal to man in rights." De Gouges's position found little sympathy among leaders of the revolution, however.

pose it. It is impossible to conceive of a legitimate association that does not have for its goal the common security, the common liberty, in short, the public good. No doubt each individual also has his own personal aims. He says to himself, "protected by the common security, I will be able to peacefully pursue my own personal projects, I will seek my happiness where I will, assured of encountering only those legal obstacles that society will prescribe for the common interest, in which I have a part, and with which my own personal interest is so usefully allied." . . .

Advantages which differentiate citizens from one another lie outside the purview of citizenship. Inequalities of wealth or ability are like the inequalities of age, sex, size, etc. In no way do they detract from the *equality* of citizenship. These individual advantages no doubt benefit from the protection of the law; but it is not the legislator's task to create them, to give privileges to some and refuse them to others. The law grants nothing; it protects what already exists until such time that what exists begins to harm the common interest. These are the only limits on individual freedom. I imagine the law as being at the center of a large globe; we the citizens without exception, stand equidistant from it on the surface and occupy equal places; all are equally dependent on the law, all present it with their liberty and their property to be protected; and this is what I call the *common rights* of citizens, by which they are all alike. All these individuals communicate with each other, enter into contracts, negotiate, always under the common guarantee of the law. If in this general activity somebody wishes to get control over the person of his neighbor or usurp his property, the common law goes into action to repress this criminal attempt and puts everyone back in their place at the same distance from the law. . . .

It is impossible to say what place the two privileged orders [the clergy and the nobility] ought to occupy in the social order: this is the equivalent of asking what place one wishes to assign to a malignant tumor that torments and undermines the strength of the body of a sick person. It must be *neutralized*. We must re-establish the health and working of all organs so thoroughly that they are no longer susceptible to these fatal schemes that are capable of sapping the most essential principles of vitality. 🙶

Source: *The French Revolution and Human Rights: A Brief Documentary History*, pp. 65, 67, 68–70. Edited, Translated, and with an Introduction by Lynn Hunt. © 1996 by Bedford/St. Martin's. Reprinted by permission of the publisher.

● **This bust, by the sculptor Pierre Jean David d'Angers, shows an aged and contemplative Sieyès reflecting, perhaps, on his key role in the outbreak and unfolding of the French Revolution.** (Erich Lessing/Art Resource, NY)

QUESTIONS FOR ANALYSIS

1. What criticism of noble privileges does Sieyès offer? Why does he believe nobles are "foreign" to the nation?

2. How does Sieyès define the nation, and why does he believe that the third estate constitutes the nation?

3. What relationship between citizens and the law does Sieyès envision? What limitations on the law does he propose?

In addition to ruling on women's rights, the National Assembly replaced the complicated patchwork of historic provinces with eighty-three departments of approximately equal size, a move toward more rational and systematic methods of administration. Monopolies, guilds, and workers' associations were prohibited, and barriers to trade within France abolished in the name of economic liberty. Thus the National Assembly applied the spirit of the Enlightenment in a thorough reform of France's laws and institutions.

The National Assembly also imposed a radical reorganization on religious life. It granted religious freedom to the small minority of French Jews and Protestants. (See "Viewpoints: The Question of Jewish Citizenship in France," page 666.) Furthermore, in November 1789 it nationalized the Catholic Church's property and abolished monasteries. The government used all former church property as collateral to guarantee a new paper currency, the assignats (A-sihg-nat), and then sold the property in an attempt to put the state's finances on a solid footing.

Imbued with the rationalism and skepticism of the eighteenth-century philosophes, many delegates distrusted popular piety and "superstitious religion." Thus

Viewpoints

The Question of Jewish Citizenship in France

• *In August 1789 the legislators of the French Revolution adopted the Declaration of the Rights of Man and of the Citizen, enshrining full legal equality under the law for French citizens. Who exactly could become a citizen and what rights they might enjoy quickly became contentious issues. After granting civil rights to Protestants in December 1789, the National Assembly began to consider the smaller but more controversial population of French Jews. Eager to become citizens, the Jews of Paris, Alsace, and Lorraine presented a joint petition to the National Assembly in January 1790. Their appeal was met with negative reactions in some quarters, including from the bishop of Nancy in Lorraine, a province on France's eastern border with a relatively large Jewish population.*

Jewish Petition to the National Assembly, January 28, 1790

❝A great question is pending before the supreme tribunal of France. *Will the Jews be citizens or not?* . . .

In general, civil rights are entirely independent from religious principles. And all men of whatever religion, whatever sect they belong to, whatever creed they practice, provided that their creed, their sect, their religion does not offend the principles of a pure and severe morality, all these men, we say, equally able to serve the fatherland, defend its interests, contribute to its splendor, should all equally have the title and the rights of citizen.

. . . Reflect, then, on the condition of the Jews. Excluded from all the professions, ineligible for all the positions, deprived even of the capacity to acquire property, not daring and not being able to sell openly the merchandise of their commerce, to what extremity are you reducing them? You do not want them to die, and yet you refuse them the means to live; you refuse them the means, and you crush them with taxes. . . .

. . . Everything is changing; the lot of the Jews must change at the same time; and the people will not be more surprised by this particular change than by all those which they see around them everyday. This is therefore the moment, the true moment to make justice triumph: attach the improvement of the lot of the Jews to the revolution.❞

La Fare, Bishop of Nancy, On the Admissibility of Jews to Full Civil and Political Rights, Spring 1790

❝Thus, Sirs, assure each Jewish individual his liberty, security, and the enjoyment of his property. You owe it to this individual who has strayed into our midst; you owe him nothing more. He is a foreigner to whom, during the time of this passage and his stay, France owes hospitality, protection and security. But it cannot and should not admit to public posts, to the administration, to the prerogatives of the family a tribe that, regarding itself everywhere as foreign, never exclusively embraces any region; a tribe whose religion, customs, and physical and moral regime essentially differ from that of all other people; a tribe whose eyes turn constantly toward the common fatherland that should one day reunite its dispersed members. . . .

There are also moral and local considerations that should, if not guide, then at least enlighten the legislation regarding the Jewish nation. . . .

The prejudices of the people against the Jews are only too well-known. From time to time, they explode into violence: recently in Alsace, some people committed the most criminal excesses against the Jews. A few months ago, similar misfortunes menaced them in Nancy. . . .

From this account it is easy to understand the habitual disposition of the people; it is a fire always ready to be lit. Any extension that a decree of the National Assembly would hasten to give to the civil existence of the Jews, before opinion has been prepared in advance and led by degrees to this change, could occasion great disaster.❞

Source: *The French Revolution and Human Rights: A Brief Documentary History*, pp. 93–96 (Jewish petition) and pp. 97–98 (La Fare). Edited, Translated, and with an Introduction by Lynn Hunt. © 1996 by Bedford/ St. Martin's. Reprinted by permission of the publisher.

QUESTIONS FOR ANALYSIS

1. On what basis do the Jews of Paris, Alsace, and Lorraine argue for their inclusion in citizenship rights? How do they describe the constraints of the Jewish population prior to the Revolution?

2. How does the Bishop of Nancy characterize the Jews' relationship to the French nation, and why does it disqualify them for citizenship? What dangers does he see in granting citizenship to French Jews?

in July 1790, with the Civil Constitution of the Clergy, they established a national church with priests chosen by voters. The National Assembly then forced the Catholic clergy to take an oath of loyalty to the new government. The pope formally condemned this attempt to subjugate the church, and only half the priests of France swore the oath. Many sincere Christians, especially those in the countryside, were also upset by these changes in the religious order. The attempt to remake the Catholic Church, like the abolition of guilds and workers' associations, sharpened the conflict between the educated classes and the common people that had been emerging in the eighteenth century.

World War and Republican France, 1791–1799

☐ Why and how did the French Revolution take a radical turn entailing terror at home and war with European powers?

When Louis XVI accepted the National Assembly's constitution in September 1791, a young provincial lawyer and delegate named Maximilien Robespierre (1758–1794) concluded that "The Revolution is over." Robespierre was right in the sense that the most constructive and lasting reforms were in place. Yet he was wrong in suggesting that turmoil had ended, for a much more radical stage lay ahead, one that would bring war with foreign powers, terror at home, and a transformation in France's government.

The International Response

The outbreak and progress of revolution in France produced great excitement and a sharp division of opinion in Europe and the United States. On the one hand, liberals and radicals saw a mighty triumph of liberty over despotism. On the other hand, conservative leaders such as British statesman Edmund Burke (1729–1797) were troubled by the aroused spirit of reform. In 1790 Burke published *Reflections on the Revolution in France*, in which he defended inherited privileges. He glorified Britain's unrepresentative Parliament and predicted that reform like that occurring in France would lead only to chaos and tyranny.

One passionate rebuttal came from a young writer in London, Mary Wollstonecraft (1759–1797). Incensed by Burke's book, Wollstonecraft (WOOL-stuhn-kraft) wrote a blistering, widely read attack, *A Vindication of the Rights of Man* (1790). Two years later, she published her masterpiece, *A Vindication of the Rights of Woman* (1792). As de Gouges had one year before her, Wollstonecraft demanded equal rights for women. She also advocated coeducation out of the belief that it would make women better wives and mothers, good citizens, and economically independent. Considered very radical for the time, the book became a founding text of the feminist movement.

The kings and nobles of continental Europe, who had at first welcomed the revolution in France as weakening a competing power, now feared its impact. In June 1791 Louis XVI and Marie Antoinette were arrested

The Capture of Louis XVI, June 1791
This painting commemorates the midnight arrest of Louis XVI and the royal family as they tried to flee France in disguise and reach counter-revolutionaries in the Austrian Netherlands. Recognized and stopped at Varennes, just forty miles from the border, the king still nearly succeeded, telling municipal officers that dangerous mobs controlled Paris and securing promises of safe passage. But within hours the local leaders reversed themselves, and by morning Louis XVI was headed back to Paris. (Bibliothèque nationale de France)

and returned to Paris after trying unsuccessfully to slip out of France. To supporters of the revolution, the attempted flight was proof that the king was treacherously seeking foreign support for an invasion of France. To the monarchs of Austria and Prussia, the arrest of a crowned monarch was unacceptable. Two months later they issued the Declaration of Pillnitz, which professed their willingness to intervene in France to restore Louis XVI's rule if necessary. It was expected to have a sobering effect on revolutionary France without causing war.

But the crowned heads of Europe misjudged the situation. The new French representative body, called the Legislative Assembly, that convened in October 1791 had completely new delegates and a different character. Still prosperous, well-educated middle-class men, the delegates were younger and less cautious than their predecessors. Many of the them belonged to the political **Jacobin club**. Such clubs had proliferated in Parisian neighborhoods since the beginning of the revolution, drawing men and women to debate the political questions of the day.

The Jacobins and other deputies reacted with patriotic fury to the Declaration of Pillnitz. They said that if the kings of Europe were attempting to incite war against France, then "we will incite a war of people against kings. . . . Ten million Frenchmen, kindled by the fire of liberty, armed with the sword, with reason, with eloquence would be able to change the face of the world and make the tyrants tremble on their thrones."[3] In April 1792 France declared war on Francis II, the Habsburg monarch.

France's crusade against tyranny went poorly at first. Prussian forces joined Austria against the French, who broke and fled at their first military encounter with this First Coalition of the foreign powers united against the revolution. The Legislative Assembly declared the country in danger, and volunteers rallied to the capital. In this wartime atmosphere, rumors of treason by the king

Areas of French Insurrection, 1793

Vendée Rebellion
Counter-revolutionary insurrections

and queen spread in Paris. On August 10, 1792, a revolutionary crowd attacked the royal palace at the Tuileries (TWEE-luh-reez), while the king and his family fled for their lives to the nearby Legislative Assembly. Rather than offering refuge, the Assembly suspended the king from all his functions, imprisoned him, and called for a legislative and constitutional assembly to be elected by universal male suffrage.

The Second Revolution and the New Republic

The fall of the monarchy marked a rapid radicalization of the revolution, a phase that historians often call the second revolution. In late September 1792 the new, popularly elected National Convention, which replaced the Legislative Assembly, proclaimed France a republic, a nation in which the people, instead of a monarch, held sovereign power.

All the members of the National Convention were republicans, and at the beginning almost all belonged to the Jacobin club of Paris. But the Jacobins themselves were increasingly divided into two bitterly opposed groups — the **Girondists** and the **Mountain**, led by Robespierre and another young lawyer, Georges Jacques Danton.

This division emerged clearly after the National Convention overwhelmingly convicted Louis XVI of treason. The Girondists accepted his guilt but did not wish to put the king to death. By a narrow majority, the Mountain carried the day, and Louis was executed on January 21, 1793, by guillotine, which the French had recently perfected. Marie Antoinette would be put to death later that year. But both the Girondists and the Mountain were determined to continue the "war against tyranny." The Prussians had been stopped at the Battle of Valmy on September 20, 1792, one day before the republic was proclaimed. French armies then invaded Savoy and captured Nice, moved into the German Rhineland, and by November 1792 were occupying the entire Austrian Netherlands (modern Belgium).

Everywhere they went, French armies of occupation chased princes, abolished feudalism, and found support among some peasants and middle-class people. But French armies also lived off the land, requisitioning food and supplies and plundering local treasures. The liberators therefore looked increasingly like foreign invaders. Meanwhile, international tensions mounted. In February 1793 the National Convention, at war with

- **Jacobin club** A political club during the French Revolution to which many of the deputies of the Legislative Assembly belonged.
- **Girondists** A moderate group that fought for control of the French National Convention in 1793.
- **Mountain** Led by Robespierre, the French National Convention's radical faction, which seized legislative power in 1793.
- **sans-culottes** The laboring poor of Paris, so called because the men wore trousers instead of the knee breeches of the aristocracy and middle class; the term came to refer to the militant radicals of the city.

Austria and Prussia, declared war on Britain, Holland, and Spain as well. Republican France was now at war with almost all of Europe.

Groups within France added to the turmoil. Peasants in western France revolted against being drafted into the army, with the Vendée region of Brittany emerging as the epicenter of revolt. Devout Catholics, royalists, and foreign agents encouraged their rebellion, and the counter-revolutionaries recruited veritable armies to fight for their cause.

In March 1793 the National Convention was locked in a life-and-death political struggle between members

of the Mountain and the more moderate Girondists. With the middle-class delegates so bitterly divided, the laboring poor of Paris once again emerged as the decisive political factor. The laboring poor and the petty traders were often known as the **sans-culottes** (san-koo-LAHT, "without breeches") because their men wore trousers instead of the knee breeches of the aristocracy and the solid middle class. They demanded radical political action to guarantee them their daily bread. The Mountain, sensing an opportunity to outmaneuver the Girondists, joined with sans-culottes activists to engineer a popular uprising. On June 2, 1793,

A PARIS BELLE.

◻ Picturing the Past

Contrasting Visions of the Sans-Culottes These two images offer profoundly different representations of a sans-culotte woman. The image on the left was created by a French artist, while the image on the right is English. The French words above the image on the right read in part, "Heads! Blood! Death! . . . I am the Goddess of Liberty! . . . Long Live the Guillotine!" (Bibliothèque nationale de France)

ANALYZING THE IMAGE How would you describe the woman on the left? What qualities does the artist seem to ascribe to her, and how do you think these qualities relate to the sans-culottes and the Revolution? How would you characterize the facial expression and attire of the woman on the right? How does the inclusion of the text contribute to your impressions of her?

CONNECTIONS What does the contrast between these two images suggest about differences between French and English perceptions of the sans-culottes and of the French Revolution? Why do you think the artists have chosen to depict women?

armed sans-culottes invaded the Convention and forced its deputies to arrest twenty-nine Girondist deputies for treason. All power passed to the Mountain.

The Convention also formed the Committee of Public Safety in April 1793 to deal with the threats from within and outside France. The committee, which Robespierre led, held dictatorial power to deal with the national emergency, allowing it to use whatever force necessary to defend the Revolution. Moderates in leading provincial cities revolted against the committee's power and demanded a decentralized government. Counter-revolutionary forces in the Vendée won significant victories, and the republic's armies were driven back on all fronts. By July 1793 only the areas around Paris and on the eastern frontier were firmly held by the central government. Defeat seemed imminent.

> " Terror is nothing more than prompt, severe inflexible justice. "
>
> **ROBESPIERRE**

Total War and the Terror

A year later, in July 1794, the central government had reasserted control over the provinces, and the Austrian Netherlands and the Rhineland were once again in French hands. This remarkable change of fortune was due to the revolutionary government's success in harnessing the explosive forces of a planned economy, revolutionary terror, and modern nationalism in a total war effort.

Robespierre and the Committee of Public Safety advanced on several fronts in 1793 and 1794, seeking to impose republican unity across the nation. First, they collaborated with the sans-culottes, who continued pressing the common people's case for fair prices and a moral economic order and who distrusted most wealthy capitalists and all aristocrats. Thus in September 1793 Robespierre and his coworkers established a planned economy with egalitarian social overtones. Rather than let supply and demand determine prices, the government set maximum allowable prices for key products. Though the state was too weak to enforce all its price regulations, it did fix the price of bread in Paris at levels the poor could afford.

The people were also put to work, mainly producing arms and munitions for the war effort. The government told craftsmen what to produce, nationalized many small workshops, and requisitioned raw materials and grain. Through these economic reforms the second revolution produced an emergency form of socialism, which thoroughly frightened Europe's propertied classes and greatly influenced the subsequent development of socialist ideology.

Second, while radical economic measures supplied the poor with bread and the armies with weapons, the **Reign of Terror** (1793–1794) enforced compliance with republican beliefs and practices. Special revolutionary courts responsible only to Robespierre's Committee of Public Safety tried "enemies of the nation" for political crimes. As a result, some forty thousand French men and women were executed or died in prison. Robespierre's Reign of Terror is therefore one of the most controversial phases of the French Revolution. Presented as a necessary measure to save the republic, the Terror was a weapon directed against all suspected of opposing the revolutionary government. As Robespierre himself put it, "Terror is nothing more than prompt, severe inflexible justice."[4] For many Europeans of the time, however, the Reign of Terror represented a frightening perversion of the ideals of 1789.

In their efforts to impose unity, the Jacobins took actions to suppress women's participation in political debate, which they perceived as disorderly and a distraction from women's proper place in the home. On October 30, 1793, the National Convention declared that "The clubs and popular societies of women, under whatever denomination are prohibited." Among those convicted of sedition was writer Olympe de Gouges, who was sent to the guillotine in November 1793.

Beyond imposing political unity by force, the Terror also sought to bring the revolution into all aspects of everyday life. The government sponsored revolutionary art and songs as well as a new series of secular holidays and open-air festivals to celebrate republican virtue and a love of nation. Moreover, the government attempted to rationalize French daily life by adopting the decimal system for weights and measures and a new calendar based on ten-day weeks. Another important element of this cultural revolution was the campaign of de-Christianization, which aimed to eliminate Catholic symbols and beliefs. Fearful of the hostility aroused in rural France, however, Robespierre called for a halt to de-Christianization measures in mid-1794.

The third and perhaps most decisive element in the French republic's victory over the First Coalition was its ability to draw on the power of patriotic dedication to a national state and a national mission. An essential part of modern nationalism, which would fully emerge throughout Europe in the nineteenth century, this commitment was something new in history. With a common language and a common tradition newly reinforced by the ideas of popular sovereignty and democ-

- **Reign of Terror** The period from 1793 to 1794, during which Robespierre's Committee of Public Safety tried and executed thousands suspected of treason and a new revolutionary culture was imposed.

- **Thermidorian reaction** A reaction to the violence of the Reign of Terror in 1794, resulting in the execution of Robespierre and the loosening of economic controls.

racy, large numbers of French people were stirred by a common loyalty. They developed an intense emotional commitment to the defense of the nation, and they saw the war against foreign opponents as a life-and-death struggle between good and evil.

The all-out mobilization of French resources under the Terror combined with the fervor of modern nationalism to create an awesome fighting machine. After August 1793 all unmarried young men were subject to the draft, and by January 1794 French armed forces outnumbered those of their enemies almost four to one.[5] Well-trained, well-equipped, and constantly indoctrinated, the enormous armies of the republic were led by young, impetuous generals. These generals often had risen from the ranks, and they personified the opportunities the revolution offered gifted sons of the people. By spring 1794 French armies were victorious on all fronts. The republic was saved.

The Thermidorian Reaction and the Directory

The success of the French armies led Robespierre and the Committee of Public Safety to relax the emergency economic controls, but they extended the political Reign of Terror. In March 1794 Robespierre's Terror wiped out many of his critics. Two weeks later Robespierre sent long-standing collaborators whom he believed had turned against him, including Danton, to the guillotine. A group of radicals and moderates in the Convention, knowing that they might be next, organized a conspiracy. They howled down Robespierre when he tried to speak to the National Convention on July 27, 1794 — a date known as 9 Thermidor according to France's newly adopted republican calendar. The next day it was Robespierre's turn to be guillotined.

As Robespierre's closest supporters followed their leader to the guillotine, the respectable middle-class lawyers and professionals who had led the liberal revolution of 1789 reasserted their authority. This period of **Thermidorian reaction**, as it was called, harkened back to the beginnings of the Revolution, rejecting the radicalism of the sans-culottes in favor of moderate policies that favored property owners. In 1795 the National Convention abolished many economic controls, let prices rise sharply, and severely restricted the local political organizations through which the sans-culottes exerted their strength.

The collapse of economic controls, coupled with runaway inflation, hit the working poor very hard. After the Convention used the army to suppress the sans-culottes' protests, the urban poor lost their revolutionary fervor. Excluded and disillusioned, they would have little interest in and influence on politics until 1830.

In 1795 the middle-class members of the National Convention wrote yet another constitution to guaran-

tee their economic position and political supremacy. As in previous elections, the mass of the population voted only for electors, whose number was cut back to men of substantial means. Electors then voted for members of a reorganized Legislative Assembly to replace the National Convention and for key officials throughout France. The new assembly also chose a five-man executive body called the Directory.

The Directory continued to support French military expansion abroad. War was no longer so much a crusade as a response to economic problems. Large, victorious French armies reduced unemployment at home. However, the French people quickly grew weary of the corruption and ineffectiveness that characterized the Directory. This general dissatisfaction revealed itself clearly in the national elections of 1797, which returned a large number of conservative and even monarchist deputies who favored peace at almost

The Execution of Robespierre Completely wooden except for the heavy iron blade, the guillotine was painted red for Robespierre's execution, a detail not captured in this black-and-white engraving of the 1794 event. Large crowds witnessed the execution in a majestic public square in central Paris, then known as the Place de la Revolution and now called the Place de la Concorde (Harmony Square). (Snark/Art Resource, NY)

any price. The members of the Directory, fearing for their skins, used the army to nullify the elections and began to govern dictatorially. Two years later Napoleon Bonaparte ended the Directory in a coup d'état (koo day-TAH) and substituted a strong dictatorship for a weak one.

Napoleon's Europe, 1799–1815

☐ Why did Napoleon Bonaparte assume control of France and much of Europe, and what factors led to his downfall?

For almost fifteen years, from 1799 to 1814, France was in the hands of a keen-minded military dictator of exceptional ability. Napoleon Bonaparte (1769–1821) realized the need to put an end to civil strife in France in order to create unity and consolidate his rule. And he did. But Napoleon saw himself as a man of destiny, and the glory of war and the dream of universal empire proved irresistible.

Napoleon's Rule of France

Born on the Mediterranean island of Corsica into an impoverished noble family, Napoleon left home and became a lieutenant in the French artillery in 1785. After a brief and unsuccessful adventure fighting for Corsican independence in 1789, he returned to France as a French patriot and a revolutionary. Rising rapidly in the new army, Napoleon was placed in command of French forces in Italy and won brilliant victories there in 1796 and 1797. His next campaign, in Egypt, was a failure, but Napoleon returned to France before the fiasco was generally known, and his reputation remained intact.

Napoleon soon learned that some prominent members of the legislature were plotting against the Directory. The dissatisfaction of these plotters stemmed not so much from the fact that the Directory was a dictatorship as from the fact that it was a weak dictatorship. To these disillusioned revolutionaries, ten years of upheaval and uncertainty had made firm rule much more appealing than liberty and popular politics.

The flamboyant thirty-year-old Napoleon, nationally revered for his heroism, was an ideal choice for the strong ruler the conspirators were seeking. Thus they and Napoleon organized a takeover. On November 9,

1799, they ousted the Directors, and the following day soldiers disbanded the legislature. Napoleon was named first consul of the republic, and a new constitution consolidating his position was overwhelmingly approved in a plebiscite in December 1799.

The essence of Napoleon's domestic policy was to use his popularity and charisma to maintain order and end civil strife. He did so by working out unwritten agreements with powerful groups in France whereby the groups received favors in return for loyal service. Napoleon's bargain with the middle class was codified in the famous Civil Code of March 1804, also known as the **Napoleonic Code**, which reasserted two of the fundamental principles of the revolution of 1789: equality of all male citizens before the law and absolute security of wealth and private property.

At the same time, Napoleon built on the bureaucracy inherited from the Revolution and the former monarchy to create a thoroughly centralized state. He consolidated his rule by recruiting disillusioned revolutionaries for the network of government officials; they depended on him and came to serve him well. Nor were members of the old nobility slighted. In 1800 and again in 1802 Napoleon granted amnesty to one hundred thousand noble émigrés on the condition that they return to France and take a loyalty oath. Members of this returning elite soon ably occupied many high posts in the expanding centralized state.

Furthermore, Napoleon applied his diplomatic skills to healing the Catholic Church in France so that it could serve as a bulwark of social stability. Napoleon and Pope Pius VII (pontificate 1800–1823) signed the Concordat of 1801. Under this agreement the pope gained the right for French Catholics to practice their religion freely, but Napoleon gained political power: his government now nominated bishops, paid the clergy, and exerted great influence over the church in France.

The domestic reforms of Napoleon's early years were his greatest achievement, and much of his legal and administrative reorganization has survived in France to this day. More generally, Napoleon's domestic initiatives gave the great majority of French people a sense of stability and national unity.

But order and unity had a price: authoritarian rule. Women, who had often participated in revolutionary politics without having legal equality, lost many of the gains they made in the 1790s. Under the new Napoleonic Code, women were regarded as dependents of either their fathers or their husbands, and they could not make contracts or have bank accounts in their own names. Napoleon aimed at re-establishing a family monarchy, where the power of the husband and father was as absolute over the wife and the children as that of Napoleon over his subjects. In other restrictions, free speech and freedom of the press were curtailed, and the occasional elections were thoroughly controlled by

Napoleonic Code French civil code promulgated in 1804 that reasserted the 1789 principles of the equality of all male citizens before the law and the absolute security of wealth and private property.

The Coronation of Napoleon, 1804 In this detail from a grandiose painting by Jacques-Louis David, Napoleon, instead of the pope, prepares to crown his wife, Josephine, in an elaborate ceremony in Notre Dame Cathedral. Napoleon, the ultimate upstart, also crowned himself. Pope Pius VII, seated glumly behind the emperor, is reduced to being a spectator. (Louvre/Réunion des Musées Nationaux/Art Resource, NY)

Napoleon and his government. After 1810 political suspects were held in state prisons, as they had been during the Terror.

Napoleon's Expansion in Europe

After coming to power in 1799 Napoleon sent peace feelers to Austria and Britain, the two remaining members of the Second Coalition that had been formed against France in 1798. When these overtures were rejected, French armies led by Napoleon decisively defeated the Austrians. In the Treaty of Lunéville (1801), Austria accepted the loss of almost all its Italian possessions, and German territory on the west bank of the Rhine was incorporated into France. The British agreed to the Treaty of Amiens in 1802, allowing France to remain in control of Holland, the Austrian Netherlands, the west bank of the Rhine, and most of the Italian peninsula.

In 1802 Napoleon was secure but still driven to expand his power. Aggressively redrawing the map of Germany so as to weaken Austria and encourage the secondary states of southwestern Germany to side with France, Napoleon tried to restrict British trade with all of Europe. He then plotted to attack Britain, but his Mediterranean fleet was destroyed by Lord Nelson at the Battle of Trafalgar on October 21, 1805. Renewed fighting had its advantages, however, for the first consul used his high status as a military leader to have himself proclaimed emperor in late 1804.

Austria, Russia, and Sweden joined with Britain to form the Third Coalition against France shortly before the Battle of Trafalgar. Yet the Austrians and the Russians were no match for Napoleon, who scored a brilliant victory over them at the Battle of Austerlitz in December 1805. Russia decided to pull back, and Austria accepted large territorial losses in return for peace as the Third Coalition collapsed.

German Confederation of the Rhine, 1806

HOLLAND

PRUSSIA

Berlin

SAXONY

Rhine R.

FRANCE

GERMAN CONFEDERATION OF THE RHINE

HELVETIAN REPUBLIC

AUSTRIAN EMPIRE

KINGDOM OF ITALY

Francisco Goya, *The Third of May 1808* Spanish master Francisco Goya created a passionate and moving indictment of the brutality of war in this painting from 1814, which depicts the close-range execution of Spanish rebels by Napoleon's forces in May 1808. Goya's painting evoked the bitterness and despair of many Europeans who suffered through Napoleon's invasions. (Erich Lessing/Art Resource, NY)

Napoleon then reorganized the German states to his liking. In 1806 he abolished many tiny German states as well as the Holy Roman Empire and established by decree the German Confederation of the Rhine, a union of fifteen German states minus Austria, Prussia, and Saxony. Naming himself "protector" of the confederation, Napoleon firmly controlled western Germany.

Napoleon's intervention in German affairs alarmed the Prussians, who mobilized their armies. In October 1806 Napoleon attacked them and won two more brilliant victories at Jena and Auerstädt, where the Prussians were outnumbered two to one. The war with Prussia, now joined by Russia, continued into the following spring. After Napoleon's larger armies won another

victory, Alexander I of Russia was ready to negotiate for peace. In the treaties of Tilsit in 1807, Prussia lost half of its population through land concessions, while Russia accepted Napoleon's reorganization of western and central Europe and promised to enforce Napoleon's economic blockade against British goods.

The Grand Empire and Its End

Increasingly, Napoleon saw himself as the emperor of Europe, not just of France. The so-called **Grand Empire** he built had three parts. The core, or first part, was an ever-expanding France, which by 1810 included Belgium, Holland, parts of northern Italy, and much German territory on the east bank of the Rhine (Map 22.2). The second part consisted of a number of dependent satellite kingdoms. The third part comprised the independent but allied states of Austria, Prussia, and Russia. After 1806 both satellites and allies were expected to support Napoleon's **Continental System**, a

• **Grand Empire** The empire over which Napoleon and his allies ruled, encompassing virtually all of Europe except Great Britain and Russia.

• **Continental System** A blockade imposed by Napoleon to halt all trade between continental Europe and Britain, thereby weakening the British economy and military.

Legend:
- French empire
- Dependent states
- Allied with Napoleon
- ✳ French victory
- ✳ French defeat

KINGDOM OF NORWAY AND DENMARK

KINGDOM OF SWEDEN

Stockholm

St. Petersburg

North Sea

Copenhagen

Baltic Sea

Napoleon's invasion of Russia, June–Sept. 1812

Borodino 1812

Moscow

SWEDISH POMERANIA

Königsberg

Tilsit Vilna

Smolensk

Maloyaroslavets 1812

GREAT BRITAIN

Hamburg Lübeck

PRUSSIA

Danzig

Friedland 1807

Neman R.

French retreat, Oct.–Dec. 1812

RUSSIAN EMPIRE

Bremen

Berlin

London

Rhine R.

WESTPHALIA

SAXONY

GRAND DUCHY OF WARSAW

Kiev

Brussels

Auerstädt 1806

Waterloo 1815

Jena 1806

Amiens

Paris

CONFEDERATION OF THE RHINE

Austerlitz 1805

Lunéville

Wagram 1804

Pressburg

Vienna

ATLANTIC OCEAN

FRANCE

WÜRTTEMBERG

Zurich

BADEN

BAVARIA

Buda Pest

AUSTRIAN EMPIRE

Marengo 1800

Milan

KINGDOM OF ITALY

ILLYRIAN PROVINCES

Danube R.

Black Sea

Genoa

Marseilles

PORTUGAL

Lisbon

Madrid

Elba

Corsica

OTTOMAN EMPIRE

SPAIN

Rome

Trafalgar 1805

Sardinia

Naples

GIBRALTAR (Gr. Br.)

Mediterranean Sea

Palermo

KINGDOM OF NAPLES

Athens

Ionian Is. (Gr. Br.)

KINGDOM OF SICILY

Malta (Gr. Br.)

0   100   200 miles
0   100   200 kilometers

▢ Mapping the Past

MAP 22.2 Napoleonic Europe in 1812 At the height of the Grand Empire in 1810, Napoleon had conquered or allied with every major European power except Britain. But in 1812, angered by Russian repudiation of his ban on trade with Britain, Napoleon invaded Russia with disastrous results. Compare this map with Map 17.2 (page 500), which shows the division of Europe in 1715.

ANALYZING THE MAP How had the balance of power shifted in Europe from 1715 to 1812? What changed, and what remained the same? What was the impact of Napoleon's wars on Germany, the Italian peninsula, and Russia?

CONNECTIONS Why did Napoleon achieve vast territorial gains where Louis XIV did not?

blockade in which no ship coming from Britain or her colonies was permitted to dock at any port that was controlled by the French. The blockade was intended to halt all trade between Britain and continental Europe, thereby destroying the British economy and its military force.

The impact of the Grand Empire on the peoples of Europe was considerable. In the areas incorporated into France and in the satellites, Napoleon abolished feudal dues and serfdom. Yet he had to put the prosperity and special interests of France first in order to safeguard his power base. Levying heavy taxes in money and men for his armies, Napoleon came to be regarded more as a conquering tyrant than as an enlightened liberator. Thus French rule sparked patriotic upheavals and encouraged the growth of reactive nationalism.

The first great revolt occurred in Spain. In 1808 a coalition of Catholics, monarchists, and patriots rebelled against Napoleon's attempts to make Spain a French satellite. French armies occupied Madrid, but the foes of Napoleon fled to the hills and waged uncompromising guerrilla warfare. Events in Spain sent a clear warning: resistance to French imperialism was growing.

Yet Napoleon pushed on. In 1810, when the Grand Empire was at its height, Britain still remained at war with France, helping the guerrillas in Spain and Portugal. The Continental System was a failure. Instead of harming Britain, the system provoked this foe to set up a counter-blockade, which created hard times for French artisans and the middle class. Perhaps looking for a scapegoat, Napoleon turned on Alexander I of Russia, who in 1811 openly repudiated Napoleon's war of prohibitions against British goods.

Napoleon's invasion of Russia began in June 1812. Originally, he planned to winter in the Russian city of Smolensk if Alexander did not sue for peace. However, after reaching Smolensk Napoleon recklessly pressed on toward Moscow (see Map 22.2). The Battle of Borodino that followed was a draw, and the Russians retreated in good order. Alexander ordered the evacuation of Moscow, which the Russians then burned in part, and he refused to negotiate. Finally, after five weeks in the scorched and abandoned city, Napoleon ordered a disastrous retreat. The Russian army, the Russian winter, and starvation cut Napoleon's army to pieces.

Leaving his troops to their fate, Napoleon raced to Paris to raise another army. Possibly he might still have saved his throne if he had been willing to accept a France reduced to its historical size — the proposal offered by Austria's foreign minister, Prince Klemens von Metternich. But Napoleon refused. Consequently, Austria and Prussia deserted Napoleon and joined Rus-

sia and Britain in the Treaty of Chaumont in March 1814, by which the four powers pledged allegiance to defeat the French emperor.

All across Europe patriots called for a "war of liberation" against Napoleon's oppression. Less than a month later, on April 4, 1814, a defeated Napoleon abdicated his throne. After this unconditional abdication, the victorious allies granted Napoleon the island of Elba off the coast of Italy as his own tiny state.

The allies also agreed to the restoration of the Bourbon dynasty under Louis XVIII (r. 1814–1824) and promised to treat France with leniency in a peace settlement. The new monarch tried to consolidate support among the people by issuing the Constitutional Charter, which accepted many of France's revolutionary changes and guaranteed civil liberties.

Yet Louis XVIII lacked the glory and magnetism of Napoleon. Hearing of political unrest in France and diplomatic tensions in Vienna, Napoleon staged a daring escape from Elba in February 1815. Landing in France, he issued appeals for support and marched on Paris. French officers and soldiers who had fought so long for their emperor responded to the call. Louis XVIII fled, and once more Napoleon took command. But Napoleon's gamble was a desperate long shot, for the allies were united against him. At the end of a frantic period known as the Hundred Days, they crushed his forces at Waterloo on June 18, 1815, and imprisoned him on the island of St. Helena, off the western coast of Africa. Louis XVIII returned to the throne, and the allies dealt more harshly with the French. As for Napoleon, he took revenge by writing his memoirs, nurturing the myth that he had been Europe's revolutionary liberator, a hero whose work had been undone by oppressive reactionaries.

The Haitian Revolution, 1791–1804

☐ How did slave revolt on colonial Saint-Domingue lead to the creation of the independent nation of Haiti in 1804?

The events that led to the creation of the independent nation of Haiti constitute the third, and perhaps most extraordinary, chapter of the revolutionary era in the Atlantic world. Prior to 1789 Saint-Domingue, the French colony that was to become Haiti, reaped huge profits through a ruthless system of slave-based plantation agriculture. News of revolution in France lit a powder keg of contradictory aspirations among white

Saint-Domingue Slave Life Although the brutal conditions of plantation slavery left little time or energy for leisure, slaves on Saint-Domingue took advantage of their day of rest on Sunday to engage in social and religious activities. The law officially prohibited slaves of different masters from mingling together, but such gatherings were often tolerated if they remained peaceful. This image depicts a fight between two slaves, precisely the type of unrest and violence feared by authorities. (Musée du Nouveau Monde, La Rochelle/Photo12.com—ARJ)

planters, free people of color, and slaves. While revolutionary authorities debated how far to extend the rights of man on Saint-Domingue, slaves took matters into their own hands, rising up to claim their freedom. Their revolt succeeded, despite invasion by the British and Spanish and Napoleon Bonaparte's bid to reimpose French control. In 1804 Haiti became the first nation in history to claim its freedom through slave revolt.

Revolutionary Aspirations in Saint-Domingue

On the eve of the French Revolution, Saint-Domingue — the most profitable of all Caribbean colonies — was even more rife with social tensions than France itself. The colony, which occupied the western third of the island of Hispaniola, was inhabited by a variety of social groups who resented and mistrusted one another.

The European population included French colonial officials, wealthy plantation owners and merchants, and poor immigrants. Vastly outnumbering the white population were the colony's five hundred thousand slaves, along with a sizable population of free people of African and mixed African and European descent. Members of this last group referred to themselves as "free coloreds" or free people of color.

The 1685 Code Noir (Black Code) that set the parameters of slavery had granted free people of color the same legal status as whites: they could own property, live where they wished, and pursue any education or career they desired. From the 1760s on, however, colonial administrators began rescinding these rights, and by the time of the French Revolution, myriad aspects of free coloreds' lives were ruled by discriminatory laws.

The political and intellectual turmoil of the 1780s, with its growing rhetoric of liberty, equality, and

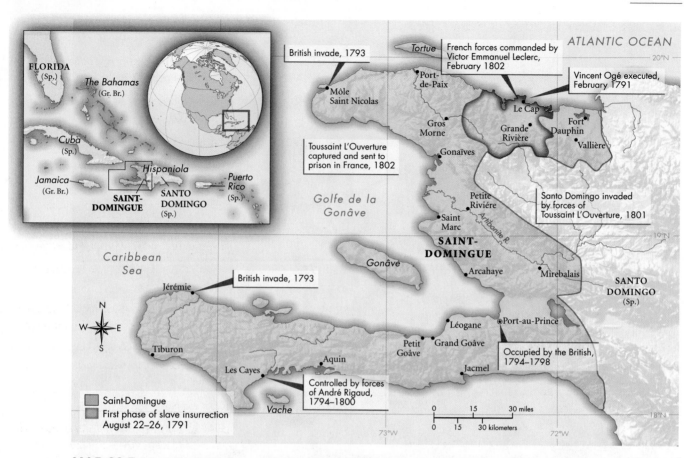

MAP 22.3 The War of Haitian Independence, 1791–1804 Neighbored by the Spanish colony of Santo Domingo, Saint-Domingue was the most profitable European colony in the Caribbean. In 1791 slave revolts erupted in the north near Le Cap, which had once been the capital. In 1770 the French had transferred the capital to Port-au-Prince, which in 1804 became capital of the newly independent Haiti.

fraternity, raised new challenges and possibilities for each of Saint-Domingue's social groups. For slaves, who constituted approximately 90 percent of the population, news of abolitionist movements in France led to hopes that the mother country might grant them freedom. Free people of color looked to reforms in Paris as a means of gaining political enfranchisement and reasserting equal status with whites. The white elite, not surprisingly, saw matters very differently. Infuriated by talk of abolition and determined to protect their way of life, they looked to revolutionary ideals of representative government for the chance to gain control of their own affairs, as had the American colonists before them.

The National Assembly frustrated the hopes of all these groups. Cowed by colonial representatives who claimed that support for free people of color would result in slave insurrection and independence, the Assembly refused to extend French constitutional safeguards to the colonies. After dealing this blow to the aspirations of slaves and free coloreds, the committee

also reaffirmed French monopolies over colonial trade, thereby angering planters as well. Like the American settlers before them, the colonists chafed under the rule of the mother country.

In July 1790 Vincent Ogé (aw-ZHAY; ca. 1750–1791), a free man of color, returned to Saint-Domingue from Paris determined to win rights for his people. He raised an army of several hundred and sent letters to the new Provincial Assembly of Saint-Domingue demanding political rights for all free citizens. But Ogé's demands were refused, so he and his followers turned to armed insurrection. After initial victories, his army was defeated, and Ogé was tortured and executed by colonial officials. Revolutionary leaders in Paris were more sympathetic to Ogé's cause. In May 1791, responding to what it perceived as partly justified grievances, the National Assembly granted political rights to free people of color born to two free parents who possessed sufficient property. When news of this legislation arrived in Saint-Domingue, the white elite was furious, and the colonial governor refused to enact it. Violence now erupted between groups of whites and free coloreds in parts of the colony.

The Outbreak of Revolt

Just as the sans-culottes helped push forward more radical reforms in France, the second stage of revolution in Saint-Domingue also resulted from decisive action from below. In August 1791 slaves, who had witnessed the confrontation between whites and free coloreds for over a year, took events into their own hands. Groups of slaves held a series of nighttime meetings to plan a mass insurrection.

Revolts began on a few plantations on the night of August 22. Within a few days the uprising had swept much of the northern plain, creating a slave army estimated at around 2,000 individuals. By August 27 it was described by one observer as "10,000 strong, divided into 3 armies, of whom 700 or 800 are on horseback, and tolerably well-armed."[6] During the next month slaves attacked and destroyed hundreds of sugar and coffee plantations.

On April 4, 1792, as war loomed with the European states, the National Assembly issued a decree extending full citizenship rights, including the right to vote, to free blacks and free people of color. As in France, voting rights and the ability to hold public office applied to men only. The Assembly hoped this measure would win the loyalty of free blacks and their aid in defeating the slave rebellion.

Warfare in Europe soon spread to Saint-Domingue (Map 22.3). Since the beginning of the slave insurrection, the Spanish colony of Santo Domingo, just to the east of Saint-Domingue, had supported rebel slaves. In early 1793 the Spanish began to bring slave leaders and their soldiers into the Spanish army. Toussaint L'Ouverture (TOO-sahn LOO-vair-toor; 1743–1803), a freed slave who had joined the revolt, was named a Spanish officer. In September the British navy blockaded the colony, and invading British troops captured French territory on the island. For the Spanish and British, revolutionary chaos provided a tempting opportunity to capture a profitable colony.

Desperate for forces to oppose France's enemies, commissioners sent by the newly elected National Convention promised freedom to slaves who fought for France. By October 1793 they had abolished slavery throughout the colony. On February 4, 1794, the Convention ratified the abolition of slavery and extended it to all French territories, including the Caribbean colonies of Martinique and Guadeloupe.

The tide of battle began to turn when Toussaint L'Ouverture switched sides, bringing his military and political skills, along with four thousand well-trained soldiers, to support the French war effort. By 1796

☐ KEY EVENTS OF THE HAITIAN REVOLUTION

1760s	Colonial administrators begin rescinding the rights of free people of color
July 1790	Vincent Ogé leads a failed rebellion to gain rights for free people of color
August 1791	Slave revolts begin
April 4, 1792	National Assembly enfranchises all free blacks and free people of color
September 1793	British troops invade Saint-Domingue
February 4, 1794	National Convention ratifies the abolition of slavery and extends it to all French territories
May 1796	Toussaint L'Ouverture is named commander of Saint-Domingue
1800	After invading the south of Saint-Domingue, L'Ouverture gains control of the entire colony
1802	French general Charles-Victor-Emmanuel Leclerc arrests L'Ouverture and deports him to France
1803	L'Ouverture dies
1804	After defeating French forces, Jean Jacques Dessalines declares the independence of Saint-Domingue and the creation of the sovereign nation of Haiti

the French had regained control of the colony, and L'Ouverture had emerged as the key leader of the combined slave and free colored forces. (See "Individuals in Society: Toussaint L'Ouverture," page 680.) In May 1796 he was named commander of the western province of Saint-Domingue (see Map 22.3). The increasingly conservative nature of the French government during the Thermidorian reaction, however, threatened to undo the gains made by former slaves and free people of color.

The War of Haitian Independence

With Toussaint L'Ouverture acting increasingly as an independent ruler of the western province of Saint-Domingue, another general, André Rigaud (1761–1811), set up his own government in the southern peninsula. Tensions mounted between L'Ouverture and Rigaud. While L'Ouverture was a freed slave of African descent, Rigaud belonged to the free colored elite. This elite resented the growing power of former slaves like

Individuals in Society

Toussaint L'Ouverture

LITTLE IS KNOWN OF THE EARLY LIFE OF
Saint-Domingue's brilliant military and political leader Toussaint
L'Ouverture. He was born in 1743 on a plantation outside Le
Cap owned by the Count de Bréda. According to tradition,
L'Ouverture was the eldest son of a captured African prince
from modern-day Benin. Toussaint Bréda, as he was then
called, occupied a privileged position among slaves. Instead of
performing backbreaking labor in the fields, he served his
master as a coachman and livestock keeper. He also learned
to read and write French and some Latin, but he was always
more comfortable with the Creole dialect.

During the 1770s the plantation manager emancipated
L'Ouverture, who subsequently leased his own small coffee
plantation, worked by slaves. He married Suzanne Simone,
who already had one son, and the couple had another son
during their marriage. In 1791 he joined the slave uprisings that
swept Saint-Domingue, and he took on the *nom de guerre*
("war name") L'Ouverture, meaning "the opening." L'Ouverture

rose to prominence among rebel slaves allied with Spain and
by early 1794 controlled his own army. A devout Catholic who
led a frugal and ascetic life, L'Ouverture impressed others with
his enormous physical energy, intellectual acumen, and air of
mystery. In 1794 he defected to the French side and led his
troops to a series of victories against the Spanish. In 1795 the
National Convention promoted L'Ouverture to brigadier general.

Over the next three years L'Ouverture successively eliminated rivals for authority on the island. First he freed himself of
the French commissioners sent to govern the colony. With a
firm grip on power in the northern province, L'Ouverture defeated
General André Rigaud in 1800 to gain control in the south. His
army then marched on the capital of Spanish Santo Domingo
on the eastern half of the island, meeting little resistance. The
entire island of Hispaniola was now under his command.

With control in his hands, L'Ouverture was confronted with
the challenge of building a post-emancipation society, the first
of its kind. The task was made even more difficult by the chaos
wreaked by war, the destruction of plantations, and
bitter social and racial tensions. For L'Ouverture the
most pressing concern was to re-establish the
plantation economy. Without revenue to pay his army,
the gains of the rebellion could be lost. He therefore
encouraged white planters to return and reclaim their
property. He also adopted harsh policies toward former
slaves, forcing them back to their plantations and
restricting their ability to acquire land. When they
resisted, he sent troops across the island to enforce
submission. L'Ouverture's 1801 constitution reaffirmed
his draconian labor policies and named L'Ouverture
governor for life, leaving Saint-Domingue as a colony in
name alone. In June 1802 French forces arrested
L'Ouverture and jailed him at Fort de Joux in France's
Jura Mountains near the Swiss border. He died of
pneumonia on April 7, 1803, leaving his lieutenant, Jean
Jacques Dessalines, to win independence for the new
Haitian nation.

QUESTIONS FOR ANALYSIS

1. Toussaint L'Ouverture was both slave and slave
   owner. How did each experience shape his life and
   actions?

2. What did L'Ouverture and Napoleon Bonaparte have
   in common? How did they differ?

 Equestrian portrait of Toussaint L'Ouverture.
(Réunion des Musées Nationaux/Art Resource, NY)

L'Ouverture, who in turn accused them of adopting the racism of white settlers. Civil war broke out between the two sides in 1799, when L'Ouverture's forces, led by his lieutenant, Jean Jacques Dessalines (1758–1806), invaded the south. Victory over Rigaud in 1800 gave L'Ouverture control of the entire colony.

This victory was soon challenged by Napoleon, who had his own plans for re-establishing slavery and using the profits as a basis for expanding French power. Napoleon ordered his brother-in-law, General Charles-Victor-Emmanuel Leclerc (1772–1802), to lead an expedition to the island to crush the new regime. In 1802 Leclerc landed in Saint-Domingue and ordered the arrest of Toussaint L'Ouverture. The rebel leader was deported to France, along with his family, where he died in 1803.

It was left to L'Ouverture's lieutenant, Jean Jacques Dessalines, to unite the resistance, and he led it to a crushing victory over French forces. On January 1, 1804, Dessalines formally declared the independence of Saint-Domingue and the creation of the new sovereign nation of Haiti, the name used by the pre-Columbian inhabitants of the island.

Haiti, the second independent state in the Americas and the first in Latin America, was born from the first successful large-scale slave revolt in history. Fearing the spread of slave rebellion to the United States, President Thomas Jefferson refused to recognize Haiti. The liberal proponents of the American Revolution thus chose to protect slavery at the expense of revolutionary ideals of universal human rights. Yet Haitian independence had fundamental repercussions for world history, helping spread the idea that liberty, equality, and fraternity must apply to all people. The next phase of Atlantic revolution soon opened in the Spanish American colonies.

CONNECTIONS

The Atlantic world was the essential context for the great revolutionary wave of the late eighteenth century. The movement of peoples, commodities, and ideas across the Atlantic Ocean in the eighteenth century created a world of common debates, conflicts, and aspirations. Moreover, the high stakes of colonial empire heightened competition among European states, leading to a series of wars that generated crushing costs for overburdened treasuries. For both the British in their North American colonies and the French at home, the desperate need for new taxes weakened government authority and opened the door to revolution. In turn, the ideals of the French Revolution inspired slaves and free people of color in Saint-Domingue, thus opening the promise of liberty, equality, and fraternity to people of all races.

The chain reaction did not end with the birth of an independent Haiti in 1804. The next chapter of liberation movements took place in Spanish America in the following decades (see Chapter 27). On the European continent throughout the nineteenth and early twentieth centuries, periodic convulsions occurred as successive generations struggled over political rights first proclaimed by the generation of 1789 (see Chapter 24). Meanwhile, as dramatic political events unfolded, a parallel economic revolution was gathering steam. This was the Industrial Revolution, originating around 1750 and accelerating through the end of the eighteenth century (see Chapter 23). After 1815 the twin forces of industrialization and democratization would combine to transform Europe and the world.

CHAPTER REVIEW

What were the factors behind the age of revolution in the Atlantic world? (p. 652)

The origins of revolutions in the Atlantic world were varied and complex. They included long-term social and economic changes, such as greater inequalities between rich and poor, that challenged the traditional privileges held by elites. Enlightenment ideals of liberty and equality inspired liberal reformers to insist on limited governments, universal human rights, and equality of opportunity under the law. However, liberals' understanding of liberty and equality often excluded women and nonwhites. The huge expenses of the Seven Years' War also opened the door to revolution by forcing the British and French governments to raise taxes and thereby provoke violent protest.

Why and how did American colonists forge a new, independent nation? (p. 656)

British efforts to raise taxes to meet debts from the Seven Years' War aroused violent protest in the American colonies. In 1774 the First Continental Congress met and rejected compromise with the home government. When the British also refused to back down, fighting broke out between the two sides. Two years later the Second Continental Congress issued the Declaration of Independence, a document that made the traditional rights of English people into universal human rights. Conflict ensued between Loyalists, who wished to remain within the British Empire, and American patriots. Eager to profit from the weakness of a mighty empire, the French, Spanish, and Dutch declared war on Britain. In 1783 the British recognized the independence of the thirteen colonies. The Constitutional Convention drafted a constitution for the new nation, but controversy soon erupted over the balance between federal and state power and the status of individual freedoms. To protect such freedoms, Congress passed the first ten amendments to the Constitution, a Bill of Rights safeguarding the individual. However, the new government did not grant women, slaves, or indigenous peoples equal rights.

How did the events of 1789 result in a constitutional monarchy in France, and what were the consequences? (p. 659)

When the Estates General gathered in 1789, delegates from the third estate, representing the common people, refused to accept the old system of one vote per estate. Instead, they declared themselves a National Assembly. Popular revolts prevented the king from intervening, and he was forced to accept the situation. The National

Assembly promulgated France's first constitution in 1791, leaving the king as head of state but limited by the powers of the National Assembly. The nobility was abolished, but only the wealthiest half of the male population could vote in elections for the National Assembly and women were not allowed to vote or hold political office. Also, to the horror of the pope and devout French Catholics, the government seized church property and imposed an oath of loyalty on priests.

Why and how did the French Revolution take a radical turn entailing terror at home and war with European powers? (p. 667)

Support for the constitutional monarchy ended with the royal family's attempted flight in June 1791. The new Legislative Assembly, comprising younger and more radical delegates led by members of the Jacobin club, declared war on Austria (which wanted Louis XVI and his queen kept in power) and proclaimed France a republic. With the execution of the royal couple and the declaration of terror as the order of the day, the French Revolution took an increasingly radical turn from the end of 1792. France was largely victorious, mostly because of the total war effort undertaken by the Jacobin leadership. To defend the Revolution against its perceived internal enemies, Jacobins eliminated political opponents and then factions within their own party. They also attempted to bring about a cultural revolution, in part by attacking Christianity and substituting secular republican festivals. The Directory that took power after the fall of Robespierre restored political equilibrium at the cost of the radical platform of social equality he had pursued.

Why did Napoleon Bonaparte assume control of France and much of Europe, and what factors led to his downfall? (p. 672)

Wearied by the weaknesses of the Directory, a group of conspirators joined forces with Napoleon Bonaparte to oust the Directors and give Napoleon

KEY TERMS

Treaty of Paris (p. 655)
Declaration of Independence (p. 657)
Antifederalists (p. 659)
Estates General (p. 660)
National Assembly (p. 661)
Jacobin club (p. 668)
Girondists (p. 668)
Mountain (p. 668)
sans-culottes (p. 669)
Reign of Terror (p. 670)
Thermidorian reaction (p. 671)
Napoleonic Code (p. 672)
Grand Empire (p. 674)
Continental System (p. 674)

control of France. His reputation as a brilliant military leader and his charisma and determination made him seem ideal to lead the country to victory over its enemies. However, Napoleon's relentless ambitions ultimately led to his downfall. Not satisfied with his successes throughout Europe, and struggling to maintain his hold on Spain and Portugal, Napoleon made the fatal mistake of attempting to invade Russia in the summer of 1812. After a disastrous retreat from Moscow, he was eventually forced to abdicate the throne in 1814.

□ How did slave revolt on colonial Saint-Domingue lead to the creation of the independent nation of Haiti in 1804? (p. 676)

The outbreak of revolution in France raised new and contradictory possibilities for the people in the French colony of Saint-Domingue. On the one hand, slaves and free people of color hoped that reforms in the mother country might lead to more rights for them. On the other hand, the white elite hoped that a representative government would help them gain more control. The revolutionary government in France waffled disastrously on colonial affairs, succeeding only in infuriating all sides. After a failed uprising by free men of color, slaves took matters into their own hands in August 1791. Their revolt, combined with the outbreak of war and the radicalization of the revolution in France, led to the enfranchisement of free men of color, the emancipation of slaves who fought for France, and the abolition of slavery throughout the colony in late 1793. Like Napoleon Bonaparte, Toussaint L'Ouverture was an unknown soldier who emerged into the political limelight out of the chaos of revolution, only to endure exile and defeat. Unlike Napoleon's quest to expand his empire, L'Ouverture's cause ultimately prevailed. After his exile, war between the French forces and the armies he had led resulted in French defeat and independence for Haiti in 1804.

SUGGESTED READING

Bell, David A. *The Cult of the Nation in France: Inventing Nationalism, 1680–1800.* 2001. Traces early French nationalism through its revolutionary culmination.
Blanning, T. C. W. *The French Revolutionary Wars (1787–1802).* 1996. A masterful account of the revolutionary wars that also places the French Revolution in its European context.
Broers, Michael. *Europe Under Napoleon.* 2002. Probes Napoleon's impact on the territories he conquered.
Calloway, Colin G. *The Scratch of a Pen: 1763 and the Transformation of North America.* 2006. A study of the dramatic impact of the Seven Years' War on the British and French colonies of North America.
Connelly, Owen. *The French Revolution and Napoleonic Era.* 1991. An excellent introduction to the French Revolution and Napoleon.

Desan, Suzanne. *The Family on Trial in Revolutionary France.* 2004. Studies the effects of revolutionary law on the family, including the legalization of divorce.
Dubois, Laurent. *Avengers of the New World: The Story of the Haitian Revolution.* 2004. An excellent and highly readable account of the revolution that transformed the French colony of Saint-Domingue into the independent state of Haiti.
Englund, Steven. *Napoleon: A Political Life.* 2004. A good biography of the French emperor.
Goulda, Eliga H., and Peter Onuf, eds. *Empire and Nation: The American Revolution in the Atlantic World.* 2005. A collection of essays placing the American Revolution in its wider Atlantic context, including studies of its impact on daily life in the new republic and the remaining British Empire.
Hunt, Lynn. *Politics, Culture, and Class in the French Revolution,* 2d ed. 2004. A pioneering examination of the French Revolution as a cultural phenomenon that generated new festivals, clothing, and songs, and even a new calendar.
Landes, John B. *Visualizing the Nation: Gender, Representation, and Revolution in Eighteenth-Century France.* 2001. Analyzes images of gender and the body in revolutionary politics.
Sutherland, Donald. *France, 1789–1815.* 1986. An overview of the French Revolution that emphasizes its many opponents as well as its supporters.
Tackett, Timothy. *When the King Took Flight.* 2003. An exciting re-creation of the royal family's doomed effort to escape from Paris.

NOTES

1. Quoted in G. Wright, *France in Modern Times,* 4th ed. (New York: W. W. Norton, 1987), p. 34.
2. G. Pernoud and S. Flaisser, eds., *The French Revolution* (Greenwich, Conn.: Fawcett, 1960), p. 61.
3. Quoted in L. Gershoy, *The Era of the French Revolution, 1789–1799* (New York: Van Nostrand, 1957), p. 150.
4. Cited in Wim Klooster, *Revolutions in the Atlantic World: A Comprehensive History* (New York and London: New York University Press, 2009), p. 74.
5. T. Blanning, *The French Revolutionary Wars, 1787–1802* (London: Arnold, 1996), pp. 116–128.
6. Quoted in Laurent Dubois, *Avengers of the New World: The Story of the Haitian Revolution* (Cambridge, Mass.: Harvard University Press, 2004), p. 97.

For practice quizzes and other study tools, visit the **Online Study Guide** at bedfordstmartins.com/mckayworld.

For primary sources from this period, see *Sources of World Societies*, **Second Edition**.

For Web sites, images, and documents related to topics in this chapter, visit **Make History** at bedfordstmartins.com/mckayworld.

• **Young Factory Worker** Children composed a substantial element of the workforce in early factories, where they toiled long hours in dangerous and unsanitary conditions. Until a mechanized process was invented at the end of the nineteenth century, boys working in glass-bottle factories, like the youth pictured here, stoked blazing furnaces with coal and learned to blow glass. (© Boume Gallery, Reigate, Surrey, UK/The Bridgeman Art Library)

23

While the revolutions of the Atlantic world and in France were opening a new political era, another revolution was beginning to transform economic and social life. The Industrial Revolution began in Great Britain around the 1780s and started to influence continental Europe after 1815. Quite possibly only the development of agriculture during Neolithic times had a comparable impact and significance. Non-European nations began to industrialize after 1860, with the United States and Japan taking an early lead.

The Industrial Revolution profoundly modified much of human experience. It changed patterns of work, transformed the social class structure and the way people thought about class, and eventually altered the international balance of political power. The Industrial Revolution also helped ordinary people gain a higher standard of living as the widespread poverty of the preindustrial world was gradually reduced.

Unfortunately, improvement in the European standard of living was limited until about 1850 for at least two reasons. First, even in Britain, only a few key industries experienced a technological revolution. Many more industries continued to use old methods. Second, rapid growth in population, which began in the eighteenth century, threatened to eat up the growth in production and to leave most individuals poorer than ever. Industrialization drew on British profits from Atlantic trade, including slavery. Even more important were the consequences of early industrialization in Britain and on the European continent, which allowed Europeans to increase their economic and political dominance over other nations. •

The Revolution in Energy and Industry
1760–1850

The Industrial Revolution in Britain

□ What were the origins of the Industrial Revolution in Britain, and how did it develop between 1780 and 1850?

Industrialization Beyond Britain

□ How after 1815 did countries outside of Britain respond to the challenge of industrialization?

Relations Between Capital and Labor

□ How did the Industrial Revolution affect people of all social classes, and what measures were taken to improve the conditions of workers?

The Industrial Revolution in Britain

□ What were the origins of the Industrial Revolution in Britain, and how did it develop between 1780 and 1850?

The Industrial Revolution began in Britain, the nation created by the formal union of Scotland, Wales, and England in 1707. The transformation in industry was something new in history, and it was unplanned. With no models to copy and no idea of what to expect, Britain pioneered not only in industrial technology but also in social relations and urban living. Just as France was the trailblazer in political change, Britain was the leader in economic development, and it must therefore command special attention.

Origins of the British Industrial Revolution

Although many aspects of the origins of the British Industrial Revolution are still matters for scholarly debate, it is generally agreed that industrial changes grew out of a long process of development. The scientific revolution and Enlightenment fostered a new worldview that embraced progress and the role of research and experimentation in understanding and mastering the natural world. In the economic realm, the seventeenth-century expansion of English woolen cloth exports throughout Europe brought commercial profits and high wages to the detriment of traditional

Industrial areas
■ Coal deposit
○ Metal goods
■ Woolen cloth
— Canals, 1800
— Navigable rivers

Cottage Industry and Transportation in Eighteenth-Century England

producers in Flanders and Italy. By the eighteenth century the expanding Atlantic economy was also serving Britain well. The mercantilist colonial empire Britain aggressively built, augmented by a strong position in Latin America and in the African slave trade, provided raw materials like cotton and a growing market for British manufactured goods (see Chapter 18).

Agriculture also played an important role in bringing about the Industrial Revolution in Britain. English farmers were second only to the Dutch in productivity in 1700, and they were continually adopting new methods of farming. The result, especially before 1760, was a period of bountiful crops and low food prices. The ordinary English family no longer had to spend almost everything it earned just to buy bread. Thus the family could spend more on manufactured goods — a razor for the man or a shawl for the woman. Moreover, in the eighteenth century the members of the average British family were redirecting their labor away from unpaid work for household consumption toward work for wages that they could spend on goods, a trend reflecting the increasing commercialization of the entire European economy. In Britain, rising urbanization and high wages both reflected these developments and spurred them forward.

As manufacturing expanded to supply both foreign and British customers, the domestic market for raw materials was well-positioned to meet the growing demands of manufacturers. In an age when it was much cheaper to ship goods by water than by land, no part of England was more than fifty miles from navigable water. Beginning in the 1770s a canal-building boom enhanced this advantage. Rivers and canals provided easy movement of England's and Wales's enormous deposits of iron and coal, resources that would be critical raw materials in Europe's early industrial age. Nor were there any tariffs within the country to hinder trade, as there were in France before 1789 and in politically fragmented Germany.

Finally, Britain had long had a large class of hired agricultural laborers, rural proletarians whose numbers were further increased by the second great round of enclosures (the division of common lands into privately held and managed properties) in the late eighteenth century. These rural wage earners were relatively mobile — compared to village-bound peasants in France and western Germany, for example — and along with cottage workers they formed a potential industrial labor force for capitalist entrepreneurs.

All these factors combined to initiate the **Industrial Revolution**, a term first coined by awed contemporaries in the 1830s to describe the burst of major inventions and technical changes they had witnessed in certain industries. This technical revolution went hand in hand with an impressive quickening in the annual rate of industrial growth in Britain. Whereas industry had grown at only 0.7 percent between 1700 and 1760 (before the Industrial Revolution), it grew at the much higher rate of 3 percent between 1801 and 1831 (when industrial transformation was in full swing).[1]

The great economic and political revolutions that shaped the modern world occurred almost simultaneously, though they began in different countries. But the Industrial Revolution was a longer process than the political upheavals of the French Revolution. It was not complete in Britain until 1850 at the earliest, and it had no real impact on continental countries until after the end of the Napoleonic wars in 1815. It spread beyond Europe in the second half of the nineteenth century.

The First Factories

The pressures to produce more goods for a growing market and to reduce the labor costs of manufacturing were directly related to the first decisive breakthrough of the Industrial Revolution: the creation of the world's first large factories in the British cotton textile industry. Technological innovations in the manufacture of cotton cloth led to a new system of production and social relationships. The putting-out system involved a merchant who loaned, or "put out," raw materials to cottage workers who processed the raw materials in their own homes and returned the finished products to the merchant.

During the eighteenth century this system was used across Europe, but most extensively in Britain. There, pressured by growing demand, the system's limitations began to outweigh its advantages for the first time. This was especially true in the British textile industry after about 1760. There was always a serious imbalance in textile production based on cottage industry: the work of four or five spinners was needed to keep one weaver steadily employed. Cloth weavers constantly had to try to find more thread and more spinners.

Moreover, deep-seated conflicts existed between merchants who put out materials and the workers who processed them. In "The Clothier's Delight, or the Rich Men's Joy and the Poor Men's Sorrow," an English popular song written about 1700, a merchant boasts of the countless tricks he used to "beat down wages":

> We heapeth up riches and treasure great store
> Which we get by griping and grinding the poor.
> And this is a way for to fill up our purse
> Although we do get it with many a curse.[2]

There were constant disputes over the weights of materials and the quality of the cloth. Merchants accused workers of stealing raw materials, and weavers complained that merchants delivered underweight bales.

• **Industrial Revolution** A term first coined in the 1830s to describe the burst of major inventions and economic expansion that took place in certain industries, such as cotton textiles and iron, between 1780 and 1850.

Woman Working a Spinning Jenny The loose cotton strands on the slanted bobbins shown in this illustration of Hargreave's spinning jenny passed up to the sliding carriage and then on to the spindles (inset) in back for fine spinning. The worker, almost always a woman, regulated the sliding carriage with one hand, and with the other she turned the crank on the wheel to supply power. By 1783 one woman could spin a hundred threads at a time. (spinning jenny: Mary Evans Picture Library/The Image Works; spindle: Picture Research Consultants & Archives)

Both were right; each tried to cheat the other, even if only in self-defense.

There was another problem, at least from the merchant-capitalist's point of view. Scattered rural labor was extremely difficult to control. Cottage workers tended to work in spurts. After they got paid on Saturday afternoon, the men in particular tended to drink and carouse for two or three days. Productivity suffered, and by the end of the week many weavers had to work feverishly to make their quota. If they did not succeed, there was little the merchant could do. The merchant-capitalist's search for more efficient methods of production intensified.

Many a tinkering worker knew that a better spinning wheel promised rich rewards. It proved hard to spin the traditional raw materials—wool and flax—with improved machines, but cotton was different. Cotton textiles had first been imported into Britain from India by the East India Company as a rare and delicate luxury for the upper classes, and by 1760 a tiny domestic cotton industry had emerged in northern England. After many experiments over a generation, a gifted carpenter and jack-of-all-trades, James Hargreaves, invented his cotton-spinning jenny about 1765. At almost the same moment, a barber-turned-manufacturer named Richard Arkwright invented (or possibly pirated) another kind of spinning machine, the water frame. These breakthroughs produced an explosion in the infant cotton textile industry in the 1780s, when it was increasing the value of its output at an unprecedented rate of about 13 percent each year. By 1790 the new machines were producing ten times as much cotton yarn as had been made in 1770.

Hargreaves's **spinning jenny** was simple, inexpensive, and powered by hand. In early models from six to twenty-four spindles were mounted on a sliding carriage, and each spindle spun a fine, slender thread. The woman moved the carriage back and forth with one hand and turned a wheel to supply power with the other. Now it was the male weaver who could not keep up with the vastly more efficient female spinner.

Arkwright's **water frame** employed a different principle. It quickly acquired a capacity of several hundred spindles and demanded much more power—waterpower. The water frame thus required large specialized mills, factories that employed as many as one

A Pioneering Silk Mill In the 1600s Italians invented a machine to spin the thread for the silk that rich people loved. Their carefully guarded secret was stolen in 1717 by John Lombe, who then built this enormous silk mill in England. But the factory production of textiles only took off when the spinning of cotton—a fabric for all classes—was mechanized in the later eighteenth century. (© The Art Gallery Collection/Alamy)

thousand workers from the very beginning. It did not completely replace cottage industry, however, for the water frame could spin only a coarse, strong thread, which was then put out for respinning on hand-powered cottage jennies. Around 1790 a hybrid machine invented by Samuel Crompton proved capable of spinning very fine and strong thread in large quantities. Gradually, all cotton spinning was concentrated in large-scale factories.

The first consequences of these revolutionary developments in the textile industry were more beneficial than is generally believed. Cotton goods became much cheaper, and they were increasingly bought by all classes. Families using cotton in cottage industry were freed from their constant search for adequate yarn from scattered part-time spinners, since all the thread needed could be spun in the cottage on the jenny or obtained from a nearby factory. The wages of weavers, now hard-pressed to keep up with the spinners, rose markedly until about 1792. They were among the best-paid workers in England. As a result, large numbers of agricultural laborers became hand-loom weavers, while mechanics and capitalists sought to invent a power loom to save on labor costs. This Edmund Cartwright achieved in 1785. But the power looms of the factories worked poorly at first, and hand-loom weavers continued to receive good wages until at least 1800.

Unfortunately, working conditions in the early cotton factories were less satisfactory than those of cottage weavers and spinners, and adult workers were reluctant to work in them. Therefore, factory owners often turned to young children who had been abandoned by their parents and put in the care of local parishes. Parish officers often "apprenticed" such

- **spinning jenny** A simple, inexpensive, hand-powered spinning machine created by James Hargreaves in 1765.
- **water frame** A spinning machine created by Richard Arkwright that had a capacity of several hundred spindles and used waterpower; it therefore required a larger and more specialized mill — a factory.

unfortunate foundlings to factory owners. The parish thus saved money, and the factory owners gained workers over whom they exercised almost the authority of slave owners. Apprenticed as young as five or six years of age, boy and girl workers were forced by law to labor for their "masters" for as many as fourteen years. Housed, fed, and locked up nightly in factory dormitories, the young workers labored thirteen or fourteen hours a day for little or no pay. Harsh physical punishment maintained brutal discipline. Hours were appalling—commonly thirteen or fourteen hours a day, six days a week. To be sure, poor children typically worked long hours and frequently outside the home for brutal masters, but the wholesale coercion of orphans as factory apprentices constituted exploitation on a truly unprecedented scale.

The creation of the world's first modern factories in the British cotton textile industry in the 1770s and 1780s, which grew out of the putting-out system of cottage production, was a major historical development. Both symbolically and substantially, the big new cotton mills marked the beginning of the Industrial Revolution in Britain. By 1831 the largely mechanized cotton textile industry accounted for fully 22 percent of the country's entire industrial production.

The Steam Engine Breakthrough

Human beings have long used their toolmaking abilities to construct machines that convert one form of energy into another for their own benefit. In the medieval period Europeans began to adopt water mills to grind their grain and windmills to pump water and drain swamps. More efficient use of water and wind in the sixteenth and seventeenth centuries enabled them to accomplish more. Nevertheless, even into the eighteenth century European society, like other areas of the world, continued to rely mainly on wood for energy, and human beings and animals continued to perform most work. This dependence meant that Europe and the rest of the world remained poor in energy and power.

The shortage of energy had become particularly severe in Britain by the eighteenth century. Wood, a basic raw material and the primary source of heat for all homes and industries, was in ever-shorter supply. Processed wood (charcoal) was the fuel that was mixed with iron ore in the blast furnace to produce pig iron. The iron industry's appetite for wood was enormous, and by 1740 the British iron industry was stagnating. Vast forests enabled Russia in the eighteenth century to become the world's leading producer of iron, much of which was exported to England.

As this early energy crisis grew worse, Britain looked to coal as an alternative to its vanishing wood. Coal was first used in Britain in the late Middle Ages as a source of heat. By 1640 most homes in London were heated with coal, and it was also used in industry to provide heat for making beer, glass, soap, and other products. The breakthrough came when industrialists began to use coal to produce mechanical energy and to power machinery.

As more coal was produced, mines were dug deeper and deeper and were constantly filling with water. Mechanical pumps, usually powered by animals walking in circles at the surface, had to be installed. Such power was expensive and bothersome. In an attempt to overcome these disadvantages, Thomas Savery in 1698 and Thomas Newcomen in 1705 invented the first primitive **steam engines**. Both engines burned coal to produce steam, which was then used to operate a pump. Although both models were extremely inefficient, by the early 1770s many of the Savery engines and hundreds of the Newcomen engines were operating successfully in English and Scottish mines.

In 1763 a gifted young Scot named James Watt (1736–1819) was drawn to a critical study of the steam engine. Watt was employed at the time by the University of Glasgow as a skilled craftsman making scientific instruments. The Scottish universities were pioneers in practical technical education, and in 1763 Watt was called on to repair a Newcomen engine being used in a physics course. After a series of observations, Watt saw that the Newcomen engine's waste of energy could be reduced by adding a separate condenser. This splendid invention, patented in 1769, greatly increased the efficiency of the steam engine.

To invent something is one thing; to make it a practical success is quite another. Watt needed skilled workers, precision parts, and capital, and the relatively advanced nature of the British economy proved essential. A partnership in 1775 with Matthew Boulton, a wealthy English industrialist, provided Watt with adequate capital and exceptional skills in salesmanship that equaled those of the renowned pottery king, Josiah Wedgwood. (See "Individuals in Society: Josiah Wedgwood," page 692.) In the craft tradition of locksmiths, tinsmiths, and millwrights, Watt found mechanics who could install, regulate, and repair his sophisticated engines. From ingenious manufacturers such as the cannonmaker John Wilkinson, Watt was gradually able to purchase precision parts. By the late 1780s the firm of Boulton and Watt had made the steam engine a practical and commercial success in Britain.

The coal-burning steam engine of Watt and his followers was the Industrial Revolution's most fundamental advance in technology. For the first time in history,

• **steam engines** A breakthrough invention by Thomas Savery in 1698 and Thomas Newcomen in 1705 that burned coal to produce steam, which was then used to operate a pump; the early models were superseded by James Watt's more efficient steam engine, patented in 1769.

James Nasmyth's Mighty Steam Hammer Nasmyth's invention was the forerunner of the modern pile driver, and its successful introduction in 1832 epitomized the rapid development of steam power technology in Britain. In this painting by the inventor himself, workers manipulate a massive iron shaft being hammered into shape at Nasmyth's foundry near Manchester. (Science & Society Picture Library, London)

humanity had, at least for a few generations, almost unlimited power at its disposal. For the first time, inventors and engineers could devise and implement all kinds of power equipment to aid people in their work.

The steam engine was quickly put to use in several industries in Britain. It drained mines and made possible the production of ever more coal to feed steam engines elsewhere. The steam-power plant began to replace waterpower in the cotton-spinning mills during the 1780s, contributing greatly to that industry's phenomenal rise. Steam also took the place of waterpower in flour mills, in the malt mills used in breweries, in the flint mills supplying the pottery industry, and in the mills exported by Britain to the West Indies to crush sugar cane.

Coal and steam power promoted important breakthroughs in other industries. The British iron industry was radically transformed. Originally, the smoke and fumes of coal burning meant that it could not be substituted for charcoal (derived from limited supplies of wood) in smelting iron. Starting around 1710, ironmakers began to use coke — a smokeless and hot-burning fuel produced by heating coal to rid it of water and impurities — to smelt pig iron. After 1770 the adoption of steam-driven bellows in blast furnaces allowed for great increases in the quantity of pig iron produced by British ironmakers. In the 1780s Henry Cort developed the puddling furnace, which allowed pig iron to be refined in turn with coke.

Cort also developed steam-powered rolling mills, which were capable of spewing out finished iron in every shape and form. The economic consequence of these technical innovations was a great boom in the British iron industry. In 1740 annual British iron production was only 17,000 tons. With the spread of coke smelting and the impact of Cort's inventions,

Individuals in Society

Josiah Wedgwood

AS THE MAKING OF CLOTH AND IRON WAS revolutionized by technical change and factory organization, so too were the production and consumption of pottery. Acquiring beautiful tableware became a craze for eighteenth-century consumers, and continental monarchs often sought prestige in building royal china works. But the grand prize went to Josiah Wedgwood, who wanted to "astonish the world."

The twelfth child of a poor potter, Josiah Wedgwood (1730–1795) grew up in the pottery district of Staffordshire in the English Midlands, where many tiny potteries made simple earthenware utensils for sale in local markets. Having grown up as an apprentice in the family business inherited by his oldest brother, Wedgwood struck off on his own in 1752. Soon manager of a small pottery, Wedgwood learned that new products recharged lagging sales. Studying chemistry and determined to succeed, Wedgwood spent his evenings experimenting with different chemicals and firing conditions.

In 1759, after five years of tireless efforts, Wedgwood perfected a beautiful new green glaze. Now established as a master potter, he opened his own factory and began manufacturing teapots and tableware finished in his green and other unique glazes, or adorned with printed scenes far superior to those being produced by competitors. Wedgwood's products caused a sensation among consumers, and his business quickly earned substantial profits. Subsequent breakthroughs, including ornamental vases imitating classical Greek models and jasperware for jewelry, contributed greatly to Wedgwood's success.

Competitors were quick to copy Wedgwood's new products and sell them at lower prices. Thus Wedgwood and his partner Thomas Bentley sought to cultivate an image of superior fashion, taste, and quality in order to develop and maintain a dominant market position. They did this by first capturing the business of the trend-setting elite. In one brilliant coup the partners first sold a very large cream-colored dinner set to Britain's queen, which they quickly christened "Queen's ware" and sold as a very expensive, must-have luxury to English aristocrats. Equally brilliant was Bentley's suave expertise in the elegant

London showroom selling Wedgwood's imitation Greek vases, which became the rage after the rediscovery of Pompeii and Herculaneum in the mid-eighteenth century.

Above all, once Wedgwood had secured his position as the luxury market leader, he was able to successfully extend his famous brand to the growing middle class, capturing an enormous mass market for his "useful ware." Thus when sales of a luxury good grew "stale," Wedgwood made tasteful modifications and sold it to the middling classes for twice the price his competitors could charge. This unbeatable combination of mass appeal and high prices brought Wedgwood great fame all across Europe and enormous wealth.

A workaholic with an authoritarian streak, Wedgwood contributed substantially to the development of the factory system. In 1769 he opened a model factory on a new canal he had promoted. With two hundred workers in several departments, Wedgwood exercised tremendous control over his workforce, imposing fines for many infractions, such as being late, drinking on the job, or wasting material. He wanted, he said, to create men who would be like "machines" that "cannot err." Yet Wedgwood also recognized the value in treating workers well. He championed a division of labor that made most workers specialists who received ongoing training. He also encouraged employment of family groups, who were housed in company row houses with long narrow backyards suitable for raising vegetables and chickens. Paying relatively high wages and providing pensions and some benefits, Wedgwood developed a high-quality labor force that learned to accept his rigorous discipline and carried out his ambitious plans.

Josiah Wedgwood (top right) perfected jasperware, a fine-grained pottery usually made in "Wedgwood blue" with white decoration. This elegant cylindrical vase (right), decorated in the form of a miniature Roman household altar, was destined for the luxury market. (portrait: Down House, Kent, Darwin Heirlooms Trust; vase: Image copyright © The Metropolitan Museum of Art/ Art Resource, NY)

QUESTIONS FOR ANALYSIS

1. How and why did Wedgwood succeed?
2. Was Wedgwood a good boss or a bad one? Why?
3. How did Wedgwood exemplify the new class of factory owners?

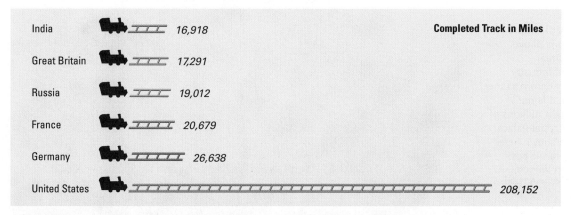

	Completed Track in Miles
India	16,918
Great Britain	17,291
Russia	19,012
France	20,679
Germany	26,638
United States	208,152

FIGURE 23.1 Railroad Track Mileage, 1890 Steam railroads were first used by the general public for shipping in England in the 1820s, and they quickly spread to other countries. The United States was an early adopter of railroads and by 1890 had surpassed all other countries in miles of track, as shown in this figure.

production had reached 260,000 tons by 1806. In 1844 Britain produced 3 million tons of iron. Once scarce and expensive, iron became the cheap, basic, indispensable building block of the economy.

The Coming of the Railroads

The coal industry had long been using plank roads and rails to move coal wagons within mines and at the surface. Rails reduced friction and allowed a horse or a human being to pull a heavier load. Thus, once a rail capable of supporting a heavy locomotive was developed in 1816, all sorts of experiments with steam engines on rails went forward. In 1825, after ten years of work, George Stephenson built an effective locomotive. In 1830 his ***Rocket*** sped down the track of the just-completed Liverpool and Manchester Railway at sixteen miles per hour. The line from Liverpool to Manchester was a financial as well as a technical success, and many private companies were quickly organized to build more rail lines. Within twenty years they had completed the main trunk lines of Great Britain (Map 23.1). Other countries were quick to follow, with the first steam-powered trains operating in the United States in the 1830s and in Brazil, Chile, Argentina, and the British colonies of Canada, Australia, and India in the 1850s (Figure 23.1).

The significance of the railroad was tremendous. It dramatically reduced the cost and uncertainty of shipping freight over land. This advance had many economic consequences. Previously, markets had tended to be small and local; as the barrier of high transportation costs was lowered, markets became larger and even nationwide. Larger markets encouraged larger factories with more sophisticated machinery in a growing number of industries. Such factories could make goods more cheaply and gradually subjected most cottage workers and many urban artisans to severe competi-

tive pressures. In all countries, the construction of railroads created a strong demand for unskilled labor and contributed to the growth of a class of urban workers.

The railroad changed the outlook and values of the entire society. The last and culminating invention of the Industrial Revolution, the railroad dramatically revealed the power and increased the speed of the new age. Racing down a track at sixteen miles per hour or by 1850 at a phenomenal fifty miles per hour was a new and awesome experience. As a French economist put it after a ride on the Liverpool and Manchester in 1833, "There are certain impressions that one cannot put into words!" Some great painters, notably Joseph M. W. Turner (1775–1851) and Claude Monet (1840–1926), succeeded in expressing this sense of power and awe. So did the massive new train stations, the cathedrals of the industrial age. Leading railway engineers such as Isambard Kingdom Brunel and Thomas Brassey, whose tunnels pierced mountains and whose bridges spanned valleys, became public idols — the astronauts of their day. Everyday speech absorbed the images of railroading. After you got up a "full head of steam," you "highballed" along. And if you didn't "go off the track," you might "toot your own whistle." The railroad fired the imagination.

Industry and Population

In 1851 London hosted an industrial fair called the Great Exhibition in the newly built **Crystal Palace**. For visitors, one fact stood out: Britain was the "workshop of the world." Britain alone produced two-thirds

- ***Rocket*** The name given to George Stephenson's effective locomotive that was first tested in 1830 on the Liverpool and Manchester Railway at sixteen miles per hour.
- **Crystal Palace** The location of the Great Exhibition in 1851 in London, an architectural masterpiece made entirely of glass and iron.

Crystal Palace Souvenir More than 6 million visitors from all over Europe marveled at the Great Exhibition of the Works of Industry of All the Nations, popularly known as the Crystal Palace Exhibition. It is no surprise that people bought millions of souvenirs picturing the Crystal Palace. The handsome depiction shown here brightened the lid of a ceramic pot. (Fitzwilliam Museum, Cambridge University, UK/ Bridgeman Giraudon/The Bridgeman Art Library)

MAP 23.1 The Industrial Revolution in England, ca. 1850 Industry concentrated in the rapidly growing cities of the north and the center of England, where rich coal and iron deposits were close to one another.

of the world's coal and more than half of its iron and cotton cloth. More generally, in 1860 Britain produced a remarkable 20 percent of the entire world's output of industrial goods, whereas it had produced only about 2 percent of the world total in 1750.[3] Experiencing revolutionary industrial change, Britain became the first industrial nation (see Map 23.1).

As the British economy significantly increased its production of manufactured goods, the gross national product (GNP) rose roughly fourfold at constant prices between 1780 and 1851. At the same time, the population of Britain boomed, growing from about 9 million in 1780 to almost 21 million in 1851. Thus, growing numbers consumed much of the increase in total production.

Although the question is still debated, many economic historians believe that rapid population growth in Great Britain was not harmful because it facilitated industrial expansion. More people meant a more mobile labor force, with a wealth of young workers in need of employment and ready to go where the jobs were. Contemporaries were much less optimistic. In his *Essay on the Principle of Population* (1798), Thomas Malthus (1766–1834) examined the dynamics of human populations. He argued that

> there are few states in which there is not a constant effort in the population to increase beyond the means of subsistence. This constant effort as constantly tends to subject the lower classes of society to distress, and to prevent any great permanent melioration of these conditions.[4]

Since, in his opinion, population would always tend to grow faster than the food supply, Malthus concluded

French Train Poster
The International Sleeping-Car Company was founded in 1872, inspired by the model of the American Pullman night trains. It quickly became the most important operator of sleeping and dining cars in Europe. The company's posters, like the one pictured here, appealed to wealthy and middle-class customers by emphasizing the luxury and spaciousness of its accommodations. The company's most famous line was the Orient Express (1883–2009), which ran from Paris to Istanbul. (Kharbine-Tapabor/The Art Archive)

that the only hope of warding off such "positive checks" to population growth as war, famine, and disease was "prudential restraint." That is, young men and women had to limit the growth of population by marrying late in life. But Malthus was not optimistic about this possibility. The powerful attraction of the sexes would cause most people to marry early and have many children.

Economist David Ricardo (1772–1823) spelled out the pessimistic implications of Malthus's thought. Ricardo's depressing **iron law of wages** posited that because of the pressure of population growth, wages would always sink to subsistence level. That is, wages would be just high enough to keep workers from starving.

Malthus, Ricardo, and their followers were proved wrong in the long run. However, until the 1820s, or even the 1840s, contemporary observers might reasonably have concluded that the economy and the total population were racing neck and neck, with the outcome very much in doubt. There was another problem as well. Perhaps workers, farmers, and ordinary people did not get their rightful share of the new wealth. Perhaps only the rich got richer, while the poor got poorer or made no progress. We turn to this great issue after looking at the process of industrialization outside of Britain.

Industrialization Beyond Britain

☐ How after 1815 did countries outside of Britain respond to the challenge of industrialization?

As new technologies and organization of labor began to revolutionize production in Britain, other countries took notice and began to emulate its example. Imitating Britain's success was hampered by the particular economic and social conditions of each country, many of whose peoples resisted attempts at drastic change. Yet by the end of the nineteenth century, several European countries as well as the United States and Japan had industrialized their economies to a considerable, but variable, degree.

The process of industrialization proceeded gradually, with uneven jerks and national and regional variations. Scholars are still struggling to explain these variations as well as the dramatic gap that emerged for the first time in history between Western and non-Western levels of economic production. These

• **iron law of wages** Theory proposed by English economist David Ricardo suggesting that the pressure of population growth prevents wages from rising above the subsistence level.

• **TABLE 23.1** Per Capita Levels of Industrialization, 1750–1913

	1750	1800	1830	1860	1880	1900	1913
Great Britain	10	16	25	64	87	100	115
Belgium	9	10	14	28	43	56	88
United States	4	9	14	21	38	69	126
France	9	9	12	20	28	39	59
Germany	8	8	9	15	25	52	85
Austria-Hungary	7	7	8	11	15	23	32
Italy	8	8	8	10	12	17	26
Russia	6	6	7	8	10	15	20
China	8	6	6	4	4	3	3
India	7	6	6	3	2	1	2

Note: All entries are based on an index value of 100, equal to the per capita level of industrialization in Great Britain in 1900. Data for Great Britain include Ireland, England, Wales, and Scotland.

Source: P. Bairoch, "International Industrialization Levels from 1750 to 1980," *Journal of European Economic History* 11 (Spring 1982): 294, U.S. Journals at Cambridge University Press. Reprinted by permission.

questions are especially important because they may offer valuable lessons for poor countries that today are seeking to improve their material condition through industrialization and economic development. The latest findings on the nineteenth-century experience are encouraging. They suggest that there were alternative paths to the industrial world and that there was and is no need to follow a rigid, predetermined British model.

National and International Variations

Comparative data on industrial production in different countries over time help give us an overview of what happened. One set of data, the work of a Swiss scholar, compares the level of industrialization on a per capita basis in several countries from 1750 to 1913. These data are far from perfect, but they reflect basic trends and are presented in Table 23.1 for closer study.

Table 23.1 presents a comparison of how much industrial product was produced, on average, for each person in a given country in a given year. All the numbers expressed in terms of a single index number of 100, which equals the per capita level of industrial goods in Great Britain (and Ireland) in 1900. Every number in the table is thus a percentage of the 1900 level in Britain and is directly comparable with other numbers. The countries are listed in roughly the order that they began to use large-scale, power-driven technology.

What does this overview tell us? First, one sees in the first column that in 1750 all countries were fairly close together, including non-Western areas such as China and India. Both China and India had been extremely important players in early modern world trade, earning high profits from exporting their luxury goods.

However, the column headed 1800 shows that Britain had opened up a noticeable lead over all countries by 1800, and that gap progressively widened as the British Industrial Revolution accelerated to 1830 and reached full maturity by 1860.

Second, the table shows that the countries of continental Europe and the United States began to emulate the British model successfully over the nineteenth century, with significant variations in the timing and in the extent of industrialization. Belgium, achieving independence from the Netherlands in 1831 and rich in iron and coal, led in adopting Britain's new technology, and it experienced a truly revolutionary surge between 1830 and 1860. France developed factory production more gradually, and most historians now detect no burst in French mechanization and no acceleration in the growth of overall industrial output that may accurately be called revolutionary. Its slow but steady growth was overshadowed by the spectacular rise of Germany and the United States after 1860 in what has been termed the "second industrial revolution." In general, eastern and southern Europe began the process of modern industrialization later than northwestern and central Europe. Nevertheless, these regions made real progress in the late nineteenth century, as growth after 1880 in Austria-Hungary, Italy, and Russia suggests.

Finally, the late but substantial industrialization in eastern and southern Europe meant that all European states as well as the United States managed to raise per capita industrial levels in the nineteenth century. These increases stood in stark contrast to the decreases that occurred at the same time in many non-Western countries, most notably in China and India as Table 23.1 shows. European countries industrialized to a greater or lesser extent even as most of the non-Western world stagnated. Japan, which is not included in this table, stands out as an exceptional area of non-Western industrial growth in the second half of the nineteenth century. After the forced opening of the country to the West in the 1850s, Japanese entrepreneurs began to adopt Western technology and manufacturing methods, resulting in a production boom by the late nineteenth century (see Chapter 26). Differential rates of wealth- and power-creating industrial development, which heightened disparities within Europe, also greatly magnified existing inequalities between Europe and the rest of the world (see Chapter 25).

The Challenge of Industrialization in Continental Europe

The different patterns of industrial development suggest that the process of industrialization was far from automatic. To be sure, throughout Europe the eighteenth century was an era of agricultural improvement, population increase, expanding foreign trade, and growing cottage industry. Thus, when the pace of British industry began to accelerate in the 1780s, continental businesses began to adopt the new methods as they proved their profitability. British industry enjoyed clear superiority, but at first the European continent was close behind.

By 1815, however, the situation was quite different. No wars in the early industrial period had been fought on British soil, so Britain did not experience nearly as much physical destruction or economic dislocation as Europe did. Rather, British industry maintained the momentum of the 1780s and continued to grow and improve between 1789 and 1815. On the European continent, by contrast, the upheavals that began with the French Revolution disrupted trade, created runaway inflation, and fostered social anxiety. War severed normal communications with Britain, severely handicapping continental efforts to use new British machinery and technology. Thus France and the rest of Europe were further behind Britain in 1815 than in 1789.

This widening gap made it more difficult, if not impossible, for other countries to follow the British pattern in energy and industry after peace was restored in 1815. Above all, in the newly mechanized industries, British goods were being produced very economically, and these goods had come to dominate world markets completely. In addition, British technology had become so advanced and complicated that very few engineers or skilled technicians outside England understood it. Moreover, the technology of steam power had grown much more expensive. It involved large investments in the iron and coal industries and, after 1830, required the existence of railroads. Continental businesspeople had great difficulty finding the large sums of money the new methods demanded, and laborers bitterly resisted the move to working in factories. All these factors slowed the spread of modern industry (Map 23.2).

After 1815, however, European countries had at least three important advantages. First, most had a rich tradition of putting-out enterprise, merchant capitalists, and skilled urban artisans. Such a tradition gave their firms the ability to adapt and survive in the face of new market conditions. Second, continental capitalists did not need to develop their own advanced technology. Instead, they could simply "borrow" the new methods developed in Great Britain, as well as the engineers and some of the financial resources they lacked. European countries such as France and Russia also had a third asset that many non-Western areas lacked in the nineteenth century: they had strong, independent governments that did not fall under foreign political control. These governments would eventually use the power of the state to promote industry and catch up with Britain.

Agents of Industrialization

The British realized the great value of their technical discoveries and tried to keep their secrets to themselves. Until 1825 it was illegal for artisans and skilled mechanics to leave Britain; until 1843 the export of textile machinery and other equipment was forbidden. Many talented, ambitious workers, however, slipped out of the country illegally and introduced the new methods abroad.

One such man was William Cockerill, a Lancashire carpenter. He and his sons began building cotton-spinning equipment in French-occupied Belgium in 1799. In 1817 the most famous son, John Cockerill, built a large industrial enterprise in Liège in southern Belgium, which produced machinery, steam engines, and then railway locomotives. He also established modern ironworks and coal mines.

Cockerill's plants in the Liège area became an industrial nerve center for the gathering and transmitting of industrial information across Europe. Many skilled British workers came to work for Cockerill, and some went on to found their own companies throughout Europe. Newcomers brought the latest industrial plans and secrets from Britain, so Cockerill could boast that ten days after an industrial advance occurred in Britain, he knew all about it in Belgium.

Thus British technicians and skilled workers were a powerful force in the spread of early industrialization. A second agent of industrialization consisted of talented entrepreneurs such as Fritz Harkort (1793–1880), a pioneer in the German machinery industry. Serving in England as a Prussian army officer during the Napoleonic wars, Harkort was impressed and enchanted with what he saw. He concluded that Germany had to match all these English achievements as

☐ Mapping the Past

MAP 23.2 Continental Industrialization, ca. 1850 Although continental countries were beginning to make progress by 1850, they still lagged far behind Britain. For example, continental railroad building was still in an early stage, whereas the British rail system was essentially complete (see Map 23.1). Coal played a critical role in nineteenth-century industrialization both as a power source for steam engines and as a raw material for making iron and steel.

ANALYZING THE MAP Locate the major exposed (that is, known) coal deposits in 1850. Which countries and areas appear rich in coal resources, and which appear poor? Is there a difference between northern and southern Europe?

CONNECTIONS What is the relationship between known coal deposits and emerging industrial areas in continental Europe? In England (see Map 23.1)?

quickly as possible. Setting up shop in the Ruhr Valley, Harkort felt an almost religious calling to build steam engines.

Lacking skilled laborers, Harkort turned to England for experienced, though expensive, mechanics. Getting materials was also difficult. He had to import the thick iron boilers that he needed from England at great cost. In spite of all these problems, Harkort succeeded in building and selling engines. His ambitious efforts over sixteen years also resulted in large financial losses for

himself and his partners. His career illustrates both the great efforts of a few important business leaders to duplicate the British achievement and the difficulty of the task.

Entrepreneurs like Harkort were obviously exceptional. Most continental businesses adopted factory technology slowly, and handicraft methods lived on. Indeed, continental industrialization usually brought substantial but uneven expansion of handicraft industry in both rural and urban areas for a time. Artisan production of luxury items grew in France as the rising income of the international middle class created increased foreign demand for silk scarves, embroidered needlework, perfumes, and fine wines.

Government Support and Corporate Banking

Another major force in the spread of industrialization throughout Europe was government, which often helped business people in continental countries to overcome some of their difficulties. **Tariff protection** was one such support, and it proved to be important. For example, after Napoleon's wars ended in 1815, France was suddenly flooded with cheaper and better British goods. The French government responded by laying high tariffs on many British imports in order to protect the French economy. After 1815 continental governments bore the cost of building roads and canals to improve transportation. They also bore to a significant extent the cost of building railroads. Belgium led the way in the 1830s and 1840s. Built rapidly as a unified network, Belgium's state-owned railroads stimulated the development of heavy industry and made the country an early industrial leader.

The Prussian government provided another kind of invaluable support. It guaranteed that the state treasury would pay the interest and principal on railroad bonds if the closely regulated private companies in Prussia were unable to do so. In France the state shouldered all the expense of acquiring and laying roadbed, including bridges and tunnels. In short, governments helped pay for railroads, the all-important leading sector in continental industrialization.

The career of German journalist and thinker Friedrich List (1789–1846) reflects government's greater role in industrialization on the European continent than in England. List considered the growth of modern industry of the utmost importance because manufacturing was a primary means of increasing people's well-being and relieving their poverty. Moreover, List was a dedicated nationalist. He wrote that the "wider the gap between the backward and advanced nations becomes, the more dangerous it is to remain behind." To promote industry was to defend the nation.

The practical policies that List focused on were railroad building and the tariff. List supported the formation of a customs union, or *Zollverein* (TSOL-fehrign), among the separate German states. Such a tariff union came into being in 1834, allowing goods to move between the German member states without tariffs, while erecting a single uniform tariff against other nations. List wanted a high protective tariff, which would encourage infant industries, allowing them to develop and eventually hold their own against their more ad-

> **"** The wider the gap between the backward and advanced nations becomes, the more dangerous it is to remain behind. **"**
>
> **FRIEDRICH LIST**

vanced British counterparts. He denounced the British doctrine of free trade as part of Britain's attempt to dominate the entire world:

> At no other epoch has the world seen a manufacturing and commercial power possessing such immense resources as those in the hands of the power which now holds sway [Britain] so consistently selfish. It is absorbing with untiring energy the manufacturing and commercial industries of the world and the important colonies, and it is making the rest of the world, like the Hindus, its serfs in all industrial and commercial relations.[5]

By the 1840s List's **economic nationalism**, designed to protect and develop the national economy, had become increasingly popular in Germany and elsewhere.

Finally, banks, like governments, also played a larger and more creative role on the continent than in Britain. Previously, almost all banks in Europe had been private. Because of the possibility of unlimited financial loss, the partners of private banks tended to be conservative and were content to deal with a few rich clients and a few big merchants. They generally avoided industrial investment as being too risky.

In the 1830s two important Belgian banks pioneered in a new direction. They received permission from the growth-oriented government to establish themselves as corporations enjoying limited liability. That is, if the bank went bankrupt, stockholders could now lose only their original investments in the bank's common stock, and they could not be forced by the courts to pay for any additional losses out of other property they owned. Limited liability helped these Belgian banks attract investors. They mobilized impressive resources for investment in big companies, became industrial banks, and successfully promoted industrial development.

Similar corporate banks became important in France and Germany in the 1850s and 1860s. Usually working in collaboration with governments, corporate

- **tariff protection** A government's way of supporting and aiding its own economy by laying high taxes on imported goods from other countries, as when the French responded to cheaper British goods flooding their country by imposing high tariffs on some imported products.
- **economic nationalism** Policies aimed at protecting and developing a country's economy.

A German Ironworks, 1845 The Borsig ironworks in Berlin mastered the new British method of smelting iron ore with coke. Germany, especially the state of Prussia, was well endowed with both iron and coal, and the rapid exploitation of these resources after 1840 transformed a poor agricultural country into an industrial powerhouse. (akg-images)

banks established and developed many railroads and many companies working in heavy industry, which were also increasingly organized as limited liability corporations.

The combined efforts of skilled workers, entrepreneurs, governments, and industrial banks meshed successfully between 1850 and the financial crash of 1873. In Belgium, Germany, and France, key indicators of modern industrial development—such as railway mileage, iron and coal production, and steam-engine capacity—increased at average annual rates of 5 to 10 percent. As a result, rail networks were completed in western and much of central Europe, and the leading continental countries mastered the industrial technologies that had first been developed in Great Britain. In the early 1870s Britain was still Europe's most industrial nation, but a select handful of countries were closing the gap that had been opened by the Industrial Revolution.

The Situation Outside of Europe

The Industrial Revolution did not extend outside of Europe prior to the 1870s, with the exception of the United States and Japan, both early adopters of British practices. In many countries, national governments and pioneering entrepreneurs did make efforts to adopt the technologies and methods of production that had proved so successful in Britain, but they fell short of transitioning to an industrial economy. For example, in Russia the imperial government brought steamships to the Volga River and a railroad to the capital, St. Petersburg, in the first decades of the nineteenth century. By mid-century ambitious entrepreneurs had established steam-powered cotton factories using imported British machines. However, these advances did not lead to overall industrialization of the country, most of whose people remained mired in rural servitude. Instead, Russia confirmed its role as provider of raw materials, especially timber and grain, to the hungry West.

Egypt similarly began an ambitious program of modernization in the first decades of the nineteenth century, which included the use of imported British technology and experts in textile manufacture and other industries (see page 770). These industries, however, could not compete with lower-priced European imports. Like Russia, Egypt fell back on agricultural exports to European markets, like sugar and cotton.

Such examples of faltering efforts at industrialization could be found in many other places in the Middle East, Asia, and Latin America. Where European governments maintained direct or indirect control, they acted to maintain colonial markets as sources for their own products, rather than encouraging the spread of industrialization. In India millions of poor textile workers lost their livelihood because they could not compete with industrially produced British cottons. The arrival of railroads in India in the mid-nineteenth century served the purpose of agricultural rather than industrial development. Latin American countries (discussed in Chapter 27) were distracted from economic concerns by the early-nineteenth-century wars of independence. By the mid-nineteenth century they had adopted steam power for sugar and coffee processing, but as elsewhere these developments led to increased reliance on agricultural crops for export, not a rise in industrial production. As in India, the arrival of cheap British cottons destroyed the pre-existing textile industry that had employed many men and women.

Relations Between Capital and Labor

☐ How did the Industrial Revolution affect people of all social classes, and what measures were taken to improve the conditions of workers?

In Britain, industrial development brought new social relations and intensified long-standing problems between capital and labor. A new group of factory owners and industrial capitalists arose. These men and women and their families strengthened the wealth and size of the middle class, which had previously been made up mainly of merchants and professional people. The demands of modern industry also created a much larger group, the factory workers.

The growth of new occupational groups in industry stimulated thinking about social relations. Often combined with reflections on the French Revolution, this thinking led to the development of a new overarching interpretation—a new paradigm—regarding social relationships. Briefly, this paradigm argued, with considerable success, that individuals were members of economically determined classes that had conflicting interests. Accordingly, the comfortable, well-educated "public" of the eighteenth century came increasingly to see itself as the middle class, and the "people" gradually transformed themselves into the modern working class. And if the new class interpretation was more of a deceptive simplification than a fundamental truth for some critics, it appealed to many because it seemed to explain what was happening. Therefore, conflicting classes existed, in part, because many individuals came to believe they existed and developed an appropriate sense of class feeling—what Marxists call **class-consciousness** (see page 721).

The New Class of Factory Owners

Early industrialists operated in a highly competitive economic system. As the careers of Watt and Harkort illustrate, there were countless production problems, and success and large profits were by no means certain. Manufacturers therefore waged a constant battle to cut their production costs and stay afloat. Much of the profit had to go back into the business for new and better machinery.

Most early industrialists drew upon their families and friends for labor and capital, but they came from a variety of backgrounds. Many, such as Harkort, were from well-established merchant families with rich networks of contacts and support. Others, such as Watt, Wedgwood, and Cockerill, were of modest means, especially in the early days. Artisans and skilled workers of exceptional ability had unparalleled opportunities. Members of ethnic and religious groups who had been discriminated against in the traditional occupations controlled by the landed aristocracy jumped at the new chances and often helped each other. Scots, Quakers, and other Protestant dissenters were tremendously important in Britain; Protestants and Jews dominated banking in Catholic France.

As factories and firms grew larger, opportunities declined, at least in well-developed industries. It became considerably harder for a gifted but poor young mechanic to start a small enterprise and end up as a wealthy manufacturer. Formal education became more important for young men as a means of success and advancement, and formal education at the advanced level was expensive. In Britain by 1830 and in France and Germany by 1860, leading industrialists were more likely to have inherited their well-established enterprises, and they were financially much more secure than their struggling parents had been. They also had a greater sense of class-consciousness; they were fully aware that ongoing industrial development had widened the gap between themselves and their workers.

The wives and daughters of successful businessmen also found fewer opportunities for active participation in Europe's business world. Rather than contributing as vital partners in a family-owned enterprise, as so many middle-class women had done, these women were increasingly valued for their ladylike gentility. By 1850 some influential women writers and most businessmen assumed that middle-class wives and daughters should steer clear of work in offices and factories. Rather, a middle-class lady should concentrate on her proper role as wife and mother, preferably in an elegant residential area far removed from ruthless commerce and the volatile working class.

• **class-consciousness** An individual's sense of class differentiation.

□ Picturing the Past

Ford Maddox Brown, *Work* This midcentury painting provides a rich and realistic visual representation of the new concepts of social class that became common by 1850. (Birmingham Museums and Art Gallery/ The Bridgeman Art Library)

ANALYZING THE IMAGE Describe the different types of work shown. What different social classes are depicted, and what kinds of work and leisure are the members of the different social classes engaged in?

CONNECTIONS What does this painting and its title suggest about the artist's opinion of the work of common laborers?

The New Factory Workers

The social consequences of the Industrial Revolution have long been hotly debated. The condition of British workers during the transformation has always generated the most controversy among historians because Britain was the first country to industrialize and because the social consequences seemed harshest there.

From the beginning, the Industrial Revolution in Britain had its critics. Among the first were the romantic poets. William Blake (1757–1827) called the early factories "satanic mills" and protested against the hard life of the London poor. William Wordsworth (1770–1850) lamented the destruction of the rural way of life and the pollution of the land and water. Some handicraft workers — notably the **Luddites**, who attacked factories in northern England in 1812 and after — smashed the new machines, which they believed were putting them out of work. Doctors and reformers wrote of problems in the factories and new towns, while Malthus and Ricardo concluded that workers would earn only enough to stay alive.

This pessimistic view was accepted and reinforced by Friedrich Engels (1820–1895), the future revolutionary and colleague of Karl Marx. After studying conditions in northern England, this young middle-class German published in 1844 *The Condition of the Working Class in England*, a blistering indictment of the middle classes. "At the bar of world opinion," he wrote, "I charge the English middle classes with mass murder, wholesale robbery, and all the other crimes in the calendar." The new poverty of industrial workers was worse than the old poverty of cottage workers and agricultural laborers, according to Engels. The culprit was industrial capitalism, with its relentless competition and constant technical change. Engels's extremely influential charge of middle-class exploitation and increasing worker poverty was embellished by Marx and later socialists.

Meanwhile, other observers believed that conditions were improving for the working people. In 1835 in his study of the cotton industry, Andrew Ure wrote that conditions in most factories were not harsh and were even quite good. Edwin Chadwick, a government official well acquainted with the problems of the working population, concluded that the "whole mass of the laboring community" was increasingly able "to buy more of the necessities and minor luxuries of life."[6] Nevertheless, those who thought conditions were getting worse for working people were probably in the majority.

Historians' studies of statistics from this period have weakened the idea that the condition of the working class got much worse with industrialization. But the most recent scholarship also confirms the view that the early years of the Industrial Revolution were hard ones for British workers. There was little or no increase in the purchasing power of the average British worker from about 1780 to about 1820. Only after 1820, and especially after 1840, did real wages rise substantially, so that the average worker earned and consumed roughly 50 percent more in real terms in 1850 than in 1770.[7] In short, there was considerable economic improvement for workers throughout Great Britain by 1850, but that improvement was hard won and slow in coming.

This important conclusion must be qualified, however. First, the number of hours in the average workweek increased. Thus, to a large extent, workers earned more because they worked more. In England nonagricultural workers labored about 250 days per year in 1760 as compared to 300 days per year in 1830, while the normal workday remained an exhausting eleven hours throughout the entire period. In 1760 nonagricultural workers still observed many religious and public holidays by not working, and many workers took Monday off. These days of leisure and relaxation declined rapidly after 1760, and by 1830 nonagricultural workers had joined landless agricultural laborers in toiling six rather than five days a week.[8]

Second, the wartime decline in the average worker's real wages and standard of living from 1792 to 1815 had a powerful negative impact on workers. These difficult war years, with more unemployment and sharply higher prices for bread, were formative years for the new factory labor force, and they colored the early experience of modern industrial life in somber tones.

Another way to consider the workers' standard of living is to look at the goods that they purchased. Again the evidence is somewhat contradictory. Speaking generally, workers ate somewhat more food of higher nutritional quality as the Industrial Revolution progressed. Diets became more varied; people ate more potatoes, dairy products, fruits, and vegetables. Clothing improved, but housing for working people probably deteriorated somewhat. In short, per capita use of specific goods supports the position that the standard of living of the working classes rose, at least moderately, after the long wars with France.

Work in Early Factories

What about working conditions? Did workers eventually earn more only at the cost of working longer and harder? Were workers exploited harshly by the new factory owners?

The first factories were cotton mills, which began functioning in the 1770s along fast-running rivers and streams and were often located in sparsely populated areas. Cottage workers in the vicinity, accustomed to the putting-out system, were reluctant to work in the new factories even when they received relatively good wages because factory work was unappealing. In a factory, workers had to keep up with the machine and follow its relentless tempo. Moreover, they had to show up every day, on time, and work long, monotonous hours under the constant supervision of demanding overseers, and they were punished systematically if they broke the work rules. For example, if a worker was late to work, or accidentally spoiled material, or nodded off late in the day, the employer imposed fines that were deducted from the weekly pay. Children and adolescents were often beaten for their infractions.

Cottage workers were not used to that kind of life and discipline. All members of the family worked hard and long, but in spurts, setting their own pace. They could interrupt their work when they wanted to. Women and children could break up their long hours of spinning with other tasks. On Saturday afternoon the head of the family delivered the week's work to the merchant manufacturer and got paid. Saturday night was a time of relaxation and drinking, especially for the men.

Also, early factories resembled English poorhouses, where totally destitute people went to live at public expense. Some poorhouses were industrial prisons, where the inmates had to work in order to receive their food and lodging. The similarity between large brick factories and large stone poorhouses increased the cottage workers' fear of factories and their hatred of factory discipline. It was cottage workers' reluctance to work in factories that prompted the early cotton mill owners

• **Luddites** Group of handicraft workers who attacked factories in northern England in 1812 and after, smashing the new machines that they believed were putting them out of work.

Workers at a U.S. Mill Female workers at a U.S. cotton mill in 1890 take a break from operating belt-driven weaving machines to pose for this photograph, accompanied by their male supervisor. The first textile mills, established in the 1820s in Massachusetts, employed local farm girls. As competition intensified, conditions deteriorated and the mills increasingly relied on immigrant women who had few alternatives to the long hours, noise, and dangers of factory work. By 1900, more than one million women worked in factories in the United States. (Courtesy of George Eastman House, International Museum of Photography and Film, GEH neg. 14250)

to turn to abandoned and pauper children for their labor. As we have seen, these owners contracted with local officials to employ large numbers of such children, who had no say in the matter. In the eighteenth century semi-forced child labor seemed necessary and was socially accepted. From our modern point of view, it was cruel exploitation and a blot on the record of the new industrial system.

Working Families and Children

By the 1790s the early pattern was rapidly changing. The use of pauper apprentices was in decline, and in 1802 it was forbidden by Parliament. Many more textile factories were being built, mainly in urban areas,

where they could use steam power rather than waterpower and attract a workforce more easily than in the countryside. As a result, people came from near and far to work in the cities, both as factory workers and as laborers, builders, and domestic servants. Yet as they took these new jobs, working people did not simply give in and accept the highly disciplined system of labor. Rather, they helped modify the system by carrying over old, familiar working traditions.

For one thing, workers often came to the mills and the mines as family units. This was how they had worked on farms and in the putting-out system. The mill or mine owner bargained with the head of the family and paid him or her for the work of the whole family. In the cotton mills, children worked for their mothers or fathers, collecting scraps and "piecing" broken threads together. In the mines, children sorted coal and worked the ventilation equipment. Their mothers hauled coal in the tunnels below the surface, while their fathers hewed with pick and shovel at the face of the seam.

The preservation of the family as an economic unit in the factories from the 1790s on made the new surroundings more tolerable, both in Great Britain and in other countries, during the early stages of industrialization. Parents disciplined their children, making firm measures socially acceptable, and directed their upbringing. The presence of the whole family meant that children and adults worked the same long hours (twelve-hour shifts were normal in cotton mills in 1800). Adult workers were not particularly interested in limiting the minimum working age or hours of their children as long as family members worked side by side. Only when technical changes threatened to place control and discipline in the hands of impersonal managers and overseers did adult workers protest against inhuman conditions in the name of their children.

Some enlightened employers and social reformers in Parliament definitely felt otherwise. They argued that more humane standards were necessary, and they used widely circulated parliamentary reports to influence public opinion. For example, Robert Owen (1771–1858), a successful manufacturer in Scotland, testified in 1816 before an investigating committee on the basis of his experience. He argued that employing children under ten years of age as factory workers was "injurious to the children, and not beneficial to the proprietors."[9] Workers also provided graphic testimony at such hearings as the reformers pressed Parliament to pass corrective laws. They scored some important successes.

Their most significant early accomplishment was the **Factory Act of 1833**. It limited the factory workday of children between nine and thirteen to eight hours and that of adolescents between fourteen and eighteen to twelve hours. Children under nine were to be enrolled in the elementary schools that factory owners were required to establish. The employment of children declined rapidly. Thus the Factory Act broke the pattern of whole families working together in the factory because efficiency required standardized shifts for all workers.

Ties of blood and kinship were important in other ways in Great Britain in the formative years between about 1790 and 1840. Many manufacturers and builders hired workers through subcontractors. They paid the subcontractors on the basis of what the subcontractors and their crews produced. Subcontractors in turn hired and fired their own workers, many of whom were friends and relations. The subcontractor might be as harsh as the greediest capitalist, but the relationship between subcontractor and work crew was close

and personal. This kind of personal relationship had traditionally existed in cottage industry and in urban crafts, and it was more acceptable to many workers than impersonal factory discipline.

Ties of kinship were particularly important for newcomers, who often traveled great distances to find work. Many urban workers in Great Britain were from Ireland. Forced out of rural Ireland by population growth and deteriorating economic conditions from 1817 on, Irish in search of jobs took what they could get. As early as 1824 most of the workers in the Glasgow cotton mills were Irish; in 1851 one-sixth of the population of Liverpool was Irish. Like many other immigrant groups held together by ethnic and religious ties, the Irish worked together, formed their own neighborhoods, and not only survived but also thrived.

The Sexual Division of Labor

The era of the Industrial Revolution witnessed major changes in the sexual division of labor. In preindustrial Europe most people worked in family units. By tradition, certain jobs were defined by gender, but many tasks might go to either sex. Family employment carried over into early factories and subcontracting, but by the 1830s it was collapsing as child labor was restricted and new attitudes emerged. A different sexual division of labor gradually arose to take its place. By 1850 the man was emerging as the family's primary wage earner, while the married woman found only limited job opportunities. Generally denied good jobs at high wages in the growing urban economy, women were expected to concentrate on housework, raising the children, and some craftwork at home.

This new pattern of **separate spheres** had several aspects. First, all studies agree that married women from the working classes were much less likely to work full-time for wages outside the house after the first child arrived, although they often earned small amounts doing putting-out handicrafts at home and taking in boarders. Second, when married women did work for wages outside the house, they usually came from the poorest families, where the husbands were poorly paid, sick, unemployed, or missing. Third, these poor married or widowed women were joined by legions of young unmarried women, who worked full-time but only in certain jobs, of which textile factory work, laundering, and domestic service were particularly important. Fourth, all women were generally confined to

- **Factory Act of 1833** English law that led to a sharp decline in the employment of children by limiting the hours that children over age nine could work and requiring younger children to attend factory-run elementary schools.

- **separate spheres** A gender division of labor with the wife at home as mother and homemaker and the husband as wage earner.

Viewpoints

Women's Role in Industrialized Europe

• *Higher wages for men during the Industrial Revolution contributed to social changes that encouraged the nineteenth-century ideology of separate spheres, which emphasized the importance of women's role of caretaker of the domestic realm. Sarah Stickney Ellis's "The Women of England: Their Social Duties and Domestic Habits," excerpted below, was one of a flood of publications offering middle-class women household advice. For the vast majority of European women and children, however, life still included hard toil. As middle-class reformers began to investigate working-class living conditions, they were shocked by what they found. The second document comes from an 1845 interview of doctors by a reformer in a German industrial city.*

Sarah Stickney Ellis, "The Women of England: Their Social Duties and Domestic Habits," 1839

"What shall I do to gratify myself—to be admired—or to vary the tenor of my existence?" are not the questions which a woman of right feelings asks awaking to the avocations of the day. Much more congenial to the highest attributes of woman's character, are inquiries such as these: "How shall I endeavor through this day to turn the time, the health, and the means permitted me to enjoy, to the best account? Is any one sick, I must visit their chamber without delay, and try to give their apartment an air of comfort, by arranging such things as the wearied nurse may not have thought of. Is any one about to set off on a journey, I must see that the early meal is spread, to prepare it with my own hands, in order that the servant, who was working late last night, may profit by unbroken rest. Did I fail in what was kind or considerate to any of the family yesterday; I will meet her this morning with a cordial welcome, and show, in the most delicate way I can, that I am anxious to atone for the past. Was any one exhausted by the last day's exertion, I will be an hour before them this morning, and let them see that their labor is so much in advance. Or, if nothing extraordinary occurs to claim my attention, I will meet the family with a consciousness that, being the least engaged of any member of it, I am consequently the most at liberty to devote myself to the general good of the whole, by cultivating cheerful conversation, adapting myself to the prevailing tone of feeling, and leading those who are least happy, to think and speak of what will make them more so."

1845 Interview Concerning the Lives of Women and Children in a German Industrial City

Question: What is your usual experience regarding the cleanliness of these classes?

Dr. Bluemner: Bad! Mother has to go out to work, and can therefore pay little attention to the domestic economy, and even if she makes an effort, she lacks time and means. A typical woman of this kind has four children, of whom she is still suckling one, she has to look after the whole household, to take food to her husband at work, perhaps a quarter of a mile away on a building site; she therefore has no time for cleaning and then it is such a small hole inhabited by so many people. The children are left to themselves, crawl about the floor or in the streets, and are always dirty; they lack the necessary clothing to change more often, and there is no time or money to wash these frequently. There are, of course, gradations; if the mother is healthy, active and clean, and if the poverty is not too great, then things are better.

Question: What is the state of health among the lower class? . . .

Dr. Kalckstein: . . . The dwellings of the working classes mostly face the yards and courts. The small quantity of fresh air admitted by the surrounding buildings is vitiated by the emanations from stables and middens [garbage heaps]. Further, because of the higher rents, people are forced to share their dwellings and to overcrowd them. The adults escape the worst influences by leaving the dwellings during the day, but the children are exposed to it with its whole force.

Sources: Sarah Stickney Ellis, "The Women of England: Their Social Duties and Domestic Habits," in Walter Arnstein, ed., *The Past Speaks*, 2d ed. (Lexington, Mass.: D. C. Heath, 1993), 2:172–175; Laura L. Frader, ed., *The Industrial Revolution: A History in Documents* (Oxford, U.K.: Oxford University Press, 2006), p. 85.

QUESTIONS FOR ANALYSIS

1. What daily tasks and duties does Sarah Stickney Ellis prescribe for the mother of the family?

2. Based on the second document, what obstacles to achieving the ideals prescribed by Stickney Ellis existed for working-class women? To what extent do the doctors seem to blame the women themselves for their situation?

low-paying, dead-end jobs. Evolving gradually, but largely in place by 1850, the new sexual division of labor in Britain constituted a major development in the history of women and of the family. (See "Viewpoints: Women's Role in Industrialized Europe," page 706.)

If the reorganization of paid work along gender lines is widely recognized, there is no agreement on its causes. One school of scholars sees little connection with industrialization and finds the answer in the deeply ingrained sexist attitudes that predated the economic transformation. These scholars stress the role of male-dominated craft unions in denying working women access to good jobs and relegating them to unpaid housework. Other scholars, stressing that the gender roles of women and men can vary enormously with time and culture, look more to a combination of economic and biological factors in order to explain the emergence of a sex-segregated division of labor.

Three ideas stand out in this more recent interpretation. First, the new and unfamiliar discipline of the clock and the machine was especially hard on married women of the laboring classes. Above all, relentless factory discipline conflicted with child care in a way that labor on the farm or in the cottage had not. A woman operating earsplitting spinning machinery could mind a child of seven or eight working beside her (until such work was outlawed), but she could no longer pace herself through pregnancy or breast-feed her baby on the job. Thus a working-class woman had strong incentives to concentrate on child care within her home if her family could afford it.

Second, running a household in conditions of primitive urban poverty was an extremely demanding job in its own right. There were no supermarkets or public transportation. Shopping and feeding the family constituted a never-ending challenge. Taking on a brutal job outside the house—a "second shift"—had limited appeal for the average married woman from the working class. Thus many women might well have accepted the emerging division of labor as the best available strategy for family survival in the industrializing society.[10]

Third, why were the young, generally unmarried women who did work for wages outside the home segregated and confined to certain "women's jobs"? No doubt the desire of males to monopolize the best opportunities and hold women down provides part of the answer. Yet as some feminist scholars have argued, sex-segregated employment was also a collective response to the new industrial system. Previously, at least in theory, young people worked under a watchful parental eye. The growth of factories and mines brought unheard-of opportunities for girls and boys to mix on the job, free of familial supervision. Such opportunities led to more unplanned pregnancies and fueled the illegitimacy explosion that had begun in the late eigh-

teenth century and that gathered force until at least 1850. Thus segregation of jobs by gender was partly an effort by older people to help control the sexuality of working-class youths.

Investigations into the British coal industry before 1842 provide a graphic example of this concern. (See "Listening to the Past: The Testimony of Young Mine Workers," page 708.) The middle-class men leading the inquiry, who expected their daughters and wives to pursue ladylike activities, often failed to appreciate the physical effort of the girls and women who dragged with belt and chain the heavy carts of coal along narrow underground passages. But they professed horror at the sight of girls and women working without shirts, which was a common practice because of the heat, and they quickly assumed the prevalence of licentious sex with the male miners, who also wore very little clothing. In fact, most girls and married women worked for related males in a family unit that provided considerable protection and restraint. Yet many witnesses from the working class also believed that the mines were inappropriate and dangerous places for women and girls. Some miners stressed particularly the danger of sexual aggression for girls working past puberty. As one explained, "I consider it a scandal for girls to work in the pits. Till they are 12 or 14 they may work very well but after that it's an abomination. . . . The work of the pit does not hurt them, it is the effect on their morals that I complain of."[11] The **Mines Act of 1842** prohibited underground work for all women and girls as well as for boys under ten.

Some women who had to support themselves protested against being excluded from coal mining, which paid higher wages than most other jobs open to working-class women. But provided they were part of families that could manage economically, the girls and the women who had worked underground were generally pleased with the law. In explaining her satisfaction in 1844, one mother of four provided real insight into why many married working women accepted the emerging sexual division of labor:

> While working in the pit I was worth to my [miner] husband seven shillings a week, out of which we had to pay 2½ shillings to a woman for looking after the younger children. I used to take them to her house at 4 o'clock in the morning, out of their own beds, to put them into hers. Then there was one shilling a week for washing; besides, there was mending to pay for, and other things. The house was not guided. The other children broke things; they did not go to school when they were sent; they would be playing about,

• **Mines Act of 1842** English law prohibiting underground work for all women and girls as well as for boys under ten.

Listening to the Past

The Testimony of Young Mine Workers

The use of child labor in British industrialization quickly attracted the attention of humanitarians and social reformers. This interest led to investigations by parliamentary commissions, which resulted in laws limiting the hours and the ages of children working in large factories. Designed to build a case for remedial legislation, parliamentary inquiries gave large numbers of workers a rare chance to speak directly to contemporaries and to historians.

The moving passages that follow are taken from testimony gathered in 1841 and 1842 by the Ashley Mines Commission. Interviewing employers and many male and female workers, the commissioners focused on the physical condition of the youth and on the sexual behavior of workers far underground. The subsequent Mines Act of 1842 sought to reduce immoral behavior and sexual bullying by prohibiting underground work for all women and girls (and for boys younger than ten).

Mr. Payne, Coal Master

❝That children are employed generally at nine years old in the coal pits and sometimes at eight. In fact, the smaller the vein of coal is in height, the younger and smaller are the children required; the work occupies from six to seven hours per day in the pits; they are not ill-used or worked beyond their strength; a good deal of depravity exists but they are certainly not worse in morals than in other branches of the Sheffield trade, but upon the whole superior; the morals of this district are materially improving; Mr. Bruce, the clergyman, has been zealous and active in endeavoring to ameliorate their moral and religious education....❞

Ann Eggley, Hurrier, 18 Years Old

❝I'm sure I don't know how to spell my name. We go at four in the morning, and sometimes at half-past four. We begin to work as soon as we get down. We get out after four, sometimes at five, in the evening. We work the whole time except an hour for dinner, and sometimes we haven't time to eat. I hurry [move coal wagons underground] by myself, and have done so for long. I know the corves [small coal wagons] are very heavy, they are the biggest corves anywhere about. The work is far too hard for me; the sweat runs off me all over sometimes. I am very tired at night. Sometimes when we get home at night we have not power to wash us, and then we go to bed. Sometimes we fall asleep in the chair. Father said last night it was both a shame and a disgrace for girls to work as we do, but there was naught else for us to do. I began to hurry when I was seven and I have been hurrying ever since. I have been 11 years in the pits. The girls are always tired. I was poorly twice this winter; it was with headache. I hurry for Robert Wiggins; he is not akin to me.... We don't always get enough to eat and drink, but we get a good supper. I have known my father go at two in the morning to work ... and he didn't come out till four. I am quite sure that we work constantly 12 hours except on Saturdays. We wear trousers and our shifts in the pit and great big shoes clinkered and nailed. The girls never work naked to the waist in our pit. The men don't insult us in the pit. The conduct of the girls in the pit is good enough sometimes and sometimes bad enough. I never went to a day-school. I went a little to a Sunday-school, but I soon gave it over. I thought it too bad to be confined both Sundays and week-days. I walk about and get the fresh air on Sundays. I have not learnt to read. I don't know my letters. I never learnt naught. I never go to church or chapel; there is no church or chapel at Gawber, there is none nearer than a mile.... I have never heard that a good man came into the world who was God's son to save sinners. I never heard of Christ at all. Nobody has ever told me about him, nor have my father and mother ever taught me to pray. I know no prayer; I never pray.❞

Patience Kershaw, Age 17

❝My father has been dead about a year; my mother is living and has ten children, five lads and five lasses; the oldest is about thirty, the youngest is four; three lasses go to mill; all the lads are colliers, two getters and three hurriers; one lives and get ill-used by other children, and their clothes torn. Then when I came home in the evening, everything was to do after the day's labor, and I was so tired I had no heart for it; no fire lit, nothing cooked, no water fetched, the house dirty, and nothing comfortable for my husband. It is all far better now, and I wouldn't go down again.[12]

The Early Labor Movement in Britain

Many kinds of employment changed slowly during and after the Industrial Revolution in Great Britain. In 1850 more British people still worked on farms than in any other occupation. The second-largest occupation was domestic service, with more than one million at home and does nothing; mother does nought but look after home.

All my sisters have been hurriers, but three went to the mill. Alice went because her legs swelled from hurrying in cold water when she was hot. I never went to day-school; I go to Sunday-school, but I cannot read or write; I go to pit at five o'clock in the morning and come out at five in the evening; I get my breakfast of porridge and milk first; I take my dinner with me, a cake, and eat it as I go; I do not stop or rest any time for the purpose; I get nothing else until I get home, and then have potatoes and meat, not every day meat. I hurry in the clothes I have now got on, trousers and ragged jacket; the bald place upon my head is made by thrusting the corves; my legs have never swelled, but sisters' did when they went to mill; I hurry the corves a mile and more under ground and back; they weigh 300 cwt.;* I hurry 11 a day; I wear a belt and chain at the workings to get the corves out; the putters [miners] that I work for are *naked* except their caps; they pull off all their clothes; I see them at work when I go up; sometimes they beat me, if I am not quick enough, with their hands; they strike me upon my back; the boys take liberties with me, sometimes, they pull me about; I am the only girl in the pit; there are about 20 boys and 15 men; all the men are naked; I would rather work in mill than in coal-pit. **99**

Isabel Wilson, Coal Putter, 38 Years Old

66 When women have children thick [fast] they are compelled to take them down early. I have been married 19 years and have had 10 bairns [children]; seven are in life. When on Sir

*An old English unit of weight equaling 112 pounds.

John's work was a carrier of coals, which caused me to miscarry five times from the strains, and was gai [very] ill after each. Putting is no so oppressive; last child was born on Saturday morning, and I was at work on the Friday night.

Once met with an accident; a coal brake my cheek-bone, which kept me idle some weeks. I have wrought below 30 years, and so has the guid man; he is getting touched in the breath now.

None of the children read, as the work is no regular. I did read once, but no able to attend to it now; when I go below lassie 10 years of age keeps house and makes the broth or stir-about. **99**

Source: *Voices of the Industrial Revolution: Selected Readings from the Liberal Economists and Their Critics*, pp. 87–90, edited by J. Bowditch and C. Ramsland. Copyright © 1961, 1989 by the University of Michigan. Reprinted by permission of the publisher.

QUESTIONS FOR ANALYSIS

1. How does Payne's testimony compare with that of Ann Eggley and Patience Kershaw?

2. Describe the work of Eggley, Kershaw, and Wilson. What strikes you most about the testimonies of these workers?

3. The witnesses were responding to questions from middle-class commissioners. What did the commissioners seem interested in? Why?

household servants, 90 percent of whom were women. Thus many old, familiar jobs outside industry lived on and provided alternatives for individual workers. This helped ease the transition to industrial civilization.

Within industry itself, the pattern of artisans working with hand tools in small shops remained unchanged in many trades, even as others were revolutionized by technological change. For example, the British iron industry was completely dominated by large-scale capitalist firms by 1850. Many large ironworks had more than one thousand people on their payrolls. Yet the firms that fashioned iron into small metal goods, such as tools, tableware, and toys, employed on average fewer than ten wage workers who used handicraft skills. Only gradually after 1850 did some owners find ways to reorganize some handicraft industries with new machines

Union Membership Certificate This handsome membership certificate belonged to Arthur Watton, a properly trained and certified papermaker of Kings Norton in Birmingham, England. Members of such unions proudly framed their certificates and displayed them in their homes, showing that they were skilled workers. (Courtesy, Sylvia Waddell)

• **Combination Acts** English laws passed in 1799 that outlawed unions and strikes, favoring capitalist business people over skilled artisans. Bitterly resented and widely disregarded by many craft guilds, the acts were repealed by Parliament in 1824.

and new patterns of work. The survival of small workshops gave many workers an alternative to factory employment.

Working-class solidarity and class-consciousness developed in small workshops as well as in large factories. In the northern factory districts, anticapitalist sentiments were frequent by the 1820s. Commenting in 1825 on a strike in the woolen center of Bradford and the support it had gathered from other regions, one paper claimed with pride that "it is all the workers of England against a few masters of Bradford."[13] Modern technology and factory organization had created a few versus the many.

The transformation of some traditional trades by organizational changes, rather than technological innovations, could by themselves also create ill will and class feeling. The classical liberal concept of economic freedom and laissez faire emerged in the late eighteenth century, and it continued to gather strength in the early nineteenth century. In 1799 Parliament passed the **Combination Acts**, which outlawed unions and strikes. In 1813 and 1814 Parliament repealed the old and often disregarded law of 1563 regulating the wages of artisans and the conditions of apprenticeship. As a result of these and other measures, certain skilled artisan workers, such as bootmakers and high-quality tailors, found aggressive capitalists ignoring traditional work rules and trying to flood their trades with unorganized women workers and children to beat down wages.

The capitalist attack on artisan guilds and work rules was bitterly resented by many craftworkers, who subsequently played an important part in Great Britain and in other countries in gradually building a modern labor movement. The Combination Acts were widely disregarded by workers. Printers, papermakers, carpenters, tailors, and other such craftsmen continued to take collective action, and societies of skilled factory workers also organized unions. Unions sought to control the number of skilled workers, to limit apprenticeship to members' own children, and to bargain with owners over wages.

They were not afraid to strike; there was, for example, a general strike of adult cotton spinners in Manchester in 1810. In the face of widespread union activity, Parliament repealed the Combination Acts in 1824, and unions were tolerated, though not fully accepted, after 1825. The next stage in the development of the British trade-union movement was the attempt to create a single large national union. This effort was led not so much by working people as by social reformers such as Robert Owen. Owen, a self-made cotton manufacturer (see page 705), had pioneered in industrial relations by combining firm discipline with concern for the health, safety, and hours of his workers. After 1815 he experimented with cooperative and socialist communities, including one at New Harmony, Indiana. Then in 1834 Owen organized one of the largest and most visionary of the early national unions, the Grand National Consolidated Trades Union.

When Owen's and other grandiose schemes collapsed, the British labor movement moved once again after 1851 in the direction of craft unions. The most famous of these was the Amalgamated Society of Engineers, which represented skilled machinists. These unions won real benefits for members by fairly conservative means and thus became an accepted part of the industrial scene.

British workers also engaged in direct political activity in defense of their own interests. After the collapse of Owen's national trade union, many working people went into the Chartist movement, which sought political democracy. The key Chartist demand — that all men be given the right to vote — became the great hope of millions of aroused people. Workers were also active in campaigns to limit the workday in factories to ten hours and to permit duty-free importation of wheat into Great Britain to secure cheap bread. Thus working people developed a sense of their own identity and played an active role in shaping the new industrial system. They were neither helpless victims nor passive beneficiaries.

The Impact of Slavery

Another mass labor force of the Industrial Revolution was made up of the millions of enslaved men, women, and children who toiled in European colonies in the Caribbean and in North and South America. Historians have long debated the extent to which revenue from slavery contributed to Britain's achievements in the Industrial Revolution. They now agree that profits from colonial plantations and slave trading were a small portion of British income in the eighteenth century and were probably more often invested in land than in industry.

Nevertheless, the impact of slavery on Britain's economy was much broader than direct profits alone. In the mid-eighteenth century the need for items to exchange for colonial cotton, sugar, tobacco, and slaves stimulated demand for British manufactured goods in the Caribbean, North America, and West Africa. Britain's dominance in the slave trade also led to the development of finance and credit institutions that would help early industrialists obtain capital for their businesses. The British Parliament abolished the slave trade in 1807 and freed all slaves in British territories in 1833, but by 1850 most of the cotton processed by British mills was supplied by the coerced labor of slaves in the southern United States. Thus, the Industrial Revolution cannot be detached from the Atlantic world and the misery of slavery it included.

CONNECTIONS

For much of its history, Europe lagged behind older and more sophisticated civilizations in China and the Middle East. There was little reason to predict that the West would one day achieve world dominance. And yet by 1800 Europe had broken ahead of the other regions of the world in terms of wealth and power, a process historians have termed "the Great Divergence."[14]

One important prerequisite for the rise of Europe was its growing control over world trade, first in the Indian Ocean in the sixteenth and seventeenth centuries and then in the eighteenth-century Atlantic world. Acquisition of New World colonies — itself the accidental result of explorers seeking direct access to the rich Afroeurasian trade world — brought Europeans new sources of wealth and raw materials as well as guaranteed markets for their finished goods. A second crucial factor in the rise of Europe was the Industrial Revolution, which by dramatically increasing the pace of production and distribution while reducing their cost, allowed Europeans to control other countries first economically and then politically. Britain dominated this process at first, but was soon followed by other European nations. By the middle of the nineteenth century the gap between Western industrial production and standards of living and those of the non-West had grown dramatically, bringing with it the economic dependence of non-Western nations, meager wages for their largely impoverished populations, and increasingly aggressive Western imperial ambitions (see Chapter 25). In the late nineteenth century non-Western countries began to experience their own processes of industrialization. Today's world is witnessing a surge in productivity in China, India, and other non-Western nations, leading some to question how long Western superiority will endure.

☐ CHAPTER REVIEW

☐ What were the origins of the Industrial Revolution in Britain, and how did it develop between 1780 and 1850? (p. 686)

As markets for manufactured goods increased both domestically and overseas, Britain was able to respond with increased production, largely because of its stable government, abundant natural resources, and flexible labor force. The first factories arose as a result of technical innovations in spinning cotton, thereby revolutionizing the textile industry. The widespread availability and affordability of cotton provided benefits for many, but also resulted in the brutal forced labor of orphaned children on a large scale. The demand for improvements in energy led to innovations and improvements in the steam engine, which transformed the iron industry, among others. In the early nineteenth century transportation of goods was greatly enhanced when railroads were built.

☐ How after 1815 did countries outside of Britain respond to the challenge of industrialization? (p. 695)

For reasons including warfare on home soil and barriers to trade, continental Europe lagged behind England in industrialization in 1815. After 1815 some continental countries, especially France, Belgium, and Germany, gradually built on England's technical breakthroughs, such as textile machinery and steam engines. Entrepreneurs set up their own factories and hired skilled urban workers from the area along with English immigrants experienced in the new technologies. England tried to limit the spread of trade secrets, and financing was difficult for early continental capitalists, but government interventions, such as tariff protection and infrastructure, were a great boon to industrialization on the European continent. In addition, newly established corporate banks worked in conjunction with governments to invest heavily in railroads and other industries. Beginning around 1850 Japan and the United States also began to rapidly industrialize, but generally the Industrial Revolution spread more slowly outside of Europe, as many countries were confined to producing agricultural goods and other

KEY TERMS

Industrial Revolution (p. 687)
spinning jenny (p. 688)
water frame (p. 688)
steam engines (p. 690)
Rocket (p. 693)
Crystal Palace (p. 693)
iron law of wages (p. 695)
tariff protection (p. 699)
economic nationalism (p. 699)
class-consciousness (p. 701)
Luddites (p. 702)
Factory Act of 1833 (p. 705)
separate spheres (p. 705)
Mines Act of 1842 (p. 707)
Combination Acts (p. 710)

raw materials to serve European markets. As a result, the gap between the industrialized West and the rest of the world widened.

☐ How did the Industrial Revolution affect people of all social classes, and what measures were taken to improve the conditions of workers? (p. 701)

The rise of modern industry had a profound impact on people and their lives, beginning in Britain in the late eighteenth century. Industrialization led to the growing size and wealth of the middle class, as factory owners took their place beside successful merchants and professional people. These early entrepreneurs at first came from diverse backgrounds, providing economic opportunities for religious and ethnic minorities, but by the middle of the nineteenth century wealthy industrial families controlled large enterprises, and it was difficult for the poor but talented person to break in. The modern industrial working class also developed during this time, filling the need for vast quantities of labor power. Rigid rules, stern discipline, and long hours weighed heavily on factory workers, and improvements in the standard of living came slowly, but they were substantial by 1850. Workers often labored as family units in early factories, but as restrictions were placed on child labor, married women withdrew increasingly from wage work and concentrated on child care and household responsibilities. At the same time many young women worked before they were married, and jobs for young workers were often separated by gender in an attempt to control sexual behavior. The era of industrialization also fostered new attitudes toward child labor, encouraged protective factory legislation, and called forth a new sense of class feeling and an assertive labor movement.

SUGGESTED READING

Cameron, Rondo, and Larry Neal. *A Concise Economic History of the World*, 4th ed. 2003. Provides an introduction to key issues related to the Industrial Revolution and has a carefully annotated bibliography.

Davidoff, Leonore, and Catherine Hall. *Family Fortunes: Men and Women of the English Middle Class, 1750–1850*, rev. ed. 2003. Examines both economic activities and cultural beliefs with great skill.

Dolan, Brian. *Wedgwood: The First Tycoon*. 2004. A comprehensive study of the famous entrepreneur.

Fuchs, Rachel G. *Gender and Poverty in Nineteenth-Century Europe*. 2005. Provides a broad comparative perspective.

Gaskell, Elizabeth. *Mary Barton*. 1848. Gaskell's famous novel offers a realistic portrayal of the new industrial society.

Goodman, Jordan, and Katrina Honeyman. *Gainful Pursuits: The Making of Industrial Europe, 1600–1914*. 1988. An excellent general treatment of European industrial growth.

Horn, Jeff. *Understanding the Industrial Revolution: Milestones in Business History*. 2007. Clear, concise, and engaging; an excellent work for students.

Kemp, Tom. *Industrialization in Europe*, 2d ed. 1985. A useful overview.

Landes, David. *Dynasties: Fortunes and Misfortunes of the World's Great Family Businesses*. 2006. A collection offering fascinating and insightful histories of famous enterprises and leading capitalists.

Pomeranz, Kenneth. *The Great Divergence: China, Europe, and the Making of the Modern World Economy*. 2000. A sophisticated reconsideration of why western Europe underwent industrialization and China did not.

Stearns, Peter N. *The Industrial Revolution in World History*, 3d ed. 2007. A useful brief survey.

Thompson, E. P. *The Making of the English Working Class*. 1963. A fascinating book in the Marxist tradition that is rich in detail and early working-class lore.

Valenze, Deborah. *The First Industrial Woman*. 1995. A gender study that reinvigorates the debate between optimists and pessimists about the consequences of industrialization in Britain.

Walton, Whitney. *France and the Crystal Palace: Bourgeois Taste and Artisan Manufacture in the 19th Century*. 1992. Examines the gradual transformation of handicraft techniques and their persistent importance in the international economy.

NOTES

1. N. F. R. Crafts, *British Economic Growth During the Industrial Revolution* (Oxford, U.K.: Oxford University Press, 1985), p. 32.

2. Quoted in P. Mantoux, *The Industrial Revolution in the Eighteenth Century* (New York: Harper & Row, 1961), p. 75.

3. P. Bairoch, "International Industrialization Levels from 1750 to 1980," *Journal of European Economic History* 11 (Spring 1982): 269–333.

4. Quoted by J. Bowditch and C. Ramsland, eds., *Voices of the Industrial Revolution* (Ann Arbor: University of Michigan Press, 1961), p. 55, from the fourth edition of Thomas Malthus, *Essay on the Principle of Population* (1807).

5. Friedrich List, *The National System of Political Economy*, trans. G. A. Matile (Philadelphia: J. B. Lippincott, 1856), p. 61; edited slightly.

6. Quoted in W. A. Hayek, ed., *Capitalism and the Historians* (Chicago: University of Chicago Press, 1954), p. 126.

7. Crafts, *British Economic Growth*, p. 95.

8. H.-J. Voth, *Time and Work in England, 1750–1830* (Oxford, U.K.: Oxford University Press, 2000), pp. 268–270; also pp. 118–133.

9. Quoted in E. R. Pike, *"Hard Times": Human Documents of the Industrial Revolution* (New York: Praeger, 1966), p. 109.

10. See especially J. Brenner and M. Rama, "Rethinking Women's Oppression," *New Left Review* 144 (March–April 1984): 33–71, and sources cited there.

11. J. Humphries, ". . . 'The Most Free from Objection' . . . : The Sexual Division of Labor and Women's Work in Nineteenth-century England," *Journal of Economic History* 47 (December 1987): 941; Pike, *"Hard Times,"* p. 266.

12. Quoted in Pike, *"Hard Times,"* p. 208.

13. Quoted in D. Geary, ed., *Labour and Socialist Movements in Europe Before 1914* (Oxford, U.K.: Berg, 1989), p. 29.

14. Kenneth Pomeranz, *The Great Divergence: China, Europe, and the Making of the Modern World Economy* (Princeton, N.J.: Princeton University Press, 2000).

For practice quizzes and other study tools, visit the **Online Study Guide** at bedfordstmartins.com/mckayworld.

For primary sources from this period, see *Sources of World Societies*, **Second Edition**.

For Web sites, images, and documents related to topics in this chapter, visit **Make History** at bedfordstmartins.com/mckayworld.

• Christabel Pankhurst, Militant Suffragette Christabel Pankhurst led the British Women's Social and Political Union, whose motto was "deeds, not words." This photo was taken in 1912 in Paris, where Pankhurst was living to avoid arrest for her increasingly violent actions to obtain the vote for women, including bombing the home of the future prime minister. Women in Britain and many other countries gained the right to vote in the years immediately after World War I. (Hulton-Deutsch Collection/Corbis)

24

Ideologies of Change in Europe

1815–1914

Europe's momentous economic and political transformation of modern times began in the late eighteenth century with the Industrial Revolution in England and then the French Revolution. Until about 1815 these economic and political revolutions were separate, involving different countries and activities and proceeding at very different paces. After peace returned in 1815, economic and political changes tended to fuse, reinforcing each other and bringing about what historian Eric Hobsbawm has incisively called the dual revolution. For instance, the growth of the industrial middle class encouraged the drive for representative government, and the demands of French workers in 1793 and 1794 eventually inspired socialists in many countries. Gathering strength, the dual revolution transformed Europe and had a powerful impact on the rest of the world.

The dual revolution also posed a tremendous intellectual challenge. The changes that were occurring fascinated observers and stimulated the growth of new ideas and powerful ideologies. The most important of these were revitalized conservatism and three ideologies of change—liberalism, nationalism, and socialism. All played critical roles in the political and social battles of the era and the great popular upheaval that eventually swept across Europe in the revolutions of 1848. These revolutions failed, however, and gave way to more sober—and more successful—nation building in the 1860s. Redrawing the political geography of central Europe and uniting first Italy and then Germany, European political leaders and middle-class nationalists also began to deal effectively with some of the problems posed by the burgeoning of urban society. Additionally, European leaders encouraged their peoples to put their faith in a responsive national state. At the same time, the triumph of nationalism promoted bitter rivalries between states and peoples, and in the twentieth century it brought an era of tragedy and decline in Europe. •

A Conservative Peace Gives Way to Radical Ideas

☐ How did the allies fashion a peace settlement in 1815, and what radical ideas emerged between 1815 and 1848?

The triumph of revolutionary economic and political forces was by no means certain as the Napoleonic era ended. The conservative aristocratic monarchies of Russia, Prussia, Austria, and Great Britain — known as the Quadruple Alliance — had finally defeated France (see Chapter 22) and reaffirmed their determination to hold France in line. But many other international questions were outstanding, and the allies agreed to meet at the **Congress of Vienna** to fashion a general peace settlement. The great challenge for political leaders in

Adjusting the Balance The Englishman below on the left uses his money to counterbalance the people that the Prussian and the fat Metternich are gaining in Saxony and Italy. Alexander I sits happily on his prize, Poland. This cartoon captures the essence of how the educated public thought about the balance-of-power diplomacy resulting in the Treaty of Vienna, the last page of which was signed and sealed in 1815 by the representatives of the various European states (left). (cartoon: Bibliothèque nationale de France; treaty: The "Final Act" of the Treaty of Vienna, established at the Congress of Vienna, 9 June 1815 [pen & ink on paper]/Archives du Ministère des Affaires Étrangères, Paris, France/Archives Charmet/The Bridgeman Art Library)

LA BALANCE POLITIQUE.

1814 was to construct a settlement that would last and not sow the seeds of another war. Their efforts were largely successful and contributed to a century unmarred by destructive generalized war (Map 24.1).

In the years following the peace settlement intellectuals and social observers sought to understand the revolutionary changes that had occurred and were still taking place. Almost all of these basic ideas were radical. In one way or another, the new ideas rejected conservatism, with its stress on tradition, a hereditary monarchy, and a strong landowning aristocracy. Radical thinkers developed and refined alternative visions — alternative ideologies — and tried to convince society to act on them.

The European Balance of Power

With the French agreeing to the restoration of the Bourbon dynasty (see Chapter 22), the allies were lenient toward that nation after Napoleon's abdication. The first Peace of Paris gave France the boundaries it possessed in 1792, which were larger than those of 1789, and France did not have to pay any war reparations.

When the four allies of the Quadruple Alliance met together at the Congress of Vienna they also agreed to raise a number of barriers against renewed French aggression. The Low Countries — Belgium and Holland — were united under an enlarged Dutch monarchy capable of opposing France more effectively. Prussia received considerably more territory along France's eastern border to stand as a "sentinel on the Rhine" against renewed French aggression. In these ways, the Quadruple Alliance combined leniency toward France with strong defensive measures.

In their moderation toward France, the allies were motivated by self-interest and traditional ideas about the balance of power. To the peacemakers, especially to Klemens von Metternich (1773–1859), Austria's foreign minister, the balance of power meant an international equilibrium of political and military forces that would discourage aggression by any combination of states or, worse, the domination of Europe by any single state. The Quadruple Alliance members, therefore, did not just sign the treaty and go home. They agreed to meet periodically to discuss their common interests and to consider appropriate measures to maintain peace in Europe. This agreement marked the beginning of the

European "congress system," which lasted long into the nineteenth century.

Coerced Conservatism After 1815

The peace settlement's domestic side was much less moderate. In 1815, under Metternich's leadership, Austria, Prussia, and Russia embarked on a crusade against the ideas and politics of the **dual revolution**. Metternich's policies dominated the entire German Confederation of thirty-eight independent German states, which the Vienna peace settlement had called into being (see Map 24.1). It was through the German

- **Congress of Vienna** A meeting of the Quadruple Alliance — Russia, Prussia, Austria, and Great Britain — and France held in 1814–1815 to fashion a general peace settlement that attempted to redraw Europe's political map after the defeat of Napoleonic France.
- **dual revolution** A term that historian Eric Hobsbawm used for the economic and political changes that tended to fuse and reinforce each other after 1815.

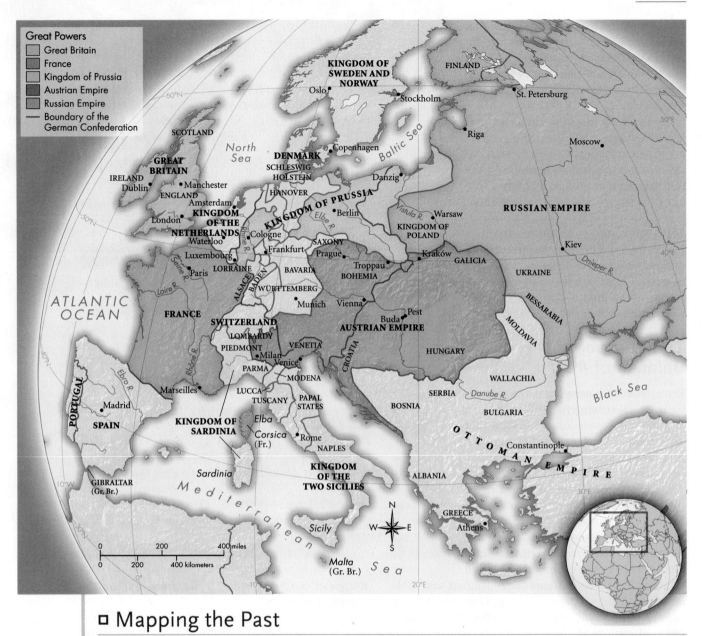

◻ Mapping the Past

MAP 24.1 Europe in 1815 In 1815 Europe contained many different states, but after the defeat of Napoleon international politics was dominated by the five Great Powers: Russia, Prussia, Austria, Great Britain, and France. (The number rises to six if one includes the Ottoman Empire.)

ANALYZING THE MAP Trace the political boundaries of each Great Power, and compare their geographical strengths and weaknesses. What territories did Prussia and Austria gain as a result of the war with Napoleon?

CONNECTIONS How did Prussia's and Austria's territorial gains contribute to the balance of power established at the Congress of Vienna? What other factors enabled the Great Powers to achieve such a long-lasting peace?

Confederation that Metternich had the repressive Carlsbad Decrees issued in 1819. These decrees required the member states to root out subversive ideas in their universities and newspapers, and a permanent committee was established to investigate and punish any liberal or radical organizations.

Born into the landed nobility, Metternich zealously defended his class and its privileges. Like many European conservatives of his time, he believed that liberalism (see page 719), as embodied in revolutionary America and France, had been responsible for a generation of war with untold bloodshed and suffering. He blamed liberal revolutionaries for stirring up the lower classes, which he believed desired nothing more than peace and quiet.

Because liberals believed that each national group had a right to establish its own independent government, the quest for national self-determination posed a grave threat to the Habsburgs' vast Austrian Empire. It was a dynastic state dominated by Germans but containing many other national groups, including Magyars (Hungarians), Czechs, Italians, Poles, Ukrainians, Slovenes, Croats, Serbs, Ruthenians, and Romanians. As a result, the multinational state that Metternich served was both strong and weak. It was strong because of its large population and vast territories; it was weak because of its many and potentially dissatisfied nationalities. In these circumstances, Metternich virtually had to oppose liberalism and nationalism, for Austria was unable to accommodate those ideologies of the dual revolution.

Liberalism and the Middle Class

The principal ideas of **liberalism**—liberty and equality—were by no means defeated in 1815. (This form of liberalism is often called "classical liberalism" and should not be confused with modern American liberalism, which usually favors government programs to meet social needs and to regulate the economy.) First realized successfully in the American Revolution and then achieved in part in the French Revolution, liberalism demanded representative government and equality before the law. The idea of liberty also meant specific individual freedoms: freedom of the press, freedom of speech, freedom of assembly, and freedom from arbitrary arrest. In Europe only France, with Louis XVIII's Constitutional Charter, and Great Britain, with its Parliament and historic rights of English men and women, had realized much of the liberal program in 1815. Even in those countries, liberalism had not fully succeeded.

Liberalism faced more radical ideological competitors in the early nineteenth century. Opponents of liberalism especially criticized its economic principles, which called for unrestricted private enterprise and no government interference in the economy. This philosophy was popularly known as the doctrine of **laissez faire** (lay-say FEHR).

Scottish philosopher Adam Smith (see page 537) posited the idea of a free economy in 1776 in opposition to mercantilism and its attempt to regulate trade. Smith argued that freely competitive private enterprise would give all citizens a fair and equal opportunity to do what they did best and would result in greater income for everyone. In early-nineteenth-century Britain this economic liberalism was embraced most en-thusiastically by business groups and thus became a doctrine associated with business interests.

In the early nineteenth century liberal political ideals also became more closely associated with narrow class interests. Early-nineteenth-century liberals favored representative government, but they generally wanted property qualifications attached to the right to vote. In practice this meant limiting the vote to well-to-do males.

As liberalism became increasingly identified with the middle class after 1815, some intellectuals and foes of conservatism felt that liberalism did not go nearly far enough. Inspired by memories of the French Revolution and the young American republic, they called for universal voting rights, at least for males, and for democracy. These democrats and republicans were more radical than the liberals, and they were more willing to endorse violent upheaval to achieve goals.

The Growing Appeal of Nationalism

Nationalism was a second radical ideology in the years after 1815—an idea destined to have an enormous influence in the modern world. In 1808, in an address to a German audience in French-occupied Berlin, the German philosopher Johann Gottlieb Fichte called on all Germans "to have that organic unity in which no member regards the fate of another as the fate of a stranger."[1] Fichte and other early advocates of the "national idea" argued that the members of each ethnic group (although the term *ethnic group* was not used at the time) had its own genius and its own cultural unity, which were manifested especially in a common language, history, and territory. In fact, such cultural unity was more a dream than a reality as local dialects abounded, historical memory divided the inhabitants of the different states as much as it unified them, and a variety of ethnic groups shared the territory of most states.

Nevertheless, European nationalists sought to make the territory of each people coincide with well-defined boundaries in an independent nation-state. It was this

- **liberalism** A philosophy whose principal ideas were equality and liberty; liberals demanded representative government and equality before the law as well as such individual freedoms as freedom of the press, freedom of speech, freedom of assembly, and freedom from arbitrary arrest.
- **laissez faire** A doctrine of economic liberalism that believed in unrestricted private enterprise and no government interference in the economy.
- **nationalism** The idea that each people had its own genius and its own specific unity, which manifested itself especially in a common language and history, and often led to the desire for an independent political state.

Building German Nationalism As popular upheaval in France spread to central Europe in March 1848, Germans from the solid middle classes came together in Frankfurt to draft a constitution for a new united Germany. (akg-images)

political goal that made nationalism so explosive in central and eastern Europe after 1815, when there were either too few states (Austria, Russia, and the Ottoman Empire) or too many (the Italian peninsula and the German Confederation), and when different peoples overlapped and intermingled.

The nationalist vision triumphed in the long run partly because the development of complex industrial and urban society required better communication between individuals and groups.[2] The development of a standardized national language that was spread through mass education created at least a superficial cultural unity. Nation-states also emerged because those who believed in the new ideology wanted to create "imagined communities," communities seeking to bind inhabitants around the abstract concept of an all-embracing national identity. Thus nationalists and leaders brought citizens together with emotionally charged symbols and ceremonies, such as ethnic festivals and flag-waving parades that celebrated the imagined nation of spiritual equals.[3]

Many of the African and Asian colonies that gained their independence in the twentieth century are ex-

amples of the imagined communities concept. During the colonial era European powers established a single language — English, French, or German, for example — as a common language of communication in their respective colonies. Many local nationalist leaders, who came from different ethnic groups within a colony, attended Christian mission schools or other schools run by the colonizer and learned a European language while adopting numerous elements of the European culture. This allowed them to communicate and plan common strategies for independence under the banner of a generally superficial national identity. Many of these leaders, such as India's Mohandas Gandhi (see page 890), even lived in Europe and witnessed the creation and promotion of national identities there firsthand.

Between 1815 and 1850 most people who believed in nationalism also believed in either liberalism or radical democratic republicanism. A common faith in the creativity and nobility of the people was perhaps the single most important reason for the linking of these two concepts. Liberals and especially democrats saw the people as the ultimate source of all good government. Early nationalists usually believed that every nation, like every citizen, had the right to exist in freedom and to develop its character and spirit. Yet early nationalists also stressed the differences among peoples, and they developed a strong sense of "we" and "they"; the "they" was often viewed as the enemy. Thus while European nationalism's main thrust was liberal and democratic, below the surface lurked ideas of national superiority and national mission that eventually led to aggression and conflict against supposedly inferior peoples in Africa and Asia, and to the great world wars of the twentieth century.

The Birth of Socialism

Socialism, the new radical doctrine after 1815, began in France. Early French socialist thinkers were acutely aware that the political revolution in France, the rise of laissez faire, and the emergence of modern industry in England were transforming society. They were disturbed because they saw these trends as fomenting selfish individualism and division within communities. There was, they believed, an urgent need for a further reorganization of society to establish cooperation and a new sense of community.

Early French socialists believed in economic planning. Inspired by the price controls and other emergency measures implemented in revolutionary France (see Chapter 22), they argued that the government should rationally organize the economy and help the poor. Socialists also believed that government should regulate private property or that private property should be abolished and replaced by state or community ownership.

One of the most influential early socialist thinkers was Henri de Saint-Simon (1760–1825). Saint-Simon optimistically proclaimed the tremendous possibilities of industrial development: "The age of gold is before us!" In his view the key to progress was proper social organization that required the "parasites"—the royal court, the aristocracy, lawyers, churchmen—to give way, once and for all, to the "doers"—the leading scientists, engineers, and industrialists. The doers would carefully plan the economy, guide it forward, and improve conditions for the poor.

Charles Fourier (1772–1837), another influential French thinker, envisaged a socialist utopia of self-sufficient communities. An early proponent of the total emancipation of women, Fourier also called for the abolition of marriage, free unions based only on love, and sexual freedom. To many people, these ideas were shocking and made the socialist program appear doubly dangerous and revolutionary.

It was left to Karl Marx (1818–1883) to establish firm foundations for modern socialism. Marx had studied philosophy at the University of Berlin before turning to journalism and economics. In 1848 the thirty-year-

> "The history of all previously existing society is the history of class struggles."
>
> **KARL MARX AND FRIEDRICH ENGELS**

old Karl Marx and the twenty-eight-year-old Friedrich Engels (1820–1895; see page 702) published *The Communist Manifesto*, which became the bible of socialism.

Early French socialists often appealed to the middle class and the state to help the poor. Marx ridiculed such appeals as naive. He argued that middle class interests and those of the industrial working class were inevitably opposed to each other. According to the *Manifesto*, the "history of all previously existing society is the history of class struggles." In Marx's view one class had always exploited the other, and, with the advent of modern industry, society was split more clearly than ever before: between the middle class—the **bourgeoisie** (boor-ZHWAH-zee)—and the modern working class—the **proletariat**.

Just as the bourgeoisie had triumphed over the feudal aristocracy, Marx predicted that the proletariat would conquer the bourgeoisie in a violent revolution. For Marx, class identity trumped national identity. While a tiny majority owned the means of production and grew richer, the ever-poorer proletariat was constantly growing in size and in class-consciousness. Marx believed that the critical moment when class conflict would result in revolution was very near, as the last lines of *The Communist Manifesto* make clear:

> Germany . . . is on the eve of a bourgeois revolution, that is bound to be . . . the prelude to an immediately following proletarian revolution. . . .
>
> Let the ruling classes tremble at a Communist revolution. The proletarians have nothing to lose but their chains. They have a world to win. WORKING MEN OF ALL COUNTRIES, UNITE!

Marx was strongly influenced by England's classical economists, who taught that labor was the source of all value. He went on to argue that profits were really wages stolen from the workers. Moreover, Marx incorporated Friedrich Engels's account of the terrible oppression of the new class of factory workers in England. Thus Marx pulled together powerful ideas and insights to create one of the great secular religions out of the intellectual ferment of the early nineteenth century.

- **socialism** A backlash against the emergence of individualism and the fragmentation of society, and a move toward international cooperation and a sense of community; the key ideas were economic planning, greater economic equality, and state regulation of property.
- **bourgeoisie** The well-educated, prosperous, middle-class groups.
- **proletariat** The Marxist term for the modern working class.

Reforms and Revolutions, 1815–1850

☐ Why in 1848 did revolutions triumph briefly throughout most of Europe, and why did they fail?

As liberal, national, and socialist forces battered the conservatism of 1815, pressure built up. In some countries change occurred gradually and peacefully, but in 1848 revolutionary political and social ideologies combined with economic crisis to produce a vast upheaval. Great Britain, France, Austria, and Prussia all experienced variations on this basic theme between 1815 and 1848.

Liberal Reform in Great Britain

The landowning aristocracy dominated eighteenth-century British society, but that class was neither closed nor rigidly defined. Basic civil rights were guaranteed, but only about 8 percent of the population could vote for representatives to Parliament. By the 1780s there was growing interest in some sort of reform, but the French Revolution threw the British aristocracy into a panic, and after 1815 it was determined to defend its ruling position.

Only in 1832 did a surge of popular protest convince the king and lords to give in. The Reform Bill of 1832 had profound significance. First, the bill moved British politics in a democratic direction and allowed the House of Commons to emerge as the all-important legislative body. Second, the new industrial areas of the country gained representation in the Commons. Third, the number of voters increased by about 50 percent. Comfortable middle-class urban groups, as well as some substantial farmers, received the vote. Thus the pressures building in Great Britain were temporarily released without revolution or civil war.

A major reform had been achieved peacefully, and continued reform within the system appeared difficult but not impossible. In 1847 the Tories passed the Ten Hours Act, which limited the workday for women and young people in factories to ten hours. Tory aristocrats continued to champion legislation regulating factory conditions. They were competing vigorously with the middle class for working-class support. This healthy competition was a crucial factor in Great Britain's peaceful evolution in the nineteenth century.

The people of Ireland did not benefit from this political competition. Long ruled as a conquered people, most of the population was made up of Irish Catholic peasants who rented their land from a tiny minority of Church of England Protestants. Ruthlessly exploited and growing rapidly in numbers, the Irish peasantry around 1800 lived under abominable conditions. The novelist Sir Walter Scott wrote:

> The poverty of the Irish peasantry is on the extreme verge of human misery; their cottages would scarce serve for pig styes even in Scotland; and their rags seem the very refuse of a sheep, and are spread over their bodies with such an ingenious variety of wretchedness that you would think nothing but some sort of perverted taste could have assembled so many shreds together.[4]

A compassionate French traveler agreed, writing that Ireland was " pure misery, naked and hungry. . . . I saw the American Indian in his forests and the black slave in his chains, and I believed that I was seeing the most extreme form of human misery; but that was before I knew the lot of poor Ireland."[5]

In spite of terrible conditions, Ireland's population continued to increase, caused in part by the extensive cultivation of the potato. The potato crop failed in 1845, 1846, 1848, and 1851 in Ireland and throughout much of Europe. Blight attacked the young plants, and the tubers rotted. The general result in Europe was high food prices, suffering, and, frequently, social upheaval. In Ireland the result was widespread starvation and mass fever epidemics. Total population losses were staggering. Fully one million emigrants fled the famine between 1845 and 1851, going primarily to the United States and Great Britain. The Great Famine, as this tragedy came to be known, intensified anti-British feeling and promoted Irish nationalism.

Revolutions in France

Louis XVIII's Constitutional Charter of 1814 protected the economic and social gains made by sections of the middle class and the peasantry in the French Revolution, and it permitted great intellectual and artistic freedom. The charter was anything but democratic, however. Only a tiny minority of males had the right to vote for the legislative deputies who, with the king and his ministers, made the nation's laws.

Although Louis Philippe (r. 1830–1848) accepted the Constitutional Charter of 1814 and titled himself merely the "king of the French people," the situation in France remained fundamentally unchanged. The vote was extended only from 100,000 to 170,000 citizens. Republicans, democrats, social reformers, and the poor of Paris were bitterly disappointed. The government's stubborn refusal to consider electoral reform heightened a sense of class injustice among shopkeepers and urban working people, and it eventually touched off a popular revolt in Paris in February 1848. Barricades went up, and Louis Philippe quickly abdicated.

The revolutionaries were firmly committed to a truly popular and democratic republic so that the common

▫ Picturing the Past

The Triumph of Democratic Republics This French illustration offers an opinion of the initial revolutionary breakthrough in 1848. The peoples of Europe, joined together around their respective national banners, are achieving republican freedom, which is symbolized by the Statue of Liberty and the discarded crowns. The woman wearing pants at the base of the statue—very radical attire—represents feminist hopes for liberation. (Musée de la Ville, Paris/Giraudon/The Bridgeman Art Library)

ANALYZING THE IMAGE How many different flags can you count and/or identify? How would you characterize the types of people marching and the mood of the crowd?

CONNECTIONS What do the angels, Statue of Liberty, and discarded crowns suggest about the artist's view of the events of 1848? Do you think this illustration was created before or after the collapse of the revolution in France? Why?

people—the peasants and the workers—could reform society with wise legislation. In practice, building such a republic meant giving the right to vote to every adult male, and this was quickly done. Revolutionary compassion and sympathy for freedom were expressed in the freeing of all slaves in French colonies, the abolition of the death penalty, and the establishment of national workshops as an alternative to capitalist employment for unemployed Parisian workers.

Yet there were profound differences within the revolutionary coalition in Paris, and the socialism promoted by radical republicans frightened not only the middle and upper classes but also the peasants, many of whom owned land. When the French masses voted for delegates to the new Constituent Assembly in late April 1848, they elected a majority of moderate republicans who opposed any further radical social measures.

After the elections this clash of ideologies—of liberal capitalism and socialism—became a clash of classes and arms. When the government dissolved the national workshops in Paris, workers rose in a spontaneous and violent uprising. Working people fought with courage, but the government had the army and the support of peasant France. After three terrible "June Days" and the death or injury of more than ten thousand people, the republican army stood triumphant in a sea of working-class blood and hatred.

The revolution in France thus ended in spectacular failure. The February coalition of the middle and working classes had in four short months become locked in mortal combat. In place of a generous democratic republic, the Constituent Assembly completed a constitution featuring a strong executive. This allowed Louis Napoleon, nephew of Napoleon Bonaparte, to win a landslide victory in the December 1848 election.

President Louis Napoleon at first shared power with a conservative National Assembly. But in 1851 Louis Napoleon dismissed the Assembly and seized power in a coup d'état. A year later he called on the French to make him hereditary emperor, and 97 percent voted

to do so in a national plebiscite. Louis Napoleon — proclaimed Emperor Napoleon III — then ruled France until 1870. Gradually his government became less authoritarian as he liberalized his empire. In 1870, on the eve of a disastrous war with Prussia (see page 729), Louis Napoleon was still seeking with some success to reconcile a strong national state with universal male suffrage and an independent National Assembly with real power.

The Revolutions of 1848 in Central Europe

Throughout central Europe the news of the upheaval in France evoked excitement and eventually revolution. Liberals demanded written constitutions, representative government, and greater civil liberties from authoritarian regimes. When governments hesitated,

Street Fighting in Berlin, 1848 This contemporary lithograph portrays a street battle on March 18, 1848, between Prussian troops loyal to King Frederick William IV and civilian men and women demonstrators. The king withdrew his troops the following day rather than kill anymore of his "beloved Berliners." Revolutionaries across Europe often dug up paving stones and used them as weapons. The tricolor flag achieved prominence during the revolution as the symbol of a united and democratic Germany. (akg-images)

popular revolts followed. Urban workers and students served as the shock troops, but they were allied with middle-class liberals and peasants. In the face of this united front, monarchs collapsed and granted almost everything. The popular revolutionary coalition then broke down as it had in France.

The revolution in the Austrian Empire began in 1848 in Hungary, where nationalistic Hungarians demanded national autonomy, full civil liberties, and universal suffrage. When Viennese students and workers also took to the streets and peasant disorders broke out, the Habsburg emperor Ferdinand I (r. 1835–1848) capitulated and promised reforms and a liberal constitution. The coalition of revolutionaries was not stable, however. When the monarchy abolished serfdom, the newly free peasants lost interest in the political and social questions agitating the cities.

The revolutionary coalition was also weakened and ultimately destroyed by conflicting national aspirations. In March the Hungarian revolutionary leaders pushed through an extremely liberal, almost democratic, constitution. But the Hungarian revolutionaries also sought to create a unified, centralized Hungarian nation. To the minority groups that formed half of the population — the Croats, Serbs, and Romanians — such unification was completely unacceptable. Each felt entitled to political autonomy and cultural independence. Likewise, Czech nationalists based in Bohemia and the city of Prague came into conflict with German nationalists. Thus conflicting national aspirations within the Austrian Empire enabled the monarchy to play off one ethnic group against the other.

The monarchy's first breakthrough came in June when the army crushed a working-class revolt in Prague. In October the predominantly peasant troops of the regular Austrian army attacked the student and working-class radicals in Vienna and retook the city. Thus the determination of Austria's aristocracy and the loyalty of its army were the final ingredients in the triumph of reaction and the defeat of revolution.

When Ferdinand I abdicated in favor of his young nephew, Franz Joseph (see page 743), only Hungary had yet to be brought under control. Another determined conservative, Nicholas I of Russia (r. 1825–1855), obligingly lent his iron hand. In June 1849, 130,000 Russian troops poured into Hungary and subdued the country. For a number of years the Habsburgs ruled Hungary as a conquered territory.

After Austria, Prussia was the largest and most influential German kingdom. Prior to 1848, the goal of middle-class Prussian liberals had been to reshape Prussia into a liberal constitutional monarchy, which would transform the German Confederation into a unified nation. The agitation following Louis Philippe's fall in France encouraged Prussian liberals to press their demands. When the artisans and factory workers in

Berlin exploded in March 1848 and joined with the middle-class liberals in the struggle against the monarchy, Prussian King Frederick William IV (r. 1840–1861) caved in. On March 21 he promised to grant Prussia a liberal constitution and to merge Prussia into a new national German state.

A self-appointed committee of liberals from various German states met in Frankfurt in May 1848 and began writing a federal constitution for a unified German state. This National Assembly completed drafting a liberal constitution in March 1849 and elected King Frederick William of Prussia emperor of the new German national state. By early 1849, however, Frederick William had reasserted his royal authority, contemptuously refusing to accept the "crown from the gutter." When Frederick William tried to get the small monarchs of Germany to elect him emperor with authoritarian power, Austria balked. Supported by Russia, Austria forced Prussia to renounce all its unification schemes in late 1850. The German Confederation was re-established. Attempts to unite the Germans — first in a liberal national state and then in a conservative Prussian empire — had failed completely.

Nation Building in Italy, Germany, and Russia

☐ How did strong leaders and nation building transform Italy, Germany, and Russia?

Louis Napoleon's triumph in 1848 and his authoritarian rule in the 1850s provided Europe's old ruling classes with a new model in politics. To what extent might the expanding urban middle classes and even portions of the working classes rally to a strong and essentially conservative national state that also promised change? This was one of the great political questions in the 1850s and 1860s. In central Europe, a resounding answer came with the national unification of Italy and Germany.

The Russian empire also experienced profound political crises in this period, but they were unlike those in Italy or Germany because Russia was already a vast multinational state built on long traditions of military conquest and absolutist rule by elites from the dominant ethnic group — the Russians. It became clear to the Russian leaders that they had to embrace the process of **modernization**, defined narrowly as the changes that enable a country to compete effectively with the leading countries at a given time.

modernization The changes that enable a country to compete effectively with the leading countries at a given time.

MAP 24.2 The Unification of Italy, 1859–1870 The leadership of Sardinia-Piedmont, nationalist fervor, and Garibaldi's attack on the kingdom of the Two Sicilies were decisive factors in the unification of Italy.

Map legend:
- Kingdom of Sardinia-Piedmont before 1859
- To Kingdom of Sardinia-Piedmont, 1859
- To Kingdom of Sardinia-Piedmont, 1860
- To Kingdom of Italy, 1866, 1870
- Major battle
- Boundary of Kingdom of Italy after unification

Cavour, Garibaldi, and the Unification of Italy

Italy had never been a united nation prior to 1850. A battleground for the Great Powers after 1494, Italy was reorganized in 1815 at the Congress of Vienna. Austria received the rich northern provinces of Lombardy and Venetia. Sardinia and Piedmont fell under the rule of an Italian monarch, and Tuscany shared north-central Italy with several smaller states. The papacy ruled over central Italy and Rome, while a branch of the Bourbons ruled Naples and Sicily. Metternich was not wrong in dismissing Italy as "a geographical expression" (Map 24.2).

After 1815 the goal of a unified Italian nation captured the imaginations of many Italians, but there was no agreement on how it could be achieved. In 1848 revolutionary efforts to form a democratic Italian republic failed, and after he was temporarily driven from Rome during the upheavals of 1848, a frightened Pope Pius IX (r. 1846–1878) turned against most modern trends, including national unification. At the same time,

Victor Emmanuel, king of independent Sardinia, retained the moderate liberal constitution granted under duress in March 1848. To the Italian middle classes Sardinia (see Map 24.2) appeared to be a liberal, progressive state ideally suited to achieve the goal of national unification.

Sardinia had the good fortune of being led by Count Camillo Benso di Cavour. Cavour came from a noble family and embraced the economic doctrines and business activities associated with the prosperous middle class. Cavour's national goals were limited and realistic. Until 1859 he sought unity only for the states of northern and perhaps central Italy in a greatly expanded kingdom of Sardinia.

In the 1850s Cavour worked to consolidate Sardinia as a liberal constitutional state capable of leading northern Italy. He worked out a secret diplomatic alliance with Napoleon III, and in July 1858 he goaded Austria into attacking Sardinia. The combined Franco-Sardinian forces were victorious, but Napoleon III decided on a compromise peace with the Austrians in July 1859. Sardinia would receive only Lombardy, the area around Milan. Cavour resigned in a rage.

Popular revolts and Italian nationalism salvaged Cavour's plans. While the war against Austria raged in the north, dedicated nationalists in central Italy had risen and driven out their rulers. Nationalist fervor seized the urban masses, and the leaders of the nationalist movement called for fusion with Sardinia. Cavour returned to power in early 1860, and the people of central Italy voted overwhelmingly to join a greatly enlarged kingdom of Sardinia. Cavour had achieved his original goal of a north Italian state (see Map 24.2).

For superpatriots such as Giuseppe Garibaldi (1807–1882), the job of unification was still only half done. A poor sailor's son, Garibaldi personified the romantic revolutionary nationalism of 1848. Having led a unit of volunteers to several victories over Austrian troops in 1859, Garibaldi emerged in 1860 as an independent force in Italian politics. (See "Individuals in Society: Giuseppe Garibaldi," page 728.)

Secretly supported by Cavour, Garibaldi conceived a bold plan to "liberate" the kingdom of the Two Sicilies. Landing on the shores of Sicily in May 1860, Garibaldi's guerrilla band of a thousand Red Shirts captured the imagination of the Sicilian peasantry, which rose in rebellion. Outwitting the royal army, Garibaldi captured Palermo, crossed to the mainland, and prepared to attack Rome and the pope. But Cavour quickly sent Sardinian forces to occupy most of the Papal States (but not Rome) and to intercept Garibaldi. When Garibaldi and Victor Emmanuel rode through Naples to cheering crowds, they symbolically sealed the union of north and south, of monarch and people.

The new kingdom of Italy, which did not include Venice until 1866 or Rome until 1870, was a parliamentary monarchy under Victor Emmanuel, neither radical nor democratic. Only a small minority of Italian males had the franchise. Despite political unity, the propertied classes and the common people were divided. A great social and cultural gap separated the progressive industrializing north from the stagnant agrarian south.

Bismarck and German Unification

In the aftermath of 1848, the German states, particularly Austria and Prussia, were locked in a political stalemate, each seeking to block the power of the other within the German Confederation. At the same time, powerful economic forces were undermining the political status quo. Modern industry was growing rapidly within the German customs union, or *Zollverein*, founded in 1834 to stimulate trade. By 1853 all the German states except Austria had joined the customs union, and a new Germany excluding Austria was becoming an economic reality.

Prussia had emerged from the upheavals of 1848 with a parliament of sorts, which was in the hands of the liberal middle class by 1859. The national uprising in Italy in 1859, however, convinced Prussia's tough-minded William I (r. 1861–1888) that political change and even war with Austria or France was possible. William I pushed to raise taxes and increase the defense budget to double the army's size. The Prussian

> "The great questions of the day will not be decided by speeches and resolutions . . . but by blood and iron."
>
> **OTTO VON BISMARCK**

parliament, reflecting the middle class's desire for a less militaristic society, rejected the military budget in 1862, and the liberals triumphed in new elections. King William then called on Count Otto von Bismarck to head a new ministry and defy the parliament.

The most important figure in German history between Martin Luther and Adolf Hitler, Otto von Bismarck (1815–1898) was above all a master of politics. Born into the Prussian landowning aristocracy, Bismarck loved power, but he was also extraordinarily flexible and pragmatic in pursuing his goals. When Bismarck took office as chief minister in 1862, he declared that the government would rule without parliamentary consent. He lashed out at the middle-class opposition: "The great questions of the day will not be decided by speeches and resolutions . . . but by blood and iron." Bismarck had the Prussian bureaucracy go right on collecting taxes even though the parliament refused to approve the budget, and he reorganized the army. For their part, the voters of Prussia continued to express their opposition by sending large liberal majorities to the parliament from 1862 to 1866.

In 1866 Bismarck launched the Austro-Prussian War with the intent of expelling Austria from German politics. The war lasted only seven weeks, and the reorganized Prussian army defeated Austria decisively at the Battle of Sadowa in Bohemia. Bismarck forced Austria to withdraw from German affairs. The mainly Protestant states north of the Main River were grouped in the new North German Confederation, led by an expanded Prussia (Map 24.3). Each state retained its own local government, but the federal government — William I and Bismarck — controlled the army and foreign affairs.

Long convinced that the old order should make peace with the liberal middle class and the nationalist movement, Bismarck asked the Prussian parliament to approve after the fact all of the government's "illegal" spending between 1862 and 1866. Most of the liberals jumped at the chance to cooperate. With German unity in sight, they legalized the government's spending. The constitutional struggle in Prussia was over, and the German middle class was accepting respectfully the monarchical authority and aristocratic superiority that Bismarck represented.

The final act in the drama of German unification followed quickly with a patriotic war with France. The apparent issue — whether a distant relative of Prussia's William I might become king of Spain — was only

Giuseppe Garibaldi

WHEN GIUSEPPE GARIBALDI (1807–1882)
visited England in 1864, he received the most triumphant welcome ever given to any foreigner. Honored and feted by politicians and high society, he also captivated the masses. An unprecedented crowd of a half-million people cheered his carriage through the streets of London. These ovations were no fluke. In his time, Garibaldi was probably the most famous and most beloved figure in the world.* How could this be?

A rare combination of wild adventure and extraordinary achievement partly accounted for his demigod status. Born in Nice, Garibaldi went to sea at fifteen and sailed the Mediterranean for twelve years. At seventeen his travels took him to Rome, and he was converted in an almost religious experience to the "New Italy, the Italy of all the Italians." As he later wrote in his best-selling *Autobiography*, "The Rome that I beheld with the eyes of youthful imagination was the Rome of the future— the dominant thought of my whole life."

Sentenced to death in 1834 for his part in a revolutionary uprising in Genoa, Garibaldi barely escaped to South America. For twelve years he led a guerrilla band in Uruguay's struggle for independence from Argentina. "Shipwrecked, ambushed, shot through the neck," he found in a tough young woman, Anna da Silva, a mate and companion in arms. Their first children nearly starved in the jungle while Garibaldi, clad in his long red shirt, fashioned a legend as a fearless freedom fighter.

After he returned to Italy in 1848, the campaigns of his patriotic volunteers against the Austrians in 1848 and 1859 mobilized democratic nationalists. The stage was set for his volunteer army to liberate Sicily against enormous odds, astonishing the world and creating a large Italian state. Garibaldi's achievement matched his legend.

A brilliant fighter, the handsome and inspiring leader was an uncompromising idealist of absolute integrity. He never drew personal profit from his exploits, continuing to milk his goats and rarely possessing more than one change of clothing. When Victor Emmanuel offered him lands and titles after his great victory in 1861, even as the left-leaning volunteers were disbanded and humiliated, Garibaldi declined, saying he could not be bought off. Returning to his farm on a tiny rocky island, he denounced the government without hesitation when he concluded that it was betraying the dream of unification with its ruthless rule in the south. Yet even after a duplicitous Italian government caused two later attacks on Rome to fail, his faith in the generative power of national unity never wavered. Garibaldi showed that ideas and ideals count in history.

Above all, millions of ordinary men and women identified with Garibaldi because they believed that he was fighting for them. They recognized him as one of their own and saw that he remained true to them in spite of his triumphs, thereby ennobling their own lives and aspirations. Welcoming runaway slaves as equals in Latin America, advocating the emancipation of women, introducing social reforms in the south, and pressing for free education and a broader suffrage in the new Italy, Garibaldi the national hero fought for freedom and human dignity. The common people understood and loved him for it.

*Denis Mack Smith, *Garibaldi: A Great Life in Brief* (New York: Alfred A. Knopf, 1956), pp. 136–147; and Denis Mack Smith, "Giuseppe Garibaldi," *History Today*, August 1991, pp. 20–26.

QUESTIONS FOR ANALYSIS

1. Why was Garibaldi so famous and popular?
2. Nationalism evolved and developed in the nineteenth century. How did Garibaldi fit into this evolution? What kind of a nationalist was he?

● **Giuseppe Garibaldi, the charismatic leader, shown in an 1856 engraving based on a photograph.** (Bettmann/Corbis)

MAP 24.3 The Unification of Germany, 1866–1871 This map shows how Prussia expanded and a new German Empire was created through two wars, the Austro-Prussian War of 1866 and the Franco-Prussian War of 1870–1871.

a diplomatic pretext. By 1870, alarmed by their powerful new neighbor on the Rhine, French leaders had decided on a war to teach Prussia a lesson.

As soon as war against France began in 1870, Bismarck had the wholehearted support of the south German states. German forces under Prussian leadership defeated Louis Napoleon's armies at Sedan on September 1, 1870. Three days later French patriots in Paris proclaimed yet another French republic and vowed to continue fighting. But after five months, in January 1871, a starving Paris surrendered, and France accepted Bismarck's harsh peace terms. By this time the south German states had agreed to join a new German Empire. As in the 1866 constitution, the Prussian king and his ministers had ultimate power in the new German Empire, and the lower house of the legislature was elected by universal male suffrage.

The Franco-Prussian War released an enormous surge of patriotic feeling in Germany. The new German Empire had become Europe's most powerful state, and most Germans were enormously proud, blissfully imagining themselves the fittest and best of the European species. Semi-authoritarian nationalism and a "new conservatism," which was based on an alliance of the propertied classes and sought the active support of the working classes, had triumphed in Germany.

The Modernization of Russia

In the 1850s Russia was a poor agrarian society with a rapidly growing population. Almost 90 percent of the population lived off the land, and serfdom was still the basic social institution. Then the Crimean War of 1853 to 1856, arising out of a dispute with France over who should protect certain Christian shrines in the Ottoman Empire, brought crisis. France and Great Britain, aided by Sardinia and the Ottoman Empire, inflicted a humiliating defeat on Russia.

Military defeat showed that Russia had fallen behind western Europe in many areas. Russia needed railroads, better armaments, and reorganization of the army if it was to maintain its international position. Moreover, the war had caused hardship and raised the specter of massive peasant rebellion. Military disaster thus forced the new tsar, Alexander II (r. 1855–1881), and his ministers along the path of rapid social change and general modernization.

The first and greatest of the reforms was the freeing of the serfs in 1861. The emancipated peasants received, on average, about half of the land. Yet they had to pay fairly high prices for their land, which was owned collectively by peasant villages. Thus the effects of the reform were limited. More successful was reform of the legal system, which established independent courts and equality before the law. Education was also liberalized somewhat, and censorship was relaxed but not removed.

Russia's greatest strides toward modernization were economic rather than political. Rapid railroad construction to 1880 enabled agricultural Russia to export grain and thus earn money for further industrialization. Industrial suburbs grew up around Moscow and St. Petersburg, and a class of modern factory workers began to take shape.

In 1881 a small group of terrorists assassinated Alexander II, and the reform era came to an abrupt end. Political modernization remained frozen until 1905, but economic modernization sped forward in the massive industrial surge of the 1890s. The key leader was Sergei Witte (suhr-GAY VIH-tuh), the energetic minister of finance. Under Witte's leadership the government doubled Russia's railroad network by the end of the century and promoted Russian industry with high protective tariffs.

By 1900 a fiercely independent Russia was catching up with western Europe and expanding its empire in Asia. By 1903 Russia had established a sphere of influence in Chinese Manchuria and was eyeing northern Korea. When the diplomatic protests of equally impe-

The Crimean War, 1853–1856

The Fruits of Terrorism
In the late 1870s a small group of revolutionaries believed that killing the tsar could destroy the Russian state. Succeeding in blowing up the reforming Alexander II after several near misses, the five assassins, including one woman, were quickly caught and hanged. Russia entered an era of reaction and harsh authoritarian rule. (Visual Connection Archive)

rialistic Japan were ignored, the Japanese launched a surprise attack on Russian forces in Manchuria in February 1904. After Japan scored repeated victories, to the amazement of self-confident Europeans, Russia was forced in September 1905 to accept a humiliating defeat.

Military disaster in East Asia brought political upheaval at home. On January 22, 1905, workers protesting for improved working conditions and higher wages were attacked by the tsar's troops outside the Winter Palace. Over one hundred were killed and around three hundred wounded. This event, known as Bloody Sunday, set off a wave of strikes, peasant uprisings, and troop mutinies across Russia. The revolutionary surge culminated in October 1905 in a paralyzing general strike, which forced the government to capitulate. The tsar, Nicholas II (r. 1894–1917), issued the **October Manifesto**, which granted full civil rights and promised a popularly elected Duma (DOO-muh; parliament) with real legislative power.

Under the new constitution Nicholas II retained great powers and the Duma had only limited authority. The middle-class liberals, the largest group in the newly elected Duma, were badly disappointed, and efforts to cooperate with the tsar's ministers soon broke down. In 1907 Nicholas II and his reactionary advisers rewrote the electoral law so as to increase greatly the weight of the propertied classes. When elections were held, the tsar could count on a loyal majority in the Duma. On the eve of World War I, Russia was partially modernized, a conservative constitutional monarchy with a peasant-based but industrializing economy.

Life in the Emerging Urban Society

☐ What was the impact of urban growth on cities, social classes, families, and ideas?

After 1850, as identification with the nation-state was becoming a basic organizing principle in Europe, urban growth rushed forward with undiminished force. In 1900 western Europe was urban and industrial as surely as it had been rural and agrarian in 1800. Rapid urban growth worsened long-standing overcrowding and unhealthy living conditions. Government leaders, city planners, reformers, and scientists worked tirelessly to address these challenges, and eventual success

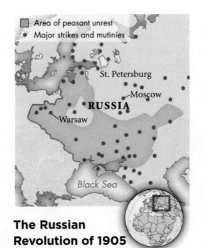

☐ Area of peasant unrest
• Major strikes and mutinies

St. Petersburg
Moscow
RUSSIA
Warsaw
Black Sea

The Russian Revolution of 1905

with urban problems encouraged people to put their faith in a responsive national state.

Taming the City

Since the Middle Ages European cities had been centers of government, culture, and large-scale commerce. They had also been congested, dirty, and unhealthy. The Industrial Revolution revealed these conditions more starkly than ever before. The steam engine freed industrialists from dependence on the energy of fast-flowing streams and rivers so that by 1800 there was every incentive to build new factories in cities, which had better shipping facilities and a large and ready workforce. Therefore, as industry grew, there was also a rapid expansion of already overcrowded and unhealthy cities.

In the 1820s and 1830s people in Britain and France began to worry about the condition of their cities. Except on the outskirts, each town or city was using every scrap of land to the full extent. Parks and open areas were almost nonexistent, and narrow houses were usually built wall to wall in long rows. Highly concentrated urban populations lived in extremely unsanitary and unhealthy conditions, with open drains and sewers flowing alongside or down the middle of unpaved streets. "Six, eight, and even ten occupying one room is anything but uncommon," wrote a Scottish doctor for a government investigation in 1842.

The urban challenge eventually brought an energetic response from a generation of reformers. The most famous early reformer was Edwin Chadwick, a British official. Chadwick was a follower of radical British philosopher Jeremy Bentham (1748–1832), whose approach to social issues, called utilitarianism, had taught that public problems ought to be dealt with on a rational, scientific basis and according to the "greatest good for the greatest number." Chadwick became convinced that disease and death actually caused poverty and that disease could be prevented by cleaning up the urban environment.

Collecting detailed reports from local officials and publishing his findings in 1842, Chadwick correctly believed that the stinking excrement of communal outhouses could be carried off by water through sewers at less than one-twentieth the cost of removing it by hand. In 1848 Chadwick's report became the basis of Great Britain's first public health law, which created a

• **October Manifesto** The result of a great general strike in Russia in October 1905, it granted full civil rights and promised a popularly elected Duma (parliament) with real legislative power.

King Cholera This 1852 drawing from *Punch* tells volumes about the unhealthy living conditions of the urban poor. In the foreground children play with a dead rat and a woman scavenges a dung heap. Cheap rooming houses provide shelter for the frightfully overcrowded population. Such conditions and contaminated water spread deadly cholera epidemics from India throughout Europe in the 1800s. The doctor's medicine chest seen here could provide patients only with opium mixtures to relieve pain and reduce intestinal swelling. (drawing: © British Library Board, P.P. 5270 vol. 23, 139; chest: Science & Society Picture Library)

national health board and gave cities broad authority to build modern sanitary systems. Such sanitary movements won dedicated supporters in the United States, France, and Germany from the 1840s on. By the 1860s and 1870s European cities were making real progress toward adequate water supplies and sewerage systems, and city dwellers were beginning to reap the reward of better health.

Early sanitary reformers were seriously handicapped by the prevailing miasmatic theory of disease — the belief that people contract disease when they breathe the bad odors of decay and putrefying excrement. In the 1840s and 1850s keen observation by doctors and public health officials suggested that contagion was spread through filth and not caused by it, thus weakening the miasmatic idea. The breakthrough was the development of the **germ theory** of disease by Louis Pasteur (1822–1895), a French chemist who began studying fermentation for brewers in 1854. Pasteur found that the growth of living organisms in a beverage could be suppressed by heating it — by pasteurization.

By 1870 the work of Pasteur and others had clearly demonstrated the connection between germs and disease. When, in the middle of the 1870s, Robert Koch and his German coworkers developed pure cultures of harmful bacteria and described their life cycles, the dam broke. Over the next twenty years researchers identified the organisms responsible for disease after disease. These discoveries led to the development of a number of effective vaccines. Surgeons also applied the germ theory in hospitals, sterilizing not only the wound but everything else — hands, instruments, clothing — that entered the operating room.

The achievements of the bacterial revolution coupled with the public health movement saved millions of lives, particularly after about 1890. In England, France, and Germany death rates declined dramatically, and the awful death sentences of the past — diphtheria, typhoid, typhus, cholera, yellow fever — became vanishing diseases in the industrializing nations.

More effective urban planning after 1850 also improved the quality of urban life. France took the lead during the rule of Napoleon III (1848–1870), who believed that rebuilding much of Paris would provide employment, improve living conditions, and glorify his empire. In the baron Georges Haussmann (1809–1884), an aggressive, impatient Alsatian whom he placed in charge of Paris, Napoleon III found an authoritarian planner capable of bulldozing both buildings and opposition. In twenty years Paris was transformed by slum clearance, new streets and housing, parks and open spaces, and good fresh water. The rebuilding of Paris stimulated modern urbanism throughout Europe, particularly after 1870.

The development of mass public transportation was also of great importance in the improvement of urban living conditions. In the 1870s many European cities authorized private companies to operate horse-drawn streetcars, which had been developed in the United States. Then in the 1890s countries in North America and Europe adopted another American transit innovation, the electric streetcar. Electric streetcars were cheaper, faster, more dependable, and more comfortable than their horse-drawn counterparts. Millions of riders hopped on board during the workweek. On weekends and holidays streetcars carried city people on outings to parks and the countryside, racetracks, and music halls.[6] Electric streetcars also gave people of modest means access to improved housing, as the still-crowded city was able to expand and become less congested.

New Social Hierarchies and the Middle Classes

By 1850 at the latest, working conditions were improving. Moreover, real wages were rising for the mass of the population, and they continued to do so until 1914. With increased wages, the rigid class structures of Old Regime Europe began to break down and, theoretically at least, open the way for social equality. Greater economic rewards for the average person did not eliminate hardship and poverty, however, nor did they significantly narrow the gap between rich and the poor. In almost every industrialized country around 1900, the richest 20 percent of households received anywhere from 50 to 60 percent of all national income, whereas the bottom 30 percent of households received 10 percent or less of all income. Thus the gap between rich and poor remained enormous and was probably almost as great in 1900 as it had been in the age of agriculture and aristocracy before the Industrial Revolution.

The great gap between rich and poor endured, in part, because industrial and urban development made society more diverse and less unified. Society had not split into two sharply defined opposing classes, as Marx had predicted. Instead, economic specialization created more new social groups than it destroyed. There developed an almost unlimited range of jobs, skills, and earnings; one group or subclass blended into another in a complex, confusing hierarchy.

The diversity and range within the urban middle class were striking as the twentieth century opened, and it is meaningful to think of a confederation of middle classes loosely united by occupations requiring mental, rather than physical, skill. As the upper middle class, composed mainly of successful business families, gained in income and progressively lost all traces of radicalism after the trauma of 1848, they were almost irresistibly drawn toward the aristocratic lifestyle. Next came the much larger, much less wealthy, and increasingly diversified middle middle class. Here one found moderately successful industrialists and merchants, professionals in law and medicine, and mid-level managers of large public and private institutions. The expansion of industry and technology created a growing demand for experts with specialized knowledge, and the most valuable of the specialties became solid middle-class professions. Engineers, architects, chemists, accountants, and surveyors first achieved professional standing in this period. At the bottom were independent shopkeepers, small traders, and tiny manufacturers—the lower middle class. Industrialization and urbanization also diversified the lower middle class and expanded the number of white-collar employees. White-collar employees were propertyless, but generally they were fiercely committed to the middle class and to the ideal of moving up in society.

Well fed and well served, the middle classes were also well housed by 1900 and were quite clothes conscious. Education was another growing expense as middle-class parents tried to provide their children with ever-more-crucial advanced education. The keystones of culture and leisure were books, music, and travel.

The middle classes were loosely united by a shared code of expected behavior and morality. This code stressed hard work, self-discipline, and personal achievement. Men and women who fell into crime or poverty were generally assumed to be responsible for their own circumstances. In short, the middle-class person was supposed to know right from wrong and to act accordingly.

The People and Occupations of the Working Classes

About four out of five Europeans belonged to the working classes at the turn of the twentieth century. Many of them were small landowning peasants and

---

• **germ theory** The idea that disease is caused by the spread of living organisms that can be controlled.

A Summer's Day in Hyde Park, 1858 John Ritchie's famous painting of Victorian England portrays the mixing of the social classes in London's Hyde Park. Middle class (bourgeoisie) ladies display their conspicuous finery, while representatives of the upper classes ride by in a fine carriage. (© Museum of London, UK/The Bridgeman Art Library)

hired farm hands. This was especially true in eastern Europe.

The urban working classes were even less unified and homogeneous than the middle classes. In the first place, economic development and increased specialization expanded the traditional range of working-class skills, earnings, and experiences. In the second place, skilled, semiskilled, and unskilled workers developed widely divergent lifestyles and cultural values, and their differences contributed to a keen sense of social status and hierarchy within the working classes.

Highly skilled workers, who made up about 15 percent of the working classes, became known as the labor aristocracy. The most "aristocratic" of the highly skilled workers were construction bosses and factory foremen, men who had often risen from the ranks and were fiercely proud of their achievement. The labor aristocracy also included members of the traditional highly skilled handicraft trades that had not yet been placed in factories, as well as new kinds of skilled workers such as shipbuilders and railway locomotive engineers. Thus the labor elite remained in a state of flux as individuals and whole crafts moved in and out of it.

Below the labor aristocracy stood the complex world of semiskilled and unskilled urban workers. A large number of the semiskilled were factory workers who earned good wages and whose relative importance in the labor force was increasing. Below the semiskilled workers was a larger group of unskilled workers that included day laborers such as longshoremen, wagon-driving teamsters, and maids. Many of these people had real skills and performed valuable services, but they were unorganized and divided, united only by the common fate of meager earnings. The same lack of unity characterized street vendors and market people—self-employed workers who competed savagely with each other and with the established lower middle class shopkeepers.

To make ends meet, many working-class wives had to join the broad ranks of working women in the "sweated industries." These industries resembled the old putting-out and cottage industries of earlier times, and they were similar to what we call sweatshops today. The women, sometimes unskilled and nearly always unorganized labor, normally worked at home and were paid by the piece. Sweating became a catch-all word denoting meager wages, hard labor, unsanitary and dangerous working conditions, and harsh treatment, often by a middleman who had subcontracted the work.

The urban working classes sought fun and recreation, and they found both. Across the face of Europe drinking remained unquestionably the favorite working class leisure-time activity. Generally, however, heavy problem drinking declined in the late nineteenth century as drinking became more public and social. Cafés and pubs became increasingly bright, friendly places.

The two other leisure-time passions of the working classes were sports and music halls. A great decline in cruel sports, such as bullbaiting and cockfighting, led to the rise of modern spectator sports, of which racing and soccer were the most popular. There was a great deal of gambling on sports events. Music halls and vaudeville theaters, the working-class counterparts of middle-class opera and classical theater, were enormously popular throughout Europe.

The Changing Family

Industrialization and the growth of modern cities also brought great changes to women's lives. These changes were particularly consequential for married women, and most women did marry in the nineteenth century.

After 1850 the work of most wives continued to become increasingly distinct and separate from that of their husbands. Husbands became wage earners in factories and offices; wives tended to stay home, manage households, and care for children. As economic conditions improved, only married women in poor families tended to work outside the home. The ideal became separate spheres (see page 705), the strict division of labor by sex. This rigid division meant that married women faced great obstacles if they needed or wanted to move into the men's world of paid employment outside the home. Well-paying jobs were off-limits to women, and a woman's wage was almost always less than a man's, even for the same work.

Middle-class women lacked legal rights and faced discrimination in education and employment. Thus organizations founded by middle-class feminists campaigned for legal equality as well as for access to higher education and professional employment. In the later nineteenth century middle-class women scored some significant victories, such as the 1882 law giving English married women full property rights. Socialist women leaders usually took a different path. They argued that the liberation of working-class women would come only with the liberation of the entire working class through revolution. In the meantime, they championed the cause of working women and won some practical improvements. In a general way these differ-

ent approaches to women's issues reflected the diversity of classes in urban society.

As the ideology and practice of rigidly separate spheres narrowed women's horizons, their control and influence in the home became increasingly strong throughout Europe in the later nineteenth century. Among the English working classes, for example, the wife generally determined how the family's money was spent. All the major domestic decisions, from the children's schooling and religious instruction to the selection of new furniture or a new apartment, were hers. (See "Listening to the Past: Mrs. Beeton's Guide for Running a Victorian Household," page 736.)

The woman's guidance of the household went hand in hand with the increased emotional importance of home and family. The home she ran was idealized as a warm shelter in a hard and impersonal urban world. Husbands and wives were expected to have emotional ties to each other, and mothers were expected to have powerful feelings toward their children. Among the middle and upper classes, marriages in the late nineteenth century were increasingly based on sentiment and sexual attraction, as money, family pressures, and financial calculation gradually declined in importance. Among the working classes, young people often began working or left home when they reached adolescence, so they had greater independence in their decisions about who to marry.

Ideas about sexuality within marriage varied. Many French marriage manuals of the late 1800s stressed that women had legitimate sexual needs, such as the "right to orgasm." In the more puritanical United States, however, sex manuals recommended sexual abstinence for unmarried men and limited sexual activity for married men. Respectable women were thought to experience no sexual pleasure at all from sexual activity, and anything vaguely sexual was to be removed from their surroundings; even the legs of pianos should be covered.

Medical doctors in both Europe and the United States began to study sexual desires and behavior more closely, and to determine what was considered "normal" and "abnormal." Same-sex attraction, labeled "homosexuality" for the first time, was identified as a "perversion." Governments seeking to promote a healthy society as a way of building up their national strength increasingly regulated prostitution, the treatment of venereal disease, and access to birth control in ways that were shaped by class and gender hierarchies. Masturbation, termed the "secret vice," became a matter of public concern in this era of growing nationalism because doctors and officials worried that it would weaken boys and men, making them incapable of defending the nation or engaging in industrial work.

Medical science also turned its attention to motherhood, and a wave of specialized books on child

Listening to the Past

Mrs. Beeton's Guide for Running a Victorian Household

The growth of the middle class in the second half of the nineteenth century resulted in sharper divisions of labor according to sex. More and more husbands were now going off each morning to their jobs in factories and offices, while their wives remained at home to manage the household. But life in a middle-class Victorian household was often quite different from the homes in which these women had been raised. Many a wife faced a steep learning curve as she learned to manage servants, purchase and use new gadgets and appliances, handle large household budgets, and present herself, her children, and her home in a comfortable and respectable middle class light.

Fortunately, there were many how-to manuals and guides that these wives could refer to for answers about nearly anything related to the home. One of the most popular of these how-to manuals in England was Mrs. Beeton's Book of Household Management. *Compiled and edited by Isabella Mary Beeton (1836–1865), this book offered advice on such wide-ranging topics as the management of children, dealing with servants, making a will, emergencies and doctors, taxes, fashion, animal husbandry, and shopkeepers. The book was also popularly referred to as "Mrs. Beeton's Cookbook" because over 900 of the 1,100 plus pages contained recipes. The excerpt that follows comes from the section on "The Mistress."*

1. As With the Commander of an Army, or the leader of any enterprise, so is it with the mistress of a household. Her spirit will be seen through the whole establishment; and just in proportion as she performs her duties intelligently and thoroughly, so will her domestics follow in her path. Of all those requirements, which more particularly belong to the feminine character, there are none which take a higher rank, in our estimation, than such as enter into a knowledge of household duties; for on these are perpetually dependent the happiness, comfort, and well-being of a family. . . .

2. Early Rising is One Of The Most Essential Qualities which enter into good Household Management, as it is not only the parent of health, but of innumerable other advantages. Indeed, when a mistress is an early riser, it is almost certain that her house will be orderly and well-managed. On the contrary, if she remain in bed till a late hour, then the domestics, who, as we have before observed, invariably partake somewhat of their mistress's character, will surely become sluggards. . . .

4. Cleanliness Is Also Indispensable To Health, and must be studied both in regard to the person and the house, and all that it contains. Cold or tepid baths should be employed every morning, unless, on account of illness or other circumstances, they should be deemed objectionable. . . .

5. Frugality And Economy Are Home Virtues, without which no household can prosper. . . . We must always remember that it is a great merit in housekeeping to manage a little well. . . . Economy and frugality must never, however, be allowed to degenerate into parsimony and meanness. . . .

14. Charity And Benevolence Are Duties which a mistress owes to herself as well as to her fellow-creatures. . . . Visiting the houses of the poor is the only practical way really to understand the actual state of each family; and although there may be difficulties in following out this plan in the metropolis and other large cities, yet in country towns and rural districts these objections do not obtain. Great advantages may result from visits paid to the poor; for there being, unfortunately, much ignorance, generally, amongst them with respect to all household knowledge, there will be opportunities for advising and instructing them, in a pleasant and unobtrusive manner, in cleanliness, industry, cookery, and good management.

15. In Marketing, That The Best Articles Are The Cheapest, may be laid down as a rule; and it is desirable, unless an experienced and confidential housekeeper be kept, that the mistress should herself purchase all provisions and stores needed for the house. If the mistress be a young wife, and not accustomed to order "things for the house," a little practice and experience will soon teach her who are the best trades people

rearing and infant hygiene instructed middle-class women on how to be better mothers. Social reformers, some of them women, attempted to instruct working-class women in this new "science of motherhood," but, often working at a "sweated" trade or caring for boarders within their own homes, poorer women had little time for new mothering practices. Similarly, when Europeans established colonial empires, the wives of missionaries and officials sometimes tried to change child-rearing practices of local peoples. They were rarely successful, and different child-rearing practices became yet another sign of colonial people's inferiority in European eyes.

Women in industrializing countries also began to limit the number of children they bore. This revolutionary reduction in family size, in which the comfortable and well-educated classes took the lead, was founded on the parents' desire to improve their ecoto deal with, and what are the best provisions to buy.

16. A Housekeeping Account-book should invariably be kept, and kept punctually and precisely. . . . The housekeeping accounts should be balanced not less than once a month; so that you may see that the money you have in hand tallies with your account of it in your diary. . . .

18. In Obtaining A Servant's Character, it is not well to be guided by a written one from some unknown quarter; but it is better to have an interview, if at all possible, with the former mistress. By this means you will be assisted in your decision of the suitableness of the servant for your place, from the appearance of the lady and the state of her house. Negligence and want of cleanliness in her and her household generally, will naturally lead you to the conclusion, that her servant has suffered from the influence of the bad example.

19. The Treatment Of Servants is of the highest possible moment, as well to the mistress as to the domestics themselves. On the head of the house the latter will naturally fix their attention; and if they perceive that the mistress's conduct is regulated by high and correct principles, they will not fail to respect her. If, also, a benevolent desire is shown to promote their comfort, at the same time that a steady performance of their duty is exacted, then their respect will not be unmingled with affection, and they will be still more solicitous to continue to deserve her favour. . . .

48. Of The Manner Of Passing Evenings At Home, there is none pleasanter than in such recreative enjoyments as those which relax the mind from its severer duties, whilst they stimulate it with a gentle delight. Where there are young people forming a part of the evening circle, interesting and agreeable pastime should especially be promoted. It is of incalculable benefit to them that their homes should possess all the attractions of healthiest amusement, comfort, and happiness; for if they do not find pleasure there, they will seek it elsewhere. It ought, therefore, to enter into the domestic policy of every parent, to make her children feel that home is the happiest place in the world; that to imbue them with this delicious home-feeling is one of the choicest gifts a parent can bestow. . . .

54. Such Are The Onerous Duties which enter into the position of the mistress of a house, and such are, happily, with a slight but continued attention, of by no means difficult performance. She ought always to remember that she is the first and the last, the Alpha and the Omega in the government of her establishment; and that it is by her conduct that its whole internal policy is regulated. 🙿

Source: Isabella Mary Beeton, ed., *Beeton's Book of House Management* (London: S.O. Beeton, 1863), pp. 1–2, 5–7, 17, 18–19.

QUESTIONS FOR ANALYSIS

1. In what ways might the mistress of the household be considered like the commander of an army?

2. How important is outward appearance—to guests, servants, and the outside world—for the Victorian mistress of a household?

3. What advice does Mrs. Beeton give for the well-being and happiness of children?

4. Some scholars consider Mrs. Beeton a feminist. Do you agree with that assessment? Why?

---

nomic and social position and that of their children. By having fewer youngsters, parents could give those they had advantages, from music lessons to expensive university education. A young German skilled worker with one child spoke for many in his class when he said, "We want to get ahead, and our daughter should have things better than my wife and sisters did."[7]

The working classes probably had more avenues of escape from such tensions than did the middle classes.

Unlike their middle-class counterparts who remained economically dependent on their families until a long education was finished or a proper marriage secured, working-class boys and girls went to work when they reached adolescence. Earning wages on their own, they could bargain with their parents for greater independence within the household, or they could leave home to live cheaply as paying lodgers in other working-class homes. Thus the young person from the working classes broke away from the family more easily when emotional ties became oppressive.

Science for the Masses

The intellectual achievements of the scientific revolution (see Chapter 18) had resulted in few practical benefits, and theoretical knowledge had also played a relatively small role in the Industrial Revolution in England. But breakthroughs in industrial technology stimulated basic scientific inquiry as researchers sought to explain how such things as steam engines and blast furnaces actually worked. The result from the 1830s onward was an explosive growth of fundamental scientific discoveries that were increasingly transformed into material improvements for the general population.

A perfect example of the translation of better scientific knowledge into practical human benefits was the work of Louis Pasteur and his followers in biology and the medical sciences (see page 732). Another was the development of the branch of physics known as thermodynamics, the relationship between heat and mechanical energy. By midcentury physicists had formulated the fundamental laws of thermodynamics, which were then applied to mechanical engineering, chemical processes, and many other fields.

The triumph of science and technology had at least three significant consequences. First, though ordinary citizens continued to lack detailed scientific knowledge, everyday experience and innumerable articles in newspapers and magazines impressed the importance of science on the popular mind. Second, as science became more prominent in popular thinking, the philosophical implications of science formulated in the Enlightenment spread to broad sections of the population. Natural processes appeared to be determined by rigid laws, leaving little room for either divine intervention

Madrid in 1900 This wistful painting of a Spanish square on a rainy day, by Enrique Martínez Cubells y Ruiz (1874–1917), includes a revealing commentary on how scientific discoveries transformed urban life. Coachmen wait atop their expensive hackney cabs for a wealthy clientele, while modern electric streetcars that carry the masses converge on the square from all directions. In this way the development of electricity brought improved urban transportation and enabled the city to expand to the suburbs. (Museo Municipal, Madrid/The Bridgeman Art Library)

or human will. Third, the methods of science acquired unrivaled prestige after 1850. For many, the union of careful experiment and abstract theory was the only reliable route to truth and objective reality.

Living in an era of rapid change, nineteenth-century thinkers in Europe were fascinated with the idea of evolution and dynamic development. The most influential of all nineteenth-century evolutionary thinkers was Charles Darwin (1809–1882). Darwin came to doubt the general belief in a special divine creation of each species of animal. (A species is generally defined as a group of organisms that can interbreed with one another and produce fertile offspring of both sexes.) Instead, he concluded, all life had gradually evolved from a common ancestral origin in an unending "struggle for survival." Darwin's theory of **evolution** is summarized in the title of his work *On the Origin of Species by the Means of Natural Selection* (1859). He argued that small variations within individuals in one species allowed them to acquire more food and better living conditions and made them more successful in reproducing, thus passing their genetic material to the next generation. When a number of individuals within a species became distinct enough that they could no longer interbreed successfully with others, they became a new species.

Ever since humans began shaping the world around them tens of thousands of years ago, they have engaged in intentional selection and selective breeding in plants and animals to produce, for example, a new color of rose, a faster racehorse, or chickens that lay more eggs. Natural selection is not intentional; it results when random variations give some individuals an advantage in passing on their genetic material. Combined with the groundbreaking work in genetics carried out by the Augustinian priest and scientist Gregor Johann Mendel (1822–1884), Darwin's theory has become one of the fundamental unifying principles of modern biology.

Darwin's theory of natural selection provoked, and continues to provoke, resistance, particularly because he extended the theory to humans. Despite the criticism, however, Darwin's theory had a powerful and many-sided influence on European thought and the European middle classes. His findings reinforced the teachings of secularists such as Marx, who scornfully dismissed religious belief in favor of agnostic or atheistic materialism. Many writers also applied the theory of biological evolution to human affairs. Herbert Spencer (1820–1903), an English philosopher, saw the human race as driven forward to ever-greater specialization and progress by a brutal economic struggle that efficiently determines the "survival of the fittest." The idea that human society also evolves, and that the stronger will become powerful and prosperous while the weaker will be conquered or remain poor became known as **Social Darwinism**. Powerful nations used this ideology to justify nationalism and expansion, and colonizers to justify imperialism. Not surprisingly, Spencer and other Social Darwinists were especially popular with the upper middle class.

Not only did science shape society, but society also shaped science. As nations asserted their differences from one another, they sought "scientific" proof for those differences, which generally meant proof of their own superiority. European and American scientists, anthropologists, and physicians measured skulls, brains, and facial angles to prove that whites were more intelligent than other races, and that northern Europeans were more advanced than southern Europeans, perhaps even a separate "Nordic race" or "Aryan race." Africans were described and depicted as "missing links" between chimpanzees and Europeans, and they were occasionally even displayed as such in zoos and fairs. This scientific racism extended to Jews, who were increasingly described as a separate and inferior race, not a religious group. In the late nineteenth century a German author coined the term "anti-Semitism" to provide a more scientific-sounding term for hostility toward Jews, describing Jews as a separate "Semitic" race (see page 744).

Cultural Shifts

The French Revolution kindled the belief that radical reconstructions of politics and society were also possible in cultural and artistic life. The most significant expression of this belief in the early nineteenth century was the romantic movement. In part a revolt against classicism and the Enlightenment, romanticism was characterized by a belief in emotional exuberance, unrestrained imagination, and spontaneity in both art and personal life. Romanticism crystallized fully in the 1790s, primarily in England and Germany, and gained strength until the 1840s. Many romantic artists of the early nineteenth century lived lives of tremendous emotional intensity. They typically led bohemian lives, wearing their hair long and uncombed in preference to powdered wigs, and rejecting the materialism of refined society. Great individualists, they believed the full development of each person's unique human potential to be the supreme purpose in life.

One of the greatest and most moving romantic painters in France, Eugène Delacroix (oe-ZHEHN

- **evolution** The idea, applied by Charles Darwin, that concluded that all life had gradually evolved from a common origin; as applied by thinkers in many fields, the idea stressed gradual change and continuous adjustment.
- **Social Darwinism** The application of the theory of biological evolution to human affairs, it sees the human race as driven to ever-greater specialization and progress by an unending economic struggle that determines the survival of the fittest.

> "Beethoven's music sets in motion the lever of fear, of awe, of horror, of suffering, and awakens just that infinite longing which is the essence of Romanticism."
>
> **ERNST HOFFMANN**

deh-luh-KWAH; 1798–1863), was a romantic master of dramatic, colorful scenes that stirred the emotions. He was fascinated with remote and exotic subjects (see *Massacre at Chios*, below). Yet he was also a passionate spokesman for freedom.

It was in music that romanticism realized most fully and permanently its goals of free expression and emotional intensity. Abandoning well-defined structures, the great romantic composers used a wide range of forms to create musical landscapes and evoke powerful emotion. The first great romantic composer is among the most famous today, Ludwig van Beethoven

(1770–1827). As one contemporary admirer wrote, "Beethoven's music sets in motion the lever of fear, of awe, of horror, of suffering, and awakens just that infinite longing which is the essence of Romanticism."

Nowhere was the break with classicism more apparent than in romanticism's general conception of nature. Classicism was not particularly interested in nature. The romantics, in contrast, were enchanted by nature. For some it was awesome and tempestuous, while others saw nature as a source of spiritual inspiration.

The study of history became a romantic passion. History was the key to a universe that was now perceived to be organic and dynamic, not mechanical and static as the Enlightenment thinkers had believed. Historical studies supported the development of national aspirations and encouraged entire peoples to seek in the past their special destinies.

Romanticism found a distinctive voice in poetry. William Wordsworth (1770–1850) was the towering

Delacroix, *Massacre at Chios*
The Greek struggle for freedom and independence won the enthusiastic support of liberals, nationalists, and romantics. The Ottoman Turks were portrayed as cruel oppressors who were holding back the course of history, as in this moving masterpiece by Delacroix. (Réunion des Musées Nationaux/Art Resource, NY)

leader of English romanticism. In 1798 Wordsworth and his fellow romantic poet Samuel Taylor Coleridge (1772–1834) published their *Lyrical Ballads,* which abandoned flowery classical conventions for the language of ordinary speech. Wordsworth described his conception of poetry as the "spontaneous overflow of powerful feeling recollected in tranquility."

Victor Hugo (1802–1885) was France's greatest romantic master in both poetry and prose. His powerful novels exemplified the romantic fascination with fantastic characters, strange settings, and human emotions. The hero of Hugo's famous *Hunchback of Notre Dame* (1831) is the great cathedral's deformed bell-ringer, a "human gargoyle" overlooking the teeming life of fifteenth-century Paris.

In central and eastern Europe, literary romanticism and early nationalism often reinforced each other. Like modern anthropologists, romantics turned their attention to peasant life and transcribed the folk songs, tales, and proverbs that the cosmopolitan Enlightenment had disdained. The brothers Jacob and Wilhelm Grimm were particularly successful at rescuing German fairy tales from oblivion. In the Slavic lands romantics played a decisive role in converting spoken peasant languages into modern written languages. The greatest of all Russian poets, Aleksander Pushkin (1799–1837), used his lyric genius to mold the modern literary language of Russia.

Beginning in the 1840s, romanticism gave way to a new artistic genre, realism, which continued to dominate Western culture and style until the 1890s. Realist writers believed that literature should depict life exactly as it is. Forsaking poetry for prose and the personal, emotional viewpoint of the romantics for strict scientific objectivity, the realists simply observed and recorded.

The major realist writers focused on creating fiction based on contemporary everyday life. Beginning with a dissection of the middle classes, from which most of them sprang, many realists eventually focused on the working classes, especially the urban working classes, which had been neglected in literature before this time. The realists put a microscope to many unexplored and taboo subjects — sex, strikes, violence, alcoholism — shocking many middle-class critics. *Madame Bovary,* by Gustave Flaubert (1821–1880), for example, describes the heroine's adulterous affairs and lavish spending as she seeks to escape a dull husband and dull existence in a small provincial village. Now considered one of the greatest novels ever written, public prosecutors charged Flaubert with obscenity when it first appeared in 1856.

The realists' claims of objectivity did not prevent the elaboration of a definite worldview. Realists such as the famous French novelist Emile Zola (1840–1902) and English novelist Thomas Hardy (1840–1928) were strict determinists. They believed that human beings, like atoms, are components of the physical world and that all human actions are caused by unalterable natural laws: heredity and environment determine human behavior; good and evil are merely social conventions.

Nationalism and Socialism, 1871–1914

☐ How did nationalism and socialism shape European politics in the decades before the Great War?

After 1871 Europe's heartland was organized into strong national states. Only on Europe's borders — in Ireland and Russia, in Austria-Hungary and the Balkans — did people still strive for national unity and independence. Nationalism served, for better or worse, as a new unifying principle. At the same time, socialist parties grew rapidly. Many prosperous and conservative citizens were troubled by the socialist movement. Governing elites manipulated national feeling to create a sense of unity to divert attention from underlying class conflicts, and increasingly channeled national sentiment in an antiliberal and militaristic direction, tolerating anti-Semitism and waging wars in non-Western lands. This policy helped manage domestic conflicts, but only at the expense of increasing the international tensions that erupted in World War I.

Trends in Suffrage

There were good reasons why ordinary people — the masses of an industrializing, urbanizing society — felt increasing loyalty to their governments in central and western Europe. More people could vote. By 1914 universal male suffrage had become the rule rather than the exception. This development had as much psychological as political significance. Ordinary men felt they were becoming "part of the system."

Women also began to demand the right to vote. The women's suffrage movement achieved its first success in the western United States, and by 1913 women could vote in twelve states. In Europe, Norway gave the vote to most women in 1914. Suffragettes had little success elsewhere before 1914, but they prepared the way for getting the vote in many countries immediately after World War I.

As the right to vote spread, politicians and parties in national parliaments usually represented the people more responsively. The multiparty system prevailing in most countries meant that parliamentary majorities were built on shifting coalitions, which gave political parties leverage to obtain benefits for their supporters. Governments also passed laws to alleviate general problems, thereby acquiring greater legitimacy and appearing more worthy of support.

The German Empire

The new German Empire was a federal union of Prussia and twenty-four smaller states. The separate states conducted much of the everyday business of government. Unifying the whole was a strong national government with a chancellor — Bismarck until 1890 — and a popularly elected parliament called the Reichstag. Although Bismarck refused to be bound by a parliamentary majority, he pragmatically sought the backing of whichever coalition of political parties would support his policies.

As for socialism, Bismarck tried to stop its growth in Germany because he feared its revolutionary language and allegiance to a movement transcending the nation-state. In 1878 he pushed through a law outlawing the Social Democrats, but he was unable to force socialism out of existence. Bismarck's essentially conservative nation-state then pioneered social measures designed to win working-class support. In 1883 the Reichstag approved a national social security system that was the first of its kind anywhere.

Under Kaiser William I (r. 1861–1888), Bismarck had, in effect, managed the domestic and foreign policies of the state. In 1890 the new emperor, William II (r. 1888–1918), eager to rule in his own right and to earn the workers' support, forced Bismarck to resign. Following Bismarck's departure, the Reichstag passed new laws to aid workers and to legalize socialist political activity. German foreign policy changed most profoundly as well, and mostly for the worse (see pages 845–846).

Although William II was no more successful than Bismarck in getting workers to renounce socialism, in the years before World War I the Social Democratic party broadened its base and adopted a more patriotic tone. German socialists identified increasingly with the German state and concentrated on gradual social and political reform.

Republican France

Although Napoleon III's reign made some progress in reducing antagonisms between classes, the Franco-Prussian war undid these efforts, and in 1871 France seemed hopelessly divided once again. The republicans who proclaimed the Third Republic in Paris refused to admit defeat. They defended Paris with great heroism for weeks, until they were starved into submission by German armies in January 1871. When na-

tional elections then sent a large majority of conservatives and monarchists to the National Assembly, France's leaders decided they had no choice but to surrender Alsace and Lorraine to Germany. The traumatized Parisians exploded in patriotic frustration and proclaimed the Paris Commune in March 1871.

Commune leaders wanted to govern Paris without interference from the conservative French countryside. The National Assembly, led by aging conservative politician Adolphe Thiers, would hear none of it. The Assembly ordered the French army into Paris and brutally crushed the Commune. Twenty thousand people died in the fighting. As in June 1848, it was Paris against the provinces, French against French. Out of this tragedy France slowly formed a new national unity before 1914.

The moderate republicans sought to preserve their creation by winning the loyalty of the next generation. Trade unions were fully legalized, and France acquired a colonial empire. More important, a series of laws between 1879 and 1886 established free compulsory elementary education for both girls and boys, thereby greatly reducing the role of parochial Catholic schools that had long been hostile to republics and to much of secular life. In France and throughout the world the general expansion of public education served as a critical nation- and nationalism-building tool in the late nineteenth century.

Although the educational reforms of the 1880s disturbed French Catholics, many of them rallied to the republic in the 1890s, and tensions between church and state eased. Unfortunately, the **Dreyfus affair** changed all that. In 1894 Alfred Dreyfus, a Jewish captain in the French army, was falsely accused and convicted of treason. In 1898 and 1899 the case split France apart. On one side was the army, which had manufactured evidence against Dreyfus, joined by anti-Semites and most of the Catholic establishment. On the other side stood the civil libertarians and most of the more radical republicans.

This battle, which eventually led to Dreyfus's being declared innocent, revived militant republican feeling against the church. Between 1901 and 1905 the government severed all ties between the state and the Catholic Church after centuries of close relations. In France only the growing socialist movement, with its very different but thoroughly secular ideology, stood in opposition to patriotic republican nationalism.

Great Britain and the Austro-Hungarian Empire

The development of Great Britain and Austria-Hungary, two leading but quite different powers, throws a powerful light on the dynamics of national-

The Traitor: Degradation of Alfred Dreyfus After being arrested and convicted in a secret court martial for treason, Captain Dreyfus bravely stood at attention during a public degradation ceremony. While the officer on duty tore off his stripes, ripped off his honors, and broke his sword in two, Dreyfus shouted out, "You are degrading an innocent man! Long live France! Long live the army!" (Private Collection/The Bridgeman Art Library)

ism in Europe before 1914. At home Britain made more of its citizens feel a part of the nation by passing consecutive voting rights bills that gave solid middle-class males the right to vote in 1832, all middle-class males and the best-paid male workers the right in the Second Reform Bill of 1867, and finally every adult male through the Third Reform Bill of 1884. Moreover, extensive social welfare measures, slow to come to Great Britain, were passed in a spectacular rush between 1906 and 1914. The Liberal Party then substantially raised taxes on the rich as part of the so-called People's Budget to pay for national health insurance, unemployment benefits, old-age pensions, and a host of other social measures. The state was integrating the urban masses socially as well as politically.

On the eve of World War I, however, the unanswered question of Ireland brought Great Britain to the brink of civil war. The terrible Irish famine fueled an Irish revolutionary movement. Thereafter the English slowly granted concessions, but refused to give Ireland self-government. In 1910 Irish nationalists in the British Parliament supported the Liberals in their battle for the People's Budget. In 1913 they received a home-rule bill for Ireland in return.

Ireland and Britain, however, still faced the prospect of civil war. The Irish Catholic majority in the southern counties wanted home rule, but the Irish Protestants in the northern counties of Ulster vowed to resist it. Unable to resolve the conflict as World War I started in August 1914, the British government postponed indefinitely the whole question of Irish home rule.

The dilemma of conflicting nationalisms in Ireland helps one appreciate how desperate the situation in the Austro-Hungarian Empire had become by the early twentieth century. Following the savage defeat of the Hungarian republic (see page 503), Hungary was ruled as a conquered territory, and Emperor Franz Joseph (r. 1848–1916) and his bureaucracy tried hard to centralize the state and Germanize the language and culture of the different nationalities.

Following its defeat by Prussia in 1866, a weakened Austria was forced to establish the so-called dual monarchy. The empire was divided in two, and the nationalistic Magyars gained virtual independence for Hungary. The two states were joined only by a shared monarch and common ministries for finance, defense, and foreign

• **Dreyfus affair** A divisive case in which Alfred Dreyfus, a Jewish captain in the French army, was falsely accused and convicted of treason. The Catholic Church sided with the anti-Semites against Dreyfus; after Dreyfus was declared innocent, the French government severed all ties between the state and the church.

affairs. Still, the disintegrating force of competing nationalisms continued unabated, and the Austro-Hungarian Empire was progressively weakened and eventually destroyed by the conflicting national aspirations of its different ethnic groups. It was these ethnic conflicts in the Balkans, the "powder keg of Europe," that touched off the Great War in 1914 (see Chapter 28).

Jewish Emancipation and Modern Anti-Semitism

Revolutionary changes in political principles and the triumph of the nation-state brought equally revolutionary changes in Jewish life in western and central Europe. Beginning in France in 1791, Jews gradually gained their civil rights, although progress was slow and uneven. In the 1850s and 1860s liberals in Austria, Italy, and Prussia pressed successfully for legal equality. In 1871 the constitution of the new German Empire abolished all restrictions on Jewish marriage, choice of occupation, place of residence, and property ownership. Exclusion from government employment and discrimination in social relations remained, however, in central Europe.

The process of emancipation presented Jews with challenges and opportunities. Traditional Jewish occupations, such as court financial agent, village moneylender, and peddler, were undermined by free-market reforms, but careers in business, the professions, and the arts were opening to Jewish talent. By 1871 a majority of Jews in western and central Europe had improved their economic situations and entered the middle classes. Most Jews identified strongly with their respective nation-states and considered themselves patriotic citizens.

Vicious anti-Semitism reappeared after the stock market crash of 1873, beginning in central Europe. Drawing on long traditions of religious intolerance, ghetto exclusion, and periodic anti-Jewish riots and expulsions, this hostility also drew on modern ideas about Jews as a separate race. Modern anti-Semitism whipped up resentment against Jewish achievement and Jewish "financial control," while fanatics claimed that the Jewish race posed a biological threat to the German people. Anti-Semitic beliefs were particularly popular among conservatives, extremist nationalists, and people who felt threatened by Jewish competition.

Anti-Semites also created modern political parties. In Austrian Vienna in the early 1890s, Karl Lueger (LOO-guhr) and his "Christian socialists" won striking electoral victories. Lueger, the popular mayor of Vienna from 1897 to 1910, combined fierce anti-Semitic rhetoric with municipal ownership of basic services. He appealed especially to the German-speaking lower middle class—and to an unsuccessful young artist named Adolf Hitler. In response to spreading anti-Semitism, a Jewish journalist named Theodor Herzl (1860–1904) turned from German nationalism to advocate Jewish political nationalism, or **Zionism**, and the creation of a Jewish state.

Before 1914 anti-Semitism was most oppressive in eastern Europe, where Jews also suffered from terrible poverty. In the Russian empire, where there was no Jewish emancipation and 4 million of Europe's 7 million Jewish people lived in 1880, officials used anti-Semitism to channel popular discontent away from the government. In 1881–1882 a wave of violent pogroms commenced in southern Russia. The police and the army stood aside for days while peasants assaulted Jews and looted and destroyed their property. Official harassment continued in the following decades, and some Russian Jews turned toward self-emancipation and the vision of a Zionist settlement in the Ottoman province of Palestine. Large numbers also emigrated to western Europe and the United States.

The Socialist Movement

Socialism appealed to large numbers of working men and women in the late nineteenth century, and the growth of socialist parties after 1871 was phenomenal. (See "Viewpoints: Socialist and Anti-Socialist Perspectives," page 745.) By 1912 the German Social Democratic Party, which espoused Marxist ideology, had millions of followers and was the Reichstag's largest party. Socialist parties also grew in other countries, and Marxist socialist parties were linked together in an international organization. In 1864 Karl Marx played an important role in founding the First International of socialists.

The First International collapsed in 1872, but in 1889 socialist leaders came together to form the Second International, which lasted until 1914. Every three years delegates from the different parties met to interpret Marxist doctrines and plan coordinated action. Yet socialism was not as radical and revolutionary in these years as it sometimes appeared. As socialist parties grew and attracted large numbers of members, they looked more and more toward gradual change and steady improvement for the working class and less and less toward revolution. Workers themselves were progressively less inclined to follow radical programs for several reasons. As workers gained the right to vote and won real benefits, their attention focused more on elections than on revolutions. Workers were also not

---

• **Zionism** The movement toward Jewish political nationhood started by Theodor Herzl.

Viewpoints

Socialist and Anti-Socialist Perspectives

• *Socialism as an ideology gained a passionate following across Europe in the middle and late 1800s. Just as ardent were the laissez-faire anti-socialists, who opposed any government interference in a country's economic or social systems.*

The following documents represent the views of a socialist and an anti-socialist. In the first, from an English socialist magazine, are present many of the key words and concepts driving the socialist movement: class, labor theory of value, the rich produce nothing, a call to foreign brethren (fellow workers), and a new social order to replace the class system. The second document comes from William Graham Sumner, a widely read Yale College professor. An ardent supporter of laissez-faire economics and of the "survival of the fittest" beliefs of Social Darwinists, he vehemently opposed socialism and communism. Here he argues against government or private efforts to help society's poor or weak.

"The Meaning of Socialism," January 1885

❝Fellow Citizens, We come before you as Revolutionists, that is, as men and women who wish to see the basis of society changed.

Why is this?

Because in the society which now exists the majority of the people is miserable and oppressed. . . . [T]he "labourers," including all those who are engaged in . . . producing food for the community, are scarcely raised above starvation, or are punished for the crime of being born poor. . . .

Those poor persons . . . are a *class*, necessary, with all its poverty and misery, to the existence, as a class, of that other *class* of rich men: for all society is based upon labour and could not exist without it; and those of its members who *do not* produce wealth must necessarily live on the labours of those who *do* produce it. Those poor people . . . form a class which . . . has one interest common to all its members, the enjoyment of the fruits of its labour, and one enemy in common, namely the *class* of rich men who produce nothing, and if they work, work only at fleecing the poor class.

So then there are two *classes*; one producing and governed, the other non-producing and governing; one the means of wealth, the other the consumers of wealth: one *Rich*, the other *Poor*.

Fellow Workers, Is it necessary that this miserable state of things should last forever?

We bid you hope . . . for the establishment of a new order of things, the Social Order, in which there will be no poor and, therefore, no rich; in which there will be no classes.

English fellow-workmen! . . . Decent and happy life for all lies ahead of us, while all around is mere squalor, disorder, discontent, and the failure of all the hopes of civilization. Come out from these dreary ruins of decaying systems, and march with us toward the new Social Order of the World.❞

William Graham Sumner, "On a New Philosophy: That Poverty Is the Best Policy," 1883

❝It is very popular to pose as a "friend of humanity," or a "friend of the working classes." Anything which has a charitable sound and a kind-hearted tone generally passes without investigation, because it is disagreeable to assail it. Sermons, essays, and orations assume a conventional standpoint with regard to the poor, the weak, etc.; and it is allowed to pass as . . . unquestioned doctrine . . . that "the rich" ought to "care for the poor." . . .

The humanitarians, philanthropists, and reformers . . . find enough which is sad and unpromising in the condition of many members of society. They see wealth and poverty side by side. They note great inequality of social position and social chances. They eagerly set about . . . to account for what they see, and to devise schemes for remedying what they do not like. In their eagerness to recommend the less fortunate classes to pity and consideration they forget all about the rights of other classes; they gloss over all the faults of the classes in question, and they exaggerate their misfortunes and their virtues. They invent new theories of property, distorting rights and perpetrating injustice, as any one is sure to do who sets about the re-adjustment of social relations with the interests of one group distinctly before his mind, and the interests of all other groups thrown into the background.

Here it may suffice to observe that, on the theories of the social philosophers to whom I have referred, we should get a new maxim of judicious living: Poverty is the best policy. If you get wealth, you will have to support other people; if you do not get wealth, it will be the duty of other people to support you.❞

Sources: The Executive Council of the Social-Democratic Federation, "The Meaning of Socialism," *To-day: The Monthly Magazine of Scientific Socialism* III (January-June 1885): 1–5, 10; William Graham Sumner, *What Social Classes Owe to Each Other* (New York and London: Harper & Brothers, 1883, 1920), pp. 16–17, 21–22, 24.

QUESTIONS FOR ANALYSIS

1. What are the positions taken by the authors? Are these positions still current today?

2. How do you think Sumner would feel about modern government programs like Social Security and Medicare? What might be his argument for or against such programs?

"The Expulsion of the Jews from Russia" So reads this postcard, correctly suggesting that Russian government officials often encouraged popular anti-Semitism and helped drive many Jews out of Russia in the late nineteenth century. The road signs indicate that these poor Jews are crossing into Germany, where they will find a grudging welcome and a meager meal at the Jolly Onion Inn. Other Jews from eastern Europe settled in France and Britain, thereby creating small but significant Jewish populations in both countries for the first time since they had expelled most of their Jews in the Middle Ages. (Alliance Israelite Universelle, Paris/Archives Charmet/ The Bridgeman Art Library)

immune to nationalistic patriotism, even as they loyally voted for socialists. Nor were workers a unified social group. Perhaps most important of all, workers' standard of living rose steadily after 1850, and the quality of life improved substantially in urban areas. Thus workers tended to become militantly moderate: they demanded gains, but they were less likely to take to the barricades in pursuit of them.

The growth of labor unions reinforced this trend toward moderation. In the early stages of industrialization, modern unions were considered subversive bodies and were generally prohibited by law. In Great Britain new unions that formed for skilled workers after 1850 avoided radical politics and concentrated on winning better wages and hours for their members through collective bargaining and compromise. Af-

ter 1890 unions for unskilled workers developed in Britain.

German unions were not granted important rights until 1869, and until the anti-socialist law was repealed in 1890 the government frequently harassed them as socialist fronts. But after most legal harassment was eliminated, union membership skyrocketed from only about 270,000 in 1895 to roughly 3 million in 1912. Genuine collective bargaining, long opposed by socialist intellectuals as a "sellout," was officially recognized as desirable by the German Trade Union Congress in 1899.

The German trade unions and their leaders were thoroughgoing revisionists. **Revisionism** was an effort by various socialists to update Marxist doctrines to reflect the realities of the time. The socialist Eduard Bernstein (1850–1932) argued in his *Evolutionary Socialism* in 1899 that Marx's predictions of ever-greater poverty for workers had been proved false. Therefore, Bernstein suggested, socialists should re-

• **revisionism** An effort by various socialists to update Marxist doctrines to reflect the realities of the time.

form their doctrines and win gradual evolutionary gains for workers through legislation, unions, and further economic development. The Second International denounced these views as heresy. Yet the revisionist gradualist approach continued to gain the tacit acceptance of many German socialists, particularly in the trade unions.

Moderation found followers elsewhere. In France the great socialist leader Jean Jaurès (1859–1914) formally repudiated revisionist doctrines in order to establish a unified socialist party, but he remained at heart a gradualist. Questions of revolutionary versus gradualist policies split Russian Marxists.

Socialist parties in other countries had clear-cut national characteristics. Russians and socialists in the Austro-Hungarian Empire tended to be the most radical. In Great Britain the socialist but non-Marxist Labour Party formally committed to gradual reform. In Spain and Italy anarchism, seeking to smash the state rather than the bourgeoisie, dominated radical thought and action.

In short, socialist policies and doctrines varied from country to country. Socialism itself was to a large extent "nationalized." This helps explain why almost all socialist leaders supported their governments when war came in 1914.

CONNECTIONS

Much of world history in the past two centuries can be seen as the progressive unfolding of the dual revolution. Europe in the nineteenth century, and Asia, Latin America, and Africa more recently, underwent interrelated economic and political transformations. Although defeated in 1848, the new political ideologies associated with the French Revolution triumphed after 1850. Nationalism, with its commitment to the nation-state, became the most dominant of the new ideologies. National movements brought about the creation of unified nation-states in two of the most fractured regions in Europe, Germany and Italy.

After 1870 nationalism and militarism, its frequent companion, touched off increased competition between the major European powers for raw materials and markets for manufactured goods. As discussed in the next chapter, during the last decades of the nineteenth century Europe colonized nearly all of Africa and large areas in Asia. In Europe itself nationalism promoted a bitter, almost Darwinian competition between states, threatening the very progress and unity it had helped to build. In 1914 the power of unified nation-states turned on itself, unleashing an unprecedented conflict among Europe's Great Powers. Chapter 28 tells the story of this First World War.

Nationalism also sparked worldwide challenges to European dominance by African and Asian leaders who fought to liberate themselves from colonialism, and it became a rallying cry in nominally independent countries like China and Japan, whose leaders sought complete independence from European and American influence and a rightful place among the world's leading nations. Chapters 25, 26, 32, and 33 explore these developments. Likewise, Chapter 34 discusses how the problems of rapid urbanization and the huge gaps between rich and poor caused by economic transformations in America and Europe in the 1800s are now the concern of policy makers in Africa, Asia, and Latin America.

Another important ideology of change, socialism, remains popular in Europe, but never accomplished more than democratically electing socialist parties to office in some countries. Marxist revolutions that took absolute control of entire countries, as in Russia, China, and Cuba, had to wait until the twentieth century.

☐ CHAPTER REVIEW

☐ How did the allies fashion a peace settlement in 1815, and what radical ideas emerged between 1815 and 1848? (p. 716)

In 1814 the victorious allied powers sought to restore peace and stability in Europe. Dealing moderately with France and wisely settling their own differences, they laid the foundations for beneficial international cooperation throughout much of the nineteenth century. Led by Metternich of Austria, the conservative powers used intervention and repression as they sought to prevent the spread of subversive ideas and radical changes in domestic politics. After 1815 ideologies of liberalism, nationalism, and socialism all developed to challenge the existing order. The principal ideas of liberalism were equality and liberty, which were expressed in representative government and civil rights. Nationalism was based on the notion that each people had its own genius and cultural unity; to this was added the idea that each people deserved its own political entity and government. The key ideas of socialism were economic planning, greater economic equality, and the state regulation of property.

☐ Why in 1848 did revolutions triumph briefly throughout most of Europe, and why did they fail? (p. 722)

The growth of liberal, nationalist, and socialist forces culminated in the liberal and nationalistic revolutions of 1848. Monarchies panicked and crumbled in the face of popular uprisings and widespread opposition that cut across class lines, and the revolutionaries triumphed, first in France and then across the continent. Very few revolutionary goals were realized. The moderate, nationalistic middle classes were unable to consolidate their initial victories. Instead, they drew back when artisans, factory workers, and radical socialists rose up to present their own, much more revolutionary demands. This retreat facilitated a resurgence of conservative forces that crushed revolution across Europe.

☐ How did strong leaders and nation building transform Italy, Germany, and Russia? (p. 725)

In Italy Cavour joined traditional diplomacy and war against Austria with nationalist uprising in central Italy to expand the constitutional monarchy in Sardinia-Piedmont. He then succeeded in merging the south and the north together in a conservative nation-state under Victor Emmanuel. In Prussia Bismarck also combined traditional statecraft with

national feeling. Ruling without the consent of parliament and reorganizing the army, Bismarck succeeded in making Prussia the dominant German state. War with France completed the unification process, expanding the power of Prussia and its king in a new German Empire, and instilling in all Germans a strong sense of national pride. In autocratic Russia, defeat in the Crimean War posed a regime-threatening crisis, which led to the emancipation of the serfs and economic modernization that featured railroad building, military improvements, and industrialization. Political reform was limited, however, and even after the revolution of 1905 led to a popularly elected Duma, the tsar retained great power.

☐ What was the impact of urban growth on cities, social classes, families, and ideas? (p. 731)

As new industrial factories and offices were built in urban areas, urban populations grew at unprecedented rates. Living conditions sharply declined until the mid-nineteenth century, when governments finally began to clean up the cities. Society also benefited from scientific advancements, including germ control and new public transportation systems that relieved overcrowding. Major changes in the class structure and family life accompanied urban growth. Family life became more stable and more loving, although a sharp separation of gender roles tended to lock women into subordinate and stereotypical roles. The class structure became more complex and diversified. The upper and middle classes expanded and gained income, and their occupations became more diverse. Ordinary people gained a new awareness and appreciation of science, and ideas such as Darwin's theory of natural selection challenged the traditional religious understanding of the world. In the realm of literature and the arts, the romantic movement reinforced the spirit of change. The movement was characterized by a belief in self-expression, imagination, and spontaneity in art as well in personal life. Romanticism gave way to realism in the 1840s, reflecting Western society's growing faith in science, material progress, and evolutionary thinking.

□ How did nationalism and socialism shape European politics in the decades before the Great War? (p. 741)

Western society became increasingly nationalistic as well as urban and industrial in the late nineteenth century. Nation-states became more responsive, and they enlisted widespread support as peaceful political participation expanded, educational opportunities increased, and social security systems took shape. More broadly, nation-states may be seen as providing a stabilizing response to the profoundly unsettling challenges of the dual revolution. Even socialism became increasingly national in orientation, gathering strength as a champion of working-class interests in domestic politics. Yet even though nationalism served to unite peoples, it also drove them apart — not only in Austria-Hungary and Ireland but also throughout Europe and the rest of the world. The national faith, which reduced social tensions within states, promoted a bitter, almost Darwinian competition between states — often most clearly visible in greatly enlarged armies and navies — and thus threatened the progress and unity it had helped to build.

SUGGESTED READING

Anderson, Bonnie S., and Judith P. Zinsser. *A History of Their Own: Women in Europe from Prehistory to the Present*, vol. 2, rev. ed. 2000. An excellent, wide-ranging survey.

Baycroft, Timothy, and Mark Hewitson, eds. *What Is a Nation? Europe 1789–1914*. 2009. A sweeping study of nationalism in all its forms and all the processes that affected its evolution.

Berend, Ivan T. *History Derailed: Central and Eastern Europe in the Long Nineteenth Century*. 2003. Focuses on industrialization and its consequences.

Berger, Stefan, ed. *A Companion to Nineteenth-Century Europe, 1789–1914*. 2006. A useful study with an up-to-date bibliography.

Clark, Linda L. *Women and Achievement in Nineteenth-Century Europe*. 2008. Examines the activities of women who sought recognition for work at home and opportunity for work outside the home.

Coontz, Stephanie. *Marriage, A History: From Obedience to Intimacy, or How Love Conquered Marriage*. 2005. A lively inquiry into the historical background to current practice.

Gildea, Robert. *Barricades and Borders: Europe, 1800–1914*, 2d ed. 1996. A recommended general study.

Kertzer, David I., and Marzio Barbagli, eds. *Family Life in the Nineteenth Century, 1789–1913*. 2002. A broad exploration of European family life and the forces that shaped it in the nineteenth century.

Malia, Martin, and Terrence Emmons. *History's Locomotives: Revolutions and the Making of the Modern World*. 2006. An ambitious comparative work of high quality.

Mann, Thomas. *Buddenbrooks*. 1901. A wonderful historical novel that traces the rise and fall of a prosperous German family over three generations.

Otis, Laura. *Literature and Science in the Nineteenth Century: An Anthology*. 2009. A fascinating selection of writings from a time when humanities and science were not considered separate disciplines.

Rapport, Mike. *1848: Year of Revolution*. 2008. A stimulating account of the revolutions that swept across Europe in 1848.

Rubinstein, W. D. *Britain's Century: Political and Social History, 1815–1905*. 1998. An excellent history with strong coverage of social questions.

Tombs, Robert. *France, 1814–1914*. 1996. An impressive survey with a useful bibliography.

Winks, Robin W., and Joan Neuberger. *Europe and the Making of Modernity: 1815–1914*. 2005. Grand narrative of the forces that shaped modern Europe from the Congress of Vienna to the Great War.

NOTES

1. J. G. Fichte, *Addresses to the German Nation*, trans. R. F. Jones and G. H. Turnbull (Chicago and London: Open Court Publishing Company, 1922), p. 4.
2. E. Gellner, *Nations and Nationalism* (Oxford, U.K.: Basil Blackwell, 1983), pp. 19–39.
3. B. Anderson, *Imagined Communities: Reflections on the Origins and Spread of Nationalism*, rev. ed. (London and New York: Verso, 1991).
4. Quoted by G. O'Brien, *The Economic History of Ireland from the Union to the Famine* (London: Longmans, Green, 1921), p. 21.
5. Ibid., pp. 23–24.
6. J. McKay, *Tramways and Trolleys: The Rise of Urban Mass Transport in Europe* (Princeton, N.J.: Princeton University Press, 1976), p. 81.
7. Quoted in R. P. Neuman, "The Sexual Question and Social Democracy in Imperial Germany," *Journal of Social History* 7 (Winter 1974): 281.

For practice quizzes and other study tools, visit the **Online Study Guide** at bedfordstmartins.com/mckayworld.

For primary sources from this period, see **Sources of World Societies, Second Edition**.

For Web sites, images, and documents related to topics in this chapter, visit **Make History** at bedfordstmartins.com/mckayworld.

• **Sengbe Pieh** Enslaved in 1839, Pieh (later known as Joseph Cinqué) led a famous revolt on the slave ship *Amistad*. He and his fellow slaves were charged with mutiny and murder, but in March 1840 the U.S. Supreme Court found them innocent because they had been illegally captured and sold. They returned to their native Sierra Leone as free men. (New Haven Colony Historical Society)

25

While industrialization and nationalism were transforming society in Europe and the neo-European countries (the United States, Canada, Australia, New Zealand, and, to an extent, South Africa), Western society itself was reshaping the world. European commercial interests went in search of new sources of raw materials and markets for their manufactured goods. At the same time, millions of Europeans and Asians picked up stakes and emigrated abroad. What began as a relatively peaceful exchange of products with Africa and Asia in the early nineteenth century had transformed by the end of the century into a frenzy of imperialist occupation and domination that had a profound impact on both the colonizers and the colonized.

Africa, Southwest Asia, and the New Imperialism

1800-1914

The political annexation of territory in the 1880s — the "new imperialism," as it is often called by historians — was the capstone of Western society's underlying economic and technological transformation. More directly, Western imperialism rested on a formidable combination of superior military might and strong authoritarian rule, and it posed a brutal challenge to African and Asian peoples. Different societies met this Western challenge in different ways and with changing tactics, as we shall see. Nevertheless, by 1914 non-Western elites in many lands were rallying their peoples and leading an anti-imperialist struggle for dignity and genuine independence that would triumph after 1945. •

Africa: From the Slave Trade to European Colonial Rule

□ What were the most significant changes in Africa during the nineteenth century, and why did they occur?

The New Imperialism, 1880–1914

□ What were the causes and consequences of European empire building after 1880?

The Islamic Heartland Under Pressure

□ How did the Ottoman Empire and Egypt try to modernize themselves, and what were the most important results?

The Expanding World Economy

□ What were the global consequences of European industrialization between 1800 and 1914?

The Great Global Migration

□ What fueled migration, and what was the general pattern of this unprecedented movement of people?

Africa: From the Slave Trade to European Colonial Rule

□ What were the most significant changes in Africa during the nineteenth century, and why did they occur?

From the beginning of the nineteenth century to the global depression of the 1930s, the different regions of Africa experienced gradual but monumental change. The long-standing transatlantic slave trade declined and practically disappeared by the late 1860s. In the early nineteenth century Islam expanded its influence in a long belt south of the Sahara, but Africa generally remained free of European political control. After about 1880 further Islamic expansion to the south stopped, but the pace of change accelerated as France and Britain led European nations in the "scramble for Africa." Africa was divided and largely conquered by Europeans, and by 1900 the foreigners were consolidating their authoritarian empires.

Trade and Social Change

The most important development in West Africa before the European conquest was the decline of the Atlantic slave trade and the simultaneous rise of the export of **palm oil** and other commodities. A major break with the past, the shift in African foreign trade marked the beginning of modern economic development in sub-Saharan Africa.

Although the trade in African people was a worldwide phenomenon, the transatlantic slave trade between Africa and the Americas became the most extensive and significant portion of it (see pages 572–580). The forced migration of millions of Africans — so cruel, unjust, and tragic — intensified after 1700, and especially after 1750 (see Figure 19.2, page 582). Increasing demand for labor resulted in rising prices for African slaves in the eighteenth century. Some African merchants and rulers who controlled exports profited, but in the long run the slave trade resulted in instability and warfare, decimated the population, and destroyed local economies.

Until 1700, and perhaps even 1750, most Europeans considered the African slave trade a legitimate business activity. After 1775 a broad campaign to abolish slavery developed in Britain. This campaign grew into one of the first peaceful mass political movements based on the mobilization of public opinion in British history. British women played a critical role in this movement, denouncing the immorality of human bondage and stressing the cruel treatment of female slaves and slave families. The abolitionist movement also argued for a transition to legitimate (non-slave) trade, to end both the transatlantic slave trade and the internal African slave systems. In 1807 Parliament declared the slave trade illegal. Britain then established the anti-slavery West Africa Squadron, using its navy to seize the ships of the slave runners, liberating the captives, and settling them in the British port of Freetown, in Sierra Leone, as well as in Liberia (Map 25.1). Freed American slaves — with the help of the American Colonization Society, a group devoted to returning freed slaves to Africa — had established the colony of Liberia in 1821–1822. They named their capital Monrovia, after America's fifth president, James Monroe, who prominently supported the enterprise.

British action had a limited impact at first. The transatlantic slave trade regained its previous massive level after Napoleon was defeated and peace returned to Europe in 1815, and the worldwide trade in enslaved

---

• **palm oil** A West African tropical product often used to make soap; the British encouraged its cultivation as an alternative to the slave trade.

Africans declined only gradually. Britain's West Africa squadron intercepted fewer than 10 percent of all slave ships, and the demand for slaves remained high on the expanding and labor-intensive sugar and coffee plantations of Cuba and Brazil until the 1850s and 1860s. In the United States the Constitution (1787) prohibited the banning of the importation of slaves before 1808, which was a twenty-year concession to the southern states for their agreeing to join the new union. By 1807 there was a passionate, sometimes violent national debate over the moral and commercial questions surrounding slavery. On March 2, 1807 President Thomas Jefferson signed into law an act that banned the importation of slaves from January 1, 1808. From that time on, natural increase (slaves having children) accounted mainly for the subsequent growth of the African American slave population before the Civil War. Strong financial incentives remained, however, for Portuguese and other European slave traders, as well as for those African rulers who relied on profits from the trade for power and influence.

As more nations joined Britain in outlawing the slave trade, the shipment of human cargo slackened along the West African coast. The decline began on the long stretch from Guinea and Senegal to the Gold Coast and present-day Nigeria by the 1830s and occurred thereafter in west-central Africa in present-day Congo and Angola (see Map 25.1). At the same time the ancient but limited shipment of slaves across the Sahara and from the East African coast into the Indian Ocean and through the Red Sea expanded dramatically. Only in the 1860s did this trade begin to decline rapidly. As a result of these shifting currents, exports of slaves from all of West Africa across the Atlantic declined from an estimated 6.5 million persons in the eighteenth century to 3.9 million in the nineteenth century. Yet total exports of slaves from all regions of sub-Saharan Africa declined less than half as fast in the same years, from 7.4 million to 6.1 million.[1] The abolitionist vision of "legitimate" commerce in tropical products quickly replacing illegal slave exports was not realized.

Nevertheless, beginning in West Africa, trade in tropical products did make steady progress, for several reasons. First, with Britain encouraging palm tree cultivation as an alternative to the slave trade, palm oil sales from West Africa to Britain surged from only one thousand tons in 1810 to more than forty thousand tons in 1855. Second, the sale of palm oil admirably served the self-interest of industrializing Europe. Manufacturers used palm oil to lubricate their giant machines, and from palm oil they made the first good, cheap soap and other cosmetics. Products made from new processes in petroleum refining supplanted palm oil in the mid- to late 1800s, but contemporary brand names like Palmolive and Lever Brothers are vestiges of the days when palm oil was king. Third, the production of peanuts for export also grew rapidly, in part because both small, independent African farmers and their families and large-scale enterprises could produce peanuts for the substantial American and European markets.

Finally, powerful West African rulers and warlords who had benefited from the Atlantic slave trade succeeded in redirecting some of their slaves into the production of legitimate goods for world markets. This was possible because slavery and slave markets remained strong in sub-Saharan Africa, as local warfare and

□ CHRONOLOGY

1805–1848	Muhammad Ali modernizes Egypt
1808–1839	Mahmud II rules Ottoman state and enacts reforms
1809	Usuman founds Sokoto caliphate
1830	France begins conquest of Algeria
1839–1876	Western-style reforms (Tanzimat) in Ottoman Empire
1860s	Transatlantic slave trade declines rapidly
1869	Completion of Suez Canal
1875	Ottoman state declares partial bankruptcy; European creditors take over
1876	Europeans take financial control in Egypt
1880	Western and central Sudan unite under Islam
1880–1900	Most of Africa falls under European rule
1880–1914	Height of new imperialism in Asia and Africa
1881	Ahmed Arabi leads revolt against foreign control of Egypt
1884–1885	Berlin Conference
1899	Kipling, "The White Man's Burden"; Amin, *The Liberation of Women*
1899–1902	South African War
1902	Conrad, *Heart of Darkness*; Hobson, *Imperialism*
1908	Young Turks seize power in Ottoman Empire

▢ Picturing the Past

Pears' Soap Advertisement Andrew Pears began making his transparent soap in London in 1789. Starting in the late 1800s, it was marketed worldwide as a product symbolizing progress in advancing Europe's "civilizing mission." In 1910 the Lever brothers, William and James, bought Pears's company and sold Pears' Soap along with their own brands, including Sunlight, Lifebuoy, and Lux. These soaps were made with palm oil from Lever plantations in the Congo and the Solomon Islands. Pears' Soap is still made today, in India. (North Wind Picture Archives/Alamy)

ANALYZING THE IMAGE Which elements or words in this advertisement suggest the Western ideal of "civilization"? Which elements or words are used to describe non-Europeans?

CONNECTIONS How might the English phrase "Cleanliness is next to Godliness" relate to this advertisement? How can Pears' Soap "lighten the white man's burden" and brighten "the dark corners of the earth"?

The first step towards lightening

The White Man's Burden

is through teaching the virtues of cleanliness.

Pears' Soap

is a potent factor in brightening the dark corners of the earth as civilization advances, while amongst the cultured of all nations it holds the highest place—it is the ideal toilet soap.

---

slave raiding continued to enslave large numbers of men, women, and children. While some enslaved captives were still sold abroad to places, like Brazil, where the slave trade remained legal, women might be kept as wives, concubines, or servants. Men were often used to transport goods, mine gold, grow crops, and serve in slave armies. For example, after the collapse of the Oyo empire in the nineteenth century, Yoruba warlords in present-day Nigeria developed palm oil plantations worked by slaves. By the 1860s and 1870s, 104 families in the city of Ibadan owned fifty thousand slaves, an average of five hundred per family.[2] As the experience of the Yoruba suggests, the slow decline of the transatlantic slave trade coincided with the most intensive use of slaves within Africa.

At the same time, a new group of African merchants—including liberated slaves from Freetown and

Monrovia who had received some Western education—did rise to handle legitimate trade, and some grew rich. Women were among the most successful of these merchants. Although there is a long tradition of the active involvement in trade of West African women, the arrival of Europeans provided new opportunities. The African wife of a European trader served as her husband's interpreter and learned all aspects of his business. When the husband died, as European men invariably did in the hot, humid, and mosquito-infested areas of tropical West Africa, the African wife inherited his commercial interests, including his inventory and his European connections. Many such widows used their considerable business acumen to make small fortunes.

By the 1850s and 1860s legitimate African traders, flanked by Western-educated African lawyers, teachers, and journalists, formed an emerging middle class in the coastal towns of West Africa. This tiny middle class provided new leadership that augured well for the region's future. Unfortunately for West Africans, in the 1880s and 1890s African business leadership gave way to imperial subordination.

Islamic Revival and Expansion in Africa

By the early eighteenth century Islam had been practiced throughout the Sudanic Savanna—the vast belt of flat grasslands across Africa below the southern fringe of the Sahara, stretching from Senegal and Gambia in the west to the mountains of Ethiopia in the east—for five hundred to a thousand years, depending on the area. The cities, political rulers, and merchants in many small states were Muslim. Yet the peasant farmers and migratory cattle raisers—the vast majority of the population—generally remained true to traditional animist practices, worshipping ancestors, local shrines, and protective spirits. Many Muslim rulers shared some of these beliefs and did not try to convert their subjects in the countryside or enforce Islamic law.

Beginning in the eighteenth century and gathering strength in the early nineteenth century, a powerful Islamic revival brought reform and revolutionary change from within to the western and eastern Sudan, until this process was halted by European military conquest at the end of the nineteenth century. In essence, Muslim scholars and fervent religious leaders arose to wage successful **jihads**, or religious wars, against both animist rulers and Islamic states that they deemed corrupt. The new reformist rulers believed that African cults and religious practice could no longer be tolerated, and they often effected mass conversions of animists to Islam.

The most important of these revivalist states, the enormous **Sokoto caliphate**, illustrates the pattern of Islamic revival in Africa. It was founded by Usuman dan Fodio (1754–1817), an inspiring Muslim teacher who first won zealous followers among both the Fulani herders and the Hausa peasants in the Muslim state of Gobir in the northern Sudan. After his religious community was attacked by Gobir's rulers, Usuman launched the jihad of 1804, one of the most important events in nineteenth-century West Africa. Usuman claimed that the Hausa rulers of Muslim Gobir "worshipped many places of idols, and trees, and rocks, and sacrificed to them," killing and plundering their subjects without any regard for Islamic law.[3] Young religious students and discontented Fulani cattle raisers formed the backbone of the fighters, who succeeded in overthrowing the Hausa rulers and inspired more jihads in the Sudan. In 1809 Usuman established the new Sokoto caliphate, which was ably consolidated by his son Muhammad Bello as a vast and enduring decentralized state (see Map 25.1).

The triumph of the Sokoto caliphate had profound consequences for Africa and the Sudan. First, the caliphate was based on Islamic history and law, which gave sub-Saharan Africa a sophisticated written constitution that earlier preliterate states had never achieved. This government of laws, rather than men, provided stability and made Sokoto one of the most prosperous regions in tropical Africa. Second, because of Sokoto and other revivalist states, Islam became much more widely and deeply rooted in sub-Saharan Africa than ever before. By 1880 the entire western and central Sudan was united in Islam. In this vast expanse Islam became an unquestioned part of everyday life and culture. Women gained greater access to education, even as veiling and seclusion became more common. Finally, Islam had always approved of slavery for non-Muslims and Muslim heretics, and "the *jihads* created a new slaving frontier on the basis of rejuvenated Islam."[4] In 1900 the Sokoto caliphate had at least 1 million and perhaps as many as 2.5 million slaves. Among all modern slave societies, only the American South had more slaves, about 4 million in 1860.

Islam also expanded in East Africa, in large part because of the efforts of Sayyid Said (r. 1804–1856), the energetic imam of Oman. Reviving his family's lordship of the African island of Zanzibar and eventually moving his capital from southern Arabia to Zanzibar in 1840, Sayyid Said (sa-EED sa-EED) and his Baluchi mercenaries (from present-day Pakistan) gained control of most of the Swahili-speaking East African coast. Said concentrated the shipment of slaves to the Ottoman Empire and Arabia through Zanzibar. In addition, he successfully encouraged Indian merchants to develop slave-based clove plantations in his territories. Thus, from the 1820s on Arab merchants and adventurers pressed far into the interior in search of slaves and ivory, converting and intermarrying with local Nyamwezi (nyahm-WAY-zee) elites and establishing small Muslim states. The Arab immigrants brought literacy, administrative skills, and increased trade and international contact, as well as the intensification of slavery, to East Africa. In 1870, before Christian missionaries and Western armies began to arrive in force, it appeared that most of the East African population would accept Islam within a generation.[5]

The Scramble for Africa, 1880–1914

Between 1880 and 1914 Britain, France, Germany, Belgium, Spain, and Italy, worried that they would not get

---

- **jihad** Religious war waged by Muslim scholars and religious leaders against both animist rulers and Islamic states that they deemed corrupt.
- **Sokoto caliphate** Founded in 1809 by Usuman dan Fodio, this African state was based on Islamic history and law.

Colonial presence, 1914

British	Belgian
French	Spanish
German	Independent African states
Italian	
Portuguese	Afrikaner republic

Colonial presence, 1878

▢ Mapping the Past

MAP 25.1 The Partition of Africa The European powers carved up Africa after 1880 and built vast political empires.

ANALYZING THE MAP What European countries were leading imperialist states in Africa, and what lands did they hold? What countries maintained political independence?

CONNECTIONS The late nineteenth century was the high point of European imperialism. What were the motives behind the rush for land and empire in Africa?

"a piece of that magnificent African cake" (in King Leopold II of Belgium's graphic phrase), scrambled for African possessions as if their national livelihoods were at stake. By 1914 only Ethiopia in northeast Africa and Liberia on the West African coast remained independent (see Map 25.1).

In addition to the general causes underlying Europe's imperialist burst after 1880 (see pages 763–767), certain events and individuals stand out. First, as the antislavery movement succeeded in shutting down the Atlantic slave trade by the late 1860s, the persistence of slavery elsewhere attracted growing attention in western Europe and the Americas. Through the publications of Protestant missionaries such as David Livingstone from Scotland and the fiery eyewitness accounts of the Catholic White Fathers missionary society (named for their white robes), antislavery activists learned of the horrors of slave raids and the suffering of thousands of innocent victims sold within Africa and through East African ports. The public was led to believe that European conquest and colonization would end this human tragedy by bringing, in Livingstone's famous phrase, "Commerce, Christianity, and Civilization" to Africa.

Leopold II of Belgium (r. 1865–1909) also played a crucial role. His agents signed treaties with African chiefs and planted Leopold's flag along the Congo River. In addition, Leopold intentionally misled leaders of the other European nations to gain their support by promising to promote Christianity and civilization in his proposed Congo Free State. By 1883 Europe had caught "African fever," and the race for territory was on.

To lay down some rules for this imperialist competition, Premier Jules Ferry of France and Chancellor Otto von Bismarck of Germany arranged a European conference on Africa in Berlin in 1884–1885. The **Berlin Conference**, to which Africans had not been invited, established the principle that European claims to African territory had to rest on "effective occupation" in order to be recognized by other states. This meant that Europeans would push relentlessly into interior regions from all sides and that no single European power would be able to claim the entire continent. A nation could establish a colony only if it had effectively taken possession of the territory through signed treaties with local leaders and had begun to develop it economically. The representatives at the conference recognized Leopold's rule over a neutral Congo state and agreed to work to stop slavery and the slave trade in Africa.

In addition to developing rules for imperialist competition, participants at the Berlin Conference also promised to end slavery and to bring Christianity and civilization to Africa. In truth, however, these ideals ran a distant second to, and were not allowed to interfere with, their primary goal of commerce — holding on

> "They shall, without distinction of creed or nation, protect and favour all religious, scientific or charitable institutions . . . which aim at instructing the natives and bringing home to them the blessings of civilization."
>
> **BERLIN CONFERENCE**

to their old markets and exploiting new ones:

All the Powers exercising sovereign rights or influence in the aforesaid territories bind themselves to watch over the preservation of the native tribes, and to care for the improvement of the conditions of their moral and material well-being, and to help in suppressing slavery, and especially the slave trade.

They shall, without distinction of creed or nation, protect and favour all religious, scientific or charitable institutions and undertakings created and organized for the above ends, or which aim at instructing the natives and bringing home to them the blessings of civilization.[6]

The Berlin Conference coincided with Germany's emergence as an imperial power. In 1884 and 1885 Bismarck's Germany established **protectorates** over a number of small African kingdoms and societies in Togoland, Kamerun, southwest Africa, and, later, East Africa (see Map 25.1). In acquiring colonies, Bismarck cooperated with France's Jules Ferry against the British. (See "Listening to the Past: A French Leader Defends Imperialism," page 764.) The French expanded into West Africa and formed a protectorate on the Congo River. As for the British, they began enlarging their West African enclaves and pushed northward from the Cape Colony and westward from the East African coast.

Pushing southward from Egypt, which the British had seized control of in 1882 (see page 772), the British were blocked in the eastern Sudan by fiercely independent Muslims, who had felt the full force of Islamic revival. In 1881 a pious local leader, Muhammad Ahmad (1844–1885), led a revolt against foreign control of Egypt. In 1885 his army massacred a British force and took the city of Khartoum, forcing the British to retreat to Cairo. Ten years later a British force returned, building a railroad to supply arms and reinforcements as it went. Finally, in 1898 these troops met their foe at Omdurman, where Sudanese Muslims armed with spears charged time and time again, only to be cut down by the

• **Berlin Conference** A meeting of European leaders held in 1884–1885 to lay down basic rules for imperialist competition in sub-Saharan Africa.

• **protectorate** An autonomous state or territory partly controlled and protected by a stronger outside power.

Brutality in the Congo No Africans suffered more violent and brutal treatment under colonial rule than those living in Belgian King Leopold the II's Congo Free State. When not having their hands, feet, or heads cut off as punishment, Africans were whipped with *chicottes*, whips made of dried hippopotamus hide. Some Congolese were literally whipped to death. (Courtesy, Anti-Slavery International, London)

recently invented machine gun. In the end eleven thousand brave but poorly armed Muslim fighters lay dead. Only twenty-eight Britons had been killed.

All European nations resorted to some violence in their colonies to retain control, subdue the population, appropriate land, and force African laborers to work long hours at physically demanding, and often dangerous, jobs. In no colony, however, was the violence and brutality worse than in Leopold II's Congo Free State. Rather than promoting Christianity and civilization as Leopold had promised, the European companies operating in the Congo Free State introduced slavery, unimaginable savagery, and terror. Missionaries and other religious leaders were not even allowed into the colony, for fear of their reporting the horrors they would witness there.

Profits in the Congo Free State came first from the ivory trade, but in the 1890s, when many of the elephant herds in the Congo had been decimated, a new cash crop arose to take ivory's place. In the mid-1880s a northern Irishman named John Dunlop developed a process to make inflatable rubber tires for his son's tricycle. Other scientific developments soon followed, and new uses for rubber were found, which caused a worldwide boom in the demand for raw rubber. As it happened, more than half of the Congo Free State possessed wild rubber vines growing thickly in the equatorial rain forest. By the mid-1890s rubber had surpassed ivory as the colony's major income producer, and Leopold and the companies he allowed to make profits in the Congo soon could not get enough of it. Violence and brutality increased exponentially as the European appetite for rubber became insatiable. Europeans and their well-armed mercenaries terrorized

entire regions, cutting off hands, feet, and heads and wiping out whole villages to make it clear to the Africans that they must either work for the Europeans or die. The African blood that was shed is recalled in the colony's frightening nickname—the "red rubber colony." In the early 1900s, human rights activists such as Edmund Morel exposed the truth about the horrific conditions in the Congo Free State, and in 1908 Leopold was forced to turn over his private territory to Belgium as a colony, the Belgian Congo. (See "Viewpoints: The Congo Free State," page 759.)

Southern Africa in the Nineteenth Century

The development of southern Africa diverged from the rest of sub-Saharan Africa in important ways. Whites settled in large numbers, modern capitalist industry took off, and British imperialists had to wage all-out war.

In 1652 the Dutch East India Company established a supply station at Cape Town for Dutch ships sailing between Amsterdam and Indonesia. The healthy, temperate climate and the sparse Khoisan population near the Cape resulted in the colony's gradual expansion. When the British took possession of the colony in the Napoleonic wars, the Cape Colony included about twenty thousand free Dutch citizens and twenty-five thousand African slaves, with substantial mixed-race communities on the northern frontier of white settlement.

After 1815 powerful African chiefdoms, Dutch settlers—first known as Boers, and then as **Afrikaners**—and British colonial forces waged a complicated three-

• **Afrikaners** Descendants of the Dutch settlers in the Cape Colony in southern Africa.

Viewpoints

The Congo Free State

• One historian estimates that between 1890 and 1910 the African population of the Congo Free State declined by nearly 10 million souls.* The public learned of the brutal conditions in the Congo through the efforts of reformers and journalists. George Washington Williams (1849–1891), an African American Baptist minister, lawyer, and historian, was dazzled, as were many others, by the noble humanitarian goals that Leopold II claimed to have for the Congo, but when he visited the Congo in 1890 he was sickened by what he saw. His public letter to King Leopold, excerpted below, offers one of the earliest firsthand accounts of the horrors of Congo. Edmund Morel (1873–1924), a British clerk, was similarly galvanized to undertake a campaign against Leopold after noticing that nearly 80 percent of the goods that his shipping firm sent to the Congo were weapons, shackles, and ammunition, while arriving ships were filled with cargoes of rubber, ivory, and other high-value goods.

George Washington Williams, "An Open Letter to His Serene Majesty Leopold II," 1890

❝Your Majesty's Government has been, and is now, guilty of waging unjust and cruel wars against natives, with the hope of securing slaves and women, to minister to the behests of the officers of your Government. . . . I have no adequate terms with which to depict to your Majesty the brutal acts of your soldiers upon such raids as these. The soldiers who open the combat are usually the bloodthirsty cannibalistic Bangalas, who give no quarter to the aged grandmother or nursing child at the breast of its mother. There are instances in which they have brought the heads of their victims to their white officers on the expeditionary steamers, and afterwards eaten the bodies of slain children. In one war two Belgian Army officers saw, from the deck of their steamer, a native in a canoe some distance away. He was not a combatant and was ignorant of the conflict . . . upon the shore, some distance away. The officers made a wager of £5 that they could hit the native with their rifles. Three shots were fired and the native fell dead, pierced through the head, and the trade canoe was transformed into a funeral barge and floated silently down the river.❞

Edmund Morel, from *King Leopold's Rule in Africa*, 1904

❝One of the most atrocious features of the persistent warfare of which year in year out the Congo territories are the scene, is the mutilation both of the dead and of the living which goes on under it. . . . The first intimation that Congo State troops were in the habit of cutting off the hands of men, women, and children in connection with the rubber traffic reached Europe through the Rev. J. B. Murphy, of the American Baptist Missionary Union, in 1895. He described how the State soldiers had shot some people on Lake Mantumba . . . , "cut off their hands and took them to the Commissaire." The survivors of the slaughter reported the matter to a missionary at Irebu, who went down to see if were true, and was quickly convinced by ocular demonstration. Among the mutilated victims was a little girl, not quite dead, who subsequently recovered. In a statement which appeared in the [London] *Times*, Mr. Murphy said, "These hands—the hands of men, women, and children—were placed in rows before the Commissary, who counted them to see that the soldiers had not wasted cartridges."❞

Sources: George Washington Williams, "An Open Letter to Leopold II, King of the Belgians and Sovereign of the Independent State of Congo, July 18, 1890," in John Hope Franklin, *George Washington Williams: A Biography* (Chicago: University of Chicago Press, 1985), pp. 245–246, 250–251; Edmund D. Morel, *King Leopold's Rule in Africa* (New York: Funk and Wagnalls, 1905), pp. 110–111.

QUESTIONS FOR ANALYSIS

1. What factors might have allowed such horrible atrocities to be committed without greater public awareness and outcry?

2. How do these two readings exemplify the theory that the colonial experience brutalized both colonized and colonizer?

*Adam Hochschild, *King Leopold's Ghost* (Boston: Houghton Mifflin, 1999), pp. 225–234.

---

cornered battle to build strong states in southern Africa. Of critical importance, the talented Zulu leader Shaka (r. 1818–1828) revolutionized African warfare and managed to create the largest and most powerful African society in southern Africa in the nineteenth century. Drafted by age groups and placed in highly disciplined regiments, Shaka's warriors perfected the use of a short stabbing spear in deadly hand-to-hand combat. The Zulu armies often destroyed their African enemies completely, sowing chaos and sending refugees fleeing in all directions. Shaka's wars also led to the consolidation of the Zulu, Tswana, Swazi, and Sotho peoples into stronger states in southern Africa. By 1880 these states were largely subdued by Dutch and British invaders, but only after many hard-fought frontier wars.

Beginning in 1834 the British gradually abolished slavery in the Cape Colony and introduced color-blind legislation (whites and blacks were equal before the law) to protect African labor. In 1836 about ten thousand Afrikaner cattle ranchers and farmers, who resented the British colonial officials and missionaries treating blacks as equals after abolishing slavery, began to make their so-called Great Trek northward into the interior. In 1845 another group of Afrikaners joined them north of the Orange River. Over the next thirty years Afrikaner and British settlers, who often fought and usually detested each other, reached a mutually advantageous division of southern Africa. The British ruled strategically valuable coastal colonies, and the Afrikaners controlled their ranch-land republics in the interior. The Zulu, the Xhosa, and other African peoples lost much of their land but remained the majority—albeit an exploited majority.

The discovery of incredibly rich deposits of diamonds in 1867 and of gold in the 1880s revolutionized the economy of southern Africa, making possible large-scale industrial capitalism and transforming the lives of all its peoples. Small-scale white and black diamond diggers soon gave way to Cecil Rhodes (1853–1902) and the powerful financiers behind his De Beers mining

company. Rhodes came from a large middle-class British family and at seventeen went to southern Africa to seek his fortune. Extraction of the deep-level gold deposits discovered in 1886 in the Afrikaners' Transvaal republic required big foreign investment, European engineering expertise, and an enormous labor force. By 1888 Rhodes's firm monopolized the world's diamond industry and earned him fabulous profits.

The "color bar" system of the diamond fields gave whites—often English-speaking immigrants—the well-paid skilled positions and put black Africans in the dangerous, low-wage jobs far below the earth's surface. Whites lived with their families in subsidized housing. African workers lived in all-male prison-like dormitories, closely watched by company guards. Southern Africa became the world's leading gold producer, pulling in black migratory workers from all over the region (as it does to this day).

The mining bonanza whetted the appetite of British imperialists led by the powerful Rhodes. Between 1889 and 1893 Rhodes used missionaries and a front company chartered by the British government to force African chiefs to accept British protectorates, and he managed to add Southern and Northern Rhodesia (modern-day Zimbabwe and Zambia) to the British

Diamond Mining in South Africa At first, both black and white miners could own and work claims at the diamond diggings, as this early photo suggests. However, as the industry expanded and was monopolized by European financial interests, white workers claimed the supervisory jobs, and blacks were limited to dangerous low-wage labor. (Hulton Archive/Corbis)

Empire. Rhodes and the imperialist clique then succeeded in starting the South African War of 1899–1902 (also known as the Anglo-Boer War), Britain's greatest imperial campaign on African soil. The British needed 450,000 troops to crush the Afrikaners, who never had more than 30,000 men in the field. Estimates of Africans who were sometimes forced and sometimes volunteered to work for one side or the other range from 15,000 to 40,000 for each side; they did everything from scouting and guard duty to heavy manual labor, driving wagons, and guarding the livestock.

The long and bitter war divided whites in South Africa, but South Africa's blacks were the biggest losers. The British had promised the Afrikaners representative government in return for surrender in 1902, and they made good on their pledge. In 1910 the Cape Colony; the former Afrikaner colony Natal (nuh-TAL), which had been annexed by the British in 1843; and the two Afrikaner republics formed a new self-governing Union of South Africa. After the peace settlement, because whites — 21.5 percent of the total population in 1910 — held almost all political power in the new union and because the Afrikaners outnumbered the English-speakers, the Afrikaners began to regain what they had lost on the battlefield. South Africa, under a joint British-Afrikaner government within the British Empire, began the creation of a modern segregated society that culminated in an even harsher system of racial separation, or apartheid, after World War II.

Colonialism's Impact After 1900

By 1900 much of black Africa had been conquered — or, as Europeans preferred to say, "pacified" — and a system of colonial administration was taking shape. In general, this system weakened or shattered the traditional social order and challenged accepted values.

The self-proclaimed political goal of the French and the British — the principal foreign powers — was to provide good government for their African subjects, especially after World War I. "Good government" meant, above all, law and order. It meant strong, authoritarian government, which maintained a small army and built up an African police force to put down rebellion, suppress ethnic warfare, and protect life and property. Good government required a modern bureaucracy capable of taxing and governing the population. Many African leaders and their peoples had chosen not to resist the invaders' superior force, and others stopped fighting and turned to other, less violent means of resisting co-

The Struggle for South Africa, 1878

lonial rule. Thus the goal of law and order was widely achieved.

Colonial governments demonstrated much less interest in providing basic social services. Expenditures on education, public health, hospitals, and other social services increased after the First World War but still remained small. Europeans feared the political implications of mass education and typically relied instead on the modest efforts of state-subsidized mission schools. Moreover, they tried to make even their poorest colonies pay for themselves. Thus salaries of government workers normally absorbed nearly all tax revenues.

Economically, the colonial goal was to draw the African interior into the world economy on terms favorable to the dominant Europeans. The key was railroads linking coastal trading centers to outposts hundreds of miles in the interior. Cheap, dependable transportation facilitated easy shipment of raw materials out and manufactured goods in. Most African railroads, generally direct lines from sources of raw materials in the interior to coastal ports, were built after 1900; fifty-two hundred miles were in operation by 1926, when attention turned to building roads for trucks. Railroads and roads had two other important outcomes: they allowed the quick movement of troops to put down local unrest, and they allowed many African peasants to earn wages for the first time.

The focus on economic development and low-cost rule explained why colonial governments were reluctant to move decisively against slavery within Africa. Officials feared that an abrupt abolition of slavery where it existed would disrupt production and lead to costly revolts by powerful slaveholding elites, especially in Muslim areas. Thus colonial regimes settled for halfway measures designed to satisfy humanitarian groups in Europe and also make all Africans, free or enslaved, participate in a market economy and work for wages. Even this cautious policy was enough for many slaves to boldly free themselves by running away, and it facilitated a rapid decline of slavery within Africa. At the same time, colonial governments often imposed head or hut taxes, payable in labor or European currency, to compel Africans to work for their white overlords. No aspect of colonialism was more despised by Africans than forced labor, widespread until about 1920. In some regions, particularly in West Africa, African peasants continued to respond freely to the new economic opportunities by voluntarily shifting to export crops on their own farms. Overall, the result of these developments was an increase in wage work and production geared to the world market and a decline in nomadic

A Missionary School A Swahili schoolboy leads his classmates in a reading lesson in Dar es Salaam in German East Africa before 1914, as portraits of Emperor William II and his wife look down on the classroom. Europeans argued that they were spreading the benefits of a superior civilization with schools like this one, which is unusually well-built and furnished because of its strategic location in the capital city. (Ullstein Bilderdienst/The Granger Collection, New York)

herding and traditional self-sufficient farming of sustainable crops.

In sum, the imposition of bureaucratic Western rule and the gradual growth of a world-oriented cash economy after 1900 had a revolutionary impact on large parts of Africa. The experiences of the Gold Coast and British East Africa, two very different African colonies, dramatically illustrate variations on the general pattern.

The British established the beginnings of the Gold Coast colony in 1821. Over the remainder of the century they extended their territorial rule inland from the coast and built up a fairly complex economy. This angered the powerful Asante kingdom in the interior, which also wanted control of the coast. After a series of Anglo-Asante wars beginning in 1824, British troops finally forced the Asante kingdom to accept British protectorate status in 1902. The large territory the British then controlled is essentially today's nation of Ghana.

Precolonial local trade was vigorous and varied, and palm oil exports were expanding. Into this sophisticated economy British colonists subsequently introduced the production of cocoa beans for the world's chocolate. Output rose spectacularly from a few hundred tons in the 1890s to 305,000 tons in 1936. Independent peasants and energetic African businessmen and businesswomen were mainly responsible for the spectacular success of cocoa-bean production. Creative African entrepreneurs even built their own roads, and they sometimes reaped big profits.

The Gold Coast also showed the way politically and culturally. The westernized black elite — relatively prosperous and well-educated lawyers, professionals, and journalists — and businesspeople took full advantage of opportunities provided by the fairly enlightened colonial regime. The black elite was the main presence in the limited local elections permitted by the British, for few permanent white settlers ventured to hot and densely populated West Africa.

Across the continent in the colony of British East Africa (modern Kenya), events unfolded differently. In West Africa Europeans had been establishing trading posts since the 1400s and carried on a complex slave trade for centuries. In East Africa there was very little European presence, other than some Portuguese, until after the scramble for Africa in the 1880s. Thus the peoples of East Africa generally remained more isolated from the Europeans than did Africans in the Gold Coast. Once the British started building their strategic railroad from the Indian Ocean across British East Africa in 1901, however, foreigners from Great Britain and India moved in to exploit the situation. Indian settlers became shopkeepers, clerks, and laborers in the towns. British settlers dreamed of turning the cool, beautiful, and fertile highlands of East Africa into a "white man's country" like Southern Rhodesia or the Union of South Africa. They dismissed the local population of peasant farmers as barbarians, fit only to toil as cheap labor on their large estates and plantations. British East Africa's blacks thus experienced much harsher colonial rule than did their fellow Africans in the Gold Coast.

The New Imperialism, 1880–1914

☐ What were the causes and consequences of European empire building after 1880?

Western expansion into Asia and Africa reached its apex between about 1880 and 1914. In those years the leading European nations continued to send streams of money and manufactured goods to both continents, and they also rushed to create or enlarge vast political empires abroad. This frantic political empire building contrasted sharply with the economic penetration of non-Western territories between 1816 and 1880, which, albeit by naked military force, had left a China or a Japan "opened" but politically independent (see Chapter 26). By contrast, the empires of the late nineteenth century recalled the old European colonial empires of the seventeenth and eighteenth centuries and led contemporaries to speak of the **new imperialism**.

Characterized by a frantic rush to plant the flag over as many people and as much territory as possible, the most spectacular manifestation of the new imperialism was the seizure of almost all of Africa, which broke sharply with previous patterns and fascinated contemporary Europeans and Americans. Although the sudden division of Africa was more striking, Europeans also extended their political control in Asia. The British expanded from their base in India, and in the 1880s the French took Indochina (modern Vietnam, Cambodia, and Laos). India and China also experienced a profound imperialist impact (see Chapter 26).

Causes of the New Imperialism

Many factors contributed to the West's late-nineteenth-century rush for territory in Africa and Asia, and it

> "[The] strongest nation has always been conquering the weaker . . . and the strongest tends to be best."
>
> **ENGLISH ECONOMIST**

is little wonder that controversies have raged over interpretation of the new imperialism. But despite complexity and controversy, basic causes are clearly identifiable.

Economic motives played an important role in the extension of political empires, especially of the British Empire. By the late 1870s France, Germany, and the United States were industrializing rapidly behind rising tariff barriers. Great Britain was losing its industrial leadership and facing increasingly tough competition in foreign markets. In this new economic situation Britain came to more highly value its old possessions, especially its vast colony in India, which it had exploited most profitably for more than a century. When in the 1880s European continental powers began to grab unclaimed territories, the British followed suit immediately. They feared that France and Germany would seal off their empires with high tariffs and that future economic opportunities would be lost forever.

The overall economic gains of the new imperialism proved limited before 1914. The new colonies were too poor to buy much, and they offered few immediately profitable investments. Nonetheless, colonies became important for political and diplomatic reasons. Each leading European country saw them as crucial to national security, military power, and international prestige. (See "Listening to the Past: A French Leader Defends Imperialism," page 764.)

Colonial rivalries reflected the increasing aggressiveness of Social Darwinian theories of brutal competition among races (see page 739). As one prominent English economist argued in 1873, the "strongest nation has always been conquering the weaker . . . and the strongest tend to be best." Thus European nations, which were seen as racially distinct parts of the dominant white race, had to seize colonies to show they were strong and virile. Moreover, since racial struggle was nature's inescapable law, the conquest of "inferior" peoples was just. Social Darwinism and harsh racial doctrines fostered imperialist expansion.

So did the industrial world's unprecedented technological and military superiority. Three aspects were crucial. First, the rapidly firing machine gun, so lethal at Omdurman in Sudan, was an ultimate weapon in many another unequal battle. Second, newly discovered

---

• **new imperialism** The late-nineteenth-century drive by European countries to create vast political empires abroad.

Listening to the Past

A French Leader Defends Imperialism

Although Jules Ferry (1832–1893) first gained political prominence as an ardent champion of secular public education, he was most famous for his empire building. While he was French premier in 1880–1881 and again in 1883–1885, France occupied Tunisia, extended its rule in Indonesia, seized Madagascar, and penetrated the Congo. Criticized by conservatives, socialists, and some left-wing republicans for his colonial expansion, Ferry defended his policies before the French National Assembly and also elaborated a philosophy of imperialism in his writings.

In a speech to the Assembly on July 28, 1883, portions of which follow, Ferry answered his critics and summarized his three main arguments with brutal honesty. Note that Ferry adamantly insisted that imperial expansion did not weaken France in its European struggle with Germany, as some opponents charged, but rather that it increased French grandeur and power. Imperialists needed the language of patriotic nationalism to be effective.

" *M. Jules Ferry*: Gentlemen, . . . I believe that there is some benefit in summarizing and condensing, in the form of arguments, the principles, the motives, and the various interests by which a policy of colonial expansion may be justified; it goes without saying that I will try to remain reasonable, moderate, and never lose sight of the major continental interests which are the primary concern of this country. What I wish to say, to support this proposition, is that in fact, just as in word, the policy of colonial expansion is a political and economic system; I wish to say that one can relate this system to three orders of ideas: economic ideas, ideas of civilization in its highest sense, and ideas of politics and patriotism.

In the area of economics, I will allow myself to place before you, with the support of some figures, the considerations which justify a policy of colonial expansion from the point of view of that need, felt more and more strongly by the industrial populations of Europe and particularly those of our own rich and hard working country: the need for export markets. Is this some kind of chimera? Is this a view of the future or is it not rather a pressing need, and, we could say, the cry of our industrial population? I will formulate only in a general way what each of you, in the different parts of France, is in a position to confirm. Yes, what is lacking for our great industry, drawn irrevocably on to the path of exportation by the [free trade] treaties of 1860, what it lacks more and more is export markets. Why? Because next door to us Germany is surrounded by barriers, because beyond the ocean, the United States of America has become protectionist, protectionist in the most extreme sense. . . .

Gentlemen, there is a second point, . . . the humanitarian and civilizing side of the question. On this point the honorable M. Camille Pellatan has jeered in his own refined and clever manner; he jeers, he condemns, and he says "What is this civilization which you impose with cannonballs? What is it but another form of barbarism? Don't these populations, these inferior races, have the same rights as you? Aren't they masters of their own houses? Have they called upon you? You come to them against their will, you offer them violence, but not civilization." There, gentlemen, is the thesis; I do not hesitate to say that this is not politics, nor is it history: it is political metaphysics. (*"Ah, Ah" on far left.*)

. . . Gentlemen, I must speak from a higher and more truthful plane. It must be stated openly that, in effect, superior races have rights over inferior races. (*Movement on many benches on the far left.*)

M. Jules Maigne: Oh! You dare to say this in the country which has proclaimed the rights of man!

M. de Guilloutet: This is a justification of slavery and the slave trade! . . .

M. Jules Ferry: I repeat that superior races have a right, because they have a duty. They have the duty to civilize inferior

---

quinine proved effective in controlling attacks of malaria, which had previously decimated Europeans in the tropics whenever they left breezy coastal enclaves and dared to venture into mosquito-infested interiors. Third, the introduction of steam power and the international telegraph permitted Western powers to

• **quinine** An agent that proved effective in controlling attacks of malaria, which had previously decimated Europeans in the tropics.

quickly concentrate their firepower in a given area when it was needed. Steamships with ever-larger cargos made round-trip journeys to far-flung colonies much more quickly and economically. Small steamboats could travel back and forth along the coast and also carry goods up and down Africa's great rivers, as portrayed in the classic American film *The African Queen*. Likewise, train cars pulled by powerful steam engines—immune to disease, unlike animals and humans—

races. . . . (*Approval from the left. New interruptions from the extreme left and from the right.*)

. . . M. Pelletan . . . then touched upon a third point, more delicate, more serious, and upon which I ask your permission to express myself quite frankly. It is the political side of the question. The honorable M. Pelletan, who is a distinguished writer, always comes up with remarkably precise formulations. I will borrow from him the one which he applied the other day to this aspect of colonial policy.

"It is a system," he says, "which consists of seeking out compensations in the Orient with a circumspect and peaceful seclusion which is actually imposed upon us in Europe."

I would like to explain myself in regard to this. I do not like this word, "compensation," and, in effect, not here but elsewhere it has often been used in a treacherous way. If what is being said or insinuated is that any government in this country, any Republican minister could possibly believe that there are in any part of the world compensations for the disasters which we have experienced [in connection with our defeat in the Franco-Prussian War of 1870–1871], an injury is being inflicted . . . and an injury undeserved by that government. (*Applause at the center and left.*) I will ward off this injury with all the force of my patriotism! (*New applause and bravos from the same benches.*)

Gentlemen, there are certain considerations which merit the attention of all patriots. The conditions of naval warfare have been profoundly altered. ("Very true! Very true!")

At this time, as you know, a warship cannot carry more than fourteen days' worth of coal, no matter how perfectly it is organized, and a ship which is out of coal is a derelict on the surface of the sea, abandoned to the first person who comes along. Thence the necessity of having on the oceans provision stations, shelters, ports for defense and revictualling. (*Applause at the center and left. Various interruptions.*) And it is for this that we needed Tunisia, for this that we needed Saigon and the Mekong Delta, for this that we need Madagascar, that we are at Diégo-Suarez and Vohemar [two Madagascar ports]

Jules Ferry, French politician and ardent imperialist. (Bettmann/Corbis)

and will never leave them! (*Applause from a great number of benches.*) Gentlemen, in Europe as it is today, in this competition of so many rivals which we see growing around us, some by perfecting their military or maritime forces, others by the prodigious development of an ever growing population; in a Europe, or rather in a universe of this sort, a policy of peaceful seclusion or abstention is simply the highway to decadence! Nations are great in our times only by means of the activities which they develop; it is not simply "by the peaceful shining forth of institutions" (*interruptions on the extreme left and right*) that they are great at this hour.

. . . [The Republican Party] has shown that it is quite aware that one cannot impose upon France a political ideal conforming to that of nations like independent Belgium and the Swiss Republic; that something else is needed for France: that she cannot be merely a free country, that she must also be a great country, exercising all of her rightful influence over the destiny of Europe, that she ought to propagate this influence throughout the world and carry everywhere that she can her language, her customs, her flag, her arms, and her genius. (*Applause at center and left.*)

Source: Speech before the French National Assembly, July 28, 1883. Reprinted in R. A. Austen, ed., *Modern Imperialism: Western Overseas Expansion and Its Aftermath, 1776–1965* (Lexington, Mass.: D. C. Heath, 1969), pp. 70–73.

QUESTIONS FOR ANALYSIS

1. What was Jules Ferry's economic argument for imperial expansion? Why had colonies recently gained greater economic value?
2. How did Ferry's critics attack the morality of foreign expansion? How did Ferry try to claim the moral high ground in his response?
3. What political arguments did Ferry advance? How would you characterize his philosophy of politics and national development?

replaced the thousands of African porters hitherto responsible for carrying raw materials from the interior to the coast. Never before — and never again after 1914 — would the technological gap between the West and the non-Western regions of the world be so great.

Social tensions and domestic political conflicts also contributed to overseas expansion. Conservative political leaders often manipulated colonial issues in order to divert popular attention from domestic conflicts and to create a false sense of national unity. Thus imperial propagandists relentlessly stressed that colonies benefited workers as well as capitalists, and they encouraged the masses to savor foreign triumphs and glory in the supposed increase in national prestige.

Finally, special-interest groups in each country were powerful agents of expansion. Shipping companies wanted lucrative subsidies. White settlers wanted more land, and missionaries and humanitarians wanted to spread religion and stop the slave trade. Military men and colonial officials foresaw rapid advancement and high-paid positions in growing empires. The actions of such groups pushed the course of empire forward.

A "Civilizing Mission"

Imperialists did not rest the case for empire solely on naked conquest and a Darwinian racial struggle or on power politics and the need for navy bases on every ocean. They developed additional arguments to satisfy their consciences and answer their critics.

A favorite idea was that Europeans and Americans could and should "civilize" supposedly primitive non-Western peoples. According to this view, Africans and Asians would receive the benefits of modern economies, cities, advanced medicine, and higher standards of living and eventually might be ready for self-government and Western democracy.

Another argument was that imperial government protected colonized peoples from ethnic warfare and the slave trade within Africa, as well as from cruder forms of exploitation by white settlers and business people. Thus the French spoke of their sacred "civiliz-

ing mission." In 1899 Rudyard Kipling (1865–1936), who wrote extensively on Anglo-Indian life and was perhaps the most influential British writer of the 1890s, exhorted Westerners to unselfish service in distant lands in his poem "The White Man's Burden":

> Take up the White Man's Burden —
> Send forth the best ye breed —
> Go bind your sons to exile
> To serve your captives' need,
> To wait in heavy harness,
> On fluttered folk and wild —
> Your new-caught, sullen peoples
> Half-devil and half-child.[7]

Written in response to America's seizure of the Philippines after the Spanish-American War, Kipling's poem and his concept of a **white man's burden** won wide acceptance among those who supported America's imperial ambitions. It was an important factor in the decision to rule, rather than liberate, the Philippines after the Spanish-American War (see page 826). Like their European counterparts, these Americans believed that their civilization had reached unprecedented heights and that they had unique benefits to bestow on all "less-advanced" peoples.

Imperialists claimed that peace and stability under European control would permit the spread of Christianity. In Africa Catholic and Protestant missionaries competed with Islam south of the Sahara, seeking converts and building schools. Many Africans' first real contact with Europeans and Americans was in mis-

Tools for Empire Building
Western technological advances aided imperialist ambitions in Africa. The Maxim gun was highly mobile and could lay down a continuous barrage that would decimate charging enemies, as in the slaughter of Muslim tribesman at the Battle of Omdurman in the Sudan. Quinine, first taken around 1850 to prevent the contraction of malaria, enabled Europeans to move safely into the African interior and overwhelm native peoples. And the development of the electromagnetic telegraph in the 1840s permitted rapid long-distance communications for the first time in history. (gun: Private Collection/Peter Newark Military Pictures/The Bridgeman Art Library; quinine: Wellcome Library, London; telegraph: John D. Jenkins, www.sparksmuseum.com)

sion schools. Some peoples, such as the Ibo in Nigeria, became highly Christianized. Such occasional successes in black Africa contrasted with the general failure of missionary efforts in the Islamic world and in much of Asia.

Critics of Imperialism

The expansion of empire aroused sharp, even bitter, critics. A forceful attack was delivered in 1902, after the unpopular South African War, by radical English economist J. A. Hobson (1858–1940) in his *Imperialism*, a work that influenced Lenin (see Chapter 28) and others. Hobson contended that the rush to acquire colonies was due to the economic needs of unregulated capitalism. Moreover, Hobson argued, the quest for empire diverted popular attention away from domestic reform and the need to reduce the great gap between rich and poor at home. These and similar arguments had limited appeal because most people were sold on the idea that imperialism was economically profitable for the homeland.

Hobson and many Western critics struck home, however, with their moral condemnation of whites imperiously ruling nonwhites. Kipling and his kind were lampooned as racist bullies whose rule rested on brutality, racial contempt, and the Maxim machine gun. Polish-born novelist Joseph Conrad (1857–1924), in *Heart of Darkness* (1902), castigated the "pure selfishness" of Europeans in "civilizing" Africa. The main character in the novel, once a liberal European scholar, is corrupted by power in Africa and turns into a savage brute.

Critics charged Europeans with applying a degrading double standard and failing to live up to their own noble ideals. At home Europeans had won or were winning representative government, individual liberties, and a certain equality of opportunity. In their empires Europeans imposed military dictatorships on Africans and Asians, forced them to work involuntarily, and discriminated against them shamelessly. Only by renouncing imperialism and giving captive peoples the freedom idealized in Western society would Europeans be worthy of their traditions.

African and Asian Resistance

To peoples in Africa and Asia, Western expansion represented a profoundly disruptive assault with many consequences. Everywhere it threatened traditional ruling classes, economies, and ways of life. Christian missionaries and European secular ideologies challenged established beliefs and values. African and Asian societies experienced crises of identity and a general pattern of reassertion, although the details of each people's story varied substantially.

Often the initial response of African and Asian rulers was to try to drive the unwelcome foreigners away, as in China and Japan (see Chapter 26). Violent antiforeign reactions exploded elsewhere again and again, but the superior military technology of the industrialized West almost invariably prevailed. In addition, European rulers gave special powers and privileges to some individuals and groups from among the local population, including traditional leaders such as chiefs, landowners, and religious figures and Western-educated professionals and civil servants. These local elites recognized the imperial power realities in which they were enmeshed, and used them to maintain or gain authority over the masses. Some concluded that the West was superior in certain ways and that it was therefore necessary to reform and modernize their societies by copying some European achievements. This process of maintaining domination through providing advantages to a select few is referred to as hegemony, and it explains why relatively small numbers of Europeans were able to maintain control over much larger populations without constant rebellion and protest. European empires were won by force, but they were maintained by cultural as well as military and political means.

Nevertheless, imperial rule was in many ways an imposing edifice built on sand. Support for European rule among the conforming and accepting millions was shallow and weak. Thus the conforming masses followed with greater or lesser enthusiasm a few determined personalities who came to oppose the Europeans. Such leaders always arose, both when Europeans ruled directly and when they manipulated native governments, for at least two basic reasons.

First, the nonconformists—the eventual anti-imperialist leaders—developed a burning desire for human dignity. They came to feel that such dignity was incompatible with foreign rule. Second, potential leaders found in the Western world the ideologies and justification for their protest. Thus they discovered liberalism, with its credo of civil liberty and political self-determination. They echoed the demands of anti-imperialists in Europe and America that the West live up to its own ideals. Above all, they found themselves attracted to the nineteenth-century Western ideology of nationalism, which asserted that every people—or at least every European people—had the right to control its own destiny (see Chapter 24). After 1917 anti-imperialist revolt would find another weapon in Lenin's version of Marxist socialism.

• **white man's burden** The idea that Europeans could and should civilize more primitive nonwhite peoples and that imperialism would eventually provide nonwhites with modern achievements and higher standards of living.

The Islamic Heartland Under Pressure

☐ How did the Ottoman Empire and Egypt try to modernize themselves, and what were the most important results?

Stretching from West Africa into southeastern Europe and across Southwest Asia all the way to the East Indies, Islamic civilization competed successfully and continuously with western Europe for centuries. But beginning in the late seventeenth century, the rising absolutist states of Austria and Russia began to challenge the greatest Muslim state, the vast Ottoman Empire, and gradually to reverse Ottoman rule in southeastern Europe. In the nineteenth century European industrialization and nation building further altered the long-standing balance of power, and Western expansion eventually posed a serious challenge to Muslims everywhere.

In close contact with Europe and under constant European pressure, the ruling elites both in the Ottoman Empire and in Egypt, a largely independent Ottoman province, led the way in trying to generate the strength to survive. The ongoing military crisis required, first of all, wrenching army reforms on Western lines in order to defend and preserve the state. These military reforms then snowballed into a series of innovations in education, which had a powerful cultural impact on Ottoman and Egyptian elites.

The results of all these pressures and the momentous changes they brought were profound and paradoxical. On the one hand, the Ottoman Empire and Egypt achieved considerable modernization on Western lines. On the other hand, these impressive accomplishments never came fast enough to offset the growing power and appetite of the West. The Islamic heartland in Southwest Asia and North Africa increasingly fell under foreign control.

Decline and Reform in the Ottoman Empire

Although the Ottoman Empire began to decline slowly after Suleiman the Magnificent in the sixteenth century (see page 592), the relationship between the Ottomans and the Europeans in about 1750 was still one of roughly equal strength. In the later eighteenth century this situation began to change quickly and radically. The Ottomans fell behind western Europe in science, industrial skill, and military technology. Absolutist Russia pushed southward between 1768 and 1774. The danger that the Great Powers of Europe would gradually conquer the Ottoman Empire and divide up its vast territories was real.

Caught up in the Napoleonic wars and losing more territory to Russia, the Ottomans were forced to grant Serbia local autonomy in 1816. In 1821 the Greeks revolted against Ottoman rule, and in 1830 they won their national independence. Facing uprisings by their Christian subjects in Europe, the Ottomans also failed to defend their Islamic provinces in North Africa. In 1830 French armies began their long and bloody conquest of the Arabic-speaking province of Algeria. By 1860 two hundred thousand French, Italian, and Spanish colonists had settled among the Muslim majority, whose number had been reduced to about 2.5 million by the war against the French and related famines and epidemics.

Ottoman weakness reflected the decline of the sultan's "slave army," the so-called janissary corps (see page 592). With time, the janissaries — boys and other slaves raised in Turkey as Muslims, then trained to serve in the elite corps of the Ottoman infantry — became a corrupt and privileged hereditary caste. They zealously pursued their own interests and refused any military innovations that might undermine their high status.

A transformation of the army was absolutely necessary to battle the Europeans more effectively and enhance the sultanate's authority within the empire. The empire was no longer a centralized military state. Instead, local governors were becoming increasingly independent, pursuing their own interests and even seeking to establish their own governments and hereditary dynasties.

The energetic sultan Selim III (r. 1789–1807) understood these realities, but when he tried to reorganize the army, the janissaries refused to use any "Christian" equipment. In 1807 they revolted, and Selim was quickly executed in a palace revolution, one of many that plagued the Ottoman state. The reform-minded Mahmud II (r. 1808–1839) proceeded cautiously, picking loyal officers and building his dependable artillery corps. In 1826 his council ordered the janissaries to drill in the European manner. As expected, the janis-

Ottoman Decline in the Balkans, 1818–1830

Belgrade

SERBIA
(Autonomous, 1816)

Danube R.

OTTOMAN EMPIRE

Ionian Is.
(Gr. Br.)

Athens

GREECE
(Independent, 1830)

Navarino Bay
1827

Mediterranean Sea

Crete

Pasha Halim Receiving Archduke Maximilian of Austria As this painting suggests, Ottoman leaders became well versed in European languages and culture. They also mastered the game of power politics, playing one European state against another and securing the Ottoman Empire's survival. The black servants on the right may be slaves from the Sudan. (Miramare Palace Trieste/Dagli Orti/The Art Archive)

saries revolted and charged the palace, where they were mowed down by the waiting artillery corps.

The destruction and abolition of the janissaries cleared the way for building a new army, but it came too late to stop the rise of Muhammad Ali, the Ottoman governor in Egypt. In 1831 his French-trained forces occupied the Ottoman province of Syria and appeared ready to depose Mahmud II. The Ottoman sultan survived, but only by begging Europe for help. Britain, Russia, and Austria intervened and negotiated a peace settlement. Having reestablished direct rule over the province of Iraq, the overconfident Ottomans were saved again in 1839 after their forces were routed trying to drive Muhammad Ali from Syria. In the last months of 1840 Russian diplomatic efforts, British and Austrian naval blockades, and threatened military action convinced Muhammad Ali to return Syria to the Ottomans. European powers preferred a weak and dependent Ottoman state to a strong and revital-

ized Muslim entity under a dynamic leader such as Muhammad Ali.

Realizing their precarious position, in 1839 liberal Ottoman statesmen launched an era of radical reforms, which lasted with fits and starts until 1876 and culminated in a constitution and a short-lived parliament. Known as the **Tanzimat** (literally, regulations or orders), these reforms were designed to remake the empire on a western European model. The new decrees called for the equality of Muslims, Christians, and Jews before the law and in business, security of life and property, and a modernized administration and military. New commercial laws allowed free importation of foreign goods, as British advisers demanded, and permitted foreign merchants to operate freely throughout an economically dependent empire. Under heavy British

• **Tanzimat** A set of radical reforms designed to remake the Ottoman Empire on a western European model.

pressure, slavery in the empire was drastically curtailed, though not abolished completely. Of great significance, growing numbers among the elite and the upwardly mobile embraced Western education, adopted Western manners and artistic styles, and accepted secular values to some extent.

Intended to bring revolutionary modernization such as that experienced by Russia under Peter the Great (see page 509) and by Japan in the Meiji era (see page 797), the Tanzimat permitted partial recovery. Yet the Ottoman state and society failed to regain its earlier strength for several reasons. First, implementation of the reforms required a new generation of well-trained and trustworthy officials, and that generation did not exist. Second, the liberal reforms failed to halt the growth of nationalism among Christian subjects in the Balkans (see Chapter 28), which resulted in crises and defeats that undermined all reform efforts. Third, the Ottoman initiatives did not curtail the appetite of Western imperialism, and European bankers gained a usurious stranglehold on Ottoman finances. In 1875 the Ottoman state had to declare partial bankruptcy and place its finances in the hands of European creditors.

Finally, the elaboration — at least on paper — of equal rights for citizens and religious communities did not create greater unity within the state. Religious disputes increased, worsened by the relentless interference of the Great Powers. This development embittered relations between the religious communities, distracted the government from its reform mission, and split Muslims into secularists and religious conservatives. Many conservative Muslims detested the religious reforms, which they saw as an irreverent departure from Islamic tradition and holy law. These Islamic conservatives became the most dependable supporters of Sultan Abdülhamid (r. 1876–1909), who abandoned the model of European liberalism in his long and repressive reign.

The combination of declining international power and conservative tyranny eventually led to a powerful resurgence of the modernizing impulse among idealistic Turkish exiles in Europe and young army officers in Istanbul. These fervent patriots, the so-called **Young Turks**, seized power in the revolution of 1908, and they forced the sultan to implement reforms. Failing to stop the rising tide of anti-Ottoman nationalism in the Balkans, the Young Turks helped to prepare the way for the birth of modern secular Turkey after the defeat and collapse of the Ottoman Empire in World War I (see pages 863–864).

• **Young Turks** Fervent patriots who seized power in the revolution of 1908, forcing the conservative sultan to implement reforms; they helped pave the way for the birth of modern secular Turkey.

Egypt: From Reform to British Occupation

The ancient land of the pharaohs had been ruled by a succession of foreigners since 525 B.C.E. and was most recently conquered by the Ottoman Turks in the early sixteenth century. In 1798 French armies under the young general Napoleon Bonaparte invaded Egypt and occupied the territory for three years as part of France's war with Britain. Into the power vacuum left by the French withdrawal stepped an extraordinary Albanian-born Turkish general, Muhammad Ali (1769–1849).

First appointed governor of Egypt by the Turkish sultan, Muhammad Ali set out to build his own state on the strength of a large, powerful army organized along European lines. In 1820–1822 the Egyptian leader conquered much of the Sudan to secure slaves for his army, and thousands of African slaves were brought to Egypt during his reign. Because many slaves died in Egyptian captivity, Muhammad Ali turned to drafting Egyptian peasants. He also reformed the government and promoted modern industry. (See "Individuals in Society: Muhammad Ali," page 771.) For a time Muhammad Ali's ambitious strategy seemed to work, but it eventually foundered when his armies occupied Syria and he threatened the Ottoman sultan Mahmud II. In the face of European military might and diplomatic entreaties, Muhammad Ali agreed to peace with his Ottoman overlords and withdrew. In return he was given unprecedented hereditary rule over Egypt and Sudan. By the time of his death in 1849, Muhammad Ali had established a strong and virtually independent Egyptian state within the Turkish empire.

To pay for a modern army and industrialization, Muhammad Ali encouraged the development of commercial agriculture geared to the European market. This development had profound social implications. Egyptian peasants had been poor but largely self-sufficient, growing food on state-owned land allotted to them by tradition. Offered the possibility of profits from export agriculture, high-ranking officials and members of Muhammad Ali's family began carving large private landholdings out of the state domain, and they forced the peasants to grow cash crops for European markets. Ownership of land became very unequal. By 1913, 12,600 large estates owned 44 percent of the land, and 1.4 million peasants owned only 27 percent. Estate owners "modernized" agriculture, to the detriment of the peasants' well-being.

Muhammad Ali's policies of modernization attracted growing numbers of Europeans to the banks of the Nile. By 1863, when Muhammad Ali's grandson Ismail began his sixteen-year rule as Egypt's khedive (kuh-DEEV), or prince, the port city of Alexandria had more than fifty thousand Europeans. Europeans served as army

Muhammad Ali

THE DYNAMIC LEADER MUHAMMAD ALI (1769–1849) stands across the history of modern Egypt like a colossus. Yet the essence of the man remains a mystery, and historians vary greatly in their interpretations of him. Sent by the Ottomans, with Albanian troops, to oppose the French occupation of Egypt in 1799, Muhammad Ali maneuvered skillfully after the French withdrawal in 1802. In 1805 he was named pasha, or Ottoman governor, of Egypt. Only the Mamluks remained as rivals. Originally an elite corps of Turkish slave-soldiers, the Mamluks had become a semifeudal military ruling class living off the Egyptian peasantry. In 1811 Muhammad Ali offered to make peace, and he invited the Mamluk chiefs and their retainers to a banquet in Cairo's Citadel. As the unsuspecting guests processed through a narrow passage, his troops opened fire, slaughtering all the Mamluk leaders.

After eliminating his foes, Muhammad Ali embarked on a program of radical reforms. He reorganized agriculture and commerce, reclaiming most of the cultivated land for the state domain, which he controlled. He also established state agencies to monopolize, for his own profit, the sale of agricultural goods. Commercial agriculture geared to exports to Europe developed rapidly, especially after the successful introduction of high-quality cotton in 1821. Canals and irrigation systems along the Nile were rebuilt and expanded.

Muhammad Ali used his growing revenues to recast his army along European lines. He recruited French officers to train the soldiers. As the military grew, so did the need for hospitals, schools of medicine and languages, and secular education. Young Turks and some Egyptians were sent to Europe for advanced study. The ruler boldly financed factories to produce uniforms and weapons, and he prohibited the importation of European goods so as to protect Egypt's infant industries. In the 1830s state factories were making one-fourth of Egypt's cotton into cloth. Above all, Muhammad Ali drafted Egyptian peasants into the military for the first time, thereby expanding his army to 100,000 men. It was this force that conquered the Ottoman province of Syria, threatened the sultan in Istanbul, and triggered European intervention. Grudgingly recognized by his Ottoman overlord as Egypt's hereditary ruler in 1841, Muhammad Ali nevertheless had to accept European and Ottoman demands to give up Syria and abolish his monopolies and protective tariffs. The old ruler then lost heart; his reforms languished, and his factories disappeared.

In the attempt to understand Muhammad Ali and his significance, many historians have concluded that he was a national hero, the "founder of modern Egypt." His ambitious state-building projects—hospitals, schools, factories, and the army—were the basis for an Egyptian reawakening and eventual independence from the Ottomans' oppressive foreign rule. Similarly, state-sponsored industrialization promised an escape from poverty and Western domination, which was foiled only by European intervention and British insistence on free trade.

A growing minority of historians question these views. They see Muhammad Ali primarily as an Ottoman adventurer. In their view, he did not aim for national independence for Egypt, but rather "intended to carve out a small empire for himself and for his children after him."* Paradoxically, his success, which depended on heavy taxes and brutal army service, led to Egyptian nationalism among the Arabic-speaking masses, but that new nationalism was directed against Muhammad Ali and his Turkish-speaking entourage. Continuing research into this leader's life will help to resolve these conflicting interpretations.

QUESTIONS FOR ANALYSIS

1. Which of Muhammad Ali's actions support the interpretation that he was the founder of modern Egypt? Which actions support the opposing view?
2. After you have studied Chapter 26, compare Muhammad Ali and the Meiji reformers in Japan. What accounts for the similarities and differences?

*K. Fahmy, *All the Pasha's Men: Mehmed Ali, His Army, and the Making of Modern Egypt* (Cambridge, U.K.: Cambridge University Press, 1997), p. 310.

• **Muhammad Ali, the Albanian-born ruler of Egypt, in 1839**
(Mary Evans Picture Library/The Image Works)

> "History confirms and demonstrates that the status of women is inseparably tied to the status of a nation."
>
> **QASIM AMIN**

officers, engineers, doctors, government officials, and police officers. Others worked in trade, finance, and shipping. Above all, Europeans living in Egypt combined with landlords and officials to continue the development of commercial agriculture geared to exports. By 1900 about two hundred thousand Europeans lived in Egypt and accounted for 2 percent of the population. As throughout the Ottoman Empire, Europeans enjoyed important commercial and legal privileges and formed an economic elite.

Ismail (r. 1863–1879) was a westernizing autocrat. Educated at France's leading military academy, he dreamed of using European technology and capital to modernize Egypt and build a vast empire in northeastern Africa. He promoted cotton production, and exports to Europe soared. Ismail also borrowed large sums, and with his support the Suez Canal was completed by a French company in 1869, shortening the voyage from Europe to Asia by thousands of miles. Cairo acquired modern boulevards and Western hotels. As Ismail proudly declared, "My country is no longer in Africa, we now form part of Europe."[8]

Major cultural and intellectual changes accompanied the political and economic ones. The Arabic of the masses, rather than the Turkish of the conquerors, became the official language, and young Egyptians educated in Europe helped spread new skills and ideas in the bureaucracy. A host of writers, intellectuals, and religious thinkers responded to the novel conditions with innovative ideas that had a powerful impact in Egypt and other Muslim societies.

Three influential figures who represented broad families of thought were especially significant. The teacher and writer Jamal al-Din al-Afghani (1838/39–1897) preached Islamic regeneration and defense against Western Christian aggression. Regeneration, he argued, required the purification of religious belief, the unity of all Muslim peoples, and a revolutionary overthrow of corrupt Muslim rulers and foreign exploiters. The more moderate Muhammad Abduh (1849–1905) also searched for Muslim rejuvenation and launched the modern Islamic reform movement, which became very important in the twentieth century. Abduh concluded that Muslims should return to the purity of the earliest, most essential doctrines of Islam and reject later additions that could limit Muslim creativity. This would permit a flexible, reasoned approach to change, social questions, and foreign ideas.

Finally, the writer Qasim Amin (1863–1908) represented those who found inspiration in the West in the late nineteenth century. In his influential book *The Liberation of Women* (1899), Amin argued forcefully that superior education for European women had contributed greatly to the Islamic world's falling far behind the West. The rejuvenation of Muslim societies required greater equality for women:

> History confirms and demonstrates that the status of women is inseparably tied to the status of a nation. Where the status of a nation is low, reflecting an uncivilized condition for that nation, the status of women is also low, and when the status of a nation is elevated, reflecting the progress and civilization of that nation, the status of women in that country is also elevated.[9]

The Suez Canal, 1869

Mediterranean Sea

Cairo • Bitter Lakes

Suez Canal

SINAI

EGYPT

Nile R.

Gulf of Suez

OTTOMAN EMPIRE

Red Sea

Egypt changed rapidly during Ismail's rule, but his projects were reckless and enormously expensive. By 1876 the Egyptian government could not pay the interest on its colossal debt. Rather than let Egypt go bankrupt and repudiate its loans, France and Great Britain intervened politically to protect the European investors who held the Egyptian bonds. They forced Ismail to appoint French and British commissioners to oversee Egyptian finances so that the Egyptian debt would be paid in full. This meant that Europeans were going to determine the state budget and in effect rule Egypt.

Foreign financial control evoked a violent nationalistic reaction among Egyptian religious leaders, intellectuals, and army officers. In 1879, under the leadership of Colonel Ahmed Arabi, they formed the Egyptian Nationalist Party. Continuing diplomatic pressure, which forced Ismail to abdicate in favor of his weak son, Tewfiq (r. 1879–1892), resulted in bloody anti-European riots in Alexandria in 1882. A number of Europeans were killed, and Tewfiq and his court had to flee to British ships for safety. The British fleet then bombarded Alexandria, and a British expeditionary force decimated Arabi's forces and occupied all of Egypt.

Egyptian Travel Guide Ismail's efforts to transform Cairo were fairly successful. As a result European tourists could more easily visit the country that their governments dominated. Ordinary Europeans were lured to exotic lands by travel books like this colorful "Official Guide" to an exhibition on Cairo held in Berlin. (Private Collection/Archives Charmet/The Bridgeman Art Library)

The British said that their occupation was temporary, but British armies remained in Egypt until 1956. They maintained the façade of the khedive's government as an autonomous province of the Ottoman Empire, but the khedive was a mere puppet. The British consul, General Evelyn Baring, later Lord Cromer, ruled the country after 1883. Baring was a paternalistic reformer, and his rule resulted in tax reforms and somewhat better conditions for peasants. Foreign bondholders received their interest payments, and Egyptian nationalists chafed under foreign rule.

In Egypt the British abandoned what some scholars have called the "imperialism of free trade," which was based on economic penetration and indirect rule. They accepted a new model for European expansion in the densely populated lands of Africa and Asia. Such expansion was based on military force, political domination, and a self-justifying ideology of beneficial reform. This model, which was also adopted in varying ways by other European colonial powers in the age of the new imperialism, was to predominate in the British colonies from the 1880s until 1914.

The Expanding World Economy

☐ What were the global consequences of European industrialization between 1800 and 1914?

The Industrial Revolution created, first in Great Britain and then in continental Europe and North America, a growing and dynamic economic system. In the course of the nineteenth century that system expanded and transformed economic relations across the face of the earth. As a result the world's total income grew as never before, and international trade boomed. Western nations used their superior military power to force non-Western nations to open their doors to Western economic interests, and the largest share of the ever-increasing gains from trade flowed to the West, resulting in a stark division between rich and poor countries.

The Rise of Global Inequality

From a global perspective, the ultimate significance of the Industrial Revolution was that it allowed those regions of the world that industrialized in the nineteenth century to increase their wealth and power enormously in comparison with those that did not. A gap between the industrializing regions and the nonindustrializing or **Third World** regions (mainly Africa, Asia, and Latin America) opened and grew steadily throughout the nineteenth century. Moreover, this pattern of uneven global development became institutionalized, built into the structure of the world economy. Thus evolved a world of haves and have-nots, with the have-not peoples and nations far outnumbering the haves.

Figure 25.1 depicts the gap between the industrializing regions (mainly Europe and North America) and the nonindustrializing Third World that opened up in the late eighteenth and the nineteenth centuries. In 1750 the average standard of living was no higher in Europe as a whole than in the rest of the world. By 1914 the average person in the wealthiest countries had an income four or five times as great (and in Great Britain nine or ten times as great) as the income of the average person in the poorest countries of Africa and Asia. The rise in average income and well-being, first in Great Britain and then in the other developed countries,

Third World A term that refers to the nonindustrialized nations of Africa, Asia, and Latin America as a single unit.

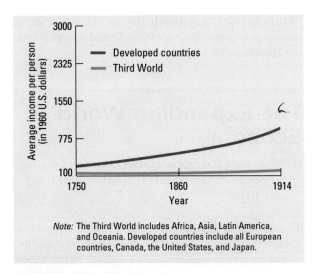

FIGURE 25.1 The Growth of Average Income per Person Worldwide, 1750–1914 (Source of data: P. Bairoch and M. Lévy-Leboyer, eds., *Disparities in Economic Development Since the Industrial Revolution*, published 1981, Macmillan Publishers.)

Note: The Third World includes Africa, Asia, Latin America, and Oceania. Developed countries include all European countries, Canada, the United States, and Japan.

reflected the rising level of industrialization in these countries before World War I.

The reasons for these enormous income disparities, which are poignant indicators of disparities in food and clothing, health and education, life expectancy, and general material well-being, have generated a great deal of debate. One school of interpretation stresses that the West used science, technology, capitalist organization, and even its critical worldview to create its wealth and greater physical well-being. Another school argues that the West used its political and economic power to steal much of its riches, continuing its rapacious colonialism in the nineteenth and twentieth centuries.

These issues are complex, and there are few simple answers. As noted in Chapter 23, the wealth-creating potential of technological improvement and more intensive capitalist organization was great. At the same time, the initial breakthroughs in the late eighteenth century rested in part on Great Britain's having already used political force to dominate a substantial part of the world economy. In the nineteenth century other industrializing countries joined with Britain to extend Western dominion over the entire world economy. Unprecedented wealth was created, but the lion's share of that new wealth flowed to the West and its propertied classes and to a tiny non-Western elite of cooperative rulers, landowners, and merchants.

The World Market

World trade was a powerful stimulus to economic development in the nineteenth century. In 1913 the value of world trade was about twenty-five times what it had been in 1800, even though prices of manufactured goods and raw materials were lower in 1913 than in 1800. In a general way, the enormous increase in international commerce summed up the growth of an interlocking world economy centered in Europe.

Great Britain played a key role in using trade to tie the world together economically. In 1815 Britain had a colonial empire, with India, Canada, Australia, and other scattered areas remaining British possessions after American independence. The technological breakthroughs of the Industrial Revolution encouraged British manufacturers to seek export markets around the world. After Parliament repealed laws restricting the importation of grain in 1846, Britain also became the world's leading importer of foreign goods. Free access to Britain's market stimulated the development of mines and plantations in Africa and Asia.

The growth of trade was facilitated by the conquest of distance. The earliest railroad construction occurred in Europe and in America north of the Rio Grande; other parts of the globe saw the building of rail lines after 1860. By 1920 about a quarter of the world's railroads were in Latin America, Asia, Africa, and Australia. Wherever railroads were built, they drastically reduced transportation costs, opened new economic opportunities, and called forth new skills and attitudes.

Much of the railroad construction undertaken in Africa, Asia, and Latin America connected seaports with inland cities and regions, as opposed to linking and developing cities and regions within a country. Thus railroads dovetailed with Western economic interests, facilitating the inflow and sale of Western manufactured goods and the export and development of local raw materials.

The power of steam also revolutionized transportation by sea. Steam power, long used to drive paddle wheelers on rivers, particularly in Russia and North America, finally began to supplant sails on the oceans of the world in the late 1860s. Lighter, stronger, cheaper steel replaced iron, which had replaced wood. Passenger and freight rates tumbled, and the shipment of low-priced raw materials from one continent to another became feasible.

The revolution in land and sea transportation helped European settlers take vast, thinly populated territories and produce agricultural products and raw materials for sale in Europe. Improved transportation enabled Asia, Africa, and Latin America to export not only the traditional tropical products — spices, dyes, tea, sugar, coffee — but also new raw materials for industry, such as jute, rubber, cotton, and coconut oil. (See "Global Trade: Indigo," page 776.)

Intercontinental trade was enormously facilitated by the Suez Canal and the Panama Canal (see page 819). Of great importance, too, was large and continual investment in modern port facilities, which made loading and unloading cheaper, faster, and more dependable. Finally, transoceanic telegraph cables inaugurated rapid communications among the financial centers of the world and linked world commodity prices in a global network.

The growth of trade and the conquest of distance encouraged Europeans to make massive foreign investments beginning about 1840. Most of the capital exported did not go to European colonies or protectorates in Asia and Africa. About three-quarters of total European investment went to other European countries, the United States and Canada, Australia and New Zealand, and Latin America. Europe found its most profitable opportunities for investment in construction of the railroads, ports, and utilities that were necessary to settle and develop the lands of extensive European expansion. Much of this investment was peaceful and mutually beneficial for lenders and borrowers. The victims were Native American Indians and Australian Aborigines, who were displaced and decimated by the diseases, liquor, and weapons of an aggressively expanding Western society (see Chapter 27).

The Great Global Migration

◻ What fueled migration, and what was the general pattern of this unprecedented movement of people?

A poignant human drama was interwoven with this worldwide economic expansion: millions of people pulled up stakes and left their ancestral lands in one of history's greatest migrations: the so-called **great migration**. In the early eighteenth century the world's population entered a period of rapid growth that continued unabated through the nineteenth and twentieth centuries. The population of Europe (including Asiatic Russia) more than doubled during the nineteenth century, from approximately 188 million in 1800 to roughly 432 million in 1900.

Between 1750 and 1900 the population of Asia followed the same general trend. China, by far the world's most populous country in the middle of the eighteenth century, increased from about 143 million in 1741 to a little more than 400 million in the 1840s, although total numbers grew more slowly in the turbulent late nineteenth century. Since population increased more slowly in Africa and Asia than in Europe, Europeans and peoples of predominately European origin jumped from about 22 percent of the world's total in 1850 to a high of about 38 percent in 1930.

The growing number of Europeans was a driving force behind emigration and Western expansion. The rapid increase in numbers led to relative overpopula-

British East African Railway Poster Europeans constructed railroads in most of their African colonies to haul raw materials from the interior to coastal ports and to transport colonial officials, white settlers, and foreign tourists. Britain's East African railroad line from Kampala, Uganda, to the Kenyan port city of Mombasa was one of the most famous and most romanticized. Indians from British India did much of the construction and then remained in Kenya to form substantial Indian communities. U.S. President Theodore Roosevelt rode this train while on his 1909 African safari. (National Archives, London/ HIP/Art Resource, NY)

tion in area after area in Europe. Thus millions of country folk went abroad as well as to nearby cities in search of work and economic opportunity. Some governments encouraged their excess populations to immigrate, even paying some of their expenses. Wars, famine, poverty, and, particularly in the case of Jews in Russia and

• **great migration** The mass movement of people from Europe in the nineteenth century; one reason that the West's impact on the world was so powerful and many-sided.

Global Trade

Indigo is the oldest and most important natural colorant, and it serves as an illustrative example of the prodigious growth of world trade in the nineteenth century. Indigo is made from the leaves of a small bush that are carefully fermented in vats; the extract is then processed into cakes of pigment. It has been highly prized since antiquity. It dyes all fabrics, does not fade with time, and yields tints ranging from light blue to the darkest purple-blue. Used primarily today as a dye for blue jeans, indigo has been used throughout history as a dye for textiles, as a pigment for painting, and for medicinal and cosmetic purposes.

Widely grown and used in Asia, indigo trickled into Europe from western India in the High Middle Ages but was very expensive. Woad—an inferior homegrown product—remained Europe's main blue dye until the opening of a direct sea route to India by the Portuguese in 1498 reconfigured the intercontinental trade in indigo, as it did for many Asian products. Bypassing Muslim traders in the Indian Ocean, first Portuguese and then Dutch and English merchants and trading companies supplied European dyers and consumers with cheaper, more abundant indigo.

In the early seventeenth century indigo became one of the British East India Company's chief articles of trade, and it was exported from India to Europe more than ever before. As European governments adopted mercantilist policies, they tried to control trade and limit the flow of gold and silver abroad for products like indigo. The result was a second transformation in the global trade in indigo.

Principal trade routes
→ Pre-1500
→ Late 16th century
→ Ca. 1700–1750
→ Early 19th century
→ Post-1900

MAP 25.2 The Indigo Trade

Europeans established indigo plantations in their American colonies, and by the first half of the eighteenth century only small quantities of indigo continued to reach Europe from peasant producers in western India. Indigo plantations in Brazil, Guatemala, Haiti and the Caribbean, and South Carolina were big capitalistic operations and frequently very profitable. They depended on slaves brought from Africa, as did the entire Atlantic economy in the eighteenth century.

In the late eighteenth century the geography of the indigo trade shifted dramatically once again: production returned to India, now largely controlled by the British. Why

Squatting next to a dye pit in northern Nigeria, a man soaks clothing in natural indigo dye, which is still used locally in parts of Africa and South Asia. (Lawrence Manning/Corbis)

did this happen? Political upheaval in the revolutionary era played a key role. American independence left South Carolina outside Britain's mercantilist system; the slave rebellion in Haiti in 1791 decimated some of the world's richest indigo producers; and Britain's continental blockades cut off Spain and France from their colonies. On the economic side, the takeoff in the British textile industry created surging demand for indigo. Thus in the 1780s the British East India Company hired experienced indigo planters from the West Indies to develop indigo production in Bengal. Leasing lands from Indian *zemindars* (landlords who doubled as tax collectors), British planters coerced Bengali peasants into growing indigo, which the planters processed in their "factories." Business expanded rapidly, as planters made—and lost—fortunes in the boom-and-bust cycles characteristic of commodity production in the nineteenth century.

In 1859 Bengali peasants revolted and received unexpected support from British officials advocating free-market contracts and recourse to the courts to settle disputes. As peasants pressed their case against the outraged planters, Indian professionals and intellectuals joined their cause. Winning freer and more equitable contracts, the rural-urban alliance created in the "Indigo Disturbances" marked a key step in the growth of nationalism in Bengal, a leading force in the subsequent drive for Indian independence.

Even as the Indigo Disturbances agitated Bengal, industrializing Europe discovered on its doorstep a completely new source of colorants: thick, black coal tar. This residue, a noxious byproduct of the destructive distillation of soft coal for the gas used in urban lighting and heating, was emerging as the basic material for the chemistry of carbon compounds and a new synthetic dye industry. British, German, and French chemists synthesized a small number of dyes between 1856 and 1869, when the first synthetic dye replaced a natural dye. Thereafter, German researchers and Germany's organic chemical companies built an interlocking global monopoly that produced more than 90 percent of the world's synthetic dyes.

Indigo was emblematic of this resounding success. Professor Adolf Bayer first synthesized indigo in 1880. But an economically viable process required many years of costly, systematic research before two leading German companies working together achieved their objective in 1897. Producers' groups in India slashed indigo prices drastically, but to no avail. Indian exports of natural indigo plummeted from nineteen thousand tons in 1895 to only one thousand tons in 1913. Synthetic indigo claimed the global market, German firms earned super profits, and Indian peasants turned to different crops. Today, nearly all the indigo produced in the world is synthetic, although limited production of natural indigo still occurs in India, as well as in parts of Africa and South America.

Steerage Passengers, 1902 Conditions for steerage passengers traveling from Europe to the Americas were cramped, as evidenced by this photo from 1902. (The Granger Collection, New York)

eastern Europe, bigotry and discrimination were also leading causes for immigrants to leave their ancestral homelands. More than 60 million people left Europe over the course of the nineteenth century, primarily for the rapidly growing "areas of European settlement"—North and South America, Australia, New Zealand, and Siberia (see Chapter 27). European emigration crested in the first decade of the twentieth century, when more than five times as many men and women departed as in the 1850s.

The European migrant was most often a small peasant landowner or a village craftsman whose traditional way of life was threatened by too little land, estate agri-culture, and cheap factory-made goods. Determined to maintain or improve their precarious status, the vast majority of migrants were young and often unmarried. Many European migrants returned home after some time abroad. One in two migrants to Argentina and probably one in three to the United States eventually returned to their native lands.

Ties of family and friendship played a crucial role in the movement of peoples. Many people from a given province or village settled together in rural enclaves or tightly knit urban neighborhoods thousands of miles away. Very often a strong individual—a businessman, a religious leader—would blaze the way, and others would follow, forming a **migration chain**.

Many young European men and women were spurred to leave by a spirit of revolt and independence. In Sweden and Norway, in Jewish Russia and Italy, these young people felt frustrated by the small privi-leged classes that often controlled both church and

- **migration chain** The movement of peoples in which one strong individual blazes the way and others follow.
- **great white walls** Discriminatory laws built by Americans and Australians to keep Asians from settling in their countries in the 1880s.

government and resisted demands for change and greater opportunity. Migration slowed when the economic situation improved at home, particularly as countries industrialized and many more occupational opportunities became available. People also stayed put when they began to win basic political and social reforms, such as the right to vote and social security.

A substantial number of Asians — especially Chinese, Japanese, Indians, and Filipinos — also responded to population pressure and rural hardship with temporary or permanent migration. At least 3 million Asians moved abroad before 1920. Most went as indentured laborers to work under incredibly difficult conditions on the plantations or in the gold mines of Latin America, southern Asia, Africa, California, Hawaii, and Australia (see Chapter 26). White estate owners often used Asians to replace or supplement blacks after the suppression of the Atlantic slave trade.

Such migration from Asia would undoubtedly have grown to much greater proportions if planters and mine owners in search of cheap labor had had their way. But usually they did not. Asians fled the plantations and gold mines as soon as possible, seeking greater opportunities in trade and towns. There they came into conflict with white settlers in areas of European settlement. These settlers demanded a halt to Asian immigration. By the 1880s Americans and Australians were building **great white walls** — discriminatory laws designed to keep Asians out.

The general policy of "whites only" in the lands of large-scale European settlement meant that Europeans and people of European ancestry reaped the main benefits of the great migration. By 1913 people in Australia, Canada, and the United States all had higher average incomes than did people in Great Britain, still Europe's wealthiest nation. This, too, was part of Western dominance in the increasingly lopsided world.

Within Asia and Africa the situation was different. Migrants from south China frequently settled in Dutch, British, and French colonies of Southeast Asia, where they established themselves as peddlers and small shopkeepers (see Chapter 26). These "overseas Chinese" gradually emerged as a new class of entrepreneurs and officeworkers. Traders from India and modern-day Lebanon performed the same function in much of sub-Saharan Africa after the European seizure in the late nineteenth century. Thus in some parts of Asia and Africa the business class was both Asian and foreign, protected and tolerated by Western imperialists who found these business people useful.

CONNECTIONS

By the end of the nineteenth century broader industrialization across Europe increased the need for raw materials and markets, and with it came a rush to create or enlarge vast political empires abroad. The new imperialism was aimed primarily at Africa and Asia, and in the years before 1914 the leading European nations not only created empires abroad, but also continued to send massive streams of migrants, money, and manufactured goods around the world. (The impact of this unprecedented migration is taken up in the next two chapters.) This political empire building contrasted sharply with the economic penetration of non-Western territories between 1816 and 1880, which had left China and Japan "opened" but politically independent, as Chapter 26 will show.

European influence also grew in the Middle East. Threatened by European military might, modernization, and Christianity, Turks and Arabs tried to implement reforms that would assure their survival and independence but also to retain key aspects of their cultures, particularly Islam. Although they made important advances in the modernization of their economies and societies, their efforts were not enough to overcome Western imperialism. With the end of World War I and the collapse of the Ottoman Empire, England and France divided much of the Middle East into colonies and established loyal surrogates as rulers in other, nominally independent countries. Chapter 29 will take up the story of these developments.

Easy imperialist victories over weak states and poorly armed non-Western peoples encouraged excessive pride and led Europeans to underestimate the fragility of their accomplishments. Imperialism also made nationalism more aggressive and militaristic. As European imperialism was dividing the world after the 1880s, the leading European states were also dividing themselves into two opposing military alliances. As Chapter 28 will show, when the two armed camps stumbled into war in 1914, the results were disastrous. World War I set the stage for a new anti-imperialist struggle in Africa and Asia for equality and genuine independence (see Chapters 32 and 33).

□ CHAPTER REVIEW

□ **What were the most significant changes in Africa during the nineteenth century, and why did they occur? (p. 752)**

European pressure in Africa contributed to the reorientation of the economy, which gradually turned from a focus on the transatlantic slave trade to the production of commodities for export. As a result, the slave trade declined steeply. A legitimate trade in African goods, including palm oil, proved profitable and led to the emergence of a small black middle class. Islam revived and expanded until about 1870. The European conquest of Africa after 1880 led to colonial empires that improved internal security and built bureaucracies, but also treated Africans as racial inferiors.

□ **What were the causes and consequences of European empire building after 1880? (p. 763)**

After 1880 a handful of Western nations seized most of Africa and parts of Asia and rushed to build authoritarian empires. The reasons for this empire building included trade rivalries, competitive nationalism in Europe, and self-justifying claims of a civilizing mission. Above all, European states had acquired unprecedented military superiority, which they used to crush resistance and impose their will.

□ **How did the Ottoman Empire and Egypt try to modernize themselves, and what were the most important results? (p. 768)**

The Ottoman Empire and Egypt introduced reforms to improve the military, provide technical and secular education, and expand personal liberties. In so doing, both countries prepared the way for modern nation-states in the twentieth century, but they failed to defend themselves from Western imperialism. The Ottoman Empire lost territory, but survived in a weakened condition. Faced with resistance by Christian nationalists and conservative Muslims, and economically hindered by Western imperialism, the modernization efforts failed to salvage the Ottoman sultan's progressive regime. Muhammad Ali was more successful, reforming the government and promoting modern industry, but Egypt went bankrupt and was conquered and ruled by Britain. Western domination was particularly bitter for most Muslims because they saw it as profaning their religion as well as taking away their political independence.

□ **What were the global consequences of European industrialization between 1800 and 1914? (p. 773)**

Between 1800 and 1914 European industrialization caused a growing gap in average income between people in the West and people in Africa, Asia, and Latin America. This new world of rich lands and poor lands experienced a prodigious increase in international trade, but most of the gains went to the Western nations, which profitably subordinated many lands to their own economic interests. Great Britain, with its colonies in Asia, Africa, and the Americas, played a key role in using trade to tie the world's markets together. Railroad construction and the development of steam power facilitated trade and made moving goods easier, and transoceanic telegraph cables allowed for rapid communication between far-flung financial centers.

□ **What fueled migration, and what was the general pattern of this unprecedented movement of people? (p. 775)**

In response to population pressures at home and economic opportunities abroad, Western nations sent forth millions of emigrants to the sparsely populated areas of European settlement in North and South America, Australia, and Asiatic Russia. Some migrants were motivated by a desire to escape oppression, though migration generally slowed when the economic situation improved at home or when social or political reform occurred. Migration from Asia was much more limited, mainly because European settlers raised high barriers to prevent the settlement of Asian immigrants.

SUGGESTED READING

Bagachi, Amiya Kumar. *Perilous Passage: Mankind and the Ascendancy of Capital.* 2005. A spirited radical critique of Western imperialism.

Conklin, Alice. *A Mission to Civilize: The French Republican Ideal and West Africa, 1895–1930.* 1997. An outstanding examination of French imperialism.

Cook, Scott B. *Colonial Encounters in the Age of High Imperialism.* 1996. A stimulating and very readable overview.

Coquery-Vidrovitch, Catherine. *Africa and the Africans in the Nineteenth Century: A Turbulent History.* 2009. English translation of a highly regarded history by a premier African scholar.

Findley, C. *The Turks in World History.* 2005. An exciting reconsideration of the Turks in long-term perspective.

Harper, Marjory, and Stephen Constantine. *Migration and Empire.* 2010. A comparative study of migration throughout the British Empire.

Headrick, D. *Tools of Empire.* 1991. Stresses technological superiority in Western expansion.

Hochschild, Adam. *King Leopold's Ghost: A Story of Greed, Terror, and Heroism in Colonial Africa.* 1999. The definitive account of King Leopold's Congo and the human rights crusaders who exposed its horrors.

Hourani, A. *A History of the Arab Peoples,* 2d ed. 2010. Brilliant on developments in the nineteenth century.

Law, Robin, ed. *From Slave Trade to "Legitimate" Commerce: The Commercial Transition in Nineteenth-Century West Africa.* 2002. Leading scholars describe the transition to legitimate trade from an African perspective.

Lovejoy, P. *Transformation in Slavery: A History of Slavery in Africa,* 2d ed. 2000. A fine synthesis of current knowledge.

Mahfouz, H. *Palace of Desire.* 1991. A great novelist's portrait of an Egyptian family before 1914.

Medard, Henri, and Shane Doyle. *Slavery in the Great Lakes Region of East Africa.* 2007. A significant contribution to the understudied story of slavery in East Africa, mainly in the nineteenth and early twentieth centuries.

Nugent, Walter. *Crossings: The Great Transatlantic Migrations, 1870–1914.* 1992. A classic study of migration history.

Wright, John. *The Trans-Saharan Slave Trade.* 2007. A well-researched study of slavery in a long-neglected region of Africa.

NOTES

1. P. Lovejoy, *Transformations in Slavery: A History of Slavery in Africa,* 2d ed. (Cambridge, U.K.: Cambridge University Press, 2000), p. 142.
2. Ibid., p. 179.
3. Quoted in J. Iliffe, *Africans: The History of a Continent* (Cambridge, U.K.: Cambridge University Press, 1995), p. 169.
4. Lovejoy, *Transformations in Slavery,* p. 15.
5. R. Oliver, *The African Experience* (New York: Icon Editions, 1991), pp. 164–166.
6. Quoted in H. Wheaton, *Elements of International Law* (London: Stevens & Sons, Limited, 1889), p. 804.
7. Rudyard Kipling, *The Five Nations* (London, 1903).
8. Quoted in Earl of Cromer, *Modern Egypt* (London, 1911), p. 48.
9. Qasim Amin, *The Liberation of Women and The New Woman* (The American University of Cairo Press, 2000), p. 6.

For practice quizzes and other study tools, visit the **Online Study Guide** at bedfordstmartins.com/mckayworld.

For primary sources from this period, see *Sources of World Societies*, **Second Edition**.

For Web sites, images, and documents related to topics in this chapter, visit **Make History** at bedfordstmartins.com/mckayworld.

• **Rammohun Roy** The expansion of British power in India posed intellectual and cultural challenges to the native elite. Among those who rose to this challenge was writer and reformer Rammohun Roy, depicted here. (V&A Images, London/Art Resource, NY)

During the nineteenth century the societies of Asia underwent enormous changes as a result of population growth, social unrest, and the looming presence of Western imperialist powers. At the beginning of the century Spain, the Netherlands, and Britain had colonies in the Philippines, modern Indonesia, and India, respectively. By the end of the century much more land—most of the southern tier of Asia, from India to the Philippines—had been made colonies of Western powers. Most of these colonies became tied to the industrializing world as exporters of agricultural products or raw materials, including timber, rubber, tin, sugar, tea, cotton, and jute. The Western presence brought benefits, especially to educated residents of major cities, where the colonizers often introduced modern public health, communications, and educational systems. Still, cultural barriers between the colonizers and the colonized were huge, and the Western presence rankled. The West relied on force to conquer and rule, and it treated non-Western peoples as racial inferiors.

Asia in the Era of Imperialism
1800–1914

Not all the countries in Asia were reduced to colonies. Although Western powers put enormous pressures on China and exacted many concessions from it, China remained politically independent. Much more impressively, Japan became the first non-Western country to use an ancient love of country to transform itself and thereby meet the many-sided challenge of Western expansion. Japan emerged from the nineteenth-century crisis stronger than any other Asian nation, becoming the first non-Western country to industrialize successfully. By the end of this period Japan had become an imperialist power itself, making Korea and Taiwan its colonies. •

India and the British Empire in Asia

☐ In what ways did India change as a consequence of British rule?

Arriving in India on the heels of the Portuguese in the seventeenth century, the British East India Company outmaneuvered French and Dutch rivals and was there to pick up the pieces as the Mughal Empire decayed during the eighteenth century (see pages 611–613). By 1757 the company had gained control over much of India. During the nineteenth century the British gov-ernment replaced the company, progressively unified the subcontinent, and harnessed its economy to British interests.

Travel and communication between Britain and India became much faster, safer, and more predictable in this period. Clipper ships with their huge sails cut the voyage from Europe to India from six to three months. By the 1850s steamships were competing with clipper ships, and they made ocean travel more predictable. After the 1869 opening of the Suez Canal, which connected the Mediterranean and Red Seas, the voyage by steamship from England to India took only three weeks. Another advance was the cables that were laid on the ocean floor in the 1860s, allowing telegrams to be sent

British and Sikh Leaders at Lahore The Sikh kingdom in the Punjab fell to the British in a brief war in 1845–1846. This painting depicts the British and Sikh representatives who negotiated the resulting treaty, which gave Britain control of the region. (Courtesy of the Trustees of the British Museum)

The Great Revolt/Great Mutiny, 1857

Under British control
Area of rebellion

from England to India. Whereas at the beginning of the nineteenth century someone in England had to wait a year or more to get an answer to a letter sent to India, by 1870 it took only a couple of months—or, if the matter was urgent, only a few hours by telegraph. Faster travel and communication aided the colonial government and foreign merchants, but they did not keep Indians from resenting British rule.

The Evolution of British Rule

In 1818 the British East India Company controlled territory occupied by 180 million Indians—more people than lived in all of western Europe and fifty times the number of people the British had lost in 1783 when the thirteen American colonies successfully overthrew British colonial control. In India the British ruled with the cooperation of local princely allies, whom they could not afford to offend. To assert their authority, the British disbanded and disarmed local armies, introduced simpler private property laws, and enhanced the powers of local princes and religious leaders, both Hindu and Muslim. The British administrators, backed by British officers and native troops, were on the whole competent and concerned about the welfare of the Indian peasants. Slavery was outlawed and banditry suppressed, and new laws designed to improve women's position in society were introduced. Sati (widow suicide) was outlawed in 1829, legal protection of widow remarriage was extended in 1856, and infanticide (disproportionately of female newborns) was banned in 1870.

The last armed resistance to British rule occurred in 1857. By that date the British military presence in India had grown to include two hundred thousand Indian sepoy troops and thirty-eight thousand British officers. The sepoys were well trained and armed with modern rifles. In 1857 groups of them, especially around Delhi, revolted in what the British called the **Great Mutiny** and the Indians called the **Great Revolt**. The sepoys' grievances were many, ranging from the use of fat from cows (sacred to Hindus) and pigs (regarded as filthy by Muslims) to grease rifle cartridges to high tax rates and the incorporation of low-caste soldiers into the army. The insurrection spread rapidly throughout northern and central India before it was finally crushed, primarily by native troops from other parts of India loyal to the British. Thereafter, although princely states

• **Great Mutiny/Great Revolt** The terms used by the British and the Indians, respectively, to describe the last armed resistance to British rule in India, which occurred in 1857.

were allowed to continue, Britain ruled India much more tightly. Moreover, the British in India acted more like an occupying power and mixed less with the Indian elite.

After 1858 India was ruled by the British Parliament in London and administered by a civil service in India, the upper echelons of which were all white. In 1900 this elite consisted of fewer than thirty-five hundred top officials for a population of 300 million. In 1877 Queen Victoria adopted the title empress of India, and her image became a common sight in India.

The Socioeconomic Effects of British Rule

The impact of British rule on the Indian economy was multifaceted. In the early stages, the British East India Company expanded agricultural production, creating large plantations. Early crops were opium to export to China (see page 793) and tea to substitute for imports from China. India gradually replaced China as the leading exporter of tea to Europe. During the nineteenth century India also exported cotton fiber, silk, sugar, jute, coffee, and other agricultural commodities to be processed elsewhere. Clearing land for tea and coffee plantations, along with massive commercial logging operations, led to extensive deforestation.

To aid the transport of goods, people, and information, the colonial administration invested heavily in India's infrastructure. By 1855 India's major cities had all been linked by telegraph and railroads, and postal service was being extended to local villages. By 1870 India had the fifth-largest rail network in the world — 4,775 miles, carrying more than 18 million passengers

a year. By 1900 the rail network had increased fivefold to 25,000 miles, and the number of passengers had increased tenfold to 188 million. By then over 370,000 Indians worked for the railroads. Irrigation also received attention, and by 1900 India had the world's most extensive irrigation system.

At the same time, Indian production of textiles suffered a huge blow. Britain imported India's raw cotton but exported machine-spun yarn and machine-woven cloth, displacing millions of Indian hand-spinners and hand-weavers. By 1900 India was buying 40 percent of Britain's cotton exports. Not until 1900 were small steps taken toward industrializing India. Local Gujaratis set up textile mills in Bombay, and the Tata family started the first steel mill in Bihar in 1911. By 1914 about a million Indians worked in factories.

As the economy expanded the standard of living of the poor did not see much improvement. Tenant farming and landlessness increased with the growth in plantation agriculture. Increases in production were eaten up by increases in population, which, as noted, had reached approximately 300 million by 1900. There was also a negative side to improved transportation. As Indians traveled more widely on the convenient trains, disease spread, especially cholera, which is transmitted by exposure to contaminated water. Pilgrims' bathing in and drinking from sacred pools and rivers worsened this problem. New sewerage and water supply systems were installed in Calcutta in the late 1860s, and the death rate there decreased, but in 1900 four out of every one thousand residents of British India still died of cholera each year.

Wooden Model of a Colonial Courtroom The judge, an officer with the British East India Company who is seated on a chair with his top hat on the table, presides over a courtroom filled with Indian assistants seated on the floor and the plaintiffs and defendants in the case standing. Notice the attention the Indian craftsman paid to the details of the dress and hats of each of the figures in this 20-inch-long wooden model. (© Victoria and Albert Museum, London/V&A Images)

The British and the Indian Educated Elite

The Indian middle class probably gained more than the poor from British rule, because they were the ones to benefit from the English-language educational system Britain established in India. (See "Viewpoints: Rammohun Roy and Thomas Babington Macauley on Education for Indians," page 788.) Missionaries also established schools with Western curricula, and 790,000 Indians were attending some 24,000 schools by 1870. High-caste Hindus came to form a new elite profoundly influenced by Western thought and culture.

By creating a well-educated, English-speaking Indian elite and a bureaucracy aided by a modern communication system, the British laid the groundwork for a unified, powerful state. Britain placed under the same general system of law and administration the various Hindu and Muslim peoples of the subcontinent who had resisted one another for centuries. It was as if Europe, with its many states and varieties of Christianity, had been conquered and united in a single great empire. University graduates tended to look on themselves as Indians more than as residents of separate states and kingdoms, a necessary step for the development of Indian nationalism.

Some Indian intellectuals sought to reconcile the values of the modern West and their own traditions. Rammohun Roy (1772–1833), who had risen to the top of the native ranks in the British East India Company, founded a college that offered instruction in Western languages and subjects. He also founded a society to reform traditional customs, especially child marriage, the caste system, and restrictions on widows. He espoused a modern Hinduism founded on the *Upanishads* (oo-PAH-nih-shahds), the ancient sacred texts of Hinduism.

The more that Western-style education was developed in India, the more the inequalities of the system became apparent to educated Indians. Indians were eligible to take the examinations for entry into the elite **Indian Civil Service**, the bureaucracy that administered the Indian government, but the exams were given in England. Since few Indians could travel such a long distance to take the test, in 1870 only 1 of the 916 members of the service was Indian. In other words, no matter how Anglicized educated Indians became, they could never become the white rulers' equals. The top jobs, the best clubs, the modern hotels, and even certain railroad compartments were sealed off to brown-skinned men and women. Most of the British elite considered the jumble of Indian peoples and castes to be racially inferior. For example, when the British Parliament in 1883 was considering a bill to allow Indian judges to try white Europeans in India, the British community rose in protest and defeated the measure.

> " However well educated and clever a native may be, and however brave he may prove himself, I believe that no rank we can bestow on him would cause him to be considered an equal of the British officer. "
>
> **LORD KITCHENER**

As Lord Kitchener, one of the most distinguished British military commanders in India, stated:

> It is this consciousness of the inherent superiority of the European which has won for us India. However well educated and clever a native may be, and however brave he may prove himself, I believe that no rank we can bestow on him would cause him to be considered an equal of the British officer.[1]

The peasant masses might accept such inequality as the latest version of age-old class and caste hierarchies, but the well-educated, English-speaking elite eventually could not. They had studied not only Milton and Shakespeare but also English traditions of democracy, liberty, and national pride.

In the late nineteenth century the colonial ports of Calcutta, Bombay, and Madras, now all linked by railroads, became centers of intellectual ferment. In these and other cities, newspapers in English and in regional languages gained influence. Lawyers trained in English law began agitating for Indian independence. By 1885, when a group of educated Indians came together to found the **Indian National Congress**, demands were increasing for the equality and self-government that Britain enjoyed and had already granted white-settler colonies such as Canada and Australia (see Chapter 27). The Congress Party called for more opportunities for Indians in the Indian Civil Service and reallocation of the government budget from military expenditures to the alleviation of poverty. They advocated unity across religious and caste lines, but most members were upper-caste, Western-educated Hindus.

Defending British possessions in India became a key element of Britain's foreign policy during the nineteenth century and led to steady expansion of the territory Britain controlled in Asia. The kingdom of Burma, to India's east, also was trying to expand, which led the British to annex Assam (located between India and Burma) in 1826, then all of Burma by 1852. Burma was

- **Indian Civil Service** The bureaucracy that administered the government of India. Entry into its elite ranks was by examinations that Indians were eligible to take but that were offered only in England.
- **Indian National Congress** A political association formed in 1885 that worked for Indian self-government.

Viewpoints

Rammohun Roy and Thomas Babington Macauley on Education for Indians

- *Opinion was divided among both British administrators and Indian intellectuals about the sort of education the colonial government should offer to Indians. In 1823 the leading Indian intellectual, Rammohun Roy (1772–1833), well-educated in both traditional Indian subjects and in English, responded negatively to a British proposal to establish a school teaching Sanskrit and Hindu literature. The matter of higher education in India was not settled until 1835, when Thomas Babington Macauley (1800–1859), in his capacity as a colonial officer, came out strongly for Western education.*

Rammohun Roy, 1823

"When this Seminary of learning was proposed, we understood that the Government in England had ordered a considerable sum of money to be annually devoted to the instruction of its Indian Subjects. We were filled with sanguine hopes that this sum would be laid out in employing European Gentlemen of talents and education to instruct the natives of India in Mathematics, Natural Philosophy, Chemistry, Anatomy, and other useful Sciences, which the Nations of Europe have carried to a degree of perfection that has raised them above the inhabitants of other parts of the world. . . .

We now find that the Government are establishing a Sanskrit school under Hindu Pundits to impart such knowledge as is already current in India. This Seminary (similar in character to those which existed in Europe before the time of Lord Bacon) can only be expected to load the minds of youth with grammatical niceties and metaphysical distinctions of little or no practicable use to the possessors or to society. The pupils will there acquire what was known two thousand years ago, with the addition of vain and empty subtleties since produced by speculative men, such as is already commonly taught in all parts of India.

The Sanskrit language, so difficult that almost a life time is necessary for its perfect acquisition, is well known to have been for ages a lamentable check on the diffusion of knowledge; and the learning concealed under this almost impervious veil is far from sufficient to reward the labour of acquiring it."

Thomas Babington Macauley, 1835

"What then shall that language [of instruction] be? One half of the committee maintain that it should be the English. The other half strongly recommend the Arabic and Sanskrit. The whole question seems to me to be which language is the best worth knowing? . . .

It will hardly be disputed, I suppose, that the department of literature in which the Eastern writers stand highest is poetry. And I certainly never met with any orientalist who ventured to maintain that the Arabic and Sanskrit poetry could be compared to that of the great European nations. But when we pass from works of imagination to works in which facts are recorded and general principles investigated, the superiority of the Europeans becomes absolutely immeasurable. . . .

It is taken for granted by the advocates of oriental learning that no native of this country can possibly attain more than a mere smattering of English. . . . They assume it as undeniable that the question is between a profound knowledge of Hindu and Arabian literature and science on the one side, and superficial knowledge of the rudiments of English on the other. This is not merely an assumption, but an assumption contrary to all reason and experience. . . . There are in this very town natives who are quite competent to discuss political or scientific questions with fluency and precision in the English language. I have heard the very question on which I am now writing discussed by native gentlemen with a liberality and an intelligence which would do credit to any member of the Committee of Public Instruction. . . .

In one point I fully agree with the gentlemen to whose general views I am opposed. I feel with them that it is impossible for us, with our limited means, to attempt to educate the body of the people. We must at present do our best to form a class who may be interpreters between us and the millions whom we govern, a class of persons Indian in blood and color, but English in tastes, in opinions, in morals and in intellect. To that class we may leave it to refine the vernacular dialects of the country, to enrich those dialects with terms of science borrowed from the Western nomenclature, and to render them by degrees fit vehicles for conveying knowledge to the great mass of the population."

Source: Bureau of Education. *Selections from Educational Records, Part I (1781–1839)*, edited by H. Sharp (Calcutta: Superintendent Government Printing, 1920; reprint: Delhi: National Archives of India, 1965), pp. 98–101, 107–117.

QUESTIONS FOR ANALYSIS

1. Are the reasons that Roy and Macauley prefer instruction in English similar?

2. What can you infer about the views of the other side? What would be the strongest reasons for establishing colleges using Indian languages?

Map showing Asia in 1914 with the following labels:

40°E, 60°E, 80°E, 100°E, 120°E, 140°E

RUSSIAN EMPIRE

Omsk, Trans-Siberian Railway, Volga R., Samara, Orenburg, SIBERIA, Lake Baikal, Irkutsk, Chita, AMUR DISTRICT (1858), Khabarovsk (1858)

Kazalinsk, OUTER MONGOLIA (Russian Influence, 1912), MANCHURIA, Harbin, Vladivostok (1860)

Batum (1878), Caspian Sea, Aral Sea, Lake Balkash, Tashkent (1864), Andizhan (1871), XINJIANG, INNER MONGOLIA, Shenyang, Sea of Japan, 40°N

Kars (1878), Baku, Krasnovodsk, Bukhara, Samarkand (1868), Tianjin, Port Arthur (Japan 1905)

OTTOMAN EMPIRE, Tehran, Ashkhabad (1881), Merv (1884), Kushka, KASHMIR (1846), Beijing, JEHOL, Weihai (Gr. Br. 1898), KOREA (1905, 1910)

RUSSIAN SPHERE (1907), AFGHANISTAN, Jiaozhou (Ger. 1898)

PERSIA, Indus R., PUNJAB, TIBET, CHINA, Nanjing, JAPANESE EMPIRE

KUWAIT (1899), BRITISH SPHERE (1907), BALUCHISTAN (1883), Delhi, HIMALAYA MTS, BHUTAN, NEPAL, ASSAM, Chongqing, Huang He R., Shanghai (Gr. Br. 1842)

ARABIA, Karachi, Ganges R., Wuhan, East China Sea, Ryukyu Is. (Jap.)

Persian Gulf, Kunming, Guangzhou (Gr. Br. 1842), Fuzhou, Formosa (Jap. 1895), Tropic of Cancer

OMAN (1891), Diu (Port. 1534), Calcutta (1786), BURMA (1852, 1885), Zhanjiang (France 1898), Macao (Port. 1557), Hong Kong (Gr. Br. 1842), 20°N

HADRAMAUT (1888), Bombay, INDIA, Yangzi R., Hanoi, Haiphong, Hainan, South China Sea

Arabian Sea, Yanaon (Fr. 1731), Bay of Bengal, Rangoon, LAOS, PACIFIC OCEAN

WEST ADEN (1903), Madras (1638), Pondicherry (Fr. 1672), Andaman Is. (Gr. Br. 1789), SIAM, Bangkok, FRENCH INDOCHINA (1859, 1907), Saigon, Manila, Philippine Is. (U.S. 1898)

Goa (Port. 1510), Karikal (Fr. 1642), CAMBODIA, BRITISH NORTH BORNEO (1886)

Ceylon, MALAYA (1874, 1909), SARAWAK (1888)

INDIAN OCEAN, Singapore (Gr. Br. 1819), Borneo, Celebes, New Guinea

Sumatra, Batavia, DUTCH EAST INDIES, Java (1619), Timor (Neth.) (Portugal 1859)

Legend:

Territories held by Western Powers
- Great Britain
- France
- Netherlands
- United States
- Russian Empire
- Japan and its territories
- Independent Asian states
- 1842 Date of colonization or occupation
- Major railroad

0 500 1,000 miles
0 500 1,000 kilometers

□ Mapping the Past

MAP 26.1 Asia in 1914 India remained under British rule, while China precariously preserved its political independence. The Dutch Empire in modern-day Indonesia was old, but French control of Indochina was a product of the new imperialism.

ANALYZING THE MAP Consider the colonies of the different powers on this map. What European countries were leading imperialist states, and what lands did they hold? Can you see places where colonial powers were likely to come into conflict with each other?

CONNECTIONS Do the sizes of the various colonial territories as seen on this map adequately reflect their importance to the countries that possessed them? If not, what else should be taken into account in thinking about the value of these sorts of colonial possessions?

then administered as a province of India. British trade between India and China went through the Strait of Malacca, making that region strategically important. Britain had taken over several Dutch territories in this region, including Java, during the Napoleonic occupation of the Netherlands (Map 26.1). After returning them to the Netherlands in 1814, Britain created its own base in the area at Singapore, later expanding into

Malaya (now Malaysia) in the 1870s and 1880s. In both Burma and Malaya, Britain tried to foster economic development, building railroads and promoting trade. Burma became a major exporter of timber and rice, Malaya of tin and rubber. So many laborers were brought into Malaya for the expanding mines and plantations that its population came to be approximately one-third Malay, one-third Chinese, and one-third Indian.

Competition for Southeast Asia

☐ Why were most but not all Southeast Asian societies reduced to colonies?

At the beginning of the nineteenth century only a small part of Southeast Asia was under direct European control. Spain administered the Philippines, and the Dutch controlled Java. By the end of the century most of the region would be in foreign hands.

The Dutch East Indies

Although Dutch forts and trading posts in the East Indies dated back to the seventeenth century, in 1816 the Dutch ruled little more than the island of Java. Thereafter they gradually brought almost all of the 3,000-mile-long archipelago under their political authority. In extending their rule, the Dutch, like the British in India, brought diverse peoples with different languages and distinct cultural traditions into a single political entity (see Map 26.1). Thus they inadvertently created the foundations of modern-day Indonesia — the world's fourth most populous nation.

Taking over the Dutch East India Company in 1799, the Dutch government modified the company's loose control of Java and gradually built a modern bureaucratic state. Javanese resistance to Dutch rule led to the bloody **Java War** (1825–1830). In 1830, after the war, the Dutch abolished the combination of tribute from rulers and forced labor from peasants that they had used to obtain spices, and they established instead a particularly exploitive policy called the Culture System. Under this system, Indonesian peasants were forced to plant a fifth of their land in export crops, especially coffee and sugar, to turn over to the Dutch as tax. The Culture System proved highly profitable for the Dutch and brought Dutch shipping and intercontinental commerce back to life. In 1870 Dutch liberals succeeded in eliminating some of the system's most coercive elements, but the practical effects were limited because Dutch and Javanese officials still worked together to make sure the flow of goods continued.

At the end of the nineteenth century the Dutch began to encourage Western education in the East Indies. The children of local rulers and privileged elites, much like their counterparts in India, encountered new ideas in Dutch-language schools. They began to question the long-standing cooperation of local elites with Dutch colonialism, and they searched for a new national identity. Thus anticolonial nationalism began to take shape in the East Indies in the early twentieth century, and it would blossom after World War I.

Mainland Southeast Asia

Unlike India and Java, mainland Southeast Asia had escaped European rule during the eighteenth century. In 1802 the **Nguyen Dynasty** came to power in Vietnam, putting an end to thirty years of peasant rebellion and civil war. For the first time in the country's history, a single Vietnamese monarchy ruled the entire country, and Vietnam's future appeared bright. Working through a centralizing scholar bureaucracy fashioned on the Chinese model, the Nguyen (gwin) Dynasty energetically built irrigation canals, roads and bridges, and impressive palaces in Hue (hway), the new capital city. In 1821 a European who had lived in India, Java, and Siam (Thailand) wrote that Hue had a "neatness, magnitude, and perfection" that made other Asian achievements look "like the works of children."[2] Yet construction placed a heavy burden on the peasants drafted to do the work, and it contributed to a resurgence of peasant uprisings.

The French Governor General and the Vietnamese Emperor The twelfth emperor of the Nguyen Dynasty, Khai Dinh (1885–1925) had to find ways to get along with the French governor general (in this picture, Albert Sarraut) if he wished to preserve his dynasty. Seen here in 1917 or 1918, he had adopted Western leather shoes but otherwise tried to keep a distinct Vietnamese identity in his dress. (Roger Viollet/Getty Images)

Roman Catholic missionaries from France posed a second, more dangerous threat to Vietnam's Confucian ruling elite. The king and his advisers believed that Christianity would undermine Confucian moral values and the unity of the Vietnamese state. In 1825 King Minh Mang (r. 1820–1841) outlawed the teaching of Christianity, and soon his government began executing Catholic missionaries and Vietnamese converts. As many as thirty thousand Vietnamese Christians were executed in the 1850s. In response, in 1859–1860 a French naval force seized Saigon and three surrounding provinces in southern Vietnam, making that part of Vietnam a French colony. In 1884–1885 France launched a second war against Vietnam and conquered the rest of the country. Laos and Cambodia were added to form French Indochina in 1887. In all three countries the local rulers were left on their thrones, but France dominated and tried to promote French culture.

After the French conquest, Vietnamese patriots continued to resist the colonial occupiers with a combination of loyalty to Confucian values and intense hatred of foreign rule. After Japan's victory over Russia in 1905 (see page 802), a new generation of nationalists saw Japan as a model for Vietnamese revitalization and freedom. They went to Japan to study and planned for anticolonial revolution in Vietnam.

In all of Southeast Asia, only Siam succeeded in preserving its independence. Siam was sandwiched between the British in Burma and the French in Indochina. Siam's very able King Chulalongkorn (r. 1868–1910) took advantage of this situation to balance the two competitors against each other and to escape the smothering embrace of both. Chulalongkorn had studied Greek and Latin and Western science and kept up with Western news by reading British newspapers from Hong Kong and Singapore. He outlawed slavery and implemented modernizing reforms that centralized the government so that it could more effectively control outlying provinces coveted by the imperialists. Independent Siam gradually developed a modern centralizing state similar to those constructed by Western imperialists in their Asian possessions.

The Philippines

The United States became one of the imperialist powers in Asia when it took the Philippines from Spain in 1898. When the Spanish established rule in the Philippines in the sixteenth century, the islands had no central government or literate culture; order was maintained by village units dominated by local chiefs. Under the Spanish, Roman Catholic churches were established, and Spanish priests able to speak the local languages became the most common intermediaries between local populations, who rarely could speak Spanish, and the new rulers. The government of Spain encouraged Spaniards to colonize the Philippines through the *encomienda* system (see page 477): Spaniards who had served the Crown were rewarded with grants giving them the exclusive right to control public affairs and collect taxes in a specific locality of the Philippines. A local Filipino elite also developed, aided by the Spanish introduction of private ownership of land. Given the great distance between Madrid and Manila, the capital of the Philippines, the local governor general, appointed by Spain, had almost unlimited powers over the courts and the military. Manila developed into an important entrepôt in the galleon trade between Mexico and China, and this trade also attracted a large Chinese community, which handled much of the trade within the Philippines.

Spain did not do much to promote education in the Philippines. In the late nineteenth century, however, wealthy Filipinos began to send their sons to study abroad, and a movement to press Spain for reforms emerged among those who had been abroad. When the Spanish cracked down on critics, a rebellion erupted in 1896 (see "Individuals in Society: José Rizal," page 792). It was settled in 1897 with Spanish promises to reform.

In 1898 war between Spain and the United States broke out in Cuba (see page 825), and in May the American naval officer Commodore George Dewey sailed into Manila Bay and sank the Spanish fleet anchored there. Dewey called on the Philippine rebels to help defeat the Spanish forces, but when the rebels declared independence, the U.S. government refused to recognize them, despite protests by American anti-imperialists. U.S. forces fought the Philippine rebels, and by the end of the insurrection in 1902 the war had cost the lives of 5,000 Americans and about 200,000 Filipinos. In the following years, the United States introduced a form of colonial rule that included public works and economic development projects, improved education and medicine, and in 1907 an elected legislative assembly.

China Under Pressure

☐ Was China's decline in the nineteenth century due more to internal problems or to Western imperialism?

In 1800 most Chinese had no reason to question the conception of China as the central kingdom. No other country had so many people; Chinese products were in great demand in foreign countries; and the borders had recently been expanded. A century later China's world standing had sunk precipitously. In 1900 foreign troops

- **Java War** The 1825–1830 war between the Dutch government and the Javanese, fought over the extension of Dutch control of the island.
- **Nguyen Dynasty** The last Vietnamese ruling house, which lasted from 1802 to 1945.

Individuals in Society

José Rizal

IN THE MID-SEVENTEENTH CENTURY, A CHINESE merchant immigrated to the Philippines and married a woman who was half Chinese, half Philippine. Because of anti-Chinese animosity, he changed his name to Mercado, Spanish for "merchant."

Mercado's direct patrilineal descendant, José Rizal (1861–1896), was born into a well-to-do family that leased a plantation from Dominican friars. Both of his parents were educated, and he was a brilliant student himself. In 1882, after completing his studies at the Jesuit-run college in Manila, he went to Madrid to study medicine. During his ten years in Europe he not only earned a medical degree in Spain and a Ph.D. in Germany but he also found time to learn several European languages and make friends with scientists, writers, and political radicals.

While in Europe, Rizal became involved with Philippine revolutionaries and contributed numerous articles to their newspaper, *La Solidaridad*, published in Barcelona. Rizal advocated making the Philippines a province of Spain, giving it representation in the Spanish parliament, replacing Spanish friars with Filipino priests, and making Filipinos and Spaniards equal before the law. He spent a year at the British Museum doing research on the early phase of the Spanish colonization of the Philippines. He also wrote two novels.

The first novel, written in Spanish, was fired by the passions of nationalism. In satirical fashion, it depicts a young Filipino of mixed blood who studies for several years in Europe before returning to the Philippines to start a modern secular school in his hometown and to marry his childhood sweetheart. The church stands in the way of his efforts, and the colonial administration proves incompetent. The novel ends with the hero being gunned down after the friars falsely implicate him in a revolutionary conspiracy. Rizal's own life ended up following this narrative surprisingly closely.

In 1892 Rizal left Europe, stopped briefly in Hong Kong, and then returned to Manila to help his family with a lawsuit. Though he secured his relatives' release from jail, he ran into trouble himself. Because his writings were critical of the power of the church, he made many enemies, some of whom had him arrested. He was sent into exile to a Jesuit mission town on the relatively primitive island of Mindanao. There he founded a school and a hospital, and the Jesuits tried to win him back to the church. He kept busy during his four years in exile, not only teaching English, science, and self-defense, but also maintaining his correspondence with scientists in Europe. When a nationalist secret society rose in revolt in 1896, Rizal, in an effort to distance himself, volunteered to go to Cuba to help in an outbreak of yellow fever. Although he had no connections with the secret society and was on his way across the ocean, Rizal was arrested and shipped back to Manila.

Tried for sedition by the military, Rizal was found guilty. When handed his death certificate, Rizal struck out the words "Chinese half-breed" and wrote "pure native." He was publicly executed by a firing squad in Manila at age thirty-five, making him a martyr of the nationalist cause.

QUESTIONS FOR ANALYSIS

1. Did Rizal's comfortable family background contribute to his becoming a revolutionary?
2. How would Rizal's European contemporaries have reacted to his opposition to the Catholic Church?

After Rizal's death, his portrait was used to inspire patriotism. (Cover of "The Filipino Teacher," December 1908. Courtesy, Museo Santisima Trinidad)

marched into China's capital to protect foreign nationals, and more and more Chinese had come to think that their government, society, and cultural values needed to be radically changed.

The Opium War

Seeing little to gain from trade with European countries, the Qing (Manchu) emperors, who had been ruling China since 1644 (see pages 626–629), permitted Europeans to trade only at the port of Guangzhou (Canton) and only through licensed Chinese merchants. Initially, the balance of trade was in China's favor. Great Britain and the other Western nations used silver to pay for tea, since they had not been able to find anything that Chinese wanted to buy. By the 1820s, however, the British had found something the Chinese would buy: opium. Grown legally in British-occupied India, opium was smuggled into China, where its use and sale were illegal. Huge profits and the cravings of addicts led to rapid increases in sales, from 4,500 chests a year in 1810 to 10,000 in 1830 and 40,000 in 1838. At this point it was China that suffered a drain of silver, since it was importing more than it was exporting.

To deal with this crisis, the Chinese government dispatched Lin Zexu to Guangzhou in 1839. He dealt harshly with Chinese who purchased opium and seized the opium stores of British merchants. Lin even wrote to Queen Victoria: "Suppose there were people from another country who carried opium for sale to England and seduced your people into buying and smoking it;

> "Suppose there were people from another country who carried opium for sale to England and seduced your people into buying and smoking it; certainly your honorable ruler would deeply hate it and be bitterly aroused."
>
> **LIN ZEXU**

certainly your honorable ruler would deeply hate it and be bitterly aroused."[3] When Lin pressured the Portuguese to expel the uncooperative British from their trading post at Macao, the British settled on the barren island of Hong Kong.

Although for years the little community of foreign merchants had accepted Chinese rules, by 1839 the British, the dominant group, were ready to flex their muscles. British merchants wanted to create a market for their goods in China and get tea more cheaply by trading closer to its source in central China. They also wanted a European-style diplomatic relationship with China, with envoys and ambassadors, commercial treaties, and published tariffs. With the encouragement of their merchants in China, the British sent an expeditionary force from India with forty-two warships, many of them leased from the major opium trader, Jardine, Matheson, and Company.

With its control of the seas, the British easily shut down key Chinese ports and forced the Chinese to negotiate. Dissatisfied with the resulting agreement, the

Treaty of Nanjing The settlement reached by Britain and China in 1842 was written in both English and Chinese. The chief negotiators of both sides signed the document, and the seals of both countries were placed on it. The Chinese seal was impressed with red ink in the traditional way, while the British used wax. (The National Archives, UK)

British sent a second, larger force, which took even more coastal cities, including Shanghai. This **Opium War** was settled at gunpoint in 1842. The resulting treaties opened five ports to international trade, fixed the tariff on imported goods at 5 percent, imposed an indemnity of 21 million ounces of silver on China to cover Britain's war expenses, and ceded the island of Hong Kong to Britain. Through the clause on **extraterritoriality**, British subjects in China became answerable only to British law, even in disputes with Chinese. The treaties also had a "most-favored nation" clause, which meant that whenever one nation extracted a new privilege from China, it was extended automatically to Britain.

The treaties satisfied neither side. China continued to refuse to accept foreign diplomats at its capital in Beijing, and the expansion of trade fell far short of Western expectations. Between 1856 and 1860 Britain and France renewed hostilities with China. Seventeen thousand British and French troops occupied Beijing and set the emperor's summer palace on fire. Another round of harsh treaties gave European merchants and missionaries greater privileges and forced the Chinese to open several more cities to foreign trade. Large areas in some of the treaty ports were leased in perpetuity to foreign powers; these were known as **concessions**.

Internal Problems

China's problems in the nineteenth century were not all of foreign origin. By 1850 China, for centuries the world's most populous country, had more than 400 million people. As the population grew, farm size shrank, forests were put to the plow, and surplus labor suppressed wages. When the best parcels of land were all occupied, conflicts over rights to water and tenancy increased. Hard times also led to increased female infanticide, as families felt that they could not afford to raise more than two or three children and

Chinese Rebellions, 1851–1911

Taiping Rebellion, 1851–1864
Boxer uprising, 1900
Revolt of 1911

saw sons as necessities. A shortage of marriageable women resulted, reducing the incentive for young men to stay near home and do as their elders told them. Some became bandits, others boatmen, carters, sedan-chair carriers, and, by the end of the century, rickshaw pullers.

These economic and demographic circumstances led to some of the most destructive rebellions in China's history. The worst was the **Taiping Rebellion** (1851–1864), in which some 20 million people lost their lives, making it one of the bloodiest wars in world history.

The Taiping (TIGH-ping) Rebellion was initiated by Hong Xiuquan (hong show-chwan; 1814–1864), a man from South China who had studied for the civil service examinations but never passed. His career as a religious leader began with visions of an old golden-bearded man and a middle-aged man who addressed him as younger brother and told him to annihilate devils. After reading a Christian tract given to him by a missionary, Hong interpreted his visions to mean he was Jesus's younger brother. He soon gathered followers, whom he instructed to destroy idols and ancestral temples, give up opium and alcohol, and renounce foot binding and prostitution. In 1851 he declared himself king of the Heavenly Kingdom of Great Peace (Taiping), an act of open insurrection.

By 1853 the Taiping rebels, as Hong's followers were known, had moved north and established their capital at the major city of Nanjing, which they held onto for a decade. From this base they set about creating a utopian society based on the equalization of landholdings and the equality of men and women. This utopia required men and women to live separately:

> It is a matter of course that we should attend to our parents and look after our wives and children, but when one first creates a new rule, the state must come first and the family last, public interests first and private interests last. . . . There must be no common mixing of the male and female groups, which would cause debauchery and violation of Heaven's command. Although to pay respects to parents and to visit wives and children occasionally are in keeping with human nature and not prohibited, yet it is only proper to converse before the door, stand a few steps apart and speak in a loud voice; one must not enter the sisters' camp or permit the mixing of men and women. Only thus, by complying with rules and commands, can we become sons and daughters of Heaven.[4]

- **Opium War** The 1839–1842 war between the British and the Chinese over limitations on trade and the importation of opium into China.
- **extraterritoriality** The legal principle that exempts individuals from local law, applicable in China because of the agreements reached after China's loss in the Opium War.
- **concessions** Large areas of Chinese treaty ports that were leased in perpetuity to foreign powers.
- **Taiping Rebellion** A massive rebellion by believers in the religious teachings of Hong Xiuquan, begun in 1851 and not suppressed until 1864.

China's First Railroad Soon after this 15-mile-long railroad was constructed near Shanghai in 1876 by the British firm of Jardine and Matheson, the provincial governor bought it in order to tear it out. Many Chinese of the period saw the introduction of railroads as harmful not only to the balance of nature but also to people's livelihoods, since the railroads eliminated jobs in transport like dragging boats along canals or driving pack horses. (Private Collection)

Christian missionaries quickly concluded that the Christian elements in Taiping doctrines were heretical and did not help the rebels. To suppress the Taipings, the Manchus had to turn to Chinese scholar-officials, who raised armies on their own, revealing that the Manchus were no longer the mighty warriors they had been when they had conquered China two centuries earlier.

The Self-Strengthening Movement

After the various rebellions were suppressed, forward-looking reformers began addressing the Western threat. Under the slogan "self-strengthening," they set about modernizing the military along Western lines, establishing arsenals and dockyards. Recognizing that guns and ships were merely the surface manifestations of the Western powers' economic strength, some of the most progressive reformers also initiated new industries, which in the 1870s and 1880s included railway lines, steam navigation companies, coal mines, telegraph lines, and cotton spinning and weaving factories. These were the same sorts of initiatives that the British were introducing in India, but China lagged behind, especially in railroads.

These measures drew resistance from conservatives, who thought copying Western practices was compounding defeat. The highly placed Manchu official Woren objected that "from ancient down to modern times" there had never been "anyone who could use mathematics to raise a nation from a state of decline or to strengthen it in times of weakness."[5] Yet knowledge of the West gradually improved with more translations

and travel in both directions. Newspapers covering world affairs began publication in Shanghai and Hong Kong. By 1880 China had embassies in London, Paris, Berlin, Madrid, Washington, Tokyo, and St. Petersburg.

Despite the enormous effort put into trying to catch up, China was humiliated yet again at the end of the nineteenth century. First came the discovery that Japan had so successfully modernized that it posed a threat to China (see pages 787–802). Then, in 1894 Japanese efforts to separate Korea from Chinese influence led to the brief Sino-Japanese War in which China was decisively defeated even though much of its navy had been purchased abroad at great expense. In the peace negotiations, China ceded Taiwan to Japan, agreed to a huge indemnity (compensation for war expenses), and gave Japan the right to open factories in China. China's helplessness in the face of aggression led to a scramble among the European powers for concessions and protectorates in China. At the high point of this rush in 1898, it appeared that the European powers might actually divide China among themselves, the way they had recently divided Africa.

Republican Revolution

China's humiliating defeat in the Sino-Japanese War in 1895 led to a renewed drive for reform. In 1898 a group of educated young reformers gained access to the twenty-seven-year-old Qing emperor. They warned him of the fate of Poland (divided by the European powers in the eighteenth century; see pages 541–542) and regaled him with the triumphs of the Meiji reformers in Japan. They proposed redesigning China as a

Hong Kong Tailors In 1872 the newspaper *Shenbao* was founded in Shanghai, and in 1884 it added an eight-page weekly pictorial supplement. Influenced by the pictorial press then popular in Europe, it depicted both news and human interest stories, both Chinese and foreign. This scene shows a tailor shop in Hong Kong where Chinese tailors use sewing machines and make women's clothes in current Western styles. To Chinese readers, men making women's clothes and placing them on bamboo forms would have seemed as peculiar as the style of the dresses. (From *Dianshizhai huabao*, a Shanghai picture magazine, 1885 or later)

constitutional monarchy with modern financial and educational systems. For three months the emperor issued a series of reform decrees. But the Manchu establishment and the empress dowager, who had dominated the court for the last quarter century, felt threatened and not only suppressed the reform movement but imprisoned the emperor as well. Hope for reform from the top was dashed.

A period of violent reaction swept the country, reaching its peak in 1900 with the uprising of a secret society that foreigners dubbed the **Boxers**. The Boxers blamed China's ills on foreigners, especially the missionaries who traveled throughout China telling the Chinese that their beliefs were wrong and their customs backward. After the Boxers laid siege to the foreign legation quar-

ter in Beijing, a dozen nations including Japan sent twenty thousand troops to lift the siege. In the negotiations that followed, China had to accept a long list of penalties, including cancellation of the civil service examinations for five years (punishment for gentry collaboration) and a staggering indemnity of 450 million ounces of silver, almost twice the government's annual revenues.

After this defeat, gradual reform lost its appeal. More and more Chinese were studying abroad and learning about Western political ideas, including democracy and revolution. The most famous was Sun Yatsen (1866–1925). Sent by his peasant family to Hawai'i, he learned English and then continued his education in Hong Kong. From 1894 on, he spent his time abroad organizing revolutionary societies and seeking financial support from overseas Chinese. He later joined forces with Chinese student revolutionaries studying in Japan, and together they attempted several times to spark rebellion. The plot that finally triggered the collapse of China's imperial system is known as the **1911 Revolution**. Army officers fearful that their connections to the revolutionaries would be exposed staged a coup and persuaded the provincial governments to secede. The powers behind the child emperor (who had as-

- **Boxers** A Chinese secret society that blamed the country's ills on foreigners, especially missionaries, and rose in rebellion in 1900.
- **1911 Revolution** The uprising that brought China's monarchy to an end.
- **gunboat diplomacy** The imposition of treaties and agreements under threat of military violence, such as the opening of Japan to trade after Commodore Perry's demands.
- **Meiji Restoration** The 1867 ousting of the Tokugawa Shogunate that "restored" the power of the Japanese emperors.

cended to the throne at the age of three in 1908) agreed to his abdication, and at the beginning of 1912 China's long history of monarchy came to an end, to be replaced by a republic modeled on Western political ideas. China had escaped direct foreign rule but would never be the same.

Japan's Rapid Transformation

☐ How was Japan able to quickly master the challenges posed by the West?

During the nineteenth century, while China's standing in the world plummeted, Japan's was rising. European traders and missionaries first arrived in Japan in the sixteenth century, but in the early seventeenth century, in part because of the remarkable success of Catholic missionaries (see pages 644–645), the Japanese government expelled them. During the eighteenth century Japan much more effectively than China kept foreign merchants and missionaries at bay. It limited trade to a single port (Nagasaki), where only the Dutch were allowed, and forbade Japanese to travel abroad. Because Japan's land and population were so much smaller than China's, the Western powers never expected much from Japan as a trading partner and did not press it as urgently. Still, the European threat was part of what propelled Japan to modernize.

The "Opening" of Japan

Wanting to play a greater role in the Pacific, the United States decided to force the Japanese to share their ports and behave as a "civilized" nation. In 1853 Commodore Matthew Perry steamed into Edo (now Tokyo) Bay and demanded diplomatic negotiations with the emperor. Some Japanese samurai (members of the warrior class) urged resistance, but senior officials knew what had happened in China and how defenseless their cities would be against naval bombardment. Under threat of **gunboat diplomacy**, and after consulting with the daimyo (major lords), the officials signed a treaty with the United States that opened two ports and permitted trade.

Japan at this time was a complex society. The emperor in Kyoto had no effective powers. For more than two hundred years real power had been in the hands of the Tokugawa shogun in Edo (see pages 631–632). The country was divided into numerous domains, each under a daimyo. Each daimyo had under him samurai, who had hereditary stipends and privileges, such as the right to wear a sword. Peasants and merchants were also le-

gally distinct classes, and in theory social mobility from peasant to merchant or merchant to samurai was impossible. After two centuries of peace, there were many more samurai than were needed to administer or defend the country, and many lived very modestly. They were proud, however, and felt humiliated by the sudden American intrusion and the unequal treaties that the Western countries imposed. Some began agitating against the shogunate under the slogan "Revere the emperor and expel the barbarians."

When foreign diplomats and merchants began to settle in Yokohama after 1858, radical samurai reacted with a wave of antiforeign terrorism and antigovernment assassinations. The Western response was swift and unambiguous. Much as the Western powers had sent troops to Beijing a few years before, they now sent an allied fleet of American, British, Dutch, and French warships to demolish key Japanese forts, further weakening the power and prestige of the shogun's government.

The Meiji Restoration

In 1867 a coalition of reform-minded daimyo led a coup that ousted the Tokugawa Shogunate. The samurai who led this coup declared a return to direct rule by the emperor, not practiced in Japan for more than six hundred years. This emperor was called the Meiji (MAY-jee) emperor and this event the **Meiji Restoration**, a great turning point in Japanese history.

The domain leaders who organized the coup, called the Meiji Oligarchs, moved the boy emperor to Tokyo castle (previously the seat of the shogun, now the imperial palace). They used the young sovereign to win over both the lords and the commoners. During the emperor's first decade on the throne, the leaders carried him around in hundreds of grand imperial processions so that he could see his subjects and they him. The emerging press also worked to keep its readers informed of the young emperor's actions and their obligations to him. Real power remained in the hands of the oligarchs.

The battle cry of the Meiji reformers had been "strong army, rich nation." How were these goals to be accomplished? In an about-face that is one of history's most remarkable chapters, the determined but flexible leaders of Meiji Japan dropped their antiforeign attacks. Convinced that they could not beat the West until they had mastered the secrets of its military and industrial might, they initiated a series of measures to reform Japan along modern Western lines. One reformer even proposed that "Japan must be reborn with America its mother and France its father."[6] In 1868 an imperial declaration promised that "Deliberative assemblies shall be widely established and all matters decided by public discussion" and that "Knowledge shall

Japan's Modernized Army A set of woodblock prints depicting the new sights of Tokyo included this illustration of a military parade ground. The soldiers' brightly colored Western-style uniforms undoubtedly helped make this a sight worth seeing. (Laurie Platt Winfrey/ The Granger Collection, New York)

be sought throughout the world so as to strengthen the foundations of imperial rule."[7] Within four years a delegation was traveling the world to learn what made the Western powers strong. Its members examined everything from the U.S. Constitution to the factories, shipyards, and railroads that made the European landscape so different from Japan's.

Japan under the shoguns had been decentralized, with most of the power over the population in the hands of the daimyos. By elevating the emperor, the oligarchs were able to centralize the government. In 1871 they abolished the domains and merged the domain armies. Following the example of the French Revolution, they dismantled the four-class legal system and declared everyone equal. This amounted to stripping the samurai (7 to 8 percent of the population) of their privileges.

First the samurai's stipends were reduced; then in 1876 the stipends were replaced by one-time grants of income-bearing bonds. Most samurai had to find work or start businesses, as the value of the bonds declined with inflation. Furthermore, samurai no longer were to wear their swords, long the symbols of their status. Even their monopoly on the use of force was eliminated: the new army recruited commoners along with samurai. Not surprisingly, some samurai rose up against their loss of privileges. In one extreme case, the rebels refused to use guns in a futile effort to retain the mystique of the sword. None of these uncoordinated uprisings made any difference.

Several leaders of the Meiji Restoration, in France on a fact-finding mission during the Franco-Prussian War of 1870–1871, were impressed by the active participation of French citizens in the defense of Paris. This contrasted with the indifference of most Japanese peasants during the battles that led to the Meiji Restoration. For Japan to survive in the hostile international environment, they concluded, ordinary people had to be trained to fight. Consequently, a conscription law, modeled on the French law, was issued in 1872. Like French law, it exempted first sons. To improve the training of soldiers, the new War College was organized along German lines, and German instructors were recruited to teach there. Young samurai were trained to form the new professional officer corps. The success of this approach was demonstrated first in 1877, when the professionally led army of draftees crushed a major rebellion by samurai.

Many of the new institutions established in the Meiji period reached down to the local level. Schools open to all were rapidly introduced after 1872. Teachers were trained in newly established teachers' colleges, where they learned to inculcate discipline, patriotism, and morality. Another modern institution that reached the local level was a national police force. In 1884 police training schools were established in every prefecture, and within a few years one- or two-man police stations were set up throughout the country. These policemen came to act as local agents of the central government. They not only dealt with crime but also enforced public health rules, conscription laws, and codes of behavior.

In time these new laws and institutions brought benefits, but at the local level they were often perceived as oppressive. Protests became very common against everything from conscription and the Western calendar to the new taxes to pay for the new schools.

In 1889 Japan became the first non-Western country to adopt the constitutional form of government. Prefectural assemblies, set up in the 1870s and 1880s, gave local elites some experience in debating political issues. The constitution, however, was handed down from above, drafted by the top political leaders and issued in the name of the emperor. A commission sent abroad to study European constitutional governments had come to the conclusion that the German constitutional monarchy would provide the best model for Japan, rather than the more democratic governments of the British, French, and Americans. Japan's new government had a two-house parliament, called the Diet. The upper house of lords was drawn largely from former daimyo and nobles, and the lower house was elected by a limited electorate (about 5 percent of the adult male population in 1890). Although Japan now had a government based on laws, it was authoritarian rather than democratic. The emperor was declared "sacred and inviolable." He had the right to appoint the prime minister and cabinet. He did not have to ask the Diet for funds because wealth assigned to the imperial house was entrusted to the Imperial Household Ministry, which was outside the government's control.

Cultural change during the Meiji period was as profound as political change. For more than a thousand years China had been the major source of ideas and technologies introduced into Japan, ranging from the writing system to Confucianism and Buddhism, tea and silk, chopsticks and soy sauce. But in the late nineteenth century China, beset by Western pressure, had become an object lesson on the dangers of stagnation rather than a model to follow. The influential author Fukuzawa Yukichi began urging Japan to pursue "civilization and enlightenment," by which he meant Western civilization. (See "Listening to the Past: Fukuzawa Yukichi, Escape from Asia," page 800.) Fukuzawa advocated learning Western languages and encouraged Japan to learn from the West in order to catch up with it. Soon Japanese were being told to conform to Western taste, eat meat, wear Western-style clothes, and drop customs that Westerners found odd, such as married women blackening their teeth.

□ Picturing the Past

Japan's First Skyscraper Meiji Japan's fascination with things Western led to the construction of Western-style buildings. Japan's first elevator made possible this twelve-story tower built in Tokyo in 1890. Situated in the entertainment district, it was filled with shops, theaters, bars, and restaurants. (Edo-Tokyo Museum. Image: TNM Image Archives/Tokyo Metropolitan Foundation for History and Culture Image Archives)

ANALYZING THE IMAGE Locate all the people in this picture. How are they dressed? What are they doing?

CONNECTIONS Keeping in mind that the building in this picture was built in 1890, what connections would you draw between the politics of the period and this visual celebration of a new style of architecture?

Industrialization

The leaders of the Meiji Restoration, wanting to strengthen Japan's military capacity, promoted industrialization. The government paid large salaries to attract foreign experts to help with industrialization, and Japanese were encouraged to go abroad to study science and engineering.

Listening to the Past

Fukuzawa Yukichi, Escape from Asia

Fukuzawa Yukichi was one of the most prominent intellectuals and promoters of westernization in Meiji Japan. His views on domestic policy were decidedly liberal, but he took a hard-line approach to foreign affairs. His ruthless criticism of Korea and China published on March 16, 1885, can be read as inviting colonialism. In 1895, ten years after writing this call to action, he rejoiced at Japan's victory over China in their conflict over Korea.

❝Civilization is like an epidemic of measles. The current measles in Tokyo, which has advanced eastwards from Nagasaki in western Japan, seems to have begun to claim more victims with the arrival of springtime. Will we be able now to find a means of checking this epidemic? It is obvious that we have no way to do so. We cannot put up effective resistance, even against an epidemic that carries with it only harm; much less against civilization, which is always accompanied by both harm and good, but by more good than harm.

Though our land of Japan is situated on the Eastern edge of Asia, the spirit of its people has already shaken off the backwardness of Asia to accept the civilization of the West. Unfortunately, however, we have two neighboring countries, one being called China, the other called Korea. The people of these two countries are no different from us Japanese people in having been brought up since olden times in the Asian culture and customs, and yet, whether because they are of another racial origin, or because, while similar in culture and customs, differ from us in the main lines of their traditional education, a comparison of the three countries, Japan, China, and Korea, reveals that the latter two resemble each other more closely than they do Japan. The people of those two countries do not know how to go about reforming and making progress, whether individually or as a country. It is not that they have not seen or heard of civilized things in the present world of facile communication; yet what their eyes and ears perceive have failed to stimulate their minds, and their emotional attachment to ancient manners and customs has changed little for the past hundreds and thousands of years. In this lively theater of civilization, where things change daily, they still speak of education in terms of Confucianism, cite humanity, justice, civility, and wisdom as their principles of school education, are completely obsessed only with outward appearance, are in reality not only ignorant of truths and principles but so extreme in their cruelty and shamelessness that for them morality is completely nonexistent, and yet are as arrogant as if they never gave a thought to self-examination.

In our view, these countries have no likelihood of maintaining their independence in the current tide of civilization's eastward advance. Let there not be the slightest doubt that, unless they are fortunate enough to have motivated men appear in their lands who, as a first step to improve the condition of their countries will plan such a great enterprise of overall reform of their governments as our Restoration was, and succeed in altering their people's minds through political reforms, those countries will meet their doom in but a few years, with their territories divided among the civilized countries of the world. The reason is that China and Korea, confronted by an epidemic of civilization comparable to measles, are impossibly trying to ward it off, despite its inevitability, by shutting themselves up in a room, with the result being that they are cutting off their supply of fresh air and asphyxiating themselves. Though mutual help

---

The government played an active role in getting railroads, mines, and factories started. Japan's coal mines had produced only 390,000 tons in 1860, but by 1900 this output had risen to 5 million tons. Early on the Japanese government decided to compete with China in the export of tea and silk to the West. Introducing the mechanical reeling of silk gave Japan a strong price advantage in the sale of silk, and Japan's total foreign trade increased tenfold from 1877 to 1900. The next stage was to develop heavy industry. The huge indemnity exacted from China in 1895 was used to establish the Yawata Iron and Steel Works. The third stage of Japan's industrialization would today be called import substitution. Factories such as cotton mills were set up to help cut the importation of Western consumer goods. By 1912 factory output accounted for 13 percent of the national product, even though only 3 percent of the labor force worked in factories, mostly small ones with fewer than fifty workers.

Most of the great Japanese industrial conglomerates known as *zaibatsu* (zigh-BAHT-dzoo), such as Mitsubishi, got their start in this period, often founded by men with government connections. Sometimes the government set up plants that it then sold to private investors at bargain prices. Successful entrepreneurs were treated as patriotic heroes.

As in Europe, the early stages of industrialization brought hardship to the countryside. Farmers often ribetween neighboring countries has been likened to the relationship between the lips and the teeth, China and Korea of today cannot be of any assistance at all to our country of Japan.

Civilized western man is not without a tendency to regard all three countries as identical because of their geographic proximity and to apply his evaluation of China and Korea to Japan also. For example, when he finds that the governments of China and Korea are old-fashioned autocracies without abiding laws, the western man will suppose Japan too to be a lawless country. When he finds that the gentlemen of China and Korea are too deeply infatuated to know what science is, the western scholar will think that Japan too is a land of Yin-Yang and the Five Elements. When the Chinese display their servility and shamelessness, they obscure the chivalrous spirit of the Japanese. When the Koreans employ cruel means of physical punishment, the Japanese too are surmised to be just as inhuman. Such examples are too numerous to count. This may be compared to the case in which most of those in a string of houses within a village or town are foolish, lawless, cruel, and inhuman; an occasional family that heeds what is just and right will be eclipsed by the other's evil and its virtue will never be noticed. It is indeed not infrequent that something similar happens in our foreign relations and indirectly interferes with them. This should be regarded a great misfortune for our country of Japan.

To plan our course now, therefore, our country cannot afford to wait for the enlightenment of our neighbors and to cooperate in building Asia up. Rather, we should leave their ranks to join the camp of the civilized countries of the West. Even when dealing with China and Korea, we need not have special scruples simply because they are our neighbors, but should behave toward them as the westerners do. One who befriends an evil person cannot avoid being involved in his notoriety. In spirit, then, we break with our evil friends of Eastern Asia. 99

Source: Centre for East Asian Cultural Studies, comp., *Meiji Japan Through Contemporary Sources*, Vol. 3, 1869–1894 (Tokyo: Centre for East Asian Cultural Studies, 1972), pp. 129–133, modified.

Fukuzawa Yukichi. (Fukuzawa Memorial Center for Modern Japanese Studies, Keio University)

QUESTIONS FOR ANALYSIS

1. What does Fukuzawa mean by "civilization"?
2. How does Fukuzawa's justification of colonialism compare to Europeans' justification of it during the same period?

oted as their incomes failed to keep up with prices or as their tax burdens grew. Workers in modern industries were no happier, and in 1898 railroad workers went on strike for better working conditions and overtime pay. Still, rice production increased, death rates dropped as public health was improved, and the population grew from about 33 million in 1868 to about 45 million in 1900.

Japan as an Imperial Power

During the course of the Meiji period, Japan became an imperial power, making Taiwan and Korea into its colonies. Taiwan had been a part of China for two centuries; Korea had been an independent country with a unified government since 668. The conflicts that led to Japanese acquisition of both of them revolved around Korea.

The Choson Dynasty had been on the throne in Korea since 1392. Chinese influence had grown over this period as the Korean elite enthusiastically embraced Confucian teachings and studied for Chinese-style civil service examinations. In the second half of the nineteenth century Korea found itself caught between China, Japan, and Russia, each trying to protect or extend its sphere of influence. Westerners also began demanding that Korea be "opened." Korea's first response was to insist that its foreign relations be handled through Beijing. Matters were complicated by the rise in the 1860s of a religious cult, the Tonghak movement, that had strong xenophobic elements. Although the government executed the cult founder in 1864, this cult continued to gain support, especially among impoverished peasants. Thus, like China in the same period, the Korean government faced simultaneous internal and external threats.

In 1871 the U.S. minister to China took five warships to try to open Korea, but left after exchanges of fire resulted in 250 Koreans dead without any progress in getting the Korean government to make concessions. Japan tried next and in 1876 forced the Korean government to sign an unequal treaty and open three ports to Japanese trade. On China's urging, Korea also signed treaties with the European powers in an effort to counterbalance Japan.

Over the next couple of decades reformers in China and Japan tried to encourage Korea to adopt its own self-strengthening movement, but Korean conservatives, including the queen (serving as regent for the child king), did their best to undo reform efforts. In 1894, when the religious cult rose in a massive revolt, both China and Japan sent military forces, claiming to come to the Korean government's aid. They ended up fighting each other instead in what is known as the Sino-Japanese War (see page 795). With Japan's decisive victory, it gained Taiwan from China and was able to make Korea a protectorate. Japan also arranged the assassination of the Korean queen in 1895.

As already noted, five years later Japan participated with the European powers in occupying Beijing to suppress the Boxer Rebellion. In this period Japan was competing aggressively with the leading European powers for influence and territory in China, particularly in the northeast (Manchuria). There Japanese and Russian imperialism met and collided. In 1904 Japan attacked Russian forces and, after its 1905 victory in the bloody **Russo-Japanese War**, emerged with a valuable foothold in China—Russia's former protectorate over Port Arthur (see Map 26.1).

Japan also steadily gained more control over Korea. In 1907, when the Korean king proved less than fully compliant, the Japanese forced him to abdicate in favor of his feeble-minded son. Korean resistance to Japan's actions was suppressed in bloody fighting, and in 1910 Korea was formally annexed as a province of Japan.

Japanese Expansion, 1875–1914

- Japan in 1875
- Territory acquired by 1910
- Sphere of Japanese influence

Japan's victories over China and Russia changed the way European nations looked at Japan. Through negotiations Japan was able to eliminate extraterritoriality in 1899 and gain control of its own tariffs in 1911. Within Japan, the success of the military in raising Japan's international reputation added greatly to its political influence.

The Movement of Peoples

☐ Why did people move much more in this period, and where did they go?

The nineteenth century was marked by extensive movement of people into, across, and out of Asia. In no earlier period had so many Europeans lived in Asia or so many Asians taken up residence in other countries. This vast migration both resulted from and helped accelerate the increasing integration of the world economy (see pages 773–775). Crossing oceans became faster and safer with the digging of the Suez and Panama Canals, which greatly shortened journeys. Foreigners had died at a high rate in tropical zones because of diseases they were not immune to; in the nineteenth century the survival rate improved as doctors found new treatments. Knowledge of foreign cultures improved. More and more people studied foreign languages. Translations of works from Western to Asian languages and vice versa made knowledge of other cultures easier to acquire, at least for the literate.

Westerners to Asia

Imperialism brought Europeans to Asia in unprecedented numbers. By the early 1900s significant expatriate communities of European and American businessmen, missionaries, and colonial civil servants had formed in most Asian countries—the largest in India. By 1863 there were already sixty-five thousand British troops in India and many more British in the civil service and commercial companies. Especially after the opening of the Suez Canal in 1869, British working in India were accompanied by their wives and children, who would return to Britain every few years on leave. By the eve of World War I, hundreds of thousands of expatriates lived in India, many since birth.

Beginning in 1809 British recruits to the British East India Company and subsequently to the Indian Civil Service were required to learn at least one Indian language fluently, but that did not mean that they mixed freely with Indians. The trend, especially after the Great Revolt of 1857 (see page 785), was for the British to live

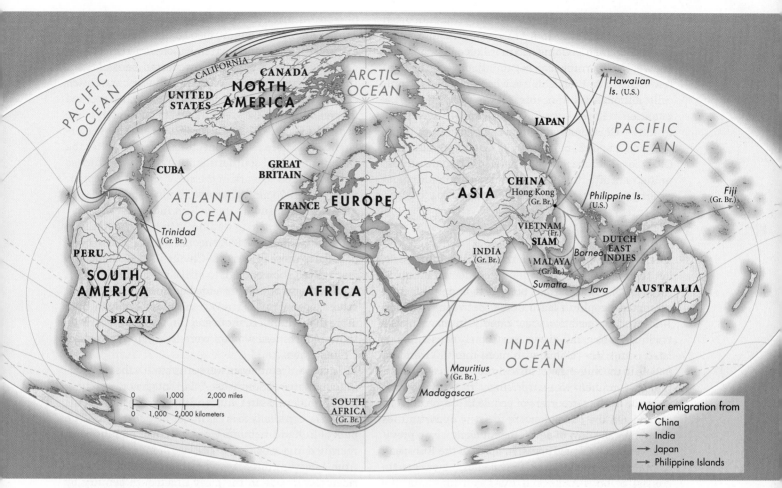

MAP 26.2 Emigration Out of Asia, 1820–1914 As steamships made crossing oceans quicker and more reliable, many people in Asia left their home countries to find new opportunities elsewhere. European imperialism contributed to this flow, especially by recruiting workers for newly established plantations or mines. Many emigrants simply wanted to work a few years to build their savings and planned to return home. Often, however, they ended up staying in their new countries and forming families there.

separately from the Indians in their own enclaves. The Indian servants who tended colonists' houses and grounds, minded their children, and did their shopping handled most of colonists' dealings with local Indians. British residents who were curious about India and wanted to make Indian friends found social intercourse difficult, especially with Muslims and higher-caste Hindus, whose social contact with outsiders was restricted by traditional rules.

China was not under colonial occupation and so did not have as many foreign civil servants and soldiers in its cities, but it did attract more missionaries than any other Asian country. After 1860, when China agreed to allow missionaries to proselytize throughout the country, missionaries came in large numbers. Unlike the British civil servants in India, missionaries had no choice but to mix with the local population, finding the best opportunities for conversion among ordinary poor Chinese. Although most missionaries devoted them-

selves to preaching, over the course of the nineteenth century more and more worked in medicine and education. By 1905 about 300 fully qualified physicians were doing medical missionary work, and 250 mission hospitals and dispensaries served about 2 million patients. Missionary hospitals in Hong Kong also ran a medical school, which trained hundreds of Chinese as physicians.

Missionaries helped spread Western learning at their schools. For their elementary schools, missionaries produced textbooks in Chinese on a full range of subjects. They also translated dozens of standard works into Chinese, especially in the natural sciences, mathematics, history, and international law. By 1906 nearly 60,000 Chinese students were attending 2,400

• **Russo-Japanese War** The 1904–1905 war between Russia and Japan fought over imperial influence and territory in northeast China (Manchuria).

Christian schools. Most of this activity was supported by contributions sent from America and Britain.

Missionaries in China had more success in spreading Western learning than in gaining converts. By 1900 fewer than a million Chinese were Christians. Ironically, although Western missionaries paid much less attention to Korea—the first missionary arrived there in 1884—Christianity took much stronger root there, and today about 25 percent of the Korean population is Christian. Catholic missionaries also had some success in Vietnam after the French occupied the country and extended protection to them.

Asian Emigration

In the nineteenth century Asians, like Europeans, left their native countries in unprecedented numbers (Map 26.2). As in Europe, both push and pull factors prompted people to leave home. Between 1750 and 1900 world population grew rapidly, in many places tripling. China and India were extremely densely populated countries—China with more than 400 million people in the mid-nineteenth century, India with more than 200 million. Not surprisingly, these two giants were the leading exporters of people in search of work or land. On the pull side were the new opportunities created by the flow of development capital into previously underdeveloped areas. In many of the European colonies in Asia and Africa the business class came to consist of both Asian and European migrants, the Asians protected and tolerated by the Western imperialists who found them useful. Asian diasporas formed in many parts of the world, with the majority in Asia itself, especially Southeast Asia.

For centuries people had emigrated from China in search of new opportunities. Chinese from the southern coastal regions came to form key components of mercantile communities throughout Southeast Asia, from Siam south to Java and east to the Philippines. Chinese often assimilated in Siam and Vietnam, but they rarely did so in Muslim areas such as Java, Catholic areas such as the Philippines, and primitive tribal areas such as northern Borneo. In these places, distinct Chinese communities emerged, usually dominated by speakers of a single Chinese dialect.

With the growth in trade that accompanied the European expansion, Chinese began to settle in the islands of Southeast Asia in larger numbers. After Singapore was founded by the British in 1819, Chinese rapidly poured in, soon to become the dominant ethnic group. In British-controlled Malaya, some Chinese built great fortunes in the tin business, while others worked in the mines. There the Chinese community included old overseas families, Malay speakers who had long lived in the Portuguese city of Malacca, and a much larger number of more recent immigrants, most of whom spoke Cantonese. Chinese also settled in the Spanish-controlled Philippines and in Dutch-controlled Indonesia, but there they suffered repeated persecutions. In Borneo early in the nineteenth century, the Dutch expropriated the mines that the Chinese had worked for generations. Elsewhere, however, the Dutch made use of the Chinese. In Java, for instance, Chinese merchants were used as tax collectors. Moreover, after the Dutch conquered southern Sumatra in 1864, Chinese were recruited to work in the sugar and tobacco plantations. By 1900 more than five hundred thousand Chinese were living in the Dutch East Indies.

Discovery of gold in California in 1848, Australia in 1851, and Canada in 1858 encouraged Chinese to book passage to those places (see Chapter 27). In California few arrived soon enough to strike gold, but they soon found other work. Thousands laid railroad tracks, and others took up mining in Wyoming and Idaho. In 1880 more than a hundred thousand Chinese men and three thousand Chinese women were living in the western United States.

Indian entrepreneurs were attracted by the burgeoning commerce of Southeast Asia, though not in quite as large numbers as the Chinese. Indians also moved outside Asia, especially to areas under British control. The bulk of Indian emigrants were **indentured laborers**, recruited under contract. The rise of indentured labor from Asia was a direct result of the outlawing of the African slave trade in the early nineteenth century by Britain and the United States. Sugar plantations in the Caribbean and elsewhere needed new sources of workers, and planters in the British colonies discovered that they could recruit Indian laborers to replace blacks. By 1870 more than half a million Indians had migrated to Mauritius (in the southern Indian Ocean, east of Madagascar) and to the British Caribbean, especially Trinidad. After the French abolished slavery in 1848, they recruited workers from India as well, with nearly eighty thousand Indians making the trip to the French Caribbean over the next half century. Later in the century, many Indians emigrated to British colonies in Africa, the largest numbers to South Africa. Indentured Indian laborers built the railroad in East Africa. Malaya, Singapore, and Fiji also received many emigrants from India.

Indentured laborers secured as substitutes for slaves were often treated little better than slaves both on the ships that delivered them and on the plantations and in the mines where they worked. After abuses of this sort were exposed, the Indian colonial government established regulations stipulating a maximum indenture period of five years, after which the migrant would be entitled to passage home. Even though government "protectors" were appointed at the ports of embarka-

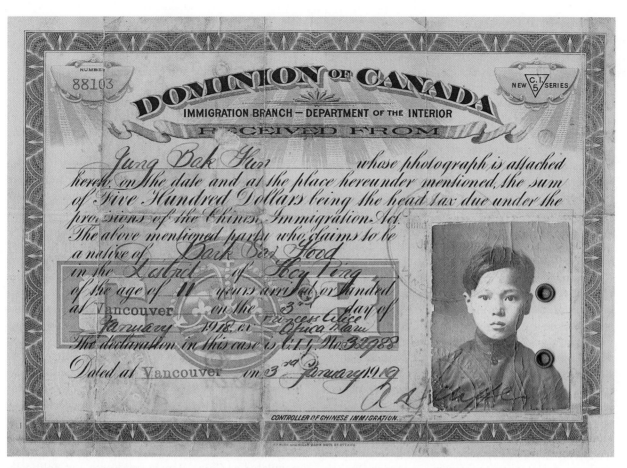

Canadian Immigration Certificate This certificate proved that the eleven-year-old boy in the photograph had a legal right to be in Canada, as the $500 head tax required for immigration of Chinese had been paid. The head tax on Chinese immigrants introduced in 1885 started at $50, but it was raised to $100 in 1900 and to $500 in 1903. Equal to about what a laborer could earn in two years, the tax succeeded in its goal of slowing the rate of Asian immigration to Canada. (Library and Archives Canada)

tion, exploitation of indentured workers continued largely unchecked. Still, many of the migrants stayed on after their indenture.

In areas outside the British Empire, China offered the largest supply of ready labor. Starting in the 1840s contractors arrived at Chinese ports to recruit labor for plantations and mines in Cuba, Peru, Hawai'i, Sumatra, South Africa, and elsewhere. In the 1840s, for example, the Spanish government actively recruited Chinese laborers for the plantations of Cuba. These workers were placed under eight-year contracts, were paid about twenty-five cents a day, and were fed potatoes and salted beef. Between 1853 and 1873 more than 130,000 Chinese laborers went to Cuba, the majority spending their lives as virtual slaves.

Chinese laborers did not have the British government to protect them and seem to have suffered even more than Indian workers. Some of the worst abuses were in Peru, where nearly a hundred thousand Chinese had arrived by 1875, lured by promoters who prom-

ised them easy riches. Instead, they were set to laying railroad tracks or working on cotton plantations or in dangerous guano pits. Those who tried to flee were forced to work in chains.

India and China sent more people abroad than any other Asian countries during this period, but they were not alone. As Japan started to industrialize, its cities could not absorb all those forced off the farms, and people began emigrating in significant numbers, many to Hawai'i and later to South America. Emigration from the Philippines also was substantial, especially after it became a U.S. territory in 1898.

Asian migration to the United States, Canada, and Australia—the primary destinations of European emigrants—would undoubtedly have been greater if it had not been so vigorously resisted by the white settlers in those regions. On the West Coast of the

> • **indentured laborers** Laborers who in exchange for passage agreed to work for a number of years, specified in a contract.

> "Passive resistance is a method of securing rights by personal suffering; it is the reverse of resistance by arms."
>
> **MOHANDAS GANDHI**

The Countries of Asia in Comparative Perspective

☐ What explains the similarities and differences in the experiences of Asian countries in this era?

United States, friction between Chinese and white settlers was fed by racist rhetoric that depicted Chinese as opium-smoking heathens. In 1882 Chinese were barred from becoming American citizens, and the immigration of Chinese laborers was suspended. In 1888 President Grover Cleveland declared the Chinese "impossible of assimilation with our people, and dangerous to our peace and welfare."[8]

Most of the Asian migrants discussed so far were illiterate peasants or business people, not members of traditional educated elites. By the beginning of the twentieth century, however, another group of Asians was going abroad in significant numbers: students. Indians and others in the British colonies usually went to Britain, Vietnamese and others in the French colonies to France, and so on. Chinese eager to master modern learning most commonly went to Japan, but others went to Europe and the United States, as did Japanese students. Most of these students traveled abroad to learn about Western science, law, and government in the hope of strengthening their own countries. On their return they contributed enormously to the intellectual life of their societies, increasing understanding of the modern Western world and also becoming the most vocal advocates of overthrowing the old order and driving out the colonial masters.

Among the most notable of these foreign-educated radicals were Mohandas Gandhi (1869–1948) and Sun Yatsen (see page 796). Sun developed his ideas about the republican form of government while studying in Hawai'i and Hong Kong. Gandhi, after studying law in Britain, took a job in South Africa, where he became involved in trying to defend the interests of the Indians who lived and worked there. He started a periodical, *Indian Opinion*, in which he gradually elaborated his idea of passive resistance. In 1909 he wrote:

Passive resistance is a method of securing rights by personal suffering; it is the reverse of resistance by arms. When I refuse to do a thing that is repugnant to my conscience, I use soul-force. For instance, the Government of the day has passed a law which is applicable to me. I do not like it. If by using violence I force the Government to repeal the law, I am employing what may be termed body-force. If I do not obey the law and accept the penalty for its breach, I use soul-force. It involves sacrifice of self.[9]

The European concept of Asia encourages us to see commonalities among the countries from India east. Although to Westerners it may seem natural to think about Japan and Indonesia as part of the same region, the world looked very different from the perspective of the peoples of these countries. The concept of Asia is handy, but we should be careful not to let it keep us from recognizing the very real differences in the historical experiences of the countries we label "Asian."

At the start of the nineteenth century the societies in this region varied much more than those of any other part of the world. In the temperate zones of East Asia the old established monarchies of China, Japan, and Korea were all densely populated and boasted long literary traditions and traditions of unified governments. They had ties to each other that dated back many centuries and shared many elements of their cultures. South of them, in the tropical and subtropical regions, cultures were more diverse. India was just as densely populated as China, Japan, and Korea, but politically and culturally less unified, with several major languages and dozens of independent rulers reigning in kingdoms large and small, not to mention the growing British presence. In both India and Southeast Asia, Islam was much more important than it was in East Asia, although there was a relatively small Muslim minority in China. All of the countries with long written histories and literate elites were at a great remove from the thinly populated and relatively primitive areas without literate cultures and sometimes even without agriculture, such as some of the islands of the Philippines and Indonesia.

The nineteenth century gave the societies of Asia more in common in that all of them in one way or another had come into contact with the expanding West (an experience that linked them to societies across the Middle East, Africa, and Latin America as well). Still, the Western powers did not treat all of the countries the same way. Western powers initially wanted manufactured goods such as Indian cotton textiles and Chinese porcelains from the more developed Asian societies. At the beginning of the nineteenth century Britain had already gained political control over large parts of India and was intent on forcing China to trade on terms more to its benefit. It paid virtually no attention to Korea and Japan, not seeing in them the same potential for profit. The less developed parts of Asia also attracted increasing Western interest, not because they could provide manufactured goods, but because they offered opportunities for Western development, much as the Americas had earlier.

The West that the societies of Asia faced during the nineteenth century was itself rapidly changing, and the steps taken by Western nations to gain power in Asia naturally also changed over time. Western science and technology were making rapid advances, which gave European armies progressively greater advantages in weaponry. The Industrial Revolution made it possible for countries that industrialized early, such as Britain, to produce huge surpluses of goods for which they had to find markets, shifting their interest in Asia from a place to buy goods to a place to sell goods. Britain had been able to profit from its colonization of India, and this profit both encouraged it to consolidate its rule and invited its European rivals to look for their own colonies. For instance, rivalry with Britain led France to seek colonies in Southeast Asia not only for its own sake but also as a way to keep Britain from extending its sphere of influence any farther.

There were some commonalities in the ways Asian countries responded to pressure from outside. In the countries with long literary traditions, often the initial response of the established elite was to try to drive the unwelcome foreigners away. This was the case in China, Japan, and Korea in particular. Violent antiforeign re-

actions exploded again and again, but the superior military technology of the industrialized West almost invariably prevailed. After suffering humiliating defeats, some Asian leaders insisted on the need to preserve their cultural traditions at all costs. Others came to the opposite conclusion that the West was indeed superior in some ways and that they would have to adopt European ideas or techniques for their own purposes. This can be seen both among Indians who acquired education in English and in many of the Meiji reformers in Japan. The struggles between the traditionalists and the westernizers were often intense. As nationalism took hold in the West, it found a receptive audience among the educated elites in Asia. How could the assertion that every people had the right to control its own destiny not appeal to the colonized?

Whether they were colonized or not, most countries in Asia witnessed the spread of new technologies between 1800 and 1914. Railroads, telegraphs, modern sanitation, and a wider supply of inexpensive manufactured goods brought fundamental changes in everyday life not only to lands under colonial rule, such as India and Vietnam, but also, if less rapidly, to places that managed to remain independent, such as China and Japan. In fact, the transformation of Japan between 1860 and 1900 was extraordinary. By 1914 Japan had urban conveniences and educational levels comparable to those in Europe.

CONNECTIONS

The nineteenth century brought Asia change on a much greater scale than did any earlier century. Much of the change was political — old political orders were ousted or reduced to tokens by new masters, often European colonial powers. Old elites found themselves at a loss when confronted by the European powers with their modern weaponry and modern armies. Cultural change was no less dramatic as the old elites pondered the differences between their traditional values and the ideas that seemed to underlie the power of the European states. In several places ordinary people rose in rebellion, probably in part because they felt threatened by the speed of cultural change. Material culture underwent major changes as elites experimented with Western dress and architecture and ordinary people had opportunities to travel on newly built railroads. Steamships, too, made long-distance travel easier, facilitating the out-migration of people seeking economic opportunities far from their countries of birth.

In the Americas, too, the nineteenth century was an era of unprecedented change and movement of people. Colonial empires were being overturned there, not imposed as they were in Asia in the same period. Another sharp contrast is that the Americas and Australia (discussed in the next chapter) were on the receiving end of the huge migrations taking place, while Asia, like Europe, was much more an exporter of people. The Industrial Revolution brought change to all these areas, though in the old countries of Asia the negative effects of this revolution were more often felt as traditional means of making a living disappeared. Intellectually, in both Asia and the Americas the ideas of nationalism and nation building shaped how people, especially the more educated, thought about the changes they were experiencing.

☐ CHAPTER REVIEW

In the nineteenth century Britain extended its rule to all of India, though often the British ruled indirectly through local princes. Britain brought many modern advances to India, such as railroads and schools. Slavery was outlawed, as was widow suicide and infanticide. Resistance to British rule took several forms. In 1857 Indian soldiers in the employ of the British rose in a huge revolt, and after Britain put down this rebellion it ruled India much more tightly. Indians who received English education turned English ideas of liberty and representative rule against the British and founded the Indian National Congress, which called for Indian independence.

☐ Why were most but not all Southeast Asian societies reduced to colonies? (p. 790)

By the end of the nineteenth century most Southeast Asian countries, from Burma to the Philippines, had been made colonies of Western powers, which developed them as exporters of agricultural products or raw materials including rubber, tin, sugar, tea, cotton, and jute. The principal exception was Siam (Thailand), whose king was able to play the English and French off against each other and institute centralizing reforms. In the Philippines more than three centuries of Spanish rule came to an end in 1898, but Spain was only replaced by another colonial power: the United States.

☐ Was China's decline in the nineteenth century due more to internal problems or to Western imperialism? (p. 791)

In the nineteenth century China's world standing declined as a result of both foreign intervention and internal unrest. The government's efforts to suppress opium imports from Britain led to military confrontation with the British and to numerous concessions that opened China to trade on Britain's terms. Within its borders, China faced unprecedented population pressure and worsening economic conditions that resulted in uprisings in several parts of the country. These rebellions proved very difficult to suppress. Further humiliations by the Western powers led to concerted efforts to modernize the military and learn other secrets of Western success, but China never quite caught up. Inspired by Western ideas of republican government, revolutionaries tried to topple the dynasty, finally succeeding in 1911–1912.

KEY TERMS

Great Mutiny/Great Revolt (p. 785)
Indian Civil Service (p. 787)
Indian National Congress (p. 787)
Java War (p. 790)
Nguyen Dynasty (p. 790)
Opium War (p. 794)
extraterritoriality (p. 794)
concessions (p. 794)
Taiping Rebellion (p. 794)
Boxers (p. 796)
1911 Revolution (p. 796)
gunboat diplomacy (p. 797)
Meiji Restoration (p. 797)
Russo-Japanese War (p. 802)
indentured laborers (p. 804)

☐ How was Japan able to quickly master the challenges posed by the West? (p. 797)

Japan was the one Asian country to quickly transform itself when confronted by the military strength of the West. It did this by overhauling its power structure. The Meiji centralized and strengthened Japan's power by depriving the samurai of their privileges, writing a constitution, instituting universal education, and creating a modern army. At the same time they guided Japan toward rapid industrialization. By the early twentieth century Japan had become an imperialist power with colonies in Korea and Taiwan.

☐ Why did people move much more in this period, and where did they go? (p. 802)

The rapid pace of political and economic change in the nineteenth century led people to move across national borders much more frequently than before. By the early 1900s significant expatriate communities of Westerners had formed in many cities in Asia. Asian students traveled to Europe, Japan, or the United States to continue their educations. Millions more left in search of work. With the end of the African slave trade, recruiters from the Americas and elsewhere went to India and China to secure indentured laborers. In other cases, ambitious young men who heard of gold strikes or other chances to get rich funded their own travels. Emigrants from China, one of the major exporters of people, sought work in such Southeast Asian territories as Malaya, Singapore, the Philippines, and Indonesia. As a consequence, Asian diasporas formed in many parts of the world.

◻ What explains the similarities and differences in the experiences of Asian countries in this era? (p. 806)

The differences between the countries of Asia at the turn of the twentieth century can be explained in several ways. The countries did not start with equivalent circumstances. Some had long traditions of unified rule; others did not. Some had manufactured goods that Western powers wanted; others offered raw materials or cheap labor. The timing of the arrival of Western powers also made a difference, especially because Western military superiority increased over time. European Great Power rivalry had a major impact, especially after 1860. Similarities in the experiences of Asian countries are also notable and include many of the benefits (and costs) of industrialization seen elsewhere in the world, such as modernizations in communication and transportation, extension of schooling, and the emergence of radical ideologies.

SUGGESTED READING

Bayly, C. A. *Indian Society and the Making of the British Empire*. 1990. A synthesis of recent research that provides a complex portrait of the interaction of Indian society and British colonial administration.

Bose, Sugata, and Ayesha Jalal. *Modern South Asia: History, Culture, Political Economy*. 1998. Incorporates recent scholarship with postcolonial perspective in a wide-ranging study.

Duus, Peter. *The Abacus and the Sword: The Japanese Penetration of Korea, 1895–1910*. 1995. Analyzes the interplay of business interests (the abacus) and military interests (the sword) in Japan's push for colonial possessions.

Fairbank, John King, and Merle Goldman. *China: A New History*, 2d ed. 2006. A treatment of China's experiences in the nineteenth century that is rich in interesting detail.

Hane, Mikiso. *Peasants, Rebels, Women and Outcastes: The Underside of Modern Japan*, 2d ed. 2003. Draws on wide-ranging sources to provide a fuller picture of Japanese history.

Hopper, Helen. *Fukuzawa Yukichi: From Samurai to Capitalist*. 2005. A brief account of the life of a key westernizing intellectual.

Irokawa, Daiichi. *The Culture of the Meiji Period*. 1988. Makes excellent use of letters, diaries, and songs to probe changes in the ways ordinary people thought during a crucial period of political change.

Kuhn, Philip A. *Chinese Among Others: Emigration in Modern Times*. 2008. A history of Chinese emigration that is global in scope and vividly written.

Masselos, Jim. *Indian Nationalism: A History*, 5th ed. 2004. A detailed account of the political movement for independence in nineteenth- and twentieth-century India.

Pruitt, Ida. *A Daughter of Han: The Autobiography of a Chinese Working Woman*. 1967. A highly revealing glimpse of Chinese society fashioned by journalist Ida Pruitt in the 1930s based on what a Chinese woman born in 1867 told Pruitt of her life.

Rowe, William T. *China's Last Empire: The Great Qing*. 2009. An overview of the Qing Empire by a major historian.

Spence, Jonathan. *God's Chinese Son*. 1997. Tells the story of the Taipings as much as possible from their own perspective.

Steinberg, David Joel, ed. *In Search of Southeast Asia: A Modern History*, rev. ed. 1987. An impressive work on Southeast Asia by seven specialists.

Walthall, Anne. *Japan: A Cultural, Social, and Political History*. 2006. A concise overview with good coverage of local society and popular culture.

NOTES

1. Quoted in K. M. Panikkar, *Asia and Western Dominance: A Survey of the Vasco da Gama Epoch of Asian History* (London: George Allen & Unwin, 1959), p. 116.
2. Quoted in D. J. Steinberg, ed., *In Search of Southeast Asia: A Modern History*, rev. ed. (Honolulu: University of Hawaii Press, 1987), p. 129.
3. Ssu-yu Teng and J. K. Fairbank, *China's Response to the West: A Documentary Survey* (New York: Atheneum, 1971), p. 26.
4. Wm. Theodore de Bary and Richard Lufrano, eds., *Sources of Chinese Tradition*, vol. 2: *From 1600* (New York: Columbia University Press, 2001).
5. Teng and Fairbank, p. 76, modified.
6. Quoted in J. W. Hall, *Japan, from Prehistory to Modern Times* (New York: Delacorte Press, 1970), p. 289.
7. R. Tsunoda, W. T. de Bary, and D. Keene, eds., *Sources of Japanese Tradition*, vol. 2 (New York: Columbia University Press, 1964), p. 137.
8. Quoted in J. D. Spence, *The Search for Modern China* (New York: W. W. Norton, 1990), p. 215.
9. Homer A. Jack, ed., *The Gandhi Reader: A Sourcebook of His Life and Writings* (Bloomington: Indiana University Press, 1956), p. 112.

For practice quizzes and other study tools, visit the **Online Study Guide** at bedfordstmartins.com/mckayworld.

For primary sources from this period, see *Sources of World Societies*, **Second Edition**.

For Web sites, images, and documents related to topics in this chapter, visit **Make History** at bedfordstmartins.com/mckayworld.

• **Ute Indian** Native Americans found their world under assault during the nineteenth century, as the United States expanded its territory and encouraged settlers to farm lands where Indians had long lived. The Ute Indian depicted here was photographed by William Gunnison Chamberlain, probably in his Denver studio in 1868. (The Granger Collection, New York)

27

In the Americas and in Australia, as in Europe, the nineteenth century was a period of nation building and industrial and commercial growth. Unlike in Europe, the century was also a time of geographical expansion and large-scale in-migration.

At the end of the eighteenth century Canada and the countries of South America remained colonies. Their European mother countries looked on the democratic experiment of the infant United States with suspicion and scorn. The island continent of Australia, remote from Europe and economically undeveloped, served as a dumping ground for English criminals. The nineteenth century brought revolutions, civil wars, and foreign invasions, among other challenges. In some countries abolishing slavery was achieved with great difficulty. Yet by 1914 all the countries were not only politically independent but also stronger and richer than they had been in 1800.

Nation Building in the Americas and Australia
1770-1914

Many issues cross-cut the histories of all these countries in the long nineteenth century: nation building, nationalism, urbanization, racism, regional separatism, new technologies, new lands to put to the plow, new trading patterns, and new constitutional governments, to name just a few. Yet the outcomes by 1914 were strikingly different. The United States had become a major industrial power and a stable democracy with a standard of living comparable to that of western Europe. Canada and Australia also had stable democratic governments and high standards of living, but their economies remained predominantly agricultural. Most of the countries of Latin America suffered political instability, and their economies did not fare as well in the emerging world trade system. •

Latin America, 1800–1914

☐ Why and how did the Spanish and Portuguese colonies of North and South America shake off European domination and develop into national states?

The United States, 1789–1914

☐ How did the United States build a large but unified nation?

Canada, from French Colony to Nation

☐ What geographical, economic, and political conditions shaped the development of Canada?

Australia, from Penal Colony to Nation

☐ What circumstances shaped the development of Australia?

The New Countries from a Comparative Perspective

☐ How and why did the new countries treated in this chapter develop differently?

Latin America, 1800–1914

☐ Why and how did the Spanish and Portuguese colonies of North and South America shake off European domination and develop into national states?

In 1800 the Spanish Empire in the Americas stretched from the headwaters of the Mississippi River in present-day Minnesota to the tip of Cape Horn in the Antarctic (see Map 27.1). In addition to large regions of South America, it encompassed large parts of the present-day United States from California to Texas. Mexico's silver mines were the richest in the world, and Mexico City had a larger population than any city in Spain. Spain believed that the great wealth of the Americas existed for its benefit, a stance that fostered bitterness and the desire for independence in the colonies. Between 1806 and 1825 the Spanish colonies in Latin America were convulsed by upheavals that ultimately resulted in their separation from Spain. Until 1898 Spain did, however, retain Cuba and Puerto Rico, its colonies in the Caribbean.

The **Creoles** — people of European descent born in the Americas (see page 549) — resented the economic and political dominance of the **peninsulares** (puh-nihn-suh-LUHR-ayz), as the colonial officials and other natives of Spain or Portugal were called. In 1800 there

Don Juan Joachin Gutierrez Altamirano Velasco, ca. 1752 In this painting by Miguel Cabrera, the pleated cuffs on Velasco's shirt, the richly embroidered and very expensive coat, the knee breeches, the tricorn hat, the plaque of titles, and the coat of arms on the wall all attest to the proud status of this member of the peninsulares, the most powerful element in colonial Mexican society. (Miguel Cabrera, Mexican, 1695–1768, oil on canvas, 81 5/16 x 53 1/2. Brooklyn Museum of Art, Museum Collection Fund, and the Dick S. Ramsay Fund 52.166.1) were about thirty thousand peninsulares and 3.5 million Creoles. Peninsulares controlled the rich export-import trade, intercolonial trade, and mining industries. The Creoles wanted to supplant the peninsulares as the ruling class and, more generally, to free themselves from Spain and Portugal. They had little interest in improving the lot of the Indians, the mestizos (meh-STEE-zohz) of mixed Spanish and Indian background, or the mulattos of mixed Spanish and African heritage.

Over the course of the nineteenth century, the countries of Latin America developed into national states. The predominant factors in this evolution were the heritage of colonial exploitation, a neocolonial economic structure, massive emigration from Europe and Asia, and the fusion of Amerindian, Caucasian, African, and Asian peoples.

The Origins of the Revolutions Against Colonial Powers

The Latin American movements for independence drew strength from unfair taxation and trade policies, Spain's declining control over its Latin American colonies, racial and class discrimination, and the spread of revolutionary ideas. By the eighteenth century the Spanish colonies had become self-sufficient producers of foodstuffs, wine, textiles, and consumer goods, though Spain maintained monopolies on alcohol and tobacco and the colonies traded with each other. In Peru, for example, domestic agriculture supported the large mining settlements, and the colony did not have to import food. Craft workshops owned by the state or by private individuals produced consumer goods for the working class; what was not manufactured locally was bought from Mexico and transported by the Peruvian merchant marine.

Spain's humiliating defeat in the War of the Spanish Succession (1701–1713; see page 501) prompted demands for sweeping reform of all of Spain's institutions, including its colonial policies and practices. To improve administrative efficiency, the enlightened monarch Charles III (r. 1759–1788) carved the region of modern Colombia, Venezuela, and Ecuador out of the vast viceroyalty of Peru; it became the new viceroyalty of New Granada with its capital at Bogotá. The Crown also created the viceroyalty of Rio de la Plata (present-day Argentina) with its capital at Buenos Aires (Map 27.1).

Additionally, Spain adopted free-trade policies (allowing trade without government interference) in order to compete with Great Britain and Holland in the great eighteenth-century struggle for empire. In Latin America these actions stimulated the production of crops that were in demand in Europe: coffee in Venezuela; sugar in the Caribbean; hides, leather, and salted beef in the Rio de la Plata viceroyalty. Between 1778 and 1788 the volume of Spain's trade with the colonies soared, possibly by as much as 700 percent.[1]

Colonial manufacturing, which had been growing steadily, suffered a heavy blow under free trade. Colonial textiles, china, and wine, for example, could not

---

• **Creoles** People of Spanish descent born in the Americas.
• **peninsulares** A term for natives of Spain and Portugal.

Before independence

Spanish colonies
- Viceroyalty of New Spain
- Viceroyalty of New Granada
- Viceroyalty of Peru and Audencia of Chile
- Viceroyalty of Rio de la Plata

Portuguese colonies
- Viceroyalty of Brazil

✕ Silver mine

In 1830
1811 Year independence gained
Colony

▫ Mapping the Past

MAP 27.1 Latin America in ca. 1780 and 1830 By 1830 almost all of Central America, South America, and the Caribbean islands had won independence. Note that the many nations that now make up Central America were unified when they first won independence from Mexico. Similarly, modern Venezuela, Colombia, and Ecuador were still joined in Gran Colombia.

ANALYZING THE MAP Compare the boundaries of the Spanish and Portuguese colonies in ca. 1780 with the boundaries of the independent states in 1830. How did these boundaries change, and which regions experienced the most breakup?

CONNECTIONS Why did Pan-Americanism fail?

compete with cheap Spanish products. In the Rio de la Plata region heavy export taxes and light import duties shattered the wine industry. Madrid's tax reforms also aggravated discontent. Like Great Britain, Spain believed its colonies should bear some of the costs of their own defense. Accordingly, Madrid raised the prices of its monopoly products—tobacco and liquor—and increased sales taxes on many items. As a result, protest movements in Latin America, like those in the thirteen North American colonies a decade earlier, claimed that the colonies were being unfairly taxed.

Political conflicts beyond the colonies also helped to drive aspirations for independence. The French Revolution and Napoleonic wars, which involved France's occupation of Spain and Britain's domination of the seas, isolated Spain from Latin America. As Spain's control over its Latin American colonies diminished, foreign traders, especially from the United States, swarmed into Spanish-American ports. In 1796 the Madrid government made exceptions to its trade restrictions for countries not engaged in the Napoleonic wars, such as the United States, thus acknowledging Spain's inability to supply the colonies with needed goods and markets.

Racial, ethnic, and class privileges also fueled discontent. At the end of the eighteenth century colonists complained bitterly that only peninsulares were appointed to the colonies' highest judicial bodies and to other positions in the colonial governments. From 1751 to 1775 only 13 percent of appointees to the judicial bodies were Creoles.[2] According to the nineteenth-century Mexican statesman and historian Lucas Alamán (1792–1853):

> This preference shown to Spaniards in political offices and ecclesiastical benefices has been the principal cause of the rivalry between the two classes; add to this the fact that Europeans possessed great wealth, which although it may have been the just reward of effort and industry, excited the envy of Americans and was considered as so much usurpation from them; consider that for all these reasons the Spaniards had obtained a decided preponderance over those born in the country; and it will not be difficult to explain the increasing jealousy and rivalry between the two groups which culminated in hatred and enmity.[3]

From a racial standpoint, the makeup of Latin American societies is one of the most complicated in the world. Because few European women immigrated to the colonies, Spanish men formed relationships with Indian and African women, while African men deprived of black women sought Indian women. The result was a population composed of every possible combination of Indian, Spanish, and African blood. Demographers

estimate that Indians still accounted for between 60 and 75 percent of the population of Latin America at the end of the colonial period, in spite of the tremendous population losses caused by the introduction of diseases in the sixteenth and seventeenth centuries. The colonies that became Peru and Bolivia had Indian majorities; the regions that became Argentina and Chile had European majorities.

Indians and black slaves toiled in the silver and gold mines of Mexico, Colombia, and Peru; in the wheat fields of Chile; in the humid, mosquito-ridden canebrakes of Mexico and the Caribbean; and in the diamond mines and coffee and sugar plantations of Brazil. Almost 40 percent of all slaves shipped from Africa went to the Caribbean, where the white elite formed a tiny minority. Also, Indians faced other difficulties. Many of them were still subject to the *repartimiento* and the *mit'a*. The law of repartimiento required Indians to buy goods solely from local tax collectors. *Mit'a* means a turn or rotation; the practice was that every seventh household in the region between Huancavelica and Potosí in the Andes took a turn working in the silver mines, with the duration of service varying.

Spanish theories of racial purity rejected people of mixed blood, particularly those of African descent. Peninsulares and Creoles reinforced their privileged status by showing contempt for people who were not white. Moreover, owners of mines, plantations, and factories had a vested interest in keeping blacks and Indians in servile positions. Nevertheless, nonwhites in Latin America did experience some social mobility in the colonial period, certainly more than nonwhites in the North American colonies experienced. A few mulattos rose in the army, some as high as the rank of colonel. The army and the church seem to have offered the greatest opportunities for social mobility. Many black slaves gained their freedom by fleeing to the jungles or mountains, where they established self-governing communities. Around the year 1800 Venezuela counted 2,400 fugitive slaves in a total population of 87,000.

A final factor contributing to rebellion were the Enlightenment ideas of Voltaire, Rousseau, and Montesquieu, which had been trickling into Latin America for decades (see Chapter 18). North American ships calling at South American ports introduced the subversive writings of Thomas Paine and Thomas Jefferson. In 1794 the Colombian Antonio Nariño translated and published the French Declaration of the Rights of Man and the Citizen. (Spanish authorities sentenced him to ten years in an African prison, but he lived to become the father of Colombian independence.) By 1800 the Creole elite throughout Latin America was familiar with liberal Enlightenment political thought, and the Creoles wanted the "rights of man" extended to themselves.

Resistance, Rebellion, and Independence

The mid-eighteenth century witnessed frequent Andean Indian rebellions against the Spaniards' harsh exploitation. In 1780, under the leadership of a descendant of the Inca rulers who took the name Tupac Amaru II, a massive insurrection exploded. Indian chieftains from the Cuzco region (see Map 27.1) gathered a powerful force of Indians and people of mixed race. Rebellion swept across highland Peru, where many Spanish officials were executed. Before peace was restored two years later, a hundred thousand people lay dead, and vast amounts of property were destroyed. Although Spanish rule was not ended, the government abolished the repartimiento system and established assemblies of local representatives in Cuzco. The revolts also raised elite fears of racial and class warfare.

As news of the rebellion of Tupac Amaru II trickled northward, it helped stimulate the 1781 Comunero Revolution in the New Granada viceroyalty (see

Triumph of Bolívar Bolívar was treated as a hero everywhere he went in South America. (akg-images)

Map 27.1). In this revolution an Indian peasant army commanded by Creole captains marched on Bogotá. Dispersed by the ruling Spanish, who made promises they did not intend to keep, the revolt in the end did little to improve the Indians' lives.

Much more than the revolts in Peru and New Granada, the successful revolution led by Toussaint L'Ouverture (1743–1803) in Haiti aroused elite fears of black revolt and class warfare (see pages 676–681 and Map 22.3). In 1804 Haiti declared its independence, becoming the second nation (after the United States) in the Western Hemisphere to achieve self-rule. The revolt was also the first successful uprising of a non-European people against a colonial power, and it sent waves of fear through the upper classes in both Europe and Latin America.

In 1808 Napoleon Bonaparte deposed the Spanish king Ferdinand VII and placed his own brother on the Spanish throne (see page 676). Since everything in Spanish America was done in the name of the king, the Creoles in Latin America argued that the removal of the legitimate king shifted sovereignty to the people — that is, to themselves. The Creoles who led the various movements for independence did not intend a radical redistribution of property or a reconstruction of society. They merely rejected the authority of the Spanish crown.

The great hero of the movement for independence was Simón Bolívar (1783–1830), a very able general who is considered the Latin American George Washington. In a letter to the governor of Jamaica in 1815, he explained his objections to Spanish rule:

> Americans today, and perhaps to a greater extent than ever before, who live within the Spanish system, occupy a position in society no better than that of serfs destined for labor, or at best they have no more status than that of mere consumers. Yet even this status is surrounded with galling restrictions, such as being forbidden to grow European crops, or to store products which are royal monopolies, or to establish factories of a type the [Iberian] Peninsula itself does not possess. To this add the exclusive trading privileges, even in articles of prime necessity, and the barriers between American provinces, designed to prevent all exchange of trade, traffic, and understanding. In short, do you wish to know what our future held? Simply the cultivation of the fields of indigo, grain, coffee, sugar cane, cacao, and cotton; cattle raising on the broad plains; hunting wild game in the jungles; digging in the earth to mine its gold which can never sate that greedy nation [Spain].[4]

Bolívar's victories over the royalist armies won him the presidency of Gran Colombia (formerly the New Granada viceroyalty) in 1819. He dreamed of a continental union and in 1826 summoned a conference of the American republics at Panama. The meeting achieved little, however. The territories of Gran Colombia splintered (see Map 27.1), and a sadly disillusioned Bolívar went into exile, saying, "America is ungovernable." Under Spain, Mexico had been united with Central America as the Viceroyalty of New Spain. In the 1830s, after independence, regional separatism resulted in New Spain's breakup into five separate countries. In South America, too, the old colonies were divided, not amalgamated. The failure of Pan-Americanism isolated individual countries, prevented collective action, and later paved the way for the political and economic intrusion of the United States and other powers.

Brazil followed a different path to independence from Portugal. When Napoleon's troops entered Portugal, the royal family fled to Brazil and made Rio de Janeiro the capital of the Portuguese Empire. The new government immediately lifted the old mercantilist restrictions and opened Brazilian ports to the ships of all friendly nations. The king returned to Portugal in 1821, leaving his son Pedro in Brazil as regent. Under popular pressure, Pedro proclaimed Brazil's independence in 1822, issued a constitution, and even led resistance against Portuguese troops. He accepted the title Emperor Pedro I (r. 1822–1834). Even though Brazil was a monarchy, Creole elites dominated society as they did elsewhere in Latin America. The reign of his successor, Pedro II (r. 1831–1889), witnessed the expansion of the coffee industry, the beginnings of the rubber industry, and massive immigration.

The Aftermath of Independence

The Latin American wars of independence, over by 1825, differed from the American Revolution in important ways. First, they lasted much longer, and outside powers provided no help, leaving those involved weary and divided. Second, many of the peninsulares returned to Europe instead of remaining in Latin America to build new nations, as most North American colonists had. Also, although the Creole elites followed the example of the United States by writing constitutions for the new Latin American governments, these governments excluded much of the population from political participation. To a large degree the local elites took over exploiting the peasantry from the old colonial elites. Small independent farmers of the sort who became common in the United States and Canada did not gain a comparable place in Latin America. The new governments also largely confirmed the wealth of the Roman Catholic Church and its authority over the people, not adopting separation of church and state.

The newly independent nations had difficulty achieving political stability when the wars of independence

LATIN AMERICA, CA. 1760–1900

1759–1788	Reign of Spain's Charles III, who instituted administrative and economic reforms
1781	Comunero Revolution in New Granada
1791–1804	Haitian Revolution
1806–1825	Latin American wars of independence against Spain
1822	Proclamation of Brazil's independence by Portugal
1826	Call by Simón Bolívar for Panama conference on Latin American union
ca. 1870–1929	Latin American neocolonialism
1876–1911	Porfirio Díaz's control of Mexico
1880–1914	Massive emigration from Europe and Asia to Latin America
1888	Emancipation of slaves in Brazil; final abolition of slavery in Western Hemisphere
1898	Spanish-American War; end of Spanish control of Cuba; transfer of Puerto Rico and the Philippines to the United States

ended. Between 1836 and 1848 Mexico lost half of its territory to the United States, and other countries, too, had difficulty defending themselves from their neighbors. (See "Viewpoints: Mexican and American Perspectives on the U.S.-Mexican War," page 818.) The Creole leaders of the revolutions had no experience in government, and the wars left a legacy of military, not civilian, leadership.

In many Latin American countries, generals ruled. In Argentina, Juan Manuel de Rosas (r. 1835–1852) assumed power amid widespread public disorder and ruled as dictator. In Mexico, liberals declared a federal republic, but incessant civil strife led to the rise of the dictator Antonio López de Santa Anna (1794–1876) in the mid-nineteenth century. Likewise in Venezuela, strongmen, dictators, and petty aristocratic oligarchs governed from 1830 to 1892. Some countries suffered constant coups d'état; in the course of the century, Bolivia had sixty and Venezuela fifty-two.

On occasion, the ruling generals were charismatic military leaders who were able to attract mass support for their governments. In Venezuela, José Antonio Páez (1790–1873) was able to present himself as a patron of the common man and maintain his popularity even though his economic policies favored the elite and he built up a personal fortune. Some rulers were of common origins. In Mexico, Benito Juarez (1806–1872) was

Viewpoints

Mexican and American Perspectives on the U.S.-Mexican War

• *In the mid-nineteenth century the United States acquired large tracts of land from Mexico, including Texas, New Mexico, Arizona, and California. The wars that were settled with these transfers were controversial even in their day, and in both Mexico and the United States some people justified government policies while others condemned them. Newspapers, which covered the events in both Mexico and the United States, played an important part in shaping opinion. Other Americans, especially those opposed to slavery and its expansion, were dubious about the war from the start.*

President of Mexico, José Joaquín de Herrera, to the Governors of the Mexican States Asking for Their Support in Accepting the Loss of Texas, December 1845

❝In order to start a war, politicians agree that three questions must be examined: 1st, that of justice, 2nd, that of availability of resources, 3rd, that of convenience. . . . If, for launching war, one would only have to consider our justice, any hesitation in this matter would be either a crime or a lack of common sense. But next come the questions of feasibility and convenience for starting and maintaining hostilities with firmness and honor and all the consequences of a war of this nature.

A foreign war against a powerful and advanced nation that possesses an impressive navy and a . . . population that increases every day because of immigrants attracted to its great . . . prosperity, would imply immense sacrifices of men and money—not to assure victory, but simply to avoid defeat. Are such sacrifices possible for the Mexican Republic in her present state of exhaustion, after so many years of error and misadventure?❞

Manuel Crescencio Rejón, Minister of the Interior and Foreign Affairs Under Two Mexican Presidents, Arguing Against Ratification of the Treaty of Guadalupe Hidalgo, 1848

❝The social advantages which would accrue to us by accepting a peace now have been exaggerated, as well as the ease with which we would be able to maintain our remaining territories. It would be necessary, in order to sustain such illusions, to underestimate the spirit of enterprise of the North American people in industrial and commercial pursuits, to misunderstand their history and their tendencies, and also to presuppose in our own spirit less resistance than we have already shown toward the sincere friends of progress. Only through such illusions might one maintain that the treaty would bring a change that would be advantageous to us—as has been claimed.❞

Walt Whitman, Editorial in the *Brooklyn Daily Eagle*, May 11, 1846

❝We are justified in the face of the world, in having treated Mexico with more forbearance than we have ever yet treated an enemy—for Mexico, though contemptible in many respects, is an enemy deserving a vigorous "lesson." . . . Let our arms now be carried with a spirit which shall teach the world that, while we are not forward for a quarrel, America knows how to crush, as well as how to expand!❞

Ulysses S. Grant in 1885 Looking Back on His Participation in the War

❝Generally the officers of the army were indifferent whether the annexation was consummated or not; but not so all of them. For myself, I was bitterly opposed to the measure, and to this day regard the war, which resulted, as one of the most unjust ever waged by a stronger against a weaker nation. It was an instance of a republic following the bad example of European monarchies, in not considering justice in their desire to acquire additional territory. . . . The occupation, separation and annexation [of Mexico] were, from the inception of the movement to its final consummation, a conspiracy to acquire territory out of which slave states might be formed for the American Union.❞

Sources: Carol and Thomas Christensen, *The U.S. Mexican War* (San Francisco: Bay Books, 1998), p. 50; Ernesto Chávez, *The U.S. War with Mexico: A Brief History with Documents* (Boston: Bedford/St. Martin's, 2008), pp. 127, 83; Ulysses S. Grant, *Memoirs*, chap. 3, accessed through Project Gutenberg, http://www.gutenberg.org/files/5860/5860-h/5860-h.htm.

QUESTIONS FOR ANALYSIS

1. What issues do the Mexican politicians raise? Do they agree on anything?

2. How does the knowledge that Whitman's piece was a newspaper editorial shape your reading of it?

3. What might the implications have been for the U.S. forces if many officers disapproved of the war the way Grant did?

something of an exception to the generalization that Creoles had a tight hold on power. A Zapotec Indian who did not learn Spanish until he was twelve, Juarez became a strong advocate of democracy. He led efforts to reduce the power of the Catholic Church and later led resistance to the "emperor" imposed by Napoleon III in 1862. Between 1858 and his death in 1872 Juarez served five terms as president of Mexico.

The economic lives of most Latin American countries were disrupted during the years of war. Mexico and Venezuela in particular suffered great destruction of farmland and animals. Armies were frequently recruited by force, and when the men were demobilized, many did not return home. The consequent population dislocation hurt agriculture and mining. Guerrilla warfare disrupted trade and communications, and the seizure of private property for military use ruined many people.

On the positive side, the push for independence speeded abolition of slavery. The destruction of agriculture in countries such as Mexico and Venezuela caused the collapse of the plantation system, and fugitive slaves could not be recaptured. Generals on both sides offered slaves their freedom in exchange for military service. Still, Cuba and Brazil, which had large slave populations, did not free their slaves until 1886 and 1888, respectively.

Although the edifice of racism persisted in the nineteenth century, Latin America offered blacks greater economic and social mobility than did the United States. One reason is that the Creole elite in Latin America approved of "whitening" — that is, they viewed race mixture as a civilizing process that diminished and absorbed the dark and "barbarous" blood of Africans and Indians. In Latin America, light-skinned people of color could rise economically and socially in a way not available to those with darker skins. (See "Listening to the Past: Mary Seacole on Her Early Life," page 822.)

Neocolonialism and Its Socioeconomic Effects

At first, political instability discouraged foreign investment in Latin America's newly independent nations. But with the general expansion of world trade after 1870 and the development of stable dictatorships, foreign investors turned to Latin America for raw materials and basic commodities to supply industrializing Europe and the United States. Modern business enterprises, often owned by foreign capitalists, led the way. These firms usually specialized in a single product that could be shipped through the growing international network of railroads, ports, and ocean freighters.

In Mexico, for example, North American capital supported the production of hemp, sugar, bananas, and rub-

ber, frequently on American-owned plantations, and British and American interests backed the development of tin, copper, and gold mining. British capital financed Argentina's railroads, meatpacking industry, and utilities; Chile's copper and nitrate industries (nitrate is used in the production of pharmaceuticals and fertilizers); and Brazil's coffee, cotton, and sugar production. By 1904 Brazil produced 76 percent of the world's coffee. The extension of railroads also attracted outside entrepreneurs. (See "Individuals in Society: Henry Meiggs, Promoter and Speculator," page 820.)

Thus, by the turn of the century, the Latin American nations were active participants in the international economic order, but foreigners controlled most of their industries, and their governments used force when they felt their economic interests were threatened. This form of economic domination is often called **neocolonialism**. Perhaps the best example was the U.S.-financed building of the Panama Canal. In 1904 Americans secured the rights to control the Panama Canal, connecting the Atlantic and Pacific Oceans, on their own terms. This monumental construction project wasn't completed until 1914 and took the lives of thousands of workers. The United States retained control of the Panama Canal Zone until 1999. In 1912 and 1926 U.S. Marines interfered in Nicaragua to bolster conservative governments; the Marines who were sent to Haiti in 1915 to protect American property stayed until 1934; and those sent to the Dominican Republic in 1916 stayed until 1924.

Another distinctive feature of neocolonialism was that each country's economy revolved around only one or two products: sugar in Cuba, nitrates and copper in Chile, meat in Argentina, coffee in Brazil. Consequently, a sharp drop in world demand for a product could devastate the export sector and with it the nation's economic well-being. For example, the outbreak of the First World War in 1914 drastically reduced exports of Latin American raw materials and imports of European manufactured goods, provoking a general economic crisis.

Many of the workers on the plantations producing export products were Indians or mestizos. In the United States and Canada, Indians were pushed out of the way when their land was taken from them. In Latin America, by contrast, many more of them were kept in place and incorporated into the social system as subordinated workers, especially on large plantations called **haciendas** (ah-see-EN-dahz).

- **neocolonialism** Term referring to the political and economic systems that perpetuated Western economic domination of nations after their political independence.
- **haciendas** Large landed estates.

Individuals in Society

Henry Meiggs, Promoter and Speculator

ALL THROUGHOUT THE AMERICAS IN THE nineteenth century opportunities beckoned. Henry Meiggs, born in upstate New York in 1811, responded to several of them, building and losing fortunes in Brooklyn, San Francisco, Chile, and Peru.

Meiggs, with only an elementary school education, began work at his father's shipyard. He soon started his own lumber business and did well until he lost everything in the financial panic of 1837. He rebuilt his business, and when gold was discovered in California in 1848, he filled a ship with lumber and sailed around Cape Horn to San Francisco, where he sold his cargo for $50,000, twenty times what he had paid for it. He then entered the lumber business, organizing crews of five hundred men to fell huge Californian redwoods and bring them to his steam sawmills. As his business flourished, he began speculating in real estate, which led to huge debts when the financial crisis of 1854 hit. In an attempt to save himself and his friends, Meiggs forged warrants for more than $900,000; when discovery of the fraud seemed imminent, he sailed with his wife and children for South America.

Although at one point Meiggs was so strapped for cash that he sold his watch, within three years of arriving in Chile, he had secured his first railway contract, and by 1867 he had built about 200 miles of rail lines in that country. In 1868 he went to Peru, which had less than 60 miles of track at the time. In the next nine years he would add 700 more.

Meiggs was not an engineer, but he was a good manager. He recruited experienced engineers from abroad and arranged purchase of foreign rolling stock, rails, and ties, acting as a promoter and developer. Much of the funding came from international investors in Peruvian bonds.

The most spectacular of the rail lines Meiggs built was Peru's Callao-Lima-Oroya line, which crosses the Andes at about seventeen thousand feet above sea level, making it the highest standard gage railway in the world. Because water was scarce in many areas along the construction site, it had to be transported up to workers, who were mostly local people. Dozens of bridges and tunnels had to be built, and casualties were high. Eight hundred people were invited to the banquet that marked the beginning of work on the Oroya Railway. Meiggs drummed up enthusiasm at the event by calling the locomotive the "irresistible battering ram of modern civilization."

In Peru Meiggs became known for his extravagance and generosity, and some charged that he bribed Peruvian officials on a large scale to get his projects approved. He was a good speaker and loved to entertain lavishly. In one example of his generosity, he distributed thousands of pesos and soles to the victims of the earthquake of 1868. He also contributed to the beautification of Lima by tearing down an old wall and putting a seven-mile-long park in its place.

Always the speculator, in 1877 Meiggs died poor, his debts exceeding his assets. He was beloved, however, and more than twenty thousand Peruvians, many of whom had labored on his projects, attended his funeral at a Catholic church in Lima.

QUESTIONS FOR ANALYSIS

1. What accounts for the changes in fortune that Meiggs experienced?
2. Were the Latin American governments that awarded contracts to Meiggs making reasonable decisions?
3. Should it matter whether Meiggs had to bribe officials to get the railroads built? Why?

The challenges in building the Callo-Lima-Oroya railroad across the Andes can be imagined from this picture of one of its many bridges. (From Elio Galessio, *Ferrocarriles del Perú: Un viaje a través de su Historia*. Reproduced with permission of the author)

Diego Rivera, *The Exploiters* The Mexican painter Diego Rivera (1886–1957) painted many large murals, using his art to convey messages of social protest. This mural was painted in 1926 for the wall of a chapel at an agricultural college in Mexico City. (*Los Explotadores*, 1926 © Banco de Mexico, Diego Rivera and Frida Kahlo Museums/2011 Artists Rights Society [ARS], New York)

The late nineteenth century witnessed ever-greater concentrations of land in ever fewer hands. In places like the Valley of Mexico in southern Mexico, a few large haciendas controlled all the land. Under the 1876–1911 dictatorship of General Porfirio Díaz, the Mexican government in 1883 passed a law allowing real estate companies (controlled by Díaz's political cronies) to survey public and "vacant" lands and to retain one-third of the land they surveyed. An 1894 law provided that land could be declared vacant if legal title to it could not be produced. Since few Indians had deeds to the land that their ancestors had worked for centuries, the door swung open to wholesale expropriation of small landholdings and entire villages. Indians who dared armed resistance were crushed by government troops and carried off to virtual slave labor. As a result of the policies of Díaz (who was overthrown in the Mexican Revolution that started in 1910), vast stretches of land—in one case, 12 million acres—came into the hands of private individuals. Debt peonage also became common: landowners paid their laborers not in cash but in vouchers redeemable only at the landowner's store, where high prices and tricky bookkeeping kept the **peons** permanently in debt.

The Impact of Immigrants from Europe, Asia, and the Middle East

In 1852 the Argentine political philosopher Juan Bautista Alberdi published *Bases and Points of Departure for Argentine Political Organization*, arguing that the development of his country depended on immigration. Indians and blacks, Alberdi maintained, lacked basic skills, and it would take too long to train them. Thus he pressed for massive immigration from the "advanced" countries of northern Europe and the United States. Alberdi's ideas won immediate acceptance and were even incorporated into the Argentine constitution, which declared that "the Federal government will encourage European immigration." Other Latin American countries adopted similar policies promoting immigration.

Although Europe was a significant source of immigrants to Latin America, so were Asia and the Middle East. For example, in the late nineteenth and early twentieth centuries large numbers of Japanese arrived in Brazil, most settling in urban areas, especially in São

peons Low-status laborers.

Listening to the Past

Mary Seacole on Her Early Life

Mary Seacole was born in Jamaica in 1805, the daughter of a Scottish soldier and a local Jamaican Creole woman. She learned folk medical treatment from her mother, who ran a boarding house, and gradually took to running hotels and to working as a nurse herself. During the Crimean War she volunteered to go to the Crimea to treat wounded soldiers. Shortly afterward, in 1857, she wrote an autobiography, an excerpt of which follows.

I was born in the town of Kingston, in the island of Jamaica, some time in the present century. . . . I am a Creole, and have good Scotch blood coursing in my veins. My father was a soldier, of an old Scotch family; and to him I often trace my affection for a camp-life, and my sympathy with what I have heard my friends call "the pomp, pride, and circumstance of glorious war." Many people have also traced to my Scotch blood that energy and activity which are not always found in the Creole race, and which have carried me to so many varied scenes: and perhaps they are right. I have often heard the term "lazy Creole" applied to my country people; but I am sure I do not know what it is to be indolent. . . .

My mother kept a boarding-house in Kingston, and was, like very many of the Creole women, an admirable doctress; in high repute with the officers of both services, and their wives, who were from time to time stationed at Kingston. It was very natural that I should inherit her tastes; and so I had from early youth a yearning for medical knowledge and practice which has never deserted me. . . .

[After returning to Kingston from a trip in 1825], I nursed my old indulgent patroness in her last long illness. After she died, in my arms, I went to my mother's house, where I stayed, making myself useful in a variety of ways, and learning a great deal of Creole medicinal art, until I couldn't find courage to say "no" to a certain arrangement timidly proposed by Mr. Seacole, but married him, and took him down to Black River, where we established a store. Poor man! He was very delicate; and before

I undertook the charge of him, several doctors had expressed most unfavorable opinions of his health. I kept him alive by kind nursing and attention as long as I could; but at last he grew so ill that we left Black River, and returned to my mother's house at Kingston.

Within a month of our arrival there he died. This was my first great trouble, and I felt it bitterly. For days I never stirred— lost to all that passed around me in a dull stupor of despair. If you had told me that the time would soon come when I should remember this sorrow calmly, I should not have believed it possible: and yet it was so. I do not think that we hot-blooded Creoles sorrow less for showing it so impetuously; but I do think that the sharp edge of our grief wears down sooner than theirs who preserve an outward demeanor of calmness, and nurse their woe secretly in their hearts. . . .

In the year 1850, the cholera swept over the island of Jamaica with terrible force. . . . While the cholera raged, I had but too many opportunities of watching its nature, and from a Dr. B—, who was then lodging in my house, received many hints as to its treatment which I afterwards found invaluable.

Early in the same year my brother had left Kingston for the Isthmus of Panama, then the great high-road to and from golden California, where he had established a considerable store and hotel. Ever since he had done so, I had found some difficulty in checking my reviving disposition to roam, and at last persuading myself that I might be of use to him (he was far from strong), I resigned my house into the hands of a cousin, and made arrangements to journey to Chagres. . . .

All my readers must know—a glance at the map will show it to those who do not—that between North America and the envied shores of California stretches a little neck of land, insignificant-looking enough on the map, dividing the Atlantic from the Pacific. By crossing this, the travellers from America avoided a long, weary, and dangerous sea voyage round Cape Horn, or an almost impossible journey by land.

But that journey across the Isthmus, insignificant in distance as it was, was by no means an easy one. It seemed as if

---

Paulo. By 1920 Brazil had the largest Japanese community in the world outside of Japan. From the Middle East, Lebanese, Turks, and Syrians also entered Brazil. Between 1850 and 1880, 144,000 South Asian laborers went to Trinidad, 39,000 to Jamaica, and smaller numbers to the islands of St. Lucia, Grenada, and St. Vincent as indentured servants under five-year contracts. Perhaps one-third returned to India, but the rest stayed, saved money, and bought small businesses or land. Cuba, the largest of the Caribbean islands (about the size of

Pennsylvania), had received 500,000 African slaves between 1808 and 1865. When slavery was abolished in 1886, some of the work in the sugar-cane fields was done by Chinese indentured servants, who followed the same pattern as the South Asian migrants who had gone to Trinidad. Likewise, the abolition of slavery in Mexico led to the arrival of thousands of Chinese bonded servants.

Immigration helped fuel urbanization, and Portuguese, Italian, French, Chinese, and Japanese imminature had determined to throw every conceivable obstacle in the way of those who should seek to join the two great oceans of the world. . . .

When, after passing Chagres, an old-world, tumble-down town, for about seven miles, the steamer reached Navy Bay, I thought I had never seen a more luckless, dreary spot. . . . It seemed as capital a nursery for ague and fever as Death could hit upon anywhere, and those on board the steamer who knew it confirmed my opinion. As we arrived a steady down-pour of rain was falling from an inky sky; the white men who met us on the wharf appeared ghostly and wraith-like, and the very negroes seemed pale and wan. The news which met us did not tempt me to lose any time in getting up the country to my brother. According to all accounts, fever and ague, with some minor diseases, especially dropsy, were having it all their own way at Navy Bay, and, although I only stayed one night in the place, my medicine chest was called into requisition. But the sufferers wanted remedies which I could not give them—warmth, nourishment, and fresh air. Beneath leaky tents, damp huts, and even under broken railway wagons, I saw men dying from sheer exhaustion. Indeed, I was very glad when, with the morning, the crowd, as the Yankees called the bands of pilgrims to and from California, made ready to ascend to Panama. . . .

It was not so easy to hire a boat as I had been led to expect. The large crowd had made the boatmen somewhat exorbitant in their demands. . . . There were several reasons why I should engage one for my own exclusive use, instead of sharing one with some of my traveling companions. In the first place, my luggage was somewhat bulky; and, in the second place, my experience of travel had not failed to teach me that Americans (even from the Northern States) are always uncomfortable in the company of colored people, and very often show this feeling in stronger ways than by sour looks and rude words. I think, if I have a little prejudice against our cousins across the Atlantic—and I do confess to a little—it is not unreasonable. I have a few shades of deeper brown upon my skin which shows me related—and I am proud of the relationship—to those poor mortals whom you once held enslaved, and whose bodies America still owns. And having this bond, and knowing what slavery is; having seen with my eyes and heard with my ears proof positive enough of its horrors—let others affect to doubt them if they will—is it surprising that I should be somewhat impatient of the airs of superiority which many Americans have endeavored to assume over me? Mind, I am not speaking of all. I have met with some delightful exceptions. "

• The first edition of Mary Seacole's *Wonderful Adventures* appeared in London in 1857 with her picture on the cover.
(© Museum of London)

Source: Mary Seacole, *Wonderful Adventures of Mrs. Seacole in Many Lands* (London: Blackwood, 1857), pp. 1–17.

QUESTIONS FOR ANALYSIS

1. How does Mary Seacole understand race?
2. How does she understand disease? What were the health problems that she saw as most serious?
3. What audience do you think Seacole is attempting to address in her autobiography?

grants gave an international flavor and a more vigorous tempo to Latin American cities. Thanks to the influx of new arrivals Rio de Janeiro, Mexico City, Montevideo, Santiago, Havana, and Buenos Aires experienced spectacular growth.

By 1914 Buenos Aires in particular had emerged as one of the most cosmopolitan cities in the world, with a population of 3.6 million. As Argentina's political capital, the city housed all its government bureaucracies and agencies. The meatpacking, food-processing, flour-milling, and wool industries were concentrated there as well. Half of all overseas tonnage passed through the city, which was also the heart of the nation's railroad network. Elegant shops near the Plaza de Mayo catered to the expensive tastes of the elite upper classes, who constituted about 5 percent of the population. By contrast, the thousands of immigrants who toiled twelve hours a day, six days a week, on docks and construction sites and in meatpacking plants were crowded into the city's one-room tenements,

Buenos Aires, 1894 When this photo was taken, Buenos Aires was already a cosmopolitan city, with a population of more than 600,000, and its streets looked much like streets in European cities of the time. (Archivo General de la Nación, Buenos Aires)

furnished with a few iron cots, a table and chairs, and maybe an old trunk.

Despite such difficult living conditions, immigrants' dreams of rapid economic success in the New World often came true. The first generation almost always did manual labor, but its sons often advanced to upper-blue-collar or white-collar jobs. The sons of successful Genoese or Neapolitan immigrants typically imitated the dress, manners, and values of the Creole elite.

Immigrants brought wide-ranging skills that helped develop industry and commerce. In Argentina, Italian and Spanish settlers stimulated the expansion of the cattle industry and the development of the wheat and shoe industries. In Brazil, Swiss immigrants built the cheese business, Italians gained a leading role in the coffee industry, and Japanese pioneered the development of the cotton industry. In Peru, Italians became influential in banking and the restaurant business, while the French dominated dressmaking as well as the jewelry and pharmaceutical businesses. Chinese laborers built the railroads, and in sections of large cities such as Lima, the Chinese came to dominate the ownership of shops and restaurants. European immigrants also brought anarchist and socialist ideas and became involved in union organizing.

The vast majority of migrants were unmarried males; seven out of ten people who landed in Argentina between 1857 and 1924 were single males between thirteen and forty years old. There, as in other South American countries, many of those who stayed sought Indian or other low-status women, leading to further racial mixing.

The creation of independent nations in Latin America did little to improve the position of the poor.

Neocolonialism had a modernizing influence on commerce and industry, but it further concentrated wealth. Spanish and Portuguese merchants who returned to the Iberian Peninsula were replaced by British and U.S. businessmen. Just as the United States waged wars against the Indians (see pages 825–827) and pushed its frontier westward, so Brazil, Venezuela, Ecuador, Peru, and Bolivia expanded into the Amazonian frontier at the expense of indigenous peoples. Likewise, Mexico, Chile, and Argentina had their "Indian wars" and frontier expansion. Racial prejudice kept most of the South American black population in a wretched socioeconomic position until well past 1914. European immigrants, rather than black plantation workers, gained the urban jobs. In 1893, 71.2 percent of the working population of São Paulo was foreign-born. Blacks continued to work cutting sugar cane and picking coffee.

The United States, 1789–1914

☐ How did the United States build a large but unified nation?

The American Revolution (see page 656) seemed to validate the Enlightenment idea that a better life on earth was possible. Americans carried an unbounded optimism about the future into the nineteenth and twentieth centuries. Until 1860 most eastern states limited voting rights to property holders or taxpayers, but suffrage was gradually expanded to include most adult white males. The movement toward popular democracy accelerated as the young nation, confident of its "manifest destiny," pushed relentlessly across the continent. As settlers moved into new territories, the industrializing North and the agricultural South came into conflict over extending slavery into these lands. The ensuing Civil War (1861–1865) cost six hundred thousand American lives — more than any other war the nation has fought. Yet the victory of the North preserved the federal system and strengthened the United States as a nation.

The years between 1865 and 1917 witnessed the transformation of the United States into a major industrial power. Immigrants settled much of the West, put the prairies to the plow, provided the labor to exploit the country's mineral resources, turned small provincial towns into sophisticated centers of ethnic and cultural diversity, and built the railroads that tied the country together. Most of the social and cultural phenomena seen in western Europe in this period (see Chapter 24) — such as improved sanitation, mass transit, faith in science, and strong identification with the nation — occurred also in the United States.

Manifest Destiny and Its Consequences for Native Americans

In an 1845 issue of the *United States Magazine and Democratic Review*, editor John L. O'Sullivan boldly declared that foreign powers were trying to prevent American annexation of Texas in order to impede "the fulfillment of our manifest destiny to overspread the continent allotted by Providence for the free development of our yearly multiplying millions." O'Sullivan was articulating a sentiment prevalent in the United States since early in its history: that God had foreordained the nation to cover the entire continent. After a large-circulation newspaper picked up the phrase **manifest destiny**, it was used on the floor of Congress and soon entered the language as a catchword for and justification of expansion.

When George Washington became president in 1789, fewer than 4 million people inhabited the thirteen states on the eastern seaboard. By the time Abraham Lincoln became the sixteenth president in 1861, the United States stretched across the continent and had 31 million inhabitants. During the colonial period, pioneers pushed westward to the Appalachian Mountains. After independence, westward movement accelerated. The eastern states claimed all the land from the Atlantic Ocean to the Mississippi River, but two forces blocked immediate expansion. The Indians, trying to save their lands, allied with the British in Canada to prevent further American encroachment. In 1794 Brit-

> **"The fulfillment of our manifest destiny [is] to overspread the continent allotted by Providence for the free development of our yearly multiplying millions."**
>
> **JOHN L. O'SULLIVAN**

ain agreed to evacuate border forts in the Northwest Territory, roughly the area north of the Ohio River and east of the Mississippi, and thereby end British support for the Indians. A similar treaty with Spain paved the way for southeastern expansion.

Events in Europe and the Caribbean led to a massive increase in American territory. In 1800 Spain ceded the Louisiana Territory — the land between the Mississippi River and the Rocky Mountains — to France. Three years later Napoleon sold it to the United States for only $12 million. Spain, preoccupied with rebellions in South America, sold the Florida Territory to the U.S. government, and beginning in 1821 American settlers poured into the Mexican territory of Texas, whose soil proved excellent for the production of cotton and sugar. Southern politicians, fearing that Texas would become a refuge for fugitive slaves, pressured President John Tyler to admit Texas to the United States. The admission of Florida as the twenty-seventh state and Texas as the twenty-eighth state in 1845 meant the absorption of large numbers of Hispanic people into the United States. Many of them had lived in those regions since the sixteenth century, long before Anglo immigration.

The acquisition of Texas's 267,339 square miles (making it a fifth larger than France) whetted American appetites for the rest of the old Spanish Empire in North America. Some expansionists even dreamed of taking Cuba and Central America.

Exploiting Mexico's political instability, President James Polk goaded Mexico into war. Mexico suffered total defeat and in the 1848 **Treaty of Guadalupe Hidalgo** surrendered its remaining claims to Texas, yielded New Mexico and California to the United States, and recognized the Rio Grande as the international border. A treaty with Great Britain in 1846 had already recognized the American settlement in the Oregon Territory, so with the new lands from Mexico the continent had been acquired. Then, in 1898 a revolt in Cuba against an incompetent Spanish administration had consequences beyond "manifest destiny." Inflamed by press reports of Spanish atrocities, public opinion swept

- **manifest destiny** The belief that God had foreordained Americans to cover the entire continent.
- **Treaty of Guadalupe Hidalgo** The 1848 treaty between the United States and Mexico in which Mexico ceded large tracts of land to the United States in exchange for $15 million.

> ❝We are deprived of membership in the human family! We have neither land, nor home, nor resting place, that can be called our own.❞
>
> **CHEROKEE CHIEF JOHN ROSS**

the United States into war. The Spanish-American War—the "splendid little war," as Secretary of State John Hay called it—lasted just ten weeks and brought U.S. control over Cuba, the Philippines, and Puerto Rico. The United States had become a colonial power.

The people who were native to this vast continent fared poorly under manifest destiny. Government officials sometimes manipulated the Indians by gathering a few chiefs, plying them with cheap whiskey, and then inducing them to hand over the tribes' hunting grounds. Sometimes officials exploited rivalries among tribes or used bribes. By these methods, William Henry Harrison, superintendent of the Indians of the Northwest Territory and a future president, got some Native Americans to cede 48 million acres (Map 27.2). He had the full backing of President Jefferson.

The policy of pushing the Indians westward across the Mississippi accelerated during Andrew Jackson's presidency (1829–1837). Thousands of Delawares, Shawnees, and Wyandots, tricked into moving from east of the Mississippi River to reservations west of Missouri, died of cholera and measles during the journey. The survivors found themselves hopelessly in debt for supplies and farming equipment. The state of Georgia, meanwhile, was nibbling away at Cherokee lands, which were theoretically protected by treaty with the U.S. government. When gold was discovered on the Cherokee lands, a gold rush took place. The Creek, Cherokee, and other tribes were rounded up, expelled, and sent beyond the western boundaries of Missouri and Arkansas. Cherokee Chief John Ross, in a 1935 letter to Congress, movingly appealed, "We are deprived of membership in the human family! We have neither land, nor home, nor resting place, that can be called our own."[5]

The mid-nineteenth century saw a steady flow of white settlers westward past the Mississippi River into the Great Plains, home to many Indians who hunted on horseback using rifles. The U.S. Army, in the name of protecting the migrants, fought the Indians, destroyed

MAP 27.2 Indian Cession of Lands to the United States, 1784–1890 Forced removal of the Creeks, Cherokees, and Chickasaws to reservations in Oklahoma led to the deaths of thousands of Native Americans on the Trail of Tears, as well as to the destruction of their cultures.

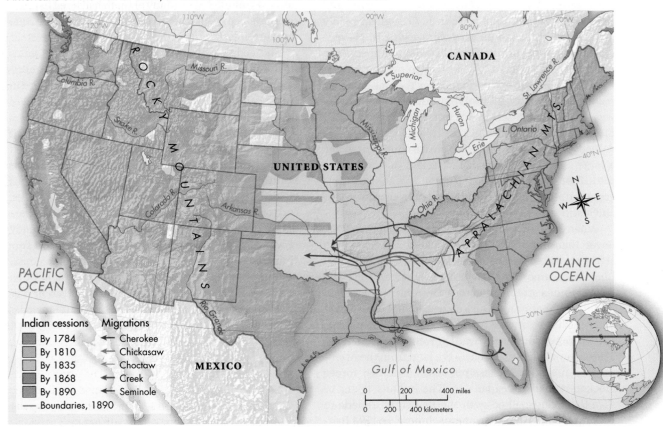

their lodges and horses, and slaughtered the buffalo on which they depended for food, shelter, and clothing. The federal government's policy was to confine indigenous people to reservations, where malnutrition and disease took a terrible toll.

Cultural differences aggravated conflict between white settlers and Native Americans. Unlike the whites, Indians did not think of land in terms of private property; they believed that land, like other resources such as air and water, belonged to everyone, that individuals or groups might hold temporary stewardship over the land but that it should be respected and treasured for future generations. In another cultural difference, white Americans, because they had a commander in chief (the president) who could give orders and expect them to be carried out, assumed that a respected Native American chief could make agreements binding on all tribes. But no chief could command all the Sioux, let alone all the Plains Indians. When a tribe or group of tribes opposed or disregarded a treaty made by a particular chief, the whites claimed that the Indians as a whole had broken the treaty.

In 1868, after pursuing a policy of total war on the Plains Indians, General W. T. Sherman brokered the Treaty of Fort Laramie. This treaty promised that the United States would close western forts and grant the Sioux and Cheyenne permanent control of their ancestral lands in the Dakotas: the Black Hills as well as the area between the Platte River and the Bighorn Mountains. A few chiefs signed; many did not. In 1874 gold was discovered in the Black Hills, and prospectors flooded into the area. By 1875 whites outnumbered Indians there, violating the terms of the treaty. During the course of the nineteenth century, while the number of white residents skyrocketed from 4.3 million to 66.8 million, the number of Indians steadily declined to a recorded 237,196 in 1900.

Women's Roles in White Settlements

Generally speaking, the settlers' lives blurred sex roles. It fell to women to make homes out of crude log cabins that had no windows or doors or out of tarpaper shacks with mud floors. Lacking cookstoves, they prepared food over open fireplaces, using all kinds of substitutes for ingredients easily available back east. To wash clothes, women had to make soap out of lye and carefully saved household ashes.

Considered the carriers of "high culture," women organized whatever educational, religious, musical, and recreational activities the settlers' society possessed. Women also had to defend their homes against prairie fires and Indian attacks. These burdens were accompanied by frequent pregnancies and, often, the need to give birth without medical help or even the support of other women. The death rate for infants and young children ran as high as 30 percent in the mid-nineteenth century. Even so, the women had large families.

Influenced by ideas then circulating in England, some women began promoting rights for women. At the Seneca Falls Convention in 1848, they demanded equal political and economic rights. Others promoted women's education and opened women's colleges. It was not until 1920, however, that women in the United States got the right to vote.

England remained an important cultural influence in other spheres besides women's rights and abolition. Many books published in London were quickly reprinted in the United States once copies arrived, and favorite English novelists such as Charles Dickens became popular in the United States as well. Education beyond the elementary level usually involved reading classics of English literature. Meanwhile, in the American South, rights to an education and other freedoms were withheld from another group of citizens: blacks.

Black Slavery in the South

In 1619, as one solution to the chronic labor shortage in North America, Dutch traders brought the first black people to Virginia as prisoners (white indentured servants who worked for a term of years was another solution). In the early eighteenth century, with the expansion of rice cultivation in the Carolinas and tobacco farming in Virginia and Maryland, planters demanded more laborers. Between 1720 and 1770, black prisoners poured into the Southern colonies, and in South Carolina they came to outnumber whites by almost two to one. From 1730 through 1760, white fears of black revolts pushed colonial legislatures to pass laws that established blacks' legal position as property of whites, enshrining the slave system in law. Racist arguments of blacks' supposed inferiority were used to justify slavery.

The American Revolution did not bring liberty to slaves. The framers of the Constitution treated private property as sacrosanct and viewed slaves as property. Antislavery sentiment was growing, however, and states from Delaware north eventually outlawed slavery. In 1809 the United States followed Britain's lead in outlawing the importation of slaves. Nevertheless, white planters and farmers had a material and psychological interest in maintaining black bondage, which brought financial profit and conferred social status and prestige.

Between 1820 and 1860, as new lands in the South and West — in Arkansas, Mississippi, Texas, and Louisiana — were put to the production of cotton and sugar, the demand for labor skyrocketed. The upper South — Maryland and Virginia — where decades of tobacco farming had reduced the fertility of the soil, supplied the slaves. Slave traders worked either independently

□ Picturing the Past

Slave Auction, 1850s In a scene outside a country tavern near a river with a Mississippi-type steamer on it, an auctioneer extols a biracial girl's qualities to a group of planters (center), while another dealer with a whip (left) brutally separates a mother from her children. The picture was intended to send an abolitionist message. (Carnegie Museum of Art, Pittsburgh. Gift of Mrs. W. Fitch Ingersoll)

ANALYZING THE IMAGE Look at the clothing the various people are wearing. What social distinctions do they convey? Is there anything else about the picture that lets you know it was intended to send an abolitionist message?

CONNECTIONS Can you think of other examples of art with social or political messages? How would this painting compare in its effectiveness?

or from firms in Charleston, Natchez, and New Orleans, the largest slave market in the United States. This period witnessed the forced migration of about 650,000 people, in many cases causing the breakup of slave families.

Despite such threats to black families, a study of the entire adult slave population of North Carolina in 1860 has shown that most slave women spent their entire adult lives in settled unions with the same hus-

band. Planters encouraged slave marriages because large slave families were in their economic interest, especially after the end of the Atlantic slave trade. As one owner put it, "marriage adds to the comfort, happiness, and health of those entering upon it, besides insuring a greater increase."[6] Evidence from all parts of the South reveals that, in spite of illiteracy, separated spouses tried to remain in touch with one another and, once slavery had been abolished, went to enormous

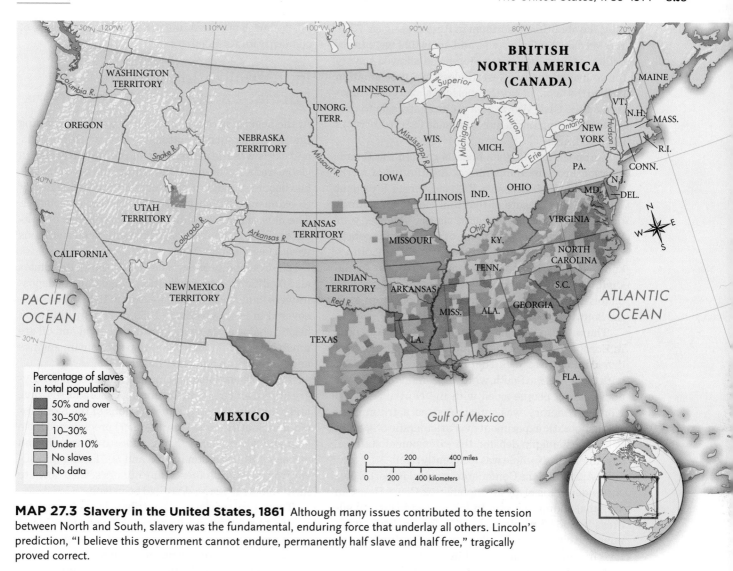

MAP 27.3 Slavery in the United States, 1861 Although many issues contributed to the tension between North and South, slavery was the fundamental, enduring force that underlay all others. Lincoln's prediction, "I believe this government cannot endure, permanently half slave and half free," tragically proved correct.

lengths to reunite their families. Typically, a slave woman had her first child around the age of nineteen. On the Good Hope plantation in South Carolina, 80 percent of slave couples had at least four children.

Blacks who were freed by their masters often went north in search of better opportunities. James Forten, a free black man (d. 1842) from Philadelphia, built a large sail-making business that employed an integrated workforce. He had a reputation as a businessman of integrity and acquired considerable wealth. But most whites of the city refused to accept him as a citizen and subjected him to verbal and physical assaults.[7]

The Civil War and Its Impact

In the 1850s westward expansion, not moral outrage, brought the controversy over slavery to a head. As Congress created new territories, the question of whether slavery would be extended to them arose again and again (Map 27.3). For years elaborate compromises were

worked out, but tensions rose, fueled by increasing differences between the North and South. On the eve of the Civil War the South was overwhelmingly agricultural, while the North controlled 90 percent of the country's industrial capacity.

Abraham Lincoln, committed to checking the spread of slavery, was elected president in 1860. To protest his victory, South Carolina seceded from the Union in December of that year. Ten Southern states soon followed South Carolina's example and formed the **Confederacy**. Its capital was at Richmond, Virginia.

Lincoln declared the seceding states' actions illegal and declared war on them to preserve the Union. The years of fighting that followed took a huge toll on both sides. Thinking that it might help end the war more quickly, Lincoln issued the Emancipation Proclamation, which became effective on January 1, 1863 (two years

Confederacy The eleven Southern states that seceded from the United States and bonded together with a capital at Richmond, Virginia.

after the abolition of serfdom in Russia; see page 730). It freed slaves only in states and areas that were in rebellion against the United States and allowed slavery for convicted felons. Nevertheless, the proclamation spelled the doom of North American slavery and transformed the Civil War from a political struggle to preserve the Union into a moral crusade for the liberty of all Americans.

European and English liberals greeted the Emancipation Proclamation with joy. A gathering of working people in Manchester, England, wrote President Lincoln: "The erasure of that foul blot upon civilization and Christianity—chattel slavery—during your Presidency will cause the name of Abraham Lincoln to be honoured and revered by posterity."[8] As Lincoln acknowledged, this was a magnanimous statement, for the Civil War hurt working people in Manchester, whose factories had closed when importation of cotton from the South stopped.

The war also had important political consequences in Europe. In 1861 British and European opinion had divided along class lines. The upper classes sympathized with the American South, while the commercial classes and working people sided with the North. Thus the Northern victory was interpreted as a triumph of the democratic experiment over aristocratic oligarchy. When parliaments debated the extension of suffrage, the American example was frequently cited.

In April 1865 the Confederate general Robert E. Lee surrendered his army at Appomattox Court House in Virginia, ending the war. In his second inaugural address in 1864 Lincoln had called for "malice toward none and charity for all." Those who came to power after Lincoln was assassinated in April 1865 were less inclined to be generous toward the South.

During Reconstruction (1865–1877), the vanquished South had to adjust to a new social and economic order without slavery. Former slaves wanted land to farm, but, lacking cash, they soon accepted the sharecropping system: sharecroppers paid landowners about half of a year's crops at harvest time in return for a cabin, food, mules, seed, tools, and land.

The Fifteenth Amendment to the U.S. Constitution outlawed denying anyone the vote "on account of race, color, or previous condition of servitude," and in the early years of Reconstruction, when Northerners were in charge, many former slaves voted. However, between 1880 and 1920, after Southerners returned to power, so-called Jim Crow laws were passed to prevent blacks from voting and to enforce rigid racial segregation.

In these racist circumstances, no institution played a more positive role in the construction of a black community than the black Protestant churches. Black preachers esteemed for their oratorical skill, organizational ability, and practical judgment became leaders of the black community. Throughout the South the black church provided support, security, and a sense of solidarity for its members.

Industrialization and the Formation of Large Corporations

At the beginning of the nineteenth century, providing raw materials such as cotton, tobacco, whale oil, pelts, and skins was the central role of the United States in global trade. By the end of the century the United States had become a major manufacturing power, due in part to extensive British investment in U.S. enterprises. The flow of British funds was a consequence of Britain's own industrialization, which generated enormous wealth (see Chapter 23).

The availability of raw materials in the United States also facilitated industrialization. Huge iron ore deposits were found near the Great Lakes in 1844; oil was discovered in Pennsylvania in 1859, and oil drilling soon began; coal was also widely available. Coal and oil are much better fuels than wood to power steam engines and to smelt iron and other metals.

The West also held precious metals, and the discovery of gold and silver in California, Colorado, Arizona, and Montana and on the reservations of the Sioux Indians of South Dakota (see page 827) precipitated huge gold and silver rushes. Even before 1900 miners had extracted $1.24 billion in gold and $901 million in silver from western mines. Many miners settled down to farm, and by 1912 the West had been won.

The federal government contributed to industrialization by turning over vast amounts of land and mineral resources to industry for development. The railroads—the foundation of industrial expansion—received 130 million acres. By 1900 the U.S. railroad system was 193,000 miles long, connected every part of the nation, and represented 40 percent of the railroad mileage of the entire world.

Between 1880 and 1920 industrial production soared. By the 1890s the United States was producing twice as much steel as Britain. Large factories replaced small ones, and Henry Ford of Detroit set up assembly lines in the automobile industry. Each person working on the line performed only one task instead of assembling an entire car. In 1910 Ford sold 10,000 cars; in 1914, a year after he inaugurated the first moving assembly line, he sold 248,000 cars. Other new machines also had a pervasive impact. Sewing machines made cheap, varied mass-produced clothing available for city people to purchase in department stores and country people through mail-order catalogues.

Even food production was industrialized. Grain elevators, introduced in 1850, made it possible to store much more grain, which could be transported by the growing rail system as needed. The new practice of canning meant that food did not have to be eaten immedi-

Oklahoma Homesteaders Beginning in 1889, Indian land in Oklahoma was offered to white settlers, who had to build a dwelling and cultivate the land for five years to gain full title to it. With trees scarce, settlers often built their houses of sod, which provided insulation but could be damaged by heavy rain. This picture of three generations of a family outside their sod house was taken in 1901. (Western History Collection, University of Oklahoma Libraries)

ately, and the development of refrigeration meant that meat could be shipped long distances. Factories turned out crackers, cookies, and breakfast cereals.

The national economy experienced repeated cycles of boom and bust in the late nineteenth century. Serious depressions in 1873, 1884, and 1893 slashed prices and threw many people out of work. Leading industrialists responded by establishing larger corporations and consolidating companies into huge conglomerates. As a result of the merger of several small oil companies, John D. Rockefeller's Standard Oil Company controlled 84 percent of the nation's oil and most American pipelines in 1898. J. P. Morgan's United States Steel monopolized the iron and steel industries, and Swift & Co. of Chicago controlled the meat-processing industry.

Immigrants and Their Reception

Immigrants were an important source of workers for the new American industries, and the United States attracted these newcomers from its founding. Before the Civil War most immigrants came from England, Ireland, and Germany. When the Irish potato crop was destroyed by a fungal disease leading to a horrific fam-

ine in 1845–1859, a million people fled overseas, the majority heading to the United States. Immigrants who arrived with nothing had to work as laborers for years, but in time many were able to acquire farms, especially if they were willing to move west as the country expanded. The Homestead Act of 1862 made land available to anyone willing to work it. From then until the end of the century, 500 million acres were put into production.

Between 1860 and 1900, 14 million additional immigrants arrived in the United States, and during the peak years between 1900 and 1914, another 14 million immigrants passed through the U.S. customs inspection station at Ellis Island in New York City. Industrial America developed on the sweat and brawn of these people. Chinese, Scandinavian, and Irish immigrants laid thirty thousand miles of railroad tracks between 1867 and 1873 and another seventy-three thousand miles in the 1880s. At the Carnegie Steel Corporation, Slavs and Italians produced one-third of the world's total steel supply in 1900. Lithuanians, Poles, Croats, Scandinavians, Irish, and blacks entered the Chicago stockyards and built the meatpacking industry. Irish immigrants continued to operate the spinning frames and knitting machines of New England's textile mills.

As in South America, immigration fed the growth of cities. In 1790 only 5.1 percent of Americans were living in centers of twenty-five hundred or more people. By 1860 this figure had risen to 19.9 percent, and by 1900 almost 40 percent were living in cities. Also by 1900, three of the largest cities in the world were in the United States — New York City with 3.4 million people, Chicago with 1.7 million, and Philadelphia with 1.4. As in Europe (see Chapter 24), cities themselves were being transformed. By the early twentieth century they had electricity, sewer systems that curbed the spread of infectious diseases, and streetcars that allowed them to expand, thus reducing crowding.

Still, the working conditions that new immigrants found were often deplorable. Industrialization had created a vast class of wage workers who depended totally on their employers for work. To keep labor costs low, employers paid workers piecemeal for the number of articles they made, and they hired women and children who could be paid much less than men. Some women textile workers earned as little as $1.56 for seventy hours of work, while men received from $7 to $9 for the same work. Because business owners fought in legislatures and courts against the installation of costly safety devices, working conditions in mines and mills were frightful. In 1913 alone, even after some safety measures had been taken, twenty-five thousand people died in industrial accidents. Between 1900 and 1917 seventy-two thousand railroad worker deaths occurred. Workers responded with strikes, violence, and, gradually, unionization.

In *How the Other Half Lives* (1890), Jacob Riis, a newspaper reporter and recent immigrant from Denmark, drew national attention to what he called "the foul core of New York's slums." Riis estimated that three hundred thousand people inhabited a single square mile on New York's Lower East Side. Overcrowding, poor sanitation, and lack of health services caused frequent epidemics. The blight of slums also increased crime, prostitution, alcoholism, and other addictions.

Nationalism carried different meanings in the United States than it did in Europe (see pages 719–721). It did not refer to an ancient people whose unique culture was tied to its language, as it did in Europe. Immigrants were expected to switch their loyalties to their new country and learn English. As in Europe, much was done to promote patriotism and bring people together through flag-waving parades and other emotionally charged symbols and ceremonies. The negative side of identification with the nation was nativist sentiment — that is, hostility to foreign and "un-American" looks, behavior, and loyalties — among native-born Americans. Some of this antagonism sprang from racism, some from old Protestant suspicions of Roman Catholicism, the faith of many of the new arrivals. Long-standing anti-Semitism also played a part. A great deal of the dislike of the foreign-born sprang from fear of economic competition. To most Americans, the Chinese with their exotic looks and willingness to work for very little seemed especially dangerous. Increasingly violent agitation against Asians

Racist Cartoon from *Harper's Weekly*, 1869 Nineteenth-century immigrants encountered terrible prejudice, as even "respectable" magazines and newspapers spewed out racism, such as this cartoon from an 1869 issue of *Harper's Weekly* that satirizes both the Irish and the Chinese as "uncivilized." The Irishman is identified by his shillelagh, a blackthorn club, here used to imply a tendency toward violence, and the Chinese man is identified by his long pigtail and his bowing, seen as a sign of his devious obsequiousness. Well into the twentieth century, being American meant being of Anglo-Saxon descent. (*Harper's Weekly*, August 28, 1869. Private Collection)

THE COMING MAN—JOHN CHINAMAN.
Uncle Sam introduces Eastern Barbarism to Western Civilization.

led to race riots in California and finally culminated in the Chinese Exclusion Act of 1882, which denied Chinese laborers entrance to the country.

The severe economic depression of the 1890s also fed resentment toward immigrants. Faced with overproduction, the rich and politically powerful owners of mines, mills, and factories fought the organization of labor unions, laid off thousands of workers, slashed wages, and ruthlessly exploited their workers. Workers in turn feared that immigrant labor would drive salaries lower.

Canada, from French Colony to Nation

☐ What geographical, economic, and political conditions shaped the development of Canada?

In 1608 the French explorer Samuel de Champlain (1567–1635) sailed down the St. Lawrence River (see Map 27.4) and established a trading post on the site of present-day Quebec. Thus began the permanent colony of New France. The fur-trading monopolies subsequently granted to Champlain by the French crown attracted settlers, and Jesuit missionaries to the Indians further increased the French population. The British, however, vigorously challenged French control of the lucrative fur trade. The mid-eighteenth-century global struggle for empire between the British and the French, known in Europe as the Seven Years' War (see pages 654–656), spilled into North America, where it was known as the French and Indian Wars. In 1759, on a field next to the city of Quebec, the English defeated the French and ended the French empire in North America. By the Treaty of Paris of 1763, France ceded Canada to Great Britain.

For the French Canadians, who in 1763 numbered about ninety thousand, the British conquest was a tragedy. British governors replaced the French, and English-speaking merchants from Britain and the thirteen American colonies to the south took over the colony's economic affairs. The Roman Catholic Church remained, however, and played a powerful role in the political and cultural, as well as the religious, life of French Canadians. Most French Canadians were farmers, though a small merchant class sold furs and imported manufactured goods.

In 1774 the British Parliament passed the Quebec Act, which granted religious freedom to French Canadians and recognized French law in civil matters, but it denied Canadians a legislative assembly, a traditional feature of British colonial government. Instead, Parliament placed power in the hands of an appointed governor and an appointed council composed of both English and French Canadians. English Canadian businessmen protested that they were being denied a basic right of Englishmen — representation.

During the American Revolution, about forty thousand Americans demonstrated their loyalty to Great Britain and its empire by moving to Canada. These "loyalists" not only altered the French-English ratio in the population but also pressed for a representative assembly. In 1791 Parliament responded with the Constitution Act, which divided the province of Quebec in two and provided for an elective assembly in each province.

Not wanting to repeat the errors made in 1776, when failure to grant the thirteen colonies autonomy provoked them to declare independence, the British gradually extended home rule to Canada, beginning in 1840. During the American Civil War (1861–1865), English-American relations were severely strained, and fear of American aggression led to **confederation**, a loose union of the provinces, each with substantial powers. In 1867 the provinces of New Brunswick and Nova Scotia joined Ontario and Quebec to form the Dominion of Canada (Map 27.4). The Dominion Cabinet was given jurisdiction over internal affairs, while Britain retained control over foreign policy. (In 1931 the British Statute of Westminster officially recognized Canadian autonomy in foreign affairs.)

Believing that the U.S. Constitution left the states too strong and helped to bring on the Civil War, the framers of the Canadian constitution created a powerful central government. The first prime minister, John A. Macdonald, vigorously pushed Canada's "manifest destiny" to absorb the entire northern part of the continent. In 1870 his government purchased the vast Northwest Territories of the Hudson's Bay Company for $1.5 million. Fearful that the sparsely settled colony of British Columbia would join the United States, Macdonald lured British Columbia into the confederation with a subsidy to pay its debts and the promise of a transcontinental railroad. Likewise, the tiny, debt-ridden maritime province of Prince Edward Island was drawn into the confederation with a large subsidy. In the five short years between 1868 and 1873, through Macdonald's imagination and drive, Canadian sovereignty stretched from coast to coast. The completion of the Canadian Pacific Railroad in 1885 led to the formation of two new prairie provinces, Alberta and Saskatchewan, which in 1905 entered the Dominion. (Only in 1949 did the island of Newfoundland renounce colonial status and join the Dominion.)

Canada was thinly populated in the nineteenth century, and by 1900 still had only a little over 5 million

confederation A relatively loose form of union, leaving the parts with substantial powers.

MAP 27.4 The Dominion of Canada, 1871 Shortly after the Dominion of Canada came into being as a self-governing nation within the British Empire in 1867, new provinces were added. Vast areas of Canada were too sparsely populated to achieve provincial status. Alberta and Saskatchewan did not become part of the Dominion until 1905, Newfoundland only in 1949.

people (as compared to 76 million in the United States). As in the United States, the native peoples were pushed aside by Canada's development plans, and their population dropped by half or more during the century, many succumbing to the newcomers' diseases. There were only about 127,000 left in 1900. French Canadians remained the largest minority in the population. Distinctively different in language, law, and religion and fiercely proud of their culture, they resisted assimilation.

Immigration picked up in the 1890s. Between 1897 and 1912, 961,000 people entered Canada from the British Isles, 594,000 from Europe, and 784,000 from the United States. Some immigrants went to work in the urban factories of Hamilton, Toronto, and Montreal. However, most immigrants from continental Europe — Poles, Germans, Scandinavians, and Russians — flooded the midwestern plains and soon transformed the prairies into one of the world's greatest grain-growing regions. Between 1891 and 1914, wheat production rock-

eted from 2 million bushels per year to 150 million bushels. Mining also was expanded, and British Columbia, Ontario, and Quebec produced large quantities of wood pulp, much of it sold to the United States. Canada's great rivers were harnessed to supply hydroelectric power for industrial and domestic use. But Canada remained a predominantly agricultural country, with less than 10 percent of its population engaged in manufacturing (and a third of them processing timber or food).

Australia, from Penal Colony to Nation

☐ What circumstances shaped the development of Australia?

In April 1770 James Cook, the English explorer, navigator, and captain of HMS *Endeavor*, dropped anchor in a wide bay about ten miles south of the present city of Sydney on the coast of eastern Australia. Because the young botanist on board the ship, Joseph Banks, subsequently discovered thirty thousand specimens of plant life in the bay, sixteen hundred of them unknown to European science, Captain Cook called the place

- **Botany Bay** A bay on the coast of eastern Australia in which numerous specimens of plant life were discovered. It later became home to a penal colony.
- **New South Wales** The name given to Australia by James Cook, the English explorer; today it is the name of the most populous of the six states of Australia.

Russian Immigrant Women in Saskatchewan These women were Doukhobors, members of a Christian religious sect who came to Canada from Russia seeking religious freedom from tsarist persecution. While most of the men took railroad jobs, the women planted the vast plains with rye, wheat, oats, and flax. Their farms and orchards flourished, and the Doukhobors played an important role in the development of western Canada. (Saskatchewan Archives Board, photo no. R-B 1964)

Botany Bay. Totally unimpressed by the flat landscape and its few naked inhabitants — the Aborigines, or native people — Cook sailed north along the coast (Map 27.5). On August 21, on a rock later named Possession Island, Cook formally claimed the entire land south of where he stood for King George III, sixteen thousand miles away. Cook called the land **New South Wales**. In accepting possession, the British crown acted on the legal fiction that Australia was *Terra Nullius*, completely unoccupied, thus entirely ignoring the native people.

Britain populated the new land with prisoners, and their labor — as well as the efforts of their descendants and new arrivals — transformed Australia into an economically viable and increasingly independent nation. Like the other nations discussed in this chapter, Australia was not free of racial discrimination.

A Distant Land Turned Penal Colony

The world's smallest continent, Australia is about half the size of Europe and almost as large as the United States (excluding Alaska and Hawai'i). It has a temperate climate and little intense cold. Three topographical zones (see Map 27.5) roughly divide the continent. The Western Plateau, a vast desert and semidesert region, covers almost two-thirds of the continent. The Central Eastern Lowlands extend from the Gulf of Carpentaria in the north to western Victoria in the south. The Eastern Highlands are a complex belt of tablelands.

When Cook arrived in Australia, about three hundred thousand Aborigines lived there. A peaceful and nomadic people who had emigrated from southern Asia millennia earlier, the Aborigines lived entirely by food gathering, fishing, and hunting. They had no agriculture. Although they used spears, bows, and arrows in hunting, they never practiced warfare as it was understood by more technologically advanced peoples such as the Mexica (Aztecs) of Mexico or the Mandinke of West Africa. When the white settlers arrived, they occupied the Aborigine lands unopposed. Like the Indians of Central and South America, the Aborigines fell victim to the white peoples' diseases and to a spiritual malaise caused by the breakdown of their tribal life. Today only about forty-five thousand pureblood Aborigines survive.

The victory of the thirteen North American colonies in 1783 inadvertently contributed to the establishment of a colony in Australia five years later. Crime in England was increasing in the 1770s and 1780s, and the transportation of felons "beyond the seas" seemed the answer to the problem of overcrowded prisons. Until the founding of the United States in 1776, the British government had shipped about one thousand convicts annually to the North American colony of Georgia. After that became impossible, the British Cabinet approved the establishment of a penal colony at Botany Bay in 1786 to serve as "a remedy for the evils likely to result from the late alarming and numerous increase of felons in this country, and more particularly in the metropolis (London)."[9] The name "Botany Bay" became

Governor Arthur's Proclamation In 1830, to communicate to Aborigines the idea of equal justice for all, the governor of Van Dieman's land (modern Tasmania) had picture boards displayed. This one shows an Aborigine being hung for killing a settler with a spear, and a settler being hung for shooting an Aborigine with a rifle. (Mitchell Library, State Library of New South Wales)

a byword for the forced and permanent exile of criminals. In May 1787 a fleet of eleven ships packed with a thousand felons and their jailers sailed for Australia. On January 28, 1788, after an eight-month voyage, it landed in Sydney Cove.

Mere survival in an alien world was the first challenge. Because the land at Botany Bay proved completely unsuited for agriculture and lacked decent water, the first governor, Arthur Phillip, moved the colony ten miles north to Port Jackson, later called Sydney. Announcing that those who did not work would not eat, Phillip set the prisoners to planting seeds. But coming from the slums of London, the convicts knew nothing of agriculture, and some were too ill or too old to work. Moreover, the colony lacked draft animals and plows. Consequently, the colony of New South Wales tottered on the brink of starvation for years.

Until the penal colony system was abolished in 1869, a total of 161,000 convicts were transported to Australia. Transportation rested on two premises: that criminals should be punished and that they should not be a financial burden on the state. Convicts became free when their sentences expired or were remitted, but few returned to England.

For the first thirty years of the penal colony, men far outnumbered women. Because the British government refused to allow wives to accompany their convict-husbands, prostitution flourished. Many women convicts, if not professional prostitutes when they left England, became such during the long voyage south. Army officers, government officials, and free immigrants chose favorite convicts as mistresses.

Officers and jailers, though descended from the middle and lower middle classes, tried to establish a colonial gentry and to impose the rigid class distinctions that they had known in England. Known as **exclusionists**, these self-appointed members of the colonial gentry tried to exclude from polite society all freed people, called **emancipists**. Deep and bitter class feeling took root.

An Economy Built on Wool, Gold, and Immigrant Labor

Governor Phillip and his successors urged the British Colonial Office to send free settlers, not just prisoners, to Australia. After the end of the Napoleonic wars in 1815 a steady stream of people relocated there. The end of the European wars also released capital for potential investment. But investment in what? What commodity could be developed and exported to England?

Immigrants explored several possibilities. Sealing seemed a good prospect, but the seal population was quickly depleted. Credit for the development of the product that was to be Australia's staple commodity for export—wool—goes to John Macarthur (1767–1834). Granted a large tract of Crown lands and assigned thirty convicts to work for him, Macarthur conducted experiments in the production of fine merino wool. In 1800 he sent sample fleeces to England to determine their quality and to attract the financial support of British manufacturers.

The report of J. T. Bigge, an able lawyer sent out in 1819 to evaluate the colony, proved decisive. Persuaded

MAP 27.5 Australia Because of the vast deserts in western Australia, cities and industries developed mainly in the east. Australia's early geographical and cultural isolation bred a sense of inferiority. Air travel, the communications revolution, and the massive importation of Japanese products and American popular culture have changed that.

by large landowners like Macarthur, Bigge reported that wool was the country's future staple. He recommended that convicts be removed from the temptations of towns and seaports and dispersed to work on the estates of men of capital. He also urged the suspension of British duties on colonial wool. The Colonial Office accepted this advice, and the pastoral economy of Australia, as the continent was beginning to be called, began.

Australia's temperate climate is ideally suited to sheep farming. Moreover, wool production requires much land and little labor — precisely the situation in Australia. In 1830 the sheep population reached a half million. After 1820 the commercial importance of Australia exceeded its significance as a penal colony, and wool exports steadily increased, from 75,400 pounds in 1821, to 2 million pounds in 1830, to 24 million pounds in 1845.

Settlers also experimented with wheat farming. Soil deficiencies and the dry climate slowed early production, but farmers eventually developed a successful white-grained winter variety, and by 1900 wheat was Australia's second most valuable crop.

Population shortage remained a problem through the nineteenth century. In its quest for British immigrants, Australia could not compete with North America. The twelve-thousand-mile journey to Australia cost between £20 and £25 and could take five weary months. By contrast, the trip to Canada or the United States cost only £5 and lasted just ten weeks. To reduce the financial disincentives, the government offered immigrants free passage. Still, in the nineteenth century over 2.5 million British immigrants went to North America and only 223,000 to Australia.

In the early nineteenth century Australia's population was concentrated on the eastern coast of the

- **exclusionists** The officers and jailers who tried to establish a colonial gentry and impose rigid class distinctions from England.

- **emancipists** The lower strata of the Australian social order in the mid-nineteenth century, made up of former convicts.

continent, but the growth of sheep farming led to the opening of the interior. The Ripon Land Regulation Act of 1831, which provided land grants, attracted free settlers, and by 1850 Australia had five hundred thousand inhabitants. The discovery of gold in Victoria in 1851 quadrupled that number in a few years. Although the government charged prospectors a very high license fee, men and women from all parts of the globe flocked to Australia to share in the fabulous wealth.

The gold rush led to an enormous improvement in transportation within Australia. People customarily traveled by horseback or on foot and used two-wheel ox-drawn carts to bring wool from inland ranches to coastal cities. Then two newly arrived Americans, Freeman Cobb and James Rutherford, built sturdy four-wheel coaches capable of carrying heavy cargo and of negotiating the bush tracks. Railroad construction, financed by British investors, began in the 1870s, and by 1890 nine thousand miles of track had been laid. The improved transportation offered by railways stimulated agricultural production.

The gold rush also provided financial backing for educational and cultural institutions. Public libraries, museums, art galleries, and universities opened in the thirty years following 1851. In keeping with the overwhelmingly British ethnic origin of most immigrants to Australia, these institutions dispensed a distinctly British culture, though a remote and provincial version.

On the negative side, the large numbers of Asians in the goldfields — in Victoria in 1857, one adult male in seven was Chinese — sparked bitter racial prejudice. Scholars date the "white Australia policy" (discussed below) to whites' hostility toward and resentment and fear of the Chinese. Although Americans numbered only about five thousand in Victoria and Asians forty thousand, Americans — with their California gold-rush experience, aggressive ways, and "democratic" frontier outlook — exercised an influence on Australian society far out of proportion to their numbers. On the U.S. Fourth of July holiday in 1852, 1854, and 1857, anti-Chinese riots occurred in the goldfields of Victoria.

"Colored peoples" (as nonwhites were called in Australia) adapted more easily than the British to the warm climate and worked for lower wages. Thus they proved essential to the country's economic development in the nineteenth century. Chinese and Japanese built the railroads and ran the market gardens near, and the shops in, the towns. Filipinos and Pacific Islanders labored in the sugar-cane fields. Afghanis and their camels controlled the carrying trade in some areas. But fear that colored labor would lower living standards and undermine Australia's distinctly British culture triumphed. The Commonwealth Immigration Restriction Act of 1901 closed immigration to Asians and established the "white Australia policy," which remained on the books until the 1970s.

The Shaping of a Government and a National Identity

In 1850 the British Parliament passed the Australian Colonies Government Act, which allowed the four most populous colonies — New South Wales, Tasmania, Victoria, and South Australia — to establish colonial legislatures, determine voting rights, and frame their own constitutions. By 1859 all but one colony was self-governing. The provincial parliament of South Australia was probably the most democratic in the world, in that it was elected by universal manhood suffrage (that is, by all adult males) and by secret ballot. Other colonies soon adopted the secret ballot. In 1902 Australia became one of the first countries in the world to give women the vote.

The Commonwealth of Australia came into existence on January 1, 1901. From the British model, Australia adopted the parliamentary form of government in which a cabinet is responsible to the House of Com-

The "Life of Emigration" Puzzle Some of the advertising designed to attract people to move to Australia was aimed at children. The 38-piece wooden puzzle depicts the life of a family moving from Britain to Australia, from their departure to clearing ground and sheering sheep. It dates to about 1840. (Photograph Courtesy of the State Library of South Australia, S.A. Memory website)

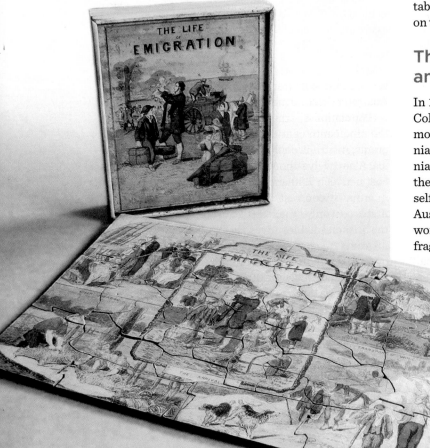

mons. From the American system, Australia took the concept of decentralized government, whereby the states and the federal government share power.

The New Countries from a Comparative Perspective

☐ How and why did the new countries treated in this chapter develop differently?

Looked at from the perspective of world history, the new countries of the Americas and Australia had much in common. All of them began as European colonies. All had indigenous populations who suffered from the arrival of Europeans. For all of them the nineteenth century was a period of nation building, and all had achieved self-rule by the end of the century. In all cases the languages of the colonial powers — English, French, Spanish, and Portuguese — became the languages of government after independence. All the new nations provided European financiers with investment opportunities, not only in the expansion of agricultural enterprises, but also in mines, transportation, and manufacturing. And by the end of the nineteenth century they all had become connected to the rest of the world through global trade. Another global current they all felt was nationalism, which in these countries meant mass identification with the country rather than with an ancient people and its language. All at one time or another allowed or encouraged immigration, and many had also imported slaves from Africa. Discrimination on the basis of ethnic origin and race was pervasive in all of them.

Despite so many similarities, the countries covered in this chapter were already very different by 1914. By then the United States had become one of the half-dozen richest and most powerful countries in the world. That could not be said of any of the others. While the United States had built a strong industrial base, the economies of most of the other countries were still predominantly agricultural. While the three English-speaking countries had established strong democratic traditions, most of the countries of Latin America were controlled by narrow elites or military strongmen, with much of the population excluded from the political process. Of the countries of Latin America, only Argentina, with its temperate climate, fertile prairies, and large influx of European immigrants approached the prosperity of the United States, Canada, or Australia.

What accounts for these differences in outcomes? That the three countries that began as British colonies ended up as stable democracies strongly suggests that their common origins mattered. Even though they obtained independence in different ways, the British tradition of representative government shaped the politi-cal culture of each of the new states. By the time they achieved independence, their citizens were already accustomed to elections and local self-government. That was not true of former Spanish or Portuguese colonies.

The United States also benefited from its size. That a single country was formed by the original thirteen colonies in North America and preserved through the Civil War gave the United States the advantages of substantial size from the beginning. In addition it had room to expand west into territory with many advantages — a temperate climate, navigable rivers, and abundant arable land and mineral resources. The expansion of the United States was made possible by the willingness of France and Spain to sell it large territories in the early years and its own willingness to aggressively pursue expansion at the expense of the Indians and Mexico. As a consequence of its original size and subsequent expansion, the United States became the largest of the new countries in population. The only country that had more land was Canada, and much of Canada's land was too far north for agriculture. If Simón Bolívar had succeeded in forming a union of the Spanish-speaking countries of South America, it might have shared some of the advantages of size that the United States had.

It was important that the United States did not long remain a supplier for Europe of raw materials and basic commodities, but was quick to industrialize. Why did the United States industrialize in the nineteenth century much more rapidly than any of the other countries of the Western Hemisphere or Australia? Many reasons can be suggested. It had ample resources such as iron, coal, petroleum, and fertile land. Also, its government put few obstacles in the way of those who built the great enterprises. At the same time, through much of the nineteenth century, the United States placed high tariffs on imports to discourage the importing of European goods and to foster its own industries. To support these industries it had no difficulty attracting both capital and immigrants from abroad. Furthermore, the United States developed a social structure that rewarded self-made men and encouraged innovation. At the beginning of the nineteenth century the most crucial advances in industrial technology were made in Europe, but by the beginning of the next century they were just as likely to come from the United States. It was the United States that introduced streetcars and Henry Ford who developed the assembly line.

Once the United States became an industrialized country, its economic advantages accelerated; its citizens had more money to buy the products of its industries, its capitalists had more income to invest, educational levels rose as the advantages of learning became clearer, it attracted more immigrants, and so on. Countries further behind could not easily catch up. In other words, by diversifying its economy early, the United States escaped the neocolonial situation.

CONNECTIONS

In the Americas and Australia the century or so leading up to World War I was a time of nation building. Colonial governments were overthrown, new constitutions were written, settlement was extended, slavery was ended, and immigrants were welcomed. On the eve of World War I, there was reason to be optimistic about the future of all these countries. Although wealth was very unevenly distributed, in most of them it was not hard to point to signs of progress: growing cities, expanding opportunities for education, modern conveniences.

World War I, the topic of the next chapter, affected these countries in a variety of ways. Those most deeply involved were Canada and Australia, which followed Britain into the war in 1914 and sent hundreds of thousands of men to fight (over 600,000 from Canada and over 300,000 from Australia), losing many in some of the bloodiest battles of the war. The United States did not join the war until 1917, but quickly mobilized several million men and in 1918 began sending soldiers and materials in huge numbers. Even countries that maintained neutrality, as all the Latin American countries other than Brazil did, felt the economic impact of the war, especially the increased demand for food and manufactured goods. For them, the war had a positive side. How the war was started, expanded, and finally concluded are the topics of the next chapter.

☐ CHAPTER REVIEW

☐ **Why and how did the Spanish and Portuguese colonies of North and South America shake off European domination and develop into national states? (p. 812)**

In Latin America dissatisfaction with Spanish colonial rule grew over the course of the eighteenth century, both on the part of the Indians and mestizos and on the part of the Creoles of European ancestry who resented the privileges granted those from Spain. The wars of independence that lasted from 1806 to 1825 ended colonial rule but also led to fragmentation of Latin America into more than a dozen separate countries. Frequently, military dictators gained political power. Many Indians and mestizos worked on haciendas, often constrained by debt peonage. Many of the large plantations produced basic commodities for the international market, dominated by foreign powers.

☐ **How did the United States build a large but unified nation? (p. 824)**

The United States was the first of the European colonies in the New World to gain its independence, and it remained a step ahead during the nineteenth century both in attracting immigrants and in industrializing. After achieving independence from British rule, settlers in the United States pushed relentlessly across the continent to fulfill their "manifest destiny," making their homes on land taken from Native Americans. Eventually, the industrializing North and the agricultural South came into conflict over extending slavery into new territories. The North's victory in the bloody Civil War assured the permanence of the Union, but

KEY TERMS

Creoles (p. 812)	Confederacy (p. 829)
peninsulares (p. 812)	confederation (p. 833)
neocolonialism (p. 819)	Botany Bay (p. 835)
haciendas (p. 819)	New South Wales (p. 835)
peons (p. 821)	exclusionists (p. 836)
manifest destiny (p. 825)	emancipists (p. 836)
Treaty of Guadalupe Hidalgo (p. 825)	

the racial inequality that had been at the core of slavery remained, and blacks continued to face discrimination. Domestic matters preoccupied the United States through most of the nineteenth century, as the country subdued the continent, tied it together with railroads, and built gigantic steel, oil, textile, food-processing, and automobile industries. Nationalist sentiment grew, and with it discrimination against immigrants.

☐ **What geographical, economic, and political conditions shaped the development of Canada? (p. 833)**

Canada's political system was shaped by the emergence of the United States to its south. Many English loyalists fled to Canada during the American Revolution, and they and other Canadians were wary about U.S. intentions. Britain, not wanting to repeat its experience with its earlier American colonies, gradually extended home rule in Canada. Adopting the British model of cabinet government and utilizing rich natural resources and immigrant labor, the provinces of Canada formed a strong federation with close economic ties to the United States. French Canadians, however, were never entirely satisfied with their situation as a minority.

☐ What circumstances shaped the development of Australia? (p. 834)

Australia is much farther from Britain than North America is, and it was colonized later. The first European settlers were forcibly transported to Australia as convicts, but by the mid-nineteenth century Australia was attracting large numbers of Irish and English immigrants and smaller numbers from other countries. As in the United States and Canada, the discovery of gold quickened the pace of immigration. Because of Australia's dry climate, agriculture concentrated on sheep raising and wheat farming. After 1850 Australia was largely self-governing, and in 1901 it established itself as a commonwealth, adopting a parliamentary system from the British and a decentralized form of government from the United States.

☐ How and why did the new countries treated in this chapter develop differently? (p. 839)

Of all the new countries of the Americas and Australia, only the United States had become a great power by 1914. Like the other countries that had begun as British colonies, the United States developed a stable democracy based on representative government. Political stability aided its rapid industrialization, which was also fostered by its rich endowment of natural resources and its ability to attract capital and immigrants. By the beginning of the twentieth century many of the countries of Latin America, by contrast, seemed trapped in neocolonial systems that kept much of their population poor.

SUGGESTED READING

Bayly, C. A. *The Birth of the Modern World*. 2003. Useful for viewing the countries of the Americas in the context of global developments.

Bender, Thomas. *A Nation Among Nations: America's Place in World History*. 2006. Shows that key events in American history are best seen in global context.

Berlin, Ira. *Many Thousands Gone: The First Two Centuries of Slavery in North America*. 1998. An excellent study that shows how varied slavery was in different times and places.

Burkholder, Mark A., and Lyman Johnson. *Colonial Latin America*, 6th ed. 2007. A broad, comprehensive survey of Latin American history in the colonial period.

Fernandez-Armesto, Felipe. *The Americas: A Hemispheric History*. 2003. Provocative and engagingly written.

Foner, Eric. *Reconstruction: America's Unfinished Revolution, 1863–1877*. 1988. A lucidly written social history that gives attention to the role of former slaves in remaking their world.

Howe, Irving. *World of Our Fathers*. 1976. A brilliant account of the lives of Jews and other immigrants in American cities.

Hughes, Robert. *The Fatal Shore*. 1987. A beautifully written account of the origins of Australia as a penal colony, drawing on diaries and letters.

Lesser, Jeffrey. *Negotiating National Identity: Immigrants, Minorities, and the Struggle for Ethnicity in Brazil*. 1999. A broad-ranging social history.

Macintyre, Stuart. *A Concise History of Australia*. 2009. A masterful work by an Australian historian.

Morton, Desmond. *A Short History of Canada*, 6th ed. 2006. A well-written popular history.

Rodriguez O., J. E. *The Independence of Spanish America*. 1998. An up-to-date treatment focusing on nation building.

Stampp, K. M. *America in 1857: A Nation on the Brink*. 1990. The best comprehensive treatment of the pre–Civil War years.

Terrill, Ross. *The Australians*. 1987. An appreciation of the Australian people and the society they made, from the first settlers to the present.

White, Richard. *"It's Your Misfortune and None of My Own": A History of the American West*. 1991. Includes environmental, urban, ethnic, and women's history, as well as the more familiar story.

NOTES

1. See B. Keen and M. Wasserman, *A Short History of Latin America* (Boston: Houghton Mifflin, 1980), pp. 109–115.
2. M. Burkholder and D. S. Chandler, *From Impotence to Authority: The Spanish Crown and the American Audiencias, 1687–1808* (Columbia: University of Missouri Press, 1977), p. 145.
3. Quoted in J. Lynch, *The Spanish-American Revolutions, 1808–1826* (New York: Norton, 1973), p. 18.
4. Simón Bolívar, *The Hope of the Universe*, trans. J. L. Salcedo-Bastardo (Paris: Unesco, 1983), p. 105. Copyright © 1983 UNESCO for the English translation. Used by permission of UNESCO.
5. Gary E. Moulton, ed., *The Papers of Chief John Ross*, vol. 1, 1807–1839 (Norman: University of Oklahoma Press, 1985).
6. H. G. Gutman, *The Black Family in Slavery and Freedom, 1750–1925* (New York: Random House, 1977).
7. See J. Winch, *A Gentleman of Color: The Life of James Forten* (New York: Oxford University Press, 2002), passim.
8. Quoted in S. E. Morison, *The Oxford History of the American People* (New York: Oxford University Press, 1965), p. 654.
9. Quoted in R. Hughes, *The Fatal Shore* (New York: Knopf, 1987), p. 66.

For practice quizzes and other study tools, visit the **Online Study Guide** at bedfordstmartins.com/mckayworld.

For primary sources from this period, see *Sources of World Societies*, **Second Edition**.

For Web sites, images, and documents related to topics in this chapter, visit **Make History** at bedfordstmartins.com/mckayworld.

• **Senegalese Soldier** A *tirailleur* (literally, "skirmisher") from French West Africa who fought in Europe during the Great War. Across the bottom of this post card image from the era, the soldier proclaimed his loyalty with the phrase "Glory to the Greater France," meaning France and its colonies. Note the two German *pickelhaube* (spike helmets) he wears on his head. (Private Collection/Archives Charmet/The Bridgeman Art Library)

28

In the summer of 1914 the nations of Europe went willingly to war. They believed they had no other choice. Both peoples and governments confidently expected a short war leading to a decisive victory. Such a war, they believed, would "clear the air," and then European society could go on as before. They were wrong. The First World War was long, indecisive, and tremendously destructive. It quickly degenerated into a senseless military stalemate lasting four years. To the shell-shocked generation of survivors, it became simply the Great War.

World War and Revolution
1914–1929

In the midst of the war, in March 1917, the war-weary Russian people rebelled against their tsar, Nicholas II, forcing him to abdicate. Moderate reformists established a provisional government, but made the fatal decision to continue the war against Germany. In November Vladimir Lenin and his communist Bolshevik party staged a second revolution, promising an end to the war. The Germans forced on the Russians a harsh peace, but for Lenin this was a small price to pay for the establishment of the first communist state in history. Few then could have realized how profoundly this event would shape the remainder of the twentieth century.

When the victorious allies, led by Great Britain, France, and the United States, gathered in Paris in 1919 to write the peace, they were well-aware of the importance of their decisions. Some came to Paris seeking revenge, some came looking for the spoils of war, and others promoted nationalist causes or sought an idealistic end to war. The process was massive and complex and in the end, few left Paris satisfied with the results. The peace and prosperity the delegates had so earnestly sought lasted barely a decade.   •

The First World War, 1914–1918

□ How did Europe's system of alliances contribute to the outbreak of World War I, and how did the conflict become a global war?

The Home Front

□ How did total war impact the home fronts of the major combatants?

The Russian Revolution

□ What factors led to the Russian Revolution, and what was its outcome?

The War's Consequences

□ What were the global consequences of the First World War?

The Search for Peace and Political Stability, 1919–1929

□ How did leaders deal with the political dimensions of uncertainty and try to re-establish peace and prosperity in the interwar years?

The Age of Anxiety

□ In what ways were the anxieties of the postwar world expressed or heightened by revolutionary ideas in modern thought, art, and science and new forms of communication?

The First World War, 1914–1918

□ How did Europe's system of alliances contribute to the outbreak of World War I, and how did the conflict become a global war?

The First World War clearly marked a great break in the course of world history. The war accelerated the growth of nationalism in Asia (see Chapter 29), and it consolidated America's position as a global power. Yet the war's greatest impact was on Europe. Drawn into war by a complicated system of alliances, the Allied and Central Powers soon found themselves in a prolonged and destructive war. Imperialism would further expand the conflict into the Middle East, Africa, and Asia, making this a global war of unprecedented scope. The young soldiers who went to war believed in the pre-1914 world of order, progress, and patriotism. Then, in soldier and writer Erich Remarque's words, the "first bombardment showed us our mistake, and under it the world as they had taught it to us broke in pieces."

MAP 28.1 European Alliances at the Outbreak of World War I, 1914 By the time war broke out, Europe was divided into two opposing alliances; the Triple Entente of Britain, France, and Russia, and the Triple Alliance of Germany, Austria-Hungary, and Italy. Italy switched sides and joined the Entente in 1915.

The Bismarckian System of Alliances

The Franco-Prussian War (see page 729) and the unification of Germany opened a new era in international relations. By 1871 France was defeated and Bismarck had made Prussia-Germany the most powerful nation in Europe. Bismarck declared Germany a "satisfied" power, having no territorial ambitions within Europe and desiring only peace.

But how to preserve the peace? Bismarck's first concern was to keep France diplomatically isolated and without military allies. His second concern was the threat to peace posed by the conflicting interests of Austria-Hungary and Russia, particularly in the Balkans, where the Ottoman Empire was losing its grip, leaving a power vacuum. To avoid Germany's being dragged into a great war between the two rival empires, Bismarck devised an alliance system to restrain both Russia and Austria-Hungary, to prevent conflict between them, and to isolate a hostile France.

Bismarck's balancing efforts infuriated Russian nationalists, leading Bismarck to conclude a defensive military alliance with Austria against Russia in 1879. Motivated by tensions with France, Italy joined Germany and Austria to form the Triple Alliance in 1882.

Bismarck's foreign policy accomplishments after 1871 were impressive, but his alliance system broke down in the 1890s. For two decades he maintained good relations with Britain and Italy while encouraging France in Africa but keeping France isolated in Europe. In 1890 the new emperor William II forced Bismarck to resign. William then refused to renew Bismarck's nonaggression pact with Russia, by which both states promised neutrality if the other was attacked. This prompted France to court Russia, offering loans, arms, and friendship. As a result, continental Europe was divided into two rival blocs (Map 28.1).

Great Britain's foreign policy became increasingly crucial. After 1891 Britain was the only uncommitted Great Power. Many Germans and some Britons felt that the racially related Germanic and Anglo-Saxon peoples were natural allies. However, the good relations that had prevailed between Prussia and Great Britain since the mid-eighteenth century gave way after 1890 to a bitter Anglo-German rivalry.

There were several reasons for this development. Commercial rivalry between Germany and Great Brit-

ain in world markets and Germany's pursuit of colonies unsettled the British. Above all, Germany's decision in 1900 to expand greatly its battle fleet challenged Britain's long-standing naval supremacy. This decision coincided with the South African War (see page 761) between the British and the Afrikaners, which revealed widespread anti-British feeling around the world. Thus British leaders prudently set about shoring up their exposed position with alliances and agreements. Britain improved its relations with the United States, concluded an alliance with Japan in 1902, and in the Anglo-French Entente of 1904 settled all outstanding colonial disputes with France.

Frustrated by Britain's closer relationship with France, Germany's leaders decided to test the entente's strength. Rather than accept the typical territorial payoff of imperial competition—a slice of French jungle somewhere in Africa or a port in Morocco—in return for French primacy in Morocco, in 1905 the Germans insisted on an international conference on the whole Moroccan question. Germany's crude bullying

MAP 28.2 The Balkans, 1878–1914 The Ottoman Empire suffered large territorial losses after the Congress of Berlin in 1878, but remained a power in the Balkans. By 1914 ethnic boundaries that did not follow political boundaries had formed, and Serbian national aspirations threatened Austria-Hungary.

forced France and Britain closer together, and Germany left the conference empty-handed.

The Moroccan crisis was something of a diplomatic revolution. Britain, France, Russia, and even the United States began to view Germany as a potential threat. At the same time, German leaders began to suspect sinister plots to encircle Germany and block its development as a world power. In 1907 Russia, battered by its disastrous war with Japan and the 1905 revolution, agreed to settle its territorial quarrels with Great Britain in Persia and Central Asia and signed the Anglo-Russian Agreement. Thus the treaty served as a catalyst for the **Triple Entente**, the alliance of Great Britain, France, and Russia in the First World War (see Map 28.1).

Germany's decision to add an enormously expensive fleet of big-gun battleships to its already expanding navy also heightened tensions. German nationalists saw a large navy as the legitimate mark of a great world power. But British leaders considered it a military challenge that forced them to spend the "People's Budget" (see page 743) on battleships rather than on social welfare. By 1909 Britain was psychologically, if not officially, in the Franco-Russian camp. Europe's leading nations were divided into two hostile blocs, both ill-prepared to deal with upheaval in the Balkans.

The Outbreak of War

In the early twentieth century a Balkans war seemed inevitable. The reason was simple: nationalism was destroying the Ottoman Empire in Europe and threatening to break up the Austro-Hungarian Empire. Western intervention in 1878 had forced the Ottoman Empire to cede most of its territory in Europe, but it retained important Balkan holdings (Map 28.2).

By 1903 Balkan nationalism was asserting itself again. Serbia led the way, becoming openly hostile to both Austria-Hungary and the Ottoman Empire. The Slavic Serbs looked to Slavic Russia for support of their national aspirations. In 1908, to block Serbian ex-

• **Triple Entente** The alliance of Great Britain, France, and Russia in the First World War.

Nationalist Opposition in the Balkans This band of well-armed and determined guerrillas from northern Albania was typical of groups fighting against Ottoman rule in the Balkans. Balkan nationalists succeeded in driving the Ottoman Turks out of most of Europe, but their victory increased tensions with Austria-Hungary and among the Great Powers. (Roger-Viollet/Getty Images)

pansion, Austria formally annexed Bosnia and Herzegovina, with their large Serbian, Croatian, and Muslim populations. Serbia erupted in rage but could do nothing without support from its ally Russia.

Then two nationalist wars, the First and Second Balkan Wars in 1912 and 1913, finally destroyed the centuries-long Ottoman presence in Europe (see Map 28.2). This sudden but long-awaited event elated the Balkan nationalists and dismayed Austria-Hungary's multinational leaders. The former hoped and the latter feared that Austria might next be broken apart.

Within this tense context, Archduke Francis Ferdinand, heir to the Austro-Hungarian throne, and his wife, Sophie, were assassinated by Serbian revolutionaries on June 28, 1914, during a state visit to the Bosnian capital of Sarajevo. Austria-Hungary's leaders held Serbia responsible and presented Serbia with an unconditional ultimatum on July 23, including demands that amounted to Austrian control of the Serbian state. When Serbia replied moderately but evasively, Austria began to mobilize and declared war on Serbia on July 28.

Of prime importance in Austria-Hungary's fateful decision was Germany's unconditional support. Emperor William II and his chancellor, Theobald von Bethmann-Hollweg, realized that war between Austria and Russia was likely, for Russia could not stand by and watch the Serbs be crushed. Yet Bethmann-Hollweg hoped that while Russia (and its ally France) would go to war, Great Britain would remain neutral.

Military plans and timetables, rather than diplomacy, soon began to dictate policy. On July 28, as Austrian armies bombarded Belgrade, Tsar Nicholas II ordered a partial mobilization against Austria-Hungary, but almost immediately found this was impossible. Russia had assumed a war with both Austria and Germany, and it could not mobilize against one without mobilizing against the other. Therefore, on July 29 Russia ordered full mobilization and in effect declared general war. The German general staff had also prepared for a two-front war. Its Schlieffen plan called for first knocking out France with a lightning attack through neutral Belgium to capture Paris before turning on Russia. On August 3 German armies invaded Belgium. Great Britain declared war on Germany the following day. In each country the great majority of the population rallied

The Schlieffen Plan

- - - Planned German offensive
→ Actual German offensive
▢ Neutral nations

GREAT BRITAIN
NETHERLANDS
BELGIUM
Brussels
GERMANY
Rhine R.
LUX.
Reims
Metz
Paris
Seine R.
Marne R.
FRANCE
0   100   200 mi.
0   100   200 km
SWITZ.

Triple Entente and allies
Central Powers and allies
Greatest extent of territory gained by Germany-Austria
German submarine war zone
Neutral nations
Farthest advance by Central Powers on date marked
Farthest advance by Entente Powers on date marked
British naval blockade
✦ Major battle

0   200   400 miles
0   200   400 kilometers

NORWAY
SWEDEN
FINLAND
Helsinki
Petrograd (St. Petersburg)
ESTONIA
LATVIA
Riga
COURLAND
LITHUANIA
Vilnius
Masurian Lakes 1914
E. PRUSSIA
RUSSIA
Moscow
Farthest Russian advance, 1914
Jutland 1916
DENMARK
Kiel
GERMANY
Berlin
Tannenberg 1914
Warsaw
Brest-Litovsk
Armistice line, December 1917
Treaty of Brest-Litovsk, March 1918
KINGDOM OF POLAND (Russia)
Kiev
March 1918
GREAT BRITAIN
Lusitania 1915
London
NETHERLANDS
BELGIUM
Armistice line, November 1918
LUXEMBOURG
ALSACE-LORRAINE
BELARUS
GALICIA
Dnieper R.
May 1915
Western front
SWITZERLAND
Aug. 1917
Caporetto 1917
AUSTRIA-HUNGARY
Vienna
Budapest
Bordeaux
FRANCE
Mar. 1918
Italian front
Po R.
TRANSYLVANIA
Black Sea
March 1918
Caspian Sea
SPAIN
Corsica
Elba
ITALY
Rome
Adriatic Sea
Sarajevo
SERBIA
MONTENEGRO
ROMANIA
Bucharest
Danube R.
BULGARIA
Constantinople
Nov. 1917
Mar. 1918
PERSIA
Balearic Is.
Sardinia
ALBANIA
1917-1918
1916
1915
Dardanelles
Gallipoli 1915
OTTOMAN EMPIRE
Middle Eastern front
IRAQ
Al Kut 1915 1916 1917
Baghdad
Basra
ALGERIA (Fr.)
Tunis
TUNISIA (Fr.)
Sicily
Malta
Balkan front
GREECE
Crete
Oct. 1918
SYRIA
Damascus
Al Aqabah 1917
Mediterranean Sea
LIBYA (It.)
EGYPT (Gr. Br.)
Cyprus
Red Sea

The Western Front

NETHERLANDS
Dover
Ostend
FLANDERS
Ghent
Antwerp
Louvain
Liège
Cologne
Ypres
Calais
Brussels
BELGIUM
Coblenz
Armistice line, November 1918
Arras
ARDENNES
LUX.
GERMANY
St. Quentin
Amiens
Somme
Sedan
ARGONNE FOREST
Compiègne
Belleau Wood
Reims
Verdun
St. Mihiel
LORRAINE
Marne I
Paris
Marne II
Chateau-Thierry
Châlons-sur-Marne
Nancy
Strasbourg
ALSACE
Epinal
FRANCE
Mulhouse
Basel
SWITZ.
English Channel

0   25   50 miles
0   25   50 kilometers

Germany, 1914
Greatest extent of territory gained by Germany, Sept. 1914
Front at beginning of 1915
German offensive, Summer 1918
✦ Major battle

MAP 28.3 The First World War in Europe
The trench war on the western front was concentrated in Belgium and northern France (inset), while the war in the east encompassed an enormous territory.

to defend its nation and enthusiastically embraced war in August 1914. Patriotic nationalism brought unity in the short run.

Stalemate and Slaughter

When the Germans invaded Belgium in August 1914, everyone believed the war would be short: "The boys will be home by Christmas." The Belgian army defended its homeland, however, and then fell back to join a rapidly landed British army corps near the Franco-Belgian border. Instead of quickly capturing Paris in a vast encircling movement, by the end of August German soldiers were advancing along an enormous front in the scorching summer heat. On September 6 the French attacked a gap in the German line at the Battle of the Marne. For three days, France threw everything into the attack. At one point, the French government desperately requisitioned all the taxis of Paris to rush reserves to the troops at the front. Finally, the Germans fell back. France had been miraculously saved (Map 28.3).

The two stalled armies now dug in behind rows of trenches, mines, and barbed wire to protect themselves from machine-gun fire. Eventually an unbroken line of parallel trenches stretched over four hundred miles from the Belgian coast to the Swiss frontier. By November 1914 the slaughter on the western front had begun in earnest. Ceaseless shelling by heavy artillery supposedly "softened up" the enemy in a given area. Then young soldiers went "over the top" of the trenches in frontal attacks on the enemy's line.

German writer Erich Remarque, who fought on the western front, described a typical attack in his great novel *All Quiet on the Western Front* (1929):

> We see men living with their skulls blown open; we see soldiers run with their two feet cut off. . . . Still the little piece of convulsed earth in which we lie is held. We have yielded no more than a few hundred yards of it as a prize to the enemy. But on every yard there lies a dead man.

The human cost of **trench warfare** was staggering; territorial gains were minuscule. The massive French and British offensives during 1915 never gained more than three miles of blood-soaked earth from the enemy. In the Battle of the Somme in the summer of 1916, the British and French gained an insignificant 125 square miles at the cost of 600,000 dead or wounded, and the Germans lost 500,000 men. In that same year the unsuccessful German campaign against Verdun cost 700,000 lives on both sides. British poet Siegfried Sassoon (1886–1967) wrote of the Somme offensive, "I am staring at a sunlit picture of Hell." (See "Viewpoints: Poetry of the Great War," page 850.) The year 1917 was equally terrible.

On the eastern front, the slaughter did not degenerate into suicidal trench warfare. With the outbreak of war, the "Russian steamroller" immediately moved into eastern Germany but suffered appalling losses against the Germans at the Battles of Tannenberg and the Masurian Lakes in August and September 1914 (see Map 28.3). With the help of German forces, the Austrians reversed the Russian advances of 1914 and forced the Russians to retreat deep into their own territory in the 1915 eastern campaign. A staggering 2.5 million Russians were killed, wounded, or taken prisoner.

These changing tides of victory and hopes of territorial gains brought neutral countries into the war. Italy, a member of the Triple Alliance since 1882, had declared its neutrality in 1914 on the grounds that Austria had launched a war of aggression. Then, in May 1915 Italy joined the Triple Entente of Great Britain, France, and Russia in return for promises of Austrian territory. In October 1914 the Ottoman Empire joined with Austria and Germany, by then known as the Central Powers. The following September Bulgaria followed the Ottoman Empire's lead in order to settle old scores with Serbia.

The War Becomes Global

In late 1914 the Ottoman Turks joined forces with Germany and Austria-Hungary. The Young Turks (see page 770) were pro-German because the Germans had helped reform the Ottoman armies before the war and had built important railroads, like the one to Baghdad. Alliance with Germany permitted the Turks to renounce the limitations on Ottoman sovereignty that the Europeans had imposed in the nineteenth century and also to settle old scores with Russia, the Turks' historic enemy.

The entry of the Ottoman Turks pulled the entire Middle East into the war and made it truly a global conflict. While Russia attacked the Ottomans in the Caucasus, the British protected their rule in Egypt. In 1915, at the Battle of Gallipoli, British forces tried to take the Dardanelles and Constantinople from the Ottoman Turks but were badly defeated. Casualties were high on both sides and included thousands of Australians and New Zealanders. Deep loyalty to the mother country led Australia to send 329,000 men and vast economic aid to Britain during the war. Over 100,000 New Zealanders also served in the war, almost a tenth of New Zealand's entire population, and they suffered a 58 percent casualty rate — one of the highest of any country in the war. Nearly 4,000 native New Zealand Maori soldiers also fought at Gallipoli and on

---

• **trench warfare** Fighting behind rows of trenches, mines, and barbed wire; used in World War I with a staggering cost in lives and minimal gains in territory.

Viewpoints

Poetry of the Great War

• *Some of the finest and most memorable literature and poetry of the twentieth century came from the generation who experienced the Great War. These are three of the most famous poems of the Great War, all written by soldiers during the war. Rupert Brooks's "The Soldier" is the most famous of a series of sonnets he wrote in 1914. Brooks died on April 23, 1915, at the age of twenty-seven while traveling with the British Mediterranean Expeditionary Force to Gallipoli. John McCrae, a Canadian doctor, published "In Flanders Fields" in December 1915. He died of pneumonia while serving at a Canadian field hospital in northern France on January 28, 1918. British poet Wilfred Owen wrote "Dulce et Decorum Est" in 1917. He was killed in battle a week before the armistice on November 4, 1918.*

Rupert Brooks, "The Soldier"

If I should die, think only this of me:
    That there's some corner of a foreign field
That is for ever England. There shall be
    In that rich earth a richer dust concealed;
A dust whom England bore, shaped, made aware,
    Gave, once, her flowers to love, her ways to roam,
A body of England's, breathing English air,
    Washed by the rivers, blest by suns of home.

And think this heart, all evil shed away,
    A pulse in the eternal mind, no less
        Gives somewhere back the thoughts by England given;
Her sights and sounds; dreams happy as her day;
    And laughter, learnt of friends; and gentleness,
        In hearts at peace, under an English heaven.

John McCrae, "In Flanders Fields"

In Flanders fields the poppies blow
    Between the crosses, row on row,
    That mark our place; and in the sky
    The larks, still bravely singing, fly
Scarce heard amid the guns below.

We are the Dead. Short days ago
We lived, felt dawn, saw sunset glow,
    Loved and were loved, and now we lie
        In Flanders Fields.

Take up our quarrel with the foe:
To you from falling hands we throw
    The torch; be yours to hold it high.
    If ye break faith, with us who die
We shall not sleep, though poppies grow
        In Flanders Fields.

Wilfred Owen, "Dulce et Decorum Est"

Bent double, like old beggars under sacks,
Knock-kneed, coughing like hags, we cursed through sludge,
Till on the haunting flares we turned our backs
And towards our distant rest began to trudge.
Men marched asleep. Many had lost their boots
But limped on, blood-shod. All went lame; all blind;
Drunk with fatigue, deaf even to the hoots
Of gas shells dropping softly behind.

Gas! Gas! Quick, boys!—An ecstasy of fumbling,
Fitting the clumsy helmets just in time;
But someone still was yelling out and stumbling,
And floundering like a man in fire or lime . . .
Dim, through the misty panes and thick green light,
As under a green sea, I saw him drowning.

In all my dreams, before my helpless sight,
He plunges at me, guttering, choking, drowning.

If in some smothering dreams you too could pace
Behind the wagon that we flung him in,
And watch the white eyes writhing in his face,
His hanging face, like a devil's sick of sin;
If you could hear, at every jolt, the blood
Come gargling from the froth-corrupted lungs,
Obscene as cancer, bitter as the cud
Of vile, incurable sores on innocent tongues—
My friend, you would not tell with such high zest
To children ardent for some desperate glory,
The old Lie: Dulce et decorum est [It is sweet and fitting
    to die]
Pro patria mori. [For one's country.]

Source: Jon Silkin, ed., *The Penguin Book of First World War Poetry*, 2d ed. revised (New York: Penguin Putnam, 1996): pp. 81–82, 85, 192–193.

QUESTIONS FOR ANALYSIS

1. Which of these poems would you describe as the most idealistic and patriotic?

2. What do you think explains the obvious antiwar nature of Owen's poem compared to the poems of Brooks and McCrae?

Henri de Groux, *The Assault, Verdun* An eerie portrayal by Belgian artist Henri de Groux (1867–1930) of French troops moving forward in a thick haze of smoke and perhaps clouds of diphosgene, a poisonous gas first used by the Germans at Verdun on June 22, 1916. (Musée des Deux Guerres Mondiales, Paris/The Bridgeman Art Library)

the western front. A highly decorated New Zealand infantryman named Ormond Burton, who served in Gallipoli and then in France, later observed that "somewhere between the landing at Anzac [a cove on the peninsula of Gallipoli] and the end of the battle of the Somme, New Zealand very definitely became a nation."[1]

The British were more successful at inciting the Arabs to revolt against their Turkish overlords. The foremost Arab leader was Hussein ibn-Ali (1856–1931), who governed much of the Ottoman Empire's territory along the Red Sea, an area known as the Hejaz (see Map 29.1, page 880). In 1915 Hussein won vague British commitments for an independent Arab kingdom. The next year he revolted against the Turks, proclaiming himself king of the Arabs. He joined forces with the British under T. E. Lawrence, who in 1917 led Arab tribesmen and Indian soldiers in a successful guerrilla war against the Turks on the Arabian peninsula. In the Ottoman province of Iraq, Britain occupied Basra in 1914 and captured Baghdad in 1917. In 1918 British armies totally smashed the old Ottoman state, drawing

primarily on imperial forces from Egypt, India, Australia, and New Zealand. Thus war brought revolutionary change to the Middle East (see pages 881–889).

Japan, allied with the British since 1902, used the war as an opportunity to seize Germany's holdings on the Shandong (Shantung) Peninsula and in 1915 forced China to accept Japanese control of Shandong and southern Manchuria. China had declared its neutrality in 1914, and these actions infuriated Chinese patriots and heightened long-standing tensions between China and Japan.

War also spread to colonies in Africa and East Asia. Instead of revolting as the Germans hoped, French and British colonial subjects generally supported the allied powers. Colonized peoples provided critical supplies and fought in Europe and in the Ottoman Empire. They also helped local British and French commanders seize Germany's colonies around the globe. More than a million Africans and Asians served in the various armies of the warring powers, with more than double that number serving as porters to carry equipment. Some of the

> **"**We black African soldiers were very sorrowful about the white man's war. . . . The reason for war was never disclosed to any soldier. . . . We just fought and fought until we got exhausted and died.**"**
>
> **INFANTRYMAN KANDE KAMARA**

most famous and bravest of these colonial troops were the Senegalese Tirailleurs (colonial riflemen). Drawn from Senegal and French West Africa, over 140,000 fought on the western front, and 31,000 of them died there.

Many of these men joined up to get clothes (uniforms), food, and money for enlisting. Others did so because colonial recruiters promised them better lives when they returned home. Most were illiterate and had no idea of why they were going or what they would experience. As one West African infantryman, Kande Kamara, later wrote:

We black African soldiers were very sorrowful about the white man's war. . . . I didn't really care who was right — whether it was the French or the Germans — I went to fight with the French army and that was all I knew. The reason for war was never disclosed to any soldier. . . . We just fought and fought until we got exhausted and died.[2]

The war had a profound impact on these colonial troops. Fighting against and killing Europeans destroyed the impression, encouraged in the colonies, that the Europeans were superhuman. New concepts like nationalism and individual freedoms — ideals for which the Europeans were supposedly fighting — were carried home to become rallying cries for future liberation struggles.

Another crucial development in the expanding conflict came in April 1917 when the United States declared war on Germany. American intervention grew out of the war at sea and sympathy for the Triple Entente. At the beginning of the war Britain and France

Indian Soldiers Convalescing in England Over 130,000 Indian soldiers served on the Western Front during the Great War, mostly during the first year of battle before being transferred to the Middle East to fight at Gallipoli and in the Mesopotamian campaign. Wounded Indian troops convalesced at the Royal Pavilion at Brighton, a former royal residence built in a faux-Oriental style that drew on several elements of Indian and Islamic architecture. In this posed piece, one of a series of photos of the Indian "martial races" distributed as postcards and used for slide-show lectures, some men sit playing cards, while others watch. Such photos reassured British and Indians alike that Britain took good care of its loyal imperial soldiers. (Royal Pavilion, Museums & Libraries, Brighton & Hove, photo ID 742)

established a naval blockade to strangle the Central Powers. No neutral cargo ship was permitted to sail to Germany. In early 1915 Germany launched a counterblockade using the new and murderously effective submarine. In May a German submarine sank the British passenger liner *Lusitania*. More than a thousand people, including 139 U.S. citizens died. President Woodrow Wilson protested vigorously. Germany was forced to restrict its submarine warfare for almost two years, or face almost certain war with the United States.

Early in 1917 the German military command—confident that improved submarines could starve Britain into submission before the United States could come to its rescue—resumed unrestricted submarine warfare. This was a reckless gamble, and the United States declared war on Germany. The United States eventually tipped the balance in favor of the Triple Entente and its allies.

The Home Front

☐ How did total war impact the home fronts of the major combatants?

The war's impact on civilians was no less massive than on the men crouched in the trenches. Total war mobilized entire populations, led to increased state power, and promoted social equality. It also led to dissent and a growing antiwar movement.

Mobilizing for Total War

In August 1914 most Europeans greeted the outbreak of hostilities enthusiastically, believing that their own nation was in the right and defending itself from aggression. Yet by mid-October generals and politicians had begun to realize that victory would require more than patriotism. Combatant countries desperately needed men and weapons. Change had to come, and fast, to keep the war machine from sputtering to a stop.

The change came through national unity governments that began to plan and control economic and social life in order to wage **total war**. Governments imposed rationing, price and wage controls, and even restrictions on workers' freedom of movement. These total war economies involved entire populations, blurring the old distinction between soldiers on the battlefield and civilians at home. (See "Listening to the Past: The Experience of War," page 854.) The ability of central governments to manage and control highly complicated economies increased and strengthened their powers, often along socialist lines.

Germany went furthest in developing a planned economy to wage total war. As soon as war began, the

Hair for the War Effort Blockaded and cut off from overseas supplies, Germany mobilized effectively to find substitutes at home. This poster calls on German women—especially young women with long, flowing tresses—to donate their hair, which was used to make rope. Children were organized by their teachers into garbage brigades to collect every scrap of useful material. (akg-images)

Jewish industrialist Walter Rathenau convinced the German government to set up the War Raw Materials Board to ration and distribute raw materials. Under Rathenau's direction, every useful material from foreign oil to barnyard manure was inventoried and rationed. Moreover, the board launched successful attempts to produce substitutes, such as synthetic rubber and synthetic nitrates, for scarce war supplies. Food was also rationed.

Following the terrible Battles of Verdun and the Somme in 1916, military leaders forced the Reichstag to accept the Auxiliary Service Law, which required all males between seventeen and sixty to work only at jobs considered critical to the war effort. Women also

---

• **total war** Practiced by countries fighting in World War I, a war in which the government plans and controls all aspects of economic and social life in order to make the greatest possible military effort.

Listening to the Past

The Experience of War

World War I was a total war: it enlisted the efforts of male and female adults and children, both at home and on the battle-field. It was a terrifying and painful experience for all those involved, not the romantic endeavor it was purported to be. The documents below offer two different wartime experiences. The first is from a letter written by a German soldier fighting in the trenches. The second is from the diary of a Viennese woman. As you read both passages, think about the different ways war and its consequences were made real for these two people.

A German Soldier Writes from the Trenches, March 1915

" *Souchez, March 11th, 1915*

"So fare you well, for we must now be parting," so run the first lines of a soldier-song which we often sang through the streets of the capital. These words are truer than ever now, and these lines are to bid farewell to you, to all my nearest and dearest, to all who wish me well or ill, and to all that I value and prize.

Our regiment has been transferred to this dangerous spot, Souchez. No end of blood has already flowed down this hill. A week ago the 142nd attacked and took four trenches from the French. It is to hold these trenches that we have been brought here. There is something uncanny about this hill-position. Already, times without number, other battalions of our regiment have been ordered here in support, and each time the company came back with a loss of twenty, thirty or more men. In the days when we had to stick it out here before, we had 22 killed and 27 wounded. Shells roar, bullets whistle; no dugouts, or very bad ones; mud, clay, filth, shell-holes so deep that one could bathe in them.

This letter has been interrupted no end of times. Shells began to pitch close to us—great English 12-inch ones—and we had to take refuge in a cellar. One such shell struck the next house and buried four men, who were got out from the ruins horribly mutilated. I saw them and it was ghastly!

Everybody must be prepared now for death in some form or other. Two cemeteries have been made up here, the losses have been so great. I ought not to write that to you, but I do so all the same, because the newspapers have probably given you quite a different impression. They tell only of our gains and say nothing about the blood that has been shed, of the cries of agony that never cease. The newspaper doesn't give any description either of *how* the "heroes" are laid to rest, though it talks about "heroes' graves" and writes poems and such-like about them. Certainly in Lens I have attended funeral-parades where a number of dead were buried in one large grave with pomp and circumstance. But up here it is pitiful the way one throws the dead bodies out of the trench and lets them lie there, or scatters dirt over the remains of those which have been torn to pieces by shells.

I look upon death and call upon life. I have not accomplished much in my short life, which has been chiefly occupied with study. I have commended my soul to the Lord God. It bears His seal and is altogether His. Now I am free to dare anything. My future life belongs to God, my present one to the Fatherland, and I myself still possess happiness and strength. "

A Viennese Woman Remembers Home Front Life

" Ten dekagrammes [3½ ounces] of horse-flesh per head are to be given out to-day for the week. The cavalry horses held in reserve by the military authorities are being slaughtered for lack of fodder, and the people of Vienna are for a change to get a few mouthfuls of meat of which they have so long been deprived. Horse-flesh! I should like to know whether my instinc-tive repugnance to horse-flesh as food is personal, or whether my dislike is shared by many other housewives. My loathing of it is based, I believe, not on a physical but on a psychological prejudice.

I overcame my repugnance, rebuked myself for being sentimental, and left the house. A soft, steady rain was falling,

worked in war factories, mines, and steel mills. Thus in Germany total war led to history's first "totalitar-ian" society.

As mature liberal democracies, France, Great Brit-ain, and the United States were much less authori-tarian in August 1914 than autocratic Russia, Ger-many, and Austria-Hungary. France and Great Britain also tended to mobilize economically for total war less rapidly and less completely than Germany, as they could import materials from their colonies and from the United States. When it became apparent that the war was not going to end quickly, however, the western allies all began to pass laws that gave their govern-ments sweeping powers over all areas of the nation's daily life — including industrial and agricultural pro-duction, censorship, education, health and welfare, the curtailment of civil liberties, labor, and foreign aliens.

In June 1915, for example, a serious shortage of shells led the British to establish a Ministry of Muni-tions that organized private industry to produce for the

A ration coupon used in the German city of Eisenberg showing Germans waiting in line for their meager rations. (akg-images)

from which I tried to protect myself with galoshes, waterproof, and umbrella. As I left the house before seven o'clock and the meat distribution did not begin until nine o'clock, I hoped to get well to the front of the queue.

No sooner had I reached the neighbourhood of the big market hall than I was instructed by the police to take a certain direction. I estimated the crowd waiting here for a meagre midday meal at two thousand at least. Hundreds of women had spent the night here in order to be among the first and make sure of getting their bit of meat. Many had brought with them improvised seats—a little box or a bucket turned upside down. No one seemed to mind the rain, although many were already wet through. They passed the time chattering, and the theme was the familiar one: What have you had to eat? What are you going to eat? One could scent an atmosphere of mistrust in these conversations: they were all careful not to say too much or to betray anything that might get them into trouble.

At length the sale began. Slowly, infinitely slowly, we moved forward. The most determined, who had spent the night outside the gates of the hall, displayed their booty to the waiting crowd: a ragged, quite freshly slaughtered piece of meat with the characteristic yellow fat. [Others] alarmed those standing at the back by telling them that there was only a very small supply of meat and that not half the people waiting would get a share of it. The crowd became very uneasy and impatient, and before the police on guard could prevent it, those standing in front organized an attack on the hall which the salesmen inside were powerless to repel. Everyone seized whatever he could lay his hands on, and in a few moments all the eatables had vanished. In the confusion stands were overturned, and the police forced back the aggressors and closed the gates. The crowds waiting outside, many of whom had been there all night and were soaked through, angrily demanded their due, whereupon the mounted police made a little charge, provoking a wild panic and much screaming and cursing. At length I reached home, depressed and disgusted, with a broken umbrella and only one galosh.

We housewives have during the last four years grown accustomed to standing in queues; we have also grown accustomed to being obliged to go home with empty hands and still emptier stomachs. Only very rarely do those who are sent away disappointed give cause for police intervention. On the other hand, it happens more and more frequently that one of the pale, tired women who have been waiting for hours collapses from exhaustion. The turbulent scenes which occurred to-day inside and outside the large market hall seemed to me perfectly natural. In my dejected mood the patient apathy with which we housewives endure seemed to me blameworthy and incomprehensible. **"**

Sources: Alfons Ankenbrand, in *German Students' War Letters*, ed. A. F. Wedd (London: Methuen, 1929), pp. 72–73; *Blockade: The Diary of an Austrian Middle-Class Woman*, 1914–1924, trans. Winifred Ray (New York: Ray Long & Richard Smith, 1932), pp. 63–68.

QUESTIONS FOR ANALYSIS

1. What is the soldier's view of the war? Would you characterize it as an optimistic or pessimistic letter?

2. What similarities and differences do you see in the experience of the Viennese woman as compared to the soldier's experience?

3. Why does the Viennese woman describe the housewives as "blameworthy" or "incomprehensible"?

war, controlled profits, allocated labor, fixed wage rates, and settled labor disputes. By December 1916 the British economy was largely planned and regulated directly by the state. The Espionage Act of June 1917 and the Sedition Act of May 1918 allowed the United States government to keeps groups like labor unions, political parties, and ethnic organizations under surveillance. Welfare systems of various kinds were also adopted in most of the belligerent countries. Many of these laws were revoked at war's end. Still, they set precedents and would be turned to again in response to the economic depressions of the 1920s and 1930s and World War II.

The Social Impact

The social impact of total war was no less profound than the economic impact, though again there were important national variations. The military's insatiable needs—nearly every belligerent power resorted to conscription to put soldiers in the field—created a

> " I am going into a munitions factory to make shells. The job will not be as well paid as domestic service . . . but it will be my bit, and every time you fire your gun you can remember I am helping to make the shells. "

PARLOR MAID TO HER BOYFRIEND LEAVING FOR THE FRONT

tremendous demand for workers. This situation — seldom, if ever, seen before 1914 — brought about momentous changes.

One such change was greater power and prestige for labor unions. Unions cooperated with war governments in return for real participation in important decisions. This entry of labor leaders into policymaking councils paralleled the entry of socialist leaders into the war governments.

Women's roles also changed dramatically. In every country, large numbers of women left home and domestic service to work in industry, transportation, and offices. As one former parlor maid is reported to have told her boyfriend as he prepared to leave for France:

> While you are at the front firing shells, I am going into a munitions factory to make shells. The job will not be as well paid as domestic service, it will not be as comfortable as domestic service; it will be much harder work, but it will be my bit, and every time you fire your gun you can remember I am helping to make the shells.[3]

Moreover, women became highly visible — not only as munitions workers but as bank tellers, mail carriers, even police officers. Women also served as nurses and doctors at the front. (See "Individuals in Society: Vera Brittain," page 857.) In general, the war greatly expanded the range of women's activities and changed attitudes toward women. Although most women were quickly let go and their jobs given back to the returning soldiers, their many-sided war effort caused Britain, Germany, and Austria to grant them the right to vote immediately after the war.

Recent scholarship has shown, however, that traditional views of gender — of male roles and female roles — remained remarkably resilient and that there was a significant conservative backlash in the postwar years. Even as the war progressed, many men, particularly soldiers, grew increasingly hostile toward women. Some were angry at mothers, wives, and girlfriends for urging them to enlist and fight in the horrible war. Suggestive posters of scantily clad women were used to remind men of the rewards they would receive for enlisting and fighting, while soldiers with wives and girlfriends back home grew increasingly convinced that they were cheating on them. Others worried that factory or farm jobs had been taken by women and that they would have no work when they returned home. Men were also concerned that if women received the vote at war's end, they would vote themselves into power. These concerns are reflected in a letter from Private G. F. Wilby, serving in East Africa, to his fiancée in London, Ethel Baxter, in August 1918:

> Whatever you do, don't go in Munitions or anything in that line — just fill a Woman's position and remain a woman. . . . I want to return and find the same loveable little woman that I left behind — not a coarse thing more of a man than a woman.[4]

War promoted social equality, blurring class distinctions and lessening the gap between rich and poor. Greater equality was reflected in full employment, rationing according to physical needs, and a sharing of hardships. Society became more uniform and more egalitarian, in spite of some war profiteering.

Growing Political Tensions

During the war's first two years many soldiers and civilians supported their governments. Belief in a just cause and patriotic nationalism united peoples behind their various national leaders. Each government employed censorship and propaganda to maintain popular support.

By spring 1916, however, people were beginning to crack under the strain of total war. In April Irish nationalists in Dublin unsuccessfully tried to take advantage of this situation and rose up against British rule in the Easter Rebellion. Strikes and protest marches over inadequate food flared up on every home front. Besides the massive mutiny of Russian soldiers in 1917 that supported the revolution, nearly half of the French infantry divisions mutinied for two months after the army suffered enormous losses in the Second Battle of the Aisne in April 1917.

The Central Powers experienced the most strain. In October 1916 a young socialist assassinated Austria's chief minister. Conflicts among nationalities grew, and both Czech and Yugoslav leaders demanded autonomous democratic states for their peoples. The strain of total war was also evident in Germany. By 1917 national political unity was collapsing and prewar social conflicts re-emerging. A coalition of socialists and Catholics in the Reichstag called for a compromise "peace without annexations or reparations." Conservatives and military leaders found such a peace unthinkable. Thus militaristic Germany, like its ally Austria-Hungary and its enemy France, began to crack in 1917. But it was Russia that collapsed first and saved the Central Powers — for a time.

Vera Brittain

ALTHOUGH THE GREAT WAR UPENDED MILLIONS of lives, it struck Europe's young people with the greatest force. For Vera Brittain (1893–1970), as for so many in her generation, the war became life's defining experience, which she captured forever in her famous autobiography, *Testament of Youth* (1933).

Brittain grew up in a wealthy business family in northern England, bristling at small-town conventions and discrimination against women. Very close to her brother Edward, two years her junior, Brittain read voraciously and dreamed of being a successful writer. Finishing boarding school and beating down her father's objections, she prepared for Oxford's rigorous entry exams and won a scholarship to its women's college. Brittain also fell in love with Roland Leighton, an equally brilliant student from a literary family and her brother's best friend. All three, along with two more close friends, Victor Richardson and Geoffrey Thurlow, confidently prepared to enter Oxford in late 1914.

When war suddenly approached in July 1914, Brittain shared with millions of Europeans a thrilling surge of patriotic support for her government, a prowar enthusiasm she later played down in her published writings. She wrote in her diary that her "great fear" was that England would declare its neutrality and commit the "grossest treachery" toward France.* She seconded Roland's decision to enlist, agreeing with her sweetheart's glamorous view of war as "very ennobling and very beautiful." Later, exchanging anxious letters in 1915 with Roland in France, Vera began to see the conflict in personal, human terms. She wondered if any victory or defeat could be worth Roland's life.

Struggling to quell her doubts, Brittain redoubled her commitment to England's cause and volunteered as an army nurse. For the next three years she served with distinction in military hospitals in London, Malta, and northern France, repeatedly torn between the vision of noble sacrifice and the reality of human tragedy. She lost her sexual inhibitions caring for mangled male bodies, and she longed to consummate her love with Roland. Awaiting his return on leave on Christmas Day in 1915, she was greeted instead with a telegram: Roland had been killed two days before.

*Quoted in the excellent study by P. Berry and M. Bostridge, *Vera Brittain: A Life* (London: Virago Press, 2001), p. 59; additional quotations are from pp. 80 and 136.

Roland's death was the first of the devastating blows that eventually overwhelmed Brittain's idealistic patriotism. In 1917, first Geoffrey and then Victor died from gruesome wounds. In early 1918, as the last great German offensive covered the floors of her war-zone hospital with maimed and dying German prisoners, the bone-weary Vera felt a common humanity and saw only more victims. A few weeks later brother Edward—her last hope—died in action. When the war ended, she was, she said, a "complete automaton," with "my deepest emotions paralyzed if not dead."

Returning to Oxford and finishing her studies, Brittain gradually recovered. She formed a deep, restorative friendship with another talented woman writer, Winifred Holtby, published novels and articles, and became a leader in the feminist campaign for gender equality. She also married and had children. But her wartime memories were always there. Finally, Brittain succeeded in coming to grips with them in *Testament of Youth*, her powerful antiwar autobiography. The unflinching narrative spoke to the experiences of an entire generation and became a runaway bestseller. Above all, perhaps, Brittain captured the ambivalent, contradictory character of the war, when millions of young people found excitement, courage, and common purpose but succeeded only in destroying their lives with their superhuman efforts and futile sacrifices. Becoming ever more committed to pacifism, Brittain opposed England's entry into World War II.

QUESTIONS FOR ANALYSIS

1. What were Brittain's initial feelings toward the war? How and why did they change as the conflict continued?

2. Why did Brittain volunteer as a nurse, as many women did? How might wartime nursing have influenced women of her generation?

3. In portraying the ambivalent, contradictory character of World War I for Europe's youth, was Brittain describing the contradictory character of all modern warfare?

• **Vera Brittain was marked forever by her wartime experiences.** (Vera Brittain Archive, William Ready Division of Archives and Research Collections, McMaster University Library)

N'OUBLIONS JAMAIS!

(Mary Evans Picture Library/The Image Works)

□ Picturing the Past

"Never Forget!" This 1915 French poster with a passionate headline dramatizes Germany's brutal invasion of Belgium in 1914. The "rape of Belgium" featured prominently—and effectively—in anti-German propaganda.

ANALYZING THE IMAGE How is neutral Belgium personified? What do you think the artist's purpose was?

CONNECTIONS How did governments use propaganda and other means to unite people for the war effort?

The Russian Revolution

□ What factors led to the Russian Revolution, and what was its outcome?

The 1917 Russian Revolution, directly related to the Great War, had a significance far beyond the wartime agonies of a single Allied or Central Power nation. The Russian Revolution opened a new era with a radically new prototype of state and society.

The Fall of Imperial Russia

Like their allies and their enemies, Russians had embraced war with patriotic enthusiasm in 1914. At the Winter Palace, while kneeling throngs sang "God Save the Tsar," Tsar Nicholas II (r. 1894–1917) vowed never to make peace as long as the enemy stood on Russian soil. For a moment Russia was united, but soon the war began to take its toll.

Unprecedented artillery barrages quickly exhausted Russia's supplies of shells and ammunition, and better-equipped German armies inflicted terrible losses — one and a half million casualties and nearly another million captured in 1915 alone. Russian soldiers were sent to the front without rifles; they were told to find their arms among the dead. The Duma, Russia's lower house of the parliament, and local governments led the effort toward full mobilization on the home front. These efforts improved the military situation, but overall Russia mobilized less effectively for total war than did the other warring nations.

The great problem was leadership. Under the constitution resulting from the 1905 revolution (see page 731), the tsar retained complete control over the bureaucracy and the army. A kindly, slightly dull-witted man, Nicholas distrusted the moderate Duma and rejected popular involvement. As a result, the Duma, the educated middle classes, and the masses became increasingly critical of the tsar's leadership. In response,

Nicholas announced in September 1915 that he was traveling to the front to lead Russia's armies.

His departure was a fatal turning point. His German-born wife, Tsarina Alexandra, took control of the government. She tried to rule absolutely in her husband's absence with an uneducated Siberian preacher, Rasputin, as her most trusted adviser. Rasputin gained her trust by claiming that he could stop the bleeding of her hemophiliac son Alexis, heir to the throne. In this atmosphere of unreality, the government slid steadily toward revolution.

In a desperate attempt to right the situation, three members of the high aristocracy murdered Rasputin in December 1916. In the meantime, food shortages worsened and morale declined. On March 8 a women's bread march in Petrograd (formerly St. Petersburg) started riots, which spread throughout the city. The tsar ordered troops to restore order, but discipline broke down, and the soldiers joined the revolutionary crowd. The Duma declared a provisional government on March 12, 1917. Three days later, Nicholas abdicated.

The Provisional Government

The **March Revolution** was joyfully accepted throughout the country. After generations of authoritarianism, the provisional government established equality before the law; freedom of religion, speech, and assembly; the right of unions to organize and strike; and other classic liberal measures. But both moderate socialist and liberal leaders of the provisional government rejected social revolution. A new government formed in May 1917, which included the socialist Alexander Kerensky, refused to confiscate large landholdings and give them to peasants, fearing that such drastic action in the countryside would only complete the disintegration of Russia's peasant army. For the patriotic Kerensky, who became prime minister in July, as for other moderate socialists, the continuation of war was still the all-important national duty.

From its first day, the provisional government had to share power with a formidable rival — the **Petrograd Soviet** (or council) of Workers' and Soldiers' Deputies. Modeled on the revolutionary soviets of 1905, the Petrograd Soviet comprised two to three thousand workers, soldiers, and socialist intellectuals. This counter- or half-government issued its own radical orders, further weakening the provisional government. Most famous of these was Army Order No. 1, issued in March 1917, which stripped officers of their authority and gave power to elected committees of common soldiers.

The order led to a total collapse of army discipline. Peasant soldiers began "voting with their feet," to use Lenin's graphic phrase. They returned to their villages

"The Russian Ruling House" This wartime cartoon captures the ominous, spellbinding power of Rasputin over Tsar Nicholas II and his wife, Alexandra. Rasputin's manipulations disgusted Russian public opinion and contributed to the monarchy's collapse. (Stock Montage)

to get a share of the land, which peasants were simply seizing from landowners in a great agrarian upheaval. Liberty was turning into anarchy in the summer of 1917, offering an unparalleled opportunity for the most radical and most talented of Russia's many socialist leaders, Vladimir Ilyich Lenin (1870–1924).

- **March Revolution** The first phase of the Russian Revolution of 1917, in which unplanned uprisings led to the abdication of the tsar and the establishment of a transitional democratic government that was then overthrown in November by Lenin and the Bolsheviks.
- **Petrograd Soviet** A counter-government that was a huge, fluctuating mass meeting of two to three thousand workers, soldiers, and socialist intellectuals.

Lenin and His Supporters Vladimir Lenin (center) with two other major figures of the Russian Revolution, Joseph Stalin (left) and Mikhail Kalinin (right). After Lenin's death in January 1924, Stalin moved to seize power and ruled the Soviet Union until his death in 1953. Kalinin was one of Lenin's earliest followers and then supported Stalin in the power struggle after Lenin's death. He was one of the few "old Bolsheviks" to survive Stalin's purges and received a large state funeral following his death from natural causes in 1946. (Gamma-Keystone/Getty Images)

Lenin and the Bolshevik Revolution

Born into the middle class, Lenin became an enemy of imperial Russia when his older brother was executed for plotting to kill the tsar in 1887. As a law student Lenin studied Marxist doctrines with religious ferocity. Exiled to Siberia for three years because of socialist agitation, after his release Lenin lived in western Europe for seventeen years and developed his own revolutionary interpretations of Marxist thought.

Three interrelated ideas were central for Lenin. First, he stressed that only violent revolution could destroy capitalism. Second, Lenin believed that a socialist revolution was possible even in a country like Russia, where capitalism was not fully developed. There the industrial working class was small, but the poor peasants were also potential revolutionaries.

Third, Lenin believed that at a given moment revolution was determined more by human leadership than by vast historical laws. He called for a highly disciplined workers' party, strictly controlled by a dedicated elite of intellectuals and full-time revolutionaries like him. This elite would not stop until revolution brought it to power.

Lenin's ideas did not go unchallenged by other Russian Marxists. At a Social Democratic Labor Party congress in London in 1903, Lenin demanded a small, disciplined, elitist party; his opponents wanted a more democratic party with mass membership. The Russian Marxists split into two rival factions. Lenin's camp was called **Bolsheviks**, or "majority group"; his opponents were Mensheviks, or "minority group."

From exile in neutral Switzerland, Lenin saw the war as a product of imperialistic rivalries and an opportunity for socialist revolution. After the March Revolution of 1917, the German government provided safe passage for Lenin across Germany and back into Russia, hoping he would undermine Russia's sagging war effort. They were not disappointed. Arriving in Petrograd on April 3, Lenin attacked at once. To the great astonishment of the local Bolsheviks, he rejected all cooperation with what he called the "bourgeois" provisional government. His slogans were radical in the extreme: "All power to the soviets"; "All land to the peasants"; "Stop the war now." Lenin was a superb tactician, and throughout the summer the Bolsheviks markedly increased their popular support, while Prime Minister Kerensky's unwavering support for the war lost him all credit with the army, the only force that might have saved him and democratic government in Russia.

In October the Bolsheviks gained a fragile majority in the Petrograd Soviet. It was Lenin's supporter Leon

• **Bolsheviks** The majority group; this was Lenin's camp of the Russian party of Marxist socialism.

Trotsky (1879–1940), an independent radical Marxist and later commander of the Red Army, who brilliantly executed the Bolshevik seizure of power. On November 6 militant Trotsky followers joined with trusted Bolshevik soldiers to seize government buildings and arrest provisional government members. At the congress of soviets a Bolshevik majority then declared that all power had passed to the soviets and named Lenin head of the new government.

The Bolsheviks came to power for three key reasons. First, by late 1917 democracy had given way to anarchy. Second, in Lenin and Trotsky the Bolsheviks had an utterly determined and truly superior leadership. Third, the Bolsheviks appealed to soldiers and urban workers who were exhausted by war and eager for socialism.

Dictatorship and Civil War

The true accomplishment of the Bolsheviks was not taking power but keeping it and conquering the chaos they had helped create. Lenin had the genius to profit from developments over which he and the Bolsheviks had no control. Since summer 1917 an unstoppable peasant revolution had swept across Russia, as peasants divided among themselves the estates of the landlords and the church. Thus Lenin's first law, which supposedly gave land to the peasants, actually merely approved what peasants were already doing. Lenin then met urban workers' greatest demand with a decree in November giving direct control of individual factories to local workers' committees.

The Bolsheviks proclaimed their regime a "provisional workers' and peasants' government," promising that a freely elected Constituent Assembly would draw up a new constitution. But after Bolshevik delegates won fewer than one-fourth of the seats in free elections in November, the Constituent Assembly met for only one day, on January 18, 1918. Bolshevik soldiers acting under Lenin's orders then permanently disbanded it.

Lenin acknowledged that Russia had lost the war with Germany and that the only realistic goal was peace at any price. That price was very high. Germany demanded that the Soviet government give up all its western territories, and a third of old Russia's population was surrendered in the Treaty of Brest-Litovsk (BREHST lih-TAWFSK), signed with Germany in March 1918. With peace, Lenin escaped the disaster of continued war and could pursue his goal of absolute political power for the Bolsheviks — now renamed Communists — within Russia.

The war's end, along with the destruction of the democratically elected Constituent Assembly, revealed Bolshevik rule as dictatorship from the capital. For the next three years "Long live the [democratic] soviets; down with the Bolsheviks" was a popular slogan. Offi-

cers of the old army organized the so-called White opposition to the Bolsheviks in southern Russia, Ukraine, Siberia, and west of Petrograd, and by the summer of 1918 the country was plunged into civil war. The Whites came from many social groups and were united only by their hatred of the Bolsheviks — the Reds. By the end of the year, White armies were on the attack. In October 1919 it appeared they might triumph as they closed in on Lenin's government from three sides. Yet they did not. The Red Army under Trotsky's command captured Vladivostok in October 1922 and that effectively marked the end of the civil war.

Lenin and the Red Army won for several reasons. Strategically, the Bolsheviks controlled the center, while the disunited Whites attacked from the fringes. Moreover, the poorly defined political program of the Whites did not unite all the foes of the Bolsheviks under a progressive democratic banner. Most important, the Communists developed a better army, an army for which the divided Whites were no match.

KEY EVENTS OF THE RUSSIAN REVOLUTION

1914	Russia enters the war
1916–1917	Tsarist government in crisis
March 1917	March Revolution; Duma declares a provisional government; tsar abdicates; Petrograd Soviet issues Army Order No. 1
April 1917	Lenin returns from exile
October 1917	Bolsheviks gain a majority in the Petrograd Soviet
November 7, 1917	Bolsheviks seize power; Lenin named head of new communist government
March 1918	Treaty of Brest-Litovsk; Trotsky becomes head of the Red Army
1918–1922	Civil war
1922	Civil war ends; Lenin and the Bolshevik-Communists take control of Russia

The Russian Civil War, 1917–1922

"You! Have You Volunteered?" A Red Army soldier makes a compelling direct appeal to the ordinary citizen and demands all-out support for the Bolshevik cause in this 1920 poster by Dmitri Moor, a popular Soviet artist. Lenin recognized the importance of visual propaganda in a vast country with limited literacy, and mass-produced posters like this one were everywhere during the civil war of 1918–1922. (Stephen White, University of Glasgow)

The Bolsheviks also mobilized the home front. Establishing **war communism** — the application of the total-war concept to a civil conflict — they seized grain from peasants, introduced rationing, nationalized all banks and industry, and required everyone to work. Although these measures contributed to a breakdown of normal economic activity, they also served to maintain labor discipline and to keep the Red Army supplied.

Revolutionary terror also contributed to the Communist victory. The old tsarist secret police was reestablished as the Cheka, which hunted down and executed thousands of real or supposed foes, including the tsar and his family. During the so-called Red Terror of 1918–1920 the Cheka sowed fear, silenced opposition, and killed tens of thousands of "class enemies."

Finally, foreign military intervention in the civil war ended up helping the Communists. The Allies sent troops to prevent war materiel that they had sent to the provisional government from being captured by the Germans. After the Soviet government nationalized all foreign-owned factories without compensation and refused to pay foreign debts, Western governments began to support White armies. While these efforts did little to help the Whites' cause, they did permit the Communists to appeal to the patriotic nationalism of ethnic Russians.

The War's Consequences

☐ What were the global consequences of the First World War?

In spring 1918 the Germans launched their last major attack against France. It failed, and Germany was defeated. Austria-Hungary and the Ottoman Empire broke apart and ceased to exist. Then, as civil war spread in Russia and as chaos engulfed much of eastern Europe, the victorious Western Allies came together in Paris to establish a lasting peace.

Laboring intensively, the allies soon worked out terms for peace with Germany and for the creation of the peacekeeping League of Nations. The 1919 peace settlement, however, turned out to be a failure. Surely this was the ultimate tragedy of the Great War that cost $332 billion and left 10 million people dead and another 20 million wounded.

The End of the War

Victory over revolutionary Russia temporarily boosted sagging German morale, and in the spring of 1918 the German army under General Ludendorff fell on France once more. For a time German armies pushed forward, coming within thirty-five miles of Paris, but they never broke through. They were stopped in July at the second Battle of the Marne, where 140,000 fresh American soldiers saw action. Adding 2 million men in arms to the war effort by August, the late but massive American intervention decisively tipped the scales in favor of Allied victory.

By September British, French, and American armies were advancing steadily on all fronts. On October 4 the German emperor formed a new, more liberal German government to sue for peace. As negotiations over an armistice dragged on, the frustrated German people rose up. On November 3 sailors in Kiel (keel) mutinied, and throughout northern Germany soldiers and workers established revolutionary councils on the Russian soviet model. Austria-Hungary surrendered to the Allies the same day. With army discipline collapsing, the German emperor abdicated and fled to Holland. Socialist leaders in Berlin proclaimed a German republic on November 9, and agreed to tough Allied terms of surrender. The armistice went into effect on November 11, 1918.

The German Revolution of November 1918 resembled the Russian Revolution of March 1917. In both countries a popular uprising toppled an authoritarian monarchy, and moderate socialists took control of the government. But when Germany's radical socialists tried to seize power, the moderate socialists called on the army to crush the attempted coup. Thus Germany had a political revolution, but without a communist second installment.

Military defeat brought political revolution to Austria-Hungary, as it had to Germany, Russia, and the Ottoman Empire (see pages 879–886). The independent states of Austria, Hungary, Czechoslovakia, and a larger Romania were created out of the Austro-Hungarian Empire (Map 28.4). A greatly expanded Serbian monarchy united the Slavs in the western Balkans and took the name Yugoslavia.

The Treaty of Versailles

The peace conference opened in the Versailles Palace near Paris in January 1919 with seventy delegates from twenty-seven nations. There were great expectations. A young British diplomat later wrote that the victors "were journeying to Paris . . . to found a new order in Europe. We were preparing not Peace only, but Eternal Peace."[5]

This idealism was strengthened by President Wilson's January 1918 peace proposal, the Fourteen Points, which stressed national self-determination and the rights of small countries and called for the creation of the **League of Nations**, a permanent international organization designed to protect member states from aggression and avert future wars.

The real powers at the conference were the United States, Great Britain, and France. Germany and Russia were excluded, and Italy's role was limited. Almost immediately the three Allies began to quarrel. President Wilson insisted that the first order of business be the creation of the League of Nations. Wilson had his way, although prime ministers Lloyd George of Great Britain and especially Georges Clemenceau of France were unenthusiastic. They were primarily concerned with punishing Germany.

The "Big Three" were soon in a stalemate over what do to with Germany. Although personally inclined to make a somewhat moderate peace with Germany, Lloyd George felt pressured for a victory worthy of the sacrifices of total war. As Rudyard Kipling summed up the general British feeling at war's end, the Germans were "a people with the heart of beasts."[6] Clemenceau also wanted revenge and lasting security for France, which, he believed, required the creation of a buffer state between France and Germany, the permanent demili-

tarization of Germany, and vast German reparations. Wilson, supported by Lloyd George, would hear none of this, and by April the conference was deadlocked on the German question.

In the end, Clemenceau agreed to a compromise. He gave up the French demand for a Rhineland buffer state in return for a formal defensive alliance with the United States and Great Britain. Both Wilson and Lloyd George also promised that their countries would come to France's aid if attacked. Thus Clemenceau appeared to win his goal of French security, as Wilson had won his of a permanent international organization.

The **Treaty of Versailles** was the first step toward re-establishing international order. Germany's colonies were given to France, Britain, and Japan as League of Nations mandates. Germany's territorial losses within Europe were minor: Alsace-Lorraine was returned to France, and parts of Germany were ceded to the new Polish state (see Map 28.4). The treaty limited Germany's army to one hundred thousand men and allowed no new military fortifications in the Rhineland.

More harshly, the Allies declared that Germany (with Austria) was responsible for the war and had therefore to pay reparations equal to all civilian damages caused by the war. These much-criticized "war-guilt" and "reparations" clauses expressed inescapable popular demands for German blood. The actual reparations figure was not set, however, and there was the clear possibility that it might be set at a reasonable level when tempers had cooled in the future.

When presented with the treaty, the German government protested vigorously, but there was no alternative. On June 28, 1919, German representatives of the ruling moderate Social Democrats and the Catholic Party signed the treaty.

The Allies concluded separate peace treaties with the other defeated powers — Austria, Hungary, Bulgaria, and Turkey. For the most part these treaties merely ratified the existing situation in east-central Europe following the breakup of the Austro-Hungarian Empire (see Map 28.4). The Ottoman Empire was broken up, and, controversially, Britain and France extended their power in the Middle East.

Despite strong French objections, Hussein ibn-Ali's son Faisal (1885–1933) attended the Versailles Peace Conference, but his efforts to secure Arab independence

- **war communism** The application of the total-war concept to a civil conflict; the Bolsheviks seized grain from peasants, introduced rationing, nationalized all banks and industry, and required everyone to work.
- **League of Nations** A permanent international organization established during the 1919 Paris peace conference to protect member states from aggression and avert future wars.
- **Treaty of Versailles** The 1919 peace settlement that ended World War I; it declared Germany responsible for the war; limited Germany's army to one hundred thousand men, and forced Germany to pay huge reparations.

Boundaries of German, Russian, and Austro-Hungarian Empires in 1914

New and reconstituted nations

Demilitarized or Allied occupation zone

□ Mapping the Past

MAP 28.4 Territorial Changes in Europe After World War I The Great War brought tremendous changes to eastern Europe. Empires were shattered, new nations were established, and a dangerous power vacuum was created by the relatively weak states established between Germany and Soviet Russia.

ANALYZING THE MAP What territory did Germany lose, and to whom? What new independent states were formed from the old Russian empire?

CONNECTIONS How were the principles of national self-determination applied to the redrawing of Europe after the war? Did this theory work out?

came to nothing. President Wilson wanted to give the Arab case serious consideration, but the British and the French were determined to rule Syria, Iraq, and Palestine as League of Nations mandates and to accept only the independence of Hussein's kingdom of Hejaz. Brushing aside Arab opposition, France received Lebanon and Syria. Britain took Iraq and Palestine, which was to include a Jewish national homeland first promised by Britain in 1917 in the Balfour Declaration (see page 882). Officially League of Nations mandates, these Allied acquisitions were one of the most imperialistic elements of the peace settlement. Another was mandating Germany's holdings in China to Japan (see page 894). The mandates system left colonial peoples in the Middle East and Asia bitterly disappointed (see Chapter 29) and demonstrated that the age of Western, and Eastern, imperialism lived on.

American Rejection of the Versailles Treaty

The 1919 peace settlement was not perfect, but for war-shattered Europe it was an acceptable beginning. Germany was punished but not dismembered. A new world organization complemented a traditional defensive alliance of victorious powers. The remaining problems could be worked out in the future. Moreover, Allied leaders wanted a quick settlement for another reason: they detested Lenin and feared his Bolshevik Revolution might spread.

There were, however, two great interrelated obstacles to such peace: Germany and the United States. Plagued by communist uprisings, reactionary plots, and popular disillusionment with losing the war, Germany's moderate socialists and their liberal and Catholic supporters faced an enormous challenge. They needed time (and luck) if they were to establish a peaceful and democratic republic. Progress in this direction required understanding yet firm treatment of Germany by the victorious Western Allies.

In the United States, there was a quick reversion to prewar preferences for isolationism, and the U.S. Senate rejected the treaty. Republican senators led by Henry Cabot Lodge believed that the treaty gave away Congress's constitutional right to declare war. In failing health, Wilson rejected all attempts at compromise and thereby ensured the treaty would never be ratified by the United States in any form and that the United States would never join the League of Nations. Moreover, the Senate refused to ratify Wilson's defensive alliance with France and Great Britain. America turned its back on Europe. Using U.S. action as an excuse, Great Britain also refused to ratify its defensive alliance with France. Betrayed by its allies, France stood alone, and the great hopes of early 1919 had turned to ashes by year's end.

The Search for Peace and Political Stability, 1919–1929

☐ How did leaders deal with the political dimensions of uncertainty and try to re-establish peace and prosperity in the interwar years?

The Versailles settlement had established a shaky truce, not a solid peace, and the pursuit of real and lasting peace in the first half of the interwar years proved difficult for many reasons. Germany hated the Treaty of Versailles. France was fearful and isolated. Britain was undependable, and the United States had turned its back on European problems. Eastern Europe was in ferment, and no one could predict the future of communist Russia. Moreover, the international economic situation was poor and was greatly complicated by war debts and disrupted patterns of trade. Yet for a time, from 1925 to late 1929, it appeared that peace and stability were within reach.

Germany and the Western Powers

Germany held the key to lasting peace, yet all Germans believed that the Treaty of Versailles represented a harsh dictated peace and should be revised or repudiated as soon as possible. Moreover, France and Great Britain disagreed over Germany. By the end of 1919 France wanted to stress the harsh elements in the Treaty of Versailles. Most of the war on the western front had been fought on French soil, and the expected costs of reconstruction, as well as of repaying war debts to the United States, were staggering. Thus the French believed that reparations from Germany were an economic necessity. Large reparation payments could hold Germany down indefinitely, and France would realize its goal of security.

The British soon felt differently. Prewar Germany had been Great Britain's second-best market, and after the war a healthy, prosperous Germany appeared to be essential to the British economy. The British were also suspicious of France's army — the largest in Europe — and the British and French were also at odds over their League of Nations mandates in the Middle East.

While France and Britain drifted in different directions, the Allied reparations commission completed its work. In April 1921 it announced that Germany had to pay the enormous sum of 132 billion gold marks ($33 billion) in annual installments of 2.5 billion gold marks. The young German republic — known as the Weimar Republic — made its first payment in 1921. Then in 1922, wracked by rapid inflation and political assassinations and motivated by hostility and arrogance as well, the Weimar Republic announced its inability to pay more and proposed a reparations moratorium for three years.

The British were willing to accept a moratorium, but the French were not. Led by their prime minister, Raymond Poincaré (1860–1934), they decided they had to either call Germany's bluff or see the entire peace settlement dissolve to France's great disadvantage.

French Occupation of the Ruhr, 1923–1925

"Hands Off the Ruhr" The French occupation of the Ruhr to collect reparations payments raised a storm of patriotic protest in Germany. This anti-French poster of 1923 turns Marianne, the personification of French virtue, into a vicious harpy. (Photo: International Institute of Social History. Collection: Imperial War Museum)

So in January 1923 armies of France and its ally Belgium occupied the Ruhr district, industrial Germany's heartland, creating the most serious international crisis of the 1920s.

Strengthened by a wave of patriotism, the German government ordered the people of the Ruhr to stop working and to nonviolently resist the French occupation. The French responded by sealing off not only the Ruhr but also the entire Rhineland from the rest of Germany, letting in only enough food to prevent starvation.

By the summer of 1923 France and Germany were engaged in a great test of wills. French armies could not collect reparations from striking workers at gun-

point. But French occupation was paralyzing Germany and its economy. Needing to support the striking Ruhr workers and their employers, the German government began to print money to pay its bills. Prices soared, and German money rapidly lost all value. Many retired and middle-class people saw their savings wiped out. Catastrophic inflation cruelly mocked the old middle-class virtues of thrift, caution, and self-reliance. Many Germans felt betrayed. They hated and blamed the Western governments, their own government, big business, the Jews, the workers, and the Communists for their misfortune. The crisis left them psychologically prepared to follow radical right-wing leaders including Adolf Hitler and the new Nazi Party.

In August 1923, as the mark fell and political unrest grew throughout Germany, Gustav Stresemann (1878–1929) became German chancellor. Stresemann adopted a compromising attitude. He called off the peaceful resistance campaign in the Ruhr and in October agreed in principle to pay reparations, but asked for a re-examination of Germany's ability to pay. Poincaré accepted. Thus, after five years of hostility and tension, Germany and France, with the help of the British and the Americans, decided to try compromise and cooperation.

Hope in Foreign Affairs

In 1924 an international committee of financial experts headed by American banker Charles G. Dawes met to re-examine reparations. The resulting **Dawes Plan** (1924) was accepted by France, Germany, and Britain. Germany's yearly reparations were reduced and linked to the level of German economic prosperity. Germany would also receive large loans from the United States to promote German recovery. In short, Germany would get private loans from the United States and pay reparations to France and Britain, thus enabling those countries to repay the large sums they owed the United States.

This circular flow of international payments was complicated and risky, but it worked for a while. Germany experienced a spectacular economic recovery. With continual inflows of American capital, Germany paid about $1.3 billion in reparations in 1927 and 1928, enabling France and Britain to pay the United States. Thus, the Americans belatedly played a part in the general economic settlement that facilitated the worldwide recovery of the late 1920s.

This economic settlement was matched by a political settlement. In 1925 European leaders met in Locarno, Switzerland. Germany and France solemnly pledged to accept their common border, and both Britain and Italy agreed to fight either France or Germany if one invaded the other. Stresemann also agreed to settle boundary disputes with Poland and Czechoslovakia by peaceful means, and France promised those countries military aid if Germany attacked them. For years a "spirit of Locarno" gave Europeans a sense of growing security and stability in international affairs.

Other developments also strengthened hopes for international peace. In 1926 Germany joined the League of Nations, and in 1928 fifteen countries signed the Kellogg-Briand Pact, initiated by French prime minister Aristide Briand and U.S. secretary of state Frank B. Kellogg. The signing states "condemned and renounced war as an instrument of national policy." The pact fostered the cautious optimism of the late 1920s and also encouraged the hope that the United States would accept its international responsibilities.

Hope in Democratic Government

European domestic politics also offered reason to hope. During the Ruhr occupation and the great inflation, Germany's republican government appeared ready to collapse. In 1923 Communists momentarily entered provincial governments, and in November an obscure politician named Adolf Hitler proclaimed a "national socialist revolution" in a Munich beer hall. Hitler's plot to seize government control was poorly organized and easily crushed. Hitler was sentenced to prison, where he outlined his theories and program in his book *Mein Kampf* (My Struggle, 1925). Throughout the 1920s, Hitler's National Socialist Party attracted support from only a few fanatical anti-Semites, ultranationalists, and disgruntled former servicemen.

The moderate businessmen who tended to dominate the various German coalition governments believed that economic prosperity demanded good relations with the Western Powers, and they supported parliamentary government at home. Elections were held regularly, and as the economy boomed, republican democracy appeared to have growing support among a majority of Germans. There were, however, sharp political divisions in the country. Many unrepentant nationalists and monarchists populated the right and the army. Members of Germany's Communist Party received directions from Moscow, and they accused the Social Democrats of betraying the revolution. The working classes were divided politically, but a majority supported the socialist, but nonrevolutionary Social Democrats.

The situation in France was similar to that in Germany. Communists and socialists battled for the workers' support. After 1924 the democratically elected government rested mainly in the hands of moderate coalitions, and business interests were well represented. France's great accomplishment was rapid rebuilding of its war-torn northern region, and good times prevailed until 1930.

Britain, too, faced challenges after 1920. The wartime trend toward greater social equality continued, however, helping maintain social harmony. The great problem was unemployment, which hovered around 12 percent throughout the 1920s. The state provided unemployment benefits and supplemented those payments with subsidized housing, medical aid, and increased old-age pensions. These and other measures kept living standards from seriously declining, defused class tensions, and pointed the way to the welfare state Britain established after World War II.

Relative social harmony was accompanied by the rise of the Labour Party. Committed to moderate, "revisionist" socialism (see page 746), the Labour Party under Ramsay MacDonald (1866–1937) governed the country in 1924 and 1929. Labour moved toward socialism gradually and democratically, so that the middle classes were not overly frightened as the working classes won new benefits.

The British Conservatives under Stanley Baldwin (1867–1947) showed the same compromising spirit on social issues, and Britain experienced only limited social unrest in the 1920s and 1930s. In 1922 Britain granted southern, Catholic Ireland full autonomy after a bitter guerrilla war, thereby removing another source of prewar friction. Thus developments in both international relations and domestic politics gave the leading democracies cause for cautious optimism in the late 1920s.

The Age of Anxiety

☐ In what ways were the anxieties of the postwar world expressed or heightened by revolutionary ideas in modern thought, art, and science and new forms of communication?

When Allied diplomats met in Paris in early 1919 with their optimistic plans for building a lasting peace, most people looked forward to happier times and a return to the familiar prewar terms of peace, prosperity, and progress. These hopes were in vain. The First World War and the Russian Revolution had mangled too many things beyond repair. Great numbers of men and women felt themselves increasingly adrift in an age of anxiety and continual crisis.

- **Dawes Plan** The product of the reparations commission, accepted by Germany, France, and Britain, that reduced Germany's yearly reparations, made payment dependent on German economic prosperity, and granted Germany large loans from the United States to promote recovery.
- *Mein Kampf* Adolf Hitler's autobiography, published in 1925, which also contains Hitler's political ideology.

Uncertainty in Philosophy and Religion

Before 1914 most people in the West still believed in Enlightenment philosophies of progress, reason, and individual rights. At the turn of the century progress was a daily reality, apparent in the rising standard of living, the taming of the city, the spread of political rights to women and workers, and the growth of state-supported social programs. Just as there were laws of science, many thinkers felt, there were laws of society that rational human beings could discover and wisely act on. The German philosopher Friedrich Nietzsche (NEE-chuh; 1844–1900) was particularly influential. In the first of his *Untimely Meditations* (1873), he argued that ever since classical Athens, the West had overemphasized rationality and stifled the passion and animal instinct that drive human activity and true creativity.

Nietzsche went on to question the values of Western society. He believed that reason, democracy, progress, and respectability were outworn social and psychological constructs that suffocated self-realization and excellence. Rejecting religion, Nietzsche claimed that Christianity embodied a "slave morality" that glorified weakness, envy, and mediocrity. Little read during his lifetime, Nietzsche attracted growing attention in the early twentieth century.

The First World War accelerated the revolt against established certainties in philosophy. Logical positivism, often associated with Austrian philosopher Ludwig Wittgenstein (VIT-guhn-shtighn; 1889–1951), rejected most concerns of traditional philosophy — from God's existence to the meaning of happiness — as nonsense, and argued that life must be based on facts and observation. Others looked to **existentialism** for answers. Highly diverse and even contradictory, existential thinkers were loosely united in a search for moral values in a world of anxiety and uncertainty. Often inspired by Nietzsche, they did not believe that a supreme being had established humanity's fundamental nature and had given life its meaning. In the words of the famous French existentialist Jean-Paul Sartre (ZHAWN-pawl SAHR-truh; 1905–1980), human beings simply exist.

The loss of faith in human reason and in continual progress led to a renewed interest in Christianity. After World War I several thinkers and theologians began to revitalize Christian fundamentals. Sometimes

described as Christian existentialists because they shared the loneliness and despair of atheistic existentialists, they stressed human beings' sinful nature, the need for faith, and the mystery of God's forgiveness.

As a result, religion became much more relevant and meaningful than it had been before the war, and intellectuals turned to religion between about 1920 and 1950. Though often of a despairing, existential variety, it was one meaningful answer to terror and anxiety. In the words of a famous Roman Catholic convert, English novelist Graham Greene, "One began to believe in heaven because one believed in hell."[7]

The New Physics

By the late nineteenth century science was one of the main pillars supporting Western society's optimistic and rationalistic worldview. Unchanging natural laws seemed to determine physical processes and permit useful solutions to more and more problems. All this was comforting, especially to people no longer committed to traditional religious beliefs. And all this was challenged by the new physics.

An important first step toward the new physics was the discovery at the end of the nineteenth century that atoms were not stable and unbreakable. Polish-born physicist Marie Curie (1867–1934) and her French husband Pierre (1859–1906) discovered that radium constantly emits subatomic particles and thus does not have a constant atomic weight. Building on this, German physicist Max Planck (1858–1947) showed in 1900 that subatomic energy is emitted in uneven little spurts, which Planck called "quanta," and not in a steady stream, as previously believed.

In 1905 the German-Jewish genius Albert Einstein (1879–1955) further undermined Newtonian physics. His theory of special relativity postulated that time and space are relative to the observer's viewpoint and that only the speed of light is constant for all frames of reference in the universe. In addition, Einstein's theory stated that matter and energy are interchangeable and that even a particle of matter contains enormous levels of potential energy.

The 1920s opened the "heroic age of physics," in the apt words of one of its leading pioneers, Ernest Rutherford (1871–1937). Breakthrough followed breakthrough. In 1919 Rutherford first split the atom. By 1944 seven subatomic particles had been identified, the most important of which was the neutron. The neutron's capacity to pass through other atoms allowed for even more intense experimental bombardment of matter, leading to chain reactions of unbelievable force. The implications of the new theories and discoveries were disturbing to millions of people in the 1920s and 1930s. The new universe was strange and troubling, and, more-

---

• **existentialism** The name given to a highly diverse and even contradictory philosophy that stresses the meaningless of existence and the search for moral values in a world of terror and uncertainty.

• **id, ego, superego** Freudian terms for the primitive, irrational unconscious (id), the rationalizing conscious that mediates what a person can do (ego), and the ingrained moral values, which specify what a person should do (superego).

Unlocking the Power of the Atom
Many of the fanciful visions of science fiction come true in the twentieth century, although not exactly as first imagined. This 1927 cartoon satirizes a professor who has split the atom and has unwittingly destroyed his building and neighborhood in the process. In the Second World War scientists harnessed the atom in bombs and decimated faraway cities and their inhabitants. (Mary Evans Picture Library/The Image Works)

over, science appeared distant from human experience and human problems.

Freudian Psychology

With physics presenting an uncertain universe so unrelated to ordinary human experience, questions about the power and potential of the human mind assumed special significance. The findings and speculations of psychologist Sigmund Freud (1856–1939) were particularly disturbing.

Before Freud, most psychologists assumed that human behavior was the result of rational thinking by the conscious mind. By analyzing dreams and hysteria, Freud developed a very different view of the human psyche. Freud concluded that human behavior was, governed by three parts of the self: the **id**, **ego**, and **superego**. The irrational unconscious, which he called the id, was driven by sexual, aggressive, and pleasure-seeking desires and was locked in constant battle with the mind's two other parts: the rationalizing conscious — the ego — which mediates what a person can do, and ingrained moral values — the superego — which specify what a person should do. Thus, for Freud human behavior was a product of a fragile compromise between instinctual drives and the controls of rational thinking and moral values. The danger for individuals was that unacknowledged drives might overwhelm the control mechanisms, leading to sexual repression, guilt, neurotic fears, and even violence.

Freudian psychology and clinical psychiatry had become an international movement by 1910, but only after 1918 did they receive popular attention. Many interpreted Freud as saying that the first requirement for mental health was an uninhibited sex life. After World War I this popular interpretation reflected and encouraged growing sexual experimentation.

Twentieth-Century Literature

Western literature was also influenced by the general intellectual climate of pessimism, relativism, and alienation. Nineteenth-century novelists had typically written as all-knowing narrators, describing realistic characters in an understandable, if sometimes harsh, society. In the twentieth century many writers adopted the limited, often confused viewpoint of a single individual. Like Freud, these novelists focused on the complexity and irrationality of the human mind.

Some novelists used the stream-of-consciousness technique with its reliance on internal monologues to explore the psyche. The most famous stream-of-consciousness novel is *Ulysses*, published by Irish novelist James Joyce (1882–1941) in 1922. Into an account of a single day in the life of an ordinary man, Joyce weaves an extended ironic parallel between his hero's aimless wanderings through Dublin's streets and pubs and the adventures of Homer's hero Ulysses on his way home from Troy. Abandoning conventional grammar and blending foreign words, puns, bits of knowledge, and scraps of memory together in bewildering confusion, the language of *Ulysses* was intended to mirror modern life itself.

Creative writers rejected the idea of progress; some even described "anti-utopias," nightmare visions of things to come. In 1918 Oswald Spengler (1880–1936) published *The Decline of the West*, in which he argues that Western civilization was in its old age and would soon be conquered by East Asia. Likewise, T. S. Eliot (1888–1965) depicts a world of growing desolation in his famous poem *The Waste Land* (1922). Franz Kafka's (1883–1924) novels *The Trial* (1925) and *The Castle* (1926) portray helpless individuals crushed by inexplicably hostile forces.

Modern Architecture, Art, and Music

Like scientists and intellectuals, creative artists rejected old forms and old values after the war. **Modernism** in architecture, art, and music meant constant experimentation and a search for new kinds of expression.

The United States, with its rapid urban growth and lack of rigid building traditions, pioneered in the new architecture. In the 1890s the Chicago School of architects, led by Louis H. Sullivan (1856–1924), used cheap steel, reinforced concrete, and electric elevators to build skyscrapers and office buildings lacking almost any exterior ornamentation. The buildings of Frank Lloyd Wright (1867–1959), another visionary American architect, were renowned for their sometimes radical design, their creative use of wide varieties of materials, and their appearance of being part of the landscape.

In Europe architectural leadership centered in German-speaking countries. In 1919 Walter Gropius (1883–1969) merged the schools of fine and applied arts at Weimar into a single interdisciplinary school, the Bauhaus. Throughout the 1920s the Bauhaus, with its stress on **functionalism** and good design for everyday life, attracted enthusiastic students from all over the world.

After 1905 art increasingly took on a nonrepresentational, abstract character. New artistic styles grew out of a revolt against French impressionism, which was characterized by an overall feeling, or impression, of light falling on a real-life scene before the artist's eyes, rather than an exact copy of objects. Though individualistic in their styles, "postimpressionists" and "expressionists" were united in their desire to depict unseen inner worlds of emotion and imagination. Artists such as the Dutch expressionist Vincent van Gogh (1853–1890) painted the moving vision of the mind's eye. Paul Gauguin (1848–1903), a French expressionist, moved to the South Pacific, where he found inspiration in Polynesian forms, colors, and legends.

In 1907 in Paris the famous Spanish painter Pablo Picasso (1881–1973), along with other artists, established cubism—an artistic approach concentrated on a complex geometry of zigzagging lines and sharply angled overlapping planes. Since the Renaissance artists had represented objects from a single viewpoint and had created unified human forms. In his first great cubist work, *Les Demoiselles d'Avignon* (1907), Picasso's figures resemble large wooden African masks, presenting a radical new view of reality with a strikingly non-Western depiction of the human form. The influence of Polynesian art on Gauguin and of carved African masks on Picasso reflected the growing importance of non-Western artistic traditions in Europe in the late nineteenth and early twentieth centuries.

About 1910 came the ultimate stage in the development of abstract, nonrepresentational art. Artists such as the Russian-born Wassily Kandinsky (1866–1944) turned away from nature completely. "The observer," said Kandinsky, "must learn to look at [my] pictures . . .

• **modernism** A variety of cultural movements at the end of the nineteenth century and beginning of the twentieth that rebelled against traditional forms and conventions of the past.

• **functionalism** The principle that buildings, like industrial products, should serve the purpose for which they were made as well as possible.

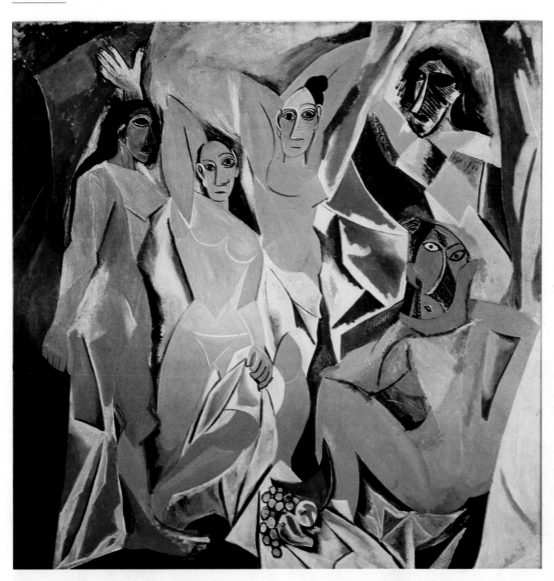

Picasso, *Les Demoiselles d'Avignon* Originating in memories of a brothel scene in Barcelona, this is one of the twentieth century's more influential paintings. Picasso abandoned unified perspective and depicted instead fragmented figures and distorted forms in his search for the magical violence of a pictorial breakthrough. The three faces on either side were inspired by African masks. (Digital image © The Museum of Modern Art/Licensed by Scala/Art Resource, NY/© 2011 Estate of Pablo Picasso/Artists Rights Society [ARS], New York)

as form and color combinations . . . as a representation of mood and not as a representation of *objects*."[8]

Radicalization accelerated after World War I. The most notable new developments were Dadaism and surrealism. Dadaism attacked all accepted standards of art and behavior, delighting in outrageous conduct. After 1924 many Dadaists were attracted to surrealism. Surrealists, such as Salvador Dalí (1904–1989), painted fantastic worlds of wild dreams and complex symbols.

Developments in modern music were strikingly parallel to those in painting. Composers, too, were attracted by the emotional intensity of expressionism. The pulsating, dissonant rhythms and the dancers' earthy representation of lovemaking in the ballet *The Rite of Spring* by composer Igor Stravinsky (1882–1971) practically caused a riot when first performed in Paris in 1913. Likewise, modernism in opera and ballet flourished. Led by Viennese composer Arnold Schönberg (SHUHN-buhrg; 1874–1951), some composers turned their backs on long-established musical conventions. As abstract painters arranged lines and color but did not draw identifiable objects, so modern composers arranged sounds without creating recognizable harmonies. Accustomed to the harmonies of classical and romantic music, audiences generally resisted modern atonal music.

Movies and Radio

Cinema and radio became major industries after World War I, and standardized commercial entertainment began to replace the traditional arts and amusements of people in villages and small towns. Moving pictures were first shown as a popular novelty in naughty peepshows and penny arcades in the 1890s, especially in Paris. The first movie houses, dating from an experiment in Los Angeles in 1902, showed short silent action films.

During the First World War the United States became the dominant force in the rapidly expanding silent-film industry, and Charlie Chaplin (1889–1978), an Englishman working in Hollywood, was unquestionably the king of the "silver screen." In his enormously popular role as a lonely tramp, complete with baggy trousers, battered derby, and an awkward, shuffling walk, Chaplin symbolized the "gay spirit of laughter in a cruel, crazy world."[9] Chaplin also demonstrated that in the hands of a genius the new medium could combine mass entertainment and artistic accomplishment.

Motion pictures also became powerful tools of indoctrination, especially in countries with dictatorial regimes. Lenin encouraged the development of Soviet film making, and beginning in the mid-1920s a series of

The International Appeal of Cinema A movie house in Havana, Cuba, in 1933 showing two American films made in 1932: *El Rey de la Plata* (*Silver Dollar*) starring Edward G. Robinson, and *6 horas de Vida* (*Six Hours to Live*) featuring Warner Baxter. The partially visible poster in the upper right is advertising *El último varon sobre la Tierra* (*The Last Man on Earth*), an American-produced Spanish-language movie staring Raul Roulien, first released in Spain in January 1933. (Image copyright © The Metropolitan Museum of Art, Gift of Arnold H. Crane, 1971(1971.646.12). © Walker Evans Archive The Metropolitan Museum Of Art/Art Resource, NY)

epic films, the most famous of which were directed by Sergei Eisenstein (1898–1948), dramatized the communist view of Russian history. In Germany Hitler turned to a talented woman filmmaker, Leni Riefenstahl (1902–2003), for a masterpiece of documentary propaganda, *The Triumph of the Will*, based on the 1934 Nazi Party rally at Nuremberg. Her film was a brilliant and all-too-powerful depiction of Germany's Nazi rebirth.

Whether foreign or domestic, motion pictures became the main entertainment of the masses worldwide until after the Second World War. Featuring glittering stars such as Ginger Rogers and Fred Astaire and the fanciful cartoons of Mickey Mouse, motion pictures offered ordinary people a temporary escape from the hard realities of international tensions, uncertainty, unemployment, and personal frustrations.

Radio also dominated popular culture after the war. The work of Guglielmo Marconi (1874–1937) in 1901 and the development of the vacuum tube in 1904 permitted the transmission of speech and music. Only in 1920, however, were the first major public broadcasts made in Great Britain and the United States. Every major country quickly established national broadcasting networks. In the United States these were privately owned and financed by advertising, as was LOR Radio Argentina, which became the first formal radio station in the world when it made its first broadcast in August 1920. In Europe, China, Japan, India, and elsewhere the typical pattern was direct government control. By the late 1930s more than three-fourths of the households in both democratic Great Britain and dictatorial Germany had at least one cheap, mass-produced radio.

Like the movies, radio was well suited for political propaganda. Dictators such as Mussolini and Hitler controlled the airwaves and could reach enormous national audiences with their frequent, dramatic speeches. In democratic countries politicians such as President Franklin Roosevelt and Prime Minister Stanley Baldwin effectively used informal "fireside chats" to bolster support.

CONNECTIONS

The Great War has continued to influence global politics and societies more than ninety years after the guns went silent in November 1918. Anyone seeking to understand the origins of many modern world conflicts must study first the intrigues and treaties and the revolutions and upheavals that were associated with this first truly world war.

The war's most obvious consequences were felt in Europe, where three empires collapsed and new states were created out of the ruins. Old European antagonisms and mistrust made the negotiation of fair and just treaties ending the war impossible, despite the best efforts of an outsider, American President Wilson, to make this a war to end all wars. In Chapter 30 we will see how the conflict contributed to a worldwide depression, the rise of totalitarian dictatorships, and a Second World War more global and destructive than the first. In the Middle East the five-hundred-year-old Ottoman Empire came to an end, allowing France and England to carve out mandated territories — including modern Iraq, Palestine/Israel, and Lebanon — that remain flashpoints for violence and political instability in the twenty-first century. Nationalism, the nineteenth-century European ideology of change, took root in Asia, partly driven by Wilson's promise of self-determination. In Chapter 29 the efforts of various nationalist leaders — Atatürk in Turkey, Gandhi in India, Mao Zedong in China, Ho Chi Minh in Vietnam, and others — to throw off colonial domination will be examined. Included there also will be a discussion of how the rise of ultranationalism in Japan led it into World War II and ultimate defeat.

America's entry into the Great War placed it on the world stage, a place it has not relinquished as a superpower in the twentieth and twenty-first centuries. Russia too eventually became a superpower, but this outcome was not so clear in 1919 as its leaders fought for survival in a vicious civil war. By the outbreak of World War II Joseph Stalin had solidified Communist power, and the Soviet Union and the United Sates would play leading roles in the defeat of totalitarianism in Germany and Japan. But at war's end, as explained in Chapter 31, the two superpowers found themselves opponents in a Cold War that lasted for much of the rest of the twentieth century.

□ CHAPTER REVIEW

□ **How did Europe's system of alliances contribute to the outbreak of World War I, and how did the conflict become a global war? (p. 844)**

Following the Franco-Prussian War of 1870–1871, German Chancellor Otto van Bismarck sought to maintain peace in Europe by negotiating a series of alliances among the various nations. When Kaiser William II became German emperor in 1888, he forced Bismarck to resign, refused to renew the Russian-German nonaggression pact, and raised tensions across Europe. He caused France and Russia to join together against the Triple Alliance of Germany, Austria, and Italy, and he also alienated Great Britain, which later joined France and Russia in an alliance known as the Triple Entente. The assassination of the heir to the Austro-Hungarian throne by a Serbian nationalist in 1914 set these alliances in motion and drew the two rival blocs into war. The war in Europe was dominated by trench warfare, and stalemate and slaughter defined both the western and eastern fronts. Imperialistic ties would broaden the war's scope significantly, bringing countries in the Middle East, Asia, and Africa into the conflict.

□ **How did total war impact the home fronts of the major combatants? (p. 853)**

The war caused an administrative revolution born of the need to mobilize entire societies and economies for total war. As a result, government power greatly increased in the West. The war effort's need for workers led to greater social equality, particularly for women who entered the workplace to fill jobs vacated by men away at the front. Labor unions grew and enjoyed greater power and prestige. Thus, even in European countries where a Communist takeover never came close to occurring, society experienced a great revolution, and socialism became a realistic economic blueprint that many countries adopted. Total war also led to increased strain at home and was manifested in strikes and a growing antiwar movement.

□ **What factors led to the Russian Revolution, and what was its outcome? (p. 858)**

After three years of horrible slaughter on the eastern front, the Russian people were tired of the ineffective autocratic rule of Tsar Nicholas II and wanted change. In March 1917 the tsar abdicated, and the reins of government were taken over by a provisional government.

Controlled by moderate social democrats, the provisional government refused to pull Russia out of the war, and the massive waste of Russian lives continued until army discipline completely collapsed in resistance to the war. This opened the way for a second Russian revolution, this one led by Vladimir Lenin and his Communist Bolshevik Party in November 1917. The Bolsheviks established a radical regime, smashed existing capitalist institutions, and stayed in power with a new kind of authoritarian rule that posed a powerful ongoing challenge to Europe and its colonial empires.

□ **What were the global consequences of the First World War? (p. 862)**

The "war to end war" brought not peace but only a fragile truce. Over the protests of the United States, France and Great Britain viewed the Versailles treaty as an opportunity to take revenge on Germany for the war. The treaty denied Germany an empire by taking away its colonies, forced Germany to destroy its army and navy, and demanded exorbitant war reparations. It also redrew the map of Europe, dissolving the Austro-Hungarian and Ottoman Empires. But the Allies failed to maintain their wartime solidarity, and Germany remained unrepentant, setting the stage for World War II. Globally, the European powers refused to extend the right of self-determination to their colonies in the Middle East, Africa, and Asia, and the mandate system created after the war would sow bitter discontent among colonized peoples.

□ **How did leaders deal with the political dimensions of uncertainty and try to re-establish peace and prosperity in the interwar years? (p. 865)**

The death and destruction caused by World War I led to political and economic disruption across Europe in the years following the war. The question of German war reparations left the Allies divided. In the 1920s moderate political leaders replaced the World War I generation and compromised to create an enduring peace and rebuild prewar prosperity. The Dawes Plan was one example of how Europe and America worked to create financial stability in Europe. For a brief period late in the decade they seemed to have succeeded: Germany experienced an economic recovery, France rebuilt its war-torn regions, and Britain's Labour Party expanded social services. Ultimately though, these measures were short-lived.

▢ In what ways were the anxieties of the postwar world expressed or heightened by revolutionary ideas in modern thought, art, and science and new forms of communication? (p. 867)

The horrors of the Great War and, particularly, the turning of new technologies to the slaughter of millions shattered the ideals of the Enlightenment and caused widespread anxiety. Beginning in the interwar years philosophers, artists, and writers portrayed these anxieties in their work — such as existentialism in philosophy, cubism and surrealism in art, functionalism in architecture, literature that explored alienation and relativism, and atonal music. Freudian psychology gained popularity and sought to prove that human behavior was basically irrational, while Einstein's new universe was "relative," containing no absolute objective reality. The new forms of communication — movies and the radio — were initially forms of escape from the world's cares, but soon became powerful tools of indoctrination for modern dictators.

SUGGESTED READING

Andelman, David A. *A Shattered Peace: Versailles 1919 and the Price We Pay Today.* 2007. Clearly written history of the Versailles Peace Conference and how it has shaped world history to the present day.

Camus, Albert. *The Stranger* and *The Plague*, 1942 and 1947. The greatest existential novelist at his unforgettable best.

Ecksteins, Modris. *Rites of Spring: The Great War and the Birth of the Modern Age.* 1989. An imaginative cultural investigation that has won critical acclaim.

Fromkin, David. *Europe's Last Summer: Who Started the Great War?* 2004. Well-argued, compulsively readable discussion of responsibility for the war by a master historian.

Fromkin, David. *A Peace to End All Peace: The Fall of the Ottoman Empire and the Creation of the Modern Middle East*, 2d ed. 2009. A brilliant account of the Middle East in the critical years between 1914 and 1922.

Gay, Peter. *Modernism: The Lure of Heresy.* 2007. A personal perspective on twentieth-century high culture by a leading intellectual and cultural historian.

Gilbert, Martin. *The First World War: A Complete History.* 1994. Comprehensive study in one volume by a major military historian.

Gorham, Deborah. *Vera Brittain: A Feminist Life.* 1996. A major study of Brittain's life.

Issacson, Walter. *Einstein: His Life and Universe.* 2007. Well-received introduction to Einstein's life and work.

Macmillan, Margaret. *Paris, 1919: Six Months That Changed the World.* 2001. A masterful account of the negotiations and the issues at the Paris Peace Conference.

Massie, Raymond. *Nicholas and Alexandra.* 1971. A moving popular biography of Russia's last royal family and the terrible health problem of the heir to the throne.

Reed, John. *Ten Days That Shook the World.* 1919. The classic eyewitness account of the Russian Revolution by a young, pro-Bolshevik American.

Smith, Bernard. *Modernism's History: A Study in Twentieth-Century Thought and Ideas.* 1998. Admirably straightforward with a global perspective.

Wade, Rex. *The Russian Revolution, 1917.* 2000. Comprehensive and accessible history of the revolution.

Young, Louise. *Japan's Total Empire: Manchuria and the Culture of Wartime Imperialism.* 1998. A fascinating pioneering work on Japanese imperialism.

NOTES

1. Quoted in Keith Sinclair, *The Growth of New Zealand Identity, 1890–1980* (Auckland, N.Z.: Longman Paul, 1987), p. 24.
2. Svetlana Palmer and Sarah Wallis, eds., *Intimate Voices from the First World War* (New York: William Morrow, 2003), p. 221.
3. Ethel Alec-Tweedie, *Women and Soldiers*, 2d ed. (London: John Lane, 1918), p. 29.
4. Janet S. K. Watson, "Khaki Girls, VADS, and Tommy's Sisters: Gender and Class in First World War Britain," *The International History Review* 19 (1997): 49.
5. Quoted in H. Nicolson, *Peacemaking 1919* (New York: Grosset & Dunlap Universal Library, 1965), pp. 8, 31–32.
6. Quoted ibid., p. 24.
7. G. Greene, *Another Mexico* (New York: Viking Press, 1939), p. 3.
8. Quoted in A. H. Barr, Jr., *What Is Modern Painting?* 9th ed. (New York: Museum of Modern Art, 1966), p. 25.
9. R. Graves and A. Hodge, *The Long Week End: A Social History of Great Britain, 1918–1939* (New York: Macmillan, 1941), p. 131.

For practice quizzes and other study tools, visit the **Online Study Guide** at bedfordstmartins.com/mckayworld.

For primary sources from this period, see *Sources of World Societies*, **Second Edition**.

For Web sites, images, and documents related to topics in this chapter, visit **Make History** at bedfordstmartins.com/mckayworld.

• **Kasturba Gandhi** Wife of Indian political leader Mohandas Gandhi, she was barely fourteen and he thirteen years old when the marriage took place. Kasturba (1869–1944) supported Gandhi through decades of struggle for Indian independence. Here she spins cotton on a *charkha*, or spinning wheel, part of Gandhi's campaign for Indians to become self-sufficient by making their own cloth and freeing themselves from imported British goods. (© Dinodia Photo Library/The Image Works)

29

Nationalism in Asia
1914–1939

From Asia's perspective the First World War was largely a European civil war that shattered Western imperialism's united front, underscored the West's moral bankruptcy, and convulsed prewar relationships throughout Asia. Most crucially, the war sped the development of modern nationalism in Asia. Before 1914 the nationalist gospel of anti-imperialist political freedom and racial equality had already won converts among Asia's westernized, educated elites. In the 1920s and 1930s it increasingly won the allegiance of the masses. As in nineteenth-century Europe, nationalism in Asia between 1914 and 1939 became a mass movement with potentially awesome power.

The modern nationalism movement was never monolithic. In Asia especially, where the new and often narrow ideology of nationalism was grafted onto old, rich, and complex civilizations, the shape and eventual outcome of nationalist movements varied enormously. Between the outbreak of the First and Second World Wars each Asian country developed a distinctive national movement rooted in its own unique culture and history. Each nation's people created their own national reawakening, which renovated thought and culture as well as politics and economics. And as in Europe, nationalist movements gave rise to conflict both within large, multiethnic states and against other independent states in Asia.

The Asian nationalist movement witnessed the emergence of two of the true giants of the twentieth century. Mohandas Gandhi in India and Mao Zedong in China both drew their support from the peasant masses in the two most populous countries in the world. Gandhi successfully used campaigns of peaceful nonviolent resistance to British colonial rule to gain Indian independence. Mao on the other hand used weapons of war to defeat his opponents and established a modern Communist state. •

The First World War's Impact on Nationalist Trends

□ Why did modern nationalism develop in Asia between the First and Second World Wars, and what was its appeal?

Nationalist Movements in the Middle East

□ How did the collapse of the Ottoman Empire in World War I shape nationalist movements in the Middle East?

Toward Self-Rule in India

□ What role did Gandhi and his campaign of militant nonviolence play in leading India to independence from the British?

Nationalist Struggles in East and Southeast Asia

□ How did nationalism shape political developments in East and Southeast Asia?

The First World War's Impact on Nationalist Trends

□ Why did modern nationalism develop in Asia between the First and Second World Wars, and what was its appeal?

Every Asian national movement sought genuine freedom from foreign imperialism. The First World War profoundly affected these aspirations by altering relations between Asia and Europe. For four years Asians watched Kipling's haughty bearers of "the white man's burden" (see page 766) vilifying and destroying each other. Japan's defeat of imperial Russia in 1905 (see page 731) had shown that an Asian power could beat a European Great Power; now for the first time Asians saw the entire West as divided and vulnerable.

Asian Reaction to the War in Europe

In China and Japan few people particularly cared who won the distant war in Europe. In British India and French Indochina enthusiasm was also limited, but the war's impact was unavoidably greater. Total war required the British and the French to draft their colonial subjects into the conflict, uprooting hundreds of thousands of Asians to fight the Germans and the Ottoman Turks. This too had major consequences. An Indian or Vietnamese soldier who fought in France and

Prince Faisal and His British Allies On board a British warship on route to the Versailles Peace Conference in 1919, Prince Faisal is flanked on his right by British officer T. E. Lawrence, popularly known as Lawrence of Arabia because of his daring campaign against the Turks. Faisal failed to win political independence for the Arabs because the British backed away from the vague pro-Arab promises they had made during the war. (Courtesy, Paul Atterbury)

came in contact there with democratic and republican ideas was less likely to accept foreign rule when he returned home.

The British and the French had made rash promises to gain the support of colonial peoples during the war. French representatives suggested to Syrian nationalists in 1917 that Syria would have self-government after the war. British leaders promised Europe's Jewish nationalists a homeland in Palestine, while promising Arab nationalists independence from the Ottoman Empire. In India the British were forced in 1917 to announce a new policy of self-governing institutions in order to counteract Indian popular unrest fanned by wartime inflation and heavy taxation. After the war the nationalist genie the colonial powers had called on refused to slip meekly back into the bottle.

U.S. President Wilson's war aims had also raised the hopes of peoples under imperial rule. In January 1918 Wilson proposed his Fourteen Points (see page 863), whose key idea was national self-determination for the peoples of Europe and the Ottoman Empire. Wilson also recommended that in all colonial questions "the interests of native populations be given equal weight with the desires of European governments," and he seemed to call for national self-rule. This subversive message had enormous appeal for educated Asians, fueling their hopes of freedom.

□ **CHRONOLOGY**

1904–1905 Russo-Japanese War ends in Russia's defeat

1916 Sykes-Picot Agreement divides Ottoman Empire; Lucknow Pact forms alliance between Hindus and Muslims in India; New Culture Movement in China begins

1917 Balfour Declaration establishes Jewish homeland in Palestine

1919 Amritsar Massacre in India; May Fourth Movement in China; Treaty of Versailles; Afghanistan achieves independence

1920 King of Syria deposed by French; Gandhi launches campaign of nonviolent resistance against British rule in India

1920s–1930s Large numbers of European Jews immigrate to Palestine; Hebrew becomes common language

1923 Sun Yatsen allies Nationalist Party with Chinese Communists; Treaty of Lausanne ends war in Turkey; Mustafa Kemal begins to modernize and secularize Turkey

1925 Reza Shah Pahlavi proclaims himself shah of Persia and begins modernization campaign

1927 Jiang Jieshi, leader of Chinese Nationalist Party, purges his Communist allies

1930 Gandhi leads Indians on march to the sea to protest the British salt tax

1931 Japan occupies Manchuria

1932 Iraq gains independence in return for military alliance with Great Britain

1934 Mao Zedong leads Chinese Communists on Long March; Philippines gain self-governing commonwealth status from United States

1937 Japanese militarists launch attack on China; Rape of Nanjing

The Mandates System

After winning the war, the Allies tried to re-establish or increase their political and economic domination in the colonial states of Asia and Africa. Although fatally weakened, Western imperialism remained very much alive in 1918, partly because President Wilson was no revolutionary. At the Versailles Peace Conference he compromised on colonial questions in order to achieve some of his European goals and the creation of the League of Nations. Also, Allied statesmen and ordinary French and British citizens quite rightly believed that their colonial empires had contributed to their ultimate victory over the Central Powers. They would not give up such valuable possessions voluntarily. If pressed, Europeans said their administration was preparing colonial subjects for eventual self-rule, but only in the distant future.

The compromise at Versailles between Wilson's vague, moralistic idealism and the European preoccupation with "good administration" was a system of League of Nations mandates over Germany's former colonies and the old Ottoman Empire. Article 22 of the League of Nations Covenant, which was part of the Treaty of Versailles, assigned territories "inhabited by peoples incapable of governing themselves" to various "developed nations." "The well-being and development of such peoples" was declared "a sacred trust of civilization." The **Permanent Mandates Commission**, whose members came from European countries with colonies, was created to oversee the developed

• **Permanent Mandates Commission** A commission created by the League of Nations to oversee the developed nations' fulfillment of their international responsibility toward their mandates.

Legend:
- Ottoman Empire in 1914
- British Protectorate in 1914
- British Mandate, with date
- French Mandate, with date
- **1923** Date of independence

▢ Mapping the Past

MAP 29.1 The Partition of the Ottoman Empire, 1914–1923 By 1914 the Ottoman Turks had been pushed out of the Balkans, and their Arab provinces were on the edge of revolt. That revolt erupted in the First World War and contributed greatly to the Ottomans' defeat. When the Allies then attempted to implement their plans, including independence for the Armenian people, Mustafa Kemal arose to forge in battle the modern Turkish state.

ANALYZING THE MAP What new countries were established as a result of the partition of the Ottoman Empire? Where were mandates established?

CONNECTIONS How might the collapse of the Ottoman Empire in World War I have contributed to the current situation in the Middle East?

nations' fulfillment of their international responsibility. Thus the League elaborated a new principle — development toward the eventual goal of self-government — but left its implementation to the colonial powers themselves.

The mandates system demonstrated that Europe was determined to maintain its imperial power and influence. Bitterly disappointed patriots throughout Asia saw France, Great Britain, and other nations — industrialized Japan was the only Asian state to obtain mandates — as grabbing Germany's colonies as spoils of war and extending the existing system of colonial rule in Muslim North Africa into the territories of the old Ottoman Empire. Yet Asian patriots did not give up. They preached national self-determination and struggled to build mass movements capable of achieving freedom and independence.

In this struggle Asian nationalists were encouraged by Soviet communism. After seizing power in 1917, Lenin declared that the Asian inhabitants of the new Soviet Union were complete equals of the Russians with a right to their own development. (In actuality this equality hardly existed, but the propaganda was effective nonetheless.) The Communists also denounced European and American imperialism and pledged to support revolutionary movements in colonial countries, even when they were primarily movements of national independence led by middle-class intellectuals instead of by revolutionary workers. Foreign political and economic exploitation was the immediate enemy, they said, and socialist revolution could wait until Western imperialism had been defeated. The example, ideology, and support of Soviet communism exerted a powerful influence in the 1920s and 1930s, particularly in China and French Indochina (see page 894).

Nationalism's Appeal

There were at least three reasons for the upsurge of nationalism in Asia. First and foremost, nationalism provided the most effective means of organizing anti-imperialist resistance both to direct foreign rule and to indirect Western domination. Second, nationalism called for fundamental changes and challenged old political and social practices and beliefs. As in Russia after the Crimean War, in Turkey after the collapse of the Ottoman Empire, and in Japan after the Meiji Restoration, the nationalist creed after World War I went hand in hand with acceptance of modernization by the educated elites. Modernization promised changes that would enable old societies to compete effectively with the world's leading nations. Educated elites thus used modernization to contest the influence and power of conservative traditionalists. Third, nationalism offered a vision of a free and prosperous future, and provided

an ideology to ennoble the sacrifices the struggle would require.

Nationalism also had a dark side. As in Europe (see page 721), Asian nationalists developed a strong sense of "we" and "they." "They" were often the enemy. European imperialists were just such a "they," and nationalist feeling generated the will to destroy European empires and challenge foreign economic domination. But, as in Europe, Asian nationalism also stimulated bitter conflicts and wars between peoples, in two different ways.

First, nationalism stimulated conflicts between relatively homogeneous peoples in large states, rallying, for example, Chinese against Japanese and vice versa. Second, it often heightened tensions between ethnic or religious groups within states, especially states with diverse populations like British India and the Ottoman Empire. Such states had been formed by authoritarian rulers and their armies and bureaucracies, very much like the Austro-Hungarian and Russian empires before 1914. When their rigid rule declined or snapped, the different nationalistic peoples might easily quarrel, seeking to divide the existing state or to dominate the enemy "they" within its borders.

Nationalism's appeal in Asia was not confined to territories under direct European rule. The extraordinary growth of international trade after 1850 had drawn millions of Asian peasants and shopkeepers into the Western-dominated world economy, disrupting local markets and often creating hostility toward European businessmen. Moreover, Europe and the United States had forced even the most solid Asian states, China and Japan, to accept unequal treaties and humiliating limitations on their sovereignty. Thus the nationalist promise of genuine economic independence and true political equality with the West appealed as powerfully in old but weak states like China as in colonial territories like British India.

Nationalist Movements in the Middle East

☐ How did the collapse of the Ottoman Empire in World War I shape nationalist movements in the Middle East?

The most flagrant attempt to expand Western imperialism occurred in the Middle East, or, more accurately, in Southwest Asia — the vast expanse that stretches eastward from the Suez Canal and Turkey's Mediterranean shores across the Tigris-Euphrates Valley and the Persian (Iranian) Plateau to the Arabian Sea and the Indus Valley (Map 29.1). There the British and the French successfully encouraged an Arab revolt in 1916 and destroyed the Ottoman Empire. Europeans then sought to replace Turks as principal rulers throughout the region, even in Turkey itself. Turkish, Arab, and Persian nationalists, as well as Jewish nationalists arriving from Europe, reacted violently. They struggled to win dignity and nationhood, and as the Europeans were forced to make concessions, they sometimes came into sharp conflict with each other, most notably in Palestine.

The Arab Revolt

Long subject to European pressure, the Ottoman Empire failed to reform and modernize in the late nineteenth century (see pages 768–770). Declining international stature and domestic tyranny led to revolutionary activity among idealistic exiles and young army officers who wanted to seize power and save the Ottoman state. These patriots, the so-called Young Turks, succeeded in the 1908 revolution, and subsequently they were determined to hold together the remnants of the vast multiethnic empire. Defeated by Bulgaria, Serbia, and Greece in the Balkan War of 1912, and stripped of practically all territory in Europe, the Young Turks redoubled their efforts in Southwest Asia. The most important of their possessions were Syria — consisting of modern-day Lebanon, Syria, Israel, the West Bank, the Gaza Strip, and Jordan — and Iraq. The Ottoman Turks also claimed the Arabian peninsula but exercised only loose control there.

For centuries the largely Arabic populations of Syria and Iraq had been tied to their Ottoman rulers by their common faith in Islam (though there were Christian Arabs as well). Yet beneath the surface, ethnic and linguistic tensions simmered between Turks and Arabs, who were as different as Chinese and Japanese.

Young Turk actions after 1908 made the embryonic "Arab movement" a reality. The majority of Young Turks promoted a narrow Turkish nationalism. They further centralized the Ottoman Empire and extended the sway of the Turkish language, culture, and race. In 1909 the Turkish government brutally slaughtered thousands of Armenian Christians, a prelude to the wholesale massacre of more than a million Armenians during the First World War. Meanwhile, Arab discontent grew.

During World War I the Turks freely aligned themselves with the Central Powers — Germany and Austria-Hungary (see page 849). As a result, the Young Turks drew all of the Middle East into what had been up to that point a European war. Arabs opposed to Ottoman rule found themselves allied with the British, who encouraged the alliance with vague promises of an independent Arab kingdom. After decisive British victories on the Arab peninsula in 1917 and 1918, Arabs rejoiced, and many patriots expected a large, unified Arab state to rise from the dust of the Ottoman collapse. Within two years, however, Arab nationalists felt bitterly betrayed by Great Britain and its allies, and this bitterness left a legacy of distrust and hatred toward the West.

Arab bitterness was partly directed at secret wartime treaties between Britain and France to divide and rule the old Ottoman Empire. In the 1916 **Sykes-Picot Agreement**, Britain and France secretly agreed that France would receive modern-day Lebanon, Syria, and much of southern Turkey, and Britain would receive Palestine, Jordan, and Iraq. The Sykes-Picot Agreement contradicted British (and later Wilsonian) promises concerning Arab independence after the war, and left Arab nationalists feeling cheated and betrayed.

A related source of Arab bitterness was Britain's wartime commitment to a Jewish homeland in Palestine. The **Balfour Declaration** of November 1917, made by the British foreign secretary Arthur Balfour, declared:

> His Majesty's Government views with favor the establishment in Palestine of a National Home for the Jewish People, and will use their best endeavors to facilitate the achievement of this object, it being clearly understood that nothing shall be done which may prejudice the civil and religious rights of existing non-Jewish communities in Palestine, or the rights and political status enjoyed by Jews in any other country.

As a careful reading reveals, the Balfour Declaration made contradictory promises to European Jews and Middle Eastern Arabs.

Some British Cabinet members believed the Balfour Declaration would appeal to German, Austrian, and American Jews and thus help the British war effort. Others sincerely supported the Zionist vision of a Jewish homeland (see page 888), but also believed that this homeland would be grateful to Britain and thus help maintain British control of the Suez Canal.

In 1914 Jews made up about 11 percent of the predominantly Arab population in the Ottoman territory that became, under British control, Palestine. The "National Home for the Jewish People" mentioned in the Balfour Declaration implied to the Arabs — and to the Zionist Jews as well — some kind of Jewish state that would be incompatible with majority rule. Moreover, a state founded on religious and ethnic exclusivity was out of keeping with both Islamic and Ottoman tradition, which had historically been more tolerant of religious diversity and minorities than had the Christian monarchs and nation-states of Europe.

• **Sykes-Picot Agreement** The 1916 secret agreement between Britain and France that divided up the Arab lands of Lebanon, Syria, southern Turkey, Palestine, Jordan, and Iraq.

• **Balfour Declaration** A 1917 statement by British foreign secretary Arthur Balfour that supported the idea of a Jewish homeland in Palestine.

The Armenian Atrocities When in 1915 some Armenians welcomed Russian armies as liberators after years of persecution, the Ottoman government ordered a genocidal mass deportation of its Armenian citizens from their homeland in the empire's eastern provinces. This photo, taken in Kharpert in 1915 by a German businessman from his hotel window, shows Turkish guards marching Armenian men off to a prison, where they will be tortured to death. A million Armenians died from murder, starvation, and disease during World War I. (Armenian Library and Museum of America Archives)

After Faisal bin Hussein's failed efforts at Versailles to secure Arab independence (see page 863), Arab nationalists met in Damascus as the General Syrian Congress in 1919 and unsuccessfully called again for political independence. (See "Listening to the Past: Resolution of the General Syrian Congress at Damascus," page 884.) Ignoring Arab opposition, the British mandate in Palestine formally incorporated the Balfour Declaration and its commitment to a Jewish national home. In March 1920 Faisal's followers met again as the Syrian National Congress and proclaimed Syria independent, with Faisal as king. A similar congress declared Iraq an independent kingdom.

Western reaction to events in Syria and Iraq was swift and decisive. A French army stationed in Lebanon attacked Syria, taking Damascus in July 1920. Faisal fled, and the French took over. Meanwhile, the British put down an uprising in Iraq with bloody fighting and established effective control there. Western imperialism appeared to have replaced Turkish rule in the Middle East (see Map 29.1).

The Turkish Revolution

At the end of the First World War, on November 12 and 13, 1918, French and then British troops entered Con-

stantinople to begin a five-year occupation of the Ottoman capital. A young English official wrote that he found the Ottoman Empire "utterly smashed." The Turks were "worn out" from the war, and without bitterness they awaited the construction of a "new system."[1] The Allies' new system was blatant imperialism, which proved harsher for the defeated Turks than for the "liberated" Arabs. A treaty forced on the helpless sultan dismembered Turkey and reduced it to a puppet state. Great Britain and France occupied parts of Turkey, and Italy and Greece claimed shares as well. There was a sizable Greek minority in western Turkey, and Greek nationalists cherished the "Great Idea" of a modern Greek empire modeled on long-dead Christian Byzantium. In 1919 Greek armies carried by British ships landed on the Turkish coast at Smyrna, met little resistance from the exhausted Turkish troops, and advanced into the interior. Turkey seemed finished.

But Turkey produced a great leader and revived to become an inspiration to the entire Middle East. Mustafa Kemal (1881–1938), considered the father of modern Turkey, was a military man sympathetic to the Young Turk movement. Kemal had distinguished himself in the Great War by directing the successful defense of the Dardanelles against British attack. After the armistice, he watched with anguish the Allies' aggression and the

Listening to the Past

Resolution of the General Syrian Congress at Damascus

Great Britain and France had agreed to divide up the Arab lands, and the British also had made conflicting promises to Arab and Jewish nationalists. However, President Wilson insisted at Versailles that the right of self-determination should be applied to the conquered Ottoman territories, and he sent an American commission of inquiry to Syria, even though the British and French refused to participate. The commission canvassed political views throughout greater Syria, and its long report with many documents reflected public opinion in the region in 1919.

To present their view to the Americans, Arab nationalists from present-day Syria, Lebanon, Israel, the West Bank, the Gaza Strip, and Jordan came together in Damascus as the General Syrian Congress, and they passed the following resolution on July 2, 1919. In addition to the Arab call for political independence, the delegates addressed the possibility of French rule under a League of Nations mandate and the establishment of a Jewish national home.

❝We the undersigned members of the General Syrian Congress, meeting in Damascus on Wednesday, July 2nd, 1919, . . . provided with credentials and authorizations by the inhabitants of our various districts, Moslems, Christians, and Jews, have agreed upon the following statement of the desires of the people of the country who have elected us to present them to the American Section of the International Commission; the fifth article was passed by a very large majority; all the other articles were accepted unanimously.

1. We ask absolutely complete political independence for Syria within these boundaries. [Describes the area including the present-day states of Syria, Lebanon, Israel, the West Bank, the Gaza Strip, and Jordan.]

2. We ask that the Government of this Syrian country should be a democratic civil constitutional Monarchy on broad decentralization principles, safeguarding the rights of minorities, and that the King be the Emir Faisal, who carried on a glorious struggle in the cause of our liberation and merited our full confidence and entire reliance.

3. Considering the fact that the Arabs inhabiting the Syrian area are not naturally less gifted than other more advanced races and that they are by no means less developed than the Bulgarians, Serbians, Greeks, and Roumanians at the beginning of their independence, we protest against Article 22 of the Covenant of the League of Nations, placing us among the nations in their middle stage of development which stand in need of a mandatory power.

4. In the event of the rejection by the Peace Conference of this just protest for certain considerations that we may not understand, we, relying on the declarations of President Wilson that his object in waging war was to put an end to the ambition of conquest and colonization, can only regard the mandate mentioned in the Covenant of the League of Nations as equivalent to the rendering of economical and technical assistance that does not prejudice our complete independence. And desiring that our country should not fall a prey to colonization and believing that the American Nation is farthest from any thought of colonization and has no political ambition in our country, we will seek the technical and economical assistance from the United States of America, provided that such assistance does not exceed 20 years.

5. In the event of America not finding herself in a position to accept our desire for assistance, we will seek this assistance from Great Britain, also provided that such assistance does not infringe the complete independence and unity of our country and that the duration of such assistance does not exceed that mentioned in the previous article.

6. We do not acknowledge any right claimed by the French Government in any part whatever of our Syrian country and refuse that she should assist us or have a hand in our country under any circumstances and in any place.

7. We oppose the pretensions of the Zionists to create a Jewish commonwealth in the southern part of Syria, known as Palestine, and oppose Zionist migration to any part of our country; for we do not acknowledge their title but consider

---

sultan's cowardice. In early 1919 he began working to unify Turkish resistance.

The sultan, bowing to Allied pressure, initially denounced Kemal, but the cause of national liberation proved more powerful. The catalyst was the Greek invasion and attempted annexation of much of western Turkey. A young Turkish woman described feelings she shared with countless others:

> After I learned about the details of the Smyrna occupation by Greek armies, I hardly opened my mouth on any subject except when it concerned the sacred struggle. . . . I suddenly ceased to exist as an individual. I worked, wrote and lived as a unit of that magnificent national madness.[2]

• **Treaty of Lausanne** The 1923 treaty that ended the Turkish war and recognized the territorial integrity of a truly independent Turkey.

them a grave peril to our people from the national, economical, and political points of view. Our Jewish compatriots shall enjoy our common rights and assume the common responsibilities.

8. We ask that there should be no separation of the southern part of Syria, known as Palestine, nor of the littoral western zone, which includes Lebanon, from the Syrian country. We desire that the unity of the country should be guaranteed against partition under whatever circumstances.

9. We ask complete independence for emancipated Mesopotamia [today's Iraq] and that there should be no economical barriers between the two countries.

10. The fundamental principles laid down by President Wilson in condemnation of secret treaties impel us to protest most emphatically against any treaty that stipulates the partition of our Syrian country and against any private engagement aiming at the establishment of Zionism in the southern part of Syria; therefore we ask the complete annulment of these conventions and agreements.

The noble principles enunciated by President Wilson strengthen our confidence that our desires emanating from the depths of our hearts, shall be the decisive factor in determining our future; and that President Wilson and the free American people will be our supporters for the realization of our hopes, thereby proving their sincerity and noble sympathy with the aspiration of the weaker nations in general and our Arab people in particular.

We also have the fullest confidence that the Peace Conference will realize that we would not have risen against the Turks, with whom we had participated in all civil, political, and representative privileges, but for their violation of our national rights, and so will grant us our desires in full in order that our political rights may not be less after the war than they were before, since we have shed so much blood in the cause of our liberty and independence.

We request to be allowed to send a delegation to represent us at the Peace Conference to defend our rights and secure the realization of our aspirations. ❞

Source: "Resolution of the General Syrian Congress at Damascus, 2 July 1919," from the *King-Crane Commission Report, in Foreign Relations of the United States: Paris Peace Conference, 1919*, 12: 780–781.

QUESTIONS FOR ANALYSIS

1. What kind of state did the delegates want?

2. How did the delegates want to modify an unwanted League of Nations mandate to make it less objectionable?

3. Did the delegates view their "Jewish compatriots" and the Zionists in different ways? Why?

Refusing to acknowledge the Allied dismemberment of their country, the Turks battled on through 1920 despite staggering defeats. The next year the Greeks advanced almost to Ankara, the nationalist stronghold in central Turkey. There Mustafa Kemal's forces took the offensive and won a great victory. The Greeks and their British allies sued for peace. The resulting **Treaty of Lausanne** (1923) abolished the hated capitulations, which since the sixteenth century had given Europe-

ans special privileges in the Ottoman Empire (see page 606) and recognized a truly independent Turkey. Turkey lost only its former Arab provinces (see Map 29.1).

Mustafa Kemal believed Turkey should modernize and secularize along Western lines. His first moves were political. Drawing on his prestige as a war hero, Kemal called on the National Assembly to depose the sultan and establish a republic. He had himself elected president and moved the capital from cosmopolitan

Mustafa Kemal Surnamed Atatürk, meaning "father of the Turks," Mustafa Kemal and his supporters imposed revolutionary changes aimed at modernizing and westernizing Turkish society and the new Turkish government. Dancing here with his adopted daughter at her high-society wedding, Atatürk often appeared in public in elegant European dress—a vivid symbol for the Turkish people of his radical break with traditional Islamic teaching and custom. (Hulton Archive/Getty Images)

ligious authorities. Profoundly influenced by the example of western Europe, Mustafa Kemal set out, like the philosophes of the Enlightenment, to limit religious influence in daily affairs. Like Russia's Peter the Great, he employed dictatorial measures rather than reason to reach his goal. Kemal decreed a revolutionary separation of church and state. Secular law codes inspired by European models replaced religious courts. State schools replaced religious schools and taught such secular subjects as science, mathematics, and social sciences.

Mustafa Kemal also struck down many entrenched patterns of behavior. Women, traditionally secluded and inferior to males in Islamic society, received the right to vote. Civil law on a European model, rather than the Islamic code, now governed marriage. Women could seek divorces, and no man could have more than one wife at a time. Men were forbidden to wear the tall red fez of the Ottoman era as headgear; government employees were ordered to wear business suits and felt hats, erasing the visible differences between Muslims and "infidel" Europeans. The old Arabic script was replaced with a new Turkish alphabet based on Roman letters, which facilitated massive government efforts to spread literacy after 1928. Finally, in 1935, family names on the European model were introduced. Before this, while Jewish and Christian citizens of the empire used surnames, Muslim Turks had not. Muslims generally used a simple formulation of "son of" with their father's name. The National Assembly granted Mustafa Kemal the surname Atatürk, which means "father of the Turks."

By his death in 1938, Atatürk and his supporters had consolidated their revolution. Government-sponsored industrialization was fostering urban growth and new attitudes, encouraging Turks to embrace business and science. Poverty persisted in rural areas, as did some religious discontent among devout Muslims. But like the Japanese after the Meiji Restoration, the Turkish people had rallied around the nationalist banner to repulse European imperialism and were building a modern secular nation-state.

Modernization Efforts in Persia and Afghanistan

In Persia (renamed Iran in 1935), strong-arm efforts to build a unified modern nation ultimately proved less successful than in Turkey. In the late nineteenth century Persia had also been subject to extreme foreign pressure, which stimulated efforts to reform the government as a means of reviving Islamic civilization. In 1906 a nationalistic coalition of merchants, religious leaders, and intellectuals revolted. The despotic shah was forced to grant a constitution and establish a national assembly, the **Majlis**. Nationalist hopes ran high.

Constantinople (now Istanbul) to Ankara in the Turkish heartland. Kemal savagely crushed the demands for independence of ethnic minorities like the Armenians and the Kurds, but he realistically abandoned all thought of winning back lost Arab territories. He then created a one-party system—partly inspired by the Bolshevik example—in order to work his will.

Kemal's most radical changes pertained to religion and culture. For centuries most believers' intellectual and social activities had been regulated by Islamic re-

• **Majlis** The national assembly established by the despotic shah of Iran in 1906.

Yet the 1906 Persian revolution was doomed to failure, largely because of European imperialism. Without consulting Iran, Britain and Russia in 1907 divided the country into spheres of influence. Britain's sphere ran along the Persian Gulf; the Russian sphere encompassed the whole northern half of Persia (see Map 29.1). Thereafter Russia intervened constantly. It blocked reforms, occupied cities, and completely dominated the country by 1912. When Russian power collapsed in the Bolshevik Revolution, British armies rushed into the power vacuum. By bribing corrupt Persians, Great Britain in 1919 negotiated a treaty allowing the installation of British "advisers" in every government department.

The Majlis refused to ratify the treaty, and the blatant attempt to make Persia a British satellite aroused the national spirit. In 1921 reaction against the British brought to power a military dictator, Reza Shah Pahlavi (1877–1944), who proclaimed himself shah in 1925 and ruled until 1941.

Inspired by Turkey's Mustafa Kemal, the patriotic, religiously indifferent Reza Shah had three basic goals: to build a modern nation, to free Persia from foreign domination, and to rule with an iron fist. The challenge was enormous. Persia was a vast, undeveloped country of deserts, mountain barriers, and rudimentary communications. The rural population was mostly poor and illiterate, and among the Persian majority were sizable ethnic minorities with their own aspirations. Furthermore, Iran's powerful religious leaders hated Western (Christian) domination but were equally opposed to a more secular, less Islamic society.

To realize his vision of a strong Persia, the energetic shah created a modern army, built railroads, and encouraged commerce. He won control over ethnic minorities such as the Kurds in the north and Arab tribesmen on the Iraqi border. He reduced the privileges granted to foreigners and raised taxes on the powerful Anglo-Persian Oil Company, which had been founded in 1909 to exploit the first great oil strike in the Middle East. Yet Reza Shah was less successful than Atatürk.

Because the European-educated elite in Persia was smaller than the comparable group in Turkey, the idea of re-creating Persian greatness on the basis of a secularized society attracted relatively few determined supporters. Many powerful religious leaders turned against Reza Shah, and he became increasingly brutal, greedy, and tyrannical, murdering his enemies and lining his pockets. His support of Hitler's Nazi Germany (discussed in Chapter 30) also exposed Persia's tenuous and fragile independence to the impact of European conflicts.

Afghanistan, meanwhile, was nominally independent in the nineteenth century, but the British imposed political restrictions and constantly meddled in the country's affairs. In 1919 the violently anti-British emir Amanullah (1892–1960) declared a holy war on the

Afghanistan Under Amanullah Khan

An Afghan Reformer
Amanullah Khan, the ruler of Afghanistan from 1919 to 1929, was inspired by Mustafa Kemal in Turkey, and he too looked to Europe for models of reform and modernization. Shown here arriving in Berlin in 1926 and accompanied by President von Hindenburg on the right, Amanullah's efforts to promote secular education and end polygamy and women's veiling incensed Islamic religious leaders and led to a fearsome backlash and his abdication. (Hulton Archive/Getty Images)

British government in India and won complete independence for the first time. Amanullah then decreed revolutionary reforms designed to hurl his primitive country into the twentieth century. The result was tribal and religious revolt, civil war, and retreat from reform. Islam remained both religion and law. A powerful but primitive patriotism enabled Afghanistan to win political independence from the West, but not to build a modern society.

Gradual Independence in the Arab States

French and British mandates established at gunpoint forced Arab nationalists to seek independence by gradual means after 1920. Arab nationalists were indirectly aided by Western taxpayers, who wanted cheap — that is, peaceful — empires. As a result, Arabs won considerable control over local affairs in the mandated states, except Palestine, though the mandates remained European satellites in international and economic affairs.

In Iraq, the British chose Faisal bin Hussein, whom the French had deposed in Syria, as king. Faisal obligingly gave British advisers broad behind-the-scenes control. The king also accepted British ownership of Iraq's oil fields, consequently giving the West a stranglehold on the Iraqi economy. Given the severe limitations imposed on him, Faisal (r. 1921–1933) proved to be an able ruler, gaining the support of his people and encouraging moderate reforms. In 1932 he secured Iraqi independence at the price of a restrictive long-term military alliance with Great Britain.

Egypt had been occupied by Great Britain since 1882 (see page 773) and had been a British protectorate since 1914. Following intense nationalist agitation after the Great War, Great Britain in 1922 proclaimed Egypt formally independent but continued to occupy the country militarily and control its politics. In 1936 the British agreed to restrict their troops to their bases in the Suez Canal Zone.

The French compromised less in their handling of their mandated Middle East territories. Following the collapse of the Ottoman Empire after World War I, the French designated Lebanon as one of several ethnic enclaves within a larger area that became part of the French mandate of Syria. They practiced a policy of divide-and-rule and generally played off ethnic and religious minorities against each other. Maronite Catholic Christians made up the majority of Lebanon's population, but there were also significant numbers of Muslims and Druzes. In 1926 Lebanon became a separate republic but remained under the control of the

French mandate. Arab nationalists in Syria finally won promises of Syrian independence in 1936 in return for a treaty of friendship with France.

In short, the Arab states gradually freed themselves from Western political mandates but not from the Western military threat or from pervasive Western influence. Of great importance, large Arab landowners and urban merchants increased their wealth and political power after 1918, and they often supported the Western hegemony, from which they benefited greatly. Western control of the newly discovered Arab oil fields helped to convince radical nationalists that economic independence and genuine freedom had not yet been achieved.

Arab-Jewish Tensions in Palestine

Relations between the Arabs and the West were complicated by the tense situation in the British mandate of Palestine, and that situation deteriorated in the interwar years. Both Arabs and Jews denounced the British, who tried unsuccessfully to compromise with both sides. Arab nationalist anger, however, was aimed primarily at Jewish settlers. The key issue was Jewish migration from Europe to Palestine.

A small Jewish community had survived in Palestine ever since the dispersal of the Jews in Roman times. But Jewish nationalism, known as Zionism, took shape in Europe in the late nineteenth century under the leadership of Theodor Herzl (see page 744). Herzl believed that only a Jewish state could guarantee Jews dignity and security. The Zionist movement encouraged the world's Jews to settle in Palestine, but until 1921 the great majority of Jewish emigrants preferred the United States.

After 1921 the situation changed radically. An isolationist United States drastically limited immigration from eastern Europe, where war and revolution had kindled anti-Semitism. Moreover, the British began honoring the Balfour Declaration despite Arab protests. Thus Jewish immigration to Palestine from turbulent Europe in the interwar years grew rapidly. In the 1930s German and Polish persecution created a mass of Jewish refugees. By 1939 the Jewish population of Palestine had increased almost fivefold since 1914 and accounted for about 30 percent of all inhabitants.

Jewish settlers in Palestine faced formidable difficulties. Although much of the land purchased by the Jewish National Fund was productive, the sellers of such land were often wealthy absentee Arab landowners who cared little for their Arab tenants' welfare. When the new Jewish owners replaced those long-time Arab tenants with Jewish settlers, Arab farmers and intellectuals burned with a sense of injustice. Moreover, most Jewish immigrants came from urban backgrounds and preferred to establish new cities like Tel

---

• **kibbutz** A Jewish collective farm on which each member shared equally in the work, rewards, and defense.

Kibbutz Children Picking Grapes Many of the early kibbutzim, such as this one at Kfar Blum in Israel's northern Galilee, were agricultural settlements that produced cotton and fruits such as grapes, oranges, and apples that were then packed and shipped around the world. They also produced most of the food eaten by the members. On the kibbutz, as these children illustrate, all did their share of the work. Collection boxes for the Zionist cause (below) date back to 1884, but donations became more standardized after the founding of the Jewish National Fund in 1901. The first Blue Box appeared in 1904, with the suggestion that a box be placed in every Jewish home around the world and contributed to as often as possible. Still in use today, Blue Box donations go for such things as the planting of forests, the establishment of parks, and the building of roads and water reservoirs in the Israeli state. (kibbutz: Courtesy, Kibbutz Kfar Blum Archives; box: Jewish National Fund Photo Archives, Jerusalem)

Aviv or to live in existing towns, where they competed with the Arabs. The land issue combined with economic and cultural friction to harden Arab protest into hatred. Anti-Jewish riots and even massacres ensued.

The British gradually responded to Arab pressure and tried to slow Jewish immigration. This effort satisfied neither Jews nor Arabs, and by 1938 the two communities were engaged in an undeclared civil war. On the eve of the Second World War, the frustrated British proposed an independent Palestine with the number of Jews permanently limited to only about one-third of the total population. Zionists felt themselves in grave danger of losing their dream of an independent Jewish state.

Nevertheless, in the face of adversity Jewish settlers from many different countries gradually succeeded in forging a cohesive community in Palestine. Hebrew, for centuries used only in religious worship, was revived as a living language to bind the Jews in Palestine together. Despite its slow beginnings, rural development achieved often remarkable results. The key unit of agricultural organization was the **kibbutz** (kih-BOOTS), a collective farm on which each member shared equally in the work, rewards, and defense. An egalitarian socialist ideology also characterized industry, which grew rapidly. By 1939 a new but old nation was emerging in the Middle East.

Toward Self-Rule in India

☐ What role did Gandhi and his campaign of militant nonviolence play in leading India to independence from the British?

The national movement in British India grew out of two interconnected cultures, Hindu and Muslim, that came to see themselves as fundamentally different in rising to challenge British rule. Nowhere has modern nationalism's power both to unify and to divide been more strikingly demonstrated than in India.

British Promises and Repression

Indian nationalism had emerged in the late nineteenth century (see page 787), and when the First World War began, the British feared revolt. Instead, Indians supported the war effort. About 1.2 million Indian soldiers and laborers voluntarily served in Europe, Africa, and the Middle East. The British government in India and the native Indian princes sent large supplies of food, money, and ammunition. In return, the British opened more good government jobs to Indians and made other minor concessions.

As the war in distant Europe ground on, however, inflation, high taxes, food shortages, and a terrible influenza epidemic created widespread suffering and discontent. The prewar nationalist movement revived stronger than ever, and moderates and radicals in the Indian National Congress Party (see page 787) joined forces. Moreover, in 1916 Hindu leaders in the Congress Party hammered out an alliance — the **Lucknow Pact** — with India's Muslim League. The League was founded in 1906 to uphold Muslim interests, as, under British rule, the once-dominant Muslim minority had fallen behind the Hindu majority. The Lucknow Pact forged a powerful united front of Hindus and Muslims and called for putting India on equal footing with self-governing British dominions like Canada, Australia, and New Zealand.

The British response was contradictory. On the one hand, the secretary of state for India made the unprecedented announcement in August 1917 that British policy in India called for the "gradual development of self-governing institutions and the progressive realization of responsible government." In late 1919 the British established a dual administration: part Indian and elected, part British and authoritarian. Such uncontroversial activities as agriculture and health were transferred from British to Indian officials who were accountable to elected provincial assemblies. More sensitive matters like taxes, police, and the courts remained solely in British hands.

Old-fashioned authoritarian rule seriously undermined the positive impact of this reform. Despite the unanimous opposition of the elected Indian members, the British in 1919 rammed the repressive Rowlatt Acts through India's Imperial Legislative Council. These acts indefinitely extended wartime "emergency measures" designed to curb unrest and root out "conspiracy." The result was a wave of rioting across India.

Under these tense conditions a crowd of some ten thousand gathered to celebrate a Sikh religious festival in an enclosed square in the Sikh holy city of Amritsar in the northern Punjab province. Unknown to the crowd, the local English commander, General Reginald Dyer, had banned all public meetings that very day. Dyer marched his native Gurkha troops into the square and, without warning, ordered them to fire into the unarmed mass at point-blank range until the ammunition ran out. Official British records of the Amritsar Massacre list 379 killed and 1,137 wounded, but these figures remain hotly contested as being too low. Tensions flared, and India stood on the verge of more violence and repression and, sooner or later, terrorism and guerrilla war. That India took a different path to national liberation was due largely to Mohandas K. Gandhi (1869–1948), the most influential Indian of modern times.

The Roots of Militant Nonviolence

By the time of Gandhi's birth in 1869, the Indian subcontinent was firmly controlled by the British. Part of the country was ruled directly by British (and subor-

British Man Fishing in India British colonial officials, such as this gentleman reposing in a wicker chair while fishing in India around 1925, enjoyed lifestyles that were often much more comfortable than would have been the case back in England. Gardeners, chauffeurs, maids, cooks, and other personal servants, like the three men helping the fisher, were commonly hired to wait on the colonists hand and foot. Some justified the lifestyle as demonstrating the refinements of civilization — part of the white man's burden. (Photograph by Ralph Ponsonby Watts/Mary Evans Picture Library/The Images Works)

dinate Indian) officials, answerable to the British Parliament in London. In each of the so-called protected states, the native prince — usually known as the maharaja — remained the titular ruler, although he was bound to the British by unequal treaties and had to accept the "advice" of the British resident assigned to his court.

Gandhi grew up in one of the small protected states north of Bombay. Gandhi's father was the well-to-do head of a large extended family. Gandhi's mother was devoted but undogmatic in religious matters, and she exercised a strong influence on her son. After his father's death, Gandhi went to study law in England, where he passed the English bar. Upon returning to India, he decided in 1893 to try a case for some wealthy Indian merchants in the colony of Natal (part of modern South Africa). It was a momentous decision.

In Natal, Gandhi took up the plight of the expatriate Indian community. White plantation owners had been importing thousands of poor Indians as indentured laborers on five-year renewable contracts since the 1860s. When Gandhi arrived there were more Indians than whites in Natal. Some of these Indians, after completing their contracts, remained in Natal as free persons and economic competitors. In response, the Afrikaner (of Dutch descent) and British settlers passed brutally discriminatory laws. Poor Indians had to work on plantations or return to India. Rich Indians, who had previously had the vote in Natal, lost that right in 1896. Gandhi undertook his countrymen's legal defense, and in 1897 a white mob almost lynched the "coolie lawyer."

Meanwhile, Gandhi was searching for a spiritual theory of social action. He studied Hindu and Christian teachings, and gradually developed a weapon for the poor and oppressed that he called **satyagraha** (suh-TYAH-gruh-huh). Gandhi conceived of satyagraha, loosely translated as "soul force," as a means of striving for truth and social justice through love and a willingness to suffer the blows of the oppressor, while trying to convert the oppressor to your views of what is true. Its tactic was active nonviolent resistance.

As the undisputed leader of South Africa's Indians before the First World War, Gandhi put his philosophy into action. When South Africa's white government severely restricted Asian immigration and internal freedom of movement, Gandhi organized a nonviolent mass resistance campaign. Thousands of Indian men and women marched in peaceful protest and withstood beatings, arrest, and imprisonment.

In 1914 South Africa's exasperated whites agreed to many of the Indians' demands. They passed a law abolishing discriminatory taxes on Indian traders, recognized the legality of non-Christian marriages, and permitted the continued immigration of free Indians. Satyagraha — militant nonviolence in pursuit of social justice — proved a powerful force in Gandhi's hands.

> "Wherein is courage required — in blowing others to pieces from behind a cannon, or with a smiling face to approach a cannon and be blown to pieces?"
>
> **GANDHI**

Gandhi's Resistance Campaign in India

In 1915 Gandhi returned to India. His reputation had preceded him: the masses hailed him as a mahatma, or "great soul" — a Hindu title of veneration for a man of great knowledge and humanity. Drawing on his South African experience because he knew Indians could not compete militarily against the British, Gandhi in 1920 launched a national campaign of nonviolent resistance to British rule. Denouncing British injustice, he urged his countrymen to boycott British goods, jobs, and honors (such as honorary titles like baron, rai, diwān, and khan, and other awards). He told peasants not to pay taxes or buy English goods, primarily cloth, or the heavily taxed liquor. Gandhi electrified the Indian people, initiating a revolution in Indian politics.

The nationalist movement had previously touched only the tiny, prosperous, Western-educated elite. Now both the illiterate masses of village India and the educated classes heard Gandhi's call for militant nonviolent resistance. It particularly appealed to the masses of Hindus who were not members of the warrior caste or the so-called military races and who were traditionally passive and nonviolent. The British had regarded ordinary Hindus as cowards. Gandhi told them that they could be courageous and even morally superior:

> What do you think? Wherein is courage required — in blowing others to pieces from behind a cannon, or with a smiling face to approach a cannon and be blown to pieces? Who is the true warrior — he who keeps death always as a bosom-friend, or he who controls the death of others? Believe me that a man devoid of courage and manhood can never be a passive resister.[3]

Gandhi made the Indian National Congress into a mass political party, welcoming members from every ethnic group and cooperating closely with the Muslim minority.

In 1922 some Indian resisters turned to violence, murdering twenty-two policemen. Savage riots broke

- **Lucknow Pact** A 1916 alliance between the Hindus leading the Indian National Congress and the Muslim League.
- **satyagraha** Loosely translated as "soul force," which Gandhi believed was the means of striving for truth and social justice through love, suffering, and conversion of the oppressor.

Gandhi Arrives in Delhi, October 1939
A small frail man, Gandhi possessed enormous courage and determination. His campaign of nonviolent resistance to British rule inspired the Indian masses and mobilized a nation. Here he arrives for talks with the British viceroy after the outbreak of World War II. (Hulton Deutsch Collection/ Corbis)

India, ca. 1930

out, and Gandhi abruptly called off his campaign. Arrested for fomenting rebellion, Gandhi told the British judge that he had committed "a Himalayan blunder to believe that India had accepted nonviolence." Released from prison after two years, Gandhi set up a commune, established a national newspaper, and set out to reform Indian society and improve the lot of the poor. He welcomed the outcaste untouchables (a caste comprised of people who worked in occupations deemed unclean or "polluting"), worked to help child widows who were denied the right to remarry and suffered discrimination, and promoted native cottage industry production. For Gandhi moral improvement, social progress, and the national movement went hand in hand. Above all, Gandhi nurtured national identity and self-respect. He also tried to instill in India's people the courage to overcome their fear of their colonial rulers and to fight these rulers with nonviolence. (See "Viewpoints: Gandhi and Mao on Revolutionary Means," page 893.)

The 1920–1922 resistance campaign left the British severely shaken, but the commission formed in 1927 to consider further steps toward self-rule included no Indian members. In the meantime, Gandhi had served two years (1922–1924) of a six-year sentence for sedition, and in his absence the Indian National Congress had splintered into various factions. Indian resentment of British rule was intense and growing throughout the 1920s, and Gandhi spent the years after his release from prison quietly trying to unite the different factions. In 1929 the radical nationalists, led by the able and aristocratic Jawaharlal Nehru (1889–1964), pushed

through the National Congress a resolution calling for virtual independence within a year. The British stiffened in their resolve against Indian independence, and Indian radicals talked of a bloody showdown.

Into this tense situation Gandhi masterfully reasserted his leadership, taking a hard line toward the British, but insisting on nonviolent methods. He organized a massive resistance campaign against the tax on salt, which gave the British a veritable monopoly on the salt that was absolutely necessary for survival in India's heat and humidity. As Gandhi shrewdly realized, the tax affected every Indian family. From March 12 to April 6, 1930, Gandhi led fifty thousand people in a spectacular march to the sea, where he made salt in defiance of the law. A later demonstration at the British-run Dharasana salt works resulted in many of the 2,500 nonviolent marchers being beaten senseless by policemen in a brutal and well-publicized encounter. Over the next months the British arrested Gandhi and sixty thousand other protesters for making and distributing salt. But the protests continued, and in 1931 the frustrated and unnerved British released Gandhi from jail and sat down to negotiate with him, as an equal, over Indian self-rule. Negotiations resulted in a new constitution, the Government of India Act, in 1935, which greatly strengthened India's parliamentary representative institutions and gave Indians some voice in the administration of British India. Although there was little Indian involvement in the drafting of the act, and it was never fully implemented, it served as a blueprint for the constitutions of India and Pakistan when they gained independence soon after World War II.

Viewpoints

Gandhi and Mao on Revolutionary Means

• India's Mohandas Gandhi and China's Mao Zedong successfully led two of the largest and most populous nations to independence in the late 1940s. Both drew much of their support from the peasant masses, among whom they both lived and worked, following very simple lifestyles, as their political power and influence grew.

Gandhi's and Mao's political philosophies could not have been more different. Gandhi believed that active nonviolent disobedience to British rule was the only way Indians could break free of British rule and gain independence. He explained his views in the following excerpts from articles that he wrote for the journal Young India *in 1921 and 1931. As shown in the second document from Mao's* Little Red Book, *Mao took the exact opposite view. He believed that "power flows from the barrel of a gun" and that violence was the only means by which the Chinese masses could rid themselves of corrupt warlords, cruel landowners, imperialist occupiers, and ruling elites.*

Mohandas Gandhi

Complete civil disobedience is rebellion without the element of violence in it. An out-and-out resister simply ignores the authority of the State. He becomes an outlaw claiming to disregard every unmoral State law. Thus, for instance, he may refuse to pay taxes, he may refuse to recognize the authority in his daily intercourse. . . . In doing all this he never uses force and never resists force when it is used against him. In fact, he invites imprisonment and other uses of force against himself. This he does because and when he finds the bodily freedom he seemingly enjoys to be an intolerable burden. He argues to himself that a State allows personal freedom only in so far as the citizen submits to its regulations. Submission to the State law is the price a citizen pays for his person liberty. Submission, therefore, to a State wholly or largely unjust is an immoral barter for liberty. . . .

A body of civil resisters is, therefore, like an army subject to all the discipline of a soldier. . . . And as a civil resistance army is or ought to be free from passion because free from the spirit of retaliation, it requires the fewest number of soldiers. Indeed, one *perfect* civil resister is enough to win the battle of Right against Wrong. [1921]

You might of course say that there can be no nonviolent rebellion and there has been none known to history. Well, it is my ambition to provide an instance, and it is my dream that my country may win its freedom through nonviolence. And, I would like to repeat to the world times without number, that I will not purchase my country's freedom at the cost of nonviolence. My marriage to nonviolence is such an absolute thing that I would rather commit suicide than be deflected from my position. I have not mentioned truth in this connection, simply because truth cannot be expressed except by nonviolence. [1931]

Mao Zedong

War is the highest form of struggle for resolving contradictions, when they have developed to a certain state, between classes, nations, states, or political groups, and it has existed ever since the emergence of private property and of classes.

The seizure of power by armed force, the settlement of the issue by war, is the central task and the highest form of revolution. This Marxist-Leninist principle of revolution holds good universally, for China and for all other countries.

According to the Marxist theory of the state, . . . whoever wants to seize and retain state power must have a strong army. Some people ridicule us as advocates of the "omnipotence of war." Yes, we are advocates of the omnipotence of revolutionary war; that is good, not bad, it is Marxist. Experience in the class struggle in the era of imperialism teaches us that it is only by the power of the gun that the working class and the laboring masses can defeat the armed bourgeoisie and landlords; in this sense we may say that only with guns can the whole world be transformed.

Sources: Mahatma Gandhi, "Young India, November 10, 1921" and "Young India, November 12, 1931," in *All Men Are Brothers: Autobiographical Reflections*, ed. Krishna Kripalani (New York: Continuum, 1997), pp. 81, 135–136. Reprinted by permission of the Navajivan Trust; Mao Tsetung, *Quotations from Chairman Mao Tsetung* (Peking: Foreign Languages Press, 1972), pp. 58, 61–63.

QUESTIONS FOR ANALYSIS

1. According to Gandhi, when should someone resort to nonviolent disobedience in opposing one's rulers?

2. According to Mao, what is the highest form of revolution? What theory does he draw on for this conclusion?

Despite his best efforts, Gandhi failed to heal a widening split between Hindus and Muslims. Indian nationalism, based largely on Hindu symbols and customs, increasingly disturbed the Muslim minority. Tempers mounted, and both sides committed atrocities. By the late 1930s Muslim League leaders were calling for the creation of a Muslim nation in British India, a "Pakistan" or "land of the pure." As in Palestine, the rise of conflicting nationalisms based on religion in India would lead to tragedy (see pages 990–993).

Nationalist Struggles in East and Southeast Asia

☐ How did nationalism shape political developments in East and Southeast Asia?

Because of the efforts of the Meiji reformers, nationalism and modernization were well developed in Japan by 1914. Japan competed politically and economically with the world's leading nations, building its own empire and proclaiming its special mission in Asia. China lagged behind initially, but after 1912 the pace of nationalist development there began to quicken.

In the 1920s the Chinese nationalist movement managed to win a large measure of political independence from the imperialist West and promoted extensive modernization. These achievements were soon undermined, however, by internal conflict and war with an expanding Japan. Nationalism also flourished elsewhere in Asia, scoring a major victory in the Philippine Islands.

The Rise of Nationalist China

The 1911 revolution that overthrew the Qing Dynasty (see page 796) opened an era of unprecedented change for Chinese society. Before the revolution many progressive Chinese realized that fundamental technological and political reforms were necessary to save the Chinese state, but most hoped to preserve the traditional core of Chinese civilization and culture. The fall of the ancient dynastic system shattered such hopes. If the emperor himself was no longer sacred, what was?

The central figure in the revolution was a seasoned and cunning military man, Yuan Shigai (Yüan Shih-k'ai). Called out of retirement to save the dynasty, Yuan (1859–1916) betrayed the Manchu leaders of the Qing Dynasty and convinced the revolutionaries that he could unite the country peacefully and prevent foreign intervention. Once elected president of the republic, however, Yuan concentrated on building his own power. In 1913 he used military force to dissolve China's parliament and ruled as a dictator. China's first modern revolution had failed.

The extent of the failure became apparent only after Yuan's death in 1916, when the central government in Beijing almost disintegrated. For more than a decade power resided in a multitude of local military leaders, the so-called warlords. Their wars, taxes, and corruption created terrible suffering.

Foreign imperialism intensified the agony of warlordism. Japan's expansion into Shandong and southern Manchuria during World War I (see page 851) angered China's growing middle class and enraged China's young patriots (Map 29.2). On May 4, 1919, five thousand students in Beijing exploded against the decision of the Versailles Peace Conference to leave the Shandong Peninsula in Japanese hands. This famous incident launched the **May Fourth Movement**, which opposed both foreign domination and warlord government.

The May Fourth Movement, which was both strongly pro-Marxist and passionately anti-imperialist, looked to the October 1917 Bolshevik Revolution in Russia as a model for its own nationalist revolution. In 1923 revolutionary leader Sun Yatsen (1866–1925) decided to ally his Nationalist Party, or Guomindang, with the Communist Third International and the newly formed Chinese Communist Party. The result was the first of many so-called national liberation fronts, in keeping with Lenin's blueprint for temporarily uniting all anticonservative, anti-imperialist forces in a common revolutionary struggle.

Sun, however, was no Communist. In his *Three Principles of the People*, elaborating on the official Nationalist Party ideology — nationalism, democracy, and people's livelihood — nationalism remained of prime importance:

> Compared to the other peoples of the world we have the greatest population and our civilization is four thousand years old; we should be advancing in the front rank with the nations of Europe and America. But the Chinese people have only family and clan solidarity, they do not have national spirit. . . . If we do not earnestly espouse nationalism and weld together our four hundred million people into a strong nation, there is a danger of China's being lost and our people being destroyed. If we wish to avert this catastrophe, we must espouse nationalism and bring this national spirit to the salvation of the country.[4]

Democracy, in contrast, had a less exalted meaning. Sun equated it with firm rule by the Nationalists, who would improve people's lives through land reform and welfare measures.

Students Demonstrating in Tiananmen Square, Beijing, Summer 1919 The news that the Versailles Peace Conference left China's Shandong Peninsula in Japanese hands brought an explosion of student protest on May 4, 1919. Student demonstrations in the capital's historic Tiananmen Square continued through June, as the May Fourth Movement against foreign domination took root and grew. (Photo from Kautz Family YMCA Archives. Reproduced with permission.)

Sun planned to use the Nationalist Party's revolutionary army to crush the warlords and reunite China under a strong central government. When Sun unexpectedly died in 1925, Jiang Jieshi (traditionally called Chiang Kai-shek; 1887–1975), the young Japanese-educated director of the party's army training school, took his place. In 1926 and 1927 Jiang led Nationalist armies in a successful attack on warlord governments in central and northern China. In 1928 the Nationalists established a new capital at Nanjing (Nanking). Foreign states recognized the Nanjing government, and superficial observers believed China to be truly reunified.

In fact, national unification was only skin-deep. China remained a vast agricultural country plagued by foreign concessions, regional differences, and a lack of modern communications. Moreover, the uneasy alliance between the Nationalist Party and the Chinese Communist Party had turned into a bitter, deadly rivalry. Justifiably fearful of Communist subversion of

the Nationalist government, Jiang decided in April 1927 to liquidate his left-wing "allies" in a bloody purge. Chinese Communists went into hiding and vowed revenge.

China's Intellectual Revolution

Nationalism was the most powerful idea in China between 1911 and 1929, but it was only one aspect of a complex intellectual revolution, generally known as the **New Culture Movement**, that hammered at

- **May Fourth Movement** A Chinese nationalist movement against foreign imperialists; it began as a student protest against the decision of the Versailles Peace Conference to leave the Shandong Peninsula in the hands of Japan.

- **New Culture Movement** An intellectual revolution, sometimes called the Chinese Renaissance, that attacked traditional Chinese, particularly Confucian, culture and promoted Western ideas of science, democracy, and individualism, from around 1916 to 1923.

MAP 29.2 The Chinese Communist Movement and the War with Japan, 1927–1938
After urban uprisings ordered by Stalin failed in 1927, Mao Zedong succeeded in forming a self-governing Communist soviet in mountainous southern China. Relentless Nationalist attacks between 1930 and 1934 finally forced the Long March to Yan'an, where the Communists were well positioned for guerrilla war against the Japanese.

traditional Chinese thought and custom, advocated cultural renaissance, and pushed China into the modern world. The New Culture Movement was founded around 1916 by young Western-oriented intellectuals in Beijing, some of whom were later involved in the May Fourth movement in 1919. These intellectuals fiercely attacked China's ancient Confucian ethics, which subordinated subjects to rulers, sons to fathers, and wives to husbands. As modernists, they provocatively advocated new and anti-Confucian virtues: individualism, democratic equality, and the critical scientific method. They also promoted the use of simple, understandable written language as a means to clear thinking and mass education. China, they said, needed a whole new culture, a radically different worldview.

Many intellectuals thought the radical worldview China needed was Marxist socialism. It too was Western in origin, "scientific" in approach, and materialist in its denial of religious belief and Confucian family ethics. But while liberalism and individualism reflected the bewildering range of Western thought since the Enlightenment, Marxist socialism offered the certainty of a single all-encompassing creed. As one young Communist intellectual exclaimed, "I am now able to impose order on all the ideas which I could not reconcile; I have found the key to all the problems which appeared to me self-contradictory and insoluble."[5]

Though undeniably Western, Marxism provided a means of criticizing Western dominance, thereby salving Chinese pride. Chinese Communists could blame

□ Picturing the Past

The Fate of a Chinese Patriot On May 30, 1925, Shanghai police opened fire on a group of Chinese demonstrators who were protesting unfair labor practices and wages and the foreign imperialist presence in their country. The police killed nine people and wounded many others, touching off nationwide and international protests and attacks on foreign offices and businesses. This political cartoon shows the fate of the Chinese patriots at the hands of warlords and foreign imperialists. (© Library of Congress, LC-USZ62-99451)

ANALYZING THE IMAGE Which figures represent Chinese warlords, foreign imperialists, and Chinese patriots? What does the cartoon suggest about the fate of the Chinese demonstrators?

CONNECTIONS Why might foreign imperialists and Chinese warlords work together to put down the demonstrations?

China's pitiful weakness on rapacious foreign capitalistic imperialism. Thus Marxism, as modified by Lenin and applied by the Bolsheviks in the Soviet Union, appeared as a means of catching up with the hated but envied West. For Chinese believers, it promised salvation soon.

Chinese Communists could and did interpret Marxism-Leninism to appeal to the masses — the peasants. Mao Zedong (Mao Tse-tung) in particular quickly recognized the impoverished Chinese peasantry's enormous revolutionary potential. (See "Viewpoints: Gandhi and Mao on Revolutionary Means," page 893.) A member of a prosperous, hard-working peasant family, Mao (1893–1976) converted to Marxist socialism in 1918. He began his revolutionary career as an urban labor organizer. In 1925 protest strikes by Chinese textile workers against their Japanese employers unexpectedly spread from the big coastal cities to rural China, prompting Mao to reconsider the peas-

ants. Investigating the rapid growth of radical peasant associations in Hunan province, Mao argued passionately in a 1927 report that

> the force of the peasantry is like that of the raging winds and driving rain. It is rapidly increasing in violence. No force can stand in its way. The peasantry will tear apart all nets which bind it and hasten along the road to liberation. They will bury beneath them all forces of imperialism, militarism, corrupt officialdom, village bosses and evil gentry.[6]

Mao's first experiment in peasant revolt — the Autumn Harvest Uprising of September 1927 — was not successful, but Mao learned quickly. He advocated equal distribution of land and broke up his forces into small guerrilla groups. After 1928 he and his supporters built up a self-governing Communist soviet, centered at Ruijin (Juichin) in southeastern China, and dug in against Nationalist attacks.

Japanese Suffragists In the 1920s Japanese women pressed for political emancipation in demonstrations like this one, but they did not receive the right to vote until 1946. Like these suffragists, some young Japanese women adopted Western fashions. Most workers in modern Japanese textile factories were women. (Time Life Pictures/Getty Images)

China's intellectual revolution also stimulated profound changes in popular culture and family life. After the 1911 revolution Chinese women enjoyed increasingly greater freedom and equality. Foot binding was outlawed and attacked as cruel and uncivilized. Arranged marriages and polygamy declined. Women gradually gained unprecedented educational and economic opportunities. Thus rising nationalism and the intellectual revolution interacted with monumental changes in Chinese family life. (See "Individuals in Society: Ning Lao, a Chinese Working Woman," page 899.)

From Liberalism to Ultranationalism in Japan

The efforts of the Meiji reformers (see page 797) to build a powerful nationalistic state and resist Western imperialism were spectacularly successful and deeply impressed Japan's fellow Asians. The Japanese, alone among Asia's peoples, had mastered modern industrial technology by 1910 and had fought victorious wars against both China and Russia. The First World War brought more triumphs. In 1915 Japan easily seized Germany's Asian holdings and held on to most of them as League of Nations mandates. The Japanese economy expanded enormously. Profits soared as Japan won new markets that wartime Europe could no longer supply.

In the early 1920s Japan made further progress on all fronts. Most Japanese nationalists believed that Japan had a semidivine mission to enlighten and protect Asia, but some were convinced that they could achieve their goal peacefully. In 1922 Japan signed a naval arms limitation treaty with the Western powers and returned some of its control over the Shandong Peninsula to China. These conciliatory moves reduced tensions in East Asia. At home Japan seemed headed toward genuine democracy. The electorate expanded twelvefold between 1918 and 1925 as all males over twenty-five won the vote. Two-party competition was intense. Japanese living standards were the highest in Asia. Literacy was universal.

Japan's remarkable rise was accompanied by serious problems. Japan had a rapidly growing population, but scarce natural resources. As early as the 1920s Japan was exporting manufactured goods in order to pay for imports of food and essential raw materials. Deeply enmeshed in world trade, Japan was vulnerable to every boom and bust. These economic realities broadened support for Japan's colonial empire. Before World War I Japanese leaders saw colonial expansion primarily in terms of international prestige and national defense. They believed that control of Taiwan, Korea, and Manchuria provided an essential "outer ring of defense" to protect the home islands from Russian attack and Anglo-American imperialism. Now, in the 1920s, Japan's colonies also seemed essential for markets, raw materials, and economic growth.

Japan's rapid industrial development also created an imbalanced "dualistic" economy. The modern sector

Individuals in Society

Ning Lao, a Chinese Working Woman

THE VOICE OF THE POOR AND UNEDUCATED IS often muffled in history. Thus *A Daughter of Han*, a rare autobiography of an illiterate working woman as told to an American friend, offers unforgettable insights into the evolution of ordinary Chinese life and family relations.

Ning Lao was born in 1867 to poor parents in the northern city of Penglai on the Shandong Peninsula. Her foot binding was delayed to age nine, "since I loved so much to run and play." When the bandages were finally drawn tight, "my feet hurt so much that for two years I had to crawl on my knees."* Her arranged marriage at age fourteen was a disaster. She found that her husband was a drug addict ("in those days everyone took opium to some extent") who sold everything to pay for his habit. Yet "there was no freedom then for women," and "it was no light thing for a woman to leave her house" and husband. Thus Ning Lao endured her situation until her husband sold their four-year-old daughter to buy opium. Taking her remaining baby daughter, she fled.

Taking off her foot bandages, Ning Lao became a beggar. Her feet began to spread, quite improperly, but she walked without pain. And the beggar's life was "not the hardest one," she thought, for a beggar woman could go where she pleased. To better care for her child, Ning Lao became a servant and a cook in prosperous households. Some of her mistresses were concubines (secondary wives taken by rich men in middle age), and she concluded that concubinage resulted in nothing but quarrels and heartache. Hot tempered and quick to take offense and leave an employer, the hard-working woman always found a new job quickly. In time she became a peddler of luxury goods to wealthy women confined to their homes.

The two unshakable values that buoyed Ning Lao were a tough, fatalistic acceptance of life—"Only fortune that comes of itself will come. There is no use to seek for it"—and devotion to her family. She eventually returned to her husband, who had mellowed, seldom took opium, and was "good" in those years. "But I did not miss him when he died. I had my newborn son and I was happy. My house was established. . . . Truly all my life I spent thinking of my family." Her lifelong devotion was reciprocated by her son and granddaughter, who cared for her well in her old age.

Ning Lao's remarkable life story encompasses both old and new Chinese attitudes toward family life. Her son moved to the capital city of Beijing, worked in an office, and had only one wife. Her

granddaughter, Su Teh, studied in missionary schools and became a college teacher and a determined foe of arranged marriages. She personified the trend toward greater freedom for Chinese women.

Generational differences also highlighted changing political attitudes. When the Japanese invaded China and occupied Beijing in 1937, Ning Lao thought that "perhaps the Mandate of Heaven had passed to the Japanese . . . and we should listen to them as our new masters." Her nationalistic granddaughter disagreed. She urged resistance and the creation of a new China, where the people governed themselves. Leaving to join the guerrillas in 1938, Su Teh gave her savings to her family and promised to continue to help them. One must be good to one's family, she said, but one must also work for the country.

QUESTIONS FOR ANALYSIS

1. Compare the lives of Ning Lao and her granddaughter. In what ways were they different and similar?
2. In a broader historical perspective, what do you find most significant about Ning Lao's account of her life? Why?

The tough and resilient Ning Lao (right) with Ida Pruitt.
(Reproduced with permission of Eileen Hsu-Belzer)

*Ida Pruitt, *A Daughter of Han: The Autobiography of a Chinese Working Woman* (New Haven, Conn.: Yale University Press, 1945), p. 22. Other quotations are from pages 83, 62, 71, 182, 166, 235, and 246.

> "Our seven hundred million brothers in China and India have no other path to independence than that offered by our guidance and protection."

JAPANESE ULTRANATIONALIST KITA IKKI

consisted of a handful of giant conglomerate firms, the **zaibatsu**, or "financial combines." Zaibatsu firms like Mitsubishi employed thousands of workers and owned banks, mines, steel mills, cotton factories, shipyards, and trading companies, all of them closely interrelated. Zaibatsu firms wielded enormous economic power and dominated the other sector of the economy, an unorganized multitude of peasant farmers and craftsmen. The result was financial oligarchy, corruption of government officials, and a weak middle class.

Behind the façade of party politics, the old and new elites — the emperor, high government officials, big businessmen, and military leaders — were jockeying savagely for the real power. Cohesive leadership, which had played such an important role in Japan's modernization by the Meiji reformers, had ceased to exist. By far the most serious challenge to peaceful progress was fanatical nationalism. As in Europe, ultranationalism first emerged in Japan in the late nineteenth century but did not flower fully until the First World War and the 1930s.

Though often vague, Japan's ultranationalists shared several fundamental beliefs. They were violently anti-Western. They rejected democracy, big business, and Marxist socialism, which they blamed for destroying the older, superior Japanese practices they wanted to restore. Reviving old myths, they stressed the emperor's godlike qualities and the samurai warrior's code of honor and obedience. Despising party politics, they assassinated moderate leaders and plotted armed uprisings to achieve their goals. Above all else, the ultranationalists preached foreign expansion. Like Western imperialists shouldering "the white man's burden," Japanese ultranationalists thought their mission was a noble one. "Asia for the Asians" was their anti-Western rallying cry. As the famous ultranationalist Kita Ikki wrote in 1923, "Our seven hundred million brothers in China and India have no other path to independence than that offered by our guidance and protection."[7]

The ultranationalists were noisy and violent in the 1920s, but it took the Great Depression of the 1930s to tip the scales decisively in their favor. The worldwide depression, which had dire consequences for many

countries (see Chapter 30), hit Japan like a tidal wave in 1930. Exports and wages collapsed; unemployment and raw suffering soared. Starving peasants ate the bark off trees and sold their daughters to brothels. The ultranationalists blamed the system, and people listened.

Japan Against China

Among those who listened with particular care were young Japanese army officers in Manchuria, the underpopulated, resource-rich province of northeastern China controlled by the Japanese army since its victory over Russia in 1905. Many junior Japanese officers in Manchuria came from the peasantry and were distressed by the stories of rural suffering they heard from home. They also knew the Japanese army's budget and prestige had declined in the prosperous 1920s.

The rise of Chinese nationalism worried the young officers most. This new political force, embodied in the Guomindang unification of China, challenged Japanese control over Manchuria. In response, junior Japanese officers in Manchuria, in cooperation with top generals in Tokyo, secretly manufactured an excuse for aggression in late 1931. They blew up some Japanese-owned railroad tracks near the city of Shenyang (Mukden) and then, with reinforcements rushed in from Korea, quickly occupied all of Manchuria in "self-defense."

In 1932 Japan proclaimed Manchuria an independent state and installed Puyi (1906–1967), the last emperor of the old Qing Dynasty, as puppet emperor. When the League of Nations condemned its aggression in Manchuria, Japan resigned in protest. Japanese aggression in Manchuria proved that the army, though reporting directly to the Japanese emperor, was an independent force subject to no outside control.

The Japanese puppet state named Manchukuo in northeast China became the model for the subsequent conquest and occupation of China and then Southeast Asia. Throughout the 1930s the Japanese worked to integrate Manchuria, along with Korea and Taiwan, into a large, self-sufficient economic bloc that provided resources, markets, and investment opportunities safe from Western power in East Asia. While exporting raw materials, state-sponsored Japanese companies in Manchuria also built steel mills and heavy industry to supply vital military goods. At home, newspapers and newsreels glorified Japan's efforts and mobilized public support for colonial empire.

For China the Japanese conquest of Manchuria was disastrous. Japanese aggression in Manchuria drew attention away from modernizing efforts. The Nationalist government promoted a massive boycott of Japanese goods but lost interest in social reform. Above all, the Nationalist government after 1931 completely neglected land reform and the Chinese peasants' grinding poverty.

• **zaibatsu** Giant conglomerate firms in Japan.
• **Long March** The 6,000-mile retreat of the Chinese Communist army to a remote region on the northwestern border of China, during which tens of thousands lost their lives.

As in many poor agricultural societies throughout history, Chinese peasants paid roughly half of their crops to their landlords as rent. Land ownership was very unequal. One study estimated that a mere 4 percent of families, usually absentee landlords living in cities, owned fully half the land. Poor peasants and farm laborers — 70 percent of the rural population — owned only one-sixth of the land. As a result, peasants were heavily in debt and chronically underfed. A contemporaneous Chinese economist spelled out the revolutionary implications: "It seems clear that the land problem in China today is as acute as that of eighteenth-century France or nineteenth-century Russia." Mao Zedong agreed.

Having abandoned land reform, partly because they themselves were often landowners, the Nationalists under Jiang Jieshi devoted their energies between 1930 and 1934 to great campaigns of encirclement and extermination of the Communists' rural power base in southeastern China. In 1934 they closed in for the kill, but, in one of the most incredible sagas of modern times, the main Communist army broke out, beat off attacks, and retreated 6,000 miles in twelve months to a remote region on the northwestern border (see Map 29.2). Of the estimated 100,000 men and women who began the **Long March**, only 8,000 to 10,000 reached the final destination. There Mao built up his forces once again, established a new territorial base, and won local peasant support by undertaking land reform.

In Japan politics became increasingly chaotic. In 1937 the Japanese military and the ultranationalists were in command. Unable to force China to cede more territory in northern China, they used a minor incident near Beijing as a pretext for a general attack. This marked the beginning of what became World War II in Asia, although Japan issued no declaration of war. The Nationalist government, which had just formed a united front with the Communists, fought hard, but Japanese troops quickly took Beijing and northern China. Taking the great port of Shanghai after ferocious combat, the Japanese launched an immediate attack up the Yangzi River (see Map 29.2).

Foretelling the horrors of World War II, the Japanese air force bombed Chinese cities and civilian populations with unrelenting fury. Nanjing, the capital, fell in December 1937. Entering the city, Japanese soldiers went berserk and committed dreadful atrocities over seven weeks. They brutally murdered an estimated

Japanese Atrocities in China In December 1937, after the fall of the Chinese capital Nanjing, Japanese soldiers went on a horrifying rampage. These Japanese recruits are using Chinese prisoners of war as live targets in a murderous bayonet drill. Other Chinese prisoners were buried alive by their Japanese captors. (Hulton Archive/Getty Images)

200,000 to 300,000 Chinese civilians and unarmed soldiers, and raped 20,000 to 80,000 Chinese women. The "Rape of Nanjing" combined with other Japanese atrocities to outrage world opinion. The Western Powers denounced Japanese aggression but, with tensions rising in Europe, took no action.

By late 1938 Japanese armies occupied sizable portions of coastal China (see Map 29.2). But the Nationalists and the Communists had retreated to the interior, and both refused to accept defeat. In 1939, as Europe edged toward another great war, China and Japan were bogged down in a savage stalemate. This undeclared war — called by historians the Second Sino-Japanese War (1937–1945) — provided a spectacular example of conflicting nationalisms.

Striving for Independence in Southeast Asia

The tide of nationalism was also rising in Southeast Asia. Like their counterparts in India, China, and Japan, nationalists in French Indochina, the Dutch East Indies, and the Philippines urgently wanted genuine political independence and freedom from foreign rule. In both French Indochina and the Dutch East Indies, they ran up against an imperialist stone wall. The obstacle to Filipino independence came from America and Japan.

The French in Indochina, as in all their colonies, refused to export the liberal policies contained in the stirring words of their own Declaration of the Rights of Man and the Citizen: liberty, equality, and fraternity (see page 653). This uncompromising attitude stimulated the growth of an equally stubborn Communist opposition under Ho Chi Minh (1890–1969), which despite ruthless repression emerged as the dominant anti-French force in Indochina.

In the East Indies — modern Indonesia — the Dutch made some concessions after the First World War, establishing a people's council with very limited lawmaking power. But in the 1930s the Dutch cracked down hard, jailing all the important nationalist leaders. Like the French, the Dutch were determined to hold on.

In the Philippines, however, a well-established nationalist movement achieved greater success. As in colonial Latin America, the Spanish in the Philippines had been indefatigable missionaries. By the late nineteenth century the Filipino population was 80 percent Catholic. Filipinos shared a common cultural heritage and a common racial origin. Education, especially for girls, was advanced for Southeast Asia, and already in 1843 a higher percentage of people could read in the Philippines than in Spain itself. Economic development helped to create a westernized elite, which turned first to reform and then to revolution in the 1890s. As in Egypt and Turkey, long-standing intimate contact with Western civilization created a strong nationalist movement at an early date.

Filipino nationalists were bitterly disillusioned when the United States, having taken the Philippines

Uncle Sam as Schoolmaster In this cartoon that first appeared on the cover of *Harper's Weekly* in August 1898, unruly students identified as a "Cuban Ex-patriot" and a "Guerilla" are being disciplined with a switch by a stern Uncle Sam as he tries to teach them self-government. The gentleman to the left reading a book is Jose Miguel Gomez, one of Cuba's revolutionary heroes, while the Filipino insurrectionist Emilio Aguinaldo is made to wear a dunce hat and stand in the corner. The two well-behaved girls to the right represent Hawai'i and Puerto Rico. (The Granger Collection, New York)

from Spain in the Spanish-American War of 1898, ruthlessly beat down a patriotic revolt and denied the universal Filipino desire for independence. The Americans claimed the Philippines were not ready for self-rule and might be seized by Germany or Britain if they could not establish a stable, secure government. As the imperialist power in the Philippines, the United States encouraged education and promoted capitalistic economic development. And as in British India, an elected legislature was given some real powers. In 1919 President Wilson even promised eventual independence, though subsequent Republican administrations saw it as a distant goal.

As in India and French Indochina, demands for independence grew. One important contributing factor was American racial attitudes. Americans treated Filipinos as inferiors and introduced segregationist practices borrowed from the American South. American racism made passionate nationalists of many Filipinos. However, it was the Great Depression that had the most radical impact on the Philippines.

The Spanish-American War in the Philippines, 1898

As the United States collapsed economically in the 1930s, the Philippines suddenly appeared to be a liability rather than an asset. American farm groups lobbied for protection from cheap Filipino sugar. To protect American jobs, labor unions demanded an end to Filipino immigration. Responding to public pressure, in 1934 Congress made the Philippines a self-governing commonwealth and scheduled independence for 1944. Sugar imports were reduced, and immigration was limited to only fifty Filipinos per year.

Like Britain and France in the Middle East, the United States was determined to hold on to its big military bases in the Philippines even as it permitted increased local self-government and promised eventual political independence. Some Filipino nationalists denounced the continued presence of U.S. fleets and armies. Others were less certain that the American presence was the immediate problem. Japan was fighting in China and expanding economically into the Philippines and throughout Southeast Asia. By 1939 a new threat to Filipino independence would come from Japan itself.

Just as nationalism drove politics and state building in Europe in the nineteenth century, so it took root across Asia in the late nineteenth and early twentieth centuries. While nationalism in Europe developed out of a desire to turn cultural unity into political reality and create imagined communities out of millions of strangers, in Asia nationalist sentiments drew their greatest energy from opposition to European imperialism and domination. Asian modernizers, aware of momentous advances in science and technology and of politics and social practices in the West, also pressed the nationalist cause by demanding an end to outdated conservative traditions that they argued only held back the development of modern, independent nations capable of throwing off Western domination and existing as equals with the West.

The nationalist cause in Asia took many forms and produced some of the most remarkable leaders of the twentieth century. In Chapter 32 we will discuss how nationalist leaders across Asia shaped the freedom struggle and the resulting independence according to their own ideological and personal visions. China's Mao Zedong is the giant among the nationalist leaders who emerged in Asia, but he replaced imperialist rule with one-party Communist rule. Gandhi's dream of a unified India collapsed with the partition of British India into Hindu India and Muslim Pakistan and Bangladesh. India and Pakistan remain bitter, and nuclear-armed, enemies today, as we will see in Chapter 34. Egypt assumed a prominent position in the Arab world after World War II under the leadership of Gamal Nasser and, after a series of wars with Israel, began to play a significant role in efforts to find a peaceful resolution to the Israeli-Palestinian conflict. That conflict, however, continues unabated as nationalist and religious sentiments inflame feelings on both sides. Ho Chi Minh eventually forced the French colonizers out of Vietnam, only to face another Western power, the United States, in a long and deadly war. As described in Chapter 32, a unified Vietnam finally gained its independence in 1975, but like China, under one-party Communist control.

Japan remained an exception to much of what happened in the rest of Asia. After a long period of isolation, the Japanese implemented an unprecedented program of modernization and westernization in the late 1800s. Japan continued to model itself after the West when it took control of former German colonies as mandated territories after the Great War and occupied territory in China, Korea, Vietnam, Taiwan, and elsewhere. In the next chapter we will see how ultranationalism drove national policy in the 1930s, ultimately leading to Japan's defeat in World War II.

CHAPTER REVIEW

□ **Why did modern nationalism develop in Asia between the First and Second World Wars, and what was its appeal? (p. 878)**

The Asian nationalist revolt against the West began before the First World War, but only after 1914 did Asian nationalist movements broaden their bases sufficiently to challenge Western domination effectively. Nationalists in Asia were roused to action by broken promises of independence, exposure to democratic and republican ideas while fighting for their colonial overlords, and the mandate system, which showed that Western imperialists did not plan to give up their colonial territories. Nationalism's appeal lay in its usefulness as a way to organize anti-imperialist resistance, its challenge to old-fashioned political and social beliefs, and its offer of a prosperous free future. Mass nationalist movements sought human dignity as well as political freedom. Generally speaking, Asian nationalists favored modernization and adopted Western techniques and ideas even as they rejected Western rule. Asian nationalists had to fight long and hard, though their struggle gained momentum from growing popular support and the encouragement of the Soviet Union.

□ **How did the collapse of the Ottoman Empire in World War I shape nationalist movements in the Middle East? (p. 881)**

The collapse of the Ottoman Empire in World War I left a power vacuum that both Western imperialists and Turkish, Arab, Persian, Jewish, and other nationalists sought to fill. The Turks, who had ruled the old Ottoman Empire, created the modern secular state of Turkey under the leadership of Mustafa Kemal. Strong leadership also played a role in the successful nationalist movements in Persia and Afghanistan. The British and French maintained various degrees of control over the League of Nations–mandated Arab states of Iraq, Syria, Lebanon, and Egypt, but lost much of their influence over the next two decades as Arab national-

KEY TERMS

Permanent Mandates Commission (p. 879)
Sykes-Picot Agreement (p. 882)
Balfour Declaration (p. 882)
Treaty of Lausanne (p. 885)
Majlis (p. 886)
kibbutz (p. 889)
Lucknow Pact (p. 890)
satyagraha (p. 891)
May Fourth Movement (p. 894)
New Culture Movement (p. 895)
zaibatsu (p. 900)
Long March (p. 901)

ists pushed for complete independence. While political independence was achieved, the concessions that Arab rulers had to make in return for independence meant continuing Western influence and the ever-present threat of military action to secure Western economic interests in the regions. The British made promises to both the Palestinians and the Jewish Zionists regarding independent homelands in Palestine, creating an impasse that deteriorated in the interwar year as European Jews migrated in ever greater numbers to Palestine.

□ **What role did Gandhi and his campaign of militant nonviolence play in leading India to independence from the British? (p. 889)**

Gandhi knew that the Indian people were not capable of fighting a military campaign against the mighty British Empire without suffering hundreds of thousands, perhaps millions, of deaths. But he realized that a few thousand British could do nothing if millions of Indians refused to cooperate or obey British laws. By employing active, nonviolent resistance, which he called satyagraha, Gandhi and his millions of Hindu and Muslim followers were able to bring British colonial rule in India to a standstill, leading to Indian independence in 1947. Regrettably, however, Gandhi was not able to control the extreme religious nationalism of the Muslims and Hindus following independence, and by the end of the 1930s Muslim separatists threatened to split off from predominantly Hindu India.

□ How did nationalism shape political developments in East and Southeast Asia? (p. 894)

Asia's nationalist movements arose out of separate historical experiences and distinct cultures. The 1911 revolution in China successfully ended the ancient dynastic system, only to see dictators and warlords seize control. The May Fourth Movement of 1919 renewed nationalist hopes, and by 1928 nationalist armies had defeated the warlords. But the direction of unified China was bitterly contested by the Nationalist Party and the Communists led by Mao Zedong. Japan, unlike China, had industrialized early and by the 1920s seemed headed toward genuine democracy. But a growing population and lack of natural resources gave rise to ultranationalists who rejected big business and Marxist socialism in favor of aggressive foreign expansion based on "Asia for Asians." Nationalist movements in Indochina and the East Indies met with little success. The Philippines did achieve independence from the United States, but as was the case for the states of the Middle East, it came at the price of long-term concessions to the U.S. military. The diversity of these nationalist movements helps explain why Asian peoples became defensive in their relations with one another while rising against Western rule. Like earlier nationalists in Europe, Asian nationalists developed a strong sense of "we" and "they"; "they" included other Asians as well as Europeans. Nationalism meant freedom, modernization, and cultural renaissance, but it nonetheless proved to be a mixed blessing.

SUGGESTED READING

Chang, Jung, and Jon Halliday. *Mao: The Unknown Story.* 2006. Very controversial biography of the Chinese leader.

Chow, Tse-tung. *The May Fourth Movement: Intellectual Revolution in Modern China.* 1960. The classic study of the Chinese intellectual revolution that began in 1919.

Erikson, Eric. *Gandhi's Truth: On the Origins of Militant Nonviolence.* 1969. A classic study of Gandhi's life and the origins of satyagraha.

Fromkin, David. *A Peace to End All Peace: The Fall of the Ottoman Empire and the Creation of the Modern Middle East.* 2001. A thorough but readable introduction to the Middle East in the early twentieth century.

Hourani, Albert, and Malise Ruthven. *History of the Arab Peoples.* 2003. One of the best single-volume histories of the Arab peoples.

Hsü, Immanuel C. Y. *The Rise of Modern China,* 6th ed. 1999. Sixth edition of a classic history of modern China.

Irokawa, Daikichi. *The Age of Hirohito: In Search of Modern Japan.* 1995. An excellent brief account by a leading Japanese historian.

Lacqueur, Walter. *A History of Zionism. From the French Revolution to the Establishment of the State of Israel.* 1972. Good general history of Zionism and the founding of Israel.

Mango, Andrew. *Atatürk.* 2000. Rich, well-researched biography of this complex Turkish leader.

Myers, Ramon H., and M. Peattie, eds. *The Japanese Colonial Expansion, 1895–1945.* 1984. Broad collection of essays covering all of Japan's colonial empire, both formal and informal.

Osborne, Milton. *Southeast Asia: An Introductory History,* 9th ed. 2005. Ninth edition of the classic introduction to the region's history.

Owen, Norman, David Chandler, and William R. Roff. *The Emergence of Southeast Asia: A New History.* 2004. Newer history looking at both individual countries and social and economic themes, including gender and ecology.

Reischauer, Edwin O. *Japan: The Story of Nation,* 4th ed. 1991. The classic history in its fourth edition by America's leading historian on Japan.

Spence, Jonathan. *The Search for Modern China.* 1990. Important study of modern China by a leading Chinese scholar.

Wolpert, Stanley. *India.* 2005. An excellent introduction to India's history.

Young, Louise. *Japan's Total Empire: Manchuria and the Culture of Wartime Imperialism.* 1998. A fascinating pioneering work on Japanese imperialism.

NOTES

1. H. Armstrong, *Turkey in Travail: The Birth of a New Nation* (London: John Lane, 1925), p. 75.
2. Quoted in Lord Kinross, *Atatürk: A Biography of Mustafa Kemal, Father of Modern Turkey* (New York: Morrow, 1965), p. 181.
3. Quoted in E. Erikson, *Gandhi's Truth: On the Origins of Militant Nonviolence* (New York: W. W. Norton, 1969), p. 225.
4. Quoted in W. T. deBary, W. Chan, and B. Watson, *Sources of Chinese Tradition* (New York: Columbia University Press, 1964), pp. 768–769.
5. Quoted in J. F. Fairbank, E. O. Reischauer, and A. M. Craig, *East Asia: Tradition and Transformation* (Boston: Houghton Mifflin, 1973), p. 774.
6. Quoted in B. I. Schwartz, *Chinese Communism and the Rise of Mao* (Cambridge, Mass.: Harvard University Press, 1951), p. 74.
7. Quoted in W. T. deBary, R. Tsunoda, and D. Keene, *Sources of Japanese Tradition,* vol. 2 (New York: Columbia University Press, 1958), p. 269.

For practice quizzes and other study tools, visit the **Online Study Guide** at bedfordstmartins.com/mckayworld.

For primary sources from this period, see *Sources of World Societies,* **Second Edition**.

For Web sites, images, and documents related to topics in this chapter, visit **Make History** at bedfordstmartins.com/mckayworld.

• **Jewish Boy in Nazi-Controlled France** Israel Lichtenstein, wearing a Jewish star, was born in Paris in 1932. His father was one of an estimated one million Jews who died in the Auschwitz concentration camp. Israel and his mother were also sent to a concentration camp, but they escaped and survived the Holocaust by going into hiding until the end of the war. Israel later immigrated to the nation of Israel. (United States Holocaust Memorial Museum, courtesy of Israel Lichtenstein)

economic situation then worsened in the recession of 1937 and 1938, and unemployment was still a staggering 10 million when war broke out in Europe in 1939. The New Deal brought fundamental reform, but it never did pull the United States out of the depression; it took the Second World War to do that.

The European Response to the Depression

The collapse of the American stock market in October 1929 set off a chain of economic downturns that hit Europe, particularly Germany and Great Britain, the hardest. Postwar Europe had come out of the Great War deeply in debt and in desperate need of investment capital to rebuild. The United States became the primary creditor and financier. Germany borrowed, for example, to pay Britain war reparations, and then Britain took that money and paid America back for its war debts and investment loans. When the American economy crashed, the whole system crashed with it.

Of all the Western democracies, the Scandinavian countries under socialist leadership responded most successfully to the challenge of the Great Depression. When the economic crisis struck in 1929, socialist governments in Sweden pioneered the use of large-scale deficits to finance public works projects and thereby maintain production and employment. Scandinavian governments also increased social welfare benefits, from old-age pensions and unemployment insurance to subsidized housing and maternity allowances. All this spending required a large bureaucracy

and high taxes. Yet both private and cooperative enterprise thrived, as did democracy. Some observers saw Scandinavia's welfare socialism as an appealing middle way between sick capitalism and cruel communism or fascism.

In Britain, Ramsay MacDonald's Labour government (1929–1931) and then, after 1931, the Conservative-dominated coalition government followed orthodox economic theory. The budget was balanced, but unemployed workers received barely enough welfare to live. Nevertheless, the economy recovered considerably after 1932. This recovery reflected the gradual reorientation of the British economy. After abandoning the gold standard in 1931 and establishing protective tariffs in 1932, Britain concentrated increasingly on the national, rather than the international, market. Old export industries, such as textiles and coal, continued to decline, but new industries, such as automobiles and electrical appliances, grew. These developments encouraged British isolationism, but often had devastating economic consequences for Britain's far-flung colonies and dominions.

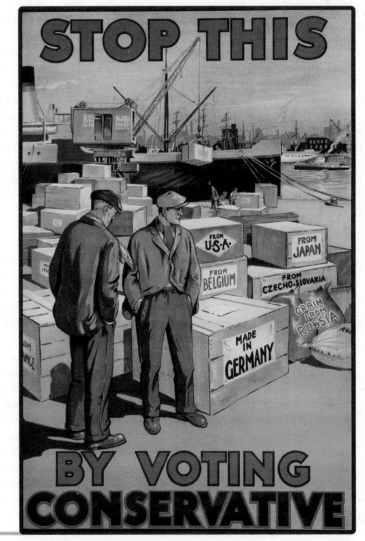

▢ Picturing the Past

British Conservative Party Poster, 1931 This campaign poster from the 1931 British general election portrays crates and bags of goods being unloaded on English docks. (Hulton Archive/Getty Images)

ANALYZING THE IMAGE Where are the goods on the dock from? What do the Conservatives want stopped?

CONNECTIONS Was this attitude toward foreign goods unique to England? What other countries held similar views? What effect did such attitudes have on the worldwide depression?

Because France was relatively less industrialized and more isolated from the world economy, the Great Depression came late. But once the depression hit France, it stayed. Decline was steady until 1935, and a short-lived recovery never brought production or employment back up to predepression levels. Economic stagnation both reflected and heightened an ongoing political crisis. Fascist-type organizations agitated against parliamentary democracy and looked to Mussolini's Italy and Hitler's Germany for inspiration. At the same time, the Communist Party and many workers looked to Stalin's Russia for guidance. Moderate republicanism's vital center was sapped from both sides.

Frightened by the fascists' growing strength at home and abroad, French Communist, Socialist, and Radical parties formed an alliance — the **Popular Front** — for the May 1936 national elections. Following its clear victory, the Popular Front government made the only real attempt to deal with France's social and economic problems of the 1930s. Inspired by Roosevelt's New Deal, the Popular Front launched a far-reaching program of social reform. Popular with workers and the lower middle class, these measures were quickly sabotaged by rapid inflation and cries of revolution from fascists and frightened conservatives. Wealthy people sneaked their money out of the country, labor unrest grew, and France entered a severe financial crisis. In June 1937, with the country hopelessly divided, the Popular Front collapsed.

Worldwide Effects

The Great Depression's magnitude was unprecedented, and its effect rippled well beyond Europe and the United States. As many of the countries and colonies of Africa, Asia, and Latin America were nearly totally dependent on one or two commodities — such as coffee beans, rubber, tin, or cocoa — for income, the implementation of protectionist trade policies by the leading industrial nations had devastating effects. The different colonies and dominions of the British Empire — particularly Australia, India, and Canada — were among the hardest hit by the Great Depression because of their close ties to the economies of Great Britain and the United States.

While Asians were affected by the Great Depression, the consequences varied greatly by country or colony and were not as severe generally as they were elsewhere in the world. That being said, where the depression did hit, it was often severe. The price of rice — Asia's staff of life and main cash crop — fell by two-thirds between 1929 and 1932. Also crippling to the

region's economies was Asia's heavy dependence on raw material exports, such as rubber and tin from Malaya for automobile production. With debts to local moneylenders fixed in value and taxes to colonial governments hardly ever reduced, many Asian peasants in the 1930s struggled under crushing debt and suffered severely.

In Japan the terrible suffering caused by the Great Depression caused ultranationalists and militarists to call for less dependence on global markets and the expansion of a self-sufficient empire. Such expansion began in 1931 when Japan invaded Chinese Manchuria, which became a major source of raw materials feeding Japanese industrial growth (see Chapter 29). Japan recovered more quickly from the Great Depression than any other major industrial power because of prompt action by the civilian democratic government, but the government and large corporations continued to be blamed for the economic downturn. This lack of confidence, combined with the collapsing international economic order, Europe's and America's increasingly isolationist and protectionist policies, and a growing admiration for Nazi Germany and its authoritarian, militaristic model of government, led by the mid-1930s to the military's toppling the civilian authorities and dictating Japan's future.

The Great Depression hit the vulnerable commodities economies of Latin America especially hard. Long dependent on foreign markets, prices and exports of Latin American commodities collapsed as Europe and the United States drastically reduced their purchases and raised tariffs to protect domestic products. Chile's exports fell by nearly 80 percent, for example, while Brazil burned millions of bags of coffee beans for which there was no longer a market. With their foreign sales plummeting, Latin American countries could not buy the industrial goods they needed from abroad. The global depression provoked a profound shift toward economic nationalism after 1930, as popularly based governments worked to reduce foreign influence and gain control of their own economies and natural resources (see page 1008). These efforts were fairly successful. By the late 1940s factories in Argentina, Brazil, and Chile could generally satisfy domestic consumer demand for the products of light industry. But as in Hitler's Germany, the deteriorating economic conditions in Brazil, Guatemala, Nicaragua, Honduras, El Salvador, Argentina, and elsewhere also gave rise to dictatorships, some of them modeled along European Fascist lines (see pages 1008–1017).

The Great Depression was the decisive turning point in the development of African nationalism. For the first time unemployment was widespread among educated Africans. African peasants and small business people who had been drawn into world trade, and who sometimes profited from booms, also felt the agony of the

---

• **Popular Front** A New Deal–inspired party in France that encouraged unions and launched a far-reaching program of social reform.

The Spread of Fascism In the 1920s and 1930s most European countries had Fascist sympathizers. The British Union of Fascists, led by Sir Oswald Mosley, modeled itself on Mussolini's nationalist Fascist Party. Its members were highly visible in their black uniforms, but they never numbered more than a few thousand and never elected a member to Parliament. Here Mosley and his Blackshirts prepare to march through London's Jewish East End in October 1936. Anti-Fascist demonstrators attacked Mosley's followers and stopped the march. (Hulton Archive/Getty Images)

decade-long bust, as did urban workers. In some areas the result was unprecedented mass protest. The Gold Coast cocoa holdups of 1930–1931 and 1937–1938 are the most famous examples (see page 1019).

Authoritarian States

◻ What was the nature of the new totalitarian dictatorships, and how did they differ from conservative authoritarian states?

Both conservative and radical dictatorships arose in Europe in the 1920s and the 1930s. Although they sometimes overlapped in character and practice, they were profoundly different in essence. Conservative authoritarian regimes were joined in this period by new and frightening radical totalitarian dictatorships.

Conservative Authoritarianism

The traditional form of antidemocratic government in world history was conservative authoritarianism. Like Russia's tsars and China's emperors, the leaders of such governments relied on obedient bureaucracies, vigilant police departments, and trustworthy armies to control society. They forbade or limited popular participation in government, and political opponents were often jailed or exiled. Yet they had neither the ability nor the desire to control many aspects of their subjects' lives. As long as the people did not try to change the system, they often had considerable personal independence.

After the First World War, authoritarianism revived, especially in Latin America and in the less-developed eastern part of Europe. By 1938 in eastern Europe only Czechoslovakia remained true to liberal political ideals. Conservative dictators also took over in Spain and Portugal.

There were several reasons for this development. These lands lacked strong traditions of self-government, and many of the new states, such as Yugoslavia, were torn by ethnic conflicts. Dictatorship appealed to nationalists and military leaders as a way to repress such tensions and preserve national unity. Large landowners and the church were still powerful forces in these predominantly agrarian areas, and they often looked to dictators to save them from progressive land reform or Communist agrarian upheaval. Although some of the conservative authoritarian regimes adopted certain Fascist characteristics in the 1930s, they were concerned more with maintaining the status quo than with mobilizing the masses or forcing society into rapid change or war.

Radical Totalitarian Dictatorships

By the mid-1930s a new kind of radical dictatorship had emerged in the Soviet Union, Germany, and, to a lesser extent, Italy. These dictatorships — termed totalitarian — violently rejected liberal values and exercised unprecedented control over the masses.

Most scholars argue that **totalitarianism** burst on the scene with the total war effort of 1914–1918 (see Chapter 28). World War I called forth a tendency to subordinate all institutions and all classes to the state in order to achieve one supreme objective: victory. As the French thinker Elie Halévy put it in 1936, the varieties of modern totalitarian tyranny — fascism, Nazism, and communism — could be thought of as "feuding brothers" with a common father: the nature of modern war.[2]

During the Russian civil war Lenin showed how a dedicated minority could achieve victory over a less-determined majority and subordinate institutions and human rights to the needs of a single group — the Communist Party — and its leader. Lenin's model of single-party dictatorship inspired imitators, including Adolf Hitler in Germany.

The modern totalitarian state reached maturity in the 1930s in the Stalinist Soviet Union and Nazi Germany. These and other totalitarian states were linked in their use of modern technology, particularly mass communication, to exercise complete political power and control over all aspects of society. Deviation from the norm, even in art or family behavior, could be a crime. This vision of a total state represented a radical revolt against liberalism.

Unlike old-fashioned authoritarianism, modern totalitarianism was based not on an elite seeking to maintain the existing social order, but on people who had become engaged in the political process for change, most notably through commitment to nationalism and socialism. Thus totalitarian societies were fully mobilized societies moving toward a goal. As soon as one goal was achieved, another arose at the leader's command. As a result totalitarianism was an unfinished revolution in which rapid, profound change imposed from above went on forever.

There were major differences between Stalin's Communist U.S.S.R. and Hitler's Nazi Germany. Most notably, Soviet communism seized private property for the state and sought to level society by crushing the middle classes. Nazi Germany also criticized big landowners and industrialists but, unlike the Communists, did not try to nationalize private property, so the middle classes survived. This difference in property and class relations led some scholars to speak of "totalitarianism of the left" — Stalinist Russia — and "totalitarianism of the right" — Nazi Germany.

The aims of Soviet Communists were ultimately international, seeking to unite the workers of the world. Fascist leaders claimed they were interested in changing state and society on a national level only. Mussolini and Hitler used the term **fascism** to describe their movements' supposedly "total" and revolutionary character. Orthodox Marxist Communists argued that the Fascists were powerful capitalists who sought to destroy the revolutionary working class and thus protect their enormous profits. So while Communists and Fascists were both committed to the overthrow of existing society, their ideologies clashed, and they were enemies.

European Fascist movements shared many characteristics, including extreme nationalism; an antisocialism aimed at destroying working-class movements; alliances with powerful capitalists and landowners; a dynamic, charismatic, and violent leader; and glorification of war and the military. Hitler and Stalin, in particular, were masters of the use of propaganda and terror. Fascists, especially in Germany, also embraced racial homogeneity, a fanatical obsession that led to the Holocaust (see page 927).

Although 1930s Japan has sometimes been called a Fascist society, most scholars disagree with this label. There were various ideological forces at work in Japan, including ultranationalism, militarism, reverence for traditional ways, and emperor worship, that contributed to the rise of a totalitarian state before the Second World War. These were all ideas that grew out of events and circumstances beginning with the Meiji Restoration in 1868 (see page 797), not from European philosophies of totalitarian government in the 1920s.

In summary, the concept of totalitarianism remains a valuable tool for historical understanding. It correctly highlights that in the 1930s Germany, the Soviet Union, and Japan made an unprecedented "total claim" on the

---

- **totalitarianism** A radical dictatorship that exercises complete political power and control over all aspects of society and seeks to mobilize the masses for action.

- **fascism** A movement characterized by extreme, often expansionist nationalism, antisocialism, a dynamic and violent leader, and glorification of war and the military.

- **five-year plan** Launched by Stalin in 1928 and termed the "revolution from above," its goal was to modernize the Soviet Union and generate a Communist society with new attitudes, new loyalties, and a new socialist humanity.

- **New Economic Policy (NEP)** Lenin's 1921 policy re-establishing limited economic freedom in an attempt to rebuild agriculture and industry in the face of economic disintegration.

beliefs and behaviors of their respective citizens.[3] As for fascism, antidemocratic, antisocialist Fascist movements sprang up all over Europe, but only in Italy and Germany (and some would say Spain under Francisco Franco) were they able to take power.

Stalin's Soviet Union

☐ How did Stalin and the Communist Party build a totalitarian order in the Soviet Union?

A master of political infighting, Joseph Stalin (1879–1953) cautiously consolidated his power and eliminated his enemies in the mid-1920s. Then in 1928, as the ruling Communist Party's undisputed leader, he launched the first **five-year plan** — the "revolution from above," as he so aptly termed it. The five-year plan marked the beginning of an attempt to transform Soviet society along socialist lines. Stalin and the Communist Party used constant propaganda, enormous sacrifice, and unlimited violence and state control to establish a dynamic, modern totalitarian state in the 1930s.

From Lenin to Stalin

By spring 1921 Lenin and the Bolsheviks had won the civil war, but they ruled a shattered and devastated land. In the face of economic disintegration, the worst famine in generations, riots by peasants and workers, and an open rebellion by previously pro-Bolshevik sailors at Kronstadt, Lenin changed course. In March 1921 he announced the **New Economic Policy (NEP)**, which re-established limited economic freedom in an attempt to rebuild agriculture and industry. Peasant producers could sell their surpluses in free markets, as could private traders and small handicraft manufacturers. Heavy industry, railroads, and banks, however, remained wholly nationalized.

The NEP was successful both politically and economically. Politically, it was a necessary but temporary compromise with the Soviet Union's overwhelming peasant majority, the only force capable of overturning Lenin's government. Economically, the NEP brought rapid recovery. In 1926 industrial output surpassed prewar levels, and peasants were producing almost as much grain as before the war.

As the economy recovered, an intense power struggle began in the Communist Party's inner circles, for Lenin left no chosen successor when he died in 1924. The principal contenders were Stalin and Leon Trotsky. Stalin was a good organizer but had no experience outside Russia. Trotsky, who had planned the 1917 takeover (see page 861) and created the Red Army, appeared to have all the advantages. Yet Stalin won because he

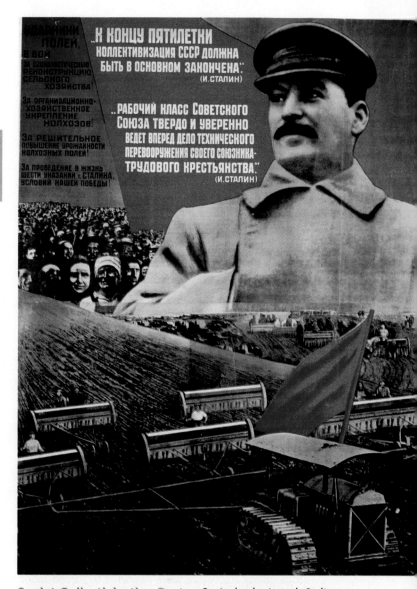

Soviet Collectivization Poster Soviet leader Joseph Stalin ordered a nationwide forced collectivization campaign from 1928 to 1933. Following communist theory, the government created large-scale collective farms by seizing land and forcing peasants to work on it. In this idealized 1932 poster, farmers are encouraged to complete the five-year plan of collectivization, while Stalin looks on approvingly. The outcome instead was a disaster. Millions of people died in the resulting human-created famine. (Deutsches Plakat Museum, Essen, Germany/Archives Charmet/The Bridgeman Art Library)

gained the support of the party, the only genuine source of power in the one-party state.

With cunning Stalin gradually achieved absolute power between 1922 and 1927. He used the moderates to crush Trotsky, and then turned against the moderates and destroyed them as well. Stalin's final triumph came at the party congress of December 1927, which condemned all "deviation from the general party line" formulated by Stalin.

The Five-Year Plans

The 1927 party congress marked the end of the NEP and the beginning of the era of socialist five-year plans. The first five-year plan had staggering economic objectives. In just five years, total industrial output was to increase by 250 percent and agricultural production by 150 percent, and one-fifth of the peasants were to give up their private plots and join socialist collective farms. By 1930 economic and social change was sweeping the country.

Stalin unleashed his "second revolution" for a variety of reasons. First, like Lenin, Stalin and his militant supporters were deeply committed to socialism as they understood it. Second, there was the old problem of catching up with the advanced and presumably hostile Western capitalist nations. "We are fifty or a hundred years behind the advanced countries," Stalin said in 1931. "We must make good this distance in ten years. Either we do it, or we shall go under."[4]

Domestically, there was the peasant problem. For centuries peasants had wanted to own the land, and finally they had it. Sooner or later, the Communists reasoned, the peasants would become conservative capitalists and threaten the regime. To resolve these issues, Stalin decided on a preventive war against the peasantry in order to bring it under the state's absolute control.

That war was **collectivization** — the forcible consolidation of individual peasant farms into large, state-controlled enterprises. Beginning in 1929 peasants were ordered to give up their land and animals and become members of collective farms. As for the kulaks, the better-off peasants, Stalin instructed party workers to "liquidate them as a class." Stripped of land and livestock, many starved or were deported to forced-labor camps for "re-education."

Since almost all peasants were poor, the term *kulak* soon meant any peasant who opposed the new system. Whole villages were often attacked. One conscience-stricken colonel in the secret police confessed to a foreign journalist:

> I am an old Bolshevik. I worked in the underground against the Tsar and then I fought in the Civil War. Did I do all that in order that I should now surround villages with machine guns and order my men to fire indiscriminately into crowds of peasants? Oh, no, no![5]

Forced collectivization led to disaster. Many peasants slaughtered their animals and burned their crops in protest. Nor were the state-controlled collective farms more productive. Grain output barely increased, and collectivized agriculture made no substantial financial contribution to Soviet industrial development during the first five-year plan.

In Ukraine Stalin instituted a policy of all-out collectivization with two goals: to destroy all expressions of Ukrainian nationalism, and to break the will of the Ukrainian peasants so they would accept collectivization and Soviet rule. Stalin began by purging Ukraine of its intellectuals and political elite, labeling them reactionary nationalists and enemies of socialism. He then set impossibly high grain quotas — up to nearly 50 percent of total production — for the collectivized farms. This grain quota had to be turned over to the government before any peasant could receive a share. The result was a terrible man-made famine in Ukraine in 1932 and 1933, which probably claimed 3 to 5 million lives.

Collectivization was a cruel but real victory for Communist ideologues. By 1938, 93 percent of peasant families had been herded onto collective farms. Regimented as state employees and dependent on the state-owned tractor stations, the collectivized peasants were no longer a political threat.

The industrial side of the five-year plans was more successful. Soviet industry produced about four times as much in 1937 as in 1928. No other major country had ever achieved such rapid industrial growth. Heavy industry led the way, and urban development accelerated: more than 25 million people migrated to cities to become industrial workers during the 1930s.

The sudden creation of dozens of new factories demanded tremendous resources. Funds for industrial expansion were collected from the people by means of heavy hidden sales taxes. Firm labor discipline also contributed to rapid industrialization. Trade unions lost most of their power, and individuals could not move without police permission. When factory managers needed more hands they were sent "unneeded" peasants from collective farms.

Foreign engineers were hired to plan and construct many of the new factories. Highly skilled American engineers, hungry for work in the depression years, were particularly important until newly trained Soviet experts began to replace them after 1932. Siberia's new steel mills were modeled on America's best. Thus Stalin's planners harnessed the skill and technology of capitalist countries to promote the surge of socialist industry.

Life and Culture in Soviet Society

Daily life was hard in Stalin's Soviet Union. Because consumption was reduced to pay for investment, there was no improvement in the average standard of living. There were constant shortages, and scarcity of housing was a particularly serious problem. A relatively lucky family received one room for all its members and

• **collectivization** Stalin's forcible consolidation of individual peasant farms into large, state-controlled enterprises.

shared both a kitchen and a toilet with others on the floor. Less fortunate people built scrap-lumber shacks in shantytowns.

Despite the hardships, many Communists saw themselves as heroically building the world's first socialist society while capitalism crumbled and Fascism rose in the West. This optimistic belief in the Soviet Union's future also attracted many disillusioned Westerners to communism in the 1930s.

On a more practical level Soviet workers received some important social benefits, such as old-age pensions, free medical services and education, and day-care centers for children. Unemployment was almost unknown. Finally, there was the possibility of personal advancement. Rapid industrialization required massive numbers of trained experts, such as skilled workers, engineers, and plant managers. Thus the Stalinist state broke with the egalitarian policies of the 1920s and provided tremendous incentives to those who acquired specialized skills. A growing technical and managerial elite joined the political and artistic elites in a new upper class, whose members were rich and powerful.

Soviet society's radical transformation profoundly affected women's lives. The Russian Revolution of 1917 immediately proclaimed complete equality of rights for women. In the 1920s divorce and abortion were made easily available, and women were urged to work outside the home. After Stalin came to power, however, he played down this trend in favor of a return to traditional family values.

The most lasting changes for women involved work and education. Peasant women continued to work on farms, and millions of women now toiled in factories and heavy construction. The more determined women entered the ranks of the better-paid specialists in industry and science. By 1950, 75 percent of all doctors in the Soviet Union were women.

Culture was thoroughly politicized through constant propaganda and indoctrination. Party activists lectured workers in factories and peasants on collective farms, while newspapers, films, and radio broadcasts recounted socialist achievements and capitalist plots. Writers and artists who could effectively combine genuine creativity and political propaganda became the darlings of the regime.

Stalinist Terror and the Great Purges

In the mid-1930s the push to build socialism and a new society culminated in ruthless police terror and a massive purging of the Communist Party. In late 1934 Stalin's number-two man, Sergei Kirov, was mysteriously murdered. Although Stalin himself probably ordered Kirov's murder, he used the incident to launch a reign of terror.

In August 1936 sixteen prominent "Old Bolsheviks" — members of the party before the Russian Revolution of 1917 — confessed to all manner of plots against Stalin in spectacular public show trials in Moscow. Then in 1937 the secret police arrested a mass of lesser party officials and newer members, torturing them and extracting confessions for more show trials. In addition to the party faithful, union officials, managers, intellectuals, army officers, and countless ordinary citizens were struck down. In all, at least 8 million people were arrested, and millions of these were executed or never returned from prisons and forced-labor camps.

Stalin recruited 1.5 million new members to take the place of those purged. Thus more than half of all Communist Party members in 1941 had joined since the purges. These new members were products of the Second Revolution of the 1930s, seeking the opportunities and rewards that party membership offered. This new generation of Stalin-formed Communists served the leader effectively until his death in 1953, and then governed the Soviet Union until the early 1980s.

Stalin's mass purges remain baffling, for most historians believe that those purged posed no threat and confessed to crimes they had not committed. Revisionist historians have challenged the long-standing interpretation that blames the great purges on Stalin's

Women Prisoners Digging a Canal Millions of Soviet citizens were sent to forced-labor prison camps from 1929 to 1953, and over 1.7 million died. Ten to 20 percent of these prisoners were women, many of them found guilty of nothing more than being married to men considered enemies of the state. In this photo women prisoners use picks and shovels to dig the canal bed of the White Sea–Baltic Sea Canal. The canal was 141 miles long, and building it took about twenty months of manual labor between 1931 and 1933. (Photo: Center for History and New Media, George Mason University. Courtesy of Russian State Documentary Film & Photo Archive at Krasnogorsk)

cruelty or madness. They argue that Stalin's fears were exaggerated but genuine and were shared by many in the party and in the general population who were bombarded daily with propaganda. Investigations and trials snowballed into a mass hysteria, a new witch-hunt.[6] In short, a popular but deluded Stalin found large numbers of willing collaborators for crime as well as for achievement.

Mussolini and Fascism in Italy

☐ How did Italian fascism develop?

Mussolini's Fascist movement and his seizure of power in 1922 were important steps in the rise of dictatorships between the two world wars. Mussolini and his supporters were the first to call themselves "fascists" — revolutionaries determined to create a new kind of totalitarian state. His dictatorship was brutal and theatrical, and it contained elements of both conservative authoritarianism and modern totalitarianism.

The Seizure of Power

In the early twentieth century Italy was a liberal state with civil rights and a constitutional monarchy. On the eve of the First World War, the parliamentary regime granted universal male suffrage. But there were serious problems. Poverty was widespread, and many peasants were more attached to their villages and local interests than to the national state. Moreover, the papacy, many devout Catholics, conservatives, and landowners remained opposed to the middle-class lawyers and politicians who ran the country largely for their own benefit. Church-state relations were often tense. Class differences were also extreme, and by 1912 the Socialist Party's radical wing led the powerful revolutionary socialist movement.[7]

World War I worsened the political situation. Having fought on the Allied side almost exclusively for purposes of territorial expansion, the parliamentary government disappointed Italian nationalists with Italy's modest gains at Versailles. Workers and peasants also felt cheated: to win their support during the war, the government had promised social and land reform, which it did not deliver after the war.

The Russian Revolution inspired and energized Italy's revolutionary socialist movement, and radical workers and peasants began occupying factories and seizing land in 1920. These actions scared and mobilized the property-owning classes. Thus by 1921 revolutionary socialists, antiliberal conservatives, and frightened property owners were all opposed — though for different reasons — to the liberal parliamentary government.

Into these crosscurrents of unrest and fear stepped Benito Mussolini (1883–1945). Mussolini began his political career as a Socialist Party leader and radical newspaper editor before World War I. Expelled from the Italian Socialist Party for supporting the war, and wounded on the Italian front in 1917, Mussolini returned home and began organizing bitter war veterans into a band of Fascists — from the Italian word for "a union of forces."

At first Mussolini's program was a radical combination of nationalist and socialist demands, including territorial expansion, workers' benefits, and land reform for peasants. As such, it competed directly with the well-organized Socialist Party and failed to get off the ground. When Mussolini saw that his violent verbal assaults on rival Socialists won him growing support from conservatives and the frightened middle classes, he shifted gears in 1920, exalting nation and race over class.

Mussolini and his private army of **Black Shirts** began to grow violent. Few people were killed, but Socialist newspapers, union halls, and local Socialist Party headquarters were destroyed. A skillful politician, Mussolini convinced his followers that they were not just opposing the "Reds" but were also making a real revolution of the little people against the established interests.

With the government breaking down in 1922, largely because of the chaos created by his Black Shirt bands, Mussolini stepped forward as the savior of order and property, demanding the existing government's resignation and his own appointment by the king. In October 1922 a large group of Fascists marched on Rome to threaten the king and force him to appoint Mussolini prime minister. The threat worked. Victor Emmanuel III (r. 1900–1946) asked Mussolini to form a new cabinet. Thus, after widespread violence and a threat of armed uprising, Mussolini seized power "legally."

The Regime in Action

In 1924 Mussolini declared his desire to "make the nation Fascist" and imposed a series of repressive measures. Press freedom was abolished, elections were fixed, and the government ruled by decree. Mussolini arrested his political opponents, disbanded all independent labor unions, and put dedicated Fascists in con-

• **Black Shirts** A private army under Mussolini that destroyed Socialist newspapers, union halls, and Socialist Party headquarters, eventually pushing Socialists out of the city governments of northern Italy.

• **Lateran Agreement** A 1929 agreement that recognized the Vatican as an independent state, with Mussolini agreeing to give the church heavy financial support in return for the pope's public support.

Mussolini Leading a Parade in Rome Benito Mussolini was a master showman who drew on Rome's ancient heritage to promote Italian fascism. He wanted a grand avenue to stage triumphal marches with thousands of troops, so he had the Way of the Imperial Forums built through the old city. Here Mussolini rides at the head of a grand parade in 1932 to inaugurate the new road, passing the Roman Coliseum, one of the focal points along the route. (Stefano Bianchetti/Corbis)

trol of Italy's schools. He created a Fascist youth movement, Fascist labor unions, and many other Fascist organizations. He trumpeted his goal in a famous slogan of 1926: "Everything in the state, nothing outside the state, nothing against the state." By year's end Italy was a one-party dictatorship under Mussolini's unquestioned leadership.

Mussolini did not complete the establishment of a modern totalitarian state. His Fascist Party never destroyed the old power structure. Interested primarily in personal power, Mussolini was content to compromise with the old conservative classes that controlled the army, the economy, and the state. He never tried to purge these classes or even move very vigorously against them. He controlled labor but left big business to regulate itself, profitably and securely. There was no land reform.

Mussolini also drew increasing support from the Catholic Church. In the **Lateran Agreement** of 1929, he recognized the Vatican as a tiny independent state and agreed to give the church heavy financial support. The pope in return urged Italians to support Mussolini's government.

Like Stalin, Hitler, and other totalitarian leaders, Mussolini favored a return of traditional roles for women. He abolished divorce and told women to stay at home and produce children. In 1938 women were limited by law to a maximum of 10 percent of the better-paying jobs in industry and government. Italian women appear not to have changed their attitudes or behavior in any important way under Fascist rule.

Mussolini's government passed no racial laws until 1938 and did not persecute Jews savagely until late in the Second World War, when Italy was under Nazi con-

trol. Nor did Mussolini establish a truly ruthless police state. Only twenty-three political prisoners were condemned to death between 1926 and 1944. Mussolini's Fascist Italy, though repressive and undemocratic, was never really totalitarian.

Hitler and Nazism in Germany

☐ Why were Hitler and his Nazi regime initially so popular, and how did their actions lead to World War II?

The most frightening dictatorship developed in Nazi Germany. A product of Hitler's evil genius as well as of Germany's social and political situation, the Nazi movement shared some of the characteristics of Mussolini's Italian model and fascism. But Nazism asserted an unlimited claim over German society and proclaimed the ultimate power of its aggressive leader, Adolf Hitler. Nazism's aspirations were truly totalitarian.

The Roots of Nazism

Nazism grew out of many complex developments, of which the most influential were extreme nationalism and racism. These two ideas captured the mind of the young Adolf Hitler (1889–1945), and he dominated Nazism until the end of World War II.

The son of an Austrian customs official, Hitler spent his childhood in small towns in Austria. He did poorly in high school and dropped out at age sixteen.

Young People in Hitler's Germany This photo from 1930 shows Hitler admiring a young boy dressed in the uniform of Hitler's storm troopers, a paramilitary organization of the Nazi Party that supported Hitler's rise to power in the 1920s and early 1930s. Only a year after the founding of the storm troopers in 1921, Hitler began to organize Germany's young people into similar paramilitary groups in an effort to militarize all of German society. The young paramilitaries became the Hitler Youth, who eventually numbered in the millions. (Popperfoto/Getty Images)

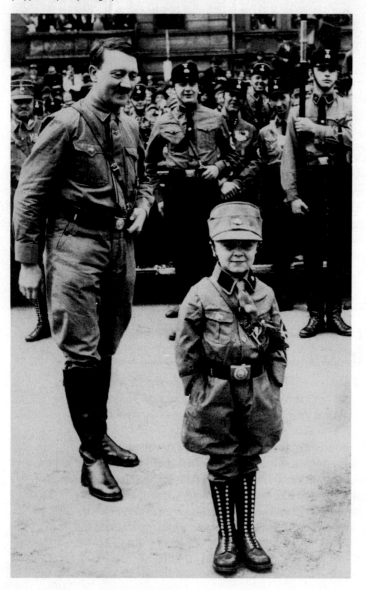

He then headed to Vienna, where he was exposed to extreme Austro-German nationalists who believed Germans to be a superior people and central Europe's natural rulers. They advocated union with Germany and violent expulsion of "inferior" peoples from the Austro-Hungarian Empire.

From these extremists Hitler eagerly absorbed virulent anti-Semitism, racism, and hatred of Slavs. He developed an unshakable belief in the crudest distortions of Social Darwinism (see page 739), the superiority of Germanic races, and the inevitability of racial conflict. The Jews, he claimed, directed an international conspiracy of finance capitalism and Marxist socialism against German culture, German unity, and the German race. Anti-Semitism and racism became Hitler's most passionate convictions.

Hitler greeted the outbreak of the Great War as a salvation. The struggle and discipline of serving as a soldier in the war gave his life meaning, and when Germany was suddenly defeated in 1918, Hitler's world was shattered. (See "Viewpoints: Hitler, Mussolini, and the Great War, page 921.) Convinced that Jews and Marxists had "stabbed Germany in the back," he vowed to fight on.

In late 1919 Hitler joined a tiny extremist group in Munich called the German Workers' Party, which promised a uniquely German "national socialism" that would abolish the injustices of capitalism and create a mighty "people's community." By 1921 Hitler had gained absolute control of this small but growing party, now renamed the National Socialist German Worker's Party, or Nazi Party. A master of mass propaganda and political showmanship, Hitler worked his audience into a frenzy with wild attacks on the Versailles treaty, the Jews, war profiteers, and Germany's Weimar Republic.

In late 1923 the Weimar Republic seemed on the verge of collapse. In 1925 the old Great War field marshal Paul von Hindenburg (1847–1934) became the second president of the young democratic Germany. Hitler, inspired by Mussolini's recent victory, attempted an armed uprising in Munich. Despite the failure of the poorly organized plot and Hitler's arrest, Nazism had been born.

Hitler's Road to Power

At his trial Hitler violently denounced the Weimar Republic, and he gained enormous publicity. From the unsuccessful revolt, Hitler concluded that he had to come to power legally through electoral competition. He used his brief prison term to dictate *Mein Kampf* (My Struggle). Here he expounded on his basic ideas on race and anti-Semitism, the notion of territorial expansion based on "living space" for Germans, and the role of the leader-dictator, called the *Führer* (FYOUR-uhr).

In the years of relative prosperity and stability between 1924 and 1929, Hitler concentrated on building

Viewpoints

Hitler, Mussolini, and the Great War

- *When the Great War ended, Private Adolf Hitler was in a hospital bed, blinded temporarily by a mustard gas shell. In his infamous autobiography,* Mein Kampf *(My Struggle), Hitler described the agonizing sense of betrayal he felt upon learning of Germany's surrender. Corporal Benito Mussolini, six years Hitler's senior, was also wounded in the war and was discharged in August 1917. Although a revolutionary socialist before the war, as was his father, Mussolini describes in his autobiography how, by war's end, he had turned completely against socialism. Although Italy was on the winning side of World War I, Mussolini felt that Italy's leaders and those who were trying to incite socialist revolution had betrayed his country.*

Adolf Hitler, *My Struggle*

"A few hours later, my eyes had turned into glowing coals, it had grown dark around me. Thus I came to the hospital ... and there I was fated to experience—the greatest villainy of the century. ...

On November 10 [1918], the pastor came to the hospital [to inform] us that the House of Hollenzollern should no longer bear the imperial crown; that the fatherland had become a "republic." But when the old gentleman tried to go on, and began to tell us that we must now end the long War, yes, that now that it was lost and we were throwing ourselves upon the mercy of the victors, our fatherland would for the future be exposed to dire oppression, that the armistice should be accepted with confidence in the magnanimity of our previous enemies—I could stand it no longer. It became impossible for me to sit still one minute more. Again everything went black before my eyes; I tottered and groped my way back to the dormitory, threw myself on my bunk and dug my burning head in to my blanket and pillow. ...

And so it had all been in vain. In vain all the sacrifices and privations; ... in vain the deaths of two millions who died. Would not the graves ... open and send the silent mud- and blood-covered heroes back as spirits of vengeance to the homeland which had cheated them with such mockery of the highest sacrifice which a man can make to his people in this world? ...

Did all this happen only so that a gang of wretched criminals could lay hands on the fatherland? ...

I, for my part, decided to go into politics."

Benito Mussolini, *My Autobiography*

"Already in January, 1919, the Socialists, slightly checked during the war, began, the moment the ink was drying on the armistice, their work of rebellion and blackmail. ... We suffered the humiliation of seeing the banners of our glorious regiments returned to their homes without being saluted, without that warm cheer of sympathy owed to those who return from victorious war. ...

I said then that never in the life of any nation on the day after victory had there been a more odious tragedy. ... In the first few months of 1919, Italy, led on by politicians ... had only one frantic wish that I could see—it was to destroy every gain of victorious struggle. Its only dedication was to a denial of the borders and soil extent of the nation. It forgot our 600,000 dead and our 1,000,000 wounded. It made waste of their generous blood. ... This attempt at matricide of the motherland was abetted by Italians of perverted intellect and by professional socialists. ...

I wrote ... Do they want to scrape the earth that was soaked with your blood and to spit on your sacrifice? Fear nothing, glorious spirits! Our task has just begun. No harm shall befall you. We shall defend the dead, and all the dead, even though we put dugouts in the public squares and trenches in the streets of our city."

Sources: Adolph Hitler, excerpts from *Mein Kampf*, translated by Ralph Manheim. Copyright © 1943, renewed 1971 by Houghton Mifflin Harcourt Publishing Company. Also published by Hutchinson. Reprinted by permission of Houghton Mifflin Harcourt Publishing Company and the Random House Group, Ltd. All rights reserved; Benito Mussolini, *My Autobiography* (New York: Charles Scribner's Sons, 1928), pp. 60–63, 65–66. Copyright 1928. Reproduced with permission of ABC-CLIO INC. in the format Textbook and Other Book via Copyright Clearance Center.

QUESTIONS FOR ANALYSIS

1. According to both Hitler and Mussolini, who was betrayed by the war's outcome in their countries?
2. How do both men plan to respond to this betrayal?

---

his Nazi Party. The Nazis remained a small splinter group until the 1929 Great Depression shattered economic prosperity. By the end of 1932 an incredible 43 percent of the labor force was unemployed. Industrial production fell by one-half between 1929 and 1932. No factor contributed more to Hitler's success than the economic crisis. Hitler began promising German voters economic as well as political and international salvation.

Hitler rejected free-market capitalism and advocated government programs to bring recovery. He pitched his speeches to middle- and lower-middle-class groups and to skilled workers. As the economy collapsed, great numbers of these people "voted their

- **Nazism** A movement born of extreme nationalism and racism and dominated by Adolf Hitler from 1933 until the end of World War II in 1945.

pocketbooks"[8] and deserted the conservative and moderate parties for the Nazis. In the 1930 election the Nazis won 6.5 million votes and 107 seats, and in July 1932 they gained 14.5 million votes — 38 percent of the total — and became the largest party in the Reichstag.

Hitler and the Nazis appealed strongly to German youth. Hitler himself was only forty in 1929, and he and most of his top aides were much younger than other leading German politicians. "National Socialism is the organized will of the youth," proclaimed the official Nazi slogan. In 1931 almost 40 percent of Nazi Party members were under thirty, compared with 20 percent of Social Democrats. National recovery, exciting and rapid change, and personal advancement made Nazism appealing to millions of German youths.

Hitler also came to power because of the breakdown of democratic government. Germany's economic collapse in the Great Depression convinced many voters that the country's republican leaders were stupid and corrupt. Disunity on the left was another nail in the republic's coffin. The Communists refused to cooperate with the Social Democrats, even though the two parties together outnumbered the Nazis in the Reichstag.

Finally, Hitler excelled in dirty backroom politics. In 1932 he succeeded in gaining support from key people in the army and big business who thought they could use him to their own advantage. Many conservative and nationalistic politicians thought similarly. Thus in January 1933 President von Hindenburg legally appointed Hitler, leader of Germany's largest party, as German chancellor.

The Nazi State and Society

Hitler quickly established an unshakable dictatorship. When the Reichstag building was partly destroyed by fire in February 1933, Hitler blamed the Communist Party, and he convinced President von Hindenburg, in poor health and displaying signs of senility, to sign dictatorial emergency acts that abolished freedom of speech and assembly and most personal liberties. He also called for new elections in an effort to solidify his political power.

When the Nazis won only 44 percent of the votes, Hitler outlawed the Communist Party and arrested its parliamentary representatives. Then on March 23, 1933, the Nazis forced through the Reichstag the so-called **Enabling Act**, which gave Hitler absolute dictatorial power for four years.

Hitler and the Nazis took over the government bureaucracy intact, installing many Nazis in top positions. Hitler next outlawed strikes and abolished independent labor unions, which were replaced by the Nazi Labor Front. Professional people — doctors and lawyers, teachers and engineers — also saw their independent organizations swallowed up in Nazi associations. Publishing houses and universities were put under Nazi control, and students and professors publicly burned forbidden books. Modern art and architecture were ruthlessly prohibited. Life became violently anti-intellectual. As the cynical Joseph Goebbels, later Nazi minister of propaganda, put it, "When I hear the word 'culture' I reach for my gun."[9] By 1934 a brutal dictatorship characterized by frightening dynamism and total obedience to Hitler was already largely in place.

In June 1934 Hitler ordered his elite personal guard — the SS — to arrest and shoot without trial roughly a thousand long-time Nazi storm troopers. Shortly thereafter army leaders surrendered their independence and swore a binding oath of "unquestioning obedience" to Adolf Hitler. The SS grew rapidly. Under Heinrich Himmler (1900–1945), the SS took over the political police, the Gestapo, and expanded its network of concentration camps.

From the beginning, German Jews were a special object of Nazi persecution. By late 1934 most Jewish lawyers, doctors, professors, civil servants, and musicians had been banned from their professions. In 1935 the infamous Nuremberg Laws classified as Jewish anyone having three or more Jewish grandparents and deprived Jews of all rights of citizenship. By 1938 roughly one-quarter of Germany's half million Jews had emigrated, sacrificing almost all their property in order to leave Germany.

In late 1938 the attack on the Jews accelerated. On November 9 and 10, 1938, the Nazis initiated a series of well-organized attacks against Jews throughout Nazi Germany and some parts of Austria. This infamous event is known as Kristallnacht, or Night of Broken Glass, after the broken glass that littered the streets following the frenzied destruction of Jewish homes, shops, synagogues, and neighborhoods by German civilians and uniformed storm troopers. U.S. Consul David Buffum reported of the Nazis in Leipzig that

> The most hideous phase of the so-called "spontaneous" action, has been the wholesale arrest and transportation to concentration camps of male German Jews between the ages of sixteen and sixty. . . . Having demolished dwellings and hurled most of the effects to the streets, the insatiably sadistic perpetrators threw many of the trembling inmates into a small stream that flows through the Zoological Park, commanding horrified spectators to spit at them, defile them with mud and jeer at their plight.[10]

Many historians consider this night the beginning of Hitler's Final Solution against the Jews (see page 927), and it now became very difficult for Jews to leave Germany.

• **Enabling Act** An act pushed through the Reichstag by the Nazis that gave Hitler absolute dictatorial power for four years.

Some Germans privately opposed these outrages, but most went along or looked the other way. Although this lack of response reflected the individual's helplessness in a totalitarian state, it also reflected the strong popular support Hitler's government enjoyed.

Hitler's Popularity

Hitler had promised the masses economic recovery — "work and bread" — and he delivered. The Nazi Party launched a large public works program to pull Germany out of the depression. Work began on highways, offices, sports stadiums, and public housing. In 1935 Germany turned decisively toward rearmament. Unemployment dropped steadily, and by 1938 the Nazis boasted of nearly full employment. The average standard of living increased moderately. Business profits rose sharply. For millions of people economic recovery was tangible evidence that Nazi promises were more than show and propaganda.

In contrast to those deemed "undesirable" (Jews, Slavs, Gypsies, Jehovah's Witnesses, Communists, and homosexuals), for ordinary German citizens, Hitler's government meant greater equality and more opportunities. In 1933 class barriers in Germany were generally high. Hitler's rule introduced changes that lowered these barriers. For example, stiff educational requirements favoring the well-to-do were relaxed. The new Nazi elite included many young and poorly educated dropouts, rootless lower-middle-class people like Hitler who rose to the top with breathtaking speed. More generally, the Nazis tolerated privilege and wealth only as long as they served party needs.

Yet few historians today believe that Hitler and the Nazis brought about a real social revolution. The well-educated classes held on to most of their advantages, and only a modest social leveling occurred in the Nazi years. Significantly, the Nazis shared with the Italian Fascists the stereotypical view of women as housewives and mothers. Only when facing labor shortages during the war did they reluctantly mobilize large numbers of German women for office and factory work. Yet low unemployment and economic recovery coupled with an aggressive propaganda effort heralding the Nazi state's successes led to broad support for the regime.

Not all Germans supported Hitler, however, and a number of German groups actively resisted him after 1933. Tens of thousands of political enemies were imprisoned, and thousands were executed. In the first years of Hitler's rule, the principal resisters were trade union Communists and Socialists, groups smashed by the expansion of the SS system after 1935. Catholic and Protestant churches produced a second group of opponents. Their efforts were directed primarily at preserving genuine religious life, however, not at overthrowing Hitler. Finally in 1938 and again during the war,

Reaching a National Audience This poster ad promotes the VE-301 receiver, "the world's cheapest radio," and claims that "All Germany listens to the Führer on the people's receiver." Constantly broadcasting official views and attitudes, the state-controlled media also put the Nazis' favorite entertainment — gigantic mass meetings that climaxed with Hitler's violent theatrical speeches — on an invisible stage for millions. (Bundesarchiv Koblenz Plak 003-022-025/Grafiker: Leonid)

some high-ranking army officers, who feared the consequences of Hitler's reckless aggression, plotted, unsuccessfully, against him.

Aggression and Appeasement, 1933–1939

After economic recovery and success establishing Nazi control of society, Hitler turned to the next item on his agenda: aggressive territorial expansion. He camouflaged his plans at first, for the Treaty of Versailles limited Germany's army to only a hundred thousand men. Thus while Hitler loudly proclaimed his peaceful intentions, Germany's withdrawal from

Hitler's Success with Aggression
This biting criticism of appeasing leaders by the cartoonist David Low appeared shortly after Hitler remilitarized the Rhineland. Appeasement also appealed to millions of ordinary citizens in Britain and France who wanted to avoid another great war at any cost. (Evening Standard/Solo Syndication)

the League of Nations in October 1933 indicated its determination to rearm. When in March 1935 Hitler established a general military draft and declared the "unequal" Versailles treaty disarmament clauses null and void, leaders in Britain, France, and Italy issued a rather tepid joint protest and warned him against future aggressive actions.

But the emerging united front against Hitler quickly collapsed. Britain adopted a policy of appeasement, granting Hitler everything he could reasonably want (and more) in order to avoid war. British appeasement, which practically dictated French policy, was motivated by the pacifism of a population still horrified by the memory of the First World War. As in Germany, many powerful British conservatives underestimated Hitler. They believed that Soviet communism was the real danger and that Hitler could be used to stop it.

In March 1936, Hitler suddenly marched his armies into the demilitarized Rhineland, brazenly violating the Treaties of Versailles and Locarno. France would not move without British support, and Britain refused to act (Map 30.1). As Britain and France opted for appeasement and the So-

Italy's Ethiopian Campaign, 1935–1936

Italian campaigns, 1935–1936

viet Union watched all developments suspiciously, Hitler found powerful allies. In 1935 the bombastic Mussolini attacked the independent African kingdom of Ethiopia. The Western Powers and the League of Nations condemned Italian aggression, but Hitler supported Italy energetically. In 1936 Italy and Germany established the so-called Rome-Berlin Axis. Japan, which wanted support for its occupation of Manchuria, also joined the Axis alliance (see page 900).

At the same time, Germany and Italy intervened in the Spanish civil war (1936–1939), where their support helped General Francisco Franco's Fascist movement defeat republican Spain. Republican Spain's only official aid in the fight against Franco came from the Soviet Union.

In late 1937 Hitler moved forward with his plans to crush Austria and Czechoslovakia as the first step in his long-contemplated drive to the east for living space. By threatening Austria with invasion, Hitler forced the Austrian chancellor in March 1938 to put local Nazis in control of the government. The next day German armies moved in unopposed, and Austria became two provinces of Greater Germany (see Map 30.1).

Simultaneously, Hitler demanded that the pro-Nazi, German-speaking territory of western Czechoslovakia—the Sudetenland—be turned over to Germany. Democratic Czechoslovakia was prepared to defend itself, but appeasement triumphed again. In September 1938 British prime minister Arthur Neville Chamberlain (1869–1940) flew to Germany three times in fourteen days. In these negotiations, Chamberlain

MAP 30.1 The Growth of Nazi Germany, 1933–1939 Until March 1939 Hitler brought ethnic Germans into the Nazi state; then he turned on the Slavic peoples, whom he had always hated. He stripped Czechoslovakia of its independence and prepared for an attack on Poland in September 1939.

and the French agreed with Hitler that the Sudetenland should be ceded to Germany immediately. Returning to London from the Munich Conference, Chamberlain told cheering crowds that he had secured "peace with honor . . . peace for our time." Sold out by the Western Powers, Czechoslovakia gave in.

Hitler's armies occupied the remainder of Czechoslovakia in March 1939. This time, there was no possible rationale of self-determination for Nazi aggression, because Hitler had seized the Czechs and Slovaks as captive peoples. When Hitler used the question of German minorities in Danzig as a pretext to confront Poland, Chamberlain declared that Britain and France would fight if Hitler attacked his eastern neighbor. Hitler did not take these warnings seriously and pressed on.

In an about-face that stunned the world, sworn enemies Hitler and Stalin signed a nonaggression pact in August 1939. Each dictator promised to remain neutral if the other became involved in war. An attached secret protocol divided eastern Europe into German and Soviet zones "in the event of a political territorial reorganization." Stalin agreed to the pact because he distrusted Western intentions, and Hitler offered territorial gain.

For Hitler, everything was now set. He told his generals on the day of the nonaggression pact, "My only fear is that at the last moment some dirty dog will come up with a mediation plan." On September 1, 1939, the Germans attacked Poland from three sides. Two days later, Britain and France, finally true to their word, declared war on Germany. The Second World War had begun.

The Second World War, 1939-1945

☐ How did Germany and Japan build empires in Europe and Asia, and how did the Allies defeat them?

World war broke out because Hitler's ambitions were essentially unlimited. Nazi soldiers scored enormous successes in Europe until late 1942, establishing a vast empire of death and destruction. Hitler's victories increased tensions in Asia between Japan, whose ambitions in Asia were equally unlimited, and the United States, and prompted Japan to attack the United States. Eventually, the mighty coalition of Britain, the United States, and the Soviet Union, which Winston Churchill called the Grand Alliance, functioned quite effectively in military terms and was determined to halt the aggressors. Thus the Nazi and Japanese empires proved short-lived.

Hitler's Empire in Europe, 1939-1942

Using planes, tanks, and trucks in the first example of a **blitzkrieg**, or "lightning war," Hitler's armies crushed Poland in four weeks. The Soviet Union quickly took its part of the booty — the eastern half of Poland and the Baltic states of Lithuania, Estonia, and Latvia. In the west French and British armies dug in; they expected another war of attrition and economic blockade. But in spring 1940 the Nazi lightning war struck again. After occupying Denmark, Norway, and Holland, German motorized columns broke through southern Belgium and into France.

As Hitler's armies poured into France, aging marshal Henri-Philippe Pétain — a national hero of the Great War — formed a new French government — the so-called Vichy (VIH-shee) government — and accepted defeat. Initially many French supported Pétain, who they believed

Vichy France, 1940

Occupied by Germany

Annexed by Germany

would stand up for them against the Germans, but as the war progressed Pétain increasingly collaborated with the Nazis. By July 1940 Hitler ruled practically all of western continental Europe; Italy was an ally, the Soviet Union a friendly neutral (Map 30.2). Only Britain, led by Winston Churchill (1874-1965), remained unconquered.

To prepare for an invasion of Britain, Germany first needed to gain control of the air. In the Battle of Britain, which began in July 1940, German planes attacked British airfields and key factories, dueling with British defenders high in the skies. In September Hitler began indiscriminately bombing British cities in an attempt to break British morale. British aircraft factories increased production, and the people of London defiantly dug in. By September Britain was beating Germany in the air war, and Hitler gave up his plans for an immediate German invasion of Britain.

Hitler now allowed his lifetime obsession of creating a vast eastern European empire for the "master race" to dictate policy. In June 1941 Germany broke the Nazi-Soviet nonaggression pact and attacked the Soviet Union. By October Leningrad was practically surrounded, Moscow was besieged, and most of Ukraine had been conquered. But the Soviets did not collapse, and when a severe winter struck German armies outfitted in summer uniforms, the invaders were stopped.

Stalled in Russia, Hitler had come to rule an enormous European empire stretching from the outskirts of Moscow to the English Channel. He now began building a **New Order** based on the guiding principle of Nazi totalitarianism: racial imperialism. Within the New Order, the Nordic peoples — the Dutch, Norwegians, and Danes — received preferential treatment, for the Germans believed they were racially related to the German "Aryan" master race. The French, an "inferior" Latin people, occupied the middle position. At the bottom of the New Order were the harshly treated "subhumans," Jews and Slavs.

Hitler envisioned a vast eastern colonial empire where Poles, Ukrainians, and Russians would be enslaved and forced to die out while Germanic peasants would resettle the abandoned lands. Himmler and the elite SS corps, supported by military commanders and German policemen, now implemented a program of destruction in the occupied territories to create a "mass settlement space" for Germans. Many Poles, captured Communists, Gypsies, and Jehovah's Witnesses were murdered in cold blood.

- **blitzkrieg** "Lightning war" using planes, tanks, and trucks, first used by Hitler to crush Poland in four weeks.
- **New Order** Hitler's program, based on the guiding principle of racial imperialism, which gave preferential treatment to the Nordic peoples above "inferior" Latin peoples and, at the bottom, "subhuman" Slavs and Jews.
- **Holocaust** The attempted systematic extermination of all European Jews and other "undesirables" by the Nazi state during World War II.

London Bomb Shelter, 1940 Hitler believed that his relentless terror bombing of London—the "blitz"—could break the will of the British people. He was wrong. The blitz caused enormous destruction, but Londoners went about their business with courage and calm determination, as this unforgettable image of people being entertained in a bomb shelter in the Tube (subway) suggests. (Bettmann/Corbis)

The Holocaust

Finally, the Nazi state condemned all European Jews to extermination in the **Holocaust**. After the fall of Warsaw in 1939 the Nazis began forcing the Jews in the occupied territories to move to urban ghettos. The remaining German Jews were sent to occupied Poland. When war with Russia broke out in 1941, forced expulsion spiraled into extermination. Himmler's SS killing squads and regular army units compelled Soviet Jews to dig giant pits, which became mass graves as the victims were lined up on the edge and cut down by machine guns. Then in late 1941 Hitler and the Nazi leadership, in some still-debated combination, ordered the SS to speed up planning for "the final solution of the Jewish question." Throughout the Nazi empire Jews were systematically arrested, packed like cattle onto freight trains, and dispatched to extermination camps.

Prelude to Murder This photo captures the terrible inhumanity of Nazi racism. Frightened and bewildered families from the soon-to-be-destroyed Warsaw Ghetto are being forced out of their homes by German soldiers for deportation to concentration camps. There they face murder in the gas chambers. (Hulton Archive/Getty Images)

☐ Axis powers and their allies
☐ Occupied by Germany and its allies
■ Extermination camp
● Major concentration camp
♦ Site of mass killing
✦ Ghetto

The Holocaust, 1941–1945

Individuals in Society

Primo Levi

MOST JEWS DEPORTED TO AUSCHWITZ WERE murdered as soon as they arrived, but the Nazis made some prisoners into slave laborers, and a few of these survived. Primo Levi (1919–1987), an Italian Jew, became one of the most influential witnesses to the Holocaust and its death camps.

Like many in Italy's small Jewish community, Levi's family belonged to the urban professional classes. The young Primo Levi graduated in 1941 from the University of Turin with highest honors in chemistry. Since 1938, when Italy introduced racial laws, he had faced growing discrimination, and two years after graduation he joined the antifascist resistance movement. Quickly captured, he was deported to Auschwitz with 650 Italian Jews in February 1944. Stone-faced SS men picked only ninety-six men and twenty-nine women to work in their respective labor camps. Levi was one of them.

Nothing had prepared Levi for what he encountered. The Jewish prisoners were kicked, punched, stripped, branded with tattoos, crammed into huts, and worked unmercifully. Hoping for some sign of prisoner solidarity in this terrible environment, Levi found only a desperate struggle of each against all and enormous status differences among prisoners. Many stunned and bewildered newcomers, beaten and demoralized by their bosses—the most privileged prisoners—collapsed and died. Others struggled to secure their own privileges, however small, because food rations and working conditions were so abominable that ordinary Jewish prisoners perished in two to three months.

Sensitive and noncombative, Levi found himself sinking into oblivion. But instead of joining the mass of the "drowned," he became one of the "saved"—a complicated surprise with moral implications that he would ponder all his life. As Levi explained in *Survival in Auschwitz* (1947), the usual road to salvation in the camps was some kind of collaboration with German power.* Savage German criminals were released from prison to become brutal camp guards; non-Jewish political prisoners competed for jobs entitling them to better conditions; and, especially troubling for Levi, a small number of Jewish men plotted and struggled for the power of life and death over other Jewish prisoners. Though not one of these Jewish bosses, Levi believed that he himself, like almost all survivors, had entered the "gray zone" of moral compromise. Only a very few superior individuals, "the stuff of saints and martyrs," survived the death camps without shifting their moral stance.

For Levi, compromise and salvation came from his profession. Interviewed by a German technocrat for the camp's synthetic rubber program, Levi performed brilliantly in scientific German and savored his triumph as a Jew over Nazi racism. Work in the warm camp laboratory offered Levi opportunities to pilfer equipment that could then be traded to other prisoners

for food and necessities. Levi also gained critical support from three saintly prisoners who refused to do wicked and hateful acts. And he counted "luck" as essential for his survival: in the camp infirmary with scarlet fever in February 1945 as advancing Russian armies prepared to liberate the camp, Levi was not evacuated by the Nazis and shot to death like most Jewish prisoners.

After the war Primo Levi was forever haunted by the nightmare that the Holocaust would be ignored or forgotten. Always ashamed that so many people whom he considered better than himself had perished, he wrote and lectured tirelessly to preserve the memory of Jewish victims and guilty Nazis. Wanting the world to understand the Jewish genocide in all its complexity so that never again would people tolerate such atrocities, he grappled tirelessly with his vision of individual choice and moral compromise in a hell designed to make the victims collaborate and persecute each other.

QUESTIONS FOR ANALYSIS

1. Describe Levi's experience at Auschwitz. How did camp prisoners treat each other? Why?
2. What does Levi mean by the "gray zone"? How is this concept central to his thinking?
3. Will a vivid historical memory of the Holocaust help prevent future genocide?

*Primo Levi, *Survival in Auschwitz: The Nazi Assault on Humanity*, rev. ed. 1958 (London: Collier Books, 1961), pp. 79–84, and *The Drowned and the Saved* (New York: Summit Books, 1988). These powerful testimonies are highly recommended.

• **Primo Levi, who never stopped thinking, writing, and speaking about the Holocaust.** (Giansanti/Corbis Sygma)

Arriving at their destination, small numbers of Jews were sent to nearby slave labor camps, where they were starved and systematically worked to death. (See "Individuals in Society: Primo Levi," page 928.) Most victims were taken to "shower rooms," which were actually gas chambers. For fifteen to twenty minutes came the terrible screams and gasping sobs of men, women, and children choking to death on poison gas. Then, only silence. Special camp workers quickly yanked the victims' gold teeth from their jaws, and the bodies were cremated. By 1945 about 6 million Jews had been murdered.

Who was responsible for this terrible crime? Some historians lay the guilt on Hitler and the Nazi leadership, arguing that ordinary Germans had little knowledge of the extermination camps, or that those who cooperated had no alternative given the brutality of Nazi terror and totalitarian control. But in recent years many studies have revealed a much broader participation of German people in the Holocaust and popular indifference (or worse) to the Jews' fate.

In most occupied countries, local non-German officials also cooperated in the arrest and deportation of Jews. As in Germany, only a few exceptional bystanders did not turn a blind eye. Catholic and Protestant church leaders protested rarely. Thus some scholars have concluded that the key for most Germans (and most people in occupied countries) was that they felt no personal responsibility for Jews and therefore were not prepared to help them. This meant that many individuals, conditioned by Nazi racist propaganda but also influenced by peer pressure and brutalizing wartime violence, were psychologically prepared to perpetrate ever-greater crimes, from mistreatment to arrest to mass murder.

Japan's Asian Empire

The Nazis did not have a monopoly on racism and brutalizing wartime violence. The Japanese, for their part, encouraged racial hatred of Westerners, giving free rein at home to the anti-Western ultranationalism that had risen in the 1920s and 1930s (see page 900): proclaiming Japan's liberating mission in Asia, glorifying the virtues of honor and sacrifice, and demanding absolute devotion to the semidivine emperor. (See "Listening to the Past: "Ultranationalist Pamphlet for Japanese Students," page 930.)

Abroad, by late 1938, 1.5 million Japanese troops were bogged down in China, holding a great swath of territory but unable to defeat the Nationalists and the Communists (see pages 900–902). In 1939, as war broke out in Europe, the Japanese redoubled their brutal efforts in China to crush peasant support for the Nationalists and the Communists. Implementing a savage policy of "kill all, burn all, destroy all," Japanese troops committed shocking atrocities, including the so-called Rape of Nanjing (see page 902). During Japan's war in China — the second Sino-Japanese War (1937–1945) — the Japanese are estimated to have killed 4 million Chinese people.

☐ EVENTS LEADING TO WORLD WAR II

1919	Treaty of Versailles is signed
1921	Hitler heads National Socialist German Worker's Party (Nazis)
1922	Mussolini seizes power in Italy
1927	Stalin takes control of the Soviet Union
1929–1939	Great Depression
1931	Japan invades Manchuria
January 1933	Hitler is appointed chancellor of Germany
March 1933	Reichstag passes the Enabling Act, granting Hitler absolute dictatorial power
October 1933	Germany withdraws from the League of Nations
1935	Nuremberg Laws deprive Jews of all rights of citizenship
March 1935	Hitler announces German rearmament
October 1935	Mussolini invades Ethiopia and receives Hitler's support
March 1936	German armies move unopposed into the demilitarized Rhineland
October 1936	Rome-Berlin Axis created
1936–1939	Spanish civil war
1937	Japan invades China
March 1938	Germany annexes Austria
September 1938	Munich Conference: Britain and France agree to German seizure of the Sudetenland from Czechoslovakia
March 1939	Germany occupies the rest of Czechoslovakia; appeasement ends in Britain
August 1939	Nazi-Soviet nonaggression pact is signed
September 1, 1939	Germany invades Poland
September 3, 1939	Britain and France declare war on Germany

Listening to the Past

Ultranationalist Pamphlet for Japanese Students

In August 1941, only four months before Japan's coordinated attack on Pearl Harbor and colonial empires in Southeast Asia, Japan's Ministry of Education issued "The Way of Subjects." Required reading for high school and university students, this twenty-page pamphlet summed up the basic tenets of Japanese ultranationalism, which had become dominant in the 1930s.

As this selection suggests, ultranationalism in Japan combined a sense of mission with intense group solidarity and unquestioning devotion to a semidivine emperor. Thus Japanese expansion into Manchuria and the war in China were part of Japan's sacred calling to protect the throne and to free Asia from Western exploitation and misrule. Of course, an unknown percentage of students (and adults) did not believe that the myths of Japan's state religion were literally true. Nevertheless, they were profoundly influenced by extremist nationalism: Japanese soldiers' determination to fight to the death was a prime indicator of that influence.

❝The way of the subjects of the Emperor issues from the policy of the Emperor and is to guard and maintain the Imperial Throne coexistent with the Heavens and the Earth. This is not an abstract principle but a way of daily practices based on history. The life and activities of the nation are all attuned to the task of strengthening the foundation of the Empire....

Modern history, in a nutshell, has been marked by the formation of unified nations in Europe and their contests for supremacy in the acquisition of colonies.... Their march into all parts of the world paved the way for their subsequent world domination politically, economically, and culturally and led them to believe that they alone were justified in their outrageous behavior....

The thoughts that have formed the foundation of Western civilization since the early modern period are individualism, liberalism, materialism, and so on. These thoughts regard the strong preying on the weak as reasonable, unstintedly promote the pursuit of luxury and pleasure, encourage materialism, and stimulate competition for acquiring colonies and securing trade, thereby leading the world to a veritable hell of fighting and bloodshed [in the First World War].... [Thereafter] a vigorous movement was started by Britain, France, and the United States to maintain the status quo by any means. Simultaneously, a movement aiming at social revolution through class conflict on the basis of thoroughgoing materialism like Communism also vigorously developed. On the other hand, Nazism and Fascism arose with great force. The basic principles of the totalitarianism in Germany and Italy are to remove the evils of individualism and liberalism.

That these [totalitarian] principles show great similarity to Eastern culture and spirit is a noteworthy fact that suggests the future of Western civilization and the creation of a new culture. Thus, the orientation of world history has made the collapse of the old world order a certainty. Japan has hereby initiated the construction of a new world order based on moral principles.

The Manchurian Affair [the Japanese invasion of Manchuria in 1931] was a violent outburst of Japanese national life long suppressed. Taking advantage of this, Japan in the glare of all the Powers made a step toward the creation of a world based on moral principles and the construction of a new order. This was a manifestation of the spirit, profound and lofty, embodied in the founding of Empire, and an unavoidable action for its national life and world mission....

The general tendency of world domination by Europe and America has begun to show signs of a change since the Russo-Japanese War of 1904–05. Japan's victory attracted the attention of the entire world, and this caused a reawakening of Asiatic countries, which had been forced to lie prostrate under British and American influence, with the result that an independence movement was started.

Hopes to be free of the shackles and bondage of Europe and America were ablaze among the nations of India, Turkey, Arabia, Thailand, Vietnam, and others. This also inspired a

In August 1940 the Japanese announced the formation of a self-sufficient Asian economic zone. Although they spoke of liberating Asia from Western imperialism and of "Asia for the Asians," their true intentions were to eventually rule over a vast Japanese empire. For the moment, however, Japan still depended on imports for essential materials like oil. Thus the Japanese sought alliances that might give them better access to these essential goods and also improve their position in Asia.

Seeking support for its war in China, in September 1940 Japan signed a formal alliance with Germany and Italy, and Vichy France granted the Japanese domination over northern French Indochina — from where they could attack southern China. The United States feared that embattled Britain would collapse if it lost new national movement in China. Amid this stormy atmosphere of Asia's reawakening, Japan has come to be keenly conscious of the fact that the stabilization of East Asia is her mission, and that the emancipation of East Asian nations rests solely on her efforts. . . .

Japan has a political mission to help various regions in the Greater East Asian Co-prosperity Sphere [the Japanese term for Japan's Asian empire], which are reduced to a state of quasi-colony by Europe and America, and rescue them from their control. Economically, this country will have to eradicate the evils of their exploitation and then set up an economic structure for coexistence and co-prosperity. Culturally, Japan must strive to fashion East Asian nations to abandon their following of European and American culture and to develop Eastern culture for the purpose of contributing to the creation of a just world. The East has been left to destruction for the past several hundred years. Its rehabilitation is not an easy task. It is natural that unusual difficulties attend the establishment of a new order and the creation of a new culture. Overcoming these difficulties will do much to help in establishing a world dominated by morality, in which all nations can cooperate and all people can secure their proper positions. . . .

In Japan, the Emperors of a line unbroken for ages eternal govern and reign over it, as the Heavens and the Earth endure, since the Imperial Foundress, Amaterasu-o-Mikami, . . . caused Her grandson Ninigi-no-Mikoto to descend on the eight great countries and She commanded him, saying: "This country, fruitful and abounding in rice, is the land over which Our descendants shall rule. Go you, therefore, down and reign over it. Under you and your offspring it shall prosper as long as the Heavens and the Earth endure." . . .

The Imperial Family is [therefore] the fountain source of the Japanese nation, and national and private lives issue from this. In the past, foreign nationals came to this country only to enjoy the benevolent rule of the Imperial Family, and became Japanese subjects spiritually and by blood. The Imperial virtues are so great and boundless that all are assimilated into one. Here is the reason for the present glorious state, in which the Emperor and his subjects are harmonized into one great unit. That the myriad subjects with one mind are glad to be unified in their devotion to the Throne is the substance of the Imperial subjects.

The way of the subjects is to be loyal to the Emperor in disregard of self. . . . To serve the Emperor is its key point. Our lives will become sincere and true when they are offered to the Emperor and the state. . . . All must be unified under the Emperor. Herein lies the significance of national life in Japan. 🙶

• **Kamikaze pilots ponder the message on the flag that they will take on their suicide mission: "All for the Emperor, we are happy to die for him."** (Photoservice Electa, Milan)

Source: "The Way of Subjects," in *Tokyo Record*, copyright 1943 by Otto D. Tolischus and renewed 1970 by Naya G. Tolischus. Reprinted by permission of Houghton Mifflin Harcourt Publishing Company.

QUESTIONS FOR ANALYSIS

1. How does "The Way of Subjects" interpret modern history? In what ways do Western thought and action threaten Japan?

2. What is Japan's mission in Asia?

3. What is the basis of Japanese sovereignty? What is the individual's proper role in society?

its Asian colonies to Japan. Applying economic sanctions in October 1940, the United States stopped scrap iron sales to Japan and later froze all Japanese assets in the United States.

Japan's invasion of southern Indochina in July 1941 further worsened relations with the United States, which viewed this aggression as a direct threat to the Philippines and the oil-rich Dutch East Indies. The United States responded by cutting off U.S. oil sales to Japan, thereby reducing Japan's oil supplies by 90 percent. Japanese leaders, increasingly convinced that war with the United States was inevitable, because Japan's fleet would run out of fuel in eighteen months, decided after much debate to launch a surprise attack on the U.S. fleet in Pearl Harbor in the Hawaiian Islands. They hoped to cripple their Pacific rival, gain time to build a

MAP 30.2 World War II in Europe and Africa, 1939–1945 The map shows the extent of Hitler's empire at its height, before the Battle of Stalingrad in late 1942 and the subsequent advances of the Allies until Germany surrendered on May 7, 1945.

defensible Asian empire, and eventually win an ill-defined compromise peace.

The Japanese attack at Pearl Harbor was a complete surprise but a limited success. On December 7, 1941, the Japanese sank or crippled every American battleship, but by chance all the American aircraft carriers were at sea and escaped unharmed. More important, Americans were humiliated by this unexpected defeat. Thus Pearl Harbor overwhelmed American isolationism and brought the United States into the war.

Hitler immediately declared war on the United States. Simultaneously, Japanese armies successfully attacked European and American colonies in Southeast Asia. Small but well-trained Japanese armies defeated larger Dutch and British armies to seize the Netherlands East Indies and the British colonies of Hong Kong, Malaya, and Singapore. After American forces surrendered the Philippines in May 1942, Japan held a vast empire in Southeast Asia and the western Pacific (Map 30.3).

□ Mapping the Past

MAP 30.3 World War II in the Pacific Japanese forces overran an enormous amount of territory in 1942, which the Allies slowly recaptured in a long, bitter struggle.

ANALYZING THE MAP Locate the extent of the Japanese empire in 1942, and compare it to the Japanese-controlled territory at surrender in 1945. Where was the fighting in the Pacific concentrated?

CONNECTIONS How was the course of the end of war in Europe different, and what does this suggest about the difficulties that the Allies faced in fighting the Japanese?

The Japanese claimed they were freeing Asians from Western imperialism, and they called their empire the Greater East Asian Co-Prosperity Sphere. By promising to create a mutually advantageous union for Asia's long-term development, the Japanese tapped currents of nationalist sentiment. Most local populations were glad to see the Western powers go, but Asian faith in "co-

prosperity" and support for Japan steadily declined as the war went on. Although the Japanese set up anticolonial governments and promised genuine independence, real power always rested with Japanese military commanders and their superiors in Tokyo. The "independent" governments established in the Philippines, French Indochina, Burma, and the Netherlands East

The War in the Philippines
U.S. and Philippine forces held out on the Bataan peninsula until April 1942, when seventy-six thousand soldiers surrendered to the Japanese military. Most of the prisoners were sick, wounded, or suffering from malnutrition, and the Japanese systematically executed many of them. Other prisoners, such as those pictured here, were marched to exhaustion without water in the blazing sun on the infamous Bataan Death March, and many were bayoneted or beaten to death. (Bettmann/Corbis)

Indies were basically shams. Moreover, the Japanese never treated local populations as equals, and the occupiers exploited local peoples for Japan's wartime needs. They cut wages, imposed supply quotas on raw materials, and drafted local people for military and labor service.

The Japanese often exhibited great cruelty toward prisoners of war and civilians. After the fall of Hong Kong in December 1941, for example, wounded prisoners were murdered, and there was a mass rape of nurses. Elsewhere Dutch, Indonesian, and perhaps as many as two hundred thousand Korean women were forced to provide sex for Japanese soldiers as "comfort women." Recurring cruel behavior aroused local populations against the invaders.

The Grand Alliance

While the Nazis and the Japanese built their empires, Great Britain, the United States (both vehemently anticommunist), and the Soviet Union (equally anticapitalist) joined together in an unlikely military pact called the Grand Alliance. Chance, rather than choice, had brought them together. Stalin had been cooperating with Hitler between August 1939 and June 1941, and only the Japanese attack on Pearl Harbor had led the United States to enter the war.

As a first step toward building an unshakable alliance, the Grand Alliance agreed on a **Europe first policy** as proposed by Winston Churchill (Chamberlain's successor as British prime minister).

Only after defeating Hitler would the Allies mount an all-out attack on Japan. To further encourage mutual trust, the Allies adopted the principle of the unconditional surrender of Germany and Japan. This policy cemented the Grand Alliance because it denied Germany and Japan any hope of dividing their foes.

The Grand Alliance's military resources were awesome. The United States possessed a unique capacity to wage global war with its large population and mighty industry, which it harnessed in 1943 to outproduce not only the Axis powers but also the rest of the world combined.[11] The British economy was totally and effectively mobilized, and the country became an important staging area for the war in Europe. As for the Soviet Union, so great was its strength that it might well have defeated Germany without Western help. In the face of the German advance, whole factories and populations were successfully evacuated to eastern Russia and Siberia. There war production was reorganized and expanded, and the Red Army was increasingly well supplied and well led. Above all, Stalin drew on the massive support of the people for what the Soviets called the "Great Patriotic War of the Fatherland."

The War in Europe, 1942–1945

Halted at the gates of Moscow and Leningrad in 1941, the Germans renewed their offensive against the Soviet Union in 1942 and attacked Stalingrad in July. The Soviet armies counterattacked, quickly surrounding the entire German Sixth Army of 300,000 men. By late

The Normandy Invasion, Omaha Beach, June 6, 1944 Airborne paratroopers landed behind German coastal fortifications around midnight, and U.S. and British forces hit several beaches at daybreak as Allied ships and bombers provided cover. U.S. troops secured full control of Omaha Beach by nightfall, but at a price of three thousand casualties. Allied air power prevented the Germans from bringing up reserves and counterattacking. (Bettmann/Corbis)

January 1943 only 123,000 soldiers were left to surrender. Hitler, who had refused to allow a retreat, suffered a catastrophic defeat. In summer 1943 the larger, better-equipped Soviet armies took the offensive and began to push the Germans back (see Map 30.2).

Not yet prepared to attack Germany directly through France, the Western Allies saw heavy fighting in North Africa (see Map 30.2). The French Vichy government allowed Germany to transport war materials and aircraft through Syria to Iraq to use against the British, and in 1941 the British had invaded Syria and Lebanon. In summer 1942 British forces defeated German and Italian armies at the Battle of El Alamein (el a-luh-MAYN) in Egypt. Shortly thereafter an Anglo-American force took control of the Vichy French colonies of Morocco and Algeria.

Having driven the Axis powers from North Africa by spring 1943, Allied forces invaded Italy. War-weary Italians deposed Mussolini, and the new Italian government accepted unconditional surrender in September 1943. Italy, it seemed, was liberated. But German commandos rescued Mussolini in a daring raid and put him at the head of a puppet government. German armies seized Rome and all of northern Italy. The allies' Italian campaign against German forces lasted

another two years and involved, in terms of infantry dead and wounded, the most costly battles of the war in western Europe. The German armies finally surrendered to the Allies on April 29, 1945. Two days earlier Mussolini — dressed in a German military uniform and trying to escape with the retreating German forces — had been captured by partisan forces. He was executed the next day.

To match the Allied war effort, Germany had applied itself to total war in 1942 and had enlisted millions of German women and millions of prisoners of war and slave laborers to work in the war industry. Between early 1942 and July 1944 German war production tripled in spite of heavy Anglo-American bombing. Terrorized at home and frightened by the prospect of unconditional surrender, the Germans fought on with suicidal stoicism.

On June 6, 1944, American and British forces under General Dwight Eisenhower landed on the beaches of Normandy, France, in history's greatest naval invasion.

• **Europe first policy** The military strategy, set forth by Churchill and adopted by Roosevelt, that called for the defeat of Hitler in Europe before the United States launched an all-out strike against Japan in the Pacific.

A Hiroshima Survivor Remembers Yasuko Yamagata was seventeen when she saw the brilliant blue-white "lightning flash" that became a fiery orange ball consuming everything that would burn. Thirty years later Yamagata painted this scene, her most unforgettable memory of the atomic attack. An incinerated woman, poised as if running with her baby clutched to her breast, lies near a water tank piled high with charred corpses. (GE15-05 drawn by Yasuko Yamagata, Hiroshima Peace Memorial Museum)

More than 2 million men and almost a half million vehicles pushed inland and broke through the German lines. In March 1945 American troops crossed the Rhine and entered Germany.

The Soviets, who had been advancing steadily since July 1943, reached the outskirts of Warsaw by August 1944. On April 26, 1945, the Red Army met American forces on the Elbe River in Germany. The Allies had closed their vise on Nazi Germany and overrun Europe. As Soviet forces fought their way into Berlin, Hitler committed suicide in his bunker, and on May 7 the remaining German commanders capitulated.

The War in the Pacific, 1942–1945

While gigantic armies clashed on land in Europe, the greatest naval battles in history decided the fate of the war in Asia. In April 1942 the Japanese devised a plan to take Port Moresby in New Guinea and also destroy U.S. aircraft carriers in an attack on Midway Island (see Map 30.3). Having broken the secret Japanese code, the Americans skillfully won a series of decisive naval victories. First, in the Battle of the Coral Sea in May 1942, an American carrier force halted the Japanese advance on Port Moresby and relieved Australia from the threat of invasion. Then, in the Battle of Midway in June 1942, American pilots sank all four of the attacking Japanese aircraft carriers and established overall naval equality with Japan in the Pacific.

Badly hampered in the ground war by the Europe first policy, the United States gradually won control of the sea and air as it geared up its war industry. By 1943 the United States was producing one hundred thousand aircraft a year, almost twice as many as Japan produced in the entire war. In July 1943 the Americans and their Australian allies opened an "island-hopping" campaign toward Japan. Pounding Japanese forces on a given island with saturation bombing, Allied units would then hit the beaches and secure victory in vicious hand-to-hand combat. By 1944 hundreds of American submarines were hunting in "wolf packs," decimating shipping and destroying economic links in Japan's far-flung, overextended empire.

The Pacific war was brutal—a "war without mercy"—and atrocities were committed on both sides.[12] Aware of Japanese atrocities in China and the Philippines, the U.S. Marines and Army troops seldom took Japanese prisoners after the Battle of Guadalcanal in August 1942, killing even those rare Japanese soldiers who offered to surrender. American forces moving across the central and western Pacific in 1943 and 1944 faced unyielding resistance, and this resistance hardened soldiers as American casualties kept rising. A product of spiraling violence, mutual hatred, and dehumanizing racial stereotypes, the war without mercy intensified as it moved toward Japan.

In June 1944 U.S. bombers began a relentless bombing campaign of the Japanese home islands. In October 1944 American forces under General Douglas MacArthur landed on Leyte Island in the Philippines. The Japanese believed they could destroy MacArthur's troops and transport ships before the main American fleet arrived. The result was the four-day Battle of Leyte Gulf, the greatest battle in naval history, with 282 ships involved. The Japanese lost 13 large warships, including 4 aircraft carriers, while the Americans lost only 3 small ships. The Japanese navy was practically finished.

In spite of massive defeats, Japanese troops continued to fight with courage and determination. Indeed, the bloodiest battles of the Pacific war took place on Iwo Jima in February 1945 and on Okinawa in June 1945. American commanders believed that the conquest of Japan might cost a million American casualties and possibly 10 to 20 million Japanese lives. In fact, Japan was almost helpless, its industry and cities largely destroyed by intense American bombing. Yet the Japanese seemed determined to fight on, ready to die for a hopeless cause.

On August 6 and 9, 1945, the United States dropped atomic bombs on Hiroshima and Nagasaki in Japan. Mass bombing of cities and civilians, one of the terrible new practices of World War II, had led to the final nightmare — unprecedented human destruction in a single blinding flash. On August 14, 1945, the Japanese announced their surrender. The Second World War, which had claimed the lives of more than 50 million soldiers and civilians, was over.

CONNECTIONS

If anyone still doubted the interconnectedness of all the world's inhabitants following the Great War, those doubts faded as events on a truly global scale touched everyone as never before in the 1930s and 1940s. First a Great Depression shook the financial foundations of the wealthiest capitalist economies and the poorest producers of raw materials and minerals. Another world war followed, bringing global death and destruction at a magnitude beyond the imaginations of even Great War survivors. At war's end, as we shall see in Chapter 34, the world's leaders revived Woodrow Wilson's idea of a League of Nations and formed the United Nations in 1946 to prevent such tragedies from ever reoccurring.

Although the United Nations was an attempt to bring nations together, the postwar world became more divided than ever. Chapter 31 will describe how two new superpowers — the United States and the Soviet Union — emerged from World War II to engage one another in the Cold War for nearly the rest of the century. Then in Chapters 32 and 33 we will see how a political Third World of nations in Asia, Africa, and Latin America emerged after the war. Many of them did so by turning the nineteenth-century European ideology of nationalism against its creators, breaking the bonds of colonialism.

Today we want to believe that the era of totalitarian dictatorship was a terrible accident, that Stalin's slave labor camps, Hitler's gas chambers, and Japan's Rape of Nanjing "can't happen again." But the cruel truth is that horrible atrocities continue to plague the world in our time. The Khmer Rouge inflicted genocide on its people in Cambodia, and civil war led to ethnically motivated atrocities in Bosnia, Rwanda, Burundi, and Sudan, recalling the horrors of the Second World War. Today's dictators, however, are losing control over access to information — historically a cornerstone of dictatorial rule — and are being challenged and even overthrown by citizens with cell phones, cameras, and Internet connections. In 2010 and 2011 ruthless dictatorial regimes in Egypt, Tunisia, Syria, Yemen, Libya, Iran, and elsewhere have found it much harder to brutally impose their will over their people when opponents have the ability to instantly expose their murderous actions to the world.

▢ CHAPTER REVIEW

▢ **What caused the Great Depression, and what were its consequences?** (p. 908)

The 1929 stock market crash in the United States resulted in a financial panic and run on banks, which in turn triggered a collapse of the international economy. The Great Depression shattered the fragile stability briefly achieved after World War I. As production declined, unemployment affected millions worldwide. Countries turned inward as they sought to cope with massive domestic problems and widespread disillusionment. Western democracies responded with relief programs, many modeled after the U.S. New Deal

KEY TERMS

New Deal (p. 910)
Popular Front (p. 912)
totalitarianism
  (p. 914)
fascism (p. 914)
five-year plan (p. 915)
New Economic Policy
  (NEP) (p. 915)
collectivization
  (p. 916)

Black Shirts (p. 918)
Lateran Agreement
  (p. 919)
Nazism (p. 920)
Enabling Act (p. 922)
blitzkrieg (p. 926)
New Order (p. 926)
Holocaust (p. 927)
Europe first policy
  (p. 934)

program, but success was generally limited. In Asia, Japan's financial woes led to aggressive empire building, as the military leadership looked for colonies that would help supply the resource-poor islands of Japan. The old liberal ideals of individual rights and responsibilities, elected government, and economic freedom, even when they managed to survive, seemed ineffective and outmoded to many, setting the stage for the rise of authoritarian and fascist regimes. In the end, only World War II would end the depression.

What was the nature of the new totalitarian dictatorships, and how did they differ from conservative authoritarian states? (p. 913)

The effects of the Great Depression, the lack of a democratic tradition, and unrest and ethnic strife led many of the budding democracies of Europe to return to traditional conservative authoritarianism. A new kind of radical dictatorship also formed in the 1920s and 1930s — specifically in Germany and the Soviet Union, and to a lesser extent in Italy, Spain, Japan, and Portugal. Like conservative authoritarian regimes, all were repressive and profoundly antiliberal. But totalitarian regimes were also exceedingly violent, asserted a total claim on the lives of their citizens, posed ambitious goals, and demanded popular support. Stalin's Russia and Hitler's Germany, in particular, exuded tremendous dynamism and awesome power. That dynamism, however, was channeled in quite different directions. Stalin and the Communist Party aimed at building their kind of socialism and the new socialist personality at home. Hitler and the Fascist Nazi elite aimed at unlimited territorial and racial aggression on behalf of a "master race"; domestic control of state and society was only a means to that end.

How did Stalin and the Communist Party build a totalitarian order in the Soviet Union? (p. 915)

After consolidating his power in the 1920s, Stalin launched the first of his five-year plans in 1928. These plans were a critical part of Stalin's efforts to totally control the Russian economy and society. Meant to introduce a "revolution from above," they were extremely ambitious efforts to modernize and industrialize the U.S.S.R. along socialist lines and to create a new socialist society. They set staggering industrial and agricultural objectives and replaced private lands with (often forced) collectivization. Labor unions were severely weakened, and foreign experts from Europe and America were brought in to lend their skill and expertise to the building of new factories and machinery in order to catch up with the more advanced capitalist nations of the West. In the 1930s Stalin implemented mass purges of the Communist Party, leading to the imprisonment and deaths of mil-

lions. In this way Stalin was able to staff the ranks of the Communist Party with young loyalists.

How did Italian fascism develop? (p. 918)

Mussolini's hatred of liberalism led him to set up the first Fascist government. Mussolini created a one-party dictatorship by abolishing press freedoms, disbanding independent trade unions, rigging elections, and ruling by decree. Mussolini allowed the old conservative classes to retain control of the economy, the army, and the state bureaucracy. He gained the support of the Roman Catholic Church by recognizing the Vatican as a tiny independent state in 1929. Racial laws were never a very significant aspect of Mussolini's rule, as they were for Hitler, and Jews were not severely persecuted until Italy came under Nazi control toward the end of World War II. Though repressive and undemocratic, Mussolini never destroyed the old power structure and allowed big business to regulate itself. Although brutal in its methods, Mussolini's regime was never truly a totalitarian state on the order of Hitler's Germany or Stalin's Soviet Union, which sought to control all aspects of society.

Why were Hitler and his Nazi regime initially so popular, and how did their actions lead to World War II? (p. 919)

Hitler and the Nazi Party drew on the humiliation of World War I and the terms of the Versailles treaty to rally support. He used this discontent to disseminate his racist sentiments about "inferior" peoples and to prey on fears of a Jewish conspiracy to harm German culture, German unity, and the German race. When the Great Depression struck, Hitler appealed to people's economic insecurity, making promises that caused voters to desert the old leaders and turn to this dynamic new voice. Popular support for Hitler's regime was initially very high, abetted by relentless propaganda, a steep drop in unemployment, and a rise in business profits and the standard of living. Hitler initially tried to camouflage his plans for aggressive territorial expansion. After he declared the Versailles treaty disarmament clause null and void, British and French leaders tried to use a policy of appeasement. On September 1, 1939, his unprovoked attack on Poland left no doubt about his intentions, and the British and French declared war, starting World War II.

How did Germany and Japan build empires in Europe and Asia, and how did the Allies defeat them? (p. 926)

Nazi armies used blitzkrieg tactics to quickly seize Poland and Germany's Western neighbors. Hitler then shifted his attention to the east, where he planned to build a New Order based on racial imperialism. The result was the Holocaust, in which millions of Jews and other "undesirables" were systematically exterminated. The Japanese also used aggressive territorial expansion to create what they called the Greater East Asian Co-Prosperity Sphere in the Pacific. As the colonies liberated from Western control soon learned, this was a sham, and "Asia for the Asians" meant nothing more than Japanese domination and brutal control. After Japan attacked Pearl Harbor, the United States entered the war. The Grand Alliance of the United States, Britain, and the Soviet Union harnessed the committed populations of these countries and, in the case of the Soviet Union and the United States, their superior war industry to outproduce and outman the overextended and far-flung empires of Japan and Germany.

SUGGESTED READING

Applebaum, Anne. *Gulag.* 2004. An excellent survey of Stalin's labor camps.

Brendon, Piers. *The Dark Valley: A Panorama of the 1930s.* 2002. Masterful, sweeping account of this tumultuous decade.

Brooker, Paul. *Twentieth Century Dictatorships: The Ideological One-Party State.* 1995. A comparative analysis.

Crowe, David M. *The Holocaust: Roots, History and Aftermath.* 2008. Analyzes the origins and ghastly implementation of Nazi racial politics.

Fitzpatrick, Sheila. *Everyday Stalinism: Ordinary Life in Extraordinary Times.* 1999. Social and cultural history.

Geyer, Michael, and Sheila Fitzpatrick. *Beyond Totalitarianism: Nazism and Stalinism Compared.* 2008. Comparative studies of the two dictatorships based on archival sources that have only recently become available to historians.

Gilbert, Martin. *The Second World War: A Complete History,* rev. ed. 2004. Massively detailed global survey.

Glantz, David M. *When Titans Clashed: How the Red Army Stopped Hitler.* 1995. Authoritative account of the eastern front in World War II.

Hasegawa, Tsuyoshi. *Racing the Enemy: Stalin, Truman and the Surrender of Japan.* 2005. Masterful diplomatic history with a controversial new account of the end of the war.

Hillberg, Raul. *The Destruction of the European Jews, 1933–1945,* rev. ed. 3 vols. 1985. A monumental classic.

Keegan, John. *The Second World War.* 1990. Broad survey by a distinguished military historian.

Kindleberger, Charles P. *The World in Depression, 1929–1939.* 1986. Perhaps the best analytical account of the global origins, events, and aftermath of the Great Depression.

Levi, Primo. *Survival at Auschwitz.* 1947. First published in English as *If This Is a Man*; a memoir and meditation on the meaning of survival.

Weinberg, Gerhard. *World at Arms: A Global History of World War II.* 1994. Global survey with a political-diplomatic emphasis.

Wright, Gordon. *The Ordeal of Total War,* rev. ed. 1997. Explores the scientific, psychological, and economic dimensions of the war.

NOTES

1. Quoted in S. B. Clough et al., eds., *Economic History of Europe: Twentieth Century* (New York: Harper & Row, 1968), pp. 243–245.
2. E. Halévy, *The Era of Tyrannies* (Garden City, N.Y.: Doubleday, 1965), pp. 265–316, esp. p. 300.
3. I. Kershaw, *The Nazi Dictatorship: Problems and Perspectives of Interpretation,* 2d ed. (London: Edward Arnold, 1989), p. 34.
4. Quoted in A. G. Mazour, *Soviet Economic Development: Operation Outstrip, 1921–1965* (Princeton, N.J.: Van Nostrand, 1967), p. 130.
5. Quoted in I. Deutscher, *Stalin: A Political Biography,* 2d ed. (New York: Oxford University Press, 1967), p. 325.
6. M. Malia, *The Soviet Tragedy: A History of Socialism in Russia, 1917–1991* (New York: Free Press, 1995), pp. 227–270.
7. R. Vivarelli, "Interpretations on the Origins of Fascism," *Journal of Modern History* 63 (March 1991): 41.
8. W. Brustein, *The Logic of Evil: The Social Origins of the Nazi Party, 1925–1933* (New Haven, Conn.: Yale University Press, 1996), pp. 52, 182.
9. Quoted in R. Stromberg, *An Intellectual History of Modern Europe* (New York: Appleton-Century-Crofts, 1966), p. 393.
10. Quoted in R. Moeller, *The Nazi State and German Society: A Brief History with Documents* (Boston: Bedford/St. Martin's, 2010), p. 108.
11. H. Willmott, *The Great Crusade: A New Complete History of the Second World War* (New York: Free Press, 1989), p. 255.
12. J. Dower, *War Without Mercy: Race and Power in the Pacific War* (New York: Pantheon, 1986).

For practice quizzes and other study tools, visit the **Online Study Guide** at bedfordstmartins.com/mckayworld.

For primary sources from this period, see *Sources of World Societies*, **Second Edition**.

For Web sites, images, and documents related to topics in this chapter, visit **Make History** at bedfordstmartins.com/mckayworld.

• **Soviet Worker Statue** An idealized, heroic Soviet worker leans forward into the new Soviet age in this example of socialist realism, an artistic style that promoted socialism and communism. Socialist realism was the only acceptable artistic style in the Soviet Union for over sixty years, as Soviet leaders condemned the art of the West as decadent and bourgeois. Statues like this one were propaganda tools glorifying the achievements of the Soviet state. (© Eduard Talaykov)

31

After the defeat of the Axis powers in Europe and Asia, recovery from this most devastating war began worldwide. Hopes of world peace quickly faded, however, when differences in Allied economic and political ideologies set aside during wartime came to the fore, pitting the democratic and capitalist countries of the United States and its allies, including Japan, against the Marxist Communist Soviet Union and its allies.

Despite the growing tensions of this global Cold War, the postwar decades witnessed remarkable growth and economic prosperity. A battered western Europe once again dug itself out from under the rubble of war and, with U.S. aid, witnessed an amazing recovery. Having avoided wartime destruction and occupation, the United States quickly converted its economies to peacetime production. After seven years of Allied occupation, Japan experienced a quick recovery that by the 1960s made it one of the world's leading economic powers. In the east, the Soviet Union sought to protect itself from future attacks from the west by occupying eastern Europe and establishing Communist dictatorships there.

Global Recovery and Division Between Superpowers
1945 to the Present

In the early 1970s the global economic boom came to an end, and domestic political stability and social harmony evaporated. The spectacular collapse of communism in eastern Europe in 1989 and the end of the Cold War reinforced global integration. The result was monumental change, especially in postcommunist eastern Europe. A similar though less dramatic transformation also occurred in the nations of western Europe as they moved toward greater unity within the European Union. •

The Division of Europe
☐ What were the causes of the Cold War?

Renaissance and Crisis in Western Europe
☐ How did western Europe recover so successfully after World War II, and how did economic decline in the 1970s and 1980s affect society?

Recovery and Reform in Soviet Eastern Europe, 1945–1991
☐ How did the Soviets try to reform society, and what were the consequences of the anticommunist revolutions of 1989?

The United States: Confrontation and Transformation
☐ What contributed to the social and political transformation of the United States in the second half of the twentieth century?

Japan's Resurgence as a World Power
☐ How did Japan recover so quickly after its total defeat in World War II to become an economic superpower?

The Post–Cold War Era in Europe
☐ What was the nature of postcommunist reconstruction in eastern Europe, and how did Europe as a whole respond to calls for increased unity?

The Division of Europe

☐ What were the causes of the Cold War?

In 1945 triumphant American and Russian soldiers embraced along the Elbe River in the heart of vanquished Germany. At home the soldiers' loved ones erupted in joyous celebration. Yet victory was flawed. The Allies could not cooperate politically in peacemaking. The United States and the Soviet Union soon found themselves at loggerheads. By the end of 1947 Europe was rigidly divided, West versus East, in a Cold War eventually waged around the world.

The Origins of the Cold War

Almost as soon as the unifying threat of Nazi Germany disappeared, the Soviet Union and the United States began to quarrel. Hostility between the Eastern and Western superpowers was the logical outgrowth of military developments, wartime agreements, and long-standing political and ideological differences dating back to World War I.

In the early phases of the Second World War, the Americans and the British made military victory their highest priority. They avoided discussion of Joseph Stalin's war aims and the shape of the eventual peace

The Big Three In 1945 a triumphant Winston Churchill, an ailing Franklin Roosevelt, and a determined Joseph Stalin met at Yalta in southern Russia to plan for peace. Cooperation soon gave way to bitter hostility. (F.D.R. Library)

Postwar Territorial Changes in Eastern Europe

Lost by Germany
Gained by Soviet Union

FINLAND
SWEDEN
ESTONIA
LATVIA
Baltic Sea
LITHUANIA
SOVIET UNION
EAST GERMANY
POLAND
UKRAINE
CZECHOSLOVAKIA
BESSARABIA
AUSTRIA
HUNGARY
ROMANIA

settlement, fearing that hard bargaining might encourage Stalin to make a separate peace with Hitler. By late 1943 decisions about the shape of the postwar world could no longer be postponed. Franklin Roosevelt, Winston Churchill, and Joseph Stalin met in Teheran, Iran, in November 1943, and there the "Big Three" reaffirmed their determination to crush Germany. Churchill argued that American and British forces should attack Germany's "soft underbelly" through the Balkans. Roosevelt, however, agreed with Stalin that a joint American-British frontal assault through France would be better. Soviet, rather than American and British, armies would then liberate eastern Europe.

When the Big Three met again in February 1945 at Yalta on the Black Sea in southern Russia, the Red Army occupied most of eastern Europe and was within a hundred miles of Berlin. American-British forces had yet to cross the Rhine into Germany. Moreover, the United States was far from defeating Japan. In short, the Soviet Union's position was strong and America's was weak. At Yalta the Big Three agreed that Germany would be divided into zones of occupation and would pay the Soviet Union heavy reparations. Stalin agreed to declare war on Japan after Germany's defeat. As for Poland and eastern Europe, the Big Three reached an ambiguous compromise: eastern European governments were to be freely elected but pro-Russian.

Almost immediately this compromise broke down. Even before the conference, Communists arriving home with the Red Army controlled Bulgaria and Poland. Elsewhere in eastern Europe, pro-Soviet "coalition" governments were formed, but key ministerial posts were reserved for Moscow-trained Communists.

At the postwar Potsdam Conference in July 1945, long-avoided differences over eastern Europe were finally debated. The compromising Roosevelt had died

MAP 31.1 Cold War Europe in the 1950s Europe was divided by an "iron curtain" during the Cold War. None of the Communist countries of eastern Europe were participants in the Marshall Plan.

and had been succeeded by the more assertive Harry Truman (1884–1972), who now demanded free elections throughout eastern Europe. Stalin refused point-blank. "A freely elected government in any of these East European countries would be anti-Soviet," he admitted simply, "and that we cannot allow."[1]

Stalin, who had lived through two enormously destructive German invasions, wanted absolute military security from Germany and its potential eastern European allies once and for all. He believed that only Communist states could be truly dependable allies. By the middle of 1945 the United States had no way to determine political developments in eastern Europe short of war, and war was out of the question. Stalin would have his way.

West Versus East

America's response to Stalin's conception of security was to "get tough." In May 1945 Truman abruptly cut off all aid to the Soviet Union. In October he declared that the United States would never recognize any government established by force against the free will of its

> **"A freely elected government in any of these East European countries would be anti-Soviet, and that we cannot allow."**
>
> **JOSEPH STALIN**

people. His declaration, however, applied only to Europe and to countries threatened by communism, not to British and French colonies in Asia and Africa, for example, or to Latin American right-wing dictatorships. America's failure to support Third World anticolonial, or liberation, movements would have tragic consequences later on, particularly in Vietnam. In March 1946 former British prime minister Churchill ominously informed an American audience that an "iron curtain" had fallen across the European continent, dividing Germany and all of Europe into two antagonistic camps (Map 31.1). (See "Viewpoints: The Cold War Begins," page 945.)

Stalin's agents quickly renewed the "ideological struggle against capitalist imperialism." France's and Italy's large, well-organized Communist Parties challenged their own governments with violent criticism and large strikes. The Soviet Union also put pressure on Iran, Turkey, and Greece, and a bitter civil war raged in China (see pages 978–979). By spring 1947 many Americans believed that Stalin was determined to export communism throughout Europe and around the world.

Viewpoints

The Cold War Begins

- *On March 5, 1946, former British prime minister Winston Churchill delivered his famous "Sinews of Peace" speech to more than forty thousand people at Westminster College in the small town of Fulton, Missouri. Giving the speech the better known name of the "iron curtain" speech, Churchill for the first time used this famous phrase that soon became ubiquitous throughout the world to describe Russia's iron grip on eastern Europe.*

  A year later, on March 12, 1947, President Harry S. Truman addressed a joint session of the United States Congress to express his concern over the Soviet occupation of eastern Europe and the threat that communism posed to other countries in Europe, particularly Greece and Turkey. In his speech Truman set forth a new doctrine for American foreign policy, moving from a policy of "détente," or friendship with the Soviet Union, to a policy that aimed to directly confront and contain communism.

Winston Churchill, "Sinews of Peace" Speech, March 5, 1946

"A shadow has fallen upon the scenes so lately lighted by the Allied victory. Nobody knows what Soviet Russia and its Communist international organization intends to do in the immediate future, or what are the limits, if any, to their expansive and proselytizing tendencies. . . . We welcome Russia to her rightful place among the leading nations of the world. . . . It is my duty however, . . . to place before you certain facts about the present position in Europe.

From Stettin in the Baltic to Trieste in the Adriatic an iron curtain has descended across the Continent. Behind that line lie all the capitals of the ancient states of Central and Eastern Europe. Warsaw, Berlin, Prague, Vienna, Budapest, Belgrade, Bucharest and Sofia, all these famous cities and the populations around them lie in what I must call the Soviet sphere, and all are subject in one form or another, not only to Soviet influence but to a very high and, in some cases, increasing measure of control from Moscow. Athens alone—Greece with its immortal glories—is free to decide its future at an election under British, American and French observation. The Russian-dominated Polish Government has been encouraged to make enormous and wrongful inroads upon Germany, and mass expulsions of millions of Germans on a scale grievous and undreamed-of are now taking place. The Communist parties, which were very small in all these Eastern States of Europe, have been raised to pre-eminence and power far beyond their numbers and are seeking everywhere to obtain totalitarian control. Police governments are prevailing in nearly every case, and so far, except in Czechoslovakia, there is no true democracy."

President Harry S. Truman, Speech to Congress, March 12, 1947

"At the present moment in world history nearly every nation must choose between alternative ways of life. The choice is too often not a free one.

One way of life is based upon the will of the majority, and is distinguished by free institutions, representative government, free elections, guarantees of individual liberty, freedom of speech and religion, and freedom from political oppression.

The second way of life is based upon the will of a minority forcibly imposed upon the majority. It relies upon terror and oppression, a controlled press and radio; fixed elections, and the suppression of personal freedoms.

I believe that it must be the policy of the United States to support free peoples who are resisting attempted subjugation by armed minorities or by outside pressures.

I believe that we must assist free peoples to work out their own destinies in their own way.

I believe that our help should be primarily through economic and financial aid, which is essential to economic stability and orderly political processes.

The world is not static, and the status quo is not sacred. But we cannot allow changes in the status quo in violation of the Charter of the United Nations by such methods as coercion, or by such subterfuges as political infiltration. . . .

The seeds of totalitarian regimes are nurtured by misery and want. They spread and grow in the evil soil of poverty and strife. They reach their full growth when the hope of a people for a better life has died. We must keep that hope alive.

The free peoples of the world look to us for support in maintaining their freedoms.

If we falter in our leadership, we may endanger the peace of the world—and we shall surely endanger the welfare of our own nation."

Sources: Winston Churchill, "Sinews of Peace" (the Iron Curtain Speech), delivered at Westminster College in Fulton, Missouri, March 5, 1946, in Robert Rhodes James, ed., *Winston S. Churchill: His Complete Speeches, 1897–1963*. Vol. VII: *1943–1949*. Reprinted with permission of Curtis Brown Ltd.; Henry Steele Commager and Milton Cantor, *Documents of American History*. Vol. II: *Since 1898*, 10th ed. (Englewood Cliffs, N.J.: Prentice Hall, 1988), pp. 527–528.

QUESTIONS FOR ANALYSIS

1. What does "shadow" refer to in the excerpt from Churchill's speech?
2. How do Churchill's speech and Truman's speech—considered by some scholars to be the opening salvos in the Cold War—use language to persuade their audiences of the Soviet threat? What democratic ideals do they call upon?
3. When Truman proposed to "support free peoples who are resisting subjugation," did he also include peoples living under colonial regimes at the time? What does this suggest about U.S. foreign policy?

The United States responded with the **Truman Doctrine**, aimed at "containing" communism to areas already occupied by the Red Army. Truman told Congress in 1947, "I believe it must be the policy of the United States to support free people who are resisting attempted subjugation by armed minorities or by outside pressure." Truman asked Congress for military aid for Greece and Turkey. Then, in June, Secretary of State George C. Marshall offered Europe economic aid—the **Marshall Plan**—to help it rebuild. Stalin refused Marshall Plan assistance for all of eastern Europe, where he had established Soviet-style Communist dictatorships. The Soviet Union's aid and support for the overthrow of the democratically elected Czechoslovakian government in February 1948 and its replacement by a Communist government shocked the U.S. Congress into action, and on April 2, 1948, it voted for the Marshall Plan.

On July 24, 1948, Stalin blocked all highway traffic through the Soviet zone of Germany to Berlin. The Western allies responded by flying hundreds of planes over the Soviet roadblocks to supply provisions to the West Berliners. After 324 days the Soviets backed down: containment seemed to work. In 1949 the United States formed an anti-Soviet military alliance of Western governments: the North Atlantic Treaty Organization (**NATO**). Stalin countered by tightening his hold on his satellites, later united in the Warsaw Pact. Europe was divided into two hostile blocs.

As tensions rose in Europe, the Cold War spread to Asia. In 1945 Korea, like Germany, was divided into Soviet and American zones of occupation, which in 1948 became Communist North Korea and anticommunist South Korea. In late 1949 the Communists triumphed in China (see page 979), frightening many Americans, who saw new evidence of a powerful worldwide Communist conspiracy. When the Russian-backed Communist forces of North Korea invaded South Korea in spring 1950, Truman sent U.S. troops to lead a twenty-nation UN coalition force.

The Korean War (1950–1953) was bitterly fought. The well-equipped North Koreans conquered most of the peninsula, but the South Korean, American, and UN troops rallied and drove their foes north to the Chinese border. At that point China intervened and pushed the South Koreans and Americans back south. In 1953 a fragile truce was negotiated, and the fighting stopped. Thus the United States extended its policy of containing communism to Asia, but drew back from invading Communist China and possible nuclear war.

The Korean War, 1950–1953

SOVIET UNION

CHINA

Chosin Reservoir

Farthest UN advance Nov. 1950

Yalu R.

NORTH KOREA

Sea of Japan

Pyongyang

Demilitarized zone 1953

38th Parallel

Seoul

Inchon landing Sept. 15, 1950

SOUTH KOREA

Yellow Sea

UN defensive line Sept. 1950

Pusan

JAPAN

→ North Korean invasion, June–Sept. 1950
→ UN offensive, Sept.–Nov. 1950
→ Communist Chinese offensive, Nov. 1950–Jan. 1951

Renaissance and Crisis in Western Europe

☐ How did western Europe recover so successfully after World War II, and how did economic decline in the 1970s and 1980s affect society?

As the Cold War divided Europe into two blocs, the future appeared bleak. Yet western Europe recovered to enjoy unprecedented economic prosperity and peaceful social transformation. Then, in the early 1970s, the cycle turned abruptly, and a downturn in the world economy hit western Europe hard.

The Postwar Challenge

After the war, economic conditions in western Europe were terrible. Runaway inflation and black markets testified to severe shortages and hardships. Many questioned whether Europe would ever recover.

Suffering was most intense in defeated Germany. The major territorial change of the war had moved the Soviet Union's border far to the west. Poland was in turn compensated for this loss to the Soviets with land taken from Germany. Thirteen million people were driven from their homes in eastern Europe and forced to resettle in a greatly reduced Germany. By spring 1947 Germany verged on total collapse and threatened to drag down the rest of Europe.

Yet western Europe began to recover. Progressive Catholics and their Christian Democrat political parties were particularly influential. In Italy Alcide De Gasperi (1881–1954) and in Germany Konrad Adenauer (1876–1967) took power, rejecting the fascism of their predecessors and placing their faith in democracy and cooperation. Socialists and Communists active in the resistance against Hitler emerged from the war with increased power and prestige, especially in France and Italy. In the immediate postwar years welfare measures such as family allowances, health insurance, and increased public housing were enacted throughout much of Europe. Social reform complemented political transformation, creating solid foundations for a great European renaissance.

There were many reasons for this amazing recovery. The United States sped the process through the

Greek Guest Workers in Germany
Thousands of Greeks immigrated to Germany after the signing of a guest worker (*Gastarbeiter*) agreement between Greece and Germany in 1961. In the 1950s and 1960s the Greek government encouraged workers, such as these Greek women working in a bottling factory in Hamburg in 1963, to emigrate because of a weak economy and high unemployment. Unlike some guest workers from countries in North Africa and the Middle East, the Greeks have generally integrated smoothly into German society. An estimated 350,000 Greeks were living in Germany in 2011. (Bildarchiv Preussischer Kulturbesitz/Art Resource, NY)

Marshall Plan, and as aid poured in, western Europe's battered economies began to turn the corner. Europe entered a period of unprecedented economic progress lasting into the late 1960s.

Western European governments also adopted a variety of successful economic and social strategies. Postwar West Germany adopted a free-market economy while maintaining the extensive social welfare network inherited from the Hitler era. The French established a new kind of planning commission that set ambitious but flexible goals for the French economy, using the nationalized banks to funnel money into key industries.

European workers also contributed to the economic turnaround. They worked hard for low wages in hope of a better future. During the Great Depression few Europeans had been able to afford many of the new consumer products. Thus in 1945 the electric refrigerator, the washing machine, and the automobile were rare luxuries, and there was great potential demand, which manufacturers moved to satisfy.

Migrant laborers from the Mediterranean basin (southern Italy, North Africa, Turkey, Greece, and Yugoslavia) also played a key role in Europe's postwar recovery. They accepted the least desirable jobs for the lowest pay. Europeans assumed that rising birthrates among the majority population would eventually fill the labor shortages, so at first they labeled the migrants "guest workers" to signal their temporary status. By the 1980s, however, as millions more migrants arrived from Europe's former colonies, it was clear that their presence would be permanent. Their full integration into European society has been incomplete, creating a backlash against them by the majority populations and a simmering anger within the immigrant communities at what seems to be their second-class citizenship.

Finally, western European nations abandoned protectionism and gradually created a large, unified market. This historic action, which stimulated the economy, was part of a larger search for European unity.

Building Europe and Decolonization

Western Europe's political recovery in the generation after 1945 was unprecedented. Democratic governments took root throughout western Europe and thrived in an atmosphere of civil liberties and individual freedom. The changes in Germany were especially profound. Konrad Adenauer, the first chancellor of postwar West Germany, was largely responsible for West Germany's remarkable recovery from near total devastation in World War II to its becoming the leading economic power in Europe. A fierce opponent of communism, Adenauer brought Germany firmly into the Western capitalist camp by developing close ties with the United States and restoring relations with Great Britain and France. Under his direction, Germany became a leading member of NATO and fully supported efforts at European unity. He also initiated dialogues

- **Truman Doctrine** U.S. policy to contain communism to areas already occupied by the Red Army.
- **Marshall Plan** American plan for providing economic aid to Europe to help it rebuild.
- **NATO** The North Atlantic Treaty Organization, an anti-Soviet military alliance of Western nations.

with important figures in Europe's Jewish community and with Israel to bring about a reconciliation of the Jewish and German peoples following the Holocaust.

A similarly extraordinary achievement was the march toward a united Europe. Many Europeans believed that only unity could forestall future European conflicts and that only a new "European nation" could reassert western Europe's influence in world affairs dominated by the United States and the Soviet Union.

The experience of close cooperation among European states for Marshall Plan aid led European federalists to turn toward economics as a way of attaining genuine unity. On May 9, 1950 (now celebrated as Europe Day), French foreign minister Robert Schuman proposed an international organization to control and integrate all European steel and coal production. France, West Germany, Italy, Belgium, the Netherlands, and Luxembourg joined together in 1952. In 1957 the six nations of the Coal and Steel Community signed the Treaty of Rome, creating the European Economic Community, popularly known as the **Common Market**. A Frenchman, Jean Monnet, was the chief architect of this plan, and he is generally recognized as the Founding Father of European unity. The treaty's primary goal was a gradual reduction of all tariffs among the six in order to create a single market almost as large as that of the United States.

The Common Market was a great success, encouraging hopes of rapid progress toward political as well as economic union. In the 1960s, however, a resurgence of more traditional nationalism in France led by Charles de Gaulle, French president from 1958 to 1969, frustrated these hopes. Viewing the United States as the main threat to genuine French (and European) independence, he withdrew all French military forces from NATO, developed France's own nuclear weapons, and refused to permit majority rule within the Common Market. De Gaulle also thwarted efforts by Denmark, Ireland, Norway, and the United Kingdom to join the Common Market. (All but Norway were finally admitted in 1973 after Georges Pompidou succeeded de Gaulle as French president.) Thus, throughout the 1960s the Common Market thrived economically but remained a union of sovereign states.

As Europe moved toward greater economic unity in the postwar era, its centuries-long overseas expansion was dramatically reversed. Between 1945 and the early 1960s almost every colonial territory gained formal independence. This rolling back of Western expansion — decolonization — marks one of world history's great turning points. The basic cause of imperial collapse

was the rising demand by Asian and African peoples for national self-determination and racial equality (see Chapters 32 and 33).

European empires had been sustained by an enormous imbalance of power between the rulers and the ruled. By 1945 that imbalance had almost vanished. Most Europeans viewed their empires after 1945 very differently than they had before 1914. Empires had rested on self-confidence and self-righteousness. The horrors of the Second World War destroyed such complacent arrogance and gave imperialism's opponents much greater influence in Europe. After 1945 many Europeans were willing to let go of their colonies more or less voluntarily and to concentrate on rebuilding at home.

European political and business leaders still wanted some ties with the former colonies, however. As a result, western European countries increased their economic and cultural ties with their former African colonies in the 1960s and 1970s. This situation led many Third World leaders and scholars to charge that western Europe and the United States had imposed a system of neocolonialism designed to perpetuate Western economic domination and undermine political independence, just as the United States had subordinated the new nations of Latin America in the nineteenth century (see pages 819–821).

The Changing Class Structure and Social Reform

A more mobile and more democratic European society developed after World War II as old class barriers relaxed. Most noticeably, the structure of the middle class changed. In the nineteenth and early twentieth centuries members of the middle class were generally independent, self-employed property owners who ran businesses or practiced professions such as law or medicine. After 1945 a new breed of managers and experts required by large corporations and government agencies replaced traditional property owners as leaders of the middle class. Members of this new middle class could give their children access to advanced education, but only rarely could they pass on the positions they had attained. Thus the new middle class, based largely on specialized skills and high levels of education, was more open, democratic, and insecure than the old propertied middle class.

The structure of the lower classes also became more flexible and open. There was a mass exodus from farms and the countryside. Meanwhile, the industrial working class ceased to expand, but job opportunities for white-collar and service employees grew rapidly. Such employees bore a greater resemblance to the new middle class of salaried specialists than to industrial workers, who were also better educated and more specialized.

• **Common Market** The European Economic Community created in 1957.

• **OPEC** The Arab-led organization of countries that export oil that helps set policies and prices on its trade.

□ Picturing the Past

Cover of *John Bull Magazine*, January 1957 Like the *Saturday Evening Post* in America, *John Bull* portrayed English life through images and stories. This cover, published twelve years after the end of World War II, shows an English household that has fully recovered from the war, with the husband coming home to two beautiful children and a lovely wife in a modern and stylish kitchen. (Private Collection/The Advertising Archives/ The Bridgeman Art Library)

ANALYZING THE IMAGE What are the members of this family doing? What clothes are they wearing, and what might this suggest about their roles within the family?

CONNECTIONS What does this magazine cover suggest about the availability of consumer goods and the desire for them after the war?

European governments also reduced class tensions with a series of social reforms. Many of these reforms — such as increased unemployment benefits and more extensive old-age pensions — strengthened existing social security measures. Other programs were new, such as state-run, comprehensive national health systems. Most countries introduced family allowances — direct government grants to parents to help them raise their children — that helped many poor families make ends meet. Maternity grants and inexpensive public housing for low-income families and individuals were also common. These and other social reforms provided a humane floor of well-being and promoted greater equality.

Economic and Social Dislocation, 1970–1990

An economic crisis in the 1970s brought the postwar economic recovery to a halt. The earliest cause was the collapse of the postwar international monetary system, which since 1945 had been based on the U.S. dollar. In 1971 the dollar's value fell sharply, and inflation accelerated worldwide. Fixed rates of exchange were abandoned, and uncertainty replaced predictability in international trade and finance.

Even more damaging was the dramatic reversal in the price and availability of energy. Cheap oil fueled the postwar boom. (See "Global Trade: Oil," page 950.) In 1971 the Arab-led Organization of Petroleum Exporting Countries — **OPEC** — decided to reverse a decline in the crude oil price by presenting a united front against the oil companies. After the Arab-Israeli war in October 1973 (see page 995), OPEC placed an embargo on oil exports, and crude oil prices quadrupled in a year.

The rise in energy prices coupled with the upheaval in the international monetary system plunged the world into its worst economic decline since the 1930s. Unemployment rose; productivity and living standards declined. By 1976 a modest recovery was in progress, but when Iranian oil production collapsed during Iran's fundamentalist Islamic revolution in 1979 (see page 995), crude oil prices doubled again. By 1985 unemployment rates in western Europe had risen to their highest levels since the Great Depression. Global recovery was painfully slow until late 1993.

Global Trade

Oil in its crude form is found as a liquid hydrocarbon located in certain rocks below the earth's crust. Although it is found throughout the world, the Persian Gulf and Caspian Sea areas contain about three-quarters of the world's proven reserves. The uses of crude oil are limited, but it may be refined into valuable products such as kerosene, gasoline, and fuel oil.

Oil has been used throughout history, although it did not become a worldwide commodity until the nineteenth century. In antiquity, the Sumerians and Babylonians mixed evaporated oil from tar pits with sand to make asphalt for waterproofing ships and paving roads. Islamic societies in the Middle East used small quantities of oil for lighting, although cooking fires were probably the main source of light.

In Europe, lamp oil—from animal fats and plants—was a luxury. The nineteenth century brought revolutionary changes in lighting, and by the 1840s manufacturers in coal-rich Europe were distilling coal into crude oil and gas for use in lighting. North America followed suit. Thus when E. L. Drake drilled the first successful American oil well in Pennsylvania in 1859, a growing demand for lamp oil already existed. The production of kerosene took off as consumers accepted the bright, clean-burning, and relatively inexpensive oil for use in their lamps.

After the late 1860s the United States exported two-thirds of its kerosene, first in wooden barrels, then in large tin cans, and finally in tankers for bulk distribution. The leading producer was John D. Rockefeller's Standard Oil, which held a monopoly on kerosene until the U.S. government

MAP 31.2 The Oil Trade, ca. 1900–1975

broke the corporation into separate companies in 1911. Most kerosene went to Europe at first, but other markets grew rapidly. In the 1870s the Baku region on the Caspian Sea introduced drilling and created a Russian refining industry. Russian capitalists fought well-publicized "oil wars" with Standard Oil for world kerosene markets.

International differences were significant. In the United States and western Europe kerosene appealed especially to farmers and urban working people, who had previously lacked decent lighting. The affluent urban classes generally continued to use coal-distilled gas until the 1880s, when electricity began to replace gas. In China peasants rejected bulk distribution and insisted on kerosene in tin cans, recycling them into valuable all-purpose containers. Russia pioneered in using oil as fuel, as the refining of heavy Baku crude yielded abundant thick "leftovers"—an excellent power source for riverboats, railroads, and factories.

" FIRST WE'LL VACATION AT THE SHORE, THEN WE'LL GO TO THE MOUNTAINS, THEN UP TO THE LAKE..... "

China's growing middle class is adopting the automobile culture of the West, which is putting more pressure on the world's dwindling supply of fossil fuels. (© 2005 Bog Englehart, The Hartford Courant)

During the twentieth century oil became a major fuel source as kerosene production declined. Until 1941 the explosive growth of automobiles in the United States was easily outpaced by the development of domestic oil fields, enabling the United States to sell one-third of all the oil consumed beyond its borders. In oil-poor Europe (Russia excepted), fuel oil loomed large as a strategic material. After 1919 the British government took control of the two oil companies in Iran and Iraq to guarantee supplies for Britain's military and industrial needs. Germany distilled coal into synthetic gasoline, and Hitler relentlessly pushed production of this very expensive alternative to free his war machine from dependence on foreign oil.

The international oil trade shifted dramatically after 1945. The United States, previously producing half the world's oil, became the world's largest importer. The Middle East, producing very modestly in the 1920s and 1930s, became the world's leading exporter. At the same time, western Europe and Japan shifted from coal to oil to drive their factories and fuel their automobiles. Nevertheless, the American and British oil companies in the Middle East expanded output so rapidly—sixteen times between 1948 and 1972—that the inflation-adjusted price for Middle Eastern oil fell substantially in these years.

Increasingly dissatisfied with their share of the profits, the main exporting countries—Iran, Iraq, Kuwait, Saudi Arabia, and Venezuela—organized the Organization of Petroleum Exporting Countries (OPEC) in 1960 to gain control of their oil resources. In 1973, during the Arab-Israeli war, OPEC engineered a fourfold price increase with enormous global consequences. The exporting states also nationalized their oil industries, reducing foreign companies to simple buyers and transporters. The oil exporters used their financial windfalls to improve health and living standards somewhat, but vast sums went for lavish spending by the elite and for overly ambitious development projects. Above all, the money went for expensive military hardware from the industrialized countries, which increased tensions and prolonged the terrible war between Iraq and Iran in the 1980s (see pages 1001–1002).

A price collapse followed the upward price revolution of the 1970s. In the 1980s and early 1990s conservation, greater efficiency, recession, environmental concerns, and significant new oil discoveries outside the Middle East eliminated much of the inflation-adjusted price increases of the 1970s. By 2002 some argued that oil was really "just another commodity." The outbreak of the Iraq War in 2003, however—followed by natural disasters such as Hurricane Katrina; instability in Nigeria, Venezuela, and other major oil-producing countries; and skyrocketing demands for oil by China and India—sent oil to nearly $150 per barrel by 2008, creating another global energy crisis.

Western Europe's welfare system prevented mass suffering through unemployment benefits and other social programs. But increased government spending was not matched by higher taxes, causing a rapid growth of budget deficits, national debts, and inflation. By the late 1970s a powerful reaction against government's ever-increasing role had set in. Growing voter dissatisfaction helped bring Conservative Margaret Thatcher (b. 1925) to power in Britain in 1979. Prime Minister Thatcher slowed government spending and privatized industry by selling off state-owned companies to private investors. Of great social significance, her government encouraged low- and moderate-income renters in state-owned housing projects to buy their apartments at rock-bottom prices. This step created a whole new class of property owners, thereby eroding the electoral base of Britain's socialist Labour Party. Other Western governments introduced austerity measures to slow the growth of public spending and the welfare state.

Individuals felt the impact of austerity, and the threat of unemployment—or underemployment in dead-end jobs—shaped the outlook of a whole generation. Students in the 1980s were serious, practical, and often conservative. As one young woman at a French university told a reporter in 1985, "Jobs are the big worry now, so everyone wants to learn something practical."[2]

Harder times also meant that more women entered or remained in the workforce after they married. Although attitudes related to personal fulfillment were one reason for the continuing increase—especially for well-educated upper-middle-class women—many wives in poor and middle-class families worked outside the home because of economic necessity.

Recovery and Reform in Soviet Eastern Europe, 1945–1991

☐ How did the Soviets try to reform society, and what were the consequences of the anticommunist revolutions of 1989?

While western Europe surged ahead economically after World War II, postwar economic recovery in eastern Europe proceeded along Soviet lines, and changes in the Soviet Union strongly influenced political and social developments. That trend remained true more than forty years later, when radical reform in the Soviet Union opened the door to popular revolution in the eastern European satellites—and ultimately to the collapse of the Soviet Union itself.

Stalin's Last Years

The "Great Patriotic War of the Fatherland" had fostered Russian nationalism and a relaxation of totalitarian terror. Having made a heroic war effort, the vast majority of the Soviet people hoped in 1945 that a grateful party and government would grant greater freedom and democracy, but even before war's end, Stalin was moving his country back toward rigid dictatorship.

As early as 1944 Communist Party members received a new slogan: "The war on Fascism ends, the war on capitalism begins."[3] Stalin's new foe provided him with an excuse for re-establishing a harsh dictatorship. He purged thousands of returning soldiers and ordinary civilians in 1945 and 1946, and he revived the terrible forced-labor camps of the 1930s. Culture and art were purged of Western influences, Orthodox Christianity again came under attack, and Soviet Jews were accused of being pro-Western and antisocialist.

Stalin reasserted his complete control of the government and society with the reintroduction of five-year plans to cope with the enormous task of economic reconstruction. Once again heavy and military industry were given top priority, and consumer goods, housing, and collectivized agriculture were neglected. Everyday life was very hard. In short, it was the 1930s all over again in the Soviet Union, although police terror was less intense.

Stalin then exported the Stalinist system to eastern Europe. Rigid ideological indoctrination, attacks on religion, and a lack of civil liberties were soon facts of life in the region's one-party states. Industry was nationalized and the middle class stripped of its possessions. Only Yugoslavia's Josip Tito (1892–1980), the popular resistance leader and Communist Party chief, could resist Soviet domination successfully, because there was no Russian army in Yugoslavia.

Limited De-Stalinization and Stagnation

In 1953 the aging Stalin died. Even as his heirs struggled for power, they realized that reforms were necessary because of the widespread fear and hatred of Stalin's political terrorism. They curbed secret police powers and gradually closed many forced-labor camps. Change was also necessary for economic reasons. Agriculture was in bad shape, and shortages of consumer goods were discouraging hard work and initiative. Moreover, Stalin's belligerent foreign policy had led directly to a strong Western alliance, isolating the Soviet Union.

The Communist Party leadership was badly split on just how much change to permit. Reformers, led by Nikita Khrushchev (1894–1971), argued for major innovations and won. Khrushchev spoke out in a "secret speech" against Stalin and his crimes at a closed session of the Twentieth Party Congress in 1956:

> It is clear that . . . Stalin showed in a whole series of cases his intolerance, his brutality, and his abuse of power. Instead of proving his political correctness and mobilizing the masses, he often chose the path of repression and physical annihilation, not only against actual enemies, but also against individuals who had not committed any crimes against the party and the Soviet Government.[4]

The liberalization of the Soviet Union—labeled **de-Stalinization** in the West—was genuine. The Communist Party jealously maintained its monopoly on political power, but Khrushchev shook up the party and brought in new members. Some resources were shifted from heavy industry and the military toward consumer goods and agriculture, and controls over workers were relaxed. The Soviet Union's low standard of living finally began to improve and continued to rise substantially throughout the booming 1960s.

De-Stalinization created great ferment among writers and intellectuals who hungered for cultural freedom. The writer Aleksandr Solzhenitsyn (1918–2008) created a sensation when his *One Day in the Life of Ivan Denisovich* was published in the Soviet Union in 1962. Solzhenitsyn's novel portrays life in a Stalinist concentration camp in grim detail and is a damning indictment of the Stalinist past.

Khrushchev also de-Stalinized Soviet foreign policy. "Peaceful coexistence" with capitalism was possible, he argued. But while Cold War tensions relaxed between 1955 and 1957, de-Stalinization stimulated rebelliousness in the eastern European satellites. Poland won greater autonomy in 1956 when extensive rioting brought in a new Communist government. Led by students and workers, the people of Budapest, Hungary, installed a liberal Communist reformer as their new chief in October 1956. After the new government promised free elections and renounced Hungary's military alliance with Moscow, Russian leaders ordered an invasion and crushed the revolution, killing around 2,700 protesters. When the United States did not come to their aid, Hungarians and most eastern Europeans concluded that their only hope was to strive for small domestic gains while following Russia obediently in foreign affairs.

In August 1961 East Germany began construction of a twenty-seven-mile wall between East and West Berlin. A ninety-mile-long barrier was also constructed between the three allied sectors of West Berlin and East Germany, thereby completely cutting off West Berlin. Officially the wall was called the "Anti-Fascist Protection Wall." In reality the Berlin Wall, which dramatically symbolized the Iron Curtain, was necessary to prevent East Germans from "voting with their feet" by defecting to the West.

By late 1962 party opposition to Khrushchev's policies had gained momentum. De-Stalinization was seen as a dangerous threat to party authority. Moreover, Khrushchev's policy toward the West was erratic and ultimately unsuccessful. When Khrushchev ordered missiles with nuclear warheads installed in Fidel Castro's Communist Cuba in 1962, U.S. president John F. Kennedy countered with a naval blockade of Cuba. After a tense diplomatic crisis Khrushchev agreed to remove the missiles. Increasingly viewed in the colorful language of the time as a bumbling buffoon, Khrushchev was removed in a bloodless coup within two years of the Cuban missile crisis.

After Leonid Brezhnev (1906–1982) and his supporters took over in 1964, they talked quietly of Stalin's "good points," stopped further liberalization, and launched a massive arms buildup, determined never to suffer Khrushchev's humiliation in the face of American nuclear superiority.

The Impact of Reform on Everyday Life

In the wake of Khrushchev's reforms, the 1960s brought modest liberalization and more consumer goods to eastern Europe, as well as somewhat greater national autonomy. In January 1968 reform elements in the Czechoslovakian Communist Party gained a majority and replaced a long-time Stalinist leader with Alexander Dubček (1921–1992), whose new government launched dramatic reforms. Dubček (DOOB-chehk) and his allies called for "socialism with a human face." The determination of the Czech reformers frightened hardline Communists who feared any easing of their totalitarian control. Thus in August 1968, five hundred thousand Russian and eastern European troops occupied Czechoslovakia, and the Czech experiment in humanizing communism came to an end. Shortly afterward, Brezhnev declared the so-called **Brezhnev Doctrine**, according to which the Soviet Union and its allies could intervene in any socialist country whenever they saw the need.

In the aftermath of intervention in Czechoslovakia, free expression and open protest disappeared. Dissidents were blacklisted or quietly imprisoned in jails or mental institutions. Unlike in the Stalinist era, though, dictatorship was collective rather than personal, and coercion replaced uncontrolled terror. This compromise seemed to suit the leaders and a majority of the

---

- **de-Stalinization** The liberalization of the post-Stalin Soviet Union, led by reformer Nikita Khrushchev during his years as the head of the Soviet Union (1953–1964).
- **Brezhnev Doctrine** Doctrine created by Leonid Brezhnev that held that the Soviet Union had the right to intervene in any socialist country whenever it saw the need.

Czechs Protest Soviet Invasion in 1968 A young Czech girl shouts "Ivan go home" at Russian soldiers sitting on tanks in Prague during the Soviet invasion of Czechoslovakia in August 1968. (Bettmann/Corbis)

people, and the Soviet Union appeared stable in the 1970s and early 1980s.

A rising standard of living for ordinary people contributed to stability, although the economic crisis of the 1970s greatly slowed the rate of improvement, and long lines and shortages persisted. The exclusive privileges enjoyed by the Communist Party elite also reinforced the system. Ambitious individuals had tremendous incentives to do as the state wished in order to gain access to special well-stocked stores, attend superior schools, and travel abroad.

Another source of stability was the enduring nationalism of ordinary Russians. Party leaders successfully identified themselves with Russian patriotism, stressing their role in saving the motherland during the Second World War and protecting it now from foreign foes, including eastern European "counter-revolutionaries." Moreover, the politically dominant Great Russians, only half of the total Soviet population, held the top positions in the Soviet Union's non-Russian republics.

Beneath this stability, however, the Soviet Union was experiencing a social revolution. A rapidly expanding urban population abandoned its old peasant ways, exchanging them for more education, better job skills,

and greater sophistication. The number of highly trained scientists, managers, and specialists expanded prodigiously, jumping fourfold between 1960 and 1985. The education that created expertise helped foster the growth of Soviet public opinion. Educated people read, discussed, and formed definite ideas about social questions ranging from environmental pollution to urban transportation. These changes set the stage for the dramatic reforms of the Gorbachev era.

The Gorbachev Era

When Brezhnev died in 1982, efforts were made to improve economic performance and to combat worker absenteeism and high-level corruption. Elected as leader in 1985, Mikhail Gorbachev (b. 1931) believed in communism, but he realized that Brezhnev's reforms would not be enough to save the failing state. Importantly, Gorbachev realized that success at home required better relations with the West. Thus Gorbachev attempted to save the Soviet system with a series of reform policies he labeled democratic socialism, or "socialism with a democratic face."

The first set of reforms was intended to transform and restructure the economy. This economic restructuring, **perestroika**, permitted freer prices, more independence for state enterprises, and the setting up of some profit-seeking private cooperatives. The reforms were rather timid, however, and when the economy stalled, Gorbachev's popular support gradually eroded.

Gorbachev's bold and far-reaching campaign of openness, or **glasnost**, was much more successful. Where censorship, dull uniformity, and outright lies had long characterized public discourse, the new frankness led

- **perestroika** Economic restructuring and reform implemented by Soviet premier Gorbachev that permitted an easing of government price controls on some goods, more independence for state enterprises, and the setting up of profit-seeking private cooperatives to provide personal services for consumers.
- **glasnost** Soviet premier Gorbachev's popular campaign for openness in the government and the media.
- **Solidarity** Led by Lech Walesa, a free and democratic Polish trade union that worked for the rights of workers and political reform.

Russia and an important power broker on the world stage. Though economically now only a middle-tier country, Russia still retains the world's second-largest nuclear arsenal. That requires the rest of the world to acknowledge and negotiate with Russia.

Postcommunist Reconstruction in Eastern Europe

Eastern Europe had many of the same problems as Russia, and developments there were similar. The postcommunist nations worked to replace state planning and socialism with market mechanisms and private property. Western-style electoral politics also took hold, and as in Russia these politics were marked by intense battles between presidents and parliaments and by weak political parties. Ordinary citizens and the elderly were the big losers, while the young and former Communist Party members were the big winners. Regional inequalities persisted. Capital cities such as Warsaw, Prague, and Budapest concentrated wealth, power, and

opportunity; provincial centers stagnated; and industrial areas declined.

Given these challenges, it is perhaps not surprising that some civilians longed for a return to the safety and stability of communism. Most eastern Europeans, however, had never fully accepted communism, primarily because they linked it to Russian imperialism and the loss of national independence. The joyous crowds that toppled Communist regimes believed they were liberating the nation as well as the individual. Thus, when communism died, nationalism was reborn, creating new difficulties in many of the former East Bloc countries.

Poland, the Czech Republic, and Hungary were the most successful in making the transition. They managed to control national and ethnic tensions that might have destroyed their postcommunist reconstruction. The popular goal of "rejoining the West" was a powerful force for moderation in these countries. They hoped to find security in NATO membership, which came in 1997, and prosperity by joining western Europe's economic union (see pages 971–972).

Putin and Democracy After the Soviet Union's collapse in 1991, Russia's new leaders instituted a number of democratic reforms. After taking office in 2000, however, Russian President Vladimir Putin, who worked as a KGB agent during the Soviet era, was accused of rolling back many of these measures, including weakening the power of the Russian parliament, curbing the freedom of the media, restricting individual freedoms, using the war on terrorism to attack opponents, and centralizing and concentrating power in the president's office. Dmitry Medvedev succeeded Putin as president in May 2008 but then appointed Putin as Russian prime minister the day after his inauguration. Putin remains the power behind the throne, with Medvedev rarely challenging any of Putin's policies. (ARIAIL © 2003 Robert Ariail. Reprinted by permission of Universal Uclick for UFS. All rights reserved.)

The great postcommunist tragedy was Yugoslavia, which under Josip Tito had been a federation of republics and regions under Communist rule. After Tito's death in 1980, power passed increasingly to the sister republics, which encouraged a revival of regional and ethnic conflicts made worse by charges of ethnically inspired massacres during World War II and a dramatic economic decline in the mid-1980s.

The revolutions of 1989 accelerated the breakup of Yugoslavia. When Serbian president Slobodan Milosevic (SLOH-buh-dayn muh-LOH-suh-vihch; 1941–2006) attempted to grab land from other republics and unite all Serbs in a "greater Serbia," a civil war broke out that eventually involved Kosovo, Slovenia, Croatia, and Bosnia-Herzegovina. The civil war unleashed ruthless brutality, with murder, rape, the destruction of villages, the herding of refugees into concentration camps,

and charges of "ethnic cleansing" — genocide — against opposing ethnic groups (Map 31.4).

Serbian aggression appalled the Western nations. From March to June 1999 the Western Powers, led by the United States, carried out heavy bombing attacks on the Serbian capital, Belgrade; on Serbian strategic sites; and on Serbian military forces. They demanded that Milosevic withdraw Serbian armies. The impoverished Serbs eventually voted the still-defiant Milosevic out of office in September 2000, and in July 2001 a new pro-Western Serbian government turned him over to a war crimes tribunal in the Netherlands to stand trial for crimes against humanity. The civil wars in the former Yugoslavia were a monument to human cruelty. But ongoing efforts to preserve peace, repatriate refugees, and try war criminals also testified to the regenerative power of liberal values and human rights.

MAP 31.4 The Breakup of Yugoslavia Yugoslavia had the most ethnically diverse population in eastern Europe. The Republic of Croatia had substantial Serbian and Muslim minorities, and Bosnia-Herzegovina had large Muslim, Serbian, and Croatian populations, none of which had a majority. In June 1991 Serbia's brutal effort to seize territory and unite all Serbs in a single state brought a tragic civil war to the region.

Srebrenica When Bosnia officially declared its independence in 1992, a brutal three-year civil war broke out between Bosniaks (predominantly, though not all, Bosnian Muslims) and Croats on the one hand and Bosnian Serbs on the other. Supported by Serbia, Bosnian Serb militias practiced ethnic cleansing in areas under their control. In July 1995 Bosnian Serb militiamen slaughtered more than 8,000 Muslim men and boys in the town of Srebrenica, Bosnia. Here a Bosnian woman weeps over the coffins of 335 bodies found in a mass grave in 2004. (Jon Jones/Sygma/Corbis)

Unity and Identity in Western Europe

The movement toward western European unity received a powerful second wind in the 1990s. French president François Mitterrand (1916–1996) and German chancellor Helmut Kohl took the lead in pushing for the monetary union of European Community members, and the Maastricht Treaty of 1992 created a single EU currency, the euro. In 1993 the European Community proudly rechristened itself the **European Union (EU)** (Map 31.5).

Western European elites generally supported this step toward economic union. They saw monetary union as a means of coping with Europe's ongoing economic problems, imposing financial discipline, cutting costs, and reducing high unemployment. These elites also saw monetary union as a step toward political unity, enabling Europe to take a more prominent role in world politics.

Not all Europeans supported economic union. Many people resented the unending flow of rules handed down by the EU's growing bureaucracy, which sought to standardize everything from cheeses to day care. Moreover, many feared that more power in the hands of distant bureaucrats would undermine popular sovereignty and democratic control. Above all, they feared that the new Europe was being created at their ex-

pense. Joining the monetary union required governments to meet stringent fiscal standards and impose budget cuts and financial austerity. The resulting reductions in health care and social benefits hit ordinary citizens and did nothing to reduce western Europe's high unemployment rate.

The movement toward union raised profound questions about the meaning of European unity and identity. Would the EU remain an exclusive Western club, or would it expand to include the postcommunist nations of eastern Europe? If some of them were included, how could Muslim Turkey's long-standing application for membership be ignored? Conversely, how could a union of twenty-five to thirty countries have any real unity? In the face of these questions, western Europeans proceeded cautiously in considering new requests for EU membership.

The highly successful introduction of the euro in January 2002 encouraged the EU to accelerate plans for an ambitious enlargement to the east. On May 1, 2004, the EU started admitting eastern European countries. By 2007 the EU had twenty-seven member states, including most of eastern Europe, and a population of nearly 500 million, making it the world's largest trading bloc. Future candidates for membership include

> • **European Union (EU)** An economic and political alliance of twenty-seven European nations.

Croatia, Macedonia, former members of the old Soviet Union, and Turkey.

A proposed EU constitution binding EU member states even closer together was scheduled to go into effect in 2007. First, however, it needed approval by voters in all member countries. In 2005 voters in France and Holland voted overwhelmingly against the constitution and threw the entire process into confusion. The rejected constitution was replaced with the Treaty of Lisbon in 2007. The new treaty kept most of the reforms contained in the original European constitution, but it reformed the political structure of the EU bureaucracy. By November 2009 all members had approved it, and the Lisbon treaty came into force on December 1, 2009, unifying what had been a profoundly divided continent just fifty years earlier.

The European Union
- Original members, 1951
- New members, 1973
- New members, 1981
- New members, 1986
- German reunification, 1990
- New members, 1995
- New members, 2004
- New members, 2007
- Candidate countries, 2011
- € Euro Zone countries, 2011

⧠ Mapping the Past

MAP 31.5 The European Union, 2011 No longer divided by ideological competition and the Cold War, much of today's Europe has banded together in a European Union.

ANALYZING THE MAP Trace the expansion of membership in the European Union. How would you characterize the most recent members? Whose membership is still pending?

CONNECTIONS Which countries are not part of the Euro Zone? What does this suggest about the euro's success in the European Union?

CONNECTIONS

In 1945 Europe lay in ruins. Two new superpowers emerged to claim the mantle of global leadership: the democratic, capitalistic United States and the communist Soviet Union, each holding diametrically opposing visions of the future world order. As each superpower worked to acquire allies in the new Cold War, other nations, particularly newly independent nations such as China and India, adopted nonaligned positions that denied the right of either the Soviet Union or the United States to determine the world's destiny (see Chapter 32). As western Europe hunkered down to address its domestic problems, the empires created at the end of the nineteenth century crumbled in the face of powerful independence movements in Asia (Chapter 32) and Africa (Chapter 33).

Western Europe and Japan, with massive aid packages from the United States, quickly recovered from the terrible destruction caused by the war and soon surged ahead economically. New industries thrived as they rebuilt infrastructures and supplied the material goods that their citizens had gone without during the global depression and the world war. But as the next chapter discusses, the economic superpower status of the United States, Europe, and Japan faced fierce new competitors from Asia, most notably China.

By the end of the twentieth century the Cold War had ended, democratic governments had replaced the former Soviet Union and its satellite states throughout eastern Europe, and a new European Union had ended the divisions that had plagued Europe for most of the century. New divisions, however, would rise to divide Europe, this time in the form of debate concerning the growing multiethnic European society, as migrants from Africa, Asia, and the economically weaker states of eastern Europe entered the European Union both legally and illegally. Chapter 34 takes up this issue and explores the economic, political, social, and environmental challenges facing the world in the twenty-first century.

CHAPTER REVIEW

□ **What were the causes of the Cold War? (p. 942)**

Ideological, political, and security differences going back to the years following the Great War began pulling the United States and the Soviet Union apart before World War II ended. A critical disagreement involved the future of eastern Europe. In his meetings with Churchill, Roosevelt, and Truman, Stalin refused to consider free elections in eastern Europe that might put in place anti-Soviet governments. The Western Allies, and especially the United States, pushed hard for free elections, but there was little they could do to stop the Soviet occupying forces from installing pro-Soviet Communist leaders in these countries. Fearing further Soviet expansion, the United States implemented a policy of containment to try to stem the spread of communism around the world. Forty years of political and military standoffs followed.

KEY TERMS

Truman Doctrine (p. 946)
Marshall Plan (p. 946)
NATO (p. 946)
Common Market (p. 948)
OPEC (p. 949)
de-Stalinization (p. 953)
Brezhnev Doctrine (p. 953)

perestroika (p. 954)
glasnost (p. 954)
Solidarity (p. 955)
Charter of Paris for a New Europe (p. 959)
Civil Rights Act (p. 961)
détente (p. 963)
"Japan, Inc." (p. 966)
European Union (EU) (p. 971)

□ **How did western Europe recover so successfully after World War II, and how did economic decline in the 1970s and 1980s affect society? (p. 946)**

Massive aid provided by the Marshall Plan jump-started recovery. Economic policies that encouraged governments to increase spending, even while incurring large deficits, were adopted by most western European countries. Workers, including many migrant laborers from the Mediterranean basin, advanced the economic turnaround by working hard for low wages. Pent-up demand for basic consumer products, like automobiles and refrigerators, encouraged economic production. Efforts to unite western Europe into a single large market helped as well to stimulate European economies. The economic decline of the 1970s brought recovery to a halt, but while unemployment rose eventually to rival that of the Great Depression, welfare systems prevented mass suffering. Increased government spending was not offset by taxes, leading to debt and a political backlash that saw new, more conservative leadership and austerity measures in many countries. To make ends meet, more women entered the workforce.

▫ How did the Soviets try to reform society, and what were the consequences of the anticommunist revolutions of 1989? (p. 952)

The Communist system in eastern Europe and the U.S.S.R. underwent tremendous changes after the death of Stalin. Khrushchev implemented a policy of de-Stalinization, which liberalized society, relaxing restrictions on workers and shifting resources from heavy industry and the military to agriculture and consumer goods. As a result, the standard of living rose. After the Cuban Missile crisis, Brezhnev stopped the program of liberalization and launched a heavy military buildup. In the 1980s public opposition to Soviet domination spread throughout the Soviet-bloc countries, fueled by Gorbachev's reform efforts, eventually leading to the revolutions of 1989 and to free elections, the restoration of civil liberties, and the institution of capitalist economies in eastern Europe.

▫ What contributed to the social and political transformation of the United States in the second half of the twentieth century? (p. 961)

American leaders generally viewed the Soviet Union and the spread of communism as the greatest dangers they faced and therefore turned their back on Third World liberation movements in order to gain the support of their western European allies in the Cold War. This stance had its most tragic consequences when the United States went to the aid of France in its efforts to hold onto its colony of Vietnam. The Vietnam War divided Americans. Students were active participants in the antiwar movement and the counterculture movement that simultaneously flourished. Liberalism triumphed in the 1960s with important civil rights legislation. The policy of containment gave way to détente in the 1970s, but after the Soviet invasion of Afghanistan and the Soviet refusal to accept the human

rights provisions of the Helsinki Accord, new, more conservative leadership again increased the military buildup. After the dissolution of the Soviet Union, the United States became the world's only superpower.

▫ How did Japan recover so quickly after its total defeat in World War II to become an economic superpower? (p. 964)

Before World War II Japan was one of the world's leading industrial nations. By the end of the war Japan lay devastated, facing what seemed like a bleak future. Allied occupation forces under the direction of General Douglas MacArthur set about helping Japan rebuild economically and develop a stable democratic government. Social and economic reforms were pushed through a new, popularly elected Diet (Japanese parliament). Article 9 of the new Japanese constitution abolished the military and renounced war. Eager to have a stable capitalist ally against communism in Asia, the United States guaranteed Japanese security with its own forces. America also poured billions of dollars into the Japanese economy, particularly during the Korean War, when Japan served as a military operations base for American forces. Japan's economic growth skyrocketed in the 1950s and 1960s, surpassing even western Europe's success in postwar recovery.

▫ What was the nature of postcommunist reconstruction in eastern Europe, and how did Europe as a whole respond to calls for increased unity? (p. 967)

The collapse of the Soviet Union and of communism there and across eastern Europe led to the adoption of liberal democracy and free market capitalism. Europe was no longer divided, and differences in political organization, human rights, and economic philosophy became less pronounced in the 1990s than at any time since 1914. Eastern Europe struggled to rejoin the West and replace the bankrupt Communist order with efficient capitalist democracies. Results varied greatly, and ordinary citizens often experienced real hardships, but no effort was made to restore economic planning or one-party rule, though a managed democracy in Russia under Putin led to a lessening of freedoms. The knitting together of Europe reached its apex in 1993 with the formation of the European Union. The introduction of a single currency — the euro — in 2002 and the signing of the Treaty of Lisbon in 2009 further solidified the economic and political unification of Europe.

SUGGESTED READING

Ash, Timothy Garton. *The Polish Revolution: Solidarity,* 3d ed. 2002. A definitive account of the role of the Solidarity movement in the Polish revolution and its subsequent fate.

Dobbs, Michael. *Down with Big Brother: The Fall of the Soviet Empire.* 1997. A superb account by a journalist who covered eastern Europe.

Eksteins, Modris. *Walking Since Daybreak: A Story of Eastern Europe, World War II, and the Heart of Our Century.* 1999. A powerful, partly autobiographical account that is highly recommended.

Gaddis, John Lewis. *The Cold War: A New History.* 2005. A concise, authoritative, and accessible account of the Cold War by one of its leading historians.

Grass, Günter. *The Tin Drum.* 1963. Nobel prize winner's exploration of the spiritual dimension of West German recovery in his world-famous novel.

Halberstam, David. *The Coldest Winter: America and the Korean War.* 2007. One of America's finest journalist-historian's last, and perhaps best, history.

Hughes, H. Stuart. *Sophisticated Rebels: The Political Culture of European Dissent, 1968–1987.* 1988. Provocatively analyzes the culture and politics of protest in Europe.

Kagan, Robert. *Of Paradise and Power: America and Europe in the New World Order.* 2004. Controversial but brilliant analysis of the post–Cold War world.

Karnow, Stanley. *Vietnam. A History,* 2d ed. 1997. One of the best and most comprehensive accounts of all sides in the war.

Kingston, Jeffrey. *Japan's Quiet Transformation: Social Change and Civil Society in the 21st Century, Politics, Economics and Society.* 2004. Leading scholar considers Japan's economic problems in the 1990s and their effects on Japanese politics and society.

Lampe, J. *Yugoslavia as History: Twice There Was a Country,* 2d ed. 2000. Judiciously and insightfully considers the history and violent collapse of Yugoslavia.

Laqueur, Walter. *Europe in Our Time: A History, 1945–1992.* 1992. Excellent comprehensive study of postwar Europe, with an extensive bibliography.

Sheehan, Neil. *A Bright and Shining Lie: John Paul Vann and America in Vietnam.* 1988. Classic account of the Vietnam War built around a biography of one of its harshest critics, Lieutenant Colonel Vann.

Urwin, Derek W. *The Community of Europe: A History of European Integration Since 1945,* 2d ed. 1995. Eloquent history of all aspects of European attempts at economic and political union since 1945.

Wapshott, Nicholas. *Ronald Reagan and Margaret Thatcher: A Political Marriage.* 2007. Particularly good analysis of their policies of economic conservatism and anticommunism in the 1980s.

NOTES

1. Quoted in N. Graebner, *Cold War Diplomacy, 1945–1960* (Princeton, N.J.: Van Nostrand, 1962), p. 17.
2. *Wall Street Journal,* June 25, 1985, p. 1.
3. Quoted in D. Treadgold, *Twentieth Century Russia,* 5th ed. (Boston: Houghton Mifflin, 1981), p. 442.
4. *Congressional Record: Proceedings and Debates* of the 84th Congress, 2nd Session (May 22, 1956–June 11, 1956), C11, Part 7 (June 4, 1956), pp. 9389–9403.
5. Regarding Gandhi's methods: see M. L. King, Jr., *Stride Toward Freedom: The Montgomery Story* (New York: Perennial Library, 1964), p. 67. Regarding evil laws: quoted in S. E. Morison et al., *A Concise History of the American Republic* (New York: Oxford University Press, 1977), p. 697.
6. Quoted in Morison, *Concise History,* p. 735.

For practice quizzes and other study tools, visit the **Online Study Guide** at bedfordstmartins.com/mckayworld.

For primary sources from this period, see *Sources of World Societies*, **Second Edition**.

For Web sites, images, and documents related to topics in this chapter, visit **Make History** at bedfordstmartins.com/mckayworld.

• **Iranian Green Revolution Protester** Iranians protest the results of the 2009 presidential election, and a young woman questions whether her vote was counted. Demonstrators returned to the streets of Iran in February 2011, as protests erupted against authoritarian regimes across North Africa and the Middle East. (Getty Images)

32

While the United States and the Soviet Union faced each other in a deadly standoff during the Cold War, most people in the so-called Third World went about their daily lives. The term *Third World* has its origins in the 1950s, when many thinkers, journalists, and politicians viewed Africa, Asia, and Latin America as a single entity, different from both the capitalist, industrialized "First World" and the Communist, industrialized "Second World." Despite differences in history and culture, most Third World countries in Africa, Asia, and Latin America — for a generation — shared many characteristics that encouraged a common consciousness and ideology. This chapter explores the characteristics of the countries in Asia and the Middle East, while Chapter 33 covers the development of the countries of Africa and Latin America.

Nearly all the countries in Asia and the Middle East experienced political or economic domination, nationalist reaction, and a struggle for genuine independence. Their peoples were thus united in their opposition to political and economic oppression in all its forms, particularly colonialism, neocolonialism, and racism. In the mid-twentieth century most Asian and Middle Eastern countries had predominately agricultural economies, earning the majority of their revenues from cash crops or natural resources, particularly oil, whose production was frequently controlled and exploited by First World countries or by multinational agribusinesses. In the second half of the twentieth century a few of these countries — most notably in the oil-rich Middle East and in East Asia, where there has been successful industrialization — became important producers and members of the global economy in their own right. In many cases, however, independence brought ethnic and religious conflict, as between the Muslims and Hindus in India, the Jews and Muslims in Palestine/Israel, the Chinese and Tibetans, and the Persians and Arabs in the Iran-Iraq War. •

Independence, Progress, and Conflict in Asia and the Middle East
1945 to the Present

The Resurgence of East Asia

☐ How did the countries of East Asia successfully recover after World War II?

New Nations and Old Rivalries in South Asia

☐ How have ethnic and religious rivalries affected the development of stable, independent states in South Asia?

Secularism and Religion at War in the Middle East

☐ In what ways has religion played a role in Middle Eastern politics since 1945?

MAP 32.1 The New States in Asia Divided primarily along religious lines into two states, British India led the way to political independence in 1947.

- **Great Leap Forward** Mao Zedong's acceleration of Chinese development in which industrial growth was to be based on small-scale backyard workshops run by peasants living in gigantic self-contained communes.

The Resurgence of East Asia

☐ How did the countries of East Asia successfully recover after World War II?

Other than Japan, most Asian countries recovered slowly after World War II. In the early 1950s the two Koreas and China were at war in the Korean peninsula, and the Vietnamese were fighting among themselves and against the French. The Nationalist Chinese in Taiwan were adjusting to life in exile from the mainland. Hong Kong, Singapore, Indonesia, South Korea, and the Philippines were recovering from years of colonial rule and Japanese occupation. Despite these challenges, over the next forty years China and the Asian "economic tigers" developed some of the largest and fastest-growing economies in the world, but liberal democracy remained elusive.

The Communist Victory in China

The Sino-Japanese War of 1937–1945 (see pages 901–902) led to the deaths of millions and created massive Chinese deficits and runaway inflation, hurting morale and ruining lives. The triumph of communism in China was due to many factors. Mao Zedong and the Communists had avoided pitched battles and concentrated on winning peasant support and forming a broad anti-Japanese coalition. By reducing rents, promising land redistribution, enticing intellectuals, and spreading propaganda, they emerged in peasant eyes as the true patriots, the genuine nationalists.

When Japan suddenly collapsed in August 1945, Communists and Nationalists both rushed to seize evacuated territory. In the last months of World War II, the Soviet Union occupied large areas of Manchuria previously held by the Japanese. When the Soviet troops left in March 1946 they allowed the Chinese Communists to seize control of key industrial areas in the north, including stockpiles of weapons left behind by the Japanese. Heavy fighting between the Communists and Nationalists broke out in Manchuria, and civil war began in earnest in April 1946. By 1948 the demoralized Nationalist forces were disintegrating before the better-led, more determined Communists. The following year Nationalist leader Jiang Jieshi and 2 million mainland Chinese fled to Taiwan, and in October 1949 Mao Zedong proclaimed the People's Republic of China (Map 32.1).

Between 1949 and 1954 the Communists consolidated their rule. They seized the vast land holdings of a minority of landlords and rich peasants and distributed the land to 300 million poor peasants. This revolutionary land reform was extremely popular and widely publicized through propaganda campaigns. Meanwhile, as Mao admitted in 1957, mass arrests led to 800,000 "class enemies" being summarily liquidated; the true figure is probably much higher. Millions more were deported to forced labor camps. All visible opposition from the old ruling groups was thus destroyed.

Claiming a new Mandate of Heaven, Mao and the Communists set out to prove that China was once again a great power. This was the real significance of China's participation in the Korean War (see page 946). From 1950 to 1953 the Chinese army's ability to fight the American "imperialists" to a bloody standstill on the Korean peninsula mobilized the masses and increased Chinese self-confidence. Fighting a war in Korea did not prevent the Chinese from also expanding their territory in the west, invading Tibet in 1950 and declaring Chinese sovereignty over the country in 1951. (See "Individuals in Society: The Dalai Lama," page 1040.)

Mao's China

Mao and the party looked to the Soviet Union for inspiration in the early 1950s. Along with the gradual collectivization of agriculture, China adopted a Soviet-style five-year plan to develop large factories and heavy industry rapidly. Russian specialists built many Chinese plants, and Soviet economic aid was considerable. The first five-year plan was successful, as undeniable economic growth followed the Communists' social revolution.

In the cultural and intellectual realms, too, the Chinese followed the Soviet example. Basic civil and political rights, which the Nationalists had seriously curtailed, were now simply abolished. Temples and churches were closed, and press freedom died. Soviet-style puritanism took hold, as the Communists quickly eradicated prostitution and drug abuse, which they had long regarded as marks of exploitation and national decline. They enthusiastically promoted Soviet Marxist ideas concerning women and the family. Full equality, work outside the home, and state-supported child care became primary goals.

In 1958 China broke from the Marxist-Leninist course of development and began to go its own way. Mao proclaimed a **Great Leap Forward** in which in-

☐ CHRONOLOGY

1947 Separation of India and Pakistan

1948 End of British mandate in Palestine; Jews proclaim state of Israel; Mohandas Gandhi assassinated

1949–1954 Mass arrests, forced-labor camps, and Communist propaganda in China

1949–present Harsh restrictions against religion and speech in China

1956 Nasser nationalizes Suez Canal Company

1958 Great Leap Forward in China

1964–1975 Vietnam War

1965 Great Proletarian Cultural Revolution in China

1967 Six-Day War in Israel

1970s–present Revival of Islamic fundamentalism in the Middle East

1975–1990 Civil war in Lebanon

1979 Islamic revolution in Iran

1980–1988 Iran-Iraq War

1987 Palestinians start the intifada

1989 Chinese military puts down student revolt in Tiananmen Square

1990–1991 Persian Gulf War

1991 Congress Party in India embraces Western capitalist reforms

2001 China joins World Trade Organization

2007 Hamas establishes Palestinian Authority government

2009 Mahmoud Ahmadinejad violently suppresses protests in Iran

2010–2011 Populist uprisings and protests across the Middle East

dustrial growth would be based on small-scale backyard workshops and steel mills run by peasants living in gigantic self-contained communes. The creation of a new socialist personality that rejected individualism and traditional Confucian family values, such as filial piety and acceptance of parental authority, was a second goal.

The intended great leap produced an economic disaster, as land in the countryside went untilled when peasants turned to industrial production. As many as 30 million people died in famines that swept the country in 1960–1961, one of the greatest human disasters in world history. When Soviet premier Nikita Khrushchev criticized Chinese policy in 1960, Mao

◻ Picturing the Past

Communist China Poster Art One of the most popular art forms in Communist China is poster art, millions of copies of which have been printed to adorn the walls of homes, offices, factories, and businesses. Although related to socialist realism in the Soviet Union (see page 940), this uniquely Chinese version contains neither abstract, modern, or bourgeois elements nor classical Chinese art styles. Like Soviet socialist realism, such posters seek to glorify the state, its leaders, and the heroes of the ongoing revolution. The two young women in this poster wear uniforms and caps bearing the Communist red star, the five points of which represent the five components of Communist society: the youth, the army, the peasants, the workers, and the intellectuals. (Courtesy, Chinese Poster Collection, University of Westminster, London)

ANALYZING THE IMAGE Who is depicted, and what are they doing? What message do you think the artist seeks to convey with this image?

CONNECTIONS What social function or application might posters such as this one have? Is this sort of expression unique to Communist societies, or can you think of examples of other types of art that promote public messages?

condemned him and his Russian colleagues as detestable "modern revisionists." The Russians abruptly cut off economic and military aid, splitting the Communist world apart.

Mao lost influence in the party after the Great Leap Forward fiasco and the Sino-Soviet split, but in 1965 he staged a dramatic comeback. Fearing that China was becoming bureaucratic, capitalistic, and "revisionist" like the Soviet Union, Mao launched the **Great Proletarian Cultural Revolution**. He sought to

purge the party and to recapture the revolutionary fervor of his guerrilla struggle (see pages 897–898). The army and the nation's young people responded enthusiastically, organizing themselves into radical cadres called **Red Guards**. Students denounced their teachers and practiced rebellion in the name of revolution. One Red Guard manifesto exulted that "Revolution is rebellion, and rebellion is the soul of Mao Tse-tung's thought."[1] Mao's thoughts, through his speeches and writings, were collected in the *Little Red Book*, which

Shaming of Enemies During the Cultural Revolution
During the Chinese Cultural Revolution in the 1960s, young Chinese militants and Red Guards attacked people identified as enemies of the Communist Party and Chairman Mao. Many of these "enemies" were intellectuals such as teachers and artists, but they could be neighbors and even parents who were considered bourgeois. Here a victim is paraded through the streets wearing a dunce cap with his crimes written on it. (Wide World Photos/AP Images)

became holy scripture to the Red Guards. Here the young Red Guards could gain inspiration from Mao's observation that

> The world is yours, as well as ours, but in the last analysis, it is yours. You young people, full of vigour and vitality, are in the bloom of life, like the sun at eight or nine in the morning. Our hope is placed on you. . . . The world belongs to you. China's future belongs to you.

And here also they could study the underlying maxim of Mao's revolution: "Every communist must grasp the truth, 'Political power grows out of the barrel of a gun.'"[2]

The Red Guards sought to erase all traces of "feudal" and "bourgeois" culture and thought. Ancient monuments and countless works of art, antiques, and books were destroyed. Party officials, professors, and intellectuals were exiled to remote villages to purify themselves with heavy labor. Universities were shut down for years. Thousands of people died, many of them executed, and millions more were sent to rural forced-labor camps. The Red Guards attracted enormous worldwide attention and served as an extreme model for the student rebellions in the West in the late 1960s (see page 962).

The Limits of Reform

Mao and the Red Guards succeeded in mobilizing the masses, shaking up the party, and creating greater so-

cial equality. But the Cultural Revolution also created growing chaos and a general crisis of confidence, especially in the cities. Persecuted intellectuals, technicians, and purged party officials launched a counterattack on the radicals and regained much of their influence by 1969. Thus China shifted to the right at the same time that Europe and the United States did. This shift opened the door to a limited but lasting reconciliation between China and the United States in 1972, facilitated by U.S. president Richard Nixon's visit that year.

After Mao's death in 1976, Deng Xiaoping (1904–1997) and his supporters initiated a series of new policies, embodied in the campaign of the "Four Modernizations": agriculture, industry, science and technology, and national defense. China's 800 million peasants experienced the most beneficial change from what Deng called China's "second revolution." Rigid collectivized agriculture had failed to provide either the peasants or the country with adequate food. Determined to modernize the economy, Deng looked to ally himself with the peasantry. China's peasants were allowed to farm the land in small family units rather than in large

• **Great Proletarian Cultural Revolution** A movement launched by Mao Zedong that attempted to purge the Chinese Communist Party of time-serving bureaucrats and recapture the revolutionary fervor of his guerrilla struggle.

• **Red Guards** Radical cadres formed by young people who would attack anyone identified as an enemy of either the Chinese Communist Party or Chairman Mao.

Chinese Students in 1989 These exuberant demonstrators in Tiananmen Square personify the idealism and optimism of China's prodemocracy movement. After some hesitation the Communist government crushed the student leaders and their supporters with tanks and executions, reaffirming its harsh, authoritarian character. (Erika Lansner/stockphoto.com)

collectives and to "dare to be rich" by producing crops of their choice. Peasants responded enthusiastically, increasing food production by more than 50 percent between 1978 and 1984.

The successful use of free markets in agriculture encouraged further economic experimentation. Foreign capitalists were allowed to open factories in southern China and to export Chinese products around the world. Private enterprise was also permitted in cities, where snack shops and a host of small businesses sprang up. China's Communist Party leaders also drew on the business talent of wealthy "overseas" Chinese in Hong Kong and Taiwan who knew the world market and needed new sources of cheap labor. The Chinese economy grew rapidly between 1978 and 1987, and per capita income doubled in these years.

Most large-scale industry remained state-owned, however, and cultural change proceeded slowly. Above all, the Communist Party zealously preserved its monopoly on political power. When the worldwide movement for greater democracy and political freedom in the late 1980s also took root in China, the government responded by banning all demonstrations and slowing the trend toward a freer economy. Inflation then soared to more than 30 percent a year. The economic reversal, the continued lack of political freedom, and the conviction that Chinese society was becoming more corrupt led China's idealistic university students to spearhead demonstrations in April 1989.

The students evoked tremendous popular support, and on May 17 more than a million people streamed into Beijing's central **Tiananmen Square** in support of their demands. The government declared martial law and ordered the army to clear the students. Masses of courageous Chinese citizens blocked the soldiers' entry into the city for two weeks, but in the early hours of June 4, 1989, tanks rolled into Tiananmen Square. At least seven hundred students died as a wave of repression, arrests, and executions descended on China.

In the months after Tiananmen Square communism fell in eastern Europe, the Soviet Union broke apart, and China's rulers felt vindicated. They believed their action had preserved Communist power, prevented chaos, and demonstrated the limits of reform. After some hesitation Deng and his successor Jiang Zemin (b. 1926) reaffirmed economic liberalization. Private enterprise and foreign investment boomed in the 1990s. Consumerism was encouraged, and the living standard rose. But critics of Communist rule were jailed, and every effort was made to ensure that the People's Army would again crush the people if ordered. Thus China coupled growing economic freedom with continued political repression.

These policies continued into the twenty-first century. In 2001, after long negotiations, China joined the World Trade Organization, giving it all the privileges and obligations of participation in the liberal global economy. Politically Communist, China now has a full-blown capitalist economy. From 1978, when Deng Xiaoping took over and launched economic reforms, through 2010, the Chinese economy grew at an average annual rate of over 9 percent, and foreign trade at an average of 16 percent. When Europe, the United States, Japan, and many other nations faced a severe economic downturn in 2008, China's economy continued to expand. Average per capita income in China has doubled every ten years, and in March 2011 China replaced Japan as the world's second largest economy after that of the United States.

But China continues to have a miserable human rights record. In 2002 current leader Hu Jintao (b. 1942) introduced modest legal reforms. He remains clearly in July 2010 and the government's slow response further weakened President Zardari's regime. The United States continues to send Pakistan massive amounts of military aid to fight the insurgents and humanitarian aid to help Pakistan recover from the floods, hoping to keep the country stable and an ally in the war in Afghanistan.

India Since Independence

Jawaharlal Nehru (1889–1964) and the Indian National Congress Party ruled India for a generation after independence and introduced major social reforms. Hindu women were granted legal equality, including the right to vote, to seek divorce, and to marry outside their castes. The constitution abolished the untouchable caste. In practice less-discriminatory attitudes toward women and untouchables evolved slowly — especially in the villages, where 85 percent of the people lived.

The Congress Party leadership tried with modest success to develop the country economically by means of democratic socialism. But population growth of about 2.4 percent per year ate up much of the increase in output. Intense poverty remained the lot of most people and encouraged widespread corruption within the bureaucracy. The Congress Party maintained neutrality in the Cold War and sought to join with newly independent states in Asia and Africa to create a "third force" of nonaligned nations, aiming for economic and cultural cooperation. This effort culminated in the Afro-Asian Conference in Bandung, Indonesia, in 1955.

Nehru's daughter, Indira Gandhi (1917–1984; no relation to Mohandas Gandhi), became prime minister in 1966 and dominated Indian political life for a generation. In 1975 she subverted parliamentary democracy and proclaimed a state of emergency. Attacking dishonest officials, black marketers, and tax evaders, she also threw the weight of the government behind a heavy-handed campaign of mass sterilization to reduce population growth. More than 7 million men were sterilized in 1976.

Many believed that Gandhi's emergency measures marked the end of the parliamentary democracy and Western liberties introduced in the last phase of British rule. But true to the British tradition, Gandhi called for free elections. She suffered a spectacular electoral defeat, largely because of the vastly unpopular sterilization campaign and her subversion of democracy. Her successors fell to fighting among themselves, and in 1980 she won an equally stunning electoral victory.

Separatist ethnic nationalism plagued Indira Gandhi's last years in office. Democratic India remained a patchwork of religions, languages, and peoples, always threatening to further divide the country along ethnic or religious lines. Most notable were the 15 million

Sikhs of the Punjab in northern India (see Map 32.2), with their own religion — founded by Guru Nanak Dev (1469–1538) — and a distinctive culture. Most Sikhs wanted greater autonomy for the Punjab, and by 1984 some Sikh radicals were fighting for independence. Gandhi cracked down hard, and she was assassinated by Sikhs in retaliation. Violence followed as Hindu mobs slaughtered over a thousand Sikhs throughout India.

Elected prime minister in 1984 by a landslide sympathy vote, one of Indira Gandhi's sons, Rajiv Gandhi (1944–1991), showed considerable skill at effecting a limited reconciliation with a majority of the Sikh population. Under his leadership the Congress Party moved away from the socialism of his mother and grandfather and he prepared the way for Finance Minister Manmohan Singh to introduce market reforms, capitalist development, and Western technology and investment from 1991 onward. These reforms were successful, and since the 1990s India's economy has experienced explosive growth.

Holding power almost continuously from 1947, the Congress Party was challenged increasingly by Hindu nationalists in the 1990s. These nationalists argued forcefully that India was based, above all, on Hindu culture and religious tradition and that these values had been badly compromised by the Western secularism of Congress Party leaders and by the historical influence of India's Muslims. Campaigning also for a strong Indian military, the Hindu nationalist party finally gained power in 1998. The new government immediately resumed testing of nuclear devices, asserting its vision of a militant Hindu nationalism. In 2004 the United Progressive Alliance (UPA), a center-left coalition dominated by the Congress Party, regained control of the government and elected Manmohan Singh (b. 1932) as prime minister. In 2009 Singh became only the second Indian prime minister since Jawaharlal Nehru to be re-elected to office after completing a full five-year term.

After Pakistan announced that it had developed nuclear weapons in 1998, relations between Pakistan and India worsened. In December 2001 the two nuclear powers seemed poised for war until intense diplomatic pressure forced them to step back from the abyss. In April 2005 both sides agreed to open business and trade relations and to work to negotiate a peaceful solution to the Kashmir dispute. Islamic and Hindu chauvinism remains strong, however, and tension between the two countries again increased dramatically in November 2008 when a Pakistan-based terrorist organization carried out a widespread shooting and bombing attack across Mumbai, India's largest city, killing 164 and wounding over 300. Tensions remain high, and nationalist and religious extremists in both countries appear willing to carry out such attacks again.

Secularism and Religion at War in the Middle East

☐ In what ways has religion played a role in Middle Eastern politics since 1945?

Throughout the vast umma (world of Islam), nationalism remained the primary political force after 1945 (Map 32.3). Anti-Western and anticommunist in most instances, Muslim nationalism generally combined a strong secular state with deep devotion to Islam. Nationalism in the Arab countries of the Middle East wore two faces. The idealistic side focused on the Pan-Arab dream of uniting all Arabs in a single nation that would be strong enough to resist the West, defeat the new state of Israel, and achieve genuine independence. Despite political and economic alliances like the Arab League, this vision floundered on intense regional, ideological, and personal rivalries. Thus a more practical Arab nationalism focused largely on nation building within former League of Nations mandates and European colonies.

In the very heart of this world of Islam, Jewish nationalists founded the state of Israel following the Second World War. The Zionist claim to a homeland came into sharp, and often violent, conflict with the rights and claims of the Palestinians. Religious differences, territorial claims, and the right to nationhood have been at the heart of the Israeli-Palestinian conflict since the early 1900s.

In the Muslim countries of the Middle East, nation building, often led by westernized elites, almost universally culminated in the creation of one-party dictatorships, corruption, and continued daily hardship for the masses. In the 1970s some Islamic preachers and devoted laypeople charged that the model of modernizing, Western-inspired nationalism had failed. These critics, labeled fundamentalists in the West, urged a return to strict Islamic principles and traditional morality. They evoked a sympathetic response among many educated Muslims as well as among villagers and city dwellers. In countries like Egypt they worked to overthrow the government, which generally resulted in their movements being banned and their leaders arrested. In countries like Lebanon and Turkey they gained some political power within the secular governments. In Iran in 1979 they overthrew the secular government and created an Islamic republic.

• **Palestine Liberation Organization (PLO)** Created in 1964, a loose union of Palestinian refugee groups opposed to Israel and working toward Palestinian home rule.

The Arab-Israeli Conflict

Before the Second World War, Arab nationalists were loosely united in their opposition to the colonial powers and to Jewish migration to Palestine. The British had granted independence to Egypt and Iraq before the war, and the French followed suit with Syria and Lebanon in 1945. In British-mandated Palestine, the situation was volatile. Jewish settlement in Palestine (see pages 888–889) was strenuously opposed by the Palestinian Arabs and the seven independent states of the newly founded Arab League (Egypt, Iraq, Jordan, Lebanon, Saudi Arabia, Syria, and Yemen). Murder and terrorism flourished, nurtured by bitterly conflicting Arab and Jewish nationalisms.

The British announced in early 1947 their intention to withdraw from Palestine in 1948. The insoluble problem of a Jewish homeland was dumped in the lap of the United Nations. In November 1947 the UN General Assembly passed a plan to partition Palestine into two separate states — one Arab and one Jewish (Map 32.4). The Jews accepted, and the Arabs rejected, the partition of Palestine.

By early 1948 an undeclared civil war was raging in Palestine. When the British mandate ended on May 14, 1948, the Jews proclaimed the state of Israel. Arab countries immediately attacked the new Jewish state, but the Israelis drove off the invaders and conquered more territory. Roughly nine hundred thousand Palestinian refugees fled or were expelled from old Palestine. The war left an enormous legacy of Arab bitterness toward Israel and its political allies, Great Britain and the United States.

In Egypt the humiliation of Arab defeat triggered a nationalist revolution. A young army colonel named Gamal Abdel Nasser (1918–1970) drove out the corrupt and pro-Western king Farouk in 1952. Nasser preached the gospel of neutralism in the Cold War, but accepted Soviet aid to demonstrate Egypt's independence of the West. Relations with Israel and the West worsened, and in 1956 Nasser nationalized the European-owned Suez Canal Company, Europe's last vestige of power in the Middle East. Outraged, the British and French joined forces with the Israelis and successfully invaded Egypt. The United States unexpectedly sided with the Soviets and forced the British, French, and Israelis to withdraw from Egypt.

Nasser's victory encouraged anti-Western radicalism, hopes of Pan-Arab political unity, and a vague "Arab socialism." Yet the Arab world remained deeply divided apart from bitter opposition to Israel and support for the right of Palestinian refugees to return to their homeland. In 1964 a loose union of Palestinian refugee groups opposed to Israel joined together, under the leadership of Yasir Arafat (1929–2004) to form the **Palestine Liberation Organization (PLO)**.

MAP 32.3 Modern Islam, ca. 2010 Although the Islamic heartland remains the Middle East and North Africa, Islam is growing steadily in Africa south of the Sahara and is the faith of heavily populated Indonesia.

On June 1, 1967, as Syrian and Egyptian armies massed on their borders, the Israelis formed a national unity government and on June 4 made the decision to go to war. The Israelis launched a surprise air strike early on June 5 and by noon had destroyed most of the Egyptian, Syrian, and Jordanian air forces. Over the next five days Israeli armies defeated Egyptian, Syrian, Jordanian, and Palestinian forces and took control of the Sinai Peninsula and the Gaza Strip from Egypt, the West Bank and East Jerusalem from Jordan, and the Golan Heights from Syria. In the Six-Day War (also known as the 1967 Arab-Israeli War), Israel proved itself to be the pre-eminent military force in the region, and it expanded the territory under its control threefold.

After the war, Israel began to build large Jewish settlements in the Gaza Strip and the West Bank, home to millions of Palestinians. On November 22, 1967, the UN Security Council adopted Resolution 242, which contained a "land for peace" formula by which Israel was called upon to withdraw from the occupied territories, and in return the Arab states were to withdraw all claims to Israeli territory, cease all hostilities, and recognize the sovereignty of the Israeli state. The resolution did not specifically mention the Palestinians, and the PLO and Syria refused to agree to it.

On Yom Kippur on October 6, 1973, the holiest day in Judaism, a coalition of Arab forces led by Syria and Egypt launched a surprise attack on Israel across the Golan Heights and the Sinai Peninsula. Despite initial setbacks, the Israelis successfully counterattacked and were less than sixty miles from Cairo and twenty-five miles from Damascus when a ceasefire ended hostilities on October 25. For the Arab world, the Yom Kippur War (or 1973 Arab-Israeli War) marked a psychological victory because of the Arab states' initial successes. The Israelis, despite having turned back the attack, now felt less invincible than they had following the Six-Day War, and the United States recognized the need to become more actively involved in mediation and peace-making. Efforts undertaken by U.S. president Jimmy Carter led to the Camp David Accords in 1979 that normalized relations between Egypt and Israel and brokered the return of the Sinai Peninsula to Egypt—the first successful realization of the UN "land for peace" formula.

MAP 32.4 Palestine, Israel, and the Middle East Since the British mandate expired on May 14, 1948, there have been five major wars and innumerable armed clashes in what was formerly Palestine (inset). Through negotiations between Israel and the PLO, Jericho and the Gaza Strip were placed under Palestinian self-rule, and Israeli troops were withdrawn in 1994. In 2010–2011 a series of populist uprisings and protests spread throughout the Middle East, toppling some regimes and leading to both uncertainty and hope for democratic reform.

The Palestinian Quest for Independence

In 1987 young Palestinians in the occupied territories of the Gaza Strip and the West Bank began the **intifada**, a prolonged campaign of rock throwing and civil disobedience against Israeli soldiers. Inspired increasingly by Islamic fundamentalists, the Palestinian uprising

eventually posed a serious challenge not only to Israel but also to the secular Palestine Liberation Organization (PLO), long led from abroad by Yasir Arafat. The result was an unexpected and mutually beneficial agreement in 1993 between Israel and the PLO. Israel agreed to recognize Arafat's organization and start a peace process that granted Palestinian self-rule in Gaza and called for self-rule throughout the West Bank in five

Israel's Wall of Separation

A Palestinian man waves as he walks across the hills near Jerusalem, where Israel's wall of separation divides Israeli and Palestinian territory. Israelis argue that the wall, made of concrete and covered with razor wire, protects them from Palestinian militants and suicide bombers. Increasingly it is described by Palestinians and others as a Berlin Wall–like structure, a symbol of Israelis forcing a separation, an Israeli version of apartheid, between the two peoples. (Kevin Frayer/AP Images)

years. In return, Arafat renounced terrorism and abandoned the long-standing demand that Israel must withdraw from all land occupied in the 1967 war.

The peace process increasingly divided Israel. In 1995 a right-wing Jewish extremist assassinated Prime Minister Yitzhak Rabin (1922–1995). In 1996 a coalition of opposition parties won a slender majority, charging the Palestinian leadership with condoning anti-Jewish terrorism. The new Israeli government limited Palestinian self-rule where it existed and expanded Jewish settlements in the West Bank. On the Palestinian side, dissatisfaction with the peace process grew. Between 1993 and 2000 the number of Jewish settlers in the West Bank doubled to two hundred thousand and Palestinian per capita income declined by 20 to 25 percent.

Failed negotiations between Arafat and Israel in 2000 unleashed an explosion of tit-for-tat violence, known as the Second Intifada, in Israel, the West Bank, and the Gaza Strip. In 2003 the Israelis began building a barrier around the West Bank, which has met with opposition from Israelis and Palestinians alike.

The death of Yasir Arafat, the PLO's long-time leader, in November 2004 marked a major turning point in the Israeli-Palestinian dispute. Mahmoud Abbas, Arafat's successor, is viewed as moderate and pragmatic, but peace talks have made very little progress since he took office. In January 2006 Hamas, a radical Sunni Muslim political party, won 72 of the 136 seats in the Palestinian legislature, seizing control from Abbas and the PLO. Considered by many in the West to be a terrorist organization, Hamas had gained widespread support from many Palestinians for the welfare programs it established in the West Bank and Gaza Strip.

Immediately after the Hamas victory, Israel, the United States, the European Union, and several other Western donor nations cut off all aid to the Palestinian Authority, the governing body of the West Bank and Gaza Strip established by the 1994 peace agreement. In June 2007 Hamas seized control of the Gaza Strip. Since then, economic and humanitarian conditions for Palestinians living in the Gaza Strip have deteriorated. In 2010, 63 percent of the 1.5 million citizens of Gaza lived below the United Nations–defined poverty line. When a "Gaza freedom flotilla" attempted to break an Israeli blockade around Gaza in May 2010, the Israeli navy intercepted the flotilla and raided the ships. Nine activists, eight of whom were Turkish nationals, were killed. This set off a worldwide condemnation of Israel's actions and severely strained relations between Israel and Turkey. Under pressure, Israel eased its blockade in 2010, allowing more humanitarian goods and food aid into Gaza, but the movement of people to and from Gaza remains restricted.

• **intifada** A popular uprising by young Palestinians against Israeli rule; the Arabic word *intifada* means "shaking off."

While Gaza remained isolated, Abbas and the Palestinian Authority formed a separate government in the West Bank. In September 2010 Israeli prime minster Benjamin Netanyahu (b. 1949) agreed to hold direct peace talks with President Abbas and the Palestinians, mediated by the U.S. Obama administration, which hoped to broker a two-state solution to the Israeli-Palestinian conflict. The peace talks broke down barely three weeks after they started, as Israel resumed construction of settlement homes in the West Bank and East Jerusalem. Thus, despite years of diplomacy, war, and stalemate, the nature of a future Palestinian state remains unresolved.

Egypt: Arab World Leader

Egypt, with its large military, its anti-imperialist rhetoric, and its support for Arab unity, was recognized as the leader of the Arab world from the time of Nasser's seizure of power in 1956 to the mid-1970s. In late 1977 Egypt's president Anwar Sadat (1918–1981) made a pathbreaking official visit to Israel, leading to a historic, though limited, peace settlement known as the Camp David Accords (see page 995). Each country gained: Egypt got back the Sinai Peninsula, which Israel had taken in the 1967 Six-Day War (see Map 32.4), and Israel obtained peace and normal relations with Egypt. Israel also kept the Gaza Strip, taken from Egypt in 1967 and home to about 1 million Palestinians. Some Arab leaders denounced Sadat's initiative as treason, and Egypt was suspended from the Arab League from 1979 to 1989.

After Sadat's assassination by Islamic radicals in 1981, Egypt's relations with Israel deteriorated, but Egypt and Israel maintained their fragile peace as Sadat's successor as president, Hosni Mubarak (b. 1928), took office in 1981. Mubarak was a consistent supporter of Israel and a mediator for peaceful relations between Israel and the Arab world. His diplomatic efforts were successful in getting Egypt readmitted to the Arab League in 1989 and getting its headquarters moved back to Cairo. Egypt is considered the closest Middle Eastern ally of the United States after Israel, and since the Camp David Accords the United States has given Egypt billions of dollars in development, humanitarian, and military aid.

Egyptian Protesters in Cairo, January 29, 2011 The Tunisian overthrow of the repressive regime of long-serving President Ben Ali on January 14, 2011, set off a wave of popular uprisings against authoritarian regimes across North Africa and the Middle East. Next to go was Egypt's Hosni Mubarak, who had ruled Egypt with an iron hand for nearly thirty years. He stepped down on February 11, 2011, after the army—including the men on the tanks in this image—joined the protesters. (Ahmed Ali/AP Images)

Domestically, however, Mubarak failed to promote significant economic development and ruled with an increasingly dictatorial hand. Prices of basic goods and foodstuffs continued to rise, while the standard of living for many Egyptians remained stagnant. Many of the government's critics charged that massive fraud and corruption funneled Egypt's wealth to a privileged few. Over 40 percent of the total population lived in poverty.

The human rights picture during Mubarak's thirty years in office was no better. Officially Egypt is a republic, but it has been ruled under an emergency law since 1967. The law suspended constitutional rights, limited freedom of expression and assembly, gave the government the right to arrest people without charge and detain prisoners indefinitely, extended police powers, legalized censorship, and allowed for the establishment of a special security court. Mubarak used the emergency law to create a wholly separate justice system in order to silence all opposition and punish, torture, and kill anyone who was perceived as a threat to his rule. Demonstrations, political organizations, and even financial donations that were not approved by the government were banned under the law. Thousands of people were arrested. In May 2010 the parliament approved the law's extension for another two years.

In December 2010 demonstrations broke out in Tunisia against the twenty-three-year authoritarian rule of President Zine Ben Ali (b. 1936), leading to his downfall on January 14, 2011. This populist revolt soon spread across North Africa and the Middle East, including to the streets of Cairo and other cities as Egyptians of all ages united in revolt against Mubarak's dictatorial rule. After three weeks of increasingly large demonstrations, coordinated through Facebook, Twitter, and other electronic communications networks, Mubarak stepped down as president on February 11, 2011.

Libya, located between Tunisia and Egypt, also witnessed a massive uprising against its dictatorial leader of forty-two years, Muammar Gaddafi (b. 1942). Gaddafi reacted much more violently and ruthlessly than either of his neighboring dictators in his effort to remain in power, using his army and air force to attack cities, neighborhoods, and rural areas held by opposition forces. As of June 2011 he retained control over the western part of the country but had lost power over several major cities in the east.

A Fractured Lebanon

With the Vichy French government unable to maintain its control over Lebanon, the mandated territory gained its independence from French rule in 1943. Lebanon prospered until the early 1970s and became a favorite tourist destination and a regional center of banking and trade. When Lebanon became an independent nation, the unwritten National Pact included an agreement that the Lebanese president would be a Christian and the prime minister a Muslim. This arrangement was based on a 1932 census that showed a Christian majority. By the late 1960s the Lebanese Muslim population had grown significantly, and Muslims were no longer content with a Christian-controlled government and military. Their long-simmering dissatisfaction and anger over the dispersal of political power came to a head in early 1975, starting with armed scrimmages between Christian and Muslim factions that resulted in the slaughter of many innocent civilians, and the escalating violence and reprisals led to a devastating fifteen-year civil war.

In the course of the war the Lebanese army disintegrated when soldiers switched their allegiance from the national government to various sectarian militias. One of these was a hard-line group known as Hezbollah, or Party of God. Hezbollah condemned the Israeli invasions of Lebanon in 1978 and 1982 aimed at eradicating the Palestine Liberation Organization's control of southern Lebanon, and had as one of its stated objectives the complete destruction of the state of Israel.

The Lebanese civil war was brutal and massively destructive. War crimes and terrorist acts were committed by all sides. Lebanon's entire infrastructure was destroyed, and Beirut in 1990 looked like the bombed-out cities of Europe after World War II. The civil war ended after Lebanon's Maronite Christian and Muslim communities agreed to a more balanced sharing of power, and by 1991 the sectarian violence had generally ceased. Israeli forces finally left Lebanon in 2000, and Syria withdrew its fifteen thousand troops, who had been sent in by the Arab League to maintain peace, in 2005.

By 2004 Hezbollah had established virtual control over much of southern Beirut and southern Lebanon, and in elections held in 2005 it won fourteen seats in the Lebanese legislature. Hezbollah members adhere to a distinct brand of Islamic theology and ideology developed by the Shi'ite Ayatollah Ruhollah Khomeini, leader of the Iranian Islamic Revolution in 1979. This connection explains the significant financial and military support that Iran provides and its powerful influence in shaping Hezbollah's policies, particularly toward Israel.

The 2006 Israel-Lebanon War

On July 12, 2006, Hezbollah's hostility toward Israel erupted into what became known as the July War in Lebanon and the Second Lebanon War in Israel. Hezbollah's continued shelling of northern Israel and Israel's seeming inability to gain a quick military victory generated mounting discontent among Israeli soldiers and civilians alike about the handling and course of the war. By early August all sides clearly desired a way out, and with the help of the United Nations Security Council, both sides agreed to a cease-fire on August 14, 2006.

Opinions about who won and who lost the war vary, but it was costly to both sides. Hezbollah declared victory, and many in the Muslim world felt pride in Hezbollah's ability to stand up to the Israeli military machine. Although Hezbollah may have won the propaganda war, there can be no doubt that the group paid dearly. It lost the elaborate infrastructure it had taken years to build in the south, and it lost the support of hundreds of thousands of Lebanese whose homes, lives, and livelihoods were destroyed by its actions. For its part, Israel also claimed victory, but it was also no better off. Many Israelis believed that indecisive leadership cost Israel a rare opportunity to destroy Hezbollah. Israelis emerged from the war deeply troubled by a new sense of vulnerability and turned to Israeli hardliners such as Benjamin Netanyahu, who was elected prime minister in the next election.

Meanwhile, efforts to rebuild Lebanon have been ongoing. The majority of Lebanese people appear to want peace, but since 2006 Hezbollah has rearmed and has reemerged as a political and military power. In May 2008 a Christian and former commander of the Lebanese armed forces, Michel Suleiman (b. 1948), became president. He formed a national unity government, which included Hezbollah parliament members, sought equal political relations with Syria, and tried to integrate Hezbollah's militia into the Lebanese army. But in early January 2011 Hezbollah pulled out of the national coalition government, causing it to collapse. In late January Suleiman appointed a Sunni businessman, Najib Mikati, as prime minister-designate. Mikati was supported by Hezbollah and its allies in parliament, leading to widespread rioting by Sunnis across Lebanon, who viewed the action as the next step in the eventual takeover of Lebanon by the Shiite Hezbollah movement.

Challenges to Turkey's Secularism

Through the remainder of the twentieth century, Turkey remained basically true to Atatürk's vision of a thoroughly modernized, secularized, Europeanized state (see pages 883–886). Islam continued to exert less influence in daily life as Turkey joined NATO in 1952

and eventually sought full membership in the European Union (EU). But Turkey remains a country on the border — seeking membership in the European Union of the West, while acknowledging its Islamic heritage and historical connections with the East. Many of its citizens lead Western lifestyles, although the population is overwhelmingly Sunni Muslim. In the twenty-first century Turks have become increasingly divided over the future of the secular state in Turkey.

Turkey is the most secular of Islamic countries. Since the 1920s Turks have maintained a strict separation of state and religion. In the 2002 elections, however, the newly formed Justice and Development Party, or AKP, scored a stunning victory, with Abdullah Gül (b. 1950) becoming president of Turkey and Recep Erdogan (b. 1954), head of the AKP, becoming prime minister. Although the AKP campaigned as a moderate, conservative, pro-Western party, many Turks are concerned that it is intent on doing away with Turkey's secular constitution and establishing an Islamic state. Erdogan has adamantly denied having a secret agenda, but his support for laws such as the banning of alcoholic beverages, the lifting of the headscarf ban in all universities, the placing of anti-secular individuals in government offices, and the awarding of government contracts to Islamic businesses plus the arrest of several secular opponents of the government have been criticized by secular parties.

Despite this opposition the AKP continues to remain popular and win elections. During its rule, the Turkish economy has seen rapid growth, and the hyperinflation that plagued the country for three decades had fallen to around 7 percent in November 2010. Turkey weathered the 2008–2009 global economic downturn better than most countries, and its stock market in 2009 rose the most in the world after Argentina's.

A second major problem facing Turkey is its handling of its minority Kurdish population (see Map 32.5 on page 1002). Many observers view the landslide victory of the AKP in the 2007 elections as having been prompted by a surge in Turkish nationalism and a resurgence of conservative Muslim influence since September 11, 2001, when the West, particularly the George W. Bush administration in the United States, demanded a "with us or against us" position from Turkey, Pakistan, and other allies in the Middle East (see pages 1041–1043). When Turkey refused to participate in the invasion of Iraq in 2003 because it worried about destabilizing fragile relations with its Kurdish citizens, many in the Bush administration labeled the Turks as "against" the United States and the war on terrorism.

As the situation in Iraq continued to deteriorate and as the Kurds in northern Iraq continued to push for more autonomy, Kurdish nationalists in Turkey increased their attacks on Turkish targets. In February and March 2008 the Turkish army began a military of-

Individuals in Society

Eva Perón

EVA PERÓN WAS ONLY THIRTY-THREE WHEN
she died of cancer on July 26, 1952, but already many Argentineans considered her a saint. The state radio broadcaster sadly announced that "today at 20:25 Eva Perón, Spiritual Leader of the Nation, entered immortality." Argentina went into official mourning; although Perón had never held an official political office, she was accorded a state funeral. Immediately following her death her corpse was embalmed, with the intention of putting it on public display forever in a planned memorial larger than the Statue of Liberty.

Often called Evita (the Spanish diminutive of Eva), she was one of five illegitimate children born near Buenos Aires to Juan Duarte and Juana Ibarguren. Duarte returned to his legitimate wife and children when Eva was a year old, leaving Juana and her children destitute and dependent on Juana's sewing for their existence. As they grew older all the children had to work, but Eva apparently also dreamed of becoming an actress.

At fifteen Eva Duarte moved to the cosmopolitan city of Buenos Aires. Although she had little formal education and no connections, she possessed great natural beauty, and soon she joined a professional theater group with which she toured nationally. She also modeled, appeared in a few movies, and then got regular employment as a character on a radio series. By 1943, although only twenty-three years old, she was one of the highest paid actresses in the country.

In 1943 Eva met widowed Colonel Juan Perón, then secretary of labor and social welfare in the military government that had seized power that year. Juan Perón had grand ambitions, intending to run for president. Eva Duarte became his partner and confidante, and she won him support among the Argentine masses. In 1945 Juan Perón and Eva Duarte were married.

A year later Perón won the presidency. Eva had gone out on the campaign trail and organized support for her husband from *los descamisados* ("the shirtless ones"), her name for Argentine's poor. When Perón assumed the presidency, Eva, though not officially appointed, became the secretary of labor. Having come from a childhood of poverty herself, she now worked tirelessly for the poor, for the working classes, and with organized labor. She instituted a number of social welfare measures and promoted a new Ministry of Health, which resulted in the creation of new hospitals and disease treatment programs. In 1948 she established the Eva Perón Welfare Foundation, which grew into an immense semiofficial welfare agency, helping the poor throughout Argentina and even contributing to victims of natural disasters in other countries.

From early on, Eva Perón had supported women's suffrage, and in September 1947 Argentine women won the right to vote.

Eva then formed the Female Perónist Party, which by 1951 had five hundred thousand members. Thousands of Argentine women have credited Eva's example as a reason for their becoming involved in politics. In 1951 she seemed ready to run for vice president beside her husband. The huge base of women, the poor, and workers assured them victory. Her declining health, however, forced her to turn down the nomination. Perón won the election by over 30 percent, but when Eva died the following year, Perón's authoritarian rule and bad economic policies lost him support, and a military junta forced him into exile.

Eva Perón's life story is an amazing one, but what happened following her death is just as extraordinary. Before the massive monument intended to hold her embalmed body could be built, the military seized power, and her body disappeared. Seventeen years later the generals finally revealed that it was in a tomb in Milan, Italy. Juan Perón, living in Spain with his third wife, had the body exhumed and brought to Spain, where he kept it in his house. Perón returned to Argentina in 1973 and won the presidential election, but died the following year. His wife, Isabel Perón, succeeded him as president. Juan and Eva's bodies were briefly displayed together at his funeral and then, finally, buried.

QUESTIONS FOR ANALYSIS

1. Why do you think Eva Perón was adored by the Argentine people when she died?
2. What were some of the welfare and government programs that Eva Perón promoted?

Source: Nicholas Fraser and Marysa Navarro, *Evita: The Real Life of Eva Perón* (New York: Norton, 1976).

• **Eva Perón waves to supporters from the balcony of the presidential palace, Casa Rosada, in Buenos Aires, on October 17, 1951.** (Clarin/AP Images)

Justice for the Victims of Chile's General Pinochet
With their faces covered with death masks, demonstrators outside Britain's High Court in 2000 hold up crosses carrying pictures of the "Disappeared"—the thousands kidnapped and allegedly murdered between 1973 and 1988 under the military dictatorship of General Pinochet. The High Court ruled against extraditing Pinochet to Spain to stand trial, but he was finally charged with torture and murder when he returned to Chile. (Dan Chung/Reuters New-Media Inc./Corbis)

movements that were trying to replicate Fidel Castro's successful revolution in Cuba.

Venezuela's economy grew throughout the twentieth century. By 1970 Venezuela was the wealthiest country in Latin America and one of the twenty richest in the world. Following the 1973 global oil crisis, oil prices skyrocketed, and Venezuela's oil revenues also soared until 1978, when the GDP began to fall. This drop was exacerbated by the collapse of global oil prices in the mid-1980s. There is still much debate over the reason for this decline following seventy years of sustained growth. One answer may be found in the government's massive public spending spree. Venezuela's leaders assumed, like the leaders of many other oil-rich countries such as Nigeria, that the price of oil would never go down. Oil money would always be available to pay off the large external debts they were accumulating. Second, the country did not invest its increased oil revenues in alternative industries that could diversify the economy and pay the bills should oil prices decline. Third, while oil revenues grew, exports of other goods and raw materials declined, leaving Venezuela again more dependent on oil. And fourth, Venezuela cut back oil production, sensing a need to horde its supplies even though new explorations had revealed massive reserves.

In the 1980s and 1990s Venezuela experienced one political crisis after another as the economy declined, poverty and crime rose, and corruption, always a problem in the country, flourished. A succession of events in the late 1980s and early 1990s—including riots in Caracas in February 1989 that left as many as three thousand dead, two attempted military coups in 1992, and the impeachment of then president Carlos Pérez for corruption in 1993—led to the election of Rafael Caldera (1916–2009) as president in 1994. Caldera had served previously as president from 1969 to 1974. One of his first acts in office was to grant a pardon to Hugo Chávez (b. 1954) for his role in the first of the 1992 military coup attempts.

Chávez succeeded Caldera as president in 1998 and immediately launched a "Bolivarian revolution," which included a new constitution, adopted in December 1999, and changed the country's official name to the Bolivarian Republic of Venezuela. The long and complicated new constitution guarantees, among other things, free education to all through college, universal suffrage, social security, free health care, a clean environment, gender equality, the right to property, and the rights of minorities, particularly Venezuela's native peoples, to maintain their traditional cultures, religions, and languages.

Chávez has labeled his efforts "socialism for the twenty-first century," and he refers to his socialist ideology as Bolivarianism. His first action was to rid the government of the old guard and to fill positions of power with his supporters. He then moved to clean up corruption and to redistribute Venezuela's oil revenues to the poor and underprivileged through social programs outlined in the constitution. Despite a 2002 coup attempt, Chávez was re-elected to a second term in December 2006. His power base has changed significantly since his first election victory, and his Bolivarian revolution has alienated most of the upper and middle classes who used to support him. To his credit, the poverty rate in Venezuela has dropped from 55 percent before he took office in 1998 to 28 percent in 2008. It is no wonder that the poorest workers continue to support him.

Since 2006 Chávez has turned more and more toward a socialist agenda and also to a position of absolute power. A referendum in February 2009 eliminated term limits, making it possible for him to remain in office indefinitely. Despite the human rights guarantees in the new constitution, various international organizations have condemned Chávez's human rights record, including the weakening of democratic institutions and the harassment or arrest of political opponents. Economically, Chávez has received much criticism for his overdependence on oil to fund the country's economy. In foreign relations Chávez has sought closer relations with other South American countries, while loudly and frequently condemning the United States, globalization, and open market economies.

The most dramatic developments in Central America occurred in Nicaragua. In 1979 a Socialist political party, the Sandinista National Liberation Front (FSLN), joined with a broad coalition of liberals, Socialists, and Marxist revolutionaries to drive long-time dictator Anastasio Somoza (1925–1980) from power. A multipartisan junta — a coalition of political leaders — then led the country from 1979 to 1985. These leaders wanted genuine political and economic independence from the United States, as well as thoroughgoing land reform, some nationalized industry, and friendly ties with Communist countries. In a general election that was universally described by impartial international observers as free and fair, the FSLN candidate Daniel Ortega (b. 1945) won the presidency for his Sandinista Party with 67 percent of the vote and took office in January 1985.

The Sandinista government and its policies infuriated the Reagan administration in the United States, which sought to overthrow it by creating a counter-revolutionary mercenary army, the Contras, and supplying it with military aid funded illegally through military weapons sales to Iran. After years of civil war, the Nicaraguan economy collapsed, and the Sandinista government's popularity eventually declined. The Sandinistas surrendered power when they were defeated in free elections by a coalition of opposition parties in 1990.

In elections in November 2006 Nicaraguans re-elected Ortega, the FSLN candidate, as president, and he continued to hold that position in 2011. He has remained an outspoken opponent of what he perceives as Western (especially American) imperialism. He has publicly praised controversial leaders such as Iranian president Mahmoud Ahmadinejad (see page 1003) and Venezuela's Hugo Chávez, and observed that capitalism was in its "death throes" during the 2008–2009 global economic crisis.

The Reagan administration also helped engineer a 1986 coup in Haiti, where "Papa Doc" Duvalier, followed by his son, "Baby Doc," had for decades ruled in one of the most repressive dictatorships in the Americas, with U.S. support. Although "Baby Doc" was forced into exile, the country experienced a period of violence and disorder until semi-fair elections were held in 1994 with the help of U.S. military intervention. Over the next ten years, however, Haiti remained unstable with a succession of disputed elections and an increase in violence and human rights abuses. A rebellion broke out in 2004 in the northern part of the country and soon spread to the capital. Then president Jean-Bertrand Aristide (who had previously served as president for eight months in 1991 and again for two years from 1994 to 1996) was forced to flee the country. A United Nations Stabilization Mission was sent to Haiti following the 2004 rebellion to preserve the peace and maintain stability.

Following a round of controversial elections in May 2006, René Préval (b. 1943) became Haiti's president. Préval had some success in improving the economy over the next two years, but in April 2008 widespread food riots broke out across the country. Préval successfully defused the demonstrations by lowering the price of rice. Minor successes in improving the economy or the prices of basic commodities lost all significance when Haiti, already the Western Hemisphere's poorest country, experienced one of the deadliest earthquakes in world history. On January 12, 2010, a catastrophic magnitude 7.0 earthquake rocked the small nation, killing perhaps as many as 316,000 people and leaving 1 to 2 million Haitians homeless. Although the initial reaction from the international community was swift and generous, a year later hundreds of thousands of Haitians continued to live in makeshift tent cities, basic services had not been restored, and there were regular outbreaks of cholera and other diseases due to the lack of clean water and proper sanitation. Widespread corruption, the absence of efficient government services, the inability to dispense relief aid effectively, and the failure of some donor nations to fulfill their monetary pledges for reconstruction have resulted in a slow recovery for this tiny island nation.

Pan-Latin American Unity

In the 1990s Latin America's popularly elected governments relaxed economic relations with other countries, moving decisively from tariff protection and economic nationalism toward free markets and international trade. In so doing, they revitalized their economies and registered solid gains. In 1994 Mexico joined with the United States and Canada in the North American Free Trade Agreement (NAFTA). Hoping to copy the success of the European Union, twelve South American countries (Brazil, Argentina, Paraguay, Uruguay, Venezuela, Bolivia, Colombia, Ecuador, Peru, Guyana, Suriname, and Chile) met in Cuzco, Peru, in December 2004 and signed the Cuzco Declaration, announcing the formation of the Union of South American Nations (UNSAN). The Constitutive Treaty formally establishing the union was signed on May 23, 2008, in Brasília, Brazil. The union is intended to provide a free-trade zone for its members and to compete economically with the United States and the European Community. In March 2011 UNSAN representatives met in Quito, Ecuador, to set in motion the formal operations of the union, electing Colombia's Maria Emma Majia and Venezuelan Ali Rodriguez as co-secretaries general of the organization.

Queen Elizabeth Visits Ghana Britain's Queen Elizabeth II pays an official visit to Ghana, the former Gold Coast colony, in 1961. Accompanying the queen at the colorful welcoming ceremony is Ghana's popular Kwame Nkrumah, who was educated in black colleges in the United States and led Ghana's breakthrough to independence in 1957. (Bettmann/Corbis)

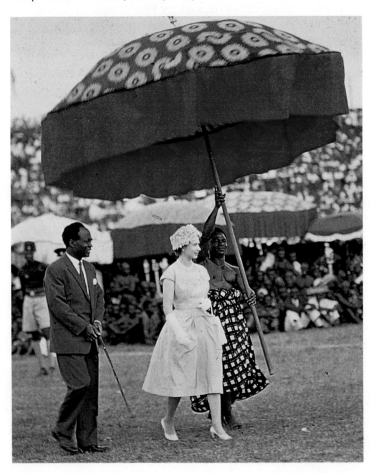

Nationalism in Sub-Saharan Africa

☐ What factors influenced decolonization in sub-Saharan Africa after World War II?

Most of sub-Saharan Africa won political independence fairly rapidly after World War II. By 1964 only Portugal's colonies and white-dominated southern Africa remained beyond the reach of African nationalists. The rise of independent states in sub-Saharan Africa resulted directly from both a reaction against Western imperialism and the growth of African nationalism.

The Growth of African Nationalism

Western intrusion was the critical factor in the development of African nationalism, as it had been in Asia and the Middle East. But two things were different about Africa. First, because the imperial system and Western education did not solidify in Africa until after 1900 (see pages 761–767), national movements began to come of age only in the 1920s and reached maturity after 1945. Second, Africa's multiplicity of ethnic groups, coupled with imperial boundaries that often bore no resemblance to existing ethnic boundaries, greatly complicated the development of political — as distinct from cultural — nationalism. Was a modern national state to be based on ethnic or clan loyalties (as it had been in France and Germany)? Was it to be a continent-wide union of all African peoples? Or would the multiethnic territories arbitrarily carved out by competing European empires become the new African nations? Only after 1945 did a tentative answer emerge.

A few educated West Africans in British colonies had articulated a kind of black nationalism before 1914. But the first real impetus came from the United States and the British West Indies. The most renowned participant in this "black nationalism" was W. E. B. Du Bois (1868–1963). The first black to receive a Ph.D. from Harvard, this brilliant writer and historian organized Pan-African congresses in Paris during the Versailles Peace Conference in 1919 and in Brussels in 1921. **Pan-Africanists** sought black solidarity and, eventually, a vast self-governing union of all African peoples. The flamboyant Jamaican-born Marcus Garvey (1887–1940) was the most influential Pan-Africanist voice in Africa. Young, educated Africans rallied to his call of "Africa for the Africans" and European expulsion from Africa.

In the 1920s many educated French and British Africans experienced a strong surge of pride and cultural nationalism. African intellectuals in Europe formulated and articulated the rich idea of *négritude*, or blackness:

racial pride, self-confidence, and joy in black creativity and the black spirit. This westernized African elite pressed for better access to government jobs, modest steps toward self-government, and an end to humiliating discrimination. They claimed the right to speak for ordinary Africans and denounced the government-supported chiefs as "Uncle Toms," yet their demands remained moderate.

The mass protests that accompanied the deprivations of the Great Depression, in particular the **cocoa holdups** of 1930–1931 and 1937–1938, proved to be the catalyst for the development of African nationalism. Cocoa completely dominated the Gold Coast's economy. As prices plummeted after 1929, cocoa farmers refused to sell their beans to the large British firms that fixed prices and monopolized the export trade. Instead, the farmers organized cooperatives to cut back production and sell their crops directly to European and American chocolate manufacturers. The cocoa holdups succeeded in mobilizing much of the population against the foreign companies and demonstrated the power of mass organization and mass protest. Mass movements for national independence were not far behind.

Achieving Independence with New Leaders

The repercussions of the Second World War in black Africa greatly accelerated the changes begun in the 1930s. Many African soldiers who served in India had been powerfully impressed by Indian nationalism. As African mines and plantations strained to meet wartime demands, towns mushroomed into cities where ramshackle housing, inflation, and shortages of consumer goods created discontent and hardship.

Western imperialism also changed. Both the British and the French acknowledged the need for rapid social and economic improvement in their colonies; for the first time both began sending money and aid on a large scale. The principle of self-government was written into the United Nations charter and was supported by Great Britain's postwar Labour government. Thus the key question for Great Britain's various African colonies was their rate of progress toward self-government. The British and the French were in no rush. But a new breed of African leader was emerging. Impatient and insistent, these spokesmen for modern African nationalism were remarkably successful: by 1964 almost all of western, eastern, and central Africa had achieved statehood, generally without much bloodshed (Map 33.2).

These new postwar African leaders formed an elite by virtue of their advanced European or American education, and they were profoundly influenced by Western thought. But compared with the interwar generation of educated Africans, they were more radical and

☐ NATIONALISM IN BLACK AFRICA

1919	Du Bois organizes first Pan-African congress
1920s	Cultural nationalism grows among Africa's educated elites
1929	Great Depression brings economic hardship and discontent
1930–1931	Gold Coast farmers organize first cocoa holdups
1939–1945	World War II accelerates political and economic change
1951	Nkrumah and Convention People's Party win national elections in Ghana (former Gold Coast)
1957	Nkrumah leads Ghana to independence
1958	De Gaulle offers commonwealth status to France's African territories; only Guinea chooses independence
1960	Nigeria becomes an independent state
1966	Ghana's Nkrumah deposed in military coup
1967	Ibos secede from Nigeria to form state of Biafra
1980	Blacks rule Zimbabwe (former Southern Rhodesia) after long civil war with white settlers
1984	South Africa's whites issue cosmetic reforms but maintain racial segregation and discrimination
1989–1990	South African government begins process of reform; black leader Nelson Mandela freed from prison
1994	Nelson Mandela elected president of South Africa

humbler in social origin. Among them were former schoolteachers, union leaders, government clerks, and unemployed students, as well as lawyers and prizewinning poets.

Postwar African leaders accepted prevailing colonial boundaries to avoid border disputes and achieve freedom as soon as possible. Sensing a loss of power, traditional rulers sometimes became the new leaders' worst political enemies. Skillfully, the new leaders channeled postwar hope and discontent into support for mass political organizations. These organizations staged gigantic protests and became political parties.

• **Pan-Africanists** People, such as W. E. B. Du Bois and Marcus Garvey, who promoted solidarity among all blacks and the eventual self-governing union of all African peoples.

• **cocoa holdups** Mass protests in the 1930s by Gold Coast producers of cocoa who refused to sell their beans to British firms and instead sold them directly to European and American chocolate manufacturers.

Viewpoints

Ghanaian and South African Leaders on Black Nationalism

• *Kwame Nkrumah led the British Gold Coast colony to independence in 1957, making it the first sub-Saharan colony to free itself from colonialism. Elected the first president of Ghana, Nkrumah is considered the father of independent Africa. His independence day speech on March 6, 1957, galvanized African nationalists across Africa, and within ten years nearly the entire continent had been liberated. One exception was South Africa, where the white apartheid regime held onto power until 1994, when Nelson Mandela became president. In May 1996 Deputy President Thabo Mbeki delivered his "I am an African" speech to celebrate the adoption of a new South African constitution that ended all discrimination.*

Kwame Nkrumah, Ghanaian Independence Day Speech

"At long last the battle has ended. And thus Ghana, your beloved country, is free forever. . . . I . . . thank the chiefs and people of this country, the youth, the farmers, the women who have so nobly fought and won this battle. I want to thank the various ex-servicemen who have also struggled with me in this mighty task of freeing our country from foreign rule and imperialism. . . .

From today, we must change our attitude—our mind. We must realize that from now on we are no more a colony but a free and independent people. But . . . that also entails hard work. I am depending upon the millions of people to help me to reshape the destiny of this county.

We are prepared to build an African nation that will be respected by every other nation in the world. . . . I can see that you are here in your millions, so that we can prove to the world that when an African is given the chance he can show the world that he is somebody. . . . We shall show the world that the African is ready to fight his own battle and that the African man is capable of managing his own affairs. . . .

We have done the battle and we again rededicate ourselves not only in the struggle to emancipate all the countries in Africa; our independence is meaningless unless it is linked up with the total liberation of the African continent.

Ghana is free forever!"

Thabo Mbeki, "I Am an African"

"On an occasion such as this, we should, perhaps, start from the beginning. So, let me begin. I am an African. . . .

I have seen what happens when one person has superiority of force over another, when the stronger appropriate to themselves the prerogative even to annul the injunction that God created all men and women in His image. I know what it signifies when race and colour are used to determine who is human and who subhuman. I have seen the destruction of all sense of self-esteem, the consequent striving to be what one is not, simply to acquire some of the benefits which those who had imposed themselves as masters had ensured that they enjoy. I have experience of the situation in which race and colour is used to enrich some and impoverish the rest. . . .

All this I know and know to be true because I am an African!

Because of that, I am also able to state this fundamental truth: that I am born of a people who are heroes and heroines. I am born of a people who would not tolerate oppression.

Whatever the setbacks of the moment, nothing can stop us now! Whatever the difficulties, Africa shall be at peace! However improbable it may sound to the sceptics, Africa will prosper!

Whoever we may be, whatever our immediate interest, however much baggage we carry from our past, however much we have been caught by the fashion of cynicism and loss of faith in the capacity of the people, let us say today: Nothing can stop us now!"

Sources: Felix M. Kiruthu, *Voices of Freedom: Great African Independence Speeches* (Colorado Springs: International Academic Publishers, 2001), pp. 27–29; Thabo Mbeki, "Statement of Deputy Resident TM Mbeki . . . on the Occasion of the Adoption . . . of 'The Republic of South Africa Constitutional Bill 1996.'" Reprinted by permission of the South African Government Information website.

QUESTIONS FOR ANALYSIS

1. What does Nkrumah believe Ghanaians must do now that they have independence?
2. What is it that gives Mbeki the confidence to say that now Africa will prosper and be at peace?
3. What does it mean to be African according to these documents?

The Opening of Parliament in Ghana As part of an ancient ritual, two medicine men pour out sacred oil and call on the gods to bless the work of the Second Parliament and President Kwame Nkrumah, standing on the right. The combination of time-honored customs and modern political institutions was characteristic of African states after they secured independence. (Wide World Photos/AP Images)

Eventually they came to power by winning the general elections that the colonial governments belatedly called to choose their successors.

Ghana Shows the Way

Perhaps the most charismatic of this generation of African leaders was Kwame Nkrumah (1909–1972). Nkrumah spent ten years studying in the United States, where he was deeply influenced by European Socialists and Marcus Garvey. He returned to the Gold Coast after the Second World War and entered politics. Under his leadership the Gold Coast — which he rechristened "Ghana" — became the first independent African state to emerge from colonialism. (See "Viewpoints: Ghanaian and South African Leaders on Black Nationalism.")

Nkrumah came to power by building a radical mass party that appealed particularly to modern elements — former servicemen, market women, union members, urban toughs, and cocoa farmers. He and his party injected the joy and enthusiasm of religious revivals into their rallies and propaganda: "Self-Government Now" was their credo, secular salvation the promise.

Rejecting halfway measures — "We prefer self-government with danger to servitude in tranquility" — Nkrumah and his Convention People's Party staged strikes and riots. Arrested, the "Deliverer of Ghana" campaigned from jail and saw his party win a smashing victory in the 1951 national elections. Called from

prison to head the transitional government, Nkrumah and his nationalist party defeated both westernized moderates and more traditional political rivals in free elections. By 1957 Nkrumah had achieved worldwide fame and influence as Ghana became independent.

After Ghana's breakthrough, independence for other African colonies followed rapidly. The main problem in some colonies, such as Algeria, was the permanent white settlers, not the colonial officials. Wherever white settlers were numerous, as in Kenya, they sought to preserve their privileged position. But only in Southern Rhodesia and South Africa were whites numerous enough to prevail for long. Southern Rhodesian whites declared independence illegally in 1965 and held out until 1980, when black nationalists won a long liberation struggle and renamed the country Zimbabwe. Majority rule in South Africa took even longer.

French-Speaking Regions

Decolonization took a somewhat different course in French-speaking Africa. The events in the French North African colony of Algeria in the 1950s and early 1960s help clarify France's attitude to its sub-Saharan black African colonies.

France tried hard to hold onto Indochina and Algeria after 1945. Predominantly Arabic speaking and Muslim, Algerian nationalists were emboldened by Nasser's great triumph in Egypt in 1952 and by France's

□ Mapping the Past

MAP 33.2 Decolonization in Africa, 1947 to the Present Most African territories achieved statehood by the mid-1960s, as European empires passed away, unlamented.

ANALYZING THE MAP How many African states achieved independence after 1945? How many experienced some sort of postcolonial conflict?

CONNECTIONS How did the imperialist legacy serve to complicate the transition to stable, independent nations in Africa and Latin America?

defeat in Indochina in 1954 (see page 988). But Algeria's large, and mostly Catholic, European population—known as the **pieds-noirs** ("black feet") because its members wore black shoes instead of sandals—was determined to keep Algeria part of France. In November 1954 Algeria's anticolonial movement, the **National Liberation Front** (FLN), began a long, bitter, and bloody war for independence. Besides being the most violent of the anticolonial wars in Africa, the war also nearly tore France apart as French anticolonialists fought with French pro-imperialists. Finally, in 1962, the FLN won, and Algeria became an independent state. An estimated 900,000 of the 1,025,000 Eu-

ropeans and indigenous Jews fled Algeria in the first few months of 1962.

While the terrible war raged on in Algeria, France upped its aid to its sub-Saharan African colonies, but independence remained a dirty word until Charles de Gaulle came to power in 1958. Seeking to head off radical nationalists and receiving the crucial support of moderate black leaders, de Gaulle chose a divide-and-rule strategy. He divided the French West Africa and French Equatorial Africa federations into thirteen separate governments, thus creating a "French commonwealth." Plebiscites were called in each territory to ratify the new arrangement. An affirmative vote meant can Republic, and Guinea-Bissau—began to pull back from the abyss. The Ivory Coast experienced years of civil war after its first-ever military coup in 1999. Rebels continue to control the country's northern half, but they and the government met and signed the Ouagadougou Agreement in March 2007, committing themselves to disarmament, reunification, and elections sometime in the future. In the meantime, Laurent Gbagbo held the presidency from October 2000 to April 2011. Gbagbo lost in elections held in November 2010 but refused to turn over the presidency to the winner, Alassane Ouattara. A tragic second civil war then broke out, which also saw military intervention by troops of the African Union, France, and the United Nations. Gbagbo was finally arrested on April 11, 2011, and Ouattara assumed the presidency.

Clearly, democracy is still a long struggle away in many African countries. Recent populist revolutions have brought down some of North Africa's one-party authoritarian rulers, but Eritrea, Ethiopia, Equatorial Guinea, Zimbabwe, and Swaziland have increasingly brutal dictatorships. Sudan's authoritarian Islamic rulers ended their long civil war with the Christians and animists in the south, only to have pro-government Arab militias attack Muslim ethnic Africans in the western Darfur region. The genocidal attacks have caused tens of thousands of deaths and an estimated 2 million refugees.

In January 2011, 98 percent of the electorate in southern Sudan voted to break away from Sudan and form a new country. If the results are upheld, the new country of South Sudan will come into being on July 9, 2011. Unlike the generally poor countries across Africa's Sahel region, South Sudan has a major revenue source: it possesses around 80 percent of Sudan's oil wells. Nearly the entire petroleum infrastructure, however, is in the north. According to the terms of the peace agreement, Sudan and South Sudan will share oil revenues equally. There remain important questions, therefore, about the transparency of the process. Many in the south worry that after the crude oil heads north to the refineries, revenues from the sale of the refined petroleum products will not be reported properly.

Congo-Kinshasa, Rwanda, and Burundi remain perilously close to the abyss of the horrendous violence that they experienced in the 1990s. The Second Congo War in Congo-Kinshasa that began in 1998 has involved nine African nations and twenty-five armed groups, and it has affected more than half of the country's 71 million people. While peace accords supposedly brought an end to the war in 2003, there has been no end to the violence in the eastern part of the country, where the war continues. By 2007 an estimated 5.4 million had died, and hundreds of thousands more have died in the four years since, making it the world's deadliest conflict

since World War II. In this war rape and sexual violence have become weapons. Although it is impossible to know precisely, observers place the number of women and young girls who have been raped by soldiers from both sides of the conflict in the tens of thousands. While the war is complex and the motivations of the many countries involved, including Rwanda, Uganda, and Burundi, are varied, possession of the Congo's abundant natural resources—including timber, diamonds, and other minerals of all kinds in great quantities—is sought by all the combatants. While the Congo is nearly the poorest country in the world, along with Burundi and Somalia, it is arguably the richest country in the world in terms of raw minerals and other natural resources, with the total mineral value estimated at $24 trillion.

Since the Somali civil war in 1991, no central government has existed to rule over this country that bends around the Horn of Africa. In effect, there is no Somalia, which has been labeled a "failed state." Somalia has some of the worst poverty and highest rates of violence in the world. Somali pirates operating off the Horn of Africa have been seriously disrupting international shipping since 2007.

Second Congo War, 1998 to the Present

Riots following the bitterly contested and questionable re-election of Mwai Kibaki (b. 1931) as president of Kenya on December 27, 2007, resulted in over 250 deaths in the first week after the election. Often considered one of Africa's most stable nations, Kenya unexpectedly erupted into chaos, with interethnic violence forcing hundreds of thousands to flee their homes. Former UN Secretary General Kofi Annan and a group of "eminent African personalities" came to Kenya to mediate an end to the election violence. They successfully promoted a power-sharing agreement known as the National Accord and Reconciliation Act 2008. Kenya remains heavily dependent on agriculture and tourism, and its tourism industry was hurt by the election violence of 2007 and the global economic downturn in 2008–2009. The economy picked up again in 2010; with significant increases in the tourism, telecommunications, transport, and agricultural export industries, Kenya's GDP grew at over 4 percent in 2010.

Many of the most stable democratic countries are in southern Africa. Botswana, South Africa, Zambia, and Namibia have all made the transition from

> "Europe is literally the creation of the Third World. The wealth which smothers her is that which was stolen from the underdeveloped peoples."
>
> **FRANTZ FANON**

colonialism to democracy. With a few stops and starts, Malawi, Nigeria, Niger, and Madagascar are also making good progress. Much of the political progress is closely linked to economic progress. As Zimbabwe's authoritarian regime under Robert Mugabe (b. 1924) has created a corrupt, immoral human rights nightmare, it has also suffered total economic collapse. More politically stable countries such as Ghana have seen their economies grow and foreign investments increase. Countries in western and central Africa may soon undergo revolutionary political and economic change as a result of the oil and natural gas boom in those regions. Chad, Mauritania, Angola, Nigeria, Gabon, São Tomé and Príncipe, Congo Brazzaville, and Equatorial Guinea could all benefit from complete economic turnarounds, and others will follow.

Interpreting the Experiences of the Emerging World

☐ How do contemporary writers seek to understand and represent the common experiences of peoples in the emerging world?

Having come of age during and after the struggle for political emancipation, numerous intellectuals embraced the vision of Third World solidarity, and some argued that genuine independence and freedom from outside control required a total break with the former colonial powers and a total rejection of Western values. This was the message of Frantz Fanon (1925–1961) in his powerful study of colonial peoples, *The Wretched of the Earth* (1961).

According to Fanon, a French-trained black psychiatrist from the Caribbean island of Martinique, decolonization is always a violent and totally consuming process whereby one "species" of men, the colonizers, is completely replaced by an absolutely different species — the colonized, the wretched of the earth. During decolonization the colonized masses mock colonial values, "insult them, and vomit them up" in a psychic purge.

Fanon believed that throughout Africa and Asia the former imperialists and their local collabora-

tors — the "white men with black faces" — remained the enemy:

> During the colonial period the people are called upon to fight against oppression; after national liberation, they are called upon to fight against poverty, illiteracy, and underdevelopment. The struggle, they say, goes on.
>
> . . . We are not blinded by the moral reparation of national independence; nor are we fed by it. The wealth of the imperial countries is our wealth too. . . . Europe is literally the creation of the Third World. The wealth which smothers her is that which was stolen from the underdeveloped peoples.[5]

Fanon's passionate, angry work became a sacred text for radicals attacking imperialism and struggling for liberation.

As countries gained independence and self-rule, some writers looked beyond wholesale rejection of the industrialized powers. They too were anti-imperialist, but often also activists and cultural nationalists who applied their talents to celebrating the rich histories and cultures of their peoples. Many did not hesitate to criticize their own leaders or fight oppression and corruption.

The Nigerian writer Chinua Achebe (b. 1930) rendered these themes with acute insight and vivid specificity in his short, moving novels. Achebe sought to restore his people's self-confidence by reinterpreting the past. For Achebe the "writer in a new nation" had first to embrace the "fundamental theme" that Africans had their own culture before the Europeans came and that it was the duty of writers to help Africans reclaim their past.

In *Things Fall Apart* (1958) Achebe achieved his goal by vividly bringing to life the men and women of an Ibo village at the beginning of the twentieth century, with all their virtues and frailties. Woven into the story are the proverbs and wisdom of a sophisticated people and the beauty of a vanishing world:

> [The white man] says that our customs are bad; and our own brothers who have taken up his religion also say that our customs are bad. How do you think we can fight when our own brothers have turned against us? The white man is very clever. He came quietly and peaceably with his religion. We were amused at his foolishness and allowed him to stay. Now he has won our brothers, and our clan can no longer act like one. He has put a knife on the things that held us together and we have fallen apart.[6]

In later novels Achebe portrays the postindependence disillusionment of many writers and intellectuals, which reflected trends in many developing nations in the 1960s and 1970s: the rulers seemed increasingly corrupted by Western luxury and estranged from the rural masses.

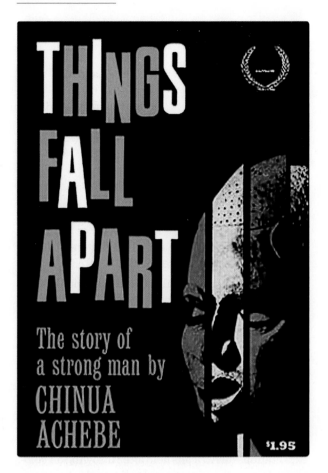

From the 1970s onward Achebe was active in the struggle for democratic government in Nigeria. In his novel *Anthills of the Savannah* (1989) he calls upon Africa to take responsibility and realize that widespread corruption is frustrating hopes of progress and genuine independence. Yet in recent essays and speeches he also returns to his earlier theme of the West's enduring low opinion of Africa — ever the "dark continent," the savage, non-Western "other world."

The Nobel Prize–winning novelist V. S. Naipaul, born in Trinidad in 1932 of Indian parents, also castigated governments in the developing countries for corruption, ineptitude, and self-deception. Another of Naipaul's recurring themes is the poignant loneliness and homelessness of people uprooted by colonialism and Western expansion.

Things Fall Apart Published in 1958, Chinua Achebe's most famous novel concerns the changing world of an Ibo village in late-nineteenth-century Africa. Achebe's powerful novels focus on complex and believable individuals caught up in the unfolding drama of colonialism, independence, and nation building in Africa. (First paperback edition cover: Chinua Achebe, *Things Fall Apart* [London: William Heinemann, 1958])

CONNECTIONS

In the last half of the twentieth century many Latin America countries broke free from their neocolonial ties with the United States and Europe. This freedom gave them the economic independence they desired to go along with the political independence they had gained in the early 1800s. Nationalist leaders in sub-Saharan Africa meanwhile were busy gathering the masses behind them to push for political independence from the colonial powers that had occupied their lands during the scramble for Africa in the late 1800s. Leaders on both continents had to decide whether to take sides in the superpower conflict of the Cold War. And when the Cold War ended, their citizens demanded more civil and human rights, democracy, and an end to corruption and rule from above.

We will see in the last chapter that the countries of Africa and Latin America played important roles in the newly formed United Nations, setting agendas in matters that were of the most concern to them: poverty, illiteracy, fair trade, globalization. The populations of these countries and those of Asia make up two-thirds of the world's citizens. In Chapter 34 we will discuss the global changes, developments, and problems that directly affect these people every day: disease, the environment, education, telecommunications, urban growth, and the agricultural revolution.

CHAPTER REVIEW

□ **What kind of government was most prevalent in Latin America during the twentieth century, and how did this change after 1980? (p. 1008)**

Politically throughout most of the twentieth century, Latin American countries were ruled by conservative, authoritarian leaders, some of them harsh and cruel dictators supported by the West. Economic nationalism was successfully practiced in countries such as Mexico and Brazil, but after the Cuban Revolution, conservatives established military rule across most of Latin America as a way to block the spread of communism. Marxist socialist reforms were implemented in Nicaragua, Chile, and Venezuela, but most successfully and thoroughly in Cuba under Fidel Castro. By the end of the 1970s only Costa Rica, Venezuela, Colombia, and Mexico had some form of democratic rule. In the 1980s much of Latin America turned toward free elections, civil liberties, and freer markets, abandoning the long-standing commitment to economic nationalism.

□ **What factors influenced decolonization in sub-Saharan Africa after World War II? (p. 1018)**

Sub-Saharan Africa decolonized rapidly after World War II, fueled by the experience of Africans during the war and by a black nationalist movement influenced by W. E. B. Du Bois. Reacting against imperialism, Pan-Africanists such as Marcus Garvey promoted the expulsion of Europeans from Africa and the eventual establishment of a unified Africa. The Great Depression and the Gold Coast cocoa holdups of the 1930s accelerated independence, and in black Africa a generation of nationalist leaders successfully guided colonial territories to self-rule by the middle of the 1960s. The father of independent Africa was Kwame Nkrumah, a Ghanaian who, like many African nationalists, had spent many years studying in the West. He returned to Ghana after World War II and led a successful independence movement against British rule. Decolonization took a different path in the countries of French-speaking Africa. While France fought a vicious war against Algerian nationalists in North Africa, it sought more peaceful separation from its black African colonies. Most of the former French colonies elected to remain French commonwealths. Decolonization in the Belgian Congo, alone among the colonies of French-speaking sub-Saharan black Africa, was violent and chaotic.

KEY TERMS

economic nationalism (p. 1008)

Cuban Revolution (p. 1011)

Pan-Africanists (p. 1018)

cocoa holdups (p. 1019)

pieds-noirs (p. 1022)

National Liberation Front (p. 1022)

Native Land Act (p. 1026)

apartheid (p. 1026)

African National Congress (ANC) (p. 1026)

□ **What are some of the common features of independent Africa since 1960? (p. 1023)**

By the mid-1960s nearly all African countries had won independence. The two largest colonial powers, Britain and France, had tried, although belatedly, to set up democratic governments in their former colonies. The new leaders of these countries, however, soon turned their backs on democracy and resorted to authoritarian one-party rule. Opposition parties were outlawed, and political opponents were jailed, sent into exile, or killed. Many of these early dictators were overthrown by military juntas, as happened, for example, in Ghana and Nigeria. Despite the high expectations all Africans held after throwing off colonial rule, most have continued to live under harsh and corrupt authoritarian governments.

□ **How do contemporary writers seek to understand and represent the common experiences of peoples in the emerging world? (p. 1032)**

Many artists in the emerging world have described the common experiences of peoples living under colonial rule and in newly independent nations. Frantz Fanon in *The Wretched of the Earth* urged Third World solidarity and a rejection of Western values. One of the most famous artists is Chinua Achebe, a Nigerian writer whose novels seek to reinterpret the past by emphasizing the African cultures that existed before the Europeans arrived and tried to force their own values on the peoples they colonized. V. S. Naipaul, like Achebe, explores the disillusionment felt by many postcolonial people with the corruption and authoritarian rule of postindependence governments. Naipaul's novels also deal with the loneliness and homelessness of people uprooted by colonialism.

SUGGESTED READING

Beck, Roger B. *The History of South Africa*. 2000. Introduction to South African history with emphasis on the twentieth century.

Collins, Robert O., and James M. Burns. *A History of Sub-Saharan Africa*. 2007. Clearly written introduction to the continent's history.

Davidson, Basil. *The Black Man's Burden: Africa and the Curse of the Nation State*. 1993. A thought-provoking reconsideration by a noted historian.

Du Bois, W. E. B. *The World and Africa*. 1947. A classic text by the distinguished black American thinker.

Kenyatta, Jomo. *Facing Mount Kenya*. 1953. Powerful commentary and autobiography by one of Africa's foremost revolutionary and political leaders.

Lowenthal, Abraham F., and Gregory F. Treverton, eds. *Latin America in a New World*. 1994. Analyzes the move toward regional cooperation and market economies.

Meade, Teresa A. *A History of Modern Latin America: 1800 to the Present*. 2009. A comprehensive history and analysis of the continent and its peoples.

Meredith, Martin. *The Fate of Africa: A History of Fifty Years of Independence*. 2006. A very accessible study of modern independent Africa that spans the entire continent.

Reid, Richard J. *A History of Modern Africa: 1800 to the Present*. 2008. A concise, clearly written history of modern Africa from independence to colonialism to independence once more.

Skidmore, Thomas, Peter Smith, and James Green. *Modern Latin America*, 9th ed. 2009. The classic study of the region.

NOTES

1. Quoted in Jonathan C. Brown, *A Brief History of Argentina*, 2d ed. (New York: Facts On File, 2010), p. 243.
2. Quoted in R. Hallett, *Africa Since 1875: A Modern History* (Ann Arbor: University of Michigan Press, 1974), pp. 378–379.
3. *Chicago Tribune*, May 3, 1994, section 1, p. 5.
4. D. Birmingham and P. Martin, eds., *History of Central Africa: The Contemporary Years Since 1960* (London: Routledge, 1998), p. 59.
5. F. Fanon, *The Wretched of the Earth* (New York: Grove Press, 1968), pp. 43, 93–94, 97, 102.
6. C. Achebe, *Things Fall Apart* (London: Heinemann, 2000), pp. 124–125.

For practice quizzes and other study tools, visit the **Online Study Guide** at bedfordstmartins.com/mckayworld.

For primary sources from this period, see *Sources of World Societies*, **Second Edition**.

For Web sites, images, and documents related to topics in this chapter, visit **Make History** at bedfordstmartins.com/mckayworld.

• **Indian UN Peacekeeper** An officer with the first all-female unit of United Nations peacekeepers stands before her troops in Liberia's capital, Monrovia, in January 2007. More than a hundred peacekeepers were stationed in Liberia following a brutal fourteen-year civil war, and the female unit has become a model for the stationing of other female UN peacekeepers at troubled spots around the globe. (Issouf Sanogo/AFP/Getty Images)

34

Communism's collapse in Europe in 1991 opened a new era in world history — one that arrived with promises of peace, democracy, and economic prosperity. Millions of people still living under repressive, authoritarian, corrupt regimes were inspired to start pressing their governments for political and human rights. (See "Individuals in Society: The Dalai Lama," page 1040.) The post-1991 optimism soon faded as new tensions, conflicts, and divisions arose. Two decades later, however, the people are again taking to the streets to demand change. Africa and the Middle East have witnessed the toppling of two dictators. Perhaps more will fall, and the promises of 1991 will finally be realized.

A New Era in World History

We live in a global age. Economic cycles, international treaties and agreements, multinational organizations, and global threats connect the world's citizens in complex networks. Every day around the world billions of individuals are confronted with similarly complex global issues that impact each of them in an immediate and personal way. As we bring our history of the world's societies to a close, let us look at our interconnected planet once again, this time focusing on ordinary people and the global changes and challenges they face.

Because people living in developing nations make up at least two-thirds of the earth's population, many of the people discussed here live in the so-called Third World, where the changes and challenges of the new millennium are perhaps greatest. We should not forget, though, that there really is no Third World. There is only a set of conditions — such as poverty, disease, hunger, and unemployment — that are at their worst in the poorest or developing countries but that exist in all countries. •

Global Unity or Continued Division?

☐ What is the multipolar nature of world politics today, and how do competing nation-states address common problems?

Global Interdependence

☐ What are some of the benefits and drawbacks of increasing global interdependence?

The Growth of Cities

☐ What factors spurred the growth of cities in Africa, Asia, and Latin America, and what were some of the main consequences of urbanization in the late twentieth century?

Science and Technology: Changes and Challenges

☐ What key technological and scientific developments have had the greatest impact on life at the beginning of the new millennium?

Social Reform and Progress

☐ What social problems facing women and children are the focus of reformers in the new millennium?

Global Unity or Continued Division?

☐ What is the multipolar nature of world politics today, and how do competing nation-states address common problems?

The end of the Cold War superpower confrontation brought dramatic changes to the global political situation. Yet nation-states, the traditional building blocks of global politics, continued to exist. An astonishing aspect of recent scientific and technological achievements is the lack of any corresponding change in the way the human race governs — or fails to govern — itself. Sovereign nation-states continue to reign supreme, reinforced by enormous military power. The embryonic growth of an effective global political organization that could protect nations from themselves appears permanently arrested, although efforts to control weapons of mass destruction, global warming, and other universal threats have sometimes led to global agreements.

The United Nations

As we have seen, the rise of the nation-state and the global triumph of nationalism have been grand themes of modern world history. The independent territorial nation-state — sometimes containing separatist ethnic groups striving for nationhood in their own right — remains the fundamental political organization in the

The United Nations in Action These soldiers are part of a French battalion serving in a United Nations peacekeeping operation in Cambodia (Kampuchea), a country wracked by war and civil conflict since 1970. United Nations forces usually provide humanitarian aid as they try to preserve fragile cease-fires after warring armies agree to stop fighting. (J. F. Roussier/Sipa Press)

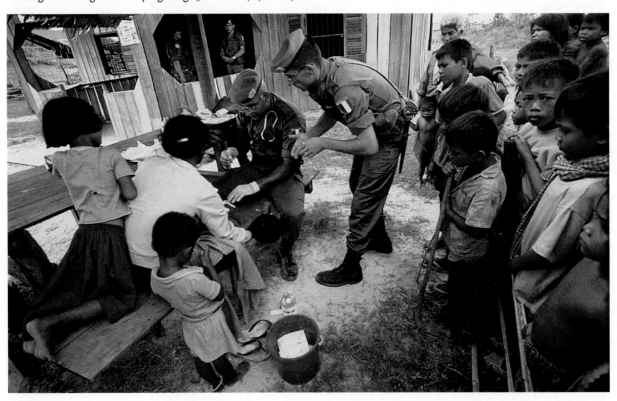

early twenty-first century. Yet as the horrors of the conflicts of the twentieth century suggested, there was a need for a form of global authority transcending sovereign states as a way to maintain peace worldwide.

With a main purpose of maintaining international peace and security, the World War II generation founded the **United Nations** in San Francisco in 1945. The UN charter prohibits any member nation from using armed force except for self-defense. The charter also gives the UN **Security Council** the authority to examine any international conflict, impose economic and political penalties on an aggressor, and use force as necessary to restore peace and security. In theory, the Security Council has the power to police the world. In practice, however, this power is severely restricted. The Security Council's five permanent members—China, France, Great Britain, Russia (formerly the Soviet Union), and the United States—have to agree on any peacekeeping action.

Every "peace-loving" state is eligible to join the United Nations and to participate in its **General Assembly**. Founded with 50 members, the General Assembly comprises 192 members in 2011. Each member state, whatever its size, has one voice and one vote on all General Assembly resolutions, but General Assembly resolutions become legally binding on states only if all five permanent members of the Security Council agree to them.

The founders of the United Nations gave voice to an emerging vision of global interdependence. According to its charter, the United Nations is "to achieve international cooperation in solving international problems of an economic, social, cultural, or humanitarian character, and in promoting and encouraging respect for human rights and for fundamental freedom for all without distinction as to race, sex, language, or religion."

During the Cold War, the original hopes for the creation of an effective world body were stymied by Security Council members, most often the Soviet Union, using their veto power to block actions they felt would harm their national interests. With the Security Council often deadlocked, the General Assembly claimed ever-greater authority. As decolonization picked up speed and the number of member states grew, a nonaligned, anticolonial African-Asian bloc emerged. Reinforced by sympathetic Latin American countries, by

the mid-1960s the bloc succeeded in organizing within the General Assembly a Third World majority that concentrated on economic and social issues.

With a large numerical majority, the developing nations succeeded in broadening the organization's mission. By the 1970s an alphabet soup of United Nations committees, specialized agencies, and affiliated international organizations were studying and promoting health, labor, agriculture, industrial development, and world trade, not to mention disarmament, control of narcotics, and preservation of endangered species.

CHRONOLOGY

1945 United Nations founded

1945–present Explosive growth of cities; rapid urbanization; increasing gap in wealth between rich and poor nations

1950s Beginning of green revolution

1970 Treaty on the Non-Proliferation of Nuclear Weapons

1980s–present HIV/AIDS global epidemic

1989 United Nations Convention on the Rights of the Child

1994 Internet becomes available to general public

1997 Chemical Weapons Convention bans the production of chemical weapons; Kyoto Protocol on global warming

2000 United Nations Millennium Project initiated

2000–2010 Warmest decade in recorded history

2001 Al-Qaeda attacks on World Trade Center and U.S. Pentagon

2003 North Korea withdraws from 1970 nonproliferation treaty; U.S.-led coalition invades Iraq; Human Genome Project completes sequencing of human genome

2004 Bombing of train station in Madrid

2005 Bombing of London subway and bus systems

2007 Assassination of Pakistani politician Benazir Bhutto

2011 U.S. begins troop drawdown in Afghanistan; bin Laden killed

---

- **United Nations** Founded in 1945, its main purpose is to maintain international peace and security; its expanded mission is to work with the international community to solve economic, social, cultural, and humanitarian problems.
- **Security Council** The UN body that has the authority to examine international conflicts, impose economic and political penalties on an aggressor, and even use force, if necessary, to restore international peace and security.
- **General Assembly** The second main body of the United Nations; each "peace-loving" state is eligible to join and participate in it.

The Dalai Lama

SHORTLY BEFORE HE DIED IN 1933, THUPTEN
Gyatso (1876–1933), the "Great Thirteenth" Dalai Lama of Tibet, had a vision of the future. He predicted that if the Tibetans did not protect their territory, their spiritual leaders would be exterminated, their property and authority would be taken away, and their people would become slaves. For fifty-seven years he had ruled over a country treated like a pawn in the "Great Game" played by Russia, Britain, and China for territory and power. He feared the Chinese the most.

After his death, a mission of high officials went in search of his successor. Tibetans believe that each succeeding Dalai Lama is the reincarnation of the previous one. In 1937 the mission came to a peasant village in northeastern Tibet to question a two-year-old boy, Tenzin Gyatso. When he passed all the tests, they took him and his family to Lhasa, the Tibetan capital. There, in 1940, he was enthroned as His Holiness the Fourteenth Dalai Lama.

In Lhasa the boy spent much of his time studying, eventually earning a doctorate in Buddhist philosophy at age twenty-five. His youth ended abruptly in October 1950, when the thirteenth Dalai Lama's vision came true: eighty thousand Chinese soldiers invaded Tibet. In November the fifteen-year-old Dalai Lama assumed full political power. In 1954 he traveled to Beijing for peace talks with Mao Zedong. Although he was impressed by Mao's promise to modernize Tibet and intrigued by socialism, he was stunned by Mao's last words to him: "But of course, religion is poison."*

This remark was deeply troubling because the Tibetans are an intensely religious people. For centuries they lived in near

● **The Dalai Lama in Germany promoting freedom for Tibet.** (Roberto Pfeill/AP Images)

isolation, practiced Buddhism, and looked to the Dalai Lama as both their political and their spiritual leader. After returning to Tibet, the Dalai Lama tried to negotiate a peaceful settlement with the Chinese, to no avail. In March 1959 the Chinese army crushed a massive demonstration in Lhasa, and the Dalai Lama had to flee for his life. The Indian prime minister, Jawaharlal Nehru, gave him political asylum, and he established a Tibetan government in exile at Dharamsala, India. More than 120,000 Tibetan refugees live there today.

Since the Chinese occupation began, all but twelve of more than six thousand monasteries in Tibet have been destroyed, and thousands of sacred treasures have been stolen or sold. An estimated three thousand political or religious prisoners are in labor camps in Tibet, and the Chinese have been directly responsible for the deaths of 1.2 million Tibetans. Over 7 million Chinese settlers have poured into Tibet. Tibetan women are routinely forced to undergo sterilization or have abortions.

To counter this destruction, the Dalai Lama has campaigned for Tibetan self-determination and basic human rights. He has established programs abroad to save the Tibetan culture and language and to shelter the refugees. There are Tibetan educational systems for refugees, a Tibetan Institute of Performing Arts, agricultural settlements for refugees, and over two hundred new monasteries to preserve Tibetan Buddhism and to train new monks. In his quest for justice, the Dalai Lama travels around the world seeking support from world leaders, institutions, and common citizens. Although he describes himself as a simple Buddhist monk, few individuals in human history have spoken for the downtrodden and oppressed and for universal justice and human dignity with such moral authority.

In December 1989 the Dalai Lama received the Nobel Peace Prize. In accepting, he said that he did so on behalf of all oppressed peoples—those who struggle for freedom and work for world peace—as well as for the people of Tibet. The prize, he said, "reaffirms our conviction that with truth, courage and determination as our weapons, Tibet will be liberated. . . . Our struggle must remain nonviolent and free of hatred."†

Source: *Freedom in Exile: The Autobiography of the Dalai Lama* (London: Little, Brown, 1990).

QUESTIONS FOR ANALYSIS

1. In what ways do Tibet's history and the Dalai Lama's life reflect many of the major issues and events of the twentieth century?
2. The world's response to China's occupation reflects what political and economic factors?

*Tenzin Gyatso, the Dalai Lama, *My Land and My People* (New York: McGraw-Hill, 1962), p. 117.

†Nobelprize.org: The Official Web Site of the Nobel Prize. The Nobel Peace Prize 1989: The 14th Dalai Lama, Acceptance Speech. http://nobelprize.org/nobel_prizes/peace/laureates/1989/lama-acceptance.html.

Without directly challenging national sovereignty, Third World members of the General Assembly pressure for international cooperation in dealing with global issues, and the world's major powers sometimes go along. In 2000 the United Nations issued the "Millennium Declaration," a plan of action identifying eight goals, such as eliminating hunger, for the United Nations and member nations to reach by 2015. (See "Listening to the Past: The United Nations Millennium Project Report," page 1042.)

Preemptive War in Iraq

As the Cold War ended, the United Nations participated in the largest joint military action taken since the Korean conflict in the early 1950s: the 1990 Persian Gulf War (see page 1002). Success in Iraq led some to believe that the United Nations could fulfill its original purpose and guarantee peace throughout the world. Failure to stop savage civil wars in Somalia in 1992 and Bosnia in the mid-1990s, however, caused the United Nations to scale back its peacekeeping ambitions.

In 2002 another crisis over Iraq brought the United Nations to the center of the world's political stage. U.S. president George W. Bush accused Iraq of rebuilding its weapons of mass destruction and claimed that the United States had the right to act preemptively to prevent a hostile attack. Iraq, impoverished by a decade of tough United Nations sanctions, gave no indication of plans to attack any of its neighbors or the United States. America's declaration of its right to stage a unilateral preemptive strike to prevent attack thus set a dangerous precedent, while raising questions about when and how the United Nations charter's stipulating the use of armed force would apply.

As 2002 ended UN inspectors found no weapons of mass destruction. France, Russia, China, Germany, and a majority of the smaller states argued for continued weapons inspections, and France threatened to veto any resolution authorizing an invasion of Iraq. Rather than risk this veto, the United States and Britain claimed that earlier Security Council resolutions provided ample authorization and on March 20, 2003, invaded Iraq.

Iraqi forces were quickly defeated, and President Bush announced an end to the war on May 1, 2003. Although the war did bring an end to Saddam Hussein's brutal rule, Iraq remained one of the most dangerous places on earth. So-called insurgents representing all three main factions in Iraq — Sunni Muslims, Shi'ite Muslims, and Kurds — carried out daily attacks on Iraqi military and police, government officials, religious leaders, and civilians. Estimates of Iraqi deaths since the war began through 2009 range from one hundred thousand to over 1 million.

Iraq, ca. 2010

Areas that are predominantly
- Sunni (ca. 36%)
- Shi'ite (ca. 60%)
- Mixed
- Kurdish

Meanwhile, the United States, Britain, and their coalition allies maintained their forces in Iraq. In the spring of 2004 stories and photographs surfaced in the world press of American soldiers abusing and

Iraqis Celebrate U.S. Withdrawal On February 27, 2009, U.S. president Barack Obama announced that only 35,000 to 50,000 American troops, out of a total of 170,000, would remain in Iraq by August 19, 2010. In this June 30, 2009, photo from the southern city of Basra, Iraqi police and soldiers celebrate the withdrawal of U.S. troops from Iraq. Iraqi forces such as these took control of Iraqi towns and cities after the Americans' departure. (AFP/Getty Images)

Listening to the Past

The United Nations Millennium Project Report

In September 2000 the United Nations issued a Millennium Declaration — a bold statement of values and an agenda of actions to be undertaken by the United Nations and its member nations to reach eight major goals relating to global poverty and hunger, disease, education, the environment, maternal health, child mortality, gender equality, and global partnerships by 2015. In the following speech delivered the previous April, Secretary-General Kofi Annan set out the broad framework for this plan of action, which became the United Nations Millennium Project. In January 2005 the United Nations issued a five-year report that summarized the results to date and offered strategies for meeting the goals by 2015.

❝ If one word encapsulates the changes we are living through, it is "globalisation." We live in a world that is interconnected as never before. . . . This has its dangers, of course. Crime, narcotics, terrorism, disease, weapons—all these move back and forth faster, and in greater numbers, than in the past. . . .

But the *benefits* of globalisation are obvious too: faster growth, higher living standards, and new opportunities—not only for individuals but also for better understanding between nations, and for common action.

One problem is that, at present, these opportunities are far from equally distributed. . . . A second problem is that, even where the global market does reach, it is not yet underpinned, as national markets are, by rules based on shared social objectives. . . .

So, . . . the overarching challenge of our times is to make globalisation mean more than bigger markets. To make a success of this great upheaval we must learn how to govern better, and—above all—how to govern better together.

We need to make our States stronger and more effective at the national level. And we need to get them working together on global issues—all pulling their weight and all having their say.

What are these global issues? I have grouped them under three headings, each of which I relate to a fundamental human freedom—freedom from want, freedom from fear, and the freedom of future generations to sustain their lives on this planet.

First, *freedom from want*. How can we call human beings free and equal in dignity when over a billion of them are struggling to survive on less than one dollar a day, without safe drinking water, and when half of all humanity lacks adequate sanitation? Some of us are worrying about whether the stock market will crash, or struggling to master our latest computer, while more than half our fellow men and women have much more basic worries, such as where their children's next meal is coming from. . . .

Many of these problems are worst in sub-Saharan Africa, where extreme poverty affects a higher proportion of the population than anywhere else, and is compounded by a higher incidence of conflict, HIV/AIDS, and other ills. I am asking the world community to make special provision for Africa's needs, and give full support to Africans in their struggle to overcome these problems. . . .

Within the next fifteen years, I believe we can halve the population of people living in extreme poverty; ensure that all children—girls and boys alike, particularly the girls—receive a full primary education; and halt the spread of HIV/AIDS. In twenty years, we can also transform the lives of one hundred million slum dwellers around the world. And I believe we should be able to offer all young people between 15 and 24 the chance of decent work. . . .

The second main heading in the Report is *freedom from fear*. Wars between States are mercifully less frequent than they used to be. But in the last decade *internal* wars have claimed more than five million lives, and driven many times that number of people from their homes. Moreover, we still live under the shadow of weapons of mass destruction.

Both these threats, I believe, require us to think of security less in terms of merely defending territory, and more in terms of protecting *people*. That means we must tackle the threat of deadly conflict at every stage in the process. . . .

[T]he best way to prevent conflict is to promote political arrangements in which all groups are fairly represented, combined with human rights, minority rights, and broad-based economic development. Also, illicit transfers of weapons, money

---

torturing prisoners at Abu Ghraib and other detention centers in Iraq, at the Guantánamo Bay naval base in Cuba, and at prisons in Afghanistan. Questions were raised about the willingness of the United States to abide by Geneva Convention standards for the human-

itarian treatment of prisoners of war and by the United Nations convention against torture.

An earthquake in world affairs, the Iraq War split the West and was partially responsible for Republican losses in the 2008 U.S. elections. Democratic presidential candidate Barack Obama campaigned on a pledge to bring American troops home. After becoming president he kept his pledge to end the American presence in Iraq by the end of 2011. In January 2011

• **middle powers** Countries not considered part of either the First World or the developing world that became increasingly assertive regional leaders after the Cold War.

or natural resources must be forced into the limelight, so we can control them better.

We must protect vulnerable people by finding better ways to enforce humanitarian and human rights law, and to ensure that gross violations do not go unpunished. National sovereignty offers vital protection to small and weak States, but it should not be a shield for crimes against humanity. In extreme cases the clash of these two principles confronts us with a real dilemma, and the Security Council may have a moral duty to act on behalf of the international community. . . .

Finally, we must pursue our disarmament agenda more vigorously. Since 1995 it has lost momentum in an alarming way. That means controlling the traffic in small arms much more tightly, but also returning to the vexed issue of nuclear weapons. . . .

The third fundamental freedom my Report addresses is one that is not clearly identified in the Charter, because in 1945 our founders could scarcely imagine that it would ever be threatened. I mean the freedom of future generations to sustain their lives on this planet. . . .

If I could sum it up in one sentence, I should say we are plundering our children's heritage to pay for our present unsustainable practices.

This must stop. We must reduce emissions of carbon and other "greenhouse gases," to put a stop to global warming. Implementing the Kyoto Protocol is a vital first step. . . .

We must face the implications of a steadily shrinking surface of cultivable land, at a time when every year brings many millions of new mouths to feed. Biotechnology may offer the best hope, but only if we can resolve the controversies and allay the fears surrounding it. . . .

We must preserve our forests, fisheries, and the diversity of living species, all of which are close to collapsing under the pressure of human consumption and destruction. In short, we need a new ethic of stewardship. We need a much better informed public, and we need to take environmental costs and benefits fully into account in our economic policy decisions. We need regulations and incentives to discourage pollution and overconsumption of nonrenewable resources, and to encourage environment-friendly practices. And we need more accurate scientific data. . . .

But, you may be asking by now, what about the United Nations? . . .

[My] Report contains a further section on renewing the United Nations. . . . But let us not forget why the United Nations matters. It matters only to the extent that it can make a useful contribution to solving the problems and accomplishing the tasks I have just outlined.

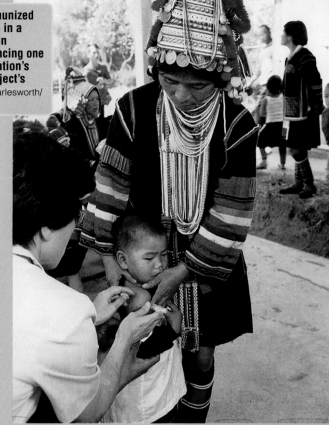

● A child is immunized against disease in a remote village in Thailand, advancing one of the United Nation's Millennium Project's goals. (Peter Charlesworth/OnAsia Images)

Those are the problems and the tasks which affect the everyday lives of our peoples. It is on how we handle *them* that the utility of the United Nations will be judged. If we lose sight of that point, the United Nations will have little or no role to play in the twenty-first century.

Let us never forget . . . that our Organisation was founded in the name of "We, the Peoples." . . . We are at the service of the world's peoples, and we must listen to them. They are telling us that our past achievements are not enough. They are telling us we must do more, and do it better. **"**

Source: Millennium Report, presented to the United Nations by Secretary-General Kofi Annan, April 3, 2000. Reproduced by permission of the United Nations Development Program.

QUESTIONS FOR ANALYSIS

1. According to Kofi Annan, what are the benefits of globalization, and what is the primary problem with it?
2. What are the three global issues and the related three fundamental freedoms that Annan hopes the Millennium Project will address?

50,000 of the one-time force of over 170,000 troops remained in Iraq.

Complexity and Violence in a Multipolar World

The sudden end of the Cold War shattered the interlocking restraints of the superpowers and their allies, removing a basic principle of global organization and order. The Cold War contributed to the ideology of Third World solidarity (see Chapter 33). Beginning in the 1980s, however, wide differences in economic performance in countries and regions undermined the whole idea of solidarity, and developing countries increasingly went their own ways.

A striking development was the growing multipolar nature of world politics. Increasingly assertive **middle powers** jockeyed for regional leadership and sometimes came into conflict. Brazil, with more than 140 million people and vast territory and resources, emerged as the dominant nation-state in South America. Mexico emerged as the leader of the Spanish-speaking Americas. France and West Germany re-emerged as strong regional powers in western Europe. Nigeria and South Africa were the leading powers in sub-Saharan Africa. Egypt and Israel were also regional powerhouses. Iran and Iraq competed and fought for dominance in the Persian Gulf. China, India, and Japan were all leading regional powers, and several other Asian countries — notably South Korea, Indonesia, Vietnam, and Pakistan — were determined to join them. The rise of these middle powers reflected the fact that most countries were small and weak, and

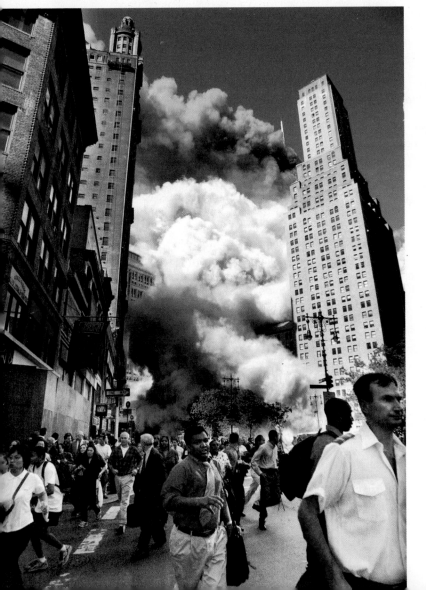

New York, September 11, 2001 Pedestrians race for safety as the World Trade Center towers collapse after being hit by jet airliners. Al-Qaeda terrorists with box cutters hijacked four aircraft and used three of them as suicide missiles to perpetrate their unthinkable crime. Heroic passengers on the fourth plane realized what was happening and forced their hijackers to crash the plane in a field. (Amy Sanetta/AP Images)

very few had the resources necessary to wield real power on even a regional scale.

Conflict and violence often bedeviled the emerging multipolar political system. In the 1990s civil wars in Bosnia, Kosovo, Rwanda, and Afghanistan killed over a million people and sent many hundreds of thousands of refugees running for their lives. Since 2000 new and continuing wars have caused millions more deaths and new refugees, particularly in Sierra Leone, Liberia, the Democratic Republic of the Congo, Uganda, Afghanistan, Burundi, Somalia, Iraq, Sudan, and Angola.

Rivalries between ethnic groups are often at the heart of the civil wars that produce so many deaths and refugees. Ethnic competition can lead to separatism — radical demands for ethnic autonomy or political independence. Only about twenty states, representing about 10 percent of the world's population, are truly homogeneous. The goal of a separate state for each self-defined people — the classic nationalist goal — could lead to endless battles and to tragedy on a global scale. The peaceful reconciliation of existing states with widespread separatist aspirations is thus a mighty challenge in the twenty-first century. The challenge of separatism seems especially great in light of the fact that civil war and terrorism often have gone hand in hand.

The Terrorist Threat

Beginning in the early 1900s and peaking in the 1960s, many nationalist movements used **terrorism** to win nationhood and political independence. This was the case in Serbia, Ireland, Israel, Cyprus, Yemen, and Algeria, among others.[1] In the post–World War II era, nationalist movements in Africa and Asia were often branded as terrorist by the imperial powers. These movements included, for example, the African National Congress in South Africa and Ho Chi Minh's Viet Minh independence movement in Vietnam. Minority ethnic groups, such as the Kurds in Turkey and the Palestinians, also attacked the powers they believed were preventing them from having their own nations. Some of the worst violence occurred in Northern Ireland, where religious differences caused Protestant and Catholic extremists to savagely attack each other's communities. Terrorist groups carried out deadly bombings, assassinations, airplane hijackings, kidnappings, and in some cases all-out war. This wave of terrorism receded in the 1980s as colonies gained independence and local and international police and security agencies became more effective in preventing attacks before they happened.

Generally successful in keeping ethnic nationalism under control in the West in the 1990s, many Europeans and most Americans believed that terrorism was primarily a problem for developing countries. In fact, terrorism had become part of a complex global pattern of violence and political conflict. As the new century opened, the global dimension of terrorism was revealed most dramatically in the United States.

On the morning of September 11, 2001, two hijacked passenger planes that departed from Boston crashed into and destroyed the World Trade Center in New York City. Shortly thereafter a third plane crashed into the Pentagon, and a fourth, believed to be headed for the White House or the U.S. Capitol, crashed into a field in rural Pennsylvania. These terrorist attacks took the lives of almost three thousand people from many countries. The United States launched a military campaign to destroy the perpetrators of the crime, Saudi-born Osama bin Laden's al-Qaeda network of terrorists and Afghanistan's reactionary Muslim government, the Taliban. Building a broad international coalition that included NATO member troops, Russia, and Pakistan, the United States joined with the faltering Northern Alliance in Afghanistan, which had been fighting the Taliban for years. In mid-November 2001 the Taliban government collapsed, and jubilant crowds in the capital of Kabul welcomed Northern Alliance soldiers as liberators. (See "Viewpoints: George W. Bush, Osama bin Laden, and the 9/11 Attacks," page 1046.)

The Taliban did not go away, however, and while bin Laden was eventually killed in May 2011, the war for control of Afghanistan continues. The Afghan government under President Hamid Karzai (b. 1957) rules tenuously from Kabul, and Taliban forces remain in the southern part of the country. The Karzai government, meanwhile, has become markedly less friendly to the United States and its allies, and critics accuse it of widespread corruption. Elections in 2009 and 2010 were marred by Taliban attacks on polling stations and claims of serious voting fraud. Karzai has become increasingly isolated, having alienated the international community, the opposition, and many of his own backers.

In December 2010 Obama significantly increased the U.S. military presence in Afghanistan, committing an additional thirty thousand forces to the sixty-eight thousand already there. The extra forces are intended to speed up the training of the Afghan Security Force so that they can take responsibility for the war. At the same time, Obama announced a troop drawdown from Afghanistan that began in 2011.

In trying to make sense of the actions of Osama bin Laden, his al-Qaeda followers, and others in this new wave of terrorism, many commentators were quick to stress the role of extreme Islamic fundamentalism as a motivating factor. But some scholars noted that recent heinous crimes had been committed by terrorists inspired by several religious faiths and sects and were by no means limited to Islamic extremists.[2] These scholars also noted that different terrorist movements needed to be examined in the context of underlying political conflicts and civil wars for meaningful understanding.

When this perspective is brought to the study of Osama bin Laden and al-Qaeda, two stages of their activities stand out. First, in the long, bitter fighting against the Soviet Union and the local Communists in Afghanistan, bin Laden and like-minded "holy warriors" developed terrorist skills and a narrow-minded, fanatical Islamic puritanism. They also developed a hatred of most existing Arab governments, which they viewed as corrupt, un-Islamic, and unresponsive to the needs of ordinary Muslims. The objects of their hostility included the absolute monarchy of oil-rich Saudi Arabia (bin Laden's country of origin), pro-Western but undemocratic Egypt, and the secular, one-party dictatorship of Saddam Hussein.

Second, when these Islamic extremists returned home and began to organize, they met the fate of many earlier Islamic extremists and were jailed or forced into exile, often in tolerant Europe. There they blamed the United States for being the supporter and corrupter of existing Arab governments, and they organized murderous plots against the United States — a proxy for the Arab rulers they could not reach. Bin Laden's network also blamed the United States for steadfastly supporting Israel and denying the claims of the Palestinians, although attempts to exploit the Israeli-Palestinian tragedy generally came later and operated mainly as an al-Qaeda recruiting tool.

Although U.S.-led forces decimated al-Qaeda camps in Afghanistan and overthrew the Taliban government, many analysts have since argued that the war on terrorism may have become more difficult as a result. Islamic extremists with only loose ties to al-Qaeda set off multiple bombs in a Madrid train station on March 11, 2004, killing 191 and wounding over 1,800. In London on July 7, 2005, 56 people were killed and more than 700 were injured by bombs detonated on three subway trains and a double-decker bus. At least three of the bombers were British citizens of Pakistani descent with unclear links to al-Qaeda. A suicide bomber who may have had links to al-Qaeda has also been blamed for the 2007 assassination of Pakistani presidential candidate Benazir Bhutto (see page 992). Thus, the war on terrorism is no longer against just the single global network of al-Qaeda. Many loosely connected cells and movements have emerged around the world, and these groups share many of the same goals but are not answerable to al-Qaeda's leadership.

Weapons of Mass Destruction

President George W. Bush justified the U.S.-led attack on Iraq in 2003 by saying that the world needed to

---

• **terrorism** The use of force or violence by a person or organized group with the intention of intimidating societies or governments, often for political purposes.

Viewpoints

George W. Bush, Osama bin Laden, and the 9/11 Attacks

• *Following the September 11, 2001, al-Qaeda attacks on the World Trade Center towers and the U.S. Pentagon, President George W. Bush addressed the U.S. Congress, telling the senators and representatives that America would respond to the attacks with a war on terror. Al-Qaeda leader Osama bin Laden initially denied any knowledge of or involvement with the attacks. Finally, in a taped statement on October 29, 2004, he accepted responsibility and described why he decided to attack the towers.*

George W. Bush, Address Before a Joint Session of Congress, September 20, 2001

"Tonight we are a country awakened to danger and called to defend freedom. Our grief has turned to anger and anger to resolution. Whether we bring our enemies to justice or bring justice to our enemies, justice will be done....

And on behalf of the American people, I thank the world for its outpouring of support. America will never ... forget the citizens of 80 other nations who died with our own: dozens of Pakistanis; more than 130 Israelis; more than 250 citizens of India; men and women from El Salvador, Iran, Mexico, and Japan; and hundreds of British citizens....

On September 11th, enemies of freedom committed an act of war against our country. Americans have known wars, ... Americans have known the casualties of war, but not at the center of a great city on a peaceful morning. Americans have known surprise attacks, but never before on thousands of civilians. All of this was brought upon us in a single day, and night fell on a different world, a world where freedom itself is under attack....

Great harm has been done to us. We have suffered great loss. And in our grief and anger, we have found our mission and our moment. Freedom and fear are at war. The advance of human freedom, the great achievement of our time and the great hope of every time, now depends on us. Our Nation—this generation—will lift a dark threat of violence from our people and our future. We will rally the world to this cause by our efforts, by our courage. We will not tire; we will not falter; and we will not fail."

Osama bin Laden, Statement Accepting Responsibility for the 9/11 Attacks, October 29, 2004

"People of America this talk of mine is for you and concerns the ideal way to prevent another Manhattan, and deals with the war and its causes and results. Before I begin, I say to you that security is an indispensable pillar of human life and that free men do not forfeit their security, contrary to Bush's claim that we hate freedom....

I say to you Allah knows that it had never occurred to us to strike the towers, but after ... we witnessed the oppression and tyranny of the American/Israeli coalition against our people in Palestine and Lebanon, it came to my mind.

The events that affected my soul in a direct way started in 1982 when America permitted the Israelis to invade Lebanon and the American Sixth Fleet helped them in that. The bombardment began and many were killed and injured and others were terrorized and displaced. I couldn't forget those moving scenes, blood and severed limbs, women and children sprawled everywhere. Houses destroyed along with their occupants and high-rises demolished over their residents, rockets raining down on our homes without mercy.... And as I looked at those demolished towers in Lebanon, it entered my mind that we should punish the oppressor in kind and that we should destroy towers in America in order that they taste some of what we tasted and so that they be deterred from killing our women and children. And that day, it was confirmed to me that oppression and the intentional killing of innocent women and children is a deliberate American policy. Destruction is freedom and democracy, while resistance is terrorism and intolerance.... So with these images ... as their background, the events of September 11th came as a reply to those great wrongs.

Should a man be blamed for defending his sanctuary? Is defending oneself and punishing the aggressor in kind objectionable terrorism? If it is such, then it is unavoidable for us."

Sources: George W. Bush, "Address Before a Joint Session of the Congress on the United States Response to the Terrorist Attacks of September 11," in *Public Papers of the Presidents of the United States: George W. Bush*, Book II, July 1 to December 31, 2001 (Washington, D.C.: Government Printing Office: 2003), pp. 1140–1144; uncredited government translation of the Osama bin Laden videotape, released October 24, 2004.

QUESTIONS FOR ANALYSIS

1. According to Bush, how did these attacks differ from attacks in America's past?

2. How does bin Laden justify the attacks as being "unavoidable for us"?

3. In what ways are Bush's and bin Laden's explanations of what freedom is similar or different?

destroy Saddam Hussein's weapons of mass destruction. As it turned out, Iraq had no weapons of mass destruction. Still, the fear that terrorists or rogue governments might acquire such weapons reflects global concern about the danger of nuclear, chemical, and biological attacks. (See "Global Trade: Arms," page 1048.)

After the bombing of Hiroshima and Nagasaki in 1945 (see page 937), the United States proposed the international control of all atomic weapons. The Soviets refused and exploded their first atomic bomb in 1949. The United States responded by exploding its first hydrogen bomb in 1952, and within ten months the Soviet Union did the same. Further scientific tests aroused worldwide fear that radioactive fallout would enter the food chain and cause leukemia, bone cancer, and genetic damage. Concerned scientists called for a ban on atomic bomb testing.

In 1963 the United States, Great Britain, and the Soviet Union signed an agreement, eventually signed by more than 150 countries, banning nuclear tests in the atmosphere. A second step toward control was the 1970 Treaty on the Non-Proliferation of Nuclear Weapons, designed to halt their spread to non-nuclear states and to reduce stockpiles of existing bombs held by the nuclear powers. It seemed that the nuclear arms race might yet be reversed.

This outcome did not come to pass. De Gaulle's France and Mao's China disregarded the test ban and by 1968 had developed their own nuclear weapons, although they later signed the nonproliferation treaty. India also developed weapons and in 1974 exploded an atomic device. Meanwhile, the nuclear arms race between the Soviet Union and the United States surged ahead after 1968, while the two sides also tried to set limits on their nuclear arsenals. The Strategic Arms Limitation Talks (SALT) in the 1970s limited the rate at which the two superpowers produced nuclear warheads, and in 1991 the United States and Russia negotiated the first Strategic Arms Reduction Treaty (START I), which eventually removed about 80 percent of existing strategic nuclear weapons. The New START treaty, signed by U.S. president Obama and Russian president Medvedev in 2010, requires the two countries to further reduce the number of their nuclear warheads by one-third.

India developed its atomic capability partly out of fear of China, which had manhandled India in a savage border war in 1962. India's nuclear blast in 1974 in turn frightened Pakistan, which regarded India as a bitter enemy, and by the mid-1980s Pakistan had the ability to produce nuclear weapons. In 1998 both India and Pakistan set off tests of their nuclear devices within weeks of each other, confirming their status as the world's sixth and seventh nuclear powers, after the United States, Russia, the United Kingdom, France,

and China. Both India and Pakistan have continued to increase their nuclear arsenals.

In the 1950s Israel began a nuclear weapons development program, and it is generally believed to have had an arsenal of nuclear weapons since the 1980s. Israel has never confirmed or denied this. Israel's apparent nuclear superiority was threatening to the Arabs. When Iraq attempted, with help from France, to develop nuclear capability in the 1980s, Israel responded suddenly, attacking and destroying the Iraqi nuclear reactor in June 1981.

The risks associated with the proliferation of nuclear weapons helped mobilize the international community and contributed to positive developments through the 1980s and 1990s. Argentina (1983), Romania (1989), Brazil (1998), South Africa (1990s), and Libya (2003) have all abandoned their nuclear weapons programs. Several of the former Soviet republics possessing nuclear arsenals, including Belarus and Kazakhstan, returned their nuclear weapons to Russia. Nuclear watch-guard agencies monitored exports of nuclear material, technology, and missiles that could carry atomic bombs. These measures encouraged confidence in global cooperation and in the nonproliferation treaty, which was extended indefinitely in 1995. The treaty had been signed by 189 countries as of 2010, including America, France, Russia, China, and the United Kingdom. Pakistan, India, North Korea, and Israel have not signed it.

Still, nuclear proliferation continues to threaten world peace. Iraq's attempt to build a bomb before the Gulf War highlighted the need for better ways to detect cheating. In 2003 the United States accused Iran of seeking to build nuclear missiles, and ongoing diplomatic efforts, economic sanctions, and other punitive measures by France, Germany, Britain, China, the United States, and Russia have failed to get Iran to place limitations on its nuclear program. There is also the threat that enriched nuclear materials will fall into the hands of terrorist organizations. In 2001 three Pakistani nuclear scientists were arrested following allegations that they had met with Taliban and al-Qaeda representatives. Just as ominously, the father of Pakistan's nuclear weapons program, Abdul Qadeer Khan, was charged in 2004 with passing on nuclear weapons expertise and technology to Iran, Libya, and North Korea.

In 2003 long-standing tensions between North Korea and the United States, which had never signed a peace treaty ending the 1950–1953 Korean War, reached crisis proportions over the question of nuclear arms on the Korean peninsula. As each side accused the other of failing to live up to a 1994 agreement, North Korea announced its intention to withdraw from the 1970 nonproliferation treaty, and in October 2006 North

Global Trade

Arms, with unprecedented destructive powers, command billions of dollars annually on the open global marketplace. On April 16, 1953, U.S. president Dwight Eisenhower spoke about the tremendous sums the Soviet Union and the United States were spending on Cold War weapons:

Every gun that is made, every warship launched, every rocket fired signifies, in the final sense, a theft from those who hunger and are not fed, those who are cold and are not clothed. The world in arms is not spending money alone. It is spending the sweat of its laborers, the genius of its scientists, the hopes of its children. . . . This is not a way of life at all, in any true sense.

In the approximately sixty years since Eisenhower's speech, the spending has never stopped, not even after the Cold War's end. In 2009 global military spending exceeded $1.53 trillion; the United States accounted for nearly half of that total. Globally in 2009 the value of all conventional arms transfer agreements to developing nations was more than $45.1 billion, and deliveries totaled $17 billion. Although those numbers have been dropping since the early 1990s, global arms manufacturing and trade remains big business.

Three different categories of arms are available on the world market. The category that generally receives the most attention is nuclear, biological, and chemical weapons. After the Soviet Union collapsed, there was widespread fear that former Soviet scientists would sell nuclear technology, toxic chemicals, or harmful biological agents from old, poorly guarded Soviet labs and stockpiles to the highest bidders. Recognizing the horrific danger such weapons represent, the world's nations have passed numerous treaties and agreements limiting their production, use, and stockpiling. The most important of these are the Treaty on the Non-Proliferation of Nuclear Weapons (1970), the Biological and Toxin Weapons Convention (1972), and the Chemical Weapons Convention (1993).

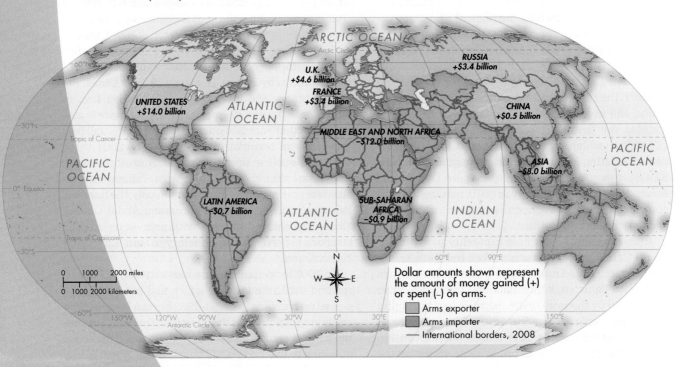

MAP 34.1 The Arms Trade

Source: Map and data from www.controlarms.org/the_issues/movers_shakers.htm, reproduced with the permission of Oxfam GB, Oxfam House, John Smith Drive, Cowley, Oxford OX4 2JY, UK, www.oxfam .org.uk. Oxfam GB does not necessarily endorse any text or activities that accompany the materials, nor has it approved the adapted text.

A second category of arms is so-called heavy conventional weapons, such as tanks, heavy artillery, jet planes, missiles, and warships. In general, worldwide demand for these weapons declined significantly after the Cold War ended. Only a few companies located in the largest industrialized nations have the scientists, the funding, and the capacity to produce them. Because the major Soviet- and Western-bloc nations had large weapon surpluses in 1991, most of the new weapons produced in this category have been made for export. In 1995 the United States for the first time produced more combat aircraft for export sales than for U.S. military use. New demand comes mainly from developing nations that are not technologically or financially capable of producing such weapons, such as Pakistan, which received fourteen F-16s in summer 2010 and has announced plans to purchase more. New or potential NATO member states have been another significant market for the United States, Great Britain, France, and Germany. In 2003, for example, the United States sold forty-eight F-16 fighter aircraft worth $3.5 billion to Poland, while Germany received $1 billion from Greece for 170 battle tanks. Many of the former Soviet-bloc countries of eastern Europe have illegally served as points of origin or transfer points for sales to embargoed nations such as North Korea and to terrorist groups such as al-Qaeda.

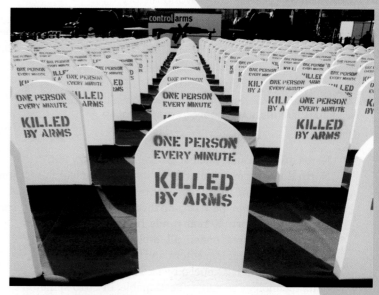

Amnesty International and Oxfam put up mock gravestones in central London in 2003 to represent the more than half million people killed on average each year by conventional light weapons.
(Jim Watson/AFP/Getty Images)

The third category is small arms and light conventional weapons (SALWs). These are almost any remotely portable weapons including automatic rifles, machine guns, pistols, antitank weapons, small howitzers and mortars, Stinger missiles and other shoulder-fired weapons, grenades, plastic explosives, land mines, machetes, small bombs, and ammunition. SALWs make up the majority of weapons exchanged in the global arms trade. They also do the most harm. Every year, they are responsible for over a half million deaths.

SALWs are popular because they have relatively long lives and are low-maintenance, cheap, easily available, highly portable, and easily concealable. Many can be used by child soldiers. Globally, there are around 650 million guns, about 60 percent of them owned by private citizens. Fifteen billion to twenty billion or more rounds of ammunition are produced annually. Despite widespread concern about terrorists obtaining nuclear or chemical weapons, terrorists on the whole favor such small conventional weapons as truck and car bombs and automatic rifles and pistols. One of the most deadly SALWs is the land mine. Over 110 million of them still lie buried in Afghanistan, Angola, Iran, and other former war zones, and they continue to kill or injure fifteen thousand to twenty thousand people a year.

Over ninety countries manufacture and sell SALWs, but the five permanent members of the UN Security Council—France, Britain, the United States, China, and Russia—dominate. The United States and Britain account for nearly two-thirds of all conventional arms deliveries, and these two nations plus France sometimes earn more income from arms sales to developing countries than they provide in aid. The total legal international trade in SALWs is estimated at about $8 billion a year; the illegal total is about $1 billion. Of course, every legal weapon can easily become an illegal one.

In 2000 UN Secretary-General Kofi Annan observed that "the death toll from small arms dwarfs that of all other weapons systems—and in most years greatly exceeds the toll of the atomic bombs that devastated Hiroshima and Nagasaki. In terms of the carnage they cause, small arms, indeed, could well be described as 'weapons of mass destruction.'"*

*Kofi A. Annan, "Freedom from Fear," in *"We the Peoples": The Role of the United Nations in the 21st Century*, ch. 4, p. 52.

> ❝In the future, warfare — highly destructive warfare — may be waged without the necessity for armies and governments, by people with little to lose.❞
>
> **BRIAN JENKINS, RAND CORPORATION SCHOLAR**

Korea tested its first nuclear device. In February 2007 North Korea agreed to shut down its major nuclear facility at Yŏngbyŏn in exchange for thousands of tons of heavy fuel oil from the West and the release of $25 million in frozen North Korean funds. In April 2009, however, North Korea ended all diplomatic talks and expelled all nuclear inspectors, and in May 2009 it successfully conducted a nuclear test. Though the success of its technology remains questionable, in 2010 some observers estimated that North Korea could possess a mid-range missile capable of reaching Japan with a nuclear warhead within five years. The case of North Korea illustrates the danger of atomic war in a multipolar world of intense regional rivalries.

Chemical and biological weapons of mass destruction created similar anxieties. Since the Geneva Protocol (1925) after World War I, the use of chemical weapons has been outlawed by international agreement, but the manufacture of these terrible weapons was none-theless permitted. In 1997 most of the world's nations signed the Chemical Weapons Convention banning the production of chemical weapons and requiring the destruction of those in existence. Inspectors received the right to make surprise searches "anytime, anywhere." As of 2010 only five countries — Angola, Egypt, North Korea, Somalia, and Syria — had not signed the agreement.

The threat of biological or nuclear weapons falling into the hands of terrorists remains a real danger. As early as 1978 Brian Jenkins, a RAND Corporation scholar, observed that

> we are approaching an age in which national governments may no longer monopolize the instruments of major destruction. The instruments of warfare once possessed only by armies will be available to gangs. . . . In the future, warfare — highly destructive warfare — may be waged without the necessity for armies and governments, by people with little to lose.[3]

Jenkins's prescient vision appears more possible than ever before. Nations think in terms of preserving themselves while destroying their enemies. But terrorists willing to become martyrs with pounds of explosives strapped to their bodies have no need for a missile to deliver a nuclear device. They will deliver it personally.

South Korean Protests Against North Korea North Korea's development of nuclear weapons has sparked angry demonstrations in the major cities of its Asian neighbors. Here a South Korean protester burns a North Korean flag and a mock atomic bomb during a rally in Seoul. (Reuters/Corbis)

Five Generations of the Yang Family This group portrait suggests the enduring Chinese commitment to close family ties. It also puts a human face on social transformation, for the great-great-grandmother has bound feet and the baby she holds will be an only child. In the 1980s the Chinese government prohibited couples from having more than one child, a major factor in China's falling birthrate. (Dermot Tatlow/Panos Pictures)

with the large operations. Agribusinesses have the advantages of economy of scale and can afford larger machines to farm larger acreages, can control all phases of the process — from producing the hybrid seeds to marketing the final product — and can take advantage of international markets.

Peasants in developing countries leave the land for many of the same reasons. The major difference in developing countries, though, is that these peasant farmers, usually illiterate, are often producing subsistence crops and are forced off the land by government troops or thugs hired by large landowners or companies to make way for large cash-crop production. The loss of land can also result from peasant families' possessing no documents proving ownership of the fields they have worked for generations. In industrialized countries like the United States, farmers who leave their land have educational and employment options. In developing countries, few options are available for illiterate peasants with no skills other than rudimentary farming.

Science and Technology: Changes and Challenges

☐ What key technological and scientific developments have had the greatest impact on life at the beginning of the new millennium?

The twentieth century was a time of rapid urbanization, but it was equally an era of amazing advances in science and technology. These advances were not always positive. The great excitement over the telephone, the automobile, electricity, and the airplane was quickly tempered in 1914 by the killing machines invented and used in the Great War. Totalitarian regimes exploited new developments in mass communication for mass propaganda. No sooner had the atom been harnessed than the United States released atomic bombs over Hiroshima and Nagasaki. Yet since World War II, scientists have made tremendous progress in medicine and communication technologies, though disease and environmental issues continue to present challenges.

The Medical Revolution

The medical revolution began in the late 1800s with the development of the germ theory of disease (see page 732) and continued rapidly after World War II. Scientists discovered vaccines for many of the most deadly diseases. Jonas Salk's development of the polio vaccine in 1952 was followed by the first oral polio vaccine (1962) and vaccines for measles (1964), mumps (1967), rubella (1970), chickenpox (1974), and hepatitis B (1981). Globally, these vaccines have saved millions of lives, especially those of children. According to the United Nations World Health Organization, medical advances reduced deaths from smallpox, cholera, and plague by more than 95 percent worldwide between 1951 and 1966.

Following independence, Asian and African countries increased the small numbers of hospitals, doctors, and nurses they had inherited from the colonial past. In addition, local people were successfully trained as paramedics to staff rural outpatient clinics that offered medical treatment, health education, and prenatal and postnatal care. Many paramedics were women, for many health problems involved childbirth and infancy, and many cultures considered it improper for a man to examine a woman's body.

The medical revolution significantly lowered death rates and lengthened life expectancies. Children became increasingly likely to survive their early years, although infant and juvenile mortality remained far higher in poor countries than in rich ones. By 1980 the average inhabitant of the developing countries could expect to live about fifty-four years; life expectancy at birth varied from forty to sixty-four years depending on the country. In industrialized countries life expectancy at birth averaged seventy-one years.

Since the 1980s medical science has continued to make remarkable advances. In 1979 the World Health Organization announced the worldwide eradication of smallpox. By this time, transplants of such organs as hearts, lungs, and kidneys had become routine, and in 1982 an American man became the first recipient of an artificial heart. Also important were advances in our understanding of DNA begun in the 1940s. In 2003 scientists working on the Human Genome Project announced that they had successfully identified, mapped, and sequenced the entire genome, or hereditary information, of human beings. This knowledge gives health care providers immense new powers for preventing, treating, and curing diseases and makes the completion of the project one of the most important scientific developments in history.

Despite these advances, there remains a wide gap in health care availability and affordability for the rich and the poor. Thousands of people die every day in the developing world from diseases and illnesses that are curable and easily treated. Between 1980 and 2000 the number of children under the age of five dying annually of diarrhea dropped by 60 percent through the global distribution of a cheap sugar-salt solution mixed in water. Still, over 1.5 million children worldwide continue to die each year from diarrhea. Deaths worldwide from HIV/AIDS are reaching epic proportions, while malaria and tuberculosis continue to be major killers of young and old alike. In 2010 tuberculosis remains the leading killer of women worldwide.

Population Change: Balancing the Numbers

A less favorable consequence of the medical revolution has been the acceleration of population growth. As in nineteenth-century Europe, a rapid decline in death rates was not immediately accompanied by a similar decline in birthrates. Women in developing countries continued to bear five to seven children each, as their mothers and grandmothers had done. The combined populations of Asia, Africa, and Latin America, which had grown relatively modestly from 1925 to 1950, increased from 1.7 billion to 3 billion between 1950 and 1975 and continues to grow at a similar rate.

Concerned about famine and starvation, some governments began pushing family planning and birth control to slow population growth. For a number of reasons these measures were not always successful. Islamic and Catholic religious teachings were hostile to birth control. Moreover, widespread cultural attitudes dictated that a "real man" keep his wife pregnant. There were also economic reasons for preferring large families. Farmers needed the help of children at planting and harvest times, and sons and daughters were a sort of social security system for their elders. By the 1970s and 1980s, however, population growth in the industrialized countries had begun to fall significantly. By the 1990s some European leaders were bemoaning birthrates in their countries that were below the 2.1 level needed to maintain a stable population.

The world's poor women also began to bear fewer children. Small countries such as Barbados, Chile, Costa Rica, Taiwan, and Tunisia led the way. Between 1970 and 1975 China followed, registering the fastest five-year birthrate decline in recorded history. Then other big countries, especially in Latin America and East Asia, experienced large declines in fertility. In 1970 the average Brazilian woman had close to 6 children; by 2005 she had 1.9. In 1970 the average woman in Bangladesh had more than 7 children; in 2005 she had 3.1.

There were several reasons for this decline in fertility among women in the developing world. Fewer babies were dying of disease or malnutrition, so couples needed fewer births to guarantee the survival of the number of children they wanted. Also, better living conditions, urbanization, and more education encouraged women to have fewer children. No wonder the most rapidly industrializing countries, such as Taiwan and South Korea, led the way in declining birthrates.

In the early 1960s the introduction of the birth control pill marked a revolution not only in birth control techniques but also in women taking control of their own fertility. Family planning was now truly possible. In the early twenty-first century more than half of the world's couples practiced birth control, up from one in eight just forty years earlier. However, male chauvinism, religious teachings, and conservative government leaders combined in many predominately Roman Catholic countries and in most Muslim countries to control the availability and distribution of birth control methods and abortion. Birth control and abortion were most accepted in North America, Protestant Europe, the Soviet Union, and East Asia, which explains why these regions had the lowest birthrates and population growth.

Although significant differences still exist between regions, projections of world population growth have declined sharply. By 2005 global birthrates had fallen to the lowest level in recorded history. The average woman in the developing world had 2.9 children, down from an average of nearly 6 babies in the 1970s. Fertility in most of the developing world could fall below the replacement level (2.1 children per woman) before 2100. The most recent estimates are that the world's population will "only" grow by 50 percent between 2000 and 2050, when it will reach about 9 billion. Over the next century it is then expected to level off at about 10 billion.

Global Epidemics

One of humanity's gravest fears in the early years of the new millennium comes from the threat posed by epidemic diseases. Outbreaks in Africa of the deadly Ebola and Marburg viruses; a worldwide outbreak of severe acute respiratory syndrome, or SARS, which began in 2002; ongoing avian, or bird, flu in Asia; and "mad-cow disease," which has wreaked havoc with meat production in several countries, have all raised the frightening specter of a global recurrence of a modern Black Death. Tuberculosis (TB) has also made a comeback and kills one person every fifteen seconds, thus claiming millions of lives every year, even though it is a curable disease. Malaria kills a million people a year worldwide, 90 percent of them in Africa.

Fighting the AIDS Epidemic in Asia A dramatic billboard warns people in Malaysia about the deadly dangers of AIDS. The billboard offers sound advice, focusing on the three primary ways by which the AIDS virus is spread. Can you "read" the three-part message? (Robert Francis/The Hutchison Library/Eye Ubiquitous)

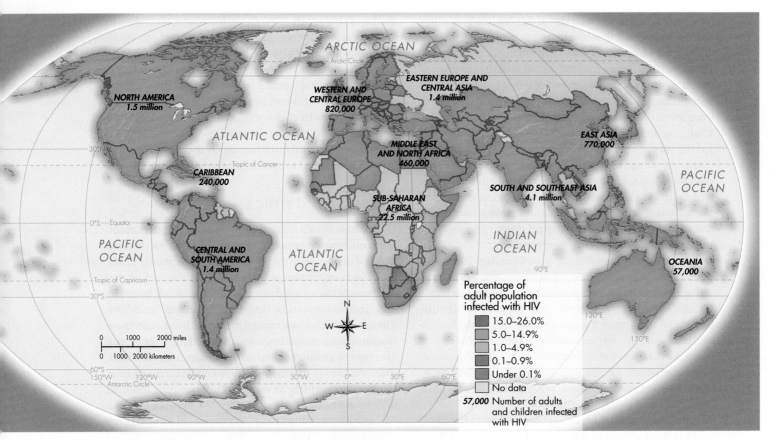

MAP 34.3 People Living with HIV/AIDS Worldwide, ca. 2010 As this map illustrates, Africa has been hit the hardest by the HIV/AIDS epidemic. It currently has fifteen to twenty times more identified cases than any other region of the world. AIDS researchers expect that in the coming decade, however, Russia and South and East Asia will overtake and then far surpass Africa in the number of infected people. (Source: Data from World Health Organization, www.whosea.org)

Few diseases in world history have been more frightening, or caused more disruption of human society, than HIV/AIDS. In 2007 the Population Division of the United Nations calculated that 36 million persons globally were infected with HIV, the virus that causes AIDS. AIDS was the world's fourth-leading cause of death.

About 90 percent of all persons who die from AIDS and 86 percent of those currently infected with HIV live in sub-Saharan Africa (Map 34.3). In Africa HIV/AIDS is most commonly spread through heterosexual sex. Widespread disease and poverty are also significant factors in that Africans already suffering from other illnesses such as malaria or tuberculosis have less resistance to HIV and less access to health care for treatment.

Another critical factor contributing to the spread of AIDS in Africa is the continued political instability of many countries — particularly those in the corridor running from Uganda to South Africa. This corridor was the scene of brutal civil and liberation wars that resulted in massive numbers of refugees, a breakdown in basic health care services, and the destruction of family and cultural networks. The populations of countries along this corridor — Uganda, Rwanda, Burundi, Zaire/Congo, Angola, Zimbabwe, Mozambique, and South Africa — have been decimated by HIV/AIDS. South Africa currently has the largest number of HIV/AIDS cases in the world. In 2010 around 10 percent of the South African population, about 5.6 million people, were living with HIV/AIDS. Of these, over 330,000 were children under fifteen years of age. An estimated 310,000 South Africans died of AIDS in 2009. Medical health experts expect that Russia, India, China, Japan, and other countries in Asia might soon overtake South Africa in reported HIV/AIDS cases.

Although HIV/AIDS has had a devastating impact on Africa, globally the epidemic is still at a relatively early stage. Changes in behavior will be critical to slowing the spread of AIDS in the developing world. Since 2001 relatively inexpensive AIDS drugs that are widely available in the West have been dispensed freely to many of those infected in Africa and Asia, but the availability of these drugs has generally failed to keep up with the increase in cases.

Environmentalism

Like disease, the environment knows no boundaries. Some voices have always expressed concern for the environment. In the eighteenth century, for example, governments became increasingly concerned about their forests as the great demand for lumber to build ships nearly destroyed the forests of Britain, Europe, the eastern United States, and later India. The United States created the first national park in the nineteenth century. The modern environmental movement began with concerns about chemical waste, rapid consumption of energy and food supplies, global deforestation, environmental degradation caused in part by sprawling megacities, and threats to wildlife. By the 1970s citizens had begun joining together in organizations such as Greenpeace and Friends of the Earth to try to preserve, restore, or enhance the natural environment.

The environmental movement is actually several different movements, each with its own agenda. American biologist and writer Rachel Carson was an early proponent of the environmental health movement. In *Silent Spring* (1962) she warned of the dangers of pesticides and pollution:

> Along with the possibility of the extinction of mankind by nuclear war, the central problem of our age has therefore become the contamination of man's total environment with such substances of incredible potential for harm — substances that accumulate in the tissues of plants and animals and even penetrate the germ cells to shatter or alter the very material of heredity upon which the shape of the future depends.[9]

Carson and others were concerned about the effects of chemicals, radiation, pollution, waste, and urban development on the environment and on human health.

The conservation movement, represented in the United States by the Sierra Club and the Audubon Society, seeks to protect the biodiversity of the planet and emphasizes the spiritual and aesthetic qualities of nature. The ecology movement consists of different groups with somewhat similar agendas, ranging from politically active Green Parties to Greenpeace. These organizations are concerned about global warming, toxic chemicals, the use of nuclear energy and nuclear weapons, genetically modified food, recycling, saving endangered species, sustainable agriculture, protecting ancient forests, and environmental justice.

Environmentalists today are especially concerned about **global warming**, the increase of global temperatures over time. The ten years to 2010 formed the warmest decade in recorded history, followed by the 1990s. The majority of the world's scientists believe that the increase began with the Industrial Revolution

> "Along with the possibility of the extinction of mankind by nuclear war, the central problem of our age has therefore become the contamination of man's total environment with such substances of incredible potential for harm."
>
> **RACHEL CARSON**

in the 1700s. The subsequent human-generated hydrocarbons produced through the burning of fossil fuels — coal, oil, natural gas — have caused a greenhouse effect.

Possible effects of global warming over the next century include a catastrophic rise in sea levels that would put many coastal cities and islands under water; ecosystem changes that may threaten various species of plants and animals; extreme and abnormal weather patterns; destruction of the earth's ozone layer, which shields the planet from harmful solar radiation; and a decline in agricultural production. Although the exact causes and consequences of global warming are being debated, the world community is so concerned that in 1997 an amendment, the Kyoto Protocol, was added to the United Nations Framework Convention on Climate Change. Countries that ratify the protocol agree to try to reduce their emissions of carbon dioxide and five other greenhouse gases. As of July 2010, 191 countries had ratified it. The most notable exception was the United States.

Mass Communication

The invention of moving pictures, the telephone, and other revolutionary new technologies between 1875 and 1900 prepared the way for a twentieth century of mass communications and the "information age." The global availability and affordability of radios and television sets in the 1950s introduced a second communications revolution. The transistor radio penetrated the most isolated hamlets of the developing world. Governments embraced radio broadcasting as a means of power, propaganda, and education. Though initially less common, television use expanded into nearly every country, even if there was just one television in a village. Governments recognized the power of the visual image to promote their ideology or leader, and a state television network became a source of national pride. By the beginning of the twenty-first century television was bringing the whole planet into the bars and

• **global warming** The belief of the majority of the world's scientists that hydrocarbons produced through the burning of fossil fuels have caused a greenhouse effect that has increased global temperatures over time.

Evidence of Global Warming The graphics indicate the change in the seasonal melt extent, in red, of the Greenland ice sheet from 1992 (left) to 2002 (right)—a significant increase in only ten years. Of greatest immediate concern to scientists is that melting polar icecaps and Greenland glaciers are releasing cold freshwater into the northern Atlantic Ocean, which could shut down the Gulf Stream that brings warm ocean currents up from the equator to warm Europe and northeastern North America. This could produce an ice age in the northern Atlantic that would drastically affect global weather patterns. (both photos: Clifford Grabhorn/AP Images)

meetinghouses of the world's villages and was having a profound, even revolutionary, impact everywhere. Alluring television images of high living standards and the excitement of urban life stirred powerful desires in young people, who copied Western materialism, migrated to the cities, and created a global youth culture.

The third, and perhaps greatest, communications revolution occurred with the first Apple personal computers in 1976, followed by the introduction of cell phones in 1985. Mass communications have exploded

since then. Cell phones allowed individuals and nations in the developing world to bypass telephone lines, installation, and other obstacles associated with landline telephone use. Africa now has over 85 million cell phone users; equivalent landline phone use would be impossible. Cell phones have become among the most widely owned consumer products worldwide.

The Internet, or World Wide Web, has had the greatest impact on human communication. First made available to the general public in 1994, the Internet and e-mail allow for instantaneous communication to anyone, anywhere with an Internet connection. The possibilities for global access to information and knowledge are seemingly infinite. Authoritarian governments

• **feminization of poverty** The issue that those living in extreme poverty are disproportionately women.

have realized the threat that the Internet and Facebook, Twitter, and other social networking services pose to their power and control. The governments of China and North Korea, for example, have spent millions of dollars trying to restrict information traveling in and out of their countries over the Internet. For the first time in history, this type of censorship may prove impossible.

Social Reform and Progress

☐ What social problems facing women and children are the focus of reformers in the new millennium?

Just as an end to slavery became the rallying cry for social reformers in the nineteenth century, modern social reformers have sought to end global inequality, racism, and sexism and to improve human and civil rights for all. We have already described many of these developments, such as the victory of the democratic movement in eastern Europe (see pages 955–961) and the

end of the racist apartheid system in South Africa (see page 1027). Much remains to be achieved, however, and nowhere is more worldwide attention being focused than on the advancement of human and civil rights for women and children.

Women: The Right to Equality

The final report for the 1995 United Nations Fourth World Conference on Women called on the world community to take action in twelve areas of critical concern to women: poverty, access to education and training, access to health care, violence against women, women and war, economic inequality with men, political inequality with men, creation of institutions for women's advancement, lack of respect for women's rights, stereotyping of women, gender inequalities and the environment, and violation of girl children's rights.[10] These are concerns that all women share, although degrees of inequality vary greatly from one country to another.

The **feminization of poverty**, the disproportionate number of women living in extreme poverty, is one of the greatest concerns facing women today. Even in the most developed countries, two out of every three

Gathering Firewood These African women in Burkina Faso bring home head-loads of wood, requiring a journey of one hour each way. In developing countries women (rarely men) make two or more such trips a week to provide fuel for cooking and heating, illustrating what has been called the "other energy crisis." As nearby forests are depleted, they must travel farther and farther to find available wood, while the denuded land becomes open to soil erosion. Women and children spend another two to three hours every day or two hauling water. (Mark Edwards/Photolibrary)

poor adults are women. In the United States, for example, half of all poor families are supported by single mothers whose average income is 23 percent lower than the poverty line. There are many causes for this phenomenon. Having principal responsibility for child care, women have less time and opportunity for work, and because they have less access to health care they are often unable to work. As male labor migration increases worldwide, the number of households headed by women increases, and thus the number of families living in poverty. Job restrictions and discrimination, plus limited education, result in women having few job options except in the "informal economy" as maids, street vendors, or prostitutes.

Despite increased access to birth control, even within developed countries, birthrates remain high among poor women, especially among poor adolescents, who make up an inordinate number of the estimated 585,000 women who die every year during pregnancy and childbirth. The poorest women usually suffer most from government policies, usually legislated by men, that restrict their access to reproductive health care.

Women have made some modest gains in the workplace, making up 38 percent of the nonfarm-sector global workforce in the early 2000s, as compared to 35 percent in 1990. But segregated labor markets remain the rule, with higher-paying jobs reserved for men. In the farm sector, women globally produce more than half of all the food that is grown and up to 80 percent of subsistence crops grown in Africa. Because this is informal labor and often unpaid, these women laborers are denied access to loans, and many of them cannot own the land they farm.

Some observers believe that violence against women is on the rise. Long part of war, rape and sexual violence were used as weapons of war during the wars in the former Yugoslavia and in Rwanda in the early 1990s. Rape and sexual violence have been subsequently labeled crimes against humanity and are considered forms of torture and genocide. Still, they have continued to be used as weapons in conflicts in Sierra Leone, Kosovo, Afghanistan, the Democratic Republic of the Congo, and elsewhere. Domestic violence appears to be on the increase in many countries, including Russia, Pakistan, Peru, and South Africa. Forced prostitution and international female slave traffic is carried on by traffickers from such countries as Ukraine, Moldova, Nigeria, Burma, and Thailand. Perhaps five thousand women a year are killed in "honor killings," when men kill their female relatives for bringing dishonor on the family's reputation, frequently because of some perceived misuse of their sexuality.

Still, some progress has been made toward equality for women. New laws have been enacted, and worldwide more girls than ever before are receiving an education. More women are now allowed to vote and to hold office, and half of all the female heads of state elected since 1900 were elected after 1990. Women also are moving across and up in the workplace, holding a wider variety of jobs and more senior positions.

Children: The Right to Childhood

In 1989 the United Nations General Assembly adopted the Convention on the Rights of the Child, which spelled out a number of rights that are due every child. These

Child Soldier in Sierra Leone
This eleven-year-old boy with a rifle slung over his shoulder is a member of the Sierra Leone army and stands guard at a checkpoint during his country's civil war. Tens of thousands of boys and girls under eighteen have been used by the militaries in more than sixty countries since 2000, either as armed combatants or informally in tasks such as spying, scouting, carrying messages, and cooking. (Brennan Linsley/AP Images)

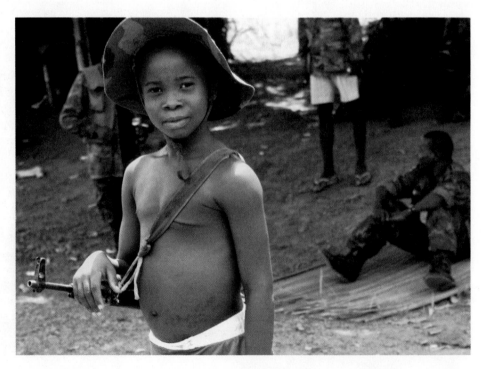

include civil and human rights and economic, social, and cultural rights. The convention has been ratified by more countries than any other human rights treaty in world history — 194 countries as of 2009. The United States and Somalia remain the only two countries in the United Nations that have not ratified it.

It is not difficult to see why such a document was necessary. Globally, a billion children live in poverty — one in every two children in the world. In the United States 16 percent of children, more than 11 million girls and boys, live in poor families with parents who earn at or below the poverty line. Worldwide, 640 million children do not have adequate shelter, 400 million do not have safe water, and 270 million receive no health care. From 10 million to 11 million children die each year before age five.

Besides poverty, the convention addresses a number of other concerns. These include children's making up half of the world's refugees, child labor and exploitation, sexual violence and sex trafficking, police abuse of street children, HIV/AIDS orphans, lack of access to education, and lack of access to adequate health care. Increasingly in the last decade, children have been recruited or kidnapped to become child soldiers, as many as 300,000 worldwide, 120,000 in Africa alone. Child sexual abuse and child soldiers have become such wide-spread problems that the United Nations wrote two additional protocols — one on the involvement of children in armed conflicts and the other on the sale of children, child pornography, and child prostitution — that were attached to the original convention and adopted in 2000.

As the twenty-first century began, nearly a billion people were unable to read a book or sign their names. Of the 100 million children without access to primary education, 60 percent or more were girls. Most of the global literacy problems are found in the developing world. Increasing economic globalization have put pressure on all governments to improve literacy rates and to improve educational opportunities for young people. Since the 1990s more and more countries have recognized the importance of providing a minimum level of basic education and have made it compulsory. Globally, four in five children now participate in lower secondary education (U.S. ninth and tenth grades), but discrepancies remain wide. Many countries have 90 to 100 percent participation in at least lower secondary education, but in Africa the rate is closer to 45 percent and is only 29 percent for upper secondary (U.S. eleventh and twelfth grades). Only when countries are stable and have prosperous economies will all children receive the education they deserve.

CONNECTIONS

After forty years of superpower confrontation, the Cold War's end brought renewed hope for global peace and prosperity. If we have learned anything since 1991, however, it is that neither peace nor prosperity come easily for the human race. New rifts and old animosities have set us at odds in ways that are just as dangerous and lethal as the Cold War differences they replaced. At the same time, as the twenty-first century enters its second decade, populist revolts in several countries across North Africa, the Middle East, and elsewhere have demonstrated that women and men are still ready to fight and die for freedom from authoritarian rule and for better lives.

A common feature of these recent revolts has been the use of the Internet, cell phones, and social networking sites. While these have proved innovative tools for political change, the most revolutionary advances in education in the developing world will also come through access to the Internet. Despite the initial costs — significant for many countries — the benefits of having even one computer connected to the Internet in each school are incalculable. Instantaneously, children get access to all the world's libraries, art galleries, museums, educational sites, and knowledge bases. Internet access does not make the playing field between rich and poor students exactly level, but it comes closer to doing so than any other development in history.

The study of world history will put these and future events in perspective. Future developments on this small planet will surely build on the many-layered foundations hammered out in the past. Moreover, the study of world history, of mighty struggles and fearsome challenges, of shining achievements and tragic failures, imparts a strong sense of life's essence: the process of change over time. Again and again we have seen how peoples and societies evolve, influenced by ideas, human passions, and material conditions. Armed with the ability to think historically, students of history are prepared to comprehend this inexorable process of change in their own lifetimes, as the world races forward toward an uncertain destiny.

☐ CHAPTER REVIEW

☐ **What is the multipolar nature of world politics today, and how do competing nation-states address common problems? (p. 1038)**

Nation-states remained the primary building blocks of political organization as the world entered the twenty-first century. But increasing interdependency and globalization led to a new multipolar nature of world politics, with a group of countries known as middle powers rising to assume regional leadership. The increasingly complex nature of world politics forced nations and peoples to come together, negotiate, and make joint global decisions more frequently than at any time in human history. The United Nations was created to maintain international peace and security, but despite some success in peacekeeping and humanitarian work, its charter has proven difficult to enforce, as the 2003 preemptive war against Iraq attests. Nuclear nonproliferation treaties and a chemical weapons ban were positive steps toward world peace, but the new wave of terrorism in the new millennium continues to challenge world security.

☐ **What are some of the benefits and drawbacks of increasing global interdependence? (p. 1051)**

Increased globalization has led to a greater degree of interdependence, as global markets and resource needs tie the countries of the world ever more closely together. Multinational corporations rapidly emerged in the early 1950s, operating across political boundaries to create a single global marketplace. Criticized for being part of a neocolonial process, multinationals bring products to developing countries but keep profits in the hand of elites at the expense of national interests. A push to industrialize developing nations in the 1950s and 1960s was successful, but Third World countries found that they could not compete with the West, and the gap between rich and poor nations widened. The green revolution dramatically increased crop yields, though profits were generally limited to larger landowners and large agribusinesses. Calls for a new international order have been complicated by the complexity of world economic systems, which consist of many distinct types of wealth and income, not just a "North" and a "South."

☐ **What factors spurred the growth of cities in Africa, Asia, and Latin America, and what were some of the main consequences of urbanization in the late twentieth century? (p. 1057)**

The phenomenal growth of cities over the past fifty years has had a tremendous impact on individuals, families, and communities. Megacities, in particular, have evolved at an astonishing pace. The reasons for this urban explosion include a tremendous spurt in population growth and people's desire to find jobs, particularly manufacturing jobs that were concentrated in the cities. People also left the countryside because they were pushed off their land or, if they were young, for the excitement of the city.

The consequences of this rapid urbanization are similar to those associated with early-twentieth-century urbanization in Europe and North America, but on a larger scale. Overcrowding and shantytowns have been some of the most visible problems. Urban social services have been overwhelmed, and cities have been unable to provide the necessary police and fire protection and adequate sanitation, running water, and electricity.

☐ **What key technological and scientific developments have had the greatest impact on life at the beginning of the new millennium? (p. 1061)**

Science and technology have significantly changed global society in the twentieth century. A medical revolution has discovered vaccines to treat some of history's most deadly diseases; artificial hearts and organ transplants have become routine. The successful mapping of human DNA offers unimaginable possibilities for the prevention, treatment, and cure of diseases. As we learn more about the environment, global warming has drawn more attention from government leaders and private citizens. Mass communication is another area where advances have been revolutionary. Many people around the world have access to the Internet and carry cell phones and other devices that make information exchange almost instantaneous.

▢ What social problems facing women and children are the focus of reformers in the new millennium? (p. 1067)

At the end of the twentieth century and the beginning of the twenty-first, social reformers have turned their attention to the advancement of human and civil rights for women and children. The feminization of poverty remains one of the greatest concerns, affecting women in both developed and developing countries. Contributing factors include child care demands, job discrimination, and high birthrates. Violence against women remains rampant, and rape and sexual violence have been used as weapons of war in many recent conflicts. Still, women have made important progress toward equality, and they are increasingly moving into more positions of power. Children suffer alongside their poor mothers, and the 1989 UN Convention on the Rights of the Child seeks to address childhood poverty, child labor exploitation, sexual violence, and lack of access to health care, among other issues facing children today. Globalization has pressured governments to provide public education, though access remains uneven.

SUGGESTED READING

Bales, Kevin. *Disposable People: New Slavery in the Global Economy*. 2004. Analysis of the economic exploitation of the world's poor.

Caircross, Frances. *The Death of Distance: How the Communications Revolution Is Changing Our Lives*. 2001. Discusses the global consequences of cell phones, communication satellites, and the Internet.

Chandler, Alfred D., and Bruce Mazlish. *Leviathans: Multinational Corporations and the New Global History*. 2005. A stimulating global perspective on multinational corporations and how they affect everyone's life.

Das, Gurcharan. *India Unbound: The Social and Economic Revolution from Independence to the Global Information Age*. 2002. India's leap into the age of modern technology and computers and the consequences for its population and the world.

Drexler, Maeline. *Secret Agents: The Menace of Emerging Infections*. 2003. Provides an overview of the global threat from infectious diseases, old and new.

Fishman, Ted C. *China, Inc.: How the Rise of the Next Superpower Challenges America and the World*. 2006. Explains the profound consequences of China's becoming the next economic superpower.

Gareis, Sven Bernhard, and Johannes Varwick. *The United Nations: An Introduction*. 2005. An up-to-date introduction to the United Nations.

Gore, Al. *An Inconvenient Truth: The Planetary Emergency of Global Warming and What We Can Do About It*. 2006. Reasoned discussion of the greatest threat to the planet in the twenty-first century, for which Gore won the Nobel Peace Prize.

Johnson-Odim, Cheryl, and Margaret Strobel, eds. *Expanding the Boundaries of Women's History: Essays on Women in the Third World*. 1992. Groundbreaking essays on women's history outside of Europe and North America.

Jones, Geoffrey. *Multinationals and Global Capitalism: From the Nineteenth to the Twenty-First Century*. 2005. A historical overview of the development of multinational corporations and a global capitalist economy.

Kasarda, John, and Allan Parnell, eds. *Third World Cities: Problems, Policies and Prospects*. 1993. Discusses the prodigious growth of Third World cities in the second half of the twentieth century.

Klare, Michael T. *Resource Wars: The New Landscape of Global Conflict*. 2002. Analyzes the conflict over vital resources and the impact on national military and economic policies.

Moaddel, Mansoor. *Islamic Modernism, Nationalism, and Fundamentalism*. 2005. A scholarly historical introduction to society and politics in the Middle East.

O'Neill, Bard. E. *Insurgency and Terrorism: From Revolution to Apocalypse*, 2d rev. ed. 2005. An excellent introduction to the nature of modern war.

O'Neill, John Terence, and Nicholas Rees. *United Nations Peacekeeping in the Post–Cold War Era*. 2005. Discusses the problems associated with United Nations peacekeeping efforts.

NOTES

1. D. Rappaport, "The Fourth Wave: September 11 in the History of Terrorism," *Current History*, December 2001, pp. 419–424.
2. Ibid.
3. Quoted in J. Fallows, "Success Without Victory," *The Atlantic Monthly* 295 (January/February 2005): 80.
4. Quoted in L. R. Brown, *Seeds of Change: The Green Revolution and Development in the 1970s* (New York: Praeger, 1970), p. 16.
5. P. Ehrlich, *The Population Bomb* (New York: Ballantine, 1968), p. 11.
6. M. ul Haq, *The Poverty Curtain: Choices for the Third World* (New York: Columbia University Press, 1976), p. 152.
7. J. Diamond, *Collapse: How Societies Choose to Fail or Survive* (New York: Viking, 2004), pp. 524–525.
8. P. Bairoch, *Economics and World History: Myths and Paradoxes* (Chicago: University of Chicago Press, 1993), p. 95.
9. R. Carson, *Silent Spring* (1962; repr., New York: Houghton Mifflin, 1994), pp. 1–3, 7–8.
10. United Nations, "Critical Areas of Concern," *Report of the Fourth World Conference on Women* (New York: United Nations Department for Policy Coordination and Sustainable Development, 1995), ch. 1, annex II, ch. 3, pp. 41–44; available at http://www.un.org/esa/gopher-data/conf/fwcw/off/a—20.en. See also Population Reference Bureau, *Women of Our World 2005* (Washington, D.C.: Population Reference Bureau, 2005) for the latest data and ten-year follow-up to the Beijing meeting.

For practice quizzes and other study tools, visit the **Online Study Guide** at bedfordstmartins.com/mckayworld.

For primary sources from this period, see *Sources of World Societies*, **Second Edition**.

For Web sites, images, and documents related to topics in this chapter, visit **Make History** at bedfordstmartins.com/mckayworld.

□ INDEX

Economic development, economic growth without, 1059
Economic liberalism, 537, 710, 723
Economic nationalism, 699
    in Latin America, 1008–1011
Economics
    of globalization, 1054–1057
    liberals on, 654
Economic sanctions, against Japan, 931
Economy. *See also* Global economy; Great Depression
    in Africa, 1031, 1032
    African slave trade and, 580
    in Asia, 977
    of "Asian Tigers," 983, 985
    of Atlantic region, 547–549, 548(m)
    of Australia, 836–838
    of Bangladesh, 991
    bazaar, 1059
    in China, 460, 625, 628, 644, 900, 979, 982
    East African, 568
    in eastern Europe, 952
    in England, 686, 909–910, 911(i)
    European unification and, 948
    in First World War, 853
    in France, 662, 670, 671, 912
    in Germany, 866–867, 912, 921–922
    global, 480–481, 967–968
    Great Depression and, 908–913
    in India, 786, 889–890
    in Islamic empires, 613
    in Italy, 912
    in Japan, 632–633, 898, 966–967
    in Japanese empire, 920
    in Latin America, 813–814, 819, 1013–1018
    in Mexico, 821
    in Middle East, 977
    mixed, 1052
    neocolonialism and, 819–821, 948
    in 1970s, 949–952
    population and, 694–695
    in Russia, 508, 730–731, 968
    after Second World War, 941, 946–947
    in 17th century, 492–493
    slavery and, 579–580, 711
    Smith on, 537
    social hierarchies and, 733
    Soviet, 915, 916, 954
    in Spain, 501
    in Third World countries, 977
    of Turkey, 1000
    underground, 1060(i)
    in United States, 830–831, 961
    in Vietnam, 988
    wealth inequalities and, 653
    worldwide, 773–775
Ecosystems, global warming and, 1065
Ecuador, 813, 814(m)
Edict of Nantes, 496
Edo. *See* Tokyo (Edo), Japan
Edo people (Benin), 556(i)

Edo period (Japan), 631, 635–639
Education. *See also* Intellectual thought; Learning; Schools
    in Africa, 1030
    in France, 742
    global advances in, 1069
    in India, 787, 788(b)
    for middle classes, 733
    in Philippines, 791
    Soviet, 954
    for women, 827
Ego, 869
Egypt, 994, 1002, 1021
    Britain and, 772–773, 888
    emergency law in, 999
    England and, 757
    First World War and, 849, 851
    France and, 672, 770, 772
    independence for, 994
    Israel and, 994, 995, 998
    modernization in, 700, 1052
    Muhammad Ali in, 769, 770, 771(b), 771(i)
    Napoleon and, 672
    in Ottoman Empire, 590
    protests in, 937
    as regional power, 1044
    Second World War in, 935
    Suez Canal and, 994
    tourism in, 773(i)
    trade and, 464
    uprising in (2011), 998(i), 999
Egyptian Nationalist Party, 772
Ehrlich, Paul, 1053
Einstein, Albert, 868
Eisenhower, Dwight D., 935–936, 961, 962, 1011, 1048(b)
Eisenstein, Sergei, 873
El Alamein, Battle of, 935
Elba, Napoleon exiled to, 676
Elbe River region, 936, 942
Elections
    demise of communism and, 968
    in France, 660
    in Nigeria, 1025(i)
    in Soviet Union, 955
    in U.S., 961, 1042
Electricity, in cities, 733, 832
Eliot, T. S., 870
Elites. *See also* Class; Nobility
    in Africa, 1019, 1023, 1024
    colonial, 478, 549
    of Communist Party, 954
    in developing countries, 1051
    Filipino, 791
    in France, 672
    in India, 787–789
    in Japan, 639
    in Korea, 643
    labor, 734
    in Latin America, 815, 817, 819
    in Persia, 887

revolutions and, 654
    in Russia, 509, 968
    in Saint-Domingue, 679
    in Songhai, 561
    in Third World, 1051, 1055, 1059
    in western Europe, 971
Elizabeth I (England), 485, 510
    revenues of, 599
    spice trade and, 608
Elizabeth II (England), 1018(i)
Ellis, Sarah Stickney, 706(b)
Ellis Island, 831
El Salvador, 912
E-mail, 1066
Emancipation, of Jews, 744
Emancipation Proclamation (U.S.), 829–830
Emancipists, in Australia, 836
Embargo
    on Cuba, 1011–1012, 1013
    on oil, 949
Emigration. *See also* Immigrants and immigration
    from Asia, 803(m), 804–806
    of German Jews, 922
    of Russian Jews, 744
Emperors. *See also* Empire(s); specific emperors
    of China, 620–621, 627–629
    of Japan, 931(b)
Empire(s). *See also* Imperialism; Islam; specific empires
    Canada and, 833
    colonial, in Africa, 755–763, 756(m)
    commercial, 480–481, 481(m)
    Hobson on, 767
    mercantilist colonial, 686
    of Napoleon, 674–676
    world economy and, 774
Empire building, new imperialism and, 766(i)
Empiricism, logical, 530
Employment
    in developing countries, 1059
    Great Depression and, 910–911
    through industrialization, 1052–1053
    after Second World War, 948
Empress dowager (China), 796
Enabling Act (Nazi Germany), 922
Enclosures, in England, 545, 686
Encomienda system, 477, 791
Encyclopedia (Diderot and d'Alembert), 536–537, 536(i)
Endangered species, 1065
Endeavor (ship), 834
Energy
    crisis over, 949, 951(b)
    Industrial Revolution and, 690–693
    new physics and, 868
    revolution in, 685
Engels, Friedrich, 702–703, 721
Engines, steam, 690–693

Republicanism, 510
  democratic, 723(*i*)
Republic of China. *See* Taiwan
Republic of South Africa. *See* South Africa
Republic of the Congo, 581
Republic of the United Provinces of the Netherlands. *See* United Provinces of the Netherlands
Reservations (American Indian), 826, 830
Resistance. *See also* Revolts and rebellions; Revolution(s)
  to British in India, 785–786, 891–892
  by Gandhi, 891–894
  in Haiti, 583
  in Latin America, 816–817
  in Turkey, 1001(*i*)
  in Vietnam, 791
  to Western imperialism, 767
Resolution 242 (UN), 995
"Resolution of the General Syrian Congress at Damascus," 884–885(*b*)
Resources. *See* Natural resources
Restoration, in England, 512–513
Reunification. *See also* Unification
  of Germany, 959
  of Vietnam, 963, 988
Revisionism, socialists and, 746–747
Revolts and rebellions. *See also* Revolution(s)
  on *Amistad,* 750(*i*)
  Arab (1916), 881–883
  Bengali (1969), 991, 991(*i*)
  by Boxers, 796
  in Brazil, 1011
  in central Europe, 724–725
  in China, 618, 626, 794, 794(*m*), 897
  in Cuba, 825
  against foreigners in Asia, 807
  in France, 496, 669
  in Haiti, 583, 1017
  by Hungarians, 503
  in Ireland, 511, 512
  in Italy, 726
  in Japan, 637
  in Latin America, 816–817
  in Mexico, 1010
  in Middle East, 998(*i*), 999
  against Napoleon, 676
  in Philippines, 791
  in Saint-Domingue, 679
  against Spain, 501
Revolution(s). *See also* Dual revolution; Industrial Revolution; Revolts and rebellions; Scientific Revolution
  in Africa, 1031
  American, 656–659
  in Atlantic world, 652–656
  in Austria-Hungary, 725
  in China (1911), 796–797, 894
  in communication, 1065–1067
  consumer, 545
  Cuban, 1011

of 1848, 722–725
  English Glorious Revolution, 513–515
  for equality and liberty, 654
  in France, 659–667, 722–723
  Gandhi and Mao on, 893(*b*)
  in Germany (1918), 863
  in Haiti, 676–681
  in Hungary (1956), 953
  in Iran (1979), 949, 994, 999, 1001
  Irish movement for, 743
  in Latin America, 813–817
  Lenin on, 860
  liberty, equality, and, 653–654
  medical, 1062
  Mexican (1910), 1009
  of 1989, 955–959, 1030
  in Persia (1906), 887
  in Russia, 731, 843, 858–861, 954, 968
  in Russian Federation (1991), 960–961
  scientific, 526–533
  in Turkey, 770, 883–886
  Velvet Revolution, 955
Revolutionary era, 651
  in America, 656–659
Revolutionary policies, Marxist, 747
Revolutionary socialists, in Italy, 918
Reza Shah Pahlavi. *See* Pahlavi family
Rhineland
  after First World War, 863
  France and, 668, 670
  Nazi invasion of, 924, 924(*i*)
Rhine River region
  France and, 673, 674
  in Second World War, 936
Rhode Island, 516
Rhodes, Cecil, 760
Rhodesia, 760
Ribeiro, Diogo, world map of, 471(*i*)
Ricardo, David, 695, 702
Ricci, Matteo, 625, 645
Rice
  in Americas, 516
  in China, 625
  in Great Depression, 912
  miracle rice, 1053
Richardson, Victor, 857(*b*)
Richelieu, Cardinal (Armand Jean du Plessis), 494, 496
Riefenstahl, Leni, 873
Rigaud, André, 679, 681
Rights. *See also* Human rights; Liberty(ies)
  in American colonies, 656, 657
  of children, 1068–1069
  for European Jews, 544
  Locke on, 513, 654
  before revolutionary era, 653–654
  in Saint-Domingue, 678, 679
  in U.S. Constitution, 659
  of women, 654, 735, 1067–1068
Right wing, totalitarianism of, 914
Riis, Jacob, 832

Rio de Janeiro, 577, 579(*i*), 823, 1008(*i*)
Rio de la Plata, 813, 815
Rio Grande River, 825
Riots. *See also* Revolts and rebellions
  in China, 626
  in Haiti, 1017
  in India, 891–892
  in Japan, 637
  in Nigeria, 1025
  in Paris, 662
Ripon Land Regulation Act (Australia, 1831), 838
Ritchie, John, 734(*i*)
Rite of Spring, The (Stravinsky), 871
Rivera, Diego, 821(*i*)
Rizal, José, 792(*b*), 792(*i*)
Roanoke colony, 516
Robespierre, Maximilien, 667, 668, 670, 671, 671(*i*)
Rockefeller, John D., 831, 950(*b*)
Rocket (locomotive), 693
Rock music, 962
Rococo style, 540
Rocroi, battle at, 501
Rodriguez, Ali, 1018
Roller mills, for sugar production, 479
Rolling mills, for iron, 691
Roman Catholic Church. *See also* Monks and monasteries; Orthodox Christianity
  birth control and, 1062, 1063
  book publication and, 550
  in Canada, 833
  in China, 804
  conversion in New World, 486(*b*), 487
  on Copernican hypothesis, 528
  Dreyfus affair and, 742, 743
  in East Asia, 644–645
  in England, 512–513
  Ethiopia and, 567
  in France, 667, 672
  in Latin America, 815, 817
  in Maryland, 516
  in Mexico, 819
  Mussolini and, 919
  in Nazi Germany, 923, 929
  in Philippines, 791
  in Poland, 955, 956(*b*)
  scientific revolution and, 533
  Thirty Years' War and, 494
  in Vietnam, 791
  White Fathers missionary society of, 757
Romance literature, in China, 624(*i*)
Romance of the Three Kingdoms, The (China), 624
Romania and Romanians, 719, 863
  in Austrian Empire, 725
  nuclear weapons and, 1047
  revolution and, 955–959
Romanov Dynasty (Russia), 508
Romanticism, 739–741
  nationalism and, 740, 741

◻ TIMELINE | A History of World Societies: An Overview

	Africa	The Americas
10,000 B.C.E.	*Homo sapiens* evolve, ca. 250,000 years ago Farming begins in Nile River Valley, ca. 9000 Domestication of cattle; plow agriculture, ca. 7000 Unification of Egypt, 3100–2660	Possible migration into Americas begins, ca. 20,000–30,000 Farming begins, ca. 8000 Maize domesticated in Mexico, ca. 3000
2500 B.C.E.	Egypt's Old Kingdom, 2660–2180 Egypt's Middle Kingdom, 2080–1640 Hyksos migrate into Egypt, 1640–1570	First cities in Peru; earliest mound building in North America, ca. 2500 Textiles become important part of Peruvian culture, ca. 2500 Farmers in southwestern North America grow maize, ca. 2000
1500 B.C.E.	Egypt's New Kingdom, ca. 1550–1070 Ironworking spreads throughout Africa, ca. 1500 B.C.E.–300 C.E. Akhenaten institutes monotheistic worship of Aton, ca. 1360	Olmec civilization in Mexico, ca. 1500–300 Earliest cities in the Andes built by Chavin people, ca. 1200
1000 B.C.E.	Political fragmentation of Egypt; rise of small kingdoms, ca. 1100–653 Bantu migrations across central and southern Africa, ca. 1000 B.C.E.–1500 C.E. Persians conquer Egypt, 525	Olmec center at San Lorenzo destroyed; power passes to La Venta, ca. 900
500 B.C.E.	Ptolemy conquers Egypt, 323	
250 B.C.E.	Scipio Africanus defeats Hannibal at Zama, 202 Meroë becomes iron-smelting center, ca. 100	Hopewell culture flourishes in North America, ca. 200 B.C.E.–600 C.E.

Asia and Oceania	Europe	Middle East
Farming begins in Yellow River Valley, ca. 9000	Farming spreads to Greece, ca. 6500	Farming begins; domestication of goats and sheep in the Fertile Crescent, ca. 9000
Domestication of cattle; plow agriculture begins, ca. 7000	Smelting of copper in Balkans, ca. 5500	Invention of pottery wheel in Mesopotamia, ca. 5000
	Farming spreads to Britain, ca. 4000	First writing in Sumeria; city-states emerge, ca. 3500
Harappan civilization, ca. 2800–1800	Minoan culture emerges, ca. 2000	Smelting of iron begins in Mesopotamia, ca. 2500
	Arrival of Greeks in peninsular Greece; founding of Mycenaean kingdom, ca. 1650	Akkadian empire, ca. 2331–2200
		Hammurabi's law code, ca. 1790
Shang Dynasty; first writing in China, ca. 1500–1050	Mycenaeans conquer Minoan Crete, ca. 1450	Hittites expand empire in Mesopotamia, ca. 1600
Vedic Age: Aryans dominate in North India; caste system develops; the *Rigveda*, ca. 1500–500	Greek Dark Age; evolution of the polis, ca. 1100–800	Moses leads Hebrews out of Egypt, ca. 1300–1200
		United Hebrew kingdom, ca. 1020–930
Early Zhou Dynasty, ca. 1050–400	Fall of Minoan and Mycenaean cultures, ca. 1000	Assyrian Empire, ca. 800–612
Upanishads, foundation of Hinduism, 750–500	Rise of Sparta and Athens, 800–500	Spread of Zoroastrianism, ca. 600–500
Life of Confucius, 551–479	Roman Republic founded, 509	Babylonian captivity of Hebrews, 587–538
Persians conquer parts of India, 513		Cyrus the Great founds Persian Empire, 550
Founding of Buddhism and Jainism, ca. 500		
Warring States period; golden age of Chinese philosophy, 403–221	Flowering of Greek art and philosophy, 500–400	Persian Empire falls to Alexander the Great, 330
Brahmanic religion develops into Hinduism, ca. 400 B.C.E.–200 C.E.	Persian wars, 499–479	Alexander the Great dies in Babylon, 323
Zhuangzi and development of Daoism, 369–268	Peloponnesian War, 431–404	
Alexander the Great invades India, 326	Roman expansion, 390–146	
Seleucus establishes Seleucid Empire, 323	Conquests of Alexander the Great, 336–323	
Mauryan Empire, ca. 322–185	Punic Wars; destruction of Carthage, 264–146	
Reign of Ashoka; Buddhism spreads in central Asia, 269–232		
Qin Dynasty unifies China; construction of Great Wall, 221–206	Late Roman republic, 133–27	
Han Dynasty, 206 B.C.E.–220 C.E.	Julius Caesar killed, 44	
Han government controls Silk Road across central Asia, 114	Octavian seizes power, rules imperial Rome as Augustus, 27 B.C.E.–14 C.E.	
Chinese armies conquer Nam Viet, 111		
Bhagavad Gita, ca. 100 B.C.E.–100 C.E.		

	Africa	The Americas
1 C.E.	Expansion of Bantu-speaking peoples into eastern and southern Africa, ca. 100	Moche civilization flourishes in Peru, ca. 100–800
200 C.E.	Aksum (Ethiopia) controls Red Sea trade, ca. 250	
300	Christianity comes to Ethiopia from Egypt, 328 Aksum accepts Christianity, ca. 350	Hohokam use irrigation to enhance farming in southwestern North America, ca. 300 Classical era in Mesoamerican and North America; Maya and other groups develop large advanced states, 300–900 Peak of Teotihuacán civilization in Mexico, ca. 450
500	Political and commercial ascendancy of Aksum, ca. 500–700 Christian missionaries convert Nubian rulers, ca. 600 Muslim conquest of Egypt; Islam introduced to Africa, 642 Height of African Mediterranean slave trade, ca. 650–1500	Peak of Maya civilization, ca. 600–900
700	Expansion of Islam into Ethiopia weakens state, 700–800 Berbers control trans-Saharan trade, ca. 700–900 Islam spreads across Sahara, 800–900 Kingdom of Ghana, ca. 900–1300	Teotihuacán destroyed, 750 Period of crop failure, disease, and war in Mesoamerica; collapse of Maya civilization, 800–1000 Toltec hegemony, ca. 980–1000
1000	Islam penetrates sub-Saharan Africa, ca. 1000–1100 Great Zimbabwe built, flourishes, ca. 1100–1400	Inca civilization in South America, ca. 1000–1500 Peak of Cahokia culture in North America, ca. 1150 Toltec state collapses, 1174
1200	Kingdom of Mali, ca. 1200–1450 Mongols conquer Baghdad; fall of Abbasid Dynasty, 1258	Cahokia's decline begins after earthquake, ca. 1200

Asia and Oceania	Europe	Middle East
Shakas and Kushans invade eastern Parthia and India, ca. 1–100	Roman Empire at greatest extent, 117	Life of Jesus, ca. 3 B.C.E.–29 C.E.
Maritime trade between Chinese and Roman ports begins, ca. 100		
Roman attacks on Parthian empire, ca. 100–200		
Chinese invent paper, 105		
Buddhism gains popularity in China, Japan, and Korea, ca. 200–600	Life of Diocletian: reforms Roman Empire; divides into western and eastern halves, 284–305	Sassanid dynasty in Persia, 226–651
Age of Division in China, 220–589		
Fall of the Parthian empire; rise of the Sassanid, ca. 226		
Three Kingdoms Period in Korea, 313–668	Life of Constantine: legalizes Christianity; founds Constantinople, 306–337	
China divides into northern and southern regimes, 316	Christianity official state religion of Roman Empire, 380	
Gupta Empire unites northern India, ca. 320–480	Germanic raids on western Europe, 400s	
Huns invade India, ca. 450	Clovis rules Gauls, ca. 481–511	
Sui Dynasty restores order in China, 581–618	Reign of Justinian; *Code* and *Digest*, 527–565	Life of Muhammad, 570–632
Prince Shōtoku introduces Chinese-style government in Japan, 604	*Rule* of Saint Benedict, 529	Publication of the Qur'an, 651
Tang Dynasty in China; cultural flowering, 618–907		Umayyad Dynasty; expansion of Islam, 661–750
Korea unified, 668		
Creation of Japan's first capital at Nara, 710	Muslims defeat Visigothic kingdom in Spain, 711	Abbasid caliphate; Islamic capital moved to Baghdad, 750–1258
Islam reaches India, 713	Christian reconquest of Spain from Muslims, 722–1492	Height of Muslim learning and creativity, ca. 800–1300
Heian era in Japan, 794–1185	Carolingians defeat Muslims at Poitiers, 732	
Khmer Empire of Cambodia founded, 802		
Koryŏ Dynasty in Korea, 935–1392	Viking, Magyar invasions, ca. 800–950	
North Vietnam gains independence from China, 939	Treaty of Verdun divides Carolingian Empire, 843	
Song Dynasty in China; invention of movable type, 960–1279		
Construction of Angkor Wat, ca. 1100–1150	Latin, Greek churches split, 1054	Seljuk Turks take Baghdad, 1055
Muslim conquests lead to decline of Buddhism in India, ca. 1100–1200	Norman Conquest of England, 1066	
China divided into Song and Jin empires, 1127	Crusades, 1095–1270	
Kamakura Shogunate in Japan, 1185–1333	Growth of trade and towns, ca. 1100–1400	
Easter Island's most prosperous period, ca. 1200–1300	Magna Carta, 1215	Mongols conquer Baghdad, 1238
Turkish sultanate at Dehli, 1206–1526	Life of Thomas Aquinas; *Summa Theologica*, 1225–1274	Ottoman Empire, 1299–1922
Peak of Khmer Empire, 1219	Mongol raids into eastern Europe; Mongols gain control of Kieven Russia, 1237–1241	
Mongol's Yuan Dynasty in China, 1234–1368		
Mongols invade Japan, 1274, 1281		
Marco Polo travels in China, ca. 1275–1292		
Mongol conquest of Song China, 1276		

	Africa	The Americas
1300	Height of Swahili city-states in East Africa, ca. 1300–1500 Mansa Musa rules Mali, ca. 1312–1337 Ibn Battuta's travels, 1325–1354	Construction of Aztec city Tenochtitlán begins, ca. 1325
1400	Songhai Empire, ca. 1464–1591 Arrival of Portuguese in Benin, 1485 Da Gama reaches East Africa; Swahili coast enters period of economic decline, 1498	Height of Inca Empire, 1438–1532 Reign of Montezuma I; height of Aztec culture, 1440–1467 Inca city of Machu Picchu built, 1450 Columbus reaches Americas, 1492
1500	Portugal dominates East Africa, ca. 1500–1600 Era of transatlantic slave trade, ca. 1500–1900 Muslim occupation of Christian Ethiopia, 1531–1543 Height of Kanem-Bornu, 1571–1603	Portuguese reach Brazil, 1500 Atlantic slave trade begins, 1518 Cortés arrives in Mexico, 1519 Aztec Empire falls, 1521 Pizarro conquers Inca Empire, 1533 First English colony in North America founded at Roanoke, 1585
1600	Dutch West India Company founded; starts to bring slave coast of West Africa under its control, 1621 Jesuit missionaries expelled from Ethiopia, 1633 Dutch East India Company settles Cape Town, 1652 Importation of slaves into Cape Colony begins, 1658	British settle Jamestown, 1607 Champlain founds first permanent French settlement at Quebec, 1608 Caribbean islands colonized by French, English, Dutch, 1612–1697 English seize New Amsterdam from Dutch, 1664
1700	Major famine in West Africa, 1738–1756	Silver production quadruples in Mexico and Peru, ca. 1700–1800 Colonial dependence on Spanish goods, ca. 1700–1800
1750	Peak of transatlantic slave trade, 1780–1820 Olaudah Equiano publishes autobiography, 1789 British seize Cape Town, 1795 Napoleon's army invades Egypt, 1798	Seven Years' War, 1756–1763 Quebec Act, 1774 American Revolution, 1775–1783 Comunero revolution in New Granada, 1781 Haitian Revolution, 1791–1804

Asia and Oceania	Europe	Middle East
Ashikaga Shogunate, 1336–1573 Mongols defeated in China, 1368 Ming Dynasty in China, 1368–1644 Timur conquers the Delhi sultanate, 1398	Hundred Years' War, ca. 1337–1453 Black Death arrives in Europe, 1347 Great Schism, 1378–1417	
Maritime trade and piracy connects East Asia and Southeast Asia with Europe, ca. 1400–1800 Zheng He's maritime expeditions to India, Middle East, Africa, 1405–1433 Reign of Sultan Mehmed II, 1451–1481	Development of movable type in Germany, ca. 1450 Italian Renaissance, ca. 1450–1521 Age of Discovery, ca. 1450–1650 Ottomans capture Constantinople; end of Byzantine Empire, 1453 Unification of Spain; Jews expelled, 1492	Ottoman Empire conquers Byzantine Empire under rule of Sultan Mehmet II, 1451–1481
Increased availability of books in China, 1500–1600 Barbur defeats Delhi sultanate; founds Mughal Empire, 1526 Japan unified under Toyotomi Hideyoshi, 1537–1598 First Christian missionaries land in Japan, 1549 Akbar expands Mughal Empire, 1556–1605 Spain founds port city of Manila in the Philippines, 1571	Michelangelo paints Sistine Chapel, 1508–1512 Luther's Ninety-five Theses, 1517 English Reformation begins, 1527 Scientific revolution, ca. 1540–1690 Council of Trent, 1545–1563 Peace of Augsburg ends religious wars in Germany, 1555 Netherlands declares independence from Spain, 1581	Safavid Empire in Persia, 1501–1722 Peak of Ottoman power; cultural flowering under Suleiman, 1520–1566 Battle of Lepanto, 1571 Height of Safavid Empire under Shah Abbas, 1587–1629
Tokogawa Shogunate in Japan, 1603–1867 Japan closes its borders, 1639 Manchus establish Qing Dynasty in China, 1644–1911 Dutch expel Portuguese in East Indies; gain control of spice trade, ca. 1660 French arrive in India, ca. 1670	Thirty Years' War, 1619–1648 Growth of absolutism in Austria and Prussia, 1620–1740 English civil war, 1642–1649 Habsburgs expel Ottomans from Hungary, 1683–1718 Revocation of Edict of Nantes, 1685 Glorious Revolution in England, 1688–1689 The Enlightenment, ca. 1690–1789	Shah Abbas captures much of Armenia from the Ottomans, 1603
Height of Edo urban culture in Japan, ca. 1700 Christian missionary work forbidden in China, 1715 Persian invaders loot Delhi, 1739 French and British fight for control of India, 1740–1763	Growth of book publishing, ca. 1700–1789 War of the Spanish Succession, 1701–1713 Peace of Utrecht, 1713	Afghans seize Isfahan from Persians, 1722
Treaty of Paris gives French colonies in India to Britain, 1763 Cook claims land in Australia for Britain, 1770 East India Act, 1784 First British convict-settlers arrive in Australia, 1788	Watt produces first steam engine, 1769 Industrial Revolution in Great Britain, ca. 1780–1850 French Revolution, 1789–1799 Romantic movement in literature and the arts, ca. 1790s–1890s National Convention declares France a republic, 1792	Ottoman ruler Selim III introduces reforms, 1761–1808

Africa	The Americas
1800	
Muhammad Ali modernizes Egypt, 1805–1848	Latin American wars of independence, 1806–1825
Slavery abolished in British Empire, 1807	Brazil wins independence, 1822
	Political instability in most Latin American countries, 1825–1870
	U.S.-Mexican War, 1846–1848
1850	
Suez Canal opens, 1869	U.S. Civil War, 1861–1865
Western and central Sudan unite under Islam, 1880	Dominion of Canada formed, 1867
European "scramble for Africa"; decline of slave trade, 1880–1900	Latin American neocolonialism, ca. 1870–1929
Battle of Omdurman, 1898	Diaz controls Mexico, 1876–1911
South African War, 1899–1902	Immigration from Europe and Asia to the Americas, 1880–1914
	Spanish-American War, 1898
1900	
Union of South Africa formed, 1910	Mexican Revolution, 1910
Native Land Act in South Africa, 1913	Panama Canal opens, 1914
Du Bois organizes first Pan-African congress, 1919	Mexico adopts constitution, 1917
1920	
Cultural nationalism in Africa, 1920s	U.S. consumer revolution, 1920s
Gold Coast farmers organize cocoa holdups, 1930–1931	Stock market crash in U.S.; Great Depression begins, 1929
	Revolutions in six South American countries, 1930
	Flowering of Mexican culture, 1930s
	New Deal begins in United States, 1933
1940	
Decolonization in Africa, 1946–1964	"Mexican miracle," 1940s–1970s
Apartheid system in South Africa, 1948–1991	Surprise attack by Japan on Pearl Harbor, 1941
	United Nations established, 1945
1950	
Egypt declared a republic; Nasser named premier, 1954	Cuban revolution, 1953–1959
French-British Suez invasion, 1956	Military rule ends in Venezuela, 1958
Morocco, Tunisia, Sudan, and Ghana gain independence, 1956–1957	Castro takes power in Cuba, 1959
France offers commonwealth status to its territories; only Guinea chooses independence, 1958	
Belgian Congo gains independence; violence follows, 1959	

Asia and Oceania	Europe	Middle East
British found Singapore, 1819	Napoleonic Europe, 1804–1814	Ottoman Empire launches Tanzimat reforms, 1839
Java War, 1825–1830	Congress of Vienna, 1814–1815	
Opium War, 1839–1842	European economic penetration of non-Western countries, ca. 1816–1880	
Treaty of Nanjing; Manchus surrender Hong Kong to British, 1842	Greece wins independence, 1830	
	Revolutions in France, Austria, and Prussia, 1848	
Taiping Rebellion, 1851–1864	Unification of Italy, 1859–1870	Crimean War, 1853–1856
Perry opens Japan to trade; Japan begins to industrialize, 1853	Freeing of Russian serfs, 1861	Ottoman state declares partial bankruptcy; European creditors take over, 1875
Great Mutiny/Revolt in India, 1857	Unification of Germany, 1866–1871	
Meiji Restoration in Japan, 1867	Massive industrialization surge in Russia, 1890–1900	
Indian National Congress, 1885		
French acquire Indochina, 1893		
Sino-Japanese War, 1894–1895		
U.S. gains Philippines, 1898		
Boxer Rebellion in China, 1900	Revolution in Russia, 1905	Young Turks seize power in Ottoman Empire, 1908
Commonwealth of Australia, 1901	World War I, 1914–1918	Turkish massacre of Armenians, 1915–1917
Russo-Japanese War, 1904–1905	Bolshevik Revolution and civil war in Russia, 1917–1922	Sykes-Picot Agreement divides Ottoman Empire, 1916
Muslim League formed, 1906	Treaty of Versailles, 1919	
Korea becomes province of Japan, 1910		Balfour Declaration establishes Jewish homeland in Palestine, 1917
Chinese revolution; fall of Qing Dynasty, 1911		
Chinese republic, 1912–1949		
Amritsar Massacre in India, 1919		
Gandhi launches nonviolent campaign against British rule in India, 1920	Mussolini seizes power in Italy, 1922	Large numbers of European Jews immigrate to Palestine, 1920s–1930s
Jiang Jieshi unites China, 1928	Stalin takes power in U.S.S.R., 1927	Turkish republic recognized; Kemal begins to modernize and secularize, 1923
Japan invades China, 1931	Great Depression, 1929–1933	Reza Shah leads Iran, 1925–1941
Mao Zedong's Long March, 1934	Hitler gains power in Germany, 1933	Iraq gains independence, 1932
Sino-Japanese War, 1937–1945	Civil war in Spain, 1936–1939	
Japan conquers Southeast Asia, 1939–1942	World War II, 1939–1945	
Japan announces "Asia for Asians"; signs alliance with Germany and Italy, 1940	Marshall Plan, 1947	Arabs and Jews at war in Palestine; Israel created, 1948
United States drops atomic bombs on Hiroshima and Nagasaki, 1945	NATO formed, 1949	
Chinese civil war; Communists win, 1945–1949	Soviet Union and Communist China sign 30-year alliance, 1949	
Philippines gain independence, 1946		
Independence and separation of India and Pakistan, 1947		
Japan begins long period of rapid economic growth, 1950	Death of Stalin, 1953	Turkey joins NATO, 1953
Korean War, 1950–1953	Warsaw Pact, 1955	Suez crisis, 1956
Vietnamese nationalists defeat French; Vietnam divided, 1954	Revolution in Hungary, 1956	
Mao announces Great Leap Forward in China, 1958	Common Market formed, 1957	

	Africa	The Americas
1960	Mali and Nigeria gain independence, 1960 Biafra declares independence from Nigeria, 1967	U.S. Alliance for Progress promotes development and reform in Latin America, 1961 Cuban missile crisis, 1962 U.S. Civil Rights Act; United States starts Vietnam War, 1964 Military dictatorship in Brazil, 1964–1985 Military takeovers lead to brutal dictatorships in Argentina, 1966, 1976
1970	Growth of Islamic fundamentalism, 1970s to present	U.S. Watergate scandal, 1972 Nixon visits China; reconciliation between U.S. and China, 1972 Military coup in Chile, 1973 Revolution in Nicaragua, 1979
1980	Blacks win long civil war with white settlers in Zimbabwe, 1980 AIDS epidemic, 1980s to present South African government opens talks with African National Congress, 1989	Democratic wave gains momentum throughout Latin America, 1980s Nationalization of Mexico's banking system, 1982 Argentina restores civilian rule, 1983 Brazilians elect first civilian government in twenty years, 1985
1990	Nelson Mandela freed in South Africa, 1990 Rwandan genocide, 1994 Second Congo War, 1998 to present	Canada, Mexico, and United States form free-trade area (NAFTA), 1994 Haiti establishes democratic government, 1994 Socialist "Bolivarian revolution" in Venezuela, 1999
2000	Civil war and genocide in Darfur, 2003 to present Mugabe increases violence against opponents after losing Zimbabwean election, 2008 Populist uprisings and protests break out in Tunisia, Egypt, and elsewhere in North Africa, 2010–2011	Terrorist attack on United States, 2001 Economic, social, and political crisis in Argentina, 2002 Formation of the Union of South American Nations, 2008 Raúl Castro succeeds his ailing brother Fidel as president of Cuba, 2008 Catastrophic earthquake in Haiti, 2010 U.S. begins troop drawdown in Afghanistan, 2011

Asia and Oceania	Europe	Middle East
Sino-Soviet split becomes apparent, 1960 Vietnam War, 1964–1975 Great Proletarian Cultural Revolution launched in China, 1965	Building of Berlin Wall, 1961 Student revolution in France, 1968 Soviet invasion of Czechoslovakia, 1968	OPEC founded, 1960 Arab-Israeli Six-Day War, 1967
Bangladesh breaks away from Pakistan, 1971 Communist victory in Vietnam War, 1975 China pursues modernization, 1976 to present	Helsinki Accord on human rights, 1975 Soviet invasion of Afghanistan, 1979	Revival of Islamic fundamentalism, 1970s to present Arab-Israeli Yom Kippur War, 1973 OPEC oil embargo, 1973 Civil war in Lebanon, 1975–1990 Islamic revolution in Iran, 1979 Camp David Accords, 1979
Japanese foreign investment surge, 1980–1992 Sikh nationalism in India, 1984 to present China crushes democracy movement, 1989	Soviet reform under Gorbachev, 1985–1991 Communism falls in eastern Europe, 1989–1990	Iran-Iraq War, 1980–1988 Palestinians start the intifada, 1987
Collapse of Japanese stock market, 1990–1992 Economic growth and political repression in China, 1990 to present Congress Party in India embraces Western capitalist reforms, 1991 Kyoto Protocol on global warming, 1997 Hong Kong returns to Chinese rule, 1997	Conservative economic policies, 1990s End of Soviet Union, 1991 Civil war in Yugoslavia, 1991–2001 Maastricht Treaty creates single currency, 1992 Creation of European Union, 1993	Persian Gulf War, 1990–1991 Israel and Palestinians sign peace agreement, 1993 Assassination of Israeli prime minster Yitzak Rabin, 1995
China joins World Trade Organization, 2001 India and Pakistan come close to all-out war, 2001 North Korea withdraws from 1970 Nuclear Non-Proliferation Treaty, 2003 Tsunami in Southeast Asia, 2004 Terrorist attack in Mumbai, India, 2008 Massive earthquake in Japan, 2011 Al-Qaeda leader Osama bin Laden killed in Pakistan, 2011	Resurgence of Russian economy under Putin, 2000–2008 Euro note enters circulation, 2002 Madrid train bombing, 2004 London subway and bus bombing, 2005	Israel begins construction of West Bank barrier, 2003 Wars in Iraq and Afghanistan, 2003 to present Hamas establishes Palestinian Authority government, 2007 Populist uprisings and protests across the Middle East, 2010–2011

THE CONTEMPORARY WORLD

Greenland
(Den.)

ICELAND

Alaska
(U.S.)

CANADA

UNITED
KINGDOM

IRELAND

FRANCE

SPAIN

PORTUGAL

UNITED STATES

ATLANTIC
OCEAN

Azores
(Port.)

Bermuda (U.K.)

MOROCCO

Canary Is.
(Sp.)

Western Sahara
(Mor.)

BAHAMAS

MEXICO

CUBA

DOMINICAN
REPUBLIC

HAITI

Hawaii (U.S.)

JAMAICA

Puerto Rico (U.S.)

ST. KITTS AND NEVIS

MAURITANIA

CAPE
VERDE

BELIZE

GUATEMALA

HONDURAS

ANTIGUA AND BARBUDA

Guadeloupe (Fr.)

DOMINICA

SENEGAL

MALI

EL SALVADOR

NICARAGUA

Martinique (Fr.)

ST. VINCENT AND THE GRENADINES

GAMBIA

COSTA RICA

ST. LUCIA

BARBADOS

GRENADA

GUINEA-BISSAU

PANAMA

VENEZUELA

TRINIDAD AND TOBAGO

GUYANA

GUINEA

SIERRA LEONE

COLOMBIA

SURINAME

French Guiana (Fr.)

LIBERIA

CÔTE D'IVOIRE

Galápagos Is.
(Ec.)

ECUADOR

BURKINA FASO

GHANA

PACIFIC OCEAN

Equator

PERU

BRAZIL

SAMOA

BOLIVIA

TONGA

PARAGUAY

Easter I.
(Chile)

CHILE

ATLANTIC
OCEAN

URUGUAY

ARGENTINA

N
W   E
S

0   1,500   3,000 miles

0   1,500   3,000 kilometers

Falkland Is.
(U.K.)

80°N

60°N

40°N

20°N

0°

20°S

40°S

60°S

80°S

160°W   140°W   120°W   100°W   80°W   60°W   40°W   20°W

ARCTIC OCEAN

NORWAY
SWEDEN
FINLAND
ESTONIA
LATVIA
LITHUANIA
DEN.
NETH.
GERMANY POLAND
BEL.
LUX.
CZ.
AUS.
SLK.
HUNG.
SWITZ.
SLN.
ITALY
CR.
B.H.
RO.
KO.
MAC.
ALB.
GREECE
SE.
ROMANIA
BULGARIA
BELARUS
UKRAINE
MOLDOVA

RUSSIAN FEDERATION

TUNISIA
MALTA
CYPRUS
ISRAEL
LEBANON
West Bank
Gaza Strip
JORDAN
LGERIA
LIBYA
EGYPT

GEORGIA
ARMENIA
TURKEY
SYRIA
IRAQ
IRAN
KUWAIT
SAUDI ARABIA
QATAR
UNITED ARAB
EMIRATES
AZERBAIJAN

KAZAKHSTAN

UZBEKISTAN
TURKMENISTAN
KYRGYZSTAN
TAJIKISTAN
AFGHANISTAN
PAKISTAN

MONGOLIA

CHINA

N. KOREA
S. KOREA
JAPAN

PACIFIC OCEAN

Taiwan

BHUTAN
NEPAL
BANGLADESH
INDIA
MYANMAR
(BURMA)
LAOS
VIETNAM
THAILAND
CAMBODIA
OMAN
BAHRAIN
YEMEN

NIGER
CHAD
SUDAN
DJIBOUTI
ERITREA
NIGERIA
BENIN
TOGO
CAMEROON
CENTRAL
AFRICAN REP.
SOUTH
SUDAN
ETHIOPIA
SOMALIA
EQ.
GUINEA
GABON
CONGO
RWANDA
UGANDA
KENYA
DEM. REP. OF
THE CONGO
BURUNDI
TANZANIA
SÃO
TOMÉ
& PRÍNCIPE
ANGOLA
ZAMBIA
MALAWI
COMOROS
SEYCHELLES

MALDIVES
SRI
LANKA

PHILIPPINES

BRUNEI
MALAYSIA
SINGAPORE
PALAU

Mariana Is.
(U.S.)
Guam
(U.S.)
MARSHALL
IS.

FEDERATED STATES
OF MICRONESIA

NAURU
KIRIBATI
TUVALU
SOLOMON
IS.

INDONESIA
PAPUA
NEW
GUINEA

INDIAN OCEAN

TIMOR
LESTE

VANUATU
FIJI

New Caledonia
(Fr.)

NAMIBIA
BOTSWANA
ZIMBABWE
MADAGASCAR
MOZAMBIQUE
SWAZILAND
SOUTH
AFRICA
LESOTHO
MAURITIUS

AUSTRALIA

NEW
ZEALAND
Tasmania
(Aust.)

ANTARCTICA

ABBREVIATIONS	
ALB.	ALBANIA
AUS.	AUSTRIA
BEL.	BELGIUM
B.H.	BOSNIA AND HERZEGOVINA
CR.	CROATIA
CZ.	CZECH REPUBLIC
DEN.	DENMARK
HUNG.	HUNGARY
KO.	KOSOVO
LUX.	LUXEMBOURG
MAC.	MACEDONIA
MO.	MONTENEGRO
NETH.	NETHERLANDS
SE.	SERBIA
SLK.	SLOVAKIA
SLN.	SLOVENIA
SWITZ.	SWITZERLAND

20°E 40°E 60°E 80°E 100°E 120°E 140°E 160°E

160°W 140°W 120°W 100°W 80°W 60°W 40°W 20°W

Arctic Circle

NORTH AMERICA

R O C K Y   M T S.

Mississippi R.

APPALACHIAN MTS.

ATLANTIC OCEAN

Gulf of Mexico

Tropic of Cancer

Caribbean Sea

PACIFIC OCEAN

Equator

Amazon R.

A N D E S   M T S.

SOUTH AMERICA

Tropic of Capricorn

ATLANTIC OCEAN

N
W   E
S

0   1,000   2,000   3,000 miles
0   1,000   2,000   3,000 kilometers

Antarctic Circle

20°E 40°E 60°E 80°E 100°E 120°E 140°E 160°E

80°N

Arctic Circle

60°N

EUROPE

ALPS

URAL MTS.

Volga R.

Ob R.

Mediterranean Sea

ASIA

GOBI

40°N

Yellow R.
(Huang He)

HIMALAYA MTS.

Yangzi R.

SAHARA

ARABIAN
DESERT

Ganges R.

Tropic of Cancer

AFRICA

Nile R.

Arabian
Sea

Bay of
Bengal

20°N

South
China
Sea

PACIFIC OCEAN

Congo R.

Equator 0°

INDIAN OCEAN

Zambezi R.

KALAHARI
DESERT

20°S

Tropic of Capricorn

AUSTRALIA

Vegetation zones

Tundra
Northern forest
Temperate forest
Temperate grassland
Desert and dry shrub
Mediterranean shrub
Mountain grassland
Tropical grassland and savanna
Tropical forest
Permanent ice cover

40°S

60°S

Antarctic Circle

80°S

◻ ABOUT THE AUTHORS

JOHN P. McKAY (Ph.D., University of California, Berkeley) is professor emeritus at the University of Illinois. He has written or edited numerous works, including the Herbert Baxter Adams Prize–winning book *Pioneers for Profit: Foreign Entrepreneurship and Russian Industrialization, 1885–1913.*

BENNETT D. HILL (Ph.D., Princeton University), late of Georgetown University, published *Church and State in the Middle Ages* and numerous articles and reviews, and was one of the contributing editors to *The Encyclopedia of World History.* He was also a Benedictine monk of St. Anselm's Abbey in Washington, D.C.

JOHN BUCKLER (Ph.D., Harvard University), late of the University of Illinois, authored *Theban Hegemony, 371–362 B.C., Philip II and the Sacred War,* and *Aegean Greece in the Fourth Century B.C.* With Hans Beck, he most recently published *Central Greece and the Politics of Power in the Fourth Century.*

PATRICIA BUCKLEY EBREY (Ph.D., Columbia University), professor of history at the University of Washington in Seattle, specializes in China. She has published many journal articles and *The Cambridge Illustrated History of China* as well as numerous monographs. In 2010 she won the Shimada Prize for outstanding work of East Asian Art History for *Accumulating Culture: The Collections of Emperor Huizong.*

ROGER B. BECK (Ph.D., Indiana University) is Distinguished Professor of African and twentieth-century world history at Eastern Illinois University. His publications include *The History of South Africa,* a translation of P. J. van der Merwe's *The Migrant Farmer in the History of the Cape Colony, 1657–1842,* and more than a hundred articles, book chapters, and reviews. He is a former treasurer and Executive Council member of the World History Association.

CLARE HARU CROWSTON (Ph.D., Cornell University) teaches at the University of Illinois, where she is currently associate professor of history. She is the author of *Fabricating Women: The Seamstresses of Old Regime France, 1675–1791,* which won the Berkshire and Hagley Prizes. She edited two special issues of the *Journal of Women's History,* has published numerous journal articles and reviews, and is a past president of the Society for French Historical Studies.

MERRY E. WIESNER-HANKS (Ph.D., University of Wisconsin–Madison) taught first at Augustana College in Illinois, and since 1985 at the University of Wisconsin–Milwaukee, where she is currently UWM Distinguished Professor in the department of history. She is the coeditor of the *Sixteenth Century Journal* and the author or editor of more than twenty books, most recently *The Marvelous Hairy Girls: The Gonzales Sisters and Their Worlds* and *Gender in History.* She is the former Chief Reader for Advanced Placement World History.

ABOUT THE COVER ART

Ito Shinsui, *Facing the Mirror* To us today this woodblock print of a Japanese woman in a bright red kimono might seem to convey the traditional side of Japanese culture. But to Japanese who saw Ito Shinsui's print the year it was made, in 1916, the departures from tradition would have been more striking, especially the deep red color and the composition, with the woman seen from behind gazing at a mirror not visible to us.